THE
INDEPENDENT
SCHOOLS
GUIDE

THE
INDEPENDENT
SCHOOLS
GUIDE

2007–2008

13TH EDITION

A FULLY COMPREHENSIVE
DIRECTORY

IN EDUCATION SINCE 1873

KOGAN
PAGE

London and Philadelphia

Publisher's note

The information supplied in this *Guide* has been published in good faith on the basis of information submitted by the schools listed. Neither Kogan Page nor Gabbitas Educational Consultants can guarantee the accuracy of the information in this *Guide* and accept no responsibility for any error or misrepresentation. All liability for loss, disappointment, negligence or other damage caused by the reliance on the information contained in this *Guide*, or in the event of bankruptcy or liquidation or cessation of trade of any company, individual or firm mentioned, is hereby excluded.

Photographs on front cover reproduced with kind permission of Wycliffe Preparatory School, Stonehouse, Gloucestershire (left), Prior Park College, Bath (centre), and Prior's Field School, Godalming, Surrey (right).

First published in 1995
This edition published in 2007

Kogan Page Ltd
120 Pentonville Road
London N1 9JN
UK

Kogan Page US
525 South 4th Street, #241
Philadelphia PA 19147
USA

© Gabbitas and Kogan Page, 2007

British Library Cataloguing in Publication Data

A CIP record for this book is available from the British Library

ISBN-10   0 7494 4948 9
ISBN-13   978 0 7494 4948 3
ISSN   1478 6893

Typeset by AJS Solutions, Dundee & Huddersfield
Printed and bound in Great Britain by Bell & Bain, Glasgow

Contents

Acknowledgements   *vii*
Foreword   *ix*
How to Use the Guide   *xi*

PART 1:
THE INDEPENDENT SECTOR

1.1	What is an Independent School?	3
1.2	The Independent Sector	9
1.3	Choosing your School	22
1.4	Coming from Overseas	28
1.5	Finding the Fees by Towry Law Financial Services Limited	33
1.6	Scholarships, Bursaries and Other Awards	37
1.7	Examinations and Qualifications in the UK	41
1.8	The Sixth Form and Beyond – a Parent's Guide	60

PART 2:
GEOGRAPHICAL DIRECTORY

2.1	Notes on Information given in the Directory Section	71
2.2	England	73
2.3	Northern Ireland	233
2.4	Scotland	236
2.5	Wales	247
2.6	Overseas Schools	254

PART 3:
SCHOOL PROFILES

3.1	England	259
3.2	Scotland	405
3.3	Continental Europe and Overseas Schools Outside Europe	413

PART 4:
REFERENCE SECTION

4.1	Index: Scholarships	419
4.2	Index: Bursaries and Reserved Entrance Awards	435
4.3	Index: Specialist Schools	447
4.4	Index: Single-Sex Schools	448
4.5	Index: Boarding Provision (Full, Weekly and Flexi-Boarding, Host Families)	457
4.6	Index: Religious Affiliation	465
4.7	Index: Schools Registered with CReSTeD (Council for the Registration of Schools Teaching Dyslexic Pupils)	474
4.8	Index: Provision for English as a Foreign Language	477
4.9	Index: Schools in Membership of the Constituent Associations of the Independent Schools Council	485
4.10	Educational Associations and Useful Addresses	498
4.11	Glossary of Abbreviations	513
4.12	Further Reading	517
4.13	Main Index	523

Acknowledgements

This Guide is the product of many hours of data collection and meticulous proof-reading by staff at Gabbitas and Kogan Page, together with cooperation and contributions from a wide-ranging team of experts. Gabbitas would like to thank all those who have helped in the preparation of this Guide, in particular Towry Law Financial Services Ltd; Wycliffe Preparatory School, Gloucestershire, Prior Park College, Bath, and Prior's Field School, Surrey for kind permission to reproduce photographs; and the educational associations, Heads and schools that have so promptly provided the information required for publication.

Gabbitas Educational Consultants Ltd
January 2007

Foreword

Gabbitas Educational Consultants

Welcome to the 13th edition of *The Independent Schools Guide*, the most comprehensive directory of independent schools in the UK. Compiled from our unique database and fully updated every year, the Guide includes nearly 2,000 schools as well as practical advice from the Gabbitas team for parents about to start their search for the right school.

The Guide's accompanying website pages offer an online school search to help you identify schools suited to your requirements as well as direct links to school websites.

Established for over 130 years, Gabbitas is uniquely placed to offer parents expert advice. Each year we help thousands of parents and students in the UK and abroad who seek personal guidance at all stages of education:

- choosing the right independent school or college;

- educational assessment;

- Sixth Form options – A levels, International Baccalaureate and vocational courses;

- university and degree choices and UCAS applications;

- alternatives to university;

- careers assessment and guidance, job searching and interview techniques.

Gabbitas also advises on transfer into the British educational system and provides guardianship services for children from overseas attending boarding schools in the UK. To find out more about Gabbitas, visit our website at www.gabbitas.co.uk or contact us at:

Gabbitas Educational Consultants
Carrington House, 126–130 Regent Street, London W1B 5EE
Tel: +44 (0)20 7734 0161 Fax: +44 (0)20 7437 1764
E-mail: admin@gabbitas.co.uk

The
British
Psychological
Society

Chartered
psychologist

GEORGE CROWTHER

BSc (Hons) MSc CPsychol AFBPsS
Chartered Educational Psychologist
Clinical & Developmental Psychologist
Education & Child Care Consultant

- Dyslexia
- Learning Difficulties
- Pre-school assessment
- Sensory or physical difficulties
- Autism/Asperger's/ASD
- Emotional & Behavioural Difficulties
- Deficits of Attention, Motor Control & Persistence (DAMP)
- Special Educational Needs Assessment
- Grammar School Selection
- Which School
- Vocational & Careers Guidance
- International Commissions
- Connexions

- Able, Gifted + Talented
- Dyspraxia/DCD
- Speech and Language Delay/Disorder
- Attention Deficit Hyperactivity Disorder (AD/HD)
- Pervasive Developmental Disorder (PDD)
- Poor School Report
- Poor SATS Results
- Special Educational Needs + Disablity Tribunal (SENDIST)
- Common Entrance
- Home Visits
- Counselling/Personal Matters
- Inclusion

Independent Professional Educational Advice

Little Hill, Colley Manor Drive, Reigate, Surrey RH2 9JS
Telephone & Fax: Reigate (+44) 01737 243286
Mobile 07710 214349

Website www.georgecrowther.co.uk
Director of Education Law Association (ELAS)
Member of Independent Tribunal Service
Single Joint Expert (SJE) Witness- The Law Society
Member of the Association for Child and Adolescen Mental Health (ACAMH)
Member of the Association of Educational Psychologists (AEP)
Member of the National Association for Gifted Children (NAGC)
Member of the National Association for Special Educational Needs (NASEN)
Member of Young Minds
Fellow of the Royal Institution of Great Britain

- -

The British Psychological Society Regulates Chartered Psychologists (CPsychol)

How to Use the Guide

About independent schools

The first part of this Guide offers extensive information about independent schools, examinations, fee-planning, scholarships and bursaries as well as guidance on choosing a school.

Researching individual schools

The main index at the back gives all page references for each school.

Selecting schools in a particular location

If you are looking for a school in a specific area, turn to the directory section (Part Two), which is arranged geographically by town and county. Schools in London are listed under their postal areas. Each entry gives the name, postal address, telephone and fax numbers and e-mail address of the school, together with the name of the Head, details of the type and age range of pupils accepted, the number of pupils, number of boarders (where applicable) and the annual fees.

Schools which have an asterisk also appear in the School Profiles section (Part Three), where advertisers provide more detailed information. These schools also have a map reference to show their exact location.

To find any other references to the school, for example to find out whether it offers scholarships, turn to the appropriate index at the back.

Scholarships, bursaries and reserved entrance awards

Many schools offer scholarships for children with a particular talent, bursaries where there is financial hardship or reserved entrance awards for children with a parent in a specific profession such as the Clergy or HM Forces. Part Four contains a complete list of schools, by county, which offer such awards.

This section is necessarily only a brief guide to awards available. More specific information can be obtained from individual schools.

Religious affiliation

The index in Part Four provides a full list of schools under appropriate headings.

Single-sex schools

For a complete list of single-sex schools, turn to Part Four.

Boarding schools

Schools with boarding provision generally offer full, weekly or flexi-boarding options. Some Sixth Form colleges, with no residential facilities, may offer accommodation with host families. The number of boarders is shown in the entries in Part Two. For an index of boarding provision by county, see Part Four.

Dyslexia

Most schools offer help, in varying degrees, for pupils with dyslexia. A list of schools registered with CReSTeD (Council for the Registration of Schools Teaching Dyslexic Pupils) appears in Part Four.

English as a foreign language

Most independent schools offer assistance to overseas pupils who require special English language tuition. A list of schools, arranged by county, appears in Part Four.

Schools accredited by the Independent Schools Council

Part Four contains an index of schools in membership of the associations listed below, which together form the Independent Schools Council (ISC). A satisfactory inspection report by the Independent Schools Inspectorate is a requirement for any school wishing to join one of these associations and for its continued accreditation as a member. For more information on the inspection of independent schools, see Part 1.1.

- Headmasters' and Headmistresses' Conference (HMC)
- Girls' Schools Association (GSA) (including the Girls' Day School Trust GDST)

- Society of Headmasters and Headmistresses of Independent Schools (SHMIS)

- Incorporated Association of Preparatory Schools (IAPS)

- Independent Schools Association (ISA).

Other associations which are constituent members of ISC but are not covered by the index are the Association of Governing Bodies of Independent Schools (AGBIS) and the Independent Schools Bursars' Association (ISBA).

School search online

Remember that you can search for schools at www.gabbitas.co.uk.

One Campus

A World of Opportunity

Regent's College is situated in central London within Regent's Park and offers a unique setting with excellent academic facilities. The campus is located just minutes away from the major shopping & financial districts of one the world's most exciting cities.

Regent's College is home to the following internationally renowned institutions.

European Business School London

ebs London

The language of business

BA (Hons) International Business

Choice of six business majors including: Law, Finance, Economics and Management

Combined with one or two languages:

Choose a language from French, German, Spanish, Italian, Russian, Japanese or Mandarin Chinese

Study abroad and work placements within blue chip organisations

RBS London

rbs REGENTS BUSINESS SCHOOL LONDON

Global business class

BA (Hons) degrees:

- International Business
- International Marketing
- International Finance &
- Accounting
- International Business with
- Design Management

A range of undergraduate business degrees and masters following an innovative British curriculum.

Regent's College, Inner Circle, Regent's Park London NW1 4NS, UK

Contact any school on: t: +44(0)20 7487 7505 **f:** +44(0)20 7487 7425 **e:** exrel@regents.ac.uk **w:** www.regents.ac.uk

British American College London

British American College London

Best of both worlds

American BA Degrees in:

- Management
- Media Communications
- International Relations
- Social Science
- Psychology

American Degrees offered in partnership with Webster University.

Part 1

The Independent Sector

1.1

What is an Independent School?

Independent schools educate about 8 per cent of the whole school population. Under the Education Act 1996 all independent schools must be registered with the Department for Education and Skills (DfES) and must meet certain regulations set by the DfES (in Wales the Welsh Office Education Department – WOED). However, independent schools are largely self-governing and are not required to comply with all legislation covering schools maintained by the State.

There is sometimes confusion over the terms used to describe independent schools. 'Public schools' generally refers to old-established schools in membership of the Headmasters' and Headmistresses' Conference (HMC). Because many of these schools date back to the days when education was a luxury, received chiefly through private tutors, the term 'public school' indicated a school which the public could attend. Most schools are now described as independent. A 'private school' simply means a school which charges fees.

How are independent schools funded?

Independent schools are usually funded by fees charged to parents. Some have generous endowments that enable them to keep fees at a lower level than might otherwise be possible. Most independent schools are run as charitable trusts under a Board of Governors. Schools with charitable status are effectively non-profit-making concerns; surplus funds are allocated at the discretion of the Governors. Often they are invested in new facilities or in scholarships or bursaries. A few schools are still privately owned.

Who is responsible for the management of an independent school?

The Board of Governors is the policy-making body for the school. It is responsible for the appointment of the Head, allocation of finances and major decisions affecting the school and its development. Governors give their time voluntarily. Often they can contribute professional expertise in education, business, finance, marketing or other areas relevant to the management of the school. The Board often includes a number of parent-governors who have children at the school.

Day-to-day responsibility for the running of the school is delegated to the Head, who is accountable to the Board of Governors and who is supported by one or more Deputy Heads. Other key figures include the Bursar, who is responsible for the school's financial management, the Director of Studies, who manages the curriculum, timetable, examinations and other academic matters, and the Registrar, who is responsible for admissions and arrangements for parents to visit the school. Many schools also have a Development Director, who is responsible for marketing and presentation.

Academic staff in independent schools are not legally required to hold teaching qualifications, but schools almost always insist on a first degree in a subject which normally forms a part of the secondary school curriculum and a Postgraduate Certificate in Education (PGCE). All schools look for enthusiastic and committed staff with flair and ability. Salary scales at independent schools tend to reflect the wide range of commitment expected of staff and are often more generous than those in the maintained sector, enabling schools to attract higher-calibre teachers. Further information on teaching in the independent sector can be found on the Gabbitas website at www.gabbitas.co.uk.

Do independent schools have to follow the National Curriculum?

Although not bound to follow the National Curriculum, most independent schools choose to do so. Almost all prepare pupils for GCSE and A level examinations (or in Scotland, for Scottish National Qualifications). An increasing number also prepare students for the International Baccalaureate Diploma. There is no requirement for independent schools to set pupils the National Tests used in the maintained sector. In practice, most schools have regular assessments throughout the year and set formal, internal exams two or three times a year, the results of which are included in the end-of-term report.

Who inspects independent schools?

While the performance of maintained schools is monitored by the Office for Standards in Education (OFSTED), most independent schools in England and Wales are inspected by the Independent Schools Inspectorate (ISI), which was established in April 2000 and works closely with OFSTED and the DfES.

The ISI is responsible for the inspection of independent schools which are members of the school associations that form the Independent Schools Council (ISC). These are: the Headmasters' and Headmistresses' Conference (HMC); the Girls' Schools Association (GSA), including the Girls' Day School Trust (GDST); the Society of Headmasters and Headmistresses of Independent Schools (SHMIS); the Incorporated Association of Preparatory Schools (IAPS); and the Independent Schools Association (ISA).

A satisfactory ISI report is a requirement for any school wishing to join one of the above associations and for its continued accreditation as a member, and from September 2003 the ISI became a body approved for the purpose of inspection.

Inspection of ISC schools in Scotland and Northern Ireland is the responsibility of the appropriate national bodies.

How often are schools inspected, and what does an inspection cover?

ISC schools are normally inspected by the ISI every six years. The aims, as published by the ISI, are to improve the quality of education provided, to raise levels of achievement by pupils and to confirm whether or not schools comply with the registration standards set by the DfES.

ISI inspections provide a comprehensive assessment of: the quality of education offered by the school, including educational experience provided, pupil's learning and achievement, spiritual, moral, social and cultural development of pupils and quality of teaching; the quality of care and relationships, including pastoral care, welfare, health and safety of pupils, quality of links with parents and the community and quality of boarding education; and the effectiveness of governance and management. Inspections usually last three or four days.

The views of parents are also assessed using a confidential questionnaire. The school receives only a statistical summary. Inspectors investigate concerns which are significant and, if they feel it appropriate to do so, make recommendations in their final report. However, they do not enter into individual correspondence with parents.

Inspection of boarding provision

ISI works in partnership with the Commission for Social Care Inspection (CSCI) for the inspection of National Boarding Standards. ISI inspections always include consideration for the impact of boarding on pupils' educational development. However, detailed inspections of boarding provision is carried out by CSCI inspectors. Teams include a CSCI lead inspector and one or more experienced and specially trained senior staff from boarding schools. Where possible ISI and CSCI inspections are conducted together. Each team will produce its own report, which is sent to all parents.

Who are the inspectors?

Inspection teams are led by a Reporting Inspector, who must be an OFSTED Registered Inspector, a recently retired Her Majesty's Inspector (HMI), a recently retired independent school Head or a highly experienced serving independent school Head. Other members of the team must also fulfil one of the above criteria or be a senior independent school teacher. All ISI inspectors must have satisfactorily completed training courses based on OFSTED principles.

What is done about the findings of the inspection?
Can parents get a copy?

As stated above, a satisfactory report is required in order for a school to take up membership of one of the associations that form the ISC or to be re-accredited for continued membership, and the ISI therefore also advises the relevant association accordingly. All parents of children at the school receive a free summary of the inspection findings and may obtain the full report free of charge on request. Reports can also be found on the ISI website at www.isinspect.org.uk.

Schools must submit a plan to their Association to remedy any deficiencies highlighted by the inspectors. The association reviews the inspection findings and the proposed action plan and may wish to arrange a further visit to the school to assess progress or offer guidance. The association may also require a follow-up inspection before membership can be confirmed or renewed.

ISI also advises the DfES whether the school meets statutory requirements, and the DfES will ask the school to submit an action plan to address any shortcomings. In cases where inspectors report that a school is failing to provide an acceptable standard of education or where the safety and welfare of pupils is in question, the DfES may ask HMI to visit the school and to monitor the situation until the concerns are resolved.

Whom do I contact if I have a complaint about my child's school?

In the first instance complaints should be referred to the Head. Parents who feel thereafter that their concerns have still not been adequately addressed can refer the matter to the Board of Governors. The ISI inspection system also allows parents to express concerns in confidence to the inspection team. If an inspection is due within the next two terms, complaints about the quality of education or safety and welfare of pupils can be addressed in writing to Durell Barns, Head of Communications, Independent Schools Inspectorate, CAP House, 9–12 Long Lane, London EC1A 9HA, e-mail: durrell@ isinspect.org.uk. At other times, concerns may be sent to Margaret Pattinson, Deputy Registrar of Schools, DfES, Mowden Hall, Staindrop Road, Darlington DL3 9BG (tel: 01325 392172; e-mail: margaret.pattinson@dfes.gov.uk). All such correspondence is treated in the strictest confidence.

Who inspects independent schools which are not members of one of the ISC constituent associations?

These schools are inspected by OFSTED at least every six years. Findings are published in a report which is available to the school, parents and wider community. Schools are given copies for distribution. Reports are also available via the OFSTED website at www.ofsted.gov.uk. The DfES may ask OFSTED to revisit a school within the six year period to review progress on any action points drawn up following the first inspection in areas where regulatory requirements had not been met. Parents' views, which are treated in confidence, also form part of the inspection. Reports refer only to the view of parents generally.

New schools must comply with the regulations before they are allowed to open. Information on the registration of new schools is available on the DfES website at www.dfes.gov.uk.

Accreditation and inspection of independent colleges

A number of independent colleges are accredited by the British Accreditation Council (BAC) (see below). Some independent Sixth Form and tutorial colleges are also in membership of the Council for Independent Further Education (CIFE) (see below). All colleges taking five or more students below the age of 16 are inspected by OFSTED on behalf of the DfES.

The British Accreditation Council (BAC)

The BAC is the main inspection and accreditation body for independent colleges accepting pupils over the age of 16. Inspections cover: premises and health and safety; administration and staffing; quality management; student welfare; and teaching and learning: delivery and resources. Accredited colleges are re-inspected every five years, with an interim visit during the intervening period. Accreditation may be refused or withdrawn if any aspect of the college does not meet the required standards for accreditation. For further information visit the website at www.the-bac.org.

Council for Independent Further Education (CIFE)

There are 21 independent Sixth Form and tutorial colleges in membership of CIFE. Member colleges offer one- and two-year A level and GCSE courses, retake courses, revision courses and also one-year foundation courses for students who wish to enter a UK university but have been educated outside the British system. At present, one college offers the International Baccalaureate programme. CIFE members are required to hold accreditation from either the BAC or ISC.

Council of International Schools (CIS)

Some international schools in the UK are accredited by CIS, a membership organization comprising international schools in all parts of the world. As part of a range of services offered to its member schools, CIS offers regular and associate schools a programme of evaluation and accreditation specially developed for international schools. Those schools that meet the standards for accreditation are given accredited status and in addition to regular monitoring must undergo a full re-evaluation every ten years.

Useful addresses

Independent Schools Inspectorate (ISI)
CAP House
9–12 Long Lane
London EC1A 9HA
Tel: 020 7600 0100
Fax: 020 7776 8849

E-mail: info@isinspect.org.uk
Website: www.isinspect.org.uk

The Chief Executive
The British Accreditation Council
44 Bedford Row
London WC1R 4LL
Tel: 020 7447 2584
Fax: 020 7447 2585
E-mail: info@the-bac.org
Website: www.the-bac.org

Council for Independent Further Education
75 Foxbourne Road
London SW17 8EN
Tel: 020 8767 8666
Fax: 020 8767 9444
E-mail: enquiries@cife.org.uk
Website: www.cife.org.uk

Council of International Schools (UK office)
21A Lavant Street
Petersfield
Hampshire GU32 3EL
Tel: (01730) 263131
Fax: (01730) 268913
E-mail: cois@cois.org
Website: www.cois.org

Office for Standards in Education (OFSTED)
Alexandra House
33 Kingsway
London WC2B 6SE
Tel: 020 7421 6800
Website: www.ofsted.gov.uk

1.2

The Independent Sector

Why choose independent education?

Variety and choice

The independent sector includes schools of many different styles and philosophies, including both the traditional and the more liberal. Each school has its own ethos and atmosphere. Schools also vary widely in size. Some are based in towns and cities. Most boarding schools have more rural locations. Some are co-educational, others are single-sex, although many boys' schools now have co-educational Sixth Forms.

A school to suit your child

Your child's academic needs are the top priority. Not all independent schools educate highly academic children, but there is always some form of selection. While some schools will only accept pupils able to keep pace with a fast-moving curriculum, there are many others which cater for a wider spectrum of ability and some which specialize in helping those in need of more individual attention in a less academic environment.

Academic success

Good independent schools enable pupils, whatever their academic ability, to achieve their best. Their success in helping children to fulfil their potential is reflected in the exam results both of highly selective schools and of schools with less competitive entry requirements where children may need more individual support and encouragement.

An all-round education

Independent schools encourage pupils to develop their strengths outside as well as inside the classroom, ensuring that special talents, in music, drama, art or sport, are nurtured and providing a range of extra-curricular activities which inspire enthusiasm for a great many wider interests.

Small classes and individual attention

Class size at the lower end of the age range normally averages 15 to 20, GCSE groups about 12 to 18 and A level between 4 and 12, although this varies from one school to another and according to subject. Most independent schools have a staff:pupil ratio which ensures that pupils receive plenty of individual attention in accordance with their needs.

St Teresa's School, Surrey p. 372

Pastoral care

Independent schools generally place great emphasis on the traditional values of tolerance and consideration for others and on personal development within a secure but disciplined environment. Pupils normally have a personal tutor who, as part of an experienced team, monitors progress and emotional welfare throughout their school career.

Excellent facilities

Many schools offer first-class facilities for teaching, accommodation, sports and all aspects of school life.

Maintaining high standards

Independent schools must meet rigorous inspection criteria. Schools in membership of any of the associations which form the Independent Schools Council must conform to strict accreditation requirements and are inspected every six years by the Independent Schools Inspectorate. Other independent schools in England and Wales are inspected by Her Majesty's Inspectorate for OFSTED (see Section 1.1).

The boarding option

About 15 per cent of all independent school pupils are boarders. Research has shown that boarders enjoy school life and welcome the special opportunities which boarding offers, including long-lasting friendships, self-reliance and immediate access to help with studies and to a full range of facilities and activities.

While traditional full boarding has declined in popularity, interest is growing in more flexible boarding arrangements. Flexi- and weekly boarding are now much more widely available, enabling pupils to spend more time with their families, while still enjoying all the benefits of boarding life. Flexi-boarding generally means an arrangement that enables pupils to board for half the week and attend as day pupils for the remainder. Most schools can also offer a bed on an occasional basis, for example before a school trip or in the event of an emergency at home.

Full boarders normally enjoy busy weekends which offer access to a range of activities. A few schools timetable lessons on Saturday mornings, although this is becoming much less common as weekly boarding becomes more popular. Schools often arrange weekend trips away, for example to centres of cultural or historical interest or for activities such as walking or sailing. Otherwise pupils may be occupied with sports fixtures, musical or theatre performances or favourite hobbies. Most attend chapel on Sundays and have free time in which to study or relax.

Accommodation in boarding schools is often of an exceptionally high standard. Pupils share well-decorated bedrooms for small groups and are encouraged to bring comforts from home such as their own duvet covers, toys and posters. Sixth Form students often have single-study bedrooms in their own accommodation block and are allowed a greater degree of freedom. Houseparents provide constant care and supervision and are there to help with any problems arising. The Housemaster or Housemistress is normally assisted by a qualified Matron and one or two assistants, depending on the number of children in the House.

Prior's Field School, Surrey p. 368

About 700 schools, including single-sex and co-educational schools, offer boarding places. Very few schools are for boarders only. Most also admit a significant number of day pupils. Whether you are looking for a boarding or a day place, it is wise to check the proportions of boarding and day pupils, since these will influence the overall ethos and character of a school. Numbers of boarders at each school are shown in Part Two. An index of boarding provision by county appears in Part Four.

State-maintained and grant-maintained boarding schools

There are 35 state-maintained schools which accept boarding pupils, although day pupils are usually in the majority. UK and EU nationals and children from outside the EU who have the right of residence in the UK can be accepted as boarders. They pay only for the cost of boarding at these schools and are not charged for tuition. This means that fees, which are generally around £2,000 a term, are much lower than those charged by independent boarding schools. For further information see the school profiles beginning on page 257 or contact the Boarding Schools' Association (see page 500).

Types of independent schools

Independent schools in the UK cover all age ranges; some offer education from nursery level through to 18, others are junior or senior only. Most are day schools, but a large number offer both boarding and day places. There is a variety of co-educational and single-sex schools; many of the latter, particularly boys' schools, offer co-education at Sixth Form level.

Age range	Type of establishment
2–7/8	**Nursery or Pre-Preparatory School**
7/8–13	**Preparatory School**
11/13–16/18	**Senior School**
16–18	**Sixth Form**

Nursery and pre-preparatory schools

Nursery education refers to schools for pupils under the age of 5, pre-preparatory education for pupils aged 5–7/8. Many preparatory schools have their own nursery and pre-prep departments.

Pupils under the age of 5 are rarely required to meet more than the very basic practical requirements for entry, although the Head will wish to meet the child in advance. Some schools also set relatively simple tests. Most schools offer entry at the beginning of each term.

The youngest children attend either mornings or afternoons only, before progressing to a full day. Emphasis is given to the development of academic, social, language and aesthetic skills through play, music, drama and handicrafts. Children may cover basic letter and number work, handwriting and spelling. Approaches vary, from traditional teaching styles to more modern methods. Montessori schools teach according to a series of principles which centre on observation of the individual needs of each child and provision of appropriate stimuli and tasks accordingly.

Francis Holland School, London p. 327

Preparatory schools

Many prep schools accept pupils from the age of 3 upwards. Entry is usually dependent upon an interview with the Head and a satisfactory report from the previous school. Some schools also set verbal or written entrance tests in English and Mathematics, although pupils entering the preparatory department of a pre-preparatory school which they already attend may be exempted from such tests. It may be difficult to join a school for the final one or two years of preparatory education when pupils are approaching Common Entrance and other entrance examinations. Schools which prepare pupils primarily for Common Entrance may test older entrants more rigorously to ensure that they have the capacity to pass at 11, 12 or 13.

When single-sex education was more common, it was usual for girls to remain at their prep school until the age of 11 and for boys to remain until 13. However, with the growth of co-education the options are now more flexible.

Most preparatory schools are preparing pupils for the Common Entrance examination, taken at 11+, 12+ or 13+ for entry to senior boarding or day schools, although some schools, particularly city day schools, set their own entrance examinations. Some parts of the country retain the old examinations for entry to local grammar schools, which require no formal preparation. The destination of school leavers and the main

Dean Close Preparatory School, Gloucestershire p. 282

academic thrust of the school may well be influenced by available provision at senior level. The Head of your child's school will want to know which senior school you have chosen when he or she reaches the last two years of prep school. Further information about Common Entrance is given on page 41.

Pupils are normally taught by class teachers until the age of about 8. After this they may be grouped according to ability. By the age of 9 or 10 there is increasing emphasis on subject teaching by specialists and close attention to the requirements of the National Curriculum, which may be complemented by other elements such as current affairs and topical studies, group projects and field trips.

Formal assessments of academic progress and achievements as well as performance in sports and other activities are made regularly. Examinations are normally held twice a year or at the end of each term. Grades are entered in the termly report for parents.

Senior schools

Senior schools generally admit pupils from 11 to 18, although some boys' schools still maintain the traditional age of entry at 13. Schools with their own preparatory department may offer a straightforward transfer into the senior school, but most demand successful completion of entrance tests. Some schools set their own entrance tests in English, Mathematics and a general paper. Many use the Common Entrance examination.

Many senior schools also offer a range of scholarships for pupils demonstrating exceptional talent and potential in academic studies, music or art. Examinations are normally held in February and March for entry in September.

Bromsgrove School, Worcestershire p. 290

St Margaret's School, London p. 341

Changing schools at 15 or 17 is not generally recommended because of the likely disruption to GCSE or A level studies, particularly if the move means a change to a different examination syllabus. If a move has to be made after age 13, it may be best to wait until after GCSEs or their equivalent have been completed.

Changing schools at 16 is quite common. Entry to the Sixth Form of most schools is dependent upon interview, together with specified results at GCSE, which will vary from one school to another. Some schools also offer scholarships at this level. Entry requirements for independent Sixth Form colleges tend to be more flexible than in schools.

Independent schools in England and Wales are not required to teach the National Curriculum or to use the National Tests, which are compulsory for state-maintained schools. However, since most are preparing students for public examinations, they generally follow the National Curriculum, complementing it with additional options or areas of study as desired. Independent schools in Scotland are free to form their own curriculum policy, but, like maintained schools in Scotland, they are normally preparing pupils for Standard and Higher examinations.

Almost all senior schools in England and Wales are preparing pupils for the General Certificate of Secondary Education (GCSEs), taken at 16, the Advanced Subsidiary (AS) and Advanced GCE (A2). In Scotland pupils are prepared for the Scottish National Qualifications.

Pupils at the lower end of the age range are often taught in sets, a method which groups children for each subject according to their ability in that subject. Streaming, which groups children according to ability on a cross-curricular basis, is used in a smaller number of schools.

The two-year GCSE course begins at 14. Most pupils take eight or nine subjects. In some cases very able children may take cer-

Kingswood School, Bath p. 398

tain GCSE examinations after one year rather than two. In Scotland pupils normally take seven to eight Standard Grade subjects.

Assessments or examinations in each subject may take place each term. Many schools operate a tutorial system under which a House tutor is assigned to each pupil to monitor social and personal development as well as academic progress. Parents receive a full report at the end of each term. In some schools, mock examinations (in preparation for GCSE, AS/A2 or Scottish equivalents) are held in the spring preceding the real examinations. These are marked internally by the school and give an indication of likely performance in the summer.

Most Sixth Form students study a combination of up to four AS levels in the first year, which are normally reduced to three subjects in the final year (A2). Some schools also offer Vocational A levels. For further details see page 44.

A few schools offer the International Baccalaureate (IB), a demanding two-year course which includes six subject groups that comprise both arts and sciences. The IB is accepted as an alternative to A levels by all British universities and as a means of entry to many universities overseas.

Some schools also run one-year courses for students who do not wish to take a full Sixth Form examination course but may wish to take a general course which includes the opportunity to take additional GCSEs, supplemented by vocational options.

Boarding schools in Scotland usually follow the English examination system, though many also offer Scottish qualifications. Higher examinations form the basis for entry to Higher Education and are offered in a wide range of subjects. Some schools also offer vocational programmes. See page 43 for details.

Pupils at Sixth Form level are encouraged to develop a more independent approach to their studies, to learn how to determine priorities and manage their time wisely. As well as timetabled lessons they normally have periods set aside for private study.

All-round education

Aside from academic studies, independent schools place great emphasis on wider activities. Many excel in areas such as sport, where pupils can develop their talents through fixtures against other schools as well as county or national school championships. Most schools recognize, however, that not all pupils enjoy team games. Many offer more individual sports, including, for example, squash, horse-riding, sailing and golf. Music, art and drama are also important aspects of the curriculum and extra-curricular activities. Many schools offer individual music lessons on a range of instruments and encourage students to play in the school orchestra or other music groups or to sing in the choir. Drama is often taught to a very high standard, with performances staged for public festivals as well as in school. Many schools offer preparation for examinations set by the Associated Board of the Royal Schools of Music and the London Academy of Music and Dramatic Art (LAMDA) and there may be regular trips to galleries, concerts, the theatre or the ballet.

Merchiston Castle School, Edinburgh p. 410

Independent Sixth Form colleges

Many students remain in the same school for A level studies, which offers the benefits of continuity and familiarity at a crucial stage of education. Others choose to move to a different school or college, for example if their preferred combination of subjects is not available or if a different type of environment is sought. Independent Sixth Form (tutorial) colleges offer an alternative option for students who are seeking a different style of education, for whom entry to a school Sixth Form is not appropriate or in situations where a mid-course transfer to an alternative mainstream school is not possible. Most colleges offer resit and short revision courses as well as full-time one-year and two-year GCSE and AS/A2 courses. Tuition is in small groups, with special emphasis given to exam technique and study skills. Attendance at lessons and coverage of academic work are strictly monitored, although the overall atmosphere within a college is usually less formal than that in schools.

Cambridge Centre for Sixth Form Studies, Cambridgeshire p. 272

Most independent colleges are located in major cities, including London, Oxford, Cambridge, Birmingham and Manchester. Most are day colleges but some offer accommodation in their own halls of residence or with local families. Some colleges provide a range of sports and extra-curricular activities, but few can offer the campus-style environment and full range of on-site facilities and activities offered by some schools.

For students who wish to pursue a more vocational route there is a variety of independent further education colleges. These tend to be much smaller than state-maintained further education colleges and specialize in specific areas such as Business, Secretarial Training, Computing or Beauty Therapy.

Pastoral care and discipline

Many independent schools, whether boarding or day, operate a House system, which divides pupils into smaller communities to ensure a good staff:pupil ratio for pastoral care. Boarders are often accommodated in small groups with resident House staff. The Housemaster or Housemistress is in charge of pastoral care and will also go through the school report with each child at the end of term. House staff monitor overall progress, keep the Head informed about each child and, in boarding schools, may be the first point of contact for parents. Many schools also allocate each pupil a personal tutor, who assists with educational guidance, keeps progress and welfare under constant review and can deal with issues arising on a day-to-day basis. The Children Act also places a legal obligation on schools to provide a statement of the policy and system of care in place for pupils. All schools are required to have a published policy on bullying.

Most schools keep rules simple, encouraging self-discipline and common sense in their pupils and giving praise for good behaviour. Sometimes children may contribute to a

House points system, being awarded points for good work, thoughtful behaviour and for showing initiative or making a particular effort. Points might be deducted for bad behaviour. Other sanctions imposed might include limitations on leaving school premises or detention. A breach of school rules with regard to smoking or alcohol may mean suspension. Breaches involving illegal drugs may mean immediate permanent exclusion. Corporal punishment is illegal in all schools.

Religion

Spiritual growth is an important aspect of life in most independent schools, whatever their affiliation. The range includes Church of England, Roman Catholic, Quaker, Methodist, Jewish and others. Most adopt an inter-denominational approach and are happy to accept children of other faiths, but parents should check with individual schools the extent to which their child, if of a faith other than the majority of pupils, would be expected to participate in school worship. An index of schools by religious affiliation starts on page 465.

Contact with parents

Every child receives a termly report which is sent home to parents. Schools also hold parents' evenings at regular intervals to allow parents to discuss with teaching and pastoral staff any issues of concern and to be fully briefed on their child's progress. The school report will also contain results of any internal exams held during the term. Parents are often invited to attend school sporting, musical or theatrical events, whether or not their child is taking part, and sometimes to help with school projects such as fundraising activities.

Educational guidance and careers assessment

The value of good educational guidance cannot be overestimated, particularly in view of the complexity and variety of options now available to school leavers and the importance of making the right choice. Some schools have a well-stocked, permanently staffed careers department and a full programme of careers guidance which includes formal assessment, talks from visiting speakers and work experience opportunities. Others may have more limited resources. For parents seeking specialist guidance from an independent source, Gabbitas offers extensive one-to-one careers assessment and advice for students aged 15+.

Special educational needs

Parents of children in need of extensive individual attention, usually those with specific learning difficulties such as dyslexia, will find that there is a large number of mainstream independent schools which offer facilities and tuition in varying degrees. Some schools may bring in a specialist teacher to assist pupils at set times during the week. Some may have specialist teachers permanently on the staff. Others may run a specially staffed department or unit. Parents interested in schools which offer provision in some form will find a number of these profiled in Part Three. More detailed information is available from the Dyslexia Institute, the British Dyslexia Association and CReSTeD (see Part Four). Many schools also offer English as a Foreign Language (EFL) support to students coming from overseas, although in most cases pupils will be expected to have a certain level of English on arrival. A list of schools offering EFL support appears in Part Four. More detailed information on special needs provision and special schools may be found in a separate Gabbitas publication, *Schools for Special Needs – A Complete Guide*, available in bookshops or direct from Gabbitas. To search for special schools online, visit www.gabbitas.co.uk.

Extra-curricular activities

Many schools offer an impressive range of options, from art appreciation to abseiling, from fencing to fishing, often at very high standards. Most schools have a range of musical activities – orchestras, choir, madrigal groups, wind ensembles, to name but a few – and offer wide-ranging opportunities for individual music tuition. Most sports form part of extra-curricular activities as well as time-tabled lessons. Other activities might include chess, badminton, canoeing, Duke of Edinburgh's Award, horse-riding, Brownies and Scout groups, ballet, cookery, gardening, trampolining, rowing, golf, billiards, furniture restoration, stamps, sailing, carpentry, model-making, DT, pottery, drama, French clubs, community service and outward bound activities. Individual schools should be happy to supply parents with a list of their activities.

Michael Hall, East Sussex p. 375

School staff – who's who?

The Board of Governors

The Board of Governors is the planning and policy-making body which controls the administration and finance of the school. Some may also be parents of children at the school. The Governors are responsible for the appointment of the Head and for all major decisions affecting the school. Governors give their time voluntarily. Many are individuals with expertise in their professional lives, for example in law or accountancy, who can contribute their knowledge for the benefit of the school.

Head

Accountable to the Governors for the safety and welfare of pupils and the competence of staff, the Head is responsible for all aspects of the day-to-day management of the school, including appointment of staff, pupil admission policy and pupil recruitment, staffing and administrative structure, curriculum content and management. As figureheads for their schools, many Heads also regard the marketing of their school as a key part of their role, although some schools now employ a Development Director specifically for the purpose. Most Heads also include several hours' teaching in the week, which helps them to keep in touch and get to know pupils individually.

Bursar

The Bursar, in conjunction with the Governors, is responsible for financial matters within the school. The Bursar also takes charge of maintenance of the grounds, premises and buildings as well as catering arrangements.

Director of Studies

Many schools have a Director of Studies, who is responsible for day-to-day curriculum matters and timetabling and for ensuring that staff are kept informed of new developments.

Registrar/Admissions Secretary

The Registrar is responsible for the admission of pupils and making arrangements for parents to visit the school and meet the Head. He or she also takes care of the practical aspects of registration and joining.

Housemaster/Housemistress

The Housemaster or Housemistress takes care of the welfare and overall progress of children in the House and is normally the first point of contact for parents. He or she will keep the Head informed of each child's progress and may often be the first to hear of any problems. Serious issues are always referred to the Head.

Subject teachers

Subject teachers are responsible for the academic progress of pupils and will produce a termly report for those taking their subject. Open evenings offer parents the opportunity to discuss any matters of concern with subject teachers.

Chaplain

The Chaplain has a special role within school. Independent of academic or disciplinary considerations, the Chaplain is responsible for the spiritual development of pupils and can often provide a sympathetic ear to children who seek guidance on issues of concern.

Matron

The Matron looks after the practical aspects of boarding life, supervising and arranging laundry. Separate Houses normally have their own Matron. She often knows children individually and can provide sympathy and support for those who feel homesick or upset.

Sister

The Sister is a qualified nurse responsible for medical arrangements. She looks after pupils who may be admitted into the sanatorium with minor ailments and may require a few days in bed. Within a boarding school, serious medical matters are always referred to the school doctor and where necessary children will be taken to hospital.

Students

Independent schools encourage their pupils to take on positions of responsibility as part of school life. Senior pupils who show good sense and have contributed to the school by their achievements in academic work, musical or sporting activities for example, may be granted suitable senior positions in recognition of their efforts. Hence an excellent sportsman may be made Games Captain or an outstanding chorister Head of Choir. Pupils with an excellent academic record or who deserve merit for other contributions may be given the post of Head Boy or Girl. Prefects have responsibility for some of the daily routines in school and are encouraged to set a good example to younger pupils.

What will it cost?

Fees vary widely, but as a general guide, in 2006/2007 parents can expect to pay annual fees of between £3,000 and £10,000 at a day preparatory school or £11,000 to £17,000 for boarding. At senior level fees range from about £6,500 to £15,000 at day schools, or £17,000 to £22,000+ for a boarding place. Fees at girls' schools tend to be marginally lower than those at boys' and co-educational schools.

Fees in independent Sixth Form colleges are usually charged per subject, with accommodation charged separately. The overall costs of tuition and accommodation for a student studying three subjects at A level are broadly in line with those charged at a senior boarding school.

Parents are normally asked to pay fees in three termly instalments, one at the start of each term, although some schools may offer a choice of payment methods. If you wish to move your child to another school, the present school will normally require a full term's notice in writing. Otherwise you may find that you are charged an additional term's fees in lieu.

Many schools also encourage parents to take out insurance against the risk of their child not being able to attend school, for example in the event of illness.

Parents may be asked to meet additional costs during the school year for school lunches, school trips, sports kit, music lessons and similar items, so it is important to check what is and what is not included in the basic termly fee and to take account of other essentials when estimating the overall costs. Boarders will also require additional items such as bedlinen and weekend wear.

If you live overseas, bear in mind that there will be other costs associated with a boarding education in the UK. These include the costs of guardianship, discussed in Part 1.4, travel and any specialist dental treatment, eye tests or spectacles which your child may need while he or she is in the UK. Your child will also need a regular supply of pocket money. Schools discourage pupils from carrying large amounts of cash, but your child will probably want to buy music or clothes as well as small treats.

Scholarships and bursaries

If your child is exceptionally talented in a specific area, there may well be scholarship opportunities which could reduce the fees by as much as 50 per cent or possibly more. If financial hardship is an issue, bursaries may be available to help top up the shortfall. The decision to grant a bursary will be taken according to individual circumstances.

Further information about planning for school fees begins on page 33. Information on scholarship and bursary opportunities begins on page 37 and a full list of schools offering scholarships and bursaries appears in Part Four (pp. 419–446).

1.3
Choosing your School

'Which is the best school?'

There is no one school which can provide the best possible education for every child. Begin by working out your child's needs, then look for schools which meet these requirements. You will undoubtedly hear differing views about individual schools but remember that you are the best judge of your own child's needs. The question to ask is 'Which school will suit my child best?'

Avoid drawing up your shortlist on the basis of published league tables. These are an unreliable guide to the suitability of schools for your child and can be misleading. Finding the right school requires a much wider approach.

When to start

For entry to preparatory school at 7 or 8, you should be thinking about your choice once your child reaches the age of about 4. This allows you to be clearer about his or her academic potential, while allowing plenty of time for your research. For entry to senior schools, most parents start to look at the options two to three years ahead.

If you are thinking about a change of school at 16, remember that your child will be expected to sit an entrance exam. These often take place in October or November for entry the following September, with the offer of a place normally conditional upon GCSE results. It is therefore important to begin your search during Year 10, ie, the first year of your child's GCSE course.

Similarly, for entry to schools in Year 10 there is normally some form of entrance exam during the preceding year, so it is wise to allow plenty of time beforehand to consider the options.

What type of school will be appropriate?

- **Single sex or co-educational:** This is really a matter of personal preference; some argue that single-sex education enables pupils to achieve at a higher level without the distraction of the opposite sex. Others believe that co-education offers a more natural environment. An index of single-sex schools appears in Part Four.

- **Day or boarding:** Boarding does not suit all children, but for those who enjoy it there are many benefits. For some children it may be a necessity. Ensure that your knowledge is up to date: most boarding schools today offer flexi-boarding or weekly boarding options which enable pupils to spend more time with their families. Some schools offer 'taster' days and weekends which enable prospective pupils to sample boarding life in advance.
- **Location:** Remember to consider the likely travelling time, particularly by car, during the morning and evening rush hours. Travel to and from school will also be required for parents' evenings, sports days and other school events. If public transport is to be used, how easy is the journey? Schools in more rural areas often offer a minibus service. Many parents of boarders, who today generally have many opportunities to go home during the term, choose schools within about two hours' drive.
- **Religious affiliation:** Would you prefer a school of a particular denomination or are you willing to include others in your choice?

Your child's needs

Academic needs are the first priority. Be realistic about your child's potential and avoid trying to gain a place at a very academic school unless you are confident of your child's ability to cope. Consider also any other interests your child may have, for example in music or sport, as well as your child's overall personality. Some children thrive in a highly active environment offering a multitude of stimuli and the company of other lively and confident youngsters. Others may benefit from being a part of a smaller school community.

Finding out

The Head of your child's present school can probably recommend suitable options, but you may also find it helpful to obtain an independent viewpoint from an educational consultant. Ask those schools which interest you to send you a prospectus. Most schools also have a website, which often has more recent news of activities and developments. Website addresses appear in Part Three of this Guide, or you can access sites for all these schools at www.gabbitas.co.uk. If you would like independent recommendations in line with your needs, contact Gabbitas.

Visiting schools

A personal visit is the only way to find out whether or not you like a particular school and will allow you to meet staff and pupils and experience the overall atmosphere. If possible, try to visit more than one school, so that you have a means of comparison. You may be invited to an Open Day, but the best time to visit is on a normal day during term time. That way you can see the day-to-day routine in place and the children at their usual activities. In most cases you will meet the Head, who will want to interview your child, following which a member of staff or senior pupil may give you a tour of the school.

In a boarding school you should also be able to meet the Housemaster or House-mistress. It is important that you feel comfortable with the Head and other staff who will be responsible for your child. Do they show a genuine interest in your child? Do they make you feel welcome?

There are a number of areas you may wish to ask about during your visit.

Academic policy and destination of leavers

- At prep level, is the school's policy appropriate for your longer-term plans? Some schools may be preparing pupils primarily for entry to senior independent schools; others may have significant numbers whose parents are interested in good local state schools. Scholarship examinations also vary in syllabus from one school to another. Since some prep schools prepare pupils for a limited range of senior schools, you may wish to find out which ones are covered.
- At secondary level, what is the school's academic pace and focus?
- Ask about subjects in which your child has a particular interest or strength. How are these taught? Are pupils encouraged to develop their knowledge and interest through special projects, trips or events?
- How many children take GCSEs and AS/A2 levels, or their equivalents?
- How many GCSE and AS/A2 level subjects are offered?
- How big is the Sixth Form?
- How many pupils stay on into the Sixth Form? If a large proportion of pupils leave after GCSE, why is this and where do they go?
- Is there any evident bias in the numbers taking certain subjects?
- What other courses are offered in the Sixth Form?
- Ask about the destinations of Sixth Form leavers. What proportion go on to university or other forms of higher education or training? In which subject areas?

Exam results

- Exam results, if you can compare them with results in previous years, are a useful measure of the school's academic performance and any trends, but take care when interpreting the figures. A 100 per cent pass rate seems impressive, but how many pupils took the exam? Some schools pre-select candidates, which inevitably improves the pass rate statistics.

Testing and assessment

- What systems are in place to monitor performance?
- How much communication is there between staff and parents?

Educational and careers guidance

- What guidance is offered to pupils choosing subjects for examination study, higher education and career options? At what stage does this begin? How is it developed as pupils progress through school?
- What experience do advisers have?
- What facilities are available? Is there a dedicated careers unit with specialist staff?
- Are there any work experience programmes in place?

Special needs

- If your child has special educational needs, exactly how will the school provide for these? What experience do staff have of meeting these needs? The same applies if your child has any special medical or dietary requirements.

Pastoral care and boarders

- How is the welfare of students monitored? How will you be kept in touch?
- If your child is to be a day pupil in a boarding school, you may wish to know whether day pupils can join in with evening and weekend activities at school.
- Many working parents may find before- and after-school care facilities attractive. Some schools, particularly city day schools, offer this service.
- Parents of boarders must have complete confidence in those who will be responsible for their child's welfare. Ask about the school's policy for the care and supervision of boarders.
- What is the routine at weekends? May pupils leave the premises?
- Who is on duty in the evenings, at night and at weekends? Are they suitably qualified and experienced?
- What happens in the event of an emergency? What is the school's responsibility?
- Do boarders receive regular medical and dental checks?
- Make sure that you are shown the boarding accommodation. Is it clean, warm and welcoming? Is there plenty of space for your child's clothes and personal effects? Is there a secure area for valuables?
- What are boarders permitted to bring to school? Some schools allow small pets.

Teaching staff

- Are staff appropriately qualified? Are they specialists in the subjects they teach?
- How many are full-time?
- Is there a high staff turnover? If so, why?
- How is teaching organized?

Extra-curricular activities

- If your child has a particular interest or strength, will the school encourage and develop it?

Discipline

- Be sure that you agree with the school's policies. How do they deal with incidents involving smoking, alcohol or drugs?
- Will you be informed of any disciplinary matter which involves your child?

Seeing the school

- What do your first impressions tell you? Are staff and pupils polite and welcoming? Is the Reception area easy to find? Are the buildings and grounds neat and well kept?
- Is there a sense of order and purpose? What are the noise levels like?
- Do the noticeboards suggest an active, enthusiastic school?
- How do pupils respond to you? Are they articulate and confident? How do they respond to teachers in class?
- How do staff respond to the Head?

Registration and confirmation

Registering your child commits neither you nor the school. Schools normally charge a non-refundable registration fee, which may be anything up to £100 for a senior school. It is wise to have your child registered at more than one school in case no place is offered or available at your first choice. You will need to make up your mind about a year before your child is due to start. Once you have formally accepted a place there is a contract between you and the school. Should you change your mind, your deposit may or may not be refundable, depending upon the terms set by the school. As with any contractual arrangement, ensure that you understand and accept the school's published terms and conditions before going ahead.

The final choice

After your visits, check the schools' performance against your original criteria. Each school will have its own strengths. Which are most important to you? Your child must also be happy with the final choice, but the decision must be yours. If you have difficulty deciding between two schools, the answer is to trust your instincts. The right school is the one which will allow your child to develop his or her full potential in the company of liked and trusted staff and pupils in an environment where he or she feels happy and at home.

1.4
Coming from Overseas

If you live overseas, the best advice is to plan ahead as far as possible and at least a year in advance. This will give you a wider choice of school and allow you time to research all the options properly and make an informed choice. Parents may find it helpful to bear in mind the following aspects.

Level of English

Most independent schools will expect your child to speak some English on arrival, although additional tuition is often available in school to improve fluency and accuracy and to ensure that your child can cope with a normal curriculum.

If your child is to board in the UK but speaks only a little or no English, he or she may benefit from a short period in one of the specialist boarding schools (often called international study centres) which prepare overseas pupils for entry into mainstream boarding schools at secondary level. A list of international study centres is given at the end of this section.

Alternatively, you may wish to arrange for your child to spend the summer at one of the UK's many language schools before joining a boarding school in September. Details of suitable courses can be obtained from reputable consultants such as Gabbitas.

Academic background

If your child has been educated within the British system, it should not be difficult to join a school in the UK, although care should be taken to avoid changing schools while a student is in the middle of GCSE or A level studies. However, if your child has not been following a British curriculum, entry to a mainstream independent school may be less straightforward. The younger your child, the easier it is likely to be for him or her to adapt to a new school environment. Prep schools may accept overseas pupils at any stage up to the final two years, when pupils are prepared for Common Entrance exams and entry may be more difficult. Senior schools, in particular, will normally look for evidence of ability and achievement comparable with pupils educated in the British system and will probably wish to test your child in English, Maths and Science before deciding whether to offer a place. Students wishing to enter the Sixth Form will probably be tested in the subjects they wish to study. Recent reports and transcripts, in translation, should also be made available to schools.

If your child has been following the International Baccalaureate (IB) programme overseas, you will find a number of schools and colleges in the UK, both state and independent, which offer the IB. Details of the IB and the schools and colleges offering it are given on pages 45–58.

Length of stay

If you are planning to live in the UK for a relatively short period, perhaps no more than a year, you may find it more appropriate for your child to attend an international school. These schools specialize in educating children whose stay is limited and who regularly move around the world with their parents. Most are day schools, though some also offer boarding provision. These schools tend to have a broad mix of nationalities and offer a curriculum, normally based either on the British or the American system, sufficiently flexible to allow a smooth transition afterwards into international schools elsewhere in the world. Many also offer the IB, as described above.

If your stay is relatively short and you plan to return home afterwards, you may be able to enter your child in one of the schools in the UK specifically for nationals of other countries who are based in the UK. France, Germany, Sweden, Norway, Greece and Japan are all represented. Your own embassy in London should be able to provide further details.

Location

If you are looking for a boarding school, try not to restrict your search too narrowly. Most schools, including those in the most beautiful and rural parts of the UK, are within easy reach of major transport links and the UK is well served by air, rail and road routes. In addition, most schools will make arrangements to have your child escorted between school and the airport and vice versa.

Visiting schools

Once you have decided on the most suitable type of school, you can obtain information on specific schools. Gabbitas can identify schools likely to meet your requirements, and arrange for you to receive prospectuses. It is essential that you visit schools before making a choice. Try to plan your visits to schools during term time. The school year in the UK begins in September and comprises three terms: early September to mid-December, early January to mid-March and early April to early July. There are also three half-term breaks, normally from two days to a week, at the end of October, in mid- to late February and at the end of May. Gabbitas can arrange a schedule of visits for you to ensure that you make the best use of your time in the UK.

Questions to ask

English language support
What level of English does the school expect? Is additional support available at school? How is this organized? Is there a qualified teacher?

Pupil mix
International schools naturally have pupils of many different nationalities at any one time. However, if you are looking to enter your child into a mainstream independent school, you may wish to find out how many other pupils of your nationality attend the school and what arrangements are made to encourage them to mix with English pupils.

Pastoral care
If your child has special dietary needs or is required to observe specific religious principles, is the school willing and able to cope? Would your child also be expected to take part in the school's normal worship?

If your child speaks little English, it can be very comforting during the early days when homesickness and minor worries arise, or in the event of an emergency, to have a member of staff on hand to whom the child can speak in his or her own language. Bear in mind, however, that fewer schools are likely to have staff who speak non-European languages.

Ask about arrangements for escorting your child to and from school at the beginning and end of term. Some schools have a minibus service to take children to railway stations and airports or will arrange a taxi where appropriate.

Guardianship

Most schools insist that boarding pupils whose parents live overseas have an appointed guardian living near the school who can offer a home for 'exeats' (weekends out of school), half-term breaks and at the beginning and end of term in case flights do not coincide exactly with school dates. A guardian may be a relative or friend appointed by parents, but it should be remembered that the arrangement may need to continue for some years and that guardianship is a substantial commitment.

For parents with no suitable contacts in the UK, schools may be able to assist in making arrangements. Alternatively there are independent organizations, including

Gabbitas, which specialize in the provision of guardianship services. Good guardian families should offer a 'home from home', looking after the interests and welfare of your child as they would their own, providing a separate room and space for study, attending school events and parents' evenings, involving your child in all aspects of family life and encouraging him or her to feel comfortable and relaxed while away from school. Some guardianship organizations are very experienced in selecting suitable families who will offer a safe and happy home to students a long way from their own parents. The range of services offered and fees charged by different providers will vary, but you should certainly look for a service which:

- personally ensures that families are visited in their homes by an experienced member of staff and that all appropriate checks are made;
- takes a genuine interest in your child's educational and social welfare and progress;
- keeps in touch with you, your child, the school and the guardian family to ensure that all is running smoothly;
- provides, as required, administrative support and assistance with visa and travel requirements, medical and dental checks and insurance, and any other matters such as the purchase of school uniform, sports kit and casual clothes.

Parents seeking a guardianship provider may like to contact AEGIS (the Association for the Education and Guardianship of International Students), of which Gabbitas is a founder member. The purpose of AEGIS is to promote best and legal practice in all areas of guardianship and to safeguard the welfare and happiness of overseas children attending educational institutions in the UK. AEGIS aims to provide accreditation for all reputable guardianship organizations. Applicants for membership are required to undergo assessment and inspection to ensure that they are adhering to the AEGIS Code of Practice and fulfilling the Membership Criteria before full membership can be granted. For further details of the Gabbitas Guardianship Service, contact Catherine Stoker on +44 (0)20 7734 0161 or visit www.gabbitas.co.uk. For further information about AEGIS, visit the website at www.aegisuk.net.

Preparing your child to come to the UK

Coming to school in a different country is an enriching and exciting experience. You can help your child to settle in more quickly by encouraging him or her to take a positive approach and to try to absorb the traditions and social customs of school and family life in the UK. After the first year, most children begin to feel more confident and comfortable in their surroundings, both at school and with their guardian family. A good guardianship organization will ensure that you and your child know what to expect from life in the UK, and that you are aware of the kind of behaviour and approach which the school and guardian family will expect from your child. They will also be able to advise on aspects such as appropriate clothes to bring for a UK climate, which may be very different from that at home. Similarly, they should be able to advise on visas, UK entry requirements and related matters.

Where to go for help

You may be able to obtain information about schools from official sources in your own country. For detailed guidance and assistance in the UK you may wish to contact an independent educational consultancy such as Gabbitas which can advise you on all aspects of education in the UK and transferring into the British system.

International study centres

For contact details, please refer to the entries in Part Two.

- The International Centre, Ackworth School, West Yorkshire
- Bedford School Study Centre, Bedfordshire
- Diana, Princess of Wales Study Centre, Riddlesworth Hall, Norfolk
- Dover College, International Study Centre, Kent
- International College, Sherborne School, Dorset
- International Study Centre at Kent College, Canterbury, Kent
- King's International Study Centre, The King's School, Ely, Cambridgeshire
- Millfield English Language School, Millfield School, Somerset
- Rossall School International Study Centre, Lancashire
- Sidcot Academic English School, Sidcot School, North Somerset
- Taunton International Study Centre, Somerset

1.5
Finding the Fees

Towry Law Financial Services Limited

How much will it cost?

Your first decision is what fees you are planning to meet. Do you have a specific school or schools in mind and if so what are the fees? Hopefully you have started planning early, which means that you are unlikely to have made a final choice of school. In this case you need to work on the average or typical fees for the type of school. This can range from day preparatory to senior boarding school. If your child was born in the latter part of the year, check that you are planning for the right period, ie don't plan to provide funds a year early, leaving a gap year at the end.

Next, you need to allow for inflation. A school's major cost is teacher and other salaries, which tend to increase in line with earnings rather than prices. Historically, earnings rise faster than prices, so even though inflation is now relatively low, it is certainly not something you can ignore.

The distinctive feature of planning for educational costs

The distinctive nature lies in the fact that you are planning for a 'known commitment'. You know that at the beginning of each term or school year you will have a bill to pay and will need to draw on your investments.

This is where the 'reward–risk' spectrum comes in. At one end, asset-backed investments offer a higher potential reward but also a degree of investment risk or potential volatility. In the longer term, such investments have been the way to achieve real growth and outpace inflation (though the past is not necessarily a guide to future performance). On the other hand, you do not want to rely on such investments if it means encashing them at the worst possible time, just after a stock market setback. Remember, because of the nature of educational planning you probably do not have any choice about when you need funds to pay a bill.

At the other end of the reward–risk spectrum are deposit accounts; just about as safe as safe can be (so long as the institution is safe), but will they even keep up with inflation?

You do not need to plump for either extreme. The answer partly depends on the period over which you are investing. If you are starting soon after birth, asset-backed investment can play a larger role, giving greater potential for real growth. Nearer the time, your holdings can be switched on a phased basis into more secure investment vehicles to lock in any gains and from which you can draw during the schooling period.

An alternative approach is 'mix and match'. A mixture of asset-backed investments and more secure ones will allow you to draw from the former in years when their values are high. In other years, you can draw from the more secure investments.

Existing investments

Your strategy should take into account any existing investments or savings that may be suitable. These may not have been taken out with school fees in mind. For example, you may have started a mortgage endowment some years ago and changed to a repayment mortgage. This would free up the endowment which could be used for school fees.

Tax-efficient investments

You can invest regular contributions or a lump sum into Individual Savings Accounts (ISAs). They are generally a good idea, especially for a higher-rate taxpayer, because the tax benefits should enhance returns. You can use ISAs for cash deposits, equities and also 'corporate bonds'. You will need to check whether 'mini' or 'maxi' ISAs are best for you. There is a limit on the contributions that can be made in each year, but both husband and wife can take out an ISA.

Rather than investing in individual shares, investors nowadays more commonly use 'collective' investments like unit trusts (or Open Ended Investment Companies – OEICs) or investment trusts. Collective funds give access to the benefits of equity investments without the investment risk inherent in investing in one or a small number of individual shares. Collective funds are a low-cost way of spreading risk by investing in a portfolio of shares, with the added advantage of professional fund management.

Investment services are now available that enable you to use your annual ISA allowance to invest in more than one fund with more than one manager. This provides additional diversification of the risk by allowing you to invest with a number of leading fund managers. It also makes a 'mix and match' approach easier. An adviser could put together a portfolio for you that mixes equities and bonds in portions to match your 'risk profile' and the length of time before fees are required, combining equities for the prospect of higher growth and bonds to provide an element of stability. With these investment services it is easy and relatively cheap to make adjustments as you go along, so as you get nearer to the fee paying period you could gradually switch from equities to bonds to lock in gains and increase the predictability of returns.

Any existing ISAs and Personal Equity Plans (PEPs) could, of course, be used as part of your planning. Not everyone is aware that you can transfer existing PEPs from one manager to another if appropriate, so that they will better meet your current objectives.

Other investment options

A range of other investment options is available. For instance, if you will be over 50 when fees (or university expenses) are required, you may be eligible to contribute more to a pension and use the benefits towards the bills (although this will of course reduce the amount available to provide retirement income).

Once you have used your ISA entitlement, you can still invest in the same underlying funds and benefit from the manager's expertise, but without the tax advantages of an ISA.

Besides with-profit bonds, insurance companies offer a number of lump-sum investment options with a range of underlying investments and risk ratings.

Expatriate parents

If you are an expatriate or offshore investor, there are offshore versions of most of the investments described above. Important considerations are your tax position whilst you are offshore, and if you will be returning to the UK during the schooling period, your UK tax position.

Late planning

If you have left it late to start planning, say within five years, you could consider the following:

- Check the school's terms for payment in advance (sometimes called composition fees schemes) as these can be attractive. Ask what happens if, for whatever reason, you switch to another school.
- Consider deposit-based schemes. Tax-efficient investments may play a part (cash ISAs).
- For other deposit accounts, consider internet or postal accounts, as they often offer better rates.
- National Savings, gilts and fixed-interest securities could also be considered.
- Loan schemes may be available whereby you arrange a 'drawdown' facility secured on your house. This assumes you have some 'free equity' (the difference between the value of the house and your mortgage) and is usually set up as a second mortgage. You can then 'drawdown' from the facility as and when you need to pay fees. Hence, you do not start paying interest sooner than necessary, keeping down the total cost. (Think carefully before securing other debts against your home. Your home may be repossessed if you do not keep up repayments on your mortgage.)

- Because of the interest payments, loan schemes are costly, so they should be regarded as a last resort and only after you have reviewed your finances to check that there is no alternative.

The need for protection

For most families, the major resource for educational expenses is the parents' earnings. Death or prolonged illness could destroy a well-laid plan and have a terrible effect on a family's standard of living and a child's education. You should therefore review your existing arrangements (whether from a company scheme or private) and make sure you are sufficiently protected.

University expenses

Although many of the same investment considerations apply, planning needs to cover living expenses plus a small proportion of the fees. There is a system of student loans.

Although university expenses are generally not as high as school fees, they have become more onerous in recent years, a trend that is likely to continue.

'Golden' rules of educational planning

- Plan as early in the child's life as possible.
- Set out what funds you need and when you need them, and plan accordingly.
- Mitigate tax on the investments wherever possible.
- Use capital if available, particularly from grandparents.
- Consult an expert, preferably an independent financial adviser.

This article briefly outlines some of the considerations and investment opportunities and does not make specific or individual recommendations. There is no one answer to suit everyone. The solution depends on a number of considerations and for a strategy tailored to your individual circumstances, seek independent financial advice.

TOWRY LAW FINANCIAL SERVICES LIMITED
Towry Law House,
Western Road,
Bracknell RG12 1TL
Tel: 0845 788 9933 (calls may be recorded)
E-mail: info@towrylaw.com

1.6

Scholarships, Bursaries and Other Awards

In addition to the many financial planning schemes available, assistance with the payment of fees may be obtainable from a variety of other sources.

Scholarships

Many senior schools offer scholarship opportunities. These are awarded, at the discretion of the school, to pupils displaying particular ability or promise, either in academic subjects, as an all-rounder or in specific areas such as music or art. Candidates are normally assessed on the basis of their performance in an examination or audition. Scholarship examinations are normally held in the February or March preceding September entry. Pupils awarded scholarships in, for example, music or art, may be required to sit the Common Entrance examination to ensure that they meet the normal academic requirements of the awarding school.

Scholarships are normally offered upon the usual age of entry to the school. Some schools also offer awards for Sixth Form entry, for example for students who have performed particularly well in the GCSE examinations. These awards may be restricted to pupils already attending the school or may also be open to prospective entrants coming from other schools.

Scholarships vary in value, although full-fee scholarships are now rarely available. Scholarships are awarded as a percentage of the full tuition fee to allow for inflation.

Fewer scholarships are available at preparatory school level. Choristers, however, are a special category. Choir schools generally offer much reduced fees for Choristers, well below the normal day fee. Help may also be available at senior schools, although in practice it is common for Choristers to gain music scholarships at their senior schools. A list of schools belonging to the Choir Schools Association appears on pp. 502–503. Details of schools specializing in the arts, dance and music appear on page 447.

Information about other music awards at independent schools is available from the Music Masters' and Mistresses' Association (MMA) at www.mma-online.org.uk. The site includes a searchable database of music awards offered by individual schools. The

MMA's annual guide to 'Music Awards at Independent Schools' is also available in printed form in music shops and libraries or by mail order from the MMA.

For a general guide to scholarships offered by individual schools, turn to the Scholarships index in Part Four.

Bursaries

Bursaries are intended primarily to ensure that children obtain provision suited to their needs and ability in cases where parents cannot afford the normal fees. They are awarded on the basis of financial hardship, rather than particular ability. All pupils applying for a bursary, however, will be required to show, normally by passing Common Entrance or the school's own entry tests, that they meet academic requirements. The size of the award is entirely at the discretion of the school.

A list of schools that offer bursaries is given in Part Four.

Reserved entrance awards

Some schools reserve awards for children with parents in a specific profession, for example in HM Forces, the clergy or in teaching. These are similar to bursaries in that the child must meet the normal entry requirements of the school, but eligibility for the award will be dependent upon fulfilment of one of the criteria stated above. Normally schools will reserve only a few places on this basis. Once a place for a specific award has been filled, it will not become available again until the pupil currently in receipt leaves the school. Hence the award may be available only once every five years or so.

A list of schools and brief summary of the reserved entrance awards offered by each is given in Part Four. The awards covered include those offered to children with one or both parents working in any of HM Forces, the Foreign Office, the medical profession, teaching, the clergy or as Christian missionaries.

Other awards

Schools may also offer concessions for brothers and sisters or for the children of former pupils.

If you are interested in the possibility of a scholarship or bursary or in other awards which might be available from schools in which you are interested, it is a good idea to advise schools accordingly when you first contact them.

The GDST Scholarship and Bursary Scheme

The GDST (Girls' Day School Trust), which comprises 26 independent girls' schools educating over 19,500 girls, has traditionally aimed to make its schools accessible to bright, motivated girls from families who could not afford a place at a GDST school without financial assistance. It has a Scholarship and Bursary Scheme specifically designed for low-income families. Grants are only awarded at GDST schools.

Most bursaries under the Scheme are awarded to girls from families with a total income of under £13,000, and it is unlikely that a bursary would be awarded in cases where total gross income exceeds £38,000. Bursaries are means-tested and may cover up to full fees. Scholarships, which are not means-tested, are awarded on merit and may cover up to half the fees. Most awards are available either on entry at 11 or for girls entering the Sixth Form. The Scheme is also designed to assist pupils already attending a GDST school whose parents face unexpected financial difficulties which could mean having to remove their daughter from the school and disrupt her education.

Awards are made at the discretion of individual school Heads rather than the Trust and requests for further information should therefore be directed to the Head of the school at which parents wish to apply for a place. A full list of GDST schools appears on page 506.

Other government grants

Assistance with the payment of fees is also offered to personnel employed by the Foreign and Commonwealth Office and by the Ministry of Defence, where a boarding education may be the only feasible option for parents whose professional lives demand frequent moves or postings overseas.

The FCO termly boarding allowance is available to FCO parents on request and is reviewed annually. Parents in need of further information should contact the FCO Personnel Services Department on 020 7238 4357.

Services personnel may seek guidance from the Service Children's Education Advisory Service, which can advise on choosing a boarding school and on the boarding allowance made. In 2006/2007 the boarding allowance is £3,695 per term for junior pupils and £4,872 per term for senior pupils. An allowance is also available for children with special educational needs. Further information may be obtained from Children's Education Advisory Service, Trenchard Lines, Upavon, Pewsey, Wiltshire SN9 6BE; Tel: 01980 618245. You may also find it helpful to visit www.army.mod.uk and www.sceschools.com.

Parents may also find it helpful to consult the list of schools offering reserved entrance awards. Some schools may be able to supplement allowances offered by employers through a reserved entrance award offered to pupils who meet the relevant criteria, eg with a parent in HM Forces.

Grant-giving Trusts

There are various educational and charitable Trusts which exist to provide help with the payment of independent school fees. Usually the criteria restrict eligibility to particular groups, for example orphans, or in cases of sudden and unforeseen financial hardship. In many cases a grant may be given only to enable a child to complete the present stage of education, eg to finish a GCSE or A Level course. Applications are normally considered on an individual basis by an appointed committee. The criteria for eligibility and for the award of a grant will vary according to individual policy. In some cases several Trusts may each contribute an agreed sum towards one individual case in order to make up the fees required. It should be noted that such Trusts receive many more applications for grants than can possibly be issued and competition is fierce. Applications for financial help purely on the grounds that parents would like an independent education for their child but cannot afford it from their own resources will be rejected. Parents are advised to consider carefully before applying for an independent school place and entering a child for the entrance examination if they cannot meet the fees unaided nor demonstrate a genuine need, as defined by the criteria published by the awarding Trusts, for an independent school education. Parents may find it helpful to consult the *Educational Grants Directory*, published by the Directory of Social Change. For further information about charitable funding contact ISC Educational Grants Advisory Service, Joint Educational Trust, 6 Lovat Lane, London EC3R 8DT; Tel: 020 7283 3445.

Local Authority grants

Grants from Local Authorities are sometimes available where a need for a child to board can be demonstrated, for example where the child has special educational needs which cannot be met in a day school environment or where travel on a daily basis is not feasible. Such grants are few in number. Awards for boarding fees at an independent school may not be granted unless it can be shown that there is no boarding place available at one of the state boarding schools, of which there are 35 nationwide.

Awards from Local Authorities are a complex issue. Parents wishing to find out more should contact the Director of Education for the Authority in which they live.

1.7
Examinations and Qualifications in the UK

Common Entrance

The Common Entrance examination forms the basis of entry to most independent senior schools, although some schools set their own entrance exams. Traditionally it is taken by boys at the age of 13 and by girls at the age of 11. However, with the growth of co-education at senior level the divisions have become less sharply defined and the examinations are open to both boys and girls.

The Common Entrance papers are set centrally by the Independent Schools Examinations Board, which comprises members of the Headmasters' and Headmistresses' Conference (HMC), the Girls' Schools Association (GSA) and the Incorporated Association of Preparatory Schools (IAPS). The papers are marked, however, by the individual schools, which have their own marking schemes and set their own entry standards. Common Entrance is not an exam which candidates pass by reaching a national standard.

The content of the Common Entrance papers has undergone regular review and the Independent Schools Examinations Board has adapted syllabuses to bring them into line with National Curriculum requirements.

Candidates are entered for Independent Schools Examinations by their junior or preparatory schools. Parents whose children attend state primary schools should apply to the Independent School Examinations Board direct, ideally four months before the scheduled examination date. Some pupils may need additional coaching for the exam if they are not attending an independent preparatory school. To be eligible, pupils must normally have been offered a place by a senior school subject to their performance in the exam. Pupils applying for scholarships may be required to pass Common Entrance before sitting the scholarship exam. Candidates normally take the exam in their own junior or preparatory school.

At 11+ the Common Entrance exam consists of papers in English, Mathematics and Science, and is designed to be suitable for all pupils, whether they attend an independent or a state school. Most pupils who take the exam at 13+ come from independent preparatory schools. Subjects are English, Mathematics, Science (compulsory); French, History, Geography, Religious Studies, German, Spanish, Latin and Greek (optional).

The examination for 13+ entry takes place in February and June. For entry at 11+ the exam is held in January. For further information on Common Entrance, or copies of past papers, contact: The General Secretary, Independent Schools Examinations Board, Jordan House, Christchurch Road, New Milton, Hampshire BH25 6QJ; Tel: 01425 621111; fax: 01425 620044; E-mail: ce@iseb.co.uk.

General Certificate of Secondary Education (GCSE)

The GCSE forms the principal means of assessing the National Curriculum at the end of compulsory schooling. GCSE courses are generally taught over the two years of Key Stage 4 of the National Curriculum from age 14.

GCSEs are assessed through a combination of coursework and terminal examination. The coursework enables pupils to gain credit from work produced during the two years of the course rather than exclusively on the basis of examination performance.

GCSE results are graded on a scale from A* to G.

Most GCSE examinations have differentiated or tiered papers that are targeted at different ranges of ability within the A*–G grade range. Nearly all large-entry GCSE subjects are examined through a foundation tier covering grades G–C and a higher tier covering grades D–A*.

Most pupils of average ability take eight or nine GCSE subjects, although some may take 10 or 11. Very able pupils may take some GCSE exams after one year. Pupils are asked to choose their subjects at 13. Schools can offer advice on those they think most suitable. GCSE (Short Course) qualifications are also available, which are designed to take only half the study time of full GCSE and are the equivalent of half a GCSE. They are graded on the same scale as a full GCSE but cover fewer topics. The GCSE (Short Course) can be used in various ways: to offer able students additional choices such as a second modern language or to offer a subject which could not otherwise be studied as a full GCSE because of other subject choices. It may also be attractive to students who need extra time in their studies and would be better suited to a two-year course devoted to a GCSE (Short Course) rather than a full GCSE. GCSEs in vocational subjects are available in the following eight subjects: Applied Art and Design; Applied Business; Applied ICT; Applied Science; Engineering; Health and Social Care; Leisure and Tourism; and Manufacturing. More information can be found on the DfES website at www.dfes.gov.uk/qualifications.

GCE A levels and GCE Advanced Subsidiary

Most A levels comprise six units. For each subject, three units form an Advanced Subsidiary level (AS) course and represent the first half of the Advanced GCE (A level) course. The remaining three units (known as A2) represent the final year's study.

Completion of all six units is required for the award of an A level. An A level grade is reached by combining AS and A2 grades. AS and A levels have UCAS (Universities and Colleges Admissions Service) point scores for the purposes of university entry. An AS level receives half the points of an A level.

Students who do not pursue a subject beyond the first year but who successfully complete the first three units will be awarded an AS. However, completion of the three A2 units on their own does not represent a qualification.

There are a few free-standing AS subjects where no corresponding A level is available. AS is designed to provide extra breadth to Sixth Form studies. Students may take four or five AS subjects in the first year of Sixth Form, but they may narrow down to three A2 units in the second year.

AS units focus on material appropriate for the first year of an A level course, and are assessed accordingly. A2 is more demanding and is assessed at full A level standard. Overall assessment is based on examinations and/or coursework and may be made at the end of the course (linear) or at stages during the course (modular). There is a compulsory 20 per cent synoptic assessment for all unitized A levels to demonstrate understanding of the course as a whole and the connections between its different elements.

The AS and A levels are graded on a scale of A to E for passes. U (unclassified) indicates a fail. Restrictions on resitting individual units were dropped from January 2004, and students are therefore able to resit units more than once. When a request is made for certification, the best attempt will count towards an award.

There is also a programme of Key Skills qualifications. The first three, covering Communication, Application of Number and Information Technology, are separate qualifications in their own right and are usually taken alongside other qualifications and groups of qualifications. They are offered at Levels 1 to 4 and the assessment consists of a portfolio of evidence and an external test. Many A level subjects offer opportunities for students to provide evidence for their Key Skills portfolio. Key Skills qualifications also attract UCAS points; for example a Level 3 in all three skills qualifications is worth 60 tariff points, the same value as an A grade AS level.

The Advanced Extension Award was designed to challenge the most able students and was first examined in 2002. It is available in 19 A level subjects with Psychology and Business examined for the first time in 2005. The AEA in Business is accessible to students studying related subjects at both Vocational A level (VCE) and GCE A level.

Vocational education and training

There are 113 awarding bodies. Many of these are sector-based and provide specific qualifications for their particular industry. However, there are also a number of key awarding bodies that provide a wide range of vocational qualifications across sectors and subjects. These include:

- Edexcel (offers BTEC qualifications);
- City & Guilds (includes Pitman qualifications);

- Cambridge International Examinations (CIE qualifications are mainly available outside of the UK and not within the national framework);
- Oxford, Cambridge and RSA Examinations;
- AQA;
- Education Development International (formerly known as LCCIEB).

Many vocational qualifications come within the National Qualifications Framework, falling into one of two broad categories, namely Vocationally-Related Qualifications and National Vocational Qualifications (NVQs). The latter are competence-based occupational qualifications and are generally taken while the candidate is in employment. The body responsible for the overall framework is the Qualifications and Curriculum Authority. In Scotland the equivalent bodies are, for the Scottish Vocational Qualifications framework (SVQ) and (GSVQ) is the Scottish Qualifications Authority.

GCSEs in Applied Subjects and GNVQs

These qualifications are designed for students who seek a course that gives a general introduction to a broad vocational area. GCSEs in applied subjects are currently all double award GCSEs and are graded from A*A* to GG.

GNVQs are still available at two levels:

Foundation: broadly equivalent to 4 GCSEs at Grade D to G or an NVQ level 1;
Intermediate: broadly equivalent to 4 GCSEs at Grade A* to C or an NVQ level 2.

Foundation and Intermediate GNVQs are being replaced by other vocational qualifications and some have already been phased out.

GCEs in Applied Subjects

Vocational A levels (VCEs) were designed as level 3 general qualifications set in the context of a broad vocational area. Like other A levels, they are usually taken over two years and students are normally expected to have achieved at least four or five GCSEs at grades A* to C or an Intermediate GNVQ. Like all A levels, the vocational A levels provide a preparation for both higher education and employment. Vocational A levels assess the students' abilities to apply their skills and understanding in a vocational context. Assessment is one-third external and two-thirds internal. From September 2005 the VCEs were redesigned with an AS/A2 structure and the title VCE was changed to GCE. VCE subject titles such as Art and Design, Business, ICT and Science (which were offered as VCE and GCE) are now known as 'GCE in Applied Art and Design' and so on.
In Scotland, General Scottish Vocational Qualifications (GSVQs) have been brought under the new National Qualifications framework. Vocational A levels and GSVQs are recognized by universities as a basis for entry to Higher Education.

As well as qualifications within the vocational framework, the Awarding Bodies offer a range of other qualifications. Further guidance may be obtained from schools, colleges and careers advisers. Alternatively, contact a reputable independent consultancy such as Gabbitas.

Scottish National Qualifications

Most schools in Scotland prepare students for Standard Grade examinations taken at 16. All students who stay on in education after Standard Grade follow a qualifications system which begins at one of five levels, depending on their examination results.

Access, Intermediate 1 and Intermediate 2 are progressive levels which a student might take to gain a better grounding in a subject before going on to take one of two higher levels: Higher and Advanced Higher. The lower three levels are not compulsory for students with aptitude, who may move straight on to study one of the Higher level courses. With the exception of Standard Grade, each National Qualification is built on units, courses and group awards:

- National Units – these are the smallest elements of a qualification and are internally assessed; most require 40 hours of study.
- Courses – National Courses are usually taken in S5 or S6 and at college. They are made up of three units each, and are assessed internally and by examination for which grades A–C are awarded.
- Scottish Group Awards (SGAs) – these are programmes of courses and units that cover 16 broad subject areas. An SGA can be obtained within one year, or worked towards over a longer period.

There are 70 subjects available, including job-orientated subjects such as Travel and Tourism and traditional ones such as Maths and English. All National Qualifications have core skills embedded in them, although it is possible to take stand-alone units, for example Problem Solving, Communication, Numeracy and Information Technology.

General Scottish Vocational Qualifications (GSVQs) have now been brought under the National Qualifications framework.

For further information contact the Scottish Qualifications Authority.

The International Baccalaureate

(Information supplied by the International Baccalaureate Organisation)

The International Baccalaureate Organisation (IBO) is a non-profit, international educational foundation registered in Switzerland that was established in 1968. The Diploma Programme, for which the IBO is best known, was developed by a group of schools seeking to establish a common curriculum and a university-entry credential for geographically mobile students. They believed that an education that emphasized critical thinking and exposure to a variety of points of view would encourage inter-cultural understanding and acceptance of others by young people. They designed a comprehensive curriculum for the last two years of secondary school that could be administered in any country and that would be recognized by universities worldwide.

Today the IBO offers three programmes to schools. The Diploma Programme is for students aged 16 to 19 in the final two years of secondary school. The Middle Years Programme, adopted in 1994, is for students aged 11 to 16. The Primary Years Programme, adopted in 1997, is for students aged 3 to 12. In August 2006 the IBO had 1,877 authorized schools in 124 countries. This number is almost evenly divided between state schools and private (including international) schools.

The Diploma Programme

The Diploma Programme (DP), for students aged 16 to 19, is a two-year course of study. Recognized internationally as a qualification for university entrance, it also allows students to fulfil the requirements of their national education system. Students share an educational experience that emphasizes critical thinking as well as inter-cultural understanding and respect for others in the global community.

The DP offers a broad and balanced curriculum in which students are encouraged to apply what they learn in the classroom to real-world issues and problems. Wherever possible, subjects are taught from an international perspective. In economics, for example, students look at economic systems from around the world. Students study six courses (including both the sciences and the humanities) selected from the following six subject groups:

Group 1   language A1
Group 2   (second language) language *ab initio*, language B, language A2, classical languages
Group 3   individuals and societies
Group 4   experimental sciences
Group 5   mathematics and computer science
Group 6   the arts

Students must also submit an extended essay, follow a course in theory of knowledge (TOK) and take part in activities to complete the creativity, action and service (CAS) requirement.

The assessment of student work in the DP is largely external. At the end of the course, students take examinations that are marked by external examiners who work closely with the IBO. The types of questions asked in the examination papers include multiple-choice questions, essay questions, data-analysis questions and case studies. Students are also graded on the extended essay and on an essay and oral presentation for the TOK course.

A smaller part of the assessment of student work is carried out within schools by DP teachers. The work that is assessed includes oral commentaries in the languages, practical experimental work in the sciences, fieldwork and investigations in the humanities, and exhibitions and performances in the arts. Examiners check the assessment of samples of work from each school to ensure that IBO standards are consistently applied. For each examination session, approximately 80 per cent of DP students are awarded the

Diploma. The majority of students register for the Diploma, but students may also register for a limited number of Diploma subjects, for each of which they are awarded a certificate with the final grade.

The Middle Years Programme (MYP)

The Middle Years Programme (MYP), for students aged 11 to 16, recognizes that students in this age group are particularly sensitive to social and cultural influences and are struggling to define themselves and their relationships to others. The programme helps students develop the skills to cope with this period of uncertainty. It encourages them to think critically and independently, to work collaboratively and to take a disciplined approach to studying.

The aim of the MYP is to give students an international perspective to help them become informed about the experiences of people and cultures throughout the world. It also fosters a commitment to help others and to act as a responsible member of the community at the local, national and international levels.

Students in the MYP study all the major disciplines, including languages, humanities, sciences, mathematics, arts, technology and physical education. The framework is flexible enough to allow a school to include subjects that are not part of the MYP curriculum but that might be required by local authorities. While the courses provide students with a strong knowledge base, they emphasize the principles and concepts of the subject and approach topics from a variety of points of view, including the perspectives of other cultures.

MYP teachers use a variety of tools to assess student progress, including oral presentations, tests, essays and projects, and they apply the assessment criteria established by the IBO to students' work. Schools may opt for official IBO certification by asking the IBO to validate their internal assessment. This is often referred to as the 'moderation system'. In this process, the IBO reviews samples of the schools' assessment of student work and checks that schools are correctly applying the MYP assessment criteria. The IBO offers guidance for teachers in the form of published examples of assessment.

The Primary Years Programme

The Primary Years Programme (PYP), for students aged 3 to 12, focuses on the development of the whole child, addressing social, physical, emotional and cultural needs. At the same time, it gives students a strong foundation in all the major areas of knowledge: mathematics, social studies, drama, language, music, visual arts, science, personal and social education, and physical education. The PYP aims to help students develop an international perspective – to become aware of and sensitive to the points of view of people in other parts of the world.

The PYP curriculum is organized around six themes:

- who we are
- where we are in place and time

- how we express ourselves
- how the world works
- how we organize ourselves
- sharing the planet.

These themes are intended to help students make sense of themselves, of other people and of the physical environment, and to give them different ways of looking at the world.

Assessment is used for two purposes: to guide teaching and to give students an opportunity to show, in a variety of ways, what they know and what they can do. In the PYP, assessment takes many forms. It ranges from completing checklists to monitor progress to compiling a portfolio of a student's work. The IBO offers schools substantial guidance for conducting assessment, including a detailed handbook and professional development workshops. Student portfolios and records of PYP exhibitions are reviewed on a regular basis by the IBO as part of programme evaluation.

For further information about the IB programmes, please contact:

International Baccalaureate Programme
Route des Morillons 15
CH-1218 Grand-Saconnex
Geneva
Switzerland
Tel: +41 22 791 7740
Fax: + 41 22 791 0277
E-mail: ibhq@ibo.org
Website: www.ibo.org

Schools authorized to offer the International Baccalaureate Organisation's Diploma Programme in the United Kingdom

ENGLAND

Bedfordshire

Bedford High School
Bromham Road
Bedford MK40 2BS
Tel: 01234 360221
Fax: 01234 353552
E-mail: ph@bedfordhigh.co.uk
IB Co-ordinator: Mr Philip Herrick

Bedford School
De Parys Avenue
Bedford MK40 7TU
Tel: 01234 362200
Fax: 01234 362283
E-mail: ib@bedfordschool.org.uk
IB Co-ordinator: Mr Adrian Johnson

Luton Sixth Form College
Bradgers Hill Road
Luton LU2 7EW
Tel: 01582 877501
E-mail: cn@lutonsfc.ac.uk
IB Co-ordinator: Mr Colin Hall

Berkshire

Slough Grammar School
Lascelles Road
Slough
Berkshire SL3 7PR
Tel: 01753 537068
Fax: 01753 538618
E-mail: ibcoordinator@
    sloughgrammar.berks.sch.uk
IB Co-ordinator: Ms Ruth Symons

Waingel's College
Denmark Avenue
Woodley
Reading RG5 4RF
Tel: 0118 969 0336
Fax: 0118 944 2843
E-mail: wilrw@
    waingels.wokingham.sch.uk
IB Co-ordinator: Mr Robert Wilkinson

Bristol

The Riding High School
High Street
Winterbourne
Bristol BS36 1JL
Tel: 01454 252000
IB Co-ordinator: Mr Rob Terol

Cambridgeshire

Deacon's School
Queen's Gardens
Peterborough PE1 2UW
Tel: 01733 562451
Fax: 01733 891601
E-mail: jdk@
    deaconschool.peterborough.sch.uk
IB Co-ordinator: Mrs Julie Kirby

Impington College
New Road
Impington
Cambridge CB4 9LX
Tel: 01223 200402
Fax: 01223 718961
E-mail: sixthform@
    impingtonvc.cambs-schools.net
IB Co-ordinator: Mrs Sandra Morton

Cornwall

The Bolitho School
Polwithen
Penzance TR18 4JR
Tel: 01736 363271
Fax: 01736 330960
E-mail:
    enquiries@bolitho.cornwall.sch.uk
IB Co-ordinator: Mr Patrick Ian Minm

Truro College
College Road
Truro
Cornwall TR1 3XX
Tel: 01872 267000
Fax: 01872 267100
E-mail: andyw@trurocollege.ac.uk
IB Co-ordinator: Mr Andy Wildin

Devon

Exeter College
Hele Road
Exeter
Devon EX4 4JS
Tel: 01392 205340
Fax: 01392 205324
E-mail: atruscott@exe-coll.ac.uk
IB Co-ordinator: Mr Andy Truscott

Dorset

Bournemouth & Poole College
North Road
Parkstone
Poole BH14 0QB
Tel: 01202 747600
Fax: 01202 465720
E-mail: ssoutherden@bpc.ac.uk
IB Co-ordinator: Ms Sara Southerden

Thomas Hardye School
Queen's Avenue
Dorchester
Dorset DT1 2ET
Tel: 01305 266004
IB Co-ordinator: Mrs Frances Anderson

Essex

Anglo-European School
Willow Green
Ingatestone
Essex CM4 0DJ
Tel: 01277 354018
Fax: 01277 355623
E-mail: strachanj@aesessex.co.uk
IB Co-ordinator: Mrs Jane Strachan

Brentwood School
Ingrave Road
Brentwood
Essex CM15 8AS
Tel: 01277 243243
IB Co-ordinator: Mr Timothy Woffenden

Felstead School
Dunmow
Essex CM6 3LL
Tel: 01371 822600
IB Co-ordinator: Mr Paul Clark

The Sixth Form College
North Hill
Colchester
Essex CO1 1SN
Tel: 01206 500700
Fax: 01206 500770
E-mail: bainess@colchsfc.ac.uk
IB Co-ordinator: Mr Stephen Christopher Baines

Gloucestershire

Cirencester College
Stroud Road
Cirencester
Gloucestershire GL7 1XA
Tel: 01285 640994
Fax: 01285 644171
E-mail: kba@cirencester.ac.uk
IB Co-ordinator: Ms Katy Albiston

Hampshire

Alton College
Old Odiham Road
Alton
Hampshire GU34 2LX
Tel: 01420 592200
Fax: 01420 592253
E-mail: martin.savery@altoncollege.ac.uk
IB Co-ordinator: Mr Martin Savery

Brockenhurst College
Lyndhurst Road
Brockenhurst
Hampshire SO42 7ZE
Tel: 01590 625555
Fax: 01590 625256
E-mail: ncousins@brock.ac.uk
IB Co-ordinator: Mr Nick Cousins

Taunton's College
Hill Lane
Southampton SO15 5RL
Tel: 02380 511811
Fax: 02380 511991
E-mail: grantw@tauntons.ac.uk
IB Co-ordinator: Mr Bill Grant

Hertfordshire

Goffs School
Goffs Lane
Cheshunt
Hertfordshire EN7 5QW
Tel: 01992 424200
Fax: 01992 424201
E-mail: gma@goffs.herts.sch.uk
IB Co-ordinator: Mr Gordon Mather

Haileybury
Hertford
Hertfordshire SG13 7NU
Tel: 01992 706205
Fax: 01992 706276
E-mail: jameshk@haileybury.com
IB Co-ordinator: Mr James Kazi

Hockerill Anglo-European School
Dunmow Road
Bishop's Stortford
Hertfordshire CM23 5HX
Tel: 01279 658451
Fax: 01279 755918
E-mail: admin.hockerill@thegrid.org.uk
IB Co-ordinator: Mrs Vicki Worsnop

Stenborough School
Stenborough Park
Watford
Hertfordshire WD25 9JT
Tel: 01923 673268
IB Co-ordinator: Mr Peter Martin

Isle of Man

King William's College
Castletown
Isle of Man IM9 1TP
Tel: 01624 822551
Fax: 01624 824207
E-mail: rene.filho@kwc.sch.im
IB Co-ordinator: Dr Rene Filho

Kent

Bexley Grammar School
Danson Lane
Welling
Kent DA16 2BL
Tel: 020 8304 8538
Fax: 020 8304 0248
E-mail: CET@bexleygs.co.uk
IB Co-ordinator: Ms Claire Tipping

The Business Academy Bexley
Yarnton Way
Erith
Kent DA18 4DW
Tel: 020 8312 4800
Fax: 020 8320 4810
E-mail: robert.burton@tba.bexley.sch.uk
IB Co-ordinator: Mr Robert Burton

Dartford Grammar School
West Hill
Dartford
Kent DA1 2HW
Tel: 01322 223039
Fax: 01322 291426
E-mail: j.maidment@
   dartfordgrammar.kent.sch.uk
IB Co-ordinator: Ms Jayne Maidment

Dartford Grammar School for Girls
Shepherds Lane
Dartford
Kent DA1 2NT
Tel: 01322 223123
Fax: 01322 294786
E-mail: ANGELA@
   dartfordgrammargirls.kent.sch.uk
IB Co-ordinator: Mrs Angela Pearson

The Leigh City Technology College
Green Street
Green Road
Pontford
Kent DA1 1QE
Tel: 01322 620400
IB Co-ordinator: Dr Colin Anderson

Maidstone Grammar School
Barton Road
Maidstone
Kent ME15 7BT
Tel: 01622 752101
Fax: 01622 753680
E-mail: keith.derrett@mgs-kent.org.uk
IB Co-ordinator: Dr Keith Derrett

The Norton Knatchbull School
Hythe Road
Ashford
Kent TN24 0QJ
Tel: 01233 620045
IB Co-ordinator: Mr Roger Baker

Sevenoaks School
Sevenoaks
Kent TN13 1HU
Tel: 01732 455133
Fax: 01732 456143
E-mail: sma@sevenoaksschool.org
IB Co-ordinator: Sue Austin

Tonbridge Grammar School
Deakin Leas
Tonbridge
Kent TN9 2JR
Tel: 01732 365125
Fax: 01732 359417
E-mail: ROSEMARYCHEETHAM@
   tgsg.kent.sch.uk
IB Co-ordinator: Ms Rosemary Cheetham

Lancashire

Rossall School
Broadway
Fleetwood
Lancashire FY7 8JW
Tel: 01253 774201
Fax: 01253 772052
E-mail: ibatrossall@hotmail.com
IB Co-ordinator: Dr Doris Dohmen

Leicestershire

Wyggeston & Queen Elizabeth I College
University Road
Leicester LE1 7RJ
Tel: 0116 223 1900
IB Co-ordinator: Mrs Ruth Fallkes

London

The Godolphin and Latymer School
Iffley Road
Hammersmith
London W6 0PG
Tel: 020 8741 1936
Fax: 020 8746 3352
E-mail: ctrimming@
   godolphinandlatymer.com
IB Co-ordinator: Mrs Caroline Trimming

Highlands School
148 Worlds End Lane
London N21 1QQ
Tel: 020 8370 1100
Fax: 020 8370 1110
E-mail: tutonk@highlands.enfield.sch.uk
IB Co-ordinator: Mr Karl Tuton

International School of London
139 Gunnersbury Avenue
London W3 8LG
Tel: 020 8992 5823
Fax: 020 8993 7012
E-mail: huwbach@btopenworld.com
IB Co-ordinator: Mr Huw Davies

King's College School
Wimbledon
Southside
Wimbledon Common
London SW19 4TT
Tel: 020 8255 5300
IB Co-ordinator: Mr Neil Tetley

St Dunstan's College
Stanstead Road
London SE6 4TY
Tel: 020 8516 7200
Fax: 020 8516 7300
E-mail: salgeo@sdmail.co.uk
IB Co-ordinator: Sue Algeo

Southbank International School
63–65 Portland Place
London W1B 1QR
Tel: 0207 436 9699
IB Co-ordinator: Ms Lori Fritz

Woodside Park School
Friern Barnet Road
Friern Barnet
London N11 3DR
Tel: 020 8368 3777
Fax: 020 8368 3220
E-mail: acobbin@wpis.org
IB Co-ordinator: Ms Alison Cobbin

Merseyside

Broadgreen High School
Queen's Drive
Liverpool L13 5UQ
Tel: 0151 228 6800
Fax: 0151 220 9256
E-mail: apatterson@
   broadgreenhigh.org.uk
IB Co-ordinator: Mr Austin Patterson

Cowley Language College
Hard Lane
St Helen's WA10 6AB
Tel: 01744 678030
IB Co-ordinator: Mr Matthew Herseth

Middlesex

ACS Hillingdon International School
108 Vine Lane
Hillingdon
Uxbridge
Middlesex UB10 0BE
Tel: 01895 259771
Fax: 01895 256974
E-mail: dwynne-jones@acs-england.co.uk
IB Co-ordinator: Mr David Wynne-Jones

North London Collegiate School
Canons
Edgware
Middlesex HA8 7RJ
Tel: 020 8952 0912
Fax: 020 8951 1391
E-mail: mburke@nlcs.org.uk
IB Co-ordinator: Mr Michael Burke

Richmond upon Thames College
Egerton Road
Twickenham
Middlesex TW2 7SJ
Tel: 020 8607 8269
Fax: 020 8891 5998
E-mail: kwildman@rutc.ac.uk
IB Co-ordinator: Mr Stephen Winfield

St Helen's School
Eastbury Road
Northwood
Middlesex HA6 3AS
Tel: 01923 843210
Fax: 01923 843211
*E-mail: mbowman@
  sthelensnorthwood.co.uk*
IB Co-ordinator: Mrs Mary Bowman

Northamptonshire

Prince William School
Herne Road
Oundle
Northamptonshire PE8 4BS
Tel: 01832 272881
Fax: 01832 274942
*E-mail: reception@
  pwschool.northants.sch.uk*
IB Co-ordinator: Ms Barbara Richards

Oxfordshire

Henley College
Deanfield Avenue
Henley-on-Thames
Oxfordshire RG9 1UH
Tel: 01491 579988
Fax: 01491 410099
E-mail: bhug@henleycol.ac.uk
IB Co-ordinator: Mrs Bridie Hughes

St Clare's
139 Banbury Road
Oxford OX2 7AL
Tel: 01865 517332
Fax: 01865 310002
E-mail: nick.lee@stclares.ac.uk
IB Co-ordinator: Mr Nick Lee

Rutland

Oakham School
Chapel Close
Oakham
Rutland LE15 6DT
Tel: 01572 758698
Fax: 01572 758623
E-mail: jr@oakham.rutland.sch.uk
IB Co-ordinator: Dr Jill Rutherford

Shropshire

Ellesmere College
Ellesmere
Shropshire SY12 9AB
Tel: 01691 622321
IB Co-ordinator: Mrs HT Scanisbrick

Surrey

ACS Cobham International School
Portsmouth Road
Cobham
Surrey KT11 1BL
Tel: 01932 867251
Fax: 01932 869791
E-mail: cworthington@acs-england.co.uk
IB Co-ordinator: Mr Craig Worthington

ACS Egham International School
London Road
Egham
Surrey TW20 0HS
Tel: 01784 430800
Fax: 01784 430153
E-mail: tstobie@acs-england.co.uk
IB Co-ordinator: Mr Tristian Stobie

King Edward's School
Witley
Godalming
Surrey GU8 5SG
Tel: 01428 686700
Fax: 01428 682850
E-mail: mehargc@kesw.surrey.sch.uk
IB Co-ordinator: Ms Christine Meharg

Kings College for the Arts and Technology
Southway
Guildford
Surrey GU2 8DU
Tel: 01483 458956
Fax: 01483 458957
E-mail: n.clay@kingscollegeguildford.com
IB Co-ordinator: Mr Nick Clay

Kings International College
Watchetts Drive
Camberley
Surrey GU15 2PQ
Tel: 01276 683539
Fax: 01276 709503
E-mail: a.reynolds@
   kings-international.co.uk
IB Co-ordinator: Ms Anne Reynolds

Marymount International School
George Road
Kingston upon Thames
Surrey KT2 7PE
Tel: 020 8949 0571
Fax: 020 8336 2485
E-mail: acdean@
   marymount.kingston.sch.uk
IB Co-ordinator: Dr Brian Johnson

TASIS The American School in England
Coldharbour Lane
Thorpe
Egham
Surrey TW20 8TE
Tel: 01932 565252
Fax: 01932 564644
E-mail: cgoldon@tasis.com
IB Co-ordinator: Mrs Chantal Goldon

Whitgift School
Haling Park
South Croydon
Surrey CR2 6YT
Tel: 020 8688 9222
Fax: 020 8760 0682
E-mail: stewartcook@totalise.co.uk
IB Co-ordinator: Mr Stewart Cook

Sussex

Ardingly College
College Road
Ardingly
Haywards Heath
West Sussex RH17 6SQ
Tel: 01444 893000
Fax: 01444 893001
E-mail: widgetcat@hotmail.com
IB Co-ordinator: Mr John Langford

Bexhill College
Penland Road
Bexhill on Sea
East Sussex TN40 2JG
Tel: 01424 214545
IB Co-ordinator: Mr Robert Hill

Hastings College of Arts and Technology
Archery Road
St Leonard's on Sea
East Sussex TN38 0HX
Tel: 01424 442222
Fax: 01424 720376
E-mail: padams@hastings.ac.uk
IB Co-ordinator: Mr Patrick Adams

Worth School
Paddockhurst Road
Turners Hill
West Sussex RH10 4SD
Tel: 01342 710222
Fax: 01342 710230
E-mail: nconnolly@worth.org.uk
IB Co-ordinator: Mr Nicholas Connolly

Tyne and Wear

Tyne Metropolitan College
Embleton Avenue
Wallsend
Tyne and Wear NE28 9NJ
Tel: 0191 229 5000
Fax: 0191 229 5301
E-mail: anne.briffa@tynemet.ac.uk
IB Co-ordinator: Ms Anne Briffa

Warwickshire

Finham Park School
Green Lane
Coventry CV3 6EA
Tel: 02476 418135
Fax: 02476 840890
E-mail: v.chandley@finhampark.co.uk
IB Co-ordinator: Mrs Victoria Chandley

Warwickshire College
Warwick New Road
Leamington Spa
Warwickshire CV32 5JE
Tel: 01926 318231
Fax: 01926 318048
E-mail: aholland@warkscol.ac.uk
IB Co-ordinator: Mr Andy Holland

West Midlands

The City Technology College
Kingshurst
PO Box 1017
Cooks Lane
Birmingham B37 6NZ
Tel: 0121 329 8300
Fax: 0121 770 0879
E-mail: julie.dent@kingshurst.ac.uk
IB Co-ordinator: Mrs Julie Dent

George Dixon International School
City Road
Edgbaston
Birmingham B17 8LF
Tel: 0121 434 4488
Fax: 0121 434 3721
E-mail: colinmac@gn.ac.org
IB Co-ordinator: Mr Colin McKenzie

The Sixth Form College, Solihull
Widney Manor Road
Solihull
West Midlands B91 3WR
Tel: 0121 704 2581
IB Co-ordinator: Mr Mike Padbury

Wiltshire

Warminster School
Church Street
Warminster
Wiltshire BD12 8PS
Tel: 01985 210100
IB Co-ordinator: Ms Olivia Bolline

Worcestershire

Malvern College
College Road
Malvern
Worcestershire WR14 3DF
Tel: 01684 581500
Fax: 01684 581617
E-mail: jpk@malcol.org
IB Co-ordinator: Mr John Knee

North Yorkshire

Harrogate Grammar School
Arthurs Avenue
Harrogate HG2 0DZ
Tel: 01423 531127
Fax: 01423 521325
E-mail: mbailey@hgs-n-yorks.sch.uk
IB Co-ordinator: Mr Michael Bailey

Scarborough College
Filey Road
Scarborough
Yorkshire YO11 3BA
Tel: 01723 360620
IB Co-ordinator: Mrs Amanda Evinger

South Yorkshire

Doncaster College
Waterdale
Doncaster
South Yorkshire DN1 3EX
Tel: 01302 553553
IB Co-ordinator: Ms Lynn Stokes

West Yorkshire

Rhodesway School
Oaks Lane
Allerton
Bradford
West Yorkshire BD15 7RU
Tel: 01274 770230
Fax: 01274 770231
E-mail: school@
    rhodesway-bradford.sch.uk
IB Co-ordinator: Mrs Marian Pearson

SCOTLAND

Aberdeenshire

The International School of Aberdeen
'Fairgirth'
296 North Deeside Road
Milltimber
Aberdeen AB13 0AB
Tel: 01224 732267
Fax: 01224 734879
E-mail: marybeth.kiley@
    isa.aberdeen.sch.uk
IB Co-ordinator: Mrs Beth Kiley

Edinburgh

Fettes College
Carrington Road
Edinburgh EH4 1QX
Tel: 0131 332 2281
IB Co-ordinator: Mr John Fern

Fife

St Leonards School
St Andrews
Fife KY16 9QJ
Tel: 01334 472126
IB Co-ordinator: Mrs Ann Scot

WALES

Cardiff

Whitchurch High School
Penlline Road
Whitchurch
Cardiff CF4 2XJ
Tel: 029 2062 9700
Fax: 029 2062 9701
E-mail: nh@whitchurch.cardiff.sch.uk
IB Co-ordinator: Ms Nicola Hansford

Conwy

Llandrillo College
Llandudno Road
Rhos-on-Sea
Colwyn Bay
Conwy LL28 4HZ
Tel: 01492 546666
Fax: 01492 543891
E-mail: m.monteith@llandrillo.ac.uk
IB Co-ordinator: Ms Melanie Monteith

Rydal Penrhos
Pwllycrochan Avenue
Colwyn Bay
Conwy LL29 7BT
Tel: 01492 530155
Fax: 01492 531872
E-mail: wynniewil@hotmail.com
IB Co-ordinator: Mr Wyn Williams

South Glamorgan

United World College of the Atlantic
St Donat's Castle
Llantwit Major
Vale of Glamorgan
CF6 7WF
Tel: 01446 799002
Fax: 01446 799013
E-mail: gareth.rees@uwc.net
IB Co-ordinator: Mr Gareth Rees

Swansea

Swansea College
Ty-coch Road
Swansea SA2 9EB
Tel: 01792 284231
IB Co-ordinator: Mrs Sue Phillips

Examining and awarding bodies: useful addresses

Assessment and Qualifications Alliance (AQA)
Devas Street
Manchester M15 6EX
Tel: 0161 953 1180
Fax: 0161 273 7572
E-mail: mailbox@aqa.org.uk
Website: www.aqa.org.uk

Stag Hill House
Guildford
Surrey GU2 7XJ
Tel: 01483 506506
Fax: 01483 300152
E-mail: postmaster@aqa.org.uk
Website: www.aqa.org.uk

Unit 10
City Business Park
Easton Road
Bristol BS5 0SP
Tel: 0117 927 3434
Fax: 0117 929 0268

31–33 Springfield Avenue
Harrogate
North Yorkshire HG1 2HW
Tel: 01423 840015
Fax: 01423 523678

City & Guilds
1 Giltspur Street
London EC1A 9DD
Tel: 020 7294 2800
Fax: 020 7294 2400
E-mail: enquiry@city-and-guilds.co.uk
Website: www.city-and-guilds.co.uk

Edexcel Foundation
One90 High Holborn
London WC1V 7BH
Tel: 0870 240 9800
Fax: 020 7190 5700
E-mail: enquiries@edexcel.org.uk
Website: www.edexcel.org.uk

OCR (Oxford, Cambridge and RSA Examinations)
9 Hills Road
Cambridge CB2 1PB
Tel: 01223 553311
Fax: 01223 460278
E-mail: helpdesk@ocr.org.uk
Website: www.ocr.org.uk

Qualifications and Curriculum Authority
Customer Relations
83 Piccadilly
London W1J 8QA
Tel: 020 7509 5555
Fax: 020 7509 6666
E-mail: info@qca.org.uk
Website: www.qca.org.uk

Scottish Qualifications Authority
The Optima Building
58 Robertson Street
Glasgow G2 8DQ
Tel: 0845 279 1000
Fax: 0845 213 5000
E-mail: customer@sqa.org.uk
Website: www.sqa.org.uk

Welsh Joint Education Committee
245 Western Avenue
Cardiff CF5 2YX
Tel: 029 2026 5000
Fax: 029 2057 5994
E-mail: info@wjec.co.uk
Website: www.wjec.co.uk

1.8

The Sixth Form and Beyond – a Parent's Guide

If you have a son or daughter studying for GCSEs or the equivalent, he or she, like most 15 and 16 year olds, is probably still some way from decisions about higher education and careers. At this stage there is, of course, plenty of room for the development of ideas and interests, and it is important to have an open mind about all the options. Some preliminary planning, however, is essential.

Choosing the right Sixth Form course is becoming increasingly important as the options at 18 become more complex. Students who have given some thought to their future plans, to their own strengths and personal qualities, will find it easier to identify broad potential career areas. This in turn will enable them to choose suitable Sixth Form and higher education options which still allow flexibility for the development of their skills and personality over the next few years. At the same time, extra-curricular activities, relevant work experience and other research will help to build up the essential personal and practical skills sought by today's employers.

Good advice is essential. Some schools have excellent careers guidance programmes and materials and may also arrange talks from visiting speakers and work experience opportunities. Others may have more limited resources. Computerized careers assessments are often used in schools. These are not designed to provide all the answers, and it is vital that they should form part of a much more extensive discussion that includes consideration of academic achievements and aspirations, attitudes, interests and any special needs.

Your son or daughter may also find it helpful to speak to an independent consultant, who can offer an objective view and perhaps a wider perspective of the possibilities.

Choosing Sixth Form options

The main options available after GCSE are: Advanced Subsidiary GCE (AS) and Advanced GCE (A2); in Scotland, National Qualifications (Highers); the International Baccalaureate (IB); and Vocational A levels (formerly Advanced GNVQs). The basic structure of these courses is covered in Part 1.7.

All can be used as a means of entry to British universities. The IB, as its name implies, is an international qualification and is also recognized for admission purposes by universities worldwide. Unlike the other options above, however, the IB Diploma course is not widely available in the UK. A list of UK schools and colleges authorized to run the IB Diploma course is given on pages 48–58.

Before making a choice, students may find it helpful to consider the following.

Subjects or areas of study

Is depth or breadth the most important factor? A levels offer a high degree of specialization. The IB is a demanding academic qualification but covers a wider range of subjects in less depth. A vocational course will probably have a focus on a particular career area such as Business, Leisure & Tourism or Information Technology.

Course load

Most students take four AS choices in the lower sixth and continue three of these subjects as A2s in the upper sixth, thus emerging from school with three full A levels and one AS in a fourth subject. Because of the diversity of the current Sixth Form programme, entry requirements vary significantly between one course and another. In some cases universities may ask for specific grades in specific subjects; in others they may seek an overall number of UCAS points. The equivalent of three A level passes remains the core requirement, with an interest in any additional qualification obtained. In this relatively uncertain climate, sixth formers should appreciate that quality is more important than quantity – in other words additional courses should not be taken if this would jeopardize the grades obtained in core subjects. Second, if they are in any doubt about the combination of A/AS levels and grades which will be acceptable to a university, they should not hesitate to contact admissions staff or seek other forms of professional advice.

Availability

Is the required course available at your child's present school or, if not, at another school or college locally? Is living away from home an option? Vocational A level courses are widely available in maintained colleges. Some vocational courses are also offered by a much smaller number of independent schools.

Assessment method and course structure

Some students prefer regular assessment through submission of coursework or projects rather than exam-based assessment. Many A level courses, traditionally assessed through a final exam, now include coursework as part of the assessment. The IB is assessed chiefly by examinations. Vocational A levels are assessed largely on coursework.

Academic ability

A level courses often demand a good deal of reading and the ability to write well-argued essays, but some students may prefer a more practical approach.

Future plans

Students aiming for a specific career should check whether their preferred options are suitable. Those still undecided should choose a programme which allows some flexibility.

Which A levels?

It is natural for students to want to continue with subjects they enjoy. Clearly, a high GCSE result suggests that a similar result may be expected at A level. This is important, of course, but students must also consider whether or not their preferred combination of subjects is suitable for higher education or career plans. It is also possible to take A level courses in subjects not previously studied.

Career choice

Some careers, typically medicine and architecture, demand a specific degree. This may limit, or sometimes dictate, the choice of A level subjects and students must be confident that they can do well in these. If career plans are undecided, it is wise to choose subjects which will leave a number of options open.

Ability

It is advisable to have achieved at least a grade B at GCSE in any subjects being considered for A level (ideally grade A in Maths, Science and Modern Languages). Some A level subjects such as Economics can be taken without any previous knowledge, but students should consider what skills are required, eg numerical, analytical or essay-writing, and whether or not it will suit them.

Different examining bodies may assess the same subject in different ways. If your son or daughter has concerns about a final exam-based assessment, he or she might consider a syllabus which offers a modular structure and a higher degree of assessment through coursework. Remember, however, that if all the subjects chosen are assessed on this basis, the workload and the pressure to meet deadlines during the course could be very heavy.

Interest

Genuine interest is essential if a student is to feel motivated throughout the two-year course and achieve high grades. Students in a dilemma over the choice between a subject they enjoy and a subject which they feel they ought to do might be well advised to opt for the former, but should check that this is suitable for their future plans. Students who are thinking of taking up a new subject, for example Psychology, may find it helpful to read a few books on the subject to test their interest before making any decisions.

Which subject combinations?

If no specific combination is demanded, how can students ensure a suitable choice? At least two subjects should be complementary, ie two arts/social sciences or two sciences. It is quite common for students to combine arts and sciences. It should be remembered that even those career areas which do not demand specific degree courses may still require certain skills, which some A level subjects will develop better than others.

If a particular degree course does not require an A level in the subject, eg Psychology, it may be better to choose a different A level subject or perhaps a complementary vocational option and so demonstrate a wider knowledge/skills base to university admissions tutors. This also avoids the risk of repeating the A level syllabus in the first year at university.

Other matters to consider include the timetabling restraints at school, which may make a certain combination impossible, in which case students may have to compromise or change to a school or college with greater flexibility, and the school's record of success in A level grades in the subjects chosen.

Where shall I study?

Staying on into the Sixth Form of the present school does have advantages, including continuity and familiarity with surroundings, staff and fellow students. It is not unusual, however, for students to change schools at 16. Some may be looking for a course, subjects or combination of subjects not available at their present school; others may simply want a change of atmosphere or a different style of education.

If a change to a different school is sought, consider the school's academic pace and examination results, its university entry record, the criteria for entry to the Sixth Form and the availability of places, the size of the Sixth Form and of the teaching groups and, where appropriate, the opportunities to develop skills or pursue interests aside from A level studies.

Independent Sixth Form or tutorial colleges offer an alternative environment and are described on page 16. There are also specialist independent colleges which focus on specific vocational areas such as business, accountancy or computing.

Maintained Sixth Form colleges offer a wide range of A levels and, increasingly, vocational options such as Vocational A levels. They may have between 500 and 1,000 students and because of their size can normally offer quite extensive facilities. However, teaching groups may be much larger than those in the independent sector.

Maintained further education colleges are located in all parts of the country and offer a vast range of A levels and vocational courses to students of all ages, many on a part-time basis. Colleges can be huge in size and may occupy several sites. Some also offer degree and diploma courses and may therefore be able to offer extensive facilities and resources, particularly for vocational studies. The age range of such colleges is much wider than in the independent sector, so it is also important to check that there is a suitable system of pastoral care for 16–18-year-olds.

There are also Apprenticeship schemes, which incorporate employment with part-time study. The best source of information on these is usually the local careers office. Such programmes have a national NVQ rating equivalent to GCSE or Sixth Form studies, depending on the level and the content.

The university challenge

Access to degree courses in the UK is now wider than ever before. Despite continuing pressures on graduate employment opportunities and the introduction of tuition fees, students entering higher education have reached record numbers.

Higher education offers a unique range of academic, career and social opportunities. However, poor preparation for university can prove disastrous. There are growing concerns about the rising number of students – currently nearly one in five – who do not complete their degree courses. The sense of having made the wrong choice is an often-cited factor.

Why does your son or daughter want to go to university? Is he or she genuinely motivated and keen to study a particular subject in depth, to qualify for a specific career, and to take advantage of all the benefits which university life offers? All these reasons are valid, but some students may apply to university largely because they feel under pressure at home and/or at school to do so. Timing is also important. Students still unsure what to study should not rush into a decision. It may be better to take a year out and to use the additional time constructively before making a choice.

Most schools encourage students to begin thinking seriously about higher education soon after entering the Sixth Form. During the spring and summer terms of the Lower Sixth, students should be doing their research. Information is available from reference guides, from the internet and from university prospectuses. Most universities organize open days, when students can visit and talk to staff and students. This means that students should be well prepared for the autumn when application forms should be sent to UCAS (the Universities and Colleges Admissions Service): by 15 October for applications that include Oxford, Cambridge or Medicine and by 15 January for all other applications (with the exception of some for Art and Design).

Support and guidance from school, from external advisers and from parents is essential throughout this period, but the final choice of course and university lies with the student, and he or she should be taking an active part in the process. So what are the key points to consider?

Which course?

Is a specific degree necessary for a specific career? In some cases, typically Medicine, yes. In many cases, however, including Law, students have more flexibility. If there are no specific requirements, prospective employers will often take account of the quality of degree obtained and the reputation of the university as much as the subject studied, and will look for other skills and qualities which match their requirements. This means that students should take a subject in which they expect to do well rather than something which they may, perhaps wrongly, believe to be 'the right thing'. It is also important to demonstrate a breadth of knowledge and skills, for example interpersonal skills, language skills, commercial awareness or an understanding of science or information technology, in addition to the subject studied. There are differing views over the importance of taking some career-related degree subjects, for example, Business Studies or Media/Communication Studies. Some employers may prefer to employ graduates with a wider education background and train them in-house. Others may prefer applicants to be able to demonstrate practical knowledge and interest. Taking the above examples, this might include work experience with a company or involvement with the university newspaper or radio station.

Sandwich courses, offered mainly in science, engineering and social sciences, include work experience as part of the course. This can help employment prospects, enhance practical skills and allow students to test their interest in a particular career before committing themselves. In some cases placements may turn into permanent positions with the same employer after graduation. Some students, however, may not want to delay graduation (a sandwich course may take an extra year), and may dislike the disruption between work and study. Many universities also offer students (and not only those taking modern language degrees) the opportunity to study abroad as part of their course.

Foundation degrees

Foundation degrees are vocational in content and focus, and offer a qualification just below the level of an Honours degree. Foundation degrees take two years' full-time study, but they can also be studied part time. They combine work experience with the traditional academic structure of a degree course and are intended to equip students with the skills required by today's employers and to enable them to go straight into their chosen career upon successful completion of the course. Each foundation degree is linked with at least one Honours degree in the same subject area, which means that those who wish to further their qualification can go on to a BA (Hons) qualification if they choose to do so. Entry to Foundation degrees is flexible in order to attract not just school leavers but also those who are already in employment and who have the right level of ability.

Specialization

Students have a choice of studying one subject (single honours) or a combination (joint honours or a modular degree). A combined course offers more breadth and the opportunity to follow complementary studies, but almost always means a heavier workload.

For students unsure about taking a subject not studied at school or going directly into a specialized field, for example Civil Engineering, a more general foundation year may be helpful in providing essential core skills before deciding on a specialization.

Checking course content

Courses with the same name may be very different in content, so it is essential to read the prospectus for details. Modern language degrees, for example, vary widely in focus. Some place particular emphasis on practical language skills and an understanding of current affairs; others may have a more traditional emphasis on literature. Course titles like Communication Studies can also mean a wide variety of things.

Entry requirements

What subjects and grades does the course specify? Is the student likely to achieve these grades or should he or she look for a course with less stringent entry requirements? Remember that published grades are given only as a guide and may be adjusted upwards or downwards when offers are made to individual students. With the variety of Sixth Form programmes being taken, Gabbitas strongly recommends students contact universities direct to find out what they may be expected to achieve. For arts A level students who wish to take a degree in a science-based subject such as Medicine or Engineering, one year conversion courses are available, but students will be expected to have good GCSE grades in Maths and Science. Many modern language courses do not require previous knowledge, although evidence of competency in another foreign language is usually essential.

Remember too that as the A level pass rate rises, admissions tutors increasingly use GCSE results as well as A level grades as an indicator of ability and level of interest in a subject.

Which university?

Quality and reputation are as important for the individual course and department as for the institution as a whole. Beware of published league tables, which will not necessarily answer your questions. Find out about the career or employment destinations of recent graduates. This information may be available direct from the university or in one of the many published handbooks. If you have in mind a particular career or employer, it may be useful to contact the recruitment department to find out their views on specific universities or degree courses. You may also want to ask the university about the teaching styles, methods of assessment and the level of supervision available.

There is, of course, much more to finding the right university than simply the course. Aspects such as accommodation (both on and off campus), location or social atmosphere can generate just as much anxiety and dissatisfaction if things go wrong and may just as likely lead to abandonment of the course.

Some students may be attracted to a collegiate style university such as Oxford, Cambridge or London. Others may prefer a self-contained campus where all academic, social and other facilities are available on-site. Some may prefer a big city environment; others a smaller, more rural location. Living costs are a further important but often neglected issue. What is the quality and frequency of local transport? Is a car necessary? How safe is the area after dark? How important is the distance from home? What other facilities are offered to cater for individual hobbies and interests?

Alternatives to university entry

Students who are not attracted by the idea of full-time study at university will find that there are a number of alternatives available. It is possible to study for a degree part time by distance learning through private institutions, or if practical skills are sought there are many short courses available in areas such as business, computer and keyboard skills, marketing and PR, and languages.

There are companies and other organizations which take on young people with A levels or the equivalent and which offer them part-time academic training leading to relevant professional qualifications, some of which are regarded as the equivalent of a first degree. Examples include the Armed Forces and Emergency Services, the Merchant Navy, retail, hotel and catering, IT, accountancy, estate agents, and certain branches of the Law.

Finding out more

There are, of course, many other options and issues which your son or daughter may want to discuss. These might include the pros and cons of taking a year out after school and how to make the best use of it, sponsorship to help finance a degree course, presenting a well-structured and effective UCAS application, interview techniques, CV writing and job applications.

Advice should be available from your child's school. Expert, independent guidance is available from Gabbitas, who can also advise students who are unhappy at university as well as recent graduates and those looking for a career move in later life. If you would like to know more about the Gabbitas Advisory and Careers Assessment Services, please telephone Richard Leathes on 020 7734 0161 or e-mail richard.leathes@gabbitas.co.uk.

Part 2

Geographical Directory

2.1

Notes on Information given in the Directory Section

Type of school

The directory comprises schools listed within the Department for Education and Skills Register of Independent Schools. Maintained schools, Foundation schools, special schools, independent further education colleges and overseas schools are not included, unless they have a profile in Part Three.

Each school is given a brief description, which explains whether the school is single-sex or co-educational. In some cases single-sex schools take small numbers of the opposite sex within a specified age range. These are indicated where appropriate, eg: Boys boarding and day 3–18 (Day girls 16–18).

Schools are described as 'boarding' (which indicates boarding pupils only), 'boarding and day', 'day and boarding' (indicating a predominance of day pupils) or 'day' only.

Number of boarders

Where appropriate these are divided into full boarders (F) and weekly boarders (W). Weekly boarding arrangements vary according to individual school policy.

Fees

All fees are given annually from September 2006 unless otherwise stated. It should be remembered, however, that some schools increase fees during the year and the figures shown may therefore be subject to change after September 2006. Where fees from September 2006 aren't available those from September 2005 are shown. Otherwise fees are available on request. Figures are shown for full boarding (FB), weekly boarding (WB) and day fees. In some instances the fees for full and weekly boarding are the same (F/WB £). A minimum and a maximum fee are given for each range. These figures are intended as a guide only. For more precise information schools should be contacted direct.

Key

* denotes that the school has a profile in Part Three;

† denotes that the school is registered with the Council for the Registration of Schools Teaching Dyslexic Pupils.

2.2
England

BEDFORDSHIRE

BEDFORD

ACORN SCHOOL
15 St Andrews Road, Bedford,
Bedfordshire MK40 2LL
Tel: (01234) 343449
Fax: (01234) 343449
Email: acornschool@
  btinternet.com
Head: Mrs M Mason
Type: Co-educational Day 2–8
No of pupils: 130
Fees: On application

BEDFORD HIGH SCHOOL
Bromham Road, Bedford,
Bedfordshire MK40 2BS
Tel: (01234) 360221
Fax: (01234) 353552
Email: admissions@
  bedfordhigh.co.uk
Head: Mrs G Piotrowska
Type: Girls Day and Boarding
7–18
No of pupils: 850
No of boarders: F143
Fees: (September 05)
FB £14319–£17019
Day £6585–£9285

**BEDFORD MODERN
SCHOOL**
Manton Lane, Bedford,
Bedfordshire MK41 7NT
Tel: (01234) 332500
Fax: (01234) 332550
Email: info@bedmod.co.uk
Head: Mr S Smith
Type: Co-educational Day 7–18
No of pupils: B1005 G200
Fees: (September 06)
Day £6486–£9093

**BEDFORD PREPARATORY
SCHOOL**
De Parys Avenue, Bedford,
Bedfordshire MK40 2TU
Tel: (01234) 362274
Fax: (01234) 362285
Email: prepinfo@
  bedfordschool.org.uk
Head: Mr C Godwin
Type: Boys Boarding and Day
7–13
No of pupils: 452
No of boarders: F23 W6
Fees: (September 06)
FB £14097–£16740
WB £13440–£16083
Day £8517–£11160

BEDFORD SCHOOL*
De Parys Avenue, Bedford,
Bedfordshire MK40 2TU
Tel: (01234) 362200
Fax: (01234) 362283
Email: registrar@
  bedfordschool.org.uk
Head: Dr I P Evans
Type: Boys Boarding and Day
7–18
No of pupils: 1105
No of boarders: F177 W81
Fees: (September 06)
FB £14097–£20703
WB £13440–£20022
Day £8517–£13167

**BEDFORD SCHOOL STUDY
CENTRE**
67 De Parys Avenue, Bedford,
Bedfordshire MK40 2TR
Tel: (01234) 362300
Fax: (01234) 362305
Email: bssc@bedfordschool.org.uk
Head: Mrs O Heffill
Type: Co-educational Boarding
10–17
No of pupils: B20 G10
No of boarders: F30
Fees: (September 06) FB £25860

DAME ALICE HARPUR SCHOOL
Cardington Road, Bedford,
Bedfordshire MK42 0BX
Tel: (01234) 340871
Fax: (01234) 344125
Email: admissions@dahs.co.uk
Head: Mrs J Berry
Type: Girls Day 7–18
No of pupils: 910
Fees: (September 05)
Day £6225–£8694

PILGRIMS PRE-PREPARATORY SCHOOL
Brickhill Drive, Bedford,
Bedfordshire MK41 7QZ
Tel: (01234) 369555
Fax: (01234) 359556
Email: pilgrims@
    harpur-trust.org.uk
Head: Mrs M Shaw
Type: Co-educational Day 0–8
No of pupils: B144 G134
Fees: On application

POLAM SCHOOL
45 Lansdowne Road, Bedford,
Bedfordshire MK40 2BU
Tel: (01234) 261864
Fax: (01234) 261194
Email: info@polamschool.co.uk
Head: Miss D Parton
Type: Co-educational Day 2–9
No of pupils: B80 G80
Fees: (September 06)
Day £2970–£4950

RUSHMOOR SCHOOL
58–60 Shakespeare Road,
Bedford, Bedfordshire MK40 2DL
Tel: (01234) 352031
Fax: (01234) 348395
Email: office@
    rushmoorschool.co.uk
Head: Mr K M Knight
Type: Co-educational Day
Boys 4–16 Girls 4–10
No of pupils: B293 G9
Fees: (September 06)
Day £3930–£8130

ST ANDREW'S SCHOOL
78 Kimbolton Road, Bedford,
Bedfordshire MK40 2PA
Tel: (01234) 267272
Fax: (01234) 355105
Email: standrews@
    standrewsschoolbedford.com
Head: Mrs J Marsland
Type: Girls Day 3–16 (Boys 3–7)
No of pupils: B38 G295
Fees: (September 05)
Day £4905–£8025

DUNSTABLE

ST GEORGE'S
28 Priory Road, Dunstable,
Bedfordshire LU5 4HR
Tel: (01582) 661471
Fax: (01582) 663605
Head: Mrs Plater
Type: Co-educational Day 2–11
No of pupils: B65 G65
Fees: On application

SCEPTRE SCHOOL
Ridgeway Avenue, Dunstable,
Bedfordshire LU5 4QL
Tel: (01582) 665900
Head: Mr Simon Wells
Type: Co-educational Day
Boys 11–17 Girls 11–18
No of pupils: B40 G66
Fees: On application

LUTON

BROADMEAD SCHOOL
Tennyson Road, Luton,
Bedfordshire LU1 3RR
Tel: (01582) 722570
Fax: (01582) 486675
Email: Broadmead1@aol.com
Head: Mr A F Compton
Type: Co-educational Day 3–11
No of pupils: B65 G65
Fees: (September 05) Day £4374

MOORLANDS SCHOOL
Leagrave Hall, Luton, Bedfordshire
LU4 9LE
Tel: (01582) 573376
Fax: (01582) 509008
Email: moorlands@
    moorlandsschool.demon.co.uk
Head: Mrs D K Attias
Type: Co-educational Day 2–11
No of pupils: B171 G180
Fees: On application

SANDY

CHILDREN'S MONTESSORI SCHOOL
Green End, Gamlingay, Sandy,
Bedfordshire SG19 3LB
Tel: (01767) 650645
Head: Mrs P L Jenkins
Type: Co-educational Day 4–9
(Nursery)
Fees: (September 06) Day £4500

SHEFFORD

EAST LODGE SCHOOL
Ampthill Road, Campton,
Shefford, Bedfordshire SG17 5BH
Tel: (01462) 812644
Fax: (01462) 815909
Email: east-lodge-school@
    supanet.com
Head: Mrs V A Green
Type: Co-educational Day 3–8
No of pupils: B25 G25
Fees: (September 05)
Day £1671–£3910

BERKSHIRE

ALDERMASTON

CEDARS SCHOOL
Church Road, Aldermaston,
Berkshire RG7 4LR
Tel: (0118) 971 4251
Head: Mrs J O'Halloran
Type: Co-educational Day 4–11
No of pupils: B25 G25
Fees: (September 06) Day £5070

ASCOT

HEATHFIELD ST MARY'S SCHOOL*
London Road, Ascot, Berkshire
SL5 8BQ
Tel: (01344) 898342
Fax: (01344) 890689
Email: registrar@
heathfieldstmarys.net
Head: Mrs F King
Type: Girls Boarding 11–18
No of boarders: F245
Fees: (September 06) FB £22890

HURST LODGE SCHOOL
Bagshot Road, Ascot, Berkshire
SL5 9JU
Tel: (01344) 622154
Fax: (01344) 627049
Email: admissions@
hurstlodgesch.co.uk
Head: Miss V S Smit
Type: Girls Day and Boarding
3–18 (Boys 3–7)
No of pupils: B25 G225
No of boarders: W25
Fees: (September 05) WB £17250
Day £5682–£10500

LICENSED VICTUALLERS' SCHOOL
London Road, Ascot, Berkshire
SL5 8DR
Tel: (01344) 882770
Fax: (01344) 890648
Email: registrar@lvs.ascot.sch.uk
Head: Mr I A Mullins and
Mr G Best
Type: Co-educational Boarding
and Day 4–18
No of pupils: B534 G385
No of boarders: F69 W120
Fees: (September 06)
F/WB £16560–£19095
Day £7770–£10860

THE MARIST PREPARATORY SCHOOL
Kings Road, Sunninghill, Ascot,
Berkshire SL5 7PS
Tel: (01344) 626137
Fax: (01344) 621566
Email: head@marist-prep.windsor-
maidenhead.sch.uk
Head: Mrs J A Peachey
Type: Girls Day 3–11
No of pupils: 247
Fees: (September 05)
Day £6300–£6405

THE MARIST SENIOR SCHOOL
Kings Road, Sunninghill, Ascot,
Berkshire SL5 7PS
Tel: (01344) 624291
Fax: (01344) 874963
Email: pa2head@
marist.ascot.org.uk
Head: Mr K McCloskey
Type: Girls Day 11–18
No of pupils: 315
Fees: (September 05) Day £8475

PAPPLEWICK SCHOOL*
Windsor Road, Ascot, Berkshire
SL5 7LH
Tel: (01344) 621488
Fax: (01344) 874639
Email: hm@papplewick.org.uk
Head: Mr T W Bunbury
Type: Boys Boarding and Day
7–13
No of pupils: 203
No of boarders: F130
Fees: (September 05) FB £17775
Day £13650

ST GEORGE'S SCHOOL*
Ascot, Berkshire SL5 7DZ
Tel: (01344) 629900
Fax: (01344) 629901
Email: office@
stgeorges-ascot.org.uk
Head: Mrs C Jordan
Type: Girls Boarding and Day
11–18
No of pupils: 270
No of boarders: F136
Fees: (September 06) FB £22650
Day £14700

ST MARY'S SCHOOL, ASCOT*
St Mary's Road, Ascot, Berkshire
SL5 9JF
Tel: (01344) 623721
Fax: (01344) 873281
Email: genenq@
st-marys-ascot.co.uk
Head: Mrs M Breen
Type: Girls Boarding and Day
11–18
No of pupils: 360
No of boarders: F345
Fees: (September 06) FB £23592
Day £16614

BRACKNELL

LAMBROOK HAILEYBURY
Winkfield Row, Bracknell,
Berkshire RG42 6LU
Tel: (01344) 882717
Fax: (01344) 891114
Email: info@
lambrook.berks.sch.uk
Head: Mr J E A Barnes
Type: Co-educational Boarding
and Day 3–13
No of pupils: B266 G146
No of boarders: W18
Fees: (September 06)
F/WB £15210–£17010
Day £7440–£12465

MEADOWBROOK MONTESSORI SCHOOL
Malt Hill, Warfield, Bracknell,
Berkshire RG42 6JQ
Tel: (01344) 890869
Fax: (01344) 890869
Email: mbrookuk@aol.com
Head: Mrs S Gunn and
Miss B O'Sullivan
Type: Co-educational Day 3–11
No of pupils: B50 G50
Fees: On application

NEWBOLD SCHOOL
Popeswood Road, Binfield,
Bracknell, Berkshire RG42 4AH
Tel: (01344) 421088
Fax: (01344) 421088
Head: Mr M Brooks
Type: Co-educational Day 3–11
No of pupils: 95
Fees: On application

CROWTHORNE

OUR LADY'S PREPARATORY SCHOOL
The Avenue, Crowthorne,
Berkshire RG45 6PB
Tel: (01344) 773394
Fax: (01344) 773394
Email: office@olps.co.uk
Head: Mrs H Robinson
Type: Co-educational Day 1–11
No of pupils: B50 G50
Fees: (September 05)
Day £2328–£5124

WELLINGTON COLLEGE*
Duke's Ride, Crowthorne,
Berkshire RG45 7PU
Tel: (01344) 444012
Fax: (01344) 444004
Email: admissions@
    wellingtoncollege.org.uk
Head: Dr A F Seldon
Type: Co-educational Boarding
and Day 13–18 (Co-ed VIth Form,
fully co-ed from 09/06)
No of pupils: B621 G131
No of boarders: F635
Fees: (September 06) FB £24195
Day £19380

MAIDENHEAD

CLAIRES COURT SCHOOL
Ray Mill Road East, Maidenhead,
Berkshire SL6 8TE
Tel: (01628) 411470
Fax: (01628) 411466
Email: Head@clairescourt.co.uk
Head: Mr J T Wilding
Type: Boys Day 11–16 (Co-ed VIth
Form)
No of pupils: 300
Fees: (September 05)
Day £7875–£9180

CLAIRES COURT SCHOOLS, RIDGEWAY
Maidenhead Thicket,
Maidenhead, Berkshire SL6 3QE
Tel: (01628) 411490
Fax: (01628) 411465
Email: Head@clairescourt.co.uk
Head: Mrs K M Rogg
Type: Boys Day 4–11
No of pupils: 231
Fees: (September 05)
Day £5895–£7875

CLAIRES COURT SCHOOLS, THE COLLEGE
1 College Avenue, Maidenhead,
Berkshire SL6 6AW
Tel: (01628) 411480
Fax: (01628) 411467
Email: Head@clairescourt.co.uk
Head: Mrs L Green
Type: Girls Day 3–16 (Boys 3–5,
co-ed VIth Form)
No of pupils: B101 G295
Fees: On application

HERRIES SCHOOL
Dean Lane, Cookham Dean,
Maidenhead, Berkshire SL6 9BD
Tel: (01628) 483350
Fax: (01628) 483329
Email: office@herries.ws
Head: Mrs A M Bradberry
Type: Co-educational Day 3–11
No of pupils: B30 G60
Fees: (September 05)
Day £4350–£6090

HIGHFIELD SCHOOL
2 West Road, Maidenhead,
Berkshire SL6 1PD
Tel: (01628) 624918
Fax: (01628) 635747
Email: office@
    highfield.berks.sch.uk
Head: Mrs C M A Lane
Type: Girls Day 3–11
No of pupils: 170
Fees: (September 06)
Day £2895–£6795

REDROOFS THEATRE SCHOOL
Littlewick Green, Maidenhead,
Berkshire SL6 3QY
Tel: (01628) 822461
Email: sam@redroofs.co.uk
Head: Ms June Rose
Type: Co-educational Day 9+
Fees: (September 05)
Day £6900–£9800

ST PIRAN'S PREPARATORY SCHOOL*
Gringer Hill, Maidenhead,
Berkshire SL6 7LZ
Tel: (01628) 594300
Fax: (01628) 594301
Email: office@stpirans.co.uk
Head: Mr J Carroll
Type: Co-educational Day 3–13
No of pupils: B225 G143
Fees: (September 06)
Day £834–£3076

WINBURY SCHOOL
Braywick Park, Hibbert Road,
Bray, Maidenhead, Berkshire
SL6 1UU
Tel: (01628) 627412
Fax: (01628) 627412
Email: info@winburyschool.co.uk
Head: Mrs P L Prewett
Type: Co-educational Day 2–8
No of pupils: B50 G50
Fees: (September 06)
Day £2910–£5055

NEWBURY

BROCKHURST AND MARLSTON HOUSE SCHOOLS
Hermitage, Newbury, Berkshire
RG18 9UL
Tel: (01635) 200293
Fax: (01635) 200190
Email: info@brockmarl.org.uk
Head: Mr D J W Fleming and
Mrs C E Riley
Type: Co-educational Boarding
and Day 3–13 (Single-sex ed)
No of pupils: B143 G90
No of boarders: F3 W70
Fees: (September 06) WB £15750
Day £7050–£11850

CHEAM SCHOOL*
Headley, Newbury, Berkshire
RG19 8LD
Tel: (01635) 268381
Fax: (01635) 269345
Email: registrar@
    cheamschool.co.uk
Head: Mr M R Johnson
Type: Co-educational Boarding
and Day 3–13
No of pupils: B221 G158
No of boarders: F10 W69
Fees: (September 06) FB £18366
Day £3570–£13599

HORRIS HILL SCHOOL
Newtown, Newbury, Berkshire
RG20 9DJ
Tel: (01635) 40594
Email: enquiries@horrishill.com
Head: Mr J H L Phillips
Type: Boys Boarding and Day
7–13
No of pupils: 125
No of boarders: F120
Fees: (September 06) FB £17850
Day £14850

MISS MORLEY'S NURSERY SCHOOL

Manor Lodge, Church Lane, Cheveley, Newbury, Berkshire RG20 8UT
Tel: (020) 7730 5797
Head: Mrs C Spence and Ms L Spence
Type: Co-educational Day 2–5
No of pupils: 42
Fees: (September 05)
Day £2700–£3000

ST GABRIEL'S SCHOOL

Sandleford Priory, Newbury, Berkshire RG20 9BD
Tel: (01635) 555680
Fax: (01635) 555698
Email: registrar@stgabriels.co.uk
Head: Mr A Jones
Type: Girls Day 3–18 (Boys 3–7)
No of pupils: B5 G499
Fees: (September 06)
Day £7095–£10125

ST MICHAELS SCHOOL

Harts Lane, Burghclere, Newbury, Berkshire RG20 9JW
Tel: (01635) 278137
Fax: (01635) 278601
Head: Father J Dreher
Type: Co-educational Boarding and Day 7–18 (Single-sex ed 13–18)
No of pupils: B37 G35
No of boarders: F20 W33
Fees: On application

THORNGROVE SCHOOL

The Mount, Highclere, Newbury, Berkshire RG20 9PS
Tel: (01635) 253172
Fax: (01635) 254135
Email: admin@ thorngroveschool.co.uk
Head: Mr N J Broughton
Type: Co-educational Day 2–13
No of pupils: B125 G99
Fees: (September 05)
Day £6795–£8340

PANGBOURNE

PANGBOURNE COLLEGE

Pangbourne, Berkshire RG8 8LA
Tel: (0118) 984 2101
Fax: (0118) 984 5443
Email: registrar@pangcoll.co.uk
Head: Mr T J Garnier
Type: Co-educational Boarding and Day 11–18
No of pupils: B294 G100
No of boarders: F193
Fees: (September 05)
FB £14955–£20595
Day £10515–£14445

READING

THE ABBEY SCHOOL

Kendrick Road, Reading, Berkshire RG1 5DZ
Tel: (0118) 987 2256
Fax: (0118) 987 1478
Email: schooloffice@ theabbey.co.uk
Head: Mrs B E Stanley
Type: Girls Day 3–18
No of pupils: 1030
Fees: (September 06)
Day £6000–£9600

ALDER BRIDGE SCHOOL

Bridge House, Mill Lane, Padworth, Reading, Berkshire RG7 4JU
Tel: (0118) 971 4471
Fax: (07092) 042631
Email: info@ alderbridge.w-berks.sch.uk
Type: Co-educational Day 3–11
No of pupils: B32 G29
Fees: On application

THE ARK SCHOOL

School Road, Padworth, Reading, Berkshire RG7 4JA
Tel: (0118) 983 4802
Fax: (0118) 983 6894
Email: office@ arkschool.fsnet.co.uk
Head: Mrs P A Oakley
Type: Co-educational Day 0–11
No of pupils: B53 G58
Fees: On application

BRADFIELD COLLEGE*

Bradfield, Reading, Berkshire RG7 6AU
Tel: (0118) 964 4510
Fax: (0118) 964 4511
Email: headmaster@ bradfieldcollege.org.uk
Head: Mr P J M Roberts
Type: Co-educational Boarding and Day 13–18
No of pupils: B455 G205
No of boarders: F580
Fees: (September 06) FB £22890
Day £18312

CHILTERN COLLEGE SCHOOL

16 Peppard Road, Caversham, Reading, Berkshire RG4 8JZ
Tel: (0118) 947 1847
Fax: (0118) 946 3218
Email: info@chilterncollege.com
Head: Mrs J Halliday
Type: Co-educational Day 4–11
No of pupils: 80
Fees: On application

CROSFIELDS SCHOOL

Shinfield, Reading, Berkshire RG2 9BL
Tel: (0118) 987 1810
Fax: (0118) 931 0806
Email: office@crosfields.com
Head: Mr J P Wansey
Type: Boys Day 4–13
No of pupils: 466
Fees: On application

DOLPHIN SCHOOL

Hurst, Reading, Berkshire RG10 0BP
Tel: (0118) 934 1277
Fax: (0118) 934 4110
Email: omnes@dolphinschool.com
Head: Mrs H Brough and Mr J Wall
Type: Co-educational Day 3–13
No of pupils: B153 G138
Fees: (September 05)
Day £4110–£8490

ELSTREE SCHOOL
Woolhampton, Reading, Berkshire
RG7 5TD
Tel: (0118) 971 3302
Fax: (0118) 971 4280
Email: secretary@
  elstreeschool.org.uk
Head: Mr S M Hill
Type: Boys Boarding and Day
3–13 (Girls 3–7)
No of pupils: B240 G20
No of boarders: F80 W10
Fees: (September 05) FB £16380
Day £6996–£12090

THE ELVIAN SCHOOL
61 Bath Road, Reading, Berkshire
RG30 2BB
Tel: (0118) 957 2861
Fax: (0118) 957 2220
Email: mansers@
  elvian.reading.sch.uk
Head: Mrs S Manser
Type: Co-educational Day 3–18
No of pupils: B151 G25
Fees: (September 06)
Day £5805–£7860

HEMDEAN HOUSE SCHOOL
Hemdean Road, Caversham,
Reading, Berkshire RG4 7SD
Tel: (0118) 947 2590
Fax: (0118) 946 4474
Email: office@
  hemdeanhouse.co.uk
Head: Mrs J Harris
Type: Co-educational Day
Boys 3–11 Girls 3–16
No of pupils: B50 G130
Fees: (September 05)
Day £3750–£5550

THE HIGHLANDS SCHOOL
Wardle Avenue, Tilehurst,
Reading, Berkshire RG31 6JR
Tel: (0118) 942 7186
Fax: (0118) 945 4953
Email: enquiries@
  highlandsschool.co.uk
Head: Mrs C A Bennett
Type: Co-educational Day
Boys 2–7 Girls 2–11
No of pupils: B39 G100
Fees: (September 06)
Day £271–£2250

LEIGHTON PARK SCHOOL
Shinfield Road, Reading, Berkshire
RG2 7ED
Tel: (0118) 987 9600
Fax: (0118) 987 9589
Email: admissions@
  leightonpark.com
Head: Mr J Dunston
Type: Co-educational Boarding
and Day 11–18
No of pupils: B302 G173
No of boarders: F75 W71
Fees: (September 06)
FB £18600–£21900
WB £16590–£19500
Day £12360–£14550

THE ORATORY PREPARATORY SCHOOL*
Goring Heath, Reading, Berkshire
RG8 7SF
Tel: (0118) 984 4511
Fax: (0118) 984 4806
Email: office@oratoryprep.co.uk
Head: Dr R J Hillier
Type: Co-educational Day and
Boarding 3–13
No of pupils: B270 G137
No of boarders: F25 W17
Fees: (September 06) FB £13845
WB £12750 Day £2985–£10050

THE ORATORY SCHOOL
Woodcote, Reading, Berkshire
RG8 0PJ
Tel: (01491) 683500
Fax: (01491) 680020
Email: enquiries@oratory.co.uk
Head: Mr C I Dytor
Type: Boys Day and Boarding
11–18
No of pupils: 400
No of boarders: F220
Fees: (September 06)
FB £16140–£22575
Day £11970–£16305

PADWORTH COLLEGE*
Padworth, Reading, Berkshire
RG7 4NR
Tel: (0118) 983 2644
Fax: (0118) 983 4515
Email: info@padworth.com
Head: Mrs L Melhuish
Type: Co-educational Boarding
and Day 13–19
No of pupils: B37 G69
No of boarders: F77 W9
Fees: (September 06) FB £18600
WB £14500 Day £7800

QUEEN ANNE'S SCHOOL*
6 Henley Road, Caversham,
Reading, Berkshire RG4 6DX
Tel: (0118) 918 7333
Fax: (0118) 918 7310
Email: admissions@qas.org.uk
Head: Mrs J Harrington
Type: Girls Boarding and Day
11–18
No of pupils: 340
No of boarders: F100 W80
Fees: (September 06) FB £22707
Day £15390

READING BLUE COAT SCHOOL*
Holme Park, Sonning-on-Thames,
Reading, Berkshire RG4 6SU
Tel: (0118) 944 1005
Fax: (0118) 944 2690
Email: vmf@
  blue-coat.reading.sch.uk
Head: Mr S J W McArthur
Type: Boys Day 11–18 (Co-ed VIth
Form)
No of pupils: B608 G54
Fees: (September 06) Day £10395

ST ANDREW'S SCHOOL
Buckhold, Pangbourne, Reading,
Berkshire RG8 8QA
Tel: (0118) 974 4276
Fax: (0118) 974 5049
Email: registrar@
  standrewspangbourne.co.uk
Head: Mr J M Snow
Type: Co-educational Day and
Boarding 3–13
No of pupils: B161 G123
Fees: (September 06) WB £14700
Day £8280

ST EDWARD'S SCHOOL
64 Tilehurst Road, Reading,
Berkshire RG30 2JH
Tel: (0118) 957 4342
Fax: (0118) 950 3736
Email: admin@stedwards.org.uk
Head: Mr P Keddie
Type: Boys Day 4–13
No of pupils: 170
Fees: (September 05)
Day £5385–£6945

ST JOSEPH'S CONVENT SCHOOL
Upper Redlands Road, Reading,
Berkshire RG1 5JT
Tel: (0118) 966 1000
Fax: (0118) 926 9932
Email: mailbox@
  st-josephs.reading.sch.uk
Head: Mrs M T Sheridan
Type: Girls Day 3–18
No of pupils: B6 G352
Fees: (September 05)
Day £4110–£8730

SANDHURST

EAGLE HOUSE*
Crowthorne Road, Sandhurst,
Berkshire GU47 8PH
Tel: (01344) 772134
Fax: (01344) 779039
Email: info@
  eaglehouseschool.com
Head: Mr Andrew Barnard
Type: Co-educational Day and
Boarding 3–13
No of pupils: B185 G83
No of boarders: F14 W8
Fees: (September 06) F/WB £15900
Day £11775

SLOUGH

ETON END PNEU
35 Eton Road, Datchet, Slough,
Berkshire SL3 9AX
Tel: (01753) 541075
Fax: (01753) 541123
Email: admin@etonend.org
Head: Mrs V M Pilgerstorfer
Type: Co-educational Day
Boys 3–7 Girls 3–11(Boys 3–7)
No of pupils: B50 G200
Fees: (September 05)
Day £3330–£6900

LANGLEY MANOR SCHOOL
St Marys Road, Langley, Slough,
Berkshire SL3 6BZ
Tel: (01753) 825368
Fax: (01753) 821451
Head: Mrs J Sculpher
Type: Co-educational Day 3–11
No of pupils: B140 G123
Fees: (September 05)
Day £5730–£5988

LONG CLOSE SCHOOL
Upton Court Road, Slough,
Berkshire SL3 7LU
Tel: (01753) 520095
Fax: (01753) 821463
Email: info@
  longcloseschool.co.uk
Head: Mrs W Holland
Type: Co-educational Day 2–16
Fees: (September 06)
Day £5130–£9060

ST BERNARD'S PREPARATORY SCHOOL
Hawtrey Close, Slough, Berkshire
SL1 1TB
Tel: (01753) 521821
Fax: (01753) 552364
Email: schooloffice@
  stbernardsprep.fsnet.co.uk
Head: Mrs M B Smith
Type: Co-educational Day 3–11
No of pupils: B125 G71
Fees: (September 05)
Day £4620–£5700

SUNNINGDALE

SUNNINGDALE SCHOOL
Sunningdale, Berkshire SL5 9PY
Tel: (01344) 620159
Fax: (01344) 873304
Email: headmaster@
  sunningdaleschool.co.uk
Head: Mr T A C N Dawson and
Mr A J N Dawson
Type: Boys Boarding 8–13
No of pupils: 100
No of boarders: F95
Fees: On application

THATCHAM

BROCKHURST & MARLSTON HOUSE PRE-PREPARATORY SCHOOL
Hermitage, Thatcham, Berkshire
RG18 9UL
Tel: (01635) 200293
Fax: (01635) 200190
Email: info@brockmarl.org.uk
Head: Mrs C Riley
Type: Co-educational Day 3–6
No of pupils: B25 G22
Fees: (September 05)
Day £3300–£6375

DOWNE HOUSE*
Cold Ash, Thatcham, Berkshire
RG18 9JJ
Tel: (01635) 200286
Fax: (01635) 202026
Email: correspondence@
  downehouse.net
Head: Mrs E McKendrick
Type: Girls Boarding and Day
11–18
No of pupils: 586
No of boarders: F565
Fees: (September 06) FB £24405
Day £17670

WINDSOR

BRIGIDINE SCHOOL WINDSOR
Queensmead, Kings Road,
Windsor, Berkshire SL4 2AX
Tel: (01753) 863779
Fax: (01753) 850278
Email: mail@brigidine.org.uk
Head: Mrs J Dunn
Type: Girls Day 3–18 (Boys 3–7)
No of pupils: B4 G248
Fees: (September 05)
Day £7110–£10755

ETON COLLEGE
Windsor, Berkshire SL4 6DW
Tel: (01753) 671249
Fax: (01753) 671248
Email: admissions@
  etoncollege.org.uk
Head: Mr A R M Little
Type: Boys Boarding 13–18
No of pupils: 1304
No of boarders: F1304
Fees: (September 06) FB £24990

ST GEORGE'S SCHOOL
Windsor Castle, Windsor,
Berkshire SL4 1QF
Tel: (01753) 865553
Fax: (01753) 842093
Email: enqs@stgwindsor.co.uk
Head: Mr J R Jones
Type: Co-educational Boarding
and Day 3–13
No of pupils: B362 G120
No of boarders: F23 W9
Fees: On application

England – Berkshire

ST JOHN'S BEAUMONT*

Priest Hill, Old Windsor, Windsor,
Berkshire SL4 2JN
Tel: (01784) 432428
Fax: (01784) 494048
Email: admissions@
    stjohnsbeaumont.co.uk
Head: Mr G Delaney
Type: Boys Boarding and Day
4–13
No of pupils: 342
No of boarders: F30 W30
Fees: (September 05) FB £17286
WB £14580 Day £5997–£11046

UPTON HOUSE SCHOOL*

115 St Leonard's Road, Windsor,
Berkshire SL4 3DF
Tel: (01753) 862610
Fax: (01753) 621950
Email: info@uptonhouse.org.uk
Head: Mrs M Collins
Type: Co-educational Day
Boys 3–7 Girls 2–11
No of pupils: B70 G170
Fees: (September 06)
Day £1220–£3300

WOKINGHAM

BEARWOOD COLLEGE*

Bearwood Road, Wokingham,
Berkshire RG41 5BG
Tel: (0118) 974 8300
Fax: (0118) 977 3186
Email: headmaster@
    bearwoodcollege.co.uk
Head: Mr S Aiano
Type: Co-educational Boarding
and Day 11–18
No of pupils: B250 G68
No of boarders: F65 W44
Fees: (September 06)
F/WB £18900–£21780
Day £11550–£13470

HOLME GRANGE SCHOOL

Heathlands Road, Wokingham,
Berkshire RG40 3AL
Tel: (0118) 978 1566
Fax: (0118) 977 0810
Email: school@holmegrange.org
Head: Mr N J Brodrick
Type: Co-educational Day 3–13
No of pupils: B150 G134
Fees: (September 05)
Day £3360–£8340

LUCKLEY-OAKFIELD SCHOOL*

Luckley Road, Wokingham,
Berkshire RG40 3EU
Tel: (0118) 978 4175
Fax: (0118) 977 0305
Email: registrar@
    luckley.wokingham.sch.uk
Head: Miss V A Davis
Type: Girls Boarding and Day
11–18
No of pupils: 304
No of boarders: F24 W8
Fees: (September 06) FB £18486
WB £17049 Day £10797

LUDGROVE

Wokingham, Berkshire RG40 3AB
Tel: (0118) 978 9881
Fax: (0118) 979 2973
Email: office@
    ludgroveschool.co.uk
Head: Mr G W P Barber
Type: Boys Boarding 8–13
No of boarders: F199
Fees: (September 06) FB £17550

WAVERLEY SCHOOL

Waverley Way, Finchampstead,
Wokingham, Berkshire RG40 4YD
Tel: (0118) 973 1121
Fax: (0118) 973 1131
Email: waverleyschool@
    waverley.wokingham.sch.uk
Head: Mr S G Melton
Type: Co-educational Day 3–11
No of pupils: B65 G63
Fees: (September 05)
Day £2530–£7080

WHITE HOUSE PREPARATORY SCHOOL

Finchampstead Road,
Wokingham, Berkshire RG40 3HD
Tel: (0118) 978 5151
Fax: (0118) 979 4716
Email: office@
    whitehouse.wokingham.sch.uk
Head: Mrs S Gillam
Type: Girls Day 2–11 (Boys 2–4)
No of pupils: B4 G116
Fees: (September 06)
Day £3807–£7449

BRISTOL

BACKWELL

FAIRFIELD SCHOOL
Fairfield Way, Backwell, Bristol
BS48 3PD
Tel: (01275) 462743
Fax: (01275) 464347
Email: secretary@
 fairfieldschool.org.uk
Head: Mrs L Barton
Type: Co-educational Day 3–11
No of pupils: B66 G75
Fees: (September 06)
Day £5400–£5925

BRISTOL

BADMINTON SCHOOL*
Westbury-on-Trym, Bristol
BS9 3BA
Tel: (0117) 905 5271
Fax: (0117) 962 8963
Email: arennie@
 badminton.bristol.sch.uk
Head: Mrs J Scarrow
Type: Girls Boarding and Day
4–18
No of pupils: 420
No of boarders: F166 W15
Fees: (September 06)
FB £15120–£22800
WB £15120–£2280
Day £5970–£12840

BRISTOL CATHEDRAL SCHOOL
College Square, Bristol BS1 5TS
Tel: (0117) 929 1872
Fax: (0117) 930 4219
Email: info@
 bristolcathedral.org.uk
Head: Mrs Anne Davey
Type: Co-educational Day 10–18
(Co-ed VIth Form)
No of pupils: B318 G70
Fees: (September 06) Day £8658

BRISTOL GRAMMAR SCHOOL
University Road, Bristol BS8 1SR
Tel: (0117) 973 6006
Fax: (0117) 946 7485
Email: headmaster@
 bgs.bristol.sch.uk
Head: Dr D J Mascord
Type: Co-educational Day 7–18
No of pupils: B808 G398
Fees: (September 05)
FB £4788–£8115

BRISTOL STEINER SCHOOL
Redland Hill House, Redland Hill,
Bristol BS6 6UX
Tel: (0117) 933 9990
Fax: (0117) 933 9999
Email: office@
 steiner.bristol.sch.uk
Head: Mr C Nelson
Type: Co-educational Day 3–14
Fees: (September 06)
Day £4020–£4416

CARMEL CHRISTIAN SCHOOL
817A Bath Road, Brislington,
Bristol BS4 5NL
Tel: (0117) 9775535
Fax: (0117) 9775678
Head: Miss S Watt
Type: Co-educational Day 4–17
No of pupils: B13 G15
Fees: On application

CLEVE HOUSE SCHOOL
254 Wells Road, Bristol BS4 2PN
Tel: (0117) 977 7218
Fax: (0117) 977 3915
Email: clevehouseschool@
 btconnect.com
Head: Mr D Lawson and Mrs E
Lawson
Type: Co-educational Day 3–11
No of pupils: B56 G65
Fees: (September 05) Day £3885

CLIFTON COLLEGE*
32 College Road, Clifton, Bristol
BS8 3JH
Tel: (0117) 315 7000
Fax: (0117) 315 7101
Email: admissions@
 clifton-college.avon.sch.uk
Head: Mr Mark Moore
Type: Co-educational Boarding
and Day 13–18
No of pupils: B444 G234
No of boarders: F269
Fees: (September 06) FB £23250
Day £15690

CLIFTON COLLEGE PRE-PREP–BUTCOMBE
Guthrie Road, Bristol BS8 3EZ
Tel: (0117) 315 7591
Fax: (0117) 315 7592
Email: wbowring@
 clifton-college.avon.sch.uk
Head: Dr W E Bowring
Type: Co-educational Day 3–8
No of pupils: B138 G80
Fees: (September 06)
Day £1760–£7860

CLIFTON COLLEGE PREPARATORY SCHOOL[†]
The Avenue, Clifton, Bristol
BS8 3HE
Tel: (0117) 315 7501
Fax: (0117) 315 7504
Email: lturley@
 clifton-college.avon.sch.uk
Head: Dr R J Acheson
Type: Co-educational Boarding
and Day 3–13
No of pupils: B397 G197
No of boarders: F47 W10
Fees: (September 06)
FB £16485–£17100
WB £15750–£16260
Day £5280–£11310

CLIFTON HIGH SCHOOL
College Road, Clifton, Bristol
BS8 3JD
Tel: (0117) 973 0201
Fax: (0117) 923 8962
Email: enquiries@
 cliftonhigh.bristol.sch.uk
Head: Mrs M C Culligan
Type: Co-educational Day and
Boarding 3–18
No of pupils: B143 G622
No of boarders: F3
Fees: On application

COLSTON'S COLLEGIATE SCHOOL
Stapleton, Bristol BS16 1BJ
Tel: (0117) 965 5207
Fax: (0117) 958 5652
Email: enquiries@
 colstons.bristol.sch.uk
Head: Mr D G Crawford
Type: Co-educational Boarding
and Day 3–18
No of pupils: B611 G257
No of boarders: F20 W40
Fees: On application

COLSTON'S GIRLS' SCHOOL
Cheltenham Road, Bristol BS6 5RD
Tel: (0117) 942 4328
Fax: (0117) 942 1052
Email: admin@
  colstonsgirls.bristol.sch.uk
Head: Mrs L A Jones
Type: Girls Day 10–18
No of pupils: 450
Fees: On application

COLSTON'S LOWER SCHOOL
Park Road, Bristol BS16 1BA
Tel: (0117) 965 5297
Fax: (0117) 965 6330
Email: schooladmin@
  colstons.bristol.sch.uk
Head: Mrs C A Aspden
Type: Co-educational Day 3–11
No of pupils: B156 G74
Fees: (September 05)
Day £4365–£6405

GRACEFIELD PREPARATORY SCHOOL
266 Overndale Road, Fishponds,
Bristol BS16 2RG
Tel: (0117) 956 7977
Fax: (0117) 956 3397
Email: enquiries@
  gracefieldschool.co.uk
Head: Mrs E Morgan
Type: Co-educational Day 4–11
No of pupils: B45 G45
Fees: (September 05) Day £2976

OVERNDALE SCHOOL
Chapel Lane, Old Sodbury, Bristol
BS37 6NQ
Tel: (01454) 310332
Head: Mrs K Winstanley
Type: Co-educational Day 1–11
No of pupils: B55 G45
Fees: On application

PROSPECT SCHOOL
Tramway Road, Brislington, Bristol
BS4 3DS
Tel: (0117) 9772271
Head: Mrs Lucy Sherrin
Type: Co-educational Day 11–17
No of pupils: B21 G20
Fees: On application

QUEEN ELIZABETH'S HOSPITAL
Berkeley Place, Clifton, Bristol
BS8 1JX
Tel: (0117) 930 3040
Fax: (0117) 929 3106
Email: headmaster@
  qehbristol.co.uk
Head: Mr S W Holliday
Type: Boys Day 7–18
No of pupils: 630
Fees: (September 06) Day £8511

THE RED MAIDS' SCHOOL
Westbury-on-Trym, Bristol
BS9 3AW
Tel: (0117) 962 2641
Fax: (0117) 962 1687
Email: admissions@
  redmaids.bristol.sch.uk
Head: Mrs I Tobias
Type: Girls Day 11–18
No of pupils: 450
Fees: (September 06) Day £7950

REDLAND HIGH SCHOOL
Redland Court, Bristol BS6 7EF
Tel: (0117) 924 5796
Fax: (0117) 924 1127
Email: admissions@
  redland.bristol.sch.uk
Head: Dr R Weeks
Type: Girls Day 3–18
No of pupils: 672
Fees: On application

ST URSULA'S HIGH SCHOOL
Brecon Road, Westbury-on-Trym,
Bristol BS9 4DT
Tel: (0117) 962 2616
Fax: (0117) 962 2616
Email: office@
  st-ursulas.bristol.sch.uk
Head: Mrs L Carter
Type: Co-educational Day 3–16
No of pupils: B165 G124
Fees: (September 06)
Day £4920–£7650

TOCKINGTON MANOR SCHOOL
Tockington, Bristol BS32 4NY
Tel: (01454) 613229
Fax: (01454) 613676
Email: admin@
  tockington.bristol.sch.uk
Head: Mr R G Tovey
Type: Co-educational Day and
Boarding 2–14
No of pupils: B168 G87
No of boarders: F14
Fees: (September 06) FB £13800
Day £6060–£10110

TORWOOD HOUSE SCHOOL
27–29 Durdham Park, Redland,
Bristol BS6 6XE
Tel: (0117) 973 6620
Fax: (0117) 973 6620
Email: emailus@
  torwoodhouse.bristol.sch.uk
Head: Mrs D Seagrove
Type: Co-educational Day 0–11
No of pupils: B100 G102
Fees: On application

CHEW MAGNA

SACRED HEART PREPARATORY SCHOOL
Winford Road, Chew Magna,
Bristol BS40 8QY
Tel: (01275) 332470
Fax: (01275) 332039
Email: info@
  sacredheartprepschool.co.uk
Head: Mrs J E Lee
Type: Co-educational Day 3–11
No of pupils: B36 G57
Fees: (September 05)
Day £960–£5130

WRAXALL

THE DOWNS SCHOOL
Wraxall, Bristol BS48 1PF
Tel: (01275) 852008
Fax: (01275) 855840
Email: office@
  thedownsschool.co.uk
Head: Mr M A Gunn
Type: Co-educational Day and
Boarding 4–13
No of pupils: B152 G67
No of boarders: W6
Fees: (September 05) WB £12900
Day £5850–£9990

BUCKINGHAMSHIRE

AMERSHAM

THE BEACON SCHOOL
Chesham Bois, Amersham,
Buckinghamshire HP6 5PF
Tel: (01494) 433654
Fax: (01494) 727849
Email: enquiries@
   beaconschool.co.uk
Head: Mr M W Spinney
Type: Boys Day 3–13
No of pupils: 430
Fees: (September 05)
Day £3630–£9870

HEATHERTON HOUSE SCHOOL
Copperkins Lane, Chesham Bois,
Amersham, Buckinghamshire
HP6 5QB
Tel: (01494) 726433
Fax: (01494) 729628
Email: admissions@
   heathertonhouse.co.uk
Head: Mr P Rushforth
Type: Girls Day 3–11 (Boys 2–5)
No of pupils: 175
Fees: (September 06)
Day £1320–£8295

AYLESBURY

ASHFOLD SCHOOL
Dorton, Aylesbury,
Buckinghamshire HP18 9NG
Tel: (01844) 238237
Fax: (01844) 238505
Email: hmsecretary@
   ashfoldschool.co.uk
Head: Mr M O M Chitty
Type: Co-educational Day and
Boarding 3–13
No of pupils: B178 G94
No of boarders: W25
Fees: (September 06) WB £13110
Day £6555–£11565

LADYMEDE
Little Kimble, Aylesbury,
Buckinghamshire HP17 0XP
Tel: (01844) 346154
Fax: (01844) 275660
Email: loffice@ladymede.com
Head: Mrs B.A. Peters
Type: Co-educational Day 3–11
No of pupils: B55 G60
Fees: (September 06)
Day £3312–£6693

BEACONSFIELD

DAVENIES SCHOOL
Beaconsfield, Buckinghamshire
HP9 1AA
Tel: (01494) 685400
Fax: (01494) 685408
Email: office@davenies.co.uk
Head: Mr A J P Nott
Type: Boys Day 4–13
No of pupils: 325
Fees: (September 05)
Day £8400–£9600

HIGH MARCH SCHOOL
23 Ledborough Lane,
Beaconsfield, Buckinghamshire
HP9 2PZ
Tel: (01494) 675186
Fax: (01494) 675377
Email: head@
   highmarch.bucks.sch.uk
Head: Mrs S J Clifford
Type: Girls Day 3–11 (Boys 3–5)
No of pupils: B12 G290
Fees: (September 06)
Day £2895–£8685

BUCKINGHAM

AKELEY WOOD LOWER SCHOOL
Lillingstone Dayrell, Buckingham,
Buckinghamshire MK18 5AN
Tel: (01280) 860182
Fax: (01280) 860194
Email: enquiries@
   akeleywoodschool.co.uk
Head: Mrs A Taylor
Type: Co-educational Day 9–11
No of pupils: B72 G83
Fees: (September 06)
Day £2500–£3800

AKELEY WOOD SCHOOL
Akeley Wood, Buckingham,
Buckinghamshire MK18 5AE
Tel: (01280) 812000
Fax: (01280) 822945
Email: enquiries@
   akeleywoodschool.co.uk
Head: Dr J Grundy
Type: Co-educational Day 3–18
No of pupils: B521 G367
Fees: (September 06)
Day £7650–£8985

STOWE SCHOOL
Stowe, Buckingham,
Buckinghamshire MK18 5EH
Tel: (01280) 818323 / 818205
Fax: (01280) 818181
Email: admissions@stowe.co.uk
Head: Dr A K Wallersteiner
Type: Co-educational Boarding
and Day 13–18
No of pupils: B502 G129
No of boarders: F550
Fees: (September 06) FB £24240
Day £17925

CHESHAM

CHESHAM PREPARATORY SCHOOL
Orchard Leigh, Chesham,
Buckinghamshire HP5 3QF
Tel: (01494) 782619
Fax: (01494) 791645
Email: secretary@
   chesham-prep.bucks.sch.uk
Head: Mr J Marjoribanks
Type: Co-educational Day 4–13
No of pupils: B212 G148
Fees: On application

FARNHAM ROYAL

CALDICOTT SCHOOL
Crown Lane, Farnham Royal,
Buckinghamshire SL2 3SL
Tel: (01753) 649300
Fax: (01753) 649325
Email: office@caldicott.com
Head: Mr S J G Doggart
Type: Boys Boarding and Day
7–13
No of pupils: 240
No of boarders: F116 W126
Fees: (September 05) FB £15966
Day £11970

DAIR HOUSE SCHOOL TRUST LTD
Bishops Blake, Beaconsfield Road,
Farnham Royal, Buckinghamshire
SL2 3BY
Tel: (01753) 643964
Fax: (01753) 642376
Email: info@dairhouse.co.uk
Head: Mr David Hopkin
Type: Co-educational Day 3–11
No of pupils: B67 G31
Fees: (September 06)
Day £2430–£7080

GERRARDS CROSS

GAYHURST SCHOOL
Bull Lane, Gerrards Cross,
Buckinghamshire SL9 8RJ
Tel: (01753) 882690
Fax: (01753) 887451
Email: gayhurst@
    gayhurst.bucks.sch.uk
Head: Mr A J Sims
Type: Boys Day 4–13
Fees: (September 05)
Day £6720–£8538

HOLY CROSS CONVENT
The Grange, Chalfont St Peter,
Gerrards Cross, Buckinghamshire
SL9 9DW
Tel: (01753) 895600
Fax: (01753) 882147
Email: enquiries@
    holy-cross.fsnet.co.uk
Head: Mrs M C Shinkwin
Type: Girls Day 3–18
No of pupils: 248
Fees: (September 05)
Day £4092–£8232

KINGSCOTE PRE-PREPARATORY SCHOOL
Oval Way, Gerrards Cross,
Buckinghamshire SL9 8PZ
Tel: (01753) 885535
Fax: (01753) 891783
Email: office@
    kingscoteschool.info
Head: Mrs S A Tunstall
Type: Boys Day 3–7
No of pupils: 130
Fees: (September 06)
Day £4543–£6810

MALTMAN'S GREEN SCHOOL
Maltmans Lane, Gerrards Cross,
Buckinghamshire SL9 8RR
Tel: (01753) 883022
Fax: (01753) 891237
Email: registrar@
    maltmansgreen.com
Head: Mrs J R Pardon
Type: Girls Day 3–11
No of pupils: 400
Fees: (September 06)
Day £6060–£9120

ST MARY'S SCHOOL
Packhorse Road, Gerrards Cross,
Buckinghamshire SL9 8JQ
Tel: (01753) 883370
Fax: (01753) 890966
Email: registrar@
    st-marys.bucks.sch.uk
Head: Mr F A Balcombe
Type: Girls Day 3–18
No of pupils: 325
Fees: (September 06)
Day £4840–£10135

THORPE HOUSE SCHOOL
Oval Way, Gerrards Cross,
Buckinghamshire SL9 8PZ
Tel: (01753) 882474
Fax: (01753) 889755
Email: office@
    thorpehouse.bucks.sch.uk
Head: Mr A F Lock
Type: Boys Day 3–16
No of pupils: 280
Fees: (September 06)
Day £3408–£10680

GREAT MISSENDEN

GATEWAY SCHOOL
1 High Street, Great Missenden,
Buckinghamshire HP16 9AA
Tel: (01494) 862407
Fax: (01494) 865787
Email: headteacher@
    gateway.bucks.sch.uk
Head: Mr S Wade
Type: Co-educational Day 2–12
No of pupils: B172 G110
Fees: (September 06)
Day £750–£7494

HIGH WYCOMBE

CROWN HOUSE SCHOOL
19 London Road, High Wycombe,
Buckinghamshire HP11 1BJ
Tel: (01494) 529927
Fax: (01494) 525693
Email: crownhouse.school@
    virgin.net
Head: Mr L Clark
Type: Co-educational Day 4–11
No of pupils: B78 G59
Fees: On application

GODSTOWE PREPARATORY SCHOOL
Shrubbery Road, High Wycombe,
Buckinghamshire HP13 6PR
Tel: (01494) 529273
Fax: (01494) 429009
Email: headmistress@
    godstowe.org
Head: Mr D St C Gainer
Type: Girls Day and Boarding
3–13 (Boys 3–8)
No of pupils: B14 G435
No of boarders: F96 W35
Fees: (September 05)
F/WB £14625–£15720
Day £6180–£10695

PIPERS CORNER SCHOOL*
Pipers Lane, Great Kingshill, High
Wycombe, Buckinghamshire
HP15 6LP
Tel: (01494) 718255
Fax: (01494) 719806
Email: school@piperscorner.co.uk
Head: Mrs V M Stattersfield
Type: Girls Day and Boarding
4–18
No of pupils: 470
No of boarders: F25 W25
Fees: On application

WYCOMBE ABBEY SCHOOL
High Wycombe, Buckinghamshire
HP11 1PE
Tel: (01494) 520381
Fax: (01494) 473836
Email: schoolsecretary@
    wycombeabbey.com
Head: Mrs P E Davies
Type: Girls Boarding 11–18 (A few
day places)
No of pupils: 547
No of boarders: F520
Fees: (September 06) FB £24600
Day £18450

MILTON KEYNES

BURY LAWN SCHOOL
Soskin Drive, Stantonbury Fields,
Milton Keynes, Buckinghamshire
MK14 6DP
Tel: (01908) 220345
Fax: (01908) 220363
Email: burylawnoffice@aol.com
Head: Mr F Roche
Type: Co-educational Day 1–18
No of pupils: B277 G214
Fees: On application

CITISCHOOL
599 Avebury Boulevard,
Milton Keynes, Buckinghamshire
MK9 3HR
Tel: (01908) 246789
Fax: (01908) 246799
Email: debbie.mack@countec.org
Head: Ms Debbie Mack
Type: Co-educational Day 15–16
No of pupils: B20 G6
Fees: On application

GROVE INDEPENDENT
SCHOOL
Redland Drive, Loughton,
Milton Keynes, Buckinghamshire
MK5 8HD
Tel: (01908) 690590
Fax: (01908) 649043
Email: office@
  groveindependentschool.co.uk
Head: Mrs D M Berkin
Type: Co-educational Day 2–13
Fees: (September 06)
Day £8952–£9228

GYOSEI INTERNATIONAL
SCHOOL UK
Japonica Lane, Willen Park,
Milton Keynes, Buckinghamshire
MK15 9JX
Tel: (01908) 690100
Fax: (01908) 690150
Head: Mr Y Mikuriya
Type: Co-educational Boarding
and Day 13–18
No of pupils: B62 G38
No of boarders: F100
Fees: On application

MILTON KEYNES
PREPARATORY SCHOOL
Tattenhoe Lane, Milton Keynes,
Buckinghamshire MK3 7EG
Tel: (01908) 642111
Fax: (01908) 366365
Email: info@mkps.co.uk
Head: Mrs H A Pauley
Type: Co-educational Day 0–11
No of pupils: B250 G250
Fees: On application

SWANBOURNE HOUSE
SCHOOL*
Swanbourne, Milton Keynes,
Buckinghamshire MK17 0HZ
Tel: (01296) 720264
Fax: (01296) 728089
Email: office@swanbourne.org
Head: Mr S D Goodhart and
Mrs J S Goodhart
Type: Co-educational Boarding
and Day 3–13
No of pupils: B225 G188
No of boarders: F28 W21
Fees: (September 06) F/WB £15300
Day £5613–£11940

THORNTON COLLEGE
CONVENT OF JESUS AND
MARY
Thornton, Milton Keynes,
Buckinghamshire MK17 0HJ
Tel: (01280) 812610
Fax: (01280) 824042
Email: registrar@
  thorntoncollege.com
Head: Miss A Williams
Type: Girls Day and Boarding
2–16 (Boys 2–4)
No of pupils: 310
No of boarders: F32 W18
Fees: (September 05)
FB £12000–£14000
WB £10950–£12525
Day £5550–£8325

NEWPORT PAGNELL

FILGRAVE SCHOOL
Filgrave, Newport Pagnell,
Buckinghamshire MK16 9ET
Tel: (01234) 711534
Email: enquiries@
  filgraveschool.org.uk
Head: Mrs S Marriott
Type: Co-educational Day 3–9
No of pupils: B20 G21
Fees: On application

PRINCES RISBOROUGH

ST TERESA'S CATHOLIC
INDEPENDENT & NURSERY
SCHOOL
Aylesbury Road, Princes
Risborough, Buckinghamshire
HP27 0JW
Tel: (01844) 345005
Fax: (01844) 345131
Email: office@
  st-teresas.bucks.sch.uk
Head: Mr R P Duigan
Type: Co-educational Day 3–11
No of pupils: B73 G68
Fees: (September 06)
Day £705–£5745

STOKE POGES

SEFTON PARK SCHOOL
School Lane, Stoke Poges,
Buckinghamshire SL2 4QA
Tel: (01753) 662482
Fax: (01753) 662168
Head: Mr S Hensby
Type: Co-educational Day 11–18
No of pupils: B63 G45
Fees: On application

England – Buckinghamshire

CAMBRIDGESHIRE

CAMBRIDGE

BELLERBYS COLLEGE & EMBASSY CES CAMBRIDGE
Queens Campus, Bateman Street, Cambridge, Cambridgeshire CB2 1LU
Tel: (01223) 363159
Fax: (01223) 307425
Email: cambridge@bellerbys.com
Head: Mr J Rushton
Type: Co-educational Boarding 14–25
No of pupils: B250 G250
No of boarders: F500
Fees: (September 06) FB £16000

CAMBRIDGE ARTS & SCIENCES (CATS)*
Round Church Street, Cambridge, Cambridgeshire CB5 8AD
Tel: (01223) 314431
Fax: (01223) 467773
Email: enquiries@catscollege.com
Head: Mrs E Armstrong and Mr H MacDonald
Type: Co-educational Boarding and Day Boys 14–23 Girls 14–24
No of pupils: B118 G152
No of boarders: F254
Fees: (September 06)
FB £17595–£25935
Day £12825–£19035

CAMBRIDGE CENTRE FOR SIXTH-FORM STUDIES*
1 Salisbury Villas, Station Road, Cambridge, Cambridgeshire CB1 2JF
Tel: (01223) 716890
Fax: (01223) 517530
Email: enquiries@ccss.co.uk
Head: Mr Neil Roskilly
Type: Co-educational Day and Boarding 15–19
No of pupils: B90 G70
No of boarders: F106
Fees: (September 06)
FB £17460–£22902
Day £8946–£14388

THE LEYS SCHOOL*
Trumpington Road, Cambridge, Cambridgeshire CB2 2AD
Tel: (01223) 508900
Fax: (01223) 505303
Email: office@theleys.net
Head: Mr Mark Slater
Type: Co-educational Boarding and Day 11–18
No of pupils: B324 G202
No of boarders: F280
Fees: (September 05)
FB £15105–£20970
Day £9570–£13425

MADINGLEY PRE-PREPARATORY SCHOOL
Cambridge Road, Madingley, Cambridge, Cambridgeshire CB3 8AH
Tel: (01954) 210309
Fax: (01233) 264169
Email: admin@ madingleyschool.co.uk
Head: Mrs P Evans
Type: Co-educational Day 3–8
No of pupils: B30 G30
Fees: (September 06) Day £6150

MPW (MANDER PORTMAN WOODWARD)
3/4 Brookside, Cambridge, Cambridgeshire CB2 1JE
Tel: (01223) 350158
Fax: (01223) 366429
Email: enquiries@ cambridge.mpw.co.uk
Head: Dr N Marriott
Type: Co-educational Day and Boarding 15–21
No of pupils: B60 G60
No of boarders: F20 W20
Fees: On application

THE PERSE SCHOOL
Hills Road, Cambridge, Cambridgeshire CB2 2QF
Tel: (01223) 403800
Fax: (01223) 403810
Email: office@perse.co.uk
Head: Mr Nigel Richardson
Type: Co-educational Day Boys 11–18 Girls 16–18
No of pupils: B590 G76
Fees: (September 06) Day £11061

THE PERSE SCHOOL FOR GIRLS
Union Road, Cambridge, Cambridgeshire CB2 1HF
Tel: (01223) 454700
Fax: (01223) 467420
Email: office@ admin.perse.cambs.sch.uk
Head: Miss P M Kelleher
Type: Girls Day 7–18
No of pupils: 668
Fees: (September 06)
Day £9090–£10680

ST ANDREW'S
2A Free School Lane, Cambridge, Cambridgeshire CB2 3QA
Tel: (01223) 360040
Fax: (01223) 467150
Email: registrar@ standrewscambridge.co.uk
Head: Mrs C Williams
Type: Co-educational Boarding and Day 14–18
No of pupils: B67 G53
No of boarders: F120
Fees: On application

ST COLETTE'S SCHOOL
Tenison Road, Cambridge, Cambridgeshire CB1 2DP
Tel: (01223) 353696
Fax: (01223) 517784
Email: stcolettes@indschool.org
Head: Mrs A C Wilson
Type: Co-educational Day 2–7
No of pupils: B60 G60
Fees: (September 06)
Day £5346–£6126

ST FAITH'S
Trumpington Road, Cambridge, Cambridgeshire CB2 2AG
Tel: (01223) 352073
Fax: (01223) 314757
Email: admissions@stfaiths.co.uk
Head: Mr C S S Drew
Type: Co-educational Day 4–13
No of pupils: B318 G196
Fees: (September 05)
Day £7305–£9225

ST JOHN'S COLLEGE SCHOOL

73 Grange Road, Cambridge,
Cambridgeshire CB3 9AB
Tel: (01223) 353532
Fax: (01223) 355846
Email: shoffice@sjcs.co.uk
Head: Mr K L Jones
Type: Co-educational Day and
Boarding 4–13
No of pupils: B270 G190
No of boarders: F40
Fees: (September 06)
FB £5244–£15732
Day £6006–£9960

ST MARY'S JUNIOR SCHOOL

1 Brookside, Cambridge,
Cambridgeshire CB2 1JE
Tel: (01223) 311666
Fax: (01223) 472168
Email: juniorschool@
   stmaryscambridge.co.uk
Head: Mrs D O'Sullivan
Type: Girls Day 4–11
No of pupils: 160
Fees: (September 06)
Day £6150–£7080

ST MARY'S SCHOOL*

Bateman Street, Cambridge,
Cambridgeshire CB2 1LY
Tel: (01223) 353253
Fax: (01223) 357451
Email: enquiries@
   stmaryscambridge.co.uk
Head: Mrs J Triffitt and
Mrs D O'Sullivan
Type: Girls Day and Boarding
4–18
No of boarders: F65 W3
Fees: (September 06) FB £20970
WB £18585 Day £10560

SANCTON WOOD SCHOOL

2 St Paul's Road, Cambridge,
Cambridgeshire CB1 2EZ
Tel: (01223) 359488
Fax: (01223) 359488
Email: sturdy@sturdy.demon.co.uk
Head: Rev J McDonald
Type: Co-educational Day 1–16
No of pupils: B105 G69
Fees: On application

ELY

THE KING'S SCHOOL ELY*

Ely, Cambridgeshire CB7 4DB
Tel: (01353) 660702
Fax: (01353) 667485
Email: admissions@
   kings-ely.cambs.sch.uk
Head: Mrs S E Freestone
Type: Co-educational Boarding
and Day 2–18
No of pupils: B518 G385
No of boarders: F194
Fees: (September 06)
FB £14175–£19410
Day £5835–£13410

HUNTINGDON

KIMBOLTON SCHOOL

Kimbolton, Huntingdon,
Cambridgeshire PE28 0EA
Tel: (01480) 860505
Fax: (01480) 860386
Email: registrar@
   kimbolton.cambs.sch.uk
Head: Mr J Belbin
Type: Co-educational Boarding
and Day 4–18 (Boarders from 11)
No of pupils: B462 G400
No of boarders: F54
Fees: (September 05) FB £16560
Day £6300–£9960

WHITEHALL SCHOOL

117 High Street, Somersham,
Huntingdon, Cambridgeshire
PE28 3EH
Tel: (01487) 840966
Fax: (01487) 840966
Email: office@
   whitehallschool.com
Head: Mr C Hutson
Type: Co-educational Day 3–11
No of pupils: B55 G55
Fees: (September 06)
Day £4131–£5361

MARCH

STATION EDUCATION CENTRE

5 Station Approach, March,
Cambridgeshire PE15 8SJ
Tel: (01354) 658768
Fax: (01354) 659356
Head: Ms Jane Breckon
Type: Co-educational Day 11–16
No of pupils: B4 G2
Fees: On application

PETERBOROUGH

PETERBOROUGH HIGH SCHOOL

Thorpe Road, Peterborough,
Cambridgeshire PE3 6JF
Tel: (01733) 343357
Fax: (01733) 355710
Email: phs@
   peterboroughhigh.co.uk
Head: Mrs S A Dixon
Type: Girls Day and Boarding
3–18 (Boys 3–11)
No of pupils: B81 G295
No of boarders: F18 W14
Fees: (September 05)
FB £15297–£16404
WB £13437–£14544
Day £6480–£8967

WISBECH

WISBECH GRAMMAR SCHOOL

North Brink, Wisbech,
Cambridgeshire PE13 1JX
Tel: (01945) 583631
Fax: (01945) 476746
Email: hmsecretary@
   wisbechgs.demon.co.uk
Head: Mr R S Repper
Type: Co-educational Day 4–18
No of pupils: B367 G342
Fees: (September 06)
Day £5910–£8700

England – Cambridgeshire

CHANNEL ISLANDS

ALDERNEY

ORMER HOUSE PREPARATORY SCHOOL
La Vallee, Alderney,
Channel Islands GY9 3XA
Tel: (01481) 823287
Fax: (01481) 824053
Email: enquiries@
 ormerhouse.com
Head: Mrs M Burridge
Type: Co-educational Day 2–13
No of pupils: B28 G24
Fees: On application

GUERNSEY

CONVENT OF MERCY
Cordier Hill, St Peter Port,
Guernsey, Channel Islands
GY1 1JH
Tel: (01481) 720729
Fax: (01481) 716339
Head: Sister C Blackburn
Type: Co-educational Day 3–7
No of pupils: B57 G46
Fees: On application

ELIZABETH COLLEGE
Guernsey, Channel Islands
GY1 2PY
Tel: (01481) 726544
Fax: (01481) 714839
Head: Dr N Argent
Type: Boys Day 2–18 (Co-ed VIth
Form)
No of pupils: 740
Fees: (September 05) Day £5400

THE LADIES' COLLEGE
Les Gravees, St Peter Port,
Guernsey, Channel Islands
GY1 1RW
Tel: (01481) 721602
Fax: (01481) 724209
Email: secretary@
 ladiescollege.education.gg
Head: Miss M E Macdonald
Type: Girls Day 4–18
No of pupils: 557
Fees: (September 05)
Day £4185–£4425

JERSEY

BEAULIEU CONVENT SCHOOL
Wellington Road, Saint Helier,
Jersey, Channel Islands JE2 4RJ
Tel: (01534) 731280
Fax: (01534) 888607
Email: secondaryadmin@
 beaulieu.sch.je
Head: Mrs R A Hill
Type: Girls Day 4–18
No of pupils: 623
Fees: On application

FCJ PRIMARY SCHOOL
Deloraine Road, St Saviour, Jersey,
Channel Islands JE2 7XB
Tel: (01534) 723063
Fax: (01534) 880353
Email: admin@fcj.sch.je
Head: Ms M Doyle
Type: Co-educational Day 4–11
No of pupils: B110 G180
Fees: On application

ST GEORGE'S PREPARATORY SCHOOL
La Hague Manor, Rue de la
Hague, St Peter, Jersey,
Channel Islands JE3 7DB
Tel: (01534) 481593
Fax: (01534) 484304
Email: admin@
 stgeorgesprep.co.uk
Head: Mr Colin Moore
Type: Co-educational Day 3–13
No of pupils: B106 G91
Fees: (September 05)
Day £3255–£10440

ST MICHAEL'S PREPARATORY SCHOOL
La Rue de la Houguette, St
Saviour, Jersey, Channel Islands
JE2 7UG
Tel: (01534) 856904
Fax: (01534) 856620
Email: ew@stmichaels.je
Head: Mr R De Figueiredo
Type: Co-educational Day 3–13
No of pupils: B167 G132
Fees: On application

VICTORIA COLLEGE
Jersey, Channel Islands JE1 4HT
Tel: (01534) 638200
Fax: (01534) 727448
Email: admin@vcj.sch.je
Head: Mr R Cook
Type: Boys Day 11–19
No of pupils: 650
Fees: On application

VICTORIA COLLEGE PREPARATORY SCHOOL
Pleasant Street, St Helier, Jersey,
Channel Islands JE2 4RR
Tel: (01534) 723468
Fax: (01534) 780596
Email: admin@vcp.sch.je
Head: Mr P Stevenson
Type: Boys Day 7–11
No of pupils: 280
Fees: (September 05) Day £3600

CHESHIRE

ALDERLEY EDGE

**ALDERLEY EDGE SCHOOL
FOR GIRLS**
Wilmslow Road, Alderley Edge,
Cheshire SK9 7QE
Tel: (01625) 583028
Fax: (01625) 590271
Email: schoolmail@aesg.co.uk
Head: Mrs K Mills
Type: Girls Day 3–18
No of pupils: 600
Fees: (September 05)
Day £4734–£7146

THE RYLEYS
Ryleys Lane, Alderley Edge,
Cheshire SK9 7UY
Tel: (01625) 583241
Fax: (01625) 581900
Email: headmaster@
ryleys.cheshire.sch.uk
Head: Mr P G Barrett
Type: Boys Day 3–13
No of pupils: 236
Fees: (September 06)
Day £4770–£8235

ALTRINCHAM

**ALTRINCHAM
PREPARATORY SCHOOL**
Marlborough Road, Bowdon,
Altrincham, Cheshire WA14 2RR
Tel: (0161) 928 3366
Fax: (0161) 929 6747
Email: admin@altprep.co.uk
Head: Mr A Potts
Type: Boys Day 4–11
No of pupils: 310
Fees: (September 06)
Day £4938–£5637

**BOWDON PREPARATORY
SCHOOL FOR GIRLS**
48 Stamford Road, Bowdon,
Altrincham, Cheshire WA14 2JP
Tel: (0161) 928 0678
Email: bps@bowdonprep.org.uk
Head: Mrs J H Tan
Type: Girls Day 2–12
No of pupils: 220
Fees: On application

CULCHETH HALL
Ashley Road, Altrincham,
Cheshire WA14 2LT
Tel: (0161) 928 1862
Fax: (0161) 929 6893
Email: admin@
culcheth-hall.org.uk
Head: Miss M A Stockwell
Type: Girls Day 2–16 (Boys 2–4)
No of pupils: B12 G203
Fees: (September 06)
Day £1860–£6960

FOREST SCHOOL
Moss Lane, Timperley,
Altrincham, Cheshire WA15 6LJ
Tel: (0161) 980 4075
Fax: (0161) 903 9275
Email: headteacher@
forestschool.co.uk
Head: Mrs E A Irons
Type: Co-educational Day 2–11
No of pupils: B86 G81
Fees: (September 06)
Day £4209–£4767

**HALE PREPARATORY
SCHOOL**
Broomfield Lane, Hale,
Altrincham, Cheshire WA15 9AS
Tel: (0161) 928 2386
Fax: (0161) 941 7934
Email: johnconnor@
b.t.connect.com
Head: Mr J Connor
Type: Co-educational Day 4–11
No of pupils: B99 G83
Fees: On application

**LORETO PREPARATORY
SCHOOL**
Dunham Road, Altrincham,
Cheshire WA14 4GZ
Tel: (0161) 928 8310
Fax: (0161) 929 5801
Email: info.loretoprep@
btconnect.com
Head: Mrs R A Hedger
Type: Girls Day 3–11 (Boys 4–7)
No of pupils: B1 G161
Fees: (September 06) Day £3960

**NORTH CESTRIAN
GRAMMAR SCHOOL**
Dunham Road, Altrincham,
Cheshire WA14 4AJ
Tel: (0161) 928 1856
Fax: (0161) 929 8657
Email: office@ncgs.co.uk
Head: Mr D G Vanstone
Type: Boys Day 11–18
No of pupils: B290 G8
Fees: (September 06) Day £6645

**ST AMBROSE PREPARATORY
SCHOOL**
Hale Barns, Altrincham, Cheshire
WA15 0HE
Tel: (0161) 903 9193
Fax: (0161) 903 8138
Email: stambroseprep.admin@
traffordlearning.org
Head: Mr M J Lochery
Type: Boys Day 4–11
No of pupils: 170
Fees: (September 06)
Day £4536–£4725

CHEADLE

CHEADLE HULME SCHOOL
Claremont Road, Cheadle Hulme,
Cheadle, Cheshire SK8 6EF
Tel: (0161) 488 3330
Fax: (0161) 488 3344
Email: headmaster@
chschool.co.uk
Head: Mr P V Dixon
Type: Boys Day 4–18
No of pupils: B706 G612
Fees: (September 06)
Day £6228–£7881

GREENBANK
Heathbank Road, Cheadle Hulme,
Cheadle, Cheshire SK8 6HU
Tel: (0161) 485 3724
Fax: (0161) 485 5519
Email: kevinphillips@
greenbank.stockport.sch.uk
Head: Mr K Phillips
Type: Co-educational Day 3–11
No of pupils: B98 G62
Fees: (September 06)
Day £3180–£5400

HULME HALL SCHOOLS
75 Hulme Hall Road, Cheadle
Hulme, Cheadle, Cheshire
SK8 6LA
Tel: (0161) 485 4638/3524
Fax: (0161) 485 5966
Email: secretary@
    hulmehallschool.co.uk
Head: Mr P Marland
Type: Co-educational Day 2–16
No of pupils: B255 G130
Fees: (September 05)
Day £3870–£6225

HULME HALL SCHOOLS
(JUNIOR DIVISION)
75 Hulme Hall Road, Cheadle
Hulme, Cheadle, Cheshire
SK8 6LA
Tel: (0161) 486 9970
Fax: (0161) 485 5966
Email: secretary@
    hulmehallschool.co.uk
Head: Mr P Marland
Type: Co-educational Day 3–11
No of pupils: B58 G32
Fees: On application

LADY BARN HOUSE
SCHOOL
Langlands, Schools Hill, Cheadle
Hulme, Cheadle, Cheshire SK8 1JE
Tel: (0161) 428 2912
Fax: (0161) 428 5798
Email: info@
    ladybarnhouse.stockport.sch.uk
Head: Mrs S Yule
Type: Co-educational Day 3–11
No of pupils: B280 G187
Fees: On application

RAMILLIES HALL SCHOOL[†]
Ramillies Avenue, Cheadle
Hulme, Cheadle, Cheshire SK8 7AJ
Tel: (0161) 485 3804
Fax: (0161) 486 6021
Email: info@ramillieshall.co.uk
Head: Miss D M Patterson and
Mrs A L Poole
Type: Co-educational Day 0–16
No of pupils: B114 G69
Fees: On application

CHESTER

ABBEY GATE COLLEGE
Saighton Grange, Saighton,
Chester, Cheshire CH3 6EN
Tel: (01244) 332077
Fax: (01244) 335510
Email: bursar@
    abbeygatecollege.co.uk
Head: Mrs L M Horner
Type: Co-educational Day 4–18
No of pupils: B242 G195
Fees: (September 06)
Day £4887–£8334

ABBEY GATE SCHOOL
Clare Avenue, Hoole, Chester,
Cheshire CH2 3HR
Tel: (01244) 319649
Email: abbeygateschool@
    talk21.com
Head: Mrs S M Fisher
Type: Co-educational Day 2–11
No of pupils: B35 G34
Fees: (September 06)
Day £4575–£4875

THE FIRS SCHOOL
45 Newton Lane, Chester,
Cheshire CH2 2HJ
Tel: (01244) 322443
Fax: (01244) 400450
Email: firsschool.admin@
    btopenworld.com
Head: Mrs M Denton
Type: Co-educational Day 4–11
No of pupils: B134 G81
Fees: (September 05) Day £4995

HAMMOND SCHOOL
Hoole Bank House, Mannings
Lane, Chester, Cheshire CH2 4ES
Tel: (01244) 305350
Fax: (01244) 305351
Email: enquiries@
    thehammondschool.co.uk
Head: Mrs M P Dangerfield
Type: Co-educational Day and
Boarding 11–18
No of pupils: B50 G170
No of boarders: F59
Fees: (September 06) FB £19275
Day £7625–£12345

THE KING'S SCHOOL
Wrexham Road, Chester, Cheshire
CH4 7QL
Tel: (01244) 689500
Fax: (01244) 689501
Email: admissions@
    kingschester.co.uk
Head: Mr T J Turvey
Type: Co-educational Day 7–18
No of pupils: B699 G117
Fees: On application

MERTON HOUSE
Abbot's Park, Off Liverpool Road,
Chester, Cheshire CH1 4BD
Tel: (01244) 377165
Fax: (01244) 374569
Email: secretary@
    mertonhousechester.co.uk
Head: Mrs A Collins
Type: Co-educational Day 3–11
No of pupils: B58 G65
Fees: On application

THE QUEEN'S SCHOOL
City Walls Road, Chester,
Cheshire CH1 2NN
Tel: (01244) 312078
Fax: (01244) 321507
Email: secretary@
    queens.cheshire.sch.uk
Head: Mrs C M Buckley
Type: Girls Day 4–18
No of pupils: 570
Fees: (September 06)
Day £5625–£8355

HOLMES CHAPEL

TERRA NOVA SCHOOL
Jodrell Bank, Holmes Chapel,
Cheshire CW4 8BT
Tel: (01477) 571251
Fax: (01477) 571646
Email: enquiries@tnschool.org
Head: Mr N Johnson
Type: Co-educational Boarding
and Day 3–13
No of pupils: B162 G121
No of boarders: F6 W20
Fees: (September 06) F/WB £12900
Day £2940–£10380

KNUTSFORD

YORSTON LODGE SCHOOL
18 St John's Road, Knutsford,
Cheshire WA16 0DP
Tel: (01565) 633177
Fax: (01565) 631245
Email: headmaster@
yorstonlodgeschool.co.uk
Head: Mr R Edgar
Type: Co-educational Day 2–11
No of pupils: B63 G61
Fees: On application

MACCLESFIELD

BEECH HALL SCHOOL
Beech Hall Drive, Tytherington,
Macclesfield, Cheshire SK10 2EG
Tel: (01625) 422192
Fax: (01625) 502424
Email: secretary@
beechhallschool.freeserve.co.uk
Head: Mr M Atkins
Type: Co-educational Day 4–13
(Kindergarten 1–5)
No of pupils: B130 G62
Fees: On application

THE KING'S SCHOOL
Macclesfield, Cheshire SK10 1DA
Tel: (01625) 260000
Fax: (01625) 260022
Email: mail@kingsmac.co.uk
Head: Dr S Coyne
Type: Co-educational Day 3–18
(Single-sex ed 11–16)
No of pupils: B800 G600
Fees: On application

NORTHWICH

CRANSLEY SCHOOL
Belmont Hall, Great Budworth,
Northwich, Cheshire CW9 6HN
Tel: (01606) 891747
Fax: (01606) 892122
Email: admin.cransleyschool@
btinternet.com
Head: Mrs G Gaunt
Type: Co-educational Day
Boys 3–11 Girls 3–16(Boys 3–11)
No of pupils: B23 G154
Fees: (September 06)
Day £3189–£7266

THE GRANGE SCHOOL
Bradburns Lane, Hartford,
Northwich, Cheshire CW8 1LU
Tel: (01606) 74007
Fax: (01606) 784581
Email: office@grange.org.uk
Head: Mr C P Jeffery
Type: Co-educational Day 4–18
No of pupils: B606 G528
Fees: (September 06)
Day £5295–£7080

SALE

CHRIST THE KING SCHOOL
The King's Centre, Raglan Road,
Sale, Cheshire M33 4AQ
Tel: (0161) 969 1906
Fax: (0161) 905 1586
Email: info@ctks.org.uk
Head: Mr D Baynes
Type: Co-educational Day 5–16
No of pupils: B25 G27
Fees: On application

FOREST PARK SCHOOL
Lauriston House, 27 Oakfield,
Sale, Cheshire M33 6NB
Tel: (0161) 973 4835
Fax: (0161) 282 9021
Email: post@
forestparkschool.freeserve.co.uk
Head: Mr L B R Groves
Type: Co-educational Day 3–11
No of pupils: B80 G60
Fees: (September 05)
Day £4086–£4473

SANDBACH

NORFOLK HOUSE PREPARATORY & KIDS CORNER NURSERY
Norfolk House, 120 Congleton
Road, Sandbach, Cheshire
CW11 1HF
Tel: (01270) 759257
Fax: (01270) 753519
Email: post@norfolkhouse.net
Head: Mrs P M Jones
Type: Co-educational Day 0–11
No of pupils: B42 G43
Fees: On application

SOUTH WIRRAL

MOSTYN HOUSE SCHOOL[†]
Parkgate, Neston, South Wirral,
Cheshire CH64 6SG
Tel: (0151) 336 1010
Fax: (0151) 353 1040
Email: enquiries@
mostynhouse.co.uk
Head: Miss S M T Grenfell
Type: Co-educational Day 4–18
No of pupils: B125 G68
Fees: (September 06)
Day £6180–£9480

STALYBRIDGE

TRINITY SCHOOL
Birbeck Street, Stalybridge,
Cheshire SK15 1SH
Tel: (0161) 303 0674
Head: Mr W R Evans
Type: Co-educational Day 4–18
No of pupils: B67 G64
Fees: On application

STOCKPORT

BRABYNS SCHOOL
34–36 Arkwright Road, Marple,
Stockport, Cheshire SK6 7DB
Tel: (0161) 427 2395
Fax: (0161) 449 0704
Email: brabyns@indschool.org
Head: Mr L Sanders
Type: Co-educational Day 2–11
No of pupils: B57 G59
Fees: On application

HILLCREST GRAMMAR SCHOOL
Beech Avenue, Stockport,
Cheshire SK3 8HB
Tel: (0161) 480 0329
Fax: (0161) 476 2814
Email: headmaster@
hillcrest.stockport.sch.uk
Head: Mr D K Blackburn
Type: Co-educational Day 3–16
No of pupils: B198 G145
Fees: On application

ORIEL BANK
Devonshire Park Road, Davenport,
Stockport, Cheshire SK2 6JP
Tel: (0161) 483 2935
Fax: (0161) 456 5990
Email: secretary@orielbank.org
Head: Mr R A Bye
Type: Girls Day 3–16
No of pupils: 180
Fees: On application

England – Cheshire

ST CATHERINE'S PREPARATORY SCHOOL
Hollins Lane, Marple Bridge, Stockport, Cheshire SK6 5BB
Tel: (0161) 449 8800
Fax: (0161) 449 8181
Email: info@stcatherinesprep. stockport.sch.uk
Head: Mrs R A Brierley
Type: Co-educational Day 3–11
No of pupils: B61 G88
Fees: (September 06) Day £4775

STELLA MARIS JUNIOR SCHOOL
St Johns Road, Heaton Mersey, Stockport, Cheshire SK4 3BR
Tel: (0161) 432 0532
Fax: (0161) 432 9440
Email: office@ stellamaris.stockport.sch.uk
Head: Mr A Whittell
Type: Co-educational Day 4–11
No of pupils: B32 G40
Fees: (September 06) Day £3855–£4290

STOCKPORT GRAMMAR SCHOOL
Buxton Road, Stockport, Cheshire SK2 7AF
Tel: (0161) 456 9000
Fax: (0161) 419 2407
Email: sgs@ stockportgrammar.co.uk
Head: Mr A H Chicken
Type: Co-educational Day 3–18
No of pupils: B792 G668
Fees: (September 06) Day £5625–£7308

WILMSLOW

POWNALL HALL SCHOOL
Carrwood Road, Wilmslow, Cheshire SK9 5DW
Tel: (01625) 523141
Fax: (01625) 525209
Email: genoffice@ pownallhall.cheshire.sch.uk
Head: Mr J J Meadmore
Type: Co-educational Day 2–11
No of pupils: B134 G65
Fees: (September 05) Day £5025–£6990

WILMSLOW PREPARATORY SCHOOL
Grove Avenue, Wilmslow, Cheshire SK9 5EG
Tel: (01625) 524246
Fax: (01625) 536660
Email: secretary@ wilmslowprep.co.uk
Head: Mrs H J Shaw
Type: Girls Day 2–11
No of pupils: 155
Fees: (September 05) Day £1854–£6540

CORNWALL

BUDE

ST PETROC'S SCHOOL
Ocean View Road, Bude, Cornwall EX23 8NJ
Tel: (01288) 352876
Fax: (01288) 352876
Email: office@stpetrocs.com
Head: Dr I T Whitehurst
Type: Co-educational Day 3–11 (Nursery from 3 mths)
No of pupils: B48 G42
Fees: (September 06) Day £4350–£6750

HAYLE

ST PIRAN'S PREPARATORY SCHOOL
14 Trelissick Road, Hayle, Cornwall TR27 4HY
Tel: (01736) 752612
Fax: (01736) 752612
Email: office@ stpirans.fsbusiness.co.uk
Head: Mr D M Wilson
Type: Co-educational Day 3–16
No of pupils: B45 G45
Fees: (September 06) Day £3990–£4980

LAUNCESTON

ST JOSEPH'S SCHOOL
St Stephen's Hill, Launceston, Cornwall PL15 8HN
Tel: (01566) 772580
Fax: (01566) 775902
Email: registrar@ stjosephs.eclipse.co.uk
Head: Dr Alan Doe
Type: Girls Day 3–16 (Boys 3–11)
No of pupils: B25 G145
Fees: On application

PAR

ROSELYON
St Blazey Road, Par, Cornwall
PL24 2HZ
Tel: (01726) 812110
Fax: (01726) 812110
Email: office@
  roselyonsch.fsnet.co.uk
Head: Mr S C Bradley
Type: Co-educational Day 2–11
No of pupils: B38 G45
Fees: (September 05)
Day £5096–£5510

PENZANCE

THE BOLITHO SCHOOL
Polwithen, Penzance, Cornwall
TR18 4JR
Tel: (01736) 363271
Fax: (01736) 330960
Email: enquiries@
  bolitho.cornwall.sch.uk
Head: Mr D Dobson
Type: Co-educational Day and
Boarding 4–18
No of pupils: B167 G137
No of boarders: F41 W45
Fees: (September 05)
FB £13800–£15900
WB £12000–£14400
Day £4500–£9000

REDRUTH

HIGHFIELDS PRIVATE SCHOOL
Cardrew Lane, Redruth, Cornwall
TR15 1SY
Tel: (01209) 210665
Fax: (01209) 210667
Email: highfieldschool@aol.com
Head: Mrs M D Haddy
Type: Co-educational Day 4–16
No of pupils: B32 G29
Fees: (September 06) Day £4200

ST IVES

ST IA SCHOOL
St Ives Road, Carbis Bay, St Ives,
Cornwall TR26 2SF
Tel: (01736) 796963
Email: betsan@
  hill3129.freeserve.co.uk
Head: Miss B R Hill
Type: Co-educational Day 3–11
No of pupils: B10 G10
Fees: (September 06)
Day £480–£500

TRURO

POLWHELE HOUSE SCHOOL
Newquay Road, Truro, Cornwall
TR4 9AE
Tel: (01872) 273011
Fax: (01872) 273011
Email: polwhele@talk21.com
Head: Mr J Mason
Type: Co-educational Day and
Boarding 3–13
No of pupils: B96 G84
No of boarders: W15
Fees: On application

TRURO HIGH SCHOOL
Falmouth Road, Truro, Cornwall
TR1 2HU
Tel: (01872) 272830
Fax: (01872) 279393
Email: admin@trurohigh.co.uk
Head: Mr M McDowell
Type: Girls Boarding and Day
3–18 (Boys 3–5)
No of pupils: B2 G463
No of boarders: F38 W10
Fees: (September 05)
FB £14901–£15429
WB £14706–£15234
Day £3405–£8184

TRURO SCHOOL
Trennick Lane, Truro, Cornwall
TR1 1TH
Tel: (01872) 272763
Fax: (01872) 223431
Email: enquiries@
  truro-school.cornwall.sch.uk
Head: Mr P K Smith
Type: Co-educational Day and
Boarding 11–18
No of pupils: B507 G315
No of boarders: F93
Fees: On application

TRURO SCHOOL PREPARATORY SCHOOL
Highertown, Truro, Cornwall
TR1 3QN
Tel: (01872) 243120
Fax: (01872) 222377
Email: enquiries@truroprep.com
Head: Mr M Lovett
Type: Co-educational Day 3–11
No of pupils: B127 G85
Fees: (September 06)
Day £1873–£2681

England – Cornwall

CUMBRIA

BARROW-IN-FURNESS

CHETWYNDE SCHOOL*
Croslands, Rating Lane,
Barrow-in-Furness, Cumbria
LA13 0NY
Tel: (01229) 824210
Fax: (01229) 871440
Email: info@
  chetwynde.cumbria.sch.uk
Head: Mrs I Nixon
Type: Co-educational Day 3–18
Fees: On application

CARLISLE

**AUSTIN FRIARS ST
MONICA'S SCHOOL**
Etterby Scaur, Carlisle, Cumbria
CA3 9PB
Tel: (01228) 528042
Fax: (01228) 810327
Email: office@
  austinfriars.cumbria.sch.uk
Head: Mr C J Lumb
Type: Co-educational Day 3–18
No of pupils: B301 G205
Fees: (September 06)
Day £4470–£9030

LIME HOUSE SCHOOL*†
Holm Hill, Dalston, Carlisle,
Cumbria CA5 7BX
Tel: (01228) 710225
Fax: (01228) 710508
Email: lhsoffice@aol.com
Head: Mr N A Rice
Type: Co-educational Boarding
and Day 4–18
No of pupils: B130 G80
No of boarders: F140 W10
Fees: On application

**WELLSPRING CHRISTIAN
SCHOOL**
Cotehill, Carlisle, Cumbria
CA4 0EA
Tel: (01228) 562023
Head: Mr A G Field
Type: Co-educational Day 3–18
No of pupils: B12 G8
Fees: On application

KENDAL

HOLME PARK SCHOOL
Hill Top, New Hutton, Kendal,
Cumbria LA8 0AE
Tel: (01539) 721245
Fax: (01539) 721245
Email: holmeparkschool@
  hotmail.com
Head: Ms V Curry
Type: Co-educational Day and
Boarding 2–12
No of pupils: B50 G15
Fees: On application

KIRKBY LONSDALE

CASTERTON SCHOOL
Kirkby Lonsdale, Cumbria LA6 2SG
Tel: (01524) 279200
Fax: (01524) 279208
Email: admissions@
  castertonschool.co.uk
Head: Dr P McLaughlin
Type: Girls Boarding and Day
3–18 (Day boys 3–11)
No of pupils: B15 G355
No of boarders: F281
Fees: On application

PENRITH

HUNTER HALL SCHOOL
Frenchfield, Penrith, Cumbria
CA11 8UA
Tel: (01768) 891291
Fax: (01768) 899161
Email: office@
  hunterhall.cumbria.sch.uk
Head: Mr A J Short
Type: Co-educational Day 3–11
No of pupils: B68 G80
Fees: (September 06) Day £5385

SEASCALE

HARECROFT HALL SCHOOL
Gosforth, Seascale, Cumbria
CA20 1HS
Tel: (01946) 725220
Fax: (01946) 725885
Email: harecroft.hall@
  btopenworld.com
Head: Mr P Block
Type: Co-educational Boarding
and Day 3–16
No of pupils: B51 G28
No of boarders: F11
Fees: (September 06)
FB £11850–£12750
WB £11400–£12150
Day £3747–£7854

SEDBERGH

SEDBERGH SCHOOL
Sedbergh, Cumbria LA10 5HG
Tel: (01539) 620535
Fax: (01539) 621301
Email: hm@sedberghschool.org
Head: Mr C H Hirst
Type: Co-educational Boarding
and Day 13–18
No of pupils: B333 G113
No of boarders: F426
Fees: (September 05) FB £20700
Day £15420

ST BEES

ST BEES SCHOOL*†
St Bees, Cumbria CA27 0DS
Tel: (01946) 828010
Fax: (01946) 828011
Email: helen.miller@
  st-bees-school.co.uk
Head: Mr P J Capes
Type: Co-educational Boarding
and Day 11–18
No of pupils: B176 G126
No of boarders: F92 W32
Fees: (September 06)
FB £15297–£21093
WB £12552–£17997
Day £9789–£12642

WIGTON

ST URSULAS CONVENT SCHOOL
Burnfoot, Wigton, Cumbria
CA7 9HL
Tel: (01697) 344359
Fax: (01697) 344420
Email: stursula@btconnect.com
Head: Mrs J Monkhouse
Type: Co-educational Day 2–11
No of pupils: B20 G31
Fees: (September 06) Day £4065

WINDERMERE

WINDERMERE ST ANNE'S*
Patterdale Road, Windermere,
Cumbria LA23 1NW
Tel: (01539) 446164
Fax: (01539) 488414
Email: admissions@
   wsaschool.com
Head: Mr A Graham
Type: Co-educational Boarding
and Day 11–18
No of pupils: B129 G145
No of boarders: F83 W44
Fees: (September 05)
FB £16005–£18000
WB £15120–£17100
Day £9000–£9966

DERBYSHIRE

BAKEWELL

ST ANSELM'S SCHOOL
Bakewell, Derbyshire DE45 1DP
Tel: (01629) 812734
Fax: (01629) 812742
Email: headmaster@anselms.co.uk
Head: Mr R J Foster
Type: Co-educational Boarding
and Day 3–13
No of pupils: B160 G120
No of boarders: F94
Fees: (September 06) FB £15540
Day £2270–£4410

CHESTERFIELD

BARLBOROUGH HALL SCHOOL*
Barlborough, Chesterfield,
Derbyshire S43 4TJ
Tel: (01246) 810511
Fax: (01246) 570605
Email: barlborough.hall@
   virgin.net
Head: Mrs W E Parkinson
Type: Co-educational Day 3–11
No of pupils: B124 G127
Fees: (September 06)
Day £4800–£6930

ST JOSEPH'S CONVENT
42 Newbold Road, Chesterfield,
Derbyshire S41 7PL
Tel: (01246) 232392
Fax: (01246) 201965
Email: info@
   st-josephs-convent-sch.org.uk
Head: Mrs B Deane
Type: Co-educational Day 2–11
No of pupils: B69 G66
Fees: On application

ST PETER & ST PAUL SCHOOL
Brambling House, Hady Hill,
Chesterfield, Derbyshire S41 0EF
Tel: (01246) 278522
Fax: (01246) 273861
Email: head@
   stpeterandstpaul.fsnet.co.uk
Head: Mr A Lamb
Type: Co-educational Day 2–11
No of pupils: B102 G107
Fees: On application

DERBY

DERBY GRAMMAR SCHOOL FOR BOYS
Rykneld Road, Littleover, Derby,
Derbyshire DE23 4BX
Tel: (01332) 523027
Fax: (01332) 518670
Email: headmaster@
   derbygrammar.co.uk
Head: Mr R D Waller
Type: Boys Day 7–18
No of pupils: 310
Fees: On application

DERBY HIGH SCHOOL
Hillsway, Littleover, Derby,
Derbyshire DE23 3DT
Tel: (01332) 514267
Fax: (01332) 516085
Email: headsecretary@
   derbyhigh.derby.sch.uk
Head: Mr C T Callaghan
Type: Co-educational Day
Boys 3–11 Girls 3–18
No of pupils: B90 G480
Fees: (September 06)
Day £5940–£7920

England – Cumbria/Derbyshire

EMMANUEL SCHOOL
Juniper Lodge, 43 Kedleston Road,
Derby, Derbyshire DE22 1FP
Tel: (01332) 340505
Fax: (01332) 299168
Email: emmanuelschool@emcf.net
Head: Mr A Townsend
Type: Co-educational Day 3–11
No of pupils: B27 G23
Fees: (September 06)
Day £1512–£2436

FOREMARKE HALL SCHOOL
Milton, Derby, Derbyshire
DE65 6EJ
Tel: (01283) 703269
Fax: (01283) 701185
Email: registrar@foremarke.org.uk
Head: Mr P Brewster
Type: Co-educational Day and
Boarding 3–13
No of pupils: B277 G155
No of boarders: F51 W29
Fees: On application

MORLEY HALL
PREPARATORY SCHOOL
Hill House, Morley Road,
Oakwood, Derby, Derbyshire
DE21 4QZ
Tel: (01332) 674501
Email: julie.lee@
morleyhall-school.co.uk
Head: Mrs R N Hassell
Type: Co-educational Day 3–11
No of pupils: B35 G37
Fees: On application

OCKBROOK SCHOOL
The Settlement, Ockbrook, Derby,
Derbyshire DE72 3RJ
Tel: (01332) 673532
Fax: (01332) 665184
Head: Miss D P Bolland
Type: Girls Day and Boarding
3–18
No of pupils: B40 G460
No of boarders: F18
Fees: On application

THE OLD VICARAGE
SCHOOL
11 Church Lane, Darley Abbey,
Derby, Derbyshire DE22 1EW
Tel: (01332) 557130
Fax: (01332) 557130
Head: Mrs S L Mclean
Type: Co-educational Day 3–11
No of pupils: B44 G44
Fees: On application

REPTON SCHOOL
Repton, Derby, Derbyshire
DE65 6FH
Tel: (01283) 559222
Fax: (01283) 559223
Email: registrar@repton.org.uk
Head: Mr R Holroyd
Type: Co-educational Boarding
and Day 13–18
No of pupils: B325 G270
No of boarders: F452
Fees: (September 06) FB £22431
Day £16647

HEANOR

MICHAEL HOUSE STEINER
SCHOOL
The Field, Shipley, Heanor,
Derbyshire DE75 7JH
Tel: (01773) 718050
Fax: (01773) 711784
Email: admin@
michaelhouseschool.co.uk
Head: Ms D Eccott
Type: Co-educational Day 4–16
No of pupils: B85 G80
Fees: On application

ILKESTON

GATEWAY CHRISTIAN
SCHOOL
Moor Lane, Dale Abbey, Ilkeston,
Derbyshire DE7 4PP
Tel: (0115) 944 0609
Fax: (0115) 944 0609
Email: admin@
gatewayschool.org.uk
Head: Mrs C Pearson
Type: Co-educational Day 3–11
No of pupils: B12 G21
Fees: On application

REPTON

ST WYSTAN'S SCHOOL
High Street, Repton, Derbyshire
DE65 6GE
Tel: (01283) 703258
Fax: (01283) 703258
Email: secretary@stwystans.org.uk
Head: Mr P Soutar
Type: Co-educational Day 2–11
No of pupils: B54 G59
Fees: (September 06)
Day £2790–£5595

SPINKHILL

MOUNT ST MARY'S
COLLEGE*
Spinkhill, Derbyshire S21 3YL
Tel: (01246) 433388
Fax: (01246) 435511
Email: headmaster@
msmcollege.com
Head: Mr P G MacDonald
Type: Co-educational Boarding
and Day 11–18
No of pupils: B257 G144
No of boarders: F62 W14
Fees: (September 06)
FB £12570–£16605
WB £10665–£14355
Day £7815–£9075

DEVON

ASHBURTON

SANDS SCHOOL
Greylands, 48 East Street,
Ashburton, Devon TQ13 7AX
Tel: (01364) 653666
Fax: (01364) 653666
Email: enquiry@
    sandsschool.demon.co.uk
Head: Mr S Bellamy
Type: Co-educational Day 11–17
No of pupils: B36 G34
Fees: (September 05) Day £6168

BARNSTAPLE

ST MICHAEL'S
Tawstock Court, Barnstaple,
Devon EX31 3HY
Tel: (01271) 343242
Fax: (01271) 346771
Email: mail@
    st-michaels-school.com
Head: Mr J W Pratt
Type: Co-educational Day 0–13
No of pupils: B114 G86
Fees: On application

WEST BUCKLAND
PREPARATORY SCHOOL
West Buckland, Barnstaple, Devon
EX32 0SX
Tel: (01598) 760629
Fax: (01598) 760546
Email: prephm@
    westbuckland.devon.sch.uk
Head: Mr A Moore
Type: Co-educational Day and
Boarding 3–11
No of pupils: B120 G110
No of boarders: F8
Fees: On application

WEST BUCKLAND SCHOOL
Barnstaple, Devon EX32 0SX
Tel: (01598) 760281
Fax: (01598) 760546
Email: headmaster@
    westbuckland.devon.sch.uk
Head: Mr J F Vick
Type: Co-educational Boarding
and Day 3–18
No of pupils: B375 G298
No of boarders: F87
Fees: (September 06)
F/WB £11640–£16575
Day £4935–£9540

BEAWORTHY

SHEBBEAR COLLEGE
Shebbear, Beaworthy, Devon
EX21 5HJ
Tel: (01409) 282000
Fax: (01409) 281784
Email: info@
    shebbearcollege.co.uk
Head: Mr R S Barnes
Type: Co-educational Boarding
and Day 3–18
No of pupils: B195 G124
No of boarders: F73 W39
Fees: (September 06)
FB £4120–£5430
WB £3400–£4450
Day £1430–£5430

BIDEFORD

EDGEHILL COLLEGE
Northdown Road, Bideford,
Devon EX39 3LY
Tel: (01237) 471701
Fax: (01237) 425981
Email: edgehill@btconnect.com
Head: Mr S Nicholson
Type: Co-educational Boarding
and Day 2–18
No of pupils: B100 G100
No of boarders: F50 W3
Fees: (September 06)
FB £14940–£16380 WB £13008
Day £4350–£9150

GRENVILLE COLLEGE[†]
Belvoir Road, Bideford, Devon
EX39 3JP
Tel: (01237) 472212
Fax: (01237) 477020
Email: registrar@
    grenvillecollege.co.uk
Head: Mr A Waters
Type: Co-educational Boarding
and Day 2–19
No of pupils: B220 G180
No of boarders: F62 W18
Fees: (September 05) FB £17985
WB £14385 Day £8985

DARTINGTON

RUDOLF STEINER SCHOOL
Hood Manor, Dartington, Devon
TQ9 6AB
Tel: (01803) 762528
Fax: (01803) 762528
Email: enquiries@
    steiner-south-devon.org
Head: Mr M Whitlock
Type: Co-educational Day 3–16
No of pupils: B139 G145
Fees: On application

EXETER

BENDARROCH SCHOOL
Aylesbeare, Exeter, Devon
EX5 2BY
Tel: (01395) 233553
Email: info@bendarroch.co.uk
Head: Mr N R Home
Type: Co-educational Day 5–13
No of pupils: B25 G25
Fees: On application

BRAMDEAN SCHOOL*
Richmond Lodge, Homefield
Road, Heavitree, Exeter, Devon
EX1 2QR
Tel: (01392) 273387
Fax: (01392) 439330
Email: info@bramdeanschool.com
Head: Miss Diane Stoneman
Type: Co-educational Boarding
and Day 3–18
No of pupils: B110 G90
No of boarders: W10
Fees: (September 06) WB £11193
Day £4110–£7497

EMMANUEL SCHOOL
36–38 Blackboy Road, Exeter,
Devon EX4 6SZ
Tel: (01392) 258150
Fax: (01392) 258150
Email: emmanuelschool@
    tiscali.co.uk
Head: Mr D Rust
Type: Co-educational Day 5–16
No of pupils: B24 G27
Fees: (September 05) Day £2784

EXETER CATHEDRAL SCHOOL
The Chantry, Palace Gate, Exeter, Devon EX1 1HX
Tel: (01392) 255298
Fax: (01392) 422718
Email: exetercs@aol.com
Head: Mr B J McDowell
Type: Co-educational Day and Boarding 3–13
No of pupils: B112 G60
No of boarders: F25 W4
Fees: On application

EXETER JUNIOR SCHOOL
Victoria Park Road, Exeter, Devon EX2 4NS
Tel: (01392) 273679
Fax: (01392) 498144
Email: admissions@
    exeterschool.org.uk
Head: Mrs A J Turner
Type: Co-educational Day 7–11
No of pupils: B97 G61
Fees: (September 06) Day £7590

EXETER SCHOOL
Victoria Park Road, Exeter, Devon EX2 4NS
Tel: (01392) 273679
Fax: (01392) 498144
Email: admissions@
    exeterschool.org.uk
Head: Mr R Griffin
Type: Co-educational Day 7–18
No of pupils: B568 G266
Fees: (September 06)
Day £7590–£8460

HYLTON KINDERGARTEN & PRE-PREPARATORY SCHOOL
13A Lyndhurst Road, Exeter, Devon EX2 4PA
Tel: (01392) 254755
Fax: (01392) 435725
Email: info@hyltonschool.co.uk
Head: Mrs R C Leveridge
Type: Co-educational Day 2–8
No of pupils: 75
Fees: On application

MAGDALEN COURT SCHOOL
Mulberry House, Victoria Park Road, Exeter, Devon EX2 4NU
Tel: (01392) 494919
Fax: (01392) 494919
Email: admin@mcs-exeter.co.uk
Head: Mr J G Bushrod
Type: Co-educational Day 2–18
No of pupils: B85 G80
Fees: On application

MARIA MONTESSORI SCHOOL
3 St Leonards Place, Exeter, Devon EX2 4LZ
Tel: (01392) 201303
Email: mmontexe@aol.com
Head: Ms Ruth Bloomfield
Type: Co-educational Day 3–7
No of pupils: B26 G37
Fees: (September 06)
Day £3770–£11580

THE MAYNARD SCHOOL
Denmark Road, Exeter, Devon EX1 1SJ
Tel: (01392) 273417
Fax: (01392) 355999
Email: office@maynard.co.uk
Head: Dr D West
Type: Girls Day 7–18
No of pupils: 485
Fees: (September 06)
Day £6873–£8601

NEW SCHOOL
The Avenue, Exminster, Exeter, Devon EX6 8AT
Tel: (01392) 496122
Fax: (01392) 496122
Head: Mrs G Redman
Type: Co-educational Day 3–8
No of pupils: B32 G31
Fees: On application

ST MARGARET'S SCHOOL
147 Magdalen Road, Exeter, Devon EX2 4TS
Tel: (01392) 273197
Fax: (01392) 251402
Email: mail@
    stmargarets-school.co.uk
Head: Miss R Edbrooke
Type: Girls Day 7–18
No of pupils: 321
Fees: (September 06)
Day £6768–£8172

ST WILFRID'S SCHOOL
29 St David's Hill, Exeter, Devon EX4 4DA
Tel: (01392) 276171
Fax: (01392) 438666
Email: office@
    stwilfrids.devon.sch.uk
Head: Mrs A E M Macdonald-Dent
Type: Co-educational Day 5–16
No of pupils: B75 G70
Fees: On application

EXMOUTH

THE DOLPHIN SCHOOL
Raddenstile Lane, Exmouth, Devon EX8 2JH
Tel: (01395) 272418
Head: Mr Bill Gott
Type: Co-educational Day 3–11
No of pupils: B43 G42
Fees: On application

ST PETER'S SCHOOL
Harefield, Lympstone, Exmouth, Devon EX8 5AU
Tel: (01395) 272148
Fax: (01395) 222410
Email: hmsec@stpetersprep.co.uk
Head: Mr R J Williams
Type: Co-educational Day and Boarding 3–13
No of pupils: B168 G72
No of boarders: W17
Fees: (September 06) WB £13500
Day £4950–£8460

HONITON

MANOR HOUSE SCHOOL
Springfield House, Honiton, Devon EX14 9TL
Tel: (01404) 42026
Fax: (01404) 41153
Email: office@
    manorhouseschoolhoniton.
    co.uk
Head: Mr S J Bage
Type: Co-educational Day 3–11
No of pupils: B85 G85
Fees: On application

NEWTON ABBOT

ABBOTSBURY SCHOOL
90 Torquay Road, Newton Abbot, Devon TQ12 2JD
Tel: (01626) 352164
Head: Mr R J Manley
Type: Co-educational Day 2–7
No of pupils: B50 G50
Fees: (September 05)
Day £795–£2634

STOVER SCHOOL
Newton Abbot, Devon TQ12 6QG
Tel: (01626) 354505
Fax: (01626) 361475
Email: mail@stover.co.uk
Head: Mrs S Bradley
Type: Co-educational Day and
Boarding 3–18
No of pupils: B130 G3300
No of boarders: F40 W38
Fees: (September 06)
FB £13395–£17685
WB £11955–£14355
Day £5418–£8550

PAIGNTON

TOWER HOUSE SCHOOL
Fisher Street, Paignton, Devon
TQ4 5EW
Tel: (01803) 557077
Fax: (01803) 557077
Email: twrhouse@aol.com
Head: Mr W M Miller
Type: Co-educational Day 2–16
No of pupils: B148 G135
Fees: On application

PLYMOUTH

FLETEWOOD SCHOOL
88 North Road East, Plymouth,
Devon PL4 6AN
Tel: (01752) 663782
Fax: (01752) 663782
Email: headteacher@
    fletewoodschool.co.uk
Head: Mr J Martin
Type: Co-educational Day 3–11
No of pupils: B35 G35
Fees: On application

KING'S SCHOOL
Hartley Road, Mannamead,
Plymouth, Devon PL3 5LW
Tel: (01752) 771789
Fax: (01752) 770826
Head: Mrs J Lee
Type: Co-educational Day 3–11
No of pupils: B75 G72
Fees: (September 06)
Day £3705–£4650

PLYMOUTH COLLEGE
Ford Park, Plymouth, Devon
PL4 6RN
Tel: (01752) 203300
Fax: (01752) 203246
Email: mail@
    plymouthcollege.com
Head: Mr S J Wormleighton
Type: Co-educational Day and
Boarding 11–18
No of pupils: B354 G258
No of boarders: F89 W10
Fees: (September 06)
FB £17886–£18543
WB £17787–£18444
Day £9108–£9765

ST DUNSTAN'S ABBEY–THE PLYMOUTH COLLEGE JUNIOR SCHOOL
The Millfields, Plymouth, Devon
PL1 3JL
Tel: (01752) 201352
Fax: (01752) 201351
Email: juniorschool@
    plymouthcollege.com
Head: Mr R P Jeynes
Type: Co-educational Day 3–11
No of pupils: B140 G127
Fees: (September 06)
Day £4461–£6741

SIDMOUTH

ST JOHN'S SCHOOL†
Broadway, Sidmouth, Devon
EX10 8RG
Tel: (01395) 513984
Fax: (01395) 514539
Email: tessasmith@
    st-johns.devon.sch.uk
Head: Mrs Tessa Smith
Type: Co-educational Day and
Boarding 2–13
No of pupils: B90 G75
No of boarders: F45 W5
Fees: (September 06)
FB £12810–£14538 WB £12810
Day £5412–£7557

TAVISTOCK

KELLY COLLEGE
Parkwood Road, Tavistock, Devon
PL19 0HZ
Tel: (01822) 813100
Fax: (01822) 612050
Email: registrar@kellycollege.com
Head: Mr M S Steed
Type: Co-educational Boarding
and Day 11–18
No of pupils: B217 G142
No of boarders: F86 W56
Fees: (September 05)
FB £17100–£20700
WB £15600–£19350
Day £9150–£12150

KELLY COLLEGE PREPARATORY SCHOOL
Hazeldon House, Parkwood Road,
Tavistock, Devon PL19 0JS
Tel: (01822) 612919
Fax: (01822) 612919
Email: admin@
    kellycollegeprep.com
Head: Mr R Stevenson
Type: Co-educational Day and
Boarding 2–11
No of pupils: B95 G85
No of boarders: F2 W8
Fees: (September 06) FB £15825
WB £14310 Day £5130–£7110

MOUNT HOUSE SCHOOL
Tavistock, Devon PL19 9JL
Tel: (01822) 612244
Fax: (01822) 610042
Email: mounthouse@aol.com
Head: Mr J R O Massey
Type: Co-educational Boarding
and Day 3–13
No of pupils: B175 G75
No of boarders: F74 W9
Fees: (September 06)
FB £13500–£15270
WB £13110–£15270
Day £5460–£11460

TEIGNMOUTH

TRINITY SCHOOL
Buckeridge Road, Teignmouth,
Devon TQ14 8LY
Tel: (01626) 774138
Fax: (01626) 771541
Email: mail@trinityschool.co.uk
Head: Mr C J Ashby
Type: Co-educational Boarding
and Day 5–19
No of pupils: B309 G206
No of boarders: F130 W3
Fees: (September 06)
FB £15345–£17565
WB £15075–£17295
Day £6210–£8430

TRINITY SCHOOL
Buckeridge Road, Teignmouth,
Devon TQ14 8LY
Tel: (01626) 774138
Fax: (01626) 771541
Email: enquiries@
   trinityschool.co.uk
Head: Mr C J Ashby and
Mr D Milnes
Type: Co-educational Day and
Boarding 3–19
No of pupils: B309 G206
No of boarders: F130 W10
Fees: (September 05)
FB £14550–£16665
WB £14280–£16395
Day £5880–£7980

TIVERTON

BLUNDELL'S PREPARATORY SCHOOL
Blundell's Road, Tiverton, Devon
EX16 4NA
Tel: (01884) 252393
Fax: (01884) 232333
Email: prep@blundells.org
Head: Mr N A Folland
Type: Co-educational Day 3–11
No of pupils: B147 G118
Fees: (September 06)
Day £1458–£7425

BLUNDELL'S SCHOOL*
Tiverton, Devon EX16 4DN
Tel: (01884) 252543
Fax: (01884) 243232
Email: registrars@blundells.org
Head: Mr I R Davenport
Type: Co-educational Boarding
and Day 11–18
No of pupils: B335 G230
No of boarders: F120 W280
Fees: (September 05)
FB £1458–£21600
WB £13170–£19005
Day £8685–£13935

TORQUAY

THE ABBEY SCHOOL
Hampton Court, St Marychurch,
Torquay, Devon TQ1 4PR
Tel: (01803) 327868
Fax: (01803) 327868
Email: mail@abbeyschool.co.uk
Head: Mrs J Joyce
Type: Co-educational Day 0–11
No of pupils: B84 G67
Fees: On application

STOODLEY KNOWLE SCHOOL
Ansteys Cove Road, Torquay,
Devon TQ1 2JB
Tel: (01803) 293160
Fax: (01803) 214757
Email: headoffice@
   stoodleyknowle.fsnet.co.uk
Head: Sister Perpetua
Type: Girls Day 2–18
No of pupils: 301
Fees: (September 06)
Day £3165–£5760

TOTNES

PARK SCHOOL
Park Road, Dartington, Totnes,
Devon TQ9 6EQ
Tel: (01803) 864588
Email: park@schooldartington.
   freeserve.co.uk
Head: Mr J Hawley-Higgs
Type: Co-educational Day 3–11
No of pupils: B29 G25
Fees: On application

ST CHRISTOPHERS SCHOOL
Mount Barton, Staverton, Totnes,
Devon TQ9 6PF
Tel: (01803) 762202
Fax: (01803) 762202
Email: office@
   st-christophers.devon.sch.uk
Head: Mrs J E Kenyon
Type: Co-educational Day 3–11
No of pupils: B60 G40
Fees: (September 06)
Day £3150–£4905

DORSET

BLANDFORD FORUM

BRYANSTON SCHOOL
Blandford Forum, Dorset
DT11 0PX
Tel: (01258) 452411
Fax: (01258) 484661
Email: headmaster@
  bryanston.co.uk
Head: Ms S J Thomas
Type: Co-educational Boarding
and Day 13–18
No of pupils: B380 G275
No of boarders: F588
Fees: On application

CLAYESMORE
PREPARATORY SCHOOL†
Iwerne Minster, Blandford Forum,
Dorset DT11 8PH
Tel: (01747) 811707
Fax: (01747) 811692
Email: prepsec@clayesmore.com
Head: Mr R Geffen
Type: Co-educational Boarding
and Day 2–13
No of pupils: B142 G92
No of boarders: F58
Fees: (September 06)
F/WB £14727–£16140
Day £5892–£11985

CLAYESMORE SCHOOL*†
Iwerne Minster, Blandford Forum,
Dorset DT11 8LL
Tel: (01747) 812122
Fax: (01747) 811343
Email: hmsec@clayesmore.com
Head: Mr M G Cooke
Type: Co-educational Boarding
and Day 13–18
No of pupils: B252 G145
No of boarders: F230
Fees: (September 06)
FB £16140–£22197
Day £11985–£16242

HANFORD SCHOOL
Childe Okeford, Blandford Forum,
Dorset DT11 8HL
Tel: (01258) 860219
Fax: (01258) 861255
Email: hanfordsch@aol.com
Head: Mr N S Mackay
Type: Girls Boarding and Day
7–13
No of pupils: 100
No of boarders: F85
Fees: (September 06) FB £15600
Day £12450

KNIGHTON HOUSE
Durweston, Blandford Forum,
Dorset DT11 0PY
Tel: (01258) 452065
Fax: (01258) 450744
Email: enquiries@
  knighton-house.co.uk
Head: Mrs C L Renton
Type: Girls Day and Boarding
3–13 (Day boys 4–7)
No of pupils: B5 G108
No of boarders: F23 W19
Fees: (September 06) F/WB £16734
Day £6363–£12573

MILTON ABBEY SCHOOL*†
Blandford Forum, Dorset
DT11 0BZ
Tel: (01258) 880484
Fax: (01258) 881194
Email: info@miltonabbey.co.uk
Head: Mr J Hughes-D'Aeth
Type: Co-educational Boarding
and Day Boys 13–18 Girls 16–18
No of pupils: B205 G21
No of boarders: F207
Fees: (September 06) FB £24030
Day £18030

BOURNEMOUTH

THE PARK SCHOOL
Queen's Park South Drive,
Bournemouth, Dorset BH8 9BJ
Tel: (01202) 396640
Fax: (01202) 392705
Email: headmaster.parkschool@
  virgin.net
Head: Mr C Cole
Type: Co-educational Day 4–11
No of pupils: B156 G116
Fees: (September 06)
Day £4500–£6375

ST MARTIN'S SCHOOL
15 Stokewood Road,
Bournemouth, Dorset BH3 7NA
Tel: (01202) 760744
Head: Mr T B T Shenton
Type: Co-educational Day 4–12
No of pupils: B50 G50
Fees: (September 06)
Day £3000–£4500

ST THOMAS GARNET'S
SCHOOL
Parkwood Road, Boscombe,
Bournemouth, Dorset BH5 2BH
Tel: (01202) 420172 /
Pre-school: (01202) 431286
Fax: (01202) 773060
Head: Mr P R Gillings
Type: Co-educational Day 0–11
No of pupils: B75 G80
Fees: On application

TALBOT HEATH
Rothesay Road, Bournemouth,
Dorset BH4 9NJ
Tel: (01202) 761881
Fax: (01202) 768155
Email: admissions@
  talbotheath.org
Head: Mrs C Dipple
Type: Girls Day and Boarding
3–18 (Boys 3–7)
No of pupils: B6 G628
No of boarders: F26 W6
Fees: On application

TALBOT HOUSE
PREPARATORY SCHOOL
8 Firs Glen Road, Bournemouth,
Dorset BH9 2LR
Tel: (01202) 510348
Fax: (01202) 775904
Email: admin.talbot@
  ntlworld.com
Head: Mrs C Oosthuizen and
Mr M Broadway
Type: Co-educational Day 3–12
No of pupils: B66 G49
Fees: On application

WENTWORTH COLLEGE*

College Road, Bournemouth,
Dorset BH5 2DY
Tel: (01202) 423266
Fax: (01202) 418030
Email: enquiries@
    wentworthcollege.com
Head: Miss S Coe
Type: Girls Boarding and Day
11–18
No of pupils: 220
No of boarders: F40 W20
Fees: (September 06) F/WB £16350
Day £10125

DORCHESTER

DORCHESTER PREPARATORY AND INDEPENDENT SCHOOLS

25/26 Icen Way, Dorchester,
Dorset DT1 1EP
Tel: (01305) 264925
Fax: (01305) 269782
Email: info@
    dorchesterprepschool.co.uk
Head: Dr C J Rattew
Type: Co-educational Day 3–18
No of pupils: B40 G40
Fees: (September 06)
Day £1560–£8400

SUNNINGHILL PREPARATORY SCHOOL

South Court, South Walks,
Dorchester, Dorset DT1 1EB
Tel: (01305) 262306
Fax: (01305) 261254
Email: sunninghillschool@
    lineone.net
Head: Mr Alan Dickey
Type: Co-educational Day 3–13
No of pupils: B97 G94
Fees: On application

POOLE

BUCKHOLME TOWERS

18 Commercial Road, Parkstone,
Poole, Dorset BH14 0JW
Tel: (01202) 742871
Fax: (01202) 740754
Email: office@
    buckholme.dorset.sch.uk
Head: Mrs S Mercer
Type: Co-educational Day 3–12
No of pupils: B70 G70
Fees: (September 05)
Day £3777–£4521

UPLANDS SCHOOL

40 St Osmund's Road, Parkstone,
Poole, Dorset BH14 9JY
Tel: (01202) 742626
Fax: (01202) 731037
Email: headteacher@
    uplands.poole.sch.uk
Head: Mrs L Shah
Type: Co-educational Day 2–16
No of pupils: B182 G102
Fees: (September 06)
Day £2625–£9225

YARRELLS SCHOOL

Yarrells House, Upton, Poole,
Dorset BH16 5EU
Tel: (01202) 622229
Fax: (01202) 620870
Email: enquiries@yarrells.co.uk
Head: Mrs N A Covell
Type: Co-educational Day 2–13
No of pupils: B87 G111
Fees: (September 06)
Day £360–£8370

SHAFTESBURY

PORT REGIS SCHOOL

Motcombe Park, Shaftesbury,
Dorset SP7 9QA
Tel: (01747) 852566
Fax: (01747) 854684
Email: office@portregis.com
Head: Mr P A E Dix
Type: Co-educational Boarding
and Day 3–13
No of pupils: B238 G187
No of boarders: F149 W120
Fees: (September 06) F/WB £19395
Day £6300–£15105

ST MARY'S SCHOOL

Shaftesbury, Dorset SP7 9LP
Tel: (01747) 854005
Fax: (01747) 851557
Email: head@
    st-marys-shaftesbury.co.uk
Head: Mrs M C McSwiggan
Type: Girls Boarding and Day
9–18
No of pupils: 324
No of boarders: F206
Fees: (September 06)
FB £18930–£19935
Day £12915–£13575

SHERBORNE

INTERNATIONAL COLLEGE, SHERBORNE SCHOOL*

Newell Grange, Sherborne, Dorset
DT9 4EZ
Tel: (01935) 814743
Fax: (01935) 816863
Email: reception@sherborne-ic.net
Head: Dr C J Greenfield
Type: Co-educational Boarding
11–17
No of pupils: B80 G50
No of boarders: F140
Fees: (September 06)
FB £26040–£28290

ST ANTONY'S LEWESTON SCHOOL

Sherborne, Dorset DT9 6EN
Tel: (01963) 210691
Fax: (01963) 210786
Email: admissions@
    leweston.dorset.sch.uk
Head: Mr A Aylward
Type: Girls Boarding and Day
2–18 (Boys 2–11)
No of pupils: B6 G315
No of boarders: F91
Fees: (September 06)
FB £12870–£19770
Day £6270–£12870

SHERBORNE PREPARATORY SCHOOL

Acreman Street, Sherborne, Dorset
DT9 3NY
Tel: (01935) 812097
Fax: (01935) 813948
Email: info@prep.sherborne.com
Head: Mr P S Tait
Type: Co-educational Day and
Boarding 3–13
No of pupils: B161 G79
No of boarders: F16 W31
Fees: (September 06)
F/WB £15810–£16530
Day £3150–£11520

SHERBORNE SCHOOL

Abbey Road, Sherborne, Dorset
DT9 3AP
Tel: (01935) 812249
Fax: (01935) 810426
Email: enquiries@sherborne.org
Head: Mr S F Eliot
Type: Boys Boarding 13–18
No of boarders: F520
Fees: (September 06) FB £24925
Day £19140

SHERBORNE SCHOOL FOR GIRLS

Bradford Road, Sherborne, Dorset
DT9 3QN
Tel: (01935) 812245
Fax: (01935) 389445
Email: enquiry@sherborne.com
Head: Mrs J Dwyer
Type: Girls Boarding and Day
11–18
No of pupils: 380
No of boarders: F350
Fees: (September 06) FB £24135
Day £17640

SWANAGE

THE OLD MALTHOUSE

Langton Matravers, Swanage,
Dorset BH19 3HB
Tel: (01929) 422302
Fax: (01929) 422154
Email: office@
  oldmalthouseschool.co.uk
Head: Dr Moira Laffey
Type: Co-educational Boarding
and Day 3–13
No of pupils: B75 G25
No of boarders: W30
Fees: (September 05) WB £14985
Day £11385

WEYMOUTH

THORNLOW PREPARATORY SCHOOL

Connaught Road, Weymouth,
Dorset DT4 0SA
Tel: (01305) 785703
Fax: (01305) 780976
Email: admin@thornlow.co.uk
Head: Mr R A Fowke
Type: Co-educational Day 3–13
No of pupils: B43 G35
Fees: (September 05) Day £1870

WIMBORNE

CANFORD SCHOOL

Wimborne, Dorset BH21 3AD
Tel: (01202) 847207
Fax: (01202) 881723
Email: admissions@canford.com
Head: Mr J D Lever
Type: Co-educational Boarding
and Day 13–18
No of pupils: B364 G238
No of boarders: F406
Fees: (September 06) FB £23400
Day £17790

CASTLE COURT PREPARATORY SCHOOL

The Knoll House, Knoll Lane,
Corfe Mullen, Wimborne, Dorset
BH21 3RF
Tel: (01202) 694438
Fax: (01202) 659063
Email: office@castlecourt.com
Head: Mr R E T Nicholl
Type: Co-educational Day 3–13
No of pupils: B203 G122
Fees: (September 06)
Day £5385–£11970

DUMPTON SCHOOL

Deans Grove House, Wimborne,
Dorset BH21 7AF
Tel: (01202) 883818
Fax: (01202) 848760
Email: secretary@dumpton.com
Head: Mr A W Browning
Type: Co-educational Day 2–13
No of pupils: B192 G115
Fees: (September 06)
Day £6225–£11225

COUNTY DURHAM

BARNARD CASTLE

BARNARD CASTLE SCHOOL

Barnard Castle, County Durham
DL12 8UN
Tel: (01833) 690222
Fax: (01833) 638985
Email: secretary@
  barneyschool.org.uk
Head: Mr D H Ewart
Type: Co-educational Boarding
and Day 4–18
No of pupils: B443 G248
No of boarders: F194
Fees: (September 05)
F/WB £11577–£15393
Day £3909–£8940

DARLINGTON

HURWORTH HOUSE SCHOOL

The Green, Hurworth-on-Tees,
Darlington, County Durham
DL2 2AD
Tel: (01325) 720645
Fax: (01325) 720122
Email: info@hurworthhouse.co.uk
Head: Mr C R T Fenwick
Type: Boys Day 3–18
No of pupils: B193 G22
Fees: On application

POLAM HALL

Grange Road, Darlington, County
Durham DL1 5PA
Tel: (01325) 463383
Fax: (01325) 383539
Email: information@
  polamhall.com
Head: Miss M Green
Type: Girls Boarding and Day
4–18
No of pupils: B8 G400
No of boarders: F41 W12
Fees: (September 06)
FB £14550–£17970
WB £14100–£17520
Day £4875–£9420

England – Dorset/County Durham

RAVENTHORPE PREPARATORY SCHOOL
96 Carmel Road North,
Darlington, County Durham
DL3 8JB
Tel: (01325) 463373
Fax: (01325) 353086
Email: admin@raventhorpe.org.uk
Head: Mrs S E L Hoiles
Type: Co-educational Day 3–11
No of pupils: B36 G20
Fees: (September 06)
Day £2940–£3810

DURHAM

THE CHORISTER SCHOOL*
The College, Durham, County
Durham DH1 3EL
Tel: (0191) 384 2935
Fax: (0191) 383 1275
Email: head@
    choristers.durham.sch.uk
Head: Mr I Hawksby
Type: Co-educational Day and
Boarding 4–13
No of pupils: B121 G56
No of boarders: F27 W3
Fees: (September 06)
F/WB £6783–£12915
Day £6060–£8340

DURHAM HIGH SCHOOL FOR GIRLS
Farewell Hall, Durham, County
Durham DH1 3TB
Tel: (0191) 384 3226
Fax: (0191) 386 7381
Email: headmistress@dhsfg.org.uk
Head: Mrs A J Templeman
Type: Girls Day 3–18
No of pupils: 592
Fees: On application

DURHAM SCHOOL
Quarryheads Lane, Durham,
County Durham DH1 4SZ
Tel: (0191) 386 4783
Fax: (0191) 383 1025
Email: enquiries@
    durhamschool.co.uk
Head: Mr N G Kern
Type: Co-educational Day and
Boarding 11–18
No of pupils: B284 G102
No of boarders: F44 W21
Fees: On application

ESSEX

BILLERICAY

ST JOHN'S SCHOOL
Stock Road, Billericay, Essex
CM12 0AR
Tel: (01277) 623070
Fax: (01277) 651288
Email: bursarstjohns@aol.com
Head: Mrs F Armour
Type: Co-educational Day 3–16
No of pupils: B260 G185
Fees: On application

BRENTWOOD

BRENTWOOD SCHOOL
Ingrave Road, Brentwood, Essex
CM15 8AS
Tel: (01277) 243243
Fax: (01277) 243299
Email: headmaster@
    brentwood.essex.sch.uk
Head: Mr D I Davies
Type: Co-educational Day and
Boarding 3–18 (Single-sex ed
11–16)
No of pupils: B889 G601
No of boarders: F52 W18
Fees: (September 06) F/WB £20265
Day £11565

HERINGTON HOUSE SCHOOL
Mount Avenue, Hutton,
Brentwood, Essex CM13 2NS
Tel: (01277) 211595
Fax: (01277) 200404
Head: Mr R Dudley-Cooke
Type: Co-educational Day 3–11
No of pupils: B43 G92
Fees: On application

URSULINE PREPARATORY SCHOOL
Old Great Ropers, Great Ropers
Lane, Warley, Brentwood, Essex
CM13 3HR
Tel: (01277) 227152
Fax: (01277) 202559
Email: rozdownes@
    ursulineprepwarley.co.uk
Head: Mrs PM Wilson
Type: Co-educational Day 3–11
No of pupils: B74 G81
Fees: (September 05)
Day £1155–£2150

WOODLANDS SCHOOLS
Warley Street, Great Warley,
Brentwood, Essex CM13 3LA
Tel: (01277) 233288
Fax: (01277) 232715
Email: ukinfo@
    woodlandsschools.co.uk
Head: Mr R O'Doherty
Type: Co-educational Day 3–11
No of pupils: B147 G134
Fees: On application

BUCKHURST HILL

BRAESIDE SCHOOL FOR GIRLS
130 High Road, Buckhurst Hill,
Essex IG9 5SD
Tel: (020) 8504 1133
Fax: (020) 8505 6675
Email: enquiries@
    braesideschool.co.uk
Head: Mrs C Naismith
Type: Girls Day 3–16
No of pupils: 212
Fees: (September 05)
Day £4650–£7320

THE DAIGLEN SCHOOL

68 Palmerston Road, Buckhurst
Hill, Essex IG9 5LG
Tel: (020) 8504 7108
Fax: (020) 8502 9608
Email: admin@
 daiglenschool.co.uk
Head: Mrs M Bradfield
Type: Co-educational Day
Boys 3–11
Fees: (September 06)
Day £6135–£6150

LOYOLA PREPARATORY SCHOOL

103 Palmerston Road, Buckhurst
Hill, Essex IG9 5NH
Tel: (020) 8504 7372
Fax: (020) 8504 7372
Email: office@loyola.essex.sch.uk
Head: Mr P G Nicholson
Type: Boys Day 3–11
No of pupils: 184
Fees: On application

CHELMSFORD

ELM GREEN PREPARATORY SCHOOL

Parsonage Lane, Little Baddow,
Chelmsford, Essex CM3 4SU
Tel: (01245) 225230
Fax: (01245) 226008
Email: admin@
 elmgreen.essex.sch.uk
Head: Ms A Milner
Type: Co-educational Day 4–11
No of pupils: B110 G110
Fees: (September 05) Day £6078

HEATHCOTE SCHOOL

Eves Corner, Danbury,
Chelmsford, Essex CM3 4QB
Tel: (01245) 223131
Fax: (01245) 224568
Email: enquiries@heathcote.co.uk
Head: Mr K Gladwin
Type: Co-educational Day 2–11
No of pupils: B96 G88
Fees: On application

NEW HALL SCHOOL

Boreham, Chelmsford, Essex
CM3 3HS
Tel: (01245) 467588
Fax: (01245) 464348
Email: registrar@
 newhallschool.co.uk
Head: Mrs K Jeffrey
Type: Co-educational Boarding
and Day 4–18 (Boys day 4–11)
No of pupils: B96 G624
No of boarders: F120
Fees: (September 05)
FB £15060–£18970
Day £6120–£12540

ST ANNE'S PREPARATORY SCHOOL

154 New London Road,
Chelmsford, Essex CM2 0AW
Tel: (01245) 353488
Fax: (01245) 353488
Email: headmistress@
 stannesprep.essex.sch.uk
Head: Mrs F Pirrie
Type: Co-educational Day 3–11
No of pupils: B70 G90
Fees: (September 06)
Day £4950–£5250

ST CEDD'S SCHOOL

Maltese Road, Chelmsford, Essex
CM1 2PB
Tel: (01245) 354380
Fax: (01245) 348635
Email: tthorogood@stcedds.org.uk
Head: Mrs B A Windley
Type: Co-educational Day 4–11
No of pupils: B155 G177
Fees: (September 06)
Day £5940–£6345

WIDFORD LODGE

Widford Road, Chelmsford, Essex
CM2 9AN
Tel: (01245) 352581
Fax: (01245) 281329
Email: enquiries@
 widfordlodge.co.uk
Head: Mr S C Trowell
Type: Co-educational Day 2–11
No of pupils: B77 G45
Fees: On application

CHIGWELL

CHIGWELL SCHOOL*

High Road, Chigwell, Essex
IG7 6QF
Tel: (020) 8501 5700
Fax: (020) 8500 6232
Email: hm@chigwell-school.org
Head: Mr D F Gibbs
Type: Co-educational Day and
Boarding 7–18
No of pupils: B405 G310
No of boarders: F40
Fees: (September 06) FB £18495
WB £16020–£17004
Day £7683–£11817

COLCHESTER

COLCHESTER HIGH SCHOOL

Wellesley Road, Colchester, Essex
CO3 3HD
Tel: (01206) 573389
Fax: (01206) 573114
Email: info@
 colchesterhighschool.co.uk
Head: Mr D E Wood
Type: Co-educational Day
Boys 3–16 Girls 3–11
No of pupils: B424 G62
Fees: (September 06)
Day £2100–£7575

HOLMWOOD HOUSE[†]

Chitts Hill, Lexden, Colchester,
Essex CO3 9ST
Tel: (01206) 574305
Fax: (01206) 768269
Email: hst@
 holmwood.essex.sch.uk
Head: Mr H S Thackrah
Type: Co-educational Day and
Boarding 4–13
No of pupils: B239 G142
No of boarders: W13
Fees: (September 06) WB £15279
Day £6630–£11814

LITTLEGARTH SCHOOL

Horkesley Park, Nayland,
Colchester, Essex CO6 4JR
Tel: (01206) 262332
Fax: (01206) 263101
Email: l.garth@virgin.net
Head: Mr P H Jones
Type: Co-educational Day 2–11
No of pupils: B178 G137
Fees: (September 05)
Day £1380–£6420

England – Essex

OXFORD HOUSE SCHOOL
2 Lexden Road, Colchester, Essex
CO3 3NE
Tel: (01206) 576686
Fax: (01206) 577670
Email: ohs@supanet.com
Head: Mr R P Spendlove
Type: Co-educational Day 2–11
No of pupils: B65 G65
Fees: (September 05)
Day £2925–£5790

ST MARY'S SCHOOL
91 Lexden Road, Colchester, Essex
CO3 3RB
Tel: (01206) 572544
Fax: (01206) 576437
Email: stmaryschoolcol@
   tinyonline.co.uk
Head: Mrs H K Vipond
Type: Girls Day 4–16
No of pupils: 450
Fees: (September 06)
Day £5535–£7725

DUNMOW

FELSTED SCHOOL
Felsted, Dunmow, Essex CM6 3LL
Tel: (01371) 822600
Fax: (01371) 822607
Email: info@felsted.org
Head: Mr S C Roberts
Type: Co-educational Boarding
and Day 13–18
No of pupils: B281 G188
No of boarders: F267
Fees: (September 06) FB £21465
Day £16065

EPPING

COOPERSALE HALL SCHOOL
Flux's Lane, off Steward's Green
Road, Epping, Essex CM16 7PE
Tel: (01992) 577133
Fax: (01992) 571544
Email: info@
   coopersalehallschool.co.uk
Head: Mr R Probyn
Type: Co-educational Day 3–11
No of pupils: B150 G110
Fees: (September 05)
Day £2070–£6600

FELSTED

FELSTED PREPARATORY SCHOOL
Braintree Road, Felsted, Essex
CM6 3JL
Tel: (01371) 822610
Fax: (01371) 822617
Email: info@felstedprep.org
Head: Mrs J M Burrett
Type: Co-educational Boarding
and Day 4–13
No of pupils: B248 G153
No of boarders: W18
Fees: (September 06) WB £15510
Day £9234–£12135

FRINTON-ON-SEA

ST PHILOMENA'S PREPARATORY SCHOOL
Hadleigh Road, Frinton-on-Sea,
Essex CO13 9HQ
Tel: (01255) 674492
Fax: (01255) 674459
Email: contactus@
   stphilomenas.com
Head: Mrs B Buck
Type: Co-educational Day 3–11
No of pupils: B67 G71
Fees: On application

HALSTEAD

GOSFIELD SCHOOL
Halstead Road, Gosfield,
Halstead, Essex CO9 1PF
Tel: (01787) 474040
Fax: (01787) 478228
Email: principal@
   gosfieldschool.org.uk
Head: Mrs C Goodchild
Type: Co-educational Day and
Boarding 2–18
No of pupils: B124 G71
No of boarders: F13 W13
Fees: On application

ST MARGARET'S SCHOOL
Gosfield Hall Park, Gosfield,
Halstead, Essex CO9 1SE
Tel: (01787) 472134
Fax: (01787) 478207
Email: enq@
   stmargaretsschool.com
Head: Mrs B Y Boyton-Corbett
Type: Co-educational Day 2–11
No of pupils: B117 G120
Fees: On application

HARLOW

ST NICHOLAS SCHOOL
Hillingdon House, Hobbs Cross
Road, Harlow, Essex CM17 0NJ
Tel: (01279) 429910
Fax: (01279) 450224
Head: Mr R Cusworth
Type: Co-educational Day 4–16
No of pupils: B180 G180
Fees: On application

HORNCHURCH

GOODRINGTON SCHOOL
17 Walden Road, Emerson Park,
Hornchurch, Essex RM11 2JT
Tel: (01708) 448349
Email: info@goodrington.org
Head: Mrs R Ellenby
Type: Co-educational Day 3–11
No of pupils: B30 G34
Fees: (September 06) Day £3360

RAPHAEL INDEPENDENT SCHOOL
Park Lane, Hornchurch, Essex
RM11 1XY
Tel: (01708) 744735
Fax: (01708) 722432
Email: raphaelschool@
   hotmail.com
Head: Mr N W Malicka
Type: Co-educational Day 4–16
No of pupils: B80 G55
Fees: (September 06)
Day £1800–£6750

ILFORD

BEEHIVE PREPARATORY SCHOOL
233 Beehive Lane, Redbridge,
Ilford, Essex IG4 5ED
Tel: (020) 8550 3224
Head: Mr C J Beasant
Type: Co-educational Day 4–11
No of pupils: B50 G45
Fees: On application

CLARKS PREPARATORY SCHOOL
81/85 York Road, Ilford, Essex
IG1 3AF
Tel: (020) 8478 6510
Fax: (020) 8553 1202
Head: Ms N C Woodman
Type: Co-educational Day 0–7
No of pupils: B46 G39
Fees: On application

CRANBROOK COLLEGE

Mansfield Road, Ilford, Essex
IG1 3BD
Tel: (020) 8554 1757
Fax: (020) 8518 0317
Email: info@
  cranbrookcollege.org.uk
Head: Mr C P Lacey
Type: Boys Day 4–16
No of pupils: 210
Fees: On application

EASTCOURT INDEPENDENT SCHOOL

1 Eastwood Road, Goodmayes,
Ilford, Essex IG3 8UW
Tel: (020) 8590 5472
Fax: (020) 8597 8313
Email: eastcourtschool@
  talk21.com
Head: Mrs C Redgrave
Type: Co-educational Day 4–11
No of pupils: B163 G177
Fees: On application

GLENARM COLLEGE

20 Coventry Road, Ilford, Essex
IG1 4QR
Tel: (020) 8554 1760
Email: head@glenarmcollege.com
Head: Mr C Perkins
Type: Co-educational Day 3–11
No of pupils: B53 G80
Fees: On application

ILFORD PREPARATORY SCHOOL

Carnegie Buildings, 785 High
Road, Ilford, Essex IG3 8RW
Tel: (020) 8599 8822
Fax: (020) 8597 2797
Email: head@ilfprep.demon.co.uk
Head: Mrs B P M Wiggs
Type: Co-educational Day 3–11
No of pupils: B100 G92
Fees: On application

ILFORD URSULINE PREPARATORY SCHOOL

2 Coventry Road, Ilford, Essex
IG1 4QR
Tel: (020) 8518 4050
Fax: (020) 8518 2060
Email: iups@ilfordursuline-
  prep.redbridge.sch.uk
Head: Mrs C Spinner
Type: Girls Day 3–11
No of pupils: 154
Fees: (September 06) Day £5937

PARK SCHOOL FOR GIRLS

20 Park Avenue, Ilford, Essex
IG1 4RS
Tel: (020) 8554 2466
Fax: (020) 8554 3003
Email: enquiries@
  parkschoolforgirls.co.uk
Head: Mrs N O'Brien
Type: Girls Day 7–18
No of pupils: 235
Fees: On application

LEIGH-ON-SEA

COLLEGE SAINT-PIERRE

16 Leigh Road, Leigh-on-sea,
Essex SS9 1LE
Tel: (01702) 474164
Fax: (01702) 474164
Email: college@
  saintpierre.fsnet.co.uk
Head: Mr K Davies
Type: Co-educational Day 2–11
No of pupils: B60 G40
Fees: On application

ST MICHAEL'S SCHOOL

198 Hadleigh Road, Leigh-on-sea,
Essex SS9 2LP
Tel: (01702) 478719
Fax: (01702) 710183
Email: info@stmichaelsschool.com
Head: Mrs L Morshead
Type: Co-educational Day 3–11
No of pupils: B150 G114
Fees: (September 06)
Day £5355–£6030

LOUGHTON

OAKLANDS SCHOOL

8 Albion Hill, Loughton, Essex
IG10 4RA
Tel: (020) 8508 3517
Fax: (020) 8508 4454
Email: info@oaklandsschool.co.uk
Head: Mrs P Simmonds
Type: Co-educational Day
Boys 2–7 Girls 2–11
No of pupils: B62 G185
Fees: (September 05) Day £3570

MALDON

MALDON COURT PREPARATORY SCHOOL

Silver Street, Maldon, Essex
CM9 4QE
Tel: (01621) 853529
Fax: (01621) 874606
Email: enquiries@
  maldoncourtschool.org
Head: Mrs L F Coyle
Type: Co-educational Day 3–11
No of pupils: B66 G57
Fees: (September 06)
Day £5737–£6039

ROCHFORD

CROWSTONE PREPARATORY SCHOOL (SUTTON ANNEXE)

Fleethall Lane, Shopland Road,
Rochford, Essex SS4 1LL
Tel: (01702) 540629
Head: Mr J P Thayer
Type: Co-educational Day 2–11
No of pupils: 110
Fees: On application

ROMFORD

GIDEA PARK COLLEGE

Balgores House, 2 Balgores Lane,
Romford, Essex RM2 5JR
Tel: (01708) 740381
Fax: (01708) 740381
Email: office@
  gideaparkcollege.co.uk
Head: Mrs V S Lee
Type: Co-educational Day 2–11
No of pupils: B86 G100
Fees: (September 06) Day £6180

IMMANUEL SCHOOL

Havering Grange Centre,
Havering Road, Romford, Essex
RM1 4HR
Tel: (01708) 764449
Head: Miss F Norcross
Type: Co-educational Day 3–16
No of pupils: B71 G54
Fees: On application

England – Essex

ST MARY'S HARE PARK SCHOOL
South Drive, Gidea Park, Romford, Essex RM2 6HH
Tel: (01708) 761220
Fax: (01708) 380255
Email: harepark@btconnect.com
Head: Mrs K Karwacinski
Type: Co-educational Day 2–11
No of pupils: B70 G84
Fees: (September 06) Day £5475

SAFFRON WALDEN

DAME JOHANE BRADBURY'S SCHOOL
Ashdon Road, Saffron Walden, Essex CB10 2AL
Tel: (01799) 522348
Fax: (01799) 516762
Email: info@djbs.org
Head: Mrs Jane Crouch
Type: Co-educational Day 3–11
No of pupils: B149 G148
Fees: (September 06)
Day £4995–£7365

FRIENDS' SCHOOL
Mount Pleasant Road, Saffron Walden, Essex CB11 3EB
Tel: (01799) 525351
Fax: (01799) 523808
Email: admin@friends.org.uk
Head: Mr G Wigley
Type: Co-educational Boarding and Day 3–18
No of pupils: B210 G160
No of boarders: F34 W30
Fees: (September 06)
FB £14220–£17970
WB £13620–£16470
Day £6720–£11520

SOUTHEND-ON-SEA

THORPE HALL SCHOOL
Wakering Road, Southend-on-Sea, Essex SS1 3RD
Tel: (01702) 582340
Fax: (01702) 587070
Email: sec@
  thorpehall.southend.sch.uk
Head: Mr D W Gibbins
Type: Co-educational Day 2–16
No of pupils: B226 G139
Fees: On application

UPMINSTER

OAKFIELDS MONTESSORI SCHOOLS LTD
Harwood Hall, Harwood Hall Lane, Corbets Tey, Upminster, Essex RM14 2YG
Tel: (01708) 220117
Fax: (01708) 227911
Email: office@
  oakfieldsmontessorischool.
  org.uk
Head: Mrs K Malandreniotis
Type: Co-educational Day 2–11
No of pupils: B82 G90
Fees: On application

WESTCLIFF-ON-SEA

CROWSTONE PREPARATORY SCHOOL
121–123 Crowstone Road, Westcliff-on-Sea, Essex SS0 8LH
Tel: (01702) 346758
Fax: (01702) 390632
Email: info@
  crowstone.southend.sch.uk
Head: Mr J P Thayer
Type: Co-educational Day 2–11
No of pupils: B120 G110
Fees: On application

ST HILDA'S SCHOOL
15 Imperial Avenue, Westcliff-on-Sea, Essex SS0 8NE
Tel: (01702) 344542
Fax: (01702) 344547
Email: sthilda15@aol.com
Head: Mrs S O'Riordan
Type: Girls Day 2–16 (Boys 2–7)
No of pupils: 180
Fees: On application

WOODFORD GREEN

AVON HOUSE[†]
490 High Road, Woodford Green, Essex IG8 0PN
Tel: (020) 8504 1749
Head: Mrs S Ferrari
Type: Co-educational Day 3–11
No of pupils: B117 G102
Fees: (September 05)
Day £5280–£6360

BANCROFT'S SCHOOL
Woodford Green, Essex IG8 0RF
Tel: (020) 8505 4821
Fax: (020) 8559 0032
Email: office@
  bancrofts.essex.sch.uk
Head: Dr P R Scott
Type: Co-educational Day 7–18
No of pupils: B492 G465
Fees: (September 06)
Day £7833–£10341

ST AUBYN'S SCHOOL
Bunces Lane, Woodford Green, Essex IG8 9DU
Tel: (020) 8504 1577
Fax: (020) 8504 2053
Email: registrar@staubyns.com
Head: Mr G James
Type: Co-educational Day 3–13
No of pupils: B286 G204
Fees: On application

WOODFORD GREEN PREPARATORY SCHOOL
Glengall Road, Woodford Green, Essex IG8 0BZ
Tel: (020) 8504 5045
Fax: (020) 8505 0639
Email: head@wgps.co.uk
Head: Mr A J Blackhurst
Type: Co-educational Day 3–11
No of pupils: B198 G186
Fees: (September 06) Day £5760

GLOUCESTERSHIRE

CHELTENHAM

AIRTHRIE SCHOOL
29 Christ Church Road,
Cheltenham, Gloucestershire
GL50 2NY
Tel: (01242) 512837
Fax: (01242) 579583
Email: mail@airthrie-school.co.uk
Head: Mrs A E Sullivan
Type: Co-educational Day 3–11
No of pupils: B90 G90
Fees: On application

BERKHAMPSTEAD SCHOOL
Pittville Circus Road, Cheltenham,
Gloucestershire GL52 2QA
Tel: (01242) 523263
Fax: (01242) 514114
Email: headberky@aol.com
Head: Mr T Owen
Type: Co-educational Day 3–11
No of pupils: B129 G128
Fees: (September 06)
Day £3708–£6411

CHELTENHAM COLLEGE
Bath Road, Cheltenham,
Gloucestershire GL53 7LD
Tel: (01242) 265600
Fax: (01242) 265630
Email: admissions@
  cheltcoll.gloucs.sch.uk
Head: Mr J S Richardson
Type: Co-educational Boarding
and Day 13–18
No of pupils: B375 G191
No of boarders: F450
Fees: (September 05) FB £23280
Day £17445

CHELTENHAM COLLEGE
JUNIOR SCHOOL
Thirlestaine Road, Cheltenham,
Gloucestershire GL53 7AB
Tel: (01242) 522697
Fax: (01242) 265620
Email: ccjs@
  cheltcoll.gloucs.sch.uk
Head: Mr N I Archdale
Type: Co-educational Boarding
and Day 3–13
No of pupils: B245 G185
No of boarders: F45
Fees: (September 05)
FB £12375–£16200
Day £5115–£12480

THE CHELTENHAM LADIES'
COLLEGE
Bayshill Road, Cheltenham,
Gloucestershire GL50 3EP
Tel: (01242) 520691
Fax: (01242) 227882
Email: enquiries@
  cheltladiescollege.org
Head: Mrs V Tuck
Type: Girls Boarding and Day
11–18
No of pupils: 850
No of boarders: F625
Fees: (September 06)
FB £23139–£26067
Day £15537–£17664

DEAN CLOSE PREPARATORY
SCHOOL*
Lansdown Road, Cheltenham,
Gloucestershire GL51 6QS
Tel: (01242) 512217
Fax: (01242) 258005
Email: dcpsoffice@
  deanclose.org.uk
Head: Rev L Browne
Type: Co-educational Boarding
and Day 2–13
No of pupils: B195 G174
No of boarders: F60
Fees: (September 06)
FB £13185–£16650
WB £9090–£12825
Day £7905–£11640

DEAN CLOSE SCHOOL*
Shelburne Road, Cheltenham,
Gloucestershire GL51 6HE
Tel: (01242) 258044
Fax: (01242) 258003
Email: registrar@deanclose.org.uk
Head: Rev T M Hastie-Smith
Type: Co-educational Boarding
and Day 13–18
No of pupils: B273 G207
No of boarders: F274
Fees: (September 06) FB £23580
Day £16665

THE RICHARD PATE
SCHOOL
Southern Road, Leckhampton,
Cheltenham, Gloucestershire
GL53 9RP
Tel: (01242) 522086
Fax: (01242) 584035
Email: hm@richardpate.co.uk
Head: Mr RA MacDonald
Type: Co-educational Day 3–11
No of pupils: B153 G135
Fees: (September 06)
Day £2370–£7110

ST EDWARD'S SCHOOL
CHELTENHAM
Cirencester Road, Cheltenham,
Gloucestershire GL53 8EY
Tel: (01242) 538600
Fax: (01242) 538160
Email: headmaster@
  stedwards.co.uk
Head: Dr A J Nash
Type: Co-educational Day 11–18
No of pupils: B258 G211
Fees: On application

CINDERFORD

ST ANTHONYS SCHOOL
93 Bellevue Road, Cinderford,
Gloucestershire GL14 2AA
Tel: (01594) 823558
Fax: (01594) 824799
Email: sister@gli42aafsnet.co.uk
Head: Sister M C McKenna
Type: Co-educational Day 3–11
No of pupils: B61 G61
Fees: On application

CIRENCESTER

HATHEROP CASTLE SCHOOL
Hatherop, Cirencester,
Gloucestershire GL7 3NB
Tel: (01285) 750206
Fax: (01285) 750430
Email: admissions@
 hatheropcastle.co.uk
Head: Mr P Easterbrook
Type: Co-educational Boarding
and Day 2–13
No of pupils: B100 G90
No of boarders: F15 W9
Fees: (September 06)
F/WB £13440–£14190
Day £5520–£9180

INGLESIDE SCHOOL
Beeches Road, Cirencester,
Gloucestershire GL7 1BN
Tel: (01285) 654046
Fax: (01285) 655073
Email: info@
 ingleside.gloucs.sch.uk
Head: Mr Mark Anderson
Type: Co-educational Day 3–11
No of pupils: B50 G56
Fees: On application

RENDCOMB COLLEGE*
Rendcomb, Cirencester,
Gloucestershire GL7 7HA
Tel: (01285) 831213
Fax: (01285) 831121
Email: info@
 rendcomb.gloucs.sch.uk
Head: Mr Gerry Holden and
Mr Martin Watson
Type: Co-educational Boarding
and Day 3–18
No of pupils: B195 G183
No of boarders: F148
Fees: (September 06)
F/WB £15045–£19500
Day £4800–£14945

GLOUCESTER

GLOUCESTERSHIRE ISLAMIC SECONDARY SCHOOL FOR GIRLS
Sinope Street, off Widden Street,
Gloucester, Gloucestershire
GL1 4AW
Tel: (01452) 300465
Email: iacademy@yahoo.co.uk
Head: Mrs C Sandall
Type: Girls Day 11–16
No of pupils: 90
Fees: On application

THE KING'S SCHOOL
Pitt Street, Gloucester,
Gloucestershire GL1 2BG
Tel: (01452) 337337
Fax: (01452) 337314
Email: office@
 thekingsschool.co.uk
Head: Mr P R Lacey
Type: Co-educational Boarding
and Day 3–18
No of pupils: B300 G220
No of boarders: W10
Fees: On application

SCHOOL OF THE LION
The Judges Lodgings, Spa Road,
Gloucester, Gloucestershire
GL1 1UY
Tel: (01452) 381601
Fax: (01452) 553331
Email: office@
 schoolofthelion.org.uk
Head: Mr N Steele
Type: Co-educational Day 3–18
No of pupils: B21 G22
Fees: On application

WYNSTONES SCHOOL
Church Lane, Whaddon,
Gloucester, Gloucestershire
GL4 0UF
Tel: (01452) 429220
Fax: (01452) 429221
Email: info@wynstones.com
Head: Mr K Power
Type: Co-educational Day and
Boarding 3–19
No of pupils: B151 G159
No of boarders: F5 W2
Fees: (September 05)
FB £9331–£9605
WB £7770–£8040
Day £2500–£5700

MORETON-IN-MARSH

THE DORMER HOUSE PNEU SCHOOL
High Street, Moreton-in-Marsh,
Gloucestershire GL56 0AD
Tel: (01608) 650758
Fax: (01608) 652238
Email: dtrembath@aol.com
Head: Ms D A Trembath
Type: Co-educational Day 2–11
No of pupils: B54 G58
Fees: On application

NAILSWORTH

ACORN SCHOOL
Church Street, Nailsworth,
Gloucestershire GL6 0BP
Tel: (01453) 836508
Fax: (01453) 836508
Head: Mr G E B Whiting
Type: Co-educational Day 3–19
No of pupils: 115
Fees: On application

STONEHOUSE

HOPELANDS SCHOOL
38 Regent Street, Stonehouse,
Gloucestershire GL10 2AD
Tel: (01453) 822164
Fax: (01453) 827288
Email: enquiries@
 hopelands.org.uk
Head: Mrs S Bradburn
Type: Co-educational Day 3–11
No of pupils: B20 G42
Fees: (September 06)
Day £4170–£4950

WYCLIFFE COLLEGE*†
Bath Road, Stonehouse,
Gloucestershire GL10 2JQ
Tel: (01453) 822432
Fax: (01453) 827634
Email: senior@wycliffe.co.uk
Head: Mrs M E Burnet Ward
Type: Co-educational Boarding
and Day 13–18
No of pupils: B271 G150
No of boarders: F252
Fees: (September 06)
FB £20520–£24960
Day £12975–£14190

WYCLIFFE PREPARATORY SCHOOL*†
Ryeford Hall, Stonehouse,
Gloucestershire GL10 2LD
Tel: (01453) 820471
Fax: (01453) 825604
Email: prep@wycliffe.co.uk
Head: Mr A Palmer
Type: Co-educational Boarding
and Day 2–13
No of pupils: B175 G145
No of boarders: F54
Fees: (September 06)
FB £11685–£14985
Day £4785–£9795

STROUD

BEAUDESERT PARK SCHOOL
Minchinhampton, Stroud,
Gloucestershire GL6 9AF
Tel: (01453) 832072
Fax: (01453) 836040
Email: office@
  beaudesert.gloucs.sch.uk
Head: Mr J P R Womersley
Type: Co-educational Boarding
and Day 4–13
No of pupils: B204 G198
No of boarders: W40
Fees: (September 06)
WB £13365–£15330
Day £6255–£11715

TETBURY

QUERNS WESTONBIRT
SCHOOL*
Tetbury, Gloucestershire GL8 8QG
Tel: (01666) 881390
Fax: (01666) 881391
Email: querns@
  westonbirt.gloucs.sch.uk
Head: Miss V James
Type: Co-educational Day 4–11
No of pupils: B35 G45
Fees: (September 06)
Day £5325–£7575

WESTONBIRT SCHOOL*
Tetbury, Gloucestershire GL8 8QG
Tel: (01666) 880333
Fax: (01666) 880364
Email: office@
  westonbirt.gloucs.sch.uk
Head: Mrs M Henderson
Type: Girls Boarding and Day
11–18
No of pupils: 234
No of boarders: F122 W32
Fees: (September 06)
F/WB £20625–£22050
Day £14100–£15300

TEWKESBURY

BREDON SCHOOL[†]
Pull Court, Bushley, Tewkesbury,
Gloucestershire GL20 6AH
Tel: (01684) 293156
Fax: (01684) 276392
Email: enquiries@
  bredonschool.co.uk
Head: Mr D J Keyte
Type: Co-educational Boarding
and Day 7–18
No of pupils: B171 G59
No of boarders: F81 W41
Fees: (September 06)
FB £4895–£6940
WB £4750–£6800
Day £1925–£4450

WOTTON-UNDER-EDGE

ROSE HILL SCHOOL
Alderley, Wotton-under-Edge,
Gloucestershire GL12 7QT
Tel: (01453) 843196
Fax: (01453) 846126
Email: office@rosehillschool.com
Head: Mr P Cawley- Wakefield
Type: Co-educational Day 3–13
No of pupils: B70 G60
Fees: (September 06)
Day £5370–£10620

SOUTH GLOUCESTERSHIRE

WINTERBOURNE

SILVERHILL SCHOOL
Swan Lane, Winterbourne,
South Gloucestershire BS36 1RL
Tel: (01454) 772156
Fax: (01454) 777141
Email: silverhill@btconnect.com
Head: Mrs J Capper and
Mr P J Capper
Type: Co-educational Day 2–11
No of pupils: B114 G117
Fees: (September 06)
Day £3900–£5240

HAMPSHIRE

ALTON

ALTON CONVENT SCHOOL
Anstey Lane, Alton, Hampshire
GU34 2NG
Tel: (01420) 82070
Fax: (01420) 541711
Email: enquiries@
alton-convent.com
Head: Mrs S Kirkham
Type: Girls Day 2–18 (Co-ed
2–11)
No of pupils: B75 G380
Fees: (September 05)
Day £4755–£7800

ANDOVER

FARLEIGH SCHOOL
Red Rice, Andover, Hampshire
SP11 7PW
Tel: (01264) 710766
Fax: (01264) 710070
Email: office@farleighschool.co.uk
Head: Fr S Everson
Type: Co-educational Boarding
and Day 3–13
No of pupils: B233 G160
No of boarders: F115
Fees: (September 05) F/WB £16155
Day £3360–£12225

ROOKWOOD SCHOOL*
Weyhill Road, Andover,
Hampshire SP10 3AL
Tel: (01264) 325900
Fax: (01264) 325909
Email: office@
rookwood.hants.sch.uk
Head: Mrs M P Langley
Type: Co-educational Day and
Boarding 3–16 (Day boys only)
No of pupils: B138 G204
No of boarders: F35
Fees: (September 06)
FB £14805–£17355
Day £5880–£9705

BASINGSTOKE

DANESHILL SCHOOL
Stratfield Turgis, Basingstoke,
Hampshire RG27 0AR
Tel: (01256) 882707
Fax: (01256) 882007
Email: office@
daneshill.hants.sch.uk
Head: Mr S V Spencer
Type: Co-educational Day 2–13
No of pupils: B124 G137
Fees: (September 06)
Day £3450–£8340

THE KING'S SCHOOL
Basingstoke Community Church,
Sarum Hill, Basingstoke,
Hampshire RG21 8SR
Tel: (01256) 467092
Fax: (01256) 473605
Head: Mr Paul Davis
Type: Co-educational Day 7–16
No of pupils: B99 G73
Fees: On application

BRAMDEAN

BROCKWOOD PARK
SCHOOL
Bramdean, Hampshire SO24 0LQ
Tel: (01962) 771744
Fax: (01962) 771875
Email: enquiry@brockwood.org.uk
Head: Mr B Taylor
Type: Co-educational Boarding
14–19
No of pupils: B27 G31
No of boarders: F58
Fees: (September 06) FB £13500

CHANDLER'S FORD

WOODHILL SCHOOL
61 Brownhill Road, Chandler's
Ford, Hampshire SO53 2EH
Tel: (023) 8026 8012
Fax: (023) 8026 8012
Head: Mrs M Dacombe
Type: Co-educational Day 3–11
No of pupils: B60 G60
Fees: On application

EASTLEIGH

THE KING'S SCHOOL
SENIOR
Lakesmere House, Allington Lane,
Fair Oak, Eastleigh, Hampshire
SO50 7DB
Tel: (023) 8060 0956
Fax: (023) 8060 0956
Email: office@
kingssenior.hants.sch.uk
Head: Mrs R Pierson
Type: Co-educational Day 11–16
No of pupils: B62 G43
Fees: On application

SHERBORNE HOUSE
SCHOOL
Lakewood Road, Chandler's Ford,
Eastleigh, Hampshire SO53 1EU
Tel: (023) 8025 2440
Fax: (023) 8025 2553
Email: info@sherbornehouse.co.uk
Head: Mrs A Entwisle
Type: Co-educational Day 2–11
No of pupils: B124 G144
Fees: (September 06)
Day £1761–£6885

FAREHAM

BOUNDARY OAK SCHOOL
Roche Court, Wickham Road,
Fareham, Hampshire PO17 5BL
Tel: (01329) 280955
Fax: (01329) 827656
Email: secretary@
boundaryoak.co.uk
Head: Mr B L Brown
Type: Co-educational Boarding
and Day 3–13
No of pupils: B166 G49
No of boarders: W25
Fees: On application

MEONCROSS SCHOOL
Burnt House Lane, Stubbington,
Fareham, Hampshire PO14 2EF
Tel: (01329) 662182
Fax: (01329) 664680
Email: meoncross@aol.com
Head: Mr C J Ford
Type: Co-educational Day 3–16
No of pupils: B225 G180
Fees: On application

WYKEHAM HOUSE SCHOOL

East Street, Fareham, Hampshire
PO16 0BW
Tel: (01329) 280178
Fax: (01329) 823964
Email: office@
    wykehamhouse.hants.sch.uk
Head: Mrs L Clarke
Type: Girls Day 2–16
No of pupils: 250
Fees: (September 06)
Day £3213–£7857

FARNBOROUGH

FARNBOROUGH HILL*

Farnborough, Hampshire
GU14 8AT
Tel: (01252) 545197
Fax: (01252) 513037
Email: devdir@
    farnborough-hill.org.uk
Head: Miss J Thomas
Type: Girls Day 11–18
No of pupils: 500
Fees: (September 06) Day £8865

SALESIAN COLLEGE

Reading Road, Farnborough,
Hampshire GU14 6PA
Tel: (01252) 893000
Fax: (01252) 893032
Email: office@
    salesian.hants.sch.uk
Head: Mr P A Wilson
Type: Boys Day 11–18
Fees: On application

FLEET

ST NICHOLAS' SCHOOL*

Redfields House, Redfields Lane,
Church Crookham, Fleet,
Hampshire GU52 0RF
Tel: (01252) 850121
Fax: (01252) 850718
Email: registrar@
    st-nicholas.hants.sch.uk
Head: Mrs A V Whatmough
Type: Girls Day 3–16 (Boys 3–7)
No of pupils: B20 G360
Fees: (September 05)
Day £3150–£8520

STOCKTON HOUSE SCHOOL

Stockton Avenue, Fleet,
Hampshire GU51 4NS
Tel: (01252) 616323
Fax: (01252) 627011
Email: stocktonialtd@
    waitrose.com
Head: Mrs S Forrest
Type: Co-educational Day 2–6
No of pupils: B30 G30
Fees: (September 06)
Day £300–£3798

FORDINGBRIDGE

FORRES SANDLE MANOR

Fordingbridge, Hampshire
SP6 1NS
Tel: (01425) 653181
Fax: (01425) 655676
Email: office@
    forressandlemanor.hants.sch.uk
Head: Mr R P J Moore
Type: Co-educational Boarding
and Day 3–13
No of pupils: B144 G129
No of boarders: F61 W35
Fees: (September 06) F/WB £16665
Day £220–£4085

GOSPORT

MARYCOURT SCHOOL

27 Crescent Road, Alverstoke,
Gosport, Hampshire PO12 2DJ
Tel: (023) 9258 1766
Fax: (023) 9258 1766
Head: Mrs J Norman
Type: Co-educational Day 3–11
No of pupils: B40 G45
Fees: On application

HAVANT

GLENHURST SCHOOL

16 Beechworth Road, Havant,
Hampshire PO9 1AX
Tel: (023) 9248 4054
Fax: (023) 9248 4054
Email: office@
    glenhurstschool.co.uk
Head: Mrs E Haines
Type: Co-educational Day 2–9
No of pupils: B40 G40
Fees: (September 05) Day £3300

HOOK

GREY HOUSE PREPARATORY SCHOOL

Mount Pleasant Road, Hartley
Wintney, Hook, Hampshire
RG27 8PW
Tel: (01252) 842353
Fax: (01252) 845527
Email: schooloffice@
    grey-house.co.uk
Head: Mrs C Allen
Type: Co-educational Day 4–11
No of pupils: B89 G52
Fees: (September 06)
Day £5412–£6663

LORD WANDSWORTH COLLEGE*

Long Sutton, Hook, Hampshire
RG29 1TB
Tel: (01256) 862201
Fax: (01256) 860363
Email: info@lordwandsworth.org
Head: Mr I G Power
Type: Co-educational Boarding
and Day 11–18
No of pupils: B347 G174
No of boarders: F46 W199
Fees: (September 06)
FB £19365–£21300
WB £19365–£20445
Day £14460–£15240

ST NEOT'S SCHOOL

Eversley, Hook, Hampshire
RG27 0PN
Tel: (0118) 973 2118
Fax: (0118) 973 9949
Email: office@st-neots-prep.co.uk
Head: Mr R J Thorp
Type: Co-educational Day and
Boarding 1–13
No of pupils: B180 G130
No of boarders: W26
Fees: (September 06) WB £13905
Day £5040–£11250

SHERFIELD SCHOOL

Reading Road,
Sherfield-on-Loddon, Hook,
Hampshire RG27 0HT
Tel: (01256) 884800
Fax: (01256) 883172
Email: info@sherfieldschool.co.uk
Head: Mr J Murphy-O'Connor and
Mrs J Tannock
Type: Co-educational Day 0–18
(Upper age increased to 18)
No of pupils: B195 G153
Fees: (September 06)
Day £5760–£10398

LEE-ON-THE-SOLENT

ST ANNE'S PRE-SCHOOL
13 Milvil Road, Lee-on-the-Solent,
Hampshire PO13 9LU
Tel: (023) 9255 0820
Email: st_annes_school@
    yahoo.co.uk
Head: Mrs A M Whitting
Type: Co-educational Day 2–8
No of pupils: B15 G15
Fees: (September 06)
Day £1710–£3990

LIPHOOK

CHURCHERS COLLEGE JUNIOR SCHOOL
Midhurst Road, Liphook,
Hampshire GU30 7HT
Tel: (01730) 236870
Fax: (01730) 722550
Head: Mrs S Rivett
Type: Co-educational Day 4–11
No of pupils: B109 G114
Fees: (September 05)
Day £5475–£5835

HIGHFIELD SCHOOL*
Highfield Lane, Liphook,
Hampshire GU30 7LQ
Tel: (01428) 728000
Fax: (01428) 728001
Email: office@
    highfieldschool.org.uk
Head: Mr P G S Evitt
Type: Co-educational Boarding
and Day 8–13
No of pupils: B110 G106
No of boarders: F85
Fees: (September 06)
FB £11700–£16650
Day £11250–£14625

LYMINGTON

HORDLE WALHAMPTON SCHOOL†
Lymington, Hampshire SO41 5ZG
Tel: (01590) 672013
Fax: (01590) 678498
Email: registrar@
    hordlewalhampton.co.uk
Head: Mr R H C Phillips
Type: Co-educational Boarding
and Day 2–13
No of pupils: B183 G143
No of boarders: F41
Fees: (September 05) F/WB £14250
Day £5415–£10830

NEW MILTON

BALLARD SCHOOL
Fernhill Lane, New Milton,
Hampshire BH25 5SU
Tel: (01425) 611153
Fax: (01425) 622099
Email: admissions@
    ballardschool.co.uk
Head: Mr S P Duckitt
Type: Co-educational Day 2–16
No of pupils: B318 G206
Fees: (September 05)
Day £1557–£9510

DURLSTON COURT
Becton Lane, Barton-on-Sea, New
Milton, Hampshire BH25 7AQ
Tel: (01425) 610010
Fax: (01425) 622731
Email: secretary@
    durlstoncourt.org.uk
Head: Mr D C Wansey
Type: Co-educational Day 2–13
No of pupils: B167 G133
Fees: (September 06)
Day £3060–£10575

PETERSFIELD

BEDALES SCHOOL
Petersfield, Hampshire GU32 2DG
Tel: (01730) 300100
Fax: (01730) 300500
Email: admissions@bedales.org.uk
Head: Mr K Budge
Type: Co-educational Boarding
and Day 13–18
No of pupils: B225 G230
No of boarders: F315
Fees: (September 06) FB £8218
Day £6372

CHURCHERS COLLEGE
Portsmouth Road, Petersfield,
Hampshire GU31 4AS
Tel: (01730) 263033
Fax: (01730) 231437
Email: enquiries@
    churcherscollege.com
Head: Mr S H Williams
Type: Co-educational Day 4–18
No of pupils: B475 G360
Fees: (September 05)
Day £5475–£8895

DITCHAM PARK SCHOOL
Ditcham Park, Petersfield,
Hampshire GU31 5RN
Tel: (01730) 825659
Fax: (01730) 825070
Email: info@ditchampark.com
Head: Mrs K S Morton
Type: Co-educational Day 4–16
No of pupils: B192 G156
Fees: (September 06)
Day £5721–£9549

DUNHURST (BEDALES JUNIOR SCHOOL)
Petersfield, Hampshire GU32 2DP
Tel: (01730) 300200
Fax: (01730) 300600
Email: dunhurst@bedales.org.uk
Head: Mr C Sanderson
Type: Co-educational Boarding
and Day 8–13
No of pupils: B90 G94
No of boarders: F53
Fees: On application

PORTSMOUTH

THE PORTSMOUTH GRAMMAR SCHOOL
High Street, Portsmouth,
Hampshire PO1 2LN
Tel: (023) 9281 9125
Fax: (023) 9236 4256
Email: admissions@pgs.org.uk
Head: Dr T R Hands
Type: Co-educational Day 2–18
No of pupils: B950 G500
Fees: (September 05)
Day £5928–£9246

ROOKESBURY PARK SCHOOL
Southwick Road, Wickham,
Portsmouth, Hampshire PO17 6HT
Tel: (01329) 833108
Fax: (01329) 835090
Email: rookesburypark@
    btconnect.com
Head: Mr P G Savage
Type: Co-educational Boarding
and Day 3–13
No of pupils: B41 G59
No of boarders: F8 W5
Fees: (September 05)
F/WB £12435–£14670
Day £5010–£9885

RINGWOOD

MOYLES COURT SCHOOL[†]
Moyles Court, Ringwood,
Hampshire BH24 3NF
Tel: (01425) 472856
Fax: (01425) 474715
Email: moylescourt@
  btinternet.com
Head: Mr R A Dean
Type: Co-educational Day and
Boarding 3–16
No of pupils: B105 G74
No of boarders: F48
Fees: On application

RINGWOOD WALDORF SCHOOL
Ashley, Ringwood, Hampshire
BH24 2NN
Tel: (01425) 472664
Type: Co-educational Day 4–14
No of pupils: B100 G100
Fees: On application

ROMSEY

HAMPSHIRE COLLEGIATE SCHOOL (EMBLEY PARK)*
Embley Park, Romsey, Hampshire
SO51 6ZE
Tel: (01794) 512206
Fax: (01794) 518737
Email: info@hampshirecs.org.uk
Head: Mr D F Chapman
Type: Co-educational Boarding
and Day 3–18
No of pupils: B300 G180
No of boarders: F30 W46
Fees: (September 05)
F/WB £8310–£16620
Day £5000–£10005

STANBRIDGE EARLS SCHOOL[†]
Stanbridge Lane, Romsey,
Hampshire SO51 0ZS
Tel: (01794) 529400
Fax: (01794) 511201
Email: admin@
  stanbridgeearls.co.uk
Head: Mr G P Link
Type: Co-educational Boarding
and Day 10–19
No of pupils: B140 G24
No of boarders: F132
Fees: (September 06)
FB £19770–£21630
Day £14730–£16035

THE STROUD SCHOOL
Highwood House, Highwood
Lane, Romsey, Hampshire
SO51 9ZH
Tel: (01794) 513231
Fax: (01794) 514432
Email: secretary@
  stroud-romsey-sch.co.uk
Head: Mr A J Dodds
Type: Co-educational Day 3–13
No of pupils: B188 G127
Fees: (September 06)
Day £2970–£10545

SOUTHAMPTON

THE GREGG SCHOOL
Townhill Park House, Cutbush
Lane, Southampton, Hampshire
SO18 2GF
Tel: (023) 8047 2133
Head: Mr R D Hart
Type: Co-educational Day 11–16
No of pupils: B200 G134
Fees: On application

KING EDWARD VI SCHOOL
Kellett Road, Southampton,
Hampshire SO15 7UQ
Tel: (023) 8070 4561
Fax: (023) 8070 5937
Email: registrar@kes.hants.sch.uk
Head: Mr A J Thould
Type: Co-educational Day 11–18
No of pupils: B624 G345
Fees: (September 05) Day £8886

KINGS PRIMARY SCHOOL
26 Quob Lane, West End,
Southampton, Hampshire
SO30 3HN
Tel: (023) 8047 2266
Fax: (023) 8047 2282
Email: kingschool@lineone.net
Head: Mr K Ford
Type: Co-educational Day 5–11
No of pupils: 120
Fees: On application

ST MARY'S COLLEGE
57 Midanbury Lane, Bitterne Park,
Southampton, Hampshire
SO18 4DJ
Tel: (023) 8067 1267
Fax: (023) 8067 7575
Email: stmarysoffice@aol.com
Head: Rev J J Davis
Type: Co-educational Day 3–18
Fees: (September 05) Day £5800

ST WINIFRED'S SCHOOL
17–19 Winn Road, Southampton,
Hampshire SO17 1EJ
Tel: (023) 8055 7352
Fax: (023) 8055 7352
Email: office@
  stwinifreds.southampton.sch.uk
Head: Mrs C A Pearcey
Type: Co-educational Day 2–11
Fees: (September 05)
Day £3600–£5040

VINE SCHOOL
Church Lane, Curdridge,
Southampton, Hampshire
SO32 2DR
Tel: (01489) 789123
Email: the@vineschool.fsnet.co.uk
Head: Mr A J Saunders
Type: Co-educational Day 3–11
No of pupils: B38 G39
Fees: On application

WOODHILL PREPARATORY SCHOOL
Brook Lane, Botley, Southampton,
Hampshire SO30 2ER
Tel: (01489) 781112
Fax: (01489) 799362
Email: m.dacombe@
  woodhill.hants.sch.uk
Head: Mrs M Dacombe
Type: Co-educational Day 3–11
No of pupils: B62 G48
Fees: On application

SOUTHSEA

MAYVILLE HIGH SCHOOL[†]
35 St Simon's Road, Southsea,
Hampshire PO5 2PE
Tel: (023) 9273 4847
Fax: (023) 9229 3649
Email: mayvillehighschoolpr@
  talk21.com
Head: Mrs L Owens and
Mr M Castle
Type: Co-educational Day 1–16
No of pupils: B210 G240
Fees: (September 06)
Day £2835–£6810

England – Hampshire

PORTSMOUTH HIGH SCHOOL GDST

Kent Road, Southsea, Hampshire
PO5 3EQ
Tel: (023) 9282 6714
Fax: (023) 9281 4814
Email: headsec@por.gdst.net
Head: Mrs J J Clough
Type: Girls Day 3–18
No of pupils: B600 G624
Fees: (September 06)
Day £4710–£7863

ST JOHN'S COLLEGE

Grove Road South, Southsea,
Hampshire PO5 3QW
Tel: (023) 9281 5118
Fax: (023) 9287 3603
Email: info@stjohnscollege.co.uk
Head: Mr N W Thorne
Type: Co-educational Boarding
and Day 2–18
No of pupils: B378 G178
No of boarders: F114
Fees: (September 06)
FB £16200–£17400
Day £5475–£7500

WINCHESTER

THE PILGRIMS' SCHOOL

3 The Close, Winchester,
Hampshire SO23 9LT
Tel: (01962) 854189
Fax: (01962) 843610
Email: info@pilgrims-school.co.uk
Head: Dr B A Rees
Type: Boys Boarding and Day
7–13
No of pupils: 200
No of boarders: F40 W25
Fees: (September 05) FB £14790
Day £11790

PRINCE'S MEAD SCHOOL

Worthy Park House, Kingsworthy,
Winchester, Hampshire SO21 1AN
Tel: (01962) 886000
Fax: (01962) 886888
Email: admin@
   princesmeadschool.org.uk
Head: Miss P Kirk
Type: Co-educational Day 3–11
No of pupils: B84 G150
Fees: (September 06)
Day £7650–£9180

ST SWITHUN'S SCHOOL

Alresford Road, Winchester,
Hampshire SO21 1HA
Tel: (01962) 835700
Fax: (01962) 835779
Email: office@stswithuns.com
Head: Dr H L Harvey
Type: Girls Boarding and Day
11–18
No of pupils: 480
No of boarders: F46 W175
Fees: (September 06) F/WB £20850
Day £12660

TWYFORD SCHOOL

Twyford, Winchester, Hampshire
SO21 1NW
Tel: (01962) 712269
Fax: (01962) 712100
Email: registrar@
   twyfordschool.com
Head: Dr D Livingstone
Type: Co-educational Day and
Boarding 3–13
No of pupils: B181 G111
No of boarders: W24
Fees: (September 06) WB £16260
Day £3465–£12585

WINCHESTER COLLEGE*

College Street, Winchester,
Hampshire SO23 9NA
Tel: (01962) 621247
Fax: (01962) 621106
Email: Admissions@
   WinchesterCollege.co.uk
Head: Dr R D Townsend
Type: Boys Boarding and Day
13–18
No of pupils: 690
No of boarders: F678
Fees: (September 06) FB £24981
Day £23730

YATELEY

YATELEY MANOR PREPARATORY SCHOOL

51 Reading Road, Yateley,
Hampshire GU46 7UQ
Tel: (01252) 405500
Fax: (01252) 405504
Email: office@yateleymanor.com
Head: Mr F G Howard
Type: Co-educational Day 3–13
No of pupils: B301 G196
Fees: (September 06)
Day £3495–£9672

HEREFORDSHIRE

BROMYARD

ST RICHARD'S
Bredenbury Court, Bromyard,
Herefordshire HR7 4TD
Tel: (01885) 482491
Fax: (01885) 488982
Email: st.dix@virgin.net
Head: Mr N Cheesman
Type: Co-educational Boarding
and Day 3–13
No of pupils: B93 G70
No of boarders: F40 W37
Fees: On application

HEREFORD

HABERDASHERS' REDCAP SCHOOL
32 Broomy Hill, Hereford,
Herefordshire HR4 0LH
Tel: (01432) 273594
Fax: (01432) 273594
Email: enquiries@
    haberdashersredcap.org
Head: Mrs A Ellis
Type: Girls Day 2–11
No of pupils: 80
Fees: On application

THE HEREFORD CATHEDRAL JUNIOR SCHOOL
28 Castle Street, Hereford,
Herefordshire HR1 2NW
Tel: (01432) 363511
Fax: (01432) 363515
Email: secretary@hcjs.co.uk
Head: Mr T R Lowe
Type: Co-educational Day 3–11
No of pupils: B190 G137
Fees: On application

THE HEREFORD CATHEDRAL SCHOOL
Old Deanery, Cathedral Close,
Hereford, Herefordshire HR1 2NG
Tel: (01432) 363522
Fax: (01432) 363525
Email: enquiry@hcsch.org
Head: Mr P A Smith
Type: Co-educational Day 11–18
No of pupils: B322 G272
Fees: On application

LEOMINSTER

LUCTON SCHOOL
Leominster, Herefordshire
HR6 9PN
Tel: (01568) 782000
Fax: (01568) 782001
Email: enquiries@luctonschool.org
Head: Mrs G Thorne
Type: Co-educational Boarding
and Day 0–16 (VIth Form from
Sept 2005)
No of pupils: B80 G72
No of boarders: F38 W15
Fees: On application

HERTFORDSHIRE

ALDENHAM

EDGE GROVE
Aldenham Village, Aldenham,
Hertfordshire WD25 8NL
Tel: (01923) 855724
Fax: (01923) 859920
Email: enquiries@
    edgegrove.indschools.co.uk
Head: Mr M T Wilson
Type: Co-educational Boarding
and Day 3–13
No of pupils: B234 G100
No of boarders: F50 W40
Fees: On application

BARNET

LYONSDOWN SCHOOL TRUST LTD
3 Richmond Road, New Barnet,
Barnet, Hertfordshire EN5 1SA
Tel: (020) 8449 0225
Fax: (020) 8441 4690
Email: enquiries@
    lyonsdownschool.co.uk
Head: Mrs L Maggs-Wellings
Type: Co-educational Day
Boys 3–7 Girls 3–11
No of pupils: B54 G158
Fees: (September 05)
Day £4929–£5424

NORFOLK LODGE NURSERY & PREPARATORY SCHOOL
Dancers Hill Road, Barnet,
Hertfordshire EN5 4RP
Tel: (020) 8447 1565
Fax: (020) 8447 1833
Email: norfolk_lodge@
    hotmail.com
Head: Mrs K Conroy
Type: Co-educational Day 1–11
No of pupils: B110 G90
Fees: On application

ST MARTHA'S SENIOR SCHOOL

Camlet Way, Hadley, Barnet,
Hertfordshire EN4 0NJ
Tel: (020) 8449 6889
Fax: (020) 8441 5632
Email: office@st-marthas.org.uk
Head: Mr J Sheridan
Type: Girls Day 11–18
No of pupils: 320
Fees: On application

SUZI EARNSHAW THEATRE SCHOOL

68 High Street, Barnet,
Hertfordshire EN5 5SJ
Tel: (020) 8441 5010
Fax: (020) 8364 9618
Email: school@
   susiearnshaw.co.uk
Head: Mr D Earnshaw
Type: Co-educational Day 11–19
No of pupils: B22 G39
Fees: (September 05)
Day £5550–£7150

BERKHAMSTED

BERKHAMSTED COLLEGIATE PREPARATORY SCHOOL

Kings Road, Berkhamsted,
Hertfordshire HP4 3YP
Tel: (01442) 358201/2
Fax: (01442) 358203
Email: info@bcschool.org
Head: Mr A J Taylor
Type: Co-educational Day 3–11
No of pupils: B229 G234
Fees: On application

BERKHAMSTED COLLEGIATE SCHOOL

Castle Street, Berkhamsted,
Hertfordshire HP4 2BB
Tel: (01442) 358000
Fax: (01442) 358040
Email: info@bcschool.org
Head: Dr P Chadwick
Type: Co-educational Day and
Boarding 11–18 (Single-sex ed
11–16)
No of pupils: B620 G418
No of boarders: F43 W4
Fees: (September 06)
F/WB £19071–£21069
Day £11340–£13338

EGERTON-ROTHESAY SCHOOL

Durrants Lane, Berkhamsted,
Hertfordshire HP4 3UJ
Tel: (01442) 865275
Fax: (01442) 864977
Email: admin@egerton2.u-net.com
Head: Mrs N Boddam-Whetham
Type: Co-educational Day 3–16
No of pupils: B255 G109
Fees: (September 05) Day £9495

HARESFOOT PREPARATORY SCHOOL

Chesham Road, Berkhamsted,
Hertfordshire HP4 2SZ
Tel: (01442) 872742
Fax: (01442) 872742
Email: haresfootschool@
   btconnect.com
Head: Mrs Carole Hawkins
Type: Co-educational Day 0–11
No of pupils: B95 G83
Fees: (September 06)
Day £420–£7200

BISHOP'S STORTFORD

BISHOP'S STORTFORD COLLEGE

Maze Green Road, Bishop's
Stortford, Hertfordshire CM23 2PJ
Tel: (01279) 838575
Fax: (01279) 836570
Email: admissions@bsc.biblio.net
Head: Mr J G Trotman
Type: Co-educational Boarding
and Day 4–18
No of pupils: B573 G427
No of boarders: F115 W106
Fees: (September 06)
FB £12120–£17397
Day £5850–£12510

HOWE GREEN HOUSE SCHOOL

Great Hallingbury, Bishop's
Stortford, Hertfordshire CM22 7UF
Tel: (01279) 657706
Fax: (01279) 501333
Email: info@
   howegreenhouseschool.co.uk
Head: Mr G R Gorton
Type: Co-educational Day 2–11
No of pupils: B101 G88
Fees: (September 06)
Day £4881–£7758

THE JUNIOR SCHOOL, BISHOP'S STORTFORD COLLEGE

Maze Green Road, Bishop's
Stortford, Hertfordshire CM23 2PH
Tel: (01279) 838607
Fax: (01279) 306110
Email: jsadmissions@
   bsc.biblio.net
Head: Mr J A Greathead
Type: Co-educational Boarding
and Day 4–13
No of pupils: B289 G208
No of boarders: F20 W21
Fees: On application

BUSHEY

IMMANUEL COLLEGE

87/91 Elstree Road, Bushey,
Hertfordshire WD23 4EB
Tel: (020) 8950 0604
Fax: (020) 8950 8687
Email: enquiries@
   immanuel.herts.sch.uk
Head: Mr P Skelker
Type: Co-educational Day 11–18
No of pupils: B262 G256
Fees: (September 06) Day £10995

LITTLE ACORNS MONTESSORI SCHOOL

Lincolnsfields Centre, Bushey Hall
Drive, Bushey, Hertfordshire
WD2 2ER
Tel: (01923) 230705
Fax: (01923) 230705
Head: Ms J Nugent and Ms R Lau
Type: Co-educational Day 2–7
No of pupils: 24
Fees: On application

LONGWOOD SCHOOL

Bushey Hall Drive, Bushey,
Hertfordshire WD23 2QG
Tel: (01923) 253715
Fax: (01923) 222760
Email: longwoodnursery@aol.com
Head: Mr M Livesey
Type: Co-educational Day 3–11
No of pupils: B63 G45
Fees: On application

THE PURCELL SCHOOL
Aldenham Road, Bushey,
Hertfordshire WD23 2TS
Tel: (01923) 331100
Fax: (01923) 331166
Email: info@purcell-school.org
Head: Mr J Tolputt
Type: Co-educational Day and
Boarding 8–18
No of pupils: B59 G109
No of boarders: F100
Fees: On application

ST HILDA'S SCHOOL
High Street, Bushey, Hertfordshire
WD23 3DA
Tel: (020) 8950 1751
Fax: (020) 8420 4523
Email: registrar@
    sthildasbushey.co.uk
Head: Mrs L Cavanagh
Type: Girls Day 3–11 (Boys 3–5)
No of pupils: B5 G120
Fees: (September 06)
Day £4245–£7800

ST MARGARET'S SCHOOL*
Merry Hill Road, Bushey,
Hertfordshire WD23 1DT
Tel: (020) 8901 0870
Fax: (020) 8950 1677
Email: admissions@
    stmargarets.herts.sch.uk
Head: Mrs Lynne Crighton
Type: Girls Boarding and Day
4–18
No of pupils: 400
No of boarders: F60
Fees: (September 05) F/WB £18885
Day £7005–£10545

BUSHEY HEATH

WESTWOOD
6 Hartsbourne Road, Bushey
Heath, Hertfordshire WD23 1JH
Tel: (020) 8950 1138
Email: westwood.school@
    virgin.net
Head: Mrs J Hill
Type: Co-educational Day 4–8
No of pupils: B36 G36
Fees: (September 06) Day £5250

ELSTREE

ALDENHAM SCHOOL*
Elstree, Hertfordshire WD6 3AJ
Tel: (01923) 858122
Fax: (01923) 854410
Email: enquiries@aldenham.com
Head: Mr J C Fowler
Type: Co-educational Boarding
and Day 3–18
No of pupils: B542 G106
No of boarders: F100 W45
Fees: (September 06)
FB £15549–£21900
WB £13023–£17997
Day £8136–£15069

**HABERDASHERS' ASKE'S
BOYS' SCHOOL**
Butterfly Lane, Elstree,
Hertfordshire WD6 3AF
Tel: (020) 8266 1700
Fax: (020) 8266 1800
Email: office@habsboys.org.uk
Head: Mr P B Hamilton
Type: Boys Day 5–18
No of pupils: 1300
Fees: (September 06)
Day £8345–£11490

**HABERDASHERS' ASKE'S
SCHOOL FOR GIRLS**
Aldenham Road, Elstree,
Hertfordshire WD6 3BT
Tel: (020) 8266 2302
Fax: (020) 8266 2303
Email: theschool@habsgirls.org.uk
Head: Mrs E J Radice
Type: Girls Day 4–18
Fees: (September 06)
Day £7905–£9420

HARPENDEN

ALDWICKBURY SCHOOL
Wheathampstead Road,
Harpenden, Hertfordshire
AL5 1AD
Tel: (01582) 713022
Fax: (01582) 767696
Email: registrar@
    aldwickbury.org.uk
Head: Mr V W Hales
Type: Boys Day and Boarding
4–13
No of pupils: 308
No of boarders: W30
Fees: (September 05)
WB £10530–£11061
Day £6539–£8445

**HARPENDEN PREPARATORY
SCHOOL**
53 Luton Road, Harpenden,
Hertfordshire AL5 2UE
Tel: (01582) 712361
Fax: (01582) 763553
Email: harpendenprep@
    lineone.net
Head: Mrs E R Broughton
Type: Co-educational Day 2–11
No of pupils: B75 G75
Fees: On application

KINGS SCHOOL
Elmfield, Ambrose Lane,
Harpenden, Hertfordshire
AL5 4DU
Tel: (01582) 767566
Fax: (01582) 765406
Email: office@thekingsschool.com
Head: Mr C J Case
Type: Co-educational Day 4–16
No of pupils: 196
Fees: On application

ST HILDA'S SCHOOL
28 Douglas Road, Harpenden,
Hertfordshire AL5 2ES
Tel: (01582) 712307
Fax: (01582) 763892
Email: office@
    st-hildasschool.herts.sch.uk
Head: Mrs F Schofield
Type: Girls Day 2–11
No of pupils: 180
Fees: (September 05)
Day £1110–£6285

HATFIELD

QUEENSWOOD SCHOOL
Shepherds Way, Brookmans Park,
Hatfield, Hertfordshire AL9 6NS
Tel: (01707) 602500
Fax: (01707) 602597
Email: registry@queenswood.org
Head: Mrs P Edgar
Type: Girls Boarding and Day
11–18
No of pupils: 416
No of boarders: F210
Fees: (September 06)
FB £19000–£22890
Day £15960–£17430

England – Hertfordshire

HEMEL HEMPSTEAD

ABBOT'S HILL SCHOOL*
Bunkers Lane, Hemel Hempstead,
Hertfordshire HP3 8RP
Tel: (01442) 240333
Fax: (01442) 269981
Email: registrar@
    abbotshill.herts.sch.uk
Head: Mrs K Lewis
Type: Girls Day 3–16 (Boys 3–7)
No of pupils: 460
Fees: (September 06)
Day £6555–£11610

LOCKERS PARK
Lockers Park Lane, Hemel
Hempstead, Hertfordshire HP1 1TL
Tel: (01442) 251712
Fax: (01442) 234150
Email: secretary@
    lockerspark.herts.sch.uk
Head: Mr D R Lees-Jones
Type: Boys Boarding and Day
7–13
No of pupils: 138
No of boarders: F37 W33
Fees: (September 05) FB £14700
Day £9195–£11895

WESTBROOK HAY
PREPARATORY SCHOOL
London Road, Westbrook Hay,
Hemel Hempstead, Hertfordshire
HP1 2RF
Tel: (01442) 256143
Fax: (01442) 232076
Email: admin@
    westbrookhay.co.uk
Head: Mr K Young
Type: Co-educational Boarding
and Day 2–13
No of pupils: B167 G83
Fees: (September 06)
Day £5625–£10350

HERTFORD

DUNCOMBE SCHOOL
4 Warren Park Road, Bengeo,
Hertford, Hertfordshire SG14 3JA
Tel: (01992) 414100
Fax: (01992) 414111
Email: admissions@
    duncombe-school.co.uk
Head: Mrs V White
Type: Co-educational Day 2–11
No of pupils: B156 G149
Fees: (September 06)
Day £2625–£8655

HAILEYBURY*
Hertford, Hertfordshire SG13 7NU
Tel: (01992) 463353
Fax: (01992) 470663
Email: registrar@haileybury.com
Head: Mr S A Westley
Type: Co-educational Boarding
and Day 11–18
No of pupils: B442 G312
No of boarders: F500
Fees: (September 06)
FB £14655–£23085
Day £11535–£17340

HEATH MOUNT SCHOOL
Woodhall Park, Watton-at-Stone,
Hertford, Hertfordshire SG14 3NG
Tel: (01920) 830230
Fax: (01920) 830357
Email: office@heathmount.org
Head: Mr H J Matthews
Type: Co-educational Boarding
and Day 3–13
No of pupils: B207 G150
No of boarders: W15
Fees: On application

ST JOSEPH'S IN THE PARK
St Mary's Lane, Hertingfordbury,
Hertford, Hertfordshire SG14 2LX
Tel: (01992) 581378
Fax: (01992) 505202
Email: admissions@
    stjosephsinthepark.co.uk
Head: Mr A Platt
Type: Co-educational Day 3–11
No of pupils: B100 G80
Fees: (September 06)
Day £1292–£3994

HITCHIN

KINGSHOTT SCHOOL
St Ippolyts, Hitchin, Hertfordshire
SG4 7JX
Tel: (01462) 432009
Fax: (01462) 421652
Email: pi@kingshott.herts.sch.uk
Head: Mr P R Ilott
Type: Co-educational Day 4–13
No of pupils: B236 G120
Fees: (September 05)
Day £6600–£8220

THE PRINCESS HELENA
COLLEGE
Preston, Hitchin, Hertfordshire
SG4 7RT
Tel: (01462) 432100
Fax: (01462) 443871
Email: head@phc.herts.sch.uk
Head: Mrs A M Hodgkiss
Type: Girls Day and Boarding
11–18
No of pupils: 215
No of boarders: F25 W60
Fees: (September 06)
F/WB £15690–£20040
Day £10980–£13875

KINGS LANGLEY

RUDOLF STEINER SCHOOL
Langley Hill, Kings Langley,
Hertfordshire WD4 9HG
Tel: (01923) 262505
Fax: (01923) 270958
Email: info@rsskl.org.uk
Type: Co-educational Day 3–19
No of pupils: B224 G189
Fees: (September 05)
Day £2790–£6300

LETCHWORTH

ST CHRISTOPHER SCHOOL
Barrington Road, Letchworth,
Hertfordshire SG6 3JZ
Tel: (01462) 650850
Fax: (01462) 481578
Email: admissions@stchris.co.uk
Head: Mr R Palmer
Type: Co-educational Boarding
and Day 2–18
No of pupils: B315 G189
No of boarders: F45
Fees: (September 06)
FB £16500–£21345
Day £2910–£12150

ST FRANCIS' COLLEGE
The Broadway, Letchworth,
Hertfordshire SG6 3PJ
Tel: (01462) 670511
Fax: (01462) 682361
Email: enquiries@
    st-francis.herts.sch.uk
Head: Miss M Hegarty
Type: Girls Boarding and Day
3–18
No of pupils: 509
No of boarders: F34 W6
Fees: (September 06)
FB £16275–£18855
WB £13245–£15855
Day £4920–£9585

POTTERS BAR

LOCHINVER HOUSE SCHOOL
Heath Road, Little Heath, Potters Bar, Hertfordshire EN6 1LW
Tel: (01707) 653064
Fax: (01707) 620030
Email: registrar@
 lochinverhouse.herts.sch.uk
Head: Mr J Gear
Type: Boys Day 4–13
No of pupils: 343
Fees: On application

ST JOHN'S PREPARATORY SCHOOL
Brownlowes, The Ridgeway, Potters Bar, Hertfordshire EN6 5QT
Tel: (01707) 657294
Fax: (020) 8363 4439
Email: stjohnssc@aol.com
Head: Mrs C Tardios
Type: Co-educational Day 4–11
No of pupils: B106 G142
Fees: (September 05)
Day £6000–£7000

STORMONT
The Causeway, Potters Bar, Hertfordshire EN6 5HA
Tel: (01707) 654037
Fax: (01707) 663295
Email: admin@
 stormont.herts.sch.uk
Head: Mrs M E Johnston
Type: Girls Day 4–11
No of pupils: 168
Fees: (September 06)
Day £8040–£8550

RADLETT

RADLETT PREPARATORY SCHOOL
Kendal Hall, Watling Street, Radlett, Hertfordshire WD7 7LY
Tel: (01923) 856812
Fax: (01923) 855880
Email: admin@
 radlett-prep.herts.sch.uk
Head: Mr W N Warren
Type: Co-educational Day 4–11
No of pupils: B265 G225
Fees: (September 06) Day £5940

RICKMANSWORTH

NORTHWOOD PREPARATORY SCHOOL
Moor Farm, Sandy Lodge Road, Rickmansworth, Hertfordshire WD3 1LW
Tel: (01923) 825648
Fax: (01923) 835802
Head: Mr T Lee
Type: Boys Day 4–13 (Girls 3–4)
No of pupils: 300
Fees: On application

RICKMANSWORTH PNEU SCHOOL
88 The Drive, Rickmansworth, Hertfordshire WD3 4DU
Tel: (01923) 772101
Fax: (01923) 776268
Email: office@
 rickmansworthpneu.co.uk
Head: Mrs C R Callegari
Type: Girls Day 3–11
No of pupils: 150
Fees: (September 06)
Day £2400–£6825

THE ROYAL MASONIC SCHOOL FOR GIRLS*
Rickmansworth Park, Rickmansworth, Hertfordshire WD3 4HF
Tel: (01923) 773168
Fax: (01923) 896729
Email: admissions@
 royalmasonic.herts.sch.uk
Head: Mrs D Rose
Type: Girls Boarding and Day 4–18
No of pupils: 785
No of boarders: F100 W55
Fees: (September 05)
FB £9675–£15720
WB £9600–£15645
Day £5445–£9705

YORK HOUSE SCHOOL
Redheath, Sarratt Road, Croxley Green, Rickmansworth, Hertfordshire WD3 4LW
Tel: (01923) 772395
Fax: (01923) 779231
Email: yhsoffice@aol.com
Head: Mr P R MacDougall
Type: Boys Day 3–13 (Co-ed 2–5)
No of pupils: B270 G15
Fees: (September 06) Day £8625

SHENLEY

MANOR LODGE SCHOOL
Rectory Lane, Ridge Hill, Shenley, Hertfordshire WD7 9BG
Tel: (01707) 642424
Fax: (01707) 645206
Email: prospectus@
 manorlodgeschool.com
Head: Mrs J M Smart
Type: Co-educational Day 4–11
No of pupils: B200 G181
Fees: (September 06)
Day £6750–£7950

ST ALBANS

BEECHWOOD PARK SCHOOL
Markyate, St Albans, Hertfordshire AL3 8AW
Tel: (01582) 840333
Fax: (01582) 842372
Email: admissions@
 beechwoodpark.herts.sch.uk
Head: Mr P C E Atkinson
Type: Co-educational Day and Boarding 4–13
No of pupils: B300 G160
No of boarders: W50
Fees: On application

HOMEWOOD PRE-PREPARATORY SCHOOL
Hazel Road, Park Street, St Albans, Hertfordshire AL2 2AH
Tel: (01727) 873542
Email: homewood@chalkface.net
Head: Mr B Cooper
Type: Co-educational Day 3–8
No of pupils: B37 G41
Fees: (September 05)
Day £2055–£6300

ST ALBANS HIGH SCHOOL FOR GIRLS*
Townsend Avenue, St Albans, Hertfordshire AL1 3SJ
Tel: (01727) 853800
Fax: (01727) 792516
Email: admissions@
 stalbans-high.herts.sch.uk
Head: Ms J C Pain
Type: Girls Day 4–18
No of pupils: 950
Fees: (September 06)
Day £7530–£9570

ST ALBANS SCHOOL*

Abbey Gateway, St Albans,
Hertfordshire AL3 4HB
Tel: (01727) 855521
Fax: (01727) 843447
Email: hm@
st-albans-school.org.uk
Head: Mr A R Grant
Type: Boys Day 11–18 (Co-ed VIth Form)
No of pupils: B739 G32
Fees: (September 06) Day £11118

ST COLUMBA'S COLLEGE

King Harry Lane, St Albans,
Hertfordshire AL3 4AW
Tel: (01727) 855185
Fax: (01727) 892024
Email: admissions@
st-columbas.herts.sch.uk
Head: Mr N J B O'Sullivan
Type: Boys Day 4–18
No of pupils: 840
Fees: (September 06)
Day £7920–£8940

STEVENAGE

REDEMPTION ACADEMY

PO BOX 352, Hertfordshire
SG1 9AG
Tel: (01438) 727370
Email: academy@
redemption-church.org.uk
Head: Rev D Neale
Type: Co-educational Day 4–18
No of pupils: B8 G11
Fees: (September 05)
Day £3600–£5400

TRING

ARTS EDUCATIONAL SCHOOL, TRING PARK*

Tring Park, Tring, Hertfordshire
HP23 5LX
Tel: (01442) 824255
Fax: (01442) 891069
Email: info@aes-tring.com
Head: Mr S Anderson
Type: Co-educational Boarding and Day 8–18
No of pupils: B55 G223
No of boarders: F214
Fees: (September 06)
FB £17355–£24510
Day £12600–£19710

FRANCIS HOUSE

Aylesbury Road, Tring,
Hertfordshire HP23 4DL
Tel: (01442) 822315
Fax: (01442) 827080
Head: Mrs Jane Billing
Type: Co-educational Day 2–11
No of pupils: B68 G63
Fees: On application

WARE

ST EDMUND'S COLLEGE

Old Hall Green, Ware,
Hertfordshire SG11 1DS
Tel: (01920) 821504
Fax: (01920) 823011
Email: admissions@
stedmundscollege.org
Head: Mr C P Long
Type: Co-educational Day and Boarding 3–18
No of pupils: B476 G257
No of boarders: F73 W37
Fees: (September 06)
FB £17340–£19830
WB £15735–£17925
Day £6750–£12225

WATFORD

ST ANDREW'S MONTESSORI SCHOOL

High Elms Lane, Watford,
Hertfordshire WD25 0JX
Tel: (01923) 681103
Fax: (01923) 681103
Email: son@care4free.net
Head: Mrs S O'Neill
Type: Co-educational Day 0–12
No of pupils: B30 G30
Fees: (September 05)
Day £1500–£12000

STANBOROUGH SCHOOL

Stanborough Park, Garston,
Watford, Hertfordshire WD25 9JT
Tel: (01923) 673268
Fax: (01923) 893943
Head: Mr S Rivers
Type: Co-educational Day and Boarding 3–16
No of pupils: B150 G150
No of boarders: F30 W20
Fees: On application

WELWYN

SHERRARDSWOOD SCHOOL

Lockleys, Welwyn, Hertfordshire
AL6 0BJ
Tel: (01438) 714282
Fax: (01438) 840616
Email: admin@
sherrardswood.plus.com
Head: Mrs L E Corry
Type: Co-educational Day 2–18
No of pupils: 310
Fees: On application

ISLE OF MAN

CASTLETOWN

THE BUCHAN SCHOOL
Arbory Road, West Hill,
Castletown, Isle of Man IM9 1RD
Tel: (01624) 820481
Fax: (01624) 820403
Email: head@buchan.sch.im
Head: Mrs Alison Hope–Hedley
Type: Co-educational Day 4–11
No of pupils: B108 G90
Fees: (September 06)
Day £6552–£8505

KING WILLIAM'S COLLEGE
Castletown, Isle of Man IM9 1TP
Tel: (01624) 820428
Fax: (01624) 820401
Email: principal@kwc.sch.im
Head: Mr P D John
Type: Co-educational Boarding
and Day 11–18
No of pupils: B191 G177
No of boarders: F78
Fees: (September 06)
FB £16806–£21105
Day £10191–£14490

ISLE OF WIGHT

RYDE

RYDE SCHOOL
Queen's Road, Ryde, Isle of Wight
PO33 3BE
Tel: (01983) 562229
Fax: (01983) 564714
Email: school.office@
   rydeschool.org.uk
Head: Dr N J England
Type: Co-educational Day and
Boarding 3–18
No of pupils: B391 G382
No of boarders: F30 W7
Fees: (September 06)
FB £16740–£17565
WB £15630–£16455
Day £4080–£8595

SHANKLIN

PRIORY SCHOOL
Alverstone Manor, Luccombe
Road, Shanklin, Isle of Wight
PO37 7JB
Tel: (01983) 861222
Head: Mrs K D'Costa
Type: Co-educational Day 2–18
No of pupils: B56 G53
Fees: On application

KENT

ASHFORD

ASHFORD SCHOOL*
East Hill, Ashford, Kent TN24 8PB
Tel: (01233) 739030
Fax: (01233) 665215
Email: registrar@
ashfordschool.co.uk
Head: Mr M R Buchanan
Type: Co-educational Day and
Boarding Boys 3–12 Girls 3–18
(Co-ed 3–11)
No of pupils: B164 G525
No of boarders: F102 W7
Fees: (September 06)
FB £20046–£21501
WB £18210–£18639
Day £5100–£11799

SPRING GROVE SCHOOL
Harville Road, Wye, Ashford, Kent
TN25 5EZ
Tel: (01233) 812337
Fax: (01233) 813390
Email: gibscan@btinternet.com
Head: Mr C A Gibbs
Type: Co-educational Day 2–11
No of pupils: B96 G105
Fees: On application

BECKENHAM

ST CHRISTOPHER'S SCHOOL
49 Bromley Road, Beckenham,
Kent BR3 5PA
Tel: (020) 8650 2200
Fax: (020) 8650 1031
Email: secretary@
stchristophersthehall.co.uk
Head: Mr A Velasco
Type: Co-educational Day 3–11
No of pupils: B142 G126
Fees: On application

BROADSTAIRS

HADDON DENE SCHOOL
57 Gladstone Road, Broadstairs,
Kent CT10 2HY
Tel: (01843) 861176
Head: Mr N Armstrong
Type: Co-educational Day 3–11
No of pupils: 150
Fees: On application

WELLESLEY HOUSE SCHOOL
Broadstairs, Kent CT10 2DG
Tel: (01843) 862991
Fax: (01843) 602068
Email: office@wellesleyhouse.org
Head: Mr S T P O'Malley
Type: Co-educational Boarding
and Day 7–13
No of pupils: B67 G44
No of boarders: F57 W38
Fees: (September 06) F/WB £16305
Day £13905

BROMLEY

ASHGROVE SCHOOL
116 Widmore Road, Bromley,
Kent BR1 3BE
Tel: (020) 8460 4143
Email: enquiries@ashgrove.org.uk
Head: Dr P Ash
Type: Co-educational Day 3–11
No of pupils: B62 G52
Fees: (September 06) Day £6660

BASTON SCHOOL
Baston Road, Hayes, Bromley,
Kent BR2 7AB
Tel: (020) 8462 1010
Fax: (020) 8462 0438
Email: admin@
bastonschool.org.uk
Head: Miss K A Greenwod
Type: Girls Day 2–16
No of pupils: 160
Fees: (September 05)
Day £6465–£8280

BICKLEY PARK SCHOOL
14/24 Page Heath Lane, Bickley,
Bromley, Kent BR1 2DS
Tel: (020) 8467 2195
Fax: (020) 8325 5511
Email: info@
bickleyparkschool.co.uk
Head: Mr P Ashley
Type: Boys Day 3–13
No of pupils: B380 G20
Fees: (September 06)
Day £3300–£10150

BISHOP CHALLONER RC
SCHOOL
228 Bromley Road, Shortlands,
Bromley, Kent BR2 0BS
Tel: (020) 8460 3546
Fax: (020) 8466 8885
Email: office@
bishopchallonerschool.com
Head: Mr J A de Waal
Type: Co-educational Day 3–18
No of pupils: B271 G139
Fees: (September 05)
Day £4920–£6990

BREASIDE PREPARATORY
SCHOOL*
41 Orchard Road, Bromley, Kent
BR1 2PR
Tel: (020) 8460 0916
Fax: (020) 8466 5664
Email: info@breaside.co.uk
Head: Mr N D Kynaston
Type: Co-educational Day 3–11
No of pupils: B142 G107
Fees: (September 05)
Day £3630–£7185

BROMLEY HIGH SCHOOL
GDST
Blackbrook Lane, Bickley,
Bromley, Kent BR1 2TW
Tel: (020) 8468 7981
Fax: (020) 8295 1062
Email: bhs@bro.gdst.net
Head: Mrs L Duggleby
Type: Girls Day 4–18
No of pupils: 912
Fees: (September 06)
Day £7632–£9810

CANTERBURY

CANTERBURY STEINER
SCHOOL
Garlinge Green, Chartham,
Canterbury, Kent CT4 5RU
Tel: (01227) 738285
Fax: (01227) 731158
Head: Mrs M McIntee
Type: Co-educational Day 4–17
No of pupils: 250
Fees: On application

JUNIOR KING'S SCHOOL
Milner Court, Sturry, Canterbury,
Kent CT2 0AY
Tel: (01227) 714000
Fax: (01227) 713171
Email: head@junior-kings.co.uk
Head: Mr P M Wells
Type: Co-educational Day and
Boarding 3–13
No of pupils: B224 G163
No of boarders: F45 W17
Fees: (September 05) F/WB £15810
Day £6900–£11700

KENT COLLEGE*
Whitstable Road, Canterbury, Kent
CT2 9DT
Tel: (01227) 763231
Fax: (01227) 787450
Email: enquiries@
    kentcollege.co.uk
Head: Mr G G Carminati
Type: Co-educational Boarding
and Day 3–18
No of pupils: B361 G291
No of boarders: F169 W5
Fees: (September 06)
FB £15750–£21570
WB £15750–£20910
Day £7590–£12630

KENT COLLEGE INFANT &
JUNIOR SCHOOL
Vernon Holme, Harbledown,
Canterbury, Kent CT2 9AQ
Tel: (01227) 762436
Fax: (01227) 763880
Email: info@vernonholme.co.uk
Head: Mr A Carter
Type: Co-educational Day and
Boarding 3–11
No of pupils: B101 G92
No of boarders: F8
Fees: (September 06) F/WB £15750
Day £7590

THE KING'S SCHOOL
Canterbury, Kent CT1 2ES
Tel: (01227) 595501
Fax: (01227) 595595
Email: headmaster@
    kings-school.co.uk
Head: Rev Canon K H Wilkinson
Type: Co-educational Boarding
and Day 13–18
No of pupils: B434 G364
No of boarders: F639
Fees: On application

ST CHRISTOPHER'S SCHOOL
New Dover Road, Canterbury,
Kent CT1 3DT
Tel: (01227) 462960
Fax: (01227) 478220
Email: enquiries@
    stchristopherscanterbury.org.uk
Head: Mr D Evans
Type: Co-educational Day 3–11
No of pupils: B60 G70
Fees: On application

ST EDMUNDS JUNIOR
SCHOOL
St Thomas's Hill, Canterbury, Kent
CT2 8HU
Tel: (01227) 475600
Fax: (01227) 471083
Email: info@stedmunds.org.uk
Head: Mr R G Bacon
Type: Co-educational Day and
Boarding 3–13
No of pupils: B160 G80
No of boarders: F30 W10
Fees: (September 05) FB £14634
Day £2244–£10302

ST EDMUND'S SCHOOL
St Thomas Hill, Canterbury, Kent
CT2 8HU
Tel: (01227) 475600
Fax: (01227) 471083
Email: headmaster@
    stedmunds.org.uk
Head: Mr J M Gladwin
Type: Co-educational Day and
Boarding 13–18
No of pupils: B165 G155
No of boarders: F85
Fees: (September 05)
FB £14634–£20931
Day £10302–£13515

ST FAITH'S AT ASH SCHOOL
5 The Street, Ash, Canterbury,
Kent CT3 2HH
Tel: (01304) 813409
Fax: (01304) 813235
Email: st-faithsatash@
    tinyworld.co.uk
Head: Mr S G I Kerruish
Type: Co-educational Day 3–11
No of pupils: B109 G91
Fees: (September 06)
Day £2850–£5661

CHISLEHURST

BABINGTON HOUSE
SCHOOL
Grange Drive, Chislehurst, Kent
BR7 5ES
Tel: (020) 8467 5537
Fax: (020) 8295 1175
Email: enquiries@
    babingtonhouse.com
Head: Miss D Odysseas
Type: Girls Day 3–16 (Boys 3–7)
No of pupils: B65 G165
Fees: On application

DARUL ULOOM LONDON
Foxbury Avenue, Perry Street,
Chislehurst, Kent BR7 6SD
Tel: (020) 8295 0637
Fax: (020) 8467 0655
Email: info@
    darululoomlondon.co.uk
Head: Mr M Musa
Type: Boys Boarding 11+
No of pupils: 160
No of boarders: F160
Fees: On application

FARRINGTONS SCHOOL*
Perry Street, Chislehurst, Kent
BR7 6LR
Tel: (020) 8467 0256
Fax: (020) 8467 5442
Email: admissions@
    farringtons.kent.sch.uk
Head: Mrs C James
Type: Co-educational Day and
Boarding Boys 3–7 Girls 3–19
No of pupils: B28 G450
No of boarders: F43 W2
Fees: (September 06) FB £17820
WB £16740 Day £9690

CRANBROOK

BEDGEBURY SCHOOL
Bedgebury Park, Goudhurst,
Cranbrook, Kent TN17 2SH
Tel: (01580) 878143
Fax: (01580) 879136
Email: registrar@
    bedgeburyschool.co.uk
Head: Mrs H Moriarty and
Mr J Lambert
Type: Girls Boarding and Day
2–18 (Boys Day 2–7)
No of pupils: B4 G293
No of boarders: F96 W49
Fees: (September 05)
F/WB £13035–£19725
Day £490–£12345

England – Kent

BENENDEN SCHOOL

Cranbrook, Kent TN17 4AA
Tel: (01580) 240592
Fax: (01580) 240280
Email: registry@
   benenden.kent.sch.uk
Head: Mrs C M Oulton
Type: Girls Boarding 11–18
No of pupils: 503
No of boarders: F503
Fees: (September 05) FB £23550

BETHANY SCHOOL†

Goudhurst, Curtisden Green,
Cranbrook, Kent TN17 1LB
Tel: (01580) 211273
Fax: (01580) 211151
Email: registrar@
   bethanyschool.org.uk
Head: Mr N Dorey
Type: Co-educational Boarding
and Day 11–18
No of pupils: B260 G90
No of boarders: F60 W60
Fees: (September 05)
F/WB £18135–£19365
Day £11658–£12270

CRANBROOK SCHOOL*

Cranbrook, Kent TN17 3JD
Tel: (01580) 711800
Fax: (01580) 711828
Email: registrar@
   cranbrook.kent.sch.uk
Head: Mrs A Daly
Type: Co-educational Day and
Boarding 13–18
No of pupils: B393 G367
No of boarders: F236
Fees: (September 06)
FB £8250–£8880

DULWICH PREPARATORY SCHOOL, CRANBROOK*

Coursehorn, Cranbrook, Kent
TN17 3NP
Tel: (01580) 712179
Fax: (01580) 715322
Email: registrar@dcpskent.org
Head: Mr S L Rigby
Type: Co-educational Day and
Boarding 3–13
No of pupils: B279 G252
No of boarders: W8
Fees: (September 06)
Day £3879–£11370

DEAL

NORTHBOURNE PARK SCHOOL

Betteshanger, Deal, Kent
CT14 0NW
Tel: (01304) 611215/8
Fax: (01304) 619020
Email: office@
   northbourne.kent.sch.uk
Head: Mr S Sides
Type: Co-educational Day and
Boarding 3–13
No of pupils: B85 G85
No of boarders: F47
Fees: (September 06)
FB £14250–£18000
WB £13350–£15225
Day £6240–£11175

DOVER

DOVER COLLEGE*†

Effingham Crescent, Dover, Kent
CT17 9RH
Tel: (01304) 205969
Fax: (01304) 242208
Email: registrar@
   dovercollege.org.uk
Head: Mr Stephen Jones
Type: Co-educational Boarding
and Day 4–18
No of pupils: B206 G154
No of boarders: F120 W13
Fees: (September 06)
FB £14970–£20550
WB £13920–£16200
Day £5055–£10170

DUKE OF YORK'S ROYAL MILITARY SCHOOL

Dover, Kent CT15 5EQ
Tel: (01304) 245024
Fax: (01304) 245019
Email: headmaster@doyrms.com
Head: Mr J A Cummings
Type: Co-educational Boarding
11–18
No of pupils: B270 G230
No of boarders: F500
Fees: (September 06)
FB £1650–£5100

FAVERSHAM

LORENDEN PREPARATORY SCHOOL

Painter's Forstal, Faversham, Kent
ME13 0EN
Tel: (01795) 590030
Fax: (01795) 538002
Email: admin@lorenden.org.uk
Head: Mr J Kirwan-Taylor
Type: Co-educational Day 3–11
No of pupils: B60 G60
Fees: (September 06)
Day £2913–£7110

GILLINGHAM

BRYONY SCHOOL

Marshall Road, Rainham,
Gillingham, Kent ME8 0AJ
Tel: (01634) 231511
Fax: (01634) 311746
Head: Mr D E Edmunds and
Mrs M P Edmunds
Type: Co-educational Day 2–11
No of pupils: B124 G118
Fees: On application

GRAVESEND

BRONTE SCHOOL

7 Pelham Road, Gravesend, Kent
DA11 0HN
Tel: (01474) 533805
Fax: (01474) 352003
Email: bronteschoolenq@aol.com
Head: Mr R A Dyson
Type: Co-educational Day 3–11
No of pupils: B72 G54
Fees: On application

COBHAM HALL*†

Cobham, Gravesend, Kent
DA12 3BL
Tel: (01474) 823371
Fax: (01474) 825906
Email: enquiries@
   cobhamhall.com
Head: Mrs H Davy
Type: Girls Boarding and Day
11–18
No of pupils: 220
No of boarders: F114 W16
Fees: (September 06)
F/WB £18000–£22800
Day £11850–£15750

CONVENT PREPARATORY SCHOOL
46 Old Road East, Gravesend,
Kent DA12 1NR
Tel: (01474) 533012
Fax: (01474) 533012
Email: sisteranne@sjcps.org
Head: Sister A C O'Connell
Type: Co-educational Day 3–11
No of pupils: B110 G105
Fees: (September 05) Day £3900

HAWKHURST

MARLBOROUGH HOUSE SCHOOL
High Street, Hawkhurst, Kent
TN18 4PY
Tel: (01580) 753555
Fax: (01580) 754281
Email: registrar@
   marlboroughhouse.kent.sch.uk
Head: Mr D N Hopkins
Type: Co-educational Day and
Boarding 3–13
No of pupils: B193 G138
Fees: (September 06)
Day £3375–£11700

ST RONAN'S SCHOOL
Water Lane, Hawkhurst, Kent
TN18 5DJ
Tel: (01580) 752271
Fax: (01580) 754882
Email: info@stronans.kent.sch.uk
Head: Mr W Trelawny-Vernon
Type: Co-educational Boarding
and Day 3–13
No of pupils: B150 G90
No of boarders: W4
Fees: On application

LONGFIELD

STEEPHILL INDEPENDENT SCHOOL*
Castle Hill, Fawkham, Longfield,
Kent DA3 7BG
Tel: (01474) 702107
Fax: (01474) 706011
Email: secretary@steephill.co.uk
Head: Mrs C Birtwell
Type: Co-educational Day 3–11
No of pupils: B54 G54
Fees: (September 05) Day £4941

MAIDSTONE

SHERNOLD SCHOOL
Hill Place, Queens Avenue,
Maidstone, Kent ME16 0ER
Tel: (01622) 752868
Fax: (01622) 752868
Email: Shernold@
   shernold.plus.com
Head: Mrs L Dack
Type: Co-educational Day 3–11
No of pupils: B52 G96
Fees: (September 06)
Day £4200–£5100

SUTTON VALENCE PREPARATORY SCHOOL
Underhill, Chart Sutton,
Maidstone, Kent ME17 3RF
Tel: (01622) 842117
Fax: (01622) 844201
Email: enquiries@
   svprep.svs.org.uk
Head: Mr A M Brooke
Type: Co-educational Day 3–11
No of pupils: B205 G173
Fees: On application

SUTTON VALENCE SCHOOL
Sutton Valence, Maidstone, Kent
ME17 3HL
Tel: (01622) 845200
Fax: (01622) 844103
Email: enquiries@svs.org.uk
Head: Mr J S Davies
Type: Co-educational Boarding
and Day 11–18
No of pupils: B373 G137
No of boarders: F60 W90
Fees: (September 06)
F/WB £17205–£22605
Day £10935–£14295

NR SEVENOAKS

COMBE BANK SCHOOL*
Combe Bank Drive, Sundridge,
Nr Sevenoaks, Kent TN14 6AE
Tel: (01959) 563720
Fax: (01959) 561997
Email: enquiries@
   combebank.kent.sch.uk
Head: Mrs R Martin
Type: Girls Day 3–18
No of pupils: B13 G348
Fees: (September 06)
Day £6825–£12225

RAMSGATE

ST LAWRENCE COLLEGE*
College Road, Ramsgate, Kent
CT11 7AE
Tel: (01843) 572931
Fax: (01843) 572917
Email: ah@slcuk.com
Head: Rev C W M Aitken
Type: Co-educational Boarding
and Day 11–18
No of pupils: B200 G125
No of boarders: F174
Fees: (September 06) F/WB £21180
Day £12405

ST LAWRENCE COLLEGE JUNIOR SCHOOL*
College Road, Ramsgate, Kent
CT11 7AF
Tel: (01843) 572931
Fax: (01843) 572917
Email: ah@slcuk.com
Head: Mr S J E Whittle
Type: Co-educational Boarding
and Day 3–11
No of pupils: B82 G55
No of boarders: F4
Fees: (September 06) F/WB £16029
Day £4845–£9891

ROCHESTER

GAD'S HILL SCHOOL*
Higham, Rochester, Kent ME3 7PA
Tel: (01474) 822366
Fax: (01474) 822977
Email: admissions@
   gadshillschool.co.uk
Head: Mr D G Craggs
Type: Co-educational Day 3–16
No of pupils: B180 G180
Fees: (September 06)
Day £5895–£6795

KING'S PREPARATORY SCHOOL
King Edward Road, Rochester,
Kent ME1 1UB
Tel: (01634) 888577
Fax: (01634) 888507
Email: walker@
   kings-school-rochester.co.uk
Head: Mr R Overend
Type: Co-educational Day and
Boarding 8–13
No of pupils: B161 G53
No of boarders: F1 W1
Fees: (September 06) F/WB £17145
Day £9825–£11130

KING'S SCHOOL ROCHESTER[†]
Satis House, Boley Hill, Rochester, Kent ME1 1TE
Tel: (01634) 888555
Fax: (01634) 888505
Email: walker@
kings-school-rochester.co.uk
Head: Dr I R Walker
Type: Co-educational Day and Boarding 4–18
No of pupils: B431 G204
No of boarders: F40 W4
Fees: (September 06)
F/WB £17145–£24210
Day £7635–£14400

ROCHESTER INDEPENDENT COLLEGE*
Star Hill, Rochester, Kent ME1 1XF
Tel: (01634) 828115
Fax: (01634) 405667
Email: admissions@
rochester-college.org
Head: Mr A Brownlow and Mr B Pain
Type: Co-educational Day and Boarding 11–21
No of pupils: B110 G110
No of boarders: F70
Fees: (September 06) FB £20850
Day £12750

ST ANDREW'S SCHOOL
24–28 Watts Avenue, Rochester, Kent ME1 1SA
Tel: (01634) 843479
Fax: (01634) 840789
Email: nkynaston@cfbt-hq.org.uk
Head: Mr N D Kynaston
Type: Co-educational Day 4–11
No of pupils: B150 G160
Fees: On application

SEVENOAKS

THE GRANVILLE SCHOOL
2 Bradbourne Park Road, Sevenoaks, Kent TN13 3LJ
Tel: (01732) 453039
Fax: (01732) 743634
Email: evans@
granville-school.co.uk
Head: Mrs J D Evans
Type: Girls Day 3–11 (Boys 3–5)
No of pupils: B10 G190
Fees: On application

THE NEW BEACON
Brittains Lane, Sevenoaks, Kent TN13 2PB
Tel: (01732) 452131
Fax: (01732) 459509
Email: admin@
newbeacon.kent.sch.uk
Head: Mr R Constantine
Type: Boys Day 4–13
No of pupils: 400
Fees: (September 05)
Day £7200–£9300

RUSSELL HOUSE SCHOOL
Station Road, Otford, Sevenoaks, Kent TN14 5QU
Tel: (01959) 522352
Fax: (01959) 524913
Email: head@
russellhouse.kent.sch.uk
Head: Mrs A Cooke
Type: Co-educational Day 2–11
No of pupils: B100 G100
Fees: (September 06)
Day £1494–£8400

ST MICHAEL'S SCHOOL
Otford Court, Otford, Sevenoaks, Kent TN14 5SA
Tel: (01959) 522137
Fax: (01959) 526044
Email: office@
stmichaels.kent.sch.uk
Head: Mr K S Crombie
Type: Co-educational Day 2–13
No of pupils: B233 G180
Fees: On application

SEVENOAKS PREPARATORY SCHOOL
Godden Green, Sevenoaks, Kent TN15 0JU
Tel: (01732) 762336
Fax: (01732) 764279
Email: admin@
sevenoaksprep.kent.sch.uk
Head: Mr P J Oldroyd
Type: Co-educational Day 2–13
No of pupils: B230 G136
Fees: (September 05)
Day £5790–£8310

SEVENOAKS SCHOOL*
Sevenoaks, Kent TN13 1HU
Tel: (01732) 455133
Fax: (01732) 456143
Email: regist@sevenoaksschool.org
Head: Mrs C L Ricks
Type: Co-educational Day and Boarding 11–18
No of pupils: B487 G494
No of boarders: F333
Fees: (September 06)
FB £22959–£24894
Day £14319–£16263

SOLEFIELD SCHOOL
Solefields Road, Sevenoaks, Kent TN13 1PH
Tel: (01732) 452142
Fax: (01732) 740388
Email: solefield.school@
btinternet.com
Head: Mr D Philps
Type: Boys Day 4–13
No of pupils: 160
Fees: (September 06)
Day £6300–£8100

WALTHAMSTOW HALL*
Hollybush Lane, Sevenoaks, Kent TN13 3UL
Tel: (01732) 451334
Fax: (01732) 740439
Email: registrar@
walthamstowhall.kent.sch.uk
Head: Mrs J Milner
Type: Girls Day 3–18
No of pupils: 490
Fees: (September 06)
Day £2965–£4080

SHEERNESS

ELLIOTT PARK SCHOOL
18–20 Marina Drive, Minster, Isle of Sheppey, Sheerness, Kent ME12 2DP
Tel: (01795) 873372
Fax: (01795) 873372
Email: elliottparkschool@
tiscali.co.uk
Head: Mr R Barson
Type: Co-educational Day 4–11
No of pupils: B30 G28
Fees: (September 05) Day £3300

SIDCUP

BENEDICT HOUSE PREPARATORY SCHOOL
1–5 Victoria Road, Sidcup, Kent
DA15 7HD
Tel: (020) 8300 7206
Fax: (020) 8309 6014
Email: Benedict.House@
btinternet.com
Head: Mrs A Brown
Type: Co-educational Day 3–11
No of pupils: B70 G70
Fees: On application

HARENC SCHOOL TRUST
167 Rectory Lane, Footscray,
Sidcup, Kent DA14 5BU
Tel: (020) 8309 0619
Fax: (020) 8309 5051
Email: info@harencschool.co.uk
Head: Miss S Woodward
Type: Boys Day 3–11
No of pupils: 160
Fees: (September 06)
Day £5373–£7044

MERTON COURT PREPARATORY SCHOOL
38 Knoll Road, Sidcup, Kent
DA14 4QU
Tel: (020) 8300 2112
Fax: (020) 8300 2112
Email: office.mertoncourt@
argonet.co.uk
Head: Mr D Price
Type: Co-educational Day 2–11
No of pupils: B180 G152
Fees: On application

WEST LODGE PREPARATORY SCHOOL
36 Station Road, Sidcup, Kent
DA15 7DU
Tel: (020) 8300 2489
Fax: (020) 8308 1905
Email: info@westlodge.org.uk
Head: Mrs S Webb
Type: Co-educational Day 3–11
No of pupils: B56 G104
Fees: (September 06)
Day £2079–£5775

TONBRIDGE

DERWENT LODGE SCHOOL FOR GIRLS
Somerhill, Tonbridge, Kent
TN11 0NJ
Tel: (01732) 352124
Fax: (01732) 363381
Email: office@
schoolsatsomerhill.com
Head: Mrs E Hill and Mr J Coakley
Type: Girls Day 7–11
No of pupils: 127
Fees: (September 05) Day £8790

FOSSE BANK MOUNTAINS SCHOOL
Noble Tree Road, Hildenborough,
Tonbridge, Kent TN11 8ND
Tel: (01732) 834212
Fax: (01732) 834884
Email: office@
fossebankschool.co.uk
Head: Mrs G Lovatt-Young
Type: Co-educational Day 3–11
No of pupils: B65 G70
Fees: On application

HILDEN GRANGE SCHOOL
62 Dry Hill Park Road, Tonbridge,
Kent TN10 3BX
Tel: (01732) 352706
Fax: (01732) 773360
Email: enquiries@
hildengrange.kent.sch.uk
Head: Mr J Withers
Type: Co-educational Day 3–13
No of pupils: B204 G100
Fees: On application

HILDEN OAKS SCHOOL
38 Dry Hill Park Road, Tonbridge,
Kent TN10 3BU
Tel: (01732) 353941
Fax: (01732) 353942
Email: secretary@hildenoaks.co.uk
Head: Mrs S A Sunderland
Type: Co-educational Day
Boys 2–7 Girls 2–11
No of pupils: B18 G140
Fees: (September 05)
Day £2580–£7170

SACKVILLE SCHOOL
Tonbridge Road, Hildenborough,
Tonbridge, Kent TN11 9HN
Tel: (01732) 838888
Fax: (01732) 836404
Email: office@
sackvilleschool.co.uk
Head: Mrs G M L Sinclair
Type: Co-educational Day 11–18
No of pupils: B181 G38
Fees: (September 05)
Day £7875–£9375

SOMERHILL PRE-PREPARATORY SCHOOL
Somerhill, Tonbridge, Kent
TN11 0NJ
Tel: (01732) 352124
Fax: (01732) 363381
Email: office@
schoolsatsomerhill.com
Head: Mrs J R Sorensen
Type: Co-educational Day 3–7
No of pupils: 278
Fees: On application

TONBRIDGE SCHOOL*
Tonbridge, Kent TN9 1JP
Tel: (01732) 304297
Fax: (01732) 363424
Email: hmsec@
tonbridge-school.org
Head: Mr T H P Haynes
Type: Boys Boarding and Day
13–18
No of pupils: 755
No of boarders: F438
Fees: (September 06) F/WB £25212
Day £18279

YARDLEY COURT
Somerhill, Tonbridge, Kent
TN11 0NJ
Tel: (01732) 352124
Fax: (01732) 363381
Email: office@
schoolsatsomerhill.com
Head: Mr J T Coakley
Type: Boys Day 7–13
Fees: (September 05)
Day £9360–£9720

TUNBRIDGE WELLS

BEECHWOOD SACRED HEART SCHOOL*
12 Pembury Road, Tunbridge Wells, Kent TN2 3QD
Tel: (01892) 532747
Fax: (01892) 536164
Email: bsh@beechwood.org.uk
Head: Mr N R Beesley
Type: Girls Boarding and Day 3–18 (Boys 3–11)
No of pupils: B85 G310
No of boarders: F55 W15
Fees: (September 06)
FB £15360–£19695
WB £13230–£17460
Day £5550–£11850

HOLMEWOOD HOUSE*
Langton Green, Tunbridge Wells, Kent TN3 0EB
Tel: (01892) 860000
Fax: (01892) 863970
Email: registrar@
holmewood.kent.sch.uk
Head: Mr A S R Corbett
Type: Co-educational Day and Boarding 3–13
No of pupils: B323 G207
No of boarders: W7
Fees: (September 06) WB £17175
Day £4640–£13635

KENT COLLEGE PEMBURY
Old Church Road, Tunbridge Wells, Kent TN2 4AX
Tel: (01892) 822006
Fax: (01892) 820221
Email: admissions@
kentcollege.kent.sch.uk
Head: Mrs A Upton
Type: Girls Boarding and Day 3–18
No of pupils: 520
No of boarders: F80 W10
Fees: (September 06)
F/WB £16230–£21120
Day £5970–£13095

THE MEAD SCHOOL
16 Frant Road, Tunbridge Wells, Kent TN2 5SN
Tel: (01892) 525837
Fax: (01892) 525837
Email: meadschool@hotmail.com
Head: Mrs A Culley
Type: Co-educational Day 3–11
No of pupils: B85 G85
Fees: On application

WEST WICKHAM

ST DAVID'S COLLEGE
Justin Hall, Beckenham Road, West Wickham, Kent BR4 0QS
Tel: (020) 8777 5852
Fax: (020) 8777 9549
Email: stdavids@dial.pipex.com
Head: Mrs A Wagstaff and Mrs S Adams
Type: Co-educational Day 4–11
No of pupils: B80 G63
Fees: (September 06)
Day £4890–£5040

WICKHAM COURT SCHOOL
Layhams Road, West Wickham, Kent BR4 9HW
Tel: (020) 8777 2942
Fax: (020) 8777 4276
Email: wickham@
schillerintschool.com
Head: Ms B Hunter
Type: Co-educational Day 2–12
No of pupils: B76 G45
Fees: (September 06)
Day £4401–£7110

WESTGATE-ON-SEA

CHARTFIELD SCHOOL
45 Minster Road, Westgate-on-Sea, Kent CT8 8DA
Tel: (01843) 831716
Fax: (01843) 221973
Email: chartfield1@btclick.com
Head: Mrs J L Prebble
Type: Co-educational Day 4–11
No of pupils: B39 G36
Fees: On application

LANCASHIRE

ACCRINGTON

HEATHLAND COLLEGE
Broadoak, Sandy Lane, Accrington, Lancashire BB5 2AN
Tel: (01254) 234284
Fax: (01254) 235398
Email: bursar@
heathlandcollege.co.uk
Head: Mrs J Harrison
Type: Co-educational Day 0–11
No of pupils: B30 G25
Fees: On application

BLACKBURN

AL-ISLAH SCHOOL
108 Audley Range, Blackburn, Lancashire BB1 1TF
Tel: (01254) 261573
Fax: (01254) 671604
Head: Mr N I Makda
Type: Co-educational Day 5–16
No of pupils: B32 G213
Fees: On application

ISLAMIYAH SCHOOL
Willow Street, Little Harwood, Blackburn, Lancashire BB1 5NQ
Tel: 01254 661259
Fax: 01254 661259
Email: z.seedat@
blackburnmail.com
Head: Mrs Zarina Seedat
Type: Girls Day 11–16
No of pupils: 250
Fees: (September 06) Day £3000

MARKAZUL ULOOM

Park Lee Road, Blackburn,
Lancashire BB2 3NY
Tel: (01254) 660026
Fax: (01254) 279406
Head: Mrs Asiya Gajaria
Type: Girls Day 11–19
No of pupils: 220
Fees: (September 06) Day £2700

QUEEN ELIZABETH'S GRAMMAR SCHOOL

West Park Road, Blackburn,
Lancashire BB2 6DF
Tel: (01254) 686300
Fax: (01254) 692314
Email: headmaster@
  qegs.blackburn.sch.uk
Head: Dr D S Hempsall
Type: Co-educational Day 3–18
No of pupils: B658 G120
Fees: (September 06)
Day £4575–£8085

RAWDHA TUL ULOOM

19 Dock Street, Blackburn,
Lancashire BB1 3AT
Tel: (01254) 670017
Email: info@
  gardenofknowledge.org
Head: Mr A W Wasway
Type: Co-educational Day 4–11
No of pupils: B49 G44
Fees: (September 06) Day £2340

TAUHEEDUL ISLAM GIRLS HIGH SCHOOL

31 Bicknell Street, Blackburn,
Lancashire BB1 7EY
Tel: (01254) 54021
Fax: (01254) 54021
Email: admin@tighs.com
Head: Mr I Patel
Type: Girls Day 11–16
No of pupils: 265
Fees: On application

WESTHOLME SCHOOL

Wilmar Lodge, Meins Road,
Blackburn, Lancashire BB2 6QU
Tel: (01254) 506070
Fax: (01254) 506080
Email: principal@
  westholmeschool.com
Head: Mrs L Croston
Type: Girls Day 3–18 (Boys 3–7)
No of pupils: B102 G987
Fees: (September 05)
Day £4080–£6438

BLACKPOOL

ARNOLD SCHOOL

Lytham Road, Blackpool,
Lancashire FY4 1JG
Tel: (01253) 346391
Fax: (01253) 336250
Email: principal@
  arnoldschool.com
Head: Mr B M Hughes
Type: Co-educational Day 2–18
No of pupils: B487 G483
Fees: (September 06)
Day £5679–£7416

LANGDALE PREPARATORY SCHOOL

95 Warbreck Drive, Blackpool,
Lancashire FY2 9RZ
Tel: (01253) 354812
Fax: (01253) 354812
Email: langdaleschool@
  btconnect.com
Head: Mr R A Rendell and
Mr P G E Clay
Type: Co-educational Day 3–11
No of pupils: B46 G46
Fees: (September 06)
Day £2750–£3600

BOLTON

BOLTON MUSLIM GIRLS SCHOOL

Swan Lane, Bolton, Lancashire
BL3 6TQ
Tel: (01204) 361103
Fax: (01204) 533220
Head: Mr I A Patel
Type: Girls Day 11–16
No of pupils: 374
Fees: On application

BOLTON SCHOOL (BOYS' DIVISION)

Chorley New Road, Bolton,
Lancashire BL1 4PA
Tel: (01204) 840201
Fax: (01204) 849477
Email: hm@boys.bolton.sch.uk
Head: Mr M E W Brooker
Type: Boys Day 7–18
No of pupils: 1106
Fees: On application

BOLTON SCHOOL (GIRLS' DIVISION)

Chorley New Road, Bolton,
Lancashire BL1 4PB
Tel: (01204) 840201
Fax: (01204) 434710
Email: info@girls.bolton.sch.uk
Head: Mrs G Richards
Type: Girls Day 4–18 (Boys 4–7)
No of pupils: B99 G1117
Fees: (September 05)
Day £5877–£7833

CLEVELANDS PREPARATORY SCHOOL

Chorley New Road, Bolton,
Lancashire BL1 5DH
Tel: (01204) 843898
Fax: (01204) 848007
Email: clevelands@indschool.org
Head: Mrs G T Mitchell
Type: Co-educational Day 2–11
No of pupils: B90 G90
Fees: (September 06) Day £5079

LORD'S COLLEGE

53 Manchester Road, Bolton,
Lancashire BL2 1ES
Tel: (01204) 523731
Head: Mrs H Seager
Type: Co-educational Day 10–17
No of pupils: B40 G35
Fees: On application

BURNLEY

ST JOSEPH'S CONVENT SCHOOL

Park Hill, Padiham Road, Burnley,
Lancashire BB12 6TG
Tel: (01282) 455622
Fax: (01282) 435375
Email: parkhillschool@aol.com
Type: Co-educational Day 3–11
No of pupils: B61 G57
Fees: (September 06) Day £3400

BURY

BURY CATHOLIC PREPARATORY SCHOOL

Arden House, 172 Manchester
Road, Bury, Lancashire BL9 9BH
Tel: (0161) 764 2346
Fax: (0161) 764 2346
Email: admin@
  burycatholicprepschool.co.uk
Head: Mrs A C Dean
Type: Co-educational Day 3–11
No of pupils: B73 G61
Fees: (September 06) Day £3720

BURY GRAMMAR SCHOOL

Tenterden Street, Bury, Lancashire
BL9 0HN
Tel: (0161) 797 2700
Fax: (0161) 763 4655
Email: info@
   burygrammarschoolboys.co.uk
Head: Mr K Richards
Type: Boys Day 7–18
No of pupils: 800
Fees: (September 05)
Day £4767–£6678

BURY GRAMMAR SCHOOL GIRLS

Bridge Road, Bury, Lancashire
BL9 0HH
Tel: (0161) 797 2808
Fax: (0161) 763 4658
Email: info@bgsg.bury.sch.uk
Head: Mrs R S Georghiou
Type: Girls Day 3–18 (Boys 4–7)
No of pupils: B88 G912
Fees: (September 06)
Day £5028–£7044

THE POTTERS HOUSE SCHOOL

6 Arley Avenue, Bury, Lancashire
BL9 5HD
Tel: (0161) 705 1885
Fax: (0161) 705 1885
Head: Mrs Catherine M Mitchell
Type: Co-educational Day 5–10
No of pupils: B6 G3
Fees: (September 06) Day £3420

CHORLEY

THE BENNETT HOUSE SCHOOL

332 Eaves Lane, Chorley,
Lancashire PR6 0DX
Tel: (01257) 267393
Fax: (01257) 262838
Email: catherine@
   bennetthouse332.fsnet.co.uk
Head: Mrs C A Mills
Type: Co-educational Day 2–8
No of pupils: B18 G17
Fees: (September 05) Day £4800

CLITHEROE

MOORLAND SCHOOL

Ribblesdale Avenue, Clitheroe,
Lancashire BB7 2JA
Tel: (01200) 423833
Fax: (01200) 429339
Email: bursar@
   moorlandschool.co.uk
Head: Mr P Smith
Type: Co-educational Boarding
and Day 4–16
No of pupils: B44 G47
No of boarders: F10 W8
Fees: On application

OAKHILL COLLEGE

Wiswell Lane, Whalley, Clitheroe,
Lancashire BB7 9AF
Tel: (01254) 823546
Fax: (01254) 822662
Email: enquiries@
   oakhillcollege.co.uk
Head: Mr M Kennedy
Type: Co-educational Day 2–16
No of pupils: B143 G137
Fees: On application

STONYHURST COLLEGE

Stonyhurst, Clitheroe, Lancashire
BB7 9PZ
Tel: (01254) 827073
Fax: (01254) 827135
Email: admissions@
   stonyhurst.ac.uk
Head: Mr A R Johnson
Type: Co-educational Boarding
and Day 13–18
No of pupils: B312 G136
No of boarders: F247 W52
Fees: (September 06) FB £22368
WB £19137 Day £13077

FLEETWOOD

ROSSALL JUNIOR SCHOOL

Fleetwood, Lancashire FY7 8JW
Tel: (01253) 774222
Fax: (01253) 774222
Email: enquiries@
   rossallcorporation.co.uk
Head: Mr J Ingham
Type: Co-educational Day and
Boarding 2–11
No of pupils: B71 G67
No of boarders: F3
Fees: On application

ROSSALL SCHOOL

Fleetwood, Lancashire FY7 8JW
Tel: (01253) 774201
Fax: (01253) 772052
Email: enquiries@
   rossallcorporation.co.uk
Head: Mr T Wilbur
Type: Co-educational Boarding
and Day 11–18
No of pupils: B242 G184
No of boarders: F180
Fees: On application

ROSSALL SCHOOL INTERNATIONAL STUDY CENTRE

Rossall School, Broadway,
Fleetwood, Lancashire FY7 8JW
Tel: (01253) 774204
Fax: (01253) 779415
Email: isc@
   rossallcorporation.co.uk
Head: Mr D Rose
Type: Co-educational Boarding
11–16
No of pupils: B60 G20
No of boarders: F80
Fees: (September 06)
FB £16876–£24000

HORWICH

RIVINGTON PARK INDEPENDENT SCHOOL

Knowle House, Rivington Lane,
Rivington, Horwich, Lancashire
BL6 7RX
Tel: (01204) 669332
Fax: (01204) 696891
Email: info@
   rivingtonparkschool.co.uk
Head: Mr Michael Ruaux
Type: Co-educational Day 1–16
No of pupils: B49 G43
Fees: (September 06)
Day £4905–£5274

LANCASTER

JAMEA AL KAUTHAR

Ashton Road, Lancaster,
Lancashire LA1 5AJ
Tel: (01524) 389898
Fax: (01524) 389333
Head: Ms Aneesa Sajid
Type: Girls Boarding 11–19
No of pupils: 392
No of boarders: F392
Fees: (September 06) FB £6000

LANCASTER STEINER SCHOOL
Lune Road, Lancaster, Lancashire
LA1 5QU
Tel: (01524) 841351
Head: Mr Mark Bamford
Type: Co-educational Day 5–14
No of pupils: B24 G24
Fees: (September 06)
Day £1450–£3400

SEDBERGH JUNIOR SCHOOL
Low Bentham, Lancaster,
Lancashire LA2 7DB
Tel: (01524) 261275
Fax: (01524) 262944
Email: hmsjs@sedberghschool.org
Head: Mr P Reynolds
Type: Co-educational Boarding
and Day 4–13
No of pupils: B79 G29
No of boarders: F27 W19
Fees: (September 05)
FB £12885–£14610
WB £11970–£13905
Day £4770–£10920

LEYLAND

STONEHOUSE SCHOOL
90 School Lane, Leyland,
Lancashire PR25 2TU
Tel: (01772) 435529
Fax: (01772) 622093
Email: welcome.stonehouse@
    fsmail.net
Head: Mrs Linda Williams
Type: Co-educational Day 4–11
No of pupils: B14 G13
Fees: (September 05) Day £3315

LYTHAM ST ANNES

KING EDWARD VII AND QUEEN MARY SCHOOL
Clifton Drive South,
Lytham St Annes, Lancashire
FY8 1DT
Tel: (01253) 784100
Fax: (01253) 784150
Email: admin@keqms.co.uk
Head: Mr R J Karling
Type: Co-educational Day 2–18
No of pupils: B369 G290
Fees: (September 05)
Day £4632–£6720

ST ANNE'S COLLEGE GRAMMAR SCHOOL
293 Clifton Drive South,
St Annes-on-Sea, Lytham St Annes,
Lancashire FY8 1HN
Tel: (01253) 725815
Fax: (01253) 782250
Email: principal@
    collgram.u-net.com
Head: Mr S R Welsby
Type: Co-educational Day and
Boarding 3–18
No of pupils: B109 G111
No of boarders: F11 W2
Fees: (September 05) FB £7000
WB £5075 Day £3885–£5625

OLDHAM

FARROWDALE HOUSE PREPARATORY SCHOOL
Farrow Street, Shaw, Oldham,
Lancashire OL2 7AD
Tel: (01706) 844533
Email: farrowdale@aol.com
Head: Mr F G Wilkinson
Type: Co-educational Day 3–11
No of pupils: B56 G57
Fees: On application

FIRWOOD MANOR PREP SCHOOL
Broadway, Chadderton, Oldham,
Lancashire OL9 0AD
Tel: (0161) 620 6570
Fax: (0161) 626 3550
Email: admin@
    firwoodmanor.org.uk
Head: Mrs P M Wild
Type: Co-educational Day 2–11
No of pupils: B79 G62
Fees: On application

GRASSCROFT INDEPENDENT SCHOOL
Lydgate Parish Hall, Stockport
Road, Lydgate, Oldham,
Lancashire OL4 4JJ
Tel: (01457) 820485
Head: Mrs J O'Hara
Type: Co-educational Day 2–7
No of pupils: 45
Fees: On application

THE HULME GRAMMAR SCHOOL FOR GIRLS
Chamber Road, Oldham,
Lancashire OL8 4BX
Tel: (0161) 624 2523
Fax: (0161) 620 0234
Email: girlsinfo@
    hulmegrammarschools.org.uk
Head: Miss M S Smolenski
Type: Girls Day 3–18
No of pupils: 571
Fees: (September 05)
Day £4377–£6735

THE OLDHAM HULME GRAMMAR SCHOOL
Chamber Road, Oldham,
Lancashire OL8 4BX
Tel: (0161) 624 4497
Fax: (0161) 652 4107
Email: boysenq@
    hulmegrammarschool.org.uk
Head: Mr K E Jones
Type: Boys Day 7–18
No of pupils: 719
Fees: On application

OLDHAM HULME KINDERGARTEN
Plum Street, Oldham, Lancashire
OL8 1TJ
Tel: (0161) 624 2947
Fax: (0161) 628 9756
Email: kindergarten@
    hulmegrammar.oldham.sch.uk
Head: Mrs A S Richards
Type: Co-educational Day 3–7
No of pupils: B46 G53
Fees: On application

SADDLEWORTH PREPARATORY SCHOOL
Huddersfield Road, Scouthead,
Oldham, Lancashire OL4 4AG
Tel: (01457) 877442
Email: info@
    saddleworthpreparatoryschool.
    org.uk
Head: Mrs L W K Hirst
Type: Co-educational Day 4–7
No of pupils: B27 G29
Fees: On application

England – Lancashire

ORMSKIRK

KINGSWOOD COLLEGE AT SCARISBRICK HALL[†]
Southport Road, Ormskirk,
Lancashire L40 9RQ
Tel: (01704) 880200
Fax: (01704) 880032
Email: admin@
  kingswoodcollege.co.uk
Head: Mr E J Borowski
Type: Co-educational Day 2–16
No of pupils: B182 G196
Fees: (September 05)
Day £3000–£6225

POULTON-LE-FYLDE

EMMANUEL CHRISTIAN SCHOOL
Singleton Hall, Lodge Lane,
Singleton, Poulton-Le-Fylde,
Lancashire FY6 8LU
Tel: (01253) 876662
Fax: (01253) 882873
Head: Mr M Derry and
Mrs P Derry
Type: Co-educational Day 4–16
No of pupils: B53 G60
Fees: On application

PRESTON

ASHBRIDGE INDEPENDENT SCHOOL
Lindle Lane, Hutton, Preston,
Lancashire PR4 4AQ
Tel: (01772) 619900
Fax: (01772) 610894
Email: admin@ashbridge.co.uk
Head: Mrs Hilary Sharples
Type: Co-educational Day 2–11
No of pupils: B154 G129
Fees: On application

HIGHFIELD PRIORY SCHOOL
Fulwood Row, Fulwood, Preston,
Lancashire PR2 6SL
Tel: (01772) 709624
Fax: (01772) 655621
Email: info@highfieldpriory.co.uk
Head: Mr D Williams
Type: Co-educational Day 2–11
No of pupils: B134 G139
Fees: (September 05)
Day £4500–£5172

KIRKHAM GRAMMAR SCHOOL
Ribby Road, Kirkham, Preston,
Lancashire PR4 2BH
Tel: (01772) 671079
Fax: (01772) 672747
Email: info@
  kirkhamgrammar.co.uk
Head: Mr D R Walker
Type: Co-educational Boarding
and Day 3–18
No of pupils: B491 G468
No of boarders: F65
Fees: (September 06) FB £4493
Day £1825–£2423

ST PIUS X PREPARATORY SCHOOL
200 Garstang Road, Fulwood,
Preston, Lancashire PR2 8RD
Tel: (01772) 719937
Fax: (01772) 787535
Email: st-pius-x@supanet.com
Head: Miss B Banks
Type: Co-educational Day 2–11
No of pupils: B136 G151
Fees: On application

ROCHDALE

BEECH HOUSE SCHOOL
184 Manchester Road, Rochdale,
Lancashire OL11 4JQ
Tel: (01706) 646309
Fax: (01706) 860685
Email: bschool119@aol.com
Head: Mr K Sartain
Type: Co-educational Day 3–16
No of pupils: B110 G110
Fees: (September 06)
Day £1770–£4459

ROCHDALE GIRLS SCHOOL
36 Taylor Street, Rochdale,
Lancashire OL12 0HX
Fax: (01706) 646642
Head: Mr A Razzak
Type: Girls Day 11–15
No of pupils: 100
Fees: On application

SALFORD

TASHBAR SCHOOL
20 Upper Park Road, Salford,
Lancashire M7 4HL
Tel: (0161) 720 8254
Fax: (0161) 720 8146
Head: Mr A Pinczewski
Type: Boys Day 2–11
No of pupils: 325
Fees: On application

STONYHURST

ST MARY'S HALL
Stonyhurst, Lancashire BB7 9PU
Tel: (01254) 826242
Fax: (01254) 827316
Email: saintmaryshall@
  stonyhurst.ac.uk
Head: Mr L A Crouch
Type: Co-educational Boarding
and Day 3–13
No of pupils: B117 G98
No of boarders: F25 W9
Fees: (September 06) FB £15762
WB £13866 Day £1829–£3646

WIGAN

KINGSWAY SCHOOL
Greenough Street, Wigan,
Lancashire WN1 3SU
Tel: (01942) 244743
Fax: (01942) 244743
Head: Mrs B Jacobs
Type: Co-educational Day 3–16
No of pupils: B30 G30
Fees: On application

LEICESTERSHIRE

ASHBY-DE-LA-ZOUCH

MANOR HOUSE SCHOOL
South Street, Ashby-de-la-Zouch,
Leicestershire LE65 1BR
Tel: (01530) 412932
Fax: (01530) 417435
Email: enquiries@
manorhouseashby.co.uk
Head: Mr I R Clews
Type: Co-educational Day 4–16
No of pupils: B94 G73
Fees: (September 06)
Day £4746–£6594

LEICESTER

AL-AQSA PRIMARY SCHOOL
The Wayne Way, Leicester,
Leicestershire LE5 4PP
Tel: (0116) 276 0953
Fax: (0116) 276 9791
Email: alaqsa@tiscali.co.uk
Head: Mr Ibrahim Hewitt
Type: Co-educational Day 3–11
Fees: (September 06)
Day £1400–£2300

AL-ISLAMIA PRIMARY
16–20 Beal Street, Leicester,
Leicestershire LE2 0AA
Tel: (0116) 251 5345
Head: Mr N Hussein
Type: Co-educational Day 5–7
No of pupils: B21 G27
Fees: (September 06) Day £3150

GRACE DIEU MANOR SCHOOL
Grace Dieu, Thringstone,
Leicester, Leicestershire LE67 5UG
Tel: (01530) 222276
Fax: (01530) 223184
Email: registrar@gracedieu.com
Head: Mr C E Foulds
Type: Co-educational Day 3–13
No of pupils: B172 G153
Fees: (September 05)
Day £5010–£8110

IRWIN COLLEGE
164 London Road, Leicester,
Leicestershire LE2 1ND
Tel: (0116) 255 2648
Fax: (0116) 285 4935
Email: registrar@
irwincollege.wireless.pipex.net
Head: Mrs L G Tonks
Type: Co-educational Boarding
and Day 14–25
No of pupils: B110 G70
No of boarders: F160
Fees: On application

LEICESTER GRAMMAR JUNIOR SCHOOL
Evington Hall, Spencefield Lane,
Leicester, Leicestershire LE5 6HN
Tel: (0116) 210 1299
Fax: (0116) 210 0432
Email: redfearnm@
leicestergrammar.org.uk
Head: Mrs M Redfearn
Type: Co-educational Day 3–11
No of pupils: B131 G117
Fees: On application

LEICESTER GRAMMAR SCHOOL
8 Peacock Lane, Leicester,
Leicestershire LE1 5PX
Tel: (0116) 222 0400
Fax: (0116) 291 0505
Email: admissions@
leicestergrammar.org.uk
Head: Mr C P M King
Type: Co-educational Day 10–18
No of pupils: B383 G305
Fees: On application

LEICESTER HIGH SCHOOL FOR GIRLS
454 London Road, Leicester,
Leicestershire LE2 2PP
Tel: (0116) 270 5338
Email: enquiries@
leicesterhigh.co.uk
Head: Mrs J Burns
Type: Co-educational Day
Girls 3–18
No of pupils: 435
Fees: (September 06)
Day £5235–£7920

LEICESTER MONTESSORI GRAMMAR SCHOOL
58 Stoneygate Road, Leicester,
Leicestershire LE2 2BN
Tel: (0116) 255 4441
Head: Mrs D Bailey
Type: Co-educational Day 3–18
No of pupils: 300
Fees: On application

LEICESTER MONTESSORI SCHOOL
194 London Road, Leicester,
Leicestershire LE1 1ND
Tel: (0116) 270 6667
Fax: (0116) 255 4440
Head: Mrs D Bailey
Type: Co-educational Day 0–18
No of pupils: B90 G100
Fees: On application

RATCLIFFE COLLEGE
Fosse Way, Ratcliffe on the
Wreake, Leicester, Leicestershire
LE7 4SG
Tel: (01509) 817000
Fax: (01509) 817004
Email: registrar@
ratcliffe.leics.sch.uk
Head: Mr P Farrar
Type: Co-educational Boarding
and Day 3–18
No of pupils: B388 G244
No of boarders: F87 W2
Fees: (September 06) FB £16911
WB £13455–£16911
Day £6012–£11229

ST CRISPIN'S SCHOOL (LEICESTER) LTD.[†]
6 St Mary's Road, Leicester,
Leicestershire LE2 1XA
Tel: (0116) 270 7648
Email: enquiries@stcrispins.co.uk
Head: Mrs D Lofthouse and Mr J
Lofthouse
Type: Co-educational Day 3–16
No of pupils: B75 G25
Fees: On application

STONEYGATE COLLEGE
2 Albert Road, Stoneygate,
Leicester, Leicestershire LE2 2AA
Tel: (0116) 270 7414
Fax: (0116) 270 7414
Email: office@
stoneygate.e7even.com
Head: Mr J C Bourlet
Type: Co-educational Day 3–11
No of pupils: B61 G70
Fees: (September 05)
Day £4185–£5385

STONEYGATE SCHOOL
London Road, Great Glen,
Leicester, Leicestershire LE8 9DJ
Tel: (0116) 259 2282
Email: stoneygate@
webleicester.co.uk
Head: Mr J H Morris
Type: Co-educational Day 3–13
No of pupils: B221 G171
Fees: On application

LOUGHBOROUGH

FAIRFIELD PREPARATORY SCHOOL
Leicester Road, Loughborough,
Leicestershire LE11 2AE
Tel: (01509) 215172
Fax: (01509) 238648
Email: admin@
fairfield.leics.sch.uk
Head: Mr R Outwin-Flinders
Type: Co-educational Day 4–11
No of pupils: B257 G236
Fees: (September 06) Day £6363

LOUGHBOROUGH GRAMMAR SCHOOL
Burton Walks, Loughborough,
Leicestershire LE11 2DU
Tel: (01509) 233233
Fax: (01509) 218436
Email: registrar@
loughgs.leics.sch.uk
Head: Mr P B Fisher
Type: Boys Day and Boarding
10–18
No of pupils: 1010
No of boarders: F38 W10
Fees: (September 06) FB £15324
WB £13512 Day £8553

LOUGHBOROUGH HIGH SCHOOL
Burton Walks, Loughborough,
Leicestershire LE11 2DU
Tel: (01509) 212348
Fax: (01509) 215720
Email: admin@
loughhs.leics.sch.uk
Head: Miss B O'Connor
Type: Girls Day 11–18
No of pupils: 590
Fees: (September 06) Day £7890

OUR LADY'S CONVENT SCHOOL
Burton Street, Loughborough,
Leicestershire LE11 2DT
Tel: (01509) 263901
Fax: (01509) 236193
Email: office@olcs.leics.sch.uk
Head: Sister S Fynn
Type: Girls Day 3–18 (Boys 3–5)
No of pupils: B7 G500
Fees: (September 06)
Day £5705–£7980

PNEU SCHOOL
8 Station Road, East Leake,
Loughborough, Leicestershire
LE12 6LQ
Tel: (01509) 852229
Fax: (01509) 852229
Email: office@
arley.pneu.eastleake.sch.uk
Head: Mrs E A Gibbs
Type: Co-educational Day 3–11
No of pupils: B36 G41
Fees: (September 06)
Day £6255–£6663

MARKET BOSWORTH

THE DIXIE GRAMMAR SCHOOL
Station Road, Market Bosworth,
Leicestershire CV13 0LE
Tel: (01455) 292244
Fax: (01455) 292151
Email: info@dixie.org.uk
Head: Mr John Wood
Type: Co-educational Day 4–18
No of pupils: B252 G249
Fees: (September 06)
Day £5325–£7485

MARKET HARBOROUGH

BROOKE HOUSE COLLEGE*
Leicester Road, Market
Harborough, Leicestershire
LE16 7AU
Tel: (01858) 462452
Fax: (01858) 462487
Email: enquiries@
brookehouse.com
Head: Mr G E I Williams
Type: Co-educational Boarding
and Day 14–19
No of pupils: B100 G80
No of boarders: F175
Fees: (September 06) FB £17550
Day £10200

LINCOLNSHIRE

ALFORD

MAYPOLE HOUSE SCHOOL
Well Vale Hall, Alford,
Lincolnshire LN13 0ET
Tel: (01507) 462764
Fax: (01507) 462681
Email: maypolehouseschool@
  hotmail.com
Head: Mrs A White
Type: Co-educational Day 3–16
No of pupils: B20 G20
Fees: On application

BOSTON

BICKER PREPARATORY SCHOOL
School Lane, Bicker, Boston,
Lincolnshire PE20 3DW
Tel: (01775) 821786
Fax: (01775) 821786
Head: Mrs S Page
Type: Co-educational Day 3–11
No of pupils: B40 G40
Fees: (September 06)
Day £3400–£3800

CONWAY PREPARATORY SCHOOL
Tunnard Street, Boston,
Lincolnshire PE21 6PL
Tel: (01205) 363150/355539
Fax: (01205) 363150
Email: conway@
  conwayschool.demon.co.uk
Head: Mr D A Wilson
Type: Co-educational Day 2–11
No of pupils: B30 G30
Fees: (September 05)
Day £543–£3690

FRISKNEY PRIVATE SCHOOL
Church Lane, Friskney, Boston,
Lincolnshire PE22 8NA
Tel: (01754) 820970
Fax: (01754) 820970
Head: Mrs D Wilcox
Type: Co-educational Day 5–10
No of pupils: B12 G7
Fees: On application

BOURNE

KIRKSTONE HOUSE SCHOOL
Main Street, Baston, Bourne,
Lincolnshire PE6 9PA
Tel: (01778) 560350
Fax: (01778) 560547
Email: kirkstone.house@
  btclick.com
Head: Miss M Pepper
Type: Co-educational Day 3–16
No of pupils: B147 G86
Fees: (September 06)
Day £4233–£7539

WITHAM HALL
Witham-on-the-Hill, Bourne,
Lincolnshire PE10 0JJ
Tel: (01778) 590222
Fax: (01778) 590606
Email: heads@withamhall.com
Head: Mr D Telfer and Mrs S Telfer
Type: Co-educational Boarding
and Day 3–13
No of pupils: B120 G115
No of boarders: W50
Fees: (September 06) F/WB £13485
Day £5985–£9855

GAINSBOROUGH

HANDEL HOUSE PREPARATORY SCHOOL
Northolme, Gainsborough,
Lincolnshire DN21 2JB
Tel: (01427) 612426
Fax: (01427) 677854
Email: headteacher@
  handelhouseschool.fsnet.co.uk
Head: Mrs V C Haigh
Type: Co-educational Day 2–11
No of pupils: B34 G33
Fees: (September 06)
Day £2430–£2925

GRANTHAM

DUDLEY HOUSE SCHOOL
1 Dudley Road, Grantham,
Lincolnshire NG31 9AA
Tel: (01476) 400184
Fax: (01476) 400184
Email: headteacher@
  dudleyhouseschool.co.uk
Head: Mrs J H Johnson
Type: Co-educational Day 3–11
No of pupils: B38 G22
Fees: (September 06) Day £3160

THE GRANTHAM PREPARATORY SCHOOL
Gorse Lane, Grantham,
Lincolnshire NG31 7UF
Tel: (01476) 593293
Fax: (01476) 593293
Email: admin@
  granthamprep.co.uk
Head: Mrs K Korcz
Type: Co-educational Day 3–11
No of pupils: B57 G52
Fees: (September 06)
Day £4392–£5640

LINCOLN

LINCOLN MINSTER SCHOOL
Hillside, Lindum Terrace, Lincoln,
Lincolnshire LN2 5RW
Tel: (01522) 551300
Fax: (01522) 551310
Email: admin@
  lincolnminsterschool.co.uk
Head: Mr C Rickart
Type: Co-educational Day and
Boarding 2–18
No of pupils: B355 G397
No of boarders: F42 W40
Fees: On application

ST MARY'S PREPARATORY SCHOOL
5 Pottergate, Lincoln, Lincolnshire
LN2 1PH
Tel: (01522) 524622
Fax: (01522) 523637
Email: office@
  st-marys-prep.lincs.sch.uk
Head: Mr M Upton
Type: Co-educational Day 2–11
No of pupils: B132 G140
Fees: On application

LOUTH

GREENWICH HOUSE INDEPENDENT SCHOOL
106 High Holme Road, Louth,
Lincolnshire LN11 0HE
Tel: (01507) 609252
Fax: (01507) 606294
Head: Mrs J M Brindle
Type: Co-educational Day 0–11
No of pupils: 150
Fees: On application

MANBY

LOCKSLEY CHRISTIAN SCHOOL
Bilney Block, Manby Park, Manby,
Lincolnshire LN11 8UT
Tel: (01507) 327859
Fax: (01507) 328512
Email: locksleychristianschool@
  hotmail.com
Head: Mrs A P Franklin
Type: Co-educational Day 3–19
No of pupils: B31 G33
Fees: (September 06) Day £4320

SKEGNESS

VIKING SCHOOL
140 Church Road North, Skegness,
Lincolnshire PE25 2QJ
Tel: (01754) 765749
Fax: (01754) 765749
Head: Mrs S Barker
Type: Co-educational Day 2–11
No of pupils: B65 G60
Fees: On application

SLEAFORD

FEN SCHOOL
Side Bar Lane, Heckington Fen,
Sleaford, Lincolnshire NG34 9LY
Tel: (01529) 460966
Head: Mrs J M Dunkley
Type: Co-educational Day 2–16
No of pupils: B14 G16
Fees: On application

SPALDING

AYSCOUGHFEE HALL SCHOOL
Welland Hall, London Road,
Spalding, Lincolnshire PE11 2TE
Tel: (01775) 724733
Fax: (01775) 724733
Email: admin@ahs.me.uk
Head: Mr B Chittick
Type: Co-educational Day 3–11
No of pupils: B80 G80
Fees: (September 06)
Day £3660–£4455

STAMFORD

COPTHILL SCHOOL
Barnack Road, Uffington,
Stamford, Lincolnshire PE9 4TD
Tel: (01780) 757506
Fax: (01780) 482938
Email: copthill@btinternet.com
Head: Mr J A Teesdale
Type: Co-educational Day 2–11
No of pupils: B149 G140
Fees: On application

STAMFORD HIGH SCHOOL
St Paul's Street, Stamford,
Lincolnshire PE9 2BQ
Tel: (01780) 484200
Fax: (01780) 484201
Email: headshs@ses.lincs.sch.uk
Head: Dr P R Mason
Type: Girls Day and Boarding
11–18
No of pupils: 640
No of boarders: F60 W5
Fees: On application

STAMFORD JUNIOR SCHOOL
Stamford, Lincolnshire PE9 2LR
Tel: (01780) 484400
Fax: (01780) 484401
Email: head@shs.lincs.sch.uk
Head: Miss E M Craig
Type: Co-educational Boarding
and Day 2–11
No of pupils: 355
Fees: On application

STAMFORD SCHOOL
St Paul's Street, Stamford,
Lincolnshire PE9 2BQ
Tel: (01780) 750300/1
Fax: (01780) 750336
Email: headss@ses.lincs.sch.uk
Head: Dr P R Mason
Type: Boys Day and Boarding
11–18
No of boarders: F75 W10
Fees: (September 06) FB £17988
WB £17940 Day £9564

WOODHALL SPA

ST HUGH'S SCHOOL
Cromwell Avenue, Woodhall Spa,
Lincolnshire LN10 6TQ
Tel: (01526) 352169
Fax: (01526) 351520
Email: sthughs-schooloffice@
  btconnect.com
Head: Mr S G Greenish
Type: Co-educational Boarding
and Day 2–13
No of pupils: B95 G80
No of boarders: F30 W50
Fees: (September 06)
FB £12945–£13200
Day £5295–£9795

NORTH EAST LINCOLNSHIRE

GRIMSBY

ST. JAMES' SCHOOL
22 Bargate, Grimsby,
North East Lincolnshire DN34 4SY
Tel: (01472) 503260
Fax: (01472) 503275
Email: enquiries@
saintjamesschool.co.uk
Head: Mrs S M Isaac
Type: Co-educational Day and
Boarding 2–18
No of pupils: B128 G108
No of boarders: F30
Fees: (September 06)
FB £10662–£14445
WB £9957–£13740
Day £3600–£8658

ST MARTIN'S PREPARATORY SCHOOL
63 Bargate, Grimsby,
North East Lincolnshire DN34 5AA
Tel: (01472) 878907
Email: info@
smpschool.fsnet.co.uk
Head: Mrs M Preston
Type: Co-educational Day 3–11
No of pupils: 224
Fees: On application

NORTH LINCOLNSHIRE

BRIGG

BRIGG PREPARATORY SCHOOL
Bigby Street, Brigg,
North Lincolnshire DN20 8EF
Tel: (01652) 653237
Fax: (01652) 658879
Email: info@
briggprepschool.co.uk
Head: Mrs P Newman
Type: Co-educational Day 3–11
No of pupils: B57 G66
Fees: On application

KEADBY

TRENTVALE PREPARATORY SCHOOL
Trentside, Keadby,
North Lincolnshire DN17 3EF
Tel: (01724) 782904
Email: trentvale@btconnect.com
Head: Mr P Wright
Type: Co-educational Day 3–11
No of pupils: B40 G40
Fees: (September 06)
Day £2520–£2670

SCUNTHORPE

LYNTON PREPARATORY SCHOOL
250 Frodingham Road,
Scunthorpe, North Lincolnshire
DN15 7NW
Tel: (01724) 850881
Fax: (01724) 850881
Email: ejbroadbent@
btconnect.com
Head: Mrs E J Broadbent
Type: Co-educational Day 3–11
No of pupils: B27 G24
Fees: (September 05)
Day £2580–£2700

LONDON

E1

AL-MIZAN SCHOOL
82–92 Whitechapel Road, London
E1 1JE
Tel: (020) 7377 0234
Fax: (020) 7377 9879
Head: Muhammad Ibn Rashid
Type: Boys Day 6–13
No of pupils: 45
Fees: On application

GREEN GABLES MONTESSORI PRIMARY SCHOOL
The Institute, 302 The Highway,
Wapping, London E1W 3DH
Tel: (020) 7488 2374
Fax: (020) 7488 2376
Email: greengablesschool@
talk21.com
Head: Mrs J Brierley
Type: Co-educational Day 0–8
No of pupils: B24 G25
Fees: On application

LONDON EAST ACADEMY
46 Whitechapel Road, London
E1 1JX
Tel: (020) 7650 3070
Fax: (020) 7650 3071
Email: admin@leacademy.com
Head: Mr A M Faradhi
Type: Boys Day 7–16
No of pupils: 124
Fees: (September 06)
Day £2400–£2650

LONDON ISLAMIC SCHOOL
18–22 Damien Street, London
E1 2HX
Tel: (020) 7265 9667
Fax: (020) 7790 5536
Head: Mr A Rouf
Type: Boys Day 11–16
No of pupils: 140
Fees: (September 06) Day £4500

MADNI GIRLS SCHOOL
Myrdle Street, London E1 1HL
Tel: (020) 7377 1992
Fax: (020) 7377 1424
Email: madni_school@
hotmail.com
Head: Mrs F R Liyawdeen
Type: Girls Day 12–18
No of pupils: 215
Fees: On application

E2

DARUL HADIS LATIFIAH
1 Cornwall Avenue, London
E2 0HW
Tel: (020) 8980 2673
Fax: (020) 8983 7942
Email: darulhadis@hotmail.co.uk
Head: Maulana M Hussain
Type: Boys Day 11–19
No of pupils: 120
Fees: (September 06)
Day £1200–£1800

GATEHOUSE SCHOOL*
Sewardstone Road, Victoria Park,
London E2 9JG
Tel: (020) 8980 2978
Fax: (020) 8983 1642
Email: admin@
gatehouseschool.co.uk
Head: Mrs Belinda Canham
Type: Co-educational Day 3–11
No of pupils: B110 G110
Fees: (September 06)
Day £5760–£7050

RIVER HOUSE MONTESSORI SCHOOL
Admin Office, 2 Printingwolde
Road, London E2 7PR
Tel: (020) 7680 1288
Fax: (020) 7488 3097
Head: Ms S Greenwood
Type: Co-educational Day 2–12
No of pupils: 25
Fees: On application

E4

NORMANHURST SCHOOL
68/74 Station Road, Chingford,
London E4 7BA
Tel: (020) 8529 4307
Fax: (020) 8524 7737
Email: info@
normanhurstschool.co.uk
Head: Mr P J Williams
Type: Co-educational Day 3–16
Fees: (September 05)
Day £5800–£8100

E5

LUBAVITCH HOUSE SCHOOL (JUNIOR BOYS)
135 Clapton Common, London
E5 9AE
Tel: (020) 8800 1044
Fax: (020) 8880 2707
Head: Rabbi D Karnowsky
Type: Boys Day 5–13
No of pupils: 131
Fees: On application

NORTH LONDON RUDOLF STEINER SCHOOL
A Steiner Waldorf Early Years
Centre, Office at: 89 Blurton Road,
London E5 0NH
Tel: (020) 8986 8968
Fax: (020) 8985 1332
Email: nlrss@talk21.com
Head: Ms G Reemer
Type: Co-educational Day 2–7
No of pupils: B26 G22
Fees: On application

PARAGON CHRISTIAN ACADEMY
233–241 Glyn Road, London
E5 0JP
Tel: (020) 8985 1119
Head: Mr G Olson
Type: Co-educational Day 3–11
No of pupils: B17 G14
Fees: On application

E7

GRANGEWOOD INDEPENDENT SCHOOL
Chester Road, Forest Gate, London
E7 8QT
Tel: (020) 8472 3552
Fax: (020) 8552 8817
Email: admin@
grangewoodschool.com
Head: Mrs C A Adams
Type: Co-educational Day 4–11
No of pupils: B42 G33
Fees: On application

QUWWATT UL ISLAM GIRLS SCHOOL
16 Chaucer Road, Forest Gate, London E7 9NB
Tel: (020) 8548 4736
Fax: (020) 8472 4411
Email: info@quwwatulislam.com
Head: Mrs B Khan
Type: Girls Day 4–13
No of pupils: 193
Fees: (September 06)
Day £4950–£5700

E8

EAST LONDON CHRISTIAN CHOIR SCHOOL
Hephzibah Christian Centre, 35–43 Beechwood Road, London E8 3DY
Tel: (0870) 020 1598
Fax: (020) 7254 5760
Email: admissions@elccs.org.uk
Head: Mr F Tobun
Type: Co-educational Day 2–16
No of pupils: B17 G18
Fees: On application

E10

NOOR UL ISLAM PRIMARY SCHOOL
135 Dawlish Road, Leyton, London E10 6QW
Tel: (020) 8558 8765
Fax: (020) 8558 5235
Email: primary@noorulislam.co.uk
Head: Mr Aslam Hansa
Type: Co-educational Day 4–11
No of pupils: B85 G80
Fees: (September 05)
Day £1875–£2100

E11

ST JOSEPH'S CONVENT SCHOOL
59 Cambridge Park, London E11 2PR
Tel: (020) 8989 4700
Fax: (020) 8989 4700
Email: stjosephswanstead@ btconnect.com
Head: Mrs C Youle
Type: Girls Day 3–11
No of pupils: 188
Fees: On application

E13

PROMISED LAND ACADEMY
St Cedds Hall, Webb Gardens, Plaistow, London E13 8SR
Tel: (020) 8471 3939
Head: Rev Allan Coote
Type: Co-educational Day 4–16
No of pupils: B7 G3
Fees: On application

E17

FOREST SCHOOL
College Place, Snaresbrook, London E17 3PY
Tel: (020) 8520 1744
Fax: (020) 8520 3656
Email: info@forest.org.uk
Head: Mr A G Boggis
Type: Co-educational Day 4–18 (Single-sex ed 7–16)
No of pupils: B600 G600
Fees: (September 06)
Day £7182–£11304

HYLAND HOUSE
896 Forest Road, Walthamstow, London E17 4AE
Tel: (020) 8520 4186
Fax: (020) 8520 1549
Head: Mrs Abbequaye
Type: Co-educational Day 3–11
No of pupils: B55 G40
Fees: On application

WALTHAMSTOW MONTESSORI SCHOOL
Penryhn Hall, Penryhn Avenue, Walthamstow, London E17 5DA
Tel: (020) 8523 2968
Head: Mrs Lorna Mahoney
Type: Co-educational Day 3–11
Fees: On application

E18

SNARESBROOK COLLEGE PREPARATORY SCHOOL
75 Woodford Road, South Woodford, London E18 2EA
Tel: (020) 8989 2394
Fax: (020) 8989 4379
Email: office@ snaresbrookcollege.org.uk
Head: Mrs L J Chiverrell
Type: Co-educational Day 3–11
No of pupils: B76 G84
Fees: On application

EC1

CHARTERHOUSE SQUARE SCHOOL
40 Charterhouse Square, London EC1M 6EA
Tel: (020) 7600 3805
Fax: (020) 7600 3805
Email: csschool@msn.com
Head: Mrs J Malden
Type: Co-educational Day 4–11
No of pupils: B90 G70
Fees: On application

DALLINGTON SCHOOL
8 Dallington Street, London EC1V 0BW
Tel: (020) 7251 2284
Fax: (020) 7336 0972
Email: postmaster@ dallingtonschool.co.uk
Head: Mrs M C Hercules
Type: Co-educational Day 3–11
No of pupils: B102 G110
Fees: (September 06)
Day £5700–£7100

THE ITALIA CONTI ACADEMY OF THEATRE ARTS
23 Goswell Road, London EC1M 7AJ
Tel: (020) 7608 0047
Head: Mr C Vote
Type: Co-educational Day 9–21
No of pupils: B45 G200
Fees: On application

EC2

CITY OF LONDON SCHOOL FOR GIRLS
St Giles' Terrace, Barbican, London EC2Y 8BB
Tel: (020) 7847 5500
Fax: (020) 7638 3212
Email: info@clsg.org.uk
Head: Dr Y Burne
Type: Girls Day 7–18
No of pupils: 675
Fees: (September 05) Day £10584

THE LYCEUM
6 Paul Street, London EC2A 4JH
Tel: (020) 7247 1588
Fax: (020) 7655 0951
Email: lyceumschool@aol.com
Head: Mr J Rowe and Mrs L Hannay
Type: Co-educational Day 3–11
Fees: (September 05) Day £8550

England – London

EC4

CITY OF LONDON SCHOOL
Queen Victoria Street, London
EC4V 3AL
Tel: (020) 7489 0291
Fax: (020) 7329 6887
Email: headmaster@clsb.org.uk
Head: Mr D Levin
Type: Boys Day 10–18
No of pupils: 871
Fees: (September 05) Day £10845

ST PAUL'S CATHEDRAL SCHOOL*
2 New Change, London
EC4M 9AD
Tel: (020) 7248 5156
Fax: (020) 7329 6568
Email: admissions@
  spcs.london.sch.uk
Head: Mr A H Dobbin
Type: Co-educational Boarding
and Day 4–13
No of pupils: B140 G86
No of boarders: F40
Fees: (September 06) FB £5688
Day £9102–£9810

N2

ANNEMOUNT SCHOOL
18 Holne Chase, Hampstead
Garden Suburb, London N2 0QN
Tel: (020) 8455 2132
Fax: (020) 8381 4010
Email: headteacher@
  annemount.co.uk
Head: Mrs G Maidment
Type: Co-educational Day 2–7
No of pupils: B50 G50
Fees: (September 06)
Day £4950–£8280

KEREM SCHOOL
Norrice Lea, London N2 0RE
Tel: (020) 8455 0909
Fax: (020) 8209 0726
Email: admin@kerem.org.uk
Head: Mrs R Goulden
Type: Co-educational Day 4–11
No of pupils: B85 G85
Fees: (September 06)
Day £6510–£6675

N3

AKIVA SCHOOL
Levy House, The Sternberg Centre,
80 East End Road, London N3 2SY
Tel: (020) 8349 4980
Fax: (020) 8349 4959
Head: Mrs S de Botton
Type: Co-educational Day 4–11
No of pupils: B81 G73
Fees: On application

PARDES GRAMMAR BOYS' SCHOOL
Hendon Lane, London N3 1SA
Tel: (020) 8343 3568
Fax: (020) 8343 4804
Head: Rabbi D Dunner
Type: Boys Day 11–17
No of pupils: 250
Fees: On application

N4

BEIS CHINUCH LEBANOS GIRLS SCHOOL
Woodberry Down Centre,
Woodberry Down, London
N4 2SH
Tel: (020) 8809 7737
Fax: (020) 8802 7996
Head: Mrs R Springer
Type: Girls Day 2–16
No of pupils: 419
Fees: On application

HOLLY PARK MONTESSORI
The Holly Park, Methodist Church,
Crouch Hill, London N4 4BY
Tel: (020) 7263 6563
Fax: (020) 7263 7022
Email: hpms@btinternet.com
Head: Mrs A Lake
Type: Co-educational Day 2–7
No of pupils: B30 G30
Fees: On application

N5

PRIMROSE INDEPENDENT SCHOOL
Congregational Church, Highbury
Quadrant, Highbury, London
N5 2TE
Tel: (020) 7424 5741
Fax: (020) 7424 5741
Email: primroseschool_1984@
  yahoo.co.uk
Head: Mrs L Grandson
Type: Co-educational Day 2–11
No of pupils: B30 G25
Fees: (September 06) Day £6000

N6

CHANNING JUNIOR SCHOOL
Fairseat, 1 Highgate High Street,
London N6 5JR
Tel: (020) 8342 9862
Fax: (020) 8348 3122
Email: fairseat@channing.co.uk
Head: Mrs J Todd
Type: Girls Day 4–11
No of pupils: 167
Fees: (September 06) Day £3390

CHANNING SCHOOL
Highgate, London N6 5HF
Tel: (020) 8340 2328
Fax: (020) 8341 5698
Email: info@channing.co.uk
Head: Mrs B Elliott
Type: Girls Day 4–18
No of pupils: 567
Fees: (September 06)
Day £10170–£11070

HIGHGATE SCHOOL
North Road, London N6 4AY
Tel: (020) 8340 1524
Fax: (020) 8340 7674
Email: admissions@
  highgateschool.org.uk
Head: Mr A S Pettitt
Type: Co-educational Day 3–18
No of pupils: B1009 G179
Fees: (September 05)
Day £10695–£12585

N10

THE MONTESSORI HOUSE SCHOOL
5 Princes Avenue, Muswell Hill,
London N10 3LS
Tel: (020) 8444 4399
Fax: (020) 8444 4399
Email: mail@
  montessori-house.co.uk
Head: Mrs L Christoforou
Type: Co-educational Day 1–6
No of pupils: B59 G40
Fees: (September 05)
Day £1000–£2500

NORFOLK HOUSE SCHOOL

10 Muswell Avenue, Muswell Hill,
London N10 2EG
Tel: (020) 8883 4584
Fax: (020) 8883 4584
Email: office@
  norfolkhouseschool.org
Head: Mr M Malley
Type: Co-educational Day 4–11
No of pupils: B50 G50
Fees: (September 06) Day £7800

N11

WOODSIDE PARK INTERNATIONAL SCHOOL[†]

6 Friern Barnet Lane, London
N11 3LX
Tel: (020) 8920 0600
Fax: (020) 8211 4605
Email: admissions@wpis.org
Head: Mr D P Rose
Type: Co-educational Day 2–19
No of pupils: B261 G144
Fees: (September 06)
Day £4365–£15900

N14

SALCOMBE PREPARATORY SCHOOL

224–226 Chase Side, Southgate,
London N14 4PL
Tel: (020) 8441 5282 / 5356
Fax: (020) 8441 5282
Email: info@salcombeprep.co.uk
Head: Mr F Steadman
Type: Co-educational Day 4–11
No of pupils: B185 G115
Fees: (September 06) Day £7056

VITA ET PAX SCHOOL

Priory Close, Green Road,
Southgate, London N14 4AT
Tel: (020) 8449 8336
Fax: (020) 8440 0483
Email: vitaetpax@lineone.net
Head: Mrs M O'Connor
Type: Co-educational Day 3–11
No of pupils: B90 G90
Fees: On application

N16

BEIS ROCHEL D'SATMAR GIRLS SCHOOL

51–57 Amhurst Park, London
N16 5DL
Tel: (020) 8800 9060
Fax: (020) 8809 7069
Head: Ms Gita Ruth Smus
Type: Girls Day 2–17
No of pupils: 831
Fees: On application

LUBAVITCH HOUSE SENIOR SCHOOL FOR GIRLS

107–115 Stamford Hill, Hackney,
London N16 5RP
Tel: (020) 8800 0022
Fax: (020) 8809 7324
Head: Rabbi S Lew
Type: Girls Day 11–18
Fees: On application

MECHINAH LIYESHIVAH ZICHRON MOSHE

86 Amhurst Park, London N16 5AR
Tel: (020) 8800 5892
Head: Rabbi M Halpern
Type: Boys Day 11–16
No of pupils: 60
Fees: On application

TALMUD TORAH BOBOV PRIMARY SCHOOL

87 Egerton Road, London N16 6UE
Tel: (020) 8809 1025
Head: Rabbi A Just
Type: Boys Day 2–13
No of pupils: 302
Fees: On application

TAWHID BOYS SCHOOL, TAWHID EDUCATIONAL TRUST

21 Cazenove Road, London
N16 6PA
Tel: (020) 8806 2999
Head: Mr Usman Mapara
Type: Boys Day 9–16
No of pupils: 129
Fees: (September 06) Day £2000

TAYYIBAH GIRLS SCHOOL

88 Filey Avenue, Stamford Hill,
London N16 6JJ
Tel: (020) 8880 0085
Fax: (020) 8249 1767
Head: Mrs N B Qureshi
Type: Girls Day 5–18
No of pupils: 247
Fees: On application

YESODEY HATORAH JEWISH SCHOOL

2–4 Amhurst Park, London
N16 5AE
Tel: (020) 8800 8612
Email: yeshatorah@aol.com
Head: Rabbi Abraham Pinter
Type: Co-educational Day 3–16
(Single-sex ed)
No of pupils: B250 G710
Fees: On application

YETEV LEV DAY SCHOOL FOR BOYS

111–115 Cazenove Road, London
N16 6AX
Tel: (020) 8806 3834
Head: Mr Delange
Type: Boys Day 3–11
No of pupils: 320
Fees: On application

N17

EXCEL PREPARATORY SCHOOL

The Annex, Selby Centre, Off
Whitehart Lane, Tottenham,
London N17 8JL
Tel: (020) 8365 1734
Head: Mrs M Jean-Marie
Type: Co-educational Day 2–12
No of pupils: B21 G17
Fees: On application

EXCELSIOR COLLEGE

Selby Centre, Selby Road,
Tottenham, London N17 8JN
Tel: 0208 365 1153
Head: Mr G Gilfillian
Type: Co-educational Day 3–11
No of pupils: B9 G3
Fees: On application

PARKSIDE PREPARATORY SCHOOL

Church Lane, Bruce Grove,
Tottenham, London N17 7AA
Tel: (020) 8808 1451
Fax: (020) 8808 1451
Email: parksideprep2002@
  aol.com
Head: Mrs M Langford
Type: Co-educational Day 3–11
No of pupils: B27 G28
Fees: On application

N21

GRANGE PARK PREPARATORY SCHOOL
13 The Chine, Grange Park,
London N21 2EA
Tel: (020) 8360 1469
Fax: (020) 8360 4869
Email: office@gpps.org.uk
Head: Mrs S R Gladwin
Type: Girls Day 4–11
No of pupils: 105
Fees: (September 06) Day £6930

KEBLE PREPARATORY SCHOOL
Wades Hill, Winchmore Hill,
London N21 1BG
Tel: (020) 8360 3359
Fax: (020) 8360 4000
Email: office@kebleprep.co.uk
Head: Mr G P McCarthy
Type: Boys Day 4–13
No of pupils: 220
Fees: (September 05)
Day £7575–£9450

PALMERS GREEN HIGH SCHOOL
104 Hoppers Road, Winchmore
Hill, London N21 3LJ
Tel: (020) 8886 1135
Fax: (020) 8882 9473
Email: office@
palmersgreen.enfield.sch.uk
Head: Mrs J C Edmundson
Type: Girls Day 3–16
No of pupils: 320
Fees: (September 06)
Day £3090–£9195

NW1

THE CAVENDISH SCHOOL*
31 Inverness Street, London
NW1 7HB
Tel: (020) 7485 1958
Fax: (020) 7267 0098
Email: admissions@
cavendish-school.co.uk
Head: Miss W Smart
Type: Girls Day 3–11
No of pupils: 150
Fees: (September 05) Day £8598

FRANCIS HOLLAND SCHOOL*
Clarence Gate, Ivor Place, London
NW1 6XR
Tel: (020) 7723 0176
Fax: (020) 7706 1522
Email: admin@fhs-nw1.org.uk
Head: Mrs V M Durham
Type: Girls Day 11–18
No of pupils: 430
Fees: (September 06) Day £11625

INTERNATIONAL COMMUNITY SCHOOL*
4 York Terrace East, Regents Park,
London NW1 4PT
Tel: (020) 7935 1206
Fax: (020) 7935 7915
Email: admissions@ics.uk.net
Head: Mr P Hurd
Type: Co-educational Day 3–18
No of pupils: B120 G120
Fees: (September 06)
Day £3547–£4649

NORTH BRIDGE HOUSE LOWER PREP SCHOOL
1 Gloucester Avenue, London
NW1 7AB
Tel: (020) 7485 0661
Fax: (020) 7284 2508
Email: lowerprep@
northbridgehouse.com
Head: Mr B Bibby
Type: Co-educational Day 8–11
No of pupils: B72 G107
Fees: (September 06) Day £10635

NORTH BRIDGE HOUSE SENIOR SCHOOL
1 Gloucester Avenue, London
NW1 7AB
Tel: (020) 7267 6266
Fax: (020) 7284 2508
Email: seniorschool@
northbridgehouse.com
Head: Miss A Ayre
Type: Co-educational Day 11–16
No of pupils: B85 G85
Fees: (September 06) Day £10635

NORTH BRIDGE HOUSE UPPER PREP SCHOOL
1 Gloucester Avenue, London
NW1 7AB
Tel: (020) 7485 9495
Fax: (020) 7284 2508
Email: upperprep@
northbridgehouse.com
Head: Mr B Bibby
Type: Boys Day 10–13
No of pupils: 94
Fees: (September 06) Day £10635

SYLVIA YOUNG THEATRE SCHOOL
Rossmore Road, Marylebone,
London NW1 6NJ
Tel: (020) 7402 0673
Fax: (020) 7723 1040
Email: info@
sylviayoungtheatreschool.co.uk
Head: Ms F E Chave
Type: Co-educational Day and
Boarding 10–16
No of pupils: B68 G88
No of boarders: W22
Fees: (September 05)
FB £10737–£13806
WB £8514–£11232
Day £5550–£7800

NW2

THE MULBERRY HOUSE SCHOOL
7 Minster Road, West Hampstead,
London NW2 3SD
Tel: (020) 8452 7340
Fax: (020) 8452 7340
Email: info@
mulberryhouseschool.com
Head: Ms B Lewis-Powell
Type: Co-educational Day 2–8
No of pupils: 200
Fees: On application

NW3

THE ACADEMY SCHOOL
2 Pilgrims Place, Rosslyn Hill,
Hampstead, London NW3 1NG
Tel: (020) 7435 6621
Head: Mr Evans
Type: Co-educational Day 6–12
No of pupils: B40 G22
Fees: On application

DEVONSHIRE HOUSE PREPARATORY SCHOOL*
2 Arkwright Road, Hampstead,
London NW3 6AE
Tel: (020) 7435 1916
Fax: (020) 7431 4787
Email: enquiries@
devonshirehouseprepschool.
co.uk
Head: Mrs S Alexander
Type: Co-educational Day
Boys 2–13 Girls 2–11
No of pupils: B293 G237
Fees: (September 06)
Day £5625–£10920

THE HALL SCHOOL
23 Crossfield Road, Hampstead,
London NW3 4NU
Tel: (020) 7722 1700
Fax: (020) 7483 0181
Email: office@hallschool.co.uk
Head: Mr Philip Lough
Type: Boys Day 4–13
No of pupils: 440
Fees: (September 06)
Day £9300–£11400

HAMPSTEAD COLLEGE OF FINE ARTS, INDEPENDENT COLLEGE*
24 Lambolle Place, Hampstead,
London NW3 4PG
Tel: (020) 7586 0312
Fax: (020) 7483 0355
Email: mail@
  hampsteadfinearts.com
Head: Ms C Cave and
Mr N Cochrane
Type: Co-educational Day 14–19
No of pupils: B60 G45
Fees: On application

HAMPSTEAD HILL PRE-PREPARATORY & NURSERY SCHOOL
St Stephen's Hall, Pond Street,
Hampstead, London NW3 2PP
Tel: (020) 7435 6262
Fax: (020) 7433 1272
Email: hampsteadhill@aol.com
Head: Mrs A Taylor
Type: Co-educational Day
Boys 2–8 Girls 2–7
No of pupils: B190 G110
Fees: (September 06)
Day £6820–£12210

HEATHSIDE PREPARATORY SCHOOL
16 New End, Hampstead, London
NW3 1JA
Tel: (020) 7794 5857
Fax: (020) 7435 6434
Email: heathside@
  school.freeserve.co.uk
Head: Ms J White and
Ms M Remus
Type: Co-educational Day 3–11
No of pupils: B64 G60
Fees: On application

HEREWARD HOUSE SCHOOL
14 Strathray Gardens, Hampstead,
London NW3 4NY
Tel: (020) 7794 4820
Fax: (020) 7794 2024
Head: Mrs L Sampson
Type: Boys Day 4–13
No of pupils: 175
Fees: (September 06)
Day £8955–£10950

LYNDHURST HOUSE PREPARATORY SCHOOL*
24 Lyndhurst Gardens,
Hampstead, London NW3 5NW
Tel: (020) 7435 4936
Email: pmg@lyndhursthouse.co.uk
Head: Mr M O Spilberg
Type: Boys Day 4–13
No of pupils: 140
Fees: (September 05)
Day £10050–£11520

MARIA MONTESSORI SCHOOL HAMPSTEAD
26 Lyndhurst Gardens,
Hampstead, London NW3 5NW
Tel: (020) 7435 3646
Fax: (020) 7431 8096
Email: info@mariamontessori.org
Head: Mrs L Lawrence
Type: Co-educational Day 2–11
No of pupils: B30 G30
Fees: On application

NORTH BRIDGE HOUSE JUNIOR SCHOOL
8 Netherhall Gardens, London
NW3 5RR
Tel: (020) 7435 2884
Fax: (020) 7794 1337
Email: junior@
  northbridgehouse.com
Head: Mrs R Allsopp
Type: Co-educational Day 6–8
No of pupils: B95 G91
Fees: (September 06) Day £10635

NORTH BRIDGE HOUSE NURSERY SCHOOL
33 Fitzjohn's Avenue, London
NW3 5JY
Tel: (020) 7435 9641
Fax: (020) 7431 7930
Email: nursery@
  northbridgehouse.com
Head: Mrs R Allsopp
Type: Co-educational Day 3–6
Fees: (September 06)
Day £2895–£10635

THE PHOENIX SCHOOL
36 College Crescent, London
NW3 5LF
Tel: (020) 7722 4433
Fax: (020) 7722 4601
Email: info@ucsphoenix.org.uk
Head: Ms J Humble
Type: Co-educational Day 3–7
No of pupils: B70 G60
Fees: On application

THE ROYAL SCHOOL, HAMPSTEAD*
65 Rosslyn Hill, Hampstead,
London NW3 5UD
Tel: (020) 7794 7708
Fax: (020) 7431 6741
Email: enquiries@
  royalschoolhampstead.net
Head: Mrs J Ebner-Landy
Type: Girls Boarding and Day
3–18
No of pupils: 240
No of boarders: F25 W7
Fees: (September 06)
FB £13050–£16200
WB £10800–£13470
Day £6510–£8160

ST ANTHONY'S PREPARATORY SCHOOL
90 Fitzjohns Avenue, Hampstead,
London NW3 6NP
Tel: (020) 7431 1066
Fax: (020) 7435 9223
Head: Mr C McGovern
Type: Boys Day 5–13
No of pupils: 288
Fees: (September 06)
Day £10605–£10905

ST CHRISTOPHER'S SCHOOL
32 Belsize Lane, London NW3 5AE
Tel: (020) 7435 1521
Fax: (020) 7431 6694
Head: Mrs F Cook
Type: Girls Day 4–11
No of pupils: 234
Fees: On application

ST MARGARET'S SCHOOL*
18 Kidderpore Gardens, London
NW3 7SR
Tel: (020) 7435 2439
Fax: (020) 7431 1308
Email: headmistress@
  st-margarets.co.uk
Head: Mrs S Meaden
Type: Girls Day 4–16
No of pupils: 143
Fees: (September 06)
Day £7965–£9180

ST MARY'S SCHOOL HAMPSTEAD
47 Fitzjohn's Avenue, London NW3 6PG
Tel: (020) 7435 1868
Fax: (020) 7794 7922
Email: headmistress@stmh.co.uk
Head: Miss A Rawlinson
Type: Co-educational Day Boys 2–7 Girls 2–11
No of pupils: B41 G244
Fees: On application

SARUM HALL
15 Eton Avenue, London NW3 3EL
Tel: (020) 7794 2261
Fax: (020) 7431 7501
Email: office@
   sarumhallschool.co.uk
Head: Mrs C J Scott
Type: Girls Day 3–11
No of pupils: 171
Fees: (September 06)
Day £6048–£10065

SOUTH HAMPSTEAD HIGH SCHOOL
3 Maresfield Gardens, London NW3 5SS
Tel: (020) 7435 2899
Fax: (020) 7431 8022
Email: senior@shhs.gdst.net
Head: Mrs J Stephen
Type: Girls Day 4–18
No of pupils: 875
Fees: (September 05)
Day £7149–£9189

SOUTHBANK INTERNATIONAL SCHOOL, HAMPSTEAD*
16 Netherhall Gardens, Hampstead, London NW3 5TH
Tel: (020) 7243 3803
Fax: (020) 7727 3290
Email: admissions@southbank.org
Head: Mr N Hughes and Mrs J Treftz
Type: Co-educational Day 3–14
No of pupils: B94 G95
Fees: (September 06)
Day £9630–£16800

TREVOR ROBERTS'
57 Eton Avenue, London NW3 3ET
Tel: (020) 7586 1444
Fax: (020) 7722 0114
Email: trsenior@btconnect.com
Head: Mr S Trevor-Roberts
Type: Co-educational Day 5–13
No of pupils: B98 G80
Fees: (September 06)
Day £8850–£11100

UNIVERSITY COLLEGE SCHOOL
Frognal, Hampstead, London NW3 6XH
Tel: (020) 7435 2215
Fax: (020) 7433 2111
Email: seniorschool@ucs.org.uk
Head: Mr K J Durham
Type: Boys Day 11–18
No of pupils: 735
Fees: (September 06) Day £13125

UNIVERSITY COLLEGE SCHOOL JUNIOR BRANCH
11 Holly Hill, Hampstead, London NW3 6QN
Tel: (020) 7435 3068
Fax: (020) 7435 7332
Email: info@ucsjb.org.uk
Head: Mr K J Douglas
Type: Boys Day 7–11
Fees: (September 06) Day £12135

THE VILLAGE SCHOOL
2 Parkhill Road, Belsize Park, London NW3 2YN
Tel: (020) 7485 4673
Fax: (020) 7267 8462
Email: admin@
   thevillageschool.co.uk
Head: Mrs F M Prior
Type: Girls Day 4–11
No of pupils: 110
Fees: (September 06) Day £9900

NW4

BETH JACOB GRAMMAR FOR GIRLS
Stratford Road, Hendon, London NW4 2AT
Tel: (020) 8203 4322
Fax: (020) 8202 8480
Head: Mrs D Steinberg
Type: Girls Day 10–16
No of pupils: 264
Fees: On application

BRAMPTON COLLEGE
Lodge House, Lodge Road, London NW4 4DQ
Tel: (020) 8203 5025
Fax: (020) 8203 0052
Email: enqs@
   bramptoncollege.com
Head: Mr B Canetti
Type: Co-educational Day 15–19
No of pupils: B131 G111
Fees: (September 06)
Day £3125–£13975

HENDON PREPARATORY SCHOOL
20 Tenterden Grove, Hendon, London NW4 1TD
Tel: (020) 8203 7727
Fax: (020) 8203 3465
Email: info@hendonprep.co.uk
Head: Mr D Baldwin
Type: Co-educational Day 4–13
No of pupils: B90 G40
Fees: (September 06)
Day £7245–£9435

LONDON JEWISH GIRLS' HIGH SCHOOL
18 Raleigh Close, Hendon, London NW4 2TA
Tel: (020) 8203 8618
Fax: (020) 8203 8618
Head: Mr Joel Rabinowitz
Type: Girls Day 11–16
No of pupils: 91
Fees: On application

OYH PRIMARY SCHOOL
Finchley Lane, Hendon, London NW4 1DJ
Tel: (020) 8202 5646
Fax: (020) 8203 7568
Head: Mr D A David
Type: Co-educational Day 3–11
No of pupils: B89 G91
Fees: On application

NW5

L'ILE AUX ENFANTS
22 Vicar's Road, London NW5 4NL
Tel: (020) 7267 7119
Head: Mr A Hadjadj
Type: Co-educational Day 3–11
No of pupils: 200
Fees: On application

NW6

AL-SADIQ AND AL-ZAHRA SCHOOLS
134 Salusbury Road, London Middlesex NW6 6PF
Tel: (020) 7372 6760
Fax: (020) 7372 2752
Email: alsadiq@btconnect.com
Head: Dr M Movahedi
Type: Co-educational Day 4–16 (Single-sex ed)
No of pupils: B181 G201
Fees: (September 06) Day £3900

BROADHURST SCHOOL
19 Greencroft Gardens, London
NW6 3LP
Tel: (020) 7328 4280
Fax: (020) 7328 9370
Email: office@
  broadhurstschool.com
Head: Miss D Berkery
Type: Co-educational Day 2–5
No of pupils: B70 G70
Fees: (September 06)
Day £6480–£10950

BRONDESBURY COLLEGE FOR BOYS
8 Brondesbury Park, London
NW6 7BT
Tel: (020) 8830 4522
Fax: (020) 8830 4523
Email: brondesburycollege@
  hotmail.com
Head: Dr N Butt
Type: Boys Day 11–16
No of pupils: 119
Fees: On application

ISLAMIA GIRLS' SCHOOL
129 Salisbury Road, London
NW6 6PE
Tel: (020) 7372 3472
Fax: (020) 7604 4061
Email: headteacher@
  islamiaschools.com
Head: Ms A Ali
Type: Girls Day 11–16
No of pupils: 125
Fees: (September 05) Day £5500

NAIMA JEWISH PREPARATORY SCHOOL
21 Andover Place, London
NW6 5ED
Tel: (020) 7328 2802
Fax: (020) 7624 0161
Head: Rabbi Dr A Levy and
Mrs K Peters
Type: Co-educational Day 3–11
No of pupils: B86 G90
Fees: On application

RAINBOW MONTESSORI JUNIOR SCHOOL
13 Woodchurch Road, West
Hampstead, London NW6 3PL
Tel: (020) 7328 8986
Fax: (020) 7624 4046
Email: rms@
  rainbowmontessori.co.uk
Head: Mrs L Madden
Type: Co-educational Day 5–12
No of pupils: B25 G29
Fees: (September 06)
Day £7695–£7800

NW7

BELMONT (MILL HILL PREPARATORY SCHOOL)
The Ridgeway, Mill Hill, London
NW7 4ED
Tel: (020) 8906 7270
Fax: (020) 8906 3519
Email: registrar@
  belmontschool.com
Head: Mrs L C Duncan
Type: Co-educational Day 7–13
No of pupils: B237 G148
Fees: On application

GOODWYN SCHOOL
Hammers Lane, Mill Hill, London
NW7 4DB
Tel: (020) 8959 3756
Fax: (020) 8906 8961
Head: Mr S W E Robertson
Type: Co-educational Day 3–11
No of pupils: B118 G107
Fees: On application

MILL HILL SCHOOL*
The Ridgeway, Mill Hill, London
NW7 1QS
Tel: (020) 8959 1221
Fax: (020) 8906 2614
Email: registrations@
  millhill.org.uk
Head: Mr W R Winfield
Type: Co-educational Boarding
and Day 13–18
No of pupils: B441 G160
No of boarders: F170
Fees: (September 05) FB £20715
Day £13206

THE MOUNT SCHOOL
Milespit Hill, Mill Hill, London
NW7 2RX
Tel: (020) 8959 3403
Fax: (020) 8959 1503
Email: admin@mountschool.com
Head: Mrs J K Jackson
Type: Girls Day 4–18
No of pupils: 400
Fees: (September 05)
Day £6885–£8085

ST MARTIN'S
22 Goodwyn Avenue, Mill Hill,
London NW7 3RG
Tel: (020) 8959 1965
Fax: (020) 8959 9065
Email: info@
  stmartinsmillhill.co.uk
Head: Mrs A Wilson
Type: Co-educational Day 3–11
No of pupils: B50 G75
Fees: (September 05) Day £4875

NW8

ABERCORN SCHOOL*
28 Abercorn Place, London
NW8 9XP
Tel: (020) 7286 4785
Fax: (020) 7266 0219
Email: a.greystoke@
  abercornschool.com
Head: Mrs A S Greystoke
Type: Co-educational Day 2–13
No of pupils: B190 G190
Fees: (September 05)
Day £5775–£10785

THE AMERICAN SCHOOL IN LONDON*
1 Waverley Place, London
NW8 0NP
Tel: (020) 7449 1200
Fax: (020) 7449 1350
Email: admissions@asl.org
Head: Dr W C Mules
Type: Co-educational Day 4–18
No of pupils: B689 G652
Fees: (September 06)
Day £15870–£19440

ARNOLD HOUSE SCHOOL
1, Loudoun Road, St John's Wood,
London NW8 0LH
Tel: (020) 7266 4840
Fax: (020) 7266 6994
Email: office@arnoldhouse.co.uk
Head: Mr N M Allen
Type: Boys Day 5–13
No of pupils: 250
Fees: (September 05) Day £11250

ST CHRISTINA'S RC PREPARATORY SCHOOL
25 St Edmunds Terrace, Regents
Park, London NW8 7PY
Tel: (020) 7722 8784
Fax: (020) 7586 3454
Email: vanda@
  stchristinasschool.co.uk
Head: Miss N Clyne Wilson
Type: Girls Day 3–11 (Boys 3–7)
No of pupils: B40 G180
Fees: On application

England – London

ST JOHNS WOOD PRE-PREPARATORY SCHOOL
St Johns Hall, Lords Roundabout,
London NW8 7NE
Tel: (020) 7722 7149
Fax: (020) 7586 6093
Email: school@dircon.co.uk
Head: Mrs H Ellis
Type: Co-educational Day 3–7
No of pupils: B30 G30
Fees: (September 05)
Day £4875–£9915

NW9

GOWER HOUSE SCHOOL
Blackbird Hill, London NW9 8RR
Tel: (020) 8205 2509
Fax: (020) 8200 6491
Head: Mr M Keane
Type: Co-educational Day 2–11
No of pupils: B120 G110
Fees: On application

ST NICHOLAS SCHOOL
22 Salmon Street, London
NW9 8PN
Tel: (020) 8205 7153
Fax: (020) 8205 9744
Email: stnich@happychild.co.uk
Head: Mrs A Gregory
Type: Co-educational Day 2–11
No of pupils: B40 G40
Fees: On application

NW10

YSGOL GYMRAEG LLUNDAIN, THE WELSH SCHOOL, LONDON
c/o Stonebridge Primary School,
Shakespeare Avenue, London
NW10 8NG
Tel: (020) 8965 3585
Email: cymraeg@
   llundain.freeserve.co.uk
Head: Mr Matthew Davies
Type: Co-educational Day 3–11
No of pupils: B10 G5
Fees: (September 05) Day £5850

NW11

BEIS HAMEDRASH ELYON
211 Golders Green Rd, London
NW11 9BY
Tel: (020) 8201 8668
Fax: (020) 8201 8769
Head: Mr Clifford Walker
Type: Boys Day 11–14
No of pupils: 45
Fees: On application

GOLDERS HILL SCHOOL
666 Finchley Road, London
NW11 7NT
Tel: (020) 8455 2589
Fax: (020) 8209 0905
Head: Mrs A Eglash
Type: Co-educational Day 2–7
No of pupils: B110 G80
Fees: On application

THE KING ALFRED SCHOOL
149 North End Road, London
NW11 7HY
Tel: (020) 8457 5200
Fax: (020) 8457 5264
Email: KAS@
   kingalfred.barnet.sch.uk
Head: Mrs D Moore
Type: Co-educational Day 4–18
No of pupils: B300 G300
Fees: (September 05)
Day £9000–£11340

SE3

BLACKHEATH HIGH SCHOOL GDST
Vanbrugh Park, Blackheath,
London SE3 7AG
Tel: (020) 8853 2929
Fax: (020) 8853 3663
Email: info@bla.gdst.net
Head: Mrs E Laws
Type: Girls Day 3–18
No of pupils: 600
Fees: (September 05)
Day £5514–£9189

BLACKHEATH PREPARATORY SCHOOL
4 St Germans Place, Blackheath,
London SE3 0NJ
Tel: (020) 8858 0692
Fax: (020) 8858 7778
Email: info@
   blackheathprepschool.com
Head: Mrs P Thompson
Type: Co-educational Day 3–11
No of pupils: B146 G156
Fees: (September 06)
Day £3705–£8025

HEATH HOUSE PREPARATORY SCHOOL
37 Wemyss Road, Blackheath,
London SE3 0TG
Tel: (020) 8297 1900
Fax: (020) 8297 1550
Email: info@
   heathhouseprepschool.com
Head: Mr I R Laslett
Type: Co-educational Day 4–11
No of pupils: B44 G38
Fees: On application

THE POINTER SCHOOL
19 Stratheden Road, Blackheath,
London SE3 7TH
Tel: (020) 8293 1331
Fax: (020) 8293 1331
Email: secretary@
   pointers-school.co.uk
Head: Mr R J S Higgins
Type: Co-educational Day 3–11
No of pupils: B87 G75
Fees: On application

SE6

ST DUNSTAN'S COLLEGE
Stanstead Road, Catford, London
SE6 4TY
Tel: (020) 8516 7200
Fax: (020) 8516 7300
Email: head@sdmail.org.uk
Head: Mrs Jane Davies
Type: Co-educational Day 4–18
No of pupils: B500 G422
Fees: (September 05)
Day £7722–£10671

SPRINGFIELD CHRISTIAN SCHOOL
145 Perry Hill, Catford, London
SE6 4LP
Tel: (020) 8291 4433
Fax: (020) 8314 4283
Head: Mr Babs Oludimu
Type: Co-educational Day
No of pupils: B45 G46
Fees: On application

SE9

ST OLAVE'S PREPARATORY SCHOOL
106–110 Southwood Road, New Eltham, London SE9 3QS
Tel: (020) 8294 8930
Fax: (020) 8294 8939
Email: office@stolaves.org.uk
Head: Mrs C P Fisher
Type: Co-educational Day 3–11
No of pupils: B126 G84
Fees: (September 06)
Day £4380–£6960

SE12

COLFE'S SCHOOL
Horn Park Lane, London
SE12 8AW
Tel: (020) 8852 2283
Fax: (020) 8297 1216
Email: head@colfes.com
Head: Mr R F Russell
Type: Co-educational Day 3–18
No of pupils: B677 G395
Fees: (September 05)
Day £7047–£10080

RIVERSTON SCHOOL
63–69 Eltham Road, London
SE12 8UF
Tel: (020) 8318 4327
Fax: (020) 8297 0514
Email: info@
  riverston.greenwich.sch.uk
Head: Mrs S E Salathiel
Type: Co-educational Day 1–16
No of pupils: B245 G130
Fees: On application

SE15

THE VILLA PRE-PREPARATORY SCHOOL
54 Lyndhurst Grove, London
SE15 5AH
Tel: (020) 7703 6216
Fax: (020) 7252 6536
Email: thevillaschool@
  hotmail.com
Head: Mrs G Quinn
Type: Co-educational Day 4–7
No of pupils: B24 G24
Fees: On application

SE16

CAVENDISH SCHOOL
Lady Gomm House, 58 Hawkstone Road, London
SE16 2PA
Tel: (020) 7349 0088
Fax: (020) 7394 1015
Head: Mrs S D Craggs
Type: Co-educational Day 11–16
No of pupils: B25 G10
Fees: (September 05) Day £20000

SE19

VIRGO FIDELIS
147 Central Hill, Upper Norwood, London SE19 1RS
Tel: (020) 8653 2169
Fax: (020) 8766 8802
Email: virgofidelis@rmplc.co.uk
Head: Mrs J M Noronha
Type: Co-educational Day 3–11
No of pupils: B121 G142
Fees: On application

SE21

DULWICH COLLEGE
Dulwich Common, London
SE21 7LD
Tel: (020) 8693 3601
Fax: (020) 8693 6319
Email: info@dulwich.org.uk
Head: Mr G G Able
Type: Boys Day and Boarding 7–18
No of boarders: F108 W22
Fees: (September 06) FB £23955
WB £23010 Day £11895

DULWICH COLLEGE PREPARATORY SCHOOL
42 Alleyn Park, Dulwich, London
SE21 7AA
Tel: (020) 8670 3217
Fax: (020) 8766 7586
Email: registrar@dcpslondon.org
Head: Mr G Marsh
Type: Boys Day and Boarding 3–13 (Girls 3–5)
No of pupils: B796 G30
No of boarders: W30
Fees: (September 06)
WB £16221–£17499
Day £3831–£11928

OAKFIELD PREPARATORY SCHOOL
125–128 Thurlow Park Road, Dulwich, London SE21 8HP
Tel: (020) 8670 4206
Fax: (020) 8766 6744
Email: cdecisneros@cfbt.com
Head: Mr A Roberts-Wray
Type: Co-educational Day 2–11
No of pupils: B302 G243
Fees: (September 06)
Day £4038–£6438

ROSEMEAD PREPARATORY SCHOOL*
70 Thurlow Park Road, London
SE21 8HZ
Tel: (020) 8670 5865
Fax: (020) 8761 9159
Email: admin@
  rosemeadprepschool.org.uk
Head: Mrs C Brown
Type: Co-educational Day 3–11
No of pupils: B131 G180
Fees: (September 06)
Day £6801–£7626

SE22

ALLEYN'S SCHOOL*
Townley Road, Dulwich, London
SE22 8SU
Tel: (020) 8557 1500
Fax: (020) 8557 1462
Email: registrar@alleyns.org.uk
Head: Dr C Diggory
Type: Co-educational Day 4–18
No of pupils: B593 G585
Fees: (September 06)
Day £9450–£11481

England – London

JAMES ALLEN'S GIRLS' SCHOOL

East Dulwich Grove, London
SE22 8TE
Tel: (020) 8693 1181
Fax: (020) 8693 7842
Email: postmaster@jags.org.uk
Head: Mrs M Gibbs
Type: Girls Day 11–18
No of pupils: 760
Fees: (September 05) Day £10305

JAMES ALLEN'S PREPARATORY SCHOOL

East Dulwich Grove, London
SE22 8TE
Tel: (020) 8693 0374
Fax: (020) 8693 8031
Email: debbie.hewlett@jags.org.uk
Head: Miss H Kahn
Type: Co-educational Day
Boys 4–7 Girls 4–11
No of pupils: B35 G265
Fees: (September 06) Day £3179

THEODORE MCLEARY PRIMARY SCHOOL

31 East Dulwich Grove, Clapham,
London SE22 8PW
Tel: (020) 8693 4200
Fax: (020) 8693 4200
Head: Mr C D Thompson
Type: Co-educational Day 5–10
No of pupils: B17 G4
Fees: On application

SE24

HERNE HILL SCHOOL

The Old Vicarage, 127 Herne Hill,
London SE24 9LY
Tel: (020) 7274 6336
Fax: (020) 7924 9510
Email: enquiries@
   hernehillschool.co.uk
Head: Mrs V Tabone
Type: Co-educational Day 3–7
No of pupils: B125 G125
Fees: (September 05)
Day £3360–£8355

SE26

SYDENHAM HIGH SCHOOL GDST

19 Westwood Hill, London
SE26 6BL
Tel: (020) 8768 8000
Fax: (020) 8768 8002
Email: info@syd.gdst.net
Head: Mrs K Pullen
Type: Girls Day 4–18
No of pupils: 678
Fees: On application

SW1

EATON HOUSE SCHOOL BELGRAVIA

3 -5 Eaton Gate, Eaton Square,
London SW1W 9BA
Tel: (020) 7730 9343
Fax: (020) 7730 1798
Email: admin@
   eatonhouseschools.com
Head: Miss L Watts
Type: Boys Day 4–8
No of pupils: 250
Fees: (September 06) Day £9600

EATON SQUARE SCHOOL

79 Eccleston Square, London
SW1V 1PP
Tel: (020) 7931 9469
Fax: (020) 7828 0164
Email: admissions@
   eatonsquare.westminster.sch.uk
Head: Mr Paul David
Type: Co-educational Day
Boys 2–13 Girls 2–11
No of pupils: B256 G236
Fees: (September 06)
Day £1695–£4200

FRANCIS HOLLAND SCHOOL

39 Graham Terrace, London
SW1W 8JF
Tel: (020) 7730 2971
Fax: (020) 7823 4066
Email: office@fhs-sw1.org.uk
Head: Miss S Pattenden
Type: Girls Day 4–18
No of pupils: 475
Fees: On application

HILL HOUSE INTERNATIONAL JUNIOR SCHOOL

17 Hans Place, London SW1X 0EP
Tel: (020) 7584 1331
Fax: (020) 7591 3938
Email: r.townend@orange.net
Head: Mr R Townend
Type: Co-educational Day 4–13
No of pupils: B610 G395
Fees: (September 06)
Day £7400–£9000

KNIGHTSBRIDGE SCHOOL

67 Pont Street, Knightsbridge,
London SW1X 0BD
Tel: (020) 7589 8730
Email: info@
   knightsbridgeschool.com
Head: Mr M Giles
Type: Co-educational Day 3–16
No of pupils: B49 G45
Fees: (September 05)
Day £7950–£10455

MORE HOUSE*

22–24 Pont Street, Chelsea,
London SW1X 0AA
Tel: (020) 7235 2855
Fax: (020) 7259 6782
Email: office@morehouse.org.uk
Head: Mr Robert Carlysle
Type: Girls Day 11–18
No of pupils: 220
Fees: On application

SUSSEX HOUSE SCHOOL

68 Cadogan Square, Chelsea,
London SW1X 0EA
Tel: (020) 7584 1741
Fax: (020) 7589 2300
Head: Mr N P Kaye
Type: Boys Day 8–13
No of pupils: 180
Fees: (September 06) Day £11610

THOMAS'S KINDERGARTEN

14 Ranelagh Grove, London
SW1W 8PD
Tel: (020) 7730 3596
Fax: (020) 7730 3596
Email: tspierenburg@
   thomas-s.co.uk
Head: Miss T Spierenburg
Type: Co-educational Day 2–4
No of pupils: B27 G27
Fees: On application

WESTMINSTER ABBEY CHOIR SCHOOL*
Dean's Yard, London SW1P 3NY
Tel: (020) 7222 6151
Fax: (020) 7222 1548
Email: headmaster@
westminster-abbey.org
Head: Mr J Milton
Type: Boys Boarding 8–13
No of pupils: 33 *No of boarders:* F33
Fees: (September 06) FB £5085

WESTMINSTER CATHEDRAL CHOIR SCHOOL
Ambrosden Avenue, London
SW1P 1QH
Tel: (020) 7798 9081
Fax: (020) 7630 7209
Email: office@choirschool.com
Head: Mr J Browne
Type: Boys Boarding and Day
8–13
No of pupils: 109
No of boarders: F31
Fees: On application

WESTMINSTER SCHOOL
17 Dean's Yard, Westminster,
London SW1P 3PB
Tel: (020) 7963 1042
Fax: (020) 7963 1043
Email: registrar@
westminster.org.uk
Head: Dr S Spurr
Type: Co-educational Boarding
and Day Boys 13–18 Girls 16–18
No of pupils: B623 G115
No of boarders: F5 W173
Fees: (September 06) F/WB £24315
Day £16842–£18264

WESTMINSTER UNDER SCHOOL
Adrian House, 27 Vincent Square,
London SW1P 2NN
Tel: (020) 7821 5788
Fax: (020) 7821 0458
Email: under.school@
westminster.org.uk
Head: Mr J P Edwards
Type: Boys Day 7–13
No of pupils: 267
Fees: On application

SW3

CAMERON HOUSE SCHOOL*
4 The Vale, Chelsea, London
SW3 6AH
Tel: (020) 7352 4040
Fax: (020) 7352 2349
Email: info@
cameronhouseschool.org
Head: Miss F Stack
Type: Co-educational Day 4–11
No of pupils: B45 G67
Fees: (September 06) Day £11685

GARDEN HOUSE SCHOOL
Turks Row, London SW3 4TW
Tel: (020) 7730 1652
Fax: (020) 7730 0470
Email: info@
gardenhouseschool.co.uk
Head: Mrs W Challen and
Mr M Giles
Type: Co-educational Day 4–11
(Co-ed nursery)
No of pupils: B134 G287
Fees: On application

JAMAHIRIYA SCHOOL
Glebe Place, London SW3 5JP
Tel: (020) 7352 6642
Fax: (020) 7352 6642
Head: Mr Alkawash
Type: Co-educational Day 5–17
No of pupils: B200 G200
Fees: On application

SW4

EATON HOUSE THE MANOR
58 Clapham Common Northside,
London SW4 9RU
Tel: (020) 7924 6000
Fax: (020) 7924 1530
Email: admin@
eatonhouseschools.com
Head: Mr S Hepher and Mrs S
Segrave (Pre-Prep)
Type: Boys Day 2–13
No of pupils: B495 G25
Fees: (September 06)
Day £9600–£11580

PARKGATE HOUSE SCHOOL*
80 Clapham Common North Side,
London SW4 9SD
Tel: (020) 7350 2452
Fax: (020) 7738 1633
Email: office@
parkgate-school.co.uk
Head: Ms C Shanley and
Mrs T Masterson
Type: Co-educational Day 2–11
No of pupils: B100 G100
Fees: (September 06)
Day £3465–£9570

SW5

COLLINGHAM INDEPENDENT GCSE AND SIXTH FORM COLLEGE*
23 Collingham Gardens, London
SW5 0HL
Tel: (020) 7244 7414
Fax: (020) 7370 7312
Email: london@collingham.co.uk
Head: Mr G Hattee
Type: Co-educational Day 14–20
No of pupils: B120 G110
Fees: (September 06)
Day £4170–£15480

SW6

AL-MUNTADA ISLAMIC SCHOOL
7 Bridges Place, Parsons Green,
London SW6 4HW
Tel: (020) 7471 8283
Fax: (020) 7371 7318
Head: Mr Z Chehimi
Type: Co-educational Day 4–11
No of pupils: B83 G93
Fees: On application

ERIDGE HOUSE PREPARATORY
1 Fulham Park Road, Fulham,
London SW6 4LJ
Tel: (020) 7471 4816
Email: office@eridgehouse.co.uk
Head: Mrs L Waring
Type: Co-educational Day 2–11
No of pupils: B50 G50
Fees: (September 06)
Day £8985–£9555

England – London

FULHAM PREP SCHOOL (PRE-PREP)
47A Fulham High Street, London SW6 3JJ
Tel: (020) 7371 9911
Fax: (020) 7371 9922
Email: admin@fulhamprep.co.uk
Head: Ms Di Steven
Type: Co-educational Day 4–7
No of pupils: B109 G98
Fees: (September 06) Day £10110

KENSINGTON PREP SCHOOL
596 Fulham Road, London SW6 5PA
Tel: (020) 7731 9300
Fax: (020) 7731 9301
Email: enquiries@kenprep.gdst.net
Head: Mrs P J F Lynch
Type: Girls Day 4–11
No of pupils: 275
Fees: (September 06) Day £9342

L'ECOLE DES PETITS
2 Hazlebury Road, London SW6 2NB
Tel: (020) 7371 8350
Fax: (020) 7736 9522
Email: admin@
  lecoledespetits.co.uk
Head: Mrs M Otten and
Mrs F Brisset
Type: Co-educational Day 2–6 (Bilingual)
No of pupils: B65 G75
Fees: (September 06)
Day £4515–£7050

SINCLAIR HOUSE SCHOOL
159 Munster Road, Fulham, London SW6 6AD
Tel: (020) 7736 9182
Fax: (020) 7371 0295
Email: info@
  sinclairhouseschool.co.uk
Head: Mrs C T M O'Sullivan
Type: Co-educational Day 2–8
No of pupils: B28 G23
Fees: On application

THOMAS'S FULHAM
Hugon Road, London Fulham, London SW6 3ES
Tel: (020) 7751 8200
Fax: (020) 7751 8201
Head: Miss Annette Dobson
Type: Co-educational Day 4–11
No of pupils: B95 G93
Fees: (September 06) Day £3465

SW7

DUFF MILLER
59 Queen's Gate, London SW7 5JP
Tel: (020) 7225 0577
Fax: (020) 7589 5155
Head: Mr C Denning
Type: Co-educational Day 14–18
No of pupils: B85 G85
Fees: On application

EATON HOUSE THE VALE SCHOOL
2 Elvaston Place, London SW7 5QH
Tel: (020) 7924 6000
Fax: (020) 7924 1530
Email: admin@
  eatonhouseschools.com
Head: Mrs S Lang
Type: Co-educational Day
Boys 4–8 Girls 4–11
No of pupils: B45 G45
Fees: (September 06) Day £9600

FALKNER HOUSE
19 Brechin Place, London SW7 4QB
Tel: (020) 7373 4501
Fax: (020) 7835 0073
Email: office@falknerhouse.co.uk
Head: Mrs A Griggs
Type: Girls Day 3–11 (Co-ed 3–4)
No of pupils: B10 G170
Fees: (September 06)
Day £5775–£11550

GLENDOWER PREPARATORY SCHOOL*
87 Queen's Gate, South Kensington, London SW7 5JX
Tel: (020) 7370 1927
Fax: (020) 7244 8308
Email: office@
  glendower.kensington.sch.uk
Head: Mrs R Bowman
Type: Girls Day 4–11
No of pupils: 182
Fees: (September 06) Day £9990

THE HAMPSHIRE SCHOOLS (KNIGHTSBRIDGE UNDER SCHOOL)
5 Wetherby Place, London SW7 4NX
Tel: (020) 7584 3297
Fax: (020) 7584 9733
Email: hampshire@indschool.org
Head: Mr A G Bray
Type: Day
No of pupils: B45 G45
Fees: On application

THE HAMPSHIRE SCHOOLS (KNIGHTSBRIDGE UPPER SCHOOL)
63 Ennismore Gardens, London SW7 1NH
Tel: (020) 7584 3297
Fax: (020) 7584 9733
Email: hampshire@indschool.org
Head: Mr A G Bray
Type: Co-educational Day 5–8
No of pupils: B48 G48
Fees: On application

LYCEE FRANCAIS CHARLES DE GAULLE
35 Cromwell Road, London SW7 2DG
Tel: (020) 7584 6322
Fax: (020) 7823 7684
Email: proviseur@
  lyceefrancais.org.uk
Head: Mr A Becherand
Type: Co-educational Day 4–19
No of pupils: B1684 G1718
Fees: On application

MANDER PORTMAN WOODWARD
90–92 Queen's Gate, London SW7 5AB
Tel: (020) 7835 1355
Fax: (020) 7259 2705
Email: london@mpw.co.uk
Head: Mr S D Boyes
Type: Co-educational Day 14+
No of pupils: B207 G170
Fees: (September 05)
Day £2102–£55796

QUEEN'S GATE SCHOOL*
133 Queen's Gate, Kensington, London SW7 5LE
Tel: (020) 7589 3587
Fax: (020) 7584 7691
Email: registrar@
  queensgate.org.uk
Head: Mrs A M Holyoak
Type: Girls Day 4–18
Fees: (September 05)
Day £8700–£10875

ST NICHOLAS PREPARATORY SCHOOL*
23 Prince's Gate, London SW7 1PT
Tel: (020) 7225 1277
Fax: (020) 7823 7557
Email: info@stnicholasprep.co.uk
Head: Mr D Wilson
Type: Co-educational Day 3–11
No of pupils: B125 G125
Fees: (September 06)
Day £6510–£10470

ST PHILIP'S SCHOOL
6 Wetherby Place, London
SW7 4ND
Tel: (020) 7373 3944
Fax: (020) 7244 9766
Email: info@stphilipschool.co.uk
Head: Mr H Biggs-Davison
Type: Boys Day 7–13
No of pupils: 111
Fees: (September 06) Day £10230

WESTMINSTER TUTORS*
86 Old Brompton Road, London
SW7 3LQ
Tel: (020) 7584 1288
Fax: (020) 7584 2637
Email: info@
    westminstertutors.co.uk
Head: Mr J J Layland
Type: Co-educational Day 14+
No of pupils: B20 G30
Fees: (September 06)
Day £13500–£21000

SW8

NEWTON PREP SCHOOL
149 Battersea Park Road, London
SW8 4BX
Tel: (020) 7720 4091
Fax: (020) 7498 9052
Email: registrar@
    newtonprep.co.uk
Head: Mr N Allen
Type: Co-educational Day 3–13
No of pupils: B290 G282
Fees: (September 05)
Day £9150–£10530

SW10

REDCLIFFE SCHOOL*
47 Redcliffe Gardens, London
SW10 9JH
Tel: (020) 7352 9247
Fax: (020) 7352 6936
Email: admissions@
    redcliffeschool.com
Head: Mrs S Bourne
Type: Co-educational Day
Boys 3–8 Girls 3–11
No of pupils: B22 G75
Fees: (September 06) Day £9000

SW11

DOLPHIN SCHOOL (INCLUDING NOAH'S ARK NURSERY SCHOOLS)
106 Northcote Road, Battersea,
London SW11 6QW
Tel: (020) 7924 3472
Fax: (020) 8265 8700
Email: admissions@
    dolphinschool.org.uk
Head: Mrs J Glen
Type: Co-educational Day 2–11
No of pupils: B84 G94
Fees: (September 06)
Day £3969–£7326

THE DOMINIE
142 Battersea Park Road, London
SW11 4NB
Tel: (020) 7720 8783
Fax: (020) 7720 8783
Email: lrdominie@aol.com
Head: Mrs L Robertson and
Miss A O'Doherty
Type: Co-educational Day 6–12
No of pupils: B15 G15
Fees: (September 06) Day £16650

EMANUEL SCHOOL
Battersea Rise, London SW11 1HS
Tel: (020) 8870 4171
Fax: (020) 8877 1424
Email: enquiries@emanuel.org.uk
Head: Mr M D Hanley-Browne
Type: Co-educational Day 10–18
No of pupils: B501 G185
Fees: (September 05) Day £10974

NORTHCOTE LODGE SCHOOL
26 Bolingbroke Grove, London
SW11 6EL
Tel: (020) 8682 8888
Fax: (020) 8682 8890
Email: info@
    northwoodschools.com
Head: Mr P Cheeseman
Type: Boys Day 8–13
No of pupils: 183
Fees: (September 05)
Day £10560–£11325

THAMES CHRISTIAN COLLEGE
Wye Street, London SW11 2HB
Tel: (020) 7228 3933
Fax: (020) 7924 1112
Email: info@
    thameschristiancollege.org.uk
Head: and Dr S Holsgrove
Type: Co-educational Day 11–16
No of pupils: B55 G45
Fees: (September 06)
Day £1000–£2850

THOMAS'S KINDERGARTEN, BATTERSEA
The Crypt, Saint Mary's Church,
Battersea Church Road, London
SW11 3NA
Tel: (020) 7738 0400
Head: Miss I Jennings
Type: Co-educational Day 2–5
No of pupils: B24 G24
Fees: On application

THOMAS'S PREPARATORY SCHOOL
28–40 Battersea High Street,
London SW11 3JB
Tel: (020) 7978 0900
Fax: (020) 7978 0901
Email: Battersea@thomas-s.co.uk
Head: Mr B V R Thomas
Type: Co-educational Day 4–13
No of pupils: B270 G215
Fees: (September 05)
Day £10365–£11715

THOMAS' PREPARATORY SCHOOL CLAPHAM
Broomwood Road, London
SW11 6JZ
Tel: (020) 7326 9300
Fax: (020) 7326 9301
Email: clapham@thomas-s.co.uk
Head: Mrs P Evelegh
Type: Co-educational Day 4–13
No of pupils: B245 G276
Fees: (September 05)
Day £9825–£11115

SW12

BALHAM PREPARATORY SCHOOL
47a Balham High Road, London
SW12 9AW
Tel: (020) 8675 7747
Fax: (020) 8675 7912
Head: Mr K Bahauddin
Type: Co-educational Day 3–16
No of pupils: 500
Fees: On application

England – London

BROOMWOOD HALL SCHOOL

74 Nightingale Lane, London
SW12 8NR
Tel: (020) 8682 8800
Fax: (020) 8675 0136
Email: broomwood@
    northwoodschools.com
Head: Mrs K A H Colquhoun
Type: Co-educational Day
Boys 4–8 Girls 4–13
No of pupils: B165 G225
Fees: On application

HORNSBY HOUSE SCHOOL

Hearnville Road, London
SW12 8RS
Tel: (020) 8673 7573
Fax: (020) 8673 6722
Email: school@
    hornsby-house.co.uk
Head: Mrs J Strong
Type: Co-educational Day 4–11
No of pupils: B161 G128
Fees: On application

THE WHITE HOUSE PREP & WOODENTOPS KINDERGARTEN

24 Thornton Road, Clapham Park,
London SW12 0LF
Tel: (020) 8674 9514
Email: office@
    whitehouseschool.com
Head: Mrs E Davies
Type: Co-educational Day 2–11
No of pupils: B60 G60
Fees: (September 05)
Day £2625–£7485

SW13

THE HARRODIAN

Lonsdale Road, London
SW13 9QN
Tel: (020) 8748 6117
Fax: (020) 8563 7327
Email: admin@harrodian.com
Head: Mr J R Hooke
Type: Co-educational Day 5–18
No of pupils: B448 G369
Fees: (September 05)
Day £9357–£13053

ST PAUL'S PREPARATORY SCHOOL

Colet Court, Lonsdale Road,
London SW13 9JT
Tel: (020) 8748 3461
Fax: (020) 8563 7361
Email: HMCC@
    stpaulsschool.org.uk
Head: Mr G J Thompson
Type: Boys Day 7–13
Fees: (September 06) Day £11331

ST PAUL'S SCHOOL

Lonsdale Road, Barnes, London
SW13 9JT
Tel: (020) 8748 9162
Fax: (020) 8746 5353
Email: hmcc@stpaulsschool.org.uk
Head: Dr Martin Stephen
Type: Boys Day and Boarding
13–18
No of boarders: F40 W40
Fees: (September 06) F/WB £21681
Day £14568

SW14

TOWER HOUSE SCHOOL

188 Sheen Lane, London
SW14 8LF
Tel: (020) 8876 3323
Fax: (020) 8876 3321
Head: Mrs J Compton-Howlett
Type: Boys Day 4–13
No of pupils: 186
Fees: On application

SW15

HURLINGHAM PRIVATE SCHOOL

122 Putney Bridge Road, Putney,
London SW15 2NQ
Tel: (020) 8874 7186
Fax: (020) 8875 0372
Email: admissions@
    hurlinghamschool.co.uk
Head: Mrs D Baker
Type: Co-educational Day 4–11
No of pupils: B95 G135
Fees: (September 05)
Day £8145–£8745

IBSTOCK PLACE SCHOOL

Clarence Lane, Roehampton,
London SW15 5PY
Tel: (020) 8876 9991
Fax: (020) 8878 4897
Email: registrar@
    ibstockplaceschool.co.uk
Head: Mrs A Sylvester Johnson
Type: Co-educational Day 3–18
No of pupils: B400 G355
Fees: (September 05)
Day £4500–£11610

LION HOUSE SCHOOL

The Old Methodist Hall,
Gwendolen Avenue, London
SW15 6EH
Tel: (020) 8780 9446
Fax: (020) 8789 3331
Email: office@
    lionhouseschool.co.uk
Head: Miss H J Luard
Type: Co-educational Day 3–8
No of pupils: B51 G54
Fees: (September 06)
Day £2985–£8895

THE MERLIN SCHOOL

4 Carlton Drive, Putney Hill,
London SW15 2BZ
Tel: (020) 8788 2769
Fax: (020) 8789 5227
Email: secretary@merlinschool.net
Head: Mrs K Prest
Type: Co-educational Day 4–8
No of pupils: 170
Fees: On application

PROSPECT HOUSE SCHOOL*

75 Putney Hill, London SW15 3NT
Tel: (020) 8780 0456
Fax: (020) 8780 3010
Email: info@prospechs.org.uk
Head: Mrs D Barratt
Type: Co-educational Day 3–11
No of pupils: B100 G100
Fees: (September 06)
Day £4800–£10410

PUTNEY HIGH SCHOOL GDST

35 Putney Hill, London SW15 6BH
Tel: (020) 8788 4886
Fax: (020) 8789 8068
Email: putneyhigh@put.gdst.net
Head: Dr D V Lodge
Type: Girls Day 4–18
No of pupils: 870
Fees: (September 06)
Day £8055–£10233

PUTNEY PARK SCHOOL*

11 Woodborough Road, Putney,
London SW15 6PY
Tel: (020) 8788 8316
Fax: (020) 8780 2376
Email: office@
putneypark.london.sch.uk
Head: Mrs Ruth Mann
Type: Co-educational Day
Boys 4–8 Girls 4–16
No of pupils: B58 G214
Fees: (September 06)
Day £2775–£3170

SW16

STREATHAM AND CLAPHAM HIGH SCHOOL

42 Abbotswood Road, London
SW16 1AW
Tel: (020) 8677 8400
Fax: (020) 8677 2001
Email: enquiry@shc.gdst-net
Head: Mrs S Mitchell
Type: Girls Day 3–18 (Boys 3–5)
No of pupils: B1 G808
Fees: On application

WALDORF SCHOOL OF SOUTH WEST LONDON

Woodfields, Abbotswood Road,
London SW16 1AP
Tel: (020) 8769 6587
Fax: (020) 8677 5334
Email: info@waldorf-swlondon.org
Head: Ms T Coutinho
Type: Co-educational Day 4–14
No of pupils: B55 G45
Fees: (September 06)
Day £3201–£4584

SW17

EVELINE DAY SCHOOL

14 Trinity Crescent, Upper
Tooting, London SW17 7AE
Tel: (020) 8672 4673
Fax: (020) 8672 7259
Head: Ms E Drut
Type: Co-educational Day 3–11
No of pupils: B34 G41
Fees: On application

FINTON HOUSE SCHOOL

171 Trinity Road, London
SW17 7HL
Tel: (020) 8682 0921
Fax: (020) 8767 5017
Email: admissions@
fintonhouse.org.uk
Head: Mr A Floyd
Type: Co-educational Day 4–11
No of pupils: B130 G180
Fees: (September 06)
Day £9225–£10200

SW18

THE ROCHE SCHOOL*

11 Frogmore, Wandsworth,
London SW18 1HW
Tel: (020) 8877 0823
Fax: (020) 8875 1156
Email: office@
therocheschool.co.uk
Head: Dr J Roche
Type: Co-educational Day 3–11
No of pupils: B88 G86
Fees: (September 06)
Day £4500–£8910

SW19

DONHEAD PREP SCHOOL

33 Edge Hill, Wimbledon, London
SW19 4NP
Tel: (020) 8946 7000
Fax: (020) 8947 1219
Email: office@donhead.org.uk
Head: Mr G C McGrath
Type: Boys Day 4–11
No of pupils: 193
Fees: (September 06) Day £6420

KING'S COLLEGE JUNIOR SCHOOL

Southside, Wimbledon Common,
London SW19 4TT
Tel: (020) 8255 5335
Fax: (020) 8255 5339
Email: jsadmissions@kcs.org.uk
Head: Mr J A Evans
Type: Boys Day 7–13
No of pupils: 460
Fees: On application

KING'S COLLEGE SCHOOL

Wimbledon Common, London
SW19 4TT
Tel: (020) 8255 5352
Fax: (020) 8255 5357
Email: admissions@kcs.org.uk
Head: Mr A C V Evans
Type: Boys Day 13–18
No of pupils: 752
Fees: (September 06) Day £13650

THE STUDY PREPARATORY SCHOOL

Camp Road, Wimbledon
Common, London SW19 4UN
Tel: (020) 8947 6969
Fax: (020) 8944 5975
Email: wilberforce@
thestudyprep.co.uk
Head: Mrs J Nicol
Type: Girls Day 4–11
No of pupils: 320
Fees: (September 06) Day £8685

WILLINGTON SCHOOL

Worcester Road, Wimbledon,
London SW19 7QQ
Tel: (020) 8944 7020
Fax: (020) 8944 9596
Email: office@
willingtonschool.co.uk
Head: Mr Graham Hill
Type: Boys Day 4–13
No of pupils: 210
Fees: (September 06)
Day £7050–£8250

WIMBLEDON COMMON PREPARATORY SCHOOL

113 Ridgway, Wimbledon,
London SW19 4TA
Tel: (020) 8946 1001
Fax: (020) 8946 1001
Email: info@
wimbledoncommonprep.co.uk
Head: Mr N J Worsey
Type: Boys Day 4–8
No of pupils: 130
Fees: (September 06)
Day £5070–£5550

WIMBLEDON HIGH SCHOOL GDST

Mansel Road, London SW19 4AB
Tel: (020) 8971 0900
Fax: (020) 8971 0901
Email: info@wim.gdst.net
Head: Mrs P H Wilkes
Type: Girls Day 4–18
No of pupils: 900
Fees: On application

England – London

SW20

HALL SCHOOL WIMBLEDON
17 The Downs (Senior School),
Wimbledon, London SW20 8HF
Tel: (020) 8879 9200
Fax: (020) 8946 0864
Email: enquiries@
    hallschoolwimbledon.co.uk
Head: Mr T Hobbs and Mr J Hobbs
Type: Co-educational Day 4–16
No of pupils: B320 G280
Fees: (September 05)
Day £7317–£9315

THE NORWEGIAN SCHOOL
28 Arterberry Road, Wimbledon,
London SW20 8AH
Tel: (020) 8947 6617/6627
Fax: (020) 8944 7345
Email: dnslondon@aol.com
Head: Mr A Larsen
Type: Co-educational Day 3–16
No of pupils: 101
Fees: On application

THE ROWANS SCHOOL
19 Drax Avenue, Wimbledon,
London SW20 0EG
Tel: (020) 8946 8220
Fax: (020) 8944 0822
Email: therowansschool@
    btinternet.com
Head: Mrs E Tyrrell
Type: Co-educational Day 3–8
No of pupils: B75 G50
Fees: (September 06)
Day £2805–£5715

URSULINE PREPARATORY SCHOOL
18 The Downs, London SW20 8HR
Tel: (020) 8947 0859
Fax: (020) 8947 0885
Email: ursulineprpsch@aol.com
Head: Mrs C Grogan
Type: Girls Day 3–11 (Boys 3–7)
No of pupils: B76 G172
Fees: On application

W1

ALBEMARLE INDEPENDENT COLLEGE
18 Dunraven Street, London
W1K 7FE
Tel: (020) 7409 7273
Fax: (020) 7629 9146
Email: admin@albemarle.org.uk
Head: Mr J Eytle and
Miss B Mellon
Type: Co-educational Day 14–19
No of pupils: B82 G73
Fees: (September 06)
Day £12000–£13440

DAVIES LAING AND DICK*
100 Marylebone Lane, London
W1U 2QB
Tel: (020) 7935 8411
Fax: (020) 7935 0755
Email: dld@dld.org
Head: Ms E Rickards
Type: Co-educational Day 14–19
No of pupils: B185 G185
Fees: (September 06)
Day £2680–£15600

GREAT BEGINNINGS MONTESSORI SCHOOL
82a Chiltern Street, Marylebone,
London W1U 5AQ
Tel: (020) 7486 2276
Head: Mrs W Innes
Type: Co-educational Day 2–6
No of pupils: B30 G30
Fees: On application

PORTLAND PLACE SCHOOL
56–58 Portland Place, London
W1B 1NJ
Tel: (020) 7307 8700
Fax: (020) 7436 2676
Email: admin@
    portland-place.co.uk
Head: Mr R Walker
Type: Co-educational Day 11–18
No of pupils: B239 G83
Fees: (September 05) Day £10950

QUEEN'S COLLEGE
43–49 Harley Street, London
W1G 8BT
Tel: (020) 7291 7000
Fax: (020) 7291 7099
Email: queens@qcl.org.uk
Head: Miss M M Connell
Type: Girls Day 11–18
No of pupils: 372
Fees: (September 05) Day £11400

QUEEN'S COLLEGE PREP SCHOOL
61 Portland Place, London
W1B 1QP
Tel: (020) 7291 0660
Fax: (020) 7291 0669
Email: tbrook@qcps.org.uk
Head: Mrs J Davies
Type: Girls Day 4–11
No of pupils: 135
Fees: On application

SOUTHBANK INTERNATIONAL SCHOOL, WESTMINSTER*
63–65 Portland Place, London
W1B 1QR
Tel: (020) 7243 3803
Fax: (020) 7727 3290
Email: admissions@southbank.org
Head: Mr N Hughes and
Mr T Hedger
Type: Co-educational Day 11–18
No of pupils: B128 G137
Fees: (September 06)
Day £16800–£18600

W2

CONNAUGHT HOUSE
47 Connaught Square, London
W2 2HL
Tel: (020) 7262 8830
Fax: (020) 7262 0781
Head: Mr & Mrs F Hampton
Type: Co-educational Day
Boys 4–8 Girls 4–11
No of pupils: B35 G35
Fees: On application

THE HAMPSHIRE SCHOOLS (KENSINGTON GARDENS)
9 Queensborough Terrace,
London W2 3TB
Tel: (020) 7584 3297
Fax: (020) 7584 9733
Email: hampshire@indschool.org
Head: Mr A G Bray
Type: Co-educational Day 4–13
No of pupils: B80 G80
Fees: On application

England – London

LANSDOWNE COLLEGE*

40–44 Bark Place, London W2 4AT
Tel: (020) 7616 4400
Fax: (020) 7616 4401
Email: education@
  lansdownecollege.com
Head: Mr H Templeton
Type: Co-educational Day 14–19
No of pupils: B105 G95
Fees: (September 06)
Day £2650–£13950

PEMBRIDGE HALL

18 Pembridge Square, London
W2 4EH
Tel: (020) 7229 0121
Fax: (020) 7792 1086
Head: Mrs E Marsden
Type: Girls Day 4–11
No of pupils: 250
Fees: (September 05) Day £11001

RAVENSTONE HOUSE PRE-PREPARATORY AND NURSERY

The Long Garden, Albion Street,
Marble Arch, London W2 2AX
Tel: (020) 7262 1190
Fax: (020) 7724 6980
Email: info@
  ravenstonehouse.co.uk
Head: Mrs A Saunders
Type: Co-educational Day 0–7
No of pupils: B50 G50
Fees: On application

WETHERBY SCHOOL*

11 Pembridge Square, London
W2 4ED
Tel: (020) 7727 9581
Fax: (020) 7221 8827
Email: learn@
  WetherbySchool.co.uk
Head: Mrs J Aviss
Type: Boys Day 4–8
No of pupils: 235
Fees: (September 05) Day £10560

W3

BARBARA SPEAKE STAGE SCHOOL

East Acton Lane, London W3 7EG
Tel: (020) 8743 1306
Fax: (020) 8743 1306
Email: cpuk@aol.com or
  speakekids3@aol.com
Head: Miss B M Speake and
Mr D R Speake
Type: Co-educational Day 3–16
No of pupils: B45 G90
Fees: (September 06)
Day £4200–£4500

INTERNATIONAL SCHOOL OF LONDON*

139 Gunnersbury Avenue, London
W3 8LG
Tel: (020) 8992 5823
Fax: (020) 8993 7012
Email: mail@islondon.com
Head: Mr A Makarem
Type: Co-educational Day
Boys 3–19 Girls 3–18
No of pupils: B163 G123
Fees: (September 06)
Day £12000–£16500

THE JAPANESE SCHOOL

87 Creffield Road, Acton, London
W3 9PU
Tel: (020) 8993 7145
Fax: (020) 8992 1224
Head: Mr F Fudo
Type: Co-educational Day 6–15
No of pupils: B320 G260
Fees: On application

KING FAHAD ACADEMY

Bromyard Avenue, East Acton,
London W3 7HD
Tel: (020) 8743 0131
Fax: (020) 8749 7085
Email: headmaster@thekfa.org.uk
Head: Mr Mansour Ghazali
Type: Co-educational Day 5–18
No of pupils: B300 G350
Fees: On application

W4

THE ARTS EDUCATIONAL SCHOOL*

Cone Ripman House, 14 Bath
Road, Chiswick, London W4 1LY
Tel: (020) 8987 6600
Fax: (020) 8987 6601
Email: head@artsed.co.uk
Head: Mr R J Luckham
Type: Co-educational Day 11–18
No of pupils: B51 G99
Fees: (September 06)
Day £9324–£10156

CHISWICK AND BEDFORD PARK PREPARATORY SCHOOL

Priory House, Priory Avenue,
Bedford Park, London W4 1TX
Tel: (020) 8994 1804
Fax: (020) 8995 3603
Email: cbpschool@aol.com
Head: Mrs C A Sunderland
Type: Co-educational Day
Boys 4–8 Girls 4–11
No of pupils: B70 G115
Fees: On application

THE FALCONS SCHOOL FOR BOYS

2 Burnaby Gardens, Chiswick,
London W4 3DT
Tel: (020) 8747 8393
Fax: (020) 8995 3903
Email: admin@falconsboys.co.uk
Head: Mr B H Evans
Type: Boys Day 3–8
No of pupils: 200
Fees: (September 05)
Day £4575–£8985

HEATHFIELD HOUSE SCHOOL

Turnham Green Church Hall,
Chiswick, London W4 4JU
Tel: (020) 8994 3385
Fax: (020) 8995 0255
Email: enquiries@
  heathfieldhouse.co.uk
Head: Mrs Caroline Goodsman
Type: Co-educational Day 4–11
Fees: (September 06)
Day £5700–£6300

ORCHARD HOUSE SCHOOL*
16 Newton Grove, Bedford Park,
London W4 1LB
Tel: (020) 8742 8544
Fax: (020) 8742 8522
Email: info@orchardhs.org.uk
Head: Mrs S A B Hobbs
Type: Co-educational Day
Boys 4–8 Girls 4–11
No of pupils: B80 G140
Fees: (September 06)
Day £4860–£10080

W5

ASTON HOUSE SCHOOL
1 Aston Road, Ealing, London
W5 2RL
Tel: (020) 8566 7300
Fax: (020) 8566 7499
Email: ahs@happychild.co.uk
Head: Mrs P Seabrook
Type: Co-educational Day 3–11
No of pupils: B75 G75
Fees: (September 05)
Day £5700–£7110

CLIFTON LODGE PREPARATORY SCHOOL*
8 Mattock Lane, Ealing, London
W5 5BG
Tel: (020) 8579 3662
Fax: (020) 8810 1332
Email: cliftonlodge@
   btinternet.com
Head: Mr D A P Blumlein
Type: Boys Day 4–13
No of pupils: 180
Fees: On application

DURSTON HOUSE
12–14 & 26 Castlebar Road,
Ealing, London W5 2DR
Tel: (020) 8991 6532
Fax: (020) 8991 6547
Email: info@
   durstonhouse.ealing.sch.uk
Head: Mr N I Kendrick
Type: Boys Day 4–13
No of pupils: 400
Fees: (September 06)
Day £7770–£10440

EALING INDEPENDENT COLLEGE*
83 New Broadway, Ealing, London
W5 5AL
Tel: (020) 8579 6668
Fax: (020) 8567 8688
Email: ealingcollege@
   btconnect.com
Head: Dr I Moores
Type: Co-educational Day
Boys 13–20 Girls 14–20
No of pupils: B45 G45
Fees: (September 06)
Day £1635–£11025

THE FALCONS SCHOOL FOR GIRLS
15 Gunnersbury Avenue, Ealing,
London W5 3XD
Tel: (020) 8992 5189
Fax: (020) 8752 1635
Email: cheath@falconsgirls.co.uk
Head: Mr B H Evans
Type: Girls Day 4–11
No of pupils: 120
Fees: On application

HARVINGTON SCHOOL
20 Castlebar Road, Ealing, London
W5 2DS
Tel: (020) 8997 1583
Fax: (020) 8810 4756
Email: admin@
   harvingtonschool.com
Head: Dr F Meek
Type: Girls Day 3–16 (Boys 3–5)
No of pupils: B14 G210
Fees: (September 05)
Day £5925–£7710

ST AUGUSTINE'S PRIORY
Hillcrest Road, Ealing, London
W5 2JL
Tel: (020) 8997 2022
Fax: (020) 8810 6501
Email: admin@
   saintaugustinespriory.org.uk
Head: Mrs F Gumley-Mason
Type: Girls Day 4–18
No of pupils: 510
Fees: On application

ST BENEDICT'S JUNIOR SCHOOL
5 Montpelier Avenue, Ealing,
London W5 2XP
Tel: (020) 8862 2050
Fax: (020) 8862 2058
Email: jssecretary@
   stbenedicts.org.uk
Head: Mr R G Simmons
Type: Co-educational Day
Boys 3–11 Girls 3–5
No of pupils: B240 G6
Fees: (September 06) Day £9240

ST BENEDICT'S SCHOOL
54 Eaton Rise, Ealing, London
W5 2ES
Tel: (020) 8862 2254
Fax: (020) 8862 2199
Email: headmaster@
   stbenedicts.org.uk
Head: Mr C J Cleugh
Type: Boys Day 11–18 (Co-ed VIth
Form)
No of pupils: B616 G40
Fees: (September 06) Day £10500

W6

BUTE HOUSE PREPARATORY SCHOOL FOR GIRLS
Luxemburg Gardens, London
W6 7EA
Tel: (020) 7603 7381
Fax: (020) 7371 3446
Email: mail@butehouse.co.uk
Head: Mrs S Salvidant
Type: Girls Day 4–11
Fees: (September 06) Day £9735

ECOLE FRANCAISE JACQUES PREVERT
59 Brook Green, London W6 7BE
Tel: (020) 7602 6871
Fax: (020) 7602 3162
Email: info@ecoleprevert.org.uk
Head: Mr R Salva
Type: Co-educational Day 4–11
No of pupils: B136 G128
Fees: On application

THE GODOLPHIN AND LATYMER SCHOOL
Iffley Road, Hammersmith,
London W6 0PG
Tel: (020) 8741 1936
Fax: (020) 8746 3352
Email: registrar@
godolphinandlatymer.com
Head: Miss M Rudland
Type: Girls Day 11–18
No of pupils: 707
Fees: On application

LATYMER PREP SCHOOL*
36 Upper Mall, Hammersmith,
London W6 9TA
Tel: (020) 8748 0303
Fax: (020) 8741 4916
Email: mlp@latymerprep.org
Head: Mr S P Dorrian
Type: Co-educational Day 7–11
Fees: (September 06) Day £11205

LATYMER UPPER SCHOOL*
King Street, Hammersmith,
London W6 9LR
Tel: (020) 8741 1851
Fax: (020) 8748 5212
Email: registrar@
latymer-upper.org
Head: Mr P J Winter
Type: Co-educational Day 11–18
No of pupils: B797 G274
Fees: (September 06) Day £12465

LE HERISSON
c/o The Methodist Church,
Rivercourt Road, Hammersmith,
London W6 9JT
Tel: (020) 8563 7664
Fax: (020) 8563 7664
Email: administration@
leherissonschool.co.uk
Head: Ms B Rios
Type: Co-educational Day 2–6
No of pupils: 64
Fees: On application

RAVENSCOURT PARK PREPARATORY SCHOOL
16 Ravenscourt Avenue, London
W6 0SL
Tel: (020) 8846 9153
Fax: (020) 8846 9413
Email: secretary@rpps.co.uk
Head: Mr R Relton
Type: Co-educational Day 4–11
No of pupils: B127 G134
Fees: (September 06) Day £10653

RAVENSCOURT THEATRE SCHOOL
Tandy House, 30–40 Dalling
Road, London W6 0JB
Tel: (020) 8741 0707
Fax: (020) 8741 1786
Head: Mr J Roper
Type: Co-educational Day 7–16
No of pupils: B39 G56
Fees: On application

ST PAUL'S GIRLS' SCHOOL
Brook Green, London W6 7BS
Tel: (020) 7603 2288
Fax: (020) 7602 9932
Email: admissions@spgs.org
Head: Ms C Faarr
Type: Girls Day 11–18
Fees: (September 06) Day £12732

W8

ABINGDON HOUSE SCHOOL
4–6 Abingdon Road, London
W8 6AF
Tel: (0845) 230 0426
Fax: (020) 7361 0751
Email: ahs@
abingdonhouseschool.co.uk
Head: Mr N Rees
Type: Co-educational Day 4–9
No of pupils: B15 G2
Fees: On application

ASHBOURNE INDEPENDENT SIXTH FORM COLLEGE*
17 Old Court Place, Kensington,
London W8 4PL
Tel: (020) 7937 3858
Fax: (020) 7937 2207
Email: admin@
ashbournecollege.co.uk
Head: Mr M J H Kirby
Type: Co-educational Day and
Boarding Boys 14–19 Girls 16–19
No of pupils: B85 G90
Fees: (September 05) Day £13500

ASHBOURNE MIDDLE SCHOOL*
17 Old Court Place, Kensington,
London W8 4PL
Tel: (020) 7937 3858
Fax: (020) 7937 2207
Email: admin@
ashbournecollege.co.uk
Head: Mr M J A Kirby and
Ms C S Brahams
Type: Co-educational Day 12–16
No of pupils: B14 G11
Fees: On application

HAWKESDOWN HOUSE SCHOOL*
27 Edge Street, Kensington,
London W8 7PN
Tel: (020) 7727 9090
Fax: (020) 7727 9988
Email: admin@hawkesdown.co.uk
Head: Mrs C J Leslie
Type: Boys Day 3–8
No of pupils: 130
Fees: (September 06)
Day £9375–£10950

THOMAS'S PREPARATORY SCHOOL
17–19 Cottesmore Gardens,
London W8 5PR
Tel: (020) 7361 6500
Fax: (020) 7361 6501
Email: Dmaine@thomas-s.co.uk
Head: Mrs D Maine
Type: Co-educational Day 4–11
No of pupils: B158 G172
Fees: (September 06)
Day £11805–£12840

W10

BALES COLLEGE
742 Harrow Road, London
W10 4AA
Tel: (020) 8960 5899
Fax: (020) 8960 8269
Email: info@balescollege.co.uk
Head: Mr W B Moore
Type: Co-educational Day and
Boarding 11–19
No of pupils: B50 G50
No of boarders: F18 W2
Fees: (September 05) F/WB £13500
Day £6150–£6855

BASSETT HOUSE SCHOOL*
60 Bassett Road, London W10 6JP
Tel: (020) 8969 0313
Fax: (020) 8960 9624
Email: info@bassetths.org.uk
Head: Mrs A Harris
Type: Co-educational Day
Boys 3–8 Girls 3–11
No of pupils: B58 G90
Fees: (September 06)
Day £5190–£10710

England – London

INSTITUTO ESPANOL VICENTE CANADA BLANCH

317 Portobello Road, London
W10 5SY
Tel: (020) 8969 2664
Fax: (020) 8968 9432
Head: Mr A Vitria
Type: Co-educational Day 4–19
No of pupils: B208 G227
Fees: On application

THE LLOYD WILLIAMSON SCHOOL*

12 Telford Road, London W10 5SH
Tel: (020) 8962 0345
Fax: (020) 8962 0345
Email: office@
   lloydwilliamson.demon.co.uk
Head: Mrs L Meyer and
Mr A Williams
Type: Co-educational Day 1–13
No of pupils: B60 G60
Fees: (September 06)
Day £8100–£11250

W11

DAVID GAME COLLEGE

69 Notting Hill Gate, London
W11 3JS
Tel: (020) 7221 6665
Fax: (020) 7243 1730
Email: nhg@
   davidgame-group.com
Head: Mr D Game
Type: Co-educational Day and
Boarding 15–25
No of pupils: B230 G220
No of boarders: F150
Fees: On application

NORLAND PLACE SCHOOL

162–166 Holland Park Avenue,
London W11 4UH
Tel: (020) 7603 9103
Fax: (020) 7603 0648
Email: office@norlandplace.com
Head: Mr P Mattar
Type: Co-educational Day
Boys 4–8 Girls 4–11
No of pupils: B90 G150
Fees: (September 06)
Day £8715–£11001

NOTTING HILL PREPARATORY SCHOOL

95 Lancaster Road, London
W11 1QQ
Tel: (020) 7221 0727
Fax: (020) 7221 0332
Email: admin@
   nottinghillprep.com
Head: Mrs J Cameron
Type: Co-educational Day 5–13
No of pupils: B93 G102
Fees: (September 06) Day £3650

SOUTHBANK INTERNATIONAL SCHOOL, KENSINGTON*

36–38 Kensington Park Road,
London W11 3BU
Tel: (020) 7243 3803
Fax: (020) 7727 3290
Email: admissions@southbank.org
Head: Mr N Hughes and
Mr G Winning
Type: Co-educational Day 3–11
No of pupils: B100 G95
Fees: (September 06)
Day £9630–£15600

TABERNACLE SCHOOL

32 St Ann's Villas, London
W11 4RS
Tel: (08702) 408207
Fax: (08702) 408207
Head: Mrs P Wilson
Type: Co-educational Day 3–18
No of pupils: B16 G31
Fees: On application

THE WALMER ROAD SCHOOL

221 Walmer Road, London
W11 4EY
Tel: (020) 7229 2928
Fax: (020) 7313 5258
Head: Mr P Moody
Type: Co-educational Day 14–16
No of pupils: B6 G1
Fees: On application

WETHERBY PREPARATORY SCHOOL*

19 Pembridge Villas, London
W11 3EP
Tel: (020) 7243 0243
Fax: (020) 7313 5244
Email: admin@
   wetherbyprep.co.uk
Head: Mr R Greenwood
Type: Boys Day 8–13
No of pupils: 84
Fees: (September 06) Day £11850

W13

AVENUE HOUSE SCHOOL*

70 The Avenue, Ealing, London
W13 8LS
Tel: (020) 8998 9981
Fax: (020) 8991 1533
Email: avenuehouseschool@
   btinternet.com
Head: Mrs C Self
Type: Co-educational Day 3–11
No of pupils: B65 G75
Fees: (September 06)
Day £4500–£7500

EALING COLLEGE UPPER SCHOOL

83 The Avenue, Ealing, London
W13 8JS
Tel: (020) 8248 2312
Fax: (020) 8248 3765
Head: Mr B Webb
Type: Day
No of pupils: B136 G2
Fees: On application

NOTTING HILL AND EALING HIGH SCHOOL GDST

2 Cleveland Road, Ealing, London
W13 8AX
Tel: (020) 8799 8400
Fax: (020) 8810 6891
Email: enquiries@nhehs.gdst.net
Head: Mrs S Whitfield
Type: Girls Day 4–18
No of pupils: 820
Fees: (September 06)
Day £7632–£9810

W14

FULHAM PREP SCHOOL (PREP DEPT)*

Prep Department, 200 Greyhound
Road, London W14 9SD
Tel: (020) 7386 2444
Fax: (020) 7386 2449
Email: prepadmin@
   fulhamprep.co.uk
Head: Mrs J Emmett
Type: Co-educational Day 7–13
No of pupils: B154 G95
Fees: (September 06) Day £11235

HOLLAND PARK PRE-PREPARATORY SCHOOL
5 & 9 Holland Road, London
W14 8HJ
Tel: (020) 7602 9066
Head: Miss K Mason and
Ms Eleni Tsakanika
Type: Co-educational Day 0–8
Fees: On application

ST JAMES INDEPENDENT SCHOOL FOR BOYS
Earsby Street, Nr. Kensington
Olympia, London W14 8SH
Tel: (020) 7348 1777
Fax: (020) 7348 1790
Email: juniorschools@
stjamesschools.co.uk
Head: Mr P Moss
Type: Boys Day 4–10
No of pupils: 117
Fees: (September 06)
Day £8070–£8550

ST JAMES INDEPENDENT SCHOOL FOR GIRLS (JUNIORS)
Earsby Street, Olympia, London
W14 8SH
Tel: (020) 7348 1777
Fax: (020) 7348 1790
Email: stjamesschools@
stjamesschools.co.uk
Head: Mr P Moss
Type: Girls Day 4–10
No of pupils: 151
Fees: (September 06)
Day £8070–£8550

ST JAMES INDEPENDENT SCHOOL FOR SENIOR GIRLS
Earsby Street, London W14 8SH
Tel: (020) 7348 1777
Fax: (020) 7348 1717
Email: enquiries@
stjamessengirls.org.uk
Head: Mrs L A Hyde
Type: Girls Day 10–18
No of pupils: 260
Fees: (September 06)
Day £9360–£9780

WC2

ROYAL BALLET SCHOOL
46 Floral Street, London
WC2E 9DA
Tel: (020) 7836 8899
Fax: (020) 7845 7080
Email: johnm@
royalballetschool.co.uk
Head: Mr N Foster
Type: Co-educational Boarding
and Day 11–18
No of pupils: B93 G109
No of boarders: F125
Fees: On application

THE URDANG ACADEMY OF BALLET
20–22 Shelton Street, London
WC2H 9JJ
Tel: (020) 7836 5709
Fax: (020) 7836 7010
Email: info@
theurdangacademy.com
Head: Miss S Goumain
Type: Co-educational Day 16–23
No of pupils: B27 G114
Fees: On application

GREATER MANCHESTER

AUDENSHAW

JOSEPH RAYNER INDEPENDENT SCHOOL
Red Hall, Audenshaw Road,
Audenshaw, Greater Manchester
M34 5HT
Tel: (0161) 355 1434
Head: Mr G Hopkinson
Type: Co-educational Day 3–11
No of pupils: B2 G12
Fees: On application

BOLTON

AL JAMIAH AL ISLAMIYYAH
Hospital Road, Bromley Cross,
Bolton, Greater Manchester
BL7 9PY
Tel: (01204) 301550
Head: Y Namji
Type: Boys Day 13–16
No of pupils: 150
Fees: On application

ECCLES

BRANWOOD PREPARATORY SCHOOL
Stafford Road, Monton, Eccles,
Greater Manchester M30 9HN
Tel: (0161) 789 1054
Fax: (0161) 789 0561
Email: mail@
branwoodschool.co.uk
Head: Mr W M Howard
Type: Co-educational Day 3–11
No of pupils: B95 G95
Fees: (September 06)
Day £3399–£4449

CLARENDON COTTAGE SCHOOL
Ivy Bank House, Half Edge Lane,
Eccles, Greater Manchester
M30 9BJ
Tel: (0161) 950 7868
Fax: (0161) 661 3822
Email: clarendon.cottage@
dial.pipex.com
Head: Mrs E Bagnall
Type: Co-educational Day 1–11
No of pupils: B120 G100
Fees: On application

MONTON PREP SCHOOL WITH MONTESSORI NURSERIES
The School House, Francis Street,
Monton, Eccles, Greater
Manchester M30 9PR
Tel: (0161) 789 0472
Head: Miss D S Bradburn
Type: Co-educational Day 2–13
No of pupils: B74 G80
Fees: On application

England – London/Greater Manchester

MANCHESTER

ABBEY COLLEGE
Cheapside, King Street,
Manchester, Greater Manchester
M2 4WG
Tel: (0161) 817 2700
Fax: (0161) 817 2705
Email: admin@
   abbeymanchester.co.uk
Head: Mrs J Thomas
Type: Co-educational Day 15–21
No of pupils: B90 G90
Fees: On application

ABBOTSFORD PREPARATORY SCHOOL
211 Flixton Road, Urmston,
Manchester, Greater Manchester
M41 5PR
Tel: (0161) 748 3261
Fax: (0161) 748 7961
Email: secretary@
   abbotsford-prep.trafford.sch.uk
Head: Mr C J Davies
Type: Co-educational Day 3–11
No of pupils: B60 G64
Fees: (September 05)
Day £4056–£4314

BRIDGEWATER SCHOOL
Drywood Hall, Worsley Road,
Worsley, Manchester, Greater
Manchester M28 2WQ
Tel: (0161) 794 1463
Fax: (0161) 794 3519
Email: admin@
   bridgewater.school.org.uk
Head: Ms G A Shannon-Little
Type: Co-educational Day 3–18
No of pupils: B268 G248
Fees: On application

CHETHAM'S SCHOOL OF MUSIC
Long Millgate, Manchester,
Greater Manchester M3 1SB
Tel: (0161) 834 9644
Fax: (0161) 839 3609
Head: Mrs C J Hickman
Type: Co-educational Boarding
and Day 8–18
No of pupils: B140 G150
No of boarders: F229
Fees: On application

KASSIM DARWISH GRAMMAR SCHOOL FOR BOYS
Hartley Hall, Alexandra Road
South, Chorlton-cum-Hardy,
Manchester, Greater Manchester
M16 8NH
Tel: (0161) 860 7676
Fax: (0161) 860 0011
Email: kdgb_ad@hotmail.com
Head: Mrs M Mohamed
Type: Boys Day 11–16
No of pupils: 166
Fees: (September 05) Day £4820

KING OF KINGS SCHOOL
142 Dantzic Street, Manchester,
Greater Manchester M4 4DN
Tel: (0161) 834 4214
Head: Mrs B Lewis
Type: Co-educational Day 3–16
No of pupils: B14 G10
Fees: On application

LIGHTHOUSE CHRISTIAN SCHOOL
193 Ashley Lane, Moston,
Manchester, Greater Manchester
M9 4NQ
Tel: (0161) 205 0957
Fax: (0161) 256 3973
Head: Mr Akintayo Akinyele
Type: Co-educational Day 2–14
No of pupils: B12 G6
Fees: On application

THE MANCHESTER GRAMMAR SCHOOL
Old Hall Lane, Manchester,
Greater Manchester M13 0XT
Tel: (0161) 224 7201
Fax: (0161) 257 2446
Email: general@mgs.org
Head: Dr C Ray
Type: Boys Day 11–18
No of pupils: 1440
Fees: (September 06) Day £7770

MANCHESTER HIGH SCHOOL FOR GIRLS
Grangethorpe Road, Manchester,
Greater Manchester M14 6HS
Tel: (0161) 224 0447
Fax: (0161) 224 2255
Email: administration@
   mhsg.manchester.sch.uk
Head: Mrs C Lee-Jones
Type: Girls Day 4–18
No of pupils: 928
Fees: (September 06)
Day £5505–£7728

MANCHESTER ISLAMIC HIGH SCHOOL
55 High Lane, Manchester,
Greater Manchester M21 9FA
Tel: (0161) 881 2127
Fax: (0161) 861 0534
Head: Mrs M Mohamed
Type: Girls Day 11–16
Fees: On application

MANCHESTER MUSLIM PREPARATORY SCHOOL
551 Wilmslow Road, Withington,
Manchester, Greater Manchester
M20 4BA
Tel: (0161) 445 5452
Fax: (0161) 445 2283
Email: muslimprepschool@
   aol.com
Head: Mrs T Amin
Type: Co-educational Day 3–11
No of pupils: B79 G104
Fees: On application

MOOR ALLERTON SCHOOL
131 Barlow Moor Road,
Manchester, Greater Manchester
M20 2PW
Tel: (0161) 445 4521
Fax: (0161) 434 5294
Email: office@moorallertonschool.
   manchester.sch.uk
Head: Mr P S Millard
Type: Co-educational Day 3–11
No of pupils: B100 G98
Fees: (September 06)
Day £5040–£5997

ST BEDE'S COLLEGE
Alexandra Park, Manchester,
Greater Manchester M16 8HX
Tel: (0161) 226 3323
Fax: (0161) 226 3813
Email: enquiries@
   stbedescollege.co.uk
Head: Mr J Byrne
Type: Co-educational Day 4–18
Fees: (September 06)
Day £4797–£7170

WILLIAM HULME'S GRAMMAR SCHOOL
Spring Bridge Road, Manchester,
Greater Manchester M16 8PR
Tel: (0161) 226 2054
Fax: (0161) 232 5544
Email: enquiries@whgs.co.uk
Head: Mr S R Patriarca
Type: Co-educational Day 3–18
No of pupils: B340 G168
Fees: (September 05)
Day £5219–£7472

WITHINGTON GIRLS' SCHOOL

Wellington Road, Fallowfield, Manchester, Greater Manchester M14 6BL
Tel: (0161) 224 1077
Fax: (0161) 248 5377
Email: office@
   withington.manchester.sch.uk
Head: Mrs J D Pickering
Type: Girls Day 7–18
No of pupils: 650
Fees: (September 06)
Day £5631–£7560

PRESTWICH

PRESTWICH PREPARATORY SCHOOL

400 Bury Old Road, Prestwich, Greater Manchester M25 1PZ
Tel: (0161) 773 1223
Head: Miss Shiels and
Mr D R Sheldon
Type: Co-educational Day 2–11
No of pupils: B60 G60
Fees: On application

SALFORD

HUBERT JEWISH HIGH SCHOOL FOR GIRLS

10 Radford Street, Salford, Greater Manchester M7 4NT
Tel: (0161) 792 2118
Head: Rabbi Y Goldblatt
Type: Girls Day 11–18
No of pupils: 165
Fees: On application

MERSEYSIDE

BIRKENHEAD

HIGHFIELD SCHOOL

96 Bidston Road, Oxton, Birkenhead, Merseyside CH43 6TW
Tel: (0151) 652 3708
Fax: (0151) 652 3708
Email: highfield.school@
   btinternet.com
Head: Mrs S Morris
Type: Co-educational Day 2–16
No of pupils: B20 G100
Fees: On application

FORMBY

CLARENCE HIGH SCHOOL

West Lane, Freshfield, Formby, Merseyside L37 7AZ
Tel: (01704) 872151
Fax: (01704) 831001
Head: Mr D McKillop
Type: Co-educational Boarding and Day 9–17
No of pupils: B45 G15
No of boarders: F30
Fees: (September 05)
WB £49890–£74010
Day £36020–£40560

LIVERPOOL

ATHERTON HOUSE SCHOOL

6 Alexandra Road, Crosby, Liverpool, Merseyside L23 7TF
Tel: (0151) 924 5578
Fax: (0151) 924 0421
Email: head@
   athertonhouse.ndo.co.uk
Head: Mrs A Apel
Type: Co-educational Day 2–11
No of pupils: B35 G40
Fees: On application

AUCKLAND COLLEGE

65–67 Parkfield Road, Liverpool, Merseyside L17 4LE
Tel: (0151) 727 0083
Head: Ms G Akaraonye
Type: Co-educational Day 7–18
No of pupils: B98 G74
Fees: On application

BEECHENHURST PREPARATORY SCHOOL

145 Menlove Avenue, Liverpool, Merseyside L18 3EE
Tel: (0151) 722 3279
Fax: (0151) 722 0697
Head: Mrs C Wright
Type: Co-educational Day 3–11
No of pupils: B55 G55
Fees: (September 05) Day £4200

CARLETON HOUSE PREPARATORY SCHOOL

Lyndhurst Road, Mossley Hill, Liverpool, Merseyside L18 8AQ
Tel: (0151) 724 4880
Fax: (0151) 724 6086
Email: carleton@
   carletonhouse.fsbusiness.co.uk
Head: Mr P Andrew
Type: Co-educational Day 4–11
No of pupils: B88 G62
Fees: (September 05) Day £4485

LIVERPOOL COLLEGE

Queens's Drive, Mossley Hill, Liverpool, Merseyside L18 8BG
Tel: (0151) 724 4000
Fax: (0151) 729 0105
Email: admin@
   liverpoolcollege.org.uk
Head: Mr J D B Christian
Type: Co-educational Day 3–18
No of pupils: B518 G355
Fees: On application

MERCHANT TAYLORS' SCHOOL

Liverpool Road, Crosby, Liverpool, Merseyside L23 0QP
Tel: (0151) 928 5759
Fax: (0151) 949 9300
Email: info@
   merchanttaylors.sefton.sch.uk
Head: Mr David Cook
Type: Boys Day 4–18
No of pupils: 830
Fees: (September 06)
Day £5211–£7254

MERCHANT TAYLORS' SCHOOL FOR GIRLS

Liverpool Road, Crosby, Liverpool,
Merseyside L23 5SP
Tel: (0151) 924 3140
Fax: (0151) 932 1461
Email: office@mtgs.co.uk
Head: Mrs L A Robinson
Type: Girls Day 4–18 (Boys 4–7)
No of pupils: 817
Fees: (September 06)
Day £5211–£7254

RUNNYMEDE ST EDWARD'S SCHOOL

North Drive, Sandfield Park,
Liverpool, Merseyside L12 1LE
Tel: (0151) 281 2300
Fax: (0151) 281 4900
Email: contact@
     runnymede-school.org.uk
Head: Miss S Carter
Type: Co-educational Day 3–11
No of pupils: B190 G140
Fees: (September 06)
Day £5300–£5600

ST MARY'S COLLEGE

Crosby, Liverpool, Merseyside
L23 5TW
Tel: (0151) 924 3926
Fax: (0151) 932 0363
Email: office@
     stmarys.lpool.sch.uk
Head: Mrs J Marsh
Type: Co-educational Day 0–18
No of pupils: B479 G402
Fees: (September 06)
Day £4587–£7176

STREATHAM HOUSE SCHOOL

Victoria Road West,
Blundellsands, Liverpool,
Merseyside L23 8UQ
Tel: (0151) 924 1514
Fax: (0151) 931 2780
Head: Mrs C Baxter
Type: Girls Day 2–16 (Boys 2–11)
No of pupils: B22 G139
Fees: On application

NEWTON-LE-WILLOWS

NEWTON BANK SCHOOL

34 High Street,
Newton-Le-Willows, Merseyside
WA12 9SN
Tel: (01925) 225979
Head: Mrs J Butler
Type: Co-educational Day 2–10
No of pupils: B25 G38
Fees: On application

PRENTON

REDCOURT- ST ANSELMS

7 Devonshire Place, Prenton,
Merseyside CH43 1TX
Tel: (0151) 652 5228
Fax: (0151) 653 5883
Email: admin@
     redcourt.wirral.sch.uk
Head: Mr K S Davey
Type: Co-educational Day 3–11
No of pupils: B118 G109
Fees: (September 06) Day £3948

PRESCOT

TOWER COLLEGE

Mill Lane, Rainhill, Prescot,
Merseyside L35 6NE
Tel: (0151) 426 4333
Fax: (0151) 426 3338
Email: towercollege@lineone.net
Head: Miss R J Oxley
Type: Co-educational Day 3–16
No of pupils: B305 G308
Fees: (September 06)
Day £4260–£5280

SOUTHPORT

SUNNYMEDE SCHOOL

4 Westcliffe Road, Birkdale,
Southport, Merseyside PR8 2BN
Tel: (01704) 568593
Fax: (01704) 551745
Email: sunnymedeschool@
     btinternet.com
Head: Mr S J Pattinson
Type: Co-educational Day 3–11
No of pupils: B65 G62
Fees: (September 06)
Day £4590–£5790

TOWER DENE PREPARATORY SCHOOL

59–76 Cambridge Road,
Southport, Merseyside PR9 9RH
Tel: (01704) 228556
Fax: (01704) 228556
Email: towerdeneschool@aol.com
Head: Mr J Preston
Type: Co-educational Day 0–11
No of pupils: B48 G52
Fees: On application

WIRRAL

AVALON PREPARATORY SCHOOL

Caldy Road, West Kirby, Wirral,
Merseyside CH48 2HE
Tel: (0151) 625 6993
Fax: (0151) 625 0332
Email: schooloffice@
     avalon-school.co.uk
Head: Dr B Scott
Type: Co-educational Day 2–11
No of pupils: B104 G102
Fees: On application

BIRKENHEAD HIGH SCHOOL GDST

86 Devonshire Place, Prenton,
Wirral, Merseyside CH43 1TY
Tel: (0151) 652 5777
Fax: (0151) 670 0639
Email: admissionssec@
     birkhs.gdst.net
Head: Mrs C H Evans
Type: Girls Day 3–18
No of pupils: 800
Fees: (September 06)
Day £4710–£7863

BIRKENHEAD SCHOOL

58 Beresford Road, Oxton, Wirral,
Merseyside CH43 2JD
Tel: (0151) 652 4014
Fax: (0151) 651 3091
Email: enquire@
     birkenheadschool.co.uk
Head: Mr D J Clark
Type: Boys Day 3–18
No of pupils: B652 G7
Fees: (September 06)
Day £6198–£8028

HESWALL PREPARATORY SCHOOL
Carberry, 28 Quarry Road East, Heswall, Wirral, Merseyside CH60 6RB
Tel: (0151) 342 7851
Fax: (0151) 342 7851
Email: hesprep@aol.com
Head: Mrs M Hannaford
Type: Co-educational Day 3–11
No of pupils: B25 G25
Fees: (September 06)
Day £1020–£4050

KINGSMEAD SCHOOL
Bertram Drive, Hoylake, Wirral, Merseyside CH47 0LL
Tel: (0151) 632 3156
Fax: (0151) 632 0302
Email: kingsmeadschool@ compuserve.com
Head: Mr J F Perry
Type: Co-educational Boarding and Day 2–16
No of pupils: B142 G241
No of boarders: F38 W4
Fees: (September 05)
FB £10650–£12390
WB £10260–£12000
Day £4605–£7290

PRENTON PREPARATORY SCHOOL
Mount Pleasant, Oxton, Wirral, Merseyside CH43 5SY
Tel: (0151) 652 3182
Fax: (0151) 653 7428
Email: enquiry@ prentonprep.co.uk
Head: Mrs N M Aloe
Type: Co-educational Day 2–11
No of pupils: B65 G87
Fees: On application

MIDDLESEX

ASHFORD

ST DAVID'S SCHOOL
Church Road, Ashford, Middlesex TW15 3DZ
Tel: (01784) 252494
Fax: (01784) 248652
Email: office@stdavidsschool.com
Head: Ms P Bristow
Type: Girls Day and Boarding 3–18
No of pupils: B10 G370
No of boarders: F25 W7
Fees: (September 05) FB £17640
WB £16290 Day £5685–£9525

EDGWARE

HOLLAND HOUSE
1 Broadhurst Avenue, Edgware, Middlesex HA8 8TP
Tel: (020) 8958 6979
Fax: (020) 8958 3591
Email: schooloffice@ hollandhouse.org.uk
Head: Mrs I Tyk
Type: Co-educational Day 4–11
No of pupils: B70 G70
Fees: On application

NORTH LONDON COLLEGIATE
Canons Drive, Edgware, Middlesex HA8 7RJ
Tel: (020) 8952 0912
Fax: (020) 8951 1391
Email: office@nlcs.org.uk
Head: Mrs B McCabe
Type: Girls Day 4–18
No of pupils: 1057
Fees: (September 06)
Day £8922–£10518

ENFIELD

ST JOHN'S SENIOR SCHOOL
North Lodge, The Ridgeway, Enfield, Middlesex EN2 8BE
Tel: (020) 8366 0035
Fax: (020) 8363 4439
Email: StJohnsSc@aol.com
Head: Mr A Tardios
Type: Co-educational Day
Boys 11–18 Girls 10–18
No of pupils: B134 G106
Fees: (September 06) Day £7320

HAMPTON

ATHELSTAN HOUSE SCHOOL
36 Percy Road, Hampton, Middlesex TW12 2LA
Tel: (020) 8979 1045
Email: admin@ athelstanhouseschool.co.uk
Head: Mrs E M Woolf
Type: Co-educational Day 3–7
No of pupils: B25 G32
Fees: On application

DENMEAD SCHOOL
41–43 Wensleydale Road, Hampton, Middlesex TW12 2LP
Tel: (020) 8979 1844
Fax: (020) 8941 8773
Email: admissions@ denmead.richmond.sch.uk
Head: Mr M T McKaughan
Type: Boys Day 2–11 (Girls 2–7)
No of pupils: B150 G20
Fees: (September 06)
Day £3498–£8085

HAMPTON SCHOOL
Hanworth Road, Hampton, Middlesex TW12 3HD
Tel: (020) 8979 5526
Fax: (020) 8941 7368
Email: headmaster@ hampton.richmond.sch.uk
Head: Mr B R Martin
Type: Boys Day 11–18
No of pupils: 1098
Fees: (September 05) Day £3530

JACK AND JILL SCHOOL
30 Nightingale Road, Hampton,
Middlesex TW12 3HX
Tel: (020) 8979 3195
Fax: (020) 8979 3195
Email: jackandjillschool@
btconnect.com
Head: Miss K S Papirnik
Type: Girls Day 3–7 (Boys 3–5)
No of pupils: B21 G124
Fees: On application

THE LADY ELEANOR HOLLES SCHOOL
102 Hanworth Road, Hampton,
Middlesex TW12 3HF
Tel: (020) 8979 1601
Fax: (020) 8941 8291
Email: office@lehs.org.uk
Head: Mrs G Low
Type: Girls Day 7–18
No of pupils: 860
Fees: (September 06)
Day £8235–£10917

TWICKENHAM PREPARATORY SCHOOL
Beveree, 43 High Street,
Hampton, Middlesex TW12 2SA
Tel: (020) 8979 6216
Fax: (020) 8979 1596
Email: office@
twickenhamprep.co.uk
Head: Mr D Malam
Type: Co-educational Day
Boys 4–13 Girls 4–11
No of pupils: B139 G135
Fees: (September 06)
Day £7260–£7770

HANWORTH

LITTLE EDEN SDA SCHOOL & EDEN HIGH SDA SCHOOL
Fortescue House, Park Road,
Hanworth, Middlesex TW13 6PN
Tel: (020) 8751 1844
Fax: (020) 8751 1844
Email: littleedensch@aol.com
Head: Mrs L A Osei
Type: Co-educational Day 3–16
No of pupils: B37 G27
Fees: On application

HARROW

ALPHA PREPARATORY SCHOOL
Hindes Road, Harrow, Middlesex
HA1 1SH
Tel: (020) 8427 1471
Fax: (020) 8424 9324
Email: sec@alpha.harrow.sch.uk
Head: Mr P J Wylie
Type: Co-educational Day 4–11
No of pupils: B90 G70
Fees: (September 06)
Day £6780–£7410

BUCKINGHAM COLLEGE SCHOOL
15 Hindes Road, Harrow,
Middlesex HA1 1SH
Tel: (020) 8427 1220
Fax: (020) 8863 0816
Email: enquiries@buckcoll.org
Head: Mr D F Bell
Type: Boys Day 11–18 (Co-ed VIth
Form)
No of pupils: B175 G1
Fees: On application

THE JOHN LYON SCHOOL
Middle Road, Harrow, Middlesex
HA2 0HN
Tel: (020) 8872 8400
Fax: (020) 8872 8455
Email: enquiries@johnlyon.org
Head: Mr K J Riley
Type: Boys Day 11–18
No of pupils: 580
Fees: (September 05) Day £10755

ORLEY FARM SCHOOL
South Hill Avenue, Harrow on the
Hill, Middlesex HA1 3NU
Tel: (020) 8869 7600
Fax: (020) 8869 7601
Email: office@
orleyfarm.harrow.sch.uk
Head: Mr I S Elliott
Type: Co-educational Day 4–13
No of pupils: B380 G90
Fees: On application

QUAINTON HALL SCHOOL
91 Hindes Road, Harrow,
Middlesex HA1 1RX
Tel: (020) 8427 1304
Fax: (020) 8861 8861
Email: admin@
quaintonhall.harrow.sch.uk
Head: Mr D P Banister
Type: Boys Day 4–13
No of pupils: 220
Fees: On application

HARROW ON THE HILL

HARROW SCHOOL
1 High Street, Harrow on the Hill,
Middlesex HA1 3HT
Tel: (020) 8872 8003
Fax: (020) 8872 8012
Email: hm@harrowschool.org.uk
Head: Mr B J Lenon
Type: Boys Boarding 13–18
No of pupils: 800
No of boarders: F800
Fees: (September 06) FB £24500

ROXETH MEAD SCHOOL
Buckholt House, 25 Middle Road,
Harrow on the Hill, Middlesex
HA2 0HW
Tel: (020) 8422 2092
Fax: (020) 8426 4974
Email: info@roxethmead.com
Head: Mrs A J Isaacs
Type: Co-educational Day 3–7
No of pupils: B26 G35
Fees: (September 06)
Day £3000–£5760

HILLINGDON

ACS HILLINGDON INTERNATIONAL SCHOOL*
Hillingdon Court, 108 Vine Lane,
Hillingdon, Middlesex UB10 0BE
Tel: (01895) 818402
Fax: (01895) 818404
Email: hillingdonadmissions@
acs-england.co.uk
Head: Mrs G Apple
Type: Co-educational Day 4–18
No of pupils: B306 G274
Fees: (September 06)
Day £7610–£15750

ST HELEN'S COLLEGE
Parkway, Hillingdon, Middlesex
UB10 9JX
Tel: (01895) 234371
Fax: (01895) 619818
Email: sthelenscoll@
easymail.rmplc.co.uk
Head: Mr D A Crehan and
Mrs G R Crehan
Type: Co-educational Day 3–11
No of pupils: B165 G175
Fees: (September 06)
Day £3450–£5940

ISLEWORTH

ASHTON HOUSE SCHOOL
50/52 Eversley Crescent,
Isleworth, Middlesex TW7 4LW
Tel: (020) 8560 3902
Fax: (020) 8568 1097
Email: principal@
ashtonhouse.com
Head: Miss M Regan
Type: Co-educational Day 3–11
No of pupils: B70 G80
Fees: (September 06)
Day £5397–£7320

NORTHWOOD

MERCHANT TAYLORS' SCHOOL
Sandy Lodge, Northwood,
Middlesex HA6 2HT
Tel: (01923) 820644
Fax: (01923) 835110
Email: admissions@mtsn.org.uk
Head: Mr S N Wright
Type: Boys Day 11–18
No of pupils: 815
Fees: (September 05) Day £11990

NORTHWOOD COLLEGE*
Maxwell Road, Northwood,
Middlesex HA6 2YE
Tel: (01923) 825446
Fax: (01923) 836526
Email: admissions@
northwoodcollege.co.uk
Head: Mrs R Mercer
Type: Girls Day 3–18
No of pupils: 805
Fees: (September 06)
Day £3041–£10317

ST HELEN'S SCHOOL*
Eastbury Road, Northwood,
Middlesex HA6 3AS
Tel: (01923) 843210
Fax: (01923) 843211
Email: enquiries@sthn.co.uk
Head: Mrs M Morris
Type: Girls Day and Boarding
3–18
No of pupils: 1153
No of boarders: F26 W3
Fees: (September 06) FB £19359
WB £18672 Day £6840–£10446

ST JOHN'S NORTHWOOD
Potter Street Hill, Northwood,
Middlesex HA6 3QY
Tel: (020) 8866 0067
Fax: (020) 8868 8770
Email: office@st-johns.org.uk
Head: Mr C R Kelly
Type: Boys Day 3–13
No of pupils: 390
Fees: (September 05)
Day £5964–£9050

ST MARTIN'S SCHOOL
40 Moor Park Road, Northwood,
Middlesex HA6 2DJ
Tel: (01923) 825740
Fax: (01923) 835452
Email: office@stmartins.org.uk
Head: Mr D T Tidmarsh
Type: Boys Day 3–13
Fees: (September 05)
Day £2955–£9135

PINNER

BUCKINGHAM COLLEGE PREPARATORY SCHOOL
458 Rayners Lane, Pinner,
Middlesex HA5 5DT
Tel: (020) 8866 2737
Fax: (020) 8868 3228
Email: enquiries@buckprep.org
Head: Mr L Smith
Type: Boys Day 4–11
No of pupils: 120
Fees: (September 06)
Day £5895–£7716

HEATHFIELD SCHOOL
Beaulieu Drive, Pinner, Middlesex
HA5 1NB
Tel: (020) 8868 2346
Fax: (020) 8868 4405
Email: enquiries@hea.gdst.net
Head: Miss C Juett
Type: Girls Day 3–18
No of pupils: 577
Fees: (September 06)
Day £5886–£9810

INNELLAN HOUSE SCHOOL
44 Love Lane, Pinner, Middlesex
HA5 3EX
Tel: (020) 8866 1855
Fax: (020) 8866 1855
Email: innellan.house@virgin.net
Head: Ms J Watkins
Type: Co-educational Day 3–7
No of pupils: B27 G41
Fees: On application

REDDIFORD
36–38 Cecil Park, Pinner,
Middlesex HA5 5HH
Tel: (020) 8866 0660
Fax: (020) 8866 4847
Email: office@reddiford.org.uk
Head: Mrs J Batt
Type: Co-educational Day 2–11
No of pupils: B180 G122
Fees: (September 06)
Day £3090–£7425

SHEPPERTON

HALLIFORD SCHOOL
Russell Road, Shepperton,
Middlesex TW17 9HX
Tel: (01932) 223593
Fax: (01932) 229781
Email: registrar@
hallifordschool.com
Head: Mr P V Cottam
Type: Boys Day 11–19 (Co-ed VIth
Form)
No of pupils: B365 G3
Fees: (September 06) Day £9225

SOUTHALL

ACORN INDEPENDENT COLLEGE
39–47 High Street, Southall,
Middlesex UB1 3HF
Tel: (020) 8571 9900
Fax: (020) 8571 9901
Email: acorncollege@
hotmail.co.uk
Head: Mrs Gladys Watt
Type: Co-educational Day 13–19
No of pupils: B88 G58
Fees: (September 06)
Day £1455–£12360

STAINES

STAINES PREPARATORY SCHOOL
3 Gresham Road, Staines,
Middlesex TW18 2BT
Tel: (01784) 450909
Fax: (01784) 464424
Email: registrar@stainesprep.co.uk
Head: Mr P Roberts
Type: Co-educational Day 3–11
No of pupils: B203 G122
Fees: (September 06)
Day £1962–£6810

England – Middlesex

STANMORE

PETERBOROUGH & ST MARGARET'S SCHOOL
Common Road, Stanmore,
Middlesex HA7 3JB
Tel: (020) 8950 3600
Fax: (020) 8421 8946
Email: psm@psmschool.org
Head: Mrs S R Watts
Type: Girls Day 4–16
No of pupils: 235
Fees: (September 05)
Day £5490–£8160

TWICKENHAM

THE MALL SCHOOL
185 Hampton Road, Twickenham,
Middlesex TW2 5NQ
Tel: (020) 8977 2523
Fax: (020) 8977 8771
Email: admissions@
  mall.richmond.sch.uk
Head: Dr J G Jeanes
Type: Boys Day 4–13
No of pupils: 300
Fees: (September 06)
Day £7440–£8610

NEWLAND HOUSE SCHOOL
Waldegrave Park, Twickenham,
Middlesex TW1 4TQ
Tel: (020) 8892 7479
Fax: (020) 8744 0399
Email: school@
  newlandhouse.co.uk
Head: Mr D J Ott
Type: Co-educational Day
Boys 4–13 Girls 4–11
No of pupils: B271 G152
Fees: (September 06)
Day £7695–£8625

ST CATHERINE'S SCHOOL
Cross Deep, Twickenham,
Middlesex TW1 4QJ
Tel: (020) 8891 2898
Fax: (020) 8744 9629
Email: info@
  stcatherineschool.com
Head: Mrs Z Braganza
Type: Girls Day 3–16 (Sixth form
in 2006)
No of pupils: 350
Fees: (September 06)
Day £6513–£8985

ST JAMES INDEPENDENT SCHOOL FOR BOYS (SENIOR)
Pope's Villa, 19 Cross Deep,
Twickenham, Middlesex
TW1 4QG
Tel: (020) 8892 2002
Fax: (020) 8892 4442
Email: admissions@
  stjamesboys.co.uk
Head: Mr David Boddy
Type: Boys Day and Boarding
10–18
No of pupils: 300
No of boarders: W28
Fees: (September 06)
WB £13215–£13635
Day £9360–£9780

SUNFLOWER MONTESSORI SCHOOL
8 Victoria Road, Twickenham,
Middlesex TW1 3HW
Tel: (020) 8891 2675
Fax: (020) 8891 1204
Email: deb@sunmont.fsnet.co.uk
Head: Mrs J Yandell and
Mrs Eileen Tiahlo
Type: Co-educational Day 2–6
No of pupils: B36 G22
Fees: (September 06)
Day £1020–£1650

WEMBLEY

BUXLOW PREPARATORY SCHOOL
5/6 Castleton Gardens, Wembley,
Middlesex HA9 7QJ
Tel: (020) 8904 3615
Fax: (020) 8904 3606
Email: buxlow@happychild.co.uk
Head: Mrs A Baines
Type: Co-educational Day 4–11
No of pupils: B50 G50
Fees: (September 06) Day £5610

ST CHRISTOPHER'S SCHOOL
71 Wembley Park Drive,
Wembley, Middlesex HA9 8HE
Tel: (020) 8902 5069
Fax: (020) 8903 5939
Email: stchris@happychild.co.uk
Head: Mr J M B Edwards
Type: Co-educational Day 4–11
No of pupils: B54 G56
Fees: (September 06)
Day £5565–£5880

NORFOLK

CROMER

BEESTON HALL SCHOOL
West Runton, Cromer, Norfolk
NR27 9NQ
Tel: (01263) 837324
Fax: (01263) 838177
Email: office@beestonhall.co.uk
Head: Mr I K MacAskill
Type: Co-educational Boarding
and Day 7–13
No of pupils: B95 G70
No of boarders: F94
Fees: (September 06) FB £15765
Day £11775

DISS

RIDDLESWORTH HALL[†]
Diss, Norfolk IP22 2TA
Tel: (01953) 681246
Fax: (01953) 688124
Email: enquiries@
   riddlesworthhall.com
Head: Mr C Campbell
Type: Co-educational Day and
Boarding Boys 2–11 Girls 2–13
(Girls only boarding)
No of pupils: B38 G123
No of boarders: F23 W15
Fees: (September 05) FB £14805
WB £13860 Day £5850–£8705

HOLT

GRESHAM'S PREPARATORY SCHOOL
Cromer Road, Holt, Norfolk
NR25 6EY
Tel: (01263) 714600
Fax: (01263) 714060
Email: prep@greshams.com
Head: Mr J H W Quick
Type: Co-educational Day and
Boarding 3–13
No of pupils: B182 G153
No of boarders: F43 W43
Fees: (September 06) F/WB £15840
Day £6000–£12150

GRESHAM'S SCHOOL
Cromer Road, Holt, Norfolk
NR25 6EA
Tel: (01263) 714500
Fax: (01263) 712028
Email: headmaster@greshams.com
Head: Mr A R Clark
Type: Co-educational Boarding
and Day 3–18
No of pupils: B400 G350
No of boarders: F285
Fees: (September 06)
FB £15840–£21705
Day £6000–£16815

HUNSTANTON

GLEBE HOUSE SCHOOL
2 Cromer Road, Hunstanton,
Norfolk PE36 6HW
Tel: (01485) 532809
Fax: (01485) 533900
Email: sjt@
   glebehouseschool.co.uk
Head: Mr J Crofts
Type: Co-educational Boarding
and Day 0–13
No of pupils: B57 G53
No of boarders: W33
Fees: (September 06)
WB £11001–£11916
Day £5796–£10011

KINGS LYNN

DOWNHAM PREP SCHOOL AND MONTESSORI NURSERY
The Old Rectory, Stow Bardolph,
Kings Lynn, Norfolk PE34 3HT
Tel: (01366) 388066
Fax: (01366) 388066
Email: secretary@
   dpsmn.norfolk.sch.uk
Head: Mrs E J Laffeaty-Sharpe
Type: Co-educational Day 2–11
No of pupils: B72 G68
Fees: (September 05)
Day £966–£5460

NORTH WALSHAM

ST NICHOLAS HOUSE KINDERGARTEN & PREP SCHOOL
Yarmouth Road, North Walsham,
Norfolk NR28 9AT
Tel: (01692) 403143
Fax: (01692) 403143
Email: stnicholas@
   yarmouth47.fsnet.co.uk
Head: Mr C Wardle
Type: Co-educational Day 3–11
No of pupils: B50 G60
Fees: On application

NORWICH

ALL SAINTS SCHOOL
School Road, Lessingham,
Norwich, Norfolk NR12 0DJ
Tel: (01692) 584999
Fax: (01692) 582083
Head: Mrs J Gardiner
Type: Co-educational Day 2–16
No of pupils: B40 G40
Fees: On application

HETHERSETT OLD HALL SCHOOL
Hethersett, Norwich, Norfolk
NR9 3DW
Tel: (01603) 810390
Fax: (01603) 812094
Email: enquiries@hohs.co.uk
Head: Mrs J M Mark
Type: Girls Boarding and Day
4–18 (Boys 4–7)
No of pupils: B11 G228
No of boarders: F28
Fees: (September 05)
FB £14250–£17700
Day £5595–£8985

LANGLEY PREPARATORY SCHOOL & NURSERY
Beech Hill, 11 Yarmouth Road,
Thorpe St Andrew, Norwich,
Norfolk NR7 0EA
Tel: (01603) 433861
Fax: (01603) 702639
Email: headmaster@
   langleyprep.norfolk.sch.uk
Head: Mr S B Marfleet
Type: Co-educational Day 2–11
No of pupils: B70 G10
Fees: On application

LANGLEY SCHOOL*

Langley Park, Loddon, Norwich,
Norfolk NR14 6BJ
Tel: (01508) 520210
Fax: (01508) 528058
Email: administration@
   langleyschool.co.uk
Head: Mr J G Malcolm
Type: Co-educational Boarding
and Day 10–18
No of pupils: B295 G180
No of boarders: F105 W30
Fees: (September 06)
FB £14700–£17700
WB £12960–£14700
Day £6705–£8700

THE NEW ECCLES HALL SCHOOL

Quidenham, Norwich, Norfolk
NR16 2NZ
Tel: (01953) 887217
Fax: (01953) 887397
Email: admin@neweccleshall.com
Head: Mr R W Allard
Type: Co-educational Day and
Boarding 4–16
No of boarders: F72
Fees: (September 06)
F/WB £12180–£14445
Day £4665–£7740

NORWICH HIGH SCHOOL FOR GIRLS GDST

Eaton Grove, 95 Newmarket
Road, Norwich, Norfolk NR2 2HU
Tel: (01603) 453265
Fax: (01603) 259891
Email: admissions@nor.gdst.net
Head: Mrs V C Bidwell
Type: Girls Day 4–18
No of pupils: 886
Fees: (September 06)
Day £5700–£7863

NORWICH SCHOOL

70 The Close, Norwich, Norfolk
NR1 4DD
Tel: (01603) 728430
Fax: (01603) 627036
Email: head.sec@
   norwich-school.org.uk
Head: Mr J B Hawkins
Type: Boys Day 7–18 (Co-ed VIth
Form)
No of pupils: B844 G84
Fees: (September 06)
Day £8820–£9165

NOTRE DAME PREPARATORY SCHOOL

147 Dereham Road, Norwich,
Norfolk NR2 3TA
Tel: (01603) 625593
Fax: (01603) 444139
Email: notredameprepschool@
   norwich147.fsnet.co.uk
Head: Mr KJ O'Herlihy
Type: Co-educational Day 3–11
No of pupils: B58 G55
Fees: (September 05)
Day £2940–£4185

ST CHRISTOPHER'S SCHOOL

George Hill, Old Catton, Norwich,
Norfolk NR6 7DE
Tel: (01603) 425179
Email: admin@stchristophers.
   connectadsl.co.uk
Head: Mrs J Higgins
Type: Co-educational Day 2–8
No of pupils: B80 G60
Fees: (September 06)
Day £780–£4683

STRETTON SCHOOL

1 Albermarle Road, Norwich,
Norfolk NR2 2DF
Tel: (01603) 451285
Fax: (01603) 458842
Email: enquiries@
   strettonschool.com
Head: Mrs Y D Barnett
Type: Co-educational Day 1–8
No of pupils: B43 G35
Fees: On application

TAVERHAM HALL

Taverham, Norwich, Norfolk
NR8 6HU
Tel: (01603) 868206
Fax: (01603) 861061
Email: enquire@
   taverhamhall.co.uk
Head: Mr W D Lawton
Type: Co-educational Boarding
and Day 1–13
No of pupils: B130 G94
No of boarders: W25
Fees: (September 05) WB £11700
Day £1500–£9900

THORPE HOUSE SCHOOL

7 Yarmouth Road, Norwich,
Norfolk NR7 0EA
Tel: (01603) 433055
Fax: (01603) 436323
Email: office@
   thorpehouseschool.com
Head: Mr A Todd
Type: Girls Day 3–16
No of pupils: 280
Fees: On application

TOWN CLOSE HOUSE PREPARATORY SCHOOL

14 Ipswich Road, Norwich,
Norfolk NR2 2LR
Tel: (01603) 620180
Fax: (01603) 618256
Email: admissions@
   townclose.com
Head: Mr Graeme Lowe
Type: Co-educational Day 3–13
No of pupils: B301 G197
Fees: (September 06)
Day £5400–£8430

WOOD DENE SCHOOL

Aylmerton Hall, Holt Road,
Aylmerton, Norwich, Norfolk
NR11 8QA
Tel: (01263) 837224
Fax: (01263) 835837
Email: mail@wood-dene.co.uk
Head: Mrs D M Taylor
Type: Co-educational Day 2–16
No of pupils: B90 G110
Fees: (September 05)
Day £2700–£5568

SWAFFHAM

SACRED HEART CONVENT SCHOOL

17 Mangate Street, Swaffham,
Norfolk PE37 7QW
Tel: (01760) 721330
Fax: (01760) 725557
Email: info@
   sacredheartschool.co.uk
Head: Sister F Ridler
Type: Co-educational Day and
Boarding Boys 3–11 Girls 3–16
No of pupils: B26 G194
No of boarders: W30
Fees: (September 05) WB £10680
Day £3576–£7200

THETFORD

**THETFORD GRAMMAR
SCHOOL**
Bridge Street, Thetford, Norfolk
IP24 3AF
Tel: (01842) 752840
Fax: (01842) 750220
Email: enquiries@
  thetfordgrammarschool.
  fsnet.co.uk
Head: Mr G J Price
Type: Co-educational Day 4–18
No of pupils: B170 G130
Fees: On application

NORTHAMPTONSHIRE

BLACKTHORN

**ST PETER'S INDEPENDENT
SCHOOL**
Lingswood Park, Blackthorn,
Northamptonshire NN3 8TA
Tel: (01604) 411745
Head: Mr G J Smith
Type: Co-educational Day 4–18
No of pupils: 170
Fees: On application

BRACKLEY

BEACHBOROUGH SCHOOL
Westbury, Brackley,
Northamptonshire NN13 5LB
Tel: (01280) 700071
Fax: (01280) 704839
Email: office@beachborough.com
Head: Mr J Whybrow
Type: Co-educational Day and
Boarding 2–13
No of pupils: B132 G95
No of boarders: W49
Fees: (September 05) Day £3744

**WINCHESTER HOUSE
SCHOOL**
Brackley, Northamptonshire
NN13 7AZ
Tel: (01280) 702483
Fax: (01280) 706400
Email: office@
  winchester-house.org
Head: Mr M S Seymour
Type: Co-educational Boarding
and Day 3–13
No of pupils: B232 G134
No of boarders: F15 W54
Fees: (September 05) FB £16065
WB £12750–£16065
Day £5565–£12150

KETTERING

ST PETER'S SCHOOL
52 Headlands, Kettering,
Northamptonshire NN15 6DJ
Tel: (01536) 512066
Fax: (01536) 416469
Email: info@st-peters.org.uk
Head: Mrs M Chapman
Type: Co-educational Day 2–11
No of pupils: B57 G78
Fees: (September 05)
Day £4416–£5874

NORTHAMPTON

**BOSWORTH INDEPENDENT
COLLEGE**
Nazareth House, Barrack Road,
Northampton, Northamptonshire
NN2 6AF
Tel: (01604) 239995
Fax: (01604) 239996
Email: info@bosworthcollege.com
Head: Mr M McQuin
Type: Co-educational Boarding
and Day 14–22
No of pupils: B179 G120
No of boarders: F221 W1
Fees: (September 06) FB £18800
WB £16000 Day £9000–£12000

**GREAT HOUGHTON
PREPARATORY SCHOOL**
Great Houghton Hall,
Northampton, Northamptonshire
NN4 7AG
Tel: (01604) 761907
Fax: (01604) 761251
Email: office@
  northamptonschool.com
Head: Mr R O Barnes
Type: Co-educational Day 3–13
No of pupils: B165 G75
Fees: (September 05)
Day £4695–£8985

England – Norfolk/Northamptonshire

MAIDWELL HALL SCHOOL
Northampton, Northamptonshire
NN6 9JG
Tel: (01604) 686234
Fax: (01604) 686659
Email: headmaster@
    maidwellhall.co.uk
Head: Mr R A Lankester
Type: Boys Boarding and Day
7–13 (Girls day only)
No of pupils: 95
No of boarders: F95
Fees: (September 06) FB £17820
Day £14250

NORTHAMPTON HIGH SCHOOL
Newport Pagnell Road,
Hardingstone, Northampton,
Northamptonshire NN4 6UU
Tel: (01604) 765765
Fax: (01604) 709418
Email: admin@
    northamptonhigh.co.uk
Head: Mrs L A Mayne
Type: Girls Day 3–18
No of pupils: 830
Fees: (September 06)
Day £6540–£8550

QUINTON HOUSE SCHOOL
Upton Hall, Upton, Northampton,
Northamptonshire NN5 4UX
Tel: (01604) 752050
Fax: (01604) 581707
Email: info@
    quintonhouseschool.co.uk
Head: Mr J R O'Leary
Type: Co-educational Day 3–18
No of pupils: B163 G162
Fees: (September 06)
Day £4413–£7281

ST MATTHEWS SCHOOL
100 Park Avenue North,
Northampton, Northamptonshire
NN3 2JB
Tel: (01604) 712647
Email: principal@
    st-matthewsschool.co.uk
Head: Mrs L Burgess
Type: Co-educational Day 2–9
No of pupils: B30 G30
Fees: (September 05)
Day £612–£5610

SPRATTON HALL
Spratton, Northampton,
Northamptonshire NN6 8HP
Tel: (01604) 847292
Fax: (01604) 820844
Email: office@sprattonhall.com
Head: Mr S Player
Type: Co-educational Day 4–13
No of pupils: B197 G192
Fees: (September 06)
Day £6150–£9300

NR PETERBOROUGH

LAXTON JUNIOR SCHOOL*
East Road, Oundle,
Nr Peterborough,
Northamptonshire PE8 4BX
Tel: (01832) 277275
Fax: (01832) 277271
Email: admissions@
    laxtonjunior.org.uk
Head: Miss S C Thomas
Type: Co-educational Day 4–11
No of pupils: B121 G103
Fees: (September 06)
Day £7365–£8085

OUNDLE SCHOOL
The Great Hall, New Street,
Oundle, Nr Peterborough,
Northamptonshire PE8 4GH
Tel: (01832) 277125
Fax: (01832) 277128
Email: registrar@oundle.co.uk
Head: Mr C M P Bush
Type: Co-educational Boarding
and Day 11–19
No of pupils: B642 G409
No of boarders: F828
Fees: (September 05)
FB £16593–£21725
Day £10785–£13185

PITSFORD

NORTHAMPTONSHIRE GRAMMAR SCHOOL
Pitsford Hall, Pitsford,
Northamptonshire NN6 9AX
Tel: (01604) 880306
Fax: (01604) 882212
Email: office@ngs-school.com
Head: Mr N R Toone
Type: Co-educational Day 3–18
No of pupils: B215 G139
Fees: (September 05)
Day £5067–£8940

TOWCESTER

SLAPTON PRE-PREPARATORY SCHOOL
Chapel Lane, Slapton, Towcester,
Northamptonshire NN12 8PE
Tel: (01327) 860158
Fax: (01327) 860158
Email: admin@slaptonpreprep.org
Head: Mrs P M Young
Type: Co-educational Day 4–8
(Pre-Prep)
No of pupils: B18 G18
Fees: (September 06) Day £6000

WELLINGBOROUGH

WELLINGBOROUGH SCHOOL
Wellingborough,
Northamptonshire NN8 2BX
Tel: (01933) 222427
Fax: (01933) 271986
Email: headmaster@
    wellingboroughschool.org
Head: Mr G R Bowe
Type: Co-educational Day 3–18
No of pupils: B496 G337
Fees: On application

NORTHUMBERLAND

ALNWICK

ROCK HALL SCHOOL
Rock, Alnwick, Northumberland
NE66 3SB
Tel: (01665) 579224
Fax: (01665) 579467
Email: rockhallschool@
   btinternet.com
Head: Mrs L A Bosanquet
Type: Co-educational Day 3–13
No of pupils: B32 G27
Fees: (September 06)
Day £4848–£6441

BERWICK-UPON-TWEED

**LONGRIDGE TOWERS
SCHOOL**
Berwick-upon-Tweed,
Northumberland TD15 2XQ
Tel: (01289) 307584
Fax: (01289) 302581
Email: admissions@lts.org.uk
Head: Mr A E Clemit
Type: Co-educational Day and
Boarding 4–18
No of pupils: B165 G160
No of boarders: F21 W12
Fees: (September 06)
FB £16320–£17550
WB £14625–£15855
Day £5235–£8385

STOCKSFIELD

MOWDEN HALL SCHOOL
Newton, Stocksfield,
Northumberland NE43 7TP
Tel: (01661) 842147
Fax: (01661) 842529
Email: lb@mowdenhall.co.uk
Head: Mr P Meadows
Type: Co-educational Boarding
and Day 3–13
No of pupils: B136 G102
No of boarders: F110 W8
Fees: On application

NOTTINGHAMSHIRE

EAST LEAKE

**ARLEY HOUSE PNEU
SCHOOL**
8 Station Road, East Leake,
Nottinghamshire LE12 6LQ
Tel: (01509) 852229
Fax: (01509) 852229
Email: office@
   arley-pneu.eastlake.sch.uk
Head: Mrs E A Gibbs
Type: Co-educational Day 3–11
No of pupils: B45 G37
Fees: (September 05)
Day £1365–£5235

MANSFIELD

**MANSFIELD PREPARATORY
SCHOOL**
Welbeck Road, Mansfield,
Nottinghamshire NG19 9LA
Tel: (01623) 420940
Head: Miss J Sparrow
Type: Co-educational Day 3–11
No of pupils: B50 G39
Fees: On application

SAVILLE HOUSE SCHOOL
11 Church Street, Mansfield
Woodhouse, Mansfield,
Nottinghamshire NG19 8AH
Tel: (01623) 625068
Fax: (01623) 659983
Email: cherubsnurseries@aol.com
Head: Mrs J Nutter
Type: Co-educational Day 3–13
No of pupils: B90 G75
Fees: (September 06) Day £2640

NEWARK

HIGHFIELDS SCHOOL
London Road, Newark,
Nottinghamshire NG24 3AL
Tel: (01636) 704103
Fax: (01636) 680919
Email: office@
   highfieldsschool.co.uk
Head: Mr D R Wood
Type: Co-educational Day 3–11
No of pupils: B92 G90
Fees: (September 06) Day £5145

WELLOW HOUSE SCHOOL
Wellow, Newark,
Nottinghamshire NG22 0EA
Tel: (01623) 861054
Fax: (01623) 836665
Email: wellowhouse@
   btinternet.com
Head: Mr P W Cook
Type: Co-educational Day and
Boarding 3–13
No of pupils: B80 G69
No of boarders: W1
Fees: (September 06) WB £10980
Day £5085–£8805

NOTTINGHAM

**ATTENBOROUGH
PREPARATORY SCHOOL**
The Strand, Attenborough,
Beeston, Nottingham,
Nottinghamshire NG9 6AU
Tel: (0115) 943 6725
Email: attprepschl@hotmail.com
Head: Mrs J Howarth
Type: Co-educational Day 4–11
No of pupils: B40 G40
Fees: (September 05)
Day £2370–£3400

COTESWOOD HOUSE SCHOOL
19 Thackeray's Lane,
Woodthorpe, Nottingham,
Nottinghamshire NG5 4HT
Tel: (0115) 967 6551
Type: Co-educational Day 3–11
No of pupils: B20 G20
Fees: On application

DAGFA HOUSE SCHOOL
57 Broadgate, Beeston,
Nottingham, Nottinghamshire
NG9 2FU
Tel: (0115) 913 8330
Fax: (0115) 913 8331
Email: enquiries@
   dagfahouse.notts.sch.uk
Head: Mr A Hampton
Type: Co-educational Day 2–16
No of pupils: B145 G105
Fees: (September 06)
Day £5430–£6585

GREENHOLME SCHOOL
392 Derby Road, Nottingham,
Nottinghamshire NG7 2DX
Tel: (0115) 978 7329
Fax: (0115) 978 1160
Email: enquiries@
   greenholmeschool.co.uk
Head: Mrs M J Nicholson
Type: Co-educational Day 3–11
No of pupils: B127 G71
Fees: (September 06)
Day £6315–£6660

GROSVENOR SCHOOL
Edwalton, Nottingham,
Nottinghamshire NG12 4BS
Tel: (0115) 923 1184
Fax: (0115) 923 5184
Email: office@
   grosvenorschool.co.uk
Head: Mr C G J Oldershaw
Type: Co-educational Day 4–13
No of pupils: B109 G62
Fees: On application

HAZEL HURST SCHOOL
400 Westdale Lane, Mapperley,
Nottingham, Nottinghamshire
NG3 6DG
Tel: (0115) 960 6759
Fax: (0115) 960 6759
Email: hazelhurst@onetel.com
Type: Co-educational Day 2–8
No of pupils: B25 G25
Fees: (September 06)
Day £3555–£3840

HOLLYGIRT SCHOOL
Elm Avenue, Nottingham,
Nottinghamshire NG3 4GF
Tel: (0115) 958 0596
Fax: (0115) 989 7929
Email: info@hollygirt.co.uk
Head: Mrs M Connolly
Type: Girls Day 3–16
No of pupils: 304
Fees: (September 06)
Day £5250–£7425

HOLLYGIRT SCHOOL
Elm Avenue, Nottingham,
Nottinghamshire NG3 4GF
Tel: (0115) 958 0596
Fax: (0115) 989 7929
Email: info@hollygirt.co.uk
Head: Mrs M Connolly
Type: Girls Day 3–16
No of pupils: 307
Fees: (September 06)
Day £5250–£7425

THE KING'S SCHOOL
Green Street, The Meadows,
Nottingham, Nottinghamshire
NG2 2LA
Tel: (0115) 953 9194
Fax: (0115) 955 1148
Email: office@thekingsschool.info
Head: Mr R Southey
Type: Co-educational Day 4–16
Fees: (September 06) Day £3336

MOUNTFORD HOUSE SCHOOL
373 Mansfield Road, Nottingham,
Nottinghamshire NG5 2DA
Tel: (0115) 960 5676
Email: enquiries@
   mountfordhouse.
   nottingham.sch.uk
Head: Mrs D Williams
Type: Co-educational Day 3–11
No of pupils: B54 G30
Fees: On application

NOTTINGHAM HIGH SCHOOL
Waverley Mount, Nottingham,
Nottinghamshire NG7 4ED
Tel: (0115) 978 6056
Fax: (0115) 924 9716
Email: info@nottinghamhigh.co.uk
Head: Mr C S Parker
Type: Boys Day 11–18
No of pupils: 841
Fees: (September 06) Day £8898

NOTTINGHAM HIGH SCHOOL FOR GIRLS GDST
9 Arboretum Street, Nottingham,
Nottinghamshire NG1 4JB
Tel: (0115) 941 7663
Fax: (0115) 924 0757
Email: enquiries@not.gdst.net
Head: Mrs S M Gorham
Type: Girls Day 4–18
No of pupils: 1078
Fees: (September 06)
Day £5700–£7863

NOTTINGHAM HIGH JUNIOR SCHOOL
Waverley Mount, Nottingham,
Nottinghamshire NG7 4ED
Tel: (0115) 845 2214
Fax: (0115) 845 2298
Email: PALLANT.PM@
   NOTTINGHAMHIGH.CO.UK
Head: Mr P M Pallant
Type: Boys Day 7–11
No of pupils: 145
Fees: (September 06) Day £7086

PLUMTREE SCHOOL
Church Hill, Plumtree,
Nottingham, Nottinghamshire
NG12 5ND
Tel: (0115) 937 5859
Fax: (0115) 937 5859
Email: plumtreeschool@
   tiscali.co.uk
Head: Mr N White
Type: Co-educational Day 3–11
No of pupils: B65 G50
Fees: (September 06)
Day £2760–£4785

ST JOSEPH'S SCHOOL
33 Derby Road, Nottingham,
Nottinghamshire NG1 5AW
Tel: (0115) 941 8356
Fax: (0115) 941 8356
Email: office@
   st-josephs.nottingham.sch.uk
Head: Mr J Crawley
Type: Co-educational Day 1–11
No of pupils: B115 G72
Fees: On application

SALTERFORD HOUSE SCHOOL

Salterford Lane, Calverton,
Nottingham, Nottinghamshire
NG14 6NZ
Tel: (0115) 965 2127
Fax: (0115) 965 2205
Email: office@
  salterfordhouseschool.co.uk
Head: Mrs M Venables
Type: Co-educational Day 2–11
No of pupils: B87 G73
Fees: (September 06)
Day £4500–£4575

TRENT COLLEGE

Long Eaton, Nottingham,
Nottinghamshire NG10 4AD
Tel: (0115) 849 4949
Fax: (0115) 849 4997
Email: enquiry@trentcollege.net
Head: Mr J S Lee
Type: Co-educational Boarding
and Day 3–18
No of pupils: B631 G452
No of boarders: F4 W124
Fees: (September 05)
WB £4063–£5644

WAVERLEY HOUSE PNEU SCHOOL

13 Waverley Street, Nottingham,
Nottinghamshire NG7 4DX
Tel: (0115) 978 3230
Fax: (0115) 978 3230
Email: wavhousepneu@
  btconnect.com
Head: Mrs H Dawes
Type: Co-educational Day 3–11
No of pupils: B39 G17
Fees: (September 06)
Day £2145–£5985

RETFORD

AL KARAM SECONDARY SCHOOL

Eaton Hall, Retford,
Nottinghamshire DN22 0PR
Tel: (01777) 706441
Fax: (01777) 711538
Email: info@alkaram.org
Head: Mr M I H Pirzada
Type: Boys Boarding 11–16
No of pupils: 140
No of boarders: F140
Fees: On application

BRAMCOTE LORNE SCHOOL*

Gamston, Retford,
Nottinghamshire DN22 0QQ
Tel: (01777) 838636
Fax: (01777) 838633
Email: enquiries.bramcotelorne@
  church-schools.com
Head: Mr R M Raistrick
Type: Co-educational Boarding
and Day 3–13
No of pupils: B114 G106
No of boarders: F24 W8
Fees: (September 06) FB £1237
WB £959 Day £1736–£2882

RANBY HOUSE SCHOOL

Retford, Nottinghamshire
DN22 8HX
Tel: (01777) 703138
Fax: (01777) 702813
Email: enquiries@
  ranbyhouseschool.co.uk
Head: Mr A C Morris
Type: Co-educational Day and
Boarding 3–13
No of pupils: B177 G147
No of boarders: F50 W10
Fees: (September 06) F/WB £13050
Day £5550–£9750

SUTTON IN ASHFIELD

LAMMAS SCHOOL

Lammas Road, Sutton in Ashfield,
Nottinghamshire NG17 2AD
Tel: (01623) 516879
Fax: (01623) 516879
Email: information@lammas.co.uk
Head: Mr C M Peck
Type: Co-educational Day 4–16
No of pupils: B90 G70
Fees: On application

WORKSOP

WORKSOP COLLEGE

Worksop, Nottinghamshire
S80 3AP
Tel: (01909) 537127
Fax: (01909) 537102
Email: headmaster@
  worksopcollege.notts.sch.uk
Head: Mr R A Collard
Type: Co-educational Boarding
and Day 13–18
No of pupils: B287 G128
No of boarders: F87 W78
Fees: On application

England – Nottinghamshire

OXFORDSHIRE

ABINGDON

ABINGDON SCHOOL
Park Road, Abingdon, Oxfordshire
OX14 IDE
Tel: (01235) 849041
Fax: (01235) 849085
Email: admissions@
  abingdon.org.uk
Head: Mr M Turner
Type: Boys Day and Boarding
11–18
No of pupils: 810
No of boarders: F70 W60
Fees: (September 06) FB £21150
WB £20040 Day £11340

COTHILL HOUSE PREPARATORY SCHOOL
Cothill, Abingdon, Oxfordshire
OX13 6JL
Tel: (01865) 390800
Fax: (01865) 390205
Email: office@cothill.oxon.sch.uk
Head: Mr N R Brooks
Type: Boys Boarding 8–13
No of boarders: F250
Fees: (September 05) FB £17400

JOSCA'S PREPARATORY SCHOOL
Kingston Road, Frilford, Abingdon,
Oxfordshire OX13 5NX
Tel: (01865) 391570
Fax: (01865) 391042
Email: enquiries@Joscas.org.uk
Head: Mr C J Davies
Type: Boys Day 4–13 (Girls 4–7)
No of pupils: B220 G1
No of boarders: W1
Fees: (September 06) FB £6360
WB £5970 Day £9270

THE MANOR PREPARATORY SCHOOL*
Faringdon Road, Abingdon,
Oxfordshire OX13 6LN
Tel: (01235) 523789
Fax: (01235) 559593
Email: registrar@manorprep.org
Head: Mr P Heyworth
Type: Co-educational Day
Boys 3–7 Girls 3–11
No of pupils: B12 G305
Fees: (September 06)
Day £3855–£8670

OUR LADY'S CONVENT JUNIOR SCHOOL
St John's Road, Abingdon,
Oxfordshire OX14 2HB
Tel: (01235) 523147
Fax: (01235) 530387
Email: office@
  ourladys-jun.oxon.sch.uk
Head: Sister J Frances
Type: Co-educational Day 3–11
No of pupils: B60 G90
Fees: (September 05) Day £1600

OUR LADY'S CONVENT SENIOR SCHOOL
Radley Road, Abingdon,
Oxfordshire OX14 3PS
Tel: (01235) 524658
Fax: (01235) 535829
Email: office@olcss.org.uk
Head: Mrs L Renwick
Type: Girls Day 11–18
No of pupils: 397
Fees: (September 05) Day £7980

RADLEY COLLEGE
Abingdon, Oxfordshire OX14 2HR
Tel: (01235) 543000
Fax: (01235) 543106
Head: Mr A W McPhail
Type: Boys Boarding 13–18
No of boarders: F625
Fees: (September 06) FB £24075

THE SCHOOL OF ST HELEN & ST KATHARINE
Faringdon Road, Abingdon,
Oxfordshire OX14 1BE
Tel: (01235) 520173
Fax: (01235) 532934
Email: info@shsk.org.uk
Head: Mrs C Hall
Type: Girls Day 9–18
No of pupils: 625
Fees: (September 06) Day £9066

BANBURY

ASH-SHIFA SCHOOL
Merton Street, Banbury,
Oxfordshire OX16 8RU
Tel: (01295) 279954
Fax: (01295) 279954
Email: info@ash-shifa.org.uk
Head: Ms F Aslam
Type: Girls Day 11–16
No of pupils: 26
Fees: (September 06) Day £4500

BLOXHAM SCHOOL[†]
Bloxham, Banbury, Oxfordshire
OX15 4PE
Tel: (01295) 720222
Fax: (01295) 721897
Email: registrar@
  bloxhamschool.com
Head: Mr M E Allbrook
Type: Co-educational Boarding
and Day 11–18
No of pupils: B262 G147
No of boarders: F211 W18
Fees: (September 06) FB £22990
WB £14885 Day £11920–£17760

THE CARRDUS SCHOOL
Overthorpe Hall, Banbury,
Oxfordshire OX17 2BS
Tel: (01295) 263733
Fax: (01295) 263733
Email: cardusschool@
  overthorpe.fsnet.co.uk
Head: Miss S Carrdus
Type: Girls Day 3–11 (Boys 3–8)
No of pupils: B29 G118
Fees: (September 06)
Day £1422–£7320

ST JOHN'S PRIORY SCHOOL
St John's Road, Banbury,
Oxfordshire OX16 5HX
Tel: (01295) 259607
Fax: (01295) 273326
Email: enquiries@
  stjohnspriory.com
Head: Mrs S Clacher
Type: Co-educational Day 2–11
No of pupils: B69 G58
Fees: (September 06)
Day £1785–£6255

SIBFORD SCHOOL[†]
Sibford Ferris, Banbury,
Oxfordshire OX15 5QL
Tel: (01295) 781200
Fax: (01295) 781204
Email: sibfordschool@
  dial.pipex.com
Head: Mr M Goodwin
Type: Co-educational Boarding
and Day 4–18
No of pupils: B249 G142
No of boarders: F33 W28
Fees: (September 06)
FB £14190–£18624
WB £12945–£17343
Day £7293–£9585

TUDOR HALL SCHOOL
Wykham Park, Banbury,
Oxfordshire OX16 9UR
Tel: (01295) 263434
Fax: (01295) 253264
Email: abrauer@
    tudorhallschool.com
Head: Miss W Griffiths
Type: Girls Boarding and Day
11–18
No of pupils: 289
No of boarders: F225
Fees: (September 06) FB £20715
Day £13356

CHIPPING NORTON

KINGHAM HILL SCHOOL*†
Kingham, Chipping Norton,
Oxfordshire OX7 6TH
Tel: (01608) 658999
Fax: (01608) 658658
Email: admissions@
    kingham-hill.oxon.sch.uk
Head: Mr M J Morris
Type: Co-educational Boarding
and Day 11–18
No of pupils: B167 G60
No of boarders: F174
Fees: (September 06)
FB £17302–£19654
Day £11349–£13298

WINDRUSH VALLEY
SCHOOL
The Green, London Lane,
Ascott-U-Wychwood, Chipping
Norton, Oxfordshire OX7 6AN
Tel: (01993) 831793
Fax: (01993) 831793
Email: windrushvalley@aol.com
Head: Mr G A Wood
Type: Co-educational Day 3–11
No of pupils: B60 G60
Fees: (September 05)
Day £3900–£4260

FARINGDON

FERNDALE PREPARATORY
SCHOOL
5–7 Bromsgrove, Faringdon,
Oxfordshire SN7 7JF
Tel: (01367) 240618
Fax: (01367) 241429
Email: ferndaleprep.school@
    talk21.com
Head: Mr Andrew Mersh
Type: Co-educational Day 3–11
No of pupils: B55 G55
Fees: (September 05)
Day £5580–£6270

ST HUGH'S SCHOOL
Carswell Manor, Faringdon,
Oxfordshire SN7 8PT
Tel: (01367) 870700
Fax: (01367) 870707
Email: registrar@st-hughs.co.uk
Head: Mr A J P Nott
Type: Co-educational Boarding
and Day 4–13
No of pupils: B157 G113
No of boarders: W35
Fees: (September 06)
WB £13845–£14775
Day £7260–£12330

HENLEY-ON-THAMES

RUPERT HOUSE
90 Bell Street, Henley-on-Thames,
Oxfordshire RG9 2BN
Tel: (01491) 574263
Fax: (01491) 573988
Email: office@
    ruperthouse.oxon.sch.uk
Head: Mrs N J Gan
Type: Co-educational Day
Boys 4–7 Girls 4–11
No of pupils: B41 G165
Fees: (September 06)
Day £3330–£7980

ST MARY'S SCHOOL
13 St Andrew's Road,
Henley-on-Thames, Oxfordshire
RG9 1HS
Tel: (01491) 573118
Email: stmarys.henley@
    btinternet.com
Head: Mrs S Bradley
Type: Co-educational Day 3–11
No of pupils: B72 G67
Fees: (September 05)
Day £1200–£6210

SHIPLAKE COLLEGE
Henley-on-Thames, Oxfordshire
RG9 4BW
Tel: (0118) 940 2455
Fax: (0118) 940 5204
Email: info@shiplake.org.uk
Head: Mr A G S Davies
Type: Co-educational Day and
Boarding Boys 13–18 Girls 16–18
(Day girls 16–18)
No of pupils: B285 G17
No of boarders: F171 W45
Fees: (September 06) FB £20760
Day £14004

OXFORD

ABACUS COLLEGE
Threeways House, George Street,
Oxford, Oxfordshire OX1 2BJ
Tel: (01865) 240111
Fax: (01865) 247259
Email: principal@
    abacuscollege.co.uk
Head: Dr R Carrington and
Mrs J Wasilewski
Type: Co-educational Boarding
and Day 16–19
No of pupils: B68 G52
No of boarders: F119
Fees: (September 06)
FB £11320–£13020
Day £6950–£8650

CHANDLINGS MANOR
SCHOOL
Bagley Wood, Kennington,
Oxford, Oxfordshire OX1 5ND
Tel: (01865) 730771
Fax: (01865) 735194
Email: office@chandlings.com
Head: Mrs J Forrest
Type: Co-educational Day 4–11
No of pupils: B242 G138
Fees: (September 05)
Day £7080–£9300

CHERWELL COLLEGE
Greyfriars, Paradise Street, Oxford,
Oxfordshire OX1 1LD
Tel: (01865) 242670
Fax: (01865) 791761
Email: secretary@
    cherwell-college.co.uk
Head: Mr A R Thompson
Type: Co-educational Boarding
and Day 16+
No of pupils: B75 G75
No of boarders: F90 W10
Fees: (September 06) F/WB £20500
Day £13750

CHRIST CHURCH
CATHEDRAL SCHOOL
3 Brewer Street, Oxford,
Oxfordshire OX1 1QW
Tel: (01865) 242561
Fax: (01865) 202945
Email: schooloffice@cccs.org.uk
Head: Mr M Bruce
Type: Boys Day 2–13 (Girls 2–4)
No of pupils: B122 G4
No of boarders: F20
Fees: (September 06)
FB £6090–£6720
Day £3075–£9870

D'OVERBROECK'S COLLEGE*

The Swan Building, 111 Banbury Road, Oxford, Oxfordshire OX2 6JX
Tel: (01865) 310000
Fax: (01865) 552296
Email: mail@doverbroecks.com
Head: Mr S Cohen
Type: Co-educational Day and Boarding 11–19 (Day only 13–16)
No of pupils: B217 G140
No of boarders: F148
Fees: (September 06)
FB £20445–£22995
Day £10650–£16215

DRAGON SCHOOL

Bardwell Road, Oxford, Oxfordshire OX2 6SS
Tel: (01865) 315405
Fax: (01865) 311664
Email: admissions@
  dragonschool.org
Head: Mr J R Baugh
Type: Co-educational Boarding and Day 4–13
No of pupils: B582 G276
No of boarders: F260
Fees: (September 06) FB £19490
Day £7350–£13560

EMMANUEL CHRISTIAN SCHOOL

Sandford Road, Littlemore, Oxford, Oxfordshire OX4 4PU
Tel: (01865) 395236
Email: admin@ecschool.org.uk
Head: Miss J P Dandy
Type: Co-educational Day 3–11
No of pupils: B23 G32
Fees: On application

GREENE'S TUTORIAL COLLEGE

45 Pembroke Street, Oxford, Oxfordshire OX1 1BP
Tel: (01865) 248308
Fax: (01865) 240700
Email: registrar@
  edward-greene.ac.uk
Head: Mr M Uffindell
Type: Co-educational Day and Boarding 7–70 (Boarding (host families))
No of pupils: B40 G40
No of boarders: F20 W20
Fees: (September 06)
FB £8260–£28280
WB £6040–£26060
Day £3080–£23100

HEADINGTON SCHOOL

Oxford, Oxfordshire OX3 7TD
Tel: (01865) 759113
Fax: (01865) 760268
Email: admissions@
  headington.org
Head: Mrs A Coutts
Type: Girls Day and Boarding 3–18 (Co-ed 3–4)
No of pupils: B8 G955
No of boarders: F125 W67
Fees: (September 06)
FB £18060–£19710
WB £17430–£18960
Day £5325–£10350

IQRA SCHOOL

Lawn Upton House, David Nicholls Close, Littlemore, Oxford, Oxfordshire OX4 4PU
Tel: (01865) 777254
Email: iqraschooloxford@
  yahoo.co.uk
Head: Mr H Ramzy and Mrs F Tenvir
Type: Girls Day 10–16
No of pupils: 80
Fees: (September 06) Day £1500

LECKFORD PLACE SCHOOL

Leckford Road, Oxford, Oxfordshire OX2 6HX
Tel: (01865) 302620
Fax: (01865) 302622
Email: corinna.hilton@
  leckfordplace.com
Head: Mr Mark Olejnik
Type: Co-educational Day 11–16
No of pupils: B70 G25
Fees: (September 06) Day £10650

MAGDALEN COLLEGE SCHOOL

Cowley Place, Oxford, Oxfordshire OX4 1DZ
Tel: (01865) 242191
Fax: (01865) 240379
Email: admissions@mcsoxford.org
Head: Mr A D Halls
Type: Boys Day 7–18
No of pupils: 680
Fees: (September 06)
Day £9294–£10572

NEW COLLEGE SCHOOL

2 Savile Road, Oxford, Oxfordshire OX1 3UA
Tel: (01865) 243657
Fax: (01865) 201277
Head: Mrs P Hindle
Type: Boys Day 4–13
No of pupils: 158
Fees: On application

OXFORD HIGH SCHOOL GDST

Belbroughton Road, Oxford, Oxfordshire OX2 6XA
Tel: (01865) 559888
Fax: (01865) 552343
Email: oxfordhigh@oxf.gdst.net
Head: Miss O F S Lusk
Type: Girls Day 3–18 (Boys 3–6)
No of pupils: B34 G894
Fees: (September 06)
Day £2355–£7863

OXFORD MONTESSORI SCHOOLS

Forest Farm, Elsfield, Oxford, Oxfordshire OX3 9UW
Tel: (01865) 358210
Fax: (01865) 358390
Email: oms.schools@
  btconnect.co.uk
Type: Co-educational Day 2–12
No of pupils: B60 G50
Fees: (September 05)
Day £4770–£6188

OXFORD TUTORIAL COLLEGE

12 King Edward Street, Oxford, Oxfordshire OX1 4HT
Tel: (01865) 793333
Fax: (01865) 793233
Email: info@otc.ac.uk
Head: Mrs F Pocock
Type: Co-educational Day and Boarding 16+
No of pupils: B70 G66
No of boarders: F45
Fees: (September 06) Day £15000

RYE ST ANTONY SCHOOL
Pullen's Lane, Oxford, Oxfordshire
OX3 0BY
Tel: (01865) 762802
Fax: (01865) 763611
Email: headmistress@
  ryestantony.co.uk
Head: Miss A M Jones
Type: Girls Boarding and Day
3–18 (Boys 3–8)
No of pupils: B20 G380
No of boarders: F60 W20
Fees: (September 05)
FB £13200–£15570
WB £12285–£14670
Day £5640–£9165

ST CLARE'S, OXFORD*
139 Banbury Road, Oxford,
Oxfordshire OX2 7AL
Tel: (01865) 552031
Fax: (01865) 513359
Email: admissions@stclares.ac.uk
Head: Mrs P Holloway
Type: Co-educational Boarding
and Day 15–20
No of pupils: B115 G125
No of boarders: F222 W3
Fees: (September 06) FB £24560
WB £24146 Day £15031

ST EDWARD'S SCHOOL
Woodstock Road, Oxford,
Oxfordshire OX2 7NN
Tel: (01865) 319200
Fax: (01865) 319202
Email: registrar@
  stedwards.oxon.sch.uk
Head: Mr A Trotman
Type: Co-educational Boarding
and Day 13–18
No of pupils: B425 G232
No of boarders: F481
Fees: (September 05) FB £22710
Day £18168

SUMMER FIELDS
Mayfield Road, Oxford,
Oxfordshire OX2 7EN
Tel: (01865) 454433
Fax: (01865) 459200
Email: schoolsec@
  summerfields.org.uk
Head: Mr R F Badham-Thornhill
Type: Boys Boarding and Day
7–13
No of pupils: 240
No of boarders: F211
Fees: (September 06) FB £17760
Day £13755

WYCHWOOD SCHOOL
74 Banbury Road, Oxford,
Oxfordshire OX2 6JR
Tel: (01865) 557976
Fax: (01865) 556806
Email: admin@
  wychwood-school.org.uk
Head: Mrs S M P Wingfield Digby
Type: Girls Boarding and Day
11–18
No of pupils: 150
No of boarders: F27 W31
Fees: On application

WALLINGFORD

**CRANFORD HOUSE
SCHOOL**
Moulsford, Wallingford,
Oxfordshire OX10 9HT
Tel: (01491) 651218
Fax: (01491) 652557
Email: admissions@
  cranfordhouse.oxon.sch.uk
Head: Mrs C Hamilton
Type: Girls Day 3–16 (Boys 3–7)
No of pupils: B58 G246
Fees: On application

**MOULSFORD
PREPARATORY SCHOOL**
Moulsford, Wallingford,
Oxfordshire OX10 9HR
Tel: (01491) 651438
Fax: (01491) 651868
Email: secretary@moulsford.com
Head: Mr M J Higham
Type: Boys Boarding and Day
5–13
No of pupils: 220
No of boarders: W51
Fees: On application

WANTAGE

ST ANDREW'S
Wallingford Street, Wantage,
Oxfordshire OX12 8AZ
Tel: (01235) 762345
Fax: (01235) 768274
Email: admin@st-andrews-
  wantage.oxon.sch.uk
Head: Mrs M Parkes
Type: Co-educational Day 3–11
No of pupils: B57 G43
Fees: (September 06)
Day £1631–£1823

ST MARY'S SCHOOL
Newbury Street, Wantage,
Oxfordshire OX12 8BZ
Tel: (01235) 773800
Fax: (01235) 760467
Email: admissions@
  stmarys.oxon.sch.uk
Head: Mrs S Sowden
Type: Girls Boarding and Day
11–18
No of pupils: 200
No of boarders: F180
Fees: (September 05) FB £21990
Day £14700

WITNEY

COKETHORPE SCHOOL*
Witney, Oxfordshire OX29 7PU
Tel: (01993) 703921
Fax: (01993) 773499
Email: admissions@
  cokethorpe.org.uk
Head: Mr D J Ettinger
Type: Co-educational Day 5–18
No of pupils: B395 G255
Fees: (September 06)
Day £7935–£12285

THE KING'S SCHOOL
12 Wesley Walk, High Street,
Witney, Oxfordshire OX8 6ZJ
Tel: (01993) 709985
Fax: (01993) 709986
Email: tks@occ.org.uk
Head: Mr K Elmitt
Type: Co-educational Day 11–16
No of pupils: B60 G50
Fees: On application

**THE KING'S SCHOOL,
PRIMARY**
New Yatt Road, Witney,
Oxfordshire OX29 6TA
Tel: (01993) 778463
Fax: (01993) 778463
Head: Mrs A Gibbon
Type: Co-educational Day 5–11
No of pupils: B60 G60
Fees: On application

England – Oxfordshire

RUTLAND

OAKHAM

BROOKE PRIORY SCHOOL
Station Approach, Oakham,
Rutland LE15 6QW
Tel: (01572) 724778
Fax: (01572) 724969
Email: info@brooke.rutland.sch.uk
Head: Mrs E Bell
Type: Co-educational Day 3–11
No of pupils: B128 G112
Fees: (September 06)
Day £4368–£5850

OAKHAM SCHOOL*
Chapel Close, Oakham, Rutland
LE15 6DT
Tel: (01572) 758758
Fax: (01572) 758595
Email: admissions@
   oakham.rutland.sch.uk
Head: Dr J A F Spence
Type: Co-educational Boarding
and Day 10–18
No of pupils: B520 G520
No of boarders: F620
Fees: (September 06)
FB £19260–£22500
WB £15660–£18090
Day £12210–£13440

UPPINGHAM

UPPINGHAM SCHOOL
Uppingham, Rutland LE15 9QE
Tel: (01572) 822216
Fax: (01572) 822332
Email: admissions@
   uppingham.co.uk
Head: Mr R S Harman
Type: Co-educational Boarding
and Day 13–18
No of pupils: B482 G268
No of boarders: F726
Fees: (September 05) FB £22500
Day £15750

WINDMILL HOUSE SCHOOL
22 Stockerston Road, Uppingham,
Rutland LE15 9UD
Tel: (01572) 823593
Fax: (01572) 822220
Head: Mrs J Taylor
Type: Co-educational Day 4–11
No of pupils: B40 G40
Fees: On application

SHROPSHIRE

BRIDGNORTH

DOWER HOUSE SCHOOL
Quatt, Bridgnorth, Shropshire
WV15 6QW
Tel: (01746) 780309
Email: info@
   dowerhouseschool.co.uk
Head: Mr A R T Ellis
Type: Co-educational Day
Boys 2–11 Girls 3–11
No of pupils: B30 G35
Fees: On application

BUCKNELL

BEDSTONE COLLEGE
Bedstone, Bucknell, Shropshire
SY7 0BG
Tel: (01547) 530303
Fax: (01547) 530740
Email: admissions@bedstone.org
Head: Mr M S Symonds
Type: Co-educational Boarding
and Day 3–18
No of pupils: B137 G99
No of boarders: F112
Fees: (September 06)
FB £12780–£18600
Day £7350–£10170

ELLESMERE

ELLESMERE COLLEGE[†]
Ellesmere, Shropshire SY12 9AB
Tel: (01691) 622321
Fax: (01691) 623286
Email: admissions.secretary@
   ellesmere.com
Head: Mr B J Wignall
Type: Co-educational Boarding
and Day 8–18
No of pupils: B389 G166
No of boarders: F88 W101
Fees: (September 06)
FB £16794–£19998
WB £16047–£16497
Day £7794–£12762

LUDLOW

MOOR PARK SCHOOL
Moor Park, Ludlow, Shropshire
SY8 4DZ
Tel: (01584) 876061
Fax: (01584) 877311
Email: head@moorpark.org.uk
Head: Mr M R Piercy
Type: Co-educational Boarding
and Day 3–13
No of pupils: B146 G116
No of boarders: F15 W30
Fees: (September 06)
F/WB £11880–£14460
Day £4305–£10590

NEWPORT

CASTLE HOUSE SCHOOL
Chetwynd End, Newport,
Shropshire TF10 7JE
Tel: (01952) 811035
Fax: (01952) 811035
Email: admin@
castlehouse.indschools.co.uk
Head: Mr R M Walden
Type: Co-educational Day 3–11
No of pupils: B40 G48
Fees: (September 05)
Day £895–£1876

OSWESTRY

MORETON HALL SCHOOL*
Weston Rhyn, Oswestry,
Shropshire SY11 3EW
Tel: (01691) 776020
Fax: (01691) 778552
Email: admin@moretonhall.com
Head: Mr J Forster
Type: Girls Boarding and Day
3–18
No of pupils: B10 G320
No of boarders: F239
Fees: (September 06)
FB £14280–£22500
Day £6270–£17850

OSWESTRY SCHOOL
Upper Brook Street, Oswestry,
Shropshire SY11 2TL
Tel: (01691) 655711
Fax: (01691) 671194
Email: enquiries@
oswestryschool.org.uk
Head: Mr P D Stockdale
Type: Co-educational Day and
Boarding 2–18
No of pupils: B238 G181
No of boarders: F105 W6
Fees: (September 05) FB £17550
WB £15450 Day £4890–£10350

OSWESTRY SCHOOL BELLAN HOUSE
Bellan House, Church Street,
Oswestry, Shropshire SY11 2ST
Tel: (01691) 653453
Fax: (01691) 680552
Email: enquiries@
oswestryschool.co.uk
Head: Mrs S L Durham
Type: Co-educational Day 2–9
No of pupils: B91 G92
Fees: On application

SHREWSBURY

ADCOTE SCHOOL FOR GIRLS
Little Ness, Shrewsbury,
Shropshire SY4 2JY
Tel: (01939) 260202
Fax: (01939) 261300
Email: secretary@
adcoteschool.co.uk
Head: Ms D J Hammond
Type: Girls Boarding and Day
4–18
No of pupils: 105
No of boarders: F35 W8
Fees: (September 05)
FB £13080–£18090
WB £11505–£16515
Day £5505–£10185

CONCORD COLLEGE
Acton Burnell Hall, Shrewsbury,
Shropshire SY5 7PF
Tel: (01694) 731631
Fax: (01694) 731389
Email: theprincipal@
concordcollegeuk.com
Head: Mr N G Hawkins
Type: Co-educational Boarding
and Day 12–21
No of pupils: B180 G180
No of boarders: F320
Fees: (September 06) FB £19980
Day £9495

KINGSLAND GRANGE
Old Roman Road, Shrewsbury,
Shropshire SY3 9AH
Tel: (01743) 232132
Fax: (01743) 352665
Email: mcjames@talk21.com
Head: Mr M C James
Type: Boys Day 4–13
No of pupils: 110
Fees: (September 06)
Day £5280–£8400

PACKWOOD HAUGH SCHOOL
Ruyton XI Towns, Shrewsbury,
Shropshire SY4 1HX
Tel: (01939) 260217
Fax: (01939) 262077
Email: head@
packwood-haugh.co.uk
Head: Mr N T Westlake
Type: Co-educational Boarding
and Day 4–13
No of pupils: B176 G112
No of boarders: F140
Fees: (September 06) FB £14985
Day £5157–£11991

PRESTFELDE PREPARATORY SCHOOL
London Road, Shrewsbury,
Shropshire SY2 6NZ
Tel: (01743) 245400
Fax: (01743) 241434
Email: office@prestfelde.net
Head: Mr J R Bridgeland
Type: Co-educational Day and
Boarding 3–13
No of pupils: B250 G85
No of boarders: F35 W10
Fees: On application

ST WINEFRIDE'S CONVENT SCHOOL
Belmont, Shrewsbury, Shropshire
SY1 1TE
Tel: (01743) 369883
Fax: (01743) 341650
Head: Sister M Felicity
Type: Co-educational Day 3–11
No of pupils: B65 G86
Fees: On application

England – Shropshire

SHREWSBURY HIGH SCHOOL GDST
32 Town Walls, Shrewsbury,
Shropshire SY1 1TN
Tel: (01743) 362872
Fax: (01743) 364942
Email: enquiries@shr.gdst.net
Head: Mrs M L R Cass
Type: Girls Day 2–18
No of pupils: 661
Fees: (September 06)
Day £4710–£7863

SHREWSBURY SCHOOL
The Schools, Shrewsbury,
Shropshire SY3 7BA
Tel: (01743) 280500
Fax: (01743) 243107
Email: enquiry@shrewsbury.org.uk
Head: Mr J Goulding
Type: Boys Boarding and Day
13–18
No of boarders: F558
Fees: (September 05) FB £22590
Day £15870

TELFORD

THE OLD HALL SCHOOL
Holyhead Road, Wellington,
Telford, Shropshire TF1 2DN
Tel: (01952) 223117
Fax: (01952) 222674
Email: enq@oldhall.co.uk
Head: Mr R J Ward
Type: Co-educational Day 3–11
No of pupils: B136 G118
Fees: On application

WREKIN COLLEGE
Wellington, Telford, Shropshire
TF1 3BH
Tel: (01952) 240131/242305
Fax: (01952) 240338
Email: info@wrekincollege.ac.uk
Head: Mr S G Drew
Type: Co-educational Boarding
and Day 11–19
No of pupils: B269 G184
No of boarders: F114
Fees: On application

WHITCHURCH

WHITE HOUSE SCHOOL
Heath Road, Whitchurch,
Shropshire SY13 2AA
Tel: (01948) 662730
Email: whitehouseschool@
btconnect.com
Head: Mrs H Clarke
Type: Co-educational Day 3–11
No of pupils: B75 G75
Fees: (September 06)
Day £1920–£2820

SOMERSET

BATH

DOWNSIDE SCHOOL
Stratton-on-the-Fosse, Radstock,
Bath, Somerset BA3 4RJ
Tel: (01761) 235100
Fax: (01761) 235105
Email: registrar@downside.co.uk
Head: Dom Leo Maidlow Davis
Type: Co-educational Boarding
and Day 9–18
No of pupils: B367 G60
No of boarders: F229
Fees: (September 05)
FB £15558–£19590
Day £9192–£10224

BRUTON

BRUTON SCHOOL FOR GIRLS
Sunny Hill, Bruton, Somerset
BA10 0NT
Tel: (01749) 814400
Fax: (01749) 812537
Email: info@brutonschool.co.uk
Head: Mr John Burrough
Type: Girls Day and Boarding
3–18
No of pupils: B6 G380
No of boarders: F80 W20
Fees: (September 06)
FB £14235–£17490
WB £12900–£15285
Day £5475–£9675

KING'S BRUTON*†
Bruton, Somerset BA10 0ED
Tel: (01749) 814200
Fax: (01749) 813426
Email: registrar@kingsbruton.com
Head: Mr N M Lashbrook
Type: Co-educational Boarding
and Day 13–18
No of pupils: B232 G94
No of boarders: F221
Fees: (September 05) FB £20100
Day £14730

BURNHAM-ON-SEA

SOUTHLEIGH KINDERGARTEN
11 Rectory Road,
Burnham-on-Sea, Somerset
TA8 2BY
Tel: (01278) 783999
Head: Mrs L Easton
Type: Co-educational Day 2–7
No of pupils: B40 G40
Fees: On application

CHARD

CHARD SCHOOL
Fore Street, Chard, Somerset
TA20 1QA
Tel: (01460) 63234
Fax: (01460) 68988
Email: headmaster@
chardschool.co.uk
Head: Mr J G Stotesbury
Type: Co-educational Day 2–11
No of pupils: B60 G60
Fees: (September 05)
Day £3618–£3897

CREWKERNE

PERROTT HILL SCHOOL
North Perrott, Crewkerne,
Somerset TA18 7SL
Tel: (01460) 72051
Fax: (01460) 78246
Email: headmaster@
  perrotthill.com
Head: Mr M J Davies
Type: Co-educational Boarding
and Day 3–13
No of pupils: B100 G80
No of boarders: F10 W25
Fees: (September 06) FB £5210
WB £4820 Day £34454–£3645

GLASTONBURY

MILLFIELD PREPARATORY SCHOOL
Edgarley Hall, Glastonbury,
Somerset BA6 8LD
Tel: (01458) 832446
Fax: (01458) 833679
Email: admissions@
  millfieldprep.com
Head: Mr K Cheney
Type: Co-educational Boarding
and Day 2–13
No of pupils: B264 G263
No of boarders: F167
Fees: On application

SHEPTON MALLET

ALL HALLOWS
Cranmore Hall, East Cranmore,
Shepton Mallet, Somerset BA4 4SF
Tel: (01749) 880227
Fax: (01749) 880709
Email: info@
  allhallows.somerset.sch.uk
Head: Mr Ian Murphy
Type: Co-educational Boarding
and Day 4–13
No of pupils: B160 G105
No of boarders: F70
Fees: (September 06) FB £15420
Day £5055–£10290

STREET

MILLFIELD SCHOOL
Butleigh Road, Street, Somerset
BA16 0YD
Tel: (01458) 442291
Fax: (01458) 447276
Email: admissions@
  millfieldschool.com
Head: Mr P M Johnson
Type: Co-educational Boarding
and Day 13–18
No of pupils: B780 G470
No of boarders: F939
Fees: On application

TAUNTON

KING'S COLLEGE
Taunton, Somerset TA1 3DX
Tel: (01823) 328200
Fax: (01823) 328202
Email: admissions@
  kings-taunton.co.uk
Head: Mr C D Ramsey
Type: Co-educational Boarding
and Day 13–18
No of pupils: B267 G148
No of boarders: F278
Fees: (September 05) FB £19980
Day £13650

KING'S HALL SCHOOL
Kingston Road, Taunton, Somerset
TA2 8AA
Tel: (01823) 285920
Fax: (01823) 285922
Email: schooloffice@
  kingshall.rmplc.co.uk
Head: Mr J K Macpherson
Type: Co-educational Boarding
and Day 3–13
No of pupils: B225 G160
No of boarders: F30 W22
Fees: (September 06)
F/WB £12000–£15600
Day £3960–£10545

QUEEN'S COLLEGE
Trull Road, Taunton, Somerset
TA1 4QS
Tel: (01823) 340830
Fax: (01823) 338430
Email: admissions@
  queenscollege.org.uk
Head: Mr C J Alcock
Type: Co-educational Day and
Boarding 3–18
No of pupils: B405 G365
No of boarders: F175
Fees: (September 05)
FB £7857–£17172
Day £3600–£11376

QUEEN'S COLLEGE JUNIOR AND PRE-PREPARATORY SCHOOLS
Trull Road, Taunton, Somerset
TA1 4QP
Tel: (01823) 272990
Fax: (01823) 323811
Email: junior.head@
  queenscollege.org.uk
Head: Mr J M Backhouse and
Mrs E Gibbs
Type: Co-educational Day and
Boarding 3–11
No of pupils: B117 G107
No of boarders: F33
Fees: On application

TAUNTON INTERNATIONAL STUDY CENTRE (TISC)
Taunton School, Taunton,
Somerset TA2 6AD
Tel: (01823) 348100
Fax: (01823) 349206
Email: tisc@tauntonschool.co.uk
Head: Mrs C G Nixon
Type: Co-educational Boarding
12–17
No of pupils: B38 G21
No of boarders: F59
Fees: (September 05)
FB £22050–£24075

England – Somerset

TAUNTON PREPARATORY SCHOOL

Staplegrove Road, Taunton,
Somerset TA2 6AE
Tel: (01823) 349250
Fax: (01823) 349202
Email: tps.enquiries@
    tauntonschool.co.uk
Head: Mr M Anderson
Type: Co-educational Day and
Boarding 3–13
No of pupils: B251 G193
No of boarders: F39
Fees: (September 05)
FB £8295–£15045
Day £4575–£9945

TAUNTON SCHOOL

Taunton, Somerset TA2 6AD
Tel: (01823) 349200/349223
Fax: (01823) 349201
Email: enquiries@
    tauntonschool.co.uk
Head: Dr J Newton
Type: Co-educational Boarding
and Day 13–18
No of pupils: B256 G194
No of boarders: F177
Fees: (September 05) FB £19200
Day £12345

WELLINGTON

WELLINGTON SCHOOL

South Street, Wellington, Somerset
TA21 8NT
Tel: (01823) 668800
Fax: (01823) 668844
Email: admin@
    wellington-school.org.uk
Head: Mr A J Rogers
Type: Co-educational Boarding
and Day 10–18
No of pupils: B456 G357
No of boarders: F155 W7
Fees: (September 05)
FB £12660–£15612
WB £9948–£12270
Day £6450–£8382

WELLS

WELLS CATHEDRAL JUNIOR SCHOOL

8 New Street, Wells, Somerset
BA5 2LQ
Tel: (01749) 834400
Fax: (01749) 834401
Email: juniorschool@
    wells-cathedral-school.com
Head: Mr N M Wilson
Type: Co-educational Boarding
and Day 3–11
No of pupils: B94 G93
No of boarders: F4 W4
Fees: On application

WELLS CATHEDRAL SCHOOL

Wells, Somerset BA5 2ST
Tel: (01749) 834200
Fax: (01749) 834201
Email: admissions@
    wells-cathedral-school.com
Head: Mrs E C Cairncross
Type: Co-educational Boarding
and Day 3–18
No of pupils: B342 G310
No of boarders: F205
Fees: On application

YEOVIL

CHILTON CANTELO SCHOOL

Chilton Cantelo, Yeovil, Somerset
BA22 8BG
Tel: (01935) 850555
Fax: (01935) 850482
Email: ccs@pavilion.co.uk
Head: Mr D S von Zeffman
Type: Co-educational Boarding
and Day 7–16
No of pupils: B230 G180
No of boarders: F210
Fees: (September 06)
FB £12555–£16125
Day £6315–£8145

HAZLEGROVE (KING'S BRUTON PREPARATORY SCHOOL)[†]

Hazlegrove House, Sparkford,
Yeovil, Somerset BA22 7JA
Tel: (01963) 440314
Fax: (01963) 440569
Email: office@hazlegrove.co.uk
Head: Mr R Fenwick
Type: Co-educational Day and
Boarding 3–13
No of pupils: B184 G141
No of boarders: F67
Fees: (September 06)
F/WB £13095–£16545
Day £5805–£11775

THE PARK SCHOOL

The Park, Yeovil, Somerset
BA20 1DH
Tel: (01935) 423514
Fax: (01935) 411257
Email: admin@parkschool.com
Head: Mr P W Bate
Type: Co-educational Day and
Boarding 3–18
No of pupils: B128 G140
No of boarders: F29 W4
Fees: (September 06)
FB £13530–£14475
WB £12930–£13845
Day £3705–£7410

BATH & NORTH EAST SOMERSET

BATH

BATH ACADEMY
27 Queen Square, Bath,
Bath & North East Somerset
BA1 2HX
Tel: (01225) 334577
Fax: (01225) 482414
Email: principal@
bathacademy.co.uk
Head: Mrs L Brown
Type: Co-educational Boarding
16–20
No of pupils: B70 G70
No of boarders: F150
Fees: (September 06) FB £13450

KING EDWARD'S JUNIOR SCHOOL
North Road, Bath,
Bath & North East Somerset
BA2 6JA
Tel: (01225) 463218
Fax: (01225) 442178
Email: juniorschhead@
kesbath.biblio.net
Head: Mr J Croker
Type: Co-educational Day 7–11
Fees: (September 05) Day £6954

KING EDWARD'S PRE-PREP SCHOOL
Weston Lane, Bath,
Bath & North East Somerset
BA1 4AQ
Tel: (01225) 421681
Fax: (01225) 428006
Email: kespp@btopenworld.com
Head: Mrs J A Siderfin
Type: Co-educational Day 3–7
No of pupils: B63 G24
Fees: On application

KING EDWARD'S SCHOOL, BATH
North Road, Bath,
Bath & North East Somerset
BA2 6HU
Tel: (01225) 464313
Fax: (01225) 481363
Email: headmaster@
kcsbath.biblio.net
Head: Mr Crispin Rowe
Type: Co-educational Day 3–18
No of pupils: B486 G177
Fees: (September 05)
Day £6525–£8910

KINGSWOOD PREPARATORY SCHOOL
College Road, Lansdown, Bath,
Bath & North East Somerset
BA1 5SD
Tel: (01225) 734460
Fax: (01225) 464434
Email: enquiries@
kingswood.bath.sch.uk
Head: Mr Marcus Cornah
Type: Co-educational Day and
Boarding 3–11
No of pupils: B173 G145
No of boarders: F7 W7
Fees: (September 05)
FB £14112–£14910 WB £11856
Day £5958–£6894

KINGSWOOD SCHOOL*
Lansdown, Bath,
Bath & North East Somerset
BA1 5RG
Tel: (01225) 734210
Fax: (01225) 734305
Email: enquiries@
kingswood.bath.sch.uk
Head: Mr G M Best
Type: Co-educational Boarding
and Day 3–18
No of pupils: B543 G417
No of boarders: F176 W43
Fees: (September 06)
FB £14889–£20592
WB £12507–£18606
Day £6285–£9234

MONKTON COMBE JUNIOR SCHOOL
Combe Down, Bath,
Bath & North East Somerset
BA2 7ET
Tel: (01225) 837912
Fax: (01225) 840312
Email: admin@
monktonjunior.org.uk
Head: Mr C J Stafford
Type: Co-educational Day and
Boarding 2–13
No of pupils: B221 G151
No of boarders: F19 W41
Fees: On application

MONKTON COMBE SCHOOL[†]
Bath, Bath & North East Somerset
BA2 7HG
Tel: (01225) 721133
Fax: (01225) 721181
Email: admissions@
monkton.org.uk
Head: Mr R P Backhouse
Type: Co-educational Boarding
and Day 2–19
No of pupils: B452 G268
No of boarders: F270
Fees: (September 06)
FB £15486–£22149
WB £14916–£20199
Day £9948–£15249

PARAGON SCHOOL, PRIOR PARK COLLEGE JUNIOR
Lyncombe House, Lyncombe
Vale, Bath,
Bath & North East Somerset
BA2 4LT
Tel: (01225) 310837
Fax: (01225) 427980
Email: office@
paragonschool.co.uk
Head: Mr D J Martin
Type: Co-educational Day 3–11
No of pupils: B116 G86
Fees: (September 05)
Day £5010–£5580

PRIOR PARK COLLEGE*
Ralph Allen Drive, Bath,
Bath & North East Somerset
BA2 5AH
Tel: (01225) 831000
Fax: (01225) 835753
Email: admissions@
priorpark.co.uk
Head: Dr G Mercer
Type: Co-educational Boarding
and Day 11–18 (Boarding from 13)
No of pupils: B298 G245
No of boarders: F120
Fees: (September 06) FB £20118
Day £10014–£11157

England – Bath and North East Somerset

THE ROYAL HIGH SCHOOL*
Lansdown Road, Bath,
Bath & North East Somerset
BA1 5SZ
Tel: (01225) 313877
Fax: (01225) 465446
Email: royalhigh@bat.gdst.net
Head: Mr J Graham-Brown
Type: Girls Boarding and Day
3–18
No of pupils: 807
No of boarders: F80 W10
Fees: (September 06) FB £15417
WB £13695 Day £7863

NORTH SOMERSET

WESTON-SUPER-MARE

ASHBROOKE HOUSE
9 Ellenborough Park North,
Weston-Super-Mare,
North Somerset BS23 1XH
Tel: (01934) 629515
Fax: (01934) 629685
Head: Mrs R Thomas
Type: Co-educational Day 3–11
No of pupils: B60 G50
Fees: On application

LANCASTER HOUSE SCHOOL
38 Hill Road, Weston-Super-Mare,
North Somerset BS23 2RY
Tel: (01934) 624116
Email: susanlewisbrent@
    supanet.com
Head: Mrs S Lewis
Type: Co-educational Day 4–11
No of pupils: B23 G23
Fees: On application

WINSCOMBE

SIDCOT SCHOOL*†
Oakridge Lane, Winscombe,
North Somerset BS25 1PD
Tel: (01934) 843102
Fax: (01934) 844181
Email: admissions@sidcot.org.uk
Head: Mr J Walmsley
Type: Co-educational Boarding
and Day 3–18
No of pupils: B286 G213
No of boarders: F127 W14
Fees: (September 06)
FB £14550–£22950 WB £16650
Day £3870–£10485

STAFFORDSHIRE

ABBOTS BROMLEY

ABBOTS BROMLEY SCHOOL FOR GIRLS
Abbots Bromley, Staffordshire
WS15 3BW
Tel: (01283) 840232
Fax: (01283) 840988
Email: registar@abbotsbromley.net
Head: Mrs P Woodhouse
Type: Girls Boarding and Day
3–18
No of pupils: 297
No of boarders: F40 W30
Fees: (September 06)
FB £15435–£19230
WB £11040–£15915
Day £5850–£11490

BREWOOD

VERNON LODGE PREPARATORY SCHOOL
School Lane, Stretton, Brewood,
Staffordshire ST19 9LJ
Tel: (01902) 850568
Fax: (01902) 850568
Email: info@vernonlodge.co.uk
Head: Mrs P Sills
Type: Co-educational Day 2–11
No of pupils: B53 G37
Fees: (September 06)
Day £5280–£5997

CANNOCK

CHASE ACADEMY
Lyncroft House, St John's Road,
Cannock, Staffordshire WS11 0UR
Tel: (01543) 501800
Fax: (01543) 501801
Email: info@chaseacademy.com
Head: Mr D R Holland
Type: Co-educational Day and
Boarding 3–18
No of pupils: B109 G82
No of boarders: F6
Fees: (September 06) FB £13650
Day £2088–£7176

LICHFIELD

LICHFIELD CATHEDRAL SCHOOL
The Palace, Lichfield, Staffordshire
WS13 7LH
Tel: (01543) 306170
Fax: (01543) 306176
Email: reception@
    lichfieldcathedralschool.com
Head: Mr P Allwood
Type: Co-educational Day and
Boarding 3–13
No of pupils: 273
No of boarders: F18 W6
Fees: On application

ST JOHN'S PREPARATORY SCHOOL
Green Gables, Longdon Hall,
Longdon Green, Lichfield,
Staffordshire WS15 4PT
Tel: (01543) 492782
Email: sjsann@aol.com
Head: Mrs A Watson
Type: Co-educational Day 3–11
No of pupils: B50 G34
Fees: (September 05)
Day £2775–£5400

NEWCASTLE-UNDER-LYME

EDENHURST SCHOOL
Westlands Avenue,
Newcastle-under-Lyme,
Staffordshire ST5 2PU
Tel: (01782) 619348
Fax: (01782) 662402
Email: headmaster@
    edenhurst.co.uk
Head: Mr N H F Copestick
Type: Co-educational Day 3–14
No of pupils: B118 G122
Fees: On application

NEWCASTLE-UNDER-LYME SCHOOL
Mount Pleasant,
Newcastle-under-Lyme,
Staffordshire ST5 1DB
Tel: (01782) 631197
Fax: (01782) 632582
Email: info@nuls.org.uk
Head: Mr R S Dillow
Type: Co-educational Day 3–18
No of pupils: B550 G550
Fees: (September 05)
Day £5340–£6984

STAFFORD

BROOKLANDS SCHOOL & LITTLE BROOKLANDS NURSERY
167 Eccleshall Road, Stafford,
Staffordshire ST16 1PD
Tel: (01785) 251399
Fax: (01785) 244379
Email: enquiries@
    brooklandsschool.com
Head: Mr D R Williams
Type: Co-educational Day 0–11
No of pupils: B57 G55
Fees: (September 06)
Day £744–£7200

ST BEDE'S SCHOOL
Bishton Hall, Wolseley Bridge,
Stafford, Staffordshire ST17 0XN
Tel: (01889) 881277
Fax: (01889) 882749
Email: admin@saintbedes.com
Head: Mr M E A McLuckie
Type: Co-educational Boarding
and Day 2–13
No of pupils: B68 G50
No of boarders: F10 W15
Fees: (September 06) F/WB £10200
Day £8325

ST DOMINIC'S SCHOOL
32 Bargate Street, Brewood,
Stafford, Staffordshire ST19 9BA
Tel: (01902) 850248
Fax: (01902) 851154
Email: enquiries@
    st-dominics-brewood.co.uk
Head: Mrs S White
Type: Girls Day 2–16 (Co-ed 2–7)
No of pupils: B5 G292
Fees: On application

STAFFORD GRAMMAR SCHOOL
Burton Manor, Stafford,
Staffordshire ST18 9AT
Tel: (01785) 249752
Fax: (01785) 255005
Email: headsec@
    staffordgs.plus.com
Head: Mr M R Darley
Type: Co-educational Day 11–18
No of pupils: B197 G160
Fees: On application

YARLET SCHOOL
Yarlet, Near Stafford, Stafford,
Staffordshire ST18 9SU
Tel: (01785) 286568
Fax: (01785) 286569
Email: headmaster@
    yarletschool.co.uk
Head: Mr R S Plant
Type: Co-educational Day and
Boarding 2–13
No of pupils: B92 G65
Fees: (September 06)
Day £5070–£8475

STOKE-ON-TRENT

ST DOMINIC'S INDEPENDENT JUNIOR SCHOOL
Hartshill Road, Stoke-on-Trent,
Staffordshire ST4 7LY
Tel: (01782) 848588
Fax: (01782) 413778
Email: saintdominics@
    btconnect.com
Head: Mr J F Butler
Type: Co-educational Day 3–11
No of pupils: B54 G46
Fees: (September 06)
Day £3399–£4272

ST JOSEPH'S PREPARATORY SCHOOL
London Road, Trent Vale,
Stoke-on-Trent, Staffordshire
ST4 5RF
Tel: (01782) 417533
Fax: (01782) 849327
Email: enquiries@
    stjosephprepschool.co.uk
Head: Mrs S D Hutchinson
Type: Co-educational Day 3–11
No of pupils: 120
Fees: On application

STONE

ST DOMINIC'S PRIORY SCHOOL
21 Station Road, Stone,
Staffordshire ST15 8EN
Tel: (01785) 814181
Fax: (01785) 819361
Email: head@
    st-dominicspriory.staffs.sch.uk
Head: Mr A Egan
Type: Girls Day 3–18 (Boys 3–11)
No of pupils: B4 G250
Fees: (September 06)
Day £4634–£7389

UTTOXETER

ABBOTSHOLME SCHOOL
Rocester, Uttoxeter, Staffordshire
ST14 5BS
Tel: (01889) 590217
Fax: (01889) 591001
Email: admissions@
  abbotsholme.co.uk
Head: Mr S Fairclough
Type: Co-educational Boarding
and Day 5–18 (Boarders from 10)
No of pupils: B171 G97
No of boarders: F55 W76
Fees: (September 06)
FB £6300–£7300
WB £4800–£6100
Day £2700–£5000

DENSTONE COLLEGE
Uttoxeter, Staffordshire ST14 5HN
Tel: (01889) 591415
Fax: (01889) 591295
Email: admissions@
  denstonecollege.org
Head: Mr D M Derbyshire
Type: Co-educational Boarding
and Day 11–18
No of pupils: B346 G178
No of boarders: F135
Fees: (September 06)
F/WB £14790–£16215
Day £7635–£9750

SMALLWOOD MANOR PREPARATORY SCHOOL
Uttoxeter, Staffordshire ST14 8NS
Tel: (01889) 562083
Fax: (01889) 568682
Email: headmaster@
  smallwoodmanor.co.uk
Head: Revd C J Cann
Type: Co-educational Day 2–11
No of pupils: B88 G63
Fees: On application

STOCKTON-ON-TEES

EAGLESCLIFFE

TEESSIDE PREPARATORY AND HIGH SCHOOL
The Avenue, Eaglescliffe,
Stockton-on-Tees TS16 9AT
Tel: (01642) 782095
Fax: (01642) 791207
Email: info@teessidehigh.co.uk
Head: Mr T A Packer
Type: Co-educational Day
Boys 3–6 Girls 3–18
No of pupils: B10 G370
Fees: (September 06)
Day £5049–£8208

NORTON

RED HOUSE SCHOOL
36 The Green, Norton,
Stockton-on-Tees TS20 1DX
Tel: (01642) 553370
Fax: (01642) 361031
Email: headmaster@r-h-s.com
Head: Mr C M J Allen
Type: Co-educational Day 3–16
No of pupils: B256 G182
Fees: On application

YARM

YARM SCHOOL
The Friarage, Yarm,
Stockton-on-Tees TS15 9EJ
Tel: (01642) 786023/781447
Fax: (01642) 789216
Email: dmd@yarmschool.org
Head: Mr D M Dunn
Type: Co-educational Day 3–18
No of pupils: B600 G350
Fees: (September 06)
Day £3954–£8718

SUFFOLK

BECCLES

THE OLD SCHOOL
Henstead, Beccles, Suffolk
NR34 7LG
Tel: (01502) 741150
Fax: (01502) 741150
Email: oldschool@btclick.com
Head: Mr M J Hewett
Type: Co-educational Day 4–11
No of pupils: B60 G45
Fees: (September 06)
Day £4350–£5460

BRANDESTON

FRAMLINGHAM COLLEGE PREPARATORY SCHOOL
Brandeston Hall, Brandeston,
Suffolk IP13 7AH
Tel: (01728) 685331
Fax: (01728) 685437
Email: office@
  brandestonhall.co.uk
Head: Mr N Woolnough
Type: Co-educational Boarding
and Day 3–13
No of pupils: B164 G110
No of boarders: F38
Fees: (September 06) FB £15429
Day £5517–£9594

BURY ST EDMUNDS

CHERRY TREES SCHOOL
Flempton Road, Risby,
Bury St Edmunds, Suffolk IP28 6QJ
Tel: (01284) 760531
Fax: (01284) 750177
Email: cherrytrees@
  cherrytrees-school.co.uk
Head: Ms W Compson
Type: Co-educational Day 0–11
No of pupils: B130 G126
Fees: On application

CULFORD SCHOOL
Bury St Edmunds, Suffolk IP28 6TX
Tel: (01284) 728615
Fax: (01284) 729146
Email: admissions@culford.co.uk
Head: Mr J Johnson-Munday
Type: Co-educational Boarding
and Day 2–18
No of pupils: B323 G253
No of boarders: F116 W58
Fees: (September 05)
FB £15204–£19698
WB £13527–£19698
Day £7131–£12837

MORETON HALL PREPARATORY SCHOOL
Mount Road, Bury St Edmunds,
Suffolk IP32 7BJ
Tel: (01284) 753532
Fax: (01284) 769197
Email: office@moretonhall.net
Head: Mr B Dunhill
Type: Co-educational Boarding
and Day 3–13
No of pupils: B64 G48
No of boarders: F3 W2
Fees: (September 06) FB £15630
WB £13800 Day £6075–£10335

SOUTH LEE PREPARATORY SCHOOL
Nowton Road, Bury St Edmunds,
Suffolk IP33 2BT
Tel: (01284) 754654
Fax: (01284) 706178
Email: office@southlee.co.uk
Head: Mr D Whipp
Type: Co-educational Day 2–13
No of pupils: B141 G150
Fees: (September 06)
Day £6360–£7920

FELIXSTOWE

FELIXSTOWE INTERNATIONAL COLLEGE
Felixstowe, Suffolk IP11 7NA
Tel: (01394) 282388
Fax: (01394) 276926
Email: felixc@rmplc.co.uk
Head: Mrs J S Lee
Type: Co-educational Boarding
9–17
No of pupils: B8 G17
No of boarders: F15
Fees: On application

HAVERHILL

BARNARDISTON HALL PREPARATORY SCHOOL[†]
Barnardiston, Haverhill, Suffolk
CB9 7TG
Tel: (01440) 786316
Fax: (01440) 786355
Email: registrar@
  barnardiston-hall.co.uk
Head: Lt Col K A Boulter
Type: Co-educational Day and
Boarding 2–13
No of pupils: B121 G128
No of boarders: F30 W16
Fees: (September 05)
FB £11655–£13500 WB £12450
Day £6900–£8850

IPSWICH

AMBERFIELD SCHOOL
Nacton, Ipswich, Suffolk IP10 0HL
Tel: (01473) 659265
Fax: (01473) 659843
Email: registrar@
  amberfield.suffolk.sch.uk
Head: Mrs H Kay
Type: Girls Day 3–16 (Boys 3–7)
No of pupils: B16 G276
Fees: (September 05)
Day £5205–£7305

IPSWICH HIGH SCHOOL GDST
Woolverstone, Ipswich, Suffolk
IP9 1AZ
Tel: (01473) 780201
Fax: (01473) 780985
Email: admissions@ihs.gdst.net
Head: Ms Elaine Purves
Type: Girls Day 3–18
No of pupils: 680
Fees: (September 06)
Day £5700–£7863

IPSWICH PREPARATORY SCHOOL
3 Ivry Street, Ipswich, Suffolk
IP1 3QW
Tel: (01473) 281302
Fax: (01473) 400068
Email: prepregistrar@
  ipswich.suffolk.sch.uk
Head: Mrs J M Jones
Type: Co-educational Day 3–11
No of pupils: B187 G117
Fees: (September 06)
Day £6258–£7062

IPSWICH SCHOOL
Henley Road, Ipswich, Suffolk
IP1 3SG
Tel: (01473) 408300
Fax: (01473) 400058
Email: registrar@
  ipswich.suffolk.sch.uk
Head: Mr I G Galbraith
Type: Co-educational Day and
Boarding 11–18
No of pupils: B519 G251
No of boarders: F26 W17
Fees: (September 06)
FB £14364–£16497
WB £13668–£15549
Day £8586–£9456

OLD BUCKENHAM HALL SCHOOL
Brettenham Park, Ipswich, Suffolk
IP7 7PH
Tel: (01449) 740252
Fax: (01449) 740955
Email: registrar@obh.co.uk
Head: Mr M A Ives
Type: Co-educational Day and
Boarding 2–13
No of pupils: B173 G95
No of boarders: F75 W37
Fees: (September 05) F/WB £15900
Day £6060–£12750

England – Suffolk

ORWELL PARK
Nacton, Ipswich, Suffolk IP10 0ER
Tel: (01473) 659225
Fax: (01473) 659822
Email: headmaster@
  orwellpark.co.uk
Head: Mr A H Auster
Type: Co-educational Boarding
and Day 3–13
No of pupils: B210 G89
No of boarders: F78 W77
Fees: (September 05)
FB £14745–£16395
Day £4515–£12780

**THE ROYAL HOSPITAL
SCHOOL***
Holbrook, Ipswich, Suffolk IP9 2RX
Tel: (01473) 326200
Fax: (01473) 326213
Email: admissions@
  royalhospitalschool.org
Head: Mr H W Blackett
Type: Co-educational Boarding
and Day 11–18 (VIth Form day
pupils)
No of pupils: B360 G257
No of boarders: F602
Fees: (September 06) FB £17754
Day £9450

ST JOSEPH'S COLLEGE
Belstead Road, Birkfield, Ipswich,
Suffolk IP2 9DR
Tel: (01473) 690281
Fax: (01473) 602409
Email: registrar@stjos.co.uk
Head: Mrs S Grant
Type: Co-educational Day and
Boarding 3–18
No of pupils: B423 G171
No of boarders: F61 W15
Fees: (September 05)

LEISTON

SUMMERHILL SCHOOL
Leiston, Suffolk IP16 4HY
Tel: (01728) 830540
Fax: (01728) 830540
Email: office@
  summerhillschool.co.uk
Head: Mrs Z S Readhead
Type: Co-educational Boarding
and Day 6–17
No of pupils: B42 G41
No of boarders: F76
Fees: On application

NEWMARKET

FAIRSTEAD HOUSE SCHOOL
Fordham Road, Newmarket,
Suffolk CB8 7AA
Tel: (01638) 662318
Fax: (01638) 561685
Email: secretary@
  fairsteadhouse.co.uk
Head: Mrs D J Buckenham
Type: Co-educational Day 3–11
No of pupils: B64 G61
Fees: (September 05)
Day £5502–£5940

SOUTHWOLD

SAINT FELIX SCHOOL
Southwold, Suffolk IP18 6SD
Tel: (01502) 722175
Fax: (01502) 722641
Email: schooladmin@
  stfelix.suffolk.sch.uk
Head: Mr David Ward
Type: Co-educational Boarding
and Day 1–18 (Boarding (girls
only) 11+)
No of pupils: B158 G231
No of boarders: F60 W15
Fees: (September 06)
FB £15000–£18900
WB £12000–£16200
Day £3900–£11400

STOWMARKET

FINBOROUGH SCHOOL†
The Hall, Great Finborough,
Stowmarket, Suffolk IP14 3EF
Tel: (01449) 773600
Fax: (01449) 773601
Email: admin@
  finborough.suffolk.sch.uk
Head: Mr J Sinclair
Type: Co-educational Boarding
and Day 2–18
No of pupils: B107 G65
No of boarders: F108 W9
Fees: On application

HILLCROFT PREPARATORY
SCHOOL†
Walnutree Manor, Haughley
Green, Stowmarket, Suffolk
IP14 3RQ
Tel: (01449) 673003
Fax: (01449) 613072
Email: office@
  hillcroft.suffolk.sch.uk
Head: Mr F Rapsey and
Mrs G Rapsey
Type: Co-educational Day 2–13
No of pupils: B46 G44
Fees: On application

SUDBURY

STOKE COLLEGE
Stoke by Clare, Sudbury, Suffolk
CO10 8JE
Tel: (01787) 278141
Fax: (01787) 277904
Email: office@stokecollege.co.uk
Head: Mr J Gibson
Type: Co-educational Day and
Boarding 3–16
No of pupils: B155 G90
No of boarders: W16
Fees: On application

WOODBRIDGE

THE ABBEY
The Prep School for Woodbridge
School, Church Street,
Woodbridge, Suffolk IP12 1DS
Tel: (01394) 382673
Fax: (01394) 383880
Email: office@
  theabbeyschool-suffolk.org.uk
Head: Mr N J Garrett
Type: Co-educational Day 4–11
No of pupils: B154 G159
Fees: (September 06)
Day £5994–£8985

FRAMLINGHAM COLLEGE*
Framlingham, Woodbridge,
Suffolk IP13 9EY
Tel: (01728) 723789
Fax: (01728) 724546
Email: admissions@
  framcollege.co.uk
Head: Mrs G M Randall
Type: Co-educational Boarding
and Day 2–18
No of pupils: B424 G269
No of boarders: F306
Fees: (September 06)
FB £15429–£19572
Day £5517–£9594

WOODBRIDGE SCHOOL
Woodbridge, Suffolk IP12 4JH
Tel: (01394) 615000
Fax: (01394) 380944
Email: office@
   woodbridge.suffolk.sch.uk
Head: Mr S Cole
Type: Co-educational Day and
Boarding 11–18
No of pupils: B360 G285
No of boarders: F40 W4
Fees: (September 06) F/WB £18954
Day £10332–£10944

SURREY

ASHTEAD

CITY OF LONDON
FREEMEN'S SCHOOL
Ashtead Park, Ashtead, Surrey
KT21 1ET
Tel: (01372) 277933
Fax: (01372) 276165
Email: headmaster@
   clfs.surrey.sch.uk
Head: Mr D C Haywood
Type: Co-educational Day and
Boarding 7–18
No of pupils: B433 G407
No of boarders: F46
Fees: (September 06) F/WB £19395
Day £9108–£12195

DOWNSEND SCHOOL,
ASHTEAD LODGE
22 Oakfield Road, Ashtead, Surrey
KT21 2RE
Tel: (01372) 273778
Fax: (01372) 273816
Email: ashteadlodge@
   downsend.co.uk
Head: Mrs K Barrett
Type: Co-educational Day 2–6
No of pupils: B35 G25
Fees: (September 06)
Day £610–£2390

BAGSHOT

HALL GROVE SCHOOL
London Road, Bagshot, Surrey
GU19 5HZ
Tel: (01276) 473059
Fax: (01276) 452003
Email: registrar@
   hallgrove.surrey.sch.uk
Head: Mr A R Graham
Type: Co-educational Day and
Boarding 4–13
No of pupils: B255 G31
No of boarders: W20
Fees: On application

BANSTEAD

GREENACRE SCHOOL FOR
GIRLS
Sutton Lane, Banstead, Surrey
SM7 3RA
Tel: (01737) 352114
Fax: (01737) 373485
Email: admin@
   greenacre.surrey.sch.uk
Head: Mrs P M Wood
Type: Girls Day 3–18
No of pupils: 410
Fees: (September 05)
Day £2850–£9120

PRIORY SCHOOL
Bolters Lane, Banstead, Surrey
SM7 2AJ
Tel: (01737) 366920
Fax: (01737) 366921
Email: office@
   priory-banstead.surrey.sch.uk
Head: Mr G D Malcolm
Type: Boys Day 2–13
No of pupils: 180
Fees: On application

CAMBERLEY

HAWLEY PLACE SCHOOL
Fernhill Road, Blackwater,
Camberley, Surrey GU17 9HU
Tel: (01276) 32028
Fax: (01276) 609695
Email: office@hawleyplace.com
Head: Mr T G Pipe and
Mrs M L Pipe
Type: Co-educational Day
Boys 2–11 Girls 2–16
No of pupils: B115 G265
Fees: (September 05)
Day £5865–£7332

LYNDHURST SCHOOL
36 The Avenue, Camberley, Surrey
GU15 3NE
Tel: (01276) 22895
Fax: (01276) 709186
Email: office@
   lyndhurstschool.com
Head: Mr S G Yeo
Type: Co-educational Day 2–12
No of pupils: B92 G80
Fees: (September 05)
Day £4845–£6330

CATERHAM

CATERHAM PREPARATORY SCHOOL
Harestone Valley Road, Caterham, Surrey CR3 6YB
Tel: (01883) 342097
Fax: (01883) 341230
Email: howard.tuckett@ caterhamschool.co.uk
Head: Mr H W G Tuckett
Type: Co-educational Day 3–11
No of pupils: B141 G131
Fees: (September 05)
Day £3423–£8817

CATERHAM SCHOOL*
Harestone Valley Road, Caterham, Surrey CR3 6YA
Tel: (01883) 343028
Fax: (01883) 347795
Email: admissions@ caterhamschool.co.uk
Head: Mr J P Thomas
Type: Co-educational Day and Boarding 11–18
No of pupils: B436 G318
No of boarders: F131 W2
Fees: (September 06)
F/WB £20502–£21609
Day £11064–£11586

ESSENDENE LODGE SCHOOL
Essendene Road, Caterham, Surrey CR3 5PB
Tel: (01883) 348349
Fax: (01883) 348349
Email: office@ essendenelodge.surrey.sch.uk
Head: Mr S J Haydock
Type: Co-educational Day 2–11
No of pupils: B71 G86
Fees: (September 05)
Day £1575–£4125

OAKHYRST GRANGE SCHOOL
160 Stanstead Road, Caterham, Surrey CR3 6AF
Tel: (01883) 343344
Fax: (01883) 342021
Email: office@ oakhyrstgrangeschool.co.uk
Head: Mrs E A Stanford
Type: Co-educational Day 3–11
No of pupils: B63 G63
Fees: (September 06)
Day £1431–£6063

CHERTSEY

SIR WILLIAM PERKINS'S SCHOOL
Guildford Road, Chertsey, Surrey KT16 9BN
Tel: (01932) 574900
Fax: (01932) 574901
Email: reg@swps.org.uk
Head: Miss S Ross
Type: Girls Day 11–18
No of pupils: 570
Fees: (September 06) Day £9960

COBHAM

ACS COBHAM INTERNATIONAL SCHOOL*
Heywood, Portsmouth Road, Cobham, Surrey KT11 1BL
Tel: (01932) 867251
Fax: (01932) 869789
Email: cobhamadmissions@ acs-england.co.uk
Head: Mr T J Lehman
Type: Co-educational Boarding and Day 2–18
No of pupils: B719 G581
No of boarders: F60 W40
Fees: (September 06)
FB £26670–£27890
WB £23600–£24820
Day £5150–£16500

FELTONFLEET SCHOOL
Cobham, Surrey KT11 1DR
Tel: (01932) 862264
Fax: (01932) 860280
Email: p.ward@feltonfleet.co.uk
Head: Mr Phil Ward
Type: Co-educational Boarding and Day 3–13
No of pupils: B228 G102
No of boarders: W22
Fees: On application

NOTRE DAME PREPARATORY SCHOOL
Burwood House, Cobham, Surrey KT11 1HA
Tel: (01932) 869991
Fax: (01932) 589480
Email: headmaster@ notredame.co.uk
Head: Mr D Plummer
Type: Girls Day 2–11 (Boys 2–5)
No of pupils: B10 G340
Fees: (September 06)
Day £3270–£8550

NOTRE DAME SENIOR SCHOOL
Burwood House, Cobham, Surrey KT11 1HA
Tel: (01932) 869990
Fax: (01932) 589481
Email: headmistress@ notredame.co.uk
Head: Mrs B Williams
Type: Girls Day 11–18
No of pupils: 375
Fees: On application

PARKSIDE SCHOOL
The Manor, Stoke D'Abernon, Cobham, Surrey KT11 3PX
Tel: (01932) 862749
Fax: (01932) 860251
Email: enquiries@ parkside-school.co.uk
Head: Mr D Aylward
Type: Boys Day 4–13 (Co-ed 2–4)
No of pupils: B390 G20
Fees: On application

REED'S SCHOOL*
Sandly Lane, Cobham, Surrey KT11 2ES
Tel: (01932) 869001
Fax: (01932) 869046
Email: admissions@ reeds.surrey.sch.uk
Head: Mr D W Jarrett
Type: Boys Boarding and Day 11–18 (Co-ed VIth Form)
No of pupils: B500 G50
No of boarders: F86
Fees: (September 06)
FB £16941–£20820
Day £12705–£15738

YEHUDI MENUHIN SCHOOL
Stoke D'Abernon, Cobham, Surrey KT11 3QQ
Tel: (01932) 864739
Fax: (01932) 864633
Email: admin@ yehudimenuhinschool.co.uk
Head: Mr N Chisholm
Type: Co-educational Boarding 8–18
No of pupils: B29 G37
No of boarders: F66
Fees: (September 05) F/WB £31410
Day £30594

CRANLEIGH

CRANLEIGH PREPARATORY SCHOOL

Horseshoe Lane, Cranleigh, Surrey
GU68 8QH
Tel: (01483) 274199
Fax: (01483) 277136
Head: Mr M W Roulston
Type: Co-educational Boarding
and Day 7–13
No of pupils: 231
No of boarders: F40
Fees: On application

CRANLEIGH SCHOOL

Horseshoe Lane, Cranleigh, Surrey
GU6 8QQ
Tel: (01483) 273666
Fax: (01483) 267398
Email: enquiry@cranleigh.org
Head: Mr G de W Waller
Type: Co-educational Boarding
and Day 13–18
No of pupils: B400 G209
No of boarders: F438
Fees: (September 06) FB £23685
Day £19305

CROYDON

CAMBRIDGE TUTORS COLLEGE

Water Tower Hill, Croydon,
Surrey CR0 5SX
Tel: (020) 8688 5284
Fax: (020) 8686 9220
Email: admin@ctc.ac.uk
Head: Mr D A Lowe
Type: Co-educational Boarding
and Day 15–22
No of pupils: B160 G150
No of boarders: F270
Fees: (September 06)
FB £16950–£18450
WB £14950–£16450
Day £12950–£14450

NEW LIFE CHRISTIAN SCHOOL

Cairo New Road, Croydon, Surrey
CR0 1XP
Tel: (020) 8680 7671
Head: Mrs E Parker and
Mrs W Emond
Type: Co-educational Day 4–11
No of pupils: 140
Fees: On application

OLD PALACE SCHOOL OF JOHN WHITGIFT

Old Palace Road, Croydon, Surrey
CR0 1AX
Tel: (020) 8688 2027
Fax: (020) 8680 5877
Email: info@
oldpalace.croydon.sch.uk
Head: Ms J Harris
Type: Girls Day 4–18
Fees: (September 05)
Day £6507–£8703

ROYAL RUSSELL SCHOOL

Coombe Lane, Croydon, Surrey
CR9 5BX
Tel: (020) 8657 4433
Fax: (020) 8657 9555
Email: headmaster@
royalrussell.croydon.sch.uk
Head: Dr J R Jennings
Type: Co-educational Boarding
and Day 3–18
No of pupils: B483 G355
No of boarders: F115 W10
Fees: (September 06)
F/WB £16410–£22200
Day £6780–£11220

TRINITY SCHOOL

Shirley Park, Croydon, Surrey
CR9 7AT
Tel: (020) 8656 9541
Fax: (020) 8655 0522
Email: admissions@
trinity.croydon.sch.uk
Head: Mr M J Bishop
Type: Boys Day 10–18
No of pupils: 890
Fees: (September 06) Day £10446

WARLINGHAM PARK SCHOOL

Chelsham Common, Warlingham,
Croydon, Surrey CR6 9PB
Tel: (01883) 626844
Fax: (01883) 625501
Email: info@
warlinghamparkschool.com
Head: Mr M R Donald
Type: Co-educational Day 2–11
No of pupils: B64 G66
Fees: (September 05)
Day £2700–£5400

DORKING

ABINGER HAMMER VILLAGE SCHOOL

Hackhurst Lane, Abinger Hammer,
Dorking, Surrey RH5 6SE
Tel: (01306) 730343
Head: Mrs C R Stansfeld
Type: Co-educational Day 4–8
No of pupils: B4 G8
Fees: On application

BELMONT SCHOOL[†]

Feldemore, Holmbury St Mary,
Dorking, Surrey RH5 6LQ
Tel: (01306) 730852/730829
Fax: (01306) 731220
Email: schooloffice@
belmont-school.org
Head: Mr D Gainer
Type: Co-educational Boarding
and Day 4–13
No of pupils: B194 G80
No of boarders: W40
Fees: On application

BOX HILL SCHOOL*

Mickleham, Dorking, Surrey
RH5 6EA
Tel: (01372) 373382
Fax: (01372) 363942
Email: enquiries@
boxhillschool.org.uk
Head: Mr M Eagers
Type: Co-educational Boarding
and Day 11–18
No of pupils: B264 G135
No of boarders: F95 W59
Fees: (September 06) FB £19350
WB £16350 Day £10050–£11700

HURTWOOD HOUSE*

Holmbury St Mary, Dorking,
Surrey RH5 6NU
Tel: (01483) 279000
Fax: (01483) 267586
Email: info@hurtwood.net
Head: Mr K R B Jackson and
Mr C M Jackson
Type: Co-educational Boarding
and Day 16–18
No of pupils: B140 G155
No of boarders: F283 W283
Fees: (September 06)
F/WB £25830–£29670
Day £17220

England – Surrey

NEW LODGE SCHOOL
Chichester Road, Dorking, Surrey
RH4 1LR
Tel: (01306) 882151
Fax: (01306) 882656
Email: office@
   newlodgeschool.com
Head: Mrs S Watt
Type: Co-educational Day 2–11
No of pupils: B95 G75
Fees: (September 06)
Day £6450–£7440

ST TERESA'S SCHOOL*
Effingham Hill, Dorking, Surrey
RH5 6ST
Tel: (01372) 452037
Fax: (01372) 450311
Email: info@stteresas.surrey.sch.uk
Head: Mrs L Falconer
Type: Girls Boarding and Day
11–18
No of pupils: 362
No of boarders: F76 W13
Fees: (September 06)
FB £19140–£19890
WB £17670–£18240
Day £10950–£11700

EAST MOLESEY

HAMPTON COURT HOUSE
Hampton Court Road, East
Molesey, Surrey KT8 9BS
Tel: (020) 8943 0889
Fax: (020) 8977 5357
Email: office@
   hamptoncourthouse.com
Head: Lady Houston-Boswall
Type: Co-educational Boarding
and Day Boys 3–17 Girls 3–16
No of pupils: B85 G70
No of boarders: W6
Fees: (September 06)
WB £14859–£15993
Day £8883–£10017

EFFINGHAM

**ST TERESA'S PREPARATORY
SCHOOL**
Grove House, Guildford Road,
Effingham, Surrey KT24 5QA
Tel: (01372) 453456
Fax: (01372) 451562
Email: prep@
   st-teresas.demon.co.uk
Head: Mrs A Stewart
Type: Girls Day and Boarding
2–11
No of pupils: 160
No of boarders: F3
Fees: On application

EGHAM

**ACS EGHAM
INTERNATIONAL SCHOOL***
Woodlee, London Road (A30),
Egham, Surrey TW20 0HS
Tel: (01784) 430800
Fax: (01784) 430626
Email: eghamadmissions@
   acs-england.co.uk
Head: Ms M Hadley
Type: Co-educational Day 2–18
No of pupils: B283 G267
Fees: (September 06)
Day £5150–£16330

BISHOPSGATE SCHOOL
Englefield Green, Egham, Surrey
TW20 0YJ
Tel: (01784) 432109
Fax: (01784) 430460
Email: admissions@
   bishopsgate.surrey.sch.uk
Head: Mr M Dunning
Type: Co-educational Day and
Boarding 2–13
No of pupils: B190 G103
No of boarders: W14
Fees: On application

EPSOM

EPSOM COLLEGE
College Road, Epsom, Surrey
KT17 4JQ
Tel: (01372) 821004
Fax: (01372) 821237
Email: admissions@
   epsomcollege.org.uk
Head: Mr S R Borthwick
Type: Co-educational Boarding
and Day 13–18
No of pupils: B498 G222
No of boarders: F99 W232
Fees: (September 05) FB £22389
WB £21477 Day £15798

EWELL CASTLE SCHOOL
Church Street, Ewell, Epsom,
Surrey KT17 2AW
Tel: (020) 8393 1413
Fax: (020) 8786 8218
Email: admissions@
   ewellcastle.co.uk
Head: Mr A J Tibble
Type: Boys Day 3–18 (Co-ed 3–11)
No of pupils: B480 G65
Fees: (September 05)
Day £2445–£8925

**KINGSWOOD HOUSE
SCHOOL**[†]
56 West Hill, Epsom, Surrey
KT19 8LG
Tel: (01372) 723590
Fax: (01372) 749081
Email: office@
   kingswoodhouse.org
Head: Mr P Brooks
Type: Boys Day 2–13
No of pupils: 210
Fees: (September 05)
Day £6150–£8175

ST CHRISTOPHER'S SCHOOL
6 Downs Road, Epsom, Surrey
KT18 5HE
Tel: (01372) 721807
Fax: (01372) 726717
Email: office@
   st-christophers.surrey.sch.uk
Head: Mrs M V Evans
Type: Co-educational Day 3–7
No of pupils: B76 G75
Fees: (September 05)
Day £2970–£5745

ESHER

CLAREMONT FAN COURT SCHOOL*

Claremont Drive, Esher, Surrey
KT10 9LY
Tel: (01372) 467841
Fax: (01372) 471109
Email: jtilson@
claremont.surrey.sch.uk
Head: Mrs P B Farrar
Type: Co-educational Day 3–18
No of pupils: B300 G300
Fees: (September 06)
Day £3228–£10800

EMBERHURST

94 Ember Lane, Esher, Surrey
KT10 8EN
Tel: (020) 8398 2933
Email: emberhurstschool@
ntlworld.com
Head: Mrs P Chadwick
Type: Co-educational Day 2–8
No of pupils: B40 G35
Fees: On application

GRANTCHESTER HOUSE

5 Hinchley Way, Hinchley Wood,
Esher, Surrey KT10 0BD
Tel: (020) 8398 1157
Fax: (020) 8398 1157
Email: enquiries@
grantchesterhouseschool.com
Head: Mrs A E Fry
Type: Co-educational Day 3–7
No of pupils: B49 G37
Fees: On application

MILBOURNE LODGE SCHOOL

43 Arbrook Lane, Esher, Surrey
KT10 9EG
Tel: (01372) 462737
Fax: (01372) 471164
Email: headmaster@
milbournelodge.co.uk
Head: Mr P MacLarnon
Type: Co-educational Day 8–13
No of pupils: B165 G35
Fees: On application

ROWAN PREPARATORY SCHOOL

6 Fitzalan Road, Claygate, Esher,
Surrey KT10 0LX
Tel: (01372) 462627
Fax: (01372) 470782
Email: office@rowan.surrey.sch.uk
Head: Mrs K Kershaw
Type: Girls Day 2–11
No of pupils: 280
Fees: (September 06)
Day £2505–£9450

EWHURST

DUKE OF KENT SCHOOL*

Peaslake Road, Ewhurst, Surrey
GU6 7NS
Tel: (01483) 277313
Fax: (01483) 273862
Email: dok.school@virgin.net
Head: Dr A Cameron
Type: Co-educational Boarding
and Day 3–13
No of pupils: B121 G60
No of boarders: F13 W18
Fees: (September 06)
FB £12810–£15330
WB £9885–£12585
Day £4785–£11295

FARNHAM

BARFIELD SCHOOL

Runfold, Farnham, Surrey
GU10 1PB
Tel: (01252) 782271
Fax: (01252) 781480
Email: admin@barfieldschool.com
Head: Mr B Hoar
Type: Co-educational Day 3–13
No of pupils: B190 G130
Fees: (September 06)
Day £6867–£10167

EDGEBOROUGH

Frensham, Farnham, Surrey
GU10 3AH
Tel: (01252) 792495
Fax: (01252) 795156
Email: office@edgeborough.co.uk
Head: Mrs M A Jackson and
Mr R A Jackson
Type: Co-educational Day and
Boarding 3–13
No of pupils: B206 G122
No of boarders: W50
Fees: (September 06)
WB £13920–£15120
Day £7215–£11775

FRENSHAM HEIGHTS SCHOOL*

Rowledge, Farnham, Surrey
GU10 4EA
Tel: (01252) 792561
Fax: (01252) 794335
Email: admissions@
frensham-heights.org.uk
Head: Mr A Fisher
Type: Co-educational Boarding
and Day 3–18
No of pupils: B256 G250
No of boarders: F100
Fees: (September 06)
FB £19350–£20970
Day £7215–£14085

MORE HOUSE SCHOOL[†]

Moons Hill, Frensham, Farnham,
Surrey GU10 3AP
Tel: (01252) 792303
Fax: (01252) 797601
Email: schooloffice@
morehouseschool.co.uk
Head: Mr B G Huggett
Type: Boys Boarding and Day
9–18
No of pupils: 260
No of boarders: F16 W85
Fees: On application

GODALMING

ALDRO SCHOOL

Lombard Street, Shackleford,
Godalming, Surrey GU8 6AS
Tel: (01483) 409020
Fax: (01483) 409010
Email: hmsec@aldro.org
Head: Mr D W N Aston
Type: Boys Boarding and Day
7–13
No of pupils: 220
No of boarders: F52
Fees: (September 05) FB £16545
Day £12810

BARROW HILLS SCHOOL

Roke Lane, Witley, Godalming,
Surrey GU8 5NY
Tel: (01428) 683639
Fax: (01428) 681906
Email: info@barrowhills.org.uk
Head: Mr M Unsworth
Type: Co-educational Day 3–13
No of pupils: B160 G105
Fees: (September 06)
Day £1675–£3265

CHARTERHOUSE
Godalming, Surrey GU7 2DX
Tel: (01483) 291501
Fax: (01483) 291507
Email: admissions@
 charterhouse.org.uk
Head: Rev J S Witheridge
Type: Boys Boarding and Day
13–18 (Co-ed VIth Form)
No of pupils: B635 G104
No of boarders: F720
Fees: (September 06) FB £25152
Day £20793

KING EDWARD'S SCHOOL WITLEY
Petworth Road, Wormley,
Godalming, Surrey GU8 5SG
Tel: (01428) 686735
Fax: (01428) 685260
Email: admissions@
 kesw.surrey.sch.uk
Head: Mr P Kerr Fulton-Peebles
Type: Co-educational Boarding
and Day 11–18
No of pupils: B295 G181
No of boarders: F263
Fees: (September 06) FB £20100
Day £14400

PRIOR'S FIELD SCHOOL*
Priorsfield Road, Hurtmore,
Godalming, Surrey GU7 2RH
Tel: (01483) 810551
Fax: (01483) 810180
Email: registrar@
 priorsfieldschool.com
Head: Mrs J Roseblade
Type: Girls Boarding and Day
11–18
No of pupils: 330
No of boarders: F38 W80
Fees: (September 06) F/WB £19185
Day £11850

ST HILARY'S SCHOOL*
Holloway Hill, Godalming, Surrey
GU7 1RZ
Tel: (01483) 416551
Fax: (01483) 418325
Email: registrar@
 sthilarysschool.com
Head: Mrs S Bailes
Type: Co-educational Day
Boys 2–7 Girls 2–11
No of pupils: B91 G197
Fees: (September 06)
Day £6645–£9600

GUILDFORD

DRAYTON HOUSE SCHOOL
35 Austen Road, Guildford, Surrey
GU1 3NP
Tel: (01483) 504707
Email: ask@draytonhouse.co.uk
Head: Mrs J Tyson-Jones
Type: Co-educational Day 3–8
(Nursery 1–3)
No of pupils: 90
Fees: On application

GUILDFORD HIGH SCHOOL
London Road, Guildford, Surrey
GU1 1SJ
Tel: (01483) 561440
Fax: (01483) 306516
Email: alex.kearney@
 church-schools.com
Head: Mrs F J Boulton
Type: Girls Day 4–18
No of pupils: 930
Fees: (September 05)
Day £5937–£10005

LANESBOROUGH
Maori Road, Guildford, Surrey
GU1 2EL
Tel: (01483) 880650
Fax: (01483) 880651
Email: secretary@
 lanesborough.surrey.sch.uk
Head: Mr M Shere
Type: Boys Day 3–13
No of pupils: 350
Fees: (September 06)
Day £6237–£8412

LONGACRE SCHOOL
Hullbrook Lane, Shamley Green,
Guildford, Surrey GU5 0NQ
Tel: (01483) 893225
Fax: (01483) 893501
Email: office@
 longacre.surrey.sch.uk
Head: Mr M Beach
Type: Co-educational Day 2–11
No of pupils: B113 G106
Fees: (September 05)
Day £4398–£8274

PEASLAKE SCHOOL
Colmans Hill, Peaslake, Guildford,
Surrey GU5 9ST
Tel: (01306) 730411
Fax: (01306) 730411
Email: info@
 peaslake.surrey.sch.uk
Head: Mrs J George
Type: Co-educational Day 3–7
No of pupils: B15 G28
Fees: On application

ROYAL GRAMMAR SCHOOL
High Street, Guildford, Surrey
GU1 3BB
Tel: (01483) 880600
Fax: (01483) 306127
Email: tmsyoung@
 rgs.guildford.co.uk
Head: Dr J M Cox
Type: Boys Day 11–18
No of pupils: 890
Fees: (September 06) Day £10470

RYDES HILL PREPARATORY SCHOOL
Aldershot Road, Guildford, Surrey
GU2 8BP
Tel: (01483) 563160
Fax: (01483) 306714
Email: enquiries@rydeshill.com
Head: Mrs J Lenahan
Type: Co-educational Day
Boys 3–7 Girls 3–11
No of pupils: B10 G150
Fees: (September 05)
Day £4470–£7485

ST CATHERINE'S SCHOOL
Station Road, Bramley, Guildford,
Surrey GU5 0DF
Tel: (01483) 899609
Fax: (01483) 899608
Email: admissions@
 stcatherines.info
Head: Mrs A M Phillips and
Mrs K Jefferies
Type: Girls Day and Boarding
4–18
No of pupils: 780
No of boarders: F24 W96
Fees: (September 06) F/WB £18315
Day £5490–£11130

TORMEAD SCHOOL
27 Cranley Road, Guildford,
Surrey GUI 2JD
Tel: (01483) 575101
Fax: (01483) 450592
Email: registrar@
 tormeadschool.org.uk
Head: Mrs S Marks
Type: Girls Day 4–18
No of pupils: 765
Fees: (September 06)
Day £4770–£10005

England – Surrey

HASLEMERE

HASLEMERE PREPARATORY SCHOOL
The Heights, Hill Road,
Haslemere, Surrey GU27 2JP
Tel: (01428) 642350
Fax: (01428) 645314
Email: office@
haslemere-prep.surrey.sch.uk
Head: Mr K J Merrick
Type: Boys Day 2–14
No of pupils: B235 G13
Fees: On application

THE ROYAL SCHOOL
Farnham Lane, Haslemere, Surrey
GU27 1HQ
Tel: (01428) 605805
Fax: (01428) 603028
Email: admissions@
royal.surrey.sch.uk
Head: Mrs L Taylor-Gooby
Type: Girls Day and Boarding
3–18 (Boys 2–4)
No of pupils: 353
No of boarders: F45 W45
Fees: (September 06)
F/WB £15672–£21060
Day £5850–£11868

ST IVES SCHOOL
Three Gates Lane, Haslemere,
Surrey GU27 2ES
Tel: (01428) 643734
Fax: (01428) 644788
Email: admin@
stiveshaslemere.com
Head: Mrs S E Cattaneo
Type: Girls Day 3–11 (Boys 3–5)
No of pupils: B5 G140
Fees: (September 05)
Day £6270–£8760

WISPERS SCHOOL FOR GIRLS
High Lane, Haslemere, Surrey
GU27 1AD
Tel: (01428) 643646
Fax: (01428) 641120
Email: secretary@wispers.org.uk
Head: Mr L H Beltran
Type: Girls Boarding and Day
11–18
No of boarders: F34 W3
Fees: (September 06) F/WB £19965
Day £12585

HINDHEAD

AMESBURY
Hazel Grove, Hindhead, Surrey
GU26 6BL
Tel: (01428) 604322
Fax: (01428) 607715
Email: enquiries@
amesburyschool.co.uk
Head: Mr N Taylor
Type: Co-educational Day 3–13
No of pupils: B210 G115
No of boarders: W10
Fees: (September 05)
Day £6420–£10200

ST EDMUND'S SCHOOL
Portsmouth Road, Hindhead,
Surrey GU26 6BH
Tel: (01428) 609875
Fax: (01428) 607898
Email: registrar@
saintedmunds.co.uk
Head: Mr A J Walliker
Type: Boys Boarding and Day
2–13 (Co-ed day 2–7)
No of pupils: B185 G5
No of boarders: W25
Fees: (September 05)
WB £9750–£14877
Day £1665–£11577

HORLEY

REDEHALL PREPARATORY SCHOOL
Redehall Road, Smallfield, Horley,
Surrey RH6 9QA
Tel: (01342) 842987
Fax: (01342) 842987
Email: enquiries@
redehall.surrey.sch.uk
Head: Mrs E Boak
Type: Co-educational Day 4–11
No of pupils: B53 G55
Fees: (September 06)
Day £2650–£2790

KINGSTON-UPON-THAMES

CANBURY SCHOOL
Kingston Hill,
Kingston-upon-Thames, Surrey
KT2 7LN
Tel: (020) 8549 8622
Fax: (020) 8974 6018
Email: head@canburyschool.co.uk
Head: Mr R Metters
Type: Co-educational Day
Boys 10–16 Girls 11–16
No of pupils: B45 G25
Fees: (September 05) Day £9675

HOLY CROSS PREPARATORY SCHOOL
George Road,
Kingston-upon-Thames, Surrey
KT2 7NU
Tel: (020) 8942 0729
Fax: (020) 8336 0764
Email: admissions@
holycrossprep.co.uk
Head: Mrs K Hayes
Type: Girls Day 4–11
No of pupils: 250
Fees: (September 05) Day £6765

KINGSTON GRAMMAR SCHOOL
London Road,
Kingston-upon-Thames, Surrey
KT2 6PY
Tel: (020) 8546 5875
Fax: (020) 8547 1499
Email: registar@
kingston-grammar.surrey.sch.uk
Head: Mr C D Baxter
Type: Co-educational Day 10–18
No of pupils: B416 G293
Fees: (September 05)
Day £10503–£10785

MARYMOUNT INTERNATIONAL SCHOOL*
George Road,
Kingston-upon-Thames, Surrey
KT2 7PE
Tel: (020) 8949 0571
Fax: (020) 8336 2485
Email: admissions@
marymountlondon.com
Head: Sister K Fagan
Type: Girls Day and Boarding
11–18
No of pupils: 230
No of boarders: F90 W10
Fees: (September 06)
FB £24150–£25650
WB £22950–£24450
Day £13750–£15250

PARK HILL SCHOOL
8 Queens Road,
Kingston-upon-Thames, Surrey
KT2 7SH
Tel: (020) 8546 5496
Fax: (020) 8546 4558
Email: admin@parkhillschool.com
Head: Mrs M D Christie
Type: Co-educational Day
Boys 3–8 Girls 3–11
No of pupils: B45 G75
Fees: On application

ROKEBY SCHOOL
George Road,
Kingston-upon-Thames, Surrey
KT2 7PB
Tel: (020) 8942 2247
Fax: (020) 8942 5707
Email: hmsec@rokeby.org.uk
Head: Mr M K Seigel
Type: Boys Day 4–13
No of pupils: 370
Fees: (September 05)
Day £6588–£9471

SURBITON HIGH SCHOOL
Surbiton Crescent,
Kingston-upon-Thames, Surrey
KT1 2JT
Tel: (020) 8546 5245
Fax: (020) 8547 0026
Email: surbiton.high@
  church-schools.com
Head: Dr J Longhurst
Type: Girls Day 4–18 (Boys 4–11)
No of pupils: B123 G1102
Fees: (September 06)
Day £6003–£10029

LEATHERHEAD

CRANMORE SCHOOL
West Horsley, Leatherhead, Surrey
KT24 6AT
Tel: (01483) 280340
Fax: (01483) 280341
Email: office@cranmoreprep.co.uk
Head: Mr A J Martin
Type: Boys Day 3–13
No of pupils: 520
Fees: (September 05)
Day £3300–£8850

DANES HILL SCHOOL[†]
Leatherhead Road, Oxshott,
Leatherhead, Surrey KT22 0JG
Tel: (01372) 842509
Fax: (01372) 844452
Email: registrar@
  daneshillschool.co.uk
Head: Mr William Murdock
Type: Co-educational Day 3–13
No of pupils: B477 G395
Fees: On application

DOWNSEND SCHOOL
1 Leatherhead Road, Leatherhead,
Surrey KT22 8TJ
Tel: (01372) 372197
Fax: (01372) 363367
Email: admin@downsend.co.uk
Head: Mr A D White
Type: Co-educational Day 6–13
No of pupils: B447 G348
Fees: (September 06)
Day £2610–£3175

DOWNSEND SCHOOL, LEATHERHEAD LODGE
13 Epsom Road, Leatherhead,
Surrey KT22 8ST
Tel: (01372) 372123
Fax: (01372) 376574
Email: leatherheadlodge@
  downsend.co.uk
Head: Mrs G Brooks
Type: Co-educational Day 2–6
No of pupils: B74 G65
Fees: (September 06)
Day £610–£2390

GLENESK SCHOOL
Ockham Road North,
East Horsley, Leatherhead, Surrey
KT24 6NS
Tel: (01483) 282329
Fax: (01483) 281489
Email: info@glenesk.co.uk
Head: Mrs S J Christie-Hall
Type: Co-educational Day 2–7
No of pupils: B74 G57
Fees: (September 06)
Day £1911–£7689

MANOR HOUSE SCHOOL
Manor House Lane, Little
Bookham, Leatherhead, Surrey
KT23 4EN
Tel: (01372) 458538
Fax: (01372) 450414
Email: admin@
  manorhouse.surrey.sch.uk
Head: Mrs A Morris
Type: Girls Day 2–16
No of pupils: 396
Fees: (September 06)
Day £3825–£10785

ST JOHN'S SCHOOL
Epsom Road, Leatherhead, Surrey
KT22 8SP
Tel: (01372) 373000
Fax: (01372) 386606
Email: secretary@
  stjohns.surrey.sch.uk
Head: Mr N J R Haddock
Type: Boys Boarding and Day
13–18 (Co-ed VIth Form)
No of pupils: B469 G57
No of boarders: F132
Fees: (September 06) FB £21660
Day £15750

LINGFIELD

LINGFIELD NOTRE DAME SCHOOL
St Piers Lane, Lingfield, Surrey
RH7 6PH
Tel: (01342) 833176
Fax: (01342) 836048
Email: office@
  lingfieldnotredame.co.uk
Head: Mrs N E Shepley
Type: Co-educational Day 2–18
No of pupils: B350 G390
Fees: (September 06)
Day £720–£8235

MITCHAM

DATE VALLEY SCHOOL
9–11 Commonside East, Mitcham,
Surrey CR4 2QA
Tel: (020) 8648 4647
Head: Mrs Razina Karim
Type: Co-educational Day 2–11
No of pupils: B40 G40
Fees: (September 06)
Day £1869–£3150

NEW MALDEN

THE STUDY SCHOOL
57 Thetford Road, New Malden,
Surrey KT3 5DP
Tel: (020) 8942 0754
Fax: (020) 8942 0754
Email: info@study.kingston.sch.uk
Head: Mrs S Mallin
Type: Co-educational Day 3–11
No of pupils: B66 G59
Fees: (September 06)
Day £1068–£2492

WESTBURY HOUSE SCHOOL
80 Westbury Road, New Malden,
Surrey KT3 5AS
Tel: (020) 8942 5885
Fax: (020) 8942 5885
Email: info@
   westburyhouse.surrey.sch.uk
Head: Mrs M T Morton
Type: Co-educational Day 3–11
No of pupils: B65 G55
Fees: (September 06)
Day £1120–£2382

OXTED

HAZELWOOD SCHOOL
Wolf's Hill, Limpsfield, Oxted,
Surrey RH8 0QU
Tel: (01883) 712194
Fax: (01883) 716135
Email: registrar@
   hazelwoodschool.com
Head: Mr Roger McDuff
Type: Co-educational Day 2–13
No of pupils: B240 G130
Fees: (September 06)
Day £3360–£10380

LAVEROCK SCHOOL
19 Bluehouse Lane, Oxted, Surrey
RH8 0AA
Tel: (01883) 714171
Fax: (01883) 722206
Email: office@laverock.fsnet.co.uk
Head: Mrs A C Paterson
Type: Girls Day 3–11
No of pupils: 145
Fees: (September 05)
Day £3060–£8235

PURLEY

LALEHAM LEA SCHOOL
29 Peaks Hill, Purley, Surrey
CR8 3JJ
Tel: (020) 8660 3351
Fax: (020) 8763 0901
Email: bursar@lalehamlea.co.uk
Head: Mrs M E McGaughrin
Type: Co-educational Day 3–11
No of pupils: B100 G50
Fees: On application

LODGE SCHOOL
11 Woodcote Lane, Purley, Surrey
CR8 3HB
Tel: (020) 8660 3179
Fax: (020) 8660 1385
Email: principal@
   lodgeschool.co.uk
Head: Miss P Maynard
Type: Girls Day 3–18 (Boys 3–11)
No of pupils: B81 G175
Fees: (September 05)
Day £4920–£8970

OAKWOOD SCHOOL & NURSERY
Godstone Road, Purley, Surrey
CR8 2AN
Tel: (020) 8668 8080
Fax: (020) 8668 2895
Email: enquiries@
   oakwoodschool.org.uk
Head: Mr C Candia
Type: Co-educational Day 2–11
No of pupils: B75 G68
Fees: (September 06)
Day £5460–£5955

ST DAVID'S SCHOOL
23 Woodcote Valley Road, Purley,
Surrey CR8 3AL
Tel: (020) 8660 0723
Fax: (020) 8645 0426
Email: office@
   stdavidsschool.co.uk
Head: Mrs L Nash
Type: Co-educational Day 3–11
No of pupils: B80 G82
Fees: (September 06)
Day £2985–£5940

WEST DENE SCHOOL
167 Brighton Road, Purley, Surrey
CR8 4HE
Tel: (020) 8660 2404
Fax: (020) 8660 1189
Email: head@
   westdeneschool.fsnet.co.uk
Head: Mr P Kelly
Type: Co-educational Day 2–11
No of pupils: B52 G62
Fees: On application

REDHILL

THE HAWTHORNS SCHOOL
Pendell Court, Bletchingley,
Redhill, Surrey RH1 4QJ
Tel: (01883) 743048
Fax: (01883) 744256
Email: office@hawthorns.com
Head: Mr T R Johns
Type: Co-educational Day 2–13
No of pupils: B333 G207
Fees: (September 06)
Day £1308–£8865

REIGATE

BURYS COURT SCHOOL
Flanchford Road, Leigh, Reigate,
Surrey RH2 8RE
Tel: (01306) 611372
Fax: (01306) 611037
Email: enquiries@
   buryscourtschool.co.uk
Head: Mr David Rowlands
Type: Co-educational Day 3–13
No of pupils: B48 G23
Fees: (September 05)

DUNOTTAR SCHOOL
High Trees Road, Reigate, Surrey
RH2 7EL
Tel: (01737) 761945
Fax: (01737) 779450
Email: info@
   dunottar.surrey.sch.uk
Head: Mrs J Hobson
Type: Girls Day 3–18
No of pupils: 418
Fees: On application

MICKLEFIELD SCHOOL
10 Somers Road, Reigate, Surrey
RH2 9DU
Tel: (01737) 242615
Fax: (01737) 248889
Email: office@
    micklefieldschool.co.uk
Head: Mrs L Rose
Type: Co-educational Day 2–11
No of pupils: B111 G164
Fees: (September 06)
Day £1035–£7290

REIGATE GRAMMAR SCHOOL
Reigate Road, Reigate, Surrey
RH2 0QS
Tel: (01737) 222231
Fax: (01737) 224201
Email: info@reigategrammar.org
Head: Mr D S Thomas
Type: Co-educational Day 11–18
No of pupils: B531 G339
Fees: (September 06) Day £11409

REIGATE ST MARY'S PREPARATORY AND CHOIR SCHOOL
Chart Lane, Reigate, Surrey
RH2 7RN
Tel: (01737) 244880
Fax: (01737) 221540
Email: hmsec@reigatestmarys.org
Head: Mr M Culverwell
Type: Co-educational Day 3–13
No of pupils: B156 G57
Fees: (September 05)
Day £1686–£7866

ROYAL ALEXANDRA AND ALBERT SCHOOL*
Gatton Park, Reigate, Surrey
RH2 0TD
Tel: (01737) 649000
Fax: (01737) 649002
Email: admissions@
    gatton-park.org.uk
Head: Mr Paul D Spencer Ellis
Type: Co-educational Boarding
and Day 7–18
No of pupils: B359 G329
No of boarders: F389
Fees: (September 06)
F/WB £10350–£11100
Day £2325–£3330

RICHMOND

BROOMFIELD HOUSE SCHOOL
10 Broomfield Road, Kew
Gardens, Richmond, Surrey
TW9 3HS
Tel: (020) 8940 3884
Fax: (020) 8332 6485
Email: office@
    broomfieldschool.com
Head: Mr N O York
Type: Co-educational Day 3–11
No of pupils: B73 G87
Fees: (September 06)
Day £3711–£9322

THE GERMAN SCHOOL
Douglas House, Petersham Road,
Richmond, Surrey TW10 7AH
Tel: (020) 8940 2510
Fax: (020) 8332 7446
Email: gerd.koehncke@
    dsLondon.org.uk
Head: Mr G Koehncke
Type: Co-educational Day 5–19
No of pupils: B320 G310
Fees: On application

KEW COLLEGE
24/26 Cumberland Road, Kew,
Richmond, Surrey TW9 3HQ
Tel: (020) 8940 2039
Fax: (020) 8332 9945
Email: KewCollege@aol.com
Head: Mrs D E Lyness
Type: Co-educational Day 3–11
No of pupils: B126 G141
Fees: (September 05)
Day £3255–£6120

KEW GREEN PREPARATORY SCHOOL*
Layton House, Ferry Lane,
Richmond, Surrey TW9 3AF
Tel: (020) 8948 5999
Fax: (020) 8948 4774
Email: secretary@kgps.co.uk
Head: Mrs M Gardener
Type: Co-educational Day 4–11
No of pupils: B140 G140
Fees: (September 06) Day £3550

KING'S HOUSE SCHOOL
68 Kings Road, Richmond, Surrey
TW10 6ES
Tel: (020) 8940 1878
Fax: (020) 8939 2501
Email: secretary1@
    kingshouse.richmond.sch.uk
Head: Mrs S Piper
Type: Boys Day 4–13
No of pupils: 380
Fees: (September 06)
Day £7590–£10263

OLD VICARAGE SCHOOL
48 Richmond Hill, Richmond,
Surrey TW10 6QX
Tel: (020) 8940 0922
Fax: (020) 8948 6834
Email: office@
    oldvicarage-richmond.co.uk
Head: Mrs J Harrison
Type: Girls Day 4–11
No of pupils: 170
Fees: (September 05)
Day £6420–£7125

ROYAL BALLET SCHOOL
White Lodge, Richmond Park,
Richmond, Surrey TW10 5HR
Tel: (020) 8392 8000
Fax: (020) 8392 8037
Email: enquiries@
    royalballetschool.co.uk
Head: Mrs P Hogg
Type: Co-educational Day and
Boarding 11–16
No of pupils: B101 G106
No of boarders: F115
Fees: On application

UNICORN SCHOOL
238 Kew Road, Kew, Richmond,
Surrey TW9 3JX
Tel: (020) 8948 3926
Fax: (020) 8332 6814
Email: enquiries@
    unicornschool.org.uk
Head: Mrs R Linehan
Type: Co-educational Day 3–11
No of pupils: B83 G89
Fees: (September 05)
Day £4395–£8040

SOUTH CROYDON

CROHAM HURST SCHOOL*
79 Croham Road, South Croydon,
Surrey CR2 7YN
Tel: (020) 8681 4078
Fax: (020) 8688 1142
Email: aparris@
  croham.surrey.sch.uk
Head: Mrs E J Abbotts
Type: Girls Day 3–18
No of pupils: 435
Fees: (September 06)
Day £5490–£9885

CROYDON HIGH SCHOOL GDST
Old Farleigh Road, Selsdon, South
Croydon, Surrey CR2 8YB
Tel: (020) 8651 5020
Fax: (020) 8657 5413
Email: info2@cry.gdst.net
Head: Miss L M Ogilvie
Type: Girls Day 3–18
No of pupils: 733
Fees: (September 06)
Day £5886–£9810

CUMNOR HOUSE SCHOOL
168 Pampisford Road, South
Croydon, Surrey CR2 6DA
Tel: (020) 8660 3445
Fax: (020) 8660 3445
Email: admin@cumnorhouse.com
Head: Mr P Clare-Hunt
Type: Boys Day 4–13
No of pupils: 360
Fees: (September 06)
Day £6690–£8040

ELMHURST SCHOOL
44–48 South Park Hill Road, South
Croydon, Surrey CR2 7DW
Tel: (020) 8688 0661
Fax: (020) 8686 7675
Email: office@elmhurstschool.net
Head: Mr B K Dighton
Type: Boys Day 4–11
No of pupils: 254
Fees: On application

SANDERSTEAD JUNIOR SCHOOL
29 Purley Oaks Road,
Sanderstead, South Croydon,
Surrey CR2 0NW
Tel: (020) 8660 0801
Fax: (020) 8763 2243
Email: aburrell26@aol.com
Head: Mrs A Barns
Type: Co-educational Day 3–12
No of pupils: B50 G50
Fees: On application

WHITGIFT SCHOOL
Haling Park, South Croydon,
Surrey CR2 6YT
Tel: (020) 8688 9222
Fax: (020) 8760 0682
Email: office@whitgift.co.uk
Head: Dr C A Barnett and
Dr J M Cox
Type: Boys Day 10–18
No of pupils: 1200
Fees: (September 06) Day £11820

SURBITON

LINLEY HOUSE
6 Berrylands Road, Surbiton,
Surrey KT5 8RA
Tel: (020) 8399 4979
Fax: (020) 8399 4979
Head: Mrs S Mallin
Type: Co-educational Day 3–7
No of pupils: B18 G17
Fees: On application

SHREWSBURY HOUSE SCHOOL
107 Ditton Road, Surbiton, Surrey
KT6 6RL
Tel: (020) 8399 3066
Fax: (020) 8339 9529
Email: office@shspost.co.uk
Head: Mr C M Ross
Type: Boys Day 7–13
No of pupils: 290
Fees: (September 06) Day £11505

SURBITON PREPARATORY SCHOOL
3 Avenue Elmers, Surbiton, Surrey
KT6 4SP
Tel: (020) 8546 5245
Fax: (020) 8390 6640
Email: surbiton.prep@
  church-schools.com
Head: Mr S J Pryce
Type: Boys Day 4–11
No of pupils: 123
Fees: (September 06)
Day £6003–£8181

SUTTON

HOMEFIELD SCHOOL*
Western Road, Sutton, Surrey
SM1 2TE
Tel: (020) 8642 0965
Fax: (020) 8642 0965
Email: administration@
  homefield.sutton.sch.uk
Head: Mr P R Mowbray and
Mr M Till
Type: Boys Day 2–13
No of pupils: 400
Fees: (September 06)
Day £3540–£8280

SEATON HOUSE SCHOOL
67 Banstead Road South, Sutton,
Surrey SM2 5LH
Tel: (020) 8642 2332
Fax: (020) 8642 2332
Email: office@
  seatonhouse.sutton.sch.uk
Head: Mrs V A Richards
Type: Girls Day 3–11 (Boys 3–5)
No of pupils: 130
Fees: (September 06)
Day £2500–£5850

STOWFORD COLLEGE†
95 Brighton Road, Sutton, Surrey
SM2 5SJ
Tel: (020) 8661 9444
Fax: (020) 8661 6136
Email: stowfordsch@
  btinternet.com
Head: Mr R J Shakespeare
Type: Co-educational Day 6–16
No of pupils: B55 G28
Fees: On application

SUTTON HIGH SCHOOL GDST
55 Cheam Road, Sutton, Surrey
SM1 2AX
Tel: (020) 8642 0594
Fax: (020) 8642 2014
Email: office@sut.gdst.net
Head: Mr S Callaghan
Type: Girls Day 3–18
No of pupils: 763
Fees: (September 06)
Day £5886–£9810

England – Surrey

TADWORTH

ABERDOUR SCHOOL
Brighton Road, Burgh Heath,
Tadworth, Surrey KT20 6AJ
Tel: (01737) 354119
Fax: (01737) 363044
Email: admin@
  aberdour.surrey.sch.uk
Head: Mr S Collins
Type: Co-educational Day 2–13
No of pupils: B160 G105
Fees: (September 06)
Day £2475–£9255

BRAMLEY SCHOOL
Chequers Lane,
Walton-on-the-Hill, Tadworth,
Surrey KT20 7ST
Tel: (01737) 812004
Fax: (01737) 819945
Email: office@
  bramleyschool.surrey.sch.uk
Head: Mrs P Burgess
Type: Girls Day 3–11
No of pupils: 120
Fees: (September 06)
Day £3450–£7545

CHINTHURST SCHOOL
Tadworth Street, Tadworth, Surrey
KT20 5QZ
Tel: (01737) 812011
Fax: (01737) 814835
Email: enquiries@
  chinthurst.surrey.sch.uk
Head: Mr T J Egan
Type: Boys Day 3–13
No of pupils: 340
Fees: (September 06)
Day £1755–£8175

THAMES DITTON

WESTON GREEN SCHOOL
Weston Green Road, Thames
Ditton, Surrey KT7 0JN
Tel: (020) 8398 2778
Fax: (020) 8398 2778
Email: info@
  westongreenschool.org.uk
Head: Mrs L Harvey
Type: Co-educational Day 2–8
No of pupils: 180
Fees: On application

THORPE

TASIS THE AMERICAN SCHOOL IN ENGLAND*
Coldharbour Lane, Thorpe, Surrey
TW20 8TE
Tel: (01932) 565252
Fax: (01932) 564644
Email: ukadmissions@tasis.com
Head: Dr J A Doran
Type: Co-educational Boarding
and Day 3–18
No of pupils: B390 G360
No of boarders: F160
Fees: (September 06) FB £24550

WALLINGTON

COLLINGWOOD SCHOOL
3 Springfield Road, Wallington,
Surrey SM6 0BD
Tel: (020) 8647 4607
Fax: (020) 8669 2884
Email: headmaster@
  collingwood.sutton.sch.uk
Head: Mr G M Barham
Type: Co-educational Day 2–11
No of pupils: B112 G64
Fees: (September 06)
Day £1515–£5385

WALTON-ON-THAMES

DANESFIELD MANOR SCHOOL
Rydens Avenue, Walton-on-
Thames, Surrey KT12 3JB
Tel: (01932) 220930
Fax: (01932) 225640
Head: Mrs L A Muggleton and Mrs
L Fidler
Type: Co-educational Day 1–11
No of pupils: B84 G85
Fees: On application

WESTWARD PREPARATORY SCHOOL
47 Hersham Road, Walton-on-
Thames, Surrey KT12 1LE
Tel: (01932) 220911
Fax: (01932) 220911
Head: Mrs P Robertson
Type: Co-educational Day 3–11
No of pupils: B70 G70
Fees: On application

WEYBRIDGE

ST GEORGE'S COLLEGE
Weybridge Road, Addlestone,
Weybridge, Surrey KT15 2QS
Tel: (01932) 839300
Fax: (01932) 839301
Email: info@
  st-georges-college.co.uk
Head: Mr J A Peake
Type: Co-educational Day 11–18
No of pupils: B525 G325
Fees: On application

ST GEORGE'S COLLEGE JUNIOR SCHOOL
Thames Street, Weybridge, Surrey
KT13 8NL
Tel: (01932) 839400
Fax: (01932) 839401
Email: jshead@
  st-georges-college.co.uk
Head: Mr A J W Hudson
Type: Co-educational Day 3–11
No of pupils: B321 G273
Fees: (September 06)
Day £3300–£8505

WINDLESHAM

WOODCOTE HOUSE SCHOOL
Snows Ride, Windlesham, Surrey
GU20 6PF
Tel: (01276) 472115
Fax: (01276) 472890
Email: info@
  woodcotehouseschool.co.uk
Head: Mr N H K Paterson
Type: Boys Boarding and Day
7–14
No of pupils: 100
No of boarders: F75
Fees: (September 06) FB £14550
Day £10425

WOKING

COWORTH-FLEXLANDS SCHOOL
Valley End, Chobham, Woking, Surrey GU24 8TE
Tel: (01276) 855707
Fax: (01276) 856043
Email: admissions@
  coworthpark.co.uk
Head: Mrs S O E Stephen and Mrs A Green
Type: Co-educational Day Boys 3–7 Girls 3–11
No of pupils: B25 G199
Fees: On application

GREENFIELD SCHOOL
Brooklyn Road, Woking, Surrey GU22 7TP
Tel: (01483) 772525
Fax: (01483) 728907
Email: principal@
  greenfield.surrey.sch.uk
Head: Ms Janis Radcliffe
Type: Co-educational Day 3–11
No of pupils: B105 G115
Fees: On application

HALSTEAD PREPARATORY SCHOOL
Woodham Rise, Woking, Surrey GU21 4EE
Tel: (01483) 772682
Fax: (01483) 757611
Email: registrar@
  halstead-school.org.uk
Head: Mrs Sabine Fellows
Type: Girls Day 3–11
No of pupils: 208
Fees: (September 05)
Day £3168–£8640

HOE BRIDGE SCHOOL*
Hoe Place, Old Woking Road, Woking, Surrey GU22 8JE
Tel: (01483) 760018
Fax: (01483) 757560
Email: enquiriesprep@
  hoebridgeschool.co.uk
Head: Mr R W K Barr
Type: Co-educational Day 2–13
No of pupils: B349 G124
Fees: (September 06)
Day £1488–£10800

OAKFIELD SCHOOL
Coldharbour Road, Pyrford, Woking, Surrey GU22 8SJ
Tel: (01932) 342465
Fax: (01932) 342745
Email: education@
  oakfieldschool.co.uk
Head: Mrs S H Goddard
Type: Co-educational Day Boys 3–7 Girls 3–16
No of pupils: B30 G150
Fees: On application

PRINS WILLEM-ALEXANDER SCHOOL
Old Woking Road, Woking, Surrey GU22 8HY
Tel: (01483) 750409
Fax: (01483) 730962
Email: info@
  prinswillemalexander.com
Head: Mr M Meines and Mr M Damhuis
Type: Co-educational Day 4–12
No of pupils: B68 G71
Fees: (September 06)
Day £7305–£11460

RIPLEY COURT SCHOOL
Rose Lane, Ripley, Woking, Surrey GU23 6NE
Tel: (01483) 225217
Fax: (01483) 223854
Email: rcshead@btconnect.com
Head: Mr A J Gough
Type: Co-educational Day 3–13
No of pupils: B170 G72
Fees: (September 06)
Day £6060–£8945

ST. ANDREW'S (WOKING) SCHOOL TRUST*
Church Hill House, Wilson Way, Horsell, Woking, Surrey GU21 4QW
Tel: (01483) 760943
Fax: (01483) 740314
Email: admin@
  st-andrews.woking.sch.uk
Head: Mr J R Evans
Type: Co-educational Day 3–13
No of pupils: B226 G67
Fees: (September 06)
Day £4080–£10470

WOLDINGHAM

WOLDINGHAM SCHOOL
Marden Park, Woldingham, Surrey CR3 7YA
Tel: (01883) 349431
Fax: (01883) 348653
Email: registrar@
  woldingham.surrey.sch.uk
Head: Miss D Vernon
Type: Girls Boarding and Day 11–18
No of pupils: 500
No of boarders: W400
Fees: (September 06) WB £22455
Day £13425

England – Surrey

EAST SUSSEX

BATTLE

BATTLE ABBEY SCHOOL*
High Street, Battle, East Sussex
TN33 0AD
Tel: (01424) 772385
Fax: (01424) 773573
Email: office@
   battleabbeyschool.com
Head: Mr R Clark
Type: Co-educational Boarding
and Day 2–18
No of pupils: B111 G115
No of boarders: F40 W2
Fees: (September 06)
F/WB £15225–£18900
Day £5550–£11475

BRIGHTON

BRIGHTON AND HOVE HIGH SCHOOL GDST
Montpelier Road, Brighton,
East Sussex BN1 3AT
Tel: (01273) 734112
Fax: (01273) 737120
Email: enquiries@bhhs.gdst.net
Head: Mrs A Greatorex
Type: Girls Day 3–18
No of pupils: 780
Fees: On application

BRIGHTON COLLEGE
Eastern Road, Brighton, East Sussex
BN2 0AL
Tel: (01273) 704200
Fax: (01273) 704204
Email: registrar@
   brightoncollege.net
Head: Dr A Seldon
Type: Co-educational Day and
Boarding 13–18
No of pupils: B470 G240
No of boarders: F55 W68
Fees: (September 05) FB £20466
WB £17976 Day £13203

BRIGHTON COLLEGE PRE-PREPARATORY SCHOOL
Sutherland Road, Brighton,
East Sussex BN2 0EQ
Tel: (01273) 704259
Fax: (01273) 704318
Email: registrar@
   brightoncollege.net
Head: Mrs S P Wicks
Type: Co-educational Day 3–8
No of pupils: B110 G85
Fees: On application

BRIGHTON COLLEGE PREP SCHOOL
Walpole Lodge, Walpole Road,
Brighton, East Sussex BN2 0EU
Tel: (01273) 704201
Fax: (01273) 704286
Email: paprep@
   brightoncollege.net
Head: Mr B Melia
Type: Co-educational Day 8–13
No of pupils: B172 G123
Fees: (September 06)
Day £9357–£11880

BRIGHTON STEINER SCHOOL LIMITED
Roedean Road, Brighton,
East Sussex BN2 5RA
Tel: (01273) 386300
Fax: (01273) 386313
Head: Ms J Firth
Type: Co-educational Day 2–16
No of pupils: 200
Fees: On application

DHARMA SCHOOL
White House, Ladies Mile Road,
Patcham, Brighton, East Sussex
BN1 8TB
Tel: (01273) 502055
Fax: (01273) 556580
Head: Mr P Murdock
Type: Co-educational Day 3–11
No of pupils: B34 G36
Fees: On application

ROEDEAN SCHOOL
Roedean Way, Brighton,
East Sussex BN2 5RQ
Tel: (01273) 603181
Fax: (01273) 680791
Email: admissions@roedean.co.uk
Head: Mrs C Shaw
Type: Girls Boarding and Day
11–18
No of pupils: 377
No of boarders: F316
Fees: On application

ST AUBYNS SCHOOL
76 High Street, Rottingdean,
Brighton, East Sussex BN2 7JN
Tel: (01273) 302170
Fax: (01273) 304004
Email: office@
   staubyns-school.org.uk
Head: Mr A G Gobat
Type: Co-educational Day and
Boarding 3–13
No of pupils: B114 G76
No of boarders: W8
Fees: (September 05) WB £14925
Day £4425–£11925

ST MARY'S HALL*
Eastern Road, Brighton, East Sussex
BN2 5JF
Tel: (01273) 606061
Fax: (01273) 620782
Email: registrar@stmaryshall.co.uk
Head: Mrs S M Meek
Type: Girls Day and Boarding
3–18 (Boys 3–8)
No of pupils: B10 G306
No of boarders: F79 W9
Fees: (September 06)
FB £14958–£18525
WB £13350–£17760
Day £2325–£11220

EASTBOURNE

EASTBOURNE COLLEGE
Old Wish Road, Eastbourne,
East Sussex BN21 4JX
Tel: (01323) 452323
Fax: (01323) 452354
Email: EDeacon@
 eastbourne-college.co.uk
Head: Mr S P Davies
Type: Co-educational Boarding
and Day 13–18
No of pupils: B382 G226
No of boarders: F290
Fees: (September 06) FB £21615
Day £14310

MOIRA HOUSE GIRLS SCHOOL
Upper Carlisle Road, Eastbourne,
East Sussex BN20 7TE
Tel: (01323) 644144
Fax: (01323) 649720
Email: info@moirahouse.co.uk
Head: Mrs L A Watson
Type: Girls Boarding and Day
3–19
No of pupils: 420
No of boarders: F110 W12
Fees: (September 06)
FB £15540–£20670
WB £15000–£18750
Day £5175–£12000

MOIRA HOUSE SCHOOL
Upper Carlisle Road, Eastbourne,
East Sussex BN20 7TE
Tel: (01323) 636800
Fax: (01323) 649720
Email: lyoung@
 moirahouse.e-sussex.sch.uk
Head: Mrs L Young
Type: Girls Day and Boarding
2–11
No of boarders: F4
Fees: (September 06)
FB £16140–£20670
WB £15000–£18750
Day £5175–£12000

ST ANDREW'S SCHOOL
Meads, Eastbourne, East Sussex
BN20 7RP
Tel: (01323) 733203
Fax: (01323) 646860
Email: office@androvian.biblio.net
Head: Mr J Griffith
Type: Co-educational Boarding
and Day 3–13
No of pupils: B236 G128
No of boarders: F16 W4
Fees: (September 05) FB £15390
WB £13650 Day £6210–£10815

ST BEDE'S PREP SCHOOL[†]
Duke's Drive, Eastbourne,
East Sussex BN20 7XL
Tel: (01323) 734222
Fax: (01323) 746437
Email: prep.school@
 stbedesschool.org
Head: Mr C P Pyemont
Type: Co-educational Boarding
and Day 2–13
No of pupils: B292 G172
No of boarders: F33 W6
Fees: (September 06) FB £16080
Day £11205

FOREST ROW

ASHDOWN HOUSE SCHOOL
Forest Row, East Sussex RH18 5JY
Tel: (01342) 822574
Fax: (01342) 824380
Email: secretary@
 ashdownhouse.com
Head: Mr A R Taylor
Type: Co-educational Boarding
8–13
No of pupils: B90 G52
No of boarders: F142
Fees: (September 05) FB £17100

GREENFIELDS SCHOOL
Priory Road, Forest Row,
East Sussex RH18 5JD
Tel: (01342) 822189
Fax: (01342) 825289
Email: grnflds@aol.com
Head: Mrs V Tupholme
Type: Co-educational Day and
Boarding 2–19
No of pupils: B85 G70
No of boarders: F30
Fees: (September 05)
F/WB £14000–£16000
Day £3300–£10000

MICHAEL HALL (STEINER WALDORF SCHOOL)*
Kidbrooke Park, Forest Row,
East Sussex RH18 5JA
Tel: (01342) 822275
Fax: (01342) 826593
Email: info@michaelhall.co.uk
Type: Co-educational Day and
Boarding 0–19
No of pupils: B300 G328
No of boarders: F15 W10
Fees: (September 06) FB £14010
WB £12965 Day £8085

HAILSHAM

ST BEDE'S SCHOOL*[†]
Upper Dicker, Hailsham,
East Sussex BN27 3QH
Tel: (01323) 843252
Fax: (01323) 442628
Email: school.office@
 stbedesschool.org
Head: Mr S W Cole
Type: Co-educational Boarding
and Day 13–19
No of pupils: B528 G317
No of boarders: F310
Fees: (September 06) FB £21165
Day £13005

HASTINGS

BUCKSWOOD SCHOOL*
Broomham Hall, Rye Road,
Guestling, Hastings, East Sussex
TN35 4LT
Tel: (01424) 813813
Fax: (01424) 812100
Email: achieve@buckswood.co.uk
Head: Mr T Fish
Type: Co-educational Day and
Boarding Boys 0–19 Girls 10–19
No of pupils: B170 G120
No of boarders: F160
Fees: (September 06) FB £17970
Day £8400

HOVE

BELLERBYS COLLEGE
44 Cromwell Road, Hove,
East Sussex BN3 3ER
Tel: (01273) 323374
Fax: (01273) 749322
Email: hove@bellerbys.com
Head: Mr N Addison
Type: Co-educational Boarding
and Day 14+
No of pupils: B270 G210
No of boarders: F390
Fees: On application

DEEPDENE SCHOOL
Hove, East Sussex BN3 4ED
Tel: (01273) 418984
Fax: (01273) 415543
Email: info@deepdeneschool.com
Head: Mrs L V Clark-Darby and
Mrs N K Gane
Type: Co-educational Day 1–8
No of pupils: B108 G122
Fees: On application

THE DRIVE PREP SCHOOL
101 The Drive, Hove, East Sussex
BN3 6GE
Tel: (01273) 738444
Fax: (01273) 738444
Email: enquiries@
    driveprep.brighton-hove.sch.uk
Head: Mrs S Parkinson
Type: Co-educational Day 3–16
No of pupils: 109
Fees: On application

THE FOLD SCHOOL
201 New Church Road, Hove,
East Sussex BN3 4ED
Tel: (01273) 410901
Email: thefoldschool@
    ntlworld.com
Head: Dr C J Drake
Type: Co-educational Day 3–11
No of pupils: B37 G38
Fees: On application

LANCING COLLEGE PREPARATORY SCHOOL AT MOWDEN
The Droveway, Hove, East Sussex
BN3 6LU
Tel: (01273) 503452
Fax: (01273) 503457
Email: info@lancingprep.co.uk
Head: Mr A Laurent
Type: Co-educational Day 3–13
No of pupils: B129 G33
Fees: (September 06)
Day £890–£3540

ST CHRISTOPHER'S SCHOOL
33 New Church Road, Hove,
East Sussex BN3 4AD
Tel: (01273) 735404
Fax: (01273) 747956
Email: office@
    stchristophershove.org.uk
Head: Mr I McIntyre
Type: Co-educational Day 4–13
No of pupils: B177 G65
Fees: (September 06)
Day £5418–£6138

STONELANDS SCHOOL OF BALLET & THEATRE ARTS
170A Church Road, Hove,
East Sussex BN3 2DJ
Tel: (01273) 770445
Fax: (01273) 770444
Email: dianacarteur@
    stonelandsschool.co.uk
Head: Mrs D Carteur
Type: Co-educational Boarding
and Day 5–16
No of pupils: B6 G44
No of boarders: F10 W10
Fees: On application

LEWES

LEWES OLD GRAMMAR SCHOOL
140 High Street, Lewes, East Sussex
BN7 1XS
Tel: (01273) 472634
Fax: (01273) 476948
Email: bursar@logs.uk.com
Head: Mr R Blewitt
Type: Co-educational Day 3–18
No of pupils: B210 G120
Fees: (September 05)
Day £4500–£8730

MAYFIELD

ST LEONARDS-MAYFIELD SCHOOL*
The Old Palace, Mayfield,
East Sussex TN20 6PH
Tel: (01435) 874600
Fax: (01435) 872627
Email: admiss@
    stlm.e-sussex.sch.uk
Head: Mrs J Dalton
Type: Girls Boarding and Day
11–18
No of pupils: 433
No of boarders: F90 W32
Fees: (September 06) F/WB £20220
Day £13425

ROBERTSBRIDGE

BODIAM MANOR SCHOOL
Bodiam, Robertsbridge, East Sussex
TN32 5UJ
Tel: (01580) 830225
Fax: (01580) 830227
Email: headmaster@
    bodiammanorschool.fsnet.co.uk
Head: Mr S Flutter
Type: Co-educational Day 2–13
No of pupils: B73 G72
Fees: On application

DARVELL SCHOOL
Darvell Bruderhof, Robertsbridge,
East Sussex TN32 5DR
Tel: (01580) 883300
Fax: (01580) 883317
Head: Mr A Meier
Type: Co-educational Day 2–14
No of pupils: B55 G55
Fees: On application

VINEHALL SCHOOL
Robertsbridge, East Sussex
TN32 5JL
Tel: (01580) 880413
Fax: (01580) 882119
Email: office@vinehallschool.com
Head: Mrs J L Robinson
Type: Co-educational Boarding
and Day 2–13
No of pupils: B226 G147
No of boarders: F50
Fees: (September 05) FB £14880
Day £11445

SEAFORD

NEWLANDS SCHOOL*†
Eastbourne Road, Sutton Avenue,
Seaford, East Sussex BN25 4NP
Tel: (01323) 892334 / 490000
Fax: (01323) 898420
Email: newlands1@msn.com
Head: Mr O T Price
Type: Co-educational Boarding
and Day 0–18 (nursery & pre-prep)
No of pupils: B70 G80
No of boarders: F10
Fees: (September 06)
FB £14985–£17850
WB £14835–£17700
Day £4950–£10875

ST LEONARDS-ON-SEA

CLAREMONT SCHOOL
Baldslow, St Leonards-on-Sea,
East Sussex TN37 7PW
Tel: (01424) 751555
Fax: (01424) 754310
Email: enquiries@
    claremontschool.co.uk
Head: Mr M Beaumont and
Mr I Culley
Type: Co-educational Day 1–14
No of pupils: B200 G200
Fees: (September 05)
Day £3900–£6750

WADHURST

BRICKLEHURST MANOR PREPARATORY
Bardown Road, Stonegate,
Wadhurst, East Sussex TN5 7EL
Tel: (01580) 200448
Fax: (01580) 200998
Email: bricklehurst@
  btconnect.com
Head: Mrs C Flowers
Type: Co-educational Day 3–11
No of pupils: B51 G70
Fees: (September 06)
Day £3135–£7350

SACRED HEART R.C. PRIMARY SCHOOL
Mayfield Lane, Durgates,
Wadhurst, East Sussex TN5 6DQ
Tel: (01892) 783414
Fax: (01892) 783510
Email: admin@
  wadhurstsacredheart.
  freeserve.co.uk
Head: Mrs H Blake
Type: Co-educational Day 3–11
No of pupils: B60 G60
Fees: (September 05)
Day £4350–£4650

WEST SUSSEX

ARUNDEL

SLINDON COLLEGE[†]
Slindon, Arundel, West Sussex
BN18 0RH
Tel: (01243) 814320
Fax: (01243) 814702
Email: registrar@
  slindoncollege.co.uk
Head: Mr I P Graham
Type: Boys Boarding and Day
9–16
No of pupils: 100
No of boarders: F20 W20
Fees: (September 06) F/WB £21075
Day £12390–£13170

BURGESS HILL

BURGESS HILL SCHOOL FOR GIRLS*
Keymer Road, Burgess Hill,
West Sussex RH15 0EG
Tel: (01444) 241050
Fax: (01444) 870314
Email: registrar@
  burgesshill-school.com
Head: Mrs A Aughwane
Type: Girls Boarding and Day
2–18
No of pupils: B50 G629
No of boarders: F51
Fees: (September 06) FB £18510
Day £5100–£10665

ST PETER'S SCHOOL
Upper St John's Road, Burgess
Hill, West Sussex RH15 8HB
Tel: (01444) 235880
Fax: (01444) 258081
Head: Mr H G Stevens
Type: Co-educational Day 2–13
No of pupils: B98 G84
Fees: On application

CHICHESTER

GREAT BALLARD SCHOOL
Eartham, Chichester, West Sussex
PO18 0LR
Tel: (01243) 814236
Fax: (01243) 814586
Email: gbschool@breathemail.net
Head: Mr R E Jennings
Type: Co-educational Boarding
and Day 2–13
No of pupils: B82 G100
No of boarders: W37
Fees: (September 06) WB £12360
Day £2415–£9990

LAVANT HOUSE
West Lavant, Chichester,
West Sussex PO18 9AB
Tel: (01243) 527211
Fax: (01243) 530490
Email: office@lavanthouse.org.uk
Head: Mrs M Scott
Type: Girls Day and Boarding
3–18
No of pupils: 159
No of boarders: F10 W10
Fees: (September 06)
F/WB £14130–£16950
Day £5310–£10710

THE LITTLEMEAD SCHOOL
Tangmere Road, Tangmere,
Chichester, West Sussex PO20 6EU
Tel: (01243) 787551
Fax: (01243) 527249
Head: Mrs S Carter
Type: Co-educational Day 0–14
No of pupils: B16 G26
Fees: On application

OAKWOOD SCHOOL
Oakwood, Chichester, West Sussex
PO18 9AN
Tel: (01243) 575209
Fax: (01243) 575433
Email: office@
  oakwoodschool.co.uk
Head: Mr J Kittermaster
Type: Co-educational Day 2–11
No of pupils: B140 G140
Fees: (September 05)
Day £920–£8880

THE PREBENDAL SCHOOL
54 West Street, Chichester,
West Sussex PO19 1RT
Tel: (01243) 782026/784828
Fax: (01243) 771821
Email: secretary.prebendal@
  btconnect.com
Head: Rev Canon G C Hall
Type: Co-educational Day and
Boarding 3–14
No of pupils: B167 G121
No of boarders: F18 W12
Fees: On application

England – East Sussex/West Sussex

**PREBENDAL SCHOOL
(NORTHGATE HOUSE)**
38 North Street, Chichester,
West Sussex PO19 1LX
Tel: (01243) 784828
Email: secretary.prebendal@
btconnect.com
Head: Mrs L M Greenall
Type: Co-educational Day 3–7
No of pupils: B53 G42
Fees: (September 05)
Day £2280–£5436

**WESTBOURNE HOUSE
SCHOOL**
Shopwyke, Chichester,
West Sussex PO20 2BH
Tel: (01243) 782739
Fax: (01243) 770759
Email: whouseoffice@rmplc.co.uk
Head: Mr B G Law
Type: Co-educational Boarding
and Day 3–13
No of pupils: B203 G161
No of boarders: F73
Fees: (September 05) FB £13470
Day £5670–£10860

COPTHORNE

COPTHORNE PREP SCHOOL
Effingham Lane, Copthorne,
West Sussex RH10 3HR
Tel: (01342) 712311
Fax: (01342) 714014
Email: office@
copthorneprep.co.uk
Head: Mr C Jones
Type: Co-educational Day and
Boarding 2–13
No of pupils: B135 G95
No of boarders: W10
Fees: (September 06) WB £13200
Day £6600–£10890

CRAWLEY

**WILLOW TREE MONTESSORI
SCHOOL**
Charlwood House, Charlwood
Road, Lowfield Heath, Crawley,
West Sussex RH11 OQA
Tel: (01293) 565544
Fax: (01293) 611705
Head: Mrs G Kerfante
Type: Co-educational Day 1–8
No of pupils: B84 G66
Fees: On application

EAST GRINSTEAD

BRAMBLETYE SCHOOL*
Lewes Road, Brambletye, East
Grinstead, West Sussex RH19 3PD
Tel: (01342) 321004
Fax: (01342) 317562
Email: admin@brambletye.com
Head: Mr H D Cocke
Type: Co-educational Boarding
and Day 3–13
No of pupils: B153 G91
No of boarders: F67
Fees: (September 06) FB £16380
Day £13450–£15600

FONTHILL LODGE
Coombe Hill Road, East Grinstead,
West Sussex RH9 4LY
Tel: (01342) 321635
Fax: (01342) 326844
Email: enquiries@
fonthill-lodge.co.uk
Head: Mrs J Griffiths
Type: Co-educational Day 2–11
(Single-sex ed 8–11)
No of pupils: B91 G99
Fees: (September 05)
Day £6060–£9390

STOKE BRUNSWICK
Ashurstwood, East Grinstead,
West Sussex RH19 3PF
Tel: (01342) 828200
Fax: (01342) 828201
Email: headmaster@
stokebrunswick.co.uk
Head: Mr R Taylor
Type: Co-educational Boarding
and Day 3–13
No of pupils: B100 G55
No of boarders: W10
Fees: (September 06) WB £13875
Day £2955–£11475

HAYWARDS HEATH

ARDINGLY COLLEGE
Haywards Heath, West Sussex
RH17 6SQ
Tel: (01444) 893000
Fax: (01444) 893001
Email: registrar@ardingly.com
Head: Mr J R Franklin
Type: Co-educational Boarding
and Day 3–18
No of pupils: B464 G289
No of boarders: F213 W14
Fees: (September 06) FB £21600
WB £11520–£13710
Day £5220–£16500

**ARDINGLY COLLEGE
JUNIOR SCHOOL**
Haywards Heath, West Sussex
RH17 6SQ
Tel: (01444) 893200
Fax: (01444) 892001
Email: mark.groome@
ardingly.com
Head: Mr M Groome
Type: Co-educational Boarding
and Day 7–13 (and pre-prep)
No of pupils: B146 G90
No of boarders: W14
Fees: (September 06)
WB £11520–£13710
Day £8340–£10500

CUMNOR HOUSE SCHOOL
Danehill, Haywards Heath,
West Sussex RH17 7HT
Tel: (01825) 790347
Fax: (01825) 790910
Email: office@cumnor.co.uk
Head: Mr C St J Heinrich
Type: Co-educational Boarding
and Day 4–13
No of pupils: B183 G151
No of boarders: F26
Fees: (September 06) FB £15345
Day £6840–£12930

GREAT WALSTEAD
East Mascalls Lane, Lindfield,
Haywards Heath, West Sussex
RH16 2QL
Tel: (01444) 483528
Fax: (01444) 482122
Email: admin@
greatwalstead.co.uk
Head: Mr H J Lowries
Type: Co-educational Day and
Boarding 2–13
No of pupils: B245 G166
No of boarders: W30
Fees: (September 05) WB £10635
Day £4800–£9885

HANDCROSS PARK SCHOOL
Handcross, Haywards Heath,
West Sussex RH17 6HF
Tel: (01444) 400526
Fax: (01444) 400527
Email: whilton@handxpark.com
Head: Mr W J Hilton
Type: Co-educational Day and
Boarding 3–13
No of pupils: B180 G120
No of boarders: W10
Fees: (September 06) WB £4836
Day £2460–£4127

TAVISTOCK & SUMMERHILL SCHOOL

Summerhill Lane, Haywards Heath, West Sussex RH16 1RP
Tel: (01444) 450256
Fax: (01444) 458251
Email: info@
   tavistockandsummerhill.co.uk
Head: Mr M Barber
Type: Co-educational Day 3–13
No of pupils: B99 G53
Fees: (September 05)
Day £4455–£8190

HORSHAM

CHRIST'S HOSPITAL

Horsham, West Sussex RH13 0YP
Tel: (01403) 211293
Fax: (01403) 211580
Email: enquiries@
   christs-hospital.org.uk
Head: Dr P C D Southern
Type: Co-educational Boarding 11–18
No of pupils: B464 G356
No of boarders: F820
Fees: (September 06) FB £19176

FARLINGTON SCHOOL*

Strood Park, Horsham, West Sussex RH12 3PN
Tel: (01403) 254967
Fax: (01403) 272258
Email: office@farlingtonschool.net
Head: Mrs J Goyer
Type: Girls Boarding and Day 4–18
No of pupils: 490
No of boarders: F32 W8
Fees: (September 06)
FB £14625–£17820
WB £14265–£17460
Day £5265–£9360

PENNTHORPE SCHOOL

Church Street, Rudgwick, Horsham, West Sussex RH12 3HJ
Tel: (01403) 822391
Fax: (01403) 822438
Email: enquiries@pennthorpe.com
Head: Mr S Moll
Type: Co-educational Day 2–14
No of pupils: B197 G109
Fees: (September 06)
Day £1194–£10674

HURSTPIERPOINT

HURSTPIERPOINT COLLEGE

College Lane, Hurstpierpoint, West Sussex BN6 9JS
Tel: (01273) 833636
Fax: (01273) 835257
Email: Info@hppc.co.uk
Head: Mr T J Manly
Type: Co-educational Boarding and Day 7–18
No of pupils: B413 G237
No of boarders: F42 W253
Fees: (September 06) FB £20970
WB £13665–£20085
Day £9450–£15855

LANCING

ARDMORE MONTESSORI SCHOOL

Wembley Gardens, Lancing, West Sussex BN15 9LA
Tel: (01903) 755583
Head: Mr N Peck
Type: Co-educational Day 2–12
No of pupils: 60
Fees: On application

LANCING COLLEGE

Lancing, West Sussex BN15 0RW
Tel: (01273) 452213
Fax: (01273) 464720
Email: admissions@
   lancing.dialnet.com
Head: Mr J Gillespie
Type: Co-educational Boarding and Day 13–18
No of pupils: B316 G122
No of boarders: F278
Fees: (September 05) FB £21885
Day £15225

MIDHURST

CONIFERS SCHOOL

Egmont Road, Midhurst, West Sussex GU29 9BG
Tel: (01730) 813243
Fax: (01730) 813382
Email: admin@conifersschool.com
Head: Mrs L R Fox
Type: Co-educational Day
Boys 3–8 Girls 3–11
No of pupils: B30 G70
Fees: (September 06)
Day £540–£7356

ST MARGARET'S SCHOOL CONVENT OF MERCY

Petersfield Road, Midhurst, West Sussex GU29 9JN
Tel: (01730) 813956
Fax: (01730) 810829
Email: smsadmin@
   conventofmercy.org
Head: Sister M Joseph Clare
Type: Co-educational Day 2–11
No of pupils: B86 G151
Fees: (September 05)
Day £1380–£5685

PEASE POTTAGE

COTTESMORE SCHOOL*

Buchan Hill, Pease Pottage, West Sussex RH11 9AU
Tel: (01293) 520648
Fax: (01293) 614784
Email: schooloffice@
   cottesmoreschool.com
Head: Mr I J Tysoe
Type: Co-educational Boarding and Day 8–13
No of pupils: B100 G50
No of boarders: F150
Fees: (September 06) FB £16680
WB £13000

PETWORTH

SEAFORD COLLEGE*

Lavington Park, Petworth, West Sussex GU27 0NB
Tel: (01798) 867392
Fax: (01798) 867606
Email: seaford@clara.co.uk
Head: Mr T J Mullins
Type: Co-educational Boarding and Day 10–18
No of pupils: B336 G160
No of boarders: F60 W114
Fees: (September 06)
FB £15510–£20070
WB £13500–£17010
Day £10560–£13170

England – West Sussex

PULBOROUGH

ARUNDALE PREPARATORY SCHOOL
Lower Street, Pulborough,
West Sussex RH20 2BX
Tel: (01798) 872520
Fax: (01798) 875202
Email: arundale@easynet.co.uk
Head: Miss K Lovejoy
Type: Co-educational Day 2–11
No of pupils: B35 G63
Fees: (September 06)
Day £2565–£8130

DORSET HOUSE SCHOOL
The Manor, Church Lane, Bury,
Pulborough, West Sussex
RH20 1PB
Tel: (01798) 831456
Fax: (01798) 831141
Email: headmaster@
    dorsethouse.w-sussex.sch.uk
Head: Mr E J D Clarke
Type: Boys Boarding and Day
3–13
No of pupils: 130
No of boarders: W30
Fees: On application

WINDLESHAM HOUSE*
Washington, Pulborough,
West Sussex RH20 4AY
Tel: (01903) 874700
Fax: (01903) 874702
Email: office@windlesham.com
Head: Mr P Forte
Type: Co-educational Boarding
and Day 4–13 (Day pre-prep 4–7)
No of pupils: B174 G104
No of boarders: F229
Fees: (September 06)
FB £16485–£16785
Day £2025–£2350

SHOREHAM-BY-SEA

SHOREHAM COLLEGE
St Julian's Lane, Shoreham-by-Sea,
West Sussex BN43 6YW
Tel: (01273) 592681
Fax: (01273) 591673
Email: info@
    shorehamcollege.co.uk
Head: Mr R K Iremonger
Type: Co-educational Day 3–16
No of pupils: B280 G144
Fees: (September 05)
Day £5400–£8850

SOMPTING

SOMPTING ABBOTTS SCHOOL
Church Lane, Sompting,
West Sussex BN15 0AZ
Tel: (01903) 235960
Fax: (01903) 210045
Email: office@
    somptingabbotts.com
Head: Mrs P M Sinclair and
Mr TR Sinclair
Type: Co-educational Day and
Boarding 3–13
No of pupils: B125 G60
No of boarders: W12
Fees: (September 06) WB £9660
Day £6030–£7695

STEYNING

THE TOWERS CONVENT SCHOOL
Henfield Road, Upper Beeding,
Steyning, West Sussex BN44 3TF
Tel: (01903) 812185
Fax: (01903) 813858
Email: admin@
    towers.w-sussex.sch.uk
Head: Mrs C Baker
Type: Girls Day and Boarding
3–16 (Boys 3–11)
No of pupils: B4 G271
No of boarders: F44 W1
Fees: (September 06)
FB £9705–£10185
WB £9225–£9705
Day £5505–£6075

TURNERS HILL

WORTH SCHOOL
Paddockhurst Road, Turners Hill,
West Sussex RH10 4SD
Tel: (01342) 710200
Fax: (01342) 710230
Email: registry@worth.org.uk
Head: Mr P Armstrong
Type: Boys Boarding and Day
11–18
No of pupils: 440
No of boarders: F291
Fees: (September 06)
FB £20190–£22437
Day £14961–£16620

WORTHING

BROADWATER MANOR SCHOOL
Broadwater Road, Worthing,
West Sussex BN14 8HU
Tel: (01903) 201123
Fax: (01903) 821777
Email: info@
    broadwatermanor.com
Head: Mrs E K Woodley
Type: Co-educational Day 2–13
No of pupils: B192 G147
Fees: On application

OUR LADY OF SION SCHOOL
Gratwicke Road, Worthing,
West Sussex BN11 4BL
Tel: (01903) 204063
Fax: (01903) 214434
Email: enquiries@
    sionschool.org.uk
Head: Mr M Scullion
Type: Co-educational Day 2–18
No of pupils: B230 G252
Fees: (September 06)
Day £5370–£8385

SANDHURST SCHOOL
101 Brighton Road, Worthing,
West Sussex BN11 2EL
Tel: (01903) 201933
Fax: (01903) 824752
Email: enquiries@
    sandhurst-school.co.uk
Head: Mrs S A Hale
Type: Co-educational Day 2–13
No of pupils: B50 G82
Fees: On application

TYNE AND WEAR

NEWCASTLE UPON TYNE

AKHURST PREPARATORY SCHOOL
The Grove, Jesmond,
Newcastle upon Tyne,
Tyne and Wear NE2 2PN
Tel: (0191) 281 2116
Fax: (0191) 281 3964
Email: akhurst@rmplc.co.uk
Head: Mr & Mrs R J Derham
Type: Co-educational Day 1–12
No of pupils: B130 G70
Fees: On application

CENTRAL NEWCASTLE HIGH SCHOOL GDST
Eskdale Terrace,
Newcastle upon Tyne,
Tyne and Wear NE2 4DS
Tel: (0191) 281 1768
Fax: (0191) 281 6192
Email: general@cnw.gdst.net
Head: Mrs H French
Type: Girls Day 3–18
No of pupils: 967
Fees: On application

DAME ALLAN'S BOYS SCHOOL
Fowberry Crescent, Fenham,
Newcastle upon Tyne,
Tyne and Wear NE4 9YJ
Tel: (0191) 275 0608
Fax: (0191) 275 1502
Email: enquiries@
   dameallans.co.uk
Head: Dr J R Hind
Type: Boys Day 8–18 (Co-ed VIth Form)
No of pupils: 510
Fees: (September 06)
Day £6039–£7674

DAME ALLAN'S GIRLS SCHOOL
Fowberry Crescent, Fenham,
Newcastle upon Tyne,
Tyne and Wear NE4 9YJ
Tel: (0191) 275 0708
Fax: (0191) 275 1502
Email: enquiries@
   dameallans.co.uk
Head: Dr J R Hind
Type: Girls Day 8–18 (Co-ed VIth Form)
No of pupils: 422
Fees: (September 06)
Day £6039–£7674

LA SAGESSE SCHOOL
North Jesmond,
Newcastle upon Tyne,
Tyne and Wear NE2 3RJ
Tel: (0191) 281 3474
Fax: (0191) 281 2721
Email: office@lsh.org.uk
Head: Miss L Clark
Type: Girls Day 3–18
Fees: On application

LINDEN SCHOOL
72 Station Road, Forest Hall,
Newcastle upon Tyne,
Tyne and Wear NE12 9BQ
Tel: (0191) 266 2943
Fax: (0191) 266 2943
Head: Mr A J Edge
Type: Co-educational Day 3–11
No of pupils: B60 G58
Fees: On application

NEWCASTLE PREPARATORY SCHOOL
6 Eslington Road, Jesmond,
Newcastle upon Tyne,
Tyne and Wear NE2 4RH
Tel: (0191) 281 1769
Fax: (0191) 281 5668
Email: enquiries@
   newcastleprepschool.org.uk
Head: Mrs M Coates
Type: Co-educational Day 3–11
No of pupils: B160 G60
Fees: (September 05)
Day £5784–£6600

NEWCASTLE SCHOOL FOR BOYS
30 West Avenue, Gosforth,
Newcastle upon Tyne,
Tyne and Wear NE3 4ES
Tel: (0191) 285 1619
Fax: (0191) 213 1105
Email: office@
   newcastleschool.co.uk
Head: Mr P M Garner
Type: Boys Day 3–13
No of pupils: 392
Fees: (September 05) Day £6855

NEWCASTLE UPON TYNE CHURCH HIGH SCHOOL
Tankerville Terrace, Jesmond,
Newcastle upon Tyne,
Tyne and Wear NE2 3BA
Tel: (0191) 281 4306
Fax: (0191) 281 0806
Email: info@churchhigh.com
Head: Mrs L G Smith
Type: Girls Day 2–18
No of pupils: 609
Fees: On application

ROYAL GRAMMAR SCHOOL
Eskdale Terrace,
Newcastle upon Tyne,
Tyne and Wear NE2 4DX
Tel: (0191) 281 5711
Fax: (0191) 212 0392
Email: hm@rgs.newcastle.sch.uk
Head: Mr J F X Miller
Type: Boys Day 8–18 (Co-ed VIth form)
No of pupils: B1067 G74
Fees: (September 05)
Day £6141–£7329

WESTFIELD SCHOOL
Oakfield Road, Gosforth,
Newcastle upon Tyne,
Tyne and Wear NE3 4HS
Tel: (0191) 285 1948
Fax: (0191) 213 0734
Email: westfield@
   westfield.newcastle.sch.uk
Head: Mrs M Farndale
Type: Girls Day 3–18
No of pupils: 370
Fees: On application

SUNDERLAND

ARGYLE HOUSE SCHOOL
19/20 Thornhill Park, Sunderland,
Tyne and Wear SR2 7LA
Tel: (0191) 510 0726
Fax: (0191) 567 2209
Email: info@
    argylehouseschool.co.uk
Head: Mr C Johnson
Type: Co-educational Day 3–16
No of pupils: B156 G81
Fees: On application

GRINDON HALL CHRISTIAN SCHOOL
Nookside, Sunderland,
Tyne and Wear SR4 8PG
Tel: (0191) 534 4444
Fax: (0191) 534 4111
Email: info@grindonhall.com
Head: Mr C J Gray
Type: Co-educational Day 3–18
(VIth Form from Sept 2005)
Fees: (September 06)
Day £2958–£5151

SUNDERLAND HIGH SCHOOL
Mowbray Road, Sunderland,
Tyne and Wear SR2 8HY
Tel: (0191) 567 4984
Fax: (0191) 510 3953
Email: info@sunderlandhigh.co.uk
Head: Dr A Slater
Type: Co-educational Day 2–18
No of pupils: B318 G257
Fees: On application

TYNEMOUTH

THE KING'S SCHOOL
Huntington Place, Tynemouth,
Tyne and Wear NE30 4RF
Tel: (0191) 258 5995
Fax: (0191) 296 3826
Email: hm@
    kings-tynemouth.co.uk
Head: Mr P J S Cantwell
Type: Co-educational Day 4–18
No of pupils: B580 G314
Fees: (September 06)
Day £5982–£7881

WHICKHAM

CHASE SCHOOL
Rectory Lane, Whickham,
Tyne and Wear NE16 4PD
Tel: (0191) 488 9432
Fax: (0191) 488 8855
Head: Mrs A Nelson
Type: Co-educational Day 4–11
No of pupils: B22 G19
Fees: On application

WARWICKSHIRE

ATHERSTONE

TWYCROSS HOUSE SCHOOL
Twycross, Atherstone,
Warwickshire CV9 3PL
Tel: (01827) 880651
Head: Mr R V Kirkpatrick
Type: Co-educational Day 8–19
No of pupils: B143 G169
Fees: On application

KENILWORTH

ABBOTSFORD SCHOOL
Bridge Street, Kenilworth,
Warwickshire CV8 1BP
Tel: (01926) 852826
Fax: (01926) 852753
Email: office@
    abbotsfordschool.co.uk
Head: Mrs J Jarvis
Type: Co-educational Day 3–11
No of pupils: B80 G56
Fees: (September 06)
Day £4200–£5250

CRACKLEY HALL SCHOOL
St Joseph's Park, Kenilworth,
Warwickshire CV8 2FT
Tel: (01926) 514444
Fax: (01926) 514455
Email: post@crackleyhall.co.uk
Head: Mrs J Le Poidevin
Type: Co-educational Day 2–11
No of pupils: B49 G76
Fees: (September 05)
Day £5295–£5460

LEAMINGTON SPA

ARNOLD LODGE SCHOOL*
Kenilworth Road, Leamington Spa,
Warwickshire CV32 5TW
Tel: (01926) 778050
Fax: (01926) 743311
Email: info@arnoldlodge.com
Head: Mrs E M Hickling
Type: Co-educational Day 3–13
No of pupils: B190 G90
Fees: (September 06)
Day £1700–£7590

EMSCOTE HOUSE SCHOOL AND NURSERY
46 Warwick Place, Leamington
Spa, Warwickshire CV32 5DE
Tel: (01926) 425067
Email: headteacher@
    emscotehouse.demon.co.uk
Head: Mrs G J Andrews
Type: Co-educational Day 2–8
No of pupils: B26 G15
Fees: (September 06)
Day £690–£1945

THE KINGSLEY SCHOOL
Beauchamp Avenue, Leamington
Spa, Warwickshire CV32 5RD
Tel: (01926) 425127
Fax: (01926) 831691
Email: admin@
    kingsley.warwickshire.sch.uk
Head: Mrs C Mannion Watson
Type: Girls Day 3–18 (Boys 2–7)
No of pupils: B2 G500
Fees: (September 06)
Day £6720–£8520

THE TERRACE SCHOOL
54 High Street, Leamington Spa,
Warwickshire CV31 1LW
Tel: (01926) 421222
Fax: (01926) 421222
Head: Mrs Celia Lowe
Type: Co-educational Day 2–13
No of pupils: B20 G20
Fees: (September 06)
Day £3350–£3900

NUNEATON

**THE DIXIE GRAMMAR
JUNIOR SCHOOL**
Temple Hall, Wellsborough,
Nuneaton, Warwickshire
CV13 6PA
Tel: (01455) 293024
Fax: (01455) 293040
Email: info@dixiejs.org.uk
Head: Mr S Barnett
Type: Co-educational Day 3–10
No of pupils: B85 G67
Fees: On application

**MILVERTON HOUSE
SCHOOL**
Holman Way, Park Street,
Attleborough, Nuneaton,
Warwickshire CV11 4NS
Tel: (024) 7664 1722
Email: reception@
   milvertonschool.com
Head: Mrs S D Latham
Type: Co-educational Day 0–11
No of pupils: B150 G150
Fees: (September 06)
Day £3750–£5550

RUGBY

BILTON GRANGE
Rugby Road, Dunchurch, Rugby,
Warwickshire CV22 6QU
Tel: (01788) 810217
Fax: (01788) 816922
Email: headmaster@
   biltongrange.co.uk
Head: Mr J P Kirk
Type: Co-educational Boarding
and Day 4–13
No of pupils: B205 G132
No of boarders: F39 W9
Fees: (September 06) F/WB £15900
Day £5865–£13005

THE CRESCENT SCHOOL
Bawnmore Road, Bilton, Rugby,
Warwickshire CV22 7QH
Tel: (01788) 521595
Fax: (01788) 816185
Email: admin@
   crescentschool.co.uk
Head: Mr R H Marshall
Type: Co-educational Day 3–11
No of pupils: B70 G87
Fees: (September 06)
Day £1855–£2040

PRINCETHORPE COLLEGE
Princethorpe, Rugby,
Warwickshire CV23 9PX
Tel: (01926) 634200
Fax: (01926) 633365
Email: post@princethorpe.co.uk
Head: Mr J M Shinkwin
Type: Co-educational Day 11–18
No of pupils: B403 G316
Fees: (September 06) Day £2570

RUGBY SCHOOL
Rugby, Warwickshire CV22 5EH
Tel: (01788) 556276
Fax: (01788) 556277
Email: registry@rugbyschool.net
Head: Mr P S J Derham
Type: Co-educational Boarding
and Day 11–18
No of pupils: B442 G338
No of boarders: F654
Fees: On application

STRATFORD-UPON-AVON

**THE CROFT PREPARATORY
SCHOOL**
Alveston Hill, Loxley Road,
Stratford-upon-Avon,
Warwickshire CV37 7RL
Tel: (01789) 293795
Fax: (01789) 414960
Email: office@croftschool.co.uk
Head: Dr P Thompson
Type: Co-educational Day 2–11
No of pupils: B237 G187
Fees: (September 06)
Day £1121–£7671

**ELFIN PRE-PREP & NURSERY
SCHOOL**
26 Evesham Place,
Stratford-upon-Avon,
Warwickshire CV37 6HT
Tel: (01789) 292571
Fax: (01789) 292450
Email: elfinschool@btinternet.com
Head: Mrs B A Buczacki
Type: Co-educational Day 2–8
No of pupils: B16 G16
Fees: (September 05)
Day £2874–£3732

**STRATFORD PREPARATORY
SCHOOL**
Church House, Old Town,
Stratford-upon-Avon,
Warwickshire CV37 6BG
Tel: (01789) 297993
Fax: (01789) 263993
Head: Mrs C Quinn
Type: Co-educational Day 2–11
No of pupils: B58 G56
Fees: On application

WARWICK

**KING'S HIGH SCHOOL,
WARWICK**
Smith Street, Warwick,
Warwickshire CV34 4HJ
Tel: (01926) 494485
Fax: (01926) 403089
Email: enquiries@
   kingshighwarwick.co.uk
Head: Mrs E Surber
Type: Girls Day 10–18
No of pupils: 596
Fees: (September 05) Day £8019

**WARWICK PREPARATORY
SCHOOL**
Bridge Field, Banbury Road,
Warwick, Warwickshire CV34 6PL
Tel: (01926) 491545
Fax: (01926) 403456
Email: info@warwick-
   prep.warwickshire.sch.uk
Head: Mrs D M Robinson
Type: Co-educational Day
Boys 3–7 Girls 3–11
No of pupils: B99 G346
Fees: On application

WARWICK SCHOOL
Myton Road, Warwick,
Warwickshire CV34 6PP
Tel: (01926) 776400
Fax: (01926) 401259
Email: enquiries@
    warwickschool.org
Head: Mr E B Halse
Type: Boys Day and Boarding
7–18
No of pupils: 1090
No of boarders: F35 W11
Fees: On application

WEST MIDLANDS

BIRMINGHAM

ABBEY COLLEGE
10 St Pauls Square, Birmingham,
West Midlands B3 1QU
Tel: (0121) 236 7474
Fax: (0121) 236 3937
Email: adminbir@
    abbeycollege.co.uk
Head: Dr C Devine
Type: Co-educational Day 13+
No of pupils: B95 G61
No of boarders: F1
Fees: On application

AL HIJRAH SCHOOL
Cherrywood Centre, Burbidge
Road, Bordesley Green,
Birmingham, West Midlands
B9 4US
Tel: (0121) 773 7979
Fax: (0121) 773 7111
Head: Mr M A K Saqib
Type: Co-educational Day 4–11
(Single sex ed)
No of pupils: B128 G128
Fees: On application

AL-BURHAN GRAMMAR
SCHOOL
28A George Street, Balsall Heath,
Birmingham, West Midlands
B12 9RG
Tel: (0121) 440 5454
Fax: (0121) 440 5454
Head: Dr Mohammad Nasrullah
Type: Girls Day 11–16
No of pupils: 85
Fees: (September 06) Day £6750

BIRCHFIELD INDEPENDENT
GIRLS SCHOOL
Beacon House, 30 Beacon Hill,
Aston, Birmingham,
West Midlands B6 6JU
Tel: (0121) 327 7707
Fax: (0121) 327 6888
Head: Mrs K Chawdhry
Type: Girls Day 11–16
No of pupils: 170
Fees: On application

THE BLUE COAT SCHOOL
Somerset Road, Edgbaston,
Birmingham, West Midlands
B17 0HR
Tel: (0121) 410 6800
Fax: (0121) 454 7757
Email: admissions@
    bluecoat.bham.sch.uk
Head: Mr A D J Browning
Type: Co-educational Day 2–11
No of pupils: B309 G202
Fees: On application

DARUL ULOOM ISLAMIC
HIGH SCHOOL & COLLEGE
521–527 Coventry Road,
Smallheath, Birmingham,
West Midlands B10 0LL
Tel: (0121) 772 6408
Fax: (0121) 773 4340
Head: Dr A A Rahim
Type: Co-educational Day and
Boarding(Single-sex ed)
No of pupils: B77 G13
No of boarders: F14
Fees: On application

EASTBOURNE HOUSE
SCHOOL
111 Yardley Road, Acocks Green,
Birmingham, West Midlands
B27 6LL
Tel: (0121) 706 2013
Fax: (0121) 706 2013
Email: admin@
    eastbournehouse.bham.sch.uk
Head: Mr P J Moynihan
Type: Co-educational Day 3–11
No of pupils: B66 G58
Fees: (September 05)
Day £2709–£3990

EDGBASTON HIGH
SCHOOL FOR GIRLS
Westbourne Road, Edgbaston,
Birmingham, West Midlands
B15 3TS
Tel: (0121) 454 5831
Fax: (0121) 454 2363
Email: genoffice@
    edgbastonhigh.bham.sch.uk
Head: Dr R Weeks
Type: Girls Day 2–18
No of pupils: 922
Fees: (September 05)
Day £3279–£7368

ELMHURST SCHOOL FOR DANCE
247–249 Bristol Road, Edgbaston, Birmingham, West Midlands
B5 7UH
Tel: (0121) 472 6655
Fax: (0121) 472 6654
Email: elmhurst@cableol.co.uk
Head: Mr J McNamara
Type: Co-educational Boarding and Day 11–19
No of pupils: B26 G159
No of boarders: F158
Fees: (September 05)
FB £16536–£17172
Day £12879–£13356

HALLFIELD SCHOOL
48 Church Road, Edgbaston, Birmingham, West Midlands
B15 3SJ
Tel: (0121) 454 1496
Fax: (0121) 454 9182
Email: admissions@ hallfield.bham.sch.uk
Head: Mr C T O'Donnell
Type: Co-educational Day 2–11
No of pupils: B327 G130
Fees: (September 06)
Day £5445–£8235

HARPER BELL SCHOOL
29 Ravenhurst Street, Birmingham, West Midlands B2 0EP
Tel: (0121) 693 7742
Fax: (0121) 693 0752
Head: Mr O F Stewart
Type: Co-educational Day 2–11
Fees: On application

HIGHCLARE SCHOOL
10 Sutton Road, Erdington, Birmingham, West Midlands
B23 6QL
Tel: (0121) 373 7400
Fax: (0121) 373 7445
Email: abbey@ highclareschool.co.uk
Head: Mrs M Viles
Type: Girls Day 1–18 (Boys 1–11 & 16–18)
No of pupils: B225 G520
Fees: (September 06)
Day £5085–£8250

HONEYBOURNE SCHOOL
621 Fox Hollies Road, Hall Green, Birmingham, West Midlands
B28 9DW
Tel: (0121) 777 3778
Email: hbsinfo@hotmail.com
Head: Mr R J Croucher
Type: Co-educational Day 2–11
No of pupils: B30 G35
Fees: On application

KING EDWARD VI HIGH SCHOOL FOR GIRLS
Edgbaston Park Road, Birmingham, West Midlands
B15 2UB
Tel: (0121) 472 1834
Fax: (0121) 471 3808
Email: admissions@kehs.co.uk
Head: Miss S H Evans
Type: Girls Day 11–18
No of pupils: 540
Fees: On application

KING EDWARD'S SCHOOL
Edgbaston Park Road, Birmingham, West Midlands
B15 2UA
Tel: (0121) 472 1672
Fax: (0121) 415 4327
Email: office@kes.bham.sch.uk
Head: Mr J A Claughton
Type: Boys Day 11–18
No of pupils: 840
Fees: (September 06) Day £8100

LAMBS CHRISTIAN SCHOOL
86–95 Bacchus Road, Winson Green, Birmingham, West Midlands B18 4QY
Tel: (0121) 554 4744
Head: Mrs Patricia Ekhuenelo
Type: Co-educational Day 4–11
No of pupils: B6 G6
Fees: On application

MANDER PORTMAN WOODWARD
17–18 Greenfield Crescent, Edgbaston, Birmingham, West Midlands B15 3AU
Tel: (0121) 454 9637
Fax: (0121) 454 6433
Email: enq@ birmingham.mpw.co.uk
Head: Mrs D Jewell
Type: Co-educational Day 14+
No of pupils: B50 G50
Fees: (September 06)
Day £2385–£13815

NORFOLK HOUSE SCHOOL
4 Norfolk Road, Edgbaston, Birmingham, West Midlands
B15 3PS
Tel: (0121) 454 7021
Fax: (0121) 454 7021
Email: office@ norfolkhouseschool.org.uk
Head: Mrs Helen Maresca
Type: Co-educational Day 3–11
No of pupils: B80 G78
Fees: On application

PRIORY SCHOOL
39 Sir Harry's Road, Edgbaston, Birmingham, West Midlands
B15 2UR
Tel: (0121) 440 0256
Fax: (0121) 440 3639
Email: enquiries@prioryschool.net
Head: Mrs E Brook
Type: Girls Day 1–18 (Co-ed 1–11)
No of pupils: B70 G230
Fees: On application

RATHVILLY SCHOOL
119 Bunbury Road, Birmingham, West Midlands B31 2NB
Tel: (0121) 475 1509
Head: Mrs D P Edwards
Type: Co-educational Day 3–11
No of pupils: B55 G65
Fees: On application

ROSSLYN SCHOOL
1597 Stratford Road, Hall Green, Birmingham, West Midlands
B28 9JB
Tel: (0121) 744 2743
Fax: (0121) 744 2743
Email: office@rosslynschool.co.uk
Head: Mrs P J Scott
Type: Co-educational Day 2–11
No of pupils: B49 G55
Fees: On application

ST GEORGE'S SCHOOL, EDGBASTON
31 Calthorpe Road, Edgbaston, Birmingham, West Midlands
B15 1RX
Tel: (0121) 625 0398
Fax: (0121) 625 3340
Email: admin@sgse.co.uk
Head: Miss H J Phillips
Type: Co-educational Day 3–18
No of pupils: B280 G140
Fees: (September 06)
Day £4080–£8025

England – West Midlands

WEST HOUSE SCHOOL
24 St James's Road, Edgbaston,
Birmingham, West Midlands
B15 2NX
Tel: (0121) 440 4097
Fax: (0121) 440 5839
Email: secretary@
    westhouseschool.demon.co.uk
Head: Mr A Lyttle
Type: Boys Day 1–11 (Girls 1–4)
No of pupils: B185 G25
Fees: (September 06)
Day £1689–£7770

**WOODSTOCK GIRLS'
SCHOOL**
11–15 Woodstock Road, Moseley,
Birmingham, West Midlands
B13 9BB
Tel: (0121) 449 9640
Head: Mrs T Anees
Type: Girls Day 11–15
No of pupils: 120
Fees: (September 05)
Day £540–£2430

COVENTRY

BABLAKE SCHOOL
Coundon Road, Coventry,
West Midlands CV1 4AU
Tel: (024) 7627 1200
Fax: (024) 7627 1290
Email: hmsec@
    bablake.coventry.sch.uk
Head: Mr J Watson
Type: Co-educational Day 11–19
No of pupils: B450 G450
Fees: (September 06) Day £7560

**CHESHUNT
PRE-PREPARATORY SCHOOL**
8 Park Road, Coventry,
West Midlands CV1 2LH
Tel: (024) 7622 1677
Fax: (024) 7623 1630
Head: Mrs F Ward
Type: Co-educational Day 3–8
No of pupils: 100
Fees: On application

**COVENTRY MUSLIM
SCHOOL**
643 Foleshill Road, Coventry,
West Midlands CV6 5JQ
Tel: (024) 7626 1803
Fax: (024) 7626 1803
Email: admin@
    coventrymuslimschool.
    freeserve.co.uk
Head: Mrs M Ashique
Type: Girls Day 4–16
No of pupils: B8 G52
Fees: On application

COVENTRY PREP SCHOOL
Kenilworth Road, Coventry,
West Midlands CV3 6PT
Tel: (024) 7627 1307
Fax: (024) 7627 1308
Email: headmaster@
    coventryprep.co.uk
Head: Mr N Lovell
Type: Co-educational Day 3–11
No of pupils: B147 G97
Fees: (September 06)
Day £6000–£8100

**DAVENPORT LODGE
SCHOOL**
21 Davenport Road, Earlsdon,
Coventry, West Midlands
CV5 6QA
Tel: (024) 7667 5051
Email: principal@
    davenportlodge.coventry.sch.uk
Head: Mrs M D Martin
Type: Co-educational Day 2–8
Fees: On application

KING HENRY VIII SCHOOL
Warwick Road, Coventry,
West Midlands CV3 6AQ
Tel: (024) 7672 1111
Fax: (024) 7672 1188
Email: info@khviii.com
Head: Mr G D Fisher
Type: Co-educational Day 7–18
No of pupils: B457 G405
Fees: On application

PATTISON COLLEGE
90 Binley Road, Coventry,
West Midlands CV3 1FQ
Tel: (024) 7645 5031
Email: pattisonsinfo@
    btconnect.com
Head: Mrs E A P Connell and
Mrs J A Satchell
Type: Co-educational Day 3–16
No of pupils: B38 G108
Fees: On application

SOLIHULL

**EVERSFIELD PREPARATORY
SCHOOL**
Warwick Road, Solihull,
West Midlands B91 1AT
Tel: (0121) 705 0354
Fax: (0121) 709 0168
Email: enquiries@eversfield.co.uk
Head: Mr K U Madden
Type: Co-educational Day 2–11
No of pupils: B191 G54
Fees: On application

KINGSWOOD SCHOOL
St James Place, Shirley, Solihull,
West Midlands B90 2BA
Tel: (0121) 744 7883
Fax: (0121) 744 1282
Email: kingswoodhm@aol.com
Head: Mr N Shaw
Type: Co-educational Day 2–11
No of pupils: B30 G20
Fees: (September 06)
Day £5070–£5685

RUCKLEIGH SCHOOL
17 Lode Lane, Solihull,
West Midlands B91 2AB
Tel: (0121) 705 2773
Fax: (0121) 704 4883
Email: admin@ruckleigh.co.uk
Head: Mrs B M Forster
Type: Co-educational Day 2–11
No of pupils: B122 G84
Fees: On application

SAINT MARTIN'S SCHOOL
Malvern Hall, Brueton Avenue,
Solihull, West Midlands B91 3EN
Tel: (0121) 705 1265
Fax: (0121) 711 4529
Email: mail@
    saintmartins-school.com
Head: Mrs J Carwithen
Type: Girls Day 3–18
No of pupils: 520
Fees: (September 05)
Day £2970–£7875

SOLIHULL SCHOOL
Warwick Road, Solihull,
West Midlands B91 3DJ
Tel: (0121) 705 4273
Fax: (0121) 711 4439
Email: enquiries@solsch.org.uk
Head: Mr P J Griffiths
Type: Co-educational Day 7–18
No of pupils: B990 G160
Fees: (September 06)
Day £6663–£8418

SUTTON COLDFIELD

THE SHRUBBERY SCHOOL
Walmley Ash Road, Walmley,
Sutton Coldfield, West Midlands
B76 1HY
Tel: (0121) 351 1582
Fax: (0121) 351 1124
Head: Mrs H Cook
Type: Co-educational Day 3–11
No of pupils: B152 G118
Fees: On application

WALSALL

ABU BAKR INDEPENDENT SCHOOL
154–160 Wednesbury Road,
Palfrey, Walsall, West Midlands
WS1 4JJ
Tel: (01922) 620618
Fax: (01922) 646175
Email: info@abubakrtrust.org
Head: Mr M Ramzan
Type: Co-educational Day 11–16
No of pupils: B60 G198
Fees: (September 06) Day £2250

EMMANUEL SCHOOL
Bath Street Centre, Bath Street,
Walsall, West Midlands WS1 3DB
Tel: (01922) 635810
Email: office@
    emmanuel.walsall.sch.uk
Head: Mr J Swain
Type: Co-educational Day 3–16
No of pupils: B27 G32
Fees: On application

HYDESVILLE TOWER SCHOOL
25 Broadway North, Walsall,
West Midlands WS1 2QG
Tel: (01922) 624374
Fax: (01922) 746169
Email: info@hydesville.com
Head: Dr Leslie Fox
Type: Co-educational Day 3–16
No of pupils: B217 G161
Fees: (September 06)
Day £4680–£8160

MAYFIELD PREPARATORY SCHOOL
Sutton Road, Walsall,
West Midlands WS1 2PD
Tel: (01922) 624107
Fax: (01299) 746908
Email: info@mayfieldprep.co.uk
Head: Mr M Coleman
Type: Co-educational Day 3–11
No of pupils: B110 G91
Fees: (September 06) Day £5925

SECOND CHANCES AT THE VINE TRUST WALSALL
33 Lower Hall Lane, Walsall,
West Midlands WS1 1RR
Tel: (01922) 621951
Fax: (01922) 621984
Email: enquiries@
    thevinetrust.co.uk
Head: Mrs R Clay
Type: Co-educational Day 14–16
Fees: On application

WOLVERHAMPTON

BIRCHFIELD SCHOOL
Albrighton, Wolverhampton,
West Midlands WV7 3AF
Tel: (01902) 372534
Fax: (01902) 373516
Email: office@
    birchfieldschool.co.uk
Head: Mr R P Merriman
Type: Co-educational Boarding
and Day Boys 4–13 Girls 4–5
No of pupils: B149 G6
No of boarders: W19
Fees: (September 06) WB £13050
Day £6060–£9705

THE DRIVE PREPARATORY SCHOOL
Wood Road, Tettenhall,
Wolverhampton, West Midlands
WV6 8RX
Tel: (01902) 751125
Fax: (01902) 741940
Head: Mr P Cochrane
Type: Co-educational Day 2–7
No of pupils: 142
Fees: On application

NEWBRIDGE PREPARATORY SCHOOL
51 Newbridge Crescent,
Tettenhall, Wolverhampton,
West Midlands WV6 0LH
Tel: (01902) 751088
Fax: (01902) 751333
Email: office@newbridge.
    wolverhampton.sch.uk
Head: Mrs B Pring
Type: Girls Day 3–11
No of pupils: 148
Fees: On application

THE ROYAL WOLVERHAMPTON JUNIOR SCHOOL
Penn Road, Wolverhampton,
West Midlands WV3 0EF
Tel: (01902) 349100
Fax: (01902) 344496
Head: Mrs M Saunders
Type: Co-educational Day and
Boarding 2–11
No of pupils: B86 G78
No of boarders: F1
Fees: (September 06) FB £18450
Day £5430–£8010

THE ROYAL WOLVERHAMPTON SCHOOL
Penn Road, Wolverhampton,
West Midlands WV3 0EG
Tel: (01902) 341230
Fax: (01902) 349119
Email: mo@
    royal.wolverhampton.sch.uk
Head: Mr T L Waters
Type: Co-educational Boarding
and Day 2–18
No of pupils: B262 G211
No of boarders: F134 W10
Fees: (September 05)
FB £17220–£19800
WB £17040–£17220
Day £5115–£9945

England – West Midlands

TETTENHALL COLLEGE[†]
Wood Road, Tettenhall,
Wolverhampton, West Midlands
WV6 8QX
Tel: (01902) 751119
Fax: (01902) 741940
Email: head@
    tettcoll.wolverhants.sch.uk
Head: Dr P C Bodkin
Type: Co-educational Boarding
and Day 2–18
No of pupils: B289 G198
No of boarders: F66 W11
Fees: (September 06)
FB £14550–£17724
WB £11808–£14748
Day £8232–£10101

**WOLVERHAMPTON
GRAMMAR SCHOOL**
Compton Road, Wolverhampton,
West Midlands WV3 9RB
Tel: (01902) 421326
Fax: (01902) 421819
Email: wgs@wgs.org.uk
Head: Dr B Trafford
Type: Co-educational Day 10–18
No of pupils: B401 G274
Fees: (September 06) Day £9144

WILTSHIRE

CALNE

**ST MARGARET'S
PREPARATORY SCHOOL**
Curzon Street, Calne, Wiltshire
SN11 0DF
Tel: (01249) 857220
Fax: (01249) 857227
Email: office@
    stmargaretsprep.org.uk
Head: Mrs K E Cordon
Type: Co-educational Day 3–11
No of pupils: B64 G118
Fees: (September 06)
Day £3600–£7350

ST MARY'S SCHOOL*
Calne, Wiltshire SN11 0DF
Tel: (01249) 857200
Fax: (01249) 857207
Email: admissions@
    stmaryscalne.org
Head: Dr H M Wright
Type: Girls Boarding and Day
11–18
No of pupils: 300
No of boarders: F250
Fees: (September 06) FB £22740
Day £15540

CHIPPENHAM

**GRITTLETON HOUSE
SCHOOL***
Grittleton, Chippenham, Wiltshire
SN14 6AP
Tel: (01249) 782434
Fax: (01249) 782669
Email: secretary@
    grittletonhouseschool.org
Head: Mrs C Whitney
Type: Co-educational Day 2–16
No of pupils: B174 G126
Fees: (September 06)
Day £5010–£7905

CORSHAM

**HEYWOOD PREPARATORY
SCHOOL**
The Priory, Priory Street, Corsham,
Wiltshire SN13 0AP
Tel: (01249) 713379
Fax: (01249) 701757
Email: principals@
    heywoodprep.com
Head: Mrs P Hall and Mr M Hall
Type: Co-educational Day 2–11
No of pupils: B94 G64
Fees: (September 06)
Day £4635–£5295

CRICKLADE

**MEADOWPARK NURSERY &
PRE-PREP SCHOOL**
Calcutt Street, Cricklade, Wiltshire
SN6 6BA
Tel: (01793) 752600
Fax: (01793) 752600
Email: mpschoffice@aol.com
Head: Mrs R Kular
Type: Co-educational Day 0–7
No of pupils: B122 G105
Fees: On application

**PRIOR PARK PREPARATORY
SCHOOL**[†]
Calcutt Street, Cricklade, Wiltshire
SN6 6BB
Tel: (01793) 750275
Fax: (01793) 750910
Email: officepriorparkprep@
    priorpark.co.uk
Head: Mr G B Hobern
Type: Co-educational Boarding
and Day 7–13
No of pupils: B111 G69
No of boarders: F23 W22
Fees: (September 06)
F/WB £12495–£13845
Day £8601–£9933

DEVIZES

DAUNTSEY'S SCHOOL*
High Street, West Lavington,
Devizes, Wiltshire SN10 4HE
Tel: (01380) 814500
Fax: (01380) 814501
Email: information@
    dauntseys.wilts.sch.uk
Head: Mr S B Roberts
Type: Co-educational Boarding
and Day 11–18
No of pupils: B391 G365
No of boarders: F282
Fees: (September 06) FB £21360
Day £12660

THE MILL SCHOOL
Whistley Road, Potterne, Devizes,
Wiltshire SN10 5TE
Tel: (01380) 723011
Fax: (01380) 736530
Email: office@mill.wilts.sch.uk
Head: Mrs L Gill
Type: Co-educational Day 4–11
No of pupils: B38 G43
Fees: (September 06)
Day £4770–£5970

MARLBOROUGH

MARLBOROUGH COLLEGE
Marlborough, Wiltshire SN8 1PA
Tel: (01672) 892300
Fax: (01672) 892307
Email: admissions@
    marlboroughcollege.org
Head: Mr N A Sampson
Type: Co-educational Boarding
13–18
No of pupils: B554 G318
No of boarders: F872
Fees: (September 05) FB £23160
Day £17370

ST ANDREW SCHOOL
Ogbourne St Andrew,
Marlborough, Wiltshire SN8 1SB
Tel: (01672) 841291
Head: Miss S Platt
Type: Co-educational Day 3–11
No of pupils: B18 G23
Fees: On application

STEPPING STONES NURSERY AND PRE-PREPARATORY SCHOOL
Oakhill Farm, Froxfield,
Marlborough, Wiltshire SN8 3JT
Tel: (01488) 681067
Fax: (01488) 681067
Head: Miss S Corfield and
Miss A Harron
Type: Co-educational Day 2–8
No of pupils: B89 G80
Fees: On application

MELKSHAM

STONAR SCHOOL*
Cottles Park, Atworth, Melksham,
Wiltshire SN12 8NT
Tel: (01225) 701740
Fax: (01225) 790830
Email: admissions@
    stonarschool.com
Head: Mrs S Shayler
Type: Girls Boarding and Day
2–18
No of pupils: B17 G400
No of boarders: F190 W80
Fees: (September 06)
F/WB £15390–£17985
Day £5190–£10125

PEWSEY

ST FRANCIS SCHOOL
Marlborough Road, Pewsey,
Wiltshire SN9 5NT
Tel: (01672) 563228
Fax: (01672) 564323
Email: admissions@
    st-francis.wilts.sch.uk
Head: Mr P W Blundell
Type: Co-educational Day 2–13
No of pupils: B156 G140
Fees: (September 05)
Day £540–£8025

SALISBURY

APPLEFORD SCHOOL†
Elston Lane, Shrewton, Salisbury,
Wiltshire SP3 4HL
Tel: (01980) 621020
Fax: (01980) 621366
Email: secretary@
    appleford.wilts.sch.uk
Head: Ms S M Wilson
Type: Co-educational Boarding
and Day 7–13
No of pupils: B69 G14
No of boarders: F10 W42
Fees: On application

AVONDALE SCHOOL
High Street, Bulford, Salisbury,
Wiltshire SP4 9DR
Tel: (01980) 632387
Email: avondale.school@
    tiscali.co.uk
Head: Mr R McNeall and
Mrs S McNeall
Type: Co-educational Day 3–11
No of pupils: B50 G50
Fees: (September 06)
Day £2790–£4710

CHAFYN GROVE SCHOOL
Bourne Avenue, Salisbury,
Wiltshire SP1 1LR
Tel: (01722) 333423
Fax: (01722) 323114
Email: info@chafyngrove.co.uk
Head: Mr E J Newton
Type: Co-educational Boarding
and Day 3–13
No of pupils: B220 G80
No of boarders: F46
Fees: (September 06)
FB £13170–£16170
Day £5925–£11985

GODOLPHIN PREPARATORY SCHOOL
Laverstock Road, Salisbury,
Wiltshire SP1 2RB
Tel: (01722) 430652
Fax: (01722) 430651
Email: prep@
    godolphin.wilts.sch.uk
Head: Mrs P White
Type: Girls Day 3–11
Fees: (September 06)
Day £1514–£2975

THE GODOLPHIN SCHOOL
Milford Hill, Salisbury, Wiltshire
SP1 2RA
Tel: (01722) 430511
Fax: (01722) 430501
Email: admissions@
    godolphin.wilts.sch.uk
Head: Miss M J Horsburgh
Type: Girls Boarding and Day
11–18
No of pupils: 440
No of boarders: F186
Fees: (September 06) FB £6832
Day £4528

LA RETRAITE SWAN
Campbell Road, Salisbury,
Wiltshire SP1 3BQ
Tel: (01722) 333094
Fax: (01722) 330868
Email: admissions@
    laraswan.co.uk
Head: Mrs R A Simmons
Type: Co-educational Day 2–16
No of pupils: B178 G165
Fees: (September 05)
Day £5145–£8745

LEADEN HALL SCHOOL
70 The Close, Salisbury, Wiltshire
SP1 2EP
Tel: (01722) 439269
Fax: (01722) 410575
Email: admin@leaden-hall.com
Head: Mrs D Watkins
Type: Girls Day and Boarding
3–11 (Boys 3–4)
No of pupils: B2 G237
No of boarders: F29
Fees: (September 05) FB £12522
Day £3435–£8850

**NORMAN COURT
PREPARATORY SCHOOL**
West Tytherley, Salisbury,
Wiltshire SP5 1NH
Tel: (01980) 862345
Fax: (01980) 862082
Email: office@normancourt.co.uk
Head: Mr K N Foyle
Type: Co-educational Boarding
and Day 3–13
No of pupils: B162 G78
No of boarders: F25 W40
Fees: (September 06) F/WB £16365
Day £5985–£12135

**SALISBURY CATHEDRAL
SCHOOL**
1 The Close, Salisbury, Wiltshire
SP1 2EQ
Tel: (01722) 555300
Fax: (01722) 410910
Email: admissions@
    salisburycathedralschool.com
Head: Mr R M Thackray
Type: Co-educational Day and
Boarding 3–13
No of pupils: B126 G86
No of boarders: F43
Fees: (September 05) FB £15180
Day £3420–£10380

SANDROYD SCHOOL
Rushmore, Tollard Royal,
Salisbury, Wiltshire SP5 5QD
Tel: (01725) 516264
Fax: (01725) 516441
Email: enquiries@sandroyd.com
Head: Mr Martin Harris
Type: Co-educational Boarding
and Day 7–13
No of pupils: B166 G12
No of boarders: F84
Fees: (September 06)
FB £13860–£17175
Day £10560–£14325

SOUTH HILLS SCHOOL
Home Farm Road, Wilton,
Salisbury, Wiltshire SP2 8PJ
Tel: (01722) 744971
Fax: (01722) 744971
Email: southhillsschool@
    btinternet.com
Head: Mrs A Proctor
Type: Co-educational Day 0–7
No of pupils: B80 G80
Fees: On application

SHRIVENHAM

PINEWOOD SCHOOL*
Bourton, Shrivenham, Wiltshire
SN6 8HZ
Tel: (01793) 782205
Fax: (01793) 783476
Email: office@
    pinewoodschool.co.uk
Head: Mr P J Hoyland
Type: Co-educational Boarding
and Day 3–13
No of pupils: B147 G149
No of boarders: W30
Fees: (September 06) FB £4770
WB £4155–£4600
Day £890–£3690

SWINDON

**MARANATHA CHRISTIAN
SCHOOL**
Queenlaines Farm,
Sevenhampton, Swindon,
Wiltshire SN6 7SQ
Tel: (01793) 762075
Fax: (01793) 783783
Head: Mr P Medlock
Type: Co-educational Day 3–18
No of pupils: B20 G20
Fees: On application

TROWBRIDGE

EMMAUS SCHOOL
School Lane, Staverton,
Trowbridge, Wiltshire BA14 6NZ
Tel: (01225) 782684
Email: info@
    emmaus-school.org.uk
Head: Mrs M Wiltshire
Type: Co-educational Day 5–16
No of pupils: B22 G23
Fees: (September 06) Day £2625

**ROUNDSTONE
PREPARATORY SCHOOL**
Courtfield House, Polebarn Road,
Trowbridge, Wiltshire BA14 7EG
Tel: (01225) 752847
Head: Mrs M E Pearce
Type: Co-educational Day 4–11
No of pupils: B54 G50
Fees: On application

WARMINSTER

**STOURBRIDGE HOUSE
SCHOOL**
Castle Street, Mere, Warminster,
Wiltshire BA12 6JQ
Tel: (01747) 860165
Fax: (01747) 861945
Email: office@
    stourbridgehouse.wilts.sch.uk
Head: Mrs E Coward
Type: Co-educational Day 3–9
No of pupils: B25 G19
Fees: (September 06)
Day £4410–£4635

WARMINSTER SCHOOL[†]
Church Street, Warminster,
Wiltshire BA12 8PJ
Tel: (01985) 210160
Fax: (01985) 210154
Email: admin@
    warminsterschool.org.uk
Head: Mr M Priestley
Type: Co-educational Boarding
and Day 3–19
No of pupils: B400 G250
No of boarders: F200
Fees: (September 06)
F/WB £13980–£17760
Day £5250–£10230

WORCESTERSHIRE

BEWDLEY

MOFFATS SCHOOL*
Kinlet Hall, Bewdley,
Worcestershire DY12
Tel: (01299) 841230
Fax: (01299) 841444
Email: office@moffats.co.uk
Head: Mr M H Daborn
Type: Co-educational Boarding
and Day 4–13
No of pupils: B46 G25
No of boarders: F25 W2
Fees: (September 06) F/WB £11835
Day £1025–£2475

MOFFATS SCHOOL
Kinlet Hall, Kinlet, Bewdley,
Worcestershire DY12 3AY
Tel: (01299) 841230
Fax: (01299) 841444
Email: office@moffats.co.uk
Head: Mr M H Daborn
Type: Co-educational Boarding
and Day 4–13
No of pupils: B46 G25
No of boarders: F25 W2
Fees: (September 06) F/WB £11835
Day £1025–£2475

BROMSGROVE

BROMSGROVE
PRE-PREPARATORY AND
NURSERY SCHOOL
Avoncroft House, Hanbury Road,
Bromsgrove, Worcestershire
B60 4JS
Tel: (01527) 873007
Fax: (01527) 873007
Email: preprep@
  bromsgrove-school.co.uk
Head: Mrs S Pickering
Type: Co-educational Day 2–7
No of pupils: B100 G79
Fees: On application

BROMSGROVE
PREPARATORY SCHOOL
Old Station Road, Bromsgrove,
Worcestershire B60 2BU
Tel: (01527) 579600
Fax: (01527) 579571
Email: admissions@
  bromsgrove-school.co.uk
Head: Mr Peter Lee-Smith
Type: Co-educational Boarding
and Day 7–13
No of pupils: B227 G178
No of boarders: F50
Fees: (September 06)
FB £1440–£17850
WB £9900–£12780
Day £7500–£9780

BROMSGROVE SCHOOL*
Worcester Road, Bromsgrove,
Worcestershire B61 7DU
Tel: (01527) 579679
Fax: (01527) 576177
Email: admissions@
  bromsgrove-school.co.uk
Head: Mr C Edwards
Type: Co-educational Boarding
and Day 13–18
No of pupils: B451 G290
No of boarders: F367
Fees: (September 05) FB £18990
Day £10560

DROITWICH SPA

DODDERHILL SCHOOL
Droitwich Spa, Worcestershire
WR9 0BE
Tel: (01905) 778290
Fax: (01905) 790623
Email: enquiries@dodderhill.co.uk
Head: Mrs J Mumby
Type: Girls Day 3–16 (Boys 3–9)
No of pupils: B20 G220
Fees: (September 06)
Day £4650–£8040

EVESHAM

GREEN HILL SCHOOL
Evesham, Worcestershire
WR11 4NG
Tel: (01386) 442364
Fax: (01386) 442364
Email: oliverlister@
  greenhillschool.co.uk
Head: Mr O Lister
Type: Co-educational Day 3–13
No of pupils: B55 G50
Fees: (September 06)
Day £4410–£5865

GREAT MALVERN

MALVERN ST JAMES*†
15 Avenue Road, Great Malvern,
Worcestershire WR14 3BA
Tel: (01684) 892288
Fax: (01684) 566204
Email: registrar@
  malvernstjames.co.uk
Head: Mrs R Hayes
Type: Girls Boarding and Day
7–18
No of pupils: 381
No of boarders: F210 W14
Fees: (September 06)
FB £7750–£8560 WB £6975
Day £2100–£3995

KIDDERMINSTER

HARTLEBURY SCHOOL
Hartlebury, Kidderminster,
Worcestershire DY11 7TE
Tel: (01299) 250258
Fax: (01299) 250379
Email: enquiries@
  hartleburyschool.com
Head: Miss C Coles
Type: Co-educational Day 4–16
No of pupils: B72 G38
Fees: On application

HEATHFIELD SCHOOL
Wolverley, Kidderminster,
Worcestershire DY10 3QE
Tel: (01562) 850204
Fax: (01562) 852609
Email: info@
    heathfieldschool.co.uk
Head: Mr Roger Brierly
Type: Co-educational Day 3–16
No of pupils: B126 G116
Fees: (September 06)
Day £1425–£8055

HOLY TRINITY SCHOOL
Birmingham Road, Kidderminster,
Worcestershire DY10 2BY
Tel: (01562) 822929
Fax: (01562) 865137
Email: office@holytrinity.co.uk
Head: Mrs Y L Wilkinson
Type: Co-educational Day
Boys 0–11 Girls 0–18
No of pupils: B44 G316
Fees: (September 05)
Day £3975–£7785

THE KNOLL SCHOOL
33 Manor Avenue, Kidderminster,
Worcestershire DY11 6EA
Tel: (01562) 822622
Fax: (01562) 865686
Email: info@knollschool.co.uk
Head: Mr N J Humphreys
Type: Co-educational Day 2–11
No of pupils: B77 G42
Fees: On application

WINTERFOLD HOUSE
Chaddesley Corbett,
Kidderminster, Worcestershire
DY10 4PW
Tel: (01562) 777234
Fax: (01562) 777078
Email: head@
    winterfoldhouse.co.uk
Head: Mr W C R Ibbetson-Price
Type: Co-educational Day 3–13
No of pupils: B220 G116
Fees: (September 06)
Day £4575–£9240

MALVERN

THE DOWNS SCHOOL
Brockhill Road, Colwall, Malvern,
Worcestershire WR13 6EY
Tel: (01684) 540277
Fax: (01684) 540094
Email: downshm@aol.com
Head: Mr A P Ramsay
Type: Co-educational Boarding
and Day 0–13
No of pupils: B70 G70
No of boarders: F20 W30
Fees: (September 06) FB £5100
Day £1625

THE ELMS
Colwall, Malvern, Worcestershire
WR13 6EF
Tel: (01684) 540344
Fax: (01684) 571174
Email: office@elmsschool.co.uk
Head: Mr L A C Ashby
Type: Co-educational Boarding
and Day 3–13
No of pupils: B111 G81
No of boarders: F86
Fees: (September 06) FB £16950
Day £5985–£15600

MADRESFIELD EARLY YEARS CENTRE
Hayswood Farm, Madresfield,
Malvern, Worcestershire
WR13 5AA
Tel: (01684) 574378
Fax: (01684) 567772
Email: meyc1to8yrs@aol.com
Head: Mrs B J Bennett
Type: Co-educational Day 1–8
No of pupils: B117 G102
Fees: (September 05)
Day £4370–£4864

MALVERN COLLEGE*
College Road, Malvern,
Worcestershire WR14 3DF
Tel: (01684) 581500
Fax: (01684) 581617
Email: srj@malcol.org
Head: Mr D Dowdles
Type: Co-educational Boarding
and Day 13–18
No of pupils: B356 G213
No of boarders: F450
Fees: (September 05)
FB £22056–£23532
Day £14619–£15072

MALVERN COLLEGE PREPARATORY AND PRE-PREP SCHOOL
Abbey Road, Malvern,
Worcestershire WR14 3HF
Tel: (01684) 581600
Fax: (01684) 581601
Email: prep@malcol.org.uk
Head: Mr P H Moody
Type: Co-educational Boarding
and Day 2–13
No of pupils: B97 G91
No of boarders: F50
Fees: (September 05)
FB £9111–£14565
Day £4374–£11004

MALVERN WELLS

THE ABBEY COLLEGE
253 Wells Road, Malvern Wells,
Worcestershire WR14 4JF
Tel: (01684) 892300
Fax: (01684) 892757
Email: enquiries@
    abbeycollege.co.uk
Head: Mr P Moere
Type: Co-educational Boarding
and Day 13+
No of pupils: B70 G50
No of boarders: F116 W4
Fees: (September 05) FB £15950
WB £11771 Day £7975

PERSHORE

BOWBROOK HOUSE SCHOOL
Peopleton, Pershore,
Worcestershire WR10 2EE
Tel: (01905) 841242
Fax: (01905) 840716
Email: enquiries@
    bowbrookhouseschool.co.uk
Head: Mr C D Allen
Type: Co-educational Day 3–16
No of pupils: B119 G63
Fees: (September 06)
Day £3690–£6840

TENBURY WELLS

SAINT MICHAEL'S COLLEGE
Oldwood Road, St Michaels,
Tenbury Wells, Worcestershire
WR15 8PH
Tel: (01584) 811300
Fax: (01584) 811221
Email: info@st-michaels.uk.com
Head: Mr S Higgins
Type: Co-educational Day and
Boarding 14–19
No of pupils: B85 G75
No of boarders: F95
Fees: (September 05)
FB £14500–£15700

WORCESTER

ABBERLEY HALL
Abberley Hall, Worcester,
Worcestershire WR6 6DD
Tel: (01299) 896275
Fax: (01299) 896875
Email: john.walker@
    abberleyhall.co.uk
Head: Mr J G W Walker
Type: Co-educational Boarding
and Day 2–13
No of pupils: B176 G90
No of boarders: F100
Fees: (September 06) FB £15600
Day £3105–£12495

THE ALICE OTTLEY SCHOOL
Britannia House, Upper Tything,
Worcester, Worcestershire
WR1 1HW
Tel: (01905) 27061
Fax: (01905) 724626
Email: enquiries@
    thealiceottleyschool.co.uk
Head: Mrs M E Chapman
Type: Girls Day 3–19
No of pupils: 543
Fees: (September 05)
Day £4398–£8685

KING'S HAWFORD
Lock Lane, Worcester,
Worcestershire WR3 7SE
Tel: (01905) 451292
Fax: (01905) 756502
Email: office@
    Kingshawford.org.uk
Head: Mr J Turner
Type: Co-educational Day 2–11
No of pupils: B168 G118
Fees: (September 06)
Day £1595–£2910

THE KING'S SCHOOL
5 College Green, Worcester,
Worcestershire WR1 2LL
Tel: (01905) 721700
Fax: (01905) 721710
Email: info@ksw.org.uk
Head: Mr T H Keyes
Type: Co-educational Day 3–18
No of pupils: B784 G588
Fees: (September 06)
Day £5145–£9429

RGS THE GRANGE
Grange Lane, Claines, Worcester,
Worcestershire WR3 7RR
Tel: (01905) 451205
Fax: (01905) 757917
Email: grange@rgsw.org.uk
Head: Mr R E Hunt
Type: Co-educational Day 2–11
No of pupils: B245 G130
Fees: (September 05)
Day £4230–£7992

RIVER SCHOOL
Oakfield House, Droitwich Road,
Worcester, Worcestershire
WR3 7ST
Tel: (01905) 457047
Fax: (01905) 754492
Head: Mr G Coyle
Type: Co-educational Day 5–16
No of pupils: B67 G82
Fees: On application

ROYAL GRAMMAR SCHOOL WORCESTER
Upper Tything, Worcester,
Worcestershire WR1 1HP
Tel: (01905) 613391
Fax: (01905) 726892
Email: office@rgsw.org.uk
Head: Mr A R Rattue
Type: Co-educational Day 11–18
No of pupils: B574 G139
Fees: (September 06) Day £8280

ST MARY'S CONVENT SCHOOL
Mount Battenhall, Worcester,
Worcestershire WR5 2HP
Tel: (01905) 357786
Fax: (01905) 351718
Email: head@stmarys.org.uk
Head: Mrs S K Cookson
Type: Girls Day 2–18 (Boys 2–8)
No of pupils: B5 G304
Fees: On application

England – Worcestershire

EAST RIDING OF YORKSHIRE

ANLABY

HULL COLLEGIATE SCHOOL
Tranby Croft, Anlaby,
East Riding of Yorkshire HU10 7EH
Tel: (01482) 657016
Fax: (01482) 655389
Email: enquiries.hull@
   church-schools.com
Head: Mr R Haworth
Type: Co-educational Day 3–18
No of pupils: B142 G339
Fees: On application

HESSLE

HESSLE MOUNT SCHOOL
Jenny Brough Lane, Hessle,
East Riding of Yorkshire HU13 0JX
Tel: (01482) 643371/641948
Fax: (01482) 643371
Email: info@
   hesslemountschool.org.uk
Head: Mrs Cutting
Type: Co-educational Day 3–8
No of pupils: 160
Fees: On application

HULL

FROEBEL HOUSE SCHOOL
5 Marlborough Avenue, Princes
Avenue, Hull,
East Riding of Yorkshire HU5 3JP
Tel: (01482) 342272
Fax: (01482) 342272
Email: froebel@
   froebel.karoo.co.uk
Head: Mrs L A Roberts
Type: Co-educational Day 4–11
No of pupils: B56 G51
Fees: On application

HYMERS COLLEGE
Hymers Avenue, Hull,
East Riding of Yorkshire HU3 1LW
Tel: (01482) 343555
Fax: (01482) 472854
Email: enquiries@
   hymers.hull.sch.uk
Head: Mr D C Elstone
Type: Co-educational Day 8–18
No of pupils: B549 G429
Fees: (September 06)
Day £5895–£7065

POCKLINGTON

POCKLINGTON
MONTESSORI SCHOOL
Bielby Lane, Pocklington,
East Riding of Yorkshire YO42 1NT
Tel: (01759) 305436
Fax: (01759) 321421
Email: info@
   montessoriandmore.co.uk
Head: Ms R Pressland
Type: Co-educational Day 0–7
No of pupils: B162 G138
Fees: On application

POCKLINGTON SCHOOL
West Green, Pocklington,
East Riding of Yorkshire YO42 2NJ
Tel: (01759) 321200
Fax: (01759) 306366
Email: enquiry@
   pocklingtonschool.com
Head: Mr N Clements
Type: Co-educational Boarding
and Day 7–18
No of pupils: B455 G356
No of boarders: F122 W20
Fees: (September 05)
FB £13995–£16332
WB £13125–£15459
Day £6192–£9213

NORTH YORKSHIRE

BEDALE

AYSGARTH PREPARATORY
SCHOOL
Bedale, North Yorkshire DL8 1TF
Tel: (01677) 450240
Fax: (01677) 450736
Email: enquiry@
   aysgarthschool.co.uk
Head: Mr C A A Goddard
Type: Boys Boarding 3–13 (Co-ed
day 3–8)
No of pupils: B148 G19
No of boarders: F67 W20
Fees: On application

HARROGATE

ASHVILLE COLLEGE
Green Lane, Harrogate,
North Yorkshire HG2 9JP
Tel: (01423) 566358
Fax: (01423) 505142
Email: ashville@ashville.co.uk
Head: Mr A Fleck
Type: Co-educational Day and
Boarding 4–18
No of pupils: B493 G316
No of boarders: F101 W19
Fees: (September 06)
FB £16080–£18300
WB £15270–£16680
Day £5430–£9330

BELMONT GROSVENOR
SCHOOL
Swarcliffe Hall, Birstwith,
Harrogate, North Yorkshire
HG3 2JG
Tel: (01423) 771029
Fax: (01423) 772600
Email: admin@
   belmontgrosvenor.co.uk
Head: Miss J Merriman
Type: Co-educational Day 2–11
No of pupils: B122 G111
Fees: (September 06)
Day £1743–£6012

BRACKENFIELD SCHOOL
128 Duchy Road, Harrogate,
North Yorkshire HG1 2HE
Tel: (01423) 508558
Fax: (01423) 524841
Email: admin@
brackenfield.n-yorks.sch.uk
Head: Mrs J Skillington
Type: Co-educational Day 2–11
No of pupils: B81 G80
Fees: (September 05)
Day £2175–£5625

HARROGATE LADIES' COLLEGE
Clarence Drive, Harrogate,
North Yorkshire HG1 2QG
Tel: (01423) 504543
Fax: (01423) 568893
Email: enquire@hlc.org.uk
Head: Dr M J Hustler
Type: Girls Boarding and Day
10–18
No of pupils: 320
No of boarders: F157 W11
Fees: (September 06) FB £18765
WB £19765 Day £11130

HARROGATE TUTORIAL COLLEGE
2 The Oval, Harrogate,
North Yorkshire HG2 9BA
Tel: (01423) 501041
Fax: (01423) 531110
Email: study@htcuk.org
Head: Mr K W Pollard
Type: Co-educational Day and
Boarding 15–20
No of pupils: B36 G34
No of boarders: F20 W20
Fees: (September 05)
FB £12950–£14450
WB £11750–£13250
Day £3500–£11850

HIGHFIELD PREPARATORY SCHOOL
Clarence Drive, Harrogate,
North Yorkshire HG1 2QG
Tel: (01423) 504543
Fax: (01423) 568893
Email: enquire@hlc.org.uk
Head: Mrs C Cameron
Type: Co-educational Day and
Boarding 4–11
No of pupils: B68 G146
Fees: (September 06)
Day £6090–£6600

MALTON

WOODLEIGH SCHOOL[†]
Langton, Malton, North Yorkshire
YO17 9QN
Tel: (01653) 658215
Fax: (01653) 658423
Head: Mr D M England
Type: Co-educational Boarding
and Day 3–13
No of pupils: B69 G49
No of boarders: F10 W25
Fees: On application

RIPON

RIPON CATHEDRAL CHOIR SCHOOL
Whitcliffe Lane, Ripon,
North Yorkshire HG4 2LA
Tel: (01765) 602134
Fax: (01765) 608760
Email: admin@
choirschool.demon.co.uk
Head: Mr C R E Pepys
Type: Co-educational Boarding
and Day 3–13
No of pupils: B62 G46
No of boarders: F19 W4
Fees: (September 06) FB £13050
Day £2355–£9735

SCARBOROUGH

BRAMCOTE SCHOOL
Filey Road, Scarborough,
North Yorkshire YO11 2TT
Tel: (01723) 373086
Fax: (01723) 364186
Email: office@
bramcoteschool.com
Head: Mr A G W Lewin
Type: Co-educational Boarding
and Day 7–13
No of pupils: B53 G50
No of boarders: F54 W33
Fees: (September 05) FB £14310
Day £9375–£10275

LISVANE, SCARBOROUGH COLLEGE JUNIOR SCHOOL
Filey Road, Scarborough,
North Yorkshire YO11 3BA
Tel: (01723) 380606
Fax: (01723) 380607
Email: lisvane@
scarboroughcoll.co.uk
Head: Mr G S Twist
Type: Co-educational Day and
Boarding 3–11
No of pupils: B69 G69
No of boarders: W2
Fees: (September 05) F/WB £12411
Day £5400–£6939

SCARBOROUGH COLLEGE & LISVANE SCHOOL
Filey Road, Scarborough,
North Yorkshire YO11 3BA
Tel: (01723) 360620
Fax: (01723) 377265
Email: admin@
scarboroughcollege.co.uk
Head: Mr T L Kirkup
Type: Co-educational Boarding
and Day 3–18
No of pupils: B289 G228
No of boarders: F41 W20
Fees: (September 05) F/WB £12411
Day £5400–£8136

SELBY

READ SCHOOL
Drax, Selby, North Yorkshire
YO8 8NL
Tel: (01757) 618248
Fax: (01757) 617432
Email: richard.hadfield@virgin.net
Head: Mr R A Hadfield
Type: Co-educational Day and
Boarding 4–18
No of pupils: B198 G135
No of boarders: F70 W2
Fees: (September 05)
FB £12600–£14490
WB £11814–£13590
Day £4710–£6696

England – North Yorkshire

SETTLE

CATTERAL HALL SCHOOL
Giggleswick, Settle,
North Yorkshire BD24 0DG
Tel: (01729) 893100
Fax: (01729) 893158
Email: catteralhall@
  giggleswick.org.uk
Head: Mr G P Boult
Type: Co-educational Boarding
and Day 7–13
No of pupils: B69 G43
No of boarders: F54
Fees: (September 06)
FB £12900–£15450
Day £12090–£14850

GIGGLESWICK SCHOOL
Giggleswick, Settle,
North Yorkshire BD24 0DE
Tel: (01729) 893000
Fax: (01729) 893150
Email: enquiries@
  giggleswick.org.uk
Head: Mr G P Boult
Type: Co-educational Boarding
and Day 13–18
No of pupils: B199 G119
No of boarders: F203
Fees: (September 06) FB £21900
Day £14850

SKIPTON

MALSIS SCHOOL
Cross Hills, Skipton,
North Yorkshire BD20 8DT
Tel: (01535) 633027
Fax: (01535) 630571
Email: admin@malsis.com
Head: Mr C J Lush
Type: Co-educational Boarding
and Day 3–13
No of pupils: B112 G48
No of boarders: F39
Fees: (September 06) FB £14940
Day £6120–£11460

THIRSK

QUEEN MARY'S SCHOOL
Baldersby Park, Topcliffe, Thirsk,
North Yorkshire YO7 3BZ
Tel: (01845) 575000
Fax: (01845) 575001
Email: admin@queenmarys.org
Head: Mr R A McKenzie Johnson
Type: Girls Boarding and Day
3–16 (Boys 3–7)
No of pupils: B11 G205
No of boarders: F14 W36
Fees: (September 06)
F/WB £13140–£15495
Day £5235–£11895

WHITBY

BOTTON VILLAGE SCHOOL
Danby, Whitby, North Yorkshire
YO21 2NJ
Tel: (01287) 661206
Type: Co-educational Day 4–14
No of pupils: B53 G41
Fees: On application

FYLING HALL SCHOOL
Robin Hood's Bay, Whitby,
North Yorkshire YO22 4QD
Tel: (01947) 880353
Fax: (01947) 881097
Email: office@fylinghall.org
Head: Dr G K Horridge
Type: Co-educational Boarding
and Day 4–19
No of pupils: B98 G88
No of boarders: F101 W9
Fees: (September 05)
FB £10335–£13650
WB £9900–£10980
Day £4185–£5685

YORK

AMPLEFORTH COLLEGE
York, North Yorkshire YO62 4EY
Tel: (01439) 766000
Fax: (01439) 788330
Email: admissions@
  ampleforth.org.uk
Head: Rev C G E Everitt
Type: Co-educational Boarding
and Day 13–18
No of pupils: B474 G87
No of boarders: F502
Fees: (September 05) FB £21450

BOOTHAM SCHOOL
Bootham, York, North Yorkshire
YO30 7BU
Tel: (01904) 623261
Fax: (01904) 652106
Email: enquiries@
  bootham.york.sch.uk
Head: Mr J Taylor
Type: Co-educational Boarding
and Day 11–18
No of pupils: B280 G172
No of boarders: F80 W40
Fees: (September 06)
FB £12300–£19500
WB £12300–£17955
Day £11280–£12150

CUNDALL MANOR SCHOOL
Helperby, York, North Yorkshire
YO6 2RW
Tel: (01423) 360200
Fax: (01423) 360754
Email: headmaster@
  cundallmanor.co.uk
Head: Mr P Phillips
Type: Co-educational Boarding
and Day 2–13
No of boarders: F30 W35
Fees: (September 05) FB £10500
Day £3489–£8997

EBOR PREPARATORY
SCHOOL
Rawcliffe Lane, York,
North Yorkshire YO30 6NP
Tel: (01904) 655021
Fax: (01904) 651666
Email: office@
  eborschool.york.sch.uk
Head: Ms S Ratcliffe
Type: Co-educational Day 3–11
No of pupils: B70 G60
Fees: On application

HOWSHAM HALL
York, North Yorkshire YO60 7PJ
Tel: (01653) 618374
Fax: (01653) 618295
Email: howsham@
  simonknock.freeserve.co.uk
Head: Mr S J Knock
Type: Co-educational Boarding
and Day 5–14
No of pupils: B60 G15
No of boarders: F40
Fees: On application

THE MINSTER SCHOOL
Deangate, York, North Yorkshire
YO1 7JA
Tel: (01904) 557230
Fax: (01904) 557232
Email: school@yorkminster.org
Head: Mr R Moore
Type: Co-educational Day 3–13
No of pupils: B100 G80
Fees: On application

THE MOUNT SCHOOL
Dalton Terrace, York,
North Yorkshire YO24 4DD
Tel: (01904) 667500
Fax: (01904) 667524
Email: enquiries@
   mount.n-yorks.sch.uk
Head: Mrs D J Gant
Type: Girls Boarding and Day
3–18
No of pupils: 456
No of boarders: F57 W14
Fees: (September 06) FB £18615
WB £17565 Day £11985

QUEEN ETHELBURGA'S COLLEGE*
Thorpe Underwood Hall,
Ouseburn, York, North Yorkshire
YO26 9SS
Tel: (0870) 742 3300
Fax: (0870) 742 3310
Email: remember@
   compuserve.com
Head: Mr S Jandrell
Type: Co-educational Boarding
and Day 2–20
No of pupils: B224 G324
No of boarders: F358 W30
Fees: (September 06)
F/WB £16605–£26895
Day £3135–£8235

QUEEN MARGARET'S SCHOOL
Escrick Park, York, North Yorkshire
YO19 6EU
Tel: (01904) 728261
Fax: (01904) 728150
Email: enquiries@
   queenmargaretsschool.co.uk
Head: Dr G A H Chapman
Type: Girls Boarding and Day
11–18
No of pupils: 365
No of boarders: F251 W85
Fees: (September 06) F/WB £19890
Day £12603

ST MARTIN'S AMPLEFORTH
Gilling Castle, Gilling East, York,
North Yorkshire YO62 4HP
Tel: (01439) 766600
Fax: (01439) 788538
Email: headmaster@
   stmartins.ampleforth.org.uk
Head: Mr N J Higham
Type: Co-educational Boarding
and Day 3–13
No of pupils: B135 G55
No of boarders: F80
Fees: (September 06) FB £15423
Day £8661

ST PETER'S SCHOOL
York, North Yorkshire YO30 6AB
Tel: (01904) 527 300
Fax: (01904) 527 302
Email: enquiries@
   st-peters.york.sch.uk
Head: Mr R I Smyth
Type: Co-educational Boarding
and Day 13–18
No of pupils: B320 G222
No of boarders: F169
Fees: (September 06)
FB £19536–£19662
Day £11376–£11667

TERRINGTON HALL
Terrington, York, North Yorkshire
YO60 6PR
Tel: (01653) 648227
Fax: (01653) 648458
Email: enquiries@
   terringtonhall.com
Head: Mr J Glen
Type: Co-educational Boarding
and Day 3–13
No of pupils: B120 G88
No of boarders: F35 W5
Fees: (September 05) F/WB £13050
Day £4500–£8800

TREGELLES
The Mount Junior School, Dalton
Terrace, York, North Yorkshire
YO24 4DD
Tel: (01904) 667513
Fax: (01904) 667524
Email: registrar@
   mount.n-yorks.sch.uk
Head: Mr M Andrews
Type: Co-educational Day 3–11
No of pupils: B59 G135
Fees: On application

England – North Yorkshire

SOUTH YORKSHIRE

BARNSLEY

BARNSLEY CHRISTIAN SCHOOL
Hope House, Blucher Street,
Barnsley, South Yorkshire S70 1AP
Tel: (01226) 211011
Fax: (01226) 211011
Email: admin@
barnsleyfellowship.fsnet.co.uk
Head: Mr G-J Barnes
Type: Co-educational Day 5–16
No of pupils: B49 G45
Fees: (September 05)
Day £2829–£3420

DONCASTER

HILL HOUSE ST MARY'S SCHOOL
65 Bawtry Road, Doncaster,
South Yorkshire DN4 7AD
Tel: (01302) 535926
Fax: (01302) 534675
Email: jharrington@
hillhousestmarys.co.uk
Head: Mr J Cusworth
Type: Co-educational Day 2–16
No of pupils: B224 G237
Fees: (September 05)
Day £5550–£7929

SYCAMORE HALL PREPARATORY SCHOOL
1 Hall Flat Lane, Balby, Doncaster,
South Yorkshire DN4 8PT
Tel: (01302) 856800
Email: sycamorehall@tiscali.co.uk
Head: Miss J Spencer
Type: Co-educational Day 3–11
No of pupils: B41 G43
Fees: On application

ROTHERHAM

RUDSTON PREPARATORY SCHOOL
59–63 Broom Road, Rotherham,
South Yorkshire S60 2SW
Tel: (01709) 837774
Fax: (01709) 837975
Email: office@rudstonschool.com
Type: Co-educational Day 2–11
No of pupils: B114 G101
Fees: (September 05) Day £4740

SHEFFIELD

ASHDELL PREPARATORY SCHOOL
266 Fulwood Road, Sheffield,
South Yorkshire S10 3BL
Tel: (0114) 266 3835
Fax: (0114) 267 1762
Email: headteacher@
ashdell-prep.sheffield.sch.uk
Head: Mrs S Williams
Type: Girls Day 4–11
No of pupils: 123
Fees: (September 05)
Day £5850–£6750

BIRKDALE SCHOOL
Oakholme Road, Sheffield,
South Yorkshire S10 3DH
Tel: (0114) 266 8409
Fax: (0114) 267 1947
Email: admissions@
birkdale.sheffield.sch.uk
Head: Mr R J Court
Type: Boys Day 4–18 (Co-ed VIth Form)
No of pupils: B730 G50
Fees: (September 05)
Day £5856–£8388

BRANTWOOD SCHOOL
1 Kenwood Bank, Sheffield,
South Yorkshire S7 1NU
Tel: (0114) 258 1747
Fax: (0114) 258 1847
Email: enquiries@
brantwoodschool.co.uk
Head: Mrs J Timmins
Type: Girls Day 3–16
No of pupils: 200
Fees: (September 06)
Day £5460–£7698

HANDSWORTH CHRISTIAN SCHOOL
231 Handsworth Road,
Handsworth, Sheffield,
South Yorkshire S13 9BJ
Tel: (0114) 243 0276
Head: Mrs P Arnott
Type: Co-educational Day 4–16
No of pupils: 144
Fees: On application

MYLNHURST RC SCHOOL & NURSERY
Button Hill, Sheffield,
South Yorkshire S11 9HJ
Tel: (0114) 236 1411
Fax: (0114) 236 1411
Email: cp_emmott@hotmail.com
Head: Mr C Emmott
Type: Co-educational Day 3–11
No of pupils: B95 G89
Fees: On application

SHEFFIELD HIGH SCHOOL GDST
10 Rutland Park, Broomhill,
Sheffield, South Yorkshire S10 2PE
Tel: (0114) 266 0324
Email: enquiries@she.gdst.net
Head: Mrs V A Dunsford
Type: Girls Day 4–18
No of pupils: 974
Fees: (September 05)
Day £5337–£7365

WESTBOURNE SCHOOL
50–54 Westbourne Road,
Sheffield, South Yorkshire
S10 2QQ
Tel: (0114) 266 0374
Fax: (0114) 267 0862
Email: jbatty@
westbourneschool.co.uk
Head: Mr J Hicks
Type: Co-educational Day 4–16
No of pupils: B224 G96
Fees: (September 06)
Day £5685–£8775

WEST YORKSHIRE

APPERLEY BRIDGE

WOODHOUSE GROVE SCHOOL
Apperley Bridge, West Yorkshire
BD10 0NR
Tel: (0113) 250 2477
Fax: (0113) 250 5290
Email: enquiries@
 woodhousegrove.co.uk
Head: Mr D C Humphreys
Type: Co-educational Boarding
and Day 11–18
No of pupils: B443 G267
No of boarders: F81 W18
Fees: (September 06)
FB £16500–£16710
WB £15150–£15360
Day £8760–£8970

BATLEY

BATLEY GRAMMAR SCHOOL
Carlinghow Hill, Batley,
West Yorkshire WF17 0AD
Tel: (01924) 474980
Fax: (01924) 471960
Email: hmsec@
 batleygrammar.co.uk
Head: Mr B Battye
Type: Co-educational Day 3–18
No of pupils: B206 G158
Fees: (September 06)
Day £5091–£7419

DALE HOUSE SCHOOL
Ruby Street, Carlinghow, Batley,
West Yorkshire WF17 8HL
Tel: (01924) 422215
Email: admin@
 dhschool.freeserve.co.uk
Head: Mrs S M G Fletcher
Type: Co-educational Day 2–11
No of pupils: B40 G43
Fees: (September 05)
Day £4050–£4350

BINGLEY

LADY LANE PARK SCHOOL
Lady Lane, Bingley, West Yorkshire
BD16 4AP
Tel: (01274) 551168
Fax: (01274) 569732
Email: secretary@
 ladylanepark.co.uk
Head: Mrs G Wilson
Type: Co-educational Day 2–11
No of pupils: B93 G88
Fees: (September 05)
Day £1541–£1636

BRADFORD

BRADFORD CHRISTIAN SCHOOL
Livingstone Road, Bolton Woods,
Bradford, West Yorkshire BD2 1BT
Tel: (01274) 595819
Fax: (01274) 620738
Email: bchristians@btconnect.com
Head: Mr P J Moon
Type: Co-educational Day 4–16
No of pupils: 197
Fees: On application

BRADFORD GIRLS' GRAMMAR SCHOOL
Squire Lane, Bradford,
West Yorkshire BD9 6RB
Tel: (01274) 545395
Fax: (01274) 482595
Email: headsec@bggs.com
Head: Mrs L J Warrington
Type: Girls Day 2–18
No of pupils: B4 G670
Fees: (September 05)
Day £5283–£8640

BRADFORD GRAMMAR SCHOOL
Keighley Road, Bradford,
West Yorkshire BD9 4JP
Tel: (01274) 553702
Fax: (01274) 548129
Email: hmsec@
 bradfordgrammar.com
Head: Mr S R Davidson
Type: Co-educational Day 6–18
No of pupils: B782 G311
Fees: (September 06)
Day £6785–£9089

BRONTE HOUSE SCHOOL
Apperley Bridge, Bradford,
West Yorkshire BD10 0PQ
Tel: (0113) 250 2811
Fax: (0113) 250 0666
Email: general.enquiries@
 brontehouse.org.uk
Head: Mr C B F Hall
Type: Co-educational Boarding
and Day 3–11
No of pupils: B170 G110
No of boarders: F5
Fees: On application

NETHERLEIGH AND ROSSEFIELD SCHOOL
Parsons Road, Heaton, Bradford,
West Yorkshire BD9 4AY
Tel: (01274) 543162
Fax: (01274) 493011
Head: Mrs M Midgley
Type: Co-educational Day 3–11
No of pupils: B110 G65
Fees: On application

OLIVE SECONDARY
8 Cunliffe Villas, Bradford,
West Yorkshire BD8 7AN
Tel: (07909) 541855
Fax: (01274) 549900
Email: info@olivesecondary.org.uk
Head: Mr Amjad Mohammed
Type: Boys Day 11–18
No of pupils: 40
Fees: (September 06) Day £4500

SHAW HOUSE SCHOOL
150–152 Wilmer Road, Heaton,
Bradford, West Yorkshire BD9 4AH
Tel: (01274) 496299
Fax: (01274) 496299
Email: shawcoll@aol.com
Head: Mr H R Williams
Type: Co-educational Day 11–18
No of pupils: B75 G45
Fees: On application

BRIGHOUSE

THE RASTRICK INDEPENDENT SCHOOL
Ogden Lane, Rastrick, Brighouse,
West Yorkshire HD6 3HF
Tel: (01484) 400344
Fax: (01484) 718318
Email: info@
rastrick-independent.co.uk
Head: Mrs S A Vaughey
Type: Co-educational Day 0–16
No of pupils: B93 G99
Fees: On application

HALIFAX

THE GLEDDINGS SCHOOL
Birdcage Lane, Halifax,
West Yorkshire HX3 0JB
Tel: (01422) 354605
Email: TheGleddings@aol.com
Head: Mrs Wilson
Type: Co-educational Day 3–11
No of pupils: B80 G80
Fees: On application

HIPPERHOLME GRAMMAR SCHOOL
Bramley Lane, Hipperholme,
Halifax, West Yorkshire HX3 8JE
Tel: (01422) 202256
Fax: (01422) 204592
Email: headmaster@
hipperholmegrammar.org.uk
Head: Dr J Scarth
Type: Co-educational Day 11–18
No of pupils: B160 G145
Fees: On application

LIGHTCLIFFE PREPARATORY
Wakefield Road, Halifax,
West Yorkshire HX3 8AQ
Tel: (01422) 201330
Fax: (01422) 204845
Email: thesecretary@
lightcliffepreparatoryschool.
co.uk
Head: Mrs J A Pickersgill
Type: Co-educational Day 2–11
No of pupils: B85 G85
Fees: (September 05)
Day £2850–£4800

HEBDEN BRIDGE

GLEN HOUSE MONTESSORI SCHOOL
Cragg Vale, Hebden Bridge,
West Yorkshire HX7 5SQ
Tel: (01422) 884682
Email: glenhouseschool@3-c.coop
Head: Ms M Scaife
Type: Co-educational Day 3–15
No of pupils: B11 G16
Fees: On application

HECKMONDWIKE

THE BRANCH CHRISTIAN SCHOOL
8–10 Thomas Street,
Heckmondwike, West Yorkshire
WF16 0NW
Tel: (01924) 235637
Fax: (01924) 411021
Head: Mr R Ward
Type: Co-educational Day 3–17
No of pupils: B8 G12
Fees: On application

HUDDERSFIELD

HUDDERSFIELD GRAMMAR SCHOOL
Royds Mount, Luck Lane, Marsh,
Huddersfield, West Yorkshire
HD1 4QX
Tel: (01484) 424549
Fax: (01484) 531835
Email: admin@huddersfield-
grammarschool.co.uk
Head: Mrs E J Jackson and
Mrs J L Straughan
Type: Co-educational Day 3–16
No of pupils: B194 G156
Fees: (September 05)
Day £4590–£5754

ISLAMIA GIRLS HIGH SCHOOL
Thornton Lodge Road, Thornton
Lodge, Huddersfield,
West Yorkshire HD1 3JQ
Tel: (01484) 432928
Head: Mr I Meer
Type: Girls Day 11–16
No of pupils: 77
Fees: On application

MOUNT SCHOOL
3 Binham Road, Edgerton,
Huddersfield, West Yorkshire
HD2 2AP
Tel: (01484) 426432
Fax: (01484) 426432
Email: info@themount.org.uk
Head: Mr N M Smith
Type: Co-educational Day 3–11
No of pupils: B75 G75
Fees: (September 06) Day £4740

MOUNTJOY HOUSE SCHOOL
63 New North Road,
Huddersfield, West Yorkshire
HD1 5ND
Tel: (01484) 429967
Fax: (01484) 362653
Email: mjhhuddersfield@aol.com
Head: Mrs C Rogers
Type: Co-educational Day 3–11
No of pupils: B43 G43
Fees: On application

ROSEMEADE SCHOOL
12 Bank End Lane, Almondbury,
Huddersfield, West Yorkshire
HD5 8ES
Tel: (01484) 421076
Fax: (01484) 652025
Email: rosemeadeschool@uk2.net
Head: Mrs H M Hebblethwaite
and Mrs C M Howson
Type: Co-educational Day 3–11
No of pupils: B40 G38
Fees: (September 05)
Day £4150–£4360

ILKLEY

GHYLL ROYD SCHOOL
Greystone Manor, Ilkley Road,
Burley in Wharfedale, Ilkley,
West Yorkshire LS29 7HW
Tel: (01943) 865575
Fax: (01943) 865574
Email: information@
ghyllroydschool.co.uk
Head: Mrs I Connor
Type: Boys Day 2–11
No of pupils: 90
Fees: On application

MOORFIELD SCHOOL
Wharfedale Lodge, Ben Rhydding
Road, Ilkley, West Yorkshire
LS29 8RL
Tel: (01943) 607285
Fax: (01943) 603186
Email: enquiries@
   moorfieldschool.co.uk
Head: Mrs J E Disley
Type: Girls Day 2–11
No of pupils: 130
Fees: (September 06) Day £924

WESTVILLE HOUSE PREPARATORY SCHOOL
Carter's Lane, Middleton, Ilkley,
West Yorkshire LS29 0DQ
Tel: (01943) 608053
Fax: (01943) 817410
Email: westville@epals.com
Head: Mr C A Holloway
Type: Co-educational Day 3–11
No of pupils: B90 G61
Fees: (September 05)
Day £3600–£6255

LEEDS

ALCUIN SCHOOL
64 Woodland Lane, Leeds,
West Yorkshire LS7 4PD
Tel: (0113) 269 1173
Email: alcuin@legend.co.uk
Head: Mr J Hipshon
Type: Co-educational Day 4–11
No of pupils: B20 G26
Fees: (September 05)
Day £3675–£4800

BROWNBERRIE SCHOOL
173–179 New Road Side,
Horsforth, Leeds, West Yorkshire
LS18 4DR
Tel: (0113) 305 3350
Head: Mr B Hargreaves
Type: Co-educational Day 11–17
No of pupils: B29 G15
Fees: On application

THE FROEBELIAN SCHOOL
Clarence Road, Horsforth, Leeds,
West Yorkshire LS18 4LB
Tel: (0113) 258 3047
Fax: (0113) 258 0173
Email: office@froebelian.co.uk
Head: Mr J Tranmer
Type: Co-educational Day 3–11
No of pupils: B93 G87
Fees: (September 06)
Day £3555–£5346

GATEWAYS SCHOOL
Harewood, Leeds, West Yorkshire
LS17 9LE
Tel: (0113) 288 6345
Fax: (0113) 288 6148
Email: gateways@
   gatewayschool.co.uk
Head: Mrs D Davidson
Type: Girls Day 3–18 (Boys 3–7)
No of pupils: B15 G490
Fees: (September 06)
Day £4653–£8442

LEEDS GIRLS' HIGH SCHOOL
Headingley Lane, Leeds,
West Yorkshire LS6 1BN
Tel: (0113) 274 4000
Fax: (0113) 275 2217
Email: enquiries@lghs.org
Head: Ms S Fishburn
Type: Girls Day 3–19
No of pupils: 990
Fees: On application

LEEDS GRAMMAR SCHOOL
Alwoodley Gates, Harrogate
Road, Leeds, West Yorkshire
LS17 8GS
Tel: (0113) 229 1552
Fax: (0113) 228 5111
Email: info@lgs.leeds.sch.uk
Head: Dr M Bailey
Type: Boys Day 4–18
No of pupils: 1380
Fees: On application

MOORLANDS SCHOOL
Foxhill Drive, Weetwood Lane,
Leeds, West Yorkshire LS16 5PF
Tel: (0113) 278 5286
Fax: (0113) 230 6548
Email: headmaster@
   moorlands-school.co.uk
Head: Mr J G Davies
Type: Co-educational Day 3–13
No of pupils: B150 G59
Fees: (September 06)
Day £3008–£7164

NEW HORIZON COMMUNITY SCHOOL
Newton Hill House, Newton Hill
Road, Leeds, West Yorkshire
LS7 4JE
Tel: (0113) 262 4001
Fax: (0113) 262 4912
Email: nhcsleeds@
   newtonhillhouse.
   wanadoo.co.uk
Head: Mrs Sakinah Dambatta
Type: Girls Day 11–16
No of pupils: 100
Fees: (September 06) Day £900

RICHMOND HOUSE SCHOOL
170 Otley Road, Leeds,
West Yorkshire LS16 5LG
Tel: (0113) 275 2670
Fax: (0113) 230 4868
Email: enquiries@rhschool.org
Head: Mr G Milne
Type: Co-educational Day 3–11
No of pupils: B163 G127
Fees: (September 05)
Day £3549–£5568

ST AGNES PNEU SCHOOL
25 Burton Crescent, Leeds,
West Yorkshire LS6 4DN
Tel: (0113) 278 6722
Email: info@st-agnes.demon.co.uk
Head: Mrs S McMeeking
Type: Co-educational Day 2–7
No of pupils: B22 G24
Fees: On application

WAKEFIELD TUTORIAL PREPARATORY SCHOOL
Commercial Street, Morley, Leeds,
West Yorkshire LS27 8HY
Tel: (0113) 253 4033
Fax: (0113) 253 3581
Email: Headteacher@
   wtschool.co.uk
Head: Mrs J A Tanner
Type: Co-educational Day 4–11
No of pupils: B25 G25
Fees: (September 06)
Day £3885–£4275

PONTEFRACT

ACKWORTH SCHOOL*
Ackworth, Pontefract,
West Yorkshire WF7 7LT
Tel: (01977) 611401
Fax: (01977) 616225
Email: admissions@
  ackworthschool.com
Head: Mr P Simpson
Type: Co-educational Boarding
and Day 4–18
No of pupils: B290 G271
No of boarders: F83
Fees: (September 05) FB £15498
Day £9354

ACKWORTH SCHOOL–INTERNATIONAL STUDY CENTRE
Ackworth, Pontefract,
West Yorkshire WF7 7LT
Tel: (01977) 611401
Fax: (01977) 616225
Email: admissions@
  ackworthschool.com
Head: Mr P J Simpson
Type: Co-educational Day and
Boarding 2–18
No of pupils: B274 G289
No of boarders: F93
Fees: (September 06) FB £15873
Day £6045–£9729

INGLEBROOK SCHOOL
Northgate Close, Pontefract,
West Yorkshire WF8 1HJ
Tel: (01977) 700120
Head: Mrs J Bellamy
Type: Co-educational Day 2–11
No of pupils: B90 G90
Fees: On application

PUDSEY

FULNECK SCHOOL†
Fulneck, Pudsey, West Yorkshire
LS28 8DS
Tel: (0113) 257 0235
Fax: (0113) 255 7316
Email: general@
  fulneckschool.co.uk
Head: Mr T Kernohan
Type: Co-educational Day and
Boarding 3–18
No of pupils: B208 G164
No of boarders: F33 W9
Fees: (September 06)
FB £13080–£15900
WB £12090–£14460
Day £2985–£8685

RISHWORTH

RISHWORTH SCHOOL
Rishworth, West Yorkshire
HX6 4QA
Tel: (01422) 822217
Fax: (01422) 820911
Email: admin@
  rishworth-school.co.uk
Head: Mr R A Baker
Type: Co-educational Day and
Boarding 3–18
No of pupils: B290 G280
No of boarders: F78 W14
Fees: (September 05)
FB £14925–£16275
WB £13575–£14850
Day £4290–£8370

WAKEFIELD

CLIFF SCHOOL
St John's Lodge, 2 Leeds Road,
Wakefield, West Yorkshire
WF1 3JT
Tel: (01924) 373597
Fax: (01924) 211137
Email: info@cliffschool.com
Head: Miss A D Gleave
Type: Co-educational Day 2–11
No of pupils: B50 G100
Fees: (September 06)
Day £2907–£8925

QUEEN ELIZABETH GRAMMAR SCHOOL
154 Northgate, Wakefield,
West Yorkshire WF1 3QX
Tel: (01924) 373943
Fax: (01924) 231603
Email: admissions@qegsss.org.uk
Head: Mr M R Gibbons
Type: Boys Day 7–18
Fees: (September 06) Day £8271

ST HILDA'S SCHOOL
Dovecote Lane, Horbury,
Wakefield, West Yorkshire
WF4 6BB
Tel: (01924) 260706
Fax: (01924) 272516
Head: Mrs J Sharpe
Type: Co-educational Day
Boys 3–7 Girls 3–11
No of pupils: B44 G89
Fees: On application

SILCOATES SCHOOL
Wrenthorpe, Wakefield,
West Yorkshire WF2 0PD
Tel: (01924) 291614
Fax: (01924) 368693
Email: hmsilcoates@aol.com
Head: Mr A P Spillane
Type: Co-educational Day 7–18
No of pupils: B377 G339
Fees: On application

SUNNY HILL HOUSE SCHOOL
Wrenthorpe Lane, Wrenthorpe,
Wakefield, West Yorkshire
WF2 0QB
Tel: (01924) 291717
Fax: (01924) 291717
Email: shhschool@aol.com
Head: Mrs H K Cushing
Type: Co-educational Day 2–7
No of pupils: B55 G44
Fees: (September 06) Day £4956

WAKEFIELD GIRLS' HIGH SCHOOL
Wentworth Street, Wakefield,
West Yorkshire WF1 2QS
Tel: (01924) 372490
Fax: (01924) 231601
Email: admissions@wghsss.org.uk
Head: Mrs P A Langham
Type: Girls Day 11–18
No of pupils: 734
Fees: (September 06) Day £8271

WAKEFIELD INDEPENDENT SCHOOL
The Nostell Centre, Doncaster
Road, Nostell, Wakefield,
West Yorkshire WF4 1QG
Tel: (01924) 865757
Fax: (01924) 865757
Email: headatwis@fsmail.net
Head: Ms K E Caryl
Type: Co-educational Day 3–16
No of pupils: B120 G100
Fees: (September 06)
Day £3900–£5835

2.3

NIR

COUNTY ANTRIM

BELFAST

BELFAST ROYAL ACADEMY
Belfast, County Antrim BT14 6JL
Tel: (028) 9074 0423
Fax: (028) 9075 0607
Email: enquiries@
bfsra.belfast.ni.sch.uk
Head: Mr W S F Young
Type: Co-educational Day 4–19
No of pupils: B772 G819
Fees: On application

CABIN HILL SCHOOL
562–594 Upper Newtownards
Road, Knock, Belfast, County
Antrim BT4 3HJ
Tel: (028) 9065 3368
Fax: (028) 9065 1966
Email: info@
cabinhill.belfast.ni.sch.uk
Head: Mrs H M Rowan
Type: Boys Day and Boarding
3–13 (Co-ed kindergarten)
No of pupils: B284 G8
No of boarders: F6 W21
Fees: On application

CAMPBELL COLLEGE
Belfast, County Antrim BT4 2ND
Tel: (028) 9076 3076
Fax: (028) 9076 1894
Email: hmoffice@
campbellcollege.co.uk
Head: Mr W D A Gribson
Type: Boys Boarding and Day
11–18
No of pupils: 800
No of boarders: F16 W24
Fees: On application

METHODIST COLLEGE
1 Malone Road, Belfast, County
Antrim BT9 6BY
Tel: (028) 9020 5205
Fax: (028) 9020 5230
Email: school@methody.org
Head: Dr T W Mulryne
Type: Co-educational Day and
Boarding 4–19
No of pupils: B1300 G1100
No of boarders: F170
Fees: On application

ROYAL BELFAST ACADEMICAL INSTITUTION
College Square East, Belfast,
County Antrim BT1 6DL
Tel: (028) 9024 0461
Fax: (028) 9023 7464
Email: prinsec@
rbai.belfast.ni.sch.uk
Head: Mr R M Ridley
Type: Boys Day 4–18
No of pupils: 1300
Fees: (September 05)
Day £690–£3100

VICTORIA COLLEGE BELFAST
Cranmore Park, Belfast, County
Antrim BT9 6JA
Tel: (028) 9066 1506
Fax: (028) 9066 6898
Email: vcbinfo@aol.com
Head: Ms P Slevin
Type: Girls Day and Boarding
4–18
No of pupils: 1029
No of boarders: F47
Fees: (September 05) F/WB £6750
Day £310

COUNTY ARMAGH

ARMAGH

THE ROYAL SCHOOL
College Hill, Armagh, County
Armagh BT61 9DH
Tel: (028) 3752 2807
Fax: (028) 3752 5014
Head: Mr P Crute
Type: Co-educational Boarding
and Day 10–19
No of pupils: B333 G336
No of boarders: F16 W65
Fees: (September 05)
FB £5500–£8300
WB £3700–£7500 Day £220–£230

COUNTY DOWN

BANGOR

**BANGOR GRAMMAR
SCHOOL**
13 College Avenue, Bangor,
County Down BT20 5HJ
Tel: (028) 9147 3734
Fax: (028) 9127 3245
Email: info@bgs.bangor.ni.sch.uk
Head: Mr S D Connolly
Type: Boys Day 11–18
No of pupils: 888
Fees: On application

**BANGOR INDEPENDENT
CHRISTIAN SCHOOL**
277A Clandeboye Road, Bangor,
County Down BT19 1AA
Tel: (028) 9145 0240
Fax: (028) 9145 0240
Email: ics.bangor@gmail.com
Head: Mrs Ruth Daly
Type: Co-educational Day 4–16
Fees: (September 06)

HOLYWOOD

**THE HOLYWOOD RUDOLF
STEINER SCHOOL**
The Highlands, 34 Croft Road,
Holywood, County Down
BT18 0PR
Tel: (028) 9042 8029
Fax: (028) 9042 8029
Email: info@
holywood-steiner.co.uk
Type: Co-educational Day 4–17
No of pupils: B86 G76
Fees: (September 06)

ROCKPORT SCHOOL
15 Rockport Road, Craigavad,
Holywood, County Down
BT18 0DD
Tel: (028) 9042 8372
Fax: (028) 9042 2608
Email: info@rockportschool.com
Head: Mrs C A Osborne
Type: Co-educational Boarding
and Day 3–16 (Boarding 7–13)
No of pupils: B111 G112
No of boarders: W16
Fees: (September 05)
WB £7395–£10245
Day £3525–£8400

COUNTY LONDONDERRY

COLERAINE

COLERAINE ACADEMICAL INSTITUTION
Castlerock Road, Coleraine,
County Londonderry BT51 3LA
Tel: (028) 7034 4331
Fax: (028) 7035 2632
Email: cai@
   coleraineai.demon.co.uk
Head: Mr L Quigg
Type: Boys Day 11–19
No of pupils: 720
Fees: On application

COUNTY TYRONE

DUNGANNON

THE ROYAL SCHOOL DUNGANNON
1 Ranfurly Road, Dungannon,
County Tyrone BT71 6EG
Tel: (028) 8772 2710
Fax: (028) 8775 2845
Email: acullen584@
   rsd.dungannon.ni.sch.uk
Head: Mr P D Hewitt
Type: Co-educational Day and
Boarding 11–19
No of pupils: B325 G325
No of boarders: F40 W5
Fees: (September 06)
F/WB £5500–£10000
Day £100–£165

SIXMILECROSS

COOLEY PRIMARY SCHOOL
90 Cooley Road, Omagh,
Sixmilecross, County Tyrone
BT79 9DH
Tel: (028) 8075 8742
Fax: (028) 8075 8744
Email: info@
   cooley.omagh.ni.sch.uk
Head: Mrs Anne Anderson and
Mrs Karen Atchison
Type: Co-educational Day 4–11
No of pupils: B62 G69
Fees: On application

2.4

SCOTLAND

ABERDEENSHIRE

ABERDEEN

ABERDEEN WALDORF SCHOOL
Craigton Road, Cults, Aberdeen,
Aberdeenshire AB15 9QD
Tel: (01224) 869932
Fax: (01224) 868366
Email: aws@talk21.com
Head: Mr P Hansmann
Type: Co-educational Day 3–16
No of pupils: B70 G55
Fees: (September 05)
Day £1500–£6700

ALBYN SCHOOL*
17–23 Queen's Road, Aberdeen,
Aberdeenshire AB15 4PB
Tel: (01224) 322408
Fax: (01224) 209173
Email: information@
   albynschool.co.uk
Head: Dr J D Halliday
Type: Co-educational Day
Boys 2–10 Girls 2–18
No of pupils: B60 G340
Fees: (September 06)
Day £5000–£8200

THE HAMILTON SCHOOL
55–57 & 80–84 Queens Road,
Aberdeen, Aberdeenshire
AB15 4YE
Tel: (01224) 317295
Fax: (01224) 317165
Email: hamilton.admin@virgin.net
Head: Ms K Taylor
Type: Co-educational Day 0–12
Fees: On application

INTERNATIONAL SCHOOL OF ABERDEEN
'Fairgirth', 296 North Deeside
Road, Milltimber, Aberdeen,
Aberdeenshire AB13 OAB
Tel: (01224) 732267
Fax: (01224) 735648
Email: admin@
   isa.aberdeen.sch.uk
Head: Dr D A Hovde
Type: Co-educational Day 3–18
No of pupils: B180 G153
Fees: (September 05)
Day £13125–£14700

ROBERT GORDONS COLLEGE
Schoolhill, Aberdeen,
Aberdeenshire AB10 1FE
Tel: (01224) 646346
Fax: (01224) 630301
Email: h.ouston@
   rgc.aberdeen.sch.uk
Head: Mr Hugh Ouston
Type: Co-educational Day 4–18
No of pupils: B910 G558
Fees: (September 05)
Day £4840–£7600

ST MARGARET'S SCHOOL FOR GIRLS
17 Albyn Place, Aberdeen,
Aberdeenshire AB10 1RU
Tel: (01224) 584466
Fax: (01224) 585600
Email: info@
   st-margaret.aberdeen.sch.uk
Head: Mrs L McKay
Type: Girls Day 3–18 (Boys 3–5)
No of pupils: B2 G365
Fees: (September 06)
Day £4650–£8112

ANGUS

DUNDEE

THE HIGH SCHOOL OF DUNDEE
Euclid Crescent, Dundee, Angus
DD1 1HU
Tel: (01382) 202921
Fax: (01382) 229822
Email: admissions@
    highschoolofdundee.co.uk
Head: Mr A M Duncan
Type: Co-educational Day 5–18
No of pupils: B546 G500
Fees: (September 06)
Day £5841–£8304

MONTROSE

LATHALLAN SCHOOL
Brotherton Castle, Johnshaven,
Montrose, Angus DD10 0HN
Tel: (01561) 362220
Fax: (01561) 361695
Email: office@lathallan.com
Head: Mr Andrew Giles
Type: Co-educational Boarding
and Day 5–13
No of pupils: B54 G44
No of boarders: W35
Fees: (September 05)
WB £9687–£12651

ARGYLL AND BUTE

HELENSBURGH

LOMOND SCHOOL
10 Stafford Street, Helensburgh,
Argyll and Bute G84 9JX
Tel: (01436) 672476
Fax: (01436) 678320
Email: admin@
    lomond-school.demon.co.uk
Head: Mr A D Macdonald
Type: Co-educational Day and
Boarding 3–19
No of pupils: B280 G282
No of boarders: F64
Fees: (September 05)
FB £15915–£16140
Day £3690–£7545

SOUTH AYRSHIRE

AYR

WELLINGTON SCHOOL
Carleton Turrets, Craigweil Road,
Ayr, South Ayrshire KA7 2XH
Tel: (01292) 269321
Fax: (01292) 272161
Email: info@wellingtonschool.org
Head: Mr M Parlour
Type: Co-educational Day 3–18
No of pupils: B270 G315
Fees: (September 05)
Day £2460–£8265

CLACKMANNANSHIRE

DOLLAR

DOLLAR ACADEMY
Dollar, Clackmannanshire
FK14 7DU
Tel: (01259) 742511
Fax: (01259) 742867
Email: rector@
   dollaracademy.org.uk
Head: Mr J S Robertson
Type: Co-educational Day and
Boarding 5–18
No of pupils: B621 G579
No of boarders: F85 W9
Fees: On application

DUMFRIES & GALLOWAY

THORNHILL

**CADEMUIR
INTERNATIONAL SCHOOL**
Crawfordton House, Moniaive,
Thornhill, Dumfries & Galloway
DG3 4HG
Tel: (01848) 200212
Fax: (01848) 200212
Email: cademuir1@aol.com
Head: Mr Ian Hornby
Type: Co-educational Day and
Boarding
No of pupils: 34
No of boarders: F33
Fees: (September 06)
FB £20700–£24600 WB £23100
Day £16500

FIFE

KIRKCALDY

SEA VIEW PRIVATE SCHOOL
102 Loughborough Road,
Kirkcaldy, Fife KY1 3DD
Tel: (01592) 652244
Fax: (01592) 655929
Email: seaviewkdy@sol.co.uk
Head: Mr Andrew Moss and
Mrs Louise Moss
Type: Co-educational Day 3–12
No of pupils: B32 G25
Fees: On application

ST ANDREWS

**ST LEONARDS SCHOOL &
VITH FORM COLLEGE**
St Andrews, Fife KY16 9QJ
Tel: (01334) 472126
Fax: (01334) 476152
Email: info@stleonards-fife.org
Head: Mr R Tims
Type: Co-educational Boarding
and Day 3–19
No of pupils: B81 G231
No of boarders: F136
Fees: On application

GLASGOW

CRAIGHOLME SCHOOL
72 St Andrews Drive,
Pollokshields, Glasgow G41 4HS
Tel: (0141) 427 0375
Fax: (0141) 427 6396
Email: principal@
craigholme.co.uk
Head: Mrs G Stobo
Type: Girls Day 3–18 (Boys 3–5)
No of pupils: B10 G520
Fees: (September 06)
Day £6165–£7860

THE GLASGOW ACADEMY
Colebrooke Street, Glasgow
G12 8HE
Tel: (0141) 334 8558
Fax: (0141) 337 3473
Email: enquiries@tga.org.uk
Head: Mr P J Brodie
Type: Co-educational Day 3–18
No of pupils: B643 G550
Fees: (September 06)
Day £2730–£8100

THE GLASGOW ACADEMY DAIRSIE
54 Newlands Road, Glasgow
G43 2JG
Tel: (0141) 632 0736
Fax: (0141) 632 1303
Email: dairsie@tga.org.uk
Head: Mrs S S McKnight
Type: Co-educational Day 3–9
No of pupils: B44 G27
Fees: (September 06)
Day £2730–£5505

GLASGOW STEINER SCHOOL
52 Lumsden Street, Glasgow
G3 8RH
Tel: (0141) 334 8855
Fax: (0141) 334 8855
Email: admin@
glasgowsteinerschool.org
Head: Ms C Rocher
Type: Co-educational Day 3–14
No of pupils: B53 G38
Fees: (September 05)
Day £1140–£4380

THE HIGH SCHOOL OF GLASGOW
637 Crow Road, Glasgow G13 1PL
Tel: (0141) 954 9628
Fax: (0141) 435 5708
Email: rector@hsog.co.uk
Head: Mr C D R Mair
Type: Co-educational Day 3–18
No of pupils: B535 G524
Fees: (September 05)
Day £2547–£7848

HUTCHESONS' GRAMMAR SCHOOL
21 Beaton Road, Glasgow
G41 4NW
Tel: (0141) 423 2933
Fax: (0141) 424 0251
Email: admissions@
hutchesons.org
Head: Dr K M Greig
Type: Co-educational Day 5–18
No of pupils: B907 G820
Fees: (September 06)
Day £6126–£7869

HUTCHESONS' LILYBANK JUNIOR SCHOOL
4 Lilybank Terrace, Glasgow
G12 8RX
Tel: (0141) 339 9127
Fax: (0141) 357 5530
Head: Mr J G Knowles
Type: Co-educational Day 3–11
No of pupils: 130
Fees: On application

KELVINSIDE ACADEMY
33 Kirklee Road, Glasgow
G12 0SW
Tel: (0141) 357 3376
Fax: (0141) 357 5401
Email: rector@
kelvinsideacademy.org.uk
Head: Mr J L Broadfoot
Type: Co-educational Day 3–18
No of pupils: B408 G220
Fees: On application

ST ALOYSIUS' COLLEGE
45 Hill Street, Glasgow G3 6RJ
Tel: (0141) 332 3190
Fax: (0141) 353 0426
Email: mail@staloysius.org
Head: Mr J E Stoer
Type: Co-educational Day 3–18
No of pupils: B661 G627
Fees: (September 05)
Day £5385–£6940

ST ALOYSIUS JUNIOR SCHOOL
56–58 Hill Street, Glasgow
G3 6RH
Tel: (0141) 331 9200
Head: Mrs F Davidson
Type: Co-educational Day 5–12
No of pupils: 431
Fees: On application

INVERCLYDE

GREENOCK

CEDARS SCHOOL OF EXCELLENCE
31 Ardgowan Square, Greenock,
Inverclyde PA16 8NJ
Tel: (01475) 723905
Fax: (01475) 723905
Email: alison@speirs.org
Type: Co-educational Day 5–14
No of pupils: 50
Fees: (September 06)
Day £3000–£3300

KILMACOLM

ST COLUMBA'S SCHOOL
Duchal Road, Kilmacolm,
Inverclyde PA13 4AU
Tel: (01505) 872238
Fax: (01505) 873995
Email: secretary@st-columbas.org
Head: Mr D Girdwood
Type: Co-educational Day 3–18
No of pupils: B361 G369
Fees: (September 06)
Day £2010–£7830

LANARKSHIRE

HAMILTON

HAMILTON COLLEGE
Bothwell Road, Hamilton,
Lanarkshire ML3 0AY
Tel: (01698) 282700
Fax: (01698) 281589
Email: principal@
   hamiltoncollege.co.uk
Head: Mr A J Leach
Type: Co-educational Day 3–18
No of pupils: B400 G400
Fees: On application

SOUTH LANARKSHIRE

RUTHERGLEN

FERNHILL SCHOOL
Fernbrae Avenue, Rutherglen,
South Lanarkshire G73 4SG
Tel: (0141) 634 2674
Fax: (0141) 631 4343
Email: info@fernhillschool.co.uk
Head: Mrs A Crammond
Type: Girls Day 4–18 (Boys 4–11)
No of pupils: B61 G270
Fees: (September 05)
Day £5250–£6750

LOTHIAN

DUNBAR

BELHAVEN HILL
Dunbar, Lothian EH42 1NN
Tel: (01368) 862785
Fax: (01368) 865225
Email: headmaster@
   belhavenhill.com
Head: Mr I M Osborne
Type: Co-educational Boarding
and Day 7–13
No of pupils: B70 G54
No of boarders: F100
Fees: (September 06) FB £15750
Day £10920

EDINBURGH

BASIL PATERSON TUTORIAL COLLEGE
66 Queen Street, Edinburgh,
Lothian EH2 4NA
Tel: (0131) 225 3802
Fax: (0131) 226 6701
Email: info@basilpaterson.co.uk
Head: Mr C Smith
Type: Co-educational Boarding
and Day 15+
No of pupils: B15 G15
No of boarders: F7
Fees: (September 06)
FB £3500–£15000
Day £2610–£13000

CARGILFIELD
Barnton Avenue West, Edinburgh,
Lothian EH4 6HU
Tel: (0131) 336 2207
Fax: (0131) 336 3179
Email: admin@cargilfield.com
Head: Mr J Elder
Type: Co-educational Boarding
and Day 3–13
No of pupils: B127 G53
No of boarders: F21
Fees: (September 05) FB £4400
WB £4200 Day £2150–£3450

CLIFTON HALL SCHOOL
Newbridge, Edinburgh, Lothian
EH28 8LQ
Tel: (0131) 333 1359
Fax: (0131) 333 4609
Email: office@cliftonhall.org.uk
Head: Mr R Grant
Type: Co-educational Day 3–11
No of pupils: B70 G70
Fees: (September 05)
Day £2850–£7500

DUNEDIN SCHOOL
5 Gilmerton Road, Edinburgh,
Lothian EH16 5TY
Tel: (0131) 664 1328
Email: staff@dunedin.edin.sch.uk
Head: Mrs S Peck and Mrs S Ford
Type: Co-educational Day 10–17
No of pupils: B10 G10
Fees: On application

THE EDINBURGH ACADEMY
42 Henderson Row, Edinburgh,
Lothian EH3 5BL
Tel: (0131) 556 4603
Fax: (0131) 624 4994
Email: rector@
   edinburghacademy.org.uk
Head: Mr J V Light
Type: Boys Day and Boarding
5–18 (Co-ed VIth Form)
No of pupils: B451 G25
No of boarders: F17 W2
Fees: On application

THE EDINBURGH RUDOLF STEINER SCHOOL
60 Spylaw Road, Edinburgh,
Lothian EH10 5BR
Tel: (0131) 337 3410
Fax: (0131) 538 6066
Email: steinersch@aol.com
Head: Mr A Farquharson
Type: Co-educational Day 3–18
No of pupils: B150 G150
No of boarders: F8 W1
Fees: On application

FETTES COLLEGE*
Carrington Road, Edinburgh,
Lothian EH4 1QX
Tel: (0131) 311 6701
Fax: (0131) 311 6714
Email: enquiries@fettes.com
Head: Mr M C B Spens
Type: Co-educational Boarding
and Day 7–18
No of pupils: B349 G261
No of boarders: F427
Fees: (September 06)
FB £16167–£22326
Day £10326–£15840

GEORGE HERIOT'S SCHOOL
Lauriston Place, Edinburgh,
Lothian EH3 9EQ
Tel: (0131) 229 7263
Fax: (0131) 229 6363
Email: admissions@
   george-heriots.com
Head: Mr A G Hector and
Mr C D Wyllie
Type: Co-educational Day 4–18
No of pupils: B886 G724
Fees: (September 06)
Day £5211–£7845

GEORGE WATSON'S COLLEGE
Colinton Road, Edinburgh, Lothian
EH10 5EG
Tel: (0131) 446 6000
Fax: (0131) 446 6090
Email: admissions@gwc.org.uk
Head: Mr Gareth Edwards
Type: Co-educational Day 3–18
No of pupils: B1214 G1083
Fees: (September 06)
Day £2364–£8163

MANNAFIELDS CHRISTIAN SCHOOL
170 Easter Road, Edinburgh,
Lothian EH7 5QE
Tel: (0131) 659 5602
Email: head@mannafields.org.uk
Head: Mr G S Ackerman
Type: Co-educational Day 5–14
Fees: On application

THE MARY ERSKINE SCHOOL
Ravelston, Edinburgh, Lothian
EH4 3NT
Tel: (0131) 347 5700
Fax: (0131) 347 5799
Email: schoolsecretary@
esmgc.com
Head: Mr J N D Gray
Type: Girls Day and Boarding
12–18 (Co-ed VIth Form)
No of boarders: F20
Fees: (September 05) FB £15045
Day £7929

MERCHISTON CASTLE SCHOOL*
Colinton, Edinburgh, Lothian
EH13 0PU
Tel: (0131) 312 2200
Fax: (0131) 441 6060
Email: admissions@
merchiston.co.uk
Head: Mr A R Hunter
Type: Boys Boarding and Day
8–18
No of pupils: 430
No of boarders: F288
Fees: (September 06)
FB £14325–£21795
Day £10005–£15585

REGIUS CHRISTIAN SCHOOL
41a South Clerk Street, Edinburgh,
Lothian EH8 8NZ
Tel: (0131) 466 8662
Email: jenny@regius.edin.sch.uk
Head: Mrs Jenny Taylor
Type: Co-educational Day
No of pupils: 16
Fees: (September 06) Day £3600

ST GEORGE'S SCHOOL FOR GIRLS
Garscube Terrace, Edinburgh,
Lothian EH12 6BG
Tel: (0131) 311 8000
Fax: (0131) 311 8120
Email: head@
st-georges.edin.sch.uk
Head: Dr J McClure
Type: Girls Day and Boarding
2–18 (Boys 2–5)
No of pupils: B19 G965
No of boarders: F40
Fees: (September 05)
FB £15630–£17550
Day £2790–£8775

ST MARGARET'S SCHOOL
East Suffolk Road, Edinburgh,
Lothian EH16 5PJ
Tel: (0131) 668 1986
Fax: (0131) 667 9814
Email: admissions@
st-margarets.sch.uk
Head: Mrs E M Davis
Type: Girls Day 1–18 (Boys 1–8)
No of pupils: B68 G472
Fees: On application

ST MARY'S MUSIC SCHOOL
Coates Hall, 25 Grosvenor
Crescent, Edinburgh, Lothian
EH12 5EL
Tel: (0131) 538 7766
Fax: (0131) 467 7289
Email: info@
st-marys-music-school.co.uk
Head: Mrs J J Rimer
Type: Co-educational Boarding
and Day 9–19
No of pupils: B31 G37
No of boarders: F25
Fees: On application

ST SERF'S SCHOOL
5 Wester Coates Gardens,
Edinburgh, Lothian EH12 5LT
Tel: (0131) 337 1015
Fax: (0131) 346 7829
Email: office@
stserfsschool.freeserve.co.uk
Head: Mrs K D Hume
Type: Co-educational Day 5–18
No of pupils: B65 G50
Fees: (September 05)
Day £4560–£6360

STEWART'S MELVILLE COLLEGE
Queensferry Road, Edinburgh,
Lothian EH4 3EZ
Tel: (0131) 311 1000
Fax: (0131) 311 1099
Email: secretary@esmgc.com
Head: Mr J N D Gray
Type: Boys Day and Boarding
12–18 (Co-ed VIth Form)
No of boarders: F21
Fees: (September 05) FB £15045
Day £7929

HADDINGTON

THE COMPASS SCHOOL
West Road, Haddington, Lothian
EH41 3RD
Tel: (01620) 822642
Fax: (01620) 822144
Email: office@
thecompassschool.co.uk
Head: Mr M Becher
Type: Co-educational Day 4–11
No of pupils: B58 G64
Fees: On application

MUSSELBURGH

LORETTO JUNIOR SCHOOL
North Esk Lodge, 1 North High
Street, Musselburgh, Lothian
EH21 6JA
Tel: (0131) 653 4570
Fax: (0131) 653 4571
Email: juniorschool@loretto.com
Head: Mr R G Selley
Type: Co-educational Boarding
and Day 3–13
No of pupils: B122 G65
No of boarders: F16 W4
Fees: (September 05)
FB £14865–£15858
Day £9825–£10521

LORETTO SCHOOL*
Linkfield Road, Musselburgh,
Lothian EH21 7RE
Tel: (0131) 653 4455
Fax: (0131) 653 4456
Email: admissions@loretto.com
Head: Mr M B Mavor
Type: Co-educational Boarding
and Day 3–18
No of pupils: B290 G213
No of boarders: F261
Fees: (September 06)
FB £15609–£22080
WB £14049–£14985
Day £4815–£14595

MORAYSHIRE

ELGIN

GORDONSTOUN SCHOOL*
Elgin, Morayshire IV30 5RF
Tel: (01343) 837837
Fax: (01343) 837808
Email: admissions@
  gordonstoun.org.uk
Head: Mr M C Pyper
Type: Co-educational Boarding
and Day 8–18
No of pupils: B344 G239
No of boarders: F482 W15
Fees: (September 06)
FB £15264–£24162 WB £12486
Day £8823–£17700

ROSEBRAE SCHOOL
Spynie, Elgin, Morayshire IV30 8XT
Tel: (01343) 544841
Fax: (01343) 544841
Email: enquiries@
  rosebrae.moray.sch.uk
Head: Mrs B MacPherson
Type: Co-educational Day 2–8
No of pupils: B32 G32
Fees: (September 05)
Day £405–£3840

PERTH AND KINROSS

CRIEFF

ARDVRECK SCHOOL
Gwydyr Road, Crieff,
Perth and Kinross PH7 4EX
Tel: (01764) 653112
Fax: (01764) 654920
Email: headmaster@
  ardvreck.org.uk
Head: Mr P Watson
Type: Co-educational Day and
Boarding 3–13
No of pupils: B80 G70
No of boarders: F105
Fees: (September 06) FB £14817
Day £9858

MORRISON'S ACADEMY
Ferntower Road, Crieff,
Perth and Kinross PH7 3AN
Tel: (01764) 653885
Fax: (01764) 655411
Email: principal@
  morrisonsacademy.org
Head: Mr S Pengelley
Type: Co-educational Day and
Boarding 3–18
No of pupils: B256 G222
No of boarders: F18 W10
Fees: (September 05)
FB £17868–£18822
WB £13758–£14712
Day £2050–£7719

DUNBLANE

QUEEN VICTORIA SCHOOL
Dunblane, Perth and Kinross
FK15 0JY
Tel: (01786) 822288
Fax: (0131) 310 2926
Email: enquiries@qvs.org.uk
Head: Mrs W E Bellars
Type: Co-educational Boarding
11–18
No of pupils: B144 G124
No of boarders: F268
Fees: (September 05) FB £1024

PERTH

CRAIGCLOWAN
PREPARATORY SCHOOL
Edinburgh Road, Perth,
Perth and Kinross PH2 8PS
Tel: (01738) 626310
Fax: (01738) 440349
Email: mbeale@btconnect.com
Head: Mr M E Beale
Type: Co-educational Day 3–13
No of pupils: B160 G145
Fees: (September 06)
Day £4500–£7400

GLENALMOND COLLEGE*
Perth, Perth and Kinross PH1 3RY
Tel: (01738) 842056
Fax: (01738) 842063
Email: registrar@
  glenalmondcollege.co.uk
Head: Mr G Woods
Type: Co-educational Boarding
and Day 12–18
No of boarders: F332
Fees: (September 06)
FB £16890–£22545
Day £11535–£15375

KILGRASTON†
Bridge of Earn, Perth,
Perth and Kinross PH2 9BQ
Tel: (01738) 812257
Fax: (01738) 813410
Email: registrar@
  kilgraston.pkc.sch.uk
Head: Mr M Farmer and
Mrs A Kelloway
Type: Girls Boarding and Day
2–18 (Boys day 2–9)
No of pupils: B6 G257
No of boarders: F96
Fees: (September 06)
FB £16485–£19935
Day £6735–£11685

STRATHALLAN SCHOOL*
Forgandenny, Perth,
Perth and Kinross PH2 9EG
Tel: (01738) 812546
Fax: (01738) 812549
Email: admissions@
strathallan.co.uk
Head: Mr B K Thompson
Type: Co-educational Boarding
and Day 10–18
No of pupils: B276 G196
No of boarders: F313
Fees: (September 06)
FB £15510–£21735
Day £9690–£14745

RENFREWSHIRE

NEWTON MEARNS

BELMONT HOUSE
Sandringham Avenue, Newton
Mearns, Renfrewshire G77 5DU
Tel: (0141) 639 2922
Fax: (0141) 639 9860
Email: admin@
belmontschool.co.uk
Head: Mr M D Shanks
Type: Co-educational Day 3–18
No of pupils: B277 G66
Fees: (September 05)
Day £3375–£7659

ROXBURGHSHIRE

MELROSE

**ST MARY'S PREPARATORY
SCHOOL**
Abbey Park, Melrose,
Roxburghshire TD6 9LN
Tel: (01896) 822517
Fax: (01896) 823550
Email: enquiries@
stmarys.newnet.co.uk
Head: Mr J Brett
Type: Co-educational Day and
Boarding 2–13
No of pupils: B57 G80
No of boarders: W21
Fees: (September 05) WB £11970
Day £7350–£10200

STIRLING

BEACONHURST SCHOOL
52 Kenilworth Road, Bridge of
Allan, Stirling FK9 4RR
Tel: (01786) 832146
Fax: (01786) 833415
Email: secretary@
  beaconhurst.stirling.sch.uk
Head: Mr I W Kilpatrick
Type: Co-educational Day 3–18
No of pupils: B205 G170
Fees: (September 06)
Day £2600–£8300

2.5

WALES

ANGLESEY

MENAI BRIDGE

TREFFOS SCHOOL
Llansadwrn, Menai Bridge,
Anglesey LL59 5SL
Tel: (01248) 712322
Fax: (01248) 715276
Email: treffos@aol.com
Head: Mrs J E Humphreys and
Dr S Humphreys
Type: Co-educational Day 0–11
No of pupils: B45 G42
Fees: (September 06)
Day £750–£1397

BRIDGEND

PORTHCAWL

ST CLARE'S SCHOOL
Clevis Lane, Newton, Porthcawl,
Bridgend CF36 5NR
Tel: (01656) 782509
Fax: (01656) 785818
Email: info@stclares-school.co.uk
Head: Mrs C M Barnard
Type: Co-educational Day 3–18
No of pupils: B156 G222
Fees: (September 06)
Day £3495–£6450

ST JOHN'S SCHOOL
Church Street, Newton,
Porthcawl, Bridgend CF36 5NP
Tel: (01656) 783404
Fax: (01656) 783535
Email: office@
stjohnsschool-porthcawl.com
Head: Mrs C A Clint
Type: Co-educational Day 3–16
Fees: (September 06)
Day £3930–£8310

CAERPHILLY

MACHEN

WYCLIF INDEPENDENT CHRISTIAN SCHOOL
Ebenezer Baptist Chapel,
Wyndham Street, Machen,
Caerphilly NP1 8PU
Tel: (01633) 441582
Fax: (01633) 441582
Head: Mr Andrew Tamplin
Type: Co-educational Day 4–16
No of pupils: B48 G51
Fees: On application

CARDIFF

CARDIFF

THE CARDIFF ACADEMY
40–41 The Parade, Roath, Cardiff
CF24 3AB
Tel: (029) 2040 9630
Fax: (029) 2045 5273
Email: 40–41@
theparade.fsbusiness.co.uk
Head: Dr S R Wilson
Type: Co-educational Day 14–18
No of pupils: B25 G25
Fees: (September 06)
Day £7050–£9000

THE CATHEDRAL SCHOOL
Cardiff Road, Llandaff, Cardiff
CF5 2YH
Tel: (029) 2056 3179
Fax: (029) 2056 7752
Email: Registrar@
cathedral-school.co.uk
Head: Mr P L Gray
Type: Co-educational Day 3–16
No of pupils: B428 G195
Fees: (September 06)
Day £5625–£8175

ELM TREE HOUSE
Clive Road, Llandaff, Cardiff
CF5 1GN
Tel: (029) 2022 3388
Fax: (029) 2022 3388
Head: Mrs C M Thomas
Type: Co-educational Day 2–11
No of pupils: B25 G95
Fees: On application

HOWELL'S SCHOOL, LLANDAFF GDST
Cardiff Road, Llandaff, Cardiff
CF5 2YD
Tel: (029) 2056 2019
Fax: (029) 2057 8879
Email: mail@how.gdst.net
Head: Mrs J Fitz
Type: Co-educational Day
Boys 16–18 Girls 3–18
No of pupils: B46 G849
Fees: (September 05)
Day £4605–£7413

KINGS MONKTON SCHOOL
6 West Grove, Cardiff CF24 3XL
Tel: (029) 2048 2854
Fax: (029) 2049 0484
Email: mail@kingsmonkton.org.uk
Head: Mr R N Griffin
Type: Co-educational Day 2–18
No of pupils: B220 G140
Fees: (September 06)
Day £4995–£6570

ST JOHN'S COLLEGE
College Green, Newport Road,
Old St Mellons, Cardiff CF3 5YX
Tel: (029) 2077 8936
Fax: (029) 20779099
Head: Dr D Neville
Type: Co-educational Day 3–18
No of pupils: B240 G200
Fees: On application

WESTBOURNE SCHOOL
Hickman Road, Penarth, Cardiff
CF64 2AJ
Tel: (029) 2070 5705
Fax: (029) 2070 9988
Email: enquiries@
westbourneschool.com
Head: Mr A Swain and
Mr K Underhill
Type: Co-educational Day 3–16
No of pupils: B103 G58
Fees: (September 06)
Day £3900–£7575

CARMARTHENSHIRE

LLANDOVERY

LLANDOVERY COLLEGE
Llandovery, Carmarthenshire
SA20 0EE
Tel: (01550) 723000
Fax: (01550) 723002
Email: mail@
  llandoverycollege.com
Head: Mr P A Hogan
Type: Co-educational Boarding
and Day 4–18
No of pupils: B206 G127
No of boarders: F135 W20
Fees: (September 06)
FB £10920–£18330
Day £5220–£11040

LLANELLI

ST MICHAEL'S SCHOOL
Bryn, Llanelli, Carmarthenshire
SA14 9TU
Tel: (01554) 820325
Fax: (01554) 821716
Head: Mr D T Sheehan
Type: Co-educational Day 3–18
No of pupils: B210 G179
No of boarders: F19
Fees: On application

CONWY

COLWYN BAY

**LYNDON PREPARATORY
SCHOOL**
Pwllycrochan Avenue,
Colwyn Bay, Conwy LL29 7BP
Tel: (01492) 530381
Fax: (01492) 539720
Email: lyndon@
  rydal-penrhos.co.uk
Head: Mr P J Bendall
Type: Co-educational Boarding
and Day 2–11
No of pupils: B146 G120
Fees: (September 06)
FB £11700–£13860
WB £10773–£12474
Day £4320–£6180

**RYDAL PENRHOS SENIOR
SCHOOL**
Pwllycrochan Avenue,
Colwyn Bay, Conwy LL29 7BT
Tel: (01492) 530155
Fax: (01492) 534072
Email: info@rydal-penrhos.com
Head: Mr M S James
Type: Co-educational Boarding
and Day 11–18 (Single-sex ed
11–16)
No of pupils: B220 G174
No of boarders: F150
Fees: On application

LLANDUDNO

ST DAVID'S COLLEGE[†]
Llandudno, Conwy LL30 1RD
Tel: (01492) 875974
Fax: (01492) 870383
Email: headmaster@
  stdavidscollege.co.uk
Head: Mr C Condrup
Type: Co-educational Boarding
and Day 11–18
No of pupils: B207 G69
No of boarders: F150 W5
Fees: (September 06)
F/WB £16647–£19551
Day £10824–£13290

DENBIGHSHIRE

DENBIGH

HOWELL'S SCHOOL
Denbigh, Denbighshire LL16 3EN
Tel: (01745) 813631
Fax: (01745) 814443
Email: enquiries@howells.org
Head: Mrs L Robinson
Type: Girls Boarding and Day
2–18
No of pupils: 300
No of boarders: F100 W30
Fees: (September 05)
F/WB £9054–£14955
Day £4185–£9570

RHYL

NORTHGATE PREPARATORY
57 Russell Road, Rhyl,
Denbighshire LL18 3DD
Tel: (01745) 342510
Email: northgateschool@
  btinternet.com
Head: Mr P G Orton
Type: Co-educational Day 4–11
No of pupils: B23 G23
Fees: On application

RUTHIN

RUTHIN SCHOOL
Mold Road, Ruthin, Denbighshire
LL15 1EE
Tel: (01824) 702543
Fax: (01824) 707141
Email: secretary@
  ruthinschool.co.uk
Head: Mr J S Rowlands
Type: Co-educational Boarding
and Day 3–18
No of pupils: B128 G52
No of boarders: F42 W5
Fees: (September 06) FB £16755
WB £13965 Day £5550–£10320

ST ASAPH

FAIRHOLME PREPARATORY SCHOOL
Mount Road, St Asaph,
Denbighshire LL17 0DH
Tel: (01745) 583505
Fax: (01745) 584332
Email: success@
  fairholmeschool.com
Head: Mrs M Cashman
Type: Co-educational Day 3–11
No of pupils: B70 G60
Fees: On application

GWYNEDD

BANGOR

HILLGROVE SCHOOL
Ffriddoedd Road, Bangor,
Gwynedd LL57 2TW
Tel: (01248) 353568
Fax: (01248) 353971
Email: headmaster@
  hillgrove.gwynedd.sch.uk
Head: Mr J G Porter
Type: Co-educational Day 3–16
No of pupils: B72 G82
Fees: (September 06)
Day £2160–£3660

ST GERARD'S SCHOOL
Ffriddoedd Road, Bangor,
Gwynedd LL57 2EL
Tel: (01248) 351656
Fax: (01248) 351204
Head: Miss A Parkinson
Type: Co-educational Day 3–18
No of pupils: B169 G184
Fees: On application

MONMOUTHSHIRE

CHEPSTOW

ST JOHN'S-ON-THE-HILL
Tutshill, Chepstow,
Monmouthshire NP16 7LE
Tel: (01291) 622045
Fax: (01291) 623932
Email: registrar@
  stjohnsonthehill.co.uk
Head: Mr I K Etchells
Type: Co-educational Boarding
and Day 2–13 (Nursery from
3 months)
No of pupils: B192 G133
No of boarders: F35 W2
Fees: On application

MONMOUTH

HABERDASHERS' MONMOUTH SCHOOL FOR GIRLS
Hereford Road, Monmouth,
Monmouthshire NP25 5XT
Tel: (01600) 711100
Fax: (01600) 711233
Email: admissions@hmsg.co.uk
Head: Dr B Despontin
Type: Girls Day and Boarding
7–18
No of pupils: 655
No of boarders: F90
Fees: (September 06) F/WB £17121
Day £9351

LLANGATTOCK SCHOOL
Llangattock-Vibon-Avel,
Monmouth, Monmouthshire
NP25 5NG
Tel: (01600) 772213
Fax: (01600) 772213
Email: admin@
  llangattockschool.co.uk
Head: Mrs Rosemary Whaley
Type: Co-educational Day 2–12
No of pupils: B53 G43
Fees: (September 06) Day £3285

MONMOUTH SCHOOL
Almshouse Street, Monmouth,
Monmouthshire NP25 3XP
Tel: (01600) 713143
Fax: (01600) 772701
Email: admissions@
  monmouthschool.org
Head: Dr S G Connors
Type: Boys Boarding and Day
7–18 (Boarding 11–18)
No of pupils: 690
No of boarders: F140
Fees: (September 06)
F/WB £13941–£16956
Day £7059–£10074

NEWPORT

NEWPORT

ROUGEMONT SCHOOL
Llantarnam Hall, Malpas Road,
Newport NP20 6QB
Tel: (01633) 820800
Fax: (01633) 855598
Email: registrar@rsch.co.uk
Head: Dr J Tribbick
Type: Co-educational Day 3–18
No of pupils: B356 G332
Fees: (September 06)
Day £5451–£8202

PEMBROKESHIRE

SAUNDERSFOOT

NETHERWOOD SCHOOL
Saundersfoot, Pembrokeshire
SA69 9BE
Tel: (01834) 811057
Fax: (01834) 811023
Email: netherwood.school@
  virgin.net
Head: Mr D H Morris
Type: Co-educational Day and
Boarding 3–18
No of pupils: B76 G59
No of boarders: F24 W4
Fees: On application

POWYS

BRECON

CHRIST COLLEGE
Brecon, Powys LD3 8AG
Tel: (01874) 615440
Fax: (01874) 615475
Email: enquiries@
  christcollegebrecon.com
Head: Mr D P Jones
Type: Co-educational Boarding
and Day 11–18
No of pupils: B185 G115
No of boarders: F172 W55
Fees: (September 06)
F/WB £14508–£18534
Day £10629–£12105

SWANSEA

SWANSEA

CRAIG-Y-NOS SCHOOL
Clyne Common, Bishopston,
Swansea SA3 3JB
Tel: (01792) 234288
Fax: (01792) 233813
Email: craigynos.school@
    btinternet.com
Head: Mr G W Fursland
Type: Co-educational Day 2–11
No of pupils: B64 G52
Fees: (September 06)
Day £3225–£4215

FFYNONE HOUSE SCHOOL
36 St James' Crescent, Swansea
SA1 6DR
Tel: (01792) 464967
Fax: (01792) 455202
Head: Mrs Edwina Jones
Type: Co-educational Day 9–18
No of pupils: B120 G129
Fees: On application

FFYNONE HOUSE SCHOOL TRUST
Oakleigh House Junior School,
38 Penlan Crescent, Uplands,
Swansea SA2 0RL
Tel: (01792) 298537
Fax: (01792) 280371
Email: jnrsec@
    ffynonetrustschools.co.uk
Head: Mrs R Ferriman
Type: Co-educational Day 3–9
No of pupils: B58 G80
Fees: (September 06)
Day £3762–£4284

2.6
Overseas Schools

FRANCE

CHAVAGNES INTERNATIONAL COLLEGE*
96 rue du Calvaire, 85250 Chavagnes-en-Paillers, France
Tel: +33 (0)2 51 42 39 82
Fax: +33 (0)2 51 42 39 83
Email: info@chavagnes.org
Head: Mr F D McDermott and Dr T E Conlon
Type: Boys Boarding and Day 9–18
No of pupils: 30
No of boarders: F26 W1
Fees: FB €13400 WB €10000 Day €7500 (various bursaries are available)

MOUGINS SCHOOL*
615 Avenue Dr Maurice Donat, Font de l'Orme, BP 401, 06251 Mougins Cedex, France
Tel: +33 (0)493 90 15 47
Fax: +33 (0)493 75 31 40
Email: information@ mougins-school.com
Head: Mr B G Hickmore
Type: Co-educational Day 3–18
No of pupils: B262 G194
Fees: Day €4100–€11250

SPAIN

KING'S COLLEGE MADRID*
Paseo de los Andes, 35, 28761
Soto de Vinuelas, Madrid, Spain
Tel: (+34) 918 034 800
Fax: (+34) 918 036 557
Email: info@kingscollege.es
Head: Mr D Johnson
Type: Co-educational Boarding
and Day 2–18
No of pupils: B780 G730
No of boarders: F25
Fees: FB €15501–€16938 DAY
€5007–€9666

SWITZERLAND

AIGLON COLLEGE*
1885 Chesieres-Villars,
Switzerland
Tel: +41 (0) 24 496 6161
Fax: +41 (0) 24 469 6162
Email: admissions@aiglon.ch
Head: Dr J Long
Type: Co-educational Day and
Boarding 9–18
No of pupils: B185 G165
Fees: FB SFr48300–SFr67800 WB
SFr42600–SFr45900 Day
SFr23000–SFr47400

Part 3

School Profiles

COUNTIES OF ENGLAND, SCOTLAND AND WALES

SCOTLAND

Moray

Highland

Aberdeenshire

Aberdeen City

1. Inverclyde
2. North Ayrshire
3. Renfrewshire
4. West Dunbartonshire
5. East Dunbartonshire
6. North Lanarkshire

7. Falkirk
8. Clackmannanshire
9. West Lothian
10. City of Edinburgh
11. Midlothian
12. East Lothian

Perth and Kinross

Angus

Fife

Argyll and Bute

Stirling

8.

4.

1. 5. 6. 9. 7. 11. 12.

3. 2. 10.

East Ayrshire

South Lanarkshire

Borders

South Ayrshire

Dumfries and Galloway

NORTHERN ENGLAND

Northumberland

Newcastle upon Tyne

Hartlepool

Stockton-on-Tees

Middlesbrough

Cumbria

Durham

York

North Yorkshire

Isle of Man

East Riding of Yorkshire

North Lincolnshire

Lancashire

West Yorkshire

North East Lincolnshire

Merseyside

G.M.

South Yorkshire

EASTERN ENGLAND

Cheshire

Derbyshire

Nottinghamshire

Lincolnshire

Rutland

WALES

Denbighshire

Flintshire

Stafford-shire

Leicester-shire

Norfolk

Conwy

Wrexham

Cambridgeshire

1. Monmouthshire
2. Torfean
3. Newport
4. Blaenau Gwent
5. Caerphilly
6. Cardiff
7. Merthyr Tydfil
8. Cynon Taff
9. Vale of Glamorgan
10. Bridgend
11. Neath Port Talbot
12. Swansea

Gwynedd

Northamptonshire

Suffolk

Shropshire

W.M.

Ceredigion

Powys

Worcestershire

Warwickshire

Bedford-shire

Hereford-shire

Buckingham-shire

Essex

HOME COUNTIES (North)

Carmarthenshire

7. 4. 1.

Gloucester-shire

Oxford-shire

Hertford-shire

12. 11. 8. 2.

10. 6.

Pembrokeshire

9.

Berkshire

CENTRAL ENGLAND

Greater London

LONDON

13. South Gloucestershire
14. Bath and North East Somerset
15. City of Bristol
16. North Somerset

15. 13.

16. 14.

Wiltshire

Somerset

Hampshire

Surrey

Kent

Devon

Dorset

West Sussex

East Sussex

Isle of Wight

HOME COUNTIES (South)

Cornwall

SOUTH WEST ENGLAND

3.1 England

MAP OF NORTHERN ENGLAND

PROFILED SCHOOLS IN NORTHERN ENGLAND

(Incorporating the counties of Cheshire, Cumbria, Derbyshire, Durham, Hartlepool, Lancashire, North East Lincolnshire, North Lincolnshire, Greater Manchester, Merseyside, Middlesbrough, Northumberland, Nottinghamshire, Staffordshire, Stockton-on-Tees, East Riding of Yorkshire, North Yorkshire, South Yorkshire, West Yorkshire)

Map   **Page**
Number   **Number**

1   Chetwynde, Barrow-in-Furness, Cumbria.. 262
2   Lime House School, Dalston, Cumbria 262
3   St Bees School, St Bees, Cumbria 263
4   Windermere St Anne's, Windermere, Cumbria 264
5   Barlborough Hall School, Chesterfield, Derbyshire 265
6   Mount St Mary's College, Spinkhill, Derbyshire................................... 265
7   The Chorister School, Durham, County Durham.................................. 266
8   Bramcote Lorne School, Retford, Nottinghamshire.............................. 267
9   Queen Ethelburga's College, York, North Yorkshire............................ 268
10   Ackworth School, Pontefract, West Yorkshire 269

England

Chetwynde School

Croslands, Rating Lane, Barrow-in-Furness, Cumbria LA13 0NY
Tel: (01229) 824210   Fax: (01229) 871440
E-mail: info@chetwynde.cumbria.sch.uk
Website: www.chetwynde.cumbria.sch.uk   www.gabbitas.co.uk

Head of School Mrs I Nixon
Founded 1938
School status Co-educational Day 3–18.
Religious denomination Inter-Denominational
Fees per annum *(day)* £5400–£6330

Chetwynde School occupies an attractive site situated near the Lake District. It has grown into a substantial and successful school with an excellent academic and outstanding sporting reputation.

The school prides itself on high academic standards based on good teaching and individual attention. The GCSE pass rate has been at or above 97 per cent five Grades A–C for over three years and the A level pass rate stands at or above 99 per cent over the same period. All our Sixth Form pupils go on to higher education. The curriculum is broad and challenging, but there is also an emphasis on music, sport and outdoor pursuits including a vibrant Duke of Edinburgh Award Scheme.

Lime House School

Holm Hill, Dalston, Carlisle, Cumbria CA5 7BX   Tel: (01228) 710225   Fax: (01228) 710508
E-mail: lhsoffice@aol.com   Website: www.limehouseschool.co.uk

Headmaster Mr N A Rice MA BA CertEd
Bursar Mrs J Fisher   **Founded** 1809
School status Independent. Co-educational
Boarding and Day 4–18. Boarders from 9.
Religious denomination Non-Denominational
Learning difficulties SNU/DYS MLD
No of pupils 210; *(full boarding)* 140; *(weekly boarding)* 10; *Girls* 80; *Boys* 130
Average class size 20

Lime House School is a fully independent co-educational boarding and day school for pupils age 3½ to 18. Our aim is to ensure that each pupil achieves his or her potential both academically and socially, with each child treated individually. Our pupils are cared for in a safe rural environment and every possible attempt is made to ensure that they develop confidence and self-esteem.

Boarding is available to all pupils, with the majority being full boarders. Each pupil's pastoral care is the shared responsibility of a residential member of staff who lives in their boarding area, a residential school matron and the pupil's form teacher.

Foreign students whose first language is not English add to the cosmopolitan atmosphere of the school. They are prepared for Cambridge English examinations and follow the same curriculum as all other students.

Games and sport form an important part of school life. All students participate and a wide range of team and individual sports is offered. Most pupils take games to GCSE level, with many continuing to A level.

We would welcome a visit to our school to see it in action. Simply contact the school and we will arrange a time convenient for you.

St Bees School

St Bees, Cumbria CA27 0DS   Tel: (01946) 828010   Fax: (01946) 828011
E-mail: helen.miller@st-bees-school.co.uk   Website: www.st-bees-school.org
All enquiries should be sent to Mrs. Helen Miller or her secretary Mrs. Cath McMullen,

Head Mr P J Capes BSc MA
Director of Marketing & Admissions Mrs H C Miller   **Founded** 1583
School status Independent. Co-educational Boarding and Day 11–18 Flexi-boarding available. Boarders from 11. Founded in 1583 – an HMC school offering places for boys and girls aged 11–18
Religious denomination Church of England
Member of BSA, HMC; **Accredited by** HMC
Learning difficulties SNU/DYC DYP DYS
Behavioural and emotional disorders RA/ADD ADHD BESD
Physical & medical conditions RA SM/EPI HEA
No of pupils 302; *(full boarding)* 92; *(weekly boarding)* 32; *(day)* 178; *Senior* 183; *Sixth Form* 119; *Girls* 126; *Boys* 176; **Teacher:pupil ratio** 1:10; **Average class size** 20; **Fees per annum** *(full boarding)* £15297–£21093; *(weekly)* £12552–£17997; *(day)* £9789–£12642

Curriculum: Very broad during the first three years: drama, music, information technology and outdoor pursuits. 16 GCSE and 17 A level courses; over 95 per cent of leavers go on to higher education. Entrance: Own examinations; Common Entrance. Sixth Form entrance requires minimum of 5 GCSEs at grade C or higher. Scholarships: Academic and music at 11+, 13+ and at 16+. Art, Music and Sport into Sixth Form. Sport and extra-curricular: Outstanding sporting record and facilities.

England

Windermere St Anne's

Patterdale Road, Windermere, Cumbria LA23 1NW
Tel: (01539) 446164   Fax: (01539) 488414   E-mail: admissions@wsaschool.com
Website: www.wsaschool.com   www.gabbitas.co.uk

Head Mr A Graham
Founded 1863
School status Co-educational Boarding and Day 11–18 Flexi-boarding available. Boarders from 8.
Religious denomination Non-Denominational
Member of BSA, SHMIS
No of pupils 274; *(full boarding)* 83; *(weekly boarding)* 44; *(day)* 149; *Girls* 145; *Boys* 129
Teacher:pupil ratio 1:6
Average class size 15
Fees per annum *(full boarding)* £16005–£18000; *(weekly)* £15120–£17100; *(day)* £9000–£9966

Windermere St Anne's is an independent boarding and day school with facilities for over 300 senior school pupils. For over 130 years the school has created a strong reputation for the individual development of pupils, from the UK and overseas, based on academic, cultural and sporting achievement, supported by close pastoral care and an international perspective.

The philosophy of the school centres around development of the individual through a balanced, full rounded approach to education. The aim is to ensure that all pupils are able to fulfil their potential. Targets are set not for the school but for each pupil and success is judged by personal achievement. This allows pupils to progress academically and develop their self-confidence and self-awareness at the same time.

A nurturing environment exists, with extremely supportive staff. This helps create a lively, caring, family atmosphere and mutual trust and respect within the school. Among the pupils, the ethos produces independence, individual responsibility, and a sense of adventure towards discovery and learning.

Windermere St Anne's has probably one of the most enviable locations for a school. In the heart of the Lake District, with views over Windermere to the fells beyond, the school is set in 80 acres of wooded parkland, with landscaped gardens and has a private lakeshore watersports centre.

The school policy is to provide equal opportunities for all pupils and each year group is divided into forms with sets in the main subjects. Class sizes are currently around 15 pupils. The curriculum comprises English, business studies, history, geography, French, mathematics, physics, chemistry, biology, music, art, drama, dance, home economics, information technology, design and technology, religious studies and physical education and games. Spanish and German are taken in Year 8. A number of scholarships are available to boys and girls for entry into all years for academic and creative disciplines.

The co-educational Junior Department, Elleray, has close links with the senior school. The children study a full range of subjects and enjoy a full activity programme after school.

Barlborough Hall School

Barlborough, Chesterfield, Derbyshire S43 4TJ   Tel: (01246) 810511   Fax: (01246) 570605
E-mail: barlborough.hall@virgin.net Website: www.barlboroughhall.co.uk www.msmcollege.com

Headteacher Mrs W E Parkinson B Ed
Founded 1939
School status Co-educational Day 3–11.
Religious denomination Roman Catholic
Member of HMC, ISCis
Accredited by HMC, ISC
Learning difficulties CA WI/DYP DYS
Physical and medical conditions RA
No of pupils 251; *(day)* 251; *Nursery* 21;
Pre-prep 92; *Prep* 138; *Girls* 127; *Boys* 124
Teacher:pupil ratio 1:16; **Average class size** 15
Fees per annum *(day)* £4800–£6930

Barlborough Hall School, preparatory school to Mount St Mary's College, is seen as one of the premier independent Catholic schools in the South Yorkshire/Derbyshire area welcoming pupils of all denominations.

Set in 300 acres of beautiful surroundings, small classes, well motivated teachers and exceptional specialist facilities, including a Technology Centre,

Science Laboratory, Art Studio, IT Suite, Theatre and indoor heated pool ensure that our pupils receive the very best educational opportunities.

The school has an excellent nursery provision (from 3yrs) in a secure and safe environment with facilities second to none.

A regular minibus service and an 'out of school club', with a full range of activities and run by qualified staff until 6.00 p.m., ensure the flexibility and peace of mind required by many working parents.

Mount St Mary's College

Spinkhill, Derbyshire S21 3YL   Tel: (01246) 433388   Fax: (01246) 435511
E-mail: headmaster@msmcollege.com   Website: www.msmcollege.com   www.gabbitas.co.uk

Head Master Mr P G MacDonald
Founded 1842
College status Independent. Co-educational Boarding and Day 11–18 Flexi-boarding available. Boarders from 11.
Religious denomination Roman Catholic
Member of HMC, ISCis
Accredited by HMC, ISC
Learning difficulties CA SC SNU/DYC DYP DYS
No of pupils 401; *(full boarding)* 62; *(weekly boarding)* 14; *(day)* 325; *Sixth Form* 101;
Girls 144; *Boys* 257
Teacher:pupil ratio 1:9; **Average class size** 18
Fees per annum *(full boarding)* £12570–£16605; *(weekly)* £10665–£14355; *(day)* £7815–£9075. Private Music lessons £26 per hour EAL lessons £1200pa £400 per term

Mount St Mary's College is a co-educational Catholic school welcoming children of all

denominations, situated in beautiful surroundings close to the M1 junction 30, with minibus service to local areas. The school offers:
* Exceptional provision for teaching and academic success
* Superb Boarding accommodation with en-suite facilities
* A unique learning experience, which provides extensive extra-curricular opportunities
* Scholarships, bursaries and Mount assisted places scheme available.

Entry: 11+ via entrance examination (February). 13+ via Common Entrance or interview. 16+ by interview and GCSE results.

England

The Chorister School

The College, Durham, County Durham DH1 3EL   Tel: (0191) 384 2935   Fax: (0191) 383 1275
E-mail: head@choristers.durham.sch.uk   Website: www.choristers.durham.sch.uk

Head Master Mr I Hawksby B A
Founded 1390
School status Independent. Co-educational
Day and Boarding 4–13 Flexi-boarding
available. Boarders from 8.
Religious denomination Church of England
Member of HMC, IAPS
Learning difficulties CA WI/DYP DYS
Behavioural and emotional disorders CA/ADD
ADHD ASP
Physical and medical conditions DS RA
WA3/EPI HEA HI
No of pupils 177; *(full boarding)* 27; *(weekly
boarding)* 3; *(day)* 140; *Pre-prep* 54; *Prep* 123;
Girls 57; *Boys* 121
Teacher:pupil ratio 1:7; **Average class size** 12
Fees per annum *(full boarding)* £6783–£12915;
(weekly) £6783–£12915; *(day)* £6060–£8340

years in the glorious surroundings of Durham
Cathedral. Our staff are of the highest calibre,
and will get to know your child as an individual,
sharing a rich and exciting curriculum in small
classes where your child will always have
personal attention.

We offer before and after-school care, after-
school clubs, full-time or flexible boarding, and
many children win scholarships to senior school
of choice.

Entry is at any time and in any year with space.
Voice Trials for the Cathedral Choir are held for
boys twice a year, and Music Scholarships may be
offered to children of at least Grade 4 standard.

Give your child the best start in life by choosing
The Chorister School spending their formative

Bramcote Lorne School

Gamston, Retford, Nottinghamshire DN22 0QQ   Tel: (01777) 838636   Fax: (01777) 838633
E-mail: enquiries.bramcotelorne@church-schools.com Website: www.bramcotelorneschool.co.uk

Headmaster Mr R M Raistrick BA (Hons) PGCE
School status Independent. Co-educational
Boarding and Day 3–13 Flexi-boarding
available.
Religious denomination Church of England
Member of IAPS, NAHT; **Accredited by** IAPS
Learning difficulties SNU/DYP DYS
Behavioural and emotional disorders CO/
ADHD ASP
Physical and medical conditions CA SM/HEA
HI IM VI
No of pupils 220; *(full boarding)* 24; *(weekly
boarding)* 8; *Girls* 106; *Boys* 114
Fees per annum *(full boarding)* £1237; *(weekly)*
£959; *(day)* £1736–£2882

Bramcote Lorne has a tradition of high standards
which challenge young people not just academically but in all areas of their development within a
spiritual framework. This ensures that every child

has the opportunity to discover talents that they
may not have realised they possessed and create
friendships and relationships which will enable
them to grow with confidence.

The school is part of United Church Schools
Trust, an organization that is renowned for its high
quality schools where every child is seen to be
important and where each child's achievements
are celebrated as a success. Our key objective is
to bring out the best in every child in an atmosphere in which they feel safe and valued, where
they are happy and challenged.

Within the setting of a small country estate on
the fringe of one of Nottinghamshire's finest
villages we enjoy excellent communications
along the A1 and the rail link to London making
the school very accessible for boarder parents.
The school operates bus routes from villages
within Nottinghamshire, Lincolnshire and South
Yorkshire.

England

Queen Ethelburga's College

Thorpe Underwood Hall, Ouseburn, York, North Yorkshire YO26 9SS
Tel: (0870) 742 3300   Fax: (0870) 742 3310   E-mail: remember@compuserve.com
Website: www.queenethelburgas.edu   www.gabbitas.co.uk

Headmaster Mr S Jandrell BA
Provost Mr Brian Martin   **Founded** 1912
College status Co-educational Boarding and
Day 2–20. Boarders from 6.
Religious denomination Church of England
Member of BHS, BSA, ISCis
Accredited by British Council, ISA, ISC
Learning difficulties RA/DYS
No of pupils 548; *(full boarding)* 358; *(weekly
boarding)* 30; *(day)* 160; *Nursery* 19; *Pre-prep*
11; *Prep* 94; *Senior* 251; *Sixth Form* 170;
Girls 324; *Boys* 224
Teacher:pupil ratio 1:10; **Average class size** 20
Fees per annum *(full boarding)* £16605–
£26895; *(weekly)* £16605–£26895; *(day)*
£3135–£8235

Broad-based curriculum following National Curriculum in key subject areas. Entry to Preparatory School by assessment and interview. Students move through to Senior School. External entry to Senior School is by test and interview. Senior students are prepared for GCSE, A levels and advanced vocational courses including Fashion and Design, Photography and Business, as well as BTEC National Diploma in Horse Studies and BHSAI for riders. Recent heavy investment has been made in living accommodation, the equestrian centre, business and computing suite, cookery area, purpose-built laboratories and lecture theatre. There is a large programme of sport and extra activities. Scholarships for academic excellence and riding competence are available.

Ackworth School

Ackworth, Pontefract, West Yorkshire WF7 7LT   Tel: (01977) 611401   Fax: (01977) 616225
E-mail: admissions@ackworthschool.com Website: www.ackworthschool.com www.gabbitas.co.uk

The Headmaster Mr P Simpson
Founded 1779
School status Co-educational Boarding and
Day 4–18.
Religious denomination Quaker
Accredited by HMC, SHMIS
No of pupils 561; *(full boarding)* 83
Girls 271; *Boys* 290
Fees per annum *(full boarding)* £15498; *(day)*
£9354

Ackworth is a boarding and day school for boys and girls aged 4 to 18. Boarding starts at 11 and boarders have well-presented accommodation in rooms for two or three. A major refurbishment of boarding accommodation has recently been completed. Ackworth has superb teaching facilities (the refurbished theatre is the latest addition), and a stable, devoted staff, who have established a tradition of excellence in academic results. Each year more than 95 per cent of Sixth Form leavers go to university. Music, drama and sporting facilities are outstanding leading to first rate sporting achievement and a fine musical and theatrical tradition. The School is friendly and welcoming.

Entry is by academic test. Academic, music and art scholarships are available.

England

MAP OF EASTERN ENGLAND

PROFILED SCHOOLS IN EASTERN ENGLAND

(Incorporating the counties of Cambridgeshire, Leicestershire, Lincolnshire, Norfolk, Northamptonshire, Suffolk)

Map Number		Page Number
1	Cambridge Arts & Sciences (CATS), Cambridge, Cambridgeshire	272
2	Cambridge Centre for Sixth Form Studies, Cambridge, Cambridgeshire	272
3	The King's School, Ely, Cambridgeshire	273
4	The Leys School, Cambridge, Cambridgeshire	273
5	St Mary's School, Cambridge, Cambridgeshire	274
6	Brooke House College, Market Harborough, Leicestershire	275
7	Oakham School, Rutland, Leicestershire	276
8	Langley School, Norwich, Norfolk	277
9	Laxton Junior School, Oundle, Northamptonshire	278
10	Framlingham College, Woodbridge, Suffolk	279
11	The Royal Hospital School, Ipswich, Suffolk	279

England

Cambridge Arts & Sciences (CATS)

Round Church Street, Cambridge, Cambridgeshire CB5 8AD
Tel: (01223) 314431   Fax: (01223) 467773   E-mail: enquiries@catscollege.com
Website: www.ceg-uk.com   www.gabbitas.co.uk

Cambridge Arts & Sciences

Director & Founder Mrs E Armstrong BA
(Hons) Dip Psych MSc
Director of Studies Mr A Sweatman BSc Pure
Mathematics
Registrar Mrs J Mullan   **Founded** 1985
School status Co-educational Boarding and
Day Boys 14–23 Girls 14–24. Boarders from 14.
Member of ISA
Accredited by BAC, British Council, ISA
Learning difficulties CA SC SNU/DYC DYP
DYS MLD
Behavioural and emotional disorders CA CO
TS/ADD ADHD ASP BESD
Physical and medical conditions AT RA/EPI
HEA HI
No of pupils 270; *(full boarding)* 254; *(day)* 16;
Girls 152; *Boys* 118
Teacher:pupil ratio 1:3; **Average class size** 3–8
Fees per annum *(full boarding)* £18315–
£25935; *(day)* £13545–£19035

Cambridge Arts & Sciences (CATS) is an independent co-educational sixth-form college located in the centre of Cambridge. CATS offer GCSE, A-level and Oxbridge University entrance examinations.

With only 270 students, tuition groups range from 3–8 ensuring classes remain intensive, dynamic and stimulating. The curriculum covers a wide range of 49 subjects and is taught within a flexible framework that can accommodate any first choice of subjects offered and which results in many students gaining places at major universities.

Cambridge Centre for Sixth-form Studies

1 Salisbury Villas, Station Road, Cambridge, Cambridgeshire CB1 2JF
Tel: (01223) 716890   Fax: (01223) 517530   E-mail: enquiries@ccss.co.uk
Website: www.ccss.co.uk   www.ccss.uk.tt (student website)
Tamsin Gray is our Admissions Coordinator

The Principal Mr Neil Roskilly BA, PGCE,
FRGS
Founded 1981
School status Independent Sixth Form College.
Co-educational Day and Boarding 15–19 Flexi-
boarding available. Boarders from 15.
Religious denomination Non-Denominational
Member of CIFE, ISA, ISCis
Accredited by ISA, ISC Registered charity.
Member of the European Council of
International Schools (ECIS)
Learning difficulties WI/DYP DYS
Behavioural and emotional disorders CO/ADD
ASP; **Physical and medical conditions** RA
No of pupils 181; *(full boarding)* 113; *(day)* 68;
Sixth Form 181; *Girls* 75; *Boys* 106
Teacher:pupil ratio 1:3; **Average class size** 4–5
Fees per annum *(full boarding)* £17460–
£22902; *(day)* £8946–£14388

We take approximately 180 students. As the College is small it is easy for new students to settle in and make friends. Two-thirds of them are boarders and the rest come from Cambridge and the surrounding area. Just over half of our students live outside the UK, from over 25 different countries.

There is a wide range of subjects to choose from, and we help students decide on the right subjects for university entrance. Although most of our students take A levels over two years, we accept some for intensive one-year courses if they have the right academic background.

The King's School Ely

Ely, Cambridgeshire CB7 4DB   Tel: (01353) 660702   Fax: (01353) 667485
E-mail: admissions@kings-ely.cambs.sch.uk   Website: www.kings-ely.cambs.sch.uk www.gabbitas.co.uk

Head Mrs S E Freestone GRSM, MEd, LRAM, ARCM
Founded 970
School status Independent. Co-educational Boarding and Day 2–18 Flexi-boarding available. Boarders from 8.
Religious denomination Church of England, Inter-Denominational
Member of HMC, IAPS, ISCis, SHMIS
Accredited by HMC, IAPS, ISC, SHMIS
Learning difficulties WI/DYS
No of pupils 903; *(full boarding)* 194; *(day)* 709; *Nursery* 51; *Pre-prep* 98; *Prep* 342; *Senior* 412; *Sixth Form* 141; *Girls* 385; *Boys* 518
Teacher:pupil ratio 1:9
Average class size 20
Fees per annum *(boarding)* £14895–£20385; *(day)* £6135–£14085

The King's School, Ely is a friendly, well-balanced and caring community known for getting the best from a broad range of abilities. Founded over 1,000 years ago, it occupies an exceptional setting beside Ely Cathedral whose boy choristers aged 8–12 are Junior School boarders. A new cathedral choir for girls aged 13–18 was established by the school in September 2006. The equivalent of a whole working-day week is devoted to sports, creative and performing arts and a unique outdoor pursuits programme: the Ely Scheme. Team sports and a range of alternatives, including golf, are offered. There is a strong rowing tradition. Everyone is encouraged to take up a musical instrument. New developments include a technology centre, library, art school, all-weather pitch, specialist Music School and Recital Hall. Junior School pupils in Years 7 and 8 enjoy newly-built acommodation including seven new classrooms, IT suite and a science laboratory. Boarding is increasingly popular and facilities are being upgraded throughout the school.

The Leys School

Trumpington Road, Cambridge, Cambridgeshire CB2 2AD   Tel: (01223) 508900
Fax: (01223) 505303   E-mail: office@theleys.net   Website: www.theleys.net

Headmaster Mr Mark Slater M.A.
School status Co-educational Boarding and Day 11–18.
Religious denomination Inter-Denominational, Methodist
Learning difficulties WI/DYS
Behavioural and emotional disorders RA/ADD ADHD
Physical and medical conditions RA/HI
No of pupils 526; *(full boarding)* 280; *Girls* 202; *Boys* 324
Fees per annum *(full boarding)* £15870–£22020; *(day)* £10050–£14100

The Leys is an Independent boarding and day school situated in the world famous university City of Cambridge. There is an academic, but caring atmosphere. Pupils are encouraged to achieve their potential. There are strong Science, Language and Mathematics departments.

Technology subjects are well-resourced. Arts subjects including Drama are popular choices up to A level. New subjects in Sixth Form include PE and Psychology. Links with the University and local industry. Modern sports complex including astro with over 20 sports offered including rugby, cricket, rowing and water polo. Scholarships available in Art, Music, Drama, Technology and Sport.

England

St Mary's School

Bateman Street, Cambridge, Cambridgeshire CB2 1LY   Tel: (01223) 353253   Fax: (01223) 357451
E-mail: enquiries@stmaryscambridge.co.uk   Website: www.stmaryscambridge.co.uk
www.gabbitas.co.uk   St Mary's Junior School   Tel: 01223 311666   Fax: 01223 472168

Headmistress (Senior School) Mrs J Triffitt MA
Founded 1898
School status Independent. Girls Day and Boarding 4–18. Boarders from 11.
Religious denomination Roman Catholic
Member of GSA; **Accredited by** GSA
Learning difficulties RA WI/DYP DYS MLD
Behavioural and emotional disorders RA/ADHD ASP
Physical and medical conditions AT CA IT SM TW WA2/EPI HEA HI IM VI; *(full boarding)* 65; *(weekly boarding)* 3; *(day)* 566
Average class size 20 in Senior School, fewer in Sixth Form
Fees per annum *(full boarding)* £20970; *(weekly)* £18585; *(day)* £10560
The above are fees for Senior School.

St Mary's is a purposeful and happy school. Founded in 1898, we provide an all-round education in a welcoming Christian community that encourages all girls to reach their full potential. We are situated in the centre of the beautiful university city of Cambridge, close to the railway station, 50 miles from London and within easy reach of four major airports. Both St Mary's Senior and Junior Schools offer an excellent academic education and a strong tradition of superlative pastoral care. In the Senior School, there is a lively programme of extra-curricular activities: rowing, yoga and a thriving Duke of Edinburgh's Award Scheme.

Brooke House College

Leicester Road, Market Harborough, Leicestershire LE16 7AU
Tel: (01858) 462452   Fax: (01858) 462487   E-mail: enquiries@brookehouse.com
Website: www.brookehouse.com   www.gabbitas.co.uk

Director Mr G E I Williams M.A.(Oxon)
Director Mr D J Williams B.A. P.G.C.E.
Founded 1967
College status Independent. Co-educational
Boarding and Day 14–19. Boarders from 14.
Religious denomination Non-Denominational
Member of CIFE; **Accredited by** BAC
Learning difficulties CA SC WI/DYC DYS
Behavioural and emotional disorders CO
Physical and medical conditions RA
No of pupils 180; *(full boarding)* 175; *(day)* 5;
Senior 30; *Sixth Form* 150; *Girls* 80; *Boys* 100
Teacher:pupil ratio 1:5; **Average class size** 8
Fees per annum *(full boarding)* £17550; *(day)*
£10200

Brooke House is a fully residential, international
college. Intensive, small-group tuition is provided
by GCSE, A level and pre-university foundation
courses. The college possesses excellent
academic facilities including science laboratories, an art and design studio and two recently
developed computer rooms. A comprehensive
programme of extra-curricular activities is organized for students' free time. Personal tutors cater
for every student's pastoral needs. The college's
full-time Universities Admissions Adviser gives
advice and guidance. Brooke House has an enviable tradition of assisting international and UK
students to gain places at the most prestigious of
universities in the UK and the USA.

England

Oakham School

Chapel Close, Oakham, Rutland LE15 6DT   Tel: (01572) 758758   Fax: (01572) 758595
E-mail: admissions@oakham.rutland.sch.uk Website: www.oakham.rutland.sch.uk ww.gabbitas.co.uk

Headmaster Dr J A F Spence BA PhD
Founded 1584
School status Independent. Co-educational
Boarding and Day 10–18. Boarders from 10.
Religious denomination Church of England
Member of BSA, HMC, ISCis
Accredited by HMC, ISC
Learning difficulties SNU/DYC DYP DYS
Behavioural and emotional disorders CO/ADD
ADHD ASP
No of pupils 1040; *(full boarding)* 620; *(day)*
469; *Prep* 351; *Senior* 724; *Sixth Form* 174;
Girls 520; *Boys* 520

Average class size 15

Fees per annum *(full boarding)* £19260–
£22500; *(weekly)* £15660–£18090; *(day)*
£12210–£13440

Founded in 1584, Oakham is a fully co-educational boarding and day school. A pioneer of full co-education over 30 years ago and one of the first schools to offer the International Baccalaureate as an alternative to AS/A2. Oakham is committed to innovation and opportunity in an atmosphere that inspires enthusiasm, self-confidence and intellectual curiosity. There are 16 houses and each pupil belongs to a small tutor group so that his or her progress can be carefully monitored, thereby ensuring that each child receives expert tuition, care and guidance.

High academic standards are achieved. In 2006, we were delighted to see by far the majority of Oakhamians fulfilling their potential at GCSE, IB or A level. New highs were achieved at GCSE with an A*/A rate of over 60% and an A*– C rate of almost 99%. At A level, an A/B rate of 77% and a pass rate of 100% again surpassed previous records. All IB students secured their diplomas, with an average points total of 36 points, and 14 students (25% of the cohort) scored more than 40 points, with 2 of them gaining maximum scores of 45. Only 5% of students worldwide achieve this!

Oakham has an excellent reputation for the quality of its musical and dramatic activities. The Art, Design & Technology Department includes as part of its staff an 'artist in residence'. Musicians and actors have performed in the United States,

Germany and most recently in South Africa. Participation in the Edinburgh Fringe Festival is an annual event. Social and cultural visits to Russia, Peru, North Africa, New Guinea, Israel and the Arctic Circle have also taken place.

Games teams compete successfully in local and national competitions. The principal games are rugby football, association football, cricket, hockey, tennis, athletics, lacrosse, swimming, shooting, squash and netball, and teams have toured Japan, Canada, the United States, Australia, New Zealand and France.

Facilities include one of the best school libraries in the country, new language and recently extended science laboratories, an information and communication technology centre, art and design centre, theatre and music school.

Normal points of entry to Oakham are at 10+, 11+, 13+, 16+ years although a few places may be available at 14+. Entrance and scholarship examinations to the Sixth Form are held in November and Junior entry exams and scholarships in January and February. Common Entrance is in June and the Oakham School entry examination for 13-year-olds is held in March. Students entering the Sixth Form will normally be offered a conditional place, pending GCSE results. A full programme of the International Baccalaureate is available as an alternative to AS/A2.

Oakham is well served by the national rail network, and motorway and trunk-road system. Co-education and the School's proximity to both London and Midland airports (there are direct rail links to both Stansted and Birmingham) make Oakham particularly well suited to families living abroad.

Langley School

Langley Park, Loddon, Norwich, Norfolk NR14 6BJ   Tel: (01508) 520210   Fax: (01508) 528058
E-mail: administration@langleyschool.co.uk Website: www.langleyschool.co.uk   www.gabbitas.co.uk

Headmaster Mr J G Malcolm BSc MA Cert Ed
Bursar Mr P J Weeks BEd(Hons) Cert Ed Cert SpLD
Founded 1910
School status Co-educational Boarding and Day 10–18. Boarders from 10.
Religious denomination Non-Denominational
Member of AGBIS, IAPS, ISBA, ISCis, SHA, SHMIS; **Accredited by** IAPS, SHMIS
Learning difficulties SNU/DYC DYP DYS
Behavioural and emotional disorders RA/ADD
Physical and medical conditions BL CA IT SM TW WA1/CP HEA IM VI W
No of pupils 475; *(full boarding)* 105; *(weekly boarding)* 30; *Nursery* 50; *Prep* 80; *Senior* 475; *Sixth Form* 130; *Girls* 180; *Boys* 295
Teacher:pupil ratio 1:8; **Average class size** 15
Fees per annum *(full boarding)* £14700–£17700; *(weekly)* £12960–£14700; *(day)* £6705–£8700

Curriculum: An experienced graduate staff employ formal teaching methods emphasising good manners, high standards of academic work and encouraging students to partake in as wide a range of experience. Currently offered are 28 GCSE, A2 and AS level subjects. Entry to the Sixth Form is selective and the majority of students take four or five subjects to AS level in L6 and three to A2 in U6. Students with specific learning difficulties or whose first language is not English can receive additional help from specialist staff.

Admission and Scholarships: At 10, 11, 12 and 13 it is normal for a student to be offered a place based on interview and satisfactory reports from their previous school or through the Common Entrance examination. At Sixth Form candidates must have completed a satisfactory GCSE course. Competitive Entrance Scholarships are offered in music, drama, art, sport, technology and for academic ability. Details can be obtained from the school.

England

Laxton Junior School

East Road, Oundle, Nr Peterborough, Northamptonshire PE8 4BX
Tel: (01832) 277275   Fax: (01832) 277271
E-mail: admissions@laxtonjunior.org.uk   Website: www.laxtonjunior.org.uk   www.gabbitas.co.uk

Headmistress Miss S C Thomas
Founded 1973
School status Independent. Co-educational
Day 4–11. .
Religious denomination Church of England
Member of IAPS, ISCis; **Accredited by** IAPS
Learning difficulties SNU/DYS
Physical and medical conditions TW WA1
No of pupils 230; *(day)* 223; *Pre-prep* 95; *Prep*
135; *Girls* 109; *Boys* 121
Average class size Max 20
Fees per annum *(day)* £7365–£8085. Lunch
included

Founded in 1973, Laxton Junior School is a co-educational day school (4–11 years), which is housed in new premises, located in the picturesque market town of Oundle, Northamptonshire. The school offers a broad and well-balanced curriculum where children are encouraged to fulfil their potential in a happy and secure environment, supported by a dedicated team of professionals.

Through the academic curriculum and caring pastoral system, the school aims to lay solid foundations in the development of well-motivated, confident and happy individuals who are always willing to give of their best on the road to high achievement.

Framlingham College

Framlingham, Woodbridge, Suffolk IP13 9EY   Tel: (01728) 723789   Fax: (01728) 724546
E-mail: admissions@framcollege.co.uk   Website: www.framlingham.suffolk.sch.uk

The Headteacher Mrs G M Randall
College status Independent. Co-educational
Boarding and Day 2–18 Flexi-boarding
available.
Religious denomination Church of England
Member of HMC, IAPS, SHMIS
Accredited by HMC
Learning difficulties SC SNU/DYC DYP DYS
Behavioural and emotional disorders ADD
ASP
Physical and medical conditions TW WA1
WA2
No of pupils 694; *(full boarding)* 299
Girls 287; *Boys* 407
Fees per annum *(full boarding)* £15429–
£19572; *(day)* £5517–£9594

magnificent rural situation, looking across to the
twelfth Century Framlingham Castle, and is within
easy striking distance of Ipswich, Cambridge,
Colchester and Norwich. The College grounds
and facilities are extensive with a state of the art
specialist Theatre and Music facility which was
opened in November 2006. The exceptional facilities create a lively academic, cultural and social
environment in which pupils are encouraged to
be industrious and ambitious and where all can
take full advantage of the rich mix of extra curricular activities on offer. At Framlingham we
believe that the academic potential of each individual is unlocked in an environment where
opportunities abound and in which a firm sense
of community prevails.

Framlingham College is a centre of all-round
excellence, providing fully co-educational boarding and day schooling from 2½–18. It enjoys a

The Royal Hospital School

Holbrook, Ipswich, Suffolk IP9 2RX   Tel: (01473) 326200   Fax: (01473) 326213
E-mail: admissions@royalhospitalschool.org   Website: www.royalhospitalschool.org
Admissions Officer-Sue Toner 01473 326210

Headmaster Mr H W Blackett MA (Oxon)
Deputy Headmaster Mr I S Wilmshurst MA
Chaplain Rev Dr CE Stewart BSc BD MTh
Founded 1715   **School status** Independent.
Co-educational Boarding and Day (11–18
years).   **Religious denomination** Christian
Member of ISCis; **Accredited by** HMC, ISC,
SHMIS The Crown Charity of Greenwich
Hospital owns and funds the school.
Bursaries and reserved entrance awards F1 F2
F3 F4 H
No of pupils 617; *(day)* 15; *Girls* 257; *Boys* 360
Teacher:pupil ratio 1:5; **Average class size** 15
Fees per annum *(full boarding)* £17754; *(day)*
£9450. Seafarer bursaries academic, sport,
music, sailing and art scholarships and special
forces rates are available

development programme including the refurbishment of all 10 boarding houses and a new music
school. Academic: 2006 GCSE pass rate 94% and
A Level 99.3% with 63% achieving A/B grades.
Extra Curriculum: including sailing at a competitive level, leisure team and individual sports,
choir, band and orchestra, music, outdoor pursuits, Combined Cadet Force, Community Action
projects, radio broadcasting, drama and dance
productions.

In September 2006 the school opened its doors to
day pupils coinciding with a multimillion pound

England

MAP OF CENTRAL ENGLAND

PROFILED SCHOOLS IN CENTRAL ENGLAND

(Incorporating the counties of Gloucestershire, Herefordshire, Oxfordshire, West Midlands, Shropshire, Warwickshire, Worcestershire)

Map Number		Page Number
1	Dean Close Preparatory School, Cheltenham, Gloucestershire	282
2	Dean Close School, Cheltenham, Gloucestershire	282
3	Rendcomb College, Cirencester, Gloucestershire	283
4	Querns Westonbirt School, Tetbury, Gloucestershire	284
5	Westonbirt School, Tetbury, Gloucestershire	284
6	Wycliffe College, Stonehouse, Gloucestershire	285
7	Wycliffe Preparatory School, Stonehouse, Gloucestershire	285
8	Cokethorpe, Witney, Oxfordshire	286
9	d'Overbroeck's College, Oxford, Oxfordshire	286
10	Kingham Hill School, Chipping Norton, Oxfordshire	287
11	The Manor Preparatory School, Abingdon, Oxfordshire	287
12	St Clare's Oxford, Oxfordshire	288
13	Moreton Hall, Oswestry, Shropshire	289
14	Arnold Lodge School, Leamington Spa, Warwickshire	290
15	Bromsgrove School, Bromsgrove, Worcestershire	290
16	Malvern College, Malvern, Worcestershire	291
17	Malvern St James, Great Malvern, Worcestershire	291
18	Moffats School, Bewdley, Worcestershire	292

England

Dean Close Preparatory School

Lansdown Road, Cheltenham, Gloucestershire GL51 6QS Tel: (01242) 512217 Fax: (01242) 258005
E-mail: dcpsoffice@deanclose.org.uk Website: www.deancloseprep.co.uk/prep www.gabbitas.co.uk

Headmaster Rev L Browne   **Founded** 1886
School status Co-educational Boarding and
Day 2–13 Flexi-boarding available. Boarders
from 7.
Religious denomination Church of England
Member of IAPS; **Accredited by** IAPS
Learning difficulties SNU/DYC DYP DYS MLD
Behavioural & emotional disorders CA/ADHD
No of pupils 369; *(full boarding)* 60; *Girls* 174;
Boys 195
Teacher:pupil ratio 1:8; **Average class size** 15
Fees per annum *(full boarding)* £13185–
£16650; *(weekly)* £9090–£12825; *(day)*
£7905–£11640

Abbey Schola Cantorum of Dean Close Prep School are available for boys aged 7–11. Academic and music scholarships and exhibitions, and sports awards are offered at 11+.

There are three boarding houses run by house parents. The number of day boarders in each house is limited to ensure a large full-time boarding community. There are also three day houses offering pastoral care of the highest order. The modern classrooms include two science laboratories, a Computer Centre and an Art and Technology Department. Other facilities include a swimming pool, climbing wall, shooting range and theatre in the Senior School. A new sports complex with extensive hall, dance studio and gym has just been opened.

Dean Close Preparatory School is a Christian family school committed to the development of the individual child in all aspects of education.

The school follows the Common Entrance base but firmly embraces the National Curriculum.

Chorister scholarships to join the Tewkesbury

Dean Close School

Shelburne Road, Cheltenham, Gloucestershire GL51 6HE
Tel: (01242) 258044   Fax: (01242) 258003   E-mail: registrar@deanclose.org.uk
Website: www.deanclose.org.uk   www.gabbitas.co.uk

Headmaster Rev T M Hastie-Smith MA Cert
Theol   **Founded** 1886
School status Independent. Co-educational
Boarding and Day 13–18. Boarders from 8.
Co-educational Independent boarding and day
Religious denomination Christian
Member of HMC; **Accredited by** HMC HMC
Learning difficulties WI/DYC DYP DYS
Behavioural and emotional disorders RA/ADD
ADHD ASP
Physical and medical conditions RA SM
No of pupils 480; *(full boarding)* 274; *(day)*
206; *Pre-prep* 112; *Prep* 300; *Senior* 261; *Sixth
Form* 220; *Girls* 207; *Boys* 273
Teacher:pupil ratio 1:9
Fees per annum *(full boarding)* £23580; *(day)*
£16665

girls and boys. The School aims to broaden the opportunities of each and every pupil through an exceptional array of facilities and coaching in sport, music, theatre and art, and offers a huge number of extra-curricular clubs and societies. Facilities include a brand new £3m sports hall, a 25-metre indoor pool, two AstroTurf pitches, an impressive 550-seat theatre, a purpose-built arts centre and a music school. A level results in 2006 generated over 74 per cent of passes at grade A or B, and at GCSE 55 per cent achieved A* or A.

Dean Close is truly co-educational, with over 30 years' experience and almost equal numbers of

Rendcomb College

Rendcomb, Cirencester, Gloucestershire GL7 7HA   Tel: (01285) 831213   Fax: (01285) 831121
E-mail: info@rendcomb.gloucs.sch.uk   Website: www.rendcombcollege.co.uk

Headmaster Mr Gerry Holden MA St Andrews PGCE FRSA
Deputy Headmaster Mr Bobby Morgan BA Hons Oxon
College status Co-educational Boarding and Day 3–18 Flexi-boarding available.
Religious denomination Church of England
Member of HMC, ISCis, SHMIS
Accredited by HMC, SHMIS
Learning difficulties WI/DYS
No of pupils 378; *(full boarding)* 148; *Girls* 183; *Boys* 195
Fees per annum *(full boarding)* £15045–£19500; *(weekly)* £15045–£19500; *(day)* £4800–£14945. Extras: School trips, fees for external exams, ind. music lessons, some activities

Set in over 200 acres of beautiful Cotswold countryside, Rendcomb College & Junior School combines the friendliness of a small school with a long tradition of outstanding academic achievement. Committed to nurturing the individual; small class sizes and a regular academic grading system ensure that every pupil achieves their full potential. Boarding accommodation is superb and every pupil from the fourth form upwards has a single, spacious study bedroom. Nearly every sixth form pupil goes to university, including Oxbridge. Rendcomb has excellent facitlies for sport drama, music, art and ICT and the extensive choice of extra-curricular activities, from riding to shooting, cookery to expedition training, develops pupils' self confidence and motivation. Rendcomb is conveniently situated for the M4 & M5 and most major airports.

England

Querns Westonbirt School

Tetbury, Gloucestershire GL8 8QG   Tel: (01666) 881390   Fax: (01666) 881391
E-mail: querns@westonbirt.gloucs.sch.uk   Website: www.querns.gloucs.sch.uk

Headmistress Miss V James BA (Hons), PGCE
School status Co-educational Day 4–11.
Religious denomination Church of England
Learning difficulties WI/DYS
Physical and medical conditions CA/CP
No of pupils 80; *(day)* 80; *Pre-prep* 29; *Prep* 51;
Girls 45; *Boys* 35
Teacher:pupil ratio 1:8; **Average class size** 10
Fees per annum *(day)* £5325–£7575

Querns Westonbirt School is a thriving co-educational day school in an idyllic Cotswold setting, where it shares a historic 250 acre private estate and extensive resources with Westonbirt School.

We offer a friendly, nurturing environment, a happy family atmosphere and small class sizes. Our staff are highly qualified, committed, kind and caring. Our pupils enjoy their education, achieving their true potential in all areas of academic, sporting and extra-curricular endeavour.

There is a strong sense of partnership between the staff, pupils and parents, which is instantly recognisable not only in the classroom but at our many social functions.

We have our own dedicated buildings and playgrounds plus access to the senior school's facilities, including Science laboratories, DT workshops, theatre, chapel, sports centre and extensive on-site sports fields.

Our leavers are prepared effectively to join the secondary school of their choice, whether in the state or independent sector, and to take advantage of the opportunities that lie ahead of them.

Applications are welcome throughout the school, subject to availability.

Westonbirt School

Tetbury, Gloucestershire GL8 8QG   Tel: (01666) 880333   Fax: (01666) 880364
E-mail: office@westonbirt.gloucs.sch.uk   Website: www.westonbirt.gloucs.sch.uk

The Headmistress Mrs M Henderson MA
(Hons), PGCE   **Founded** 1928
School status Girls Boarding and Day 11–18
Flexi-boarding available. Boarders from 11.
Religious denomination Church of England
Member of GSA, ISCis; **Accredited by** ISC
Learning difficulties SNU/DYC DYP DYS
No of pupils 234; *(full boarding)* 122; *(weekly boarding)* 32; *(day)* 80; *Senior* 167; *Sixth Form* 67
Teacher:pupil ratio 1:8; **Average class size** 15
Fees per annum *(full boarding)* £20625–£22050; *(weekly)* £20625–£22050; *(day)* £14100–£15300

Westonbirt School is more than just a school – it is like a large, happy family, and for many pupils it is like their second home.

Regardless of their background or nationality, they develop into confident, interesting and well-balanced individuals. They fulfil their potential in

every respect, whatever their natural level of ability, without the pressures of an academic hothouse. Virtually all the girls achieve the public exam results required to gain entry to the university or art college of their choice. They also have a very active extra-curricular programme, particularly in sport, music, art and drama, and a busy social programme.

We offer the best of both worlds to boarders and day girls, who mix together freely. With the ethos and resources of a boarding school, we also welcome day girls to stay one night a week free of charge and for additional nights, as required. All join together in the same houses maximising opportunities for friendship groups.

Applications are welcome throughout the school, from 11+ to 16+, subject to availability.

Wycliffe College

Bath Road, Stonehouse, Gloucestershire GL10 2JQ   Tel: (01453) 822432   Fax: (01453) 827634
E-mail: senior@wycliffe.co.uk Website: www.wycliffe.co.uk www.gabbitas.co.uk, www.crested.org.uk

Head Mrs M E Burnet Ward MA (Hons)
Head of Preparatory School Mr A Palmer B Ed
Founded 1882
College status Co-educational Boarding and Day 13–18 Flexi-boarding available.
Religious denomination Inter-Denominational
Member of CReSTeD, GSA, HMC, IAPS, ISBA, ISCis, SHA; **Accredited by** GSA, HMC
Learning difficulties SNU/DYP DYS
Behavioural and emotional disorders TOU
Physical and medical conditions RA
No of pupils 421; (full boarding) 252; (day) 168; Girls 150; Boys 271
Teacher:pupil ratio 1:7; **Average class size** 12
Fees per annum (full boarding) £20520–£24960; (day) £12975–£14190. The maximum boarding fees include ESOL lessons

Wycliffe is situated in sixty acres of parkland on the edge of the Cotswolds. There has been much investment over the last five years and these new facilities enable pupils to achieve the very best results. The focus is on individual learning and there is a wide range of AS courses including psychology, media studies, theatre studies, Japanese and ICT as well as the traditional subjects. Music and drama play a large part in school life and a wide variety of sport is available, including rugby, soccer, hockey, cricket, netball, rowing, squash and basketball. Pastoral care is excellent and pupils each have their own tutor. A warm and friendly welcome awaits visitors.

Wycliffe Preparatory School

Ryeford Hall, Stonehouse, Gloucestershire GL10 2LD   Tel: (01453) 820471   Fax: (01453) 825604
E-mail: prep@wycliffe.co.uk   Website: www.wycliffe.co.uk

Headmaster Mr A Palmer
School status Independent. Co-educational Boarding and Day 2–13. Boarders from 7.
Religious denomination Inter-Denominational
Member of BSA, CReSTeD, IAPS
Accredited by IAPS
Learning difficulties CA SNU/DYC DYP DYS
Behavioural and emotional disorders RA/ADD
Physical and medical conditions CA RA SM/EPI HEA
No of pupils 320; (full boarding) 54; (day) 266; Nursery 30; Pre-prep 64; Prep 226; Girls 145; Boys 175
Teacher:pupil ratio 1:18; **Average class size** 18
Fees per annum (full boarding) £11685–£14985; (day) £4785–£9795

At Wycliffe Preparatory School our aim is to educate pupils to become confident and capable of dealing with the challenges that lie ahead of them; to achieve academically in a happy and caring environment, but also to contribute to sport, music, art and drama, as well as other activities which make the school such a special place.

Academic achievements at Wycliffe Preparatory School are also high and the school prides itself on enabling every child to reach his or her full academic and personal potential. Scholarships, both academic and non-academic, are available for entry at 11+. Forces bursaries are also offered.

Morning and afternoon créche in the Pre-Prep and an extended day with supervised prep and evening activities in the Prep School enable the necessary flexibility for working parents.

An excellent pastoral care system ensures that the academic progress and welfare of the children are monitored very carefully.

Cokethorpe School

Witney, Oxfordshire OX29 7PU   Tel: (01993) 703921   Fax: (01993) 773499
E-mail: admissions@cokethorpe.org.uk   Website: www.cokethorpe.org.uk   www.gabbitas.co.uk

Headmaster Mr D J Ettinger BA, MA, PGCE
Registrar Mrs F M Rutland MA
Founded 1957
School status Independent. Co-educational
Day 5–18.
Religious denomination Inter-Denominational
Member of AGBIS, ISBA, ISCis, SHMIS
Learning difficulties SNU/DYS MLD
Physical and medical conditions AT RA TW/EPI
HEA HI VI
No of pupils 650; *(day)* 650; *Prep* 145; *Senior*
405; *Sixth Form* 100; *Girls* 255; *Boys* 395
Teacher:pupil ratio 1:10; **Average class size** 17
Fees per annum *(day)* £7935–£12285

Set in beautiful Oxfordshire parkland, Cokethorpe offers a broad and exciting education to girls and boys aged from 5 to 18. A network of buses brings pupils from a wide area, classes are small and there is an unparalleled range of extra-curricular activities. Expectations and aspirations are high, with many academic, sporting and other achievements, notably meteoric rises in GCSE and A level results in the last three years,and Value Added scores amongst the very best in the country, which have established Cokethorpe among the best independent schools in the area.

d'Overbroeck's College

The Swan Building, 111 Banbury Road, Oxford, Oxfordshire OX2 6JX
Tel: (01865) 310000   Fax: (01865) 552296   E-mail: mail@doverbroecks.com
Website: www.doverbroecks.com   www.gabbitas.co.uk
For entry at age 11 or 13 contact Leckford Place School 01865 302620

Principal Mr S Cohen
Founded 1977
College status Independent. Co-educational
Day and Boarding 11–19 (Day only 13–16).
Boarders from 16. Entry at age 11+ and 13+
into Leckford Place School; entry at 16+ into
the d'Overbroeck's Sixth Form
Religious denomination Non-Denominational
Member of ISA, ISCis, SHMIS
Accredited by ISA, SHMIS
Learning difficulties DYS MLD
Behavioural and emotional disorders CO/ADD
Physical and medical conditions RA/HEA
No of pupils 357; *(full boarding)* 148; *(day)*
209; *Senior* 124; *Sixth Form* 233; *Girls* 140;
Boys 217
Teacher:pupil ratio 1:7; **Average class size** 7
Fees per annum *(full boarding)* £20445–
£22995; *(day)* £10650–£16215

The College's approach in the Sixth Form is characterized by small classes, a very high level of support and encouragement and an unusual degree of flexibility in the range and combinations of subjects. The teaching is highly interactive and our aim is to make the whole learning process and sixth form experience enjoyable. In 2006, 55 per cent of our entries achieved grade A at A level. Our students go on to good universities; this year 11% of our Upper Sixth gained a place at Oxford or Cambridge University. We offer specialist Medical and Oxbridge programmes.

Kingham Hill School

Kingham, Chipping Norton, Oxfordshire OX7 6TH
Tel: (01608) 658999   Fax: (01608) 658658   E-mail: admissions@kingham-hill.oxon.sch.uk
Website: www.kingham-hill.oxon.sch.uk   www.gabbitas.co.uk

Headmaster Mr M J Morris B.Ed (Hons), BA
Admissions Mrs K A Harvey
Marketing Consultant Mr S King
Founded 1886   **School status** Independent.
Co-educational Boarding and Day 11–18 Flexi-boarding available. Boarders from 11.
Religious denomination Christian
Member of AGBIS, BSA, CReSTeD, ISBA, ISCis, SHA, SHMIS; **Accredited by** ISC, SHMIS Membership of AEGIS
Learning difficulties CA SNU/DYC DYP DYS
Behavioural and emotional disorders CO RA/ADD
Physical and medical conditions RA SM WA3/HEA
No of pupils 227; *(full boarding)* 174; *(day)* 53; *Senior* 177; *Sixth Form* 50; *Girls* 60; *Boys* 167
Teacher:pupil ratio 1:7; **Average class size** 15
Fees per annum *(full boarding)* £16402–£18754; *(day)* £10449–£12398

SpLD per term: £1184. ESOL per term £1250.

Kingham Hill School is a thriving mixed boarding/day school for 250 pupils aged 11–18 years. Beautifully situated, it has offered many generations of students the best possible opportunity to flourish, enjoying their formative years and becoming successful, responsible and well-rounded adults.

The Headmaster and his dedicated staff team ensure that the school's special qualities benefit all.

- Christian values that permeate school life
- Added value that enables so many to exceed all expectations
- Family-style boarding houses and superb pastoral care

The Manor Preparatory School

Faringdon Road, Abingdon, Oxfordshire OX13 6LN   Tel: (01235) 523789   Fax: (01235) 559593
E-mail: registrar@manorprep.org   Website: www.manorprep.org

Headmaster Mr P Heyworth MA PGCE
Deputy Head Mrs A G Barnes B Ed ISI inspector
Founded 1907
School status Co-educational Day Boys 3–7 Girls 3–11.
Religious denomination Church of England
Member of AGBIS, IAPS, ISBA, ISCis, SATIPS; **Accredited by** IAPS, ISC Nursery also OFSTED accredited
Learning difficulties CA WI/DYC DYP DYS
Behavioural and emotional disorders CA
Physical and medical conditions AT CA SM TW WA2/HI
No of pupils 317; *Girls* 305; *Boys* 12
Teacher:pupil ratio 1:9, 1:12
Average class size 18
Fees per annum *(day)* £3855–£8670

Renowned for academic excellence and with a broad curriculum The Manor has superb facilities, including award-winning classrooms and three IT suites, set in extensive grounds. A thriving music department boasts two orchestras, 4 choirs, various ensembles and a jazz band. The Manor holds the 'Gold Activemark' award from Sport England for its 'commitment to promoting the benefits of physical activity and sport.'

Extra-curricular clubs and before and after school care are available. There are also sessions for pre-nursery children.

Lively, experienced staff encourage all pupils to contribute positively to the school community, to show consideration towards other people, to have a disciplined approach to work – and above all to have fun! They leave us happy, fully prepared and confident to take the next step in their education.

England

St Clare's, Oxford

139 Banbury Road, Oxford, Oxfordshire OX2 7AL   Tel: (01865) 552031   Fax: (01865) 513359
E-mail: admissions@stclares.ac.uk   Website: www.stclares.ac.uk   www.gabbitas.co.uk

Principal Mrs P Holloway MSc (Oxon) BSc, PGCE, Dip PM
Founded 1953
School status Independent Sixth Form College. Co-educational Boarding and Day 15–20 Flexi-boarding available. Boarders from 15.
Religious denomination Non-Denominational
Member of ARELS, CASE, CIS, IBO, LISA
Accredited by British Council
Learning difficulties RA
Behavioural and emotional disorders CO ST TS
Physical and medical conditions SM
No of pupils 240; *(full boarding)* 222; *(weekly boarding)* 3; *(day)* 15; *Sixth Form* 240
Girls 125; *Boys* 115
Teacher:pupil ratio 1:7; **Average class size** 7
Fees per annum *(full boarding)* £24560; *(weekly)* £24146; *(day)* £15031

We are the longest established provider of the International Baccalaureate Diploma in England with a mission to advance international education and understanding. The IB Diploma is a two year course giving access to fine universities all over the world. Our students regularly win places at Oxford, Cambridge, LSE and other leading UK Universities as well as Harvard, Yale and Stanford in the USA. We also offer a Pre-IB course for students who are not ready to embark on the Diploma programme.

We are a co-educational day and boarding college occupying substantial premises in the elegant residential area of North Oxford. Around 40 different nationalities are represented of which about 20% are from Britain. The atmosphere at the college is informal and friendly encouraging personal responsibility and international friendships. Our students live in comfortable college houses under the care of a resident warden and all meals are served in the college dining room. There is also a student coffee bar, The Sugar House, which provides snacks at lunchtime and in the evening.

IB students choose six academic subjects including modern languages, science, mathematics and humanities. They also complete a research project, follow a course in critical thinking and take part in extra-curricular activities. The final mark is an average of performance in each subject. The maximum score on the IB is 45 points. The new UCAS tariff equates an IB score of 45 to six and a half A grades at A level. In 2006 our average score was 33.5 points which equates to 4 A grades at A level.

Each of our students is assigned a personal tutor who oversees welfare and progress at regular, individual weekly meetings. Our teachers are selected for their strong academic backgrounds and IB teaching experience. Many are involved in IB curriculum development and examining. We regularly assist schools who are introducing the IB and run teacher training workshops for teachers from around the world.

We provide an extensive programme of social, cultural, service and sporting activities and our students are encouraged to take full advantage of the opportunities that Oxford provides. Apart from more traditional sports, our activities staff organise regular overseas trips as well as activities nearer home such as climbing in Wales, canoeing in Scotland and the popular Duke of Edinburgh Award.

Acceptance is on the basis of academic results, school reports and an interview. Scholarships are available. Almost all our students proceed to higher education in Britain or elsewhere in the world. Our two highly qualified, full time Academic Advisers help all students with university choice, application and interview skills as well as providing comprehensive careers advice.

Moreton Hall School

Weston Rhyn, Oswestry, Shropshire SY11 3EW
Tel: (01691) 773671   Fax: (01691) 778552
E-mail: admin@moretonhall.com
Website: www.moretonhall.org   www.gabbitas.co.uk

The Principal Mr J Forster B.A.
Founded 1913
School status Independent. Girls Boarding and Day 3–18. Boys 3–8 Boarders from 8. Safe, caring environment in N.Shropshire. Excellent EFL Language Centre. New boarding accommodation.
Religious denomination Non-denominational
Member of AGBIS, BSA, GSA, ISCis, SHA
Learning difficulties SNU/DYC DYP DYS MLD
Behavioural and emotional disorders CO ST
Physical and medical conditions IT SM TW WA3/HEA
No of pupils 330; *(full boarding)* 239; *(day)* 91; *Nursery* 28; *Pre-prep* 20; *Prep* 37; *Senior* 171; *Sixth Form* 102; *Girls* 320; *Boys* 10
Teacher:pupil ratio 1:8
Average class size 15
Fees per annum *(full boarding)* £14280–£22500; *(day)* £6270–£17850

Curriculum: Going well beyond the National Curriculum, some 20 subjects are available at GCSE, ranging from the traditional academic subjects such as Latin and the sciences, to practical subjects such as drama, dance and physical education. Modern languages available include French, German and Spanish. A levels in history of art, human biology, business studies and theatre studies extend the range of the curriculum. Information technology is a compulsory subject up to Sixth Form, optional thereafter.

Entry requirements: Girls are admitted to the school, normally in September, at the ages of 11–13, either by Common Entrance or by the school's entrance examination, which is held at the end of January each year. Sixth Form entrance is by interview, and numbers are limited. Girls and boys can start the school at 3. Boys stay to the age of 8. There is also a nursery.

Academic and leisure facilities: Moreton Hall has recently completed an ambitious building and refurbishment programme. The new laboratories, information technology rooms and Art Design

Centre are housed within a short distance of the central classroom, careers and library complex. An exceptionally well-equipped sports centre comprising a sports hall and floodlit tennis courts, all-weather surface along with heated swimming pool, nine-hole golf course and playing fields, are set in one hundred acres of beautiful parkland at the foot of the Berwyn Hills. The school offers a wide range of sporting options, including lacrosse, netball, hockey, cricket, tennis and athletics. Sailing and riding are also popular. Moreton Enterprises, a Sixth Form managed group of companies, offers the girls real business experience. A radio station and recording studio were opened in 1997.

Scholarships: A number of scholarships and bursaries are awarded to girls entering at 11, 13 and the Lower Sixth or to assist a pupil in the school to complete her education. Awards for music, drama, art and for outstanding sporting talent are made at 11+, 12+, 13+ and 16+.

Boarding facilities: Younger girls are housed in the Norton-Roberts building under the supervision of resident houseparents. Boarding houses at Moreton Hall are all linked informally with houses at Shrewsbury School, meeting regularly for musical, dramatic and social occasions. An outstanding Sixth Form boarding house opened in September 2003, with en-suite facilities.

England

Arnold Lodge School

Kenilworth Road, Leamington Spa, Warwickshire CV32 5TW   Tel: (01926) 778050
Fax: (01926) 743311   E-mail: info@arnoldlodge.com   Website: info@arnoldlodge.com
Leamington Spa has excellent road,rail and air links to Birmingham, London and beyond.

Principal Mrs E M Hickling MA
Founded 1864
School status Independent. Co-educational
Day 3–13. French, ICT, Music and PE taught by
specialist teachers from Reception onwards
Religious denomination Christian
Member of IAPS, ISCis
Accredited by IAPS, ISC
No of pupils 280; *(day)* 280; *Nursery* 35;
Pre-prep 75; *Prep* 170; *Girls* 90; *Boys* 190
Teacher:pupil ratio 1:11; **Average class size** 14
Fees per annum *(day)* £1700–£7590
Fees include healthy lunch cooked on site.

Situated in the heart of Leamington Spa, Arnold
Lodge is the only co-educational school in South
Warwickshire offering education from Kindergarten to year 8.The school has a broad and balanced
curriculum, strong pastoral care and a caring
ethos. There are a wide range of extra curricular
activities available including musical ensembles,
an academy of dance and drama, sports and chess
club.

The school provides after school care and
holiday clubs, which have been highly praised
by Ofsted. Pupils from years 4 to 8 benefit from
playing sporting fixtures against other independent schools.

Bromsgrove School

Worcester Road, Bromsgrove, Worcestershire B61 7DU
Tel: (01527) 579679   Fax: (01527) 576177   E-mail: admissions@bromsgrove-school.co.uk
Website: www.bromsgrove-school.co.uk   www.gabbitas.co.uk

Headmaster Mr C Edwards MA Oxon
Assistant Head Miss R Scannell BA
Founded 1553
School status Independent. Co-educational
Boarding and Day 13–18. Boarders from 7.
Religious denomination Church of England
Member of BSA, HMC, IAPS, ISCis
Accredited by HMC, IAPS
Learning difficulties WI/DYP DYS
Behavioural and emotional disorders RA
Physical and medical conditions RA
No of pupils 741; *(full boarding)* 367; *(day)*
374; *Girls* 290; *Boys* 451
Teacher:pupil ratio 1:9; **Average class size** 20
Fees per annum *(full boarding)* £19950; *(day)*
£10770

International airport is 35 minutes away and London Heathrow just 2 hours by car. The school is
opportunity oriented and provides a very wide
range of academic, extra-curricular and sporting
activities.

Bromsgrove School, though unashamedly academic, is not as selective at 13 as its very high
league table position suggests.

Entry between ages 7 and 11 is based on assessment tests and at 13 on interview and tests, or
Common Entrance. Entry into the Sixth Form is
dependent on results at GCSE.

Bromsgrove School, a self-contained campus near
the town of Bromsgrove, is easily accessible from
the national motorway network; Birmingham

Malvern College

College Road, Malvern, Worcestershire WR14 3DF   Tel: (01684) 581500   Fax: (01684) 581617
E-mail: srj@malcol.org   Website: www.malcol.org   www.gabbitas.co.uk

Headmaster Mr D Dowdles
Founded 1865
College status Co-educational Boarding and Day 13–18.
Religious denomination Church of England
Member of CASE, HMC
Accredited by HMC, ISC
Learning difficulties SNU/DYP DYS MLD
Physical and medical conditions RA/EPI HEA
No of pupils 569; *(full boarding)* 450; *(day)* 119; *Girls* 213; *Boys* 356
Teacher:pupil ratio 1:8
Fees per annum *(full boarding)* £22056–£23532; *(day)* £14619–£15072; Pre-prep *(boarding)* £8,595; *(day)* £4,125–£5,460; Prep *(boarding)* £11,415–£13,740; *(day)* £8,130–£10,380; Senior *(boarding)* £21,015–£21,990; *(day)* £13,935–£16,080

Malvern College is a thriving co-educational boarding and day school set on a beautiful 260 acre campus. The College has an excellent reputation for pastoral care and pupils leave the school as confident, mature young men and women.

In a recent Independent Schools Inspection Report the inspector noted that 'Relationships among pupils and between them and the hard-working staff are excellent'.

The school is ranked in the top 50 in Britain in The Times 2006 academic league tables and offers a choice between the International Baccalaureate and A levels in the Sixth Form. Whilst retaining best traditional values Malvern College is modern and innovative in its approach.

Malvern St James

15 Avenue Road, Great Malvern, Worcestershire WR14 3BA   Tel: (01684) 892288
Fax: (01684) 566204 E-mail: registrar@malvernstjames.co.uk Website: www.malvernstjames.co.uk

Headmistress Mrs R Hayes BA Hons MA PGCE FRGS
Founded 01/09/06
School status Independent. Girls Boarding and Day 7–18. Malvern St James welcomes boarders aged 9–18 and day girls aged 7–18.
Religious denomination Church of England
Member of BSA, GSA, ISBA, ISCis, NAHT, SHA; **Accredited by** GSA
Learning difficulties CA SNU/DYC DYP DYS MLD
Behavioural and emotional disorders CA CO RA ST/ADD ASP AUT
Physical and medical conditions DS SM TW WA3/HEA
No of pupils 381; *(full boarding)* 210; *(weekly boarding)* 14; *(day)* 157; *Girls* 381
Teacher:pupil ratio 1:6
Fees per annum *(full boarding)* £7750–£8560; *(weekly)* £6975; *(day)* £2100–£3995

Pupils at Malvern St James enjoy a range of high-quality facilities designed to make the most of their learning experience and the School is committed to promoting facilities that support a forward-looking curriculum. This is evident in the state-of-the-art Science Centre, multimedia Language Centre, and Modern Drama Studio built early in 2006.

Admission is through the schools own examination, or through Common Entrance examination. The school offers Academic Entrance Scholarships and Exhibitions, as well as Scholarships in Art, Music, and Physical Education.

Moffats School

Kinlet Hall, Bewdley, Worcestershire DY12   Tel: (01299) 841230   Fax: (01299) 841444
E-mail: office@moffats.co.uk   Website: www.moffats.co.uk

Headmaster Mr M H Daborn MA (Cantab) (QTS)   **Founded** 1934
School status Independent. Co-educational Boarding and Day 4–13 Flexi-boarding available.
Religious denomination Church of England
Member of BSA, ISA, ISCis
Accredited by ISA, ISC
Learning difficulties WI/DYP DYS
Physical and medical conditions RA WA3/HEA HI
No of pupils 71; *(full boarding)* 25; *(weekly boarding)* 2; *Pre-prep* 11; *Prep* 60; *Girls* 25; *Boys* 46
Teacher:pupil ratio 1:7; **Average class size** 12
Fees per annum *(full boarding)* £11835; *(weekly)* £11835; *(day)* £1025–£2475

Set in a beautiful Georgian house on the Shropshire–Worcestershire border, Moffats provides a happy, safe environment valuing childhood. This family-run school has an ethos that children should receive unlimited encouragement in all they do, and that high academic standards are maintained without expecting more than each child's natural capacity. Good manners, kindness and respect for others are greatly valued. Small classes ensure high attention, so that each individual, whether a bright pupil or one needing more assistance, progresses at the right pace, receiving as much help as is needed.

The school's 108-acre grounds provide space not only for daily sports but also for riding, a popular option. The school carefully maintains a balance between class work and other activities, promoting cultural awareness, strengthening self-confidence and ensuring a sense of fun. Prime importance is given to the development of communication skills. Pupils regularly gain distinctions in annual ESB examinations. The school runs two choirs.

MAP OF THE HOME COUNTIES (NORTH)

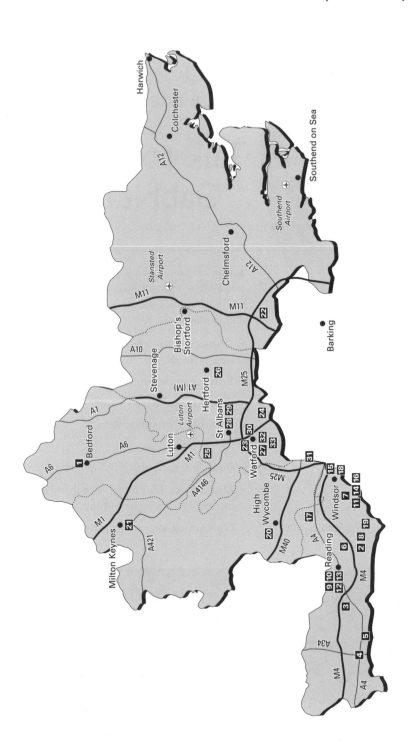

PROFILED SCHOOLS IN THE HOME COUNTIES (NORTH)

(Incorporating the counties of Bedfordshire, Berkshire, Buckinghamshire, Essex, Hertfordshire, Middlesex)

Map Number		Page Number
1	Bedford School, Bedford, Bedfordshire	296
2	Bearwood College, Wokingham, Berkshire	297
3	Bradfield College, Bradfield, Berkshire	297
4	Cheam School, Newbury, Berkshire	298
5	Downe House, Thatcham, Berkshire	298
6	Eagle House School, Sandhurst, Berkshire	299
7	Heathfield St Mary's School, Ascot, Berkshire	300
8	Luckley-Oakfield School, Wokingham, Berkshire	301
9	The Oratory Preparatory School, Reading, Berkshire	301
10	Padworth College, Reading, Berkshire	302
11	Papplewick School, Ascot, Berkshire	302
12	Queen Anne's School, Reading, Berkshire	303
13	Reading Blue Coat School, Reading, Berkshire	303
14	St George's School, Ascot, Berkshire	304
15	St John's Beaumont, Windsor, Berkshire	304
16	St Mary's School, Ascot, Berkshire	305
17	St Piran's Preparatory School, Maidenhead, Berkshire	305
18	Upton House, Windsor, Berkshire	306
19	Wellington College, Crowthorne, Berkshire	306

Map Number		Page Number
20	Pipers Corner School, High Wycombe, Buckinghamshire	307
21	Swanbourne House School, Milton Keynes, Buckinghamshire	307
22	Chigwell School, Chigwell, Essex	308
23	Abbot's Hill, Hemel Hempstead, Hertfordshire	309
24	Aldenham School, Elstree, Hertfordshire	309
25	Arts Educational School, Tring Park, Tring, Hertfordshire	310
26	Haileybury, Hertford, Hertfordshire	311
27	Royal Masonic School for Girls, Rickmansworth, Hertfordshire	311
28	St Albans High School for Girls, St Albans, Hertfordshire	312
29	St Albans School, St Albans, Hertfordshire	312
30	St Margaret's School, Bushey, Hertfordshire	313
31	ACS Hillingdon International School, Hillingdon, Middlesex	314
32	Northwood College, Northwood, Middlesex	314
33	St Helen's School for Girls, Northwood, Middlesex	315

England

Bedford School

De Parys Avenue, Bedford, Bedfordshire MK40 2TU   Tel: (01234) 362200   Fax: (01234) 362283
E-mail: registrar@bedfordschool.org.uk   Website: www.bedfordschool.org.uk

Head Master Dr I P Evans OBE MA PhD
CChem FRSC   **Founded** 1552
School status Independent. Boys Boarding and
Day 7–18 Flexi-boarding available in the Prep
School. Boarders from 7
Religious denomination Church of England
Member of HMC, ISCis
Accredited by International Study Centre
accredited by British Council
Learning difficulties SNU/DYC DYP DYS
Behavioural and emotional disorders CO/ADD
ADHD ASP
Physical and medical conditions SM TW/HEA
HI VI
No of pupils 1105; *(full boarding)* 177; *(weekly
boarding)* 81; *(day)* 847; *Prep* 452; *Senior* 653;
Sixth Form 290; *Boys* 1105
Teacher:pupil ratio 1:20 (1:10 Yrs 11 & 12)
Fees per annum *(full boarding)* £14097–
£20703; *(weekly)* £13440–£20022; *(day)*
£8517–£13167

Every day is packed with challenge and diversity. There is a strong sense of community with an easy mix of boarders and day boys who all enjoy the outstanding sports and social facilities. In this stimulating and supportive atmosphere every boy is encouraged to achieve more than he ever thought possible.

Every detail is geared towards the particular needs of boys. In small classes boys are inspired to develop a thirst for knowledge, to question, and ultimately develop the skills necessary for University and beyond. Academic excellence is our primary aim and our success is demonstrated by our consistently outstanding results at GCSE, A level and in the International Baccalaureate.

Bearwood College

Bearwood Road, Wokingham, Berkshire RG41 5BG   Tel: (0118) 974 8300   Fax: (0118) 977 3186
E-mail: headmaster@bearwoodcollege.co.uk   registrar@bearwoodcollege.co.uk
Website: www.bearwoodcollege.co.uk   www.gabbitas.co.uk

Headmaster Mr S Aiano MA (Cantab) PGCE
Second Master Mr R P Ryall BA PGCE FRGS
Director of Studies Mr I M Smith BA MA PGCE
NPQH   **Founded** 1827
College status Co-educational Boarding and
Day 11–18.
Religious denomination Church of England
Member of BSA, ISCis, SHA, SHMIS;
Accredited by British Council, SHMIS
Learning difficulties SNU/DYS MLD
Behavioural and emotional disorders ADHD
Physical and medical conditions AT SM
TW/EPI HEA
No of pupils 318; *(full boarding)* 65; *(weekly boarding)* 44; *(day)* 209; *Prep* 61; *Senior* 183;
Sixth Form 74; *Girls* 68; *Boys* 250
Teacher:pupil ratio 1:8; **Average class size** 18
Fees per annum *(full boarding)* £18900–£21780; *(weekly)* £18900–£21780; *(day)* £11550–£13470

Bearwood College has opened a Pre-prep School (age 5 to 7 years) this September, following the success of our Nursery for children of 3 months to 5 years. We plan to open our Prep School in 2008 providing the full age range to 18 years. All pupils are encouraged to perform to their best, both academically and outside the classroom. A generous staff:pupil ratio ensures small classes, allowing real focus on each pupil. Pastoral care is given a high priority. Our pupils continue to achieve strongly in all areas. All children participate in an exciting programme of extra-curricular activities and outdoor pursuits. We are close to London and the motorway network, and within easy reach of Heathrow and Gatwick airports, and 45 minutes from London by train.

Bradfield College

Bradfield, Reading, Berkshire RG7 6AU   Tel: (0118) 964 4510   Fax: (0118) 964 4511
E-mail: headmaster@bradfieldcollege.org.uk   Website: www.bradfieldcollege.org.uk

Head Mr P J M Roberts MA (Oxon)
Founded 1850
College status Independent. Co-educational
Boarding and Day 13–18
Religious denomination Church of England
Member of BSA, HMC, ISCis
Accredited by BSA HMC
Learning difficulties SNU/DYS
No of pupils 680; *(full boarding)* 600; *(day)* 80;
Sixth Form 300; *Girls* 225; *Boys* 455
Teacher:pupil ratio 1:8; **Average class size** 16
Fees per annum *(full boarding)* £22890; *(day)* £18312

Exhibitions and Art/Music/DT awards at 13+. Sixth Form entry is by our own internal assessments, which lead to the offer of places in the December preceding the year of entry. The College is effectively the village and is situated close to Junction 12 of the M4 and within easy reach of Reading Station and Heathrow Airport. The College offers an all-round education based on superb facilities and a young and dynamic staff. The boarding houses offer single and double bedsits.

Curriculum: A wide selection of subjects at GCSE is extended at A level with exciting additions such as Economics, Business Studies, Film Studies, Textiles, Music Technology, Psychology and PE. All pupils in the Sixth Form go on to university.

Entry requirements and procedures: Entrance at 13+ by Common Entrance. Scholarships,

England

Cheam School

Headley, Newbury, Berkshire RG19 8LD   Tel: (01635) 268381   Fax: (01635) 269345
E-mail: registrar@cheamschool.co.uk   Website: www.cheamschool.co.uk   www.gabbitas.co.uk

Headmaster Mr M R Johnson B.Ed
Founded 1645
School status Independent. Co-educational Boarding and Day 3–13 Flexi-boarding available. Boarders from 8.
Religious denomination Church of England
Member of AGBIS, BSA, IAPS, ISBA
Accredited by ISC
Learning difficulties SC SNU/DYP DYS MLD
Behavioural and emotional disorders CO
Physical and medical conditions RA SM WA2/HEA
No of pupils 379; *(full boarding)* 10; *(weekly boarding)* 69; *(day)* 300; *Nursery* 18; *Pre-prep* 72; *Prep* 289; *Girls* 158; *Boys* 221
Average class size 18 maximum
Fees per annum *(full boarding)* £18366; *(day)* £3570–£13599. Minimum fee relates to 5 weekly sessions in Nursery

Curriculum: Children are prepared in small classes (maximum 18) for Common Entrance and scholarships to all major public schools. The syllabus covers and exceeds National Curriculum requirements. Those with special needs are well catered for.

Entry requirements: By interview. Two scholarships are offered annually.

Academic and leisure facilities: Excellent facilities set in a stimulating yet secure 80-acre estate. New classroom block, Music School and refurbished Chapel, completed September 2001. Modern science block (1996); dedicated IT, Art and Design departments; superb sporting facilities include squash court and 9-hole golf course. New indoor sports centre (completed Sep 2003).

Pastoral care and boarding facilities: Each child is under the watchful eye of two house tutors and a form teacher; resident staff and matrons supervise boarders in comfortable dormitories. Separate girls' boarding accommodation. Nursery and pre-prep on site.

Downe House

Cold Ash, Thatcham, Berkshire RG18 9JJ   Tel: (01635) 200286   Fax: (01635) 202026
E-mail: correspondence@downehouse.net   Website: www.downehouse.net   www.gabbitas.co.uk

Headmistress Mrs E McKendrick BA
Founded 1907
School status Independent. Girls Boarding and Day 11–18. Boarders from 11.
Religious denomination Church of England
Member of AGBIS, BSA, GSA, ISBA, ISCis
Accredited by GSA
Learning difficulties SNU/DYP DYS
Behavioural and emotional disorders RA
Physical and medical conditions RA/HEA HI
No of pupils 586; *(full boarding)* 565; *(day)* 21; *Senior* 412; *Sixth Form* 174; *Girls* 586
Teacher:pupil ratio 1:7
Fees per annum *(full boarding)* £24405; *(day)* £17670

grade B or above for an A level course. Scholarships at 11+, 12+, 13+ and Sixth Form.

The School is only 5 miles from Newbury, with easy access to the motorway network, London and Heathrow Airport. It has an excellent academic record, with nearly all pupils going on to university.

Curriculum: A wide selection of subjects is available at both GCSE and A level. Girls are also prepared for university entrance.

Entry requirements and procedures: By Common Entrance and assessment. Seven passes at

Academic and leisure facilities: Sixth Form complex with study-bedrooms. Extensive refurbishment of all boarding houses. Significant expenditure on ICT, with voicemail and e-mail for every girl. New Sports Hall and Performing Arts Centre, and indoor swimming pool. One term spent in France in 12+ year.

Leith's Food and Wine Certificate is offered in the Sixth Form.

Eagle House

Crowthorne Road, Sandhurst, Berkshire GU47 8PH   Tel: (01344) 772134   Fax: (01344) 779039
E-mail: info@eaglehouseschool.com   Website: www.eaglehouseschool.com

Headmaster Mr Andrew Barnard BA Hons P.G.C.E.   **Founded** 1820
School status Independent. Co-educational Day and Boarding 3–13 Flexi-boarding available. Boarders from 8.
Religious denomination Church of England
Member of BSA, IAPS, ISCis, NAHT, SATIPS;
Accredited by IAPS, ISC
Learning difficulties CA SNU/DYP DYS
Behavioural and emotional disorders RA/ADD ADHD
Physical and medical conditions SL SM TW WA1/HEA
No of pupils 268; *(full boarding)* 14; *(weekly boarding)* 8; *(day)* 246; *Nursery* 27; *Pre-prep* 59; *Prep* 182; *Girls* 83; *Boys* 185
Teacher:pupil ratio 1:6; **Average class size** 14
Fees per annum *(full boarding)* £15900; *(weekly)* £15900; *(day)* £11775. Pre-Prep – £7200 (Rec/Year 1) £7350 (Year 2) Nursery – £4245 (5 mornings)

At Eagle House every child is unique. From 3 to 13, girls and boys develop in a friendly, creative and expressive environment. Working closely with parents, Eagle House nurtures the individual talents of every child, so that they grow in self-esteem and confidence, through their success in academic subjects, sports, art, music and drama. The school believes in rewards and praise for good work and exemplary behaviour to encourage high standards and good citizenship.

Eagle House benefits from superb facilities and small class sizes and dedicated staff ensure that all children have the best academic start possible. The high sporting achievements of the pupils is testament to the opportunities and coaching offered by the school. A diverse activities programme is enjoyed by all pupils helping to give them an all round education. With boarding opportunities from Year 3 and late stay facilities for all children, Eagle House caters for the busy lives families lead.

England

Heathfield St Mary's School

London Road, Ascot, Berkshire SL5 8BQ   Tel: (01344) 898342   Fax: (01344) 890689
E-mail: registrar@heathfieldstmarys.net Website: www.heathfieldstmarys.net   www.gabbitas.co.uk

Headmistress Mrs F King BA(Oxon)
MA(London) MBA(Hull)
Deputy Headmistress Miss R Appleyard BA
Hons (London), PGCE (London
Deputy Head (academic) Mrs U Stevens BA
London   **Founded** 1899
School status Independent. Girls Boarding
11–18. Boarders from 11.
Religious denomination Christian
Member of BSA, GSA, IAPS, ISCis, SHA
Accredited by GSA, IAPS, ISC
Learning difficulties CA SNU/DYC DYP DYS
Behavioural and emotional disorders CO
ST/ADD ADHD ASP
Physical and medical conditions SM WA3/HEA
No of pupils *(full boarding)* 225; *Senior* 140;
Sixth Form 85
Fees per annum *(full boarding)* £22890

Heathfield St Mary's is an all girls' full boarding school offering a relevant and inspiring education. Set in spacious surroundings on the outskirts of Ascot, the school is 40 minutes from London and 25 minutes from Heathrow. The original Georgian house has been extended over the years and facilities now include a fully equipped science block, 2 computer suites with internet access for all girls, art studios, a superb sports hall, indoor swimming pool and an Upper-Sixth complex. The school has a beautiful late Victorian chapel.

Heathfield St Mary's is comfortable but competitive and academically rigorous too. Emphasis is always on individual achievement and depth, an ethos underlined by excellent, highly qualified teachers. The staff:pupil ratio is 1:6. While the more traditional subject combinations remain most popular, there is also excellence in art, drama, music and sport. Twenty four subjects are offered up to AS and A level including economics, business studies, theatre studies and critical thinking. Academic results are consistently impressive and all girls go on to higher education.

Boarding accommodation is excellent, two-thirds of the pupils having single bedrooms. All rooms are light, airy and appropriately personalised by the girls. The Upper Sixth live in a separate, self-contained complex which encourages them to prepare for the relative independence of university. Pastoral care throughout the school is recognized as outstanding, with year heads, tutors, two resident SRNs and four heads of house all playing their part.

Two ICT suites are used in a wide variety of academic areas as well as outside lessons. The Sports Hall and 25m indoor heated swimming pool are always a hive of activity. There are weekday societies and activities after school and whole school activities at the weekend, also frequent museum and theatre trips to London and elsewhere, workshops, field trips and work experience abroad for linguists. At Heathfield St Mary's the day does not finish at 4 pm, nor the week on Friday.

Entry for the majority of pupils is at 11; a few girls join at 12 or 13 or come into the Lower Sixth for AS and A level studies. Junior entrants take our entrance papers and also the appropriate Common Entrance examination. Entry into the Lower Sixth is via predicted GCSE grades, tests in intended AS and A level subjects and interview. A number of academic, music and art scholarships at Junior entry and to the Sixth Form are awarded each year. Our Scholarship Day is held in early November.

Luckley-Oakfield School

Luckley Road, Wokingham, Berkshire RG40 3EU   Tel: (0118) 978 4175   Fax: (0118) 977 0305
E-mail: registrar@luckley.wokingham.sch.uk
Website: www.luckley.wokingham.sch.uk   www.gabbitas.co.uk

Headmistress Miss V A Davis ARCS BSc
Founded 1918
School status Independent. Girls Boarding and Day 11–18 Flexi-boarding available. Boarders from 11.
Religious denomination Church of England
Member of AGBIS, BSA, GSA
Accredited by GSA
Learning difficulties WI/DYP DYS
Physical and medical conditions WA3
No of pupils 304; *(full boarding)* 24; *(weekly boarding)* 8; *(day)* 272; *Senior* 258; *Sixth Form* 46; *Girls* 304
Teacher:pupil ratio 1:8; **Average class size** 18
Fees per annum *(full boarding)* £18486; *(weekly)* £17049; *(day)* £10797

Luckley-Oakfield provides a welcoming and comfortable setting for studies, recreation and friendships. It prides itself on excellent GCSE and A level results as well as successes in music, drama and the Duke of Edinburgh's Award Scheme and outstanding value-added results recognised nationally. Facilities include an IT centre, sports hall, covered swimming pool, Sixth Form house and new Jubilee Library building. Pupils are backed by a high standard of pastoral care, which has long been synonymous with the name of the school. These values are encompassed within the Christian principles upon which life at Luckley is based.

The Oratory Preparatory School

Goring Heath, Reading, Berkshire RG8 7SF   Tel: (0118) 984 4511   Fax: (0118) 984 4806
E-mail: office@oratoryprep.co.uk   Website: www.oratoryprep.co.uk   www.gabbitas.co.uk

Headmaster Dr R J Hillier MA, PhD, PGCE
Founded 1859
School status Co-educational Day and Boarding 3–13 Flexi-boarding available.
Religious denomination Roman Catholic
Member of IAPS
Learning difficulties CA WI/DYC DYP DYS
Behavioural and emotional disorders RA/ADD
Physical & medical conditions CA WA1/HEA HI
No of pupils 407; *(full boarding)* 25; *(weekly boarding)* 17; *Pre-prep* 116; *Prep* 291; *Girls* 137; *Boys* 270
Average class size 16
Fees per annum *(full boarding)* £13845; *(weekly)* £12750; *(day)* £2985–£10050

The Oratory Preparatory School is a Catholic day and boarding school for boys and girls from 3 to 13 which welcomes children of all denominations and faiths. A large proportion of boys goes on each year to The Oratory School. There are currently 116 in the pre-preparatory department and 291 in the preparatory school.

Our aim is to discover and develop the potential latent in every child. To this end, we are proud of their achievements not only in the academic sphere, at Common Entrance and Scholarship, but also on the sports field and in music, art and drama.

Recent developments include a purpose-built classroom block, well-equipped library, 300-seat theatre and music school. An indoor swimming-pool complex is currently under construction and due for completion in Summer 2007.

England

Padworth College

Padworth, Reading, Berkshire RG7 4NR   Tel: (0118) 983 2644   Fax: (0118) 983 4515
E-mail: info@padworth.com   Website: www.padworth.com

The Principal Mrs L Melhuish   **Founded** 1963
College status Independent. Co-educational
Boarding and Day 13–19 Flexi-boarding
available. Boarders from 13.
Religious denomination Non-Denominational
Member of ARELS; **Accredited by** BAC, British
Council Member of English UK
No of pupils 106; *(full boarding)* 77; *(weekly
boarding)* 9; *(day)* 20; *Senior* 41; *Sixth Form* 65;
Girls 69; *Boys* 37
Teacher:pupil ratio 1:4; **Average class size** 5
Fees per annum *(full boarding)* £18600;
(weekly) £14500; *(day)* £7800

Padworth College is a distinctive co-educational
day and boarding school for students aged 13–19
from the UK and overseas offering a wide range of
courses leading to GCSE, AS, A Level, University
Access and ESOL qualifications.

Outstanding academic results are achieved as a
consequence of high quality teaching and small
classes. Excellent pastoral care is provided by the
committed team of house staff who also organise
the broad extra-curricular programme. Our International Study Centre offers full-time English
courses at all levels which can be combined with
academic study for overseas students. Students
can be accepted at any point in the year and
may stay for any length of time. Modern
classrooms and science laboratories are complemented by a newly-equipped IT room, wireless
network and art studio with excellent resources.
Other facilities include an outdoor swimming
pool, tennis, basketball and volleyball courts.

Padworth is only 45 minutes by road from Heathrow. Visitors to the College are welcome.

Papplewick School

Windsor Road, Ascot, Berkshire SL5 7LH   Tel: (01344) 621488   Fax: (01344) 874639
E-mail: hm@papplewick.org.uk   Website: www.papplewick.org.uk   www.gabbitas.co.uk

Head Mr T W Bunbury B.A.(Hons) P.G.C.E.
Founded 1947
School status Independent. Boys Boarding and
Day 7–13. Boarders from 7. Years 3–5 boarders
may go home on Saturday nights. Years 6–8
boarders may go home on Sundays.
Religious denomination Church of England
Member of IAPS, ISCis, NAHT, SATIPS, BSA
Learning difficulties WI/DYS MLD
Behavioural and emotional disorders RA/ADD
Physical and medical conditions RA
No of pupils 203; *(full boarding)* 130; *Boys* 203
Teacher:pupil ratio 1:8
Average class size 13
Fees per annum *(full boarding)* £18660; *(day)*
£14334

Curriculum: All main subjects are studied. ICT is
taught throughout the school, as are art, design
and technology. Outstanding teaching towards
scholarships and Common Entrance passes is
balanced with music, PE and a wide range of
competitive sports and games. Magnificent new
Sports Hall, Music School and indoor Swimming
Pool.

Entry requirements: Parental choice and interview followed by placing test. It is essential to
register boys well in advance of their sixth
birthday.

Papplewick enjoys a spacious rural location on
the edge of Windsor Great Park. Convenient links
with M4, M3, M25, Heathrow and Gatwick. The
quality of care and the dedication of staff are
outstanding and remain Papplewick's special
hallmark.

Learning difficulties: WI/DYS
Behavioural and emotional disorders: RA
Physical and medical conditions: RA

Queen Anne's School

6 Henley Road, Caversham, Reading, Berkshire RG4 6DX   Tel: (0118) 918 7333
Fax: (0118) 918 7310   E-mail: admissions@qas.org.uk   Website: www.qas.org.uk www.gabbitas.co.uk

The Headmistress Mrs J Harrington
Founded 1894
School status Girls Boarding and Day 11–18
Flexi-boarding available.
Religious denomination Church of England
No of pupils 340; *(full boarding)* 100; *(weekly boarding)* 80; *Girls* 340
Teacher:pupil ratio 1:7.4
Average class size 16–18
Fees per annum *(full boarding)* £22707; *(day)* £15390. Overnight accommodation £30 per night for day girls

Situated on an attractive 35 acre campus in Caversham, north of the River Thames, Reading. Easy access to London, the South-East and Heathrow Airport. Entry at 11, 12, 13, 16 and into the Sixth Form, either by Common Entrance or the school's own examination. Academic, music, drama, art, sport and Sixth Form scholarships are available.

School facilities include: a performing arts centre, well-stocked library, extensive science laboratories, modern languages centre, a large music department, IT department as well as excellent sports facilities including the Morgan Sports Centre and heated indoor swimming pool. Recently refurbished boarding accommodation with separate Sixth Form houses.

At Queen Anne's, girls have the space and the opportunity to grow and learn in the security of a single-sex environment. With a host of extra-curricular activities and an excellent academic record, girls are fully prepared for university life and successful careers.

Reading Blue Coat School

Holme Park, Sonning-on-Thames, Reading, Berkshire RG4 6SU
Tel: (0118) 944 1005   Fax: (0118) 944 2690   E-mail: vmf@blue-coat.reading.sch.uk
Website: www.blue-coat.reading.sch.uk   www.gabbitas.co.uk

Headmaster Mr S J W McArthur BSc MA
FCollP   **Founded** 1646
School status Boys Day 11–18 (Co-ed VIth Form).Co-educational Sixth Form
Religious denomination Church of England
Member of AGBIS, HMC, SHMIS
No of pupils 662; *Senior* 465; *Sixth Form* 197; *Girls* 54; *Boys* 608
Fees per annum *(day)* £10395

Set in 46 acres of attractive parkland including a boathouse and direct access to the Thames, Blue Coat provides a stimulating and friendly atmosphere in which each pupil can realise their full intellectual, physical and creative potential. To enable students to reach attainable goals the school provides close attention to their progress by good teaching and careful assessment.

The School sets great store by the philosophy that a good education is much more than a formal academic training consequently whilst academic excellence is our goal, co-curricular activities play an important part of Blue Coat life. A wide range of sports are offered; CCF, D of E Awards Scheme, Sports Leadership Award and Public Speaking are some of the many activities that thrive at school.

Music and drama have a strong tradition; a number of concerts and drama productions being staged regularly. Over a third of pupils play musical instruments.

England

St George's School

Ascot, Berkshire SL5 7DZ   Tel: (01344) 629900   Fax: (01344) 629901
E-mail: office@stgeorges-ascot.org.uk   Website: www.stgeorges-ascot.org.uk   www.gabbitas.co.uk

Headmistress Mrs C Jordan MA PGCE
Founded 1877
School status Independent. Girls Boarding and Day 11–18 Flexi-boarding available.
Religious denomination Church of England
Member of GSA
Learning difficulties WI/DYC DYP DYS
Behavioural and emotional disorders RA/ADHD ASP
Physical and medical conditions HL RA SM/HEA VI
No of pupils 270; *(full boarding)* 136; *(day)* 134; *Girls* 270
Fees per annum *(full boarding)* £22650; *(day)* £14700

St George's School, Ascot, is located in the Berkshire countryside. It is situated between the M3, M4 and M25 motorways, allowing for easy access to London, Heathrow and Gatwick. Entry is by examination and, while broadstream, the academic results are outstanding. The average result in 2006 was 3 As at A2 Level and A at AS Level.

Boarders and day girls benefit from the caring and personal attention of a dedicated teaching and pastoral staff. The main faith is Church of England, but girls from any denomination are welcome. Extra-curricular activities are many and include music, drama, debating, voluntary service, Duke of Edinburgh's Award and photography. Sport is excellent and includes lacrosse, tennis, swimming, gymnastics, squash and fitness exercising.

St George's, Ascot, is committed to the development of the individual and her talents, to the best of her ability.

St John's Beaumont

Priest Hill, Old Windsor, Windsor, Berkshire SL4 2JN   Tel: (01784) 432428   Fax: (01784) 494048
E-mail: admissions@stjohnsbeaumont.co.uk   Website: www.stjohnsbeaumont.org.uk

Acting Headmaster Mr G Delaney
Founded 1888
School status Boys Boarding and Day 4–13.
Religious denomination Roman Catholic
Member of AGBIS, BSA, IAPS, ISCis
Accredited by IAPS, ISC
Physical & medical conditions IT SM TW WA2
No of pupils 342; *(full boarding)* 30; *(weekly boarding)* 30; *(day)* 282; *Boys* 342
Teacher:pupil ratio 1:8; **Average class size** 17
Fees per annum *(full boarding)* £17286; *(weekly)* £14580; *(day)* £5997–£11046

St John's Beaumont is a Roman Catholic school founded in 1888 by the Society of Jesus. Set in grounds of over 100 acres on the edge of Old Windsor are the imposing, spacious, bright purpose-built premises designed by J F Bentley, architect of Westminster Cathedral. The school has outstanding academic, creative and sporting facilities. Several new facilities have recently opened, including a science and technology block, art and craft block and indoor swimming pool. A new music school opened in 2000 and an information and communication technology centre opened in April 2003. In 2004 wireless technology was made available in classrooms, enabling access to individual laptops. On top of their daily curriculum schedules, each member of staff offers an extra activity after school. These include chess, pottery, art and various sports, which are played every day.

St Mary's School, Ascot

St Mary's Road, Ascot, Berkshire SL5 9JF   Tel: (01344) 623721   Fax: (01344) 873281
E-mail: admissions@st-marys-ascot.co.uk Website: www.st-marys-ascot.co.uk   www.gabbitas.co.uk

Headmistress Mrs M Breen MSc. BSc.
Founded 1885
School status Independent. Girls Boarding and
Day 11–18. Boarders from 11.
Religious denomination Roman Catholic
Member of BSA, GSA, ISCis
Accredited by GSA
Learning difficulties WI/DYS
Physical and medical conditions RA SM
WA2/EPI HEA HI
No of pupils 360; *(full boarding)* 345; *(day)* 15;
Senior 259; *Sixth Form* 101; *Girls* 360
Teacher:pupil ratio 1:7; **Average class size** 16
Fees per annum *(full boarding)* £23592; *(day)*
£16614

St Mary's is a selective independent Roman Catholic boarding school for girls aged 11–18 years. The school is situated in 55 acres close to the M3, M4 and M25 motorways and within easy access of London and the airports. Entry at 11+, 13+ and 16+ is subject to the School's own entry procedure. Facilities are excellent as are examination results, with 97 per cent AB grades at A level and 100 per cent A*–C grades at GCSE (2006).

We are a friendly, stable and caring community, proud of our academic and sporting achievements and dedicated to bringing out the full potential of each of our pupils. We are committed to full boarding, with spaces for a few day pupils living nearby. We offer a stimulating range of extra-curricular activities which take place in the evenings and throughout the weekend.

St Piran's Preparatory School

Gringer Hill, Maidenhead, Berkshire SL6 7LZ   Tel: (01628) 594300   Fax: (01628) 594301
E-mail: office@stpirans.co.uk   Website: www.stpirans.co.uk   www.gabbitas.co.uk

Head Master Mr J Carroll BA Hons BPhiled
PGCE   **Founded** 1805
School status Co-educational Day 3–13.
Religious denomination Church of England
Member of IAPS, ISBA, ISCis, NAHT, SATIPS;
Accredited by IAPS
Learning difficulties WI/DYC DYP DYS MLD
Behavioural and emotional disorders RA/ADD
ADHD ASP
Physical and medical conditions AT RA SM
WA3/EPI HEA HI VI
No of pupils 368; *(day)* 368; *Nursery* 66;
Pre-prep 105; *Prep* 169; *Senior* 28; *Girls* 143;
Boys 225; **Average class size** 18
Fees per annum *(day)* £2502–£9228

Curriculum: National Curriculum subjects up to Year 8. French is offered from Reception to Year 8. German and Spanish are options for seniors.

Sport: A comprehensive range for all pupils. Facilities include a sports hall, indoor swimming pool, all-weather pitch, dance studio, music room, ICT suite and new learning resource centre.

Facilities: Excellent facilities. Fully networked ICT department, PCs in classrooms and a new learning resource centre. We have three specialist teachers for those who need additional support. Trampolining, drama, games and crafts, among others, are activities for Year 5 to Year 8 at the end of the day.

Entry requirements: Entry is by interview, school report and, where necessary, a short assessment if entry is higher up in the school. The school has expanded to a three-form entry at age 7+.

England

Upton House School

115 St Leonard's Road, Windsor, Berkshire SL4 3DF   Tel: (01753) 862610   Fax: (01753) 621950
E-mail: info@uptonhouse.org.uk   Website: www.uptonhouse.org.uk   www.gabbitas.co.uk

Headmistress Mrs M Collins BA (Hons) PGCE
Founded 1936
School status Independent. Co-educational
Day Boys 3–7 Girls 2–11.
Religious denomination Church of England
Member of IAPS; **Accredited by** IAPS
Learning difficulties SNU/DYP DYS MLD
Behavioural and emotional disorders CA RA
ST TS/ADD
Physical and medical conditions CA IT RA SM
TW/EPI HEA
No of pupils 240; *Girls* 170; *Boys* 70
Teacher:pupil ratio 1:6; **Average class size** 17
Fees per annum *(day)* £1220–£3300

Upton House School is a thriving community of
240 children and 40 staff in the heart of historic
Windsor. It is dedicated to a caring philosophy for
all its children, allowing each to develop their
talents and, at the same time, to learn the importance of helping others in the wider world.

A very full syllabus is offered and we take
particular pride in making the whole learning
process fun – with a range of extra-curricular
activities, off-site visits, after-school clubs, dramatic productions, summer camps, etc.

For further information or a copy of our
prospectus, please contact the Secretary, Mrs
Jill Gilmour on (01753) 862610 or at info@
uptonhouse.org.uk or www.uptonhouse.org.uk.

Wellington College

Duke's Ride, Crowthorne, Berkshire RG45 7PU   Tel: (01344) 444012   Fax: (01344) 444004
E-mail: admissions@wellingtoncollege.org.uk   Website: www.wellingtoncollege.org.uk

Headmaster Dr A F Seldon MA PhD FRSA
MBA FRHisS
The Second Master Mr R I H B Dyer BA
Director of Admissions Mr R J W Walker MA
(Cantab)   **Founded** 1853
College status Independent FE College.
Co-educational Boarding and Day 13–18
Flexi-boarding available. Boarders from 13.
Dr Anthony Seldon became Head in January
2006.
Religious denomination Church of England
Member of AGBIS, BSA, HMC, ISBA, ISCis,
Round_Square; **Accredited by** HMC
Learning difficulties RA/DYC DYP DYS
Behavioural and emotional disorders RA/ADD
ADHD
No of pupils 752; *(full boarding)* 635; *(day)*
117; *Girls* 131; *Boys* 621
Teacher:pupil ratio 1:8; **Average class size** 16
Fees per annum *(full boarding)* £24195; *(day)*
£19380

Wellington College is one of
the country's leading independent schools. It stands in
an attractive 400-acre
woodland estate.

A sensible priority is
given to academic study
(98 per cent of leavers go
on to take degree courses),
but the highest standards are
also achieved in other
aspects of school life, including sport, art, technology, writing, music and drama. Extra-
curricular activities are important, as they develop
self-confidence and provide experience in team-
work, initiative and leadership.

Wellington provides a well-disciplined, Christian framework within which pupils have a wide
range of opportunities to fulfil their personal
potential.

Pipers Corner School

Pipers Lane, Great Kingshill, High Wycombe, Buckinghamshire HP15 6LP
Tel: (01494) 718255   Fax: (01494) 719806
E-mail: school@piperscorner.co.uk
Website: www.gabbitas.co.uk

Headmistress Mrs V M Stattersfield MA(Oxon) PGCE
Founded 1930
School status Girls Day and Boarding 4–18 Flexi-boarding available.
Religious denomination Church of England
No of pupils 470; *(full boarding)* 25; *(weekly boarding)* 25; *Girls* 470
Fees per annum *(full boarding)* £14640–£17685; *(weekly)* £14415–£17460; *(day)* £5130–£10695

Set in 36 acres of the beautiful Chilterns, our spacious campus, with its outstanding facilities, is only half an hour from Heathrow and less than an hour from London.

Pipers is not only for girls with academic, artistic or sporting talent who hit the headlines or gain Oxbridge places (although ours do!). It is just as proud of students with average abilities who strive to do their best and achieve more than they ever thought they would. Every success is valued. We provide a challenging and well-balanced curriculum. Girls achieve high standards and are well prepared for higher education.

In boarding, the atmosphere is calm and relaxed, with the emphasis on family values and with friendly, well-ordered supervision. An exciting variety of weekend activities is organized for the girls.

Entry requirements: Preparatory Department by interview and report; Senior School by entrance examination, interview and report.

Scholarships: Academic and service bursaries and Sixth Form scholarships are available.

Swanbourne House School

Swanbourne, Milton Keynes, Buckinghamshire MK17 0HZ Tel: (01296) 720264 Fax: (01296) 728089
E-mail: office@swanbourne.org   Website: www.swanbourne.org   www.gabbitas.co.uk

Head Mr S D Goodhart BEd (Hons)
Founded 1920
School status Independent. Co-educational Boarding and Day 3–13 Flexi-boarding available. Boarders from 7.
Religious denomination Church of England
Member of BSA, IAPS, ISBA, SATIPS
Accredited by IAPS
Learning difficulties WI/DYS MLD
Behavioural and emotional disorders RA
Physical and medical conditions SM/HEA
No of pupils 413; *(full boarding)* 28; *(weekly boarding)* 21; *(day)* 364; *Nursery* 45; *Pre-prep* 123; *Prep* 275; *Girls* 188; *Boys* 225
Fees per annum *(full boarding)* £15300; *(weekly)* £15300; *(day)* £5613–£11940
Sliding scale depending on age

Swanbourne House is a successful IAPS preparatory school from which academic scholarships and awards in arts/sport and music are won every

year. There are many opportunities for personal development through activities, sport, the arts, holiday clubs and trips abroad.

Pupils have a form tutor in addition to a Housemaster and are prepared for Public School through leadership training, Public School Induction, socials, first aid, personal advice, taking responsibility and study skills.

Facilities: Laboratory, computer rooms, Astro-Turf, comfortable boarding house, Design and Art Centre, language lab, library, amphitheatre, sports hall and a swimming pool.

Entry is by a familiarization day and short assessment test.

England

Chigwell School

High Road, Chigwell, Essex IG7 6QF   Tel: (020) 8501 5700   Fax: (020) 8500 6232
E-mail: hm@chigwell-school.org   Website: www.chigwell-school.org   www.gabbitas.co.uk

Headmaster Mr D F Gibbs B.A.
Founded 1629
School status Co-educational Day and
Boarding 7–18 Flexi-boarding available.
Boarders from 15.
Religious denomination Church of England
Member of HMC, IAPS
Accredited by HMC, IAPS, ISC
Learning difficulties RA
No of pupils 715; *(full boarding)* 40; *(day)* 675;
Prep 338; *Senior* 377; *Sixth Form* 178;
Girls 310; *Boys* 405
Teacher:pupil ratio 1:3
Average class size 10 (Sixth Form); 20 (Junior
School)
Fees per annum *(full boarding)* £17961;
(weekly) £16020–£17004; *(day)* £7683–
£11817

The oldest major co-educational independent school in the West Essex and East London area, founded in 1629, set in 70 acres of green belt while on the Central Line and bus routes, Chigwell has a fine reputation for academic excellence and extra-curricular achievements. In the last three years A Level results have been above 70% at A and B grades with 10% gaining Oxbridge places and over 60% reaching the leading Russell Group Universities. Excellent range of extra-curricular activities, particular strengths in sport, drama and music. Facilities include an outstanding Drama Centre, Music School and Arts Centre.

Abbot's Hill School

Bunkers Lane, Hemel Hempstead, Hertfordshire HP3 8RP   Tel: (01442) 240333
Fax: (01442) 269981 E-mail: registrar@abbotshill.herts.sch.uk Website: www.abbotshill.herts.sch.uk

Headmistress Mrs K Lewis
Founded 1912
School status Independent. Girls Day 3–16
(Boys 3–4).
Religious denomination Church of England
Member of AHIS, GSA, ISCis
Accredited by GSA, IAPS, ISC
Learning difficulties CA SNU/DYC DYP DYS
Behavioural and emotional disorders CO/ASP
BESD
Physical and medical conditions IT SM/EPI
HEA HI VI
No of pupils 460; *(day)* 460; *Girls* 460
Average class size 15–18
Fees per annum *(day)* £6555–£11610

A thriving, vibrant, high-achieving school, Abbot's Hill is set in 76 acres of parkland on the edge of Hemel Hempstead, Hertfordshire.

We are justly proud of our academic record but never stray from our prime objective: to educate the whole person, to achieve his or her highest personal, social and educational potential. Every pupil benefits from being known personally by the Headmistress and teaching staff in a warm and enabling environment.

The school and its dedicated staff offer excellent facilities and a wide range of subjects and extra-curricular activities.

Aldenham School

Elstree, Hertfordshire WD6 3AJ   Tel: (01923) 858122   Fax: (01923) 854410
E-mail: enquiries@aldenham.com   Website: www.aldenham.com

Headmaster Mr J C Fowler MA
Founded 1597
School status Independent co-educational
Boarding and Day 3–18 Flexi-boarding
available. Boarders from 11
Religious denomination Church of England,
Inter-Denominational
Member of AGBIS, BSA, CASE, HMC, IAPS,
ISCis; **Accredited by** HMC, IAPS, ISA, ISC
No of pupils 648; *(full boarding)* 100; *(weekly boarding)* 45; *(day)* 503; *Nursery* 25; *Pre-prep* 56; *Prep* 75; *Senior* 333; *Sixth Form* 159; *Girls* 106; *Boys* 542
Teacher:pupil ratio 1:8; **Average class size** 20
Fees per annum *(full boarding)* £15549–£21900; *(weekly)* £13023–£17997; *(day)* £8136–£15069

Aldenham stands in a 100+ acre site with modern state-of-the-art facilities.

The curriculum includes the arts, sciences and humanities, music technology, business studies, theatre studies and sports science. Personal tutors are provided.

An extensive games and activities programme includes football, hockey, basketball, squash, sailing and cricket. Strong Music and Drama departments stage regular productions. The Learning Support department encourages able pupils with dyslexia and dyscalculia and provides specialist English lessons for overseas students (ESL). Awards for academic potential, sport, music (including Organ Scholarship), art and technology are available.

England

Arts Educational School, Tring Park

Tring Park, Tring, Hertfordshire HP23 5LX
Tel: (01442) 824255   Fax: (01442) 891069
E-mail: info@aes-tring.com
Website: www.aes-tring.com

The Headmaster Mr S Anderson M.A. (contact)
B.Mus, ARCM
Founded 1919
School status Co-educational Boarding and
Day 8–18.
Religious denomination Non-Denominational
Member of BSA, ISA, SHA, SHMIS
Learning difficulties WI/DYS MLD
Physical and medical conditions SM
No of pupils 278; *(full boarding)* 214; *(day)* 64;
Prep 7; *Senior* 161; *Sixth Form* 110
Girls 223; *Boys* 55
Fees per annum *(full boarding)* £17355–
£24510; *(day)* £12600–£19710

Tring Park offers exciting educational opportunities for pupils who show talent in one or more of the Performing Arts and we are committed to ensuring that all pupils fulfil their potential. The School is set in 17 acres of attractive and secluded parkland and the main house was formerly a Rothschild Mansion.

The School accommodates over two hundred boarders and over eighty day pupils and aims to provide an environment ideally suited to the teaching of the Performing Arts, combined with academic study to the highest level.

Tring Park is part of the Music and Dance Scheme, funded and administered by the DfES, and places are awarded annually under this scheme for talented classical dancers. A number of Dance and Drama Awards are available for the Sixth Form dance course.

Up to the age of fourteen all pupils study Dance, Music and Drama combined with a full and vigorous academic curriculum. The pupils all study eight or nine GCSE subjects combined with the Dance or Performance Foundation Course. In the Sixth Form pupils study 3 or 4 'A' Levels combined with the Dance, Musical Theatre or Drama Course. Academic study receives equal emphasis and the department provides a broad and balanced curriculum for all pupils. Following

success in the 'A' Level examinations, many of our Sixth Form pupils proceed to higher vocational or academic studies at universities and colleges. For others, the opportunity to perform becomes a reality immediately.

For those entering the Dance Course, we believe in training the whole dancer in body, mind and in artistic understanding. Dancers are encouraged to fulfil their own individual potential and each pupil's progress is monitored carefully.

Sixth Form pupils joining the Drama Course will undertake an intensive and wide-ranging preparation for either direct entry into the theatre, further training at drama school or, with appropriate A Levels, higher education on a relevant degree course.

The Musical Theatre Course for Sixth Form pupils is designed to extend the skills of the all-round performer and to focus them in this popular entertainment area.

Throughout the School, pupils have frequent opportunities to present work in the Markova Theatre and there are regular public shows given by junior and senior pupils. The range of work undertaken provides pupils with the opportunity to become versatile and able to communicate skilfully, whatever the chosen field.

Individual appointments are made to visit the School and auditions are held on a regular basis.

Haileybury

Hertford, Hertfordshire SG13 7NU   Tel: (01992) 463353   Fax: (01992) 470663
E-mail: registrar@haileybury.com   Website: www.haileybury.com   www.gabbitas.co.uk

The Master Mr S A Westley MA
Registrar Mrs E Alexander BA
Founded 1862
School status Independent. Co-educational
Boarding and Day 11–18 Flexi-boarding
available. Boarders from 11.
Religious denomination Church of England
Member of HMC; **Accredited by** HMC
Learning difficulties RA SNU/DYC DYP DYS
Behavioural & emotional disorders CO/ASP AUT
Physical and medical conditions WA2/HEA W
No of pupils 754; *(full boarding)* 500; *(day)*
254; *Senior* 647; *Sixth Form* 298; *Girls* 312;
Boys 442
Teacher:pupil ratio 1:7; **Average class size** 16
Fees per annum *(full boarding)* £14655–
£23085; *(day)* £11535–£17340

Boys and girls, mostly boarding, admitted at 11
into the Lower School, at 13 into the Main School,
and also into the Sixth Form.

Magnificent classical buildings are complemented by modern, state-of-the art developments. Set
in 500 rural acres and situated 20 miles north of
central London, Haileybury combines high academic standards with broad-ranging excellence in
art, music, drama and sport. The school is pleased
to offer International Baccalaureate alongside A
levels. Please contact the Registrar for further
details.

The Royal Masonic School for Girls

Rickmansworth Park, Rickmansworth, Hertfordshire WD3 4HF
Tel: (01923) 773168   Fax: (01923) 896729   E-mail: admissions@royalmasonic.herts.sch.uk
Website: www.royalmasonic.herts.sch.uk   www.gabbitas.co.uk
For further details about the School, please contact Mrs G Braiden, Admissions Secretary.

The Headmistress Mrs D Rose MA (Cantab)
Admissions Secretary Mrs G Braiden
Founded 1788
School status Girls Boarding and Day 4–18
Flexi-boarding available.
Religious denomination Non-Denominational
Member of BSA, GSA
Physical and medical conditions HEA HI
No of pupils 785; *(full boarding)* 100; *(weekly
boarding)* 55; *(day)* 631; *Pre-prep* 50; *Prep* 134;
Senior 426; *Sixth Form* 174; *Girls* 785
Teacher:pupil ratio 1:12
Average class size 18–20
Fees per annum *(full boarding)* £9675–£15720;
(weekly) £9600–£15645; *(day)* £5445–£9705

RMS offers an exceptionally wide-ranging curriculum in a supportive and friendly environment,
where the highest standards prevail. Our girls

receive individual
attention and are
given the confidence
to succeed.

The school has
outstanding facilities
and occupies a stunning 315-acre site. An
impressive sports hall, indoor swimming pool,
squash, tennis and netball courts, and hockey
pitches maintain sporting excellence.

Rickmansworth is close to the M25 and London
is easily accessible.

Boarding pupils are cared for in well-appointed
and spacious houses. In each house there is a
balanced number of boarders and day pupils.

Admission is by the school's own entrance
examination and interview. A number of generous scholarships are available.

England

St Albans High School for Girls

Townsend Avenue, St Albans, Hertfordshire AL1 3SJ   Tel: (01727) 853800   Fax: (01727) 792516
E-mail: admissions@stalbans-high.herts.sch.uk   Website: www.sahs.org.uk   www.gabbitas.co.uk

Headmistress Ms J C Pain MA MA MBA
Founded 1889
School status Independent. Girls Day 4–18.
Religious denomination Church of England
Member of GDST, GSA, ISCis
Accredited by GSA
Learning difficulties SNU/DYS MLD
Physical and medical conditions TW WA2/W
No of pupils 950; *(day)* 950; *Pre-prep* 123; *Prep* 187; *Senior* 469; *Sixth Form* 167; *Girls* 950
Fees per annum *(day)* £7530–£9570
Fees Lunch included for infants (Yrs 1–2)

Curriculum: A broad and balanced academic education is provided to include National Curriculum subjects and others. Teaching methods are modern and extensive use is made of resources such as computers and audio-video equipment. Public examination results at GCSE and A level are of a consistently high standard and, for the vast majority, degree courses follow.

Entry requirements and examinations: Entry is by examination at 4, 5, 7, 11 and 16, with intermediate ages being subject to vacancies.

Academic and leisure facilities: A wide range of extra-curricular activities is offered, with sport, music and drama featuring strongly. Facilities for physical education include playing fields and a sports hall adjoining a brand new complex comprising 25 metre indoor pool, fitness suite and dance studio.

Scholarships/bursaries: Academic and music scholarships are available on entry at 11. Further academic scholarships are available at 16.

St Albans School

Abbey Gateway, St Albans, Hertfordshire AL3 4HB   Tel: (01727) 855521   Fax: (01727) 843447
E-mail: hm@st-albans-school.org.uk   Website: www.st-albans.herts.sch.uk   www.gabbitas.co.uk

The Headmaster Mr A R Grant
Founded 948
School status Boys Day 11–18 (Co-ed VIth Form).Co-educational Sixth Form
Religious denomination Non-Denominational
Member of HMC
No of pupils 772; *Girls* 33; *Boys* 739
Fees per annum *(day)* £11118

Following the abolition of the Government's Assisted Places Scheme, the school is able to offer some assistance with fees in certain circumstances of proven need, from its own endowed bursary fund. All bursaries are means-tested. A variable number of academic scholarships worth up to 50 per cent of the annual fees are awarded on academic merit at 11+, 13+ and 16+. Scholarships for music and art are offered at 13+. Bursaries towards music tuition are provided for pupils from each year in the school. Further details of all awards are available from the Head.

The school is a registered charity and aims to provide an excellent education, enabling pupils to achieve the highest standard of academic success according to ability, and to develop their character and personality so as to become caring and self-disciplined adults.

St Margaret's School

Merry Hill Road, Bushey, Hertfordshire WD23 1DT   Tel: (020) 8901 0870   Fax: (020) 8950 1677
E-mail: admissions@stmargarets.herts.sch.uk   Website: www.stmargaretsbushey.org.uk
www.gabbitas.co.uk   A great education and lasting friendships Set in over 70 acres of parkland
Yet less than an hour from Marble Arch and Heathrow

Headteacher Mrs Lynne Crighton BA (Hons)
Founded 1749
School status Independent. Girls Boarding and
Day 4–18 Flexi-boarding available. Boarders
from 11.
Religious denomination Church of England
Member of BSA, GSA
No of pupils 400; *(full boarding)* 60; *(day)* 340;
Pre-prep 36; *Prep* 61; *Senior* 225; *Sixth
Form* 78; *Girls* 400
Fees per annum *(full boarding)* £18885;
(weekly) £18885; *(day)* £7005–£10545
Fees All fees include lunch for day girls

Established in 1749, St Margaret's educates girls
aged 4 to 18 years. The school is set in over 70
acres of parkland yet is less than an hour from
Marble Arch and Heathrow. We provide a first
class education that delivers an enviable record of
success at all public examinations within a supportive, caring community that encourages lasting
friendships. The original buildings have been
extended and upgraded considerably in the past
decade, including a £3 million sports centre,
which opened in 2002. There is a wide range of
sporting and cultural activities, with language
exchange visits, choir, orchestra, speech and
drama, ballet, judo, the Duke of Edinburgh's
Award Scheme and World Challenge expeditions.
A number of scholarships and bursaries are
available.

England

ACS Hillingdon International School

Hillingdon Court, 108 Vine Lane, Hillingdon, Middlesex UB10 0BE
Tel: (01895) 818402   Fax: (01895) 818404
E-mail: hillingdonadmissions@acs-england.co.uk   Website: www.acs-england.co.uk

Head of School Mrs G Apple
Dean of Admissions Mrs D Fontanes-Halliday
Founded 1967
School status Co-educational Day 4–18.
International Baccalaureate (IB) World School,
also US Advanced Placement (AP) & high
school diploma
Religious denomination Non-Denominational
Member of CIS, IBO, IBSCA, ISA, LISA, NEASC
NEAS&C and inspected by the Independent
Schools Inspectorate on behalf of OFSTED.
No of pupils 580; *(day)* 580; *Girls* 274;
Boys 306
Teacher:pupil ratio 1:9; **Average class size** 20
Fees per annum *(day)* £7610–£15750

ACS Hillingdon International School ranks among
the top independent schools in the UK. Its students have consistently achieved diploma scores
well above international results which has led to
placements in top universities including London
School of Economics, Oxford University, Imperial
College London, University College London, University of Warwick, the School of Oriental and
African Studies and the Royal Academy of Music.
Occupying an 11-acre site, ACS Hillingdon is
situated in a Grade II listed stately mansion with
a modern wing accommodating classrooms, computer labs, an integrated IT network, libraries,
cafeteria, a gymnasium and an auditorium. The
school also has separate early-childhood pavi-
lions and a new music centre with a digital
recording studio, rehearsal rooms, practice studios and a computer lab for music technology.

Northwood College

Maxwell Road, Northwood, Middlesex HA6 2YE   Tel: (01923) 825446   Fax: (01923) 836526
E-mail: admissions@northwoodcollege.co.uk   Website: www.northwoodcollege.co.uk

Head Mistress Mrs R Mercer BA Hons
College status Girls Day 3–18.
Religious denomination Non-Denominational
Member of GSA, ISCis
Accredited by GSA, ISC
Learning difficulties WI/DYP DYS
Physical and medical conditions RA/HEA HI
IM VI
No of pupils 805; *Nursery* 32; *Pre-prep* 103;
Prep 165; *Senior* 381; *Sixth Form* 124; *Girls* 805
Fees per annum *(day)* £3041–£10317

Why choose Northwood College?

One of the ways we achieve our excellent
results in through our unique Thinking Skills Programme. Run in both the Junior and Senior
Schools, this programme teaches the girls to
understand and develop the way they learn. Year
by year, it builds their reasoning skills, improves
their creativity and gives them strategies for
tackling complex decisions. It also shows them
that learning is fun.

We are very proud of what the Thinking
Programme helps our girls achieve. It's just one
of the ways we equip them with skills for life.

To find out what else we can offer your daughter, come to an Open Day or phone us for a
personal tour of the School.

Northwood College – a Thinking School.

St Helen's School

Eastbury Road, Northwood, Middlesex HA6 3AS   Tel: (01923) 843210   Fax: (01923) 843211
E-mail: enquiries@sthn.co.uk   Website: www.StHelensNorthwood.co.uk

Headteacher Mrs M Morris BA
Deputy Head Mr P Tiley BSc
Deputy Head Mrs J Dewhurst BA
Founded 1899
School status Independent. Girls Day and
Boarding 3–18. Boarders from 11.
Religious denomination Christian
Member of GSA, ISCis
Learning difficulties WI/DYP DYS
Behavioural and emotional disorders CO
Physical & medical conditions TW/HEA HI VI
No of pupils 1153; *(full boarding)* 26; *(weekly boarding)* 3; *(day)* 1153; *Nursery* 48; *Pre-prep* 179; *Prep* 247; *Senior* 490; *Sixth Form* 189; *Girls* 1153
Teacher:pupil ratio 1:10; **Average class size** 21
Fees per annum *(full boarding)* £19359; *(weekly)* £18672; *(day)* £6840–£10446

St Helen's School is a highly academic school. Pupils achieve outstanding GCSE and A level results and go to excellent universities of their first choice. The International Baccalaureate Diploma is offered alongside A levels in the Sixth Form. Staff are subject specialists who to inspire a love of their subjects. Girls study two modern foreign languages together with Latin. Science is taught throughout as three separate subjects. Excellent specialist facilities exist for science, design and technology, art, drama, modern languages, music and ICT. Our grounds offer opportunities for a range of sporting activities, several of which are pursued to national standard.

England

MAP OF LONDON

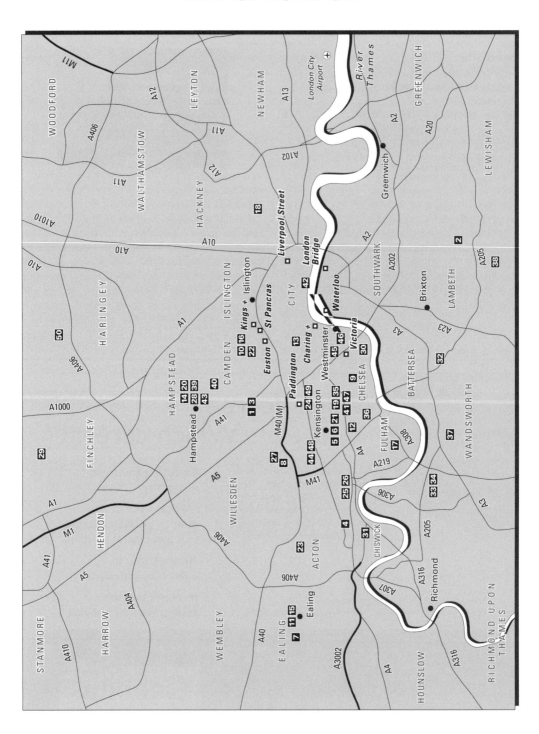

PROFILED SCHOOLS IN LONDON

Map Number		Page Number
1	Abercorn School, NW8	318
2	Alleyn's School, SE22	318
3	The American School in London, NW8	319
4	The Arts Educational School, W4	319
5	Ashbourne Independent Sixth Form College, W8	320
6	Ashbourne Middle School, W8	320
7	Avenue House, W13	321
8	Bassett House School, W10	322
9	Cameron House, SW3	323
10	The Cavendish School, NW1	323
11	Clifton Lodge Preparatory School, W5	324
12	Collingham Independent GCSE and Sixth Form College, SW5	324
13	Davies, Laing & Dick (DLD), W1	325
14	Devonshire House Preparatory School, NW3	326
15	Ealing Independent College, W5	327
16	Francis Holland School, NW1	327
17	Fulham Prep School, W14	328
18	Gatehouse School, E2	328
19	Glendower Preparatory School, SW7	329
20	Hampstead College of Fine Arts, Independent College, NW3	329
21	Hawkesdown House, W8	330
22	International Community School, NW1	331
23	International School of London, W3	331
24	Lansdowne College, W2	332
25	Latymer Prep School, W6	333
26	Latymer Upper School, W6	333
27	The Lloyd Williamson School, W10	334
28	Lyndhurst House Preparatory School, NW3	334
29	Mill Hill School, NW7	335
30	More House School, SW1X	336
31	Orchard House School, W4	322
32	Parkgate House School, SW4	336
33	Prospect House School, SW15	322
34	Putney Park School, SW15	337
35	Queen's Gate School, SW7	337
36	Redcliffe School, SW10	338
37	The Roche School, SW18	338
38	Rosemead Preparatory School, SE21	339
39	The Royal School, Hampstead, NW3	340
40	St Margaret's, NW3	341
41	St Nicholas Preparatory School, SW7	342
42	St Paul's Cathedral School, EC4M	342
43	Southbank International School, Hampstead, NW3	343
44	Southbank International School, Kensington, W11	343
45	Southbank International School, Westminster, W1	344
46	Westminster Abbey Choir School, SW1P	344
47	Westminster Tutors, SW7	345
48	Wetherby Preparatory School, W11	346
49	Wetherby School, W2	346
50	Woodside Park International School, N11	347

England

Abercorn School

28 Abercorn Place, London NW8 9XP
Tel: (020) 7286 4785   Fax: (020) 7266 0219
E-mail: a.greystoke@abercornschool.com   Website: www.abercornschool.com

The Headmistress Mrs A S Greystoke BA
School status Co-educational Day 2–13.
Religious denomination Non-Denominational
No of pupils 380
Girls 190; *Boys* 190
Fees per annum *(day)* £5775–£10785

Abercorn School

The Nursery and younger children are housed in a gracious Victorian mansion in leafy St John's Wood. Year 2 and older children are based in the magnificent listed building formerly occupied by the Marylebone Grammar School. Abercorn has the enviable reputation for developing young children into individuals with the confidence, self-discipline and talents to achieve across the curriculum. Whilst emphasis is placed upon basic skills in literacy and numeracy, the children are also taught and encouraged to participate in music, sport, computing, art and design technology.

French is taught throughout the age groups and Latin from age 9.

Enthusiastic, qualified staff produce excellent academic results in a happy atmosphere. Communication between the School and parents is encouraged in all aspects of school life.

Alleyn's School

Townley Road, Dulwich, London SE22 8SU   Tel: (020) 8557 1500   Fax: (020) 8557 1462
E-mail: registrar@alleyns.org.uk   Website: www.alleyns.org.uk

Headmaster Dr C Diggory BSc, MA, EdD, CMath, FIMA, FRSA
Senior Deputy Head Mr MG Longmore MA, FRSA
Deputy Head Mrs J M Helm BSc, FRSA
Founded 1619   **School status** Independent. Co-educational Day 4–18.
Religious denomination Church of England
Member of HMC, IAPS, SHA
Accredited by HMC, IAPS
Learning difficulties WI/DYC DYP DYS
Behavioural and emotional disorders CO/ADD ADHD ASP TOU
Physical and medical conditions RA SM TW/EPI HEA HI VI
No of pupils 1178; *(day)* 1178; *Girls* 585; *Boys* 593; **Teacher:pupil ratio** 1:9
Average class size Juniors (under 11); 21, Seniors (11–16); 20–25 Sixth Form; 12
Fees per annum *(day)* £9450–£11481

Alleyn's has been committed to providing co-educational excellence for nearly thirty years, as the best framework for boys and girls to achieve their full potential and to develop life-long skills in preparation for university, the world of work and life in general. We aim to achieve high academic success and expect high standards from all our pupils, who are cared for within a culture of strong pastoral care which promotes and values the widest possible range of co-curricular activities. Drama is very strong (National Youth Theatre was founded at Alleyn's), as is Art and Music. Sport is also much valued with many County honours, but 'sport for all' is the aim.

The American School in London

1 Waverley Place, London NW8 0NP   Tel: (020) 7449 1200   Fax: (020) 7449 1350
E-mail: admissions@asl.org   Website: www.asl.org

Head of School Dr W C Mules
Founded 1951
School status Independent. Co-educational
Day 4–18.
Religious denomination Non-Denominational
Member of CASE, CIS, NAIS, CIS, ERB
Accredited by MSA (USA), CIS
Behavioural and emotional disorders CO
Physical and medical conditions SM
No of pupils 1341; *Girls* 652; *Boys* 689
Fees per annum *(day)* £15870–£19440

The American School in London is a co-educational, non-profit institution which offers an outstanding American education. The curriculum leads to an American high school diploma, and a strong Advanced Placement programme enables students to enter the top universities in the USA, the UK and other countries.

The core curriculum of English, maths, science and social studies is enriched with courses in modern languages, computing, fine arts and physical education. Small classes allow teachers to focus on individuals; students are encouraged to take an active role in learning to develop the skills necessary for independent critical thinking and expression. Many extra-curricular activities, including sports, music, drama and community service, are available for students of all ages.

The American School in London welcomes students of all nationalities, including non-English speakers below the age of 10, who meet the scholastic standards. Entry is at any time throughout the year.

The Arts Educational School

Cone Ripman House, 14 Bath Road, Chiswick, London W4 1LY   Tel: (020) 8987 6600
Fax: (020) 8987 6601 E-mail: head@artsed.co.uk Website: www.artsed.co.uk www.gabbitas.co.uk

Headmaster Mr R J Luckham BSc (Hons),
MBIM   **Founded** 1919
School status Independent (special).
Co-educational Day 11–18. Specialises in
Performing Arts but strong on Academics.
Religious denomination Inter-Denominational
Member of ISA, ISCis, SHA
Accredited by ISA, ISC
Learning difficulties CA RA/DYS
No of pupils 150; *(day)* 150; *Senior* 110; *Sixth
Form* 40; *Girls* 99; *Boys* 51
Teacher:pupil ratio 1:7; **Average class size** 12
Fees per annum *(day)* £9324–£10156. No
school scholarships available.

The Arts Educational School (London) provides a stimulating academic curriculum that prepares pupils for the full range of GCSE examinations. In addition, it is a leader in the provision of study and training for Music, Dance and Drama. Pupils are taught in small groups in dedicated subject areas by highly trained specialist staff. To accommodate the arts training there is an extended timetable for all pupils in the senior school (8.30 a.m.–5.30 p.m.).

Many of the school's graduates go on to higher education, professional training and illustrious careers in the world of the performing and creative arts.

England

Ashbourne Independent Sixth Form College

17 Old Court Place, Kensington, London W8 4PL   Tel: (020) 7937 3858   Fax: (020) 7937 2207
E-mail: admin@ashbournecollege.co.uk Website: www.ashbournecollege.co.uk www.gabbitas.co.uk

The Principal Mr M J H Kirby MSc
Vice Principal Ms C S R Brahams BA Hons
(Durham), MA, PGCE
Founded 1981
College status Co-educational Day and
Boarding Boys 14–19 Girls 16–19. Boarders
from 16.
Religious denomination Non-Denominational
No of pupils 175; *(day)* 155; *Girls* 90; *Boys* 85
Average class size 8
Fees per annum *(day)* £13500

Wonderfully situated near Kensington Gardens, Ashbourne is a few minutes away from many of London's greatest attractions. The wide-ranging curriculum embraces both the traditional and the modern. Professor John Foreman, FRCP, oversees Ashbourne's flagship Medical School programme that has helped medical students achieve a 64 per cent success rate over the past three years. There is also an excellent programme for media, including drama, film, fashion, photography, art and graphics.

Class sizes are restricted, reflecting the importance placed on individual attention communication and feedback. Ashbourne believes that high expectations are the key to academic achievement, and encourages and supports students accordingly. We have recently implemented a system of Personal Tutors to enable students to be supported throughout their Sixth Form including their application to UCAS.

Ashbourne Middle School

17 Old Court Place, Kensington, London W8 4PL   Tel: (020) 7937 3858   Fax: (020) 7937 2207
E-mail: admin@ashbournecollege.co.uk
Website: www.ashbournecollege.co.uk   www.gabbitas.co.uk

Principal Mr M J A Kirby MSc, BApSc
Founded 1981
School status Co-educational Day 12–16.
Religious denomination Non-Denominational
Member of CIFE
Accredited by BAC, British Council
No of pupils 25; *Girls* 11; *Boys* 14
Average class size 8
Fees per annum *(day)* £13500

Wonderfully situated near Kensington Gardens, Ashbourne is a few minutes away from many of London's greatest attractions.

Class sizes are restricted to a maximum of ten, reflecting the importance placed on individual attention, communication and feedback. Staff-student relations are personable and informal yet provide discipline and encourage independence and self-reliance.

Our pupils are encouraged to take nine GCSE's, mainly concentrating on traditional subjects; however, they may also take art and design, ICT, photography and Business Studies. In addition to their studies, pupils play sport and are frequently accompanied on trips to the theatre, exhibitions and museums. The College strongly encourages academic success and most students stay on for the Sixth Form.

Ashbourne believes that high expectations are the key to academic achievement, and encourages and supports students accordingly.

The Pastoral Head of the Middle School is Ms Breanne Amy.

Avenue House School

70 The Avenue, Ealing, London W13 8LS   Tel: (020) 8998 9981   Fax: (020) 8991 1533
E-mail: avenuehouseschool@btinternet.com   Website: www.avenuehouse.com

Principal Mrs C Self
Admissions Miss N Jory
School status Independent. Co-educational
Day 3–11.
Religious denomination Non-Denominational
Member of IAPS; **Accredited by** IAPS
Physical and medical conditions SM
No of pupils 140; *(day)* 140; *Girls* 75; *Boys* 65
Average class size 17
Fees per annum *(day)* £4500–£7500

The Preparatory School curriculum, while aware of the National Curriculum, is based on the need to prepare pupils for the relevant public examination of the parents' choice. In conjunction with the traditional academic subjects the children are taught French, music, PE, gymnastics, art and drama. The school has its own small library. We also have the latest in laptop computers for all classes, with a wireless broadband internet connection installed throughout.

England

Bassett House School

60 Bassett Road, London W10 6JP   Tel: (020) 8969 0313   Fax: (020) 8960 9624
E-mail: info@bassetths.org.uk   Website: www.bassetths.org.uk

Head Mrs A Harris BEd(Lond) CEPLF(Caen)
Founded 1947
School status Independent. Co-educational
Day, Boys 3–8, Girls 3–11.
Religious denomination Non-Denominational
Member of IAPS; **Accredited by** IAPS
Learning difficulties WI/DYS
Behavioural and emotional disorders ST
Physical and medical conditions IT TW/HEA VI
No of pupils 148; *(day)* 148; *Nursery* 17;
Pre-prep 93; *Prep* 38; *Girls* 90; *Boys* 58
Teacher:pupil ratio 1:6

Average class size 16–18
Fees per annum *(day)* £5190–£10710

Bassett House School is situated in a large Victorian house in North Kensington, which was recently rebuilt to very high standards. Boys leave the school aged 8 for prep schools specializing in preparation for senior school examinations at 13+. Girls are prepared for senior school examinations at 11+. The school is equipped with a science and IT lab, gym/theatre and school hall, music room and art room.

Orchard House School

16 Newton Grove, Bedford Park, London W4 1LB   Tel: (020) 8742 8544   Fax: (020) 8742 8522
E-mail: info@orchardhs.org.uk   Website: www.orchardhs.org.uk

Headmistress Mrs S A B Hobbs
BA(Hons)(Exeter) PGCE MontDip
School status Independent. Co-educational
Day Boys 4–8 Girls 4–11.
Religious denomination Non-Denominational
Member of IAPS, ISBA
Accredited by IAPS
No of pupils 220
Girls 140; *Boys* 80
Fees per annum *(day)* £4860–£10080

Orchard House School occupies a substantial Norman Shaw house in the conservation area of Bedford Park, Chiswick, with a large garden and recreational area. Boys leave the school at age 8+ for prep schools specializing in preparation for boys' senior school examinations at 13+. Girls are prepared for senior school examinations at 11+. The school has its own sports area and is equipped with a science and IT lab, music room and art room.

Prospect House School

75 Putney Hill, London SW15 3NT   Tel: (020) 8780 0456   Fax: (020) 8780 3010
E-mail: info@prospecths.org.uk   Website: www.prospecths.org.uk

Headmistress Mrs D Barratt MEd (Newcastle)
Founded 1991
School status Co-educational Day 3–11.
Religious denomination Non-Denominational
Member of IAPS
Accredited by IAPS
Learning difficulties SNU
No of pupils 200
Girls 100; *Boys* 100
Teacher:pupil ratio 1:8
Average class size 18
Fees per annum *(day)* £4800–£10410

Prospect House School is a member of House Schools Group and has sister schools at Bassett House School in Kensington and Orchard House School in Chiswick. It is based in an imposing Victorian house opposite Putney Heath. Boys and girls are prepared for examinations at senior school at 11+. The school enjoys a large garden and all-weather sports area. It is also equipped with a maths and IT lab, gym/theatre and school hall, music rooms and art room. Music is a popular key option. The school is highly staffed and equipped. Academic results have been strong.

Cameron House School

4 The Vale, Chelsea, London SW3 6AH

Tel: (020) 7352 4040   Fax: (020) 7352 2349   E-mail: info@cameronhouseschool.org

Website: www.cameronhouseschool.org   www.gabbitas.co.uk

The Headmistress Miss F Stack BA (Hons) PGCE Mont Dip   **Founded** 1985
School status Independent. Co-educational Day 4–11.
Religious denomination Church of England
Member of IAPS, ISCis, NAHT, SATIPS, CReSTeD; **Accredited by** IAPS, ISC
Learning difficulties CA SNU/DYC DYP DYS
Behavioural and emotional disorders ST/ADD
Physical and medical conditions CA RA/VI
No of pupils 112; *(day)* 112; *Pre-prep* 60; *Prep* 52; *Girls* 67; *Boys* 45
Teacher:pupil ratio 1:9; **Average class size** 18
Fees per annum *(day)* £11685
The school operates a sibling discount

Cameron House aims to produce academically confident pupils who appreciate the virtues of courtesy, good manners and kindness, and are positive-minded and confident. Our highly qualified and dedicated teaching staff create a stimulating environment in which initiative and individual objectives can flourish.

The curriculum is broadly based and designed to cultivate a wide range of interests, though emphasis is placed on the core curriculum. Essential disciplines are balanced with aesthetic and practical activities such as speech and drama, debating and French. The school is well equipped with its own class libraries, and a dedicated IT room with a bank of mobile laptops.

Pupils discover their talents through a wide variety of optional clubs after school. Children are encouraged to join the Choirs to develop singing talent.

The learning process necessarily focuses on public exams. For boys these can take place at any time after the age of eight. Girls are prepared for the entrance exam to independent London day or country boarding schools.

The Cavendish School

31 Inverness Street, London NW1 7HB

Tel: (020) 7485 1958   Fax: (020) 7267 0098   E-mail: admissions@cavendish-school.co.uk

Website: www.cavendishschool.co.uk   www.gabbitas.co.uk

For all enquiries please contact the Admissions Secretary, Mrs Frances Jones, as above

Acting Headmistress Miss W Smart BSc (Hons) Dip   **Founded** 1875
School status Girls Day 3–11.
Religious denomination Christian
Member of AGBIS, IAPS, ISBA, ISCis
Accredited by ISC
No of pupils 150; *Nursery* 17; *Pre-prep* 17; *Prep* 116; *Girls* 150
Teacher:pupil ratio 1:8; **Average class size** 20
Fees per annum *(day)* £8598. Nursery from £4,758–£9,480 All fees include lunches and outings

Parents seeking a happy, well-resourced, academic girls' preparatory school should consider The Cavendish School – an independent preparatory and pre-preparatory day school for girls between the ages of three and eleven years and a limited number of boys in the pre-prep. We have a caring family atmosphere based on Christian values, founded in the Catholic tradition. We welcome children of all faiths and none.

The school aims to stimulate the children's attainment of sound academic standards whilst also encouraging the development of their creative skills, confidence and happiness. Particular attention is paid to each pupil's individual needs. Throughout the school the pupil's progress is carefully monitored so that, in consultation with parents, talents may be developed or difficulties overcome with supplementary specialist teaching.

A highly favourable staff-pupil ratio is a feature of this programme. A broad range of subjects and extra-curricular activities, ballet, BAYS science, gymnastics and games is taught by highly qualified experienced staff. An after-school care facility is provided along with flexible nursery arrangements.

England

Clifton Lodge Preparatory School

8 Mattock Lane, Ealing, London W5 5BG
Tel: (020) 8579 3662   Fax: (020) 8810 1332   E-mail: cliftonlodge@btinternet.com

Principal Mr D A P Blumlein BA
School status Boys Day 4–13.
Religious denomination Christian
No of pupils 180; *Boys* 180
Fees per annum *(day)* £7140–£7800

Clifton Lodge is a school that stands for standards: standards of proper behaviour, and standards of personal achievement. We believe that boys want to be successful in life and this they can obtain only by hard work, confidence in their own ability and a properly disciplined approach, whatever the activity. Clifton Lodge seeks at all times to impart these values.

The School is geared to give much individual attention, with boys being able to work at their own level, enabling them to realise their own potential.

The curriculum is based on the need to prepare boys for entry to public school at 13+ through the Common Entrance examination, public school scholarships or other equivalent examinations, and Clifton Lodge is justifiably proud of its excellent record to success in these.

Whereas this provides the core of the academic programme, we consider it essential to educate all pupils as broadly as possible and much time is also given to music (regular choral and instrumental recitals are given), sport (football, rugby, cricket, tennis, athletics, etc) and drama, these avenues providing boys with valuable opportunities to develop further talents and to build up their self-confidence.

The School is of Christian denomination and the daily assembly, attended by the whole community, is based around these ideas.

Choral scholarships: the School has an established choral tradition and choristerships to the value of one third of the basic fees are available to boys who become full choristers.

Collingham Independent GCSE and Sixth Form College

23 Collingham Gardens, London SW5 0HL   Tel: (020) 7244 7414   Fax: (020) 7370 7312
E-mail: london@collingham.co.uk   Website: www.collingham.co.uk

The Principal Mr G Hattee
Founded 1975
College status Co-educational Day 14–20.
Religious denomination Non-Denominational
Accredited by BAC
Learning difficulties DYC DYP DYS
Physical and medical conditions AT RA
No of pupils 230; *Girls* 110; *Boys* 120
Teacher:pupil ratio 1:3
Average class size 5
Fees per annum *(day)* £4170–£15480

- Supportive environment
- Expert tuition
- Rigorous academic standards
- Individual learning programmes
- Small class size

Davies Laing and Dick

100 Marylebone Lane, London W1U 2QB
Tel: (020) 7935 8411   Fax: (020) 7935 0755
E-mail: dld@dld.org
Website: www.dld.org   www.gabbitas.co.uk

Principal Ms E Rickards MA PGCE
Founded 1931
School status Independent. Co-educational
Day 15–19. Boarders from 16.
Religious denomination Non-Denominational
Member of ISA
Accredited by BAC, ISA
Learning difficulties DYS
No of pupils 370; *(day)* 367; *Sixth Form* 367
Girls 185; *Boys* 185
Average class size 5
Fees per annum *(day)* £2500–£16000

Davies Laing and Dick (DLD) is a co-educational London day school accepting pupils from the ages of 15 to 19. There are over 330 students in the Sixth Form studying A levels from a choice of 43 subjects. Two thirds are doing A Levels in the normal way over a two-year period. Another large group joins DLD at the start of Upper Sixth. There are no subject restrictions at A Level. GCSE intensive courses are taught over a one year period. The average class size is 5. Supplementary lessons in English as a foreign language are taken by 6% of the student body.

DLD is housed in two linked buildings in Marylebone, both newly refurbished and very well equipped buildings. There are three laboratories, two IT classrooms, a library for private study with an IT annexe, a GCSE study area, an eighty-seat theatre which is also used to screen films. There is a recording studio and a film edit suite. Many classrooms are equipped with interactive whiteboards. Students are able to access work done in class, teachers' notes and homework assignments remotely via the DLD Virtual School.

Extra-curricular activities include sport, DLD youth theatre, set design, film making, the DLD house band, concerts, French club, life drawing classes, fund raising and Activities Week, which takes place at the end of June. The school day finishes at 4.40pm: most activities take place after this.

While the atmosphere at DLD is more informal than in mainstream independent schools, rules regarding academic performance are strictly enforced. Those who do not hand in work on time are required to attend Supervised Study at the end of the day. Lateness to lessons is not tolerated. There are fortnightly tests in each subject and three weekly reports. Parents receive five reports each year and there are two parents' evenings.

The teaching staff are highly qualified and chosen not just for their expertise but also for their ability to relate positively to young people. The college aims to make learning interesting, active and rigorous. While clear guidelines are very important to ensure pupils establish a good working routine, the college believes strongly that pupils respond best when there is a culture of encouragement. Effort, progress, achievement and courtesy are regularly acknowledged and formally rewarded.

England

Devonshire House Preparatory School

2 Arkwright Road, Hampstead, London NW3 6AE
Tel: (020) 7435 1916   Fax: (020) 7431 4787
E-mail: enquiries@devonshirehouseprepschool.co.uk
Website: www.devonshirehouseschool.co.uk   www.gabbitas.co.uk

Headmistress Mrs S Alexander BA (Hons)
PGCE
Founded 1989
School status Independent. Co-educational
Day Boys 2–13 Girls 2–11.
Religious denomination Non-Denominational
Member of ISA
Accredited by ISA, ISC
Learning difficulties SC WI/DYP DYS
Behavioural and emotional disorders RA
Physical and medical conditions RA/EPI HEA
HI
No of pupils 530; *(day)* 530
Girls 237; *Boys* 293
Fees per annum *(day)* £5625–£10920

Curriculum: Early literacy and numeracy are very important and the traditional academic subjects form the core curriculum. Specialist teaching and the combined sciences form an increasingly important part of the timetable as the children grow older. Expression in all forms of communication is encouraged, with classes also having lessons in art, music, drama, French, and information and design technology. Much encouragement is given to pupils to help to widen their horizons and broaden their interests. The school fosters a sense of responsibility amongst the pupils.

Entry requirements: The offer of places is subject to availability and to an interview. Children wishing to enter the school over the age of six will normally be required to take a formal written test.

Academic and leisure facilities: The school is situated in fine premises in the heart of Hampstead with their own walled grounds. The aim is to achieve high academic standards whilst developing enthusiasm and initiative throughout a wide range of interests. It is considered essential to encourage pupils to develop their own individual personalities and a good sense of personal responsibility.

Scholarships: The school offers academic and music scholarships.

Ealing Independent College

83 New Broadway, Ealing, London W5 5AL   Tel: (020) 8579 6668   Fax: (020) 8567 8688
E-mail: ealingcollege@btconnect.com   Website: www.ealingindependentcollege.com

Principal Dr I Moores BSc, PhD
College status Independent Sixth Form College.
Co-educational Day
Religious denomination Non-Denominational
Accredited by BAC
No of pupils 95; *GCSE* 25; *Sixth Form* 70;
Girls 47; *Boys* 48
Fees per annum *(day)* £1635–£11025

Founded in 1992, Ealing Independent College is accredited by the British Accreditation Council and the Department for Education and Skills. Regular inspections ensure that a high quality of teaching and learning is maintained.

Most students are preparing for entry onto degree courses at major universities. The College has a reputation for helping students onto Medical, Dental, Pharmacy, Business, ICT and Law courses through one- or two-year A-level programmes. At GCSE students follow KS4 through a one- or two-year programme. Students are admitted from Year 9 upwards. The results at both GCSE and A-level are very good for a non-selective school.

The College has well equipped laboratories and a new computer suite. The spacious Study Room is supervised and provides a quiet place for independent learning.

Francis Holland School

Clarence Gate, Ivor Place, London NW1 6XR   Tel: (020) 7723 0176   Fax: (020) 7706 1522
E-mail: admin@fhs-nw1.org.uk   Website: www.francisholland.org.uk

Head Mistress Mrs V M Durham
School status Girls Day 11–18.
Religious denomination Church of England
Member of GSA, IAPS, ISA, ISCis, SHA;
Accredited by GSA, IAPS, ISA
Learning difficulties RA/DYP DYS MLD
Behavioural and emotional disorders RA
Physical and medical conditions RA/HI
No of pupils 430; *Girls* 430
Fees per annum *(day)* £11625

Francis Holland, Clarence Gate, is a happy, academic day school for girls aged 11–18. Within a friendly and supportive atmosphere, pupils achieve excellent examination results. The ethos of the school emphasises courtesy and altruistic behaviour at all times. As part of their curriculum, sixth formers attend weekly lectures from visiting guest speakers, many of them prominent in public life. Sport, drama and music make a particularly strong contribution to the school's lively extra-curricular schedule. The school has its own swimming pool and uses Regent's Park for tennis, hockey, rounders and netball. There are two school orchestras, several choirs and a jazz band. The school runs more than sixty clubs and societies, such as history and politics, ju-jitsu, cookery, water polo, wildlife photography, gymnastics, yoga, kick-boxing and pet club. Charitable initiatives are strongly encouraged and the whole school undertakes an annual sponsored walk for charity in Regent's Park.

England

Fulham Prep School (Prep Dept)

Prep Department, 200 Greyhound Road, London W14 9SD   Tel: (020) 7386 2444
Fax: (020) 7386 2449   E-mail: prepadmin@fulhamprep.co.uk   Website: www.fulhamprep.co.uk
Pre-Prep (4+–7+) based at 47A Fulham High Street London SW6 3JJ

Principal & Head of Prep School Mrs J Emmett
Head of Pre-Prep Ms D Steven
Founded 1996
School status Independent. Co-educational
Day 7–13.
Religious denomination Non-Denominational
No of pupils 249; *Pre-prep* 207; *Prep* 249;
Girls 95; *Boys* 154
Teacher:pupil ratio 1:9; **Average class size** 16
Fees per annum *(day)* £11235

FULHAM PREP SCHOOL

Curriculum: In the Pre-Prep School, the curriculum, though broadly based, lays particular emphasis on the early acquisition of the traditional basic skills of reading, writing and numeracy. We do not prepare children for 7+ and 8+ exams. The curriculum in the Prep School is based on the demands of the 11+ and 13+ Common Entrance exams.

Entry requirements: The school is non-selective at the Reception stage, while entry into other years is by Assessment in maths and English. Siblings of current pupils are given priority.

Academic and other facilities: Academic achievement is strong but we also put a lot of emphasis on all-round development, providing an extensive range of activities featuring Sport, Music, Art and Drama. The school has two choirs and an orchestra. A wide range of lunchtime and after-school clubs is offered each term.

Gatehouse School

Sewardstone Road, Victoria Park, London E2 9JG
Tel: (020) 8980 2978   Fax: (020) 8983 1642
E-mail: admin@gatehouseschool.co.uk
Website: www.gatehouseschool.co.uk

The Headmistress Mrs Belinda Canham JP
BA(Hons) PGCE (Froebel)
Founded 1948
School status Independent. Co-educational
Day 3–11.We have a broad access entry and achieve places in top London independent secondary schools.
Religious denomination Christian
Learning difficulties SNU
No of pupils 220; *(day)* 220; *Nursery* 50;
Pre-prep 100; *Prep* 70
Girls 110; *Boys* 110
Average class size 18
Fees per annum *(day)* £5760–£7050

Founded in May 1948 by Phyllis Wallbank, a pioneer of educational development, in the gatehouse of St Bartholomew of the Great Priory Church, West Smithfield. The school was then a pioneer of much that is now generally accepted in education.

Gatehouse's policy is: Children of any race, colour, creed, background and intellect shall be accepted as students and work side by side without streaming or any kind of segregation with the aim that each child shall get to know and love God, and to develop their own uniqueness of personality to enable them to appreciate the world and the world to appreciate them.

Gatehouse is now located in Sewardstone Road close to Victoria Park, where it continues to follow the education philosophy of Phyllis Wallbank.

Glendower Preparatory School

87 Queen's Gate, South Kensington, London SW7 5JX   Tel: (020) 7370 1927   Fax: (020) 7244 8308
E-mail: office@glendower.kensington.sch.uk   www.gabbitas.co.uk

Head Mistress Mrs R Bowman BA PGCE
Founded 1895
School status Independent. Girls Day 4–11.
Girls Day only
Religious denomination Non-Denominational
No of pupils 182; *Girls* 182
Average class size 16
Fees per annum *(day)* £9990

Why Choose Glendower for your daughter?

Our School is small in numbers, 182 pupils, aged between 4 and 11, but high in expectation and achievement. We aim to provide a stimulating environment in which each girl is valued and can enjoy developing her particular talents to the full, whether it be in art, music, sport, drama or other social activities. In the family atmosphere of Glendower, girls acquire the confidence to develop their talents to the utmost of their ability and gain the solid academic foundations necessary for competitive entry into a leading London day school or boarding school. We are a happy school!

For further details please contact the school office.

Hampstead College of Fine Arts, Independent College

24 Lambolle Place, Hampstead, London NW3 4PG
Tel: (020) 7586 0312   Fax: (020) 7483 0355
E-mail: mail@hampsteadfinearts.com
Website: www.hampsteadfinearts.com

Principal Ms C Cave C F A (Oxon)
Principal Mr N Cochrane C F A (Oxon)
Founded 1978
College status Independent. Co-educational
Day 14–19.
No of pupils 105; *Girls* 45; *Boys* 60
Fees per annum *(day)* £12750

Hampstead College of Fine Arts is a specialist college in the arts and humanities for A level and GCSE. We are situated in Belsize Park and each of the three departments, A level, Art and GCSE has its own specially designed building.

Hampstead College of Fine Arts has approximately 100 students and is high in expectation and achievement. Classes are small to encourage discussion and maximum attention. Each student is supported by a personal tutor and has timetabled weekly meetings and fortnightly reports. The college consistently achieves excellent results with students achieving high examination passes, university and art school acceptance and success in professional careers.

We provide an excellent opportunity to study in a friendly and stimulating atmosphere: a bridge between school and university. All of our tutors are highly qualified university or art school graduates, with over 70 per cent serving as examiners, moderators or advisers for public examinations.

England

Hawkesdown House School

27 Edge Street, Kensington, London W8 7PN
Tel: (020) 7727 9090   Fax: (020) 7727 9988
E-mail: admin@hawkesdown.co.uk
Website: www.hawkesdown.co.uk   www.gabbitas.co.uk

Headmistress Mrs C J Leslie BA Cert Ed
Founded 2001
School status Independent. Boys Day 3–8.
Member of IAPS
Accredited by IAPS, ISC
No of pupils 130; *(day)* 125; *Nursery* 8;
Pre-prep 122; *Boys* 130
Fees per annum *(day)* £9375–£10950

Hawkesdown House is an independent school for boys from the ages of three to eight. In December 2003, the Headmistress was the first Head of a free standing pre-preparatory school to be elected to IAPS (Incorporated Association of Preparatory Schools). Early literacy and numeracy are of prime importance and the traditional academic subjects form the core curriculum. A balanced education helps all aspects of learning and a wide range of interests is encouraged. The School finds and fosters individual talents in each pupil. Boys are prepared for entry at eight to the main London and other preparatory schools. The Headmistress places the greatest importance on matching boys happily and successfully to potential schools and spends time with parents ensuring that the transition is smooth and free of stress.

Sound and thorough early education is important for success, and also for self-confidence. The thoughtful and thorough teaching and care at Hawkesdown House ensures high academic standards and promotes initiative, kindness and courtesy. Hawkesdown is a school with fun and laughter, where boys develop their own personalities together with a sense of personal responsibility.

The School provides an excellent traditional education, with the benefits of modern technology, in a safe, happy and caring atmosphere. Many of the boys coming to the School live within walking distance and the School, although just five years old, has rapidly become an important part of the Kensington community.

There are clear expectations and the boys are encouraged by positive motivation and by the recognition and praise of their achievements, progress and effort. Individual attention and pastoral care for each of the boys is of great importance.

Hawkesdown House has a fine building in Edge Street, off Kensington Church Street.

Parents who would like further information or to visit the School and meet the Headmistress, should contact the School Office for a prospectus or an appointment.

International Community School

4 York Terrace East, Regents Park, London NW1 4PT   Tel: (020) 7935 1206   Fax: (020) 7935 7915
E-mail: admissions@ics.uk.net   Website: www.ics.uk.net

Head of School Mr P Hurd BSc PGCSE
Director of Admissions Ms R Threlfall BSc
PGCSE MA MA
Assistant Director of Admissions Miss A
Dabholkar BA (HONS) MSc
Founded 1979
School status Co-educational Day 3–18.
Religious denomination Non-Denominational
Member of ARELS, CIS, IBO, LISA
Accredited by British Council, DfES
Learning difficulties CA SC SNU/DOW DYC
DYP DYS MLD PMLD SLD SP&LD
Behavioural and emotional disorders ST/ADD
ADHD ASP AUT
No of pupils 240; *Girls* 120; *Boys* 120
Teacher:pupil ratio 1:8; **Average class size** 16
Fees per annum *(day)* £3547–£4649
Additional fees for student support services

ICS is a small friendly central London school for students aged 2½ to 18 years. Children and faculty are from 65 countries (including the UK) and form a dynamic learning community.

A large team of assistants and specialists support class teachers. The school has a strong pastoral care/welfare reputation and classes are kept to a maximum of 18 students. Environmental, sports and language visits to overseas destinations and to our outdoor education centre in Suffolk feature every holiday.

Throughout ICS there is a specialist English for Education department, providing intensive English for students year-round. A strong Special Educational Needs department supports students in all areas of the school.

International School of London

139 Gunnersbury Avenue, London W3 8LG
Tel: (020) 8992 5823   Fax: (020) 8993 7012
E-mail: mail@islondon.com
Website: www.ISLondon.com

Director Mr A Makarem
Founded 1972
School status Independent. Co-educational
Day Boys 3–19 Girls 3–18.
Religious denomination Non-Denominational
Member of CIS, IBO, IBSCA, LISA
Accredited by CIS
Learning difficulties DYS
No of pupils 286; *Girls* 123; *Boys* 163
Fees per annum *(day)* £12000–£16500

The International School of London (ISL) accepts students of all nationalities from pre-school age up to the International Baccalaureate Diploma.

ISL is implementing the IB Primary Years Programme (PYP) throughout all the primary classes, from early childhood (3 years old) to Year Six (10 years old). Using the PYP we provide students with an International Curriculum which focuses on developing the whole child.

The secondary curriculum follows the IB Middle Years Programme and the full IB Diploma. Comprehensive and integrated English as a Second Language programmes are available at all ages. Students can also follow courses in 20 home languages including Arabic, Danish, Dutch, Hindi, Italian, Japanese, Portuguese and Spanish.

To join ISL parents will need to provide the Admissions Office with a completed application form and previous school records. Most students join ISL in September, but we admit students throughout the year, provided that we have places available.

We offer door-to-door transport covering west, central and south London.

England

Lansdowne College

40–44 Bark Place, London W2 4AT   Tel: (020) 7616 4400   Fax: (020) 7616 4401
E-mail: education@lansdownecollege.com Website: www.lansdownecollege.com www.gabbitas.co.uk

Principal Mr H Templeton FCCA
Vice-Principal Mr G Hunter BA FRSA
Founded 1976
College status Independent Sixth Form College with GCSE Department from Year 10. Co-educational Day 14–19.
Religious denomination Non-Denominational
Member of CIFE
Accredited by BAC, British Council
Learning difficulties RA/DYC DYP DYS
Behavioural and emotional disorders RA/ADD ADHD
Physical and medical conditions RA/EPI HEA
No of pupils 200; *Senior* 30; *Sixth Form* 170; *Girls* 95; *Boys* 105
Teacher:pupil ratio 1:7; **Average class size** 8
Fees per annum *(day)* £2650–£13950
Scholarships and bursaries covering part fees (up to a maximum of 50%)are available

Lansdowne College is housed in a modern, spa-cious building with excellent facilities, including a 200-seater hall, in a quiet residential road, one minute's walk from Kensington Gardens and Hyde Park.

The College is renowned for the warm, supportive atmosphere provided by our staff and students together. Our students thrive on a mixture of expert tuition, hard work and pastoral care, and, as young adults, benefit from an environment that, while maintaining academic rigour and discipline, provides a relaxed and friendly atmosphere, allowing each student to achieve his or her full potential.

At Lansdowne we offer all the subjects on the school curriculum and many others that are not. Teaching is in small groups for both A level and GCSE students. We have an expanding GCSE department and we also offer one-term and one-year A level retake courses, alongside traditional A level courses.

Latymer Prep School

LATYMER

36 Upper Mall, Hammersmith, London W6 9TA   Tel: (020) 8748 0303
Fax: (020) 8741 4916   E-mail: mlp@latymerprep.org
Website: www.latymerprep.org   www.gabbitas.co.uk

Principal Mr S P Dorrian BA
Founded 1995
School status Independent. Co-educational
Day 7–11.
Religious denomination Non-Denominational
Member of IAPS, SATIPS; **Accredited by** ISC
Learning difficulties SNU/DYP DYS
Behavioural and emotional disorders CO
Physical and medical conditions WA3/IM;
(day) 165
Average class size 20
Fees per annum *(day)* £11205

Curriculum: Children are taught the full range of subjects following National Curriculum guidelines, but to an advanced standard. Classes are small, which allows for close monitoring and evaluation of each pupil's progress and well-being.

Entry requirements and procedures: The school is academically selective and entry to the school is by assessment in maths, English and verbal reasoning. Visits for prospective parents occur throughout the Autumn term and can be arranged by telephoning for an appointment.

Academic and leisure facilities: Academic achievement is strong, but in addition there is an extensive range of activities featuring sport, music, art and drama. The school has a large choir and its own orchestra.

The school is well resourced, sharing catering, sport and theatre facilities with the Upper School.

Sports include contact and touch rugby, soccer, cricket, tennis, hockey, gymnastics and dance. There is also a thriving swimming club (the school has its own indoor pool). Karate, Mandarin and a whole range of clubs take place after school.

Latymer Upper School

King Street, Hammersmith, London W6 9LR   Tel: (020) 8741 1851   Fax: (020) 8748 5212
E-mail: registrar@latymer-upper.org   Website: www.latymer-upper.org   www.gabbitas.co.uk

Head Mr P J Winter MA (Oxon)
Founded 1624
School status Independent. Co-educational
Day 11–18.
Religious denomination Non-Denominational
Member of HMC; **Accredited by** HMC
Learning difficulties SNU/DYP DYS
No of pupils 1071; *Girls* 274; *Boys* 797
Teacher:pupil ratio 1:10; **Average class size** 22
Fees per annum *(day)* £12465

Latymer conducts competitive examinations, and interviews are held for entry at 7, 11 and 13, and at 16 for the Sixth Form. Scholarships of up to half fees are awarded each year for art, drama and sport in the Sixth Form. Scholarships of up to half fees are awarded annually at 11+, 13+ and 16+ for music. Exhibitions for art, drama, music and sport and fixed-sum awards are available at 11+, 13+ and 16+.

A full range of academic subjects is offered to GCSE and AS/A2 level. Science is taught as separate subjects by subject specialists.

The school has a strong tradition of excellent pastoral care. Teams of form tutors deliver a coherent programme promoting involvement in the community, charity work, and the personal, social and academic development of their form.

Music and drama play a large part in the life of the school. There are several orchestras and choirs and concerts are given each term. The £4 million Latymer Arts Centre (including a 300-seat theatre) opened in January 2000.

The school has a boathouse in the grounds with direct river access, a large sports hall and an indoor swimming pool on site.

The Duke of Edinburgh's Award Scheme flourishes in the school, with several boys and girls achieving the Gold Award each year.

England

The Lloyd Williamson School

12 Telford Road, London W10 5SH   Tel: (020) 8962 0345   Fax: (020) 8962 0345   E-mail:
office@lloydwilliamson.demon.co.uk   Website: www.lloydwilliamsonschools.co.uk
Lucy Meyer (Proprietor and Co-Principal); Aaron Williams (Co-Principal); Emma Cole (Administrator)

Co-Principal Mrs L Meyer
Administrator Miss E Cole   **Founded** 1999
School status Independent. Co-educational
Day 1–13. Small co-eduactional, village style
school in the heart of west London – next to
Portobello Road.
Learning difficulties CA/DYS MLD
Behavioural and emotional disorders ADHD
ASP AUT
Physical and medical conditions CA/CP HEA
HI IM VI
No of pupils 120; *Nursery* 55; *Pre-prep* 24;
Prep 41; *Girls* 60; *Boys* 60
Teacher:pupil ratio 1:5; **Average class size** 15
Fees per annum *(day)* £8100–£11250

The Lloyd Williamson Schools are small, family
run co-educational, village style schools located
in the heart of west London, close to the vibrant,
urban setting that is Portobello Road.

We offer quality, affordable education with
extended hours from 7.30 a.m.–6 p.m. and open
fifty weeks of the year. The school has exclusive
use of a secure, purpose built adventure centre and
children participate in local competitive sporting
leagues throughout the academic year. A cohe-
sive, dedicated staff deliver a comprehensive
curriculum based on the knowledge and approach
to learning expected in a progressive independent
school. We are proud to be a stimulating, supportive, multi-cultural and multi-ability school.

Lyndhurst House Preparatory School

24 Lyndhurst Gardens, Hampstead, London NW3 5NW   Tel: (020) 7435 4936
E-mail: pmg@lyndhursthouse.co.uk   Website: www.lyndhursthouse.co.uk
A large detached Victorian red-brick building with its own playground in a quiet side street.

Headmaster Mr M O Spilberg MA
Founded 1952
School status Boys Day 4–13. A small, friendly
school with an intimate feel and high
expectations.
Religious denomination Non-Denominational
Member of IAPS, ISCis, NAHT, SATIPS
Accredited by IAPS, ISC
Learning difficulties CA
No of pupils 140; *(day)* 140; *Pre-prep* 20; *Prep*
120; *Boys* 140
Teacher:pupil ratio 1:8.4
Average class size 12
Fees per annum *(day)* £10770–£12270

With the opening of our new Pre-Prep department, there are now entry points at 4+, 5+, 6+,
7+, 8+ and 11+ subject to interview and availability.

Mill Hill School

The Ridgeway, Mill Hill, London NW7 1QS
Tel: (020) 8959 1221   Fax: (020) 8906 2614
E-mail: registrations@millhill.org.uk   Website: www.millhill.org.uk

Headmaster Mr W R Winfield
School status Co-educational Boarding and Day 13–18.
No of pupils 601; *(full boarding)* 170
Girls 160; *Boys* 441
Fees per annum *(full boarding)* £20715; *(day)* £13206

Founded in 1807, Mill Hill School offers education to boys and girls aged 13 to 18 years. The schools occupy a magnificent parkland site of 120 acres, only 10 miles from central London and within easy reach of Heathrow Airport and other transport links. The boarders form the heart of a vibrant, open and cosmopolitan community where the contribution of every child is valued.

Curriculum: Mill Hill School offers exciting teaching methods set against a traditional background. At age 13 pupils follow a broad curriculum in which the core subjects are separately streamed by ability. GCSE French may be taken in the second year but all other subjects are taken in the third year.

In the Lower Sixth, pupils take a one-year course to AS level in four subjects. In the Upper Sixth they continue with three of these to A level. Pupils are specially prepared in all subjects for Oxford and Cambridge.

Academic performance: The School has achieved excellent public examination results year on year. Notable strengths are history, art, science, modern languages and business education. In 2004, the three-year average pass rate was another school record, with over 98 per cent of entries graded A-E and over 59 per cent graded A–B. The A–E pass rate for AS level was also a school record at over 95 per cent. At GCSE, 123 pupils achieved an A*–C pass rate, with 76 per cent A* to B and 41 per cent A* or A grades. Academic and careers guidance is provided throughout a pupil's career at the school, with particular care taken over AS and A level and university course choices. More than 95 per cent of our leavers go on to university.

Drama, art, multi-media and IT: Mill Hill has an outstanding reputation for music, drama and art. Over the past four years the school has opened a new drama centre, along with new facilities for art/design and music. The school has over 200 computers and is a leader in IT and internet communication.

Sports and other extra-curricular activities: Historically great sports achievers, we offer over 26 sporting disciplines, and are frequent participants in national and overseas inter-school contests. Extra-curricular activities include a Community Service group and a Combined Cadet Force, along with a wide range of other clubs and societies. Key developments for 2003/2004 include a new Sixth Form Centre, a new indoor swimming pool and a refurbishment programme for one of the classroom blocks.

European initiative: We are leaders in developing an integrated European education policy.

Scholarships: The school offers a range of academic, sports and music scholarships and bursary awards.

Entrance examinations: Entrance at 13+ and 14+ is by tests and interviews and a head's confidential reference. Entrance at 16+ is by interview and school reference and is normally conditional on GCSE performance. Entrance and scholarship examinations are held in January.

For further information please contact the Admissions Office.

England

More House

22–24 Pont Street, Chelsea, London SW1X 0AA   Tel: (020) 7235 2855   Fax: (020) 7259 6782
E-mail: office@morehouse.org.uk   Website: www.morehouse.org.uk

Acting Head Mr Shane Fletcher
Founded 1953
School status Girls Day 11–18.
Religious denomination Roman Catholic
Member of GSA
No of pupils 220; *Girls* 220
Teacher:pupil ratio 1:6
Average class size 18
Fees per annum *(day)* £9780. Includes all meals and books and certain school trips.

More House was founded in 1953 at the request of parents wanting a central London Catholic day school for their daughters. The School is a Catholic Foundation, which accepts pupils of all faiths. It is an Educational Trust with a Board of Governors drawn partly from present and past parents.

Despite our smaller size we offer a full range of academic subjects up to GCSE and A level. Girls go on to a range of prestigious universities to follow courses including medicine, law, history, art, modern languages, drama, mathematics, classics, economics and biochemistry.

Extra-curricular activities include running, swimming, fencing, choirs, orchestra, art, drama, photography, mathematics competitions, public speaking and dance. Girls are encouraged to become involved in a range of activities, although the younger girls also benefit from supervised homework after school.

Two full Scholarships and smaller awards are made on entry to Year 7 and Sixth Form for academic and musical excellence. Occasional scholarships may be awarded at other levels of entry on academic grounds.

Parkgate House School

80 Clapham Common North Side, London SW4 9SD   Tel: (020) 7350 2452   Fax: (020) 7738 1633
E-mail: office@parkgate-school.co.uk   Website: www.parkgate-school.co.uk

Principal Ms C Shanley   **Founded** 1987
School status Co-educational Day 2–11.
Religious denomination Non-Denominational
Member of SATIPS
Learning difficulties WI/DYC DYS
Behavioural and emotional disorders CO ST TS
Physical and medical conditions CA IT SM TW WA2/EPI HEA
No of pupils 200; *Girls* 100; *Boys* 100
Teacher:pupil ratio 1:5; **Average class size** 18
Fees per annum *(day)* £3465–£9570

Parkgate House School is an independent school educating over 200 children aged from two to 11 years. Residing in an historic Georgian Grade II listed building overlooking Clapham Common, the school is supported by an impressive staff of over forty teaching professionals.

Children receive focussed attention in one of three specialised areas: the Montessori Nursery for two to four year olds; the Pre-Preparatory Department for those aged four to seven and the Preparatory Department for the seven to 11 age range.

At any age, children enjoy an expansive, high-quality curriculum, which is further enhanced by an established after school programme including choir, IT, drama, French, sport and horse riding.

A recent Ofsted report praised Parkgate House as 'a very good school with a friendly and welcoming atmosphere and an attractive learning environment'.

Putney Park School

11 Woodborough Road, Putney, London SW15 6PY   Tel: (020) 8788 8316   Fax: (020) 8780 2376
E-mail: office@putneypark.london.sch.uk   Website: www.putneypark.london.sch.uk

Headmistress Mrs Ruth Mann BSc (Hons), PGCE
Founded 1953
School status Co-educational Day Boys 4–8 Girls 4–16.
Religious denomination Inter-Denominational
Member of ISCis; **Accredited by** ISA
Learning difficulties SNU/DYP DYS MLD SP&LD
Behavioural and emotional disorders RA/AUT
Physical and medical conditions RA
No of pupils 272; *Prep* 174; *Senior* 97; *Girls* 214; *Boys* 58
Average class size 22
Fees per annum *(day)* £2775–£3170

Putney Park School, established in 1953, and now in the second generation of the Tweedie-Smith family ownership, is situated in a Conservation Area and consists of four delightful Edwardian houses with a welcoming, family atmosphere.

The aim of the School is to provide a sound education in a happy atmosphere.

Pupils are offered a broad curriculum to enable them to develop their creativity and individual talents to their full potential. Pupils thrive in the caring and supportive environment. The school prepares boys for entry to other schools including Colet Court and King's College, Wimbledon at 7+ and 8+. Girls are prepared for entry to other schools, particularly Putney High, Bute House and Wimbledon High at 7+ and 11+.

Queen's Gate School

133 Queen's Gate, Kensington, London SW7 5LE   Tel: (020) 7589 3587   Fax: (020) 7584 7691
E-mail: registrar@queensgate.org.uk   Website: www.queensgate.org.uk

Principal Mrs A M Holyoak CertEd
Founded 1891
School status Girls Day 4–18.
Religious denomination Non-Denominational
Member of GSA
Learning difficulties WI/DYS; *(day)* 422
Fees per annum *(day)* £8700–£10875

Curriculum and academic life: The curriculum is rich, varied, well balanced and as wide as possible during the years leading to the GCSE examinations, and is frequently reviewed to take into account new approaches to teaching and scientific and technological change.

All girls sit GCSE examinations in English Language, English Literature, mathematics, a modern language, and a science, and have the option of taking courses in additional science subjects, the humanities, modern languages, classics, business studies, computer studies, art and design, graphic design, music and drama.

Entry requirements and procedures: Junior School: Girls enter the preliminary form aged four without formal testing. Girls wishing to enter after this take tests in maths and English. Girls in Year 6 are required to pass the London Day Schools Consortium 11+ Examination before moving up into the Senior School. Senior School: Girls sit the London Day Schools Consortium Examination at 11+ and the School's own entrance examinations at 12+, 13+ and 16+. Sixth Form: Girls entering the Sixth Form are required to have at least 5 GCSE passes, grades A–C, with at least an A grade in those subjects they wish to pursue to A2. They are expected to study 4–5 A/S levels and to continue three of those subjects to A2.

Scholarships: One 8+ scholarship (external and internal), two internal Sixth Form scholarships.

England

Redcliffe School

47 Redcliffe Gardens, London SW10 9JH   Tel: (020) 7352 9247   Fax: (020) 7352 6936   E-mail: admissions@redcliffeschool.com   Website: www.redcliffeschool.com   www.gabbitas.co.uk

Headmistress Mrs S Bourne BSc Hons PGCE
Founded 1948
School status Independent. Co-educational
Day Boys 3–8 Girls 3–11. Additional spaces
available in September 2007 due to expansion
Religious denomination Christian
Member of AGBIS, IAPS; **Accredited by** IAPS
Learning difficulties WI/DYP DYS
Behavioural and emotional disorders RA
Physical and medical conditions RA WA3/HEA
No of pupils 97; *Nursery* 12; *Girls* 75; *Boys* 22
Average class size 12
Fees per annum *(day)* £9000. Between £3360–£5040 for nursery

Redcliffe School, founded in 1948, is an established and growing Nursery and Preparatory school situated in Chelsea and easily accessible from all parts of central and west London.

Registration information for all classes may be obtained from the School Office. Redcliffe School Trust is a registered charity. (Charity No: 312716).

The Roche School

11 Frogmore, Wandsworth, London SW18 1HW   Tel: (020) 8877 0823   Fax: (020) 8875 1156
E-mail: office@therocheschool.co.uk   Website: www.therocheschool.co.uk

Headmaster Dr J Roche BSc PhD
Head of Lower School Miss J Calabrini
BA.Hons & Mont Dip
Head of Nursery Schools Mrs G Emery
BA.Hons & Mont Dip
Founded 1983
School status Independent. Co-educational
Day 3–11.
Religious denomination Non-Denominational
Learning difficulties CA SC WI/DOW DYP
DYS MLD
Behavioural and emotional disorders ADD
ADHD ASP AUT
Physical and medical conditions RA/IM
No of pupils 174; *Nursery* 15; *Pre-prep* 53;
Prep 106; *Girls* 86; *Boys* 88
Teacher:pupil ratio 1:9 for reception 1:18 from
year 2; **Average class size** 16
Fees per annum *(day)* £4500–£8910
Bursaries available

DRAMA: NARNIA

Ofsted: "The Roche School fulfils its aims in creating a very caring and happy family environment in which pupils do well. Academic achievement is high"

- Plenty of sport, art, drama, French and music
- Good teaching which matches children's needs.

Rosemead Preparatory School

70 Thurlow Park Road, London SE21 8HZ
Tel: (020) 8670 5865   Fax: (020) 8761 9159   E-mail: admin@rosemeadprepschool.org.uk
Website: www.rosemeadprepschool.org.uk   www.gabbitas.co.uk

Head Teacher Mrs C Brown Cert. Ed., Dip. Ed., Dip.SpLD
Founded 1942
School status Independent. Co-educational Day 3–11.
Religious denomination Non-Denominational
Member of AGBIS, ISA, ISBA, ISCis, NAHT;
Accredited by ISA
Learning difficulties SNU/DYS
No of pupils 311; *Nursery* 31; *Pre-prep* 132; *Prep* 147; *Girls* 180; *Boys* 131
Teacher:pupil ratio 1:12
Average class size 18
Fees per annum *(day)* £6801–£7626

Rosemead is a well-established preparatory school with a fine record of academic achievement. Children are prepared for entrance to independent London day schools at age 11 years, many gaining awards and scholarships. The school has a happy, family atmosphere with boys and girls enjoying a varied, balanced curriculum which includes maths, English, science, French, information and communication technology, arts and humanities. Music and drama are strong subjects with tuition available in most orchestral instruments and various music groups meeting frequently. A full programme of physical education includes gymnastics, most major games, dance and (from age 6) swimming. Classes make regular visits to places of interest. Two residential field study courses are arranged for the junior pupils along with various school trips. Main entry to the school is at Nursery (age 3), following informal assessment, and at National Curriculum Year 3, following a formal assessment. The school is administered by a board of governors elected annually by the parents.

England

The Royal School, Hampstead

65 Rosslyn Hill, Hampstead, London NW3 5UD   Tel: (020) 7794 7708   Fax: (020) 7431 6741
E-mail: enquiries@royalschoolhampstead.net   Website: www.royalschoolhampstead.net
www.gabbitas.co.uk   Nursery website: www.royalschool-nursery.net

Headmistress Mrs J Ebner-Landy B.Ed (Hons)
Cantab, MA (Lon) PG Dip Couns, Cert FP
Founded 1855
School status Girls independent day and
boarding school. Age range: 3–18. Weekly and
flexi-boarding available.
Religious denomination Non-Denominational
Member of AGBIS, ISA, GSA, BSA, ISBA
Accredited by ISA Artsmark
Learning difficulties SC/DYS MLD
Behavioural and emotional disorders ADD
Physical and medical conditions HEA HI
No of pupils 220; *(full boarding)* 19; *(weekly
boarding)* 9; *(day)* 192; *Nursery* 8; *Pre-prep* 42;
Prep 36; *Senior* 111; *Sixth Form* 23; *Girls* 220
Teacher:pupil ratio 1:9; **Average class size** 13
Fees per annum *(full boarding)* £13050–
£16200; *(weekly)* £10800–£13470; *(day)*
£6510–£8160

The school was founded in 1855, originally for the
daughters of soldiers serving in the Crimean War.
It is now a day and boarding school for 260 girls
from 3–18 years, with boarders from 11 years.

The school is situated in pleasant surroundings
only 250m from Hampstead Village Centre. It has
comfortable modern boarding accommodation
and spacious, light classrooms with panoramic
views over London. The development of the
school continues with two recently refurbished
science laboratories, upgraded boarding accommodation, a Sixth Form Study Centre, and an Early
Years Unit.

The school's aim is to provide an excellent
education based on individual attention, in a
happy, positive and secure environment, to allow
each girl to develop her full potential and to
become a self-confident, responsible young adult
with a clear sense of duty towards others.

Curriculum: Girls follow a balanced curriculum, including 2 modern languages and 3
Sciences, leading to GCSE, AS and A2. The performing and visual arts are a particular strength of
the school, and charity work and life enrichment
programmes are important aspects of the school's

ethos which feature strongly throughout the
school. The school is consistently placed amongst
the highest positions in the Value Added Key
Stage 3 to GCSE Performance Tables. EFL is also
offered. The Sixth Form has its own self-contained
Study Centre with computer workstations, common room and kitchen. A maximum of 15 girls
per year are offered a personal approach to education and a wide life enrichment programme
including local community projects, overseas visits and affiliation with business and universities.

Extra-curricular activities feature widely in the
school's routine programme, and includes the
Duke of Edinburgh's Award scheme, karate,
drama, art, music, ballet, dance and a wide range
of games and sports.

Boarding: The school offers a homely and
friendly boarding environment where girls thrive.
Each new boarder is assigned a 'buddy' who acts
as a companion and helper. Communication
between parents and staff is welcomed and
encouraged. Weekly boarding is a popular
option; 'flexi-boarding' and 'sleep-overs' can be
arranged when required.

Entry requirements: Junior School: in-class
assessment. Senior School: examinations based
on National Curriculum (Maths, English and
Reasoning). Previous school reports required for
all pupils.

Bursaries and academic, music and art scholarships: Means tested bursaries are awarded
throughout all year groups including boarding.
Scholarships are awarded at Early Years, KS1,
Year 7 and 12.

St Margaret's School

18 Kidderpore Gardens, London NW3 7SR
Tel: (020) 7435 2439   Fax: (020) 7431 1308
E-mail: headmistress@st-margarets.co.uk
Website: www.st-margarets.co.uk   www.gabbitas.co.uk

Headmistress Mrs S Meaden BA, MBA, PGCE
Founded 1884
School status Independent. Girls Day 4–16.
Religious denomination Church of England
Member of AGBIS, ISA
Accredited by ISA, ISC
Learning difficulties RA/DYC DYP DYS MLD
No of pupils 143; *(day)* 143; *Prep* 67; *Senior* 76; *Girls* 143
Teacher:pupil ratio 1:7
Average class size 14
Fees per annum *(day)* £7965–£9180

St Margaret's offers a high standard of teaching in small classes. Pupils follow the National Curriculum. French begins in the infant classes, and in the senior school Spanish, Russian and classical civilisation are offered in addition to the core National Curriculum subjects. All girls go on to full-time Sixth Form education. Recent leavers are now studying at South Hampstead High School, Francis Holland, Channing, Camden School for Girls, and Fine Arts College.

The girls frequently visit London theatres, art galleries and concert halls. Extra-curricular activities include netball, drama clubs, self-defence, batik classes, yoga, and junior and senior choirs. Girls may have individual instrumental and speech and drama lessons.

Entrance is by interview at ages 4, 5 and 6, and by interview and written test from the age of 7. A prospectus is available from the school and Suzanne Meaden is happy to see parents at any time.

England

St Nicholas Preparatory School

23 Prince's Gate, London SW7 1PT   Tel: (020) 7225 1277   Fax: (020) 7823 7557
E-mail: info@stnicholasprep.co.uk Website: www.stnicholasprep.co.uk www.cognitaschools.co.uk

Headmaster Mr D Wilson BEd MA Dip TEFL
Founded 1968
School status Co-educational Day 3–11.
Member of NAHT
Learning difficulties SNU/DYS
Behavioural & emotional disorders ADD ASP
Physical and medical conditions WA3
No of pupils 250; *Girls* 125; *Boys* 125
Teacher:pupil ratio 1:10; **Average class size** 16
Fees per annum *(day)* £6510–£10470

At Prince's Gate, overlooking Hyde Park, Nursery and Reception classes have been in existence since 1968, offering a child-centred approach to learning using the Montessori method in classes of around 20 children. In 1998 the school developed its facilities to offer a broad-based, traditional programme of education to prepare pupils for entrance examinations to all the leading senior schools at 7+, 8+ and 11+. The school has a fully equipped science room, two networked suites of personal computers and 12 wireless laptops, an outstanding library, and also benefits from its own gymnasium and ballet floor. The academic programme is based on the National Curriculum of England and Wales, and includes a full range of sports, music and arts, providing a balanced and challenging curriculum. We take full advantage of being within walking distance of museums and other famous places of interest.

St Paul's Cathedral School

2 New Change, London EC4M 9AD
Tel: (020) 7248 5156   Fax: (020) 7329 6568
E-mail: admissions@spcs.london.sch.uk
Website: www.spcs.london.sch.uk

Head Master Mr A H Dobbin
Founded 1123
School status Co-educational Boarding and Day 4–13. Boarders from 7
Religious denomination Church of England
No of pupils 226; *(full boarding)* 40; *(day)* 185; *Girls* 86; *Boys* 140
Average class size 18
Fees per annum *(full boarding)* £5688; *(day)* £9102–£9810

Governed by the Dean and Chapter, the original residential choir school now includes non-chorister day boys and girls from age 4–13.

Curriculum: A broad curriculum leads to scholarship and Common Entrance examinations at 13 and the school has an excellent record in placing pupils in senior schools of their choice, many with scholarships. A wide variety of sport and musical instrument tuition is offered. Choristers receive an outstanding choral training as members of the renowned St Paul's Cathedral Choir.

Facilities: The refurbishment of the school's facilities has provided a separate Pre-Preparatory Department, improved classrooms and new boarding facilities for the choristers.

Admission: Children are interviewed and tested before September entry at 4+ or 7+ years old. Voice trials and tests for choristers are held three times a year for boys of nearly 7 years and upwards.

Southbank International School, Hampstead

16 Netherhall Gardens, Hampstead, London NW3 5TH
Tel: (020) 7243 3803   Fax: (020) 7727 3290
E-mail: admissions@southbank.org
Website: www.southbank.org   www.gabbitas.co.uk

Head Mr N Hughes
School status Co-educational Day 3–11.
Member of IBO, IBSCA, ISCis, LISA
Accredited by CIS, ISC, MSA (USA)
Learning difficulties WI/DYP DYS
Behavioural and emotional disorders RA/ADD
Physical and medical conditions CA IT RA
WA2/CP HEA HI
No of pupils 200; *(day)* 200
Girls 100; *Boys* 100
Average class size 16
Fees per annum *(day)* £9630–£16800

The Hampstead branch of Southbank International School serves pupils from 3 to 11 years from over 30 countries including the UK. The school is in a new, purpose-built property. The International Baccalaureate Primary (IBPYP) programme is taught. Further details are available on the school website. Students completing the Primary Years programme are eligible to transfer to the Middle and High School at the new Westminster campus.

Learning difficulties: WI/DYP DYS

Behavioural and emotional disorders: RA/ADD

Physical and medical conditions: CA IT RA WA2/CP HEA HI

Southbank International School, Kensington

36–38 Kensington Park Road, London W11 3BU
Tel: (020) 7243 3803   Fax: (020) 7727 3290
E-mail: admissions@southbank.org
Website: www.southbank.org

Head Mr N Hughes
School status Co-educational Day 3–11.
Repeat from previous publication
Member of IBO, ISCis, LISA
Accredited by ISC
Learning difficulties SNU WI/DYP DYS MLD
Behavioural and emotional disorders RA/ADD
Physical and medical conditions WA3
No of pupils 200; *Girls* 100; *Boys* 100
Fees per annum *(day)* £9630–£15600

Southbank Kensington is a designated Primary School for children aged 3 to 11 years. Students are from over 20 countries including the UK. The International Baccalaureate Primary Years programme (IBPYP) is taught. Further details are available on the school website. Students completing the Primary Years Programme are eligible to transfer to the Middle School in the new Westminster campus.

England

Southbank International School, Westminster

63–65 Portland Place, London W1B 1QR
Tel: (020) 7243 3803   Fax: (020) 7727 3290
E-mail: admissions@southbank.org   Website: www.southbank.org

Head Mr N Hughes
School status Co-educational Day 11–18
Member of CIS, IBO, IBSCA, ISCis, LISA;
Accredited by ISC
Learning difficulties WI/DYP DYS MLD
Behavioural and emotional disorders RA/
ADHD
No of pupils 275; *Girls* 142; *Boys* 135
Average class size 16
Fees per annum *(day)* £16800–£18600

Southbank Westminster, Portland Place (11–16) is the location for the Middle and High School, with IB Diploma Students (16–18) having dedicated facilities in the new annexe in Fitzrovia. Students come from around 56 countries including the UK. The International Baccalaureate Middle Years programme (IBMYP) and IB Diploma are taught. The IB Diploma is a rigorous A level alternative now recognized worldwide for university entrance requirement. Further details are available on the school website.

Westminster Abbey Choir School

Dean's Yard, London SW1P 3NY
Tel: (020) 7222 6151   Fax: (020) 7222 1548
E-mail: headmaster@westminster-abbey.org   Website: www.westminster-abbey.org

Head Mr J Milton
School status Independent. Boys Boarding 8–
13 Flexi-boarding available.
Religious denomination Church of England
No of pupils 33; *(full boarding)* 33; *Boys* 33
Fees per annum *(full boarding)* £5085

Westminster Abbey Choir School offers a unique opportunity for musical boys between the ages of 7 and 13.

The Abbey is one of most famous churches in the world, with a colourful history dating back over a thousand years. Today its choir school is the only remaining school in Britain exclusively for choristers.

The 30 or so boys live, work and play in the precincts of the Abbey, surrounded by trees and the peace of Dean's Yard and yet right in the heart of one of the most exciting and diverse cities in the world. Every day during term time they sing in one of the world's great choirs, playing a central part in daily services and in national and state occasions.

It is an outstanding opportunity for boys from all backgrounds who enjoy singing and would relish being part of a small, close-knit team. All schools claim to be unique, but this school is indeed quite unlike any other.

Every boy receives a generous scholarship, including free tuition on two musical instruments throughout his five-year career, so no one should be discouraged from applying on financial grounds.

We are looking for promise and potential rather than experience. If you have a son of about 7 or 8 who shows musical promise do please contact us for a prospectus.

Westminster Tutors

86 Old Brompton Road, London SW7 3LQ   Tel: (020) 7584 1288   Fax: (020) 7584 2637
E-mail: info@westminstertutors.co.uk   Website: www.westminstertutors.co.uk

Principal Mr J J Layland BSc ARCS
Founded 1934
School status Independent. Co-educational
Day 14+ for full time GCSE and A-Level
students. Flexi-boarding available. We tutor all
ages for CE, Scholarship, GCSE and A-Level.
Learning difficulties WI/DYP DYS
No of pupils 40; *(day)* 20; *Girls* 20; *Boys* 20
Teacher:pupil ratio 1:1; **Average class size** 3
Fees per annum *(day)* £13500–£21000
Fees The fees quoted are for 3 & 5 A-Levels.

Westminster Tutors has been widely known and highly respected since its establishment in 1934. We are a small co-educational college with a friendly atmosphere and excellent examination results in a wide range of subjects. Our small teaching groups allow tutors to pay special attention to the particular needs of students and help them achieve their potential. Classes combine hard work with lively discussions, and students have access to study rooms and computers. There are also common rooms where students and staff can mingle freely during breaks.

We offer regular and intensive A-level and GCSE courses and preparation for Common Entrance. Private tuition at all levels is available throughout the year. We have been preparing students for entrance to top Universities, including Oxford and Cambridge, for seven decades.

England

Wetherby Preparatory School

19 Pembridge Villas, London W11 3EP
Tel: (020) 7243 0243   Fax: (020) 7313 5244
E-mail: admin@wetherbyprep.co.uk

Head Teacher Mr R Greenwood BSc FTCL ARCM
Founded 2004
School status Independent. Boys Day 8–13. We currently have Year 4, 5 and 6 pupils, having opened in September 2004.
Religious denomination Christian
Learning difficulties WI/DYS
Physical and medical conditions RA
No of pupils 84; *(day)* 84; *Prep* 84; *Boys* 84
Teacher:pupil ratio 1:16
Average class size 12–18
Fees per annum *(day)* £11850

Following on with the traditions of the pre-preparatory, Wetherby School, Wetherby Preparatory has grown quickly to gain a place in the London Independent sector. Well-qualified, dedicated teachers inspire the boys in a nurturing, fun-filled environment, instilling traditional values including hard work and good manners.

Wetherby School

11 Pembridge Square, London W2 4ED   Tel: (020) 7727 9581   Fax: (020) 7221 8827
E-mail: learn@WetherbySchool.co.uk   Website: www.alphaplusgroup.co.uk

Head Mistress Mrs J Aviss MA London
Founded 1951
School status Boys Day 4–8.Wetherby Preparatory boys 8–13,11 Pembridge Villas W11 3EP automatic entry Pre-Prep boys.
Religious denomination Non-Denominational
Learning difficulties WI/DYP DYS
Physical and medical conditions RA/HEA
No of pupils 235; *Pre-prep* 235; *Boys* 235
Teacher:pupil ratio 1:10; **Average class size** 21
Fees per annum *(day)* £10560

Wetherby School is an independent school for boys aged 4 to 8½ years. The school is based in a freehold, double-fronted listed building of the Italian Ornate style dating back to 1849. It overlooks the beautiful Pembridge Square gardens, where the boys enjoy playtime each day.

There is no test on entry; places are offered on interview with the parents and the Head Teacher.

Expectations of the boys are good social skills, discipline and the ability to interact with their peer group in a confident and caring manner. The school prides itself on attention to detail; each child is valued as an individual and this is implemented through a high teacher:pupil teaching ratio.

Wetherby is a traditional school; high academic standards prevail and the boys enjoy a healthy balance between this and many other curriculum activities that are offered during the school day. Sports and the Arts have a particularly high profile within the school. Wetherby offers excellent facilities for IT, library, indoor gym and individual specialist teaching if required. In addition, the school is well known for the home cooked healthy lunches it provides.

The school operates a sibling policy, though early registration is advised. Please contact the Administrator's office in the first instance.

Woodside Park International School

6 Friern Barnet Lane, London N11 3LX   Tel: (020) 8920 0600   Fax: (020) 8211 4605
E-mail: admissions@wpis.org   Website: www.wpis.org

Head Mr D P Rose MA(Ed),BA,Cert Ed,LPSH
School status Co-educational Day 2–19.
Boarders from 16.
Religious denomination Non-Denominational
Member of CReSTeD, IBO, ISCis, LISA;
Accredited by CIS, IAPS, ISA, ISC
Learning difficulties SNU/MLD
Physical and medical conditions SL
No of pupils 405; *Girls* 144; *Boys* 261
Fees per annum *(day)* £4365–£15900

Woodside Park International School provides a unique school environment where all areas of achievement are celebrated and where our students take pride in being members of a thriving school community. It is an accredited International Baccalaureate World School authorised to teach all three of the IB Programmes – Primary Years Programme (PYP), Middle Years Programme (MYP) and the Diploma programme. It combines the very best features of a traditional curriculum with opportunities for discovery, inquiry and extended learning. Children are challenged to think, learn, take risks and discover new things in a happy and caring environment. The school also encourages and enables students to become responsible and successful members of a diverse world community.

With an emphasis on individual progress and talent, the school prepares students well for life beyond school: higher education, business, family, society; wherever in the world the student might be now, or might choose to go.

England

MAP OF THE HOME COUNTIES (SOUTH)

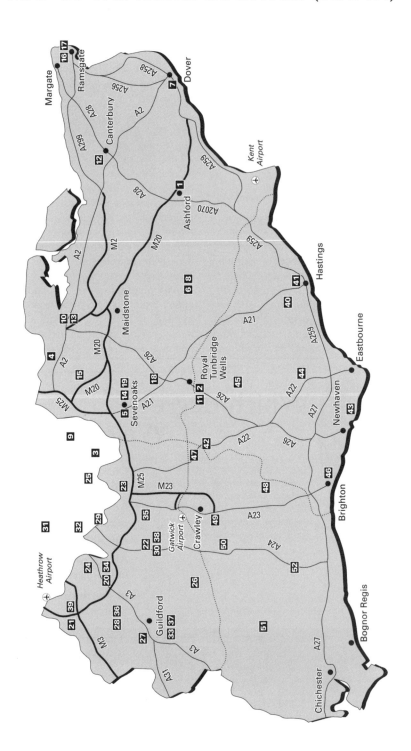

PROFILED SCHOOLS IN THE HOME COUNTIES (SOUTH)

(Incorporating the counties of Kent, Surrey, East Sussex, West Sussex)

Map Number		Page Number
1	Ashford School, Ashford, Kent	350
2	Beechwood Sacred Heart, Tunbridge Wells, Kent	350
3	Breaside Preparatory School, Bromley, Kent	351
4	Cobham Hall, Gravesend, Kent	351
5	Combe Bank School, Sevenoaks, Kent	352
6	Cranbrook School, Cranbrook, Kent	352
7	Dover College, Dover, Kent	353
8	Dulwich Preparatory School, Cranbrook, Kent	353
9	Farringtons School, Chislehurst, Kent	354
10	Gad's Hill School, Rochester, Kent	354
11	Holmewood House School, Tunbridge Wells, Kent	355
12	Kent College, Canterbury, Kent	355
13	Rochester Independent College, Rochester, Kent	356
14	Sevenoaks School, Sevenoaks, Kent	356
15	Steephill Independent College, Longfield, Kent	357
16	St Lawrence College, Ramsgate, Kent	358
17	St Lawrence College Junior School, Ramsgate, Kent	358
18	Tonbridge School, Tonbridge, Kent	359
19	Walthamstow Hall, Sevenoaks, Kent	359
20	ACS Cobham International School, Cobham, Surrey	360
21	ACS Egham International School, Egham, Surrey	360
22	Box Hill School, Dorking, Surrey	361
23	Caterham School, Caterham, Surrey	361
24	Claremont Fan Court School, Esher, Surrey	362
25	Croham Hurst School, South Croydon, Surrey	363
26	Duke of Kent School, Ewhurst, Surrey	363
27	Frensham Heights, Farnham, Surrey	364
28	Hoe Bridge School, Woking, Surrey	364
29	Homefield Preparatory School, Sutton, Surrey	365
30	Hurtwood House, Dorking, Surrey	366
31	Kew Green Preparatory School, Richmond, Surrey	367
32	Marymount International School, Kingston upon Thames, Surrey	367
33	Prior's Field School, Godalming, Surrey	368
34	Reed's School, Cobham, Surrey	369
35	Royal Alexandra and Albert School, Reigate, Surrey	370
36	St Andrew's (Woking) School Trust, Woking, Surrey	370
37	St Hilary's School, Godalming, Surrey	371
38	St Teresa's School, Dorking, Surrey	372
39	TASIS The American School in England, Thorpe, Surrey	373
40	Battle Abbey School, Battle, East Sussex	374
41	Buckswood School, Hastings, East Sussex	374
42	Michael Hall (Steiner Waldorf School), Forest Row, East Sussex	375
43	Newlands School, Seaford, East Sussex	376
44	St Bede's Schools, Hailsham, East Sussex	377
45	St Leonards-Mayfield School, Mayfield, East Sussex	378
46	St Mary's Hall, Brighton, East Sussex	379
47	Brambletye, East Grinstead, West Sussex	380
48	Burgess Hill School for Girls, Burgess Hill, West Sussex	381
49	Cottesmore School, Pease Pottage, West Sussex	382
50	Farlington School, Horsham, West Sussex	383
51	Seaford College, Petworth, West Sussex	384
52	Windlesham House, Pulborough, West Sussex	385

England

Ashford School

East Hill, Ashford, Kent TN24 8PB   Tel: (01233) 739030   Fax: (01233) 665215
E-mail: registrar@ashfordschool.co.uk   Website: www.ashfordschool.co.uk

Head Mr M R Buchanan BSc. Hons
Founded 1898
School status Independent. Co-educational
Day and Boarding Boys 3–12 Girls 3–18(Co-ed
3–11) Flexi-boarding available. Boarders from
10. From September 2007 Boys will be able to
enrol in the Sixth Form and also into Boarding
Religious denomination Inter-Denominational
Member of BSA, IAPS, ISCis, SHMIS
Learning difficulties WI/DYP DYS MLD
Behavioural and emotional disorders RA/
ADHD ASP
Physical and medical conditions RA WA3/VI
No of pupils 689; *(full boarding)* 102; *(weekly
boarding)* 7; *(day)* 587; *Nursery* 67; *Pre-prep*
110; *Prep* 165; *Senior* 228; *Sixth Form* 119;
Girls 525; *Boys* 164
Average class size 15
Fees per annum *(full boarding)* £20046–
£21501; *(weekly)* £18210–£18639; *(day)*
£5100–£11799

A new chapter has begun in the long history of
Ashford School as it opens its doors to boys as
well as girls. Parents choose Ashford School for
many reasons: high achievement leading to the
best UK and overseas universities, close attention
to the needs of the individual, an orderly, challenging and supportive environment, a wide range of
co-curricular activities and energetic, specialist
teachers that are supported by extensive resources
and inventive leadership.

If boarding is what you are after there are two
high quality boarding houses catering for children
from 11–18 years. Both provide shared rooms of
two or three children or in individual study bedrooms with en-suite bathrooms. An international
flavour pervades the boarding houses and the
diversity of cultures provides a stimulating term-
time home. With no lessons on Saturday there is
plenty of time to make use of the school facilities
or participate in a variety of visits to London,
Canterbury or elsewhere.

Beechwood Sacred Heart School

12 Pembury Road, Tunbridge Wells, Kent TN2 3QD   Tel: (01892) 532747   Fax: (01892) 536164
E-mail: bsh@beechwood.org.uk   Website: www.beechwood.org.uk   www.gabbitas.co.uk

Headmaster Mr N R Beesley MA (Oxon)
Founded 1915
School status Independent. Girls Boarding and
Day 3–18 (Boys 3–11) Flexi-boarding
available. Boarders from 10.
Religious denomination Roman Catholic
Member of BSA, GSA, ISCis
Accredited by GSA
Learning difficulties WI/DYC DYP DYS
Behavioural and emotional disorders RA/ADD
ASP AUT; **Physical and medical conditions** AT
RA SM/EPI HEA
No of pupils 397; *(full boarding)* 55; *(weekly
boarding)* 15; *(day)* 130; *Nursery* 34; *Prep* 199;
Senior 198; *Sixth Form* 55; *Girls* 310; *Boys* 87
Teacher:pupil ratio 1:9; **Average class size** 15
Fees per annum *(full boarding)* £19695;
(weekly) £17460; *(day)* £11850. Fees per term
(full boarding) £6,565; (weekly) £5,820; (day)
£3,950

Beechwood is a
happy, friendly
school, firmly com-
mitted to the single-
sex education of
girls at secondary
level, as we believe
that this provides
for them a secure
environment in which their educational and pastoral needs can be met most effectively.

Curriculum: A broad curriculum is followed;
small classes and committed staff produce excellent examination results at all levels. Government
league tables for 2005 and 2006 placed Beechwood as the top girls' school in Kent for added
value at GCSE. At A level, 100% pass rate and
77% A and B grades were achieved by our Sixth
Formers who all gained places in higher education at universities, including Oxbridge.

Breaside Preparatory School

41 Orchard Road, Bromley, Kent BR1 2PR   Tel: (020) 8460 0916   Fax: (020) 8466 5664
E-mail: info@breaside.co.uk   Website: www.breaside.co.uk   www.cognitaschools.co.uk

Headmaster Mr N D Kynaston
Founded 1950
School status Co-educational Day 3–11.
Religious denomination Non-Denominational
Member of IAPS; **Accredited by** IAPS
Learning difficulties CA SNU/DYP DYS
Behavioural and emotional disorders RA
Physical and medical conditions IT RA/HEA
No of pupils 249; *Girls* 107; *Boys* 142
Average class size 20
Fees per annum *(day)* £3630–£7185

Breaside is a co-educational school with a well-established reputation for friendliness and high achievement. On the Chislehurst side of Bromley, it is easily reached from many parts of South East London.

Curriculum A strong emphasis is placed on individual attention in small classes. Children are prepared for all senior schools and those with additional promise sit scholarships. The broadly based curriculum aims to help children fulfil their potential. French is taught from Reception and pupils are able to participate in the many games, clubs and activities. The school is well-resourced and enjoys the support of belonging to Cognita Schools Ltd.

Entry requirements Interview and test after five years of age. The school is well worth a visit to experience the busy, caring environment created by our dedicated staff.

Cobham Hall

Cobham, Gravesend, Kent DA12 3BL   Tel: (01474) 823371   Fax: (01474) 825906
E-mail: enquiries@cobhamhall.com   Website: www.cobhamhall.com   www.gabbitas.co.uk

Headmistress Mrs H Davy MA (Oxon)
Registrar Mrs S Ferrers
Head of Sixth Form Mr A Pinchin MA (Cantab)
Founded 1962
School status Independent. Girls Boarding and Day 11–18 Flexi-boarding available.
Religious denomination Inter-Denominational
Member of BSA, CReSTeD, GSA, ISCis, Round_Square; **Accredited by** GSA, ISC
Learning difficulties SNU/DYC DYP DYS
Physical and medical conditions HI
No of pupils 220; *(full boarding)* 114; *(weekly boarding)* 16; *(day)* 90; *Girls* 220
Teacher:pupil ratio 1:6; **Average class size** 15
Fees per annum *(full boarding)* £18000–£22800; *(weekly)* £18000–£22800; *(day)* £11850–£15750

One of Britain's leading girls' schools, Cobham Hall promotes excellence in all subjects and enables the majority of students to proceed to higher education. Specialist help is provided for dyslexic students and our EFL Department offers overseas students English language support.

The school is housed in a beautiful 16th century mansion set in landscaped parkland of 150 acres with a purpose-built classroom block, modern boarding houses, an indoor swimming pool and sports centre.

Membership of Round Square, an affiliation which unites schools around the world, provides the opportunity for international exchanges.

Cobham Hall is situated 25 miles from central London, with easy access to international airports.

England

Combe Bank School

Combe Bank Drive, Sundridge, Nr Sevenoaks, Kent TN14 6AE
Tel: (01959) 563720   Fax: (01959) 561997
E-mail: enquiries@combebank.kent.sch.uk   Website: www.combebank.kent.sch.uk

The Headmistress Mrs R Martin M.ED. NPQH
FRSA **Founded** 1924
School status Girls Day 3–18.
Religious denomination Roman Catholic
Member of GSA; **Accredited by** GSA
Learning difficulties RA/DYC DYP DYS
Behavioural and emotional disorders ASP
Physical & medical conditions SL TW/EPI HEA
No of pupils 361; *(day)* 361; *Nursery* 30;
Pre-prep 15; *Prep* 135; *Senior* 144; *Sixth
Form* 37; *Girls* 348; *Boys* 13
Fees per annum *(day)* £6825–£12225

Combe Bank school is a thriving, Independent girls school ranging from 3 to 18 years of age. With small classes, excellent facilities, and first rate teaching, the girls achieve admirable exam results. With outstanding Key stage two SATS results in English and Maths, 100% pass rate at GCSE and A level, and a 100% university success rate.

The school has excellent ICT facilities with over 200 fully networked computers and video conferencing facilities. Our £1.7 million sports complex, houses a 25 metre pool, a fitness Suite, and a large multi purpose sports hall, along with five outdoor tennis/netball courts. We are also a leading Duke of Edinburgh award scheme school. For our sixth formers we have a purpose built centre.

With our school buses travelling in from Bromley, Borough Green, Oxted, and Sevenoaks, it is now easy for parents from further afield to look at Combe Bank as a viable prospect for their girls. We are also only 10 minutes drive from the centre of Sevenoaks.

Cranbrook School

Cranbrook, Kent TN17 3JD   Tel: (01580) 711800   Fax: (01580) 711828
E-mail: registrar@cranbrook.kent.sch.uk Website: www.cranbrookschool.co.uk www.gabbitas.co.uk

Headteacher Mrs A Daly MA   **Founded** 1518
School status State (Voluntary-aided).
Co-educational Day and Boarding 13–18.
Boarders from 13. Co-educational boarding
and day.
Religious denomination Non-Denominational
Member of BSA, ISBA
Learning difficulties RA/DYP DYS
Behavioural & emotional disorders RA/ADD ASP
Physical and medical conditions RA SM/EPI
No of pupils 760; *(full boarding)* 236; *(day)*
524; *Sixth Form* 300; *Girls* 367; *Boys* 393
Average class size 30
Fees per annum *(full boarding)* £8580–£9240

Cranbrook is a selective co-educational boarding and day Science Specialist school offering a superb all-round education at a very reasonable cost, with a wide range of extra-curricular activities in a small country town setting in the beautiful Kentish Weald. High academic standards of 99

per cent A-C grades at GCSE and 100 per cent pass rate (67 per cent A/B grades) at A level. Over 95 per cent of students go on to university.

Music, art and drama thrive and teams compete at the highest levels in all major sports. Musical activities include an orchestra and choral society; many productions for music and drama are held in our superb 400-seat theatre. Cranbrook has fine facilities for the creative arts, including a new Performing Arts Centre, which includes a state-of-the-art recording studio, a new Sixth Form centre and a design/technology centre. Team and individual sports are an important part of Cranbrook life and the school has plentiful playing fields, a swimming pool, a sports hall and Astro-Turf pitches. Teams play at the highest levels locally and nationally.

Entry at 13+ and 16+ is by interview and examination. Details from the Registrar, Cranbrook School. Cranbrook School (VA) exists to promote education in Cranbrook.

Dover College

Effingham Crescent, Dover, Kent CT17 9RH   Tel: (01304) 205969   Fax: (01304) 242208
E-mail: registrar@dovercollege.org.uk   Website: www.dovercollege.org.uk   www.gabbitas.co.uk

The Headmaster Mr Stephen Jones MSc MLitt
FRSA   **Founded** 1871
College status Independent. Co-educational
Boarding and Day 4–18 Flexi-boarding
available. Boarders from 11.
Religious denomination Church of England
Member of BSA, CReSTeD, ISCis, SHMIS
Accredited by GSA, ISC, SHMIS International
Study Centre on site
Learning difficulties WI/DYP DYS
Behavioural and emotional disorders CO/ADD
ADHD
Physical and medical conditions RA SM/EPI
HEA HI
No of pupils 360; *(full boarding)* 120; *(weekly
boarding)* 13; *(day)* 227; *Pre-prep* 70; *Senior*
191; *Sixth Form* 99; *Girls* 154; *Boys* 206
Teacher:pupil ratio 1:8
Average class size GCSE 15–20; A level 10–15
Fees per annum *(full boarding)* £14970–
£20550; *(weekly)* £13920–£16200; *(day)*

£5055–£10170
Sibling/HM Forces bursaries available.
International Study Centre on site

Dover College is a small dynamic school, where
pupils are given the opportunity to fulfil their
potential within a happy, caring environment.
Pupils benefit enormously from small classes,
excellent teaching and from the breadth of education on offer. Music, art, drama and sport are an
integral part of the curriculum. Scholarships are
also available from 11+.

Dulwich Preparatory School, Cranbrook

Coursehorn, Cranbrook, Kent TN17 3NP   Tel: (01580) 712179   Fax: (01580) 715322
E-mail: registrar@dcpskent.org   Website: www.dcpskent.org   www.gabbitas.co.uk

Headmaster Mr S L Rigby BA PGCE
Founded 1939
School status Co-educational Day and
Boarding 3–13 Flexi-boarding available.
Boarders from 9.
Religious denomination Church of England
Member of IAPS; **Accredited by** IAPS
Learning difficulties CA SNU/DYP DYS
Behavioural & emotional disorders ADHD ASP
Physical & medical conditions IT RA/EPI HEA IM
No of pupils 531; *(weekly boarding)* 8; *(day)*
523; *Nursery* 20; *Pre-prep* 119; *Prep* 384;
Girls 252; *Boys* 279; **Average class size** 20
Fees per annum *(day)* £3879–£11370
Boarding now charged on daily basis £30 per
night

The school is fully co-educational, taking pupils
on a first come, first served basis. There is a strong
academic tradition enabling children to achieve
scholarships to top senior schools. Up-to-date

teaching has achieved notable successes in music
and art. Entry is at 3+ and 4; by assessment from 7+
onwards.
Curriculum
National Curriculum followed. Usual subjects
taught, plus French, art, DT, drama, IT, music and
physical education.
Examinations offered
Pupils prepare for 11+, Common Entrance and
scholarships.
Academic and leisure facilities
Music School, IT & CDT centre, new theatre
and art rooms. Astroturf, athletics track, playing
fields, tennis courts, sports hall complex, two
swimming pools.
Boarding facilities
Regular and part-boarding from age nine in two
houses. Boarding charged nightly. Six to eight
pupils in each dormitory. Gifted children catered
for. Remedial and dyslexia help given. Several
trained staff.

England

Farringtons School

Perry Street, Chislehurst, Kent BR7 6LR   Tel: (020) 8467 0256   Fax: (020) 8467 5442
E-mail: admissions@farringtons.kent.sch.uk   Website: www.farringtons.org.uk www.gabbitas.co.uk

Headmistress Mrs C James MA
Registrar Mrs F Vail   **Founded** 1911
School status Independent. Co-educational
Day and Boarding Boys 3–7 Girls 3–19 Flexi-
boarding available. Boarders from 11.
Religious denomination Methodist
Member of BSA, GSA, ISCis; **Accredited by**
British Council, GSA, ISC
Learning difficulties SNU/DYP DYS MLD
Behavioural and emotional disorders RA
Physical & medical conditions RA/EPI HEA HI VI
No of pupils 478; *(full boarding)* 43; *(weekly
boarding)* 2; *(day)* 433; *Nursery* 24; *Prep* 204;
Senior 207; *Sixth Form* 67; *Girls* 450; *Boys* 28
Average class size 16 (juniors), 20 (seniors)
Fees per annum *(full boarding)* £17820;
(weekly) £16740; *(day)* £9690

Farringtons School has a wide ability intake and a commitment to stretch every pupil to the very best of his or her ability. We are proud of the way we educate our pupils, combining traditional values with the skills required for the 21st century.

We have a range of facilities, including a new computer suite, impressive sports hall with dance studio and weights room, a technology centre and a swimming pool. Our boarding facilities have just been refurbished, giving girls comfortable study-bedrooms all freshly decorated with new carpets, curtains and modern furniture.

Farringtons School is situated on a beautiful 25-acre site in a peaceful Kent village: yet it is a mere 12 miles from central London. It is also ideally located close to airports and the M25.

Gad's Hill School

Higham, Rochester, Kent ME3 7PA   Tel: (01474) 822366   Fax: (01474) 822977
E-mail: admissions@gadshillschool.co.uk   Website: www.gadshill.org   www.gabbitas.co.uk

Headmaster Mr D G Craggs B.Sc, MA, NPQH
Admissions Sec Mrs S Fitzgerald
Founded 1924
School status Independent. Co-educational
Day 3–16.Co-educational Indpendent day only
Religious denomination Non-Denominational
Member of ISA; **Accredited by** ISA, ISC ISA ISC
Learning difficulties SNU/DYS
Physical and medical conditions RA SM WA3
No of pupils 360; *(day)* 360; *Nursery* 20;
Pre-prep 60; *Prep* 100; *Senior* 180; *Girls* 180;
Boys 180
Teacher:pupil ratio 1:10; **Average class size** 20
Fees per annum *(day)* £5895–£6795

Once the home of Charles Dickens, Gad's Hill School is surrounded by beautiful grounds, playing fields and countryside.

At Gad's we believe that education is primarily about 'learning for life' and that while academic success is a priority, it is only a part of what makes Gad's so successful. Excellent teaching, enthusiastic students and staff, and our friendly, close community all help to ensure that our children achieve success in life.

School days, according to perceived wisdom, are supposed to be 'the happiest days of your life'. Children who enjoy school are much more likely to learn productively and to achieve success, and therefore it will be no surprise that one of our priorities is to ensure that all of our pupils are happy. At Gad's Hill you will find that small classes, picturesque surroundings and a positive approach help to produce an environment where your child will thrive and succeed.

Holmewood House

Langton Green, Tunbridge Wells, Kent TN3 0EB   Tel: (01892) 860000   Fax: (01892) 863970
E-mail: registrar@holmewood.kent.sch.uk Website: www.holmewood.kent.sch.uk www.gabbitas.co.uk

The Headmaster Mr A S R Corbett MA PGCE
Founded 1945
School status Co-educational Day and
Boarding 3–13 Flexi-boarding available.
Boarders from 9.
Religious denomination Inter-Denominational
Member of IAPS, ISBA, ISCis
Accredited by IAPS
Learning difficulties SNU/DYP DYS MLD
Behavioural and emotional disorders CA CO
ST TS/ASP
Physical and medical conditions CA SM/EPI
HEA HI VI
No of pupils 530; *(weekly boarding)* 7; *(day)*
523; *Nursery* 36; *Pre-prep* 145; *Prep* 349;
Girls 207; *Boys* 323
Teacher:pupil ratio 1:8; **Average class size** 15
Fees per annum *(weekly)* £17175; *(day)*
£4640–£13635

Holmewood House is renowned for its highly

qualified staff, superb facilities and broad curriculum (covering all aspects of the National Curriculum, Common Entrance and scholarship examinations to independent schools), resulting in outstanding academic results. We encourage all children to achieve their true potential in a warm and friendly atmosphere by fostering confidence and enthusiasm.

Set in 22 acres of beautiful grounds, Holmewood is a happy busy place, where every child is considered unique. We have strong Sport, Music, Drama and Art departments and offer a wide range of activities so all our children find something to inspire them.

We offer weekly and flexi-boarding. Form teachers are responsible for pastoral care and a tutor system for the older children ensures that each child is cared for and guided in all matters during their time at school.

Essentially non-selective, but all children are assessed prior to entry.

Kent College

Whitstable Road, Canterbury, Kent CT2 9DT   Tel: (01227) 763231   Fax: (01227) 787450
E-mail: enquiries@kentcollege.co.uk   Website: www.kentcollege.com   www.gabbitas.co.uk
Junior School website: www.kentcollege.com/junior

Head Mr G G Carminati MA, FRSA
Deputy Head Mr J G Waltho MA
Founded 1885   **College status** Independent.
Co-educational Boarding and Day 3–18 Flexi-boarding available. Boarders from 7.
Religious denomination Methodist
Member of HMC, IAPS, ISCis
Accredited by HMC, IAPS, ISC
Learning difficulties SNU/DYP DYS
Behavioural and emotional disorders CO
ST/ADD ASP AUT
Physical & medical conditions SM TW/HEA HI
No of pupils 652; *(full boarding)* 169; *(weekly boarding)* 5; *(day)* 478; *Nursery* 34; *Pre-prep* 159; *Senior* 295; *Sixth Form* 164; *Girls* 291; *Boys* 361; **Average class size** 15
Fees per annum *(full boarding)* £15750–£21570; *(weekly)* £15750–£20910; *(day)* £7590–£12630. Fees for attending the International Study Centre are £8,170 per term

(boarding) and £5,190 (day)

Kent College is a vibrant co-educational boarding and day school, taking children from 3 to18 years. We offer full, weekly and flexible boarding, small classes and a broad curriculum that allows all students to fulfil their potential. The visual and performing arts have a high profile, as does sport, and the school also has its own farm, and an International Study Centre and Dyslexic Unit. A superb new Music Centre opened in 2006.

Rochester Independent College

Star Hill, Rochester, Kent ME1 1XF
Tel: (01634) 828115   Fax: (01634) 405667   E-mail: admissions@rochester-college.org
Website: www.schoolcanbedifferent.org   www.gabbitas.co.uk

Co Principal Mr A Brownlow MA Hons, MPhil
Founded 1985
College status Co-educational Day and
Boarding 11–21 Flexi-boarding available.
Boarders from 16   **Accredited by** BAC
Learning difficulties DYP DYS
Behavioural and emotional disorders RA
No of pupils 220; *(full boarding)* 70; *Girls* 110;
Boys 110
Fees per annum *(full boarding)* £20850; *(day)*
£12750

Rochester Independent College is a progressive alternative to traditional private education for day and boarding students. The focus is on examination success and progression to university in a lively, supportive and informal atmosphere. Students achieve A level and GCSE results that often exceed their expectations. There is no uniform, no bells ring and everybody is on first name terms.

For many of our students the College is the first place where they have been engaged by education and have found the freedom to be themselves. We believe that that confidence and self-esteem is best fostered in a warm, informal atmosphere of trust, honesty, and mutual respect between students and teachers.

The College is not academically selective and direct entry is possible into any school year.

Sevenoaks School

Sevenoaks, Kent TN13 1HU   Tel: (01732) 455133   Fax: (01732) 456143   E-mail:
regist@sevenoaksschool.org   Website: www.sevenoaksschool.org   www.gabbitas.co.uk

Head Mrs C L Ricks MA   **Founded** 1432
School status Independent. Co-educational
Day and Boarding 11–18. Boarders from 11.
Religious denomination Inter-Denominational
Member of BSA, HMC, IBO, ISCis
Accredited by HMC, ISC
Learning difficulties WI/DYP DYS
Behavioural and emotional disorders CO RA
Physical & medical conditions SM WA2/HEA W
No of pupils 981; *(full boarding)* 333; *(day)*
648; *Senior* 569; *Sixth Form* 412; *Girls* 494;
Boys 487
Teacher:pupil ratio 1:10; **Average class size** 15
Fees per annum *(full boarding)* £22959–
£24894; *(day)* £14319–£16263. Higher fees
shown are for direct entrants to the Sixth Form.

Sevenoaks is a co-educational, independent, day and boarding school, situated next to the 1,000 acres of Knole Park, 30 minutes from central London and Gatwick Airport, and an hour from

Heathrow. Approximately one-third of the 980 students are boarders. Pupils worldwide enter at 11, 13 or 16, taking GCSEs and the International Baccalaureate. Sevenoaks aspires to high academic standards – all students proceed to Oxbridge and major universities – while providing excellent facilities for sport and co-curricular activities. More than 50 scholarships are awarded annually for academic excellence, art, music and all-round ability. Prospectus and further details are available from the Registrar.

Steephill Independent School

Castle Hill, Fawkham, Longfield, Kent DA3 7BG   Tel: (01474) 702107   Fax: (01474) 706011
E-mail: secretary@steephill.co.uk   Website: www.steephill.co.uk

Headteacher Mrs C Birtwell BSc. MBA PGCE
Bursar Mrs Nicola Kiley   **Founded** 1935
School status Independent. Co-educational
Day 3½–11.
Religious denomination Church of England
Accredited by ISA
Learning difficulties CA WI/DYS MLD
Behavioural and emotional disorders RA ST
Physical and medical conditions RA TW WA2
No of pupils 108; *Girls* 54; *Boys* 54
Teacher:pupil ratio 1:12; **Average class size** 14
Fees per annum *(day)* £3932

Steephill is an independent day school which takes pupils from 3 ½ to 11 years old. It is situated in the beautiful Fawkham Valley countryside in a quiet lane looking over the 13th century village church. The school was founded in 1935 by Miss Eileen Bignold, who established its excellent reputation for high academic standards. These have been continued by the Educational Trust, which was formed in 1990 to run the school through a Board of Governors. Our small classes bring out the best in young children, who receive all the help and encouragemnet they need from Steephill's qualified and experienced teachers. With just a maximum of 16 pupils in a class, each child benefits from the individual attention necessary to achieve his or her full potential. As a small school the staff, parents and children all know each other and this contributes to our happy, family atmosphere.

England

St Lawrence College

College Road, Ramsgate, Kent CT11 7AE   Tel: (01843) 572931   Fax: (01843) 572917
E-mail: ah@slcuk.com   Website: www.slcuk.com

Headmaster Rev C W M Aitken BA (Durham)
Founded 1879
College status Independent. Co-educational
Boarding and Day 11–18. Boarders from 11.
Religious denomination Church of England
Member of HMC, ISCis; **Accredited by** HMC
Learning difficulties CA SNU/DYC DYP DYS
MLD
Behavioural and emotional disorders ST/ADD
ADHD ASP
Physical and medical conditions WA3/HEA VI
No of pupils 325; *(full boarding)* 174; *(day)*
151; *Nursery* 23; *Pre-prep* 35; *Prep* 79; *Senior*
225; *Sixth Form* 100; *Girls* 125; *Boys* 200
Teacher:pupil ratio 1:8; **Average class size** 15
Fees per annum *(full boarding)* £21180;
(weekly) £21180; *(day)* £12405

over the world and has some of the finest boarding accommodation in the country.

The newly opened Kirby House accommodates students aged 11 and 12 in modern five-bedded dormitories with en-suite facilities. Senior students are accommodated in recently refurbished five-bedded dormitories, double and single rooms. Outstanding results are achieved by the most academic students who progress to many of the top universities. The school is also highly regarded as a centre of excellence for 'value added'. The school is close to the channel tunnel and the port of Dover and has excellent transport links to London and Europe. Gatwick and Heathrow airports are within easy reach.

Walk through the historic arch at St Lawrence College in Kent and you will immediately feel at home. The school welcomes students from all

St Lawrence College Junior School

College Road, Ramsgate, Kent CT11 7AF   Tel: (01843) 572931   Fax: (01843) 572917
E-mail: ah@slcuk.com   Website: www.slcuk.com   www.gabbitas.co.uk

Head of the Junior School Mr S J E Whittle BA
(Hons)   **Founded** 1884
College status Independent. Co-educational
Boarding and Day 3–11 Flexi-boarding
available. Boarders from 7.
Religious denomination Church of England
Member of IAPS, ISCis; **Accredited by** IAPS
Learning difficulties SNU/DYC DYP DYS MLD
Behavioural and emotional disorders ST/ADD
ADHD ASP
Physical and medical conditions RA WA3/EPI
HEA VI
No of pupils 137; *(full boarding)* 4; *(day)* 133;
Nursery 23; *Pre-prep* 35; *Prep* 79; *Girls* 55;
Boys 82
Teacher:pupil ratio 1:8; **Average class size** 15
Fees per annum *(full boarding)* £16029;
(weekly) £16029; *(day)* £4845–£9891

Christian values, in which all children are encouraged to fulfil their potential. Academic expectations are high, but realistic and open-minded, and pupils are provided with a wide range of opportunities.

A dedicated team of teachers aims to find something special in everyone. And, as members of the wider College community, pupils get the best of both worlds: the peace and security of a self-contained, family environment, along with access to the Senior School's spacious grounds and outstanding facilities.

Pay us a visit, and see for yourself! A warm welcome is guaranteed.

St. Lawrence College Junior School offers a caring, supportive atmosphere, based on traditional

Tonbridge School

Tonbridge, Kent TN9 1JP   Tel: (01732) 304297   Fax: (01732) 363424
E-mail: admissions@tonbridge-school.org
Website: www.tonbridge-school.co.uk   www.gabbitas.co.uk

Headmaster Mr T H P Haynes BA
Admissions Registrar Mr D M Robins MA
Founded 1553
School status Independent. Boys Boarding and Day 13–18.
Religious denomination Church of England
Member of BSA, HMC; **Accredited by** ISC
Learning difficulties SNU/DYP DYS
Behavioural & emotional disorders CO/ADHD
Physical and medical conditions AT SM WA3/HEA
No of pupils 755; *(full boarding)* 438; *(day)* 317; *Boys* 755; **Teacher:pupil ratio** 1:8
Fees per annum *(full boarding)* £25212; *(weekly)* £25212; *(day)* £18279

Tonbridge School was founded in 1553 and today occupies an extensive site of about 150 acres on the northern edge of Tonbridge. Academic standards are high. The 2005 *Good Schools Guide* says of Tonbridge School: 'One of the very best, outstanding in everything that really counts'. The 2006 A level results included 94.5 per cent A and B grades and a 100 per cent pass rate. Over 20 per cent of leavers go to Oxbridge. Facilities are outstanding for sport, music, drama, art and technology. Both boarders and day boys benefit from strong pastoral support based in the seven boarding houses and five day houses. Generous scholarships are available.

Walthamstow Hall

Hollybush Lane, Sevenoaks, Kent TN13 3UL   Tel: (01732) 451334   Fax: (01732) 740439
E-mail: registrar@walthamstowhall.kent.sch.uk
Website: www.walthamstow-hall.co.uk   www.gabbitas.co.uk

The Headmistress Mrs J Milner MA (Oxon)
Founded 1838
School status Independent. Girls Day 3–18. Plus small number of girls accepted at 2½ years.
Religious denomination Inter-Denominational
Member of AGBIS, GSA, IAPS, ISCis
Accredited by GSA, IAPS, ISC
Learning difficulties WI/DYP DYS
Physical & medical conditions SL SM TW/HEA
No of pupils 494; *(day)* 494; *Nursery* 12; *Pre-prep* 82; *Prep* 207; *Senior* 287; *Sixth Form* 78; *Girls* 494; **Average class size** 16
Fees per annum *(day)* £2965–£4080

We are a selective, independent day school for girls, offering excellent facilities with a caring and supportive environment from Kindergarten to Sixth Form. Set in beautiful grounds in the centre of town, with good transport links and minibus services, we offer a broad and varied curriculum with many extra-curricular activities. The combination of first-class teachers and small class sizes means that each child is given a high level of personal attention, enabling them to reach their full potential. We have our own theatre, swimming pool and extensive sports grounds. Girls have many opportunities to excel in music, art, drama and sport, with some of our teams competing at national and international level. Entry is at 3+, 4+, 7+, 11+, 13+ and 16+. In the Sixth Form there are over 23 subjects to choose from and girls benefit from small tutor groups with specialist staff. Scholarships and bursaries available.

England

ACS Cobham International School

Heywood, Portsmouth Road, Cobham, Surrey KT11 1BL Tel: (01932) 867251 Fax: (01932) 869789
E-mail: cobhamadmissions@acs-england.co.uk   Website: www.acs-england.co.uk

Head of School Mr T J Lehman
Dean of Admissions Mrs E Allis
Founded 1967
School status Independent. Co-educational.
Day ages 2–18. Boarding ages 12–18.
Religious denomination Non-Denominational
Member of CIS, IBO, IBSCA, ISA, ISCis, LISA,
NEASC NEAS&C and inspected by the
Independent Schools Inspectorate (ISI) on
behalf of OFSTED.
No of pupils 1300; *(full boarding)* 60; *(weekly boarding)* 40; *(day)* 1200; *Girls* 581; *Boys* 719
Teacher:pupil ratio 1:9; **Average class size** 20
Fees per annum *(full boarding)* £26670–
£27890; *(weekly)* £23600–£24820; *(day)*
£5150–£16500. £5150 for Rising 3; £7610 for
full-day PreKindergarten

Offering both the International Baccalaureate (IB)
Diploma and American Advanced Placement
(AP) courses, ACS Cobham graduates attend leading universities throughout the world including
Cambridge, Harvard, Oxford and the London
School of Economics. Situated on a 128-acre site,
the ACS Cobham campus has excellent sports
facilities with on-site soccer and rugby fields,
softball and baseball diamonds, an all-weather
Olympic-sized track, tennis courts, a six-hole golf
course and a sports centre which houses a basket-
ball/volleyball show court, 25-metre competition-
class swimming pool, dance studio, fitness suite
and cafeteria. A Co-educational boarding house
provides separate-wing accommodation for 110
students aged between 12 and 18. The two-per-
son rooms have ensuite facilities and internet
connections. The school's Early Childhood programme was rated outstanding in every category
in its recent ISI report.

ACS Egham International School

Woodlee, London Road (A30), Egham, Surrey TW20 0HS   Tel: (01784) 430800 Fax: (01784) 430626
E-mail: eghamadmissions@acs-england.co.uk   Website: www.acs-england.co.uk

Head of School Ms M Hadley
Dean of Admissions Ms J Love
Founded 1967
School status Co-educational Day ages 2–18.
International Baccalaureate (IB) World School,
with IB Middle Years and Primary Years
Programmes and high school diploma
Religious denomination Non-Denominational
Member of CIS, IBO, IBSCA, ISA, ISCis, LISA,
NEASC NEAS&C and inspected by the
Independent Schools Inspectorate (ISI) on
behalf of OFSTED.
No of pupils 550; *(day)* 550
Girls 267; *Boys* 283
Teacher:pupil ratio 1:9; **Average class size** 16
Fees per annum *(day)* £5150–£16330

ACS Egham International School is the UK's most
successful young International Baccalaureate (IB)
school. Its students have consistently achieved
100 per cent pass rates and diploma score
averages well above international results. This has
led to placements in top universities worldwide.
Additionally, the school is one of only 3 schools
offering the IB Primary Years Programme (PYP),
the Middle Years Programme (MYP) and the IB
Diploma as well as an American High School
Diploma. Situated on a 20-acre site ACS Egham
has students from 29 nationalities speaking 19
languages, all seeking a world-class education.
With a wireless network on campus, the school
operates a comprehensive information technology programme supported by extensive use of
laptops and individual data technology storage
units.

Box Hill School

Mickleham, Dorking, Surrey RH5 6EA   Tel: (01372) 373382   Fax: (01372) 363942
E-mail: enquiries@boxhillschool.org.uk Website: www.boxhillschool.org.uk   www.gabbitas.co.uk

Headmaster Mr M Eagers MA
Registrar Mrs K Hammond   **Founded** 1959
School status Independent. Co-educational
Boarding and Day 11–18 Flexi-boarding
available. Boarders from 11.
Religious denomination Non-Denominational
Member of AGBIS, BSA, ISA, ISBA, ISCis,
Round_Square, SHA, SHMIS
Accredited by British Council, ISC, SHMIS
British Council, ISC, SHMIS
Learning difficulties CA SNU/DYC DYP DYS
Behavioural & emotional disorders ADD ADHD
Physical & medical conditions CA IT SM TW
WA2/HEA IM
No of pupils 399; *(full boarding)* 95; *(weekly
boarding)* 59; *(day)* 245; *Senior* 284; *Sixth
Form* 115; *Girls* 135; *Boys* 264
Teacher:pupil ratio 1:8.5; **Average class size** 18
Fees per annum *(full boarding)* –£19350;
(weekly) –£16350; *(day)* £10050–£11700
Fees (ISC per annum) £16,350–£19,350

Box Hill School is a co-educational independent day and boarding school for 11–18 year olds located in Mickleham, Surrey, and convenient to central London, Gatwick and Heathrow airports. It is small and friendly and places a great emphasis on pastoral care so that students experience balanced academic, social and emotional growth.

Overseas students are fully integrated into the social and academic life of the school. They enjoy social and cultural activities while being carefully guided on a course of study either in the mainstream school or in our International Study Centre.

Students and leavers of the school are well-rounded and poised to become leaders and socially responsible individuals capable of making a positive contribution to society.

Caterham School

Harestone Valley Road, Caterham, Surrey CR3 6YA   Tel: (01883) 343028   Fax: (01883) 347795
E-mail: admissions@caterhamschool.co.uk Website: www.caterhamschool.co.uk

Headmaster Mr R A E Davey MA
Founded 1811   **School status** Independent.
Co-educational Day and Boarding 11–18 Flexi-
boarding available. Boarders from 11.
Religious denomination United Reformed
Church
Member of AGBIS, BSA, HMC, IAPS, ISCis,
SHA
Learning difficulties SNU/DYC DYP DYS MLD
Behavioural and emotional disorders CO
ST/ADD ADHD ASP AUT
Physical and medical conditions AT SM TW
WA2/EPI HEA HI IM VI W
No of pupils 754; *(full boarding)* 131; *(weekly
boarding)* 2; *(day)* 623; *Nursery* 20; *Pre-prep*
28; *Prep* 224; *Senior* 513; *Sixth Form* 241;
Girls 318; *Boys* 436
Teacher:pupil ratio 1:10; **Average class size** 20
Fees per annum *(full boarding)* £20502–
£21609; *(weekly)* £20502–£21609; *(day)*
£11064–£11586

We aim to provide an excellent all-round education so that every pupil can achieve their full potential academically and socially.

Excellent A-level results enable over 90% of pupils to accept a place at their first choice university. The school also offers a wide range of extra-curricular activities enabling the students to develop their skills and interests. Over a year there are 18 different sports, 14 music groups and 32 various clubs and societies.

England

Claremont Fan Court School

Claremont Drive, Esher, Surrey KT10 9LY
Tel: (01372) 467841   Fax: (01372) 471109
E-mail: jtilson@claremont.surrey.sch.uk
Website: www.claremont-school.co.uk   www.gabbitas.co.uk
Junior School: abutler@claremont.surrey.sch.uk

Principal Mrs P B Farrar
Founded 1922
School status Co-educational Day 3–18.
Christian, all denominations welcome
Religious denomination Christian Science
Member of ISCis, SHMIS
Learning difficulties CA SNU/DYP DYS
Behavioural and emotional disorders ST/
ADHD
Physical and medical conditions AT CA RA SL
TW WA2/HI IM W
No of pupils 600; *Girls* 300; *Boys* 300
Fees per annum *(day)* £3228–£10800

The School is situated in the Claremont Estate, one of the premier historic sites in the country. The original house and the famous landscape garden were first laid out by Sir John Vanbrugh for the Duke of Newcastle early in the 18th century. Later Capability Brown built the present Palladian mansion for Clive of India and landscaped the grounds in his typical manner. For over a century Claremont was a royal residence and played an important part in Queen Victoria's early years.

Aims: An excellent academic programme with small class sizes provides the pupils with a wide and varied curriculum. High personal expectations and moral values are established and developed within small classes in a happy, positive environment free from the excessive pressures sometimes placed on young people today.

Curriculum: The expectation of high academic achievement and personal growth is established in the junior years. The syllabus follows National Curriculum guidelines but our expectations of attainment are well beyond the national levels. Over the next three years there will be a phased development into e-learning through the introduction of laptops for every child from Year 4 to

Year 10. Classrooms have been specially designed for collaborative, independent learning and most have been fitted with interactive white boards. The academic programme in Senior School ensures that all pupils attain the highest qualifications of which they are capable for entry into university or college.

Students also have a strong tradition of excellence in technology, drama, music, art and sport. Facilities include five ICT suites, a fully equipped design and technology studio, and a workshop. Major drama productions are performed in the Joyce Grenfell Centre for the Performing Arts. The Music Department benefits from excellent music technology facilities.

A new fully equipped Sports Centre and Gymnasium have recently enhanced sports at Claremont. Teams compete regularly with neighbouring schools, with individuals competing at county and national levels.

Entry to the School: Applications for entry into the School are welcome at all levels. Main intakes are at 3+, 4+, 7+, 11+ and Sixth Form.

Scholarships: Academic scholarships are available at Years 3, 7, 9 and Sixth Form. Music, Art, Drama and Sport scholarships are also available.

Croham Hurst School

79 Croham Road, South Croydon, Surrey CR2 7YN   Tel: (020) 8681 4078   Fax: (020) 8688 1142
E-mail: aparris@croham.surrey.sch.uk   Website: www.crohamhurst.com   www.gabbitas.co.uk

Headmistress Mrs E J Abbotts BA MEd NPQH
Registrar Mrs A J Parris DipM MCIM
Founded 1899
School status Independent. Girls Day 3–18.
Religious denomination Christian
Member of AGBIS, GSA, ISBA, ISCis, SHA
Accredited by GSA, ISC
Learning difficulties WI/DYC DYP DYS
Behavioural and emotional disorders CO/ADD
ADHD
Physical and medical conditions SM/HEA HI VI
No of pupils 435; *(day)* 435; *Nursery* 12;
Pre-prep 15; *Prep* 115; *Senior* 240; *Sixth
Form* 53; *Girls* 435
Teacher:pupil ratio 1:10; **Average class size** 16
Fees per annum *(day)* £5490–£9885
Lunches are taken by all girls up to Year 10 and
are charged additionally on the bills.

Croham Hurst provides a modern and challenging education for girls aged 3–18. Occupying an attractive site close to green belt woodland, Croham Hurst is easily accessible by public transport. Extensive facilities include a new Sixth Form centre and new Art Department both completed Summer 2006. PE, Music and Academic scholarships are available as bursaries.

Duke of Kent School

Peaslake Road, Ewhurst, Surrey GU6 7NS   Tel: (01483) 277313   Fax: (01483) 273862
E-mail: dok.school@virgin.net   Website: www.dukeofkentschool.org.uk   www.gabbitas.co.uk

Headmaster Dr A Cameron
Founded 1976
School status Independent. Co-educational
Boarding and Day 3–13 Flexi-boarding
available. Boarders from 7.
Religious denomination Non-Denominational
Member of BSA, ISCis; **Accredited by** IAPS
Learning difficulties SNU/DYS
Physical and medical conditions RA/HEA
No of pupils 181; *(full boarding)* 13; *(weekly
boarding)* 18; *(day)* 157; *Nursery* 10; *Pre-prep*
30; *Prep* 148; *Girls* 60; *Boys* 121
Teacher:pupil ratio 1:8; **Average class size** 14
Fees per annum *(full boarding)* £12810–
£15330; *(weekly)* £9885–£12585; *(day)*
£4785–£11295

A happy and caring co-educational day and boarding school situated in a beautiful location in the Surrey hills with easy access to Gatwick, Heathrow and major stations. Pupils are prepared for entry to many leading public schools and a full range of music and sport is offered and played in the extensive facilities.

Curriculum: All main subjects required for Common Entrance and public school scholarships plus art, music, drama, CDT, computer studies and a structured games and activity programme.

Entry: Placement tests and interviews. Bursaries and scholarships available.

Frensham Heights School

Rowledge, Farnham, Surrey GU10 4EA   Tel: (01252) 792561   Fax: (01252) 794335
E-mail: admissions@frensham-heights.org.uk
Website: www.frensham-heights.org.uk   www.gabbitas.co.uk

Headmaster Mr A Fisher
Founded 1925
School status Co-educational Boarding and Day 3–18. Co-educational independent junior and senior boarding and day
Religious denomination Non-Denominational
Member of AGBIS, HMC, ISCis
No of pupils 506; *(full boarding)* 100; *Pre-prep* 55; *Prep* 155; *Senior* 200; *Sixth Form* 86; *Girls* 250; *Boys* 256
Fees per annum *(full boarding)* £19350–£20970; *(day)* £7215–£14085

Frensham Heights is a fully co-educational HMC boarding (full or weekly) and day school of 496 pupils aged between 3 and 18. The School's philosophy endorses liberal values and promotes strong personal relationships and respect for the individual. It achieves distinguished results in the performing and creative arts. Classes are small and academic results are excellent. New facilities include a sixth form complex, opened September 2006, a multi-award winning Performing Arts Centre, a Music School, an indoor sports hall, modern science laboratories, a fully equipped ICT Suite, a newly renovated library and an adventure centre for outdoor education. The school is situated in beautiful grounds near Farnham, 45 minutes from Heathrow and Gatwick airports.

Hoe Bridge School

Hoe Place, Old Woking Road, Woking, Surrey GU22 8JE
Tel: (01483) 760018   Fax: (01483) 757560   E-mail: enquiriesprep@hoebridgeschool.co.uk
Website: www.hoebridgeschool.co.uk   www.gabbitas.co.uk

Head Mr R W K Barr
Pre-prep-Head Mrs L M Renfrew
Founded 1987
School status Co-educational Day 2–13.
Religious denomination Non-Denominational
Member of IAPS; **Accredited by** IAPS
Learning difficulties WI/DYP DYS
Behavioural and emotional disorders CA/ADD
Physical and medical conditions RA WA3
No of pupils 473; *Nursery* 44; *Pre-prep* 154; *Prep* 275; *Girls* 124; *Boys* 349
Teacher:pupil ratio 1:10; **Average class size** 19
Fees per annum *(day)* £1488–£10800

The Pre-Preparatory Department is for children aged 2½ to 7. It is an attractive purpose-built school with its own play areas in landscaped grounds and with its own Nursery Unit.

The Prep School prepares boys and girls between the ages of 7 and 14 for the scholarship and Common Entrance requirements of all senior independent schools. The curriculum includes those subjects, games and activities necessary for a child's development.

The grounds afford facilities for all games and outdoor pursuits, including rugby, soccer, hockey, netball, basketball, cricket, athletics, tennis and swimming. It also has four all-weather tennis courts providing ample space for all sports.

A 17th century mansion forms the heart of the school but extensive architect-designed buildings have been added. These include laboratories, changing rooms, classrooms and a multi-purpose Sports Hall.

The school has a Design and Music Centre set in a restored 17th century tower and stable block. This provides superb facilities for art, design technology, information technology and music. ICT is networked throughout the school and there are two computer suites.

Homefield School

Western Road, Sutton, Surrey SM1 2TE   Tel: (020) 8642 0965   Fax: (020) 8642 0965
E-mail: administration@homefield.sutton.sch.uk   Website: www.homefield.sutton.sch.uk

Head Master Mr P R Mowbray MA Cant
Assistant Headteacher Mrs J Goodman MA
PGCE
Assistant Headteacher Mrs S B White MA LLB
PGCE   **Founded** 1870
School status Independent. Boys Day 2–13.
Please note that the age of entry is 2½
Religious denomination Non-Denominational
Member of IAPS, ISCis; **Accredited by** IAPS,
ISC last inspected in February 2006
Learning difficulties WI/DYC DYP DYS MLD
Behavioural and emotional disorders RA/ADD
Physical and medical conditions SL TW
WA2/HEA
No of pupils 400; *(day)* 400; *Nursery* 70;
Pre-prep 130; *Prep* 200; *Boys* 400
Teacher:pupil ratio 1:10; **Average class size** 17
Fees per annum *(day)* £3540–£8280
Fees Nursery vouchers accepted

Homefield is a Preparatory school for 400 boys

aged 2½ to 13, housed in an extensive purpose-built complex complemented by a spacious state of the art Early Years' Unit and a 2-acre adjoining playing field.

Rated by The Sunday Times Parent Power as '*Amongst the best performing schools in Great London*', Homefield is renowned for its family atmosphere, small class sizes, the fulfilment of individual potential, the openness of communication, the provision of specialist teaching at the earliest appropriate opportunity and its all round academic, musical, dramatic and sporting achievements.

Daily minibuses to and from Wimbledon and other areas, breakfast club and after school club facilities.

England

Hurtwood House

Holmbury St Mary, Dorking, Surrey RH5 6NU   Tel: (01483) 279000   Fax: (01483) 267586
E-mail: info@hurtwood.net   Website: www.hurtwoodhouse.com   www.gabbitas.co.uk

The Headmaster Mr K R B Jackson MA
Founded 1970
School status Independent Sixth Form College.
Co-educational Boarding and Day 16–18.
Boarders from 16.
Religious denomination Non-Denominational
Member of ARELS, BSA, ISA, ISCis
Accredited by BAC, British Council, ISA, ISC

No of pupils 295; *(full boarding)* 283; *(weekly boarding)* 283; *(day)* 12; *Sixth Form* 295; *Girls* 155; *Boys* 140
Teacher:pupil ratio 1:6
Average class size 10
Fees per annum *(full boarding)* £25830–£29670; *(weekly)* £25830–£29670; *(day)* £17220

THE SCHOOL WITH THE BEST PERFORMANCE

HURTWOOD HOUSE

For further details, please contact:

**Richard Jackson,
Hurtwood House,
Holmbury St Mary,
Dorking, Surrey, RH5 6NU**

**T: 01483 279000
F: 01483 267586**

E: info@hurtwood.net

www.hurtwoodhouse.com

Hurtwood House has the biggest and best Drama and Media Departments in England, with superb professional facilities. It is also hugely successful academically and came top of the league table this year and last year as *the best co-educational boarding school in the UK*. Uniquely, our 300 boarding students join us after GCSE, when they are ready for the fresh challenge of a sixth-form where life is as exciting and stimulating as it is at university. Structured and secure, innovative and dynamic, Hurtwood House is one of England's most successful and exciting schools.

Kew Green Preparatory School

Layton House, Ferry Lane, Richmond, Surrey TW9 3AF Tel: (020) 8948 5999 Fax: (020) 8948 4774
E-mail: secretary@kgps.co.uk   Website: www.kgps.co.uk

Head Mrs M Gardener PGCE
Founded 2004
School status Co-educational Day 4–11.
Religious denomination Non-Denominational
Member of IAPS, ISCis
Accredited by IAPS, ISC
Learning difficulties CA SNU/DYC DYP DYS MLD
Behavioural and emotional disorders CA CO ST TS/ADD CB
Physical and medical conditions CA IT TW
No of pupils 280; *(day)* 280; *Prep* 280; *Girls* 140; *Boys* 140
Teacher:pupil ratio 1:7; **Average class size** 20
Fees per annum *(day)* £3550

Kew Green Preparatory School provides an education of the highest quality. Unlike many private schools, LPS Ltd is owned by fully qualified and experienced teachers who understand that effective learning is achieved without pressure in a warm and nurturing environment. We are committed to co-education, opposed to 'cramming', and work on the basis of keeping pupils from age 4 to secondary transfer at 11 years. Within this timescale we are able to allow children to develop at their own pace whilst providing a rich curriculum. We strive to inculcate in our pupils a proper self-esteem and respect for others. Above all, we want our children to be clamouring at our gates every morning and to show a marked reluctance to leave at the end of the day!

Marymount International School

George Road, Kingston-upon-Thames, Surrey KT2 7PE Tel: (020) 8949 0571   Fax: (020) 8336 2485
E-mail: admissions@marymountlondon.com
Website: www.marymountlondon.com www.gabbitas.co.uk

Headmistress Sister K Fagan RSHM
Academic Dean Dr B Johnson PhD
Founded 1955
School status Independent. Girls age 11–18 Day and Boarding 11–18 Flexi-boarding available. Boarders from age 11.
Religious denomination Roman Catholic
Member of CIS, GSA, IBO, ISCis, LISA, SHA;
Accredited by CIS, GSA, ISC, MSA (USA)
Learning difficulties RA SC SNU/DYC DYS MLD
No of pupils 230; *(full boarding)* 90; *(weekly boarding)* 10; *(day)* 130; *Senior* 230; *Sixth Form* 100; *Girls* 230
Teacher:pupil ratio 1:7
Average class size 10–12
Fees per annum *(full boarding)* £24150–£25650; *(weekly)* £22950–£24450; *(day)* £13750–£15250

Curriculum: International Baccalaureate (IB) and College Preparatory. 98 per cent of our students enter university.

Entry requirements: Application form and reports or transcripts for previous three years, together with teacher recommendations.

Boarding facilities: Three boarding houses cater for our students and a wide range of activities are provided, to encourage community spirit.

England

Prior's Field School

Priorsfield Road, Hurtmore, Godalming, Surrey GU7 2RH
Tel: (01483) 810551   Fax: (01483) 810180   E-mail: registrar@priorsfieldschool.com
Website: www.priorsfieldschool.com   www.gabbitas.co.uk
Prior's Field is situated just south of Guildford on the A3 and within easy reach of London airports

Headmistress Mrs J Roseblade MA
Founded 1902
School status Independent. Girls Boarding and
Day 11–18. Boarders from 11.
Religious denomination Non-Denominational
Member of AGBIS, BSA, GSA, ISBA, ISCis;
Accredited by GSA, ISC
Learning difficulties WI/DYC DYP DYS
Behavioural & emotional disorders CO/ADHD
Physical and medical conditions HL SM TW
WA3/EPI HEA HI VI
No of pupils 330; (full boarding) 38; (weekly
boarding) 80; (day) 212; Girls 330
Teacher:pupil ratio 1:7; **Average class size** 17
Fees per annum (full boarding) £19185;
(weekly) £19185; (day) £11850

At Prior's Field we achieve the balance between working hard and offering a friendly, vibrant environment with a huge range of opportunities, activities and clubs. A tradition of high academic standards, excellent academic results and small classes, ensures individual attention and encourages confidence and high achievement for every girl. A wide choice of A level subjects enables students to gain places at top universities including Oxbridge.

Excellent boarding facilities including single rooms for year 10 and some en-suite rooms for sixth form. Scholarships available – open days and trial boarding weekends take place each term.

Reed's School

Sandly Lane, Cobham, Surrey KT11 2ES
Tel: (01932) 869001   Fax: (01932) 869046   E-mail: admissions@reeds.surrey.sch.uk
Website: www.reeds.surrey.sch.uk   www.gabbitas.co.uk

Headmaster Mr D W Jarrett
Founded 1813
School status Boys Boarding and Day 11–18
(Co-ed VIth Form).Girls' Sixth Form
Religious denomination Church of England
Member of SHMIS
Accredited by HMC
No of pupils 550; *(full boarding)* 86
Girls 50; *Boys* 500
Teacher:pupil ratio 1:8
Average class size 20 (Yrs 7–11) 14 (Yrs 12–13
Fees per annum *(full boarding)* £16941–
£20820; *(day)* £12705–£15738
Minimum relates to years 7–8
Maximum to years 9–13
There is no fee reduction for weekly boarding

The Headmaster is assisted by a permanent full-time teaching staff of 60+, including a school chaplain, and pupils are prepared for GCSE, AS and A level examinations with a variety of boards. Up to the beginning of GCSE courses, the school broadly follows the National Curriculum. At GCSE all pupils take English, English literature, maths, a modern language, ICT, science and 2–3 option subjects; most pupils take 10 subjects in all. A wide range of AS and A level options are available.

Registration and entry: Pupils may be registered at any time but, for 13+, registrations must be received at least two years in advance of entry date. Entry is at ages 11+, 12+, 13+ and Sixth Form. Entry at 11+ and 12+ is by special examination, while at 13+ it is normally by Common Entrance or Common Scholarship. Sixth Form entry is determined by entry tests in November, school report and interview. Foundation bursaries are available to children who meet the specific criteria. For information on this please contact the school.

Scholarships: Academic, music, art, drama, sport and all-round scholarships up to the value of half fees are offered each year for pupils entering at 11+, 13+ and Sixth Form. In addition Design Technology scholarships are available for 13+ and Sixth Form applicants.

Facilities: Nine science laboratories and specialist classrooms for all subjects, including outstanding facilities for art, graphic design, photography and printing, music and music technology, technology and ICT. Full facilities for rugby, hockey, cricket, tennis, squash and swimming, including a sports hall, swimming pool, two artificial hockey pitches, nine tennis courts and an indoor tennis centre. A new Music School opened in 2001 and in 2005 four biology laboratories and five classrooms were opened together with extended Day Pupil facilities. There are three separate boarding houses: The Close for 11 and 12+, School House for 13–16 and a Sixth Form house.

There is an ongoing development programme and new girls accommodation and a lecture theatre have just been completed.

Ethos: While the ethos of the school is directed towards academic achievement, Reed's offers an extensive range of opportunities to each pupil through its Activities Curriculum. Reed's is also distinctive in that the school has an international dimension through its partnership with the Rijnlands Lyceum for Dutch-speaking pupils. Pupils participate in the Duke of Edinburgh's Award Scheme, the CCF, major sports (rugby, hockey and cricket), and a whole host of options which extend from the martial arts to dance and archery. In addition, the school is developing partnerships with the Lawn Tennis Association and the British Ski Academy as a centre of excellence for tennis and skiing.

Through creating the highest quality of opportunities Reed's genuinely seeks to identify the talents of each individual, thereby enabling every pupil to leave the school with the qualities necessary to be high achievers in their chosen careers. The school is situated just off the A3 in 40 acres of Surrey heathland within easy reach of Heathrow and Gatwick airports. Application should be made to the Registrar/Admissions Secretary: admissions@reeds.surrey.sch.uk.

England

Royal Alexandra and Albert School

Gatton Park, Reigate, Surrey RH2 0TD   Tel: (01737) 649000   Fax: (01737) 649002
E-mail: admissions@gatton-park.org.uk   Website: www.gatton-park.org.uk

Headmaster Mr Paul D Spencer Ellis BA MPhil NPQH   **Founded** 1758
School status State (Voluntary-aided). Co-educational Boarding and Day 7–18 Flexi-boarding available. Boarders from 7.
Religious denomination Church of England
Member of BSA, SHA, SHMIS
Accredited by SHMIS SBSA – State Boarding Schools Association
No of pupils 688; *(full boarding)* 389; *(day)* 299; *Prep* 146; *Senior* 542; *Sixth Form* 33; *Girls* 329; *Boys* 359
Teacher:pupil ratio 1:14.3
Average class size 24
Fees per annum *(full boarding)* £10350–£11100; *(weekly)* £10350–£11100; *(day)* £2325–£3330

This is a true boarding school in the sense that the majority of pupils are boarders. We have Saturday lessons and longer holidays, and run a vast range of sporting and other activities in the afternoons, evenings and at weekends.

Admission is by confidential reference from the current school and interview, together with some diagnostic tests, but is restricted to citizens of the UK and other EU countries and those with the right of residence in the UK.

Set in 260 acres of parkland, yet close to London, we have an excellent range of facilities including a sports hall, riding school, indoor swimming pool, drama studio, chapel, new music centre and 11 boarding houses, most of which have been recently refurbished to a very high standard.

St. Andrew's (Woking) School Trust

Church Hill House, Wilson Way, Horsell, Woking, Surrey GU21 4QW
Tel: (01483) 760943   Fax: (01483) 740314   E-mail: admin@st-andrews.woking.sch.uk
Website: www.st-andrews.woking.sch.uk   www.gabbitas.co.uk

The Headmaster Mr J R Evans BEd (Hons) Ad Dip Ed Man
Deputy Head Mr A K Perks MSc BSc
Founded 1938
School status Independent. Co-educational Day 3–13.
Religious denomination Church of England
Member of IAPS; **Accredited by** ISC
Learning difficulties CA WI/DYS MLD
Behavioural and emotional disorders RA/ADD ADHD
Physical and medical conditions RA SM
No of pupils 293; *(day)* 293; *Nursery* 31; *Pre-prep* 91; *Prep* 171; *Girls* 67; *Boys* 226
Teacher:pupil ratio 1:9
Average class size 14
Fees per annum *(day)* £4080–£10470

Curriculum: Children are prepared for Common Entrance and scholarships to a wide range of senior schools, with top awards won every year. Specialist teaching facilities for all subjects including science, computing, music and ADT. The curriculum is broad and appropriate to children of all abilities. The school places great emphasis on music and the Arts.

Academic and leisure activities: There is a sports hall, all-weather tennis and netball courts, heated pool and ample grounds for games. Major games are soccer, hockey, cricket, swimming, tennis, athletics, netball and rounders. In addition the children do rugby, cross-country and basketball.

Activities programme: Children can be supervised at school from 8.00 a.m. and, through our extensive after-school activities programme, until 6.00/6.30 p.m. most evenings during the week.

Entry requirements: Entry test for children over 6. The school has a number of scholarships and bursaries available at 7+ and 11+.

St Hilary's School

Holloway Hill, Godalming, Surrey GU7 1RZ   Tel: (01483) 416551   Fax: (01483) 418325
E-mail: registrar@sthilarysschool.com   Website: www.sthilarysschool.com

The Headmistress Mrs S Bailes BA (Hon) MA PGCE
Founded 1927
School status Co-educational Day Boys 2–7 Girls 2–11.
Religious denomination Non-Denominational
Member of AHIS, IAPS, ISCis, SATIPS
Accredited by IAPS
Learning difficulties CA SNU/DYP DYS
Physical and medical conditions CA HL IT/HEA
No of pupils 288; *(day)* 288; *Nursery* 73; *Pre-prep* 107; *Prep* 108; *Girls* 197; *Boys* 91
Teacher:pupil ratio 1:9; **Average class size** 16
Fees per annum *(day)* £6645–£9600

Visit St Hilary's and leave doors open for the future. As Headmistress, Mrs Susan Bailes remarks: "Our aim is to provide a happy, secure environment and to unlock a love of learning, which will last for ever." If you want the best for your child, where he or she is treated as an individual in small classes with dedicated staff, encouraged to grow in self-esteem while receiving a firm academic foundation, then choose St Hilary's School.

Boys and girls can join our impressive Nursery from 2 ½ and receive a head start. Scholarships are also available. We are proud of our independence and the successes of our pupils. Facilities include an all-weather pitch and superb ICT suite along with vibrant extra-curricular provision.

England

St Teresa's School

Effingham Hill, Dorking, Surrey RH5 6ST   Tel: (01372) 452037   Fax: (01372) 450311
E-mail: info@stteresas.surrey.sch.uk   Website: www.stteresasschool.com   www.gabbitas.co.uk

Head-Senior Mrs L Falconer BSc
Prep Head Mrs A M Stewart MA (Hons), PGCE
Founded 1928
School status Independent. Girls Boarding and Day 11–18 Flexi-boarding available. Boarders from 8. Entrance exam to Y7–9 in Jan each year. In 2006 100% Alevel pass rate, 100% gained 5 or more A*–C GCSEs
Religious denomination Roman Catholic
Member of BSA, GSA, ISCis
Accredited by GSA
Learning difficulties SNU/DYC DYP DYS
Behavioural and emotional disorders CO/ADHD
Physical and medical conditions SM
No of pupils 362; *(full boarding)* 76; *(weekly boarding)* 13; *(day)* 273; *Senior* 362; *Sixth Form* 85; *Girls* 362
Teacher:pupil ratio 1:8
Average class size 20
Fees per annum *(full boarding)* £19140–£19890; *(weekly)* £17670–£18240; *(day)* £10950–£11700

St Teresa's is a thriving girls school situated in 48 acres of beautiful parkland in the Surrey Hills, with good road and rail links to London and 45 minutes from both Heathrow and Gatwick airports. Since its establishment in 1928, the school facilities have been continually expanded and updated to high contemporary standards. A magnificent new indoor swimming pool complex opened in 2004 and a £3 million Performing Arts Theatre Hall in 2005.

St Teresa's is a community of almost 500 girls, including around 80 boarders, who enjoy first class care in a flexible boarding system with a programme of weekend activities. Although a Catholic foundation, St Teresa's welcomes girls of all denominations and everyone is encouraged to respect one another in a happy, caring Christian environment. The school is particularly sensitive to the differing needs and latent talents of each individual girl and adopts a 'can do' attitude, stimulating, supporting and developing each girl's interests and talents.

Girls in the Preparatory School benefit from specialist subject teachers and assume responsibility in their last year through a School Council. They can take advantage of an extended day, including breakfast and homework supervision and the 19 extra-curricular activities and clubs on offer.

Entrance to the Senior School is at 11+, but girls are also warmly welcomed at 12+ and 13+. Scholarships are available at all these entry points and in the Sixth Form. There are 60+ extra-curricular activities on offer and girls are encouraged to develop their life skills through the Duke of Edinburgh's Award Scheme, the Young Enterprise Scheme, World Challenge and work experience.

St Teresa's offers a very broad curriculum with 25 subjects at A level. All girls go on to higher education: many to first rank universities, including Oxbridge, others to the best art schools, drama schools and music colleges.

TASIS The American School in England

Coldharbour Lane, Thorpe, Surrey TW20 8TE   Tel: (01932) 565252   Fax: (01932) 564644
E-mail: ukadmissions@tasis.com   Website: www.tasis.com   www.gabbitas.co.uk
Ofsted inspected TASIS in 2004 and praised its programs and the overall tone of the School.

Headmaster Dr J A Doran PhD
Director of Admissions Mrs B Thorburn-Riseley
BSc MSc Dip RSA Grad CIPD
Founded 1976
School status Independent. Co-educational
Boarding and Day 3–18. Boarders from 14.
Religious denomination Non-Denominational
Member of CASE, CIS, IBO, IBSCA, LISA,
NAIS, NEASC; **Accredited by** CIS Also a
member of The Association of Boarding
Schools (TABS), an American organization.
Behavioural and emotional disorders CO
Physical and medical conditions SM TW
WA2/HEA
No of pupils 750; *(full boarding)* 160; *(day)*
590; *Nursery* 12; *Pre-prep* 261; *Prep* 157;
Senior 155; *Sixth Form* 175; *Girls* 360;
Boys 390
Teacher:pupil ratio 12:1; **Average class size** 15
Fees per annum *(full boarding)* £24550
£95 application fee £750 one-time
development fee

TASIS The American School in England, frequently cited as the premier American school in
the United Kingdom, is now into its third decade
of offering international and American college-
preparatory curriculum to day students from
grades Nursery through to 13 and to boarding
students from grades 9–13. Located on a beautiful
historic estate of Georgian mansions and 17th
century cottages some 18 miles south-west of
London, TASIS combines an excellent academic
programme, which includes the International
Baccalaureate, Advanced Placement courses,
and the traditional high school course of study.
The school offers exceptional facilities for art,
drama, music, computers, and sports. Small
classes and over 100 dedicated, experienced teachers provide individualised attention and an
outstanding environment for learning.

The school's international student enrolment is
drawn from all corners of the world.

TASIS England embraces three divisions: Lower
School (Nursery–Grade 5; ages 3–10), Middle
School (Grades 6–8; ages 11–13), and Upper

School (Grades 9–13; ages 14–18). Students in
each division regularly benefit from the opportunity to work closely with visiting artists, actors,
musicians and sports professionals. The comprehensive athletics programme includes intramurals
in the Lower School and interscholastic games for
Middle School, and Junior Varsity and Varsity
teams in the Upper School. Throughout the year,
students enjoy numerous field trips, weekend
activities, and travel throughout the UK and
abroad.

The combination of well-equipped facilities
and a strong traditional academic programme
has given TASIS its valued reputation both in
England and abroad. Each year TASIS students
are offered places at some of the finest universities
within the UK, US, Canada, Europe, and other
parts of the world.

Admissions decisions for the academic school
year are made on a rolling basis upon receipt of a
completed application form together with the
application fee, three teachers' recommendations, and three years of transcripts.
Standardized test scores and a student questionnaire are required. An interview is recommended
unless distance is a prohibiting factor. For additional information, please contact Mrs Bronwyn
Thorburn-Riseley, Director of Admissions (ukad-
missions@tasis.com).

TASIS England also offers Summer Programmes
for day and boarding students from ages 12 to 18.
Local and international students participate in:
intensive courses for high school credit, enrichment programmes, theatre workshops, ESL,
TOEFL, and SAT Review. Students also enjoy
extensive sports activities and travel, both international and within the UK. For more information
please contact Faie Gilbert, Director of Summer
Admissions (uksummer@tasis.com).

England

Battle Abbey School

High Street, Battle, East Sussex TN33 0AD   Tel: (01424) 772385   Fax: (01424) 773573
E-mail: office@battleabbeyschool.com   Website: www.battleabbeyschool.com www.gabbitas.co.uk

Head Mr R Clark   **Founded** 1922
School status Independent. Co-educational
Boarding and Day 2–18 Flexi-boarding
available. Boarders from 11. 2006: 100% Six
GCSE subjects at A*–C. 54% at A*/A.99%
A-Level passes, with 49% A/B grades.
Religious denomination Non-Denominational
Learning difficulties CA SC WI/DYC DYP DYS
Behavioural and emotional disorders RA
ST/ADHD ASP AUT
Physical and medical conditions RA SM
WA3/HEA VI
No of pupils 226; *(full boarding)* 40; *(weekly*
boarding) 2; *(day)* 185; *Nursery* 22; *Prep* 75;
Senior 159; *Sixth Form* 55; *Girls* 115; *Boys* 111
Fees per annum *(full boarding)* £15225–
£18900; *(weekly)* £15225–£18900; *(day)*
£5550–£11475

Battle Abbey School, which occupies one of the
most famous historical sites in the world – that of
the 1066 Battle of Hastings, is an independent,
co-educational school for pupils from 2 ½ to 18.
Boarders are accepted from the age of 8. The
school is large enough to encourage healthy competition and to develop the social skills and
awareness of others, learnt by being part of a
lively community, but it is small enough to have
many of the attributes of a large family. Teaching
classes are small throughout the school, allowing
individual attention and the opportunity for all
pupils to achieve their maximum potential. A
new Performing Arts Centre was opened in the
Summer of 2005.

Buckswood School

Broomham Hall, Rye Road, Guestling, Hastings, East Sussex TN35 4LT
Tel: (01424) 813813   Fax: (01424) 812100   E-mail: achieve@buckswood.co.uk
Website: www.buckswood.co.uk   www.gabbitas.co.uk

Director Mr T Fish
Registrar Miss Fiona Wratten
School status Independent. Co-educational
Day and Boarding Boys 0–19 Girls 10–19
Flexi-boarding available. Boarders from 10.
Religious denomination Non-Denominational
Member of ARELS
Accredited by British Council
Learning difficulties WI/DYS MLD
No of pupils 290; *(full boarding)* 160; *(day)*
130; *Senior* 220; *Sixth Form* 70; *Girls* 120;
Boys 170
Teacher:pupil ratio 1:8; **Average class size** 16
Fees per annum *(full boarding)* £17970; *(day)*
£8400. £60 registration £600 Deposit
(boarding) £200 Deposit (day)

contributes something special to their children's
education. Its size allows the School to preserve a
more home-like atmosphere, where the care and
welfare of students is a priority.

Buckswood follows the British Curriculum, and
small classes for GCSE and A levels ensure pupils
receive more individual attention.

We have a large campus near the seaside town
of Hastings with a swimming pool, horse riding,
large sports grounds and new tennis courts –
sports and activities play an important part of a
Buckswood all-round education.

A truly international educational environment
awaits your child at Buckswood. Parents select
Buckswood because they know it is a school that

Michael Hall (Steiner Waldorf School)

Kidbrooke Park, Forest Row, East Sussex RH18 5JA   Tel: (01342) 822275   Fax: (01342) 826593
E-mail: info@michaelhall.co.uk   Website: www.michaelhall.co.uk   www.gabbitas.co.uk

Founded 1925
School status Co-educational Day and Boarding 0–19 Flexi-boarding available.
Religious denomination Christian
No of pupils 628; *(full boarding)* 15; *(weekly boarding)* 10; *Girls* 328; *Boys* 300
Fees per annum *(full boarding)* £14010; *(weekly)* £12965; *(day)* £8085

**Protecting the right to childhood.
Creating abilities for life.**

Offering a structured and imaginative approach and an international curriculum, Michael Hall has gained wide recognition as a creative and compassionate alternative to more traditional avenues of education.

* Full age range from pre-school to university entrance
* Unique international curriculum based on child development

* Languages from age six
* GCSE, AS & A2 level
* Arts, crafts, sport, sciences and humanities
* Intensive English courses for foreign students
* Over 620 day and boarding pupils
* Set in rural Sussex, within reach of main cultural centres

England

Newlands School

Eastbourne Road, Sutton Avenue, Seaford, East Sussex BN25 4NP
Tel: (01323) 892334 / 490000   Fax: (01323) 898420
E-mail: newlands1@msn.com   Website: www.newlands-school.com   www.gabbitas.co.uk

Headmaster Mr O T Price BEd (Hons)
Founded 1854
School status Independent. Co-educational
Boarding and Day 0–18 (nursery & pre-prep).
Religious denomination Inter-Denominational
Member of CReSTeD, IAPS, ISA, ISCis, SATIPS;
Accredited by IAPS, ISA, ISC
Learning difficulties SNU/DYC DYP DYS
Physical and medical conditions SM
No of pupils 150; *(full boarding)* 10; *(day)* 140;
Nursery 20; *Pre-prep* 10; *Prep* 60; *Senior* 50;
Sixth Form 10; *Girls* 80; *Boys* 70
Teacher:pupil ratio 1:8; **Average class size** 15
Fees per annum *(full boarding)* £14985–
£17850; *(weekly)* £14835–£17700; *(day)*
£4950–£10875

Newlands is a friendly, happy school with a strong academic tradition. Classes are small and a pupil's progress is monitored carefully. A high quality teaching ensures the pupils achieve excellent examination results. The wide range of activities available make it possible for every pupil to achieve success and confidence in one field or another.

Location Newlands is situated on one 21-acre campus in a pleasant coastal town surrounded by an area of outstanding natural beauty. Good communication links exist with Gatwick (37 miles), Heathrow (78 miles) and London (65 miles).

High academic standards At Newlands, we expect pupils to attain optimum results in external examinations, as is evident by our strong academic record. A level and GCSE results show year-on-year improvement.

The arts flourish with thriving music, drama, dance and art departments. There is a strong choral tradition and annual dramatic productions. A Theatre Arts Course is available to students who wish to specialize in dance, drama, music and art within an academic environment.

Entry requirements Interview and school reports are required.

Scholarships Academic, drama, sport, music, art and theatre arts scholarships are available for the Preparatory and Manor parts of the school.

We also prepare Preparatory pupils for scholarships to Newlands Manor at 13 years. There is a generous discount for service families as fees are in line with the BSA.

Academic and sports facilities Our facilities include five high-tech computer rooms, science laboratories, a large art studio, a language laboratory, a design technology workshop, an assembly hall/theatre and a music room.

There are the equivalent of eight football pitches, a heated indoor swimming pool, a hard playing surface for three tennis/netball courts, a gymnasium, and a .22 rifle range. There are many opportunities for sports, including soccer, hockey, rugby, netball, cricket, athletics, volleyball, basketball, squash, rounders, badminton, tennis, horse-riding and cross-country running. A new multi-purpose hall is appropriate for most indoor games as well as other activities.

Accelerated Learning Unit This nationally renowned centre has specialist teachers who provide one-to-one tuition for gifted pupils, dyslexic pupils and those learning English as a foreign language. All members of staff are fully qualified with diplomas in Special Education Needs or Certificate/Diplomas in Teaching English as a Foreign Language.

The centre is approved by CReSTeD, having a category B listing, supported by the British Dyslexia Association and the Dyslexia Institute.

Gifted pupils receive intensive tuition in their area of giftedness, so that they can achieve success at an earlier age.

Study skills and examination techniques are taught in order to prepare pupils for their GCSE and A level courses.

Newlands International College, a specialist language school for students whose first language is not English, was opened in September 2005 to prepare students for entry into the mainstream school or directly into higher education.

St Bede's School

Upper Dicker, Hailsham, East Sussex BN27 3QH   Tel: (01323) 843252   Fax: (01323) 442628
E-mail: school.office@stbedesschool.org   Website: www.stbedesschool.org   www.gabbitas.co.uk

Headmaster Mr S W Cole
Head (Prep School) Mr C Pyemont
Founded 1978 & 1895
School status Independent. Co-educational
Boarding and Day Senior 13–19. Boarders from
13. Prep 2–13. Boarders from 8.
Religious denomination Inter-Denominational
Member of AGBIS, CReSTeD, IAPS, ISCis,
SHMIS; **Accredited by** IAPS, SHMIS
Learning difficulties SNU/DYP DYS MLD
Behavioural and emotional disorders CO/ADD
ADHD ASP
Physical and medical conditions SM/EPI W
No of pupils Senior, 845; *(full boarding)* 310;
(day) 535; *Girls* 317; *Boys* 528
Prep, No of pupils 450; *(full boarding)* 39; *(day)*
411; *Girls* 201; *Boys* 203
Teacher:pupil ratio 1:8
Average class size 16 – GCSE, 12 – A LEVEL
Fees per annum *(full boarding)* £21165; *(day)*
£13005 (not including Pre-prep)

At the Senior School, students spend the first year following a widely based curriculum prior to making their choice from the 30 GCSE (Key Stage 4) subjects offered. Similarly at AS and A level, 30 subjects are offered, including media studies, theatre studies and pure and applied mathematics. The school also offers a number of Advanced Vocational Courses (AVCEs), a professional dance course and specialist coaching in tennis and swimming.

Facilities: Both schools have imaginatively converted and added to their original Edwardian buildings to provide excellent teaching and sporting facilities. Each site provides an indoor sports centre, indoor swimming pool, EFL centre, art, design and technology studios and an impressive computer network. In addition the Senior School has a drama studio, riding stables, a practice golf course, and ceramics and graphic design studios.

St Bede's is one of Britain's leading independent co-educational schools. The school is proudly and purposefully non-selective and the generous staffing ratio of 1:8 enables outstanding results to be achieved. The Senior School is located on a separate campus to the Pre-prep and Prep Schools, which gives students a change of teaching staff and environment as well as the opportunity to mature.

Location: The Senior School is found at the heart of the village of Upper Dicker, based on a small country estate set in beautiful countryside. The Prep School is situated nearby on the seafront in Eastbourne. Both schools are easily accessible by road and rail from London's airports and Channel seaports. Transport to and from school can be arranged for boarders and a school bus service is available for day students.

Curriculum: St Bede's provides an extremely wide-ranging and flexible programme. In the early years at the Prep School there is a strong emphasis on literacy and numeracy as well as skills such as languages and computing. Academic standards are high and all students are prepared for Common Entrance and Scholarship exams.

Sporting and club activities: Both schools are particularly strong in football, tennis, cricket, squash and swimming. The Prep School has a very strong games-playing tradition and encourages students of all abilities to participate in sport. At the Senior School games are organized as part of an extensive club activities programme which takes place every day. In all there are over 140 club activities, ranging from all kinds of sport and outdoor pursuits to activities within the fields of art, drama, music, journalism, science, agriculture and technology.

Scholarships and bursaries: A generous number of academic, art, music, dance, drama, and sports scholarships are available at both schools and scholarships may be awarded to those entering the Sixth Form.

Learning difficulties: SNU/DYC DYP DYS

Behavioural and emotional disorders: CO/ADD ADHD ASP

Physical and medical conditions: SM/EPI

St Leonards-Mayfield School

The Old Palace, Mayfield, East Sussex TN20 6PH   Tel: (01435) 874600   Fax: (01435) 872627
E-mail: admiss@stlm.e-sussex.sch.uk   Website: www.stlm.e-sussex.sch.uk

Headmistress Mrs J Dalton BA PGCE
Founded 1846
School status Independent. Girls Boarding and
Day 11–18 Flexi-boarding available. Boarders
from 11. 80 pupils flexi-board
Religious denomination Roman Catholic
Member of AGBIS, GSA, ISBA
Accredited by GSA
Learning difficulties WI/DYC DYP DYS
Behavioural and emotional disorders CO
Physical and medical conditions AT CA RA SM
TW/HEA
No of pupils 433; *(full boarding)* 90; *(weekly
boarding)* 32; *(day)* 311; *Senior* 322; *Sixth
Form* 111; *Girls* 433
Teacher:pupil ratio 1:8; **Average class size** 18
Fees per annum *(full boarding)* £20220;
(weekly) £20220; *(day)* £13425. Flexi-boarding
£38 per night

St Leonards-Mayfield School are celebrating the

publication of their ISI Inspection Report in which
it is deemed that 'the quality of the educational
experience provided for the girls is outstanding'.

The conclusions of the inspection are best sum-
marised in statements like 'the school is
outstandingly successful in achieving its aim to
realise the unique potential of each individual'
and 'the school is an exemplary model of the
dynamic effects which can be achieved by an
education based on faith and love'.

St Mary's Hall

Eastern Road, Brighton, East Sussex BN2 5JF   Tel: (01273) 606061   Fax: (01273) 620782
E-mail: registrar@stmaryshall.co.uk   Website: www.stmaryshall.co.uk   www.gabbitas.co.uk

Head Mrs S M Meek MA
Founded 1836
School status Independent. Girls Day and Boarding 3–18 (Boys 3–8) Flexi-boarding available. Girls 3–18, Boys 3–8, independent, pre-prep, prep and senior boarding and day
Religious denomination Church of England
Member of AGBIS, BSA, GSA, IAPS, ISCis, SHA; **Accredited by** GSA, ISC
Learning difficulties CA/DYS MLD
Behavioural and emotional disorders ASP
No of pupils 316; *(full boarding)* 79; *(weekly boarding)* 9; *(day)* 228; *Nursery* 17; *Pre-prep* 18; *Prep* 57; *Senior* 166; *Sixth Form* 58; *Girls* 306; *Boys* 10
Teacher:pupil ratio 1:15 average
Average class size 12–20.
Fees per annum *(full boarding)* £14958–£18525; *(weekly)* £13350–£17760; *(day)* £2325–£11220

Established in 1836 St Mary's Hall is one of the oldest schools for girls in Britain. Situated on extensive grounds overlooking the sea, St Mary's Hall is very much a city school. London is 55 minutes away by train, Heathrow Airport easily accessible, and Gatwick Airport only a 40-minute drive away.

Our aim is to develop personal qualities necessary to make a positive contribution to a changing and unpredictable world. This requires each individual in the community to be ready for lifelong learning, to be adaptable, to have the courage to face challenges, to acquire transferable skills, to be able to work independently and as part of a team, and to show self-discipline, commitment, flexibility and openness to change.

At St Mary's Hall, we encourage a culture of learning, respect, knowledge and achievement, focus upon the individual development of each pupil and prepare our pupils for life as young responsible adults. Great emphasis is placed on establishing sound personal relationships. Support and advice is given to integrate every student in the school community at all levels.

A wide range of subjects is on offer throughout the school at GCSE and A Level and each pupil's programme is carefully monitored to suit the individual. There are many extra-curricular opportunities, which aim to give every pupil a chance to 'shine' in some respect with activities ranging from sport to the arts.

There are two boarding houses: Venn House which was modernized three years ago and Elliott House which opened in September 2006. Elliott House houses our Senior and Sixth Form boarders primarily in single study bedrooms close to individual shower rooms. St Mary's Hall offers boarding from as early as the age of 8.

Facilities include an indoor 25-metre heated swimming pool; netball and tennis courts; four large and two small laboratories; libraries; the Art House includes two pottery kilns and a darkroom: a studio theatre and a School Chapel. There are two design-technology rooms and two ICT suites. The Sixth Form Centre provides an attractive, spacious common room, a Study and IT area, a coffee bar and a wireless network system providing internet and intranet access.

Our pupils come from the local community, as well as from around the world. Our cultural diversity is an asset. We have an ESL Department for our overseas students. A team of talented and caring ESL specialist provides tailor-made tuition to allow a seamless integration of all nationalities into St Mary's Hall.

England

Brambletye School

Lewes Road, Brambletye, East Grinstead, West Sussex RH19 3PD
Tel: (01342) 321004   Fax: (01342) 317562   E-mail: admin@brambletye.com
Website: www.brambletye.com   www.gabbitas.co.uk

The Headmaster Mr H D Cocke
Founded 1919
School status Co-educational Boarding and
Day 3–13. Boarders from 7.
Religious denomination Church of England
Member of AGBIS, BSA, IAPS, ISBA, ISCis,
SATIPS; **Accredited by** IAPS
Learning difficulties WI/DYC DYP DYS
Behavioural & emotional disorders RA/ADHD
Physical and medical conditions RA SM/HEA
No of pupils 244; *(full boarding)* 67; *(day)* 177;
Nursery 6; *Pre-prep* 62; *Prep* 176; *Girls* 91;
Boys 153
Teacher:pupil ratio 1:7; **Average class size** 16
Fees per annum *(full boarding)* £16380; *(day)*
£13450–£15600; Nursery £4020–£5610 Pre-
Prep £6390

Brambletye is situated in 140-acre grounds. It has
a new sports hall and pre-preparatory building,
theatre, art department, indoor swimming pool,
hard tennis courts, 6-hole golf course, computer
centre and library.

Children may start as boarders or day pupils,
but there is an expectation that all pupils will
board in their final three years. Our generous
exeat system means that, on average, there is a
leave-out weekend every fortnight.

Music awards are available each year in the
spring, details of which, along with the School
Prospectus, can be obtained on application to the
Headmaster's Secretary.

Burgess Hill School for Girls

Keymer Road, Burgess Hill, West Sussex RH15 0EG
Tel: (01444) 241050   Fax: (01444) 870314
E-mail: registrar@burgesshill-school.com
Website: www.burgesshill-school.com   www.gabbitas.co.uk   Junior School – tel 01444 233167

Headmistress Mrs A Aughwane BSc (Hons) CertEd
Founded 1906
School status Independent. Girls Boarding and Day 2–18 Flexi-boarding available. Boarders from 11.Girls' independent boarding and day. Flexi-boarding available.
Religious denomination Inter-Denominational
Member of GSA
Accredited by GSA GSA
Learning difficulties RA/DYP DYS
Physical and medical conditions HL SM TW WA3/HEA HI
No of pupils 679; *(full boarding)* 51; *(day)* 523; *Nursery* 100; *Prep* 187; *Senior* 293; *Sixth Form* 94; *Girls* 629; *Boys* 50
Teacher:pupil ratio 1:18
Average class size 20 max
Fees per annum *(full boarding)* £18510; *(day)* £5100–£10665

Burgess Hill School stands in 14 acres of beautiful grounds close to the centre of the town and is a 20-minute drive from Gatwick Airport.

The excellent facilities include a fully equipped science block, a technology laboratory, a learning resources centre, an art & design studio, a textiles centre, a music centre and a drama studio. The Sixth Form have their own centre with individual study areas, common rooms and an HE centre holding extensive careers advice.

The main aim of the school is to challenge the students to achieve goals well beyond their own expectations in all the activities they pursue. We educate for life and develop consideration for others, a love of learning, self-esteem and self-discipline. The curriculum is broad and challenging and relevant to the needs of young people. There is a wide choice of subjects both at GCSE and at A level.

There are well-appointed boarding houses adjoining the school grounds. The rooms and common rooms are spacious, light and pleasantly furnished, and the atmosphere is informal and friendly.

The school also runs a daily bus service to and from a number of outlying districts, including Turners Hill, Henfield, Cowfold, Lewes, Uckfield, Newick, East Grinstead and Worthing.

For further details please contact the Registrar.

England

Cottesmore School

Buchan Hill, Pease Pottage, West Sussex RH11 9AU
Tel: (01293) 520648   Fax: (01293) 614784
E-mail: schooloffice@cottesmoreschool.com
Website: www.cottesmoreschool.com   www.gabbitas.co.uk

Head Mr I J Tysoe BA
PA to Headmaster Miss J A Scola
Head of Admissions Miss J A Scola
Founded 1894
School status Independent. Co-educational
Boarding and Day 8–13 Flexi-boarding
available. Boarders from 7–13.
Religious denomination Church of England
Member of IAPS, ISCis
Accredited by IAPS, ISC
Learning difficulties SNU/DYP DYS
Behavioural and emotional disorders RA ST
Physical and medical conditions AT RA SM TW
WA3/HEA IM
No of pupils 150; *(full boarding)* 150; *Prep* 150
Girls 50; *Boys* 100
Teacher:pupil ratio 1:9
Average class size 12
Fees per annum *(full boarding)* £16680;
(weekly) from £12500

Cottesmore is a boarding school situated ten minutes from Gatwick Airport and one hour from Central London and Heathrow Airport. Boys and girls are taught together and are fully prepared for Common Entrance and Scholarship examinations. There is a strong musical tradition with children learning a variety of instruments; there are three Choirs and a School Orchestra. Sport plays a major part in school life which includes, Rugby, Football, Cricket, Hockey, Netball, Rounders, Swimming, Golf, Riding and Athletics. There are a number of Hobbies and other Activities available such as Dance, Craft, Cooking, Chess and model making to name but a few! The boys and girls lead a full and varied life and are all encouraged to take part in as wide a variety of activities as possible. Weekends are a vital part of the school life and are made busy and fun for all.

Farlington School

Strood Park, Horsham, West Sussex RH12 3PN   Tel: (01403) 254967   Fax: (01403) 272258
E-mail: office@farlingtonschool.net   Website: www.farlingtonschool.net   www.gabbitas.co.uk

Headmistress Mrs J Goyer   **Founded** 1896
School status Girls Boarding and Day 4–18
Flexi-boarding available.
Religious denomination Church of England
Member of BSA, GSA, IAPS
Learning difficulties CA RA/DYP DYS
Behavioural and emotional disorders CO/
ADHD
Physical and medical conditions CA RA TW/
HEA IM
No of pupils 490; *(full boarding)* 32; *(weekly boarding)* 8; *Pre-prep* 56; *Prep* 130; *Senior* 248; *Sixth Form* 56; *Girls* 490
Average class size 15 (fewer in Sixth Form)
Fees per annum *(full boarding)* £14625–£17820; *(weekly)* £14265–£17460; *(day)* £5265–£11205

Entry requirements and procedures: our own exam and interview.

Examination results 2006: 100 per cent A level pass rate; 90 per cent A to C. GCSE: 94 per cent A* to C;

Academic and leisure facilities: new sports hall, new library, new Sixth Form Centre, new prep building; new computer facilities. Science building with five large laboratories, and interactive white boards. All-weather pitch, outdoor heated swimming pool and student-run farm.

Scholarships: music, art, drama, PE, academic, Sixth Form.

Boarding facilities: weekly, full and flexi in small, friendly boarding house.

Curriculum: broadly-based academic curriculum. Wide range of subjects offered at GCSE; 22 subjects at A level and AS level.

England

Seaford College

Lavington Park, Petworth, West Sussex GU27 0NB   Tel: (01798) 867392   Fax: (01798) 867606
E-mail: seaford@clara.co.uk   Website: www.seaford.org   www.gabbitas.co.uk

The Headmaster Mr T J Mullins BA
Founded 1884
College status Independent. Co-educational Boarding and Day 10–18 Flexi-boarding available. Boarders from 10.
Religious denomination Church of England
Member of HMC, SHMIS
Accredited by HMC, SHMIS
Learning difficulties SNU/DYP DYS MLD
Physical and medical conditions SL TW WA2 WA3/CP HEA W
No of pupils 496; *(full boarding)* 60; *(weekly boarding)* 114; *(day)* 322; *Senior* 389; *Sixth Form* 107; *Girls* 160; *Boys* 336
Teacher:pupil ratio 1:9
Average class size 15–20
Fees per annum *(full boarding)* £15510–£20070; *(weekly)* £13500–£17010; *(day)* £10560–£13170. Flexi-boarding available for day pupils.

Seaford College was founded in 1884 and is a fully co-educational school for boarding and day pupils aged 10–18. Situated within 400 acres at the foot of the South Downs, the College is close to the historic town of Petworth and just seven miles from the closest railway station. Heathrow and Gatwick airports are within an hour's drive. Pupils may board weekly or full-time and a bus service collects day pupils from a wide area.

Curriculum: A wide range of subjects is offered at GCSE and a wide choice of A level options are available to the large Sixth Form. Ninety-six per cent of leavers go on to university.

Entry requirements and procedures: Entrance to the Junior House at 10+ and 11+ is based on a trial day and Ability test. Entrance to the Senior school at 13+ is based on similar lines, along with Common Entrance Examination results. Sixth Form entry is dependent on GCSE results and an interview. Overseas pupils must pass an English exam set by the College and past academic achievements will also be taken into account.

Academic and leisure facilities: The College boasts an impressive and successful Art, Design and Technology Centre.

Outstanding sports facilities including 6 rugby pitches, an artificial hockey pitch of international standard and a new 9-hole golf course and driving range, along with staff who have coached at international level, have helped the College gain an excellent sporting record. The hockey and rugby teams have toured South Africa, Australia, Canada and New Zealand and our pupils have played at county and national level.

Music and drama feature strongly in the life of the College. The Chapel Choir enjoys an international reputation and they have sung for Her Majesty Queen Elizabeth, the Queen Mother as well as touring America, Russia, France and South America.

Scholarships: Scholarships are offered for Academic, Design and Technology, Music (instrumental or choral), Sport or Art but must be accompanied by a good all-round academic standard. Value: £500. Parents who require further discount from the fees may apply for a bursary, which will be 'means-tested'.

Bursaries: Bursaries are available to Forces families and siblings.

Boarding facilities: Boys aged 13–17 are divided between two houses with separate boarding and day accommodation. The older boys have individual studies and the younger boys sleep in rooms of two or three. Second-year A level students are accommodated in a separate house, offering more privileges and responsibility and helping with the transition from the protection of school life to the relative freedom of university. The girls' boarding house, comprising dormitories for pre-GCSE girls, and single and twin rooms for lower sixth is located in the Mansion House. Dormitory facilities are provided in the Junior House for girls and boys aged 10–13.

For further information and a prospectus please contact the Admissions Secretary on 01798 867456 or jmackay@seaford.org.

Windlesham House

Washington, Pulborough, West Sussex RH20 4AY   Tel: (01903) 874700   Fax: (01903) 874702
E-mail: office@windlesham.com   Website: www.windlesham.com   www.gabbitas.co.uk

Acting Headmaster Mr P Forte MA (Oxon)
Founded 1837
School status Independent. Co-educational
Boarding and Day 4–13 (Day pre-prep 4–7).
Boarders from 7. From Sept 07 children joining
at Pre-Prep level (4+ to 7+) can remain as day
children up to age 13.
Religious denomination Church of England
Member of BSA, IAPS, ISBA, ISCis, SATIPS
Accredited by IAPS
Learning difficulties CA SNU WI/DYC DYP
DYS MLD SLD
Behavioural and emotional disorders CO RA
ST/ADD
Physical and medical conditions CA HL IT RA
SM WA3/HI
No of pupils 278; *(full boarding)* 229; *(day)* 49;
Pre-prep 33; *Prep* 245; *Girls* 104; *Boys* 174
Teacher:pupil ratio 1:7; **Average class size** 16
Fees per annum *(full boarding)* £16485–
£16785; *(day)* £2025–£2350

Curriculum: Broad curriculum enables children to
discover and develop their personal strengths and
talents. Strong academic record and emphasis on
creative arts, drama, music and sport.

Entrance requirements: No entrance examination. Flexible entrance policy.

Academic/leisure facilities: Recently upgraded
science labs, ICT, dorms and classrooms. Theatre/
sports hall, swimming pool (indoor), gymnasium,
dance/drama studio, tennis courts, AstroTurf
pitch, climbing wall, 8-hole golf course, extensive
playing fields and grounds (60 acres).

Boarding: This is very much a family school
with a warm, friendly, child-centred atmosphere.

England

MAP OF SOUTH WEST ENGLAND

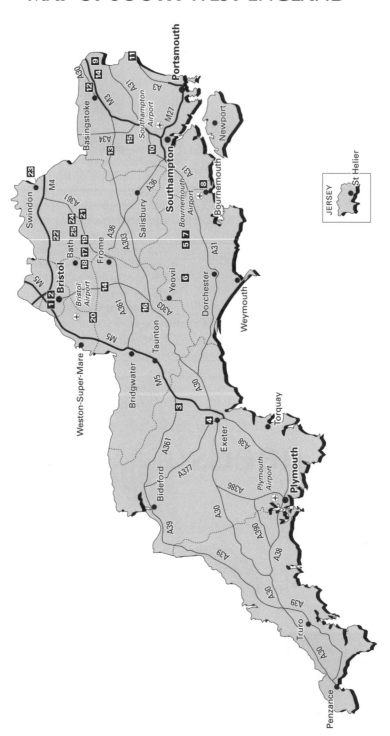

PROFILED SCHOOLS IN SOUTH WEST ENGLAND

(Incorporating the counties of Bath and North East Somerset, City of Bristol, Cornwall, Devon, Dorset, South Gloucestershire, Hampshire, Isle of Wight, Somerset, North Somerset, Wiltshire)

Map Number		Page Number
1	Badminton School, Westbury-on-Trym, Bristol	388
2	Clifton College, Clifton, Bristol	388
3	Blundell's School, Tiverton, Devon	389
4	Bramdean School, Exeter, Devon	389
5	Clayesmore School, Blandford Forum, Dorset	390
6	International College, Sherborne School, Sherborne, Dorset	391
7	Milton Abbey School, Blandford Forum, Dorset	392
8	Wentworth College, Bournemouth, Dorset	392
9	Farnborough Hill, Farnborough, Hampshire	393
10	Hampshire Collegiate School (Embley Park), Romsey, Hampshire	393
11	Highfield School, Liphook, Hampshire	394
12	Lord Wandsworth College, Hook, Hampshire	394
13	Rookwood School, Andover, Hampshire	395
14	St Nicholas' School, Church Crookham, Hampshire	395
15	Winchester College, Winchester, Hampshire	396
16	King's Bruton, Bruton, Somerset	397
17	Kingswood School, Bath, Somerset	398
18	Prior Park College, Bath, Somerset	399
19	The Royal High School, Bath, Somerset	399
20	Sidcot School, Winscombe, North Somerset	400
21	Dauntsey's School, Devizes, Wiltshire	401
22	Grittleton House School, Chippenham, Wiltshire	401
23	Pinewood School, Shrivenham, Wiltshire	402
24	St Mary's School, Calne, Wiltshire	402
25	Stonar School, Melksham, Wiltshire	403

England

Badminton School

Westbury-on-Trym, Bristol BS9 3BA   Tel: (0117) 905 5271   Fax: (0117) 962 8963
E-mail: arennie@badminton.bristol.sch.uk   Website: www.badminton.bristol.sch.uk

The Headmistress Mrs J Scarrow
Director of Marketing Mrs H Lightwood BA
and Dip Marketing
Director of Boarding Mrs J Dowling MA
Founded 1858
School status Girls Boarding and Day 4–18
Flexi-boarding available. Boarders from 7.
Religious denomination Non-Denominational
Member of BSA, GSA, IAPS, ISCis
Accredited by GSA, IAPS
Learning difficulties RA/DYS
Behavioural and emotional disorders RA
Physical and medical conditions RA/HI VI
No of pupils 420; *(full boarding)* 166; *(day)*
242; *Prep* 100; *Senior* 220; *Sixth Form* 100;
Girls 420
Teacher:pupil ratio Depends on age of child
Average class size 14 in JS and 16 in SS
Fees per annum *(full boarding)* £15120–
£22800; *(weekly)* £15120–£2280; *(day)*
£5970–£12840

Badminton School is an independent boarding, weekly boarding and day school, located on a 20-acre campus in the heart of the attractive University City of Bristol.

The school is currently ranked 5th in the national league table and around 20% of girls go onto Oxford and Cambridge.

The community spirit of the school also encourages girls to develop as individuals. By the time they leave school, the girls are confident and caring team players.

Clifton College

32 College Road, Clifton, Bristol BS8 3JH   Tel: (0117) 315 7000   Fax: (0117) 315 7101
E-mail: admissions@clifton-college.avon.sch.uk
Website: www.cliftoncollegeuk.com   www.gabbitas.co.uk

Head Master Mr Mark Moore MA
Director of Admissions Mr Philip Hallworth
MA MEd   **Founded** 1862
College status Independent. Co-educational
Boarding and Day 13–18 Flexi-boarding
available.
Religious denomination Church of England
Member of HMC
Learning difficulties SNU/DYC DYP DYS
Behavioural and emotional disorders CO
RA/ADD ASP
Physical and medical conditions RA WA3/HEA
No of pupils 678; *(full boarding)* 269; *(day)*
409; *Nursery* 28; *Pre-prep* 192; *Prep* 375;
Senior 384; *Sixth Form* 294; *Girls* 234;
Boys 444
Teacher:pupil ratio 1:8; **Average class size** 20
Fees per annum *(full boarding)* £23250; *(day)*
£15690

Clifton offers a broad and flexible curriculum with an unusually large number of subjects on offer. Entry at 13+ is by Common Entrance or ability tests. Scholarships are available at 11 (prep school), 13 and 16 for academic, art, music, sport and all-round abilities. The School occupies a superb site in what has been described as 'the handsomest suburb in Europe'.

Blundell's School

Tiverton, Devon EX16 4DN   Tel: (01884) 252543   Fax: (01884) 243232
E-mail: registrars@blundells.org   Website: www.blundells.org   www.gabbitas.co.uk

Head Master 2004 Mr I R Davenport BA
Founded 1604
School status Co-educational Boarding and
Day 11–18 Flexi-boarding available.
Religious denomination Church of England
Member of BSA, HMC, ISCis
Accredited by HMC, ISC
Learning difficulties SNU/DYS
Behavioural and emotional disorders CO
Physical and medical conditions SM TW
No of pupils 565; *(full boarding)* 120; *(weekly boarding)* 280; *(day)* 165; *Senior* 390; *Sixth Form* 175; *Girls* 230; *Boys* 335
Teacher:pupil ratio 1:11; **Average class size** 14
Fees per annum *(full boarding)* £14580–£21600; *(weekly)* £13170–£19005; *(day)* £8685–£13935

Blundell's, a key West Country school, combines balance, excellence, space and tradition to provide a unique package for 11–18-year-old day and boarding pupils.

All traditional subjects are offered at A level, plus Theatre Studies, Music, Art, Business Studies, Psychology, Photography and Sports Science. Supplementary courses and lectures are also provided at all levels.

A level entry requires a minimum of 5 GCSEs, interview and report from present school. At 11+ and 13+ pupils must sit Blundell's Entrance Test or Common Entrance.

Examinations offered: GCSE, A level, Music. Scholarships: 11+, 13+ and Sixth Form: academic, sport, music, art and all-rounder.

Boarders are supported by a strong house structure and live in a family environment guided by their Houseparents and Tutors.

Bramdean School

Richmond Lodge, Homefield Road, Heavitree, Exeter, Devon EX1 2QR   Tel: (01392) 273387
Fax: (01392) 439330   E-mail: info@bramdeanschool.com   Website: www.bramdeanschool.com

Headmistress Miss Diane Stoneman NAHT
Soccer Coach Mr J Martin Former Barcelona
Coach FC BSc
National Cricket Coach Mr K Brown Former
Vice-Captain MCC Lords
School status Independent. Co-educational
Boarding and Day 3–18 Flexi-boarding available.
Religious denomination Inter-Denominational
Member of NAHT
Learning difficulties WI/DYS
Physical and medical conditions SM/HEA
No of pupils 200; *(weekly boarding)* 10;
Girls 90; *Boys* 110
Teacher:pupil ratio 8:1; **Average class size** 18
Fees per annum *(weekly)* £10662; *(day)*
£4398–£7497. Kindergarten £1370 per term
(less grant)

Bramdean established in 1901. Bramdean is a traditional School with a modern approach offering a high level of education with experienced and qualified graduate staff. The school aims to fulfill the potential of each pupil it accepts and supply a varied range of opportunities for personal success both inside and outside the classroom.

At Bramdean we encourage our pupils to be tolerant, respectful and considerate to the needs of others. Classes are kept to a sensible size, maximum of 18. Pupils progress through the school according to ability and this approach has culminated in pupils achieving fine examination results over the years.

Excellent boarding facilities, homely atmosphere, resident Matron RGN.

Excellent games facilities for boys and girls plus state of the art indoor floodlit coaching area.

Clayesmore School

Iwerne Minster, Blandford Forum, Dorset DT11 8LL   Tel: (01747) 812122   Fax: (01747) 811343
E-mail: hmsec@clayesmore.com   Website: www.clayesmore.com

The Headmaster Mr M G Cooke BEd (Hons) FCollP
Head of Clayesmore Prep Mr R D H Geffen BEd (Hons)
School status Independent. Co-educational Boarding and Day 13–18. Boarders from 8. Senior School, Prep School, Pre-Prep and Nursery for children aged 2½–18 years.
Religious denomination Church of England
Member of CReSTeD, HMC, IAPS, ISCis, SATIPS, SHMIS
Accredited by HMC, IAPS, SHMIS
Learning difficulties SNU/DYC DYS
Physical & medical conditions AT RA SM/HEA
No of pupils 397; *(full boarding)* 230; *(day)* 167; *Nursery* 34; *Pre-prep* 30; *Prep* 184; *Senior* 397; *Sixth Form* 112; *Girls* 145; *Boys* 252
Teacher:pupil ratio 1:10
Average class size 18–20
Fees per annum *(full boarding)* £16140–£22197; *(day)* £11985–£16242

'This is a school on a roll' *Good Schools Guide*, 2006

An HMC school, Clayesmore has rapidly expanded in recent years and invested heavily in brand new academic buildings as well as new boarding facilities. However, amidst the quality, excellent exam results and status expected of an HMC school, Clayesmore still maintains its 'small school' family ethos. The result is a harmonious and tremendously happy atmosphere which feeds into the academic, cultural and sporting success of its pupils.

Located alongside the Senior School on the same beautiful countryside campus, is the Prep School where pupils also thrive on the individual attention they receive. This helps motivate and inspire them to achieve the highest standards in the broadest sense. Therefore, Clayesmore is truly a family school, where brothers and sisters of all ages can be together and for those looking for a happy and caring boarding environment, that is surely of inestimable value. The fundamental work ethic ensures that Clayesmore can deliver its principal aim of 'discovering and developing the unique gifts of every girl and boy' and all the pupils enjoy a busy and exciting life beyond the curriculum too.

International College, Sherborne School

Newell Grange, Sherborne, Dorset DT9 4EZ
Tel: (01935) 814743   Fax: (01935) 816863
E-mail: reception@sherborne-ic.net
Website: www.sherborne-ic.net   www.gabbitas.co.uk

The Principal Dr C J Greenfield
Founded 1977
College status Co-educational Boarding 11–17.
Member of BSA, COBISEC, ISA
Accredited by ISA
Learning difficulties MLD
Behavioural and emotional disorders TOU
Physical and medical conditions SM TW WA2
No of pupils 130; *(full boarding)* 130
Girls 50; *Boys* 80
Teacher:pupil ratio 1: 3
Average class size 6 students
Fees per annum *(full boarding)* £26040–
£28290

The International College is unique. It was established in 1977 (as the International Study Centre) to prepare boys – and later girls – from non-British educational backgrounds so that they could function successfully in traditional British boarding schools. Typically these boys and girls spend one year at the International College before moving on to a traditional British boarding school where the majority of students are British. Those students who join in Year 10 (usually around 14 or 15 years old) and start a two-year course leading towards GCSE examinations must stay at the school for the duration of the course.

The college has three major tasks:

* concentrated improvement in spoken and written English;
* academic preparation in English in the full range of curriculum subjects;
* a good introduction to British educational procedures and the British way of life.

The arrangements of the college are designed to achieve these tasks. Classes are small, usually between six and eight students to each teacher. All teachers are not only experienced specialists in their own subject, but also have additional training in teaching the English language.

Characteristics: The teaching facilities at the International College include modern classrooms, eight science laboratories, an art studio, a computer centre and a library with internet access. The college uses the extensive sporting, musical and theatre facilities at Sherborne School including a 25-metre indoor swimming pool.

The International College has gained an unrivalled reputation for providing the very best start to British independent education for children from overseas. Through a carefully supervised programme of study, students gain a sound working knowledge of the main British curriculum subjects such as mathematics, the sciences and humanities. The college has high standards of discipline and pastoral care. Most weekends there is a busy programme that ensures students are fully occupied on Saturday and Sunday.

England

Milton Abbey School

Blandford Forum, Dorset DT11 0BZ
Tel: (01258) 880484   Fax: (01258) 881194
E-mail: info@miltonabbey.co.uk   Website: www.miltonabbey.co.uk

The Headmaster Mr J Hughes-D'Aeth BA PGCE
Admissions Mrs D Morant BEd Hons
Founded 1954
School status Independent. Co-educational
Boarding and Day Boys 13–18 Girls 16–18.
Boarders from 13.
Religious denomination Church of England
Member of CReSTeD, ISCis, SHMIS
Accredited by SHMIS
Learning difficulties CA SNU/DYC DYP DYS
Behavioural and emotional disorders ADD
ADHD
Physical and medical conditions CA IT SM/
HEA HI
No of pupils 226; *(full boarding)* 207
Girls 21; *Boys* 205
Average class size 15
Fees per annum *(full boarding)* £24030; *(day)*
£18030

Milton Abbey is a very personal place – a school in which everybody genuinely knows everyone. We have achieved what other, bigger schools strive in vain to achieve: an intimate community in which achievement in any area of school life is never rated more highly than quality of character. No one is overlooked. Everyone is famous.

Wentworth College

College Road, Bournemouth, Dorset BH5 2DY   Tel: (01202) 423266   Fax: (01202) 418030
E-mail: enquiries@wentworthcollege.com   Website: www.wentworthcollege.com www.gabbitas.co.uk

Headmistress Miss S Coe BA Hons PGCE FRGS
Deputy Head Mrs F Langridge BSc Hons
Director of Studies Mr C Hancock BEd Cert ED
Founded 1871
College status Independent. Girls Boarding and
Day 11–18 Flexi-boarding available. Boarders
from 11.
Religious denomination Inter-Denominational
Member of GSA, ISCis
Accredited by GSA, ISC
Learning difficulties SNU/DYC DYP DYS
Behavioural & emotional disorders ADD ASP
Physical & medical conditions AT RA WA3/HEA
No of pupils 220; *(full boarding)* 40; *(weekly boarding)* 20; *Girls* 220
Fees per annum *(full boarding)* £16350;
(weekly) £16350; *(day)* £10125

her to reach her full potential. We aim to develop happy, confident young women who are proud of their academic success and personal achievement, and who leave equipped for adult life.

Situated in beautiful grounds on a cliff top just 200 metres from Bournemouth's award-winning beaches and close to the New Forest, the school offers well-equipped teaching and excellent sports facilities. We have a dedicated Sixth Form study centre and offer numerous extra-curricular activities.

Wentworth College provides a stimulating and caring environment with committed teachers who respond to the needs of every girl, helping

Farnborough Hill

Farnborough, Hampshire GU14 8AT   Tel: (01252) 545197   Fax: (01252) 513037
E-mail: devdir@farnborough-hill.org.uk   Website: www.farnborough-hill.org.uk

Headmistress Miss J Thomas MA PGCE
Development Director Mrs C Duffin BA FCIM
Founded 1889
School status Independent. Girls Day 11–18.
Religious denomination Roman Catholic
Member of AGBIS, GSA, ISCis
Accredited by GSA, ISC
Learning difficulties SNU/DYC DYP DYS
Behavioural and emotional disorders CO/ADD ADHD
Physical and medical conditions RA SM/EPI HEA HI
No of pupils 500; *(day)* 500; *Girls* 500
Teacher:pupil ratio 1:10; **Average class size** 22
Fees per annum *(day)* £8865

Farnborough Hill is an independent, Roman Catholic day school, which welcomes girls of all Christian denominations and of other faiths. Farnborough Hill is entirely committed to providing an environment that inspires in all its students warmth, friendship and enthusiasm for life and learning. Academic standards are high. However, the school offers much more than a narrow academic curriculum. The vision of 'educating the whole person' means that opportunities are provided for the spiritual, academic, emotional, physical, moral and social development of each pupil. Girls learn to accept and value themselves as individuals and to develop independence of thought and action. A spirit of friendliness pervades the school and visitors comment on the palpable feeling of happiness. This relaxed atmosphere enables students to work hard, play hard and give of their best at all times.

Hampshire Collegiate School (Embley Park)

Embley Park, Romsey, Hampshire SO51 6ZE   Tel: (01794) 512206   Fax: (01794) 518737
E-mail: info@hampshirecs.org.uk   Website: www.hampshirecs.org.uk   www.embleypark.org.uk

Principal Mr D F Chapman BA (Dunelm)
Deputy Head Mr Roy Macartney BA, MA(Ed)
Founded 1946
School status Independent. Co-educational Boarding and Day 3–18 Flexi-boarding available. Boarders from 11.
Religious denomination Church of England
Member of AGBIS, BSA, IAPS, SHA, SHMIS
Learning difficulties SNU/DYP DYS
Behavioural and emotional disorders RA/ADD ADHD
Physical & medical conditions SM WA2/HEA W
No of pupils 480; *(full boarding)* 30; *(weekly boarding)* 46; *Girls* 180; *Boys* 300
Teacher:pupil ratio 1:<20; *(classes)* 1:15
Average class size 18
Fees per annum *(full boarding)* £8310–£16620; *(weekly)* £8310–£16620; *(day)* £5000–£10005

Embley is a broad-ability school with an IQ threshold of 100, but still achieves, by small classes and setting in key subjects, approximately 90 per cent entry to higher education (Oxbridge 7 per cent). The Senior School sets its own entry test, but Common Entrance is used at 13+. At GCSE a core curriculum is offered but separate subject sciences and two languages can still be attempted. Business Studies with IT, PE and Drama are alternative humanity options. At A level, 22 subjects are offered. New facilities include a new junior school (£2.5 million), purpose-built science laboratories and a 7,000 square-foot sports hall. Scholarships available; also bursaries (HM Forces, clergy, teachers, single parents, and hardship cases).

England

Highfield School

Highfield Lane, Liphook, Hampshire GU30 7LQ   Tel: (01428) 728000   Fax: (01428) 728001
E-mail: office@highfieldschool.org.uk   Website: www.highfieldschool.org.uk   www.gabbitas.co.uk
Pre-Prep Brookham School at the same address as Highfield. Tel. No. 01428 722005

The Headmaster Mr P G S Evitt MA
Head of Pre-Prep Mrs D E Gardiner Cert Ed
MEd
Founded 1907
School status Independent. Co-educational
Boarding and Day 8–13. Brookham Pre-Prep
and Highfield Prep offer Co-educational
Boarding and Day education from 3+ to 13+
Religious denomination Church of England
Member of IAPS, ISCis, NAHT
Accredited by IAPS, ISC
Learning difficulties CA SNU/DYP DYS MLD
Behavioural and emotional disorders CO
RA/ASP
Physical and medical conditions RA SM/HEA
No of pupils 216; *(full boarding)* 85; *(day)* 131;
Pre-prep 135; *Prep* 216; *Girls* 106; *Boys* 110
Teacher:pupil ratio 1:9
Average class size 16

Fees per annum *(full boarding)* £11700–
£16650; *(day)* £11250–£14625

Highfield is a co-educational day and boarding
school founded in 1907 and set in 175 acres of
superb grounds on the Hampshire/Sussex border.
Highfield children are prepared for Common
Entrance and scholarships to all the major senior
schools. The broad curriculum includes ICT, PE
and DT and the school's excellent tradition in
music, drama and art is reflected in the number
of scholarships gained recently. The school has
built new facilities for Science, Maths, English and
ICT. All the major sports are offered and over 50
activities take place in the evenings, lunchtimes
and at weekends.

Lord Wandsworth College

Long Sutton, Hook, Hampshire RG29 1TB   Tel: (01256) 862201   Fax: (01256) 860363
E-mail: info@lordwandsworth.org   Website: www.lordwandsworth.org

Headmaster Mr I G Power MA
Director of Admissions Mrs M P Hicks
Founded 1922
College status Co-educational Boarding and
Day 11–18 Flexi-boarding available. Boarders
from 11.
Religious denomination Non-Denominational
Member of BSA, HMC, ISCis, SHMIS
Accredited by HMC, ISC, SHMIS
Learning difficulties SNU/DYS
Behavioural & emotional disorders RA/ADD ASP
Physical & medical conditions RA SM/EPI HEA
No of pupils 521; *(full boarding)* 46; *(weekly
boarding)* 199; *(day)* 276; *Senior* 387; *Sixth
Form* 134; *Girls* 174; *Boys* 347
Teacher:pupil ratio 1:10; **Average class size** 18
Fees per annum *(full boarding)* £19365–
£21300; *(weekly)* £19365–£20445; *(day)*
£14460–£15240
Fees Flexi boarding £35 per night

Lord Wandsworth College Offers:
- A safe and secure environment
- A high level of pastoral care
- Excellent exam results which consistently
  exceed individual expectations
- Outstanding facilities for both academic and
  co-curricular activities
- An unpretentious, caring, happy and relaxed
  atmosphere
- A broad, balanced education

Rookwood School

Weyhill Road, Andover, Hampshire SP10 3AL   Tel: (01264) 325900   Fax: (01264) 325909
E-mail: office@rookwood.hants.sch.uk Website: www.rookwood.hants.sch.uk www.gabbitas.co.uk

Headmistress Mrs M P Langley BSc (Hons)
Founded 1934
School status Independent. Co-educational
Day and Boarding 3–16 (Day boys only) Flexi-
boarding available. Boarders from 8. Rated
No.1 in Hampshire at GCSE in 2005/among
top 50 independent schools at GCSE in 2006
(The Times)
Religious denomination Non-Denominational
Member of BSA, ISA, ISCis, SHA
Accredited by ISA
Learning difficulties CA WI/DYP DYS
Behavioural & emotional disorders RA/ADHD
ASP
Physical & medical conditions CA RA/HEA HI
No of pupils 342; *(full boarding)* 35; *(day)* 307;
Nursery 33; *Pre-prep* 52; *Prep* 119; *Senior* 138;
Girls 204; *Boys* 138
Average class size 14
Fees per annum *(full boarding)* £14805–
£17355; *(day)* £5880–£9705

Rookwood School was described in the latest ISI
report as an 'outstandingly happy and successful
school'.

The school is non-selective, yet the Senior
School's excellent GCSE results are testament to
the high academic standards achieved in small
classes taught by experienced subject specialists.
In recent years 100% of candidates gained at least
5 A*–C grades. The school also prepares pupils for
the Common Entrance examination.

St Nicholas' School

Redfields House, Redfields Lane, Church Crookham, Fleet, Hampshire GU52 0RF
Tel: (01252) 850121   Fax: (01252) 850718   E-mail: registrar@st-nicholas.hants.sch.uk
Website: www.st-nicholas.hants.sch.uk   www.gabbitas.co.uk

Headmistress Mrs A V Whatmough BA(Hons)
Cert Ed
Founded 1935
School status Independent. Girls Day 3–16
(Boys 3–7). Co-educational (girls only 7–16)
independent pre-prep, prep and senior day
Religious denomination Church of England
Member of GSA, ISCis
Accredited by GSA, ISC
No of pupils 380; *(day)* 380; *Nursery* 20;
Pre-prep 80; *Prep* 110; *Senior* 170; *Girls* 360;
Boys 20
Fees per annum *(day)* £3150–£8520

At St Nicholas' School we believe that the best
education is a partnership between teachers,
pupils and parents. By creating a supportive environment, the personal and academic potential of
each pupil can be developed. Classes are small
and facilities are excellent. The personal and

academic progress of each individual is monitored carefully and should any help be needed,
it is available. The secure base laid at St Nicholas'
gives students a wide range of choice for the next
stage of their education. The fact that they are
welcome wherever they go is a tribute to the work
of the school.

Winchester College

College Street, Winchester, Hampshire SO23 9NA
Tel: (01962) 621247   Fax: (01962) 621106   E-mail: Admissions@WinchesterCollege.co.uk
Website: www.winchestercollege.org   www.gabbitas.co.uk

Headmaster Dr R D Townsend MA DPhil
Registrar Dr A P Wolters BSc PhD CChem MRSC
Bursar Mr J E Hynam MPhil BEd ACP
Founded 1382
College status Independent. Boys Boarding and Day 13–18.
Religious denomination Church of England
Member of AGBIS, HMC, ISCis, SHA
Accredited by HMC
Learning difficulties DYP DYS
No of pupils 690; *(full boarding)* 678; *(day)* 12; *Boys* 690
Teacher:pupil ratio 1:8
Fees per annum *(full boarding)* £24981; *(day)* £23730

Winchester College is a boarding school for boys aged 13–18. It was founded in 1382 by William of Wykeham, Bishop of Winchester and Chancellor to Richard II, and has the longest unbroken history of any school in the country. Its setting is one of unrivalled beauty and spaciousness.

Winchester enjoys an international reputation for its outstanding academic record. This can be seen not just in its excellent examination results but also in the quality of the intellectual training it provides. Nearly all of it pupils go on to good universities and about 45 each year win places at Oxford or Cambridge.

The high academic standards are matched by similar achievements in music, art, drama and a wide range of sporting activities. The school has extensive playing fields and generous provision for pupils to develop their cultural and athletic interests.

Most of the boys in the school are boarders, but day boys are accepted.

Generous academic and music awards are offered annually to boys entering the school at age 13 and 16. Financial help with the fees is available to all candidates on a means-tested basis.

13+ academic scholarships and exhibitions: The examination of candidates for scholarships and exhibitions is held at the college in early May; about 15 scholarships and about 6 exhibitions are offered. Scholarships have a basic value of 25 per cent of the full fee. Exhibitions are also awarded on the same exam. Candidates must be under 14 and at least 12 on 1 September in the year in which they sit the exam. Entry forms, which must be returned by March, are available from the Master in College, Winchester College, College Street, Winchester SO23 9NA.

Sixth Form academic awards: The entrance examination for both awards and places takes place at the college early in the Spring term. Up to four scholarships with a maximum value of 25 per cent of the full fee are offered. Entry forms, which must be returned by mid-November the previous year, are obtainable from the Registrar (address as above).

Details of music awards can also be obtained from Winchester College Music School, Culver Road, Winchester SO23 9JF; Tel: (01962) 621122.

King's Bruton

Bruton, Somerset BA10 0ED   Tel: (01749) 814200   Fax: (01749) 813426
E-mail: registrar@kingsbruton.com   Website: www.kingsbruton.com   www.gabbitas.co.uk

Headmaster Mr N M Lashbrook BA
Founded 1519
School status Independent. Co-educational
Boarding and Day 13–18.
Religious denomination Church of England
Member of CReSTeD, HMC, ISCis
Accredited by HMC
Learning difficulties SNU/DYC DYP DYS
Behavioural and emotional disorders ADD
ADHD ASP
Physical and medical conditions RA/HEA VI
No of pupils 326; *(full boarding)* 221; *(day)*
105; *Senior* 326; *Sixth Form* 146; *Girls* 94;
Boys 232
Teacher:pupil ratio 1:8; **Average class size** 15
Fees per annum *(full boarding)* £20100; *(day)*
£14730

The King's Senior School is situated in the small Somerset town of Bruton. Founded in the early 16th century, the school combines historic buildings with more recent development. The Preparatory School lies in 220 acres of parkland at Sparkford, 8 miles away. Both schools foster a close community within which all members are given the opportunity to achieve their academic, spiritual, social, aesthetic and physical potential. The schools have a lively, purposeful and friendly atmosphere where everyone is able to flourish within a supportive and disciplined framework.

England

Kingswood School

Lansdown, Bath, Bath & North East Somerset BA1 5RG   Tel: (01225) 734210   Fax: (01225) 734305
E-mail: enquiries@kingswood.bath.sch.uk Website: www.kingswood.bath.sch.uk www.gabbitas.co.uk
Contact our Admissions Office for information about Scholarships and bursaries.

Head Master Mr G M Best MA
Prep School Head Mr Marcus Cornah
Founded 1748
School status Co-educational Boarding and
Day 3–18 Flexi-boarding available. Boarders
from 7. A Kingswood pupil will take much
more than good results to university. Happiness
and excellence!
Religious denomination Methodist
Member of BSA, HMC, IAPS, ISBA, ISCis;
Accredited by British Council, HMC, IAPS
Learning difficulties MILD DYP DYS
Physical and medical conditions RA/HEA HI
No of pupils 960; *(full boarding)* 176; *(weekly
boarding)* 43; *(day)* 780; *Nursery* 32; *Pre-prep*
109; *Prep* 183; *Senior* 636; *Sixth Form* 180;
Girls 417; *Boys* 543
Teacher:pupil ratio 1:9
Average class size 22 (Senior School)
Fees per annum *(full boarding)* £14889–
£20592; *(weekly)* £12507–£18606; *(day)*
£6285–£9234. Includes all text books, personal
accident (including dental) and personal effects
insurance.

Kingswood School is set within 215 acres of
beautiful parkland overlooking the world heritage
City of Bath. It offers a caring environment in
which high academic standards are attained with
a strong emphasis being placed upon 'all-round'
education. This is delivered not only through a
wide variety of over 100 extra-curricular activities, but also through a lively and dynamic
curriculum that is broad and balanced.

The School's facilities include not only extensive classrooms, laboratories and ICT facilities,
but also a Music School with recording studio, a
'state of the art' theatre and drama studio, and
extensive sports facilities including a floodlit Astro
Turf pitch. New for 2006 the School has opened a
multi-media library and resource centre. All the
boarding houses have been upgraded and offer an
excellent homely environment with high-quality
furnishings and facilities.

The Senior School offers education for boys and
girls between the ages of 11 and 18. The younger

pupils aged 11 and 12 have their own 'junior
house' within the senior school campus, enabling
them to enjoy the extra care normally associated
with the best prep schools, whilst simultaneously
experiencing the benefits of the senior school
facilities and its curriculum. At 13+ they enter
one of six senior houses, which provide a strong
caring community in which friendships can flourish. The Sixth Form has a purpose-built Study
Centre with an array of extra facilities, including
a Higher Education and Careers suite.

The school consistently achieves very high
results, with 100 per cent pass rates at GCSE
and A level. In addition, it attempts to ensure that
students develop their other talents to equal
effect, enabling over 90 per cent of its students
to attend the university of their first choice.

Inspection reports have praised Kingswood
School for the commitment and dedication of its
teaching staff. The relationships between staff and
pupils are one of the factors most commented
upon by parents and the generation of life-long
friendships is very much a part of what the school
encourages.

The school is the oldest Methodist educational
establishment in the world. It welcomes pupils
from every faith and none. Christian values
permeate Kingswood School's philosophy and
ethos, and all members of the School community
are encouraged to behave in a way that reflects
the best Christian values, creating a love of life
and learning in all its pupils.

Scholarships and Special Talent awards are
available. HM Forces Remissions (20 per cent)
and some Bursaries are also offered.

A Kingswood pupil will be taking much more
than good results to university. Please come and
meet us to see at first hand all that Kingswood has
to offer your children.

Prior Park College

Ralph Allen Drive, Bath, Bath & North East Somerset BA2 5AH
Tel: (01225) 831000   Fax: (01225) 835753   E-mail: admissions@priorpark.co.uk
Website: www.priorpark.co.uk   www.gabbitas.co.uk

Headmaster Dr G Mercer KSG, MA
Registrar Dr M Ruxton BSc Phd
Founded 1831
College status Independent. Co-educational
Boarding and Day 11–18 (Boarding from 13)
Flexi-boarding available. Boarders from 13.
Religious denomination Roman Catholic
Member of CIS, HMC, ISCis
Accredited by CIS, HMC
Learning difficulties RA/DYP DYS
Physical and medical conditions SM WA3/VI
No of pupils 543; *(full boarding)* 120; *(day)*
423; *Senior* 543; *Sixth Form* 171; *Girls* 245;
Boys 298
Teacher:pupil ratio 1:9; **Average class size** 20
Fees per annum *(full boarding)* £20118; *(day)*
£10014–£11157. Fees include lunch and
supervised prep.

educational, Christian community where an excellent work ethic mixes seamlessly with outstanding enrichment opportunities. Positive teaching encourages excellent academic results at GCSE and A Level and 99% of students go on to higher education at good universities. Recent new facilities include a major refurbishment of the indoor heated swimming pool, a new ICT centre and classroom extension and a new Mackintosh Dance studio. The Combined Cadet Force, Duke of Edinburgh's Award Scheme and Prior Concern, our own community service programme, sporting excellence and sport for all offer further opportunities for every pupil.

Prior Park is a friendly, well-established co-

The Royal High School

Lansdown Road, Bath, Bath & North East Somerset BA1 5SZ   Tel: (01225) 313877
Fax: (01225) 465446   E-mail: royalhigh@bat.gdst.net
Website: www.gdst.net/royalhighbath   www.gabbitas.co.uk

Headmaster Mr J Graham-Brown BA (Hons)
M.Phil.
Head of Junior School Mrs Helen Fathers BA
(Hons)
School status Independent. Girls Boarding and
Day 3–18 Flexi-boarding available. Boarders
from 11.(GDST school)
Religious denomination Non-Denominational
Member of GDST, GSA
Learning difficulties DYP DYS
No of pupils 811; *(full boarding)* 80; *(weekly
boarding)* 10; *(day)* 727; *Nursery* 18; *Pre-prep*
48; *Prep* 150; *Senior* 482; *Sixth Form* 127;
Girls 811; **Average class size** 22
Fees per annum *(full boarding)* –£15417;
(weekly) –£13695; *(day)* –£7863

As one of the 28 members of the Girls' Day School Trust, we belong to an organisation that is renowned for providing a high quality, all-round

education at an affordable cost to girls of academic promise. We are unique among Trust schools in offering the enriching experience of boarding, giving parents more flexibility as circumstances and preferences change. Recent developments include fully refurbished boarding accommodation, a new sports hall and astroturf pitches, additional ICT suites and new science facilities. We are proud of our strong academic tradition and our girls' achievements.

Sidcot School

Oakridge Lane, Winscombe, North Somerset BS25 1PD Tel: (01934) 843102   Fax: (01934) 844181
E-mail: admissions@sidcot.org.uk   Website: www.sidcot.org.uk   www.gabbitas.co.uk

The Headmaster Mr J Walmsley BSc
Deputy Head Mrs E Burgess BSc BEd
Bursar Mr T Synge BA FCA   **Founded** 1699
School status Independent. Co-educational
Boarding and Day 3–18 Flexi-boarding
available.   **Religious denomination** Quaker
Member of BSA, CReSTeD, ISA, ISBA, ISCis,
SHA, SHMIS; **Accredited by** British Council
Learning difficulties CA SNU/DYS
Behavioural and emotional disorders RA/ADD
ADHD ASP BESD CB
Physical and medical conditions SM TW
WA2/EPI HEA
No of pupils 499; *(full boarding)* 127; *(weekly boarding)* 14; *(day)* 358; *Nursery* 15; *Pre-prep* 46; *Prep* 79; *Senior* 234; *Sixth Form* 125; *Girls* 213; *Boys* 286
Teacher:pupil ratio 1:15; **Average class size** 15
Fees per annum *(full boarding)* £14550–£22950; *(weekly)* £16650; *(day)* £3870–£10485

Sidcot School is a thriving independent co-educational day and boarding school situated in 150 acres of beautiful countryside on the edge of the Mendip Hills, close to Bristol, Bath and Wells.

Sidcot offers a blend of excellent traditional and state-of-the-art facilities. It is well equipped with academic facilities, a new learning resource and Sixth Form centre, excellent computer facilities, sports hall complex with heated swimming pool, extensive playing fields and a riding centre.

Our Quaker philosophy means that we value all children whatever their abilities. Our students gain excellent exam results but also develop as caring and confident individuals. Happy children learn, and small classes and good working relationships between staff and students make for a positive and inclusive atmosphere.

Academic, music, sports and Sixth Form scholarships are available. Quaker bursaries are available for members of the Society of Friends. We welcome pupils of all faiths or none.

Dauntsey's School

High Street, West Lavington, Devizes, Wiltshire SN10 4HE
Tel: (01380) 814500   Fax: (01380) 814501
E-mail: information@dauntseys.wilts.sch.uk   Website: www.dauntseys.wilts.sch.uk

Head Master Mr S B Roberts MA
Registrar Mr A S Whitney BA JP
Founded 1542
School status Independent. Co-educational Boarding and Day 11–18.
Religious denomination Inter-Denominational
Member of BSA, HMC
Accredited by HMC, ISC
Learning difficulties WI/DYS
Behavioural and emotional disorders CO
Physical and medical conditions SL SM TW WA1/W
No of pupils 756; *(full boarding)* 282; *(day)* 474; *Senior* 518; *Sixth Form* 233; *Girls* 365; *Boys* 391
Teacher:pupil ratio 1:9
Average class size Around 20 up to GCSE, 8–12 in Sixth Form
Fees per annum *(full boarding)* £21360; *(day)* £12660

Dauntsey's is a very happy and successful co-educational independent school. Excellent facilities are available for academic work, music, drama, art and sport. There are several new buildings: a new five-studio art school, a new library and IT suite, a major science development and a brand new senior girls' boarding house.

Outward-bound activities flourish and include a very active sailing club, which sails the famous Jolie Brise (winner of the Tall Ships' Race on several occasions).

There is an emphasis on pastoral care and Christian values, though worship is not narrowly denominational. There is a flexible system of exeats for boarders. Careers advice is thorough and there is a programme of work experience. Virtually all the pupils go on to university and each year several go to Oxbridge. Visitors are always welcome. Please contact the Registrar for a prospectus and details of the entry procedure.

Grittleton House School

Grittleton, Chippenham, Wiltshire SN14 6AP   Tel: (01249) 782434   Fax: (01249) 782669
E-mail: secretary@grittletonhouseschool.org   Website: www.grittletonhouseschool.org

Headmistress Mrs C Whitney
Bursar Mr J Shipp
Founded 1951
School status Independent. Co-educational Day 2–16.
Religious denomination Non-Denominational
Learning difficulties WI/DYS
No of pupils 300; *(day)* 300; *Nursery* 21; *Pre-prep* 44; *Prep* 68; *Senior* 167; *Girls* 126; *Boys* 174
Teacher:pupil ratio 1:14
Average class size 15
Fees per annum *(day)* £5385–£8355. Please note fees will be reviewed in January 2007

Grittleton House School is unique. Set in the beautiful Wiltshire countryside, it offers an unequalled chance for children to experience the very best in education. Its 'whole school' philosophy caters for children from Nursery age to GCSE level, in a secure and happy environment, where the children flourish, meeting the challenges that come their way with enthusiasm.

Staff at Grittleton support, inspire – cajole when necessary – and the pupils respond by achieving the best possible results they can. Last year's 11th year achieved excellent results at GCSE, and in the Lower School SATS grades were at the highest level. Please contact the School Secretary on 01249 782434 for a prospectus, a copy of our recent excellent Ofsted report and any further information you may require.

Pinewood School

Bourton, Shrivenham, Wiltshire SN6 8HZ   Tel: (01793) 782205   Fax: (01793) 783476
E-mail: office@pinewoodschool.co.uk   Website: www.pinewood.oxon.sch.uk www.gabbitas.co.uk

Headmaster Mr P J Hoyland
Deputy Head Mr C Acheson-Gray
Founded 1875
School status Independent. Co-educational
Boarding and Day 3–13 Flexi-boarding
available.
Religious denomination Church of England
Member of IAPS; **Accredited by** IAPS
Learning difficulties SNU/DYP DYS MLD
Behavioural and emotional disorders RA
Physical and medical conditions WA3
No of pupils 296; *(weekly boarding)* 30; *(day)*
266; *Nursery* 22; *Pre-prep* 73; *Prep* 201;
Girls 149; *Boys* 147
Fees per annum *(full boarding)* £4770; *(weekly)*
£4155–£4600; *(day)* £890–£3690

Pinewood offers a quality, family-based, co-educational environment where children are encouraged to think for themselves and a strong emphasis is placed on self-reliance, manners, trust and a regard for others. Resources include a purpose-built Music School and Junior Forms' wing, a flourishing Pre-prep and Nursery, art and design workshops, research and reference library and ICT rooms. Excellent academic results are achieved through a mixture of traditional and forward-thinking. Outside trips are frequent and visiting speakers prominent. Music and drama are encouraged. Sport is keenly coached, and matches are played at all levels on our picturesque playing fields, which incorporate a nine-hole golf course. There is a wide range of activities and clubs both for day-children and, in the evenings, for boarders.

St Mary's School

Calne, Wiltshire SN11 0DF
Tel: (01249) 857200   Fax: (01249) 857207
E-mail: admissions@stmaryscalne.org
Website: www.stmaryscalne.org

Headmistress Dr H M Wright MA(Oxon) MA
(Leics), EdD, FRSA
Founded 1873
School status Independent. Girls Boarding and
Day 11–18.
Religious denomination Church of England
Member of GSA
Accredited by British Council, GSA, ISA
Learning difficulties SNU/DYP DYS
Behavioural and emotional disorders CO
Physical and medical conditions RA SM WA2
WA3/EPI HEA HI IM
No of pupils 300; *(full boarding)* 250; *(day)* 50;
Girls 300
Teacher:pupil ratio 8
Average class size 14
Fees per annum *(full boarding)* £22740; *(day)*
£15540

St Mary's Calne is one of the top achieving girls' schools in the UK, featuring regularly at the top of the school league tables. The school has a stimulating and exciting cutting edge curriculum and prides itself on educating successful young women for the 21st century. It benefits additionally from outstanding drama and sporting facilities in a rural location which is nonetheless only just over an hour from London by train.

Stonar School

Cottles Park, Atworth, Melksham, Wiltshire SN12 8NT   Tel: (01225) 701740   Fax: (01225) 790830
E-mail: admissions@stonarschool.com   Website: www.stonarschool.com   www.gabbitas.co.uk

Head Mrs S Shayler BSc Hons MA
Founded 1895
School status Independent. Girls Boarding and
Day 2–18 Flexi-boarding available. Boarders
from 8.
Religious denomination Inter-Denominational
Member of BSA, GSA, ISCis, SHA
Accredited by GSA, ISC
Learning difficulties CA WI/DYC DYP DYS
MLD
Behavioural and emotional disorders CA CO
Physical and medical conditions AT CA RA
SM/EPI HEA VI
No of pupils 417; *(full boarding)* 190; *(weekly*
boarding) 80; *(day)* 210; *Nursery* 45; *Pre-prep*
23; *Prep* 69; *Senior* 217; *Sixth Form* 60;
Girls 400; *Boys* 17
Teacher:pupil ratio 1:9; **Average class size** 14
Fees per annum *(full boarding)* £15390–
£17985; *(weekly)* £15390–£17985; *(day)*
£5190–£10125

Stonar School, set in over 80 acres of parkland
within easy reach of the city of Bath, offers a
high-quality, effective, single-sex education for
girls 2–18.

Facilities are excellent with an on-site equestrian centre, swimming pool, theatre, sports hall
and AstroTurf as well as a purpose-built music
suite and art studio. A new nursery building was
opened in 2002 and new science accommodation
was finished in 2004.

England

Gabbitas Guardianship

Caring for your child at boarding school in the UK

Established for nearly 30 years, Gabbitas Guardianship provides an outstanding level of personal care for students from all over the world.

- **Careful selection of a guardian family**

- **Guidance on the best schools**

- **Monitoring progress and welfare**

- **Advice on all stages of education**

- **Management of travel arrangements, passport and visa formalities and finances**

- **Arrangements for guardians to attend parent-teacher meetings and school events**

- **Arrangements for purchase of school uniform and other items**

AEGIS
ENSURING QUALITY IN GUARDIANSHIP

Gabbitas is fully accredited by AEGIS (Association for the Education and Guardianship of International Students)

Gabbitas Educational Consultants
126-130 Regent Street,
London W1B 5EE

Contact Catherine Stoker
Tel: +44 (0)20 7734 0161
Email: guardian@gabbitas.co.uk

or visit www.gabbitas.co.uk

Gabbitas

IN EDUCATION SINCE 1873

3.2 Scotland

MAP OF SCOTLAND

PROFILED SCHOOLS IN SCOTLAND

(Incorporating the counties of Aberdeen City, Aberdeenshire, Angus, Argyll and Bute, East Ayrshire, North Ayrshire, South Ayrshire, Borders, City of Edinburgh, Dumfries and Galloway, East Dunbartonshire, West Dunbartonshire, Falkirk, Fife, Highland, Inverclyde, East Lothian, Midlothian, Moray, Perth and Kinross, Renfrewshire, Stirling, South Lanarkshire, West Lothian)

Map Number		Page Number
1	Albyn School, Aberdeen, Aberdeenshire	408
2	Fettes College, Edinburgh, Lothian	409
3	Loretto School, Musselburgh, Lothian	409
4	Merchiston Castle School, Edinburgh, Midlothian	410
5	Gordonstoun School, Elgin, Moray	411
6	Glenalmond College, Perth, Perth and Kinross	412
7	Strathallan School, Perth, Perth and Kinross	412

Scotland

Albyn School

17–23 Queen's Road, Aberdeen, Aberdeenshire AB15 4PB   Tel: (01224) 322408 Fax: (01224) 209173
E-mail: information@albynschool.co.uk   Website: www.albynschool.co.uk   www.gabbitas.co.uk

Headmaster Dr JD Halliday BA.PhD
Founded 1867
School status Independent. Co-educational
Day Boys 2–10 Girls 2–18. Co-educational
nurseries for children aged 12 weeks–5 years
old
Religious denomination Non-Denominational
Member of GSA, HAS, ISBA, SCIS, SHA
Learning difficulties SNU/DYP DYS
Physical and medical conditions CA IT RA TW/
EPI HEA HI
No of pupils 400; *(day)* 450; *Nursery* 80;
Pre-prep 40; *Prep* 200; *Senior* 210; *Sixth
Form* 30; *Girls* 340; *Boys* 60
Teacher:pupil ratio 1:8; **Average class size** 15
Fees per annum *(day)* £5000–£8200

This summer Albyn School achieved the best Higher pass rate of all schools in Scotland. Last year the School was best in Scotland for Advanced Highers.

Recently the school has invested in new science facilities and a nursery for babies and toddlers. In 2005 the decision was taken to move from a single sex girls' to a fully co-educational school. The first boys were enrolled in the primary school in August 2005. Albyn's new £3 million, purpose-built primary school is already under construction and is due to open in August 2007. Albyn now has boys in classes up to P6. They will work their way through the school forging a co-educational school behind them. However, the secondary school will remain girls only until 2008.

Fettes College

Carrington Road, Edinburgh, Lothian EH4 1QX   Tel: (0131) 311 6701   Fax: (0131) 311 6714
E-mail: enquiries@fettes.com   Website: www.fettes.com

Headmaster Mr M C B Spens MA
Admissions Secretary Mrs H F Marshall
Founded 1870
College status Independent. Co-educational Boarding and Day 7–18. Boarders from 7.
Religious denomination Inter-Denominational
Member of AGBIS, BSA, HAS, HMC, IAPS, IBO, ISBA, SCIS; **Accredited by** HMC, IAPS
Learning difficulties SC/DYS MLD
Behavioural and emotional disorders RA
Physical and medical conditions WA2/EPI HEA
No of pupils 610; *(full boarding)* 427; *(day)* 183; *Prep* 143; *Senior* 467; *Sixth Form* 190; *Girls* 261; *Boys* 349
Teacher:pupil ratio 1:8; **Average class size** 15
Fees per annum *(full boarding)* £16167–£22326; *(day)* £10326–£15840

Fettes College is one of the UK's pre-eminent co-educational boarding schools situated in extensive grounds close to the heart of Edinburgh. Our mission is to develop broadly educated, confident and thoughtful individuals.

Academically excellent, Fettes is the leading A Level school in Scotland with over 80% achieving grades A or B at A Level. Unique to Scotland, Fettes offers A Levels alongside the International Baccalaureate Diploma allowing each pupil choice of curriculum to suit their strengths. Fettes has a high rate of entry into University (98%), including up to 15 students a year to Oxford and Cambridge.

All major sports are offered with excellent outdoor and indoor facilities plus a wide range of extra-curricular activities available. Charitable work and community service plays an important role in school life. A new Upper Sixth Co-educational boarding house is due for completion by September 2007 and is designed to act as the conduit between school and university.

The Fettes College Charitable Trust exists to provide high quality education for boys and girls. Charity No. SCO 17489.

Loretto School

Linkfield Road, Musselburgh, Lothian EH21 7RE   Tel: (0131) 653 4455   Fax: (0131) 653 4456
E-mail: admissions@loretto.com   Website: www.loretto.com
Junior School 0131 653 4570 email juniorschool@loretto.com

Headmaster Mr M B Mavor C.V.O.
Founded 1827
School status Independent. Co-educational Boarding and Day 3–18 Flexi-boarding available. Boarders from 8.
Religious denomination Non-Denominational
Member of BSA, HMC, IAPS, ISCis, SCIS
Accredited by HMC, IAPS, ISC
Learning difficulties SC
No of pupils 503; *(full boarding)* 261; *(day)* 242; *Nursery* 28; *Pre-prep* 52; *Prep* 121; *Senior* 302; *Sixth Form* 136; *Girls* 213; *Boys* 290
Teacher:pupil ratio 1:9
Average class size 10–15
Fees per annum *(full boarding)* £15609–£22080; *(weekly)* £14049–£14985; *(day)* £4815–£14595. Flexi-boarding packages available. Weekly boarding only in junior school. Scholarships available

Loretto provides an all-round education for 500 children (3–18). Renowned for its music, drama and art including a state-of-the-art recording studio and theatre facilities.

There is a relaxed family atmosphere and emphasis on the development of the whole person, mind, body and spirit – through academic study, the arts, extra-curricular and sporting activities.

GCSEs and A Levels offered. In 2006, 73% of students achieved grades A or B at A Level.

Extracurricular activities are many making full use of Loretto's Golf Academy, sports hall, indoor swimming pool and arts complex.

Merchiston Castle School

Colinton, Edinburgh, Lothian EH13 0PU   Tel: (0131) 312 2200   Fax: (0131) 441 6060
E-mail: admissions@merchiston.co.uk   Website: www.merchiston.co.uk   www.gabbitas.co.uk

Head Mr A R Hunter BA   **Founded** 1833
School status Independent. Boys Boarding and
Day 8–18. Boarders from 8.
Religious denomination Inter-Denominational
Member of BSA, HMC, ISBA, ISCis, SCIS,
IBSCA; **Accredited by** HMC, ISC
Learning difficulties SNU/DYP DYS MLD
Behavioural and emotional disorders ADHD
Physical and medical conditions RA
No of pupils 430; (full boarding) 288; (day)
142; Prep 104; Senior 173; Sixth Form 153;
Boys 430; **Teacher:pupil ratio** 1:9
Average class size (under 11) 15; (11–16) 16;
(Sixth Form) 9
Fees per annum (full boarding) £14325–
£21795; (day) £10005–£15585

Set in 100 acres of parkland Merchiston is a school renowned for academic and sporting excellence.

Merchiston offers a full range of GCSEs, A levels and Highers. In 2006, 77 per cent of A level candidates gained A and B grades, while at GCSE 59 per cent of grades were awarded at A and A*; 88 per cent of pupils achieved a place at their first choice of university. Regular winners of national engineering, electronic and mathematics prizes. Sporting achievements include pupils participating at international level. Strongly featured music department with prestigious school choir and pipe band.

Integral Junior department (8–12 years). Strong links with two girls' schools. Junior teaching centre, refurbished science labs, modern IT suite, Music School and library. Indoor pool and sports hall. Extensive co-curricular activities. Admission though school's own exam. Scholarships and bursaries available.

Gordonstoun School

Elgin, Morayshire IV30 5RF   Tel: (01343) 837837   Fax: (01343) 837808
E-mail: admissions@gordonstoun.org.uk   Website: www.gordonstoun.org.uk   www.gabbitas.co.uk

The Principal Mr M C Pyper BA
Director of Admissions Mr C J Barton BEd
Founded 1934   **School status** Independent.
Co-educational Boarding and Day 8–18.
Boarders from 8.
Religious denomination Non-Denominational
Member of BSA, ISBA, Round_Square, SCIS;
Accredited by British Council Also member of
ISCO; **Learning difficulties** SC SNU/DYC DYP
DYS MLD; **Behavioural and emotional
disorders** CO RA/ADD; **Physical and medical
conditions** RA SM/HEA
No of pupils 583; *(full boarding)* 482; *(weekly
boarding)* 15; *(day)* 86; *Prep* 100; *Senior* 191;
Sixth Form 292; *Girls* 239; *Boys* 344
Teacher:pupil ratio 1:7
Average class size 12–15 at GCSE level
Fees per annum *(full boarding)* £15264–
£24162; *(weekly)* £12486; *(day)* £8823–
£17700. Weekly boarding available for Junior
School only

Set in a magnificent estate, Gordonstoun and its
Junior School, Aberlour House, lie between the
sea and mountains in beautiful countryside. It is
well located for easy access to international airports as well as mainline railway stations.

The School's distinctive, holistic ethos is based
on internationalism, challenge, responsibility and
service and aims to prepare students to make a
positive contribution to society. Offering a broad,
integrated curriculum, Gordonstoun combines
study for GCSE and AS/A-Level with sporting,
creative and outdoor education, including the
School's unique sail training programme, to help
students encompass the School motto, Plus est en
Vous (There is more in you).

Scotland

Glenalmond College

Perth, Perth and Kinross PH1 3RY   Tel: (01738) 842056   Fax: (01738) 842063
E-mail: registrar@glenalmondcollege.co.uk
Website: www.glenalmondcollege.co.uk www.gabbitas.co.uk

The Warden Mr G Woods MA PGCE
Registrar J M B Poulter   **Founded** 1847
College status Co-educational Boarding and
Day 12–18. Boarders from 12.
Religious denomination Episcopelian
Member of BSA, HMC, SCIS
Accredited by HMC
Learning difficulties DYS MLD
Physical and medical conditions WA3/HEA
No of pupils 396; *(full boarding)* 332; *(day)* 64;
Senior 229; *Sixth Form* 167
Teacher:pupil ratio 1:10; **Average class size** 16
Fees per annum *(full boarding)* £16890–
£22545; *(day)* £11535–£15375

Full range of subjects to GCSE, A level in Sixth
Form. Very strong music, art, theatre.

Splendid facilities for technology and there are
excellent computing opportunities, including
new internet access throughout the school. Golf
course, salmon river, artificial ski-slope, indoor
and outdoor shooting, skiing and water sports
enhance a wide range of sports facilities. There
is a new second AstroTurf pitch, a new science
block and a new IT resource centre. Glenalmond
is also strong on public speaking and debating.
There are good European links.

Easy access to Glasgow and Edinburgh and to
airports. Art, music and academic scholarships
and all-rounder awards. Bursaries are available
for service children and clergy children.

The college is a registered charity providing
quality education for boys and girls.

Strathallan School

Forgandenny, Perth, PH2 9EG   Tel: (01738) 812546   Fax: (01738) 812549   E-mail:
admissions@strathallan.co.uk   Website: www.strathallan.co.uk

The Headmaster Mr B K Thompson MA
Founded 1913
School status Independent. Co-educational
Boarding and Day 10–18. Boarders from 10.
Religious denomination Non-Denominational
Member of AGBIS, BSA, HAS, HMC, ISA,
ISBA, SCIS, SHA
Accredited by British Council, HMC, ISA, ISC
No of pupils 476; *(full boarding)* 317; *(day)*
159; *Prep* 64; *Senior* 412; *Sixth Form* 208;
Girls 198; *Boys* 278
Teacher:pupil ratio 1:7; **Average class size** 10
Fees per annum *(full boarding)* £15510–
£21735; *(day)* £9690–£14745

Strathallan is a boarding school (70 per cent of
pupils are full boarders) that caters for pupils from
all round the world. With pupils from the local
area to throughout Scotland and the UK as well as
foreign nationals and Scots who live abroad, it is a
Scottish school with an international outlook.

Academically, Strathallan is one of the stron-
gest schools in the country, with excellent GCSE
and A level results. Outside the classroom,
Strathallan prides itself on providing opportunities
for all pupils to excel in the widest range of areas.
Its size makes it possible for everyone to feel very
much part of the community and to take part in all
its activities. Particular emphasis is placed on the
pastoral care provided in the boarding houses, the
positive relationship between teachers and pupils,
and the small classes. Pupils also benefit from
teaching, sport and extra-curricular activities of
the highest standard.

3.3 Schools in Continental Europe and Overseas Schools Outside Europe

MAP OF SCHOOLS IN CONTINENTAL EUROPE AND OVERSEAS SCHOOLS OUTSIDE EUROPE

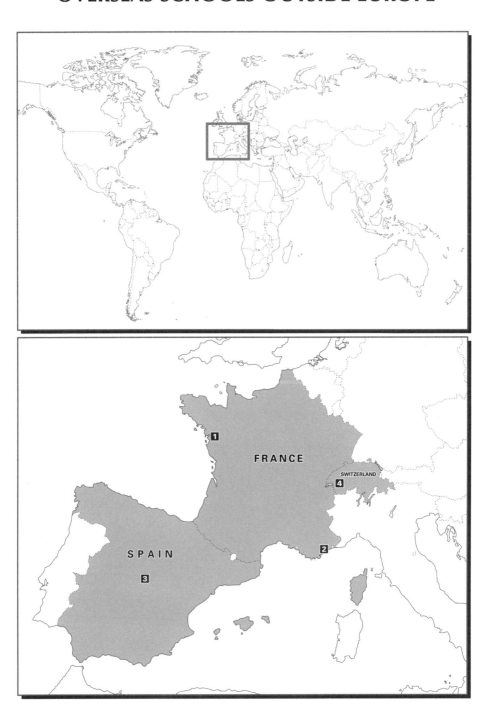

PROFILED SCHOOLS IN CONTINENTAL EUROPE AND OVERSEAS SCHOOLS OUTSIDE EUROPE

Map
Number

Page
Number

1	Chavagnes International College, Chavagnes-en-Paillers France	416
2	Mougins School, Mougins, France	416
3	King's College, Madrid, Spain	417
4	Aiglon College, Chesières, Switzerland	418

Continental Europe and Overseas Schools Outside Europe

Chavagnes International College

96 rue du Calvaire, 85250 Chavagnes-en-Paillers Tel: +33 (0)2 51 42 39 82 Fax: +33 (0)2 51 42 39 83
E-mail: info@chavagnes.org   Website: www.chavagnes.org
The College is 40 minutes from Nantes International Airport, served by Ryanair, B.A. and Air France.

Principal Mr F D McDermott M.A. (Hons)
Headmaster Dr T E Conlon
Chaplain Rev J. P. Pilon B.A., M.A.
Founded September 2002
College status Independent. Boys Boarding and Day 9–18 Flexi-boarding available. Boarders from 9. Flexible about age of entry. Boys sit examinations early if ready.
Religious denomination Roman Catholic
Member of SHA Affiliated to local Catholic Education Directorate
Learning difficulties CA SC WI/DYP DYS MLD
Physical and medical conditions RA TW WA2
No of pupils 30; *(full boarding)* 26; *(weekly boarding)* 1; *(day)* 3; *Prep* 11; *Senior* 19; *Boys* 30
Teacher:pupil ratio 3:1; **Average class size** 8
Fees FB €13400 WB €10000 DAY €7500 (various bursaries are available)

The College provides a solid academic, cultural, spiritual and moral foundation for boys. Founded in 2002 with ten pupils, we now have thirty and a proven track record of university entrance, including Oxbridge. All sit GCSEs and A-levels. Most are British and aim to attend British universities.

Facilities include a beautiful neo-gothic chapel, laboratory, theatre, library, playing fields, tennis and basketball courts, computer suite, four pianos, church organ, table tennis, table football and billiards. Additional activities include rowing, riding, fishing, boxing, chess, Chapel choir, debating, drama, music groups and instrumental lessons.

Mougins School

615 Avenue Dr Maurice Donat, Font de l'Orme, BP 401, 06251 Mougins Cedex,
Tel: +33 (0) 4 93 90 15 47   Fax: +33 (0) 4 93 75 31 40   E-mail: information@mougins-school.com
Website: www.mougins-school.com   www.gabbitas.co.uk

Headmaster Mr B G Hickmore
Deputy Head Ms Jane Hart
Primary School Co-ordinator Mrs Ann Edwards
Founded 1964
School status Independent. Co-educational Day 3–18. Co-educational independent pre-prep Reception/EY), prep (Forms 1–6), senior (Forms 7–11) and Sixth Form (Forms 12–13) day only
Religious denomination Non-Denominational
Member of COBISEC
Learning difficulties CA SC/DYS MLD
Behavioural and emotional disorders RA/ADD AUT
Physical and medical conditions TW WA1/CP
No of pupils 456; *(day)* 456; *Nursery* 15; *Pre-prep* 21; *Prep* 153; *Senior* 267; *Sixth Form* 71; *Girls* 194; *Boys* 262
Teacher:pupil ratio 1:13; **Average class size** 22
Fees *(day)* €4100–€11250

Mougins School is situated on the Côte d'Azur, north of Cannes and west of Nice, on a purpose-built campus. Facilities include a library, three science laboratories, IT centre, two art studios, music room, gymnasium, all weather football pitch and dining room.

The School accepts students aged three to eighteen representing over thirty nationalities. The School follows the British curriculum modified to meet the needs of an international market with examinations in IGCSE, AS and A Level.

The caring family atmosphere complements the high quality of the teaching and helps to enhance the academic, cultural and physical development of our students. We offer a comprehensive education that produces excellent results, not only academically but also in the sporting and artistic domains, leading to entry to the world's leading universities.

King's College Madrid

Paseo de los Andes, 35, 28761 Soto de Vinuelas, Madrid, Spain
Tel: (+34) 918 034 800   Fax: (+34) 918 036 557   E-mail: info@kingscollege.es
Website: www.kingscollege.es   www.gabbitas.co.uk

Head Master Mr D Johnson B.Ed. Hons, MSc. (Oxon)
Founded 1969
College status Independent. Co-educational Boarding and Day 2–18. Boarders from 11.
Religious denomination Non-Denominational
Member of COBISEC, HMC, NABSS
Accredited by ISC, Spanish Ministry of Education
No of pupils 1510; *(full boarding)* 25; *(day)* 1485; *Prep* 935; *Senior* 426; *Sixth Form* 149; *Girls* 730; *Boys* 780
Teacher:pupil ratio 1:13; **Average class size** 25
Fees FB €15501–€16938 Day €5007–€9666

Founded in 1969, King's College is the largest British school in Spain and the first to have had full UK accreditation through the Independent Schools Inspectorate.

It is a co-educational day and boarding school following the English National Curriculum which prepares pupils for IGCSE and GCE A levels and offers a wide range of subjects at both levels. There are optional Spanish studies and preparation for Spanish University entrance examinations.

With 1,510 pupils of more than 38 nationalities, the school has a complement of over 100 fully qualified teachers. All academic staff have British qualifications, except the Spanish teachers and some who teach modern languages. The average length of stay of the staff is over seven years.

The school has a reputation for high academic standards and excellent examination results with students going on to universities in Britain, USA, and Spain amongst others. An Oxbridge preparatory group works with the most able students to prepare university applications. There is a very experienced Careers and University Entrance Advisory Department for all students.

The main school for pupils from 2 to 18 years (Pre-Nursery to Year 13) stands on a 12 acre site, surrounded by countryside but well connected to Madrid. A second Infant School in the centre of Madrid caters for children between the ages of 3 to 6 years (Nursery to Year 2).In September 2007 a third site will be opening in La Moraleja for pupils aged 3 to 14 years (Nursery to Year 9).

The school has its own catering service and offers three-course midday meals. There is an optional bus service with a modern fleet of 18 vehicles covering Madrid and outlying areas.

The main school offers the following facilities:

Academic facilities: Seven science laboratories, three multimedia computer centres, two libraries, two music rooms, art studio, etc. Recent additions include a purpose-built Early Learning Centre, an auditorium with seating for over 350 people and a music school for individual tuition.

Sports facilities: Gymnasium, judo room, fitness centre, 25-metre heated indoor swimming pool, eleven-a-side and five-a-side football pitches, floodlit multi-sports area, tennis courts, stables and riding school.

Boarding facilities: There are boarding facilities for boys and girls with rooms for one to two pupils over the age of 11. At present the Residence is home to pupils from the UK, Russia, Jamaica, Japan as well as students from expatriate families living in Spain. Resident pupils enjoy access to many of the sports facilities at the weekends and after school.

Optional activities: Music, ballet, handicrafts, performing arts, judo, violin, riding, swimming and tennis are all offered as optional classes.

Admission: The procedure for admission varies according to the age of the pupil. Importance is given to previous school records and from age 7 to 16 years candidates are required to sit entrance tests in mathematics and English.

Aiglon College

1885 Chesieres-Villars, Switzerland
Tel: +41 (0) 24 496 6161   Fax: +41 (0) 24 469 6162
E-mail: admissions@aiglon.ch
Website: www.aiglon.ch   www.gabbitas.co.uk

Principle Dr J Long BA(Hons) MA MTh Dphil
DipRE DiTS
Founded 1949
College status Independent. Co-educational
Day and Boarding 9–18. Boarders from 9.
Co-educational independent prep, junior and
senior boarding and day
Religious denomination Non-Denominational
Member of CASE, COBISEC, IAPS, NEASC,
Round_Square
Accredited by HMC, IAPS, ECIS, NEASC,
ADISR, Parents League of NY
No of pupils 350; *(day)* 60; *Pre-prep* 22; *Prep*
60; *Senior* 25; *Sixth Form* 110
Girls 165; *Boys* 185
Teacher:pupil ratio 1:6
Average class size 12
Fees FB SFr48300–SFr67800 WB SFr42600–
SFr45900 Day SFr23000–SFr47400

Aiglon College offers a well-rounded education in a secure and friendly international community on a 25-acre campus within an Alpine ski village. It is an independent, non-profit, co-educational, international boarding school with an enrolment of over 60 nationalities. The school is registered as a charitable trust in Switzerland, the UK, USA, Netherlands and Canada. There are eight boarding houses, each with its own houseparents and tutors offering a high degree of pastoral care.

The academic programme is demanding and prepares students for British GCSE and A-level examinations as well as the American College Board. Courses are taught in English except in the first two years of the Junior School (ages 9–11) where the emphasis is based on French and English. The school offers an ESL (English as a Second Language) programme for all non-English speakers aged 10–12.

Facilities include a new computer centre, world languages centre, eight science laboratories, library and outstanding art and music departments. The school is also a centre for the College Board, TOEFL and some AICE exams at subsidiary levels. Aiglon's graduates are currently enrolled in leading international universities and colleges.

Sports and expeditions form an essential component of a well-rounded approach to the development of the students' personality and character. The wide range of sports include skiing, basketball, tennis, soccer, athletics, gymnastics, swimming and volleyball. Expeditions take place at weekends and activities include camping, climbing and skiing under expert and qualified supervision. Service and responsibility are fostered through social service and through the Round Square organisation.

During vacations, Aiglon offers a Summer School and a Languages and Snowsports programme which combine expert language tuition with fun outdoor activities. There is also a selection of adult courses.

Part 4

Reference Section

4.1

Scholarships

The following is based on information provided by schools. The entry age, where given, is the age at which scholarships are available to pupils. Please note that for each school, not every scholarship listed is offered at all the stated entry ages. Further details of scholarships available at individual schools may be found in Part Three: School Profiles. The abbreviations are as follows:

A Art
AA Academic ability
D Drama
G Games

I Instrumental music/Choral
O All round ability
S Science
6 VIth Form entry

ENGLAND

BEDFORDSHIRE

Bedford High School, Bedford	AA I O
Bedford Modern School, Bedford	
Entry age: 11+	A D G I
Bedford Preparatory School, Bedford	AA
Bedford School, Bedford	6 AA D G I
Moorlands School, Luton Entry age: 7+	A AA I O

BERKSHIRE

The Abbey School, Reading Entry age: 11+, 16+	6 AA I
The Ark School, Reading Entry age: 7	A AA I
Bearwood College, Wokingham	
Entry age: 11/13	6 A AA D G I O S
Bradfield College, Reading	
Entry age: 13+, 16+	6 A AA G I O
Brigidine School Windsor, Windsor	
Entry age: 11, 16	6 A AA D G I
Brockhurst and Marlston House Schools, Newbury	A AA D G I O S
Cheam School, Newbury	AA
Claires Court School, Maidenhead	6 A AA D G I O
Claires Court Schools, Ridgeway, Maidenhead	A AA D G I O

Claires Court Schools, The College, Maidenhead	6 A AA D G I O
Dolphin School, Reading	A AA D G I O
Downe House, Thatcham	6 A AA G I
Eagle House, Sandhurst	AA I
Elstree School, Reading Entry age: 7	AA
The Elvian School, Reading Entry age: 11+	6 A AA G I
Eton College, Windsor	6 AA I
Heathfield St Mary's School, Ascot	6 A AA D G I
Hemdean House School, Reading	AA I O
Highfield School, Maidenhead	AA
Holme Grange School, Wokingham	
Entry age: 11+	AA O
Horris Hill School, Newbury	AA O
Hurst Lodge School, Ascot	
Entry age: various	6 A AA D I O
Langley Manor School, Slough	AA G I O
Leighton Park School, Reading	
Entry age: 12, 14, 17	6 A AA I O
Licensed Victuallers' School, Ascot	6 A AA G I
Luckley-Oakfield School, Wokingham	
Entry age: 11	6 AA I
The Marist Senior School, Ascot	
Entry age: 11	6 A AA D G I O
The Oratory Preparatory School, Reading	AA G I

The Oratory School, Reading
    Entry age: 11+, 13+   6 A AA D G I O
Padworth College, Reading Entry age: 14, 16   6 A AA
Pangbourne College, Pangbourne
    Entry age: 11+, 13+, 16+   6 A AA D G I O S
Papplewick School, Ascot Entry age: 7–11   A AA G I O
Queen Anne's School, Reading
    Entry age: 11, 12, 13+, 16+   6 A AA D G I O
Reading Blue Coat School, Reading   A AA I
St Edward's School, Reading   AA O
St Gabriel's, Newbury Entry age: 11, 16   6 A AA G I
St George's School, Ascot
    Entry age: 11+, 16+   A AA D I
St George's School, Windsor Entry age: 7+, 9+   AA I
St Joseph's Convent School, Reading   6 AA D G I
St Mary's School, Ascot, Ascot   6 A AA I S
St Piran's Preparatory School, Maidenhead A AA G I O
Thorngrove School, Newbury   AA G I O
Upton House School, Windsor   A AA
Wellington College, Crowthorne   6 A AA D G I O

BRISTOL

Badminton School
    Entry age: 11+, 13+, 16+   6 A AA I O
Bristol Cathedral School
    Entry age: 11+, 13+, 16+   6 AA G I
Bristol Grammar School
    Entry age: 7, 11, 13, 16   6 A AA D I O S
Clifton College Entry age: 13+, 16+   6 A AA G I O
Clifton College Pre-Prep – Butcombe   O
Clifton College Preparatory School
    Entry age: 11+   AA G I O
Clifton High School Entry age: 11+, 13+, 16+ 6 AA G I
Colston's Collegiate School   6 A AA D G I O
Colston's Girls' School   6 A AA I O S
The Downs School, Wraxall Entry age: 8+   A AA G I O
Fairfield School, Backwell   AA
Queen Elizabeth's Hospital
    Entry age: 11, 13, 16   6 AA I S
The Red Maids' School
    Entry age: 11+,13+, 16+   6 AA G I O
Redland High School Entry age: 7, 11, 16   6 A AA I
Sacred Heart Preparatory School, Chew Magna
    Entry age: 3+, 11+   O
St Ursula's High School   AA
Torwood House School   O

BUCKINGHAMSHIRE

Bury Lawn School, Milton Keynes   6 AA
Davenies School, Beaconsfield   A AA G I O
Gateway School, Great Missenden   O
Godstowe Preparatory School, High Wycombe
    Entry age: 8, 11   AA
High March School, Beaconsfield Entry age: 8   AA
Holy Cross Convent, Gerrards Cross
    Entry age: 11+, 16+   6 AA I O
Ladymede, Aylesbury Entry age: 7+   AA O
Milton Keynes Preparatory School,
    Milton Keynes   A AA G I
Pipers Corner School, High Wycombe   6 I

St Mary's School, Gerrards Cross
    Entry age: 11/16+   6 AA I
Stowe School, Buckingham
    Entry age: 13, 16   6 A AA G I O
Swanbourne House School, Milton Keynes
    Entry age: 11+   AA G I
Thornton College Convent of Jesus and Mary,
    Milton Keynes Entry age: 11   AA
Thorpe House School, Gerrards Cross   AA
Wycombe Abbey School, High Wycombe 6 AA I

CAMBRIDGESHIRE

Bellerbys College & Embassy CES Cambridge,
    Cambridge   AA O
Cambridge Centre for Sixth-Form Studies,
    Cambridge   6 AA O
Kimbolton School, Huntingdon   6 A AA G I O
The King's School Ely, Ely Entry age: 11+ 6 A AA D G I
The Leys School, Cambridge
    Entry age: 11, 13, 16   6 A AA D G I O
MPW (Mander Portman Woodward),
    Cambridge   6 AA O
The Perse School, Cambridge   6 A AA I
The Perse School for Girls, Cambridge   6 I
Peterborough High School, Peterborough
    Entry age: 11, 17   6 A AA I O
St Faith's, Cambridge Entry age: 7+   AA
St John's College School, Cambridge   I
St Mary's School, Cambridge   6 AA I
Sancton Wood School, Cambridge   D O
Wisbech Grammar School, Wisbech   I

CHANNEL ISLANDS

Elizabeth College, Guernsey   I O
Ormer House Preparatory School, Alderney AA
St George's Preparatory School, Jersey
    Entry age: 7+   A AA G I O S
St Michael's Preparatory School, Jersey   AA
Victoria College, Jersey   AA I S

CHESHIRE

Abbey Gate College, Chester
    Entry age: 11+, 16+   6 AA I
Abbey Gate School, Chester   AA
Alderley Edge School for Girls,
    Alderley Edge   6 A AA G I
Brabyns School, Stockport   AA
Cransley School, Northwich
    Entry age: 11+   A AA G I O S
Culcheth Hall, Altrincham   AA
The Grange School, Northwich   6 AA I
Hammond School, Chester   AA D I
Hulme Hall Schools, Cheadle   AA
The King's School, Macclesfield   AA I
Merton House, Chester   AA G
Mostyn House School, South Wirral
    Entry age: 7, 11   AA G O
North Cestrian Grammar School, Altrincham AA
Oriel Bank, Stockport   I

The Ryleys, Alderley Edge   AA O
Stockport Grammar School, Stockport Entry age: 11+   I
Terra Nova School, Holmes Chapel   A AA D G I O S

CORNWALL

The Bolitho School, Penzance
  Entry age: 10+, 13+   6 A AA I O
Polwhele House School, Truro   AA I
Roselyon, Par   AA I O
St Joseph's School, Launceston
  Entry age: 7+, 11+   AA G I O
St Petroc's School, Bude Entry age: 7+   A AA D G I O S
Truro High School, Truro
  Entry age: 11+, 16+   6 A AA G I

CUMBRIA

Austin Friars St Monica's School, Carlisle
  Entry age: 11+   AA G I
Casterton School, Kirkby Lonsdale   6 A AA D G I O S
Chetwynde School, Barrow-in-Furness   6 AA G I O
Harecroft Hall School, Seascale   AA
Holme Park School, Kendal Entry age: 7+   AA D G O S
Lime House School, Carlisle   AA G O
St Bees School, St Bees   6 A AA G I
Sedbergh School, Sedbergh
  Entry age: 13+, 16+, 17+   6 A AA D G I O
Windermere St Anne's, Windermere
  Entry age: 11+, 13+, 16+   6 A AA D G I O

DERBYSHIRE

Derby Grammar School for Boys, Derby   6 AA I
Derby High School, Derby
  Entry age: 11/16   6 AA G I O
Foremarke Hall School, Derby   A AA D G I
Mount St Mary's College, Spinkhill
  Entry age: 11+, 15+   6 AA G I O
Ockbrook School, Derby   A AA D G I
Repton School, Derby
  Entry age: 13+, 16+   6 A AA D G I O
St Wystan's School, Repton Entry age: 7+   AA G I O

DEVON

The Abbey School, Torquay   AA O
Blundell's School, Tiverton
  Entry age: 11, 13, 16   6 A AA G I O
Bramdean School, Exeter Entry age: 7/11   AA D G I
Trinity School, Teignmouth   6 A AA D G I O
Edgehill College, Bideford   6 A AA D G I O
Exeter Cathedral School, Exeter
  Entry age: 7/12+   AA I O
Exeter Junior School, Exeter
  Entry age: 7+   AA
Exeter School, Exeter
  Entry age: 7, 11, 12, 13   6 A AA I S
Grenville College, Bideford
  Entry age: 11, 12, 13, 16+   6 A AA D G I O S

Kelly College, Tavistock
  Entry age: 11, 13, 16   6 A AA G I O
The Maynard School, Exeter   6 A G I O
Mount House School, Tavistock   AA G I
Plymouth College, Plymouth
  Entry age: 11, 13, 16   6 A AA G I
St Margaret's School, Exeter   6 A AA D I
St Michael's, Barnstaple   A AA D G I O
St Peter's School, Exmouth   AA G I O
St Wilfrid's School, Exeter Entry age: 7   O
Shebbear College, Beaworthy
  Entry age: 11+, 13+, 16+   6 A AA D G I O
St Christophers School, Totnes   O
Stoodley Knowle School, Torquay   O
Stover School, Newton Abbot   6 A AA G I O
Tower House School, Paignton
  Entry age: 11   A AA D G I O S
Trinity School, Teignmouth   6 A AA D G I O S
West Buckland Preparatory School, Barnstaple   AA O
West Buckland School, Barnstaple   6 AA G I O

DORSET

Bryanston School, Blandford Forum
  Entry age: 13, 16   6 A AA G I O
Canford School, Wimborne   6 A AA D G I
Castle Court Preparatory School, Wimborne   AA I
Clayesmore Preparatory School,
  Blandford Forum   A AA G I O
Clayesmore School, Blandford Forum   6 A AA I O
Dorchester Preparatory and Independent
  Schools, Dorchester   6 A AA D G I O S
Dumpton School, Wimborne Entry age: 7   AA O
Hanford School, Blandford Forum   I
Knighton House, Blandford Forum   A AA D G I O
Milton Abbey School, Blandford Forum   6 A AA D G I
The Old Malthouse, Swanage Entry age: 7+ A AA G I O
The Park School, Bournemouth   AA I O
Port Regis School, Shaftesbury   A AA G I O
St Antony's Leweston School, Sherborne
  Entry age: 7–13, 16   6 A AA D G I S
St Martin's School, Bournemouth   AA
St Mary's School, Shaftesbury
  Entry age: 11+, 13+, 16+   6 A AA I
Sherborne Preparatory School, Sherborne   AA G I
Sherborne School, Sherborne
  Entry age: 13+, 16+   6 A AA D G I
Sherborne School for Girls, Sherborne   6 A AA I O
Talbot Heath, Bournemouth   6 A AA D G I O
Thornlow Preparatory School, Weymouth   AA G
Uplands School, Poole Entry age: 11+, 12+, 13+   AA
Wentworth College, Bournemouth   6 A AA D G I
Yarrells School, Poole   AA I O

COUNTY DURHAM

Barnard Castle School, Barnard Castle   6 A AA G I
The Chorister School, Durham   I
Durham High School For Girls, Durham
  Entry age: 11, 16   6 A AA G I
Durham School, Durham
  Entry age: 11–16   6 A AA G I O

Hurworth House School, Darlington	AA G O
Polam Hall, Darlington	
Entry age: 7, 11, 13, 16	6 AA G I O
Raventhorpe Preparatory School, Darlington	O

ESSEX

Bancroft's School, Woodford Green	
Entry age: 11, 16	6 AA I
Brentwood School, Brentwood	
Entry age: 11, 16	6 A AA D G I O
Chigwell School, Chigwell	A AA D I O
Colchester High School, Colchester	AA
College Saint-Pierre, Leigh-on-Sea	O
Crowstone Preparatory School, Westcliff-on-Sea	O
The Daiglen School, Buckhurst Hill	AA
Felsted Preparatory School, Felsted	AA I
Felsted School, Dunmow	6 A AA D I O
Friends' School, Saffron Walden	
Entry age: 11, 13, 16	6 A AA G I
Gosfield School, Halstead	6 AA D G I O
Herington House School, Brentwood	D G I O
Holmwood House, Colchester	A AA G I O
Loyola Preparatory School, Buckhurst Hill	AA
New Hall School, Chelmsford	
Entry age: 11, 13, 16	6 A AA D I O
Park School for Girls, Ilford	AA
St Aubyn's School, Woodford Green	AA
St Hilda's School, Westcliff-on-Sea	O
St Margaret's School, Halstead Entry age: 8+	AA I
St Mary's School, Colchester Entry age: 11+	O
St Nicholas School, Harlow	6 A AA G I
Thorpe Hall School, Southend-on-Sea	
Entry age: 7/11	AA

GLOUCESTERSHIRE

Berkhampstead School, Cheltenham	AA G I
Bredon School, Tewkesbury	A AA G O
Cheltenham College, Cheltenham	
Entry age: 13, 16	6 A AA G I O S
Cheltenham College Junior School, Cheltenham	
Entry age: 11+	A AA G I O
The Cheltenham Ladies' College,	
Cheltenham	6 A AA G I
Dean Close Preparatory School, Cheltenham	AA G I O
Dean Close School, Cheltenham	
Entry age: 11+, 13+, 16+	6 A AA G I O
Hatherop Castle School, Cirencester	
Entry age: 7+	AA D G I O
The King's School, Gloucester	6 A AA G I O
Rendcomb College, Cirencester	
Entry age: 11, 13, 16	6 A AA D G I
The Richard Pate School, Cheltenham	
Entry age: 7+	AA
Rose Hill School, Wotton-under-Edge	A AA D G I O
St Edward's School Cheltenham,	
Cheltenham	6 A AA D G I
Westonbirt School, Tetbury	6 A AA D G I O S
Wycliffe College, Stonehouse	6 A AA D G I O
Wycliffe Preparatory School, Stonehouse	
Entry age: 11	A AA D G I

SOUTH GLOUCESTERSHIRE

Silverhill School, Winterbourne	O

HAMPSHIRE

Alton Convent School, Alton Entry age: 11/16	6 AA I
Ballard School, New Milton Entry age: 7	A AA G I O
Bedales School, Petersfield	6 A AA I
Boundary Oak School, Fareham	AA I
Brockwood Park School, Bramdean	O
Churchers College, Petersfield	6 AA I
Ditcham Park School, Petersfield Entry age: 11	AA I
Dunhurst (Bedales Junior School), Petersfield	I
Durlston Court, New Milton Entry age: Over 7	
in September of year of entry	A AA G I
Farleigh School, Andover	AA O
Farnborough Hill, Farnborough	6 AA G I
The Gregg School, Southampton	AA I
Hampshire Collegiate School (Embley Park),	
Romsey	6 A AA D G I O S
Highfield School, Liphook	AA
Hordle Walhampton School, Lymington	AA I O
King Edward VI School, Southampton	
Entry age: 11+, 13+	AA I
Lord Wandsworth College, Hook	
Entry age: 11+, 13+, 16+	6 A AA D I O
Marycourt School, Gosport Entry age: 7	O
Mayville High School, Southsea	A AA D G I
Meoncross School, Fareham Entry age: 11	AA
The Pilgrims' School, Winchester	I
The Portsmouth Grammar School,	
Portsmouth	6 A AA D G I O
Portsmouth High School GDST,	
Southsea Entry age: 11+, 13+, 16+	6 A AA D G I
Prince's Mead School, Winchester	A AA G I
Rookesbury Park School, Portsmouth	AA I
Rookwood School, Andover	AA G I
St John's College, Southsea	6 AA G I O
St Mary's College, Southampton	AA
St Neot's School, Hook	O
St Nicholas' School, Fleet Entry age: 11, 13	AA I O
St Swithun's School, Winchester	
Entry age: 11+, 13+, 16+	6 AA I
Sherborne House School, Eastleigh	A AA G I O
Sherfield School, Hook	AA D G I O
Stockton House School, Fleet	AA O
The Stroud School, Romsey	A AA D G I O
Winchester College, Winchester	
Entry age: 13, 16	6 AA I
Wykeham House School, Fareham	AA
Yateley Manor Preparatory School, Yateley	
Entry age: 7+	A AA G I O

HEREFORDSHIRE

The Hereford Cathedral School, Hereford	6 A AA I
Lucton School, Leominster	
Entry age: 11, 13, 16	6 A AA D G I O S
St Richard's, Bromyard	AA

HERTFORDSHIRE

Abbot's Hill School, Hemel Hempstead	
Entry age: 11	A AA G I O
Aldenham School, Elstree	A AA G I O
Arts Educational School, Tring Park, Tring	D I O
Berkhamsted Collegiate Preparatory School,	
Berkhamsted	AA
Berkhamsted Collegiate School,	
Berkhamsted	6 A AA G I
Bishop's Stortford College, Bishop's Stortford	
Entry age: 11+, 13+, 16+	6 A AA I O
Egerton-Rothesay School, Berkhamsted	
Entry age: 5+, 16+	A AA G I
Haberdashers' Aske's Boys' School, Elstree	
Entry age: 11, 13	AA I
Haberdashers' Aske's School for Girls, Elstree	AA I
Haileybury, Hertford Entry age: 11, 13, 16	6 A AA I O
Haresfoot Preparatory School, Berkhamsted	A AA D I
Heath Mount School, Hertford	
Entry age: 7+, 11+	A AA
Immanuel College, Bushey Entry age: 11/16	6 A AA I
The Junior School, Bishop's Stortford College,	
Bishop's Stortford	A AA I O
Lockers Park, Hemel Hempstead	A AA G I O
The Princess Helena College, Hitchin	
Entry age: 11–18	6 A AA D G I
The Purcell School, Bushey	I
Queenswood School, Hatfield	6 AA D G I
The Royal Masonic School for Girls, Rickmansworth	
Entry age: 7, 11, 16	6 A AA D G I O
St Albans High School for Girls, St Albans	
Entry age: 11+, 13+, 16+	6 I O
St Albans School, St Albans Entry age: 11+,	
13+, 16+	6 A AA I
St Andrew's Montessori School, Watford	AA I O
St Christopher School, Letchworth	6 AA
St Columba's College, St Albans	
Entry age: 11+/13+	6 AA I
St Edmund's College, Ware	6 A AA G I
St Francis' College, Letchworth	6 AA G I
St Joseph's in the Park, Hertford	O
St Margaret's School, Bushey	6 AA I O S
Sherrardswood School, Welwyn	6 AA O
Stanborough School, Watford	AA G I
Westbrook Hay Preparatory School,	
Hemel Hempstead Entry age: 8+	AA G O
York House School, Rickmansworth	AA G

ISLE OF MAN

King William's College, Castletown	6 A AA G I O

ISLE OF WIGHT

Ryde School, Ryde	6 AA I

KENT

Ashford School, Ashford	6 A AA D G I O
Babington House School, Chislehurst	AA D G I O
Baston School, Bromley	AA O

Beechwood Sacred Heart School, Tunbridge Wells	
Entry age: 11+, 13+	6 A AA D G I O S
Benenden School, Cranbrook	
Entry age: 11, 13, 16	6 A AA G I
Bethany School, Cranbrook	
Entry age: 11+, 13+, 16+	6 A AA D G I
Bickley Park School, Bromley	AA G I
Bishop Challoner RC School, Bromley	
Entry age: 11+	AA I
Breaside Preparatory School, Bromley	
Entry age: 7+	AA
Bromley High School GDST, Bromley	
Entry age: 11/16+	6 A AA G I
Cobham Hall, Gravesend	6 A AA D G I O S
Combe Bank School, Nr Sevenoaks	
Entry age: 7+	6 AA G I
Cranbrook School, Cranbrook	I
Darul Uloom London, Chislehurst	AA G O S
Derwent Lodge School for Girls, Tonbridge	AA
Dover College, Dover Entry age: 11,	
13, 16	6 A AA G I O
Duke of York's Royal Military School,	
Dover	6 A AA G I
Elliott Park School, Sheerness	O
Farringtons School, Chislehurst	6 A AA G I
Gad's Hill School, Rochester	
Entry age: 11	A AA D G I O
Haddon Dene School, Broadstairs	O
Hilden Grange School, Tonbridge	AA I
Holmewood House, Tunbridge Wells	AA
Kent College, Canterbury Entry age: 11,	
13, 16+	6 A AA G I O
Kent College Pembury, Tunbridge Wells	
Entry age: 11, 13, 16	6 A AA D G I O
King's Preparatory School, Rochester	AA I
The King's School, Canterbury	6 A AA I
King's School Rochester, Rochester	6 A AA G I
Merton Court Preparatory School, Sidcup	AA D G I O
Northbourne Park School, Deal	A AA G I O
Rochester Independent College,	
Rochester	6 A AA D I O S
Sackville School, Tonbridge	6 A AA D G I
St Christopher's School, Canterbury	O
St Edmunds Junior School, Canterbury	
Entry age: 11	AA G I O
St Edmund's School, Canterbury	
Entry age: 11+, 13+, 16+	6 A AA D G I O
St Lawrence College Junior School, Ramsgate	AA G O
St Lawrence College, Ramsgate	
Entry age: 8, 11, 13, 16	6 A AA G I O
St Michael's School, Sevenoaks Entry age: 7	AA G I O
St Ronan's School, Hawkhurst Entry age: 11	AA
Sevenoaks School, Sevenoaks Entry age: 11+,	
13+, 16+	6 A AA G I O
Solefield School, Sevenoaks	I
Spring Grove School, Ashford	
Entry age: 7+	A AA D G I O S
Sutton Valence School, Maidstone	
Entry age: 11+, 13+, 16+	6 A AA D G I O
Tonbridge School, Tonbridge	
Entry age: 13+, 16+	6 A AA D G I
Walthamstow Hall, Sevenoaks	
Entry age: 11+, 13+, 16+	6 A AA D I

Wellesley House School, Broadstairs	AA G I
Yardley Court, Tonbridge	AA O

LANCASHIRE

Arnold School, Blackpool	
Entry age: 11+, 16+	6 A AA D G I O
Bury Grammar School, Bury	6 AA
Bury Grammar School Girls, Bury Entry age: 11	AA
Clevelands Preparatory School, Bolton	AA O
Firwood Manor Prep School, Oldham	AA O
Heathland College, Accrington	AA I
The Hulme Grammar School for Girls, Oldham	AA
King Edward VII and Queen Mary School,	
Lytham St Annes Entry age: 11, 16	6 AA G I
Kingswood College at Scarisbrick Hall,	
Ormskirk	AA G I
Kirkham Grammar School, Preston	6 AA G I
Queen Elizabeth's Grammar School, Blackburn	
Entry age: 11+	AA S
Rossall Junior School, Fleetwood	6 A AA G I O
Rossall School, Fleetwood Entry age: 11,	
13, 16	6 A AA G I O S
St Anne's College Grammar School,	
Lytham St Annes	6 AA
St Joseph's Convent School, Burnley	I
St Mary's Hall, Stonyhurst	A AA I
Sedbergh Junior School, Lancaster	
Entry age: 11	A AA D G I O
Stonyhurst College, Clitheroe	
Entry age: 13, 16	6 A AA I O
Westholme School, Blackburn	6 A AA I

LEICESTERSHIRE

Brooke House College, Market Harborough	6 AA G O
The Dixie Grammar School, Market Bosworth	
Entry age: 10, 11, 14, 16	6 A AA G I
Grace Dieu Manor School, Leicester	AA
Irwin College, Leicester Entry age: 14, 16	AA
Leicester Grammar School, Leicester	6 A AA G I O
Leicester High School For Girls, Leicester	6 AA I
Loughborough Grammar School, Loughborough	
Entry age: 10+, 11+, 13+, 16+	6 AA I
Loughborough High School, Loughborough	AA I
Ratcliffe College, Leicester Entry age: 11+,	
13+, 16+	6 AA I
St Crispin's School (Leicester) Ltd., Leicester	
Entry age: 7+, 11+, 13+	AA G
Stoneygate School, Leicester	AA

LINCOLNSHIRE

Copthill School, Stamford Entry age: 11	AA
Fen School, Sleaford Entry age: 7	AA
Kirkstone House School, Bourne	A AA G I O
Lincoln Minster School, Lincoln	6 AA G I
Maypole House School, Alford	AA O
Stamford High School, Stamford	6 A AA I O
Stamford School, Stamford	6 A AA I
Witham Hall, Bourne	AA O

NORTH EAST LINCOLNSHIRE

St. James' School, Grimsby	6 AA G I O

LONDON

Abercorn School, NW8	O
Albemarle Independent College, W1K	
Entry age: 14+, 19+	AA
Alleyn's School, SE22 Entry age: 11+, 16+	6 A AA G I
Ashbourne Independent Sixth Form College,	
W8	6 A AA D G I O S
Ashbourne Middle School, W8	
Entry age: 13/16	6 A AA D O S
Belmont (Mill Hill Preparatory School),	
NW7 Entry age: 11	AA D I S
Blackheath High School GDST, SE3	
Entry age: 11+/16+	6 A AA I
Blackheath Preparatory School, SE3	AA
Brampton College, NW4	AA
Broomwood Hall School, SW12	A AA O
Channing School, N6	6 AA I
City of London School, EC4V	
Entry age: 11+, 13+, 16+	6 AA I
City of London School for Girls, EC2Y	
Entry age: 11, 16	6 A AA I
Clifton Lodge Preparatory School, W5	I
Colfe's School, SE12	6 A AA G I
Connaught House, W2 Entry age: 6, 8	A AA I O
Davies Laing and Dick, W1U	6 AA O
Devonshire House Preparatory School, NW3	AA I
Dulwich College, SE21	6 A AA G I
Durston House, W5	AA
Ealing College Upper School, W13	6 AA
Ealing Independent College, W5	AA
Eaton House The Manor, SW4	
Entry age: 8+	A AA G I O
Eaton Square School, SW1V	O
Emanuel School, SW11	6 A AA D G I O
Forest School, E17	6 A AA D I S
Francis Holland School, NW1	6 I
Francis Holland School, SW1W	
Entry age: 11+, 16+	6 AA I
Fulham Prep School (Prep Dept), W14	A AA G I
Garden House School, SW3	AA I O
The Godolphin and Latymer School, W6	I
Hall School Wimbledon, SW20	A AA D G I O
The Hampshire School	
(Kensington Gardens), W2	AA G I O
The Hampshire Schools	
(Knightsbridge Under School), SW7	AA I O
The Hampshire Schools	
(Knightsbridge Upper School), SW7	AA I O
Hampstead College of Fine Arts,	
Independent College, NW3	6 O
Hampstead Hill Pre-Preparatory & Nursery School,	
NW3	O
Harvington School, W5	D I
Heathside Preparatory School, NW3	AA
Hendon Preparatory School, NW4	AA G O
Highgate School, N6	AA I
Hill House International Junior School, SW1X	
Entry age: 11	A I

Hurlingham Private School, SW15 Entry age: 7+	O
Ibstock Place School, SW15	6 I
The Italia Conti Academy of Theatre Arts, EC1M	D
James Allen's Girls' School, SE22	
Entry age: 11+, 16+	6 A AA G I
Keble Preparatory School, N21 Entry age: 11	AA G O
King's College Junior School, SW19	AA I
King's College School, SW19	6 A AA I
Knightsbridge School, SW1X	AA
Lansdowne College, W2 Entry age: 14+, 16+	6 AA O
Latymer Prep School, W6	AA
Latymer Upper School, W6	6 A D G I
Lycee Francais Charles de Gaulle, SW7	6 AA
The Lyceum, EC2A	I
Mander Portman Woodward, SW7	6 AA
More House, SW1X	6 AA I
The Mount School, NW7	6 AA I
Newton Prep School, SW8	AA
Normanhurst School, E4 Entry age: 11	AA
North Bridge House Lower Prep School, NW1	AA I
North Bridge House Senior School, NW1	I
Northcote Lodge School, SW11	AA
Notting Hill and Ealing High School GDST, W13	
Entry age: 11+, 16+	6 A AA D I O
Orchard House School, W4	AA
Palmers Green High School, N21 Entry age: 11+	AA I
Parkgate House School, SW4	AA I O
The Pointer School, SE3	AA D G O
Portland Place School, W1B	A AA I
Prospect House School, SW15	AA O
Putney High School GDST, SW15	
Entry age: 11+, 16+	6 A AA D G I S
Queen's College, W1G	6 A AA I
Queen's Gate School, SW7	6 O
Riverston School, SE12	AA G I O
The Roche School, SW18 Entry age: 7	AA
The Royal School, Hampstead, NW3	
Entry age: 7, 16	A AA I
St Augustine's Priory, W5	6 I O
St Benedict's Junior School, W5	I
St Benedict's School, W5 Entry age: 11+	AA G
St Christopher's School	AA
St Margaret's School, NW3	AA
St Mary's School Hampstead, NW3	A AA G I
St Paul's Cathedral School, EC4M	I
St Paul's Girls' School, W6	6 A AA I
St Paul's Preparatory School, SW13	AA I
St Paul's School, SW13	6 AA I
Sinclair House School, SW6	O
South Hampstead High School, NW3	6 AA I
Southbank International School, Westminster, W1B	6
Streatham and Clapham High School, SW16	
Entry age: 11, 16	6 AA I S
Sussex House School, SW1X	I
Sydenham High School GDST, SE26	
Entry age: 11/16+	6 AA I
Sylvia Young Theatre School, NW1	
Entry age: 10–14	D I
The Lloyd Williamson School, W10	O
Thomas's Preparatory School, SW11	O
University College School, NW3	AA I
Virgo Fidelis, SE19 Entry age: 7–11	AA
Welsh School of London, NW10	O

Westminster Abbey Choir School, SW1P	I
Westminster Cathedral Choir School, SW1P	I
Westminster School, SW1P	6 AA I
Westminster Tutors, SW7	6 AA O
Westminster Under School, SW1P Entry age: 11+	I
The White House Prep & Woodentops Kindergarten, SW12	AA
Willington School, SW19	AA
Wimbledon High School GDST, SW19	6 AA I S
Woodside Park International School, N11	6 A AA D G I O

GREATER MANCHESTER

Abbey College, Manchester	6 AA
Branwood Preparatory School, Eccles	O
Bridgewater School, Manchester	
Entry age: 11/16+	6 AA
Chetham's School of Music, Manchester	I
Manchester High School for Girls, Manchester	
Entry age: 11, 16	6 AA I
St Bede's College, Manchester	6 AA I
William Hulme's Grammar School, Manchester	
Entry age: 11/16+	6 AA I

MERSEYSIDE

Avalon Preparatory School, Wirral Entry age: 7	AA
Birkenhead High School GDST, Wirral	6 AA I
Birkenhead School, Wirral	6 AA I
Kingsmead School, Wirral Entry age: 7/11+	AA G I
Liverpool College, Liverpool	6 AA G I O
Merchant Taylors' School, Liverpool	6 AA G
Merchant Taylors' School for Girls, Liverpool	6 AA O
Runnymede St Edward's School, Liverpool	I
St Mary's College, Liverpool	
Entry age: 11/16+	6 A AA G I
Streatham House School, Liverpool	AA
Tower College, Prescot Entry age: 7, 11	AA I
Tower Dene Preparatory School, Southport	
Entry age: 5, 7	A AA G O

MIDDLESEX

Buckingham College Preparatory School, Pinner	AA
Buckingham College School, Harrow	6 AA
Halliford School, Shepperton	
Entry age: 11+	6 A AA G I
Hampton School, Hampton	
Entry age: 11+, 13	A AA G I O
Harrow School, Harrow on the Hill	
Entry age: 13, 16	6 A AA G I
Heathfield School, Pinner	6 AA I
The John Lyon School, Harrow	6 A AA D G I
The Lady Eleanor Holles School, Hampton	6 AA I
Merchant Taylors' School, Northwood	6 AA I
North London Collegiate, Edgware	6 AA I
Northwood College, Northwood	
Entry age: 11+, 16+	6 A AA G I
St Catherine's School, Twickenham	
Entry age: 11	A AA G I

St David's School, Ashford
Entry age: 11+, 16+   6 A AA G I O
St Helen's School, Northwood   6 A AA D G I
Sunflower Montessori School, Twickenham   I

NORFOLK

All Saints School, Norwich   AA I
Glebe House School, Hunstanton   A AA G I O
Gresham's Preparatory School, Holt   A AA D G I O
Gresham's School, Holt   6 A AA D G I
Hethersett Old Hall School, Norwich   6 AA O
Langley Preparatory School & Nursery, Norwich   AA I
Langley School, Norwich Entry age: 11,
13, 16   6 A AA D G I O
The New Eccles Hall School, Norwich
Entry age: 8   AA I O
Norwich High School for Girls GDST, Norwich   6 AA I
Norwich School, Norwich Entry age: 9+,
11+, 16+   6 AA I S
Sacred Heart Convent School, Swaffham
Entry age: 11+   A AA D G I O
Taverham Hall, Norwich   AA G I
Thetford Grammar School, Thetford
Entry age: 16+   6 AA I
Town Close House Preparatory School, Norwich
Entry age: 7+   G I
Wood Dene School, Norwich   A AA D

NORTHAMPTONSHIRE

Beachborough School, Brackley Entry age: 8–11 AA I O
Bosworth Independent College, Northampton 6 AA O S
Great Houghton Preparatory School,
Northampton   A AA I
Maidwell Hall School, Northampton   A I
Northampton High School, Northampton
Entry age: 11, 13, 16   6 A AA D G I
Northamptonshire Grammar School, Pitsford   6 AA I
Oundle School, Nr Peterborough   6 A AA D I O
Quinton House School, Northampton   6 AA O
Winchester House School, Brackley   A AA G I O

NORTHUMBERLAND

Longridge Towers School, Berwick-upon-Tweed
Entry age: 9, 11, 13, 16   6 AA G I
Mowden Hall School, Stocksfield   AA

NOTTINGHAMSHIRE

Bramcote Lorne School, Retford   A AA G I O
Coteswood House School, Nottingham   A AA D G I O
Hollygirt School, Nottingham Entry age: 11+   AA I
Hollygirt School, Nottingham   AA I
Nottingham High School, Nottingham   6 AA
Nottingham High School for Girls GDST,
Nottingham   O
Ranby House School, Retford Entry age: 11+ AA G I O
Rodney School, Newark   AA D
Trent College, Nottingham   6 A AA D G I

Wellow House School, Newark   A AA G I O
Worksop College, Worksop   6 A AA G I O

OXFORDSHIRE

Abacus College, Oxford   O
Abingdon School, Abingdon   6 A AA I O
Bloxham School, Banbury
Entry age: 11, 13, 16   6 A AA G I O
Christ Church Cathedral School, Oxford   I
Cokethorpe School, Witney   6 A AA D G I O
Cranford House School, Wallingford   I O
d'Overbroeck's College, Oxford   6 A AA D I S
Ferndale Preparatory School, Faringdon   AA
Headington School, Oxford
Entry age: 11, 13, 16   6 A AA D G I
Josca's Preparatory School, Abingdon   AA
Kingham Hill School, Chipping Norton
Entry age: 11+, 13+   6 A AA D G I O
Leckford Place School, Oxford   A AA D I
Magdalen College School, Oxford
Entry age: 7+, 13+, 16+   A AA G I
New College School, Oxford Entry age: 8   I
Our Lady's Convent Senior School, Abingdon 6 A AA I
Oxford High School GDST, Oxford   6 A AA G I
Oxford Tutorial College, Oxford   AA
Radley College, Abingdon Entry age: 13+ 6 A AA D I O
Rye St Antony School, Oxford   6 AA O
St Andrew's, Wantage   AA
St Clare's, Oxford, Oxford Entry age: 16+   6 AA O
St Edward's School, Oxford   6 A AA D G I O
St Mary's School, Wantage Entry age: 11,
13, 16   6 A AA D G I O S
The School of St Helen & St Katharine,
Abingdon   6 AA I
Shiplake College, Henley-on-Thames
Entry age: 13+, 16+   6 A AA D G I
Sibford School, Banbury   6 A AA I O
Tudor Hall School, Banbury
Entry age: 11, 13, 16   A AA D G I
Wychwood School, Oxford   6 A AA I S

RUTLAND

Oakham School, Oakham   6 A AA D G I O S
Uppingham School, Uppingham   6 A AA I O

SHROPSHIRE

Adcote School for Girls, Shrewsbury   6 AA
Bedstone College, Bucknell   6 A AA G I O
Concord College, Shrewsbury   6 AA O S
Dower House School, Bridgnorth
Entry age: 7, 8, 9   AA G O
Ellesmere College, Ellesmere   6 A AA D G I O S
Kingsland Grange, Shrewsbury Entry age: 7–11   AA G I
Moor Park School, Ludlow   AA O
Moreton Hall School, Oswestry
Entry age: 11+, 13+, 16+   6 A AA D G I O
The Old Hall School, Telford   AA I
Oswestry School, Oswestry Entry age: 9+,
11+, 13+, 16+   6 A AA G I O

Oswestry School Bellan House, Oswestry AA I O
Packwood Haugh School, Shrewsbury A AA G I
Prestfelde Preparatory School, Shrewsbury
 Entry age: 7+, 11+ AA I O
Shrewsbury High School GDST, Shrewsbury 6 AA I
Shrewsbury School, Shrewsbury 6 A AA I O
Wrekin College, Telford Entry age: 11,
 13, 16 6 A AA G I O

SOMERSET

All Hallows, Shepton Mallet Entry age: 11+ A AA G I O
Bruton School for Girls, Bruton
 Entry age: 11+, 13+, 16+ 6 A AA D G I O S
Chilton Cantelo School, Yeovil O
Downside School, Bath 6 A AA G I O
Hazlegrove (King's Bruton Preparatory School),
 Yeovil AA G I
King's Bruton, Bruton 6 A AA D I O
King's College, Taunton 6 A AA D G I O S
King's Hall, Taunton AA G I
Millfield Preparatory School, Glastonbury
 Entry age: 7–13 A AA G I O
Millfield School, Street Entry age: 13,
 14, 16 6 A AA G I O
The Park School, Yeovil Entry age: 8–18+ 6 A AA D I
Perrott Hill School, Crewkerne A AA D G I O
Queen's College Junior and Pre-Preparatory
 Schools, Taunton AA G I O
Queen's College, Taunton 6 A AA D G I
Taunton Preparatory School, Taunton
 Entry age: 11+ AA G I
Taunton School, Taunton 6 AA G I O
Wellington School, Wellington
 Entry age: 10+, 11+, 13+, 16+ 6 AA I
Wells Cathedral Junior School, Wells
 Entry age: 8–11 AA I
Wells Cathedral School, Wells Entry age: 11,
 13, 16 6 AA I S

BATH & NORTH EAST SOMERSET

King Edward's School, Bath, Bath
 Entry age: 11–18 6 A AA D G I
Kingswood School, Bath 6 A AA D G I O
Monkton Combe Junior School, Bath AA
Monkton Combe School, Bath 6 A AA D G I O
Paragon School, Prior Park College Junior,
 Bath AA G I O
Prior Park College, Bath 6 A AA D G I O
The Royal High School, Bath
 Entry age: 11/16+ 6 A AA D G I

NORTH SOMERSET

Sidcot School, Winscombe 6 A AA I O

STAFFORDSHIRE

Abbots Bromley School for Girls,
 Abbots Bromley Entry age: 11/16+ 6 A AA D G I

Abbotsholme School, Uttoxeter
 Entry age: 11+, 13+, 16+ 6 A AA D G I O
Chase Academy, Cannock Entry age: 3+,
 18+ AA G I O
Denstone College, Uttoxeter Entry age: 11,
 13, 16 6 A AA D G I O
Edenhurst School, Newcastle-under-Lyme O
Lichfield Cathedral School, Lichfield
 Entry age: 7, 9, 11 A AA D G I O
Newcastle-under-Lyme School,
 Newcastle-under-Lyme 6 AA G
St Dominic's Independent Junior School,
 Stoke-on-Trent Entry age: 8+ AA
St Dominic's Priory School, Stone A AA D I O
St Dominic's School, Stafford
 Entry age: 11, 12 AA D G I
Stafford Grammar School, Stafford 6 A AA D G I O
Vernon Lodge Preparatory School, Brewood AA O
Yarlet School, Stafford Entry age: 11+ A AA D G I O

STOCKTON-ON-TEES

Teesside Preparatory and High School,
 Eaglescliffe 6 AA
Yarm School, Yarm Entry age: 7+, 11+, 16+ 6 AA I S

SUFFOLK

Amberfield School, Ipswich Entry age: 11/13+ A AA I
Cherry Trees School, Bury St Edmunds AA
Culford School, Bury St Edmunds 6 A AA D G I S
Fairstead House School, Newmarket AA
Felixstowe International College, Felixstowe AA O
Finborough School, Stowmarket 6 A AA G I O
Framlingham College, Woodbridge 6 A AA D G I O S
Framlingham College Preparatory School,
 Brandeston Entry age: 11+/13+ A AA D I O
Hillcroft Preparatory School, Stowmarket AA G I
Ipswich High School GDST, Ipswich
 Entry age: 11+ 6 AA I
Ipswich School, Ipswich
 Entry age: 11, 13, 16 6 A AA G I O
Moreton Hall Preparatory School,
 Bury St Edmunds A AA D G I
Orwell Park, Ipswich Entry age: 7+ A AA I O
The Royal Hospital School, Ipswich
 Entry age: 11+ 6 A AA G I O
Saint Felix School, Southwold
 Entry age: 11, 13, 16 6 A AA D G I
St Joseph's College, Ipswich 6 AA G I O
South Lee Preparatory School, Bury St Edmunds
 Entry age: 8+, 11+ AA O
Stoke College, Sudbury AA I
Woodbridge School, Woodbridge 6 A AA D G I O

SURREY

Aberdour, Tadworth AA
Amesbury, Hindhead AA G I
Barfield School, Farnham AA G I O
Belmont School, Dorking AA
Box Hill School, Dorking 6 A AA D G I O

Bramley School, Tadworth Entry age: 7+	AA
Cambridge Tutors College, Croydon	6 AA
Canbury School, Kingston-upon-Thames	AA O
Caterham School, Caterham	6 A AA D G I O S
Charterhouse, Godalming	6 A AA G I O
City of London Freemen's School, Ashtead	6 A AA D G I
Claremont Fan Court School, Esher	6 A AA D G I
Cranleigh Preparatory School, Cranleigh	AA I
Cranleigh School, Cranleigh	
Entry age: 13+, 16+	6 A AA I O
Croham Hurst School, South Croydon	
Entry age: 11+, 16+	6 AA G I
Croydon High School GDST, South Croydon	6 AA G I
Cumnor House School, South Croydon	AA G I
Danes Hill School, Leatherhead	AA
Duke of Kent School, Ewhurst	
Entry age: 7+, 10+, 11+	AA O
Dunottar School, Reigate Entry age: 11, 14, 16	6 AA I
Edgeborough, Farnham	O
Epsom College, Epsom Entry age: 13+,	
16+	6 A AA D G I O
Essendene Lodge School, Caterham	AA O
Ewell Castle School, Epsom Entry age: 11+,	
13+, 16+	6 A AA G I O
Feltonfleet School, Cobham	A AA I O
Frensham Heights School, Farnham	A AA D G I O
Greenacre School for Girls, Banstead	6 A AA D G I O
Guildford High School, Guildford	6 AA I
Hampton Court House, East Molesey	AA I
Haslemere Preparatory School,	
Haslemere	A AA D G I O
Hawley Place School, Camberley	
Entry age: 7, 11	A AA D G I O
The Hawthorns School, Redhill	AA I O
Hazelwood School, Oxted	AA D G I O
Hoe Bridge School, Woking Entry age: 7+	AA O
Homefield School, Sutton	AA G O
Hurtwood House, Dorking Entry age: 16	6 D O S
King Edward's School Witley,	
Godalming	6 A AA G I O S
Kingston Grammar School,	
Kingston-upon-Thames	6 A AA G I
Kingswood House School, Epsom	AA G
Lanesborough, Guildford Entry age: 8+	I
Lingfield Notre Dame School, Lingfield	
Entry age: 11+	6 AA O
Lodge School, Purley	AA I
Lyndhurst School, Camberley	AA
Manor House School, Leatherhead	
Entry age: 7+, 11+	A AA D G I
Marymount International School,	
Kingston-upon-Thames Entry age: 11, 16	AA
Milbourne Lodge School, Esher	AA
New Lodge School, Dorking	O
Notre Dame Preparatory School, Cobham	O
Notre Dame Senior School, Cobham	6 AA
Oakfield School, Woking Entry age: 7+, 11+	AA I O
Old Palace School of John Whitgift, Croydon	AA I
Prior's Field School, Godalming	
Entry age: 11, 16	6 A AA D G I
Reed's School, Cobham	6 A AA D G I O
Reigate Grammar School, Reigate	6 AA I O

Reigate St Mary's Preparatory and Choir School,	
Reigate Entry age: 8+	I
Ripley Court School, Woking	A AA D G I O
Rokeby School, Kingston-upon-Thames	A AA G I
Royal Grammar School, Guildford	
Entry age: 11+/13+	A AA I
Royal Russell School, Croydon	
Entry age: 11+/16	6 A AA D I
The Royal School, Haslemere	
Entry age: 11+, 13+, 16+	6 A AA D G I O
St. Andrew's (Woking) School Trust, Woking	
Entry age: 7+	A AA G I O
St Catherine's School, Guildford	
Entry age: 11/16+	6 A AA G I O
St Edmund's School, Hindhead	
Entry age: 7/8	A AA G I O
St George's College, Weybridge	6 A AA I O
St Hilary's School, Godalming	A AA D I
St Ives School, Haslemere	A AA D G I O
St John's School, Leatherhead Entry age: 13+,	
16+	6 A AA G I O
St Teresa's School, Dorking	6 A AA D G I O
Seaton House School, Sutton	AA
Sir William Perkins's School, Chertsey	6 AA I
Stowford College, Sutton Entry age: 11, 14	AA G O
Surbiton High School,	
Kingston-upon-Thames	6 A AA G I
Sutton High School GDST, Sutton	
Entry age: 11+, 16+	6 A AA D G I O
Tormead School, Guildford	6 A AA I
Trinity School, Croydon Entry age: 10+,	
11+, 13+, 16+	6 A AA G I O
West Dene School, Purley Entry age: 7	I
Whitgift School, South Croydon	
Entry age: 10–13, 16	6 A AA D G I O
Wispers School for Girls, Haslemere	A AA D G I
Woldingham School, Woldingham	
Entry age: 11+	6 A AA D G I
Woodcote House School, Windlesham	A AA G I O
Yehudi Menuhin School, Cobham	I

EAST SUSSEX

Battle Abbey School, Battle	
Entry age: 13/16+	6 AA D G O
Bellerbys College, Hove	6 AA
Bricklehurst Manor Preparatory, Wadhurst	AA
Brighton and Hove High School GDST, Brighton	6 AA
Brighton College, Brighton	
Entry age: 13+, 16+	6 A AA D G I O
Brighton College Prep School, Brighton	
Entry age: 11+	AA O
Buckswood School, Hastings	AA G I
Claremont School, St Leonards-on-Sea	A AA D G I O
Eastbourne College, Eastbourne	
Entry age: 13, 16	6 A AA D G I S
The Fold School, Hove Entry age: 3+	AA I
Lewes Old Grammar School, Lewes	6 AA I O
Lancing College Preparatory School at	
Mowden, Hove Entry age: 7+, 11+	AA
Moira House Girls School, Eastbourne	6 AA D G I O
Moira House School, Eastbourne	O
Newlands School, Seaford	6 A AA D G I O

Roedean School, Brighton
    Entry age: 11+, 12+, 13+, 16+   6 A AA D G I S
St Andrew's School, Eastbourne   A AA D G I O
St Aubyns School, Brighton   A AA G I O
St Bede's Prep School, Eastbourne   A AA D G I
St Bede's School, Hailsham   6 A AA D G I
St Leonards-Mayfield School, Mayfield
    Entry age: 11, 13, 16   6 A AA G I
St Mary's Hall, Brighton   6 A AA D G I
Stonelands School of Ballet & Theatre Arts, Hove   D O
Vinehall School, Robertsbridge   AA I O

WEST SUSSEX

Ardingly College, Haywards Heath
    Entry age: 7+, 11+, 13+, 16+   6 A AA D G I O S
Ardingly College Junior School,
    Haywards Heath Entry age: 11+   A AA G I
Arundale Preparatory School, Pulborough
    Entry age: 7–11   A AA G I O
Brambletye School, East Grinstead Entry age: 9+   I
Burgess Hill School for Girls,
    Burgess Hill   6 A AA D G I O
Conifers School, Midhurst   A AA G I O
Copthorne Prep School, Copthorne   A AA G I
Dorset House School, Pulborough   AA I
Farlington School, Horsham   6 A AA D G I O
Great Ballard School, Chichester
    Entry age: 7   A AA D G I O
Great Walstead, Haywards Heath
    Entry age: 7–11   AA D G I
Handcross Park School, Haywards Heath
    Entry age: 7–11   AA G I
Hurstpierpoint College, Hurstpierpoint   6 A AA D G I O
Lancing College, Lancing   6 A AA G I O
Lavant House, Chichester Entry age: 11, 13   6 AA
Oakwood School, Chichester   AA O
Our Lady of Sion School, Worthing   6 AA
The Prebendal School, Chichester Entry age: 7   I
Seaford College, Petworth Entry age: 10+,
    11+, 13+   6 A AA G I
Shoreham College, Shoreham-by-Sea   AA G I O
Slindon College, Arundel Entry age: 10   AA O
Stoke Brunswick, East Grinstead   AA I O
Tavistock & Summerhill School,
    Haywards Heath   AA
The Towers Convent School, Steyning   AA D I O
Westbourne House School, Chichester   I
Windlesham House, Pulborough   AA G I O
Worth School, Turners Hill
    Entry age: 11, 13, 16   6 A AA I

TYNE AND WEAR

Central Newcastle High School GDST,
    Newcastle upon Tyne Entry age: 11+, 16+   6 AA
Dame Allan's Boys School, Newcastle upon Tyne   6 AA
Dame Allan's Girls School, Newcastle upon Tyne
    Entry age: 11   6 AA I
The King's School, Tynemouth
    Entry age: 11+   6 A AA I O
La Sagesse School, Newcastle upon Tyne   AA O

Newcastle School for Boys, Newcastle upon Tyne   AA
Newcastle Upon Tyne Church High School,
    Newcastle upon Tyne   AA I
Sunderland High School, Sunderland   6 AA I
Westfield School, Newcastle upon Tyne   6 A AA G I O

WARWICKSHIRE

Abbotsford School, Kenilworth Entry age: 7   AA
Bilton Grange, Rugby Entry age: 8+   AA G I O
The Croft Preparatory School,
    Stratford-upon-Avon Entry age: 8   AA
King's High School, Warwick, Warwick   6 AA I
The Kingsley School, Leamington Spa   6 A AA D I
Princethorpe College, Rugby
    Entry age: 11/18+   6 A AA G I O
Rugby School, Rugby   6 A AA G I
Warwick School, Warwick   6 A AA I

WEST MIDLANDS

Abbey College, Birmingham   6 AA O
Al Hijrah School, Birmingham   AA
Bablake School, Coventry   6 A AA I O
Birchfield School, Wolverhampton
    Entry age: 11   A AA G I O
The Blue Coat School, Birmingham
    Entry age: 7+   AA I O
Coventry Prep School, Coventry Entry age: 7+   A AA I O
Edgbaston High School for Girls, Birmingham
    Entry age: 11+   6 AA G I
Elmhurst School for Dance, Birmingham   6
Eversfield Preparatory School, Solihull   AA
Highclare School, Birmingham
    Entry age: 11/16+   6 A AA G I O
Hydesville Tower School, Walsall   AA G I O
King Edward VI High School for Girls,
    Birmingham   AA
King Edward's School, Birmingham
    Entry age: 11+, 13+, 16+   6 AA I
King Henry VIII School, Coventry   6 A AA I O
Norfolk House School, Birmingham   AA
Priory School, Birmingham
    Entry age: 11, 16   6 A AA D I
The Royal Wolverhampton School,
    Wolverhampton   6 AA G I
St George's School, Edgbaston, Birmingham
    Entry age: 11+   6 AA I O
Saint Martin's School, Solihull
    Entry age: 11+, 16+   6 AA I
Solihull School, Solihull   6 A AA D I S
Tettenhall College, Wolverhampton
    Entry age: 11   6 A AA G I O
Wolverhampton Grammar School, Wolverhampton
    Entry age: 11+, 13+, 16+   6 AA I O S

WILTSHIRE

Chafyn Grove School, Salisbury   A AA D G I O
Dauntsey's School, Devizes
    Entry age: 11+, 13+, 16+   6 A AA D G I O S
Godolphin Preparatory School, Salisbury   AA

The Godolphin School, Salisbury   6 A AA G I O
Grittleton House School, Chippenham   A AA D G I S
La Retraite Swan, Salisbury Entry age: 7, 11, 14A AA G I
Leaden Hall School, Salisbury   AA
Marlborough College, Marlborough
    Entry age: 13+, 16+   6 A AA G I O
Norman Court Preparatory School, Salisbury
    Entry age: 7, 8, 11   A AA D G I O
Pinewood School, Shrivenham Entry age: 11+   AA O
St Francis School, Pewsey   A AA G I O
St Mary's School, Calne Entry age: 11+,
    13+, 16+   6 A AA I O
Salisbury Cathedral School, Salisbury
    Entry age: 7, 10   A AA D G I
Sandroyd School, Salisbury   AA I O
Stonar School, Melksham   6 A AA D G I O
Warminster School, Warminster
    Entry age: 7, 9, 11, 13, 16   6 A AA D G I O

WORCESTERSHIRE

Abberley Hall, Worcester Entry age: 8+   AA
The Abbey College, Malvern Wells   6 AA O S
The Alice Ottley School, Worcester   6 A AA G I
Bromsgrove Preparatory School, Bromsgrove
    Entry age: 11+   AA I O
Bromsgrove School, Bromsgrove   6 A AA D G I O
Dodderhill School, Droitwich Spa
    Entry age: 11+   AA I
The Downs School, Malvern   A AA D G I O
The Elms, Malvern   AA G I O
Hartlebury School, Kidderminster   A AA D G I S
Malvern College Preparatory and Pre-Prep
    School, Malvern   A AA D G I O
Holy Trinity School, Kidderminster   6 AA I O S
King's Hawford, Worcester Entry age: 7+, 8+   AA
The King's School, Worcester   6 AA I
The Knoll School, Kidderminster   AA
Malvern College, Malvern   6 A AA D G I O
Malvern St James, Great Malvern
    Entry age: 11+, 12+, 13+, 16+   6 A AA G I
Moffats School, Bewdley   A AA D G O S
Moffats School, Bewdley   A AA D G I O S
RGS The Grange, Worcester   AA
Royal Grammar School Worcester, Worcester   A AA I
St Mary's Convent School, Worcester
    Entry age: 11+, 16+   A AA G I
Saint Michael's College, Tenbury Wells   6 AA O S
Winterfold House, Kidderminster   A AA G I O

EAST RIDING OF YORKSHIRE

Hull Collegiate School, Anlaby Entry age: 11   6 AA
Pocklington School, Pocklington   6 AA I O

NORTH YORKSHIRE

Ampleforth College, York Entry age: 13, 16   6 AA I O
Ashville College, Harrogate
    Entry age: 11–18   6 A AA D G I O
Aysgarth Preparatory School, Bedale   I

Belmont Grosvenor School, Harrogate   AA
Bootham School, York Entry age: 11+,
    13+, 16+   6 AA I O
Bramcote School, Scarborough   AA G I O
Catteral Hall School, Settle Entry age: 10, 11   AA G I O
Cundall Manor School, York   AA G I
Fyling Hall School, Whitby   6 AA G I O
Giggleswick School, Settle
    Entry age: 13, 16   6 A AA D G I O
Harrogate Ladies' College, Harrogate
    Entry age: 11+, 16+   6 AA I O
Harrogate Tutorial College, Harrogate
    Entry age: 15+   6 AA O
Howsham Hall, York   AA G O
Lisvane, Scarborough College Junior School,
    Scarborough Entry age: 7–9   AA
Malsis School, Skipton   AA I O
The Minster School, York   I
The Mount School, York   6 A AA D G I O S
Queen Ethelburga's College, York
    Entry age: 11   6 A AA D G I O S
Queen Margaret's School, York   6 A AA I O
Queen Mary's School, Thirsk   A AA G I
Read School, Selby Entry age: 11+, 13+, 16+   6 A AA I
Ripon Cathedral Choir School, Ripon   AA I
St Martin's Ampleforth, York Entry age: 7/12+ AA G I O
St Peter's School, York Entry age: 13/16+   6 AA I O
Scarborough College & Lisvane School,
    Scarborough   6 A AA I
Terrington Hall, York   A AA D G I O
Woodleigh School, Malton   A AA D G I

SOUTH YORKSHIRE

Birkdale School, Sheffield Entry age: 11, 16   6 AA I S
Hill House St Mary's School, Doncaster   A AA G I O
Sheffield High School GDST, Sheffield
    Entry age: 11, 16   6 AA I O
Westbourne School, Sheffield   AA G I O

WEST YORKSHIRE

Ackworth School, Pontefract   A AA I
Ackworth School - International Study Centre,
    Pontefract   6 A AA I
Bradford Girls' Grammar School, Bradford   I
Bradford Grammar School, Bradford Entry age: 11+   I
Bronte House School, Bradford Entry age: 9   AA
The Froebelian School, Leeds   AA
Fulneck School, Pudsey   6 A AA G I O
Gateways School, Leeds Entry age: 11   6 A AA D G I
Ghyll Royd School, Ilkley Entry age: 7   AA
Hipperholme Grammar School, Halifax
    Entry age: 16+   6 AA
Huddersfield Grammar School, Huddersfield   AA I
Leeds Girls' High School, Leeds   6 AA I
Leeds Grammar School, Leeds Entry age: 11+,
    16+   6 AA I
Queen Elizabeth Grammar School, Wakefield   6 AA I
Richmond House School, Leeds Entry age: 7/8   AA
Rishworth School, Rishworth
    Entry age: 11, 16   6 AA D G I O

Shaw House School, Bradford	AA O
Silcoates School, Wakefield	
Entry age: 11	6 A AA D G I O S
Wakefield Girls' High School, Wakefield	6 AA

Wakefield Independent School, Wakefield	AA
Wakefield Tutorial Preparatory School, Leeds	O
Woodhouse Grove School, Apperley Bridge	AA D G I O

NORTHERN IRELAND

COUNTY ANTRIM

Campbell College, Belfast	A AA I
Methodist College, Belfast	6 I

COUNTY TYRONE

The Royal School Dungannon, Dungannon	
Entry age: 11–16	AA G I

SCOTLAND

ABERDEENSHIRE

Albyn School, Aberdeen	A AA G I
Robert Gordons College, Aberdeen	6 AA G I O
St Margaret's School for Girls, Aberdeen	AA I

ANGUS

Lathallan School, Montrose	A AA D G I O

ARGYLL AND BUTE

Lomond School, Helensburgh	
Entry age: 11, 16	6 AA I

CLACKMANNANSHIRE

Dollar Academy, Dollar	A I

FIFE

St Leonards School & VIth Form College, St Andrews	6 A AA D G I

GLASGOW

Craigholme School Entry age: 12	AA
The Glasgow Academy Entry age: 11+	6 AA
The High School of Glasgow	AA
Kelvinside Academy	6 AA
St Aloysius' College	AA

LANARKSHIRE

Hamilton College, Hamilton	AA I

LOTHIAN

Cargilfield, Edinburgh	AA I O
The Edinburgh Academy, Edinburgh	6 A AA I
Fettes College, Edinburgh	6 A AA I O
George Heriot's School, Edinburgh	
Entry age: 11+	6 A AA D G I
George Watson's College, Edinburgh	6 AA G I S
Loretto Junior School, Musselburgh	
Entry age: 10/11	A AA D G O
Loretto School, Musselburgh	6 A AA D G I O
The Mary Erskine School, Edinburgh	6 AA I
Merchiston Castle School, Edinburgh	6 A AA I O
St Margaret's School, Edinburgh	6 A AA D G I
St Mary's Music School, Edinburgh Entry age: 9+	I
Stewart's Melville College, Edinburgh	AA I

MORAYSHIRE

Gordonstoun School, Elgin	
Entry age: 9	6 A AA D G I O

PERTHSHIRE

Ardvreck School, Crieff	AA
Glenalmond College, Perth	
Entry age: 12, 13, 16	6 A AA I O
Kilgraston, Perth	6 A AA G I O
Morrison's Academy, Crieff	6 AA
Strathallan School, Perth	
Entry age: 10+, 16+	6 A AA I O

ROXBURGHSHIRE

St Mary's Preparatory School, Melrose	O

STIRLING

Beaconhurst School	AA D O

WALES

BRIDGEND

St Clare's School, Porthcawl
    Entry age: 11+, 13+,16+   AA
St John's School, Porthcawl   AA G O

CARDIFF

The Cardiff Academy   AA
The Cathedral School Entry age: 11   AA G I
Howell's School, Llandaff GDST
    Entry age: 11, 16   6 AA I
Kings Monkton School   6 A AA G I

CARMARTHENSHIRE

Llandovery College, Llandovery
    Entry age: 11+, 17+   6 A AA D G I O
St Michael's School, Llanelli   6 AA D G I O

CONWY

Lyndon Preparatory School,
    Colwyn Bay   6 A AA D G I O S
Rydal Penrhos Senior School, Colwyn Bay   6 AA G I
St David's College, Llandudno
    Entry age: 11   6 A AA G I O

DENBIGHSHIRE

Howell's School, Denbigh Entry age: 11   6 A AA D G I
Ruthin School, Ruthin Entry age: 11   6 A AA D G I O S

MONMOUTHSHIRE

Haberdashers' Monmouth School For Girls,
    Monmouth   6 AA I
Llangattock School, Monmouth   O
Monmouth School, Monmouth
    Entry age: 11, 13, 16   6 AA G I
St John's-on-the-Hill, Chepstow   A AA D G I O

NEWPORT

Rougemont School   AA

PEMBROKESHIRE

Netherwood School, Saundersfoot
    Entry age: 11, 12, 13   AA

POWYS

Christ College, Brecon
    Entry age: 11, 13, 16   6 A AA G I O S

SWANSEA

Ffynone House School Entry age: 11 6 A AA D G I O S
Ffynone House School Trust   6 A AA D G I

4.2

Bursaries and Reserved Entrance Awards

The following is compiled from information provided by schools. For further information please contact the school direct. The abbreviations used are as follows:

E   Christian Missionary or full-time worker
F1   The Royal Navy
F2   The Royal Marines
F3   The Army
F4   The Royal Air Force

FO Foreign Office
H   Financial or domestic hardship
M   Medical profession
T   Teaching profession
+   The Clergy

ENGLAND

BEDFORDSHIRE

Bedford High School, Bedford	F1 F2 F3 F4 H
Bedford Modern School, Bedford	H
Bedford Preparatory School, Bedford	F1 F2 F3 F4 H
Bedford School, Bedford	+ F1 F2 F3 F4 H T
Dame Alice Harpur School, Bedford	H
Moorlands School, Luton	H T

BERKSHIRE

The Abbey School, Reading Entry age: 11+, 16+	H
The Ark School, Reading Entry age: 5+	H T
Bearwood College, Wokingham	+ E F1 F3 F4 H
Brigidine School Windsor, Windsor Entry age: 11	H
Dolphin School, Reading	H T
Elstree School, Reading Entry age: 7	+ E H T
Eton College, Windsor	H
Heathfield St Mary's School, Ascot Entry age: 11+, 13+, 16+	+ F1 F2 F3 F4 FO
Hemdean House School, Reading Entry age: 11+	H
Highfield School, Maidenhead Entry age: 7+, 12+	H
Horris Hill School, Newbury	F1 F2 F3 F4
Hurst Lodge School, Ascot	F1 F2 F3 F4
Lambrook Haileybury, Bracknell	T
Leighton Park School, Reading	H
Licensed Victuallers' School, Ascot	F1 F2 F3 F4
Luckley-Oakfield School, Wokingham	F1 F2 F3 F4 H
The Oratory Preparatory School, Reading	F1 F2 F3 F4 H
The Oratory School, Reading Entry age: 11+, 13+	F1 F2 F3 F4 FO H T
Padworth College, Reading	F1 F2 F3 F4 FO H
Pangbourne College, Pangbourne	F1 F2 F3 F4 H
Queen Anne's School, Reading	+
Reading Blue Coat School, Reading	H T
St Andrew's School, Reading	+
St Gabriel's, Newbury	+
St George's School, Ascot Entry age: 11+, 16+	H
St Joseph's Convent School, Reading	H
St Michaels School, Newbury	H

St Piran's Preparatory School, Maidenhead   E H T
Sunningdale School, Sunningdale   T
Upton House School, Windsor   H
Wellington College, Crowthorne   F1 F2 F3 F4 H
White House Preparatory School, Wokingham   + H

BRISTOL

Badminton School   F1 F2 F3 F4 H
Bristol Cathedral School Entry age: 11+, 13+, 16+   H
Bristol Grammar School   H
Clifton College   + F1 F2 F3 F4 H T
Clifton College Preparatory School   + F1 F2 F3 F4
Clifton High School Entry age: 11+, 13+, 16+   H
Colston's Collegiate School   F1 F2 F3
Colston's Girls' School   H
The Downs School, Wraxall
    Entry age: 8+   + F1 F2 F3 H
Fairfield School, Backwell   H
Overndale School   H
Queen Elizabeth's Hospital Entry age: 11, 13, 16   H
The Red Maids' School   H
Redland High School Entry age: 11, 16   H
Tockington Manor School   T

BUCKINGHAMSHIRE

Akeley Wood School, Buckingham   H
Ashfold School, Aylesbury   + E F1 F2 F3 F4
The Beacon School, Amersham   H
Bury Lawn School, Milton Keynes   H
Caldicott School, Farnham Royal   H T
Davenies School, Beaconsfield   H
Gayhurst School, Gerrards Cross   + E H
Godstowe Preparatory School, High Wycombe
    Entry age: 8,11   T
High March School, Beaconsfield   H T
Holy Cross Convent, Gerrards Cross   + H
Ladymede, Aylesbury   H
Maltman's Green School, Gerrards Cross   H
Milton Keynes Preparatory School, Milton Keynes H
Pipers Corner School, High Wycombe   F1 F2 F3 F4
St Mary's School, Gerrards Cross   + H
Stowe School, Buckingham   E H
Swanbourne House School, Milton Keynes
    Entry age: 11+   + F1 F2 F3 F4
Thornton College Convent of Jesus and Mary,
    Milton Keynes Entry age: 8, 11   F1 F2 F3 F4 H
Thorpe House School, Gerrards Cross   H T

CAMBRIDGESHIRE

Bellerbys College & Embassy CES Cambridge,
    Cambridge   H
Cambridge Arts & Sciences (CATS), Cambridge   H
Cambridge Centre for Sixth-Form Studies,
    Cambridge   F1 F2 F3 H
Kimbolton School, Huntingdon   H
The King's School Ely, Ely
    Entry age: 11+   + F1 F2 F3 F4 H
The Leys School, Cambridge
    Entry age: 11, 13, 16   F1 F2 F3 F4 H

Madingley Pre-Preparatory School, Cambridge   H
MPW (Mander Portman Woodward), Cambridge   H
The Perse School for Girls, Cambridge Entry age: 11   H
Peterborough High School,
    Peterborough   F1 F2 F3 F4 H
St John's College School, Cambridge   H
St Mary's School, Cambridge   H
Sancton Wood School, Cambridge   H T
Wisbech Grammar School, Wisbech   H

CHANNEL ISLANDS

Ormer House Preparatory School, Alderney   H
St George's Preparatory School, Jersey Entry age: 7   H T
St Michael's Preparatory School, Jersey   + H
Victoria College, Jersey   H

CHESHIRE

Abbey Gate College, Chester Entry age: 11+, 16+   H
Alderley Edge School for Girls, Alderley Edge   H
Beech Hall School, Macclesfield   + E H
Cheadle Hulme School, Cheadle Entry age: 11, 16   H
Culcheth Hall, Altrincham   H
The Grange School, Northwich   H
Hillcrest Grammar School, Stockport   H
Hulme Hall Schools, Cheadle   H T
The King's School, Chester Entry age: 11, 16   H
The King's School, Macclesfield   H
Mostyn House School, South Wirral Entry age: 4   H
North Cestrian Grammar School, Altrincham   H
Oriel Bank, Stockport   H
Pownall Hall School, Wilmslow   + T
The Queen's School, Chester   H
Ramillies Hall School, Cheadle   F1 F2 F3 F4
The Ryleys, Alderley Edge   H
Stockport Grammar School, Stockport
    Entry age: 11+   H
Terra Nova School, Holmes Chapel   + E F1 F2 F3 F4 H
Wilmslow Preparatory School, Wilmslow   H T
Yorston Lodge School, Knutsford   +

CORNWALL

The Bolitho School, Penzance
    Entry age: 10+,13+   + F1 F2 F3 F4 H
Polwhele House School, Truro   + H T
Roselyon, Par   H
St Joseph's School, Launceston Entry age: 7+, 11+   H
St Petroc's School, Bude   + F1 F2 F3 F4 H T
Truro High School, Truro Entry age: 11+, 16+   + E H
Truro School Preparatory School, Truro
    Entry age: 7+   H

CUMBRIA

Austin Friars St Monica's School, Carlisle   H
Casterton School, Kirkby Lonsdale   E H T
Chetwynde School, Barrow-in-Furness   H
Harecroft Hall School, Seascale   + F1 F2 F3 F4 H
Hunter Hall School, Penrith   H

Lime House School, Carlisle	E F1 F2 F3 FO H T
St Bees School, St Bees	+ F1 F2 F3 F4 H
St Ursulas Convent School, Wigton	H
Sedbergh School, Sedbergh	
Entry age: 13+, 16+, 17+	+ E F1 F2 F3 F4 H T
Wellspring Christian School, Carlisle	E H
Windermere St Anne's, Windermere	
Entry age: 11+, 13+, 16+	H

DERBYSHIRE

Barlborough Hall School, Chesterfield	H
Derby Grammar School for Boys, Derby	H
Derby High School, Derby	+ H
Foremarke Hall School, Derby	F1 F2 F3 F4 H
Michael House Steiner School, Heanor	H
Mount St Mary's College, Spinkhill	
Entry age: 11+	F2 F3 F4 FO H
Repton School, Derby	
Entry age: 13+, 16+	F1 F2 F3 F4 H
St Anselm's School, Bakewell	
Entry age: 7	+ F1 F2 F3 F4
St Wystan's School, Repton	H

DEVON

Blundell's School, Tiverton	
Entry age: 11, 13, 16	F1 F2 F3 F4 FO H
Bramdean School, Exeter Entry age: 7	FO H
Trinity School, Teignmouth	F1 F2 F3 F4 H
Edgehill College, Bideford	+ E F1 F2 F3 F4 H
Emmanuel School, Exeter	H
Exeter Cathedral School, Exeter	
Entry age: 7+	F1 F2 F3 F4 H
Exeter Junior School, Exeter	H
Exeter School, Exeter Entry age: 7, 8, 11, 12, 13, 16	H
Grenville College, Bideford	+ F1 F2 F3 F4 H T
Kelly College, Tavistock	
Entry age: 11, 13, 16	E F1 F2 F3 F4 H T
Kelly College Preparatory School,	
Tavistock	F1 F2 F3 F4
The Maynard School, Exeter	H
Mount House School, Tavistock	T
Park School, Totnes	H
Plymouth College, Plymouth	H
St John's School, Sidmouth Entry age: 8	F1 F2 F3 F4 H
St Margaret's School, Exeter	E H
St Michael's, Barnstaple	+ F1 F2 F3 F4 H T
St Wilfrid's School, Exeter	H
Sands School, Ashburton	H
Shebbear College, Beaworthy	+ E F1 F2 F3 F4 H T
St Christophers School, Totnes	H
Stover School, Newton Abbot	+ F1 F2 F3 F4 FO H
Tower House School, Paignton Entry age: 11	H
Trinity School, Teignmouth	+ F1 F2 F3 F4 H M T
West Buckland Preparatory School, Barnstaple	H
West Buckland School, Barnstaple	H

DORSET

Bryanston School, Blandford Forum	H
Castle Court Preparatory School, Wimborne	+ E H

Clayesmore Preparatory School,	
Blandford Forum	+ F1 F2 F3 F4 H
Clayesmore School, Blandford Forum	F1 F2 F3 F4
Dorchester Preparatory and Independent	
Schools, Dorchester	H
Dumpton School, Wimborne	H
Knighton House, Blandford Forum	F1 F2 F3 F4 FO H T
Milton Abbey School, Blandford Forum	F1 F2 F3 F4 H T
The Park School, Bournemouth	H
Port Regis School, Shaftesbury	
Entry age: 7+, 12+	F1 F2 F3 F4 T
St Antony's Leweston School, Sherborne	H
St Martin's School, Bournemouth	E
Sherborne Preparatory School, Sherborne	F1 F2 F3 F4 H
Sherborne School, Sherborne	F1 F2 F3 F4 H
Sherborne School for Girls, Sherborne	H
Talbot Heath, Bournemouth	H
Uplands School, Poole	H
Wentworth College, Bournemouth	F1 F2 F3 F4
Yarrells School, Poole	F1 F2 H

COUNTY DURHAM

Barnard Castle School, Barnard Castle	F1 F2 F3 F4
The Chorister School, Durham	+ H
Durham High School For Girls, Durham	+ H
Durham School, Durham	
Entry age: 11–18	F1 F2 F3 F4 H
Hurworth House School, Darlington	H
Polam Hall, Darlington	F1 F2 F3 F4 H

ESSEX

Bancroft's School, Woodford Green Entry age: 11	H
Brentwood School, Brentwood Entry age: 11–18	H T
Chigwell School, Chigwell	H T
Cranbrook College, Ilford	T
Dame Johane Bradbury's School, Saffron Walden	H
Felsted Preparatory School, Felsted	+ F1 F2 F3 F4 H
Felsted School, Dunmow	F1 F2 F3
Friends' School, Saffron Walden	F1 F3 F4
Holmwood House, Colchester	H
Littlegarth School, Colchester	H
New Hall School, Chelmsford Entry age: 11	F1 F2 F4
St Hilda's School, Westcliff-on-Sea	H
St Michael's School, Leigh-on-Sea	+ E T
St Nicholas School, Harlow	H T
Thorpe Hall School, Southend-on-Sea	H

GLOUCESTERSHIRE

Berkhampstead School, Cheltenham	H
Bredon School, Tewkesbury	F1 F2 F3 F4
Cheltenham College, Cheltenham	F1 F2 F3 F4
Cheltenham College Junior School,	
Cheltenham	F1 F2 F3 F4
The Cheltenham Ladies' College, Cheltenham	H
Dean Close Preparatory School,	
Cheltenham	+ E F1 F2 F3 F4 H
Dean Close School, Cheltenham	+ E F1 F2 F3 F4 H T
Hatherop Castle School, Cirencester	H
Ingleside PNEU School, Cirencester	H

The King's School, Gloucester   + F1 F2 F3 F4 H T
Rendcomb College, Cirencester   F1 F2 F3 F4
Rose Hill School, Wotton-under-Edge   F1 F2 F3 F4 H T
St Edward's School Cheltenham, Cheltenham   H
School of the Lion, Gloucester   E H
Westonbirt School, Tetbury   + F1 F2 F3 F4 FO H T
Wycliffe College, Stonehouse   F1 F2 F3 F4 H T
Wycliffe Preparatory School,
   Stonehouse   F1 F2 F3 F4 FO H T
Wynstones School, Gloucester   H

HAMPSHIRE

Ballard School, New Milton   H T
Bedales School, Petersfield Entry age: 13+, 16+   H
Churchers College, Petersfield   H
Daneshill School, Basingstoke   T
Dunhurst (Bedales Junior School), Petersfield   H
Durlston Court, New Milton   H
Farnborough Hill, Farnborough   H
Forres Sandle Manor, Fordingbridge   F1 F2 F3 F4
The Gregg School, Southampton   H
Hampshire Collegiate School (Embley Park),
   Romsey   + F1 F2 F3 F4 FO H T
Highfield School, Liphook
   Entry age: 7+, 12+   + E F1 F2 F3 F4
Hordle Walhampton School, Lymington   H
King Edward VI School, Southampton
   Entry age: 11+, 13+   H
Lord Wandsworth College, Hook   F1 F3 F4 H
Mayville High School, Southsea   H
The Pilgrims' School, Winchester   H
The Portsmouth Grammar School, Portsmouth   H T
Portsmouth High School GDST, Southsea   H
Rookesbury Park School, Portsmouth   F1 F2 F3 H
St Neot's School, Hook Entry age: 5+   H
St Nicholas' School, Fleet   +
St Swithun's School, Winchester Entry age: 11–18   H
Salesian College, Farnborough   H
Sherborne House School, Eastleigh Entry age: 5–11   H
Sherfield School, Hook   H
Stanbridge Earls School, Romsey   H
Stockton House School, Fleet   H
Winchester College, Winchester Entry age: 13, 16   H
Wykeham House School, Fareham   H

HEREFORDSHIRE

The Hereford Cathedral School,
   Hereford   + F1 F2 F3 F4 H T
Lucton School, Leominster   E H
St Richard's, Bromyard   F1 F2 F3 F4

HERTFORDSHIRE

Abbot's Hill School, Hemel Hempstead   T
Aldenham School, Elstree   H
Berkhamsted Collegiate Preparatory School,
   Berkhamsted   H
Berkhamsted Collegiate School,
   Berkhamsted   F3 H M T

Bishop's Stortford College,
   Bishop's Stortford   F1 F3 F4 H T
Edge Grove, Aldenham
   Entry age: 7+   E F1 F2 F3 F4 FO H T
Egerton-Rothesay School, Berkhamsted   H
Haberdashers' Aske's Boys' School, Elstree
   Entry age: 11, 13   H
Haberdashers' Aske's School for Girls, Elstree   + H
Haileybury, Hertford   H
Harpenden Preparatory School, Harpenden   H
The Junior School, Bishop's Stortford College,
   Bishop's Stortford   H
Lockers Park, Hemel Hempstead   F1 F2 F3 T
The Princess Helena College, Hitchin + E F1 F2 F3 F4 H
The Purcell School, Bushey   H
Queenswood School, Hatfield   H
The Royal Masonic School for Girls, Rickmansworth
   Entry age: 11+   F1 F2 F3 F4 H
St Albans High School for Girls, St Albans   + H
St Albans School, St Albans
   Entry age: 11+, 13+, 16+   H
St Andrew's Montessori School, Watford   H T
St Christopher School, Letchworth   H
St Columba's College, St Albans   H
St Edmund's College, Ware   + F1 F2 F3 F4 H T
St Francis' College, Letchworth   H
St Margaret's School, Bushey   + H
Stormont, Potters Bar   H
Westbrook Hay Preparatory School,
   Hemel Hempstead   H
York House School, Rickmansworth   H T

ISLE OF MAN

King William's College, Castletown   + F1 F2 F3 F4 H T

ISLE OF WIGHT

Ryde School, Ryde   H

KENT

Ashford School, Ashford   + F1 F3 F4 H
Baston School, Bromley   H
Beechwood Sacred Heart School, Tunbridge Wells
   Entry age: 11+, 13+   E F1 F2 F3 F4 FO H
Benenden School, Cranbrook Entry age: 11–18   H
Bethany School, Cranbrook   + E F1 F2 F3 F4 H
Bickley Park School, Bromley   H T
Bromley High School GDST, Bromley   H
Cobham Hall, Gravesend   F1 F2 F3 F4 H
Combe Bank School, Nr Sevenoaks   H
Dover College, Dover   F1 F2 F3 F4
Elliott Park School, Sheerness   H
Farringtons School, Chislehurst   + E F1 F2 F3 F4
Gad's Hill School, Rochester   H
The Granville School, Sevenoaks   H
Hilden Grange School, Tonbridge   H
Junior King's School, Canterbury   +
Kent College, Canterbury Entry age: 11+,
   13+, 16+   + H
Kent College Pembury, Tunbridge Wells   F1 F2 F3 F4

King's Preparatory School, Rochester   + E F1 F2 F3 F4 H
King's School Rochester, Rochester   + F1 F2 F3 F4 H
Lorenden Preparatory School, Faversham
   Entry age: 7+   H
Marlborough House School, Hawkhurst   T
Merton Court Preparatory School, Sidcup   H T
Northbourne Park School, Deal   + E F1 F2 F3 F4 H
Rochester Independent College, Rochester   H
Sackville School, Tonbridge   H
St Christopher's School, Canterbury
   Entry age: 3–11   H
St Edmunds Junior School,
   Canterbury   + F1 F2 F3 F4 FO
St Edmund's School, Canterbury
   Entry age: 11+, 13+, 16+   + F1 F2 F3 F4 FO H
St Lawrence College Junior School,
   Ramsgate   + E F1 F2 F3 F4 H T
St Lawrence College, Ramsgate   + E F1 F2 F3 F4 H T
St Michael's School, Sevenoaks   H
Sevenoaks Preparatory School, Sevenoaks   T
Sevenoaks School, Sevenoaks Entry age: 11+   H
Solefield School, Sevenoaks   H T
Sutton Valence School, Maidstone
   Entry age: 11+, 13+, 16   H T
Tonbridge School, Tonbridge Entry age: 13+,
   14+, 16+   H
Walthamstow Hall, Sevenoaks Entry age: 11+,
   13+, 16+   + E H
Wellesley House School, Broadstairs   + H T
Yardley Court, Tonbridge   H

LANCASHIRE

Arnold School, Blackpool   H
Beech House School, Rochdale   H
Bolton School (Boys' Division), Bolton   H
Bolton School (Girls' Division), Bolton
   Entry age: 11, 16   H
Bury Grammar School, Bury   H
Bury Grammar School Girls, Bury   H
Heathland College, Accrington   H
The Hulme Grammar School for Girls, Oldham   H
Kingswood College at Scarisbrick Hall, Ormskirk   H T
Kirkham Grammar School, Preston   H
Moorland School, Clitheroe   F1 F2 F3 F4
The Oldham Hulme Grammar School, Oldham   H
Queen Elizabeth's Grammar School, Blackburn
   Entry age: 11+   H
Rossall Junior School, Fleetwood   + F3
Rossall School, Fleetwood Entry age: 11   + F1 F2 F3
St Anne's College Grammar School,
   Lytham St Annes   F1 F2 F3 F4 FO
Sedbergh Junior School, Lancaster   F1 F2 F3 F4 H
Stonyhurst College, Clitheroe   H

LEICESTERSHIRE

Leicester Grammar School, Leicester
   Entry age: 11, 18   H
Leicester High School For Girls, Leicester   H
Loughborough Grammar School, Loughborough
   Entry age: 10–18   + F1 F2 F3 F4 H

Loughborough High School, Loughborough   H
Manor House School, Ashby-de-la-Zouch   H
Ratcliffe College, Leicester   F1 F2 F3 F4
St Crispin's School (Leicester) Ltd., Leicester
   Entry age: 3+, 7+, 13+, 16+   H
Stoneygate School, Leicester   + E H

LINCOLNSHIRE

Fen School, Sleaford Entry age: 4–5   E F1 F2 F3 F4
Kirkstone House School, Bourne   H
Maypole House School, Alford   H
St Hugh's School, Woodhall Spa   F1 F2 F3 F4 T
Stamford High School, Stamford   H
Stamford School, Stamford   H
Witham Hall, Bourne   H T

NORTH EAST LINCOLNSHIRE

St. James' School, Grimsby   + F1 F2 F4 FO H T

NORTH LINCOLNSHIRE

Brigg Preparatory School, Brigg   +

LONDON

Albemarle Independent College, W1K
   Entry age: 14+, 19+   H
Alleyn's School, SE22   H
The American School in London, NW8   H
Arnold House School, NW8   H
The Arts Educational School, W4   H
Ashbourne Independent Sixth Form College,
   W8   + FO H M T
Ashbourne Middle School, W8   + F4 FO H M T
Bales College, W10   H
Belmont (Mill Hill Preparatory School), NW7   H
Blackheath High School GDST, SE3   H
Channing School, N6   H
City of London School, EC4V Entry age: 11+,
   13+, 16+   H T
City of London School for Girls, EC2Y   H
Colfe's School, SE12   H
Collingham Independent GCSE and Sixth Form
   College, SW5   FO H T
Dallington School, EC1V   H
Davies Laing and Dick, W1U   H
Dolphin School (Including Noah's Ark Nursery
   Schools), SW11   + E H
Dulwich College, SE21 Entry age: 11, 13   H
Dulwich College Preparatory School, SE21
   Entry age: 7–8   H
Ealing College Upper School, W13   H
Emanuel School, SW11   H
Forest School, E17   +
Francis Holland School, NW1   + H
Francis Holland School, SW1W
   Entry age: 11+   + E FO H
Garden House School, SW3   H
The Godolphin and Latymer School, W6   H

Hampstead College of Fine Arts, Independent
    College, NW3   H
Hampstead Hill Pre-Preparatory & Nursery
    School, NW3 Entry age: 4+   H
Hereward House School, NW3   +
Highgate School, N6 Entry age: 11+, 13+   H
Hill House International Junior School, SW1X   T
Hurlingham Private School, SW15   H
International School of London, W3   H
James Allen's Girls' School, SE22   H
Kerem School, N2   H
King Fahad Academy, W3   H
King's College Junior School, SW19   H
King's College School, SW19   H
Knightsbridge School, SW1X   H
Lansdowne College, W2 Entry age: 14+, 16+   H
Latymer Upper School, W6   H
Lyndhurst House Preparatory School, NW3   H
Mander Portman Woodward, SW7   FO T
More House, SW1X   H
Naima Jewish Preparatory School, NW6   H
The Norwegian School, SW20   F1 F2 F3 F4 FO
Notting Hill and Ealing High School GDST, W13   H
Palmers Green High School, N21 Entry age: 11+   H
The Pointer School, SE3   + E F1 F2 F3 H
Putney High School GDST, SW15   H
Queen's College, W1G   H
Riverston School, SE12   + H
The Roche School, SW18   H
Royal Ballet School, WC2E   H
The Royal School, Hampstead, NW3
    Entry age: 3–18   F1 F3 F4 H
St Benedict's School, W5 Entry age: 11+   H
St James Independent School for Boys, W14   H
St James Independent School for Senior Girls, W14   H
St James Independent School for Girls (Juniors), W14   H
St Johns Wood Pre-Preparatory School, NW8   H
St Margaret's School, NW3   H
St Mary's School Hampstead, NW3   H
St Paul's Cathedral School, EC4M   H
St Paul's Girls' School, W6   H
St Paul's Preparatory School, SW13   H
St Paul's School, SW13   H
Sarum Hall, NW3   H
Sinclair House School, SW6   H
South Hampstead High School, NW3   H
Streatham and Clapham High School, SW16
    Entry age: 11, 13, 16   H
Sydenham High School GDST, SE26   H
Sylvia Young Theatre School, NW1 Entry age: 10–14   H
Thames Christian College, SW11   + E
University College School, NW3   H
Westminster Cathedral Choir School, SW1P   H
Westminster School, SW1P   H
Westminster Tutors, SW7   H
Westminster Under School, SW1P   H
The White House Prep & Woodentops Kindergarten,
    SW12   H
Willington School, SW19   H
Woodside Park International School, N11   H

GREATER MANCHESTER

Abbey College, Manchester   M
Bridgewater School, Manchester Entry age: 11   H
The Manchester Grammar School, Manchester
    Entry age: 11   H
Manchester High School for Girls, Manchester
    Entry age: 11   H
Monton Prep School with Montessori Nurseries,
    Eccles   H T
St Bede's College, Manchester   H
William Hulme's Grammar School, Manchester   H
Withington Girls' School, Manchester   H

MERSEYSIDE

Avalon Preparatory School, Wirral   H
Birkenhead High School GDST, Wirral   H
Birkenhead School, Wirral   H
Highfield School, Birkenhead   H
Kingsmead School, Wirral   + E F1 F2 F3 F4 H
Liverpool College, Liverpool   + E F1 F2 F3 F4 H M
Merchant Taylors' School, Liverpool   H
Merchant Taylors' School for Girls, Liverpool   H
St Mary's College, Liverpool   H
Streatham House School, Liverpool   H
Sunnymede School, Southport   H T
Tower Dene Preparatory School, Southport
    Entry age: 5   F1 F2 F3 F4 FO H M T

MIDDLESEX

ACS Hillingdon International School, Hillingdon   + H
Alpha Preparatory School, Harrow   T
Halliford School, Shepperton   H
Hampton School, Hampton Entry age: 11+, 13   H T
Harrow School, Harrow on the Hill   + H
Heathfield School, Pinner   H
The John Lyon School, Harrow   H
The Lady Eleanor Holles School, Hampton   H
The Mall School, Twickenham   H
Merchant Taylors' School, Northwood   H T
Newland House School, Twickenham   H
North London Collegiate, Edgware   H
Quainton Hall School, Harrow Entry age: 4+   H T
St David's School, Ashford   F1 F2 F3 H
St Helen's School, Northwood   F1 F2 F3 F4 H
St James Independent School for Boys (Senior),
    Twickenham   H
Staines Preparatory School, Staines   H
Sunflower Montessori School, Twickenham   E

NORFOLK

Beeston Hall School, Cromer   H
Glebe House School, Hunstanton   + T
Gresham's Preparatory School, Holt   F1 F2 F3 F4 H
Gresham's School, Holt   H
Hethersett Old Hall School, Norwich   + F1 F2 F3 F4
Langley Preparatory School & Nursery,
    Norwich   F1 F2 F3 F4 H

Langley School, Norwich Entry age: 10+,
  11+, 13+, 16+   E F1 F2 F3 F4 FO H
The New Eccles Hall School,
  Norwich   + F1 F2 F3 F4 H
Norwich High School for Girls GDST, Norwich   H
Norwich School, Norwich Entry age: 11+, 12+, 16+   H
Riddlesworth Hall, Diss   F1 F2 F3 F4 H
Sacred Heart Convent School, Swaffham   E H T
Taverham Hall, Norwich   F1 F2 F3 F4
Thetford Grammar School, Thetford   H
Wood Dene School, Norwich   H

NORTHAMPTONSHIRE

Beachborough School, Brackley   H
Bosworth Independent College,
  Northampton   F1 F2 F3 F4 H
Great Houghton Preparatory School,
  Northampton   + H T
Maidwell Hall School, Northampton   F2 F4
Northampton High School, Northampton
  Entry age: 11+   H
Northamptonshire Grammar School, Pitsford   H
Oundle School, Nr Peterborough   H T
Quinton House School, Northampton   H
St Peter's School, Kettering   H

NORTHUMBERLAND

Longridge Towers School,
  Berwick-upon-Tweed   F1 F2 F3 F4 H
Mowden Hall School, Stocksfield   F1 F2 F3 F4 H T

NOTTINGHAMSHIRE

Bramcote Lorne School, Retford   + H
Grosvenor School, Nottingham   + F1 F2 F3 F4
The King's School, Nottingham   H
Nottingham High Junior School, Nottingham   H
Nottingham High School, Nottingham
  Entry age: 11 + 16   H
Nottingham High School for Girls GDST,
  Nottingham   H
Ranby House School, Retford
  Entry age: 11+   F1 F2 F3 F4
Rodney School, Newark   H
Trent College, Nottingham   F1 F2 F3 F4 H
Wellow House School, Newark   H
Worksop College, Worksop   + E F1 F2 H

OXFORDSHIRE

Abingdon School, Abingdon   H
Bloxham School, Banbury   + E F1 F2 F3 F4 H T
The Carrdus School, Banbury Entry age: 3–11   H T
Cherwell College, Oxford   F1 F2 F3 H
Cokethorpe School, Witney   H
Cranford House School, Wallingford   H
Dragon School, Oxford   H
Emmanuel Christian School, Oxford Entry age: 5   H

Headington School, Oxford Entry age: 11+,
  12+, 13+, 16+   +
Josca's Preparatory School, Abingdon   H
Kingham Hill School,
  Chipping Norton   + E F1 F2 F3 F4 FO H T
Magdalen College School, Oxford   H
The Manor Preparatory School, Abingdon   H
Our Lady's Convent Senior School, Abingdon   H
Oxford High School GDST, Oxford   H
Oxford Tutorial College, Oxford   H
Radley College, Abingdon   H
Rye St Antony School, Oxford   F1 F2 F3 F4
St Andrew's, Wantage   H
St Clare's, Oxford, Oxford   H
St Edward's School, Oxford   + F1 F2 F3 F4
St Mary's School, Wantage   + F1 F2 F3 F4 H
The School of St Helen & St Katharine, Abingdon   H
Sibford School, Banbury   F1 F2 F3 F4 H
Windrush Valley School, Chipping Norton   H
Wychwood School, Oxford   H

RUTLAND

Oakham School, Oakham   H
Uppingham School, Uppingham   H

SHROPSHIRE

Adcote School for Girls, Shrewsbury   + F1 F2 F3 F4 H
Bedstone College, Bucknell   H
Dower House School, Bridgnorth   H
Ellesmere College, Ellesmere   + H T
Kingsland Grange, Shrewsbury   H T
Moor Park School, Ludlow   F1 F2 F3 F4 H
Moreton Hall School, Oswestry
  Entry age: 11+, 13+, 16+   E F1 F2 F3 F4 FO H T
Oswestry School, Oswestry   F1 F2 F3 H T
Oswestry School Bellan House,
  Oswestry   + F1 F2 F3 F4 T
Packwood Haugh School,
  Shrewsbury   + F1 F2 F3 F4 H T
Prestfelde Preparatory School,
  Shrewsbury   F1 F2 F3 F4 H T
Shrewsbury High School GDST, Shrewsbury   H
Shrewsbury School, Shrewsbury   H
Wrekin College, Telford   F1 F2 F3 F4 H T

SOMERSET

All Hallows, Shepton Mallet Entry age: 11+   H
Bruton School for Girls, Bruton   F1 F2 F3 F4 H
Chard School, Chard   H
Downside School, Bath Entry age: 11+, 13+, 16+   F3 H
Hazlegrove (King's Bruton Preparatory School),
  Yeovil   F1 F2 F3 F4 H
King's Bruton, Bruton   + F2 F4 H
King's College, Taunton   + E F1 F2 F3 H
King's Hall, Taunton   + F1 F2 F3 F4
Millfield Preparatory School, Glastonbury
  Entry age: 7–13   F1 F4 H
Millfield School, Street   F1 F2 F3 F4 H

The Park School, Yeovil
Entry age: 8–18 + E F1 F2 F3 F4
Perrott Hill School, Crewkerne + F1 F2 F3 F4 FO H T
Queen's College, Taunton F1 F2 F3 F4 H
Queen's College Junior and Pre-Preparatory
Schools, Taunton + F1 F2 F3 F4 H
Taunton Preparatory School, Taunton
Entry age: 11 + F1 F2 F3 F4 H
Taunton School, Taunton E F1 F2 F3 F4
Wellington School, Wellington
Entry age: 10+, 11+, 13+, 16+ F1 F2 F3 F4 H T
Wells Cathedral Junior School, Wells + H
Wells Cathedral School, Wells F1 F2 F3 F4 H

BATH & NORTH EAST SOMERSET

King Edward's School, Bath, Bath H
Kingswood Preparatory School, Bath + F1 F2 F3 F4
Kingswood School, Bath + E F1 F2 F3 F4 FO H
Monkton Combe Junior School, Bath E
Monkton Combe School, Bath + E F1 F2 F3 F4 H T
Paragon School, Prior Park College Junior, Bath H
Prior Park College, Bath F1 F2 F3 F4 H
The Royal High School, Bath
Entry age: 11+,16+ F1 F2 F3 F4 H

NORTH SOMERSET

Sidcot School, Winscombe H

STAFFORDSHIRE

Abbots Bromley School for Girls,
Abbots Bromley + F1 F3 F4 H
Brooklands School & Little Brooklands Nursery,
Stafford H
Chase Academy, Cannock F1 F2 F3 F4 H
Denstone College, Uttoxeter + F1 F2 F3 F4 H T
Edenhurst School, Newcastle-under-Lyme + T
Lichfield Cathedral School, Lichfield
Entry age: 3, 7 + F1 F2 F3 F4 H
Newcastle-under-Lyme School,
Newcastle-under-Lyme H
St Dominic's Priory School, Stone H
St Dominic's School, Stafford H
Stafford Grammar School, Stafford H
Yarlet School, Stafford Entry age: 7 F1 F2 F3 F4 H T

STOCKTON-ON-TEES

Teesside Preparatory and High School, Eaglescliffe H
Yarm School, Yarm Entry age: 7+, 11+, 16+ H

SUFFOLK

Amberfield School, Ipswich H
Barnardiston Hall Preparatory School,
Haverhill + F1 F2 F3 F4
Culford School, Bury St Edmunds F1 F2 F3 F4 H
Framlingham College, Woodbridge F1 F2 F3 F4 H

Framlingham College Preparatory School,
Brandeston F1 F2 F3 F4 H
Hillcroft Preparatory School, Stowmarket H
Ipswich High School GDST, Ipswich
Entry age: 11–18 H
Ipswich School, Ipswich Entry age: 11,
13, 16 F1 F3 F4 H
Moreton Hall Preparatory School,
Bury St Edmunds F1 F2 F3 F4 H T
Old Buckenham Hall School, Ipswich + E F1 F2 F3 F4
Orwell Park, Ipswich F1 F2 F3 F4 H T
The Royal Hospital School, Ipswich
Entry age: 11–14, 16 F1 F2 F3 F4 H
Saint Felix School, Southwold F1 F3 F4 FO H T
St Joseph's College, Ipswich H
Stoke College, Sudbury H
Woodbridge School, Woodbridge H

SURREY

Aberdour, Tadworth H
ACS Cobham International School, Cobham + H
ACS Egham International School, Egham + H
Aldro School, Godalming H
Amesbury, Hindhead T
Box Hill School, Dorking + F1 F2 F3 F4 H T
Bramley School, Tadworth Entry age: 7+ H
Cambridge Tutors College, Croydon H
Canbury School, Kingston-upon-Thames H
Caterham Preparatory School, Caterham
Entry age: 10+ + H
Caterham School, Caterham + F1 F2 F3 F4 FO H
Charterhouse, Godalming H
Coworth-Flexlands School, Woking +
Cranleigh School, Cranleigh H T
Croham Hurst School, South Croydon
Entry age: 11+ 16+ H
Croydon High School GDST, South Croydon H
Drayton House School, Guildford H
Duke of Kent School, Ewhurst
Entry age: 7+, 10+, 11+ F1 F2 F3 F4
Dunottar School, Reigate H
Edgeborough, Farnham F1 F2 F3 F4 H
Epsom College, Epsom Entry age: 13+, 16+ M
Essendene Lodge School, Caterham H
Ewell Castle School, Epsom H
Feltonfleet School, Cobham H
Frensham Heights School, Farnham H
Glenesk School, Leatherhead H
Greenacre School for Girls, Banstead H
Guildford High School, Guildford
Entry age: 11+, 16+ + H
Halstead Preparatory School, Woking H
Haslemere Preparatory School, Haslemere T
Hawley Place School, Camberley H
The Hawthorns School, Redhill + H
Hazelwood School, Oxted Entry age: 7+, 11+ H
Holy Cross Preparatory School,
Kingston-upon-Thames H T
King Edward's School Witley, Godalming
Entry age: 11–18 + E F1 F2 F3 F4 H T
King's House School, Richmond H
Kingston Grammar School, Kingston-upon-Thames H

Kingswood House School, Epsom	+ H T
Lingfield Notre Dame School, Lingfield	
Entry age: 11+	H
Lyndhurst School, Camberley	H
Marymount International School,	
Kingston-upon-Thames	H
New Lodge School, Dorking	H
Notre Dame Preparatory School, Cobham	H
Oakfield School, Woking Entry age: 7	H T
Oakwood School & Nursery, Purley	H
Prior's Field School, Godalming	F1 F2 F3 F4 H T
Reed's School, Cobham	H
Reigate Grammar School, Reigate	H
Ripley Court School, Woking Entry age: 7	H T
Royal Alexandra and Albert School, Reigate	+ H
Royal Grammar School, Guildford	H
Royal Russell School, Croydon	F1 F2 F3 F4 FO
The Royal School, Haslemere	
Entry age: 11+, 13+, 16+	+ F1 F2 F3 F4 H T
St. Andrew's (Woking) School Trust, Woking	H
St David's School, Purley	H
St Edmund's School, Hindhead	H T
St Hilary's School, Godalming	H
St Ives School, Haslemere	H
St John's School, Leatherhead Entry age: 13+, 16+	+
St Teresa's School, Dorking	T
Sanderstead Junior School, South Croydon	H
Shrewsbury House School, Surbiton	T
Sir William Perkins's School, Chertsey	H
Stowford College, Sutton	E H
Surbiton High School, Kingston-upon-Thames	+ H
Sutton High School GDST, Sutton	
Entry age: 11+, 16+	H
TASIS The American School in England, Thorpe	H
Trinity School, Croydon Entry age: 10+, 11+, 13+	H
Warlingham Park School, Croydon	H
Whitgift School, South Croydon	
Entry age: 10–13, 16	H
Wispers School for Girls, Haslemere	F1 F2 F3 F4 H
Woodcote House School, Windlesham	H T
Yehudi Menuhin School, Cobham	H

EAST SUSSEX

Ashdown House School, Forest Row	+ T
Battle Abbey School, Battle	F1 F2 F3 F4 M T
Bricklehurst Manor Preparatory, Wadhurst	H
Brighton and Hove High School GDST, Brighton	H
Brighton College, Brighton	+ F3 H T
Buckswood School, Hastings	H
Eastbourne College, Eastbourne	H
The Fold School, Hove	H
Lancing College Preparatory School at Mowden,	
Hove	+ H
Moira House Girls School,	
Eastbourne	E F1 F2 F3 F4 H T
Moira House School, Eastbourne	H T
Newlands School, Seaford	F1 F2 F3 F4
Roedean School, Brighton Entry age: 11+,	
12+, 13+, 16+	H
Sacred Heart R.C. Primary School, Wadhurst	H
St Andrew's School, Eastbourne	F1 F2 F3 F4
St Aubyns School, Brighton	+ H T

St Christopher's School, Hove	H
St Leonards-Mayfield School, Mayfield	H
St Mary's Hall, Brighton	+ E F1 F2 F3 F4 H
Vinehall School, Robertsbridge	F1 F2 F3 F4 H

WEST SUSSEX

Ardingly College, Haywards Heath	H
Ardingly College Junior School, Haywards Heath	H
Arundale Preparatory School, Pulborough	H
Burgess Hill School for Girls, Burgess Hill	H
Christ's Hospital, Horsham	+ F1 F2 F4 H
Conifers School, Midhurst	H T
Copthorne Prep School, Copthorne	H T
Cottesmore School, Pease Pottage	H
Dorset House School, Pulborough	FO H T
Farlington School, Horsham	+ F1 F2 F3 H
Fonthill Lodge, East Grinstead	H
Great Ballard School, Chichester	F1 F2 F3 F4
Great Walstead, Haywards Heath	+ E H T
Handcross Park School, Haywards Heath	
Entry age: 7–11	H T
Lancing College, Lancing	H T
Lavant House, Chichester	H
Our Lady of Sion School, Worthing	H
Pennthorpe School, Horsham	H
The Prebendal School, Chichester Entry age: 7	H
St Peter's School, Burgess Hill	H
Seaford College, Petworth Entry age: 10+,	
11+, 13+	F1 F2 F3 F4 H
Shoreham College, Shoreham-by-Sea	+ H
Slindon College, Arundel Entry age: 10	F1 F2 F3 F4 H
Sompting Abbotts School, Sompting	T
Stoke Brunswick, East Grinstead	H
Tavistock & Summerhill School, Haywards Heath	H
The Towers Convent School, Steyning	H T
Windlesham House, Pulborough	F1 F2 F3 F4 FO H

TYNE AND WEAR

Central Newcastle High School GDST,	
Newcastle upon Tyne Entry age: 11+, 16+	H
Dame Allan's Boys School, Newcastle upon Tyne	H
Dame Allan's Girls School, Newcastle upon Tyne	H
Grindon Hall Christian School, Sunderland	+ E T
The King's School, Tynemouth Entry age: 4, 11	+ E H
La Sagesse School, Newcastle upon Tyne	H
Newcastle Preparatory School, Newcastle upon Tyne	H
Newcastle Upon Tyne Church High School,	
Newcastle upon Tyne	+
Sunderland High School, Sunderland	E H
Westfield School, Newcastle upon Tyne	H

WARWICKSHIRE

Bilton Grange, Rugby Entry age: 8+	+ F1 F2 F3 F4 H T
King's High School, Warwick, Warwick	H
The Kingsley School, Leamington Spa	H
Rugby School, Rugby	H
Warwick School, Warwick	H

WEST MIDLANDS

Abbey College, Birmingham	H
Bablake School, Coventry	H
Birchfield School, Wolverhampton	F4 H T
The Blue Coat School, Birmingham	H
Edgbaston High School for Girls, Birmingham	H
Elmhurst School for Dance, Birmingham	F1 F3 F4 H
Eversfield Preparatory School, Solihull	+
Highclare School, Birmingham	H
King Edward VI High School for Girls, Birmingham	H
King Edward's School, Birmingham	
Entry age: 11+, 16+	H
King Henry VIII School, Coventry	H
Newbridge Preparatory School, Wolverhampton	+
Pattison College, Coventry	H
Priory School, Birmingham	H
The Royal Wolverhampton Junior School,	
Wolverhampton	F1 F3 H
The Royal Wolverhampton School, Wolverhampton	
Entry age: 11+	F1 F2 F3 F4 H
St George's School, Edgbaston, Birmingham	+ H
Solihull School, Solihull	+
Tettenhall College, Wolverhampton	+ F1 F2 F3 F4
West House School, Birmingham	H T
Wolverhampton Grammar School, Wolverhampton	
Entry age: 11+, 13+, 16+	H

WILTSHIRE

Chafyn Grove School, Salisbury	F1 F2 F3 F4 H T
The Godolphin School, Salisbury	F1 F2 F3 F4
La Retraite Swan, Salisbury	H
Leaden Hall School, Salisbury	+
Marlborough College, Marlborough	
Entry age: 13+, 16+	+
Norman Court Preparatory School,	
Salisbury	F1 F2 F3 F4
Pinewood School, Shrivenham	H
Prior Park Preparatory School, Cricklade	F1 F2 F3 F4
St Francis School, Pewsey	H
St Mary's School, Calne	+ H
South Hills School, Salisbury	H
Stonar School, Melksham	F1 F2 F3 F4
Warminster School, Warminster	F1 F2 F3 F4 H

WORCESTERSHIRE

Abberley Hall, Worcester Entry age: 8+	F1 F2 F3 F4 H
The Abbey College, Malvern Wells	H
The Alice Ottley School, Worcester	+
Bromsgrove Preparatory School,	
Bromsgrove	F1 F2 F3 F4 H
Bromsgrove School, Bromsgrove	F1 F2 F3 F4 H T
The Downs School, Malvern	+ F1 F2 F3 F4 FO H M T
The Elms, Malvern	F1 F2 F3 F4 H T
Hartlebury School, Kidderminster	H
King's Hawford, Worcester	+
The King's School, Worcester	H
Malvern College, Malvern	F1 F2 F3 F4 H T
Malvern College Preparatory and Pre-Prep School,	
Malvern	F1 F2 F3 FO
Malvern St James, Great Malvern	
Entry age: 11+, 12+, 13+, 16+	F1 F2 F3 F4 H T
Moffats School, Bewdley	+ E F1 F2 F3 F4 FO H M T
River School, Worcester	H
Royal Grammar School Worcester, Worcester	H
St Mary's Convent School, Worcester	
Entry age: 11+, 16+	H
Winterfold House, Kidderminster	H

EAST RIDING OF YORKSHIRE

Hull Collegiate School, Anlaby Entry age: 11	H
Hymers College, Hull	H
Pocklington School, Pocklington	F1 F2 F3 F4 H

NORTH YORKSHIRE

Ampleforth College, York	H
Ashville College, Harrogate	
Entry age: 7	+ E F1 F2 F3 F4 H T
Aysgarth Preparatory School, Bedale	F1 F2 F3 F4 H T
Belmont Grosvenor School, Harrogate	+ F1 F2 F3 F4
Bootham School, York Entry age: 11+,	
13+, 16+	H
Bramcote School, Scarborough	E F1 F2 F3 F4 FO H T
Catteral Hall School, Settle	F1 F2 F3 F4 T
Cundall Manor School, York	F1 F2 F3 F4 FO
Giggleswick School, Settle	
Entry age: 13, 16	F1 F2 F3 F4 H T
Harrogate Ladies' College, Harrogate	+ E F1 F3 F4 H T
Harrogate Tutorial College,	
Harrogate	F1 F2 F3 F4 FO H T
Highfield Preparatory School,	
Harrogate	+ E F1 F2 F3 F4 T
Howsham Hall, York	+ H T
Malsis School, Skipton	F1 F2 F3 F4 H T
The Mount School, York	H
Queen Ethelburga's College, York	
Entry age: 11	+ F1 F2 F3 F4 FO M T
Queen Margaret's School, York	+ F1 F2 F3
Queen Mary's School, Thirsk	+ F1 F2 F3 F4 H T
Read School, Selby Entry age: 11+, 13+, 16+	H
Ripon Cathedral Choir School, Ripon	F1 F2 F3 F4 H
St Martin's Ampleforth, York	F1 F2 F3 F4
St Peter's School, York Entry age: 13,	
14, 16	+ F1 F2 F3 F4 H
Scarborough College & Lisvane School,	
Scarborough	F2 F3 F4 H
Terrington Hall, York	+ F1 F2 F3 F4 T
Woodleigh School, Malton	F1 F2 F3

SOUTH YORKSHIRE

Ashdell Preparatory School, Sheffield Entry age: 4	H
Birkdale School, Sheffield	+ H
Brantwood School, Sheffield	H
Handsworth Christian School, Sheffield	H
Rudston Preparatory School, Rotherham	H T
Sheffield High School GDST, Sheffield	
Entry age: 11–18	H
Westbourne School, Sheffield	H

WEST YORKSHIRE

Ackworth School, Pontefract	H
Alcuin School, Leeds	H
Batley Grammar School, Batley	H
Bradford Girls' Grammar School, Bradford	H
Bradford Grammar School, Bradford	
Entry age: 11+, 13+, 16+	H
Bronte House School, Bradford	
Entry age: 7+, 8+	F1 F2 F3 H
The Froebelian School, Leeds	H
Fulneck School, Pudsey	+ E F1 F2 F3 F4 H
Gateways School, Leeds	H
Hipperholme Grammar School, Halifax	H
Huddersfield Grammar School, Huddersfield	H

Leeds Girls' High School, Leeds	H
Leeds Grammar School, Leeds Entry age: 11+,16+	H
Moorlands School, Leeds	H
Queen Elizabeth Grammar School, Wakefield	H
Richmond House School, Leeds Entry age: 7/8	H T
Rishworth School, Rishworth	H
Shaw House School, Bradford	H T
Silcoates School, Wakefield	
Entry age: 11	+ E F1 F2 F3 F4 FO H M T
Wakefield Girls' High School, Wakefield	
Entry age: 11+-16+	H
Woodhouse Grove School,	
Apperley Bridge	+ F1 F2 F3 F4 H

NORTHERN IRELAND

COUNTY ANTRIM

Cabin Hill School, Belfast	F3
Methodist College, Belfast	+
Royal Belfast Academical Institution, Belfast	H

COUNTY ARMAGH

The Royal School, Armagh	+

COUNTY DOWN

The Holywood Rudolf Steiner School, Holywood	H

COUNTY LONDONDERRY

Coleraine Academical Institution, Coleraine	+ E

COUNTY TYRONE

The Royal School Dungannon, Dungannon Entry age:	
11–16	+ E F1 F2 F3 F4

SCOTLAND

ABERDEENSHIRE

Aberdeen Waldorf School, Aberdeen	H
International School of Aberdeen, Aberdeen	H
Robert Gordons College, Aberdeen	H
St Margaret's School for Girls, Aberdeen	H

ANGUS

The High School of Dundee, Dundee	H
Lathallan School, Montrose	F1 F2 F3 F4 H

SOUTH AYRSHIRE

Wellington School, Ayr	H

FIFE

St Leonards School & VIth Form College,	
St Andrews	+ F1 F2 F3 F4 H T
Sea View Private School, Kirkcaldy	H

GLASGOW

Craigholme School Entry age: 12	H
The Glasgow Academy Entry age: 11+	+ H
The High School of Glasgow	H
Hutchesons' Grammar School	H
St Aloysius' College	H

LOTHIAN

Belhaven Hill, Dunbar Entry age: 8+	H T
Cargilfield, Edinburgh	F1 F2 F3 F4
Clifton Hall School, Edinburgh	
Entry age: 3	F1 F2 F3 F4 H
The Compass School, Haddington	H
The Edinburgh Academy, Edinburgh	H
Fettes College, Edinburgh	F1 F3 F4 H T
George Heriot's School, Edinburgh	H
George Watson's College, Edinburgh	H
Loretto School, Musselburgh	F1 F2 F3 F4 H T
The Mary Erskine School, Edinburgh	H
Merchiston Castle School, Edinburgh	F1 F2 F3 F4
St George's School for Girls, Edinburgh	H
St Margaret's School, Edinburgh	F1 F2 F3 F4 H
Stewart's Melville College, Edinburgh	H

MORAYSHIRE

Gordonstoun School, Elgin Entry age: 9	F1 F2 H
Rosebrae School, Elgin	H

PERTHSHIRE

Ardvreck School, Crieff	F1 F2 F3 F4
Craigclowan Preparatory School, Perth	H T
Glenalmond College, Perth	E F1 F2 F3 F4 H T

Kilgraston, Perth	F1 F2 F3 F4 H T
Morrison's Academy, Crieff	H
Queen Victoria School, Dunblane	F1 F2 F3 F4
Strathallan School, Perth	F1 F2 F3 F4 H T

STIRLING

Beaconhurst School	H

WALES

BRIDGEND

St John's School, Porthcawl	H

CARDIFF

The Cathedral School	H
Elm Tree House	H
Howell's School, Llandaff GDST	H

CARMARTHENSHIRE

Llandovery College, Llandovery Entry age: 11+, 17+	E F1 F2 F3 F4 H T
St Michael's School, Llanelli	H

CONWY

Lyndon Preparatory School, Colwyn Bay	E F1 F2 F3 F4 H
Rydal Penrhos Senior School, Colwyn Bay	F3
St David's College, Llandudno	+ E F1 F2 F3 F4 H

DENBIGHSHIRE

Howell's School, Denbigh Entry age: 11	F1 F2 F3 F4 FO
Ruthin School, Ruthin Entry age: 5	F1 F2 F3 F4 H

GWYNEDD

Hillgrove School, Bangor	E

MONMOUTHSHIRE

Haberdashers' Monmouth School For Girls, Monmouth	F1 F2 F3 F4 H
Llangattock School, Monmouth	H
Monmouth School, Monmouth Entry age: 11, 13, 16	F1 F2 F3 F4 H T
St John's-on-the-Hill, Chepstow	F1 F2 F3 F4 H

NEWPORT

Rougemont School	H

PEMBROKESHIRE

Netherwood School, Saundersfoot	H

POWYS

Christ College, Brecon Entry age: 11+, 13+, 16	+ F1 F3 F4 H T

SWANSEA

Ffynone House School	H
Ffynone House School Trust	H

4.3

Specialist Schools

Schools in the directory which specialize in the theatre, dance or music are listed below. For full details about entrance requirements and the curriculum, parents are advised to contact schools direct.

Arts Schools

The Arts Educational School, Hertfordshire
The Arts Educational Schools, London W4
Barbara Speake Stage School, London W3
The Italia Conti Academy of Theatre Arts, London EC1
Pattison College, Coventry
Ravenscourt Theatre School, London W6
Sylvia Young Theatre School, London NW1

Dance Schools

Elmhurst School for Dance, Birmingham
Hammond School, Chester
Royal Ballet School, London WC2E
Stonelands School of Ballet & Theatre Arts, East Sussex
The Urdang Academy of Ballet, London WC2

Music Schools

Chetham's School of Music, Manchester
The Purcell School, Bushey
St Mary's Music School, Edinburgh
Yehudi Menuhin School, Cobham

4.4

Single-Sex Schools

Note: * denotes a co-educational school that educates boys and girls separately, either within a specific age range or throughout the school. For details consult the school listings in Part 2.

BOYS

ENGLAND

BEDFORDSHIRE

Bedford Preparatory School, Bedford	7–13
Bedford School, Bedford	7–18

BERKSHIRE

*Brockhurst and Marlston House Schools, Newbury	3–13
Claires Court School, Maidenhead	11–16 (Co-ed VIth Form)
Claires Court Schools, Ridgeway, Maidenhead	4–11
Crosfields School, Reading	4–13
Elstree School, Reading	3–13 (Girls 3–7)
Eton College, Windsor	13–18
Horris Hill School, Newbury	7–13
Ludgrove, Wokingham	8–13
The Oratory School, Reading	11–18
Papplewick School, Ascot	7–13
Reading Blue Coat School, Reading	11–18 (Co-ed VIth Form)
St Edward's School, Reading	4–13
St John's Beaumont, Windsor	4–13
*St Michaels School, Newbury	7–18 (Single-sex ed 13–18)
Sunningdale School, Sunningdale	8–13

BRISTOL

Queen Elizabeth's Hospital	7–18

BUCKINGHAMSHIRE

The Beacon School, Amersham	3–13
Caldicott School, Farnham Royal	7–13
Davenies School, Beaconsfield	4–13
Gayhurst School, Gerrards Cross	4–13
Kingscote Pre-Preparatory School, Gerrards Cross	3–7
Thorpe House School, Gerrards Cross	3–16

CHANNEL ISLANDS

Elizabeth College, Guernsey	2–18 (Co-ed VIth Form)
Victoria College, Jersey	11–19
Victoria College Preparatory School, Jersey	7–11

CHESHIRE

Altrincham Preparatory School, Altrincham	4–11
Cheadle Hulme School, Cheadle	4–18
*The King's School, Macclesfield	3–18 (Single-sex ed 11–16)
North Cestrian Grammar School, Altrincham	11–18
The Ryleys, Alderley Edge	3–13
St Ambrose Preparatory School, Altrincham	4–11

DERBYSHIRE

Derby Grammar School for Boys, Derby	7–18

DORSET

Sherborne School, Sherborne	13–18

COUNTY DURHAM

Hurworth House School, Darlington	3–18

ESSEX

*Brentwood School, Brentwood	3–18 (Single-sex ed 11–16)
Cranbrook College, Ilford	4–16
Loyola Preparatory School, Buckhurst Hill	3–11

HAMPSHIRE

The Pilgrims' School, Winchester	7–13

Salesian College, Farnborough   11–18
Winchester College, Winchester   13–18

HERTFORDSHIRE

Aldwickbury School, Harpenden   4–13
*Berkhamsted Collegiate School, Berkhamsted   11–18
   (Single-sex ed 11–16)
Haberdashers' Aske's Boys' School, Elstree   5–18
Lochinver House School, Potters Bar   4–13
Lockers Park, Hemel Hempstead   7–13
Northwood Preparatory School,
   Rickmansworth   4–13 (Girls 3–4)
St Albans School, St Albans   11–18 (Co-ed VIth Form)
St Columba's College, St Albans   4–18
York House School, Rickmansworth   3–13 (Co-ed 2–5)

KENT

Bickley Park School, Bromley   3–13
Darul Uloom London, Chislehurst   11–18
Harenc School Trust, Sidcup   3–11
The New Beacon, Sevenoaks   4–13
Solefield School, Sevenoaks   4–13
Tonbridge School, Tonbridge   13–18
Yardley Court, Tonbridge   7–13

LANCASHIRE

Bolton School (Boys' Division), Bolton   7–18
Bury Grammar School, Bury   7–18
The Oldham Hulme Grammar School, Oldham   7–18
Tashbar School, Salford   2–11

LEICESTERSHIRE

Loughborough Grammar School, Loughborough   10–18

LINCOLNSHIRE

Stamford School, Stamford   11–18

LONDON

Al-Mizan School, E1   6–13
*Al-Sadiq and Al-Zahra Schools, NW6   4–16
Arnold House School, NW8   5–13
Beis Hamedrash Elyon, NW11   11–14
Brondesbury College For Boys, NW6   11–16
City of London School, EC4V   10–18
Clifton Lodge Preparatory School, W5   4–13
Darul Hadis Latifiah, E2   11–19
Donhead Prep School, SW19   4–11
Dulwich College, SE21   7–18
Dulwich College Preparatory School,
   SE21   3–13 (Girls 3–5)
Durston House, W5   4–13
Eaton House School Belgravia, SW1W   4–8
Eaton House The Manor, SW4   2–13
The Falcons School for Boys, W4   3–8

*Forest School, E17   4–18 (Single-sex ed 7–16)
The Hall School, NW3   4–13
Hawkesdown House School, W8   3–8
Hereward House School, NW3   4–13
Keble Preparatory School, N21   4–13
King's College Junior School, SW19   7–13
King's College School, SW19   13–18
London East Academy, E1   7–16
London Islamic School, E1   11–16
Lubavitch House School (Junior Boys), E5   5–13
Lyndhurst House Preparatory School, NW3   4–13
Mechinah Liyeshivah Zichron Moshe, N16   11–16
North Bridge House Upper Prep School, NW1   10–13
Northcote Lodge School, SW11   8–13
Pardes Grammar Boys' School, N3   11–17
St Anthony's Preparatory School, NW3   5–13
St Benedict's School, W5   11–18 (Co-ed VIth Form)
St James Independent School for Boys, W14   4–10
St Paul's Preparatory School, SW13   7–13
St Paul's School, SW13   13–18
St Philip's School, SW7   7–13
Sussex House School, SW1X   8–13
Talmud Torah Bobov Primary School, N16   2–13
Tawhid Boys School, Tawhid Educational Trust,
   N16   9–16
Tower House School, SW14   4–13
University College School, NW3   11–18
University College School Junior Branch, NW3   7–11
Westminster Abbey Choir School, SW1P   8–13
Westminster Cathedral Choir School, SW1P   8–13
Westminster Under School, SW1P   7–13
Wetherby Preparatory School, W11   8–13
Wetherby School, W2   4–8
Willington School, SW19   4–13
Wimbledon Common Preparatory School, SW19   4–8
*Yesodey Hatorah Jewish School, N16   3–16
Yetev Lev Day School for Boys, N16   3–11

GREATER MANCHESTER

Al Jamiah Al Islamiyyah, Bolton   13–16
Kassim Darwish Grammar School for Boys,
   Manchester   11–16
The Manchester Grammar School, Manchester   11–18

MERSEYSIDE

Birkenhead School, Wirral   3–18
Merchant Taylors' School, Liverpool   4–18

MIDDLESEX

Buckingham College Preparatory School, Pinner   4–11
Buckingham College School,
   Harrow   11–18 (Co-ed VIth Form)
Denmead School, Hampton   2–11 (Girls 2–7)
Halliford School, Shepperton   11–19 (Co-ed VIth Form)
Hampton School, Hampton   11–18
Harrow School, Harrow on the Hill   13–18
The John Lyon School, Harrow   11–18
The Mall School, Twickenham   4–13
Merchant Taylors' School, Northwood   11–18

Quainton Hall School, Harrow   4–13
St James Independent School for Boys (Senior),
   Twickenham   10–18
St John's Northwood, Northwood   3–13
St Martin's School, Northwood   3–13

NORFOLK

Norwich School, Norwich   7–18 (Co-ed VIth Form)

NORTHAMPTONSHIRE

Maidwell Hall School,
   Northampton   7–13 (Girls day only)

NOTTINGHAMSHIRE

Al Karam Secondary School, Retford   11–16
Nottingham High Junior School, Nottingham   7–11
Nottingham High School, Nottingham   11–18

OXFORDSHIRE

Abingdon School, Abingdon   11–18
Christ Church Cathedral School,
   Oxford   2–13 (Girls 2–4)
Cothill House Preparatory School, Abingdon   8–13
Josca's Preparatory School, Abingdon   4–13 (Girls 4–7)
Magdalen College School, Oxford   7–18
Moulsford Preparatory School, Wallingford   5–13
New College School, Oxford   4–13
Radley College, Abingdon   13–18
Summer Fields, Oxford   7–13

SHROPSHIRE

Kingsland Grange, Shrewsbury   4–13
Shrewsbury School, Shrewsbury   13–18

SURREY

Aldro School, Godalming   7–13
Charterhouse, Godalming   13–18 (Co-ed VIth Form)
Chinthurst School, Tadworth   3–13
Cranmore School, Leatherhead   3–13
Cumnor House School, South Croydon   4–13
Elmhurst School, South Croydon   4–11
Ewell Castle School, Epsom   3–18 (Co-ed 3–11)
Haslemere Preparatory School, Haslemere   2–14
Homefield School, Sutton   2–13
King's House School, Richmond   4–13
Kingswood House School, Epsom   2–13
Lanesborough, Guildford   3–13
More House School, Farnham   9–18

Parkside School, Cobham   4–13 (Co-ed 2–4)
Priory School, Banstead   2–13
Reed's School, Cobham   11–18 (Co-ed VIth Form)
Rokeby School, Kingston-upon-Thames   4–13
Royal Grammar School, Guildford   11–18
St Edmund's School, Hindhead   2–13 (Co-ed day 2–7)
St John's School, Leatherhead   13–18 (Co-ed VIth Form)
Shrewsbury House School, Surbiton   7–13
Surbiton Preparatory School, Surbiton   4–11
Trinity School, Croydon   10–18
Whitgift School, South Croydon   10–18
Woodcote House School, Windlesham   7–14

WEST SUSSEX

Dorset House School, Pulborough   3–13
*Fonthill Lodge, East
   Grinstead   2–11 (Single-sex ed 8–11)
Slindon College, Arundel   9–16
Worth School, Turners Hill   11–18

TYNE AND WEAR

Dame Allan's Boys School, Newcastle upon Tyne   8–18
   (Co-ed VIth Form)
Newcastle School for Boys, Newcastle upon Tyne   3–13
Royal Grammar School,
   Newcastle upon Tyne   8–18 (Co-ed VIth form)

WARWICKSHIRE

Warwick School, Warwick   7–18

WEST MIDLANDS

*Al Hijrah School, Birmingham   4–11
*Darul Uloom Islamic High School & College,
   Birmingham   -
King Edward's School, Birmingham   11–18
West House School, Birmingham   1–11 (Girls 1–4)

NORTH YORKSHIRE

Aysgarth Preparatory School,
   Bedale   3–13 (Co-ed day 3–8)

SOUTH YORKSHIRE

Birkdale School, Sheffield   4–18 (Co-ed VIth Form)

WEST YORKSHIRE

Ghyll Royd School, Ilkley   2–11
Leeds Grammar School, Leeds   4–18
Olive Secondary, Bradford   11–18
Queen Elizabeth Grammar School, Wakefield   7–18

NORTHERN IRELAND

COUNTY ANTRIM

Cabin Hill School, Belfast   3–13 (Co-ed kindergarten)

Campbell College, Belfast   11–18

Royal Belfast Academical Institution, Belfast   4–18

COUNTY DOWN

Bangor Grammar School, Bangor   11–18

COUNTY LONDONDERRY

Coleraine Academical Institution, Coleraine   11–19

SCOTLAND

LOTHIAN

The Edinburgh Academy, Edinburgh   5–18 (Co-ed VIth Form)

Merchiston Castle School, Edinburgh   8–18

Stewart's Melville College,
  Edinburgh   12–18 (Co-ed VIth Form)

WALES

CONWY

*Rydal Penrhos Senior School,
  Colwyn Bay   11–18 (Single-sex ed 11–16)

MONMOUTHSHIRE

Monmouth School, Monmouth   7–18 (Boarding 11–18)

GIRLS

ENGLAND

BEDFORDSHIRE

Bedford High School, Bedford   7–18
Dame Alice Harpur School, Bedford   7–18
St Andrew's School, Bedford   3–16 (Boys 3–7)

BERKSHIRE

The Abbey School, Reading   3–18
Brigidine School Windsor, Windsor   3–18 (Boys 3–7)
*Brockhurst and Marlston House Schools,
  Newbury   3–13
Claires Court Schools, The College,
  Maidenhead   3–16 (Boys 3–5, co-ed VIth Form)
Downe House, Thatcham   11–18
Heathfield St Mary's School, Ascot   11–18
Highfield School, Maidenhead   3–11
Hurst Lodge School, Ascot   3–18 (Boys 3–7)
Luckley-Oakfield School, Wokingham   11–18
The Marist Senior School, Ascot   11–18
The Marist Preparatory School, Ascot   3–11
Queen Anne's School, Reading   11–18
St Gabriel's, Newbury   3–18 (Boys 3–7)
St George's School, Ascot   11–18
St Joseph's Convent School, Reading   3–18

St Mary's School, Ascot, Ascot   11–18
*St Michaels School,
  Newbury   7–18 (Single-sex ed 13–18)
White House Preparatory School,
  Wokingham   2–11 (Boys 2–4)

BRISTOL

Badminton School   4–18
Colston's Girls' School   10–18
The Red Maids' School   11–18
Redland High School   3–18

BUCKINGHAMSHIRE

Godstowe Preparatory School,
  High Wycombe   3–13 (Boys 3–8)
Heatherton House School, Amersham   3–11 (Boys 2–5)
High March School, Beaconsfield   3–11 (Boys 3–5)
Holy Cross Convent, Gerrards Cross   3–18
Maltman's Green School, Gerrards Cross   3–11
Pipers Corner School, High Wycombe   4–18
St Mary's School, Gerrards Cross   3–18

Thornton College Convent of Jesus and Mary,
  Milton Keynes   2–16 (Boys 2–4)
Wycombe Abbey School, High Wycombe   11–18

CAMBRIDGESHIRE

The Perse School for Girls, Cambridge   7–18
Peterborough High School,
  Peterborough   3–18 (Boys 3–11)
St Mary's Junior School, Cambridge   4–11
St Mary's School, Cambridge   4–18

CHANNEL ISLANDS

Beaulieu Convent School, Jersey   4–18
The Ladies' College, Guernsey   4–18

CHESHIRE

Alderley Edge School for Girls, Alderley Edge   3–18
Bowdon Preparatory School For Girls, Altrincham   2–12
Culcheth Hall, Altrincham   2–16 (Boys 2–4)
*The King's School,
  Macclesfield   3–18 (Single-sex ed 11–16)
Loreto Preparatory School, Altrincham   3–11 (Boys 4–7)
Oriel Bank, Stockport   3–16
The Queen's School, Chester   4–18
Wilmslow Preparatory School, Wilmslow   2–11

CORNWALL

St Joseph's School, Launceston   3–16 (Boys 3–11)
Truro High School, Truro   3–18 (Boys 3–5)

CUMBRIA

Casterton School, Kirkby
  Lonsdale   3–18 (Day boys 3–11)

DERBYSHIRE

Ockbrook School, Derby   3–18

DEVON

The Maynard School, Exeter   7–18
St Margaret's School, Exeter   7–18
Stoodley Knowle School, Torquay   2–18

DORSET

Hanford School, Blandford Forum   7–13
Knighton House, Blandford Forum   3–13 (Day boys 4–7)
St Antony's Leweston School,
  Sherborne   2–18 (Boys 2–11)
St Mary's School, Shaftesbury   9–18
Sherborne School for Girls, Sherborne   11–18
Talbot Heath, Bournemouth   3–18 (Boys 3–7)
Wentworth College, Bournemouth   11–18

COUNTY DURHAM

Durham High School For Girls, Durham   3–18
Polam Hall, Darlington   4–18

ESSEX

Braeside School for Girls, Buckhurst Hill   3–16
*Brentwood School,
  Brentwood   3–18 (Single-sex ed 11–16)
Ilford Ursuline Preparatory School, Ilford   3–11
Park School for Girls, Ilford   7–18
St Hilda's School, Westcliff-on-Sea   2–16 (Boys 2–7)
St Mary's School, Colchester   4–16

GLOUCESTERSHIRE

The Cheltenham Ladies' College, Cheltenham   11–18
Gloucestershire Islamic Secondary
  School For Girls, Gloucester   11–16
Westonbirt School, Tetbury   11–18

HAMPSHIRE

Alton Convent School, Alton   2–18 (Co-ed 2–11)
Farnborough Hill, Farnborough   11–18
Portsmouth High School GDST, Southsea   3–18
St Nicholas' School, Fleet   3–16 (Boys 3–7)
St Swithun's School, Winchester   11–18
Wykeham House School, Fareham   2–16

HEREFORDSHIRE

Haberdashers' Redcap School, Hereford   2–11

HERTFORDSHIRE

Abbot's Hill School,
  Hemel Hempstead   3–16 (Boys 3–7)
*Berkhamsted Collegiate School,
  Berkhamsted   11–18 (Single-sex ed 11–16)
Haberdashers' Aske's School for Girls, Elstree   4–18
The Princess Helena College, Hitchin   11–18
Queenswood School, Hatfield   11–18
Rickmansworth PNEU School, Rickmansworth   3–11
The Royal Masonic School for Girls,
  Rickmansworth   4–18
St Albans High School for Girls, St Albans   4–18
St Francis' College, Letchworth   3–18
St Hilda's School, Bushey   3–11 (Boys 3–5)
St Hilda's School, Harpenden   2–11
St Margaret's School, Bushey   4–18
St Martha's Senior School, Barnet   11–18
Stormont, Potters Bar   4–11

KENT

Babington House School, Chislehurst   3–16 (Boys 3–7)
Baston School, Bromley   2–16
Bedgebury School, Cranbrook   2–18 (Boys day 2–7)

Beechwood Sacred Heart School,
  Tunbridge Wells   3–18 (Boys 3–11)
Benenden School, Cranbrook   11–18
Bromley High School GDST, Bromley   4–18
Cobham Hall, Gravesend   11–18
Combe Bank School, Nr Sevenoaks   3–18
Derwent Lodge School for Girls, Tonbridge   7–11
The Granville School, Sevenoaks   3–11 (Boys 3–5)
Kent College Pembury, Tunbridge Wells   3–18
Walthamstow Hall, Sevenoaks   3–18

LANCASHIRE

Bolton Muslim Girls School, Bolton   11–16
Bolton School (Girls' Division), Bolton   4–18 (Boys 4–7)
Bury Grammar School Girls, Bury   3–18 (Boys 4–7)
The Hulme Grammar School for Girls, Oldham   3–18
Islamiyah School, Blackburn   11–16
Jamea Al Kauthar, Lancaster   11–19
Markazul Uloom, Blackburn   11–19
Rochdale Girls School, Rochdale   11–15
Tauheedul Islam Girls High School, Blackburn 11–16
Westholme School, Blackburn   3–18 (Boys 3–7)

LEICESTERSHIRE

Loughborough High School, Loughborough   11–18
Our Lady's Convent School,
  Loughborough   3–18 (Boys 3–5)

LINCOLNSHIRE

Stamford High School, Stamford   11–18

LONDON

*Al-Sadiq and Al-Zahra Schools, NW6   4–16
Beis Chinuch Lebanos Girls School, N4   2–16
Beis Rochel D'Satmar Girls School, N16   2–17
Beth Jacob Grammar for Girls, NW4   10–16
Blackheath High School GDST, SE3   3–18
Bute House Preparatory School for Girls, W6   4–11
The Cavendish School, NW1   3–11
Channing Junior School, N6   4–11
Channing School, N6   4–18
City of London School for Girls, EC2Y   7–18
The Falcons School for Girls, W5   4–11
Falkner House, SW7   3–11 (Co-ed 3–4)
*Forest School, E17   4–18 (Single-sex ed 7–16)
Francis Holland School, NW1   11–18
Francis Holland School, SW1W   4–18
Glendower Preparatory School, SW7   4–11
The Godolphin and Latymer School, W6   11–18
Grange Park Preparatory School, N21   4–11
Harvington School, W5   3–16 (Boys 3–5)
Islamia Girls' School, NW6   11–16
James Allen's Girls' School, SE22   11–18
Kensington Prep School, SW6   4–11
London Jewish Girls' High School, NW4   11–16
Lubavitch House Senior School for Girls, N16 11–18
Madni Girls School, E1   12–18

More House, SW1X   11–18
The Mount School, NW7   4–18
Notting Hill and Ealing High School GDST, W13 4–18
Palmers Green High School, N21   3–16
Pembridge Hall, W2   4–11
Putney High School GDST, SW15   4–18
Queen's College, W1G   11–18
Queen's College Prep School, W1B   4–11
Queen's Gate School, SW7   4–18
Quwwatt Ul Islam Girls School, E7   4–13
The Royal School, Hampstead, NW3   3–18
St Augustine's Priory, W5   4–18
St Christina's RC Preparatory School,
  NW8   3–11 (Boys 3–7)
St Christopher's School, NW3   4–11
St James Independent School for Girls (Juniors),
  W14   4–10
St James Independent School for Senior Girls,
  W14   10–18
St Joseph's Convent School, E11   3–11
St Margaret's School, NW3   4–16
St Paul's Girls' School, W6   11–18
Sarum Hall, NW3   3–11
South Hampstead High School, NW3   4–18
Streatham and Clapham High School,
  SW16   3–18 (Boys 3–5)
The Study Preparatory School, SW19   4–11
Sydenham High School GDST, SE26   4–18
Tayyibah Girls School, N16   5–18
Ursuline Preparatory School, SW20   3–11 (Boys 3–7)
The Village School, NW3   4–11
Wimbledon High School GDST, SW19   4–18
*Yesodey Hatorah Jewish School, N16   3–16

GREATER MANCHESTER

Hubert Jewish High School for Girls, Salford   11–18
Manchester High School for Girls, Manchester   4–18
Manchester Islamic High School, Manchester   11–16
Withington Girls' School, Manchester   7–18

MERSEYSIDE

Birkenhead High School GDST, Wirral   3–18
Merchant Taylors' School for Girls,
  Liverpool   4–18 (Boys 4–7)
Streatham House School, Liverpool   2–16 (Boys 2–11)

MIDDLESEX

Heathfield School, Pinner   3–18
Jack and Jill School, Hampton   3–7 (Boys 3–5)
The Lady Eleanor Holles School, Hampton   7–18
North London Collegiate, Edgware   4–18
Northwood College, Northwood   3–18
Peterborough & St Margaret's School, Stanmore   4–16
St Catherine's School,
  Twickenham   3–16 (Sixth form in 2006)
St David's School, Ashford   3–18
St Helen's School, Northwood   3–18

NORFOLK

Hethersett Old Hall School, Norwich   4–18 (Boys 4–7)
Norwich High School for Girls GDST, Norwich   4–18
Thorpe House School, Norwich   3–16

NORTHAMPTONSHIRE

Northampton High School, Northampton   3–18

NOTTINGHAMSHIRE

Hollygirt School, Nottingham   3–16
Hollygirt School, Nottingham   3–16
Nottingham High School for Girls GDST,
    Nottingham   4–18

OXFORDSHIRE

Ash-Shifa School, Banbury   11–16
The Carrdus School, Banbury   3–11 (Boys 3–8)
Cranford House School, Wallingford   3–16 (Boys 3–7)
Headington School, Oxford   3–18 (Co-ed 3–4)
IQRA School, Oxford   10–16
Our Lady's Convent Senior School, Abingdon   11–18
Oxford High School GDST, Oxford   3–18 (Boys 3–6)
Rye St Antony School, Oxford   3–18 (Boys 3–8)
St Mary's School, Wantage   11–18
The School of St Helen & St Katharine, Abingdon   9–18
Tudor Hall School, Banbury   11–18
Wychwood School, Oxford   11–18

SHROPSHIRE

Adcote School for Girls, Shrewsbury   4–18
Moreton Hall School, Oswestry   3–18
Shrewsbury High School GDST, Shrewsbury   2–18

SOMERSET

Bruton School for Girls, Bruton   3–18

BATH & NORTH EAST SOMERSET

The Royal High School, Bath   3–18

STAFFORDSHIRE

Abbots Bromley School for Girls, Abbots Bromley   3–18
St Dominic's Priory School, Stone   3–18 (Boys 3–11)
St Dominic's School, Stafford   2–16 (Co-ed 2–7)

SUFFOLK

Amberfield School, Ipswich   3–16 (Boys 3–7)
Ipswich High School GDST, Ipswich   3–18

SURREY

Bramley School, Tadworth   3–11
Croham Hurst School, South Croydon   3–18
Croydon High School GDST, South Croydon   3–18
Dunottar School, Reigate   3–18
Greenacre School for Girls, Banstead   3–18
Guildford High School, Guildford   4–18
Halstead Preparatory School, Woking   3–11
Holy Cross Preparatory School,
    Kingston-upon-Thames   4–11
Laverock School, Oxted   3–11
Lodge School, Purley   3–18 (Boys 3–11)
Manor House School, Leatherhead   2–16
Marymount International School,
    Kingston-upon-Thames   11–18
Notre Dame Preparatory School, Cobham   2–11 (Boys 2–5)
Notre Dame Senior School, Cobham   11–18
Old Palace School of John Whitgift, Croydon   4–18
Old Vicarage School, Richmond   4–11
Prior's Field School, Godalming   11–18
Rowan Preparatory School, Esher   2–11
The Royal School, Haslemere   3–18 (Boys 2–4)
St Catherine's School, Guildford   4–18
St Ives School, Haslemere   3–11 (Boys 3–5)
St Teresa's Preparatory School, Effingham   2–11
St Teresa's School, Dorking   11–18
Seaton House School, Sutton   3–11 (Boys 3–5)
Sir William Perkins's School, Chertsey   11–18
Surbiton High School,
    Kingston-upon-Thames   4–18 (Boys 4–11)
Sutton High School GDST, Sutton   3–18
Tormead School, Guildford   4–18
Wispers School for Girls, Haslemere   11–18
Woldingham School, Woldingham   11–18

EAST SUSSEX

Brighton and Hove High School GDST, Brighton   3–18
Moira House Girls School, Eastbourne   3–19
Moira House School, Eastbourne   2–11
Roedean School, Brighton   11–18
St Leonards-Mayfield School, Mayfield   11–18
St Mary's Hall, Brighton   3–18 (Boys 3–8)

WEST SUSSEX

Burgess Hill School for Girls, Burgess Hill   2–18
Farlington School, Horsham   4–18
*Fonthill Lodge,
    East Grinstead   2–11 (Single-sex ed 8–11)
Lavant House, Chichester   3–18
The Towers Convent School, Steyning   3–16 (Boys 3–11)

TYNE AND WEAR

Central Newcastle High School GDST,
    Newcastle upon Tyne   3–18
Dame Allan's Girls School, Newcastle upon Tyne   8–18
    (Co-ed VIth Form)
La Sagesse School, Newcastle upon Tyne   3–18

Newcastle Upon Tyne Church High School,
Newcastle upon Tyne   2–18
Westfield School, Newcastle upon Tyne   3–18

WARWICKSHIRE

King's High School, Warwick, Warwick   10–18
The Kingsley School, Leamington Spa   3–18 (Boys 2–7)

WEST MIDLANDS

*Al Hijrah School, Birmingham   4–11
Al-Burhan Grammar School, Birmingham   11–16
Birchfield Independent Girls School, Birmingham   11–16
Coventry Muslim School, Coventry   4–16
*Darul Uloom Islamic High School & College,
Birmingham   -
Edgbaston High School for Girls, Birmingham   2–18
Highclare School,
Birmingham   1–18 (Boys 1–11 & 16–18)
King Edward VI High School for Girls,
Birmingham   11–18
Newbridge Preparatory School, Wolverhampton   3–11
Priory School, Birmingham   1–18 (Co-ed 1–11)
Saint Martin's School, Solihull   3–18
Woodstock Girls' School, Birmingham   11–15

WILTSHIRE

Godolphin Preparatory School, Salisbury   3–11
The Godolphin School, Salisbury   11–18
Leaden Hall School, Salisbury   3–11 (Boys 3–4)
St Mary's School, Calne   11–18
Stonar School, Melksham   2–18

WORCESTERSHIRE

The Alice Ottley School, Worcester   3–19
Dodderhill School, Droitwich Spa   3–16 (Boys 3–9)
Malvern St James, Great Malvern   7–18
St Mary's Convent School, Worcester   2–18 (Boys 2–8)

EAST RIDING OF YORKSHIRE

Hull High School, Anlaby   3–18 (Boys 3–11)

NORTH YORKSHIRE

Harrogate Ladies' College, Harrogate   10–18
The Mount School, York   3–18
Queen Margaret's School, York   11–18
Queen Mary's School, Thirsk   3–16 (Boys 3–7)

SOUTH YORKSHIRE

Ashdell Preparatory School, Sheffield   4–11
Brantwood School, Sheffield   3–16
Sheffield High School GDST, Sheffield   4–18

WEST YORKSHIRE

Bradford Girls' Grammar School, Bradford   2–18
Gateways School, Leeds   3–18 (Boys 3–7)
Islamia Girls High School, Huddersfield   11–16
Leeds Girls' High School, Leeds   3–19
Moorfield School, Ilkley   2–11
New Horizon Community School, Leeds   11–16
Wakefield Girls' High School, Wakefield   11–18

NORTHERN IRELAND

COUNTY ANTRIM

Victoria College Belfast, Belfast   4–18

SCOTLAND

ABERDEENSHIRE

St Margaret's School for Girls, Aberdeen 3–18 (Boys 3–5)

GLASGOW

Craigholme School   3–18 (Boys 3–5)

SOUTH LANARKSHIRE

Fernhill School, Rutherglen   4–18 (Boys 4–11)

LOTHIAN

The Mary Erskine School,
Edinburgh   12–18 (Co-ed VIth Form)
St George's School for Girls, Edinburgh 2–18 (Boys 2–5)
St Margaret's School, Edinburgh   1–18 (Boys 1–8)

PERTHSHIRE

Kilgraston, Perth   2–18 (Boys day 2–9)

WALES

CONWY

*Rydal Penrhos Senior School,
   Colwyn Bay   11–18 (Single-sex ed 11–16)

DENBIGHSHIRE

Howell's School, Denbigh   2–18

MONMOUTHSHIRE

Haberdashers' Monmouth School For Girls,
   Monmouth   7–18

4.5

Boarding Provision (Full, Weekly and Flexi-Boarding, Host Families)

The schools and colleges listed below offer boarding/residential accommodation. Full boarding is indicated by 'F', weekly boarding by 'W'. Many schools now offer Flexi-boarding (Fl), ie pupils may board for part of the week or on an occasional basis. Please note that in some cases independent Sixth Form colleges may offer accommodation with host families (H) or in hostels. For further details please contact schools direct.

ENGLAND

BEDFORDSHIRE

Bedford High School, Bedford	F
Bedford Preparatory School, Bedford	F W Fl
Bedford School, Bedford	F W Fl
Bedford School Study Centre, Bedford	F

BERKSHIRE

Bearwood College, Wokingham	F W
Bradfield College, Reading	F
Brockhurst and Marlston House Schools, Newbury	W Fl
Cheam School, Newbury	F W Fl
Downe House, Thatcham	F
Eagle House, Sandhurst	F W Fl
Elstree School, Reading	F Fl
Eton College, Windsor	F
Heathfield St Mary's School, Ascot	F
Horris Hill School, Newbury	F
Hurst Lodge School, Ascot	W Fl
Lambrook Haileybury, Bracknell	W Fl
Leighton Park School, Reading	F W Fl
Licensed Victuallers' School, Ascot	F W
Luckley-Oakfield School, Wokingham	F W Fl
Ludgrove, Wokingham	F
The Oratory Preparatory School, Reading	F Fl
The Oratory School, Reading	F
Padworth College, Reading	F W Fl
Pangbourne College, Pangbourne	F W Fl
Papplewick School, Ascot	F

Queen Anne's School, Reading	F Fl
St Andrew's School, Reading	W Fl
St George's School, Ascot	F Fl
St George's School, Windsor	F W Fl
St John's Beaumont, Windsor	F W
St Mary's School, Ascot, Ascot	F
St Michaels School, Newbury	F W Fl
Sunningdale School, Sunningdale	F
Wellington College, Crowthorne	F Fl

BRISTOL

Badminton School	F W Fl
Clifton College	F Fl
Clifton College Preparatory School	F W
Clifton High School	F W Fl
Colston's Collegiate School	F Fl
The Downs School, Wraxall	F W Fl
Tockington Manor School	F Fl

BUCKINGHAMSHIRE

Ashfold School, Aylesbury	W Fl
Caldicott School, Farnham Royal	F
Godstowe Preparatory School, High Wycombe	F W
Gyosei International School UK, Milton Keynes	
Pipers Corner School, High Wycombe	F W Fl
Stowe School, Buckingham	F
Swanbourne House School, Milton Keynes	F W Fl

Thornton College Convent of Jesus and Mary,
  Milton Keynes   F W Fl
Wycombe Abbey School, High Wycombe   F

CAMBRIDGESHIRE

Bellerbys College & Embassy CES Cambridge,
  Cambridge   F
Cambridge Arts & Sciences (CATS), Cambridge   F H
Cambridge Centre for Sixth-Form Studies,
  Cambridge   F W Fl
Kimbolton School, Huntingdon   F Fl
The King's School Ely, Ely   F W Fl
The Leys School, Cambridge   F
MPW (Mander Portman Woodward), Cambridge   Fl
Peterborough High School, Peterborough   F W Fl
St Andrew's, Cambridge   Fl
St John's College School, Cambridge   F Fl
St Mary's School, Cambridge   F W H

CHESHIRE

Hammond School, Chester   F W
Terra Nova School, Holmes Chapel   F W Fl

CORNWALL

The Bolitho School, Penzance   F W Fl
Polwhele House School, Truro   W Fl
Truro High School, Truro   F W Fl
Truro School, Truro   F Fl

CUMBRIA

Casterton School, Kirkby Lonsdale   F Fl
Harecroft Hall School, Seascale   F W Fl
Holme Park School, Kendal   Fl
Lime House School, Carlisle   F W
St Bees School, St Bees   F W Fl
Sedbergh School, Sedbergh   F
Windermere St Anne's, Windermere   F W Fl

DERBYSHIRE

Foremarke Hall School, Derby   F W Fl
Mount St Mary's College, Spinkhill   F W Fl
Ockbrook School, Derby   F W Fl
Repton School, Derby   F
St Anselm's School, Bakewell   F

DEVON

Blundell's School, Tiverton   F W Fl
Bramdean School, Exeter   W Fl
Trinity School, Teignmouth   F W
Edgehill College, Bideford   F W Fl
Exeter Cathedral School, Exeter   F W Fl
Grenville College, Bideford   F W
Kelly College, Tavistock   F W Fl
Kelly College Preparatory School, Tavistock   F W Fl

Mount House School, Tavistock   F W
Plymouth College, Plymouth   F W
St John's School, Sidmouth   F W Fl
St Peter's School, Exmouth   W Fl
Shebbear College, Beaworthy   F W Fl
Stover School, Newton Abbot   F W Fl H
Trinity School, Teignmouth   F W
West Buckland Preparatory School, Barnstaple   F Fl
West Buckland School, Barnstaple   F W Fl

DORSET

Bryanston School, Blandford Forum   F
Canford School, Wimborne   F
Claysmore Preparatory School,
  Blandford Forum   F W Fl
Claysmore School, Blandford Forum   F W
Hanford School, Blandford Forum   F
International College, Sherborne School, Sherborne   F
Knighton House, Blandford Forum   F W Fl
Milton Abbey School, Blandford Forum   F
The Old Malthouse, Swanage   W
Port Regis School, Shaftesbury   F W
St Antony's Leweston School, Sherborne   F Fl
St Mary's School, Shaftesbury   F
Sherborne Preparatory School, Sherborne   F W Fl
Sherborne School, Sherborne   F
Sherborne School for Girls, Sherborne   F
Talbot Heath, Bournemouth   F W Fl
Wentworth College, Bournemouth   F W Fl

COUNTY DURHAM

Barnard Castle School, Barnard Castle   F W Fl
The Chorister School, Durham   F W Fl
Durham School, Durham   F W Fl
Polam Hall, Darlington   F W Fl

ESSEX

Brentwood School, Brentwood   F W
Chigwell School, Chigwell   F W Fl
Felsted Preparatory School, Felsted   W Fl
Felsted School, Dunmow   F Fl
Friends' School, Saffron Walden   F W Fl
Gosfield School, Halstead   F Fl
Holmwood House, Colchester   W Fl
New Hall School, Chelmsford   F Fl

GLOUCESTERSHIRE

Beaudesert Park School, Stroud   W Fl
Bredon School, Tewkesbury   F W Fl
Cheltenham College, Cheltenham   F
Cheltenham College Junior School, Cheltenham   F Fl
The Cheltenham Ladies' College, Cheltenham   F
Dean Close Preparatory School, Cheltenham   F Fl
Dean Close School, Cheltenham   F
Hatherop Castle School, Cirencester   F Fl
The King's School, Gloucester   W Fl
Rendcomb College, Cirencester   F W Fl

Westonbirt School, Tetbury	F W Fl
Wycliffe College, Stonehouse	F Fl H
Wycliffe Preparatory School, Stonehouse	F W
Wynstones School, Gloucester	F W Fl H

HAMPSHIRE

Bedales School, Petersfield	F
Boundary Oak School, Fareham	W Fl
Brockwood Park School, Bramdean	F
Dunhurst (Bedales Junior School), Petersfield	F Fl
Farleigh School, Andover	F W Fl
Forres Sandle Manor, Fordingbridge	F W Fl
Hampshire Collegiate School (Embley Park), Romsey	F W Fl
Highfield School, Liphook	F
Hordle Walhampton School, Lymington	F W
Lord Wandsworth College, Hook	F W Fl
Moyles Court School, Ringwood	F
The Pilgrims' School, Winchester	F W
Rookesbury Park School, Portsmouth	F W Fl
Rookwood School, Andover	F Fl
St John's College, Southsea	F Fl
St Neot's School, Hook	W Fl
St Swithun's School, Winchester	F W
Stanbridge Earls School, Romsey	F
Twyford School, Winchester	W Fl H
Winchester College, Winchester	F

HEREFORDSHIRE

Lucton School, Leominster	F W Fl
St Richard's, Bromyard	F W Fl

HERTFORDSHIRE

Aldenham School, Elstree	F W Fl
Aldwickbury School, Harpenden	W Fl
Arts Educational School, Tring Park, Tring	F
Beechwood Park School, St Albans	W Fl
Berkhamsted Collegiate School, Berkhamsted	F W Fl
Bishop's Stortford College, Bishop's Stortford	F Fl
Edge Grove, Aldenham	F Fl
Haileybury, Hertford	F Fl
Heath Mount School, Hertford	W Fl
The Junior School, Bishop's Stortford College, Bishop's Stortford	F W
Lockers Park, Hemel Hempstead	F Fl
The Princess Helena College, Hitchin	F W Fl
The Purcell School, Bushey	F
Queenswood School, Hatfield	F Fl
The Royal Masonic School for Girls, Rickmansworth	F W Fl
St Christopher School, Letchworth	F W Fl
St Edmund's College, Ware	F W Fl
St Francis' College, Letchworth	F W Fl
St Margaret's School, Bushey	F W Fl
Stanborough School, Watford	F W Fl
Westbrook Hay Preparatory School, Hemel Hempstead	Fl

ISLE OF MAN

King William's College, Castletown	F Fl

ISLE OF WIGHT

Ryde School, Ryde	F W Fl

KENT

Ashford School, Ashford	F W Fl
Bedgebury School, Cranbrook	F W
Beechwood Sacred Heart School, Tunbridge Wells	F W Fl
Benenden School, Cranbrook	F
Bethany School, Cranbrook	F W
Cobham Hall, Gravesend	F W Fl
Cranbrook School, Cranbrook	F
Darul Uloom London, Chislehurst	F
Dover College, Dover	F W Fl
Duke of York's Royal Military School, Dover	F
Dulwich Preparatory School, Cranbrook, Cranbrook	W Fl
Farringtons School, Chislehurst	F W Fl
Holmewood House, Tunbridge Wells	W Fl
Junior King's School, Canterbury	F W Fl
Kent College, Canterbury	F W Fl
Kent College Infant & Junior School, Canterbury	F W Fl
Kent College Pembury, Tunbridge Wells	F W Fl
King's Preparatory School, Rochester	F W Fl
The King's School, Canterbury	F
King's School Rochester, Rochester	F W
Marlborough House School, Hawkhurst	Fl
Northbourne Park School, Deal	F W Fl
Rochester Independent College, Rochester	F Fl
St Edmunds Junior School, Canterbury	F Fl
St Edmund's School, Canterbury	F Fl
St Lawrence College Junior School, Ramsgate	F W Fl
St Lawrence College, Ramsgate	F
St Ronan's School, Hawkhurst	Fl
Sevenoaks School, Sevenoaks	F
Sutton Valence School, Maidstone	F W Fl
Tonbridge School, Tonbridge	F W
Wellesley House School, Broadstairs	F W

LANCASHIRE

Jamea Al Kauthar, Lancaster	F
Kirkham Grammar School, Preston	F W Fl
Moorland School, Clitheroe	F W Fl
Rossall Junior School, Fleetwood	F Fl
Rossall School, Fleetwood	F Fl
Rossall School International Study Centre, Fleetwood	F
St Anne's College Grammar School, Lytham St Annes	F W Fl H
St Mary's Hall, Stonyhurst	F W Fl
Sedbergh Junior School, Lancaster	F W Fl
Stonyhurst College, Clitheroe	F W

LEICESTERSHIRE

Brooke House College, Market Harborough	F
Irwin College, Leicester	F
Loughborough Grammar School, Loughborough	F W Fl
Ratcliffe College, Leicester	F W Fl

LINCOLNSHIRE

Lincoln Minster School, Lincoln	F W Fl
St Hugh's School, Woodhall Spa	F W
Stamford High School, Stamford	F W Fl
Stamford Junior School, Stamford	F W
Stamford School, Stamford	F W Fl
Witham Hall, Bourne	F W Fl

NORTH EAST LINCOLNSHIRE

St. James' School, Grimsby	F W Fl

LONDON

Ashbourne Independent Sixth Form College, W8	F
Bales College, W10	
David Game College, W11	
Dulwich College, SE21	F W
Dulwich College Preparatory School, SE21	W
Mill Hill School, NW7	F
Royal Ballet School, WC2E	F
The Royal School, Hampstead, NW3	F W Fl
St Paul's Cathedral School, EC4M	F
St Paul's School, SW13	F W Fl
Sylvia Young Theatre School, NW1	F W H
Westminster Abbey Choir School, SW1P	F Fl
Westminster Cathedral Choir School, SW1P	F
Westminster School, SW1P	W

GREATER MANCHESTER

Chetham's School of Music, Manchester	F

MERSEYSIDE

Clarence High School, Formby	
Kingsmead School, Wirral	F W Fl

MIDDLESEX

Harrow School, Harrow on the Hill	F
St David's School, Ashford	F W
St Helen's School, Northwood	F W
St James Independent School for Boys (Senior), Twickenham	W

NORFOLK

Beeston Hall School, Cromer	F
Glebe House School, Hunstanton	W Fl
Gresham's Preparatory School, Holt	F W Fl
Gresham's School, Holt	F W Fl
Hethersett Old Hall School, Norwich	F Fl
Langley School, Norwich	F W
The New Eccles Hall School, Norwich	F W Fl
Riddlesworth Hall, Diss	F W Fl
Sacred Heart Convent School, Swaffham	F W
Taverham Hall, Norwich	W

NORTHAMPTONSHIRE

Beachborough School, Brackley	Fl
Bosworth Independent College, Northampton	F W H
Maidwell Hall School, Northampton	F
Oundle School, Nr Peterborough	F
Winchester House School, Brackley	F W Fl

NORTHUMBERLAND

Longridge Towers School, Berwick-upon-Tweed	F W Fl
Mowden Hall School, Stocksfield	F W

NOTTINGHAMSHIRE

Al Karam Secondary School, Retford	F Fl
Bramcote Lorne School, Retford	F W Fl
Ranby House School, Retford	F W Fl
Rodney School, Newark	Fl
Trent College, Nottingham	W Fl
Wellow House School, Newark	W Fl
Worksop College, Worksop	F W Fl

OXFORDSHIRE

Abacus College, Oxford	F
Abingdon School, Abingdon	F W
Bloxham School, Banbury	F W Fl
Cherwell College, Oxford	F W H
Cothill House Preparatory School, Abingdon	F
d'Overbroeck's College, Oxford	F H
Dragon School, Oxford	F
Greene's Tutorial College, Oxford	F W Fl H
Headington School, Oxford	F W Fl
Kingham Hill School, Chipping Norton	F W Fl
Moulsford Preparatory School, Wallingford	W
Oxford Tutorial College, Oxford	H
Radley College, Abingdon	F
Rye St Antony School, Oxford	F W Fl
St Clare's, Oxford, Oxford	F W Fl
St Edward's School, Oxford	F
St Hugh's School, Faringdon	W Fl
St Mary's School, Wantage	F
Shiplake College, Henley-on-Thames	F W
Sibford School, Banbury	F W Fl
Summer Fields, Oxford	F
Tudor Hall School, Banbury	F
Wychwood School, Oxford	F W Fl

RUTLAND

Oakham School, Oakham	F
Uppingham School, Uppingham	F

SHROPSHIRE

Adcote School for Girls, Shrewsbury	F W Fl H
Bedstone College, Bucknell	F
Concord College, Shrewsbury	F
Ellesmere College, Ellesmere	F W Fl
Moor Park School, Ludlow	F W Fl
Moreton Hall School, Oswestry	F H
Oswestry School, Oswestry	F W Fl
Packwood Haugh School, Shrewsbury	F
Prestfelde Preparatory School, Shrewsbury	F Fl
Shrewsbury School, Shrewsbury	F
Wrekin College, Telford	F Fl

SOMERSET

All Hallows, Shepton Mallet	F W Fl
Bruton School for Girls, Bruton	F W Fl
Chilton Cantelo School, Yeovil	F Fl
Downside School, Bath	F W
Hazlegrove (King's Bruton Preparatory School), Yeovil	F W Fl
King's Bruton, Bruton	F
King's College, Taunton	F
King's Hall, Taunton	F W Fl
Millfield Preparatory School, Glastonbury	F
Millfield School, Street	F
The Park School, Yeovil	F W H
Perrott Hill School, Crewkerne	F W Fl
Queen's College Junior and Pre-Preparatory Schools, Taunton	F
Queen's College, Taunton	F Fl
Taunton International Study Centre (TISC), Taunton	F
Taunton Preparatory School, Taunton	F Fl
Taunton School, Taunton	F
Wellington School, Wellington	F W Fl
Wells Cathedral Junior School, Wells	F W Fl
Wells Cathedral School, Wells	F Fl

BATH & NORTH EAST SOMERSET

Bath Academy, Bath	F Fl H
Kingswood Preparatory School, Bath	F W Fl
Kingswood School, Bath	F W Fl
Monkton Combe Junior School, Bath	F W Fl
Monkton Combe School, Bath	F W
Prior Park College, Bath	F W Fl
The Royal High School, Bath	F W Fl

NORTH SOMERSET

Sidcot School, Winscombe	F W Fl

STAFFORDSHIRE

Abbots Bromley School for Girls, Abbots Bromley	F W Fl
Abbotsholme School, Uttoxeter	F W Fl
Chase Academy, Cannock	F
Denstone College, Uttoxeter	F W
Lichfield Cathedral School, Lichfield	F W Fl

St Bede's School, Stafford	F W Fl
Yarlet School, Stafford	Fl

SUFFOLK

Barnardiston Hall Preparatory School, Haverhill	F W Fl
Culford School, Bury St Edmunds	F W Fl
Felixstowe International College, Felixstowe	F
Finborough School, Stowmarket	F W Fl
Framlingham College, Woodbridge	F W Fl
Framlingham College Preparatory School, Brandeston	F W Fl
Ipswich School, Ipswich	F W Fl
Moreton Hall Preparatory School, Bury St Edmunds	F W Fl
Old Buckenham Hall School, Ipswich	F W
Orwell Park, Ipswich	F W Fl
The Royal Hospital School, Ipswich	F
Saint Felix School, Southwold	F W Fl
St Joseph's College, Ipswich	F W Fl
Stoke College, Sudbury	W Fl
Summerhill School, Leiston	Fl
Woodbridge School, Woodbridge	F W Fl

SURREY

ACS Cobham International School, Cobham	F W
Aldro School, Godalming	F
Belmont School, Dorking	W Fl
Bishopsgate School, Egham	W Fl
Box Hill School, Dorking	F W Fl
Cambridge Tutors College, Croydon	H
Caterham School, Caterham	F W Fl
Charterhouse, Godalming	F
City of London Freemen's School, Ashtead	F W Fl
Cranleigh Preparatory School, Cranleigh	
Cranleigh School, Cranleigh	F
Duke of Kent School, Ewhurst	F W Fl
Edgeborough, Farnham	W Fl
Epsom College, Epsom	F W
Feltonfleet School, Cobham	W Fl
Frensham Heights School, Farnham	F
Hall Grove School, Bagshot	W Fl
Hampton Court House, East Molesey	W Fl
Hurtwood House, Dorking	F W
King Edward's School Witley, Godalming	F Fl
Marymount International School, Kingston-upon-Thames	F W Fl H
More House School, Farnham	
Prior's Field School, Godalming	F W
Reed's School, Cobham	F
Royal Alexandra and Albert School, Reigate	F W Fl
Royal Ballet School, Richmond	
Royal Russell School, Croydon	F W Fl
The Royal School, Haslemere	F W Fl
St Catherine's School, Guildford	F W Fl
St Edmund's School, Hindhead	W Fl
St John's School, Leatherhead	F
St Teresa's Preparatory School, Effingham	F W Fl
St Teresa's School, Dorking	F W Fl
TASIS The American School in England, Thorpe	F
Wispers School for Girls, Haslemere	F W

Woldingham School, Woldingham	F W
Woodcote House School, Windlesham	F
Yehudi Menuhin School, Cobham	F Fl

EAST SUSSEX

Ashdown House School, Forest Row	F
Battle Abbey School, Battle	F W Fl
Bellerbys College, Hove	F
Brighton College, Brighton	F W Fl
Buckswood School, Hastings	F W Fl
Eastbourne College, Eastbourne	F
Greenfields School, Forest Row	F W Fl
Michael Hall (Steiner Waldorf School), Forest Row	F W Fl
Moira House Girls School, Eastbourne	F W Fl
Moira House School, Eastbourne	F W Fl
Newlands School, Seaford	F W
Roedean School, Brighton	Fl
St Andrew's School, Eastbourne	F W Fl
St Aubyns School, Brighton	W Fl
St Bede's Prep School, Eastbourne	F W Fl
St Bede's School, Hailsham	F W
St Leonards-Mayfield School, Mayfield	F W Fl
St Mary's Hall, Brighton	F W Fl
Stonelands School of Ballet & Theatre Arts, Hove	F Fl
Vinehall School, Robertsbridge	F

WEST SUSSEX

Ardingly College, Haywards Heath	F W Fl
Ardingly College Junior School, Haywards Heath	Fl
Brambletye School, East Grinstead	F
Burgess Hill School for Girls, Burgess Hill	F Fl
Christ's Hospital, Horsham	F
Copthorne Prep School, Copthorne	W Fl
Cottesmore School, Pease Pottage	F Fl
Cumnor House School, Haywards Heath	F Fl
Dorset House School, Pulborough	W Fl
Farlington School, Horsham	F W Fl
Great Ballard School, Chichester	W Fl
Great Walstead, Haywards Heath	W Fl
Handcross Park School, Haywards Heath	W Fl
Hurstpierpoint College, Hurstpierpoint	F W Fl
Lancing College, Lancing	F Fl
Lavant House, Chichester	F W Fl
The Prebendal School, Chichester	F W Fl
Seaford College, Petworth	F W Fl
Slindon College, Arundel	F W Fl
Sompting Abbotts School, Sompting	W Fl
Stoke Brunswick, East Grinstead	W Fl
The Towers Convent School, Steyning	F W Fl
Westbourne House School, Chichester	F Fl
Windlesham House, Pulborough	F
Worth School, Turners Hill	F W

WARWICKSHIRE

Bilton Grange, Rugby	F W Fl
Rugby School, Rugby	F
Warwick School, Warwick	F W Fl

WEST MIDLANDS

Birchfield School, Wolverhampton	W
Darul Uloom Islamic High School & College, Birmingham	F
Elmhurst School for Dance, Birmingham	F
The Royal Wolverhampton Junior School, Wolverhampton	F
The Royal Wolverhampton School, Wolverhampton	F W Fl
Tettenhall College, Wolverhampton	F W

WILTSHIRE

Appleford School, Salisbury	F W
Chafyn Grove School, Salisbury	F W Fl
Dauntsey's School, Devizes	F
The Godolphin School, Salisbury	F Fl
Leaden Hall School, Salisbury	F Fl
Marlborough College, Marlborough	F
Norman Court Preparatory School, Salisbury	F W Fl
Pinewood School, Shrivenham	F W Fl
Prior Park Preparatory School, Cricklade	F W Fl
St Mary's School, Calne	F
Salisbury Cathedral School, Salisbury	F Fl
Sandroyd School, Salisbury	F
Stonar School, Melksham	F W Fl H
Warminster School, Warminster	F W Fl

WORCESTERSHIRE

Abberley Hall, Worcester	F Fl
The Abbey College, Malvern Wells	Fl
Bromsgrove Preparatory School, Bromsgrove	F W Fl
Bromsgrove School, Bromsgrove	F
The Downs School, Malvern	F W Fl
The Elms, Malvern	F Fl
Malvern College, Malvern	F
Malvern College Preparatory and Pre-Prep School, Malvern	F Fl
Malvern St James, Great Malvern	F W
Moffats School, Bewdley	F W Fl
Moffats School, Bewdley	F W Fl
Saint Michael's College, Tenbury Wells	F

EAST RIDING OF YORKSHIRE

Pocklington School, Pocklington	F W

NORTH YORKSHIRE

Ampleforth College, York	F
Ashville College, Harrogate	F W
Aysgarth Preparatory School, Bedale	F W Fl
Bootham School, York	F W Fl
Bramcote School, Scarborough	F W Fl
Catteral Hall School, Settle	F Fl
Cundall Manor School, York	F
Fyling Hall School, Whitby	F W
Giggleswick School, Settle	F
Harrogate Ladies' College, Harrogate	F W Fl
Harrogate Tutorial College, Harrogate	F W Fl H

Highfield Preparatory School, Harrogate	F W Fl
Howsham Hall, York	F Fl
Lisvane, Scarborough College Junior School, Scarborough	F W
Malsis School, Skipton	F
The Mount School, York	F W Fl
Queen Ethelburga's College, York	F
Queen Margaret's School, York	F W
Queen Mary's School, Thirsk	F W Fl
Read School, Selby	F W Fl
Ripon Cathedral Choir School, Ripon	F W Fl
St Martin's Ampleforth, York	F Fl
St Peter's School, York	F
Scarborough College & Lisvane School, Scarborough	F W Fl

Terrington Hall, York	F W Fl
Woodleigh School, Malton	F W Fl

WEST YORKSHIRE

Ackworth School, Pontefract	F W
Ackworth School - International Study Centre, Pontefract	F W Fl
Bronte House School, Bradford	F W Fl
Fulneck School, Pudsey	F W Fl
Rishworth School, Rishworth	F W Fl
Woodhouse Grove School, Apperley Bridge	F W

NORTHERN IRELAND

COUNTY ANTRIM

Cabin Hill School, Belfast	Fl
Campbell College, Belfast	F W Fl
Methodist College, Belfast	F
Victoria College Belfast, Belfast	F W Fl

COUNTY ARMAGH

The Royal School, Armagh	F W Fl

COUNTY DOWN

Rockport School, Holywood	W Fl

COUNTY TYRONE

The Royal School Dungannon, Dungannon	F W Fl

SCOTLAND

ANGUS

Lathallan School, Montrose	W Fl

ARGYLL AND BUTE

Lomond School, Helensburgh	F H

CLACKMANNANSHIRE

Dollar Academy, Dollar	F W Fl

DUMFRIES & GALLOWAY

Cademuir International School, Thornhill	F

FIFE

St Leonards School & VIth Form College, St Andrews	F Fl

LOTHIAN

Basil Paterson Tutorial College, Edinburgh	H
Belhaven Hill, Dunbar	F
Cargilfield, Edinburgh	F W Fl

The Edinburgh Academy, Edinburgh	Fl
Fettes College, Edinburgh	F
Loretto Junior School, Musselburgh	F W Fl
Loretto School, Musselburgh	F W Fl
The Mary Erskine School, Edinburgh	F W
Merchiston Castle School, Edinburgh	F
St George's School for Girls, Edinburgh	F Fl
St Mary's Music School, Edinburgh	F
Stewart's Melville College, Edinburgh	F W Fl

MORAYSHIRE

Gordonstoun School, Elgin	F W

PERTHSHIRE

Ardvreck School, Crieff	F
Glenalmond College, Perth	F
Kilgraston, Perth	F W Fl
Morrison's Academy, Crieff	F W Fl
Queen Victoria School, Dunblane	F
Strathallan School, Perth	F

ROXBURGHSHIRE

St Mary's Preparatory School, Melrose	W Fl

WALES

CARMARTHENSHIRE

Llandovery College, Llandovery   F W Fl

CONWY

Lyndon Preparatory School, Colwyn Bay   F W Fl
Rydal Penrhos Senior School, Colwyn Bay   F Fl
St David's College, Llandudno   F W Fl

DENBIGHSHIRE

Howell's School, Denbigh   F W Fl
Ruthin School, Ruthin   F W Fl

MONMOUTHSHIRE

Haberdashers' Monmouth School For Girls,
    Monmouth   F W Fl
Monmouth School, Monmouth   F W Fl
St John's-on-the-Hill, Chepstow   F W Fl

PEMBROKESHIRE

Netherwood School, Saundersfoot   F W Fl

POWYS

Christ College, Brecon   F W Fl

4.6

Religious Affiliation

The following index lists all schools specifying a particular denomination. However, it should be noted that this is intended as a guide only and that many of the schools listed also welcome children of other faiths. Schools which claim to be non- or inter-denominational are not listed. Parents should check precise details with individual schools. A full list of each school's entries elsewhere in the book is given in the main index at the back.

BUDDHIST

Dharma School, Brighton

CHRISTIAN

Abinger Hammer Village School, Dorking
Alderley Edge School for Girls, Alderley Edge
All Saints School, Norwich
Amberfield School, Ipswich
Ardvreck School, Crieff
The Ark School, Reading
Arnold Lodge School, Leamington Spa
Ashdell Preparatory School, Sheffield
Ashfold School, Aylesbury
Avon House, Woodford Green
Avondale School, Salisbury
Bangor Independent Christian School, Bangor
Barnsley Christian School, Barnsley
Benedict House Preparatory School, Sidcup
Berkhamsted Collegiate Preparatory School, Berkhamsted
Berkhamsted Collegiate School, Berkhamsted
Blundell's Preparatory School, Tiverton
Bowbrook House School, Pershore
Bradford Christian School, Bradford
The Branch Christian School, Heckmondwike
Bromley High School GDST, Bromley
Broomwood Hall School, SW12
Brownberrie School, Leeds
Carmel Christian School
Castle Court Preparatory School, Wimborne
Castle House School, Newport
Caterham Preparatory School, Caterham
The Cavendish School, NW1

Cedars School, Aldermaston
Chard School, Chard
Chase Academy, Cannock
Christ the King School, Sale
Clifton Lodge Preparatory School, W5
The Crescent School, Rugby
Croham Hurst School, South Croydon
The Daiglen School, Buckhurst Hill
Dale House School, Batley
Dame Alice Harpur School, Bedford
Danes Hill School, Leatherhead
Darvell School, Robertsbridge
Dean Close School, Cheltenham
Derby Grammar School for Boys, Derby
Derwent Lodge School for Girls, Tonbridge
Ditcham Park School, Petersfield
Dolphin School (Including Noah's Ark Nursery Schools), SW11
The Dolphin School, Exmouth
Dower House School, Bridgnorth
Downham Prep School and Montessori Nursery, Kings Lynn
East London Christian Choir School, E8
Egerton-Rothesay School, Berkhamsted
Emmanuel Christian School, Oxford
Emmanuel School, Derby
Emmanuel School, Exeter
Emmanuel School, Walsall
Emmaus School, Trowbridge
Eversfield Preparatory School, Solihull
Exeter Junior School, Exeter
Exeter School, Exeter
Ffynone House School Trust
Filgrave School, Newport Pagnell

Fosse Bank Mountains School, Tonbridge
Francis House, Tring
The Froebelian School, Leeds
Gatehouse School, E2
Gateway Christian School, Ilkeston
Ghyll Royd School, Ilkley
Glenarm College, Ilford
Godolphin Preparatory School, Salisbury
Gracefield Preparatory School
Grangewood Independent School, E7
Great Walstead, Haywards Heath
Grey House Preparatory School, Hook
Guildford High School, Guildford
Hamilton College, Hamilton
Handsworth Christian School, Sheffield
Haslemere Preparatory School, Haslemere
Heath House Preparatory School, SE3
Heathfield St Mary's School, Ascot
Herne Hill School, SE24
Heswall Preparatory School, Wirral
Hillgrove School, Bangor
Holy Trinity School, Kidderminster
Honeybourne School, Birmingham
Howell's School, Denbigh
Hydesville Tower School, Walsall
Jack and Jill School, Hampton
Josca's Preparatory School, Abingdon
Joseph Rayner Independent School, Audenshaw
King of Kings School, Manchester
The King's School, Nottingham
King's School, Plymouth
The King's School, Witney
The King's School, Primary, Witney
The King's School Senior, Eastleigh
Kingham Hill School, Chipping Norton
Kings Primary School, Southampton
Kings School, Harpenden
Kingsmead School, Wirral
Kingston Grammar School, Kingston-upon-Thames
Kingsway School, Wigan
La Retraite Swan, Salisbury
La Sagesse School, Newcastle upon Tyne
Lady Barn House School, Cheadle
Lambs Christian School, Birmingham
Langley Manor School, Slough
Laverock School, Oxted
Leicester Grammar School, Leicester
Lightcliffe Preparatory, Halifax
Lighthouse Christian School, Manchester
Lincoln Minster School, Lincoln
Lingfield Notre Dame School, Lingfield
Lisvane, Scarborough College Junior School, Scarborough
Locksley Christian School, Manby
Lorenden Preparatory School, Faversham
Lucton School, Leominster
The Lyceum, EC2A
Mannafields Christian School, Edinburgh
Maranatha Christian School, Swindon
Maypole House School, Alford
The Mead School, Tunbridge Wells
Meadowpark Nursery & Pre-Prep School, Cricklade
Michael Hall (Steiner Waldorf School), Forest Row
Monton Prep School with Montessori Nurseries, Eccles

Mountjoy House School, Huddersfield
New Life Christian School, Croydon
Norfolk House Preparatory & Kids Corner Nursery, Sandbach
Norfolk House School, Birmingham
Norwich School, Norwich
Paragon Christian Academy, E5
The Park School, Yeovil
Plymouth College, Plymouth
The Pointer School, SE3
The Portsmouth Grammar School, Portsmouth
The Potters House School, Bury
Priory School, Shanklin
Promised Land Academy, E13
Prospect School
The Rastrick Independent School, Brighouse
Red House School, Norton
Redcliffe School, SW10
Regius Christian School, Edinburgh
Richmond House School, Leeds
Rickmansworth PNEU School, Rickmansworth
River School, Worcester
Roundstone Preparatory School, Trowbridge
The Royal Hospital School, Ipswich
Sacred Heart Preparatory School, Chew Magna
St Aubyn's School, Woodford Green
St Christophers School, Totnes
St David's College, Llandudno
St Dominic's School, Stafford
St Francis' College, Letchworth
St George's School, Edgbaston, Birmingham
St Helen's School, Northwood
St Hilda's School, Westcliff-on-Sea
St Ia School, St Ives
St John's Senior School, Enfield
St Joseph's College, Ipswich
St Mary's Preparatory School, Lincoln
St Matthews School, Northampton
St Michael's School, Leigh-on-Sea
Sceptre School, Dunstable
School of the Lion, Gloucester
Second Chances at The Vine Trust Walsall, Walsall
Sedbergh Junior School, Lancaster
Sefton Park School, Stoke Poges
Sherborne Preparatory School, Sherborne
Springfield Christian School, SE6
Stonehouse School, Leyland
Stoneygate College, Leicester
Stowford College, Sutton
Sunflower Montessori School, Twickenham
Sunninghill Preparatory School, Dorchester
Tabernacle School, W11
The Terrace School, Leamington Spa
Thomas's Kindergarten, SW1W
Thomas's Preparatory School, W8
Thorpe Hall School, Southend-on-Sea
Trent College, Nottingham
Trinity School, Croydon
Trinity School, Stalybridge
Twickenham Preparatory School, Hampton
Uplands School, Poole
Victoria College, Jersey
Vine School, Southampton

Wakefield Tutorial Preparatory School, Leeds
Warlingham Park School, Croydon
Warwick Preparatory School, Warwick
Wellspring Christian School, Carlisle
Weston Green School, Thames Ditton
Wetherby Preparatory School, W11
Wickham Court School, West Wickham
Woodford Green Preparatory School, Woodford Green
Worksop College, Worksop
Yardley Court, Tonbridge
Yarm School, Yarm

CHRISTIAN SCIENCE

Claremont Fan Court School, Esher

CHURCH IN WALES

Albemarle Independent College, W1K
The Cathedral School
Christ College, Brecon
Ffynone House School
Llandovery College, Llandovery
Monmouth School, Monmouth

CHURCH OF ENGLAND

The Abbey, Woodbridge
Abbey Gate College, Chester
Abbey Gate School, Chester
The Abbey School, Reading
Abbot's Hill School, Hemel Hempstead
Abbots Bromley School for Girls, Abbots Bromley
Abbotsbury School, Newton Abbot
Abingdon School, Abingdon
Acorn School, Nailsworth
Adcote School for Girls, Shrewsbury
Airthrie School, Cheltenham
Aldenham School, Elstree
Aldro School, Godalming
Aldwickbury School, Harpenden
The Alice Ottley School, Worcester
Alleyn's School, SE22
Amesbury, Hindhead
Ardingly College, Haywards Heath
Ardingly College Junior School, Haywards Heath
Arnold House School, NW8
Ashdown House School, Forest Row
Aysgarth Preparatory School, Bedale
Ballard School, New Milton
Bancroft's School, Woodford Green
Barfield School, Farnham
Barnardiston Hall Preparatory School, Haverhill
Baston School, Bromley
Beachborough School, Brackley
The Beacon School, Amersham
Bearwood College, Wokingham
Beaudesert Park School, Stroud
Bedford Preparatory School, Bedford
Bedford School, Bedford
Bedstone College, Bucknell
Beech Hall School, Macclesfield

Beechenhurst Preparatory School, Liverpool
Beechwood Park School, St Albans
Beeston Hall School, Cromer
Belmont School, Dorking
Benenden School, Cranbrook
Berkhampstead School, Cheltenham
Bethany School, Cranbrook
Bilton Grange, Rugby
Birchfield School, Wolverhampton
Bloxham School, Banbury
The Blue Coat School, Birmingham
Blundell's School, Tiverton
Bodiam Manor School, Robertsbridge
The Bolitho School, Penzance
Bradfield College, Reading
Brambletye School, East Grinstead
Bramcote Lorne School, Retford
Bramcote School, Scarborough
Bredon School, Tewkesbury
Brentwood School, Brentwood
Brigg Preparatory School, Brigg
Brighton College, Brighton
Brighton College Pre-preparatory School, Brighton
Brighton College Prep School, Brighton
Bristol Cathedral School
Broadwater Manor School, Worthing
Brockhurst & Marlston House Pre-Preparatory School,
  Thatcham
Brockhurst and Marlston House Schools, Newbury
Bromsgrove Pre-preparatory and Nursery School,
  Bromsgrove
Bromsgrove Preparatory School, Bromsgrove
Bromsgrove School, Bromsgrove
Bronte School, Gravesend
Broomfield House School, Richmond
Bryanston School, Blandford Forum
Buckingham College Preparatory School, Pinner
Burys Court, Reigate
Caldicott School, Farnham Royal
Cameron House School, SW3
Canford School, Wimborne
Casterton School, Kirkby Lonsdale
Chafyn Grove School, Salisbury
Chandlings Manor School, Oxford
Charterhouse, Godalming
Cheam School, Newbury
Cheltenham College, Cheltenham
Cheltenham College Junior School, Cheltenham
Chigwell School, Chigwell
Chilton Cantelo School, Yeovil
The Chorister School, Durham
Christ Church Cathedral School, Oxford
Christ's Hospital, Horsham
Claremont School, St Leonards-on-Sea
Clayesmore Preparatory School, Blandford Forum
Clayesmore School, Blandford Forum
Clifton College
Clifton College Preparatory School
Colfe's School, SE12
Colston's Collegiate School
Conifers School, Midhurst
Conway Preparatory School, Boston
Coopersale Hall School, Epping

Copthorne Prep School, Copthorne
Cothill House Preparatory School, Abingdon
Cottesmore School, Pease Pottage
Coventry Prep School, Coventry
Cranford House School, Wallingford
Cranleigh Preparatory School, Cranleigh
Cranleigh School, Cranleigh
The Croft Preparatory School, Stratford-upon-Avon
Cumnor House School, Haywards Heath
Cumnor House School, South Croydon
Cundall Manor School, York
Dair House School Trust Ltd, Farnham Royal
Daneshill School, Basingstoke
Dean Close Preparatory School, Cheltenham
Deepdene School, Hove
Denmead School, Hampton
Denstone College, Uttoxeter
Derby High School, Derby
The Dormer House PNEU School, Moreton-in-Marsh
Dorset House School, Pulborough
Dover College, Dover
Downe House, Thatcham
The Downs School, Wraxall
Dragon School, Oxford
Duke of York's Royal Military School, Dover
Dulwich College, SE21
Dulwich College Preparatory School, SE21
Dulwich Preparatory School, Cranbrook, Cranbrook
Dumpton School, Wimborne
Duncombe School, Hertford
Durham High School For Girls, Durham
Durham School, Durham
Durlston Court, New Milton
Eagle House, Sandhurst
Eastbourne College, Eastbourne
Edenhurst School, Newcastle-under-Lyme
Edge Grove, Aldenham
Edgeborough, Farnham
Elizabeth College, Guernsey
Ellesmere College, Ellesmere
Elmhurst School for Dance, Birmingham
The Elms, Malvern
Elstree School, Reading
The Elvian School, Reading
Emanuel School, SW11
Epsom College, Epsom
Eton College, Windsor
Eton End PNEU, Slough
Ewell Castle School, Epsom
Exeter Cathedral School, Exeter
Fairfield School, Backwell
Fairholme Preparatory School, St Asaph
Farlington School, Horsham
Felixstowe International College, Felixstowe
Felsted Preparatory School, Felsted
Felsted School, Dunmow
Feltonfleet School, Cobham
Fen School, Sleaford
Fonthill Lodge, East Grinstead
Foremarke Hall School, Derby
Forest School, E17
Forres Sandle Manor, Fordingbridge
Framlingham College, Woodbridge

Framlingham College Preparatory School, Brandeston
Francis Holland School, NW1
Francis Holland School, SW1W
Gayhurst School, Gerrards Cross
Giggleswick School, Settle
Glebe House School, Hunstanton
The Godolphin School, Salisbury
Godstowe Preparatory School, High Wycombe
Great Ballard School, Chichester
Grenville College, Bideford
Gresham's Preparatory School, Holt
Gresham's School, Holt
Haberdashers' Aske's Boys' School, Elstree
Haberdashers' Aske's School for Girls, Elstree
Haileybury, Hertford
The Hall School, NW3
Hallfield School, Birmingham
Halstead Preparatory School, Woking
Hammond School, Chester
Hampshire Collegiate School (Embley Park), Romsey
Handcross Park School, Haywards Heath
Hanford School, Blandford Forum
Harrogate Ladies' College, Harrogate
Harrow School, Harrow on the Hill
Hatherop Castle School, Cirencester
Hazelwood School, Oxted
Hazlegrove (King's Bruton Preparatory School), Yeovil
Headington School, Oxford
Heath House Preparatory School, SE3
Heath Mount School, Hertford
Heathland College, Accrington
Hemdean House School, Reading
The Hereford Cathedral Junior School, Hereford
The Hereford Cathedral School, Hereford
Hethersett Old Hall School, Norwich
Highfield Preparatory School, Harrogate
Highfield School, Liphook
Highgate School, N6
Hilden Grange School, Tonbridge
Hilden Oaks School, Tonbridge
Hillcroft Preparatory School, Stowmarket
Holme Grange School, Wokingham
Holme Park School, Kendal
Hordle Walhampton School, Lymington
Hull Collegiate School, Anlaby
Hurlingham Private School, SW15
Hurstpierpoint College, Hurstpierpoint
Innellan House School, Pinner
Ipswich School, Ipswich
James Allen's Girls' School, SE22
James Allen's Preparatory School, SE22
Junior King's School, Canterbury
Kelly College, Tavistock
Kelly College Preparatory School, Tavistock
King Edward's School, Birmingham
King William's College, Castletown
King's Bruton, Bruton
King's College, Taunton
King's College Junior School, SW19
King's College School, SW19
King's Hall, Taunton
King's Hawford, Worcester
King's Preparatory School, Rochester

The King's School, Canterbury
The King's School, Chester
The King's School, Gloucester
The King's School, Macclesfield
The King's School, Worcester
The King's School Ely, Ely
King's School Rochester, Rochester
Kingscote Pre-Preparatory School, Gerrards Cross
Kingshott School, Hitchin
Kingsland Grange, Shrewsbury
The Kingsley School, Leamington Spa
The Knoll School, Kidderminster
The Lady Eleanor Holles School, Hampton
Lambrook Haileybury, Bracknell
Lancing College Preparatory School at Mowden, Hove
Lanesborough, Guildford
Lavant House, Chichester
Laxton Junior School, Nr Peterborough
Leicester Grammar Junior School, Leicester
Leicester Grammar School, Leicester
Leicester High School For Girls, Leicester
Lichfield Cathedral School, Lichfield
The Littlemead School, Chichester
Liverpool College, Liverpool
Lockers Park, Hemel Hempstead
Luckley-Oakfield School, Wokingham
Ludgrove, Wokingham
Maidwell Hall School, Northampton
Malvern College, Malvern
Malvern College Preparatory and Pre-Prep School,
    Malvern
Malvern St James, Great Malvern
The Manor Preparatory School, Abingdon
Marlborough College, Marlborough
Marlborough House School, Hawkhurst
Meadowbrook Montessori School, Bracknell
Merchant Taylors' School, Northwood
Merton Court Preparatory School, Sidcup
Merton House, Chester
Micklefield School, Reigate
Milbourne Lodge School, Esher
Milton Abbey School, Blandford Forum
The Minster School, York
Moffats School, Bewdley
Monkton Combe Junior School, Bath
Monkton Combe School, Bath
Moorland School, Clitheroe
Moreton Hall School, Oswestry
Morley Hall Preparatory School, Derby
Moulsford Preparatory School, Wallingford
Mount House School, Tavistock
Mowden Hall School, Stocksfield
Netherwood School, Saundersfoot
The New Beacon, Sevenoaks
New College School, Oxford
New Lodge School, Dorking
New School, Exeter
Newcastle Upon Tyne Church High School,
    Newcastle upon Tyne
Norman Court Preparatory School, Salisbury
Northampton High School, Northampton
Northbourne Park School, Deal
Northcote Lodge School, SW11

Northwood Preparatory School, Rickmansworth
Oakham School, Oakham
Oakwood School, Chichester
Old Buckenham Hall School, Ipswich
The Old Hall School, Telford
The Old Malthouse, Swanage
Old Palace School of John Whitgift, Croydon
The Old School, Beccles
Old Vicarage School, Richmond
Oriel Bank, Stockport
Orley Farm School, Harrow
Oswestry School Bellan House, Oswestry
Oundle School, Nr Peterborough
Packwood Haugh School, Shrewsbury
Pangbourne College, Pangbourne
Papplewick School, Ascot
Park Hill School, Kingston-upon-Thames
Peaslake School, Guildford
Pennthorpe School, Horsham
Perrott Hill School, Crewkerne
Peterborough & St Margaret's School, Stanmore
Peterborough High School, Peterborough
Pilgrims Pre-Preparatory School, Bedford
The Pilgrims' School, Winchester
Pinewood School, Shrivenham
Pipers Corner School, High Wycombe
Plumtree School, Nottingham
Pocklington School, Pocklington
The Prebendal School, Chichester
Prebendal School (Northgate House), Chichester
Prestfelde Preparatory School, Shrewsbury
Prince's Mead School, Winchester
The Princess Helena College, Hitchin
Quainton Hall School, Harrow
Queen Anne's School, Reading
Queen Ethelburga's College, York
Queen Margaret's School, York
Queen Mary's School, Thirsk
Queen's College, W1G
Queen's College Prep School, W1B
Querns Westonbirt School, Tetbury
Radley College, Abingdon
Ranby House School, Retford
Rathvilly School, Birmingham
Ravenscourt Theatre School, W6
Read School, Selby
Reading Blue Coat School, Reading
Reddiford, Pinner
Reed's School, Cobham
Reigate St Mary's Preparatory and Choir School, Reigate
Rendcomb College, Cirencester
Repton School, Derby
Riddlesworth Hall, Diss
Ripon Cathedral Choir School, Ripon
Rishworth School, Rishworth
Rock Hall School, Alnwick
Rodney School, Newark
Roedean School, Brighton
Rose Hill School, Wotton-under-Edge
Roselyon, Par
Rossall Junior School, Fleetwood
Rossall School, Fleetwood
Rosslyn School, Birmingham

Roxeth Mead School, Harrow on the Hill
Royal Alexandra and Albert School, Reigate
Royal Russell School, Croydon
The Royal School, Haslemere
The Royal Wolverhampton Junior School,
    Wolverhampton
The Royal Wolverhampton School, Wolverhampton
Rugby School, Rugby
Rushmoor School, Bedford
Russell House School, Sevenoaks
Ryde School, Ryde
Sackville School, Tonbridge
Saddleworth Preparatory School, Oldham
St Agnes PNEU School, Leeds
St Albans High School for Girls, St Albans
St Andrew's School, Eastbourne
St Andrew's School, Reading
St. Andrew's (Woking) School Trust, Woking
St Anselm's School, Bakewell
St Aubyns School, Brighton
St Bees School, St Bees
St Catherine's School, Guildford
St Christopher's School
St Christopher's School, Epsom
St Christopher's School, Hove
St David's School, Ashford
St David's School, Purley
St Edmunds Junior School, Canterbury
St Edmund's School, Canterbury
St Edmund's School, Hindhead
St Edward's School, Oxford
St Francis School, Pewsey
St Gabriel's, Newbury
St George's School, Ascot
St George's School, Windsor
St Hilda's School, Harpenden
St Hilda's School, Wakefield
St Hugh's School, Faringdon
St Hugh's School, Woodhall Spa
St Ives School, Haslemere
St. James' School, Grimsby
St John's College School, Cambridge
St John's Northwood, Northwood
St John's School, Leatherhead
St John's-on-the-Hill, Chepstow
St Lawrence College Junior School, Ramsgate
St Lawrence College, Ramsgate
St Margaret's School, Bushey
St Margaret's School, Exeter
St Margaret's School, Halstead
St Margaret's School, NW3
St Martin's School, Bournemouth
St Martin's School, Northwood
St Mary's College, Southampton
St Mary's Hall, Brighton
St Mary's School, Calne
St Mary's School, Gerrards Cross
St Mary's School, Wantage
St Michael's, Barnstaple
St Michael's School, Leigh-on-Sea
St Michael's School, Sevenoaks
St Neot's School, Hook
St Nicholas' School, Fleet

St Paul's Cathedral School, EC4M
St Paul's Preparatory School, SW13
St Paul's School, SW13
St Peter's School, Kettering
St Peter's School, York
St Petroc's School, Bude
St Piran's Preparatory School, Maidenhead
St Ronan's School, Hawkhurst
St Swithun's School, Winchester
St Wilfrid's School, Exeter
St Wystan's School, Repton
Salisbury Cathedral School, Salisbury
Sancton Wood School, Cambridge
Sanderstead Junior School, South Croydon
Sandroyd School, Salisbury
Sarum Hall, NW3
Saville House School, Mansfield
The School of St Helen & St Katharine, Abingdon
Seaford College, Petworth
Sedbergh School, Sedbergh
Shaw House School, Bradford
Sherborne Preparatory School, Sherborne
Sherborne School, Sherborne
Sherborne School for Girls, Sherborne
Shernold School, Maidstone
Sherrardswood School, Welwyn
Shiplake College, Henley-on-Thames
Shoreham College, Shoreham-by-Sea
Shrewsbury House School, Surbiton
Shrewsbury School, Shrewsbury
Slapton Pre-Preparatory School, Towcester
Smallwood Manor Preparatory School, Uttoxeter
Snaresbrook College Preparatory School, E18
Solefield School, Sevenoaks
Solihull School, Solihull
Sompting Abbotts School, Sompting
Spratton Hall, Northampton
Stamford School, Stamford
Steephill Independent School, Longfield
Stepping Stones Nursery and Pre-Preparatory School,
    Marlborough
Stoke Brunswick, East Grinstead
Stoneygate School, Leicester
Stourbridge House School, Warminster
Stover School, Newton Abbot
Stowe School, Buckingham
The Stroud School, Romsey
The Study School, New Malden
Sunderland High School, Sunderland
Sunningdale School, Sunningdale
Surbiton High School, Kingston-upon-Thames
Surbiton Preparatory School, Surbiton
Sussex House School, SW1X
Sutton Valence Preparatory School, Maidstone
Sutton Valence School, Maidstone
Swanbourne House School, Milton Keynes
Talbot Heath, Bournemouth
Taverham Hall, Norwich
Thomas's Kindergarten, Battersea, SW11
Thomas's Preparatory School, SW11
Thomas' Preparatory School Clapham, SW11
Thorpe House School, Gerrards Cross
Tockington Manor School

Tonbridge School, Tonbridge
Town Close House Preparatory School, Norwich
Trevor Roberts', NW3
Truro High School, Truro
Tudor Hall School, Banbury
Twyford School, Winchester
Uppingham School, Uppingham
Upton House School, Windsor
Vinehall School, Robertsbridge
Wakefield Independent School, Wakefield
Warminster School, Warminster
Warwick School, Warwick
Wellesley House School, Broadstairs
Wellington College, Crowthorne
Wellington School, Wellington
Wells Cathedral Junior School, Wells
Wells Cathedral School, Wells
West Buckland Preparatory School, Barnstaple
West Buckland School, Barnstaple
Westbourne House School, Chichester
Westbrook Hay Preparatory School, Hemel Hempstead
Westminster Abbey Choir School, SW1P
Westminster School, SW1P
Westminster Under School, SW1P
Westonbirt School, Tetbury
Widford Lodge, Chelmsford
Winchester College, Winchester
Winchester House School, Brackley
Windlesham House, Pulborough
Wisbech Grammar School, Wisbech
Witham Hall, Bourne
Wood Dene School, Norwich
Woodbridge School, Woodbridge
Woodleigh School, Malton
Worksop College, Worksop
Wrekin College, Telford
Wycombe Abbey School, High Wycombe
Wykeham House School, Fareham
Yateley Manor Preparatory School, Yateley
York House School, Rickmansworth
Yorston Lodge School, Knutsford

CHURCH OF SCOTLAND

The Glasgow Academy

EPISCOPELIAN

Glenalmond College, Perth

GREEK ORTHODOX

Knightsbridge School, SW1X

JEWISH

Akiva School, N3
Beis Hamedrash Elyon, NW11
Beis Rochel D'Satmar Girls School, N16
Hubert Jewish High School for Girls, Salford
Immanuel College, Bushey

Kerem School, N2
London Jewish Girls' High School, NW4
Lubavitch House School (Junior Boys), E5
Lubavitch House Senior School for Girls, N16
Mechinah Liyeshivah Zichron Moshe, N16
Naima Jewish Preparatory School, NW6
OYH Primary School, NW4
Pardes Grammar Boys' School, N3
Talmud Torah Bobov Primary School, N16
Tashbar School, Salford
Yesodey Hatorah Jewish School, N16
Yetev Lev Day School for Boys, N16

METHODIST

Ashville College, Harrogate
Bronte House School, Bradford
Culford School, Bury St Edmunds
Edgehill College, Bideford
Farringtons School, Chislehurst
Kent College, Canterbury
Kent College Infant & Junior School, Canterbury
Kent College Pembury, Tunbridge Wells
Kingswood Preparatory School, Bath
Kingswood School, Bath
The Leys School, Cambridge
Lyndon Preparatory School, Colwyn Bay
Queen's College, Taunton
Queen's College Junior and Pre-Preparatory Schools,
    Taunton
Rydal Penrhos Senior School, Colwyn Bay
St Crispin's School (Leicester) Ltd., Leicester
Shebbear College, Beaworthy
Truro School Preparatory School, Truro
Woodhouse Grove School, Apperley Bridge

MORAVIAN

Fulneck School, Pudsey

MUSLIM

Abu Bakr Independent School, Walsall
Al Hijrah School, Birmingham
Al Karam Secondary School, Retford
Al-Burhan Grammar School, Birmingham
Al-Islamia Primary, Leicester
Al-Mizan School, E1
Al-Muntada Islamic School, SW6
Balham Preparatory School, SW12
Birchfield Independent Girls School, Birmingham
Bolton Muslim Girls School, Bolton
Brondesbury College For Boys, NW6
Coventry Muslim School, Coventry
Darul Hadis Latifiah, E2
Darul Uloom Islamic High School & College, Birmingham
Date Valley School, Mitcham
Gloucestershire Islamic Secondary School For Girls,
    Gloucester
IQRA School, Oxford
Islamia Girls High School, Huddersfield
Islamia Girls' School, NW6

Islamic Shakhsiyah Foundation, Walthamstow
Islamiyah School, Blackburn
Jamahiriya School, SW3
Jamea Al Kauthar, Lancaster
Jamiah Madaniyah Primary School, Forest Gate
King Fahad Academy, W3
London East Academy, E1
London Islamic School, E1
Madni Girls School, E1
Manchester Islamic High School, Manchester
Markazul Uloom, Blackburn
New Horizon Community School, Leeds
Noor Ul Islam Primary School, E10
Quwwatt Ul Islam Girls School, E7
Rawdha Tul Uloom, Blackburn
Rochdale Girls School, Rochdale
Tawhid Boys School, Tawhid Educational Trust, N16
Tayyibah Girls School, N16

QUAKER

Ackworth School, Pontefract
Ackworth School - International Study Centre, Pontefract
Bootham School, York
Friends' School, Saffron Walden
Leighton Park School, Reading
The Mount School, York
Sibford School, Banbury
Sidcot School, Winscombe
Tregelles, York

ROMAN CATHOLIC

All Hallows, Shepton Mallet
Alton Convent School, Alton
Ampleforth College, York
Austin Friars St Monica's School, Carlisle
Barlborough Hall School, Chesterfield
Barrow Hills School, Godalming
Beechwood Sacred Heart School, Tunbridge Wells
Bishop Challoner RC School, Bromley
Brigidine School Windsor, Windsor
Bury Catholic Preparatory School, Bury
Carleton House Preparatory School, Liverpool
Claires Court Schools, The College, Maidenhead
Combe Bank School, Nr Sevenoaks
Convent of Mercy, Guernsey
Cranmore School, Leatherhead
Donhead Prep School, SW19
Downside School, Bath
Farleigh School, Andover
Farnborough Hill, Farnborough
FCJ Primary School, Jersey
Fernhill School, Rutherglen
Grace Dieu Manor School, Leicester
Holy Cross Convent, Gerrards Cross
Holy Cross Preparatory School, Kingston-upon-Thames
Ilford Ursuline Preparatory School, Ilford
Kilgraston, Perth
Laleham Lea School, Purley
Loreto Preparatory School, Altrincham
Loyola Preparatory School, Buckhurst Hill

The Marist Preparatory School, Ascot
The Marist Senior School, Ascot
Marymount International School, Kingston-upon-Thames
Moor Park School, Ludlow
More House, SW1X
More House School, Farnham
Moreton Hall Preparatory School, Bury St Edmunds
Mount St Mary's College, Spinkhill
Mylnhurst RC School & Nursery, Sheffield
New Hall School, Chelmsford
Notre Dame Preparatory School, Cobham
Notre Dame Preparatory School, Norwich
Notre Dame Senior School, Cobham
Oakhill College, Clitheroe
Oakwood School & Nursery, Purley
The Oratory Preparatory School, Reading
The Oratory School, Reading
Our Lady's Convent Junior School, Abingdon
Our Lady's Convent School, Loughborough
Our Lady's Convent Senior School, Abingdon
Our Lady's Preparatory School, Crowthorne
Princethorpe College, Rugby
Prior Park College, Bath
Prior Park Preparatory School, Cricklade
Priory School, Birmingham
Ratcliffe College, Leicester
Redcourt- St Anselms, Prenton
Runnymede St Edward's School, Liverpool
Rye St Antony School, Oxford
Sacred Heart Convent School, Swaffham
Sacred Heart R.C. Primary School, Wadhurst
St Aloysius' College
St Ambrose Preparatory School, Altrincham
St Anthony's Preparatory School, NW3
St Anthonys School, Cinderford
St Antony's Leweston School, Sherborne
St Augustine's Priory, W5
St Bede's College, Manchester
St Bede's School, Stafford
St Benedict's Junior School, W5
St Benedict's School, W5
St Bernard's Preparatory School, Slough
St Catherine's Preparatory School, Stockport
St Catherine's School, Twickenham
St Christina's RC Preparatory School, NW8
St Columba's College, St Albans
St Dominic's Priory School, Stone
St Edmund's College, Ware
St Edward's School Cheltenham, Cheltenham
St George's College, Weybridge
St George's College Junior School, Weybridge
St Gerard's School, Bangor
St John's Beaumont, Windsor
St John's College, Southsea
St Joseph's Convent, Chesterfield
St Joseph's Convent School, Burnley
St Joseph's Convent School, E11
St Joseph's Convent School, Reading
St Joseph's Preparatory School, Stoke-on-Trent
St Joseph's School, Nottingham
St Leonards-Mayfield School, Mayfield
St Margaret's School Convent of Mercy, Midhurst
St Martha's Senior School, Barnet

St Martin's Ampleforth, York
St Mary's College, Liverpool
St Mary's Convent School, Worcester
St Mary's Hall, Stonyhurst
St Mary's Hare Park School, Romford
St Mary's Junior School, Cambridge
St Mary's School, Ascot, Ascot
St Mary's School, Cambridge
St Mary's School, Shaftesbury
St Mary's School Hampstead, NW3
St Michaels School, Newbury
St Philip's School, SW7
St Philomena's Preparatory School, Frinton-on-Sea
St Pius X Preparatory School, Preston
St Richard's, Bromyard
St Teresa's Catholic Independent & Nursery School,
    Princes Risborough
St Teresa's Preparatory School, Effingham
St Teresa's School, Dorking
St Thomas Garnet's School, Bournemouth
St Ursula's High School
St Winefride's Convent School, Shrewsbury
Salesian College, Farnborough
Sinclair House School, SW6
Stella Maris Junior School, Stockport
Stonyhurst College, Clitheroe
Thornton College Convent of Jesus and Mary,
    Milton Keynes

The Towers Convent School, Steyning
Trinity School, Teignmouth
Ursuline Preparatory School, Brentwood
Ursuline Preparatory School, SW20
Virgo Fidelis, SE19
Vita Et Pax School, N14
Westminster Cathedral Choir School, SW1P
Winterfold House, Kidderminster
Woldingham School, Woldingham
Worth School, Turners Hill

SEVENTH DAY ADVENTIST

Dudley House School, Grantham
Fletewood School, Plymouth
Hyland House, E17
Newbold School, Bracknell
Stanborough School, Watford

UNITED REFORMED CHURCH

Caterham School, Caterham
The Firs School, Chester
Silcoates School, Wakefield
Sunny Hill House School, Wakefield

4.7

Schools Registered with CReSTeD (Council for the Registration of Schools Teaching Dyslexic Pupils)

Registered charity number 1052103
Information provided by CReSTeD

CReSTeD (the Council for the Registration of Schools Teaching Dyslexic Pupils) produces a twice yearly register of schools that provide for dyslexic children. The aim is to help parents and those who advise them to choose a school that has been approved to published criteria. CReSTeD was established in 1989 – its main supporters are the British Dyslexia Association and The Dyslexia Institute. Schools wishing to be included in the Register are visited by a CReSTeD consultant whose report is considered by the CReSTeD Council before registration can be finalised.

Consulting the Register should enable parents to decide which schools they wish to approach for further information. Dyslexic students have a variety of difficulties and so have a wide range of special needs. An equally wide range of teaching approaches is necessary. CReSTeD has therefore grouped schools together under four broad categories, which are designed to help parents match their child's needs to an appropriate philosophy and provision.

The four categories of the schools are described below:

SPECIALIST PROVISION SCHOOLS – SP

The school is established primarily to teach pupils with dyslexia. The curriculum and timetable are designed to meet specific needs in a holistic, co-ordinated manner with a significant number of staff qualified in teaching dyslexic pupils.

DYSLEXIA UNIT – DU

The school has a designated unit or centre that provides specialist tuition on a small group or individual basis, according to need. The unit or centre is an adequately resourced teaching area under the management of a senior specialist teacher, who co-ordinates the work of other specialist teachers and ensures ongoing liaison with all mainstream teachers. This senior specialist teacher will probably have head of department status, and will certainly have significant input into the curriculum design and delivery.

SPECIALIST CLASSES – SC

Schools where dyslexic pupils are taught in separate classes within the school for some lessons, most probably English and mathematics. These are taught by teachers with qualifications in teaching dyslexic pupils. These teachers are deemed responsible for communicating with the pupils' other subject teachers.

WITHDRAWAL SYSTEMS – WS

Schools where dyslexic pupils are withdrawn from appropriately selected lessons for specialist tuition from a teacher qualified in teaching dyslexic pupils. There is ongoing communication between mainstream and specialist teachers.

Note: **Qualified** means holding a BDA recognized qualification in the teaching of dyslexic pupils.

The list below includes those schools registered with CReSTeD which are listed elsewhere in this guide. For a full list of schools registered with CReSTeD, including specialist schools and maintained schools, contact CReSTeD on 01242 604852 or by email at admin@crested.org.uk, or by writing to The Administrator, CReSTeD, Greygarth, Littleworth, Winchcombe, Cheltenham, GL54 5BT. Alternatively, visit the website at www.crested.org.uk.

DYSLEXIA UNIT

Avon House, Woodford Green
Barnardiston Hall, Havershill
Bedgebury School, Cranbrook
Bethany School, Cranbrook
Bloxham School, Banbury
Bredon School, Tewkesbury
Clayesmore Preparatory School, Blandford Forum
Clayesmore School, Blandford Forum
Clifton College Preparatory School
Cobham Hall, Gravesend
Danes Hill School, Leatherhead
Ellesmere College, Ellesmere
Finborough School, Stowmarket
Fulneck School, Pudsey
Grenville College, Bideford
Hazlegrove (King's Bruton Preparatory School), Yeovil
Hillcroft Preparatory School, Stowmarket
Holmwood House, Colchester
Hordle Walhampton School, Lymington

King's Bruton, Bruton
King's School Rochester, Rochester
Kingham Hill School, Chipping Norton
Kingswood College at Scarisbrick Hall, Ormskirk
Kingswood House School, Epsom
Lime House School, Carlisle
Malvern St James, Great Malvern
Mayville High School, Southsea
Monkton Combe School, Bath
Mostyn House School, South Wirral
Moyles Court School, Ringwood
Newlands School, Seaford
Ramillies Hall School, Cheadle
Riddlesworth Hall, Diss
St Bede's Prep School, Eastbourne
St Bede's School, Hailsham
St Bees School, St Bees
St David's College, Llandudno
St John's School, Sidmouth
Sibford School, Banbury
Sidcot School, Winscombe

Slindon College, Arundel
Stanbridge Earls School, Romsey
Stowford College, Sutton
Tettenhall College, Wolverhampton
Warminster School, Warminster
Wycliffe College & Preparatory School, Stonehouse
Wycliffe Preparatory School, Stonehouse

SPECIALIST CLASSES

Belmont School, Dorking
Bruern Abbey, Chesterton
St Crispin's School (Leicester) Ltd., Leicester

WITHDRAWAL SYSTEM

Centre Academy, SW11
Dover College, Dover
Kilgraston (A Sacred Heart School), Perth
Malvern College Preparatory and Pre-Prep School,
    Malvern
Milton Abbey School, Blandford Forum
Prior Park Preparatory School, Cricklade
Woodleigh School, Malton
Woodside Park International School, N11
Ysgol Rhydygors, Carmarthen

4.8

Provision for English as a Foreign Language

This index is intended as a general guide only and is compiled upon the basis of information given to Gabbitas by schools. Parents should note that there are wide variations in provision and are advised to contact individual schools for further details.

Schools listed below with a 'U' have a dedicated English language unit or offer intensive initial tuition for students whose first language is not English. Schools with no 'U' displayed offer one-to-one English language tuition, or arrange this tuition, according to need, for students whose first language is not English.

Parents may also wish to refer to the list of International Study Centres on page 00.

ENGLAND

BEDFORDSHIRE

Acorn School, Bedford
Bedford School, Bedford

BERKSHIRE

The Ark School, Reading
Bearwood College, Wokingham U
Bradfield College, Reading U
Brockhurst & Marlston House Pre-Preparatory School, Thatcham
Brockhurst and Marlston House Schools, Newbury
Cedars School, Aldermaston
Cheam School, Newbury
Claires Court School, Maidenhead
Claires Court Schools, Ridgeway, Maidenhead
Dolphin School, Reading
Eagle House, Sandhurst
Elstree School, Reading
The Elvian School, Reading
Heathfield St Mary's School, Ascot
Highfield School, Maidenhead
Holme Grange School, Wokingham
Horris Hill School, Newbury
Hurst Lodge School, Ascot
Leighton Park School, Reading U

Licensed Victuallers' School, Ascot
Luckley-Oakfield School, Wokingham
The Oratory Preparatory School, Reading
The Oratory School, Reading U
Padworth College, Reading U
Papplewick School, Ascot
Queen Anne's School, Reading
St Gabriel's, Newbury
St George's School, Ascot
St John's Beaumont, Windsor U
St Joseph's Convent School, Reading
Upton House School, Windsor
Waverley School, Wokingham
White House Preparatory School, Wokingham
Winbury School, Maidenhead

BRISTOL

Badminton School
Clifton College U
Clifton College Preparatory School U
The Downs School, Wraxall
Gracefield Preparatory School
Queen Elizabeth's Hospital
The Red Maids' School
St Ursula's High School U

Tockington Manor School   U
Torwood House School

BUCKINGHAMSHIRE

Akeley Wood School, Buckingham
Caldicott School, Farnham Royal
Godstowe Preparatory School, High Wycombe   U
Grove Independent School, Milton Keynes
Holy Cross Convent, Gerrards Cross
Ladymede, Aylesbury
Maltman's Green School, Gerrards Cross
Milton Keynes Preparatory School, Milton Keynes
Pipers Corner School, High Wycombe
Stowe School, Buckingham
Swanbourne House School, Milton Keynes
Thornton College Convent of Jesus and Mary,
    Milton Keynes
Thorpe House School, Gerrards Cross

CAMBRIDGESHIRE

Bellerbys College & Embassy CES Cambridge,
    Cambridge   U
Cambridge Arts & Sciences (CATS), Cambridge   U
Cambridge Centre for Sixth-Form Studies, Cambridge
Kimbolton School, Huntingdon
The King's School Ely, Ely   U
The Leys School, Cambridge   U
Madingley Pre-Preparatory School, Cambridge
MPW (Mander Portman Woodward), Cambridge   U
Peterborough High School, Peterborough   U
St Mary's School, Cambridge   U
Sancton Wood School, Cambridge

CHANNEL ISLANDS

St George's Preparatory School, Jersey

CHESHIRE

Abbey Gate School, Chester
Cransley School, Northwich
Culcheth Hall, Altrincham
The Firs School, Chester
Forest Park School, Sale
Hale Preparatory School, Altrincham   U
Loreto Preparatory School, Altrincham
Mostyn House School, South Wirral   U
The Queen's School, Chester
The Ryleys, Alderley Edge
Terra Nova School, Holmes Chapel
Wilmslow Preparatory School, Wilmslow

CORNWALL

The Bolitho School, Penzance   U
St Ia School, St Ives
Truro School, Truro

CUMBRIA

Harecroft Hall School, Seascale
Holme Park School, Kendal
St Bees School, St Bees   U
Sedbergh School, Sedbergh   U
Windermere St Anne's, Windermere   U

DERBYSHIRE

Derby High School, Derby
Mount St Mary's College, Spinkhill   U
Repton School, Derby   U
St Anselm's School, Bakewell

DEVON

Blundell's School, Tiverton
Bramdean School, Exeter
Edgehill College, Bideford   U
Exeter Cathedral School, Exeter
Grenville College, Bideford   U
Kelly College, Tavistock   U
The Maynard School, Exeter
Mount House School, Tavistock
Plymouth College, Plymouth   U
St Dunstan's Abbey - The Plymouth College Junior
    School, Plymouth
St John's School, Sidmouth   U
Shebbear College, Beaworthy   U
Stover School, Newton Abbot   U
Tower House School, Paignton
Trinity School, Teignmouth   U
West Buckland School, Barnstaple   U

DORSET

Bryanston School, Blandford Forum
Clayesmore Preparatory School, Blandford Forum
Clayesmore School, Blandford Forum
Dorchester Preparatory and Independent Schools,
    Dorchester
International College, Sherborne School, Sherborne   U
Milton Abbey School, Blandford Forum
The Old Malthouse, Swanage
Port Regis School, Shaftesbury   U
St Antony's Leweston School, Sherborne
St Mary's School, Shaftesbury
Sherborne Preparatory School, Sherborne
Sherborne School, Sherborne
Sherborne School for Girls, Sherborne   U
Talbot Heath, Bournemouth
Wentworth College, Bournemouth   U
Yarrells School, Poole

COUNTY DURHAM

Durham School, Durham
Polam Hall, Darlington   U

ESSEX

Brentwood School, Brentwood	U
Chigwell School, Chigwell	U
College Saint-Pierre, Leigh-on-Sea	
Elm Green Preparatory School, Chelmsford	U
Felsted Preparatory School, Felsted	
Felsted School, Dunmow	U
Friends' School, Saffron Walden	U
New Hall School, Chelmsford	U
Oaklands School, Loughton	
St John's School, Billericay	
St Margaret's School, Halstead	U
St Mary's School, Colchester	
Thorpe Hall School, Southend-on-Sea	

GLOUCESTERSHIRE

Bredon School, Tewkesbury	U
Cheltenham College, Cheltenham	
Cheltenham College Junior School, Cheltenham	
The Cheltenham Ladies' College, Cheltenham	
Dean Close Preparatory School, Cheltenham	U
Dean Close School, Cheltenham	U
Hatherop Castle School, Cirencester	
Rendcomb College, Cirencester	
Rose Hill School, Wotton-under-Edge	
Westonbirt School, Tetbury	U
Wycliffe College, Stonehouse	U
Wycliffe Preparatory School, Stonehouse	U
Wynstones School, Gloucester	

HAMPSHIRE

Bedales School, Petersfield	
Brockwood Park School, Bramdean	U
Glenhurst School, Havant	
Hampshire Collegiate School (Embley Park), Romsey	
Highfield School, Liphook	
Hordle Walhampton School, Lymington	
Lord Wandsworth College, Hook	
Mayville High School, Southsea	U
Rookesbury Park School, Portsmouth	
St John's College, Southsea	
St Mary's College, Southampton	
St Nicholas' School, Fleet	
Sherborne House School, Eastleigh	
Stanbridge Earls School, Romsey	
Twyford School, Winchester	
Woodhill School, Chandler's Ford	
Wykeham House School, Fareham	

HEREFORDSHIRE

Lucton School, Leominster

HERTFORDSHIRE

Aldenham School, Elstree	
Arts Educational School, Tring Park, Tring	
Bishop's Stortford College, Bishop's Stortford	
Haileybury, Hertford	
Lockers Park, Hemel Hempstead	
The Princess Helena College, Hitchin	
Queenswood School, Hatfield	U
The Royal Masonic School for Girls, Rickmansworth	
St Andrew's Montessori School, Watford	
St Christopher School, Letchworth	
St Edmund's College, Ware	U
St Francis' College, Letchworth	U
St Margaret's School, Bushey	U
Stanborough School, Watford	U

ISLE OF MAN

King William's College, Castletown

ISLE OF WIGHT

Ryde School, Ryde

KENT

Ashford School, Ashford	
Bedgebury School, Cranbrook	U
Beechwood Sacred Heart School, Tunbridge Wells	U
Benenden School, Cranbrook	
Bethany School, Cranbrook	U
Bromley High School GDST, Bromley	
Cobham Hall, Gravesend	U
Dover College, Dover	U
Dulwich Preparatory School, Cranbrook, Cranbrook	
Farringtons School, Chislehurst	U
Harenc School Trust, Sidcup	
Holmewood House, Tunbridge Wells	
Junior King's School, Canterbury	U
Kent College, Canterbury	U
Kent College Infant & Junior School, Canterbury	U
Kent College Pembury, Tunbridge Wells	
Northbourne Park School, Deal	U
Rochester Independent College, Rochester	U
St Christopher's School, Canterbury	U
St Edmunds Junior School, Canterbury	
St Edmund's School, Canterbury	
St Lawrence College Junior School, Ramsgate	U
St Lawrence College, Ramsgate	U
St Michael's School, Sevenoaks	
Sevenoaks School, Sevenoaks	
Sutton Valence School, Maidstone	
Tonbridge School, Tonbridge	
Walthamstow Hall, Sevenoaks	
Wellesley House School, Broadstairs	
West Lodge Preparatory School, Sidcup	

LANCASHIRE

Bolton School (Girls' Division), Bolton	
Clevelands Preparatory School, Bolton	
Kingswood College at Scarisbrick Hall, Ormskirk	
Kirkham Grammar School, Preston	
Langdale Preparatory School, Blackpool	
Rossall School, Fleetwood	U

Rossall School International Study Centre,
   Fleetwood   U
St Anne's College Grammar School,
   Lytham St Annes   U
Stonyhurst College, Clitheroe   U

LEICESTERSHIRE

Brooke House College, Market Harborough   U
Irwin College, Leicester   U
Leicester Grammar School, Leicester   U
Ratcliffe College, Leicester   U
St Crispin's School (Leicester) Ltd., Leicester

LINCOLNSHIRE

Copthill School, Stamford
Kirkstone House School, Bourne
Stamford School, Stamford

NORTH EAST LINCOLNSHIRE

St. James' School, Grimsby   U

LONDON

Albemarle Independent College, W1K   U
The American School in London, NW8   U
Ashbourne Independent Sixth Form College, W8
Ashbourne Middle School, W8
Aston House School, W5
Bales College, W10
Barbara Speake Stage School, W3
Brampton College, NW4   U
Cameron House School, SW3
Collingham Independent GCSE and Sixth Form
   College, SW5
Connaught House, W2
Davies Laing and Dick, W1U   U
Donhead Prep School, SW19
Ealing Independent College, W5
Eaton House School Belgravia, SW1W
Eaton House The Manor, SW4
Eaton House The Vale, SW7
Eaton House The Vale School, SW7
Eaton Square School, SW1V
Finton House School, SW17
Francis Holland School, SW1W
Gatehouse School, E2
Hall School Wimbledon, SW20
Heath House Preparatory School, SE3
Heathside Preparatory School, NW3
Hendon Preparatory School, NW4   U
Hill House International Junior School, SW1X   U
International Community School, NW1   U
International School of London, W3   U
Kerem School, N2
Knightsbridge School, SW1X
Lansdowne College, W2
Le Herisson, W6   U
Lion House School, SW15

Mander Portman Woodward, SW7   U
The Mount School, NW7   U
North Bridge House Senior School, NW1
North Bridge House Upper Prep School, NW1
Parkgate House School, SW4
Primrose Independent School, N5
Putney Park School, SW15
Ravenscourt Park Preparatory School, W6
Riverston School, SE12
The Roche School, SW18
The Rowans School, SW20
The Royal School, Hampstead, NW3
St Augustine's Priory, W5
St Johns Wood Pre-Preparatory School, NW8
St Margaret's School, NW3
St Martin's, NW7
St Mary's School Hampstead, NW3
St Olave's Preparatory School, SE9
Southbank International School, Hampstead, NW3   U
Southbank International School, Kensington, W11   U
Southbank International School, Westminster, W1B   U
The Study Preparatory School, SW19
Sylvia Young Theatre School, NW1
Thames Christian College, SW11   U
The Lloyd Williamson School, W10
Thomas's Fulham, SW6
Thomas's Preparatory School, W8   U
Welsh School of London, NW10
Westminster Tutors, SW7
Wetherby Preparatory School, W11
Willington School, SW19
Woodside Park International School, N11

GREATER MANCHESTER

Clarendon Cottage School, Eccles
St Bede's College, Manchester
Withington Girls' School, Manchester

MERSEYSIDE

Heswall Preparatory School, Wirral
Kingsmead School, Wirral
Liverpool College, Liverpool
Merchant Taylors' School for Girls, Liverpool

MIDDLESEX

ACS Hillingdon International School, Hillingdon   U
Denmead School, Hampton
Halliford School, Shepperton
Harrow School, Harrow on the Hill
Little Eden SDA School & Eden High SDA School,
   Hanworth
The Mall School, Twickenham
St Christopher's School, Wembley
St Helen's School, Northwood   U
Staines Preparatory School, Staines
Sunflower Montessori School, Twickenham

NORFOLK

Beeston Hall School, Cromer
Gresham's Preparatory School, Holt
Gresham's School, Holt
Hethersett Old Hall School, Norwich
Langley School, Norwich   U
The New Eccles Hall School, Norwich   U
Norwich High School for Girls GDST, Norwich
Notre Dame Preparatory School, Norwich
Riddlesworth Hall, Diss   U
St Nicholas House Kindergarten & Prep School,
    North Walsham   U
Taverham Hall, Norwich   U

NORTHAMPTONSHIRE

Bosworth Independent College, Northampton   U
Maidwell Hall School, Northampton
Northamptonshire Grammar School, Pitsford
Quinton House School, Northampton

NORTHUMBERLAND

Longridge Towers School, Berwick-upon-Tweed

NOTTINGHAMSHIRE

Dagfa House School, Nottingham
Greenholme School, Nottingham
Ranby House School, Retford

OXFORDSHIRE

Abacus College, Oxford   U
Abingdon School, Abingdon
Bloxham School, Banbury   U
Cherwell College, Oxford
Christ Church Cathedral School, Oxford
Cokethorpe School, Witney
Cothill House Preparatory School, Abingdon
d'Overbroeck's College, Oxford   U
Dragon School, Oxford
Greene's Tutorial College, Oxford
Headington School, Oxford
IQRA School, Oxford   U
Josca's Preparatory School, Abingdon
Kingham Hill School, Chipping Norton   U
Leckford Place School, Oxford
New College School, Oxford
Our Lady's Convent Senior School, Abingdon
Oxford Tutorial College, Oxford   U
Rye St Antony School, Oxford
St Clare's, Oxford, Oxford   U
St Mary's School, Wantage   U
The School of St Helen & St Katharine, Abingdon
Shiplake College, Henley-on-Thames
Sibford School, Banbury   U
Summer Fields, Oxford

RUTLAND

Oakham School, Oakham

SHROPSHIRE

Adcote School for Girls, Shrewsbury
Bedstone College, Bucknell   U
Dower House School, Bridgnorth
Ellesmere College, Ellesmere   U
Kingsland Grange, Shrewsbury
Moor Park School, Ludlow
Moreton Hall School, Oswestry   U
Oswestry School, Oswestry   U
Packwood Haugh School, Shrewsbury
St Winefride's Convent School, Shrewsbury
Shrewsbury School, Shrewsbury
Wrekin College, Telford

SOMERSET

All Hallows, Shepton Mallet
Bruton School for Girls, Bruton   U
Chard School, Chard
Chilton Cantelo School, Yeovil
Downside School, Bath
Hazlegrove (King's Bruton Preparatory School),
    Yeovil
King's Bruton, Bruton
King's College, Taunton
King's Hall, Taunton
Millfield Preparatory School, Glastonbury   U
Millfield School, Street   U
The Park School, Yeovil
Perrott Hill School, Crewkerne
Queen's College, Taunton   U
Taunton International Study Centre (TISC), Taunton   U
Taunton Preparatory School, Taunton   U
Taunton School, Taunton   U
Wellington School, Wellington   U
Wells Cathedral School, Wells   U

BATH & NORTH EAST SOMERSET

Bath Academy, Bath   U
Kingswood Preparatory School, Bath
Kingswood School, Bath   U
Monkton Combe School, Bath   U
Prior Park College, Bath
The Royal High School, Bath

NORTH SOMERSET

Sidcot School, Winscombe   U

STAFFORDSHIRE

Abbots Bromley School for Girls, Abbots Bromley
Denstone College, Uttoxeter
Lichfield Cathedral School, Lichfield
St Bede's School, Stafford   U
St Dominic's School, Stafford

SUFFOLK

Culford School, Bury St Edmunds
Felixstowe International College, Felixstowe   U
Framlingham College, Woodbridge   U
Framlingham College Preparatory School, Brandeston   U
Ipswich School, Ipswich
Moreton Hall Preparatory School, Bury St Edmunds
Orwell Park, Ipswich
The Royal Hospital School, Ipswich   U
Saint Felix School, Southwold
Summerhill School, Leiston   U
Woodbridge School, Woodbridge   U

SURREY

Aberdour, Tadworth
ACS Cobham International School, Cobham   U
ACS Egham International School, Egham   U
Aldro School, Godalming
Amesbury, Hindhead
Box Hill School, Dorking   U
Cambridge Tutors College, Croydon   U
Canbury School, Kingston-upon-Thames   U
Caterham School, Caterham
Charterhouse, Godalming
Chinthurst School, Tadworth
City of London Freemen's School, Ashtead
Croham Hurst School, South Croydon
Croydon High School GDST, South Croydon
Epsom College, Epsom
Ewell Castle School, Epsom
Grantchester House, Esher
Greenacre School for Girls, Banstead
Hampton Court House, East Molesey
Hawley Place School, Camberley
Hoe Bridge School, Woking
Hurtwood House, Dorking
Kew Green Preparatory School, Richmond   U
King Edward's School Witley, Godalming   U
King's House School, Richmond
Lodge School, Purley
Longacre School, Guildford
Marymount International School,
    Kingston-upon-Thames   U
New Lodge School, Dorking
Notre Dame Preparatory School, Cobham
Old Palace School of John Whitgift, Croydon
Park Hill School, Kingston-upon-Thames   U
Prior's Field School, Godalming   U
Royal Ballet School, Richmond
Royal Russell School, Croydon   U
The Royal School, Haslemere   U
St Catherine's School, Guildford
St David's School, Purley
St Hilary's School, Godalming
St John's School, Leatherhead   U
St Teresa's School, Dorking   U
Stowford College, Sutton
Surbiton High School, Kingston-upon-Thames
Surbiton Preparatory School, Surbiton
Sutton High School GDST, Sutton
TASIS The American School in England, Thorpe   U

Westbury House School, New Malden
Woldingham School, Woldingham   U
Woodcote House School, Windlesham
Yehudi Menuhin School, Cobham   U

EAST SUSSEX

Ashdown House School, Forest Row
Battle Abbey School, Battle   U
Brighton College, Brighton   U
Brighton College Prep School, Brighton
Buckswood School, Hastings   U
Eastbourne College, Eastbourne   U
Greenfields School, Forest Row   U
Lancing College Preparatory School at Mowden,
    Hove
Moira House Girls School, Eastbourne   U
Moira House School, Eastbourne
Newlands School, Seaford   U
Roedean School, Brighton   U
St Andrew's School, Eastbourne   U
St Aubyns School, Brighton
St Leonards-Mayfield School, Mayfield   U
St Mary's Hall, Brighton   U
Stonelands School of Ballet & Theatre Arts, Hove
Vinehall School, Robertsbridge

WEST SUSSEX

Ardingly College, Haywards Heath
Ardingly College Junior School, Haywards Heath
Arundale Preparatory School, Pulborough
Brambletye School, East Grinstead
Burgess Hill School for Girls, Burgess Hill
Cottesmore School, Pease Pottage
Dorset House School, Pulborough
Great Ballard School, Chichester
Hurstpierpoint College, Hurstpierpoint
Lavant House, Chichester
Seaford College, Petworth
Slindon College, Arundel
The Towers Convent School, Steyning
Windlesham House, Pulborough   U
Worth School, Turners Hill

TYNE AND WEAR

Central Newcastle High School GDST,
    Newcastle upon Tyne
Grindon Hall Christian School, Sunderland   U
The King's School, Tynemouth
Sunderland High School, Sunderland
Westfield School, Newcastle upon Tyne

WARWICKSHIRE

Abbotsford School, Kenilworth   U
Arnold Lodge School, Leamington Spa
Bilton Grange, Rugby
The Kingsley School, Leamington Spa
Princethorpe College, Rugby
Rugby School, Rugby

WEST MIDLANDS

Birchfield School, Wolverhampton
The Blue Coat School, Birmingham
Coventry Prep School, Coventry
Highclare School, Birmingham
Mander Portman Woodward, Birmingham
Priory School, Birmingham
The Royal Wolverhampton School, Wolverhampton   U
St George's School, Edgbaston, Birmingham
Tettenhall College, Wolverhampton   U

WILTSHIRE

Chafyn Grove School, Salisbury
Dauntsey's School, Devizes
Grittleton House School, Chippenham
Norman Court Preparatory School, Salisbury
Prior Park Preparatory School, Cricklade
St Margaret's Preparatory School, Calne
St Mary's School, Calne   U
Sandroyd School, Salisbury
Stonar School, Melksham
Warminster School, Warminster   U

WORCESTERSHIRE

Abberley Hall, Worcester   U
Bowbrook House School, Pershore
Bromsgrove Preparatory School, Bromsgrove   U
Bromsgrove School, Bromsgrove   U
The Downs School, Malvern
Malvern College, Malvern   U
Malvern College Preparatory and Pre-Prep School,
  Malvern
Malvern St James, Great Malvern   U
Moffats School, Bewdley
Moffats School, Bewdley
Saint Michael's College, Tenbury Wells   U

EAST RIDING OF YORKSHIRE

Pocklington School, Pocklington

NORTH YORKSHIRE

Ashville College, Harrogate
Bootham School, York
Brackenfield School, Harrogate
Bramcote School, Scarborough
Catteral Hall School, Settle
Fyling Hall School, Whitby
Giggleswick School, Settle
Harrogate Ladies' College, Harrogate   U
Harrogate Tutorial College, Harrogate   U
Howsham Hall, York
The Mount School, York
Queen Ethelburga's College, York   U
Queen Margaret's School, York
Read School, Selby
St Martin's Ampleforth, York
Scarborough College & Lisvane School, Scarborough
Terrington Hall, York

SOUTH YORKSHIRE

Ashdell Preparatory School, Sheffield
Brantwood School, Sheffield
Sheffield High School GDST, Sheffield

WEST YORKSHIRE

Ackworth School, Pontefract   U
Ackworth School - International Study Centre,
  Pontefract   U
Batley Grammar School, Batley
Fulneck School, Pudsey   U
Gateways School, Leeds
New Horizon Community School, Leeds
The Rastrick Independent School, Brighouse
Richmond House School, Leeds
Rishworth School, Rishworth   U
Woodhouse Grove School, Apperley Bridge   U

NORTHERN IRELAND

COUNTY ANTRIM

Victoria College Belfast, Belfast

COUNTY ARMAGH

The Royal School, Armagh   U

COUNTY TYRONE

The Royal School Dungannon, Dungannon   U

SCOTLAND

ABERDEENSHIRE

International School of Aberdeen, Aberdeen   U
St Margaret's School for Girls, Aberdeen

GLASGOW

Hutchesons' Grammar School

LOTHIAN

Basil Paterson Tutorial College, Edinburgh	U
Belhaven Hill, Dunbar	U
Clifton Hall School, Edinburgh	
The Edinburgh Rudolf Steiner School, Edinburgh	U
Fettes College, Edinburgh	U
George Watson's College, Edinburgh	
Loretto Junior School, Musselburgh	U
Loretto School, Musselburgh	
Merchiston Castle School, Edinburgh	U
St George's School for Girls, Edinburgh	U
St Serf's School, Edinburgh	

MORAYSHIRE

Gordonstoun School, Elgin

PERTHSHIRE

Craigclowan Preparatory School, Perth	
Glenalmond College, Perth	
Kilgraston, Perth	U
Morrison's Academy, Crieff	
Strathallan School, Perth	

WALES

BRIDGEND

St Clare's School, Porthcawl

CARDIFF

The Cardiff Academy	
Kings Monkton School	
Westbourne School	U

CARMARTHENSHIRE

Llandovery College, Llandovery	U

CONWY

Lyndon Preparatory School, Colwyn Bay	
Rydal Penrhos Senior School, Colwyn Bay	
St David's College, Llandudno	U

DENBIGHSHIRE

Fairholme Preparatory School, St Asaph

Howell's School, Denbigh	U
Ruthin School, Ruthin	U

MONMOUTHSHIRE

Monmouth School, Monmouth	
St John's-on-the-Hill, Chepstow	

PEMBROKESHIRE

Netherwood School, Saundersfoot

POWYS

Christ College, Brecon	U

SWANSEA

Ffynone House School

4.9

Schools in Membership of the Constituent Associations of the Independent Schools Council

The schools listed below are all in membership of the Independent Schools Council in the UK. Please note that ISC-accredited special schools and overseas schools are not included. The constituent associations of the ISC include:

Association of Governing Bodies of Independent Schools (AGBIS)
The Girls' Schools Association (GSA)
The Headmasters' and Headmistresses' Conference (HMC)
The Incorporated Association of Preparatory Schools (IAPS)
The Independent Schools Association (ISA)
The Independent Schools' Bursars Association (ISBA)
The Society of Headmasters and Headmistresses of Independent Schools (SHMIS)

Further information about ISC can be found in Part 1.1.

ENGLAND

BEDFORDSHIRE

Bedford High School, Bedford
Bedford Modern School, Bedford
Bedford Preparatory School, Bedford
Bedford School, Bedford
Dame Alice Harpur School, Bedford
Moorlands School, Luton
Pilgrims Pre-Preparatory School, Bedford
Rushmoor School, Bedford
St Andrew's School, Bedford

BERKSHIRE

The Abbey School, Reading
Bearwood College, Wokingham
Bradfield College, Reading
Brigidine School Windsor, Windsor

Brockhurst and Marlston House Schools, Newbury
Cheam School, Newbury
Claires Court School, Maidenhead
Claires Court Schools – Ridgeway, Maidenhead
Crosfields School, Reading
Dolphin School, Reading
Downe House, Thatcham
Eagle House, Sandhurst
Elstree School, Reading
The Elvian School, Reading
Eton College, Windsor
Eton End PNEU, Slough
Heathfield St Mary's School, Ascot
Hemdean House School, Reading
Herries School, Maidenhead
Highfield School, Maidenhead
The Highlands School, Reading
Holme Grange School, Wokingham

Horris Hill School, Newbury
Hurst Lodge School, Ascot
Lambrook Haileybury, Bracknell
Leighton Park School, Reading
Licensed Victuallers' School, Ascot
Long Close School, Upton
Luckley-Oakfield School, Wokingham
Ludgrove, Wokingham
The Marist Preparatory School, Ascot
The Marist Senior School, Ascot
The Oratory Preparatory School, Reading
The Oratory School, Reading
Pangbourne College, Pangbourne
Papplewick School, Ascot
Queen Anne's School, Reading
Reading Blue Coat School, Reading
St Andrew's School, Reading
St Bernard's Preparatory School, Slough
St Edward's School, Reading
St Gabriel's School, Newbury
St George's School, Ascot
St George's School, Windsor
St John's Beaumont, Windsor
St Joseph's Convent School, Reading
St Mary's School, Ascot
St Piran's Preparatory School, Maidenhead
Sunningdale School, Sunningdale
Upton House School, Windsor
Waverley School, Wokingham
Wellington College, Crowthorne
White House Preparatory School, Wokingham
Winbury School, Maidenhead

BRISTOL

Badminton School, Bristol
Bristol Cathedral School, Bristol
Bristol Grammar School, Bristol
Clifton College, Bristol
Clifton College Preparatory School, Bristol
Clifton College Pre-Prep, Bristol
Clifton High School, Bristol
Colston's Collegiate School, Bristol
Colston's Girls' School, Bristol
Colston's Lower School, Bristol
The Downs School, Bristol
Fairfield School, Bristol
Queen Elizabeth's Hospital, Bristol
The Red Maids' School, Bristol
Redland High School, Bristol
Sacred Heart Preparatory School, Chew Magna
St Ursula's High School, Bristol
Tockington Manor School, Bristol

BUCKINGHAMSHIRE

Ashfold School, Aylesbury
The Beacon School, Amersham
Bury Lawn School, Milton Keynes
Caldicott School, Farnham Royal
Chesham Preparatory School, Chesham
Crown House School, High Wycombe

Dair House School Trust Ltd, Farnham Royal
Davenies School, Beaconsfield
Gateway School, Great Missenden
Gayhurst School, Gerrards Cross
Godstowe Preparatory School, High Wycombe
Heatherton House School, Amersham
High March School, Beaconsfield
Kingscote Pre-Preparatory School, Gerrards Cross
Ladymede, Aylesbury
Maltman's Green School, Gerrards Cross
Milton Keynes Preparatory School, Milton Keynes
Pipers Corner School, High Wycombe
St Mary's School, Gerrards Cross
St Teresa's Catholic Independent & Nursery School, Princes Risborough
Stowe School, Buckingham
Swanbourne House School, Milton Keynes
Thornton College Convent of Jesus and Mary, Milton Keynes
Thorpe House School, Gerrards Cross
Wycombe Abbey School, High Wycombe

CAMBRIDGESHIRE

Cambridge Arts & Sciences (CATS), Cambridge
Cambridge Centre for Sixth Form Studies, Cambridge
Horlers Pre-Preparatory School, Cambridge
Kimbolton School, Huntingdon
The King's School Ely, Ely
The Leys School, Cambridge
The Perse School, Cambridge
The Perse School for Girls, Cambridge
Peterborough High School, Peterborough
St Colette's School, Cambridge
St Faith's, Cambridge
St John's College School, Cambridge
St Mary's Junior School, Cambridge
St Mary's School, Cambridge
Whitehall School, Huntingdon
Wisbech Grammar School, Wisbech

CHANNEL ISLANDS

Elizabeth College, Guernsey
The Ladies' College, Guernsey
St Michael's Preparatory School, Jersey
Victoria College, Jersey
Victoria College Preparatory School, Jersey

CHESHIRE

Abbey Gate College, Chester
Abbey Gate School, Chester
Alderley Edge School for Girls, Alderley Edge
Altrincham Preparatory School, Altrincham
Beech Hall School, Macclesfield
Brabyns School, Stockport
Cheadle Hulme School, Cheadle
Cransley School, Northwich
Culcheth Hall, Altrincham
The Firs School, Chester
Forest Park School, Sale

Forest School, Altrincham
The Grange School, Northwich
Greenbank, Cheadle
Hale Preparatory School, Altrincham
Hammond School, Chester
Hillcrest Grammar School, Stockport
Hulme Hall Schools, Cheadle
Hulme Hall Schools (Junior Division), Cheadle
The King's School, Chester
The King's School, Macclesfield
Lady Barn House School, Cheadle
Loreto Preparatory School, Altrincham
Mostyn House School, South Wirral
North Cestrian Grammar School, Altrincham
Pownall Hall School, Wilmslow
The Queen's School, Chester
Ramillies Hall School, Cheadle
The Ryleys, Alderley Edge
St Catherine's Preparatory School, Stockport
Stockport Grammar School, Stockport
Terra Nova School, Holmes Chapel
Wilmslow Preparatory School, Wilmslow

CORNWALL

The Bolitho School, Penzance
Polwhele House School, Truro
Roselyon, Par
St Joseph's School, Launceston
Treliske, Truro
Truro High School, Truro
Truro School, Truro

COUNTY DURHAM

Barnard Castle School, Barnard Castle
Bow School, Durham
The Chorister School, Durham
Durham High School For Girls, Durham
Durham School, Durham
Polam Hall, Darlington

CUMBRIA

Austin Friars St Monica's School, Carlisle
Casterton School, Kirkby Lonsdale
Chetwynde School, Barrow-in-Furness
Harecroft Hall School, Seascale
Lime House School, Carlisle
St Bees School, St Bees
Sedbergh School, Sedbergh
Windermere St Anne's, Windermere

DERBYSHIRE

Derby Grammar School for Boys, Derby
Derby High School, Derby
Foremarke Hall School, Derby
Mount St Mary's College, Spinkhill
Ockbrook School, Derby
Repton School, Derby

St Anselm's, Bakewell
St Wystan's School, Repton

DEVON

Blundell's Preparatory School, Tiverton
Blundell's School, Tiverton
Edgehill College, Bideford
Exeter Cathedral School, Exeter
Exeter School, Exeter
Grenville College, Bideford
Kelly College, Tavistock
Kelly College Preparatory School, Tavistock
Manor House School, Honiton
The Maynard School, Exeter
Mount House School, Tavistock
Plymouth College, Plymouth
St John's School, Sidmouth
St Margaret's School, Exeter
St Michael's, Barnstaple
St Peter's School, Exmouth
Shebbear College, Beaworthy
St Dunstan's Abbey-Plymouth College Junior School,
   Plymouth
Stover School, Newton Abbot
Trinity School, Teignmouth
West Buckland School, Barnstaple

DORSET

Bryanston School, Blandford Forum
Canford School, Wimborne
Castle Court Preparatory School, Wimborne
Clayesmore Preparatory School, Blandford Forum
Clayesmore School, Blandford Forum
Dorchester Preparatory School, Dorchester
Dumpton School, Wimborne
Hanford School, Blandford Forum
International College, Sherborne School, Sherborne
Knighton House, Blandford Forum
Milton Abbey School, Blandford Forum
The Old Malthouse, Swanage
The Park School, Bournemouth
Port Regis School, Shaftesbury
St Antony's Leweston Schools, Sherborne
St Mary's School, Shaftesbury
Sherborne Preparatory School, Sherborne
Sherborne School, Sherborne
Sherborne School for Girls, Sherborne
Sunninghill Preparatory School, Dorchester
Talbot Heath, Bournemouth
Thornlow Preparatory School, Weymouth
Uplands School, Poole
Wentworth College, Bournemouth
Yarrells School, Poole

ESSEX

Alleyn Court Preparatory School, Southend-on-Sea
Bancroft's School, Woodford Green
Braeside School for Girls, Buckhurst Hill
Brentwood School, Brentwood

Chigwell School, Chigwell
Colchester High School, Colchester
Coopersale Hall School, Epping
Cranbrook College, Ilford
Crowstone Preparatory School, Westcliff-on-Sea
The Daiglen School, Buckhurst Hill
Dame Johane Bradbury's School, Saffron Walden
Elm Green Preparatory School, Chelmsford
Felsted Preparatory School, Dunmow
Felsted School, Dunmow
Friends' School, Saffron Walden
Glenarm College, Ilford
Gosfield School, Halstead
Heathcote School, Chelmsford
Holmwood House, Colchester
Ilford Ursuline Preparatory School, Ilford
Littlegarth School, Colchester
Loyola Preparatory School, Buckhurst Hill
Maldon Court Preparatory School, Maldon
New Hall School, Chelmsford
Oaklands School, Loughton
Oxford House School, Colchester
Park School for Girls, Ilford
Raphael Independent School, Romford
St Anne's Preparatory School, Chelmsford
St Aubyn's School, Woodford Green
St Cedd's School, Chelmsford
St Hilda's School, Westcliff-on-Sea
St John's School, Billericay
St Margaret's School, Halstead
St Mary's School, Colchester
St Michael's School, Leigh-on-Sea
St Nicholas School, Harlow
St Philomena's Preparatory School, Frinton-on-Sea
Thorpe Hall School, Southend-on-Sea
Ursuline Preparatory School, Brentwood
Widford Lodge, Chelmsford
Woodford Green Preparatory School, Woodford Green
Woodlands School, Brentwood

GLOUCESTERSHIRE

The Abbey School, Tewkesbury
Beaudesert Park School, Stroud
Berkhampstead School, Cheltenham
Bredon School, Tewkesbury
Cheltenham College, Cheltenham
Cheltenham College Junior School, Cheltenham
The Cheltenham Ladies' College, Cheltenham
Dean Close Preparatory School, Cheltenham
Dean Close School, Cheltenham
Hatherop Castle School, Cirencester
The King's School, Gloucester
Rendcomb College, Cirencester
The Richard Pate School, Cheltenham
Rose Hill School, Wotton-under-Edge
St Edward's School, Cheltenham
Westonbirt School, Tetbury
Wycliffe College, Stonehouse
Wycliffe Preparatory School, Stonehouse

HAMPSHIRE

Alton Convent School, Alton
Ballard School, New Milton
Bedales School, Petersfield
Boundary Oak School, Fareham
Churchers College, Petersfield
Daneshill School, Basingstoke
Ditcham Park School, Petersfield
Dunhurst (Bedales Junior School), Petersfield
Durlston Court, New Milton
Farleigh School, Andover
Farnborough Hill, Farnborough
Forres Sandle Manor, Fordingbridge
The Gregg School, Southampton
Hampshire Collegiate School, Embley Park, Romsey
Highfield School, Liphook
Hordle Walhampton School, Lymington
King Edward VI School, Southampton
Kingscourt School, Catherington
Lord Wandsworth College, Hook
Mayville High School, Southsea
Meoncross School, Fareham
Moyles Court School, Ringwood
The Pilgrims' School, Winchester
The Portsmouth Grammar School, Portsmouth
Portsmouth High School GDST, Southsea
Prince's Mead School, Winchester
Rookesbury Park School, Portsmouth
Rookwood School, Andover
St John's College, Southsea
St Neot's School, Hook
St Nicholas' School, Fleet
St Swithun's School, Winchester
St Winifred's School, Southampton
Salesian College, Farnborough
Sherborne House School, Eastleigh
Stanbridge Earls School, Romsey
The Stroud School, Romsey
Twyford School, Winchester
Winchester College, Winchester
Wykeham House School, Fareham
Yateley Manor Preparatory School, Yateley

HEREFORDSHIRE

Haberdashers' Redcap School, Hereford
The Hereford Cathedral Junior School, Hereford
The Hereford Cathedral School, Hereford
Lucton School, Leominster
St Richard's, Bromyard

HERTFORDSHIRE

Abbot's Hill School, Hemel Hempstead
Aldenham School, Elstree
Aldwickbury School, Harpenden
Arts Educational School, Tring Park, Tring
Beechwood Park School, St Albans
Berkhamsted Collegiate Preparatory School, Berkhamsted
Berkhamsted Collegiate School, Berkhamsted
Bishop's Stortford College, Bishop's Stortford
CKHR Immanuel College, Bushey

Duncombe School, Hertford
Edge Grove, Aldenham
Egerton-Rothesay School, Berkhamsted
Francis House, Tring
Haberdashers' Aske's Boys' School, Elstree
Haberdashers' Aske's School for Girls, Elstree
Haileybury, Hertford
Haresfoot Preparatory School, Berkhamsted
Heath Mount School, Hertford
Homewood Pre-Preparatory School, St Albans
Howe Green House School, Bishop's Stortford
Immanuel College, Bushey
Kingshott School, Hitchin
Lochinver House School, Potters Bar
Lockers Park, Hemel Hempstead
Manor Lodge School, Radlett
Northwood Preparatory School, Rickmansworth
The Princess Helena College, Hitchin
The Purcell School, Bushey
Queenswood School, Hatfield
Rickmansworth PNEU School, Rickmansworth
The Royal Masonic School for Girls, Rickmansworth
St Albans High School for Girls, St Albans
St Albans School, St Albans
St Christopher School, Letchworth
St Columba's College, St Albans
St Edmund's College, Ware
St Francis' College, Letchworth
St Hilda's School, Bushey
St Hilda's School, Harpenden
St Margaret's School, Bushey
Sherrardswood School, Welwyn
Stanborough School, Watford
Stormont, Potters Bar
Westbrook Hay Preparatory School, Hemel Hempstead
York House School, Rickmansworth

ISLE OF MAN

The Buchan School, Castletown
King William's College, Castletown

ISLE OF WIGHT

Ryde School, Ryde

KENT

Ashford School, Ashford
Babington House School, Chislehurst
Baston School, Bromley
Bedgebury School, Cranbrook
Beechwood Sacred Heart School, Tunbridge Wells
Benenden School, Cranbrook
Bethany School, Cranbrook
Bickley Park School, Bromley
Bishop Challoner RC School, Bromley
Bromley High School GDST, Bromley
Bronte School, Gravesend
Cobham Hall, Gravesend
Combe Bank School, Sevenoaks
Derwent Lodge School for Girls, Tonbridge

Dover College, Dover
Duke of York's Royal Military School, Dover
Dulwich Preparatory School, Cranbrook, Cranbrook
Farringtons School, Chislehurst
Friars School, Ashford
Gad's Hill School, Rochester
The Granville School, Sevenoaks
Harenc School Trust, Sidcup
Hilden Grange School, Tonbridge
Hilden Oaks School, Tonbridge
Holmewood House, Tunbridge Wells
Junior King's School, Canterbury
The Junior School, St Lawrence College, Ramsgate
Kent College, Canterbury
Kent College Infant & Junior School, Canterbury
Kent College Pembury, Tunbridge Wells
King's Preparatory School, Rochester
The King's School, Canterbury
King's School Rochester, Rochester
Marlborough House School, Hawkhurst
The Mead School, Tunbridge Wells
The New Beacon, Sevenoaks
Northbourne Park School, Deal
Rose Hill School, Tunbridge Wells
Russell House School, Sevenoaks
Sackville School, Tonbridge
St David's College, West Wickham
St Edmunds Junior School, Canterbury
St Edmund's School, Canterbury
St Lawrence College, Ramsgate
St Mary's Westbrook, Folkestone
St Michael's School, Sevenoaks
St Ronan's, Hawkhurst
Sevenoaks Preparatory School, Sevenoaks
Sevenoaks School, Sevenoaks
Solefield School, Sevenoaks
Steephill School, Longfield
Sutton Valence Preparatory School, Maidstone
Sutton Valence School, Maidstone
Tonbridge School, Tonbridge
Walthamstow Hall, Sevenoaks
Wellesley House School, Broadstairs
West Lodge Preparatory School, Sidcup
Yardley Court, Tonbridge

LANCASHIRE

Arnold School, Blackpool
Bolton School (Boys' Division), Bolton
Bolton School (Girls' Division), Bolton
Bury Grammar School, Bury
Bury Grammar School Girls, Bury
Clevelands Preparatory School, Bolton
Highfield Priory School, Preston
The Hulme Grammar School for Girls, Oldham
King Edward VII and Queen Mary School,
    Lytham St Annes
Kingswood College at Scarisbrick Hall, Ormskirk
Kirkham Grammar School, Preston
The Oldham Hulme Grammar School, Oldham
Queen Elizabeth's Grammar School, Blackburn
Rossall Junior School, Fleetwood
Rossall School, Fleetwood

St Mary's Hall, Stonyhurst
St Pius X Preparatory School, Preston
Stonyhurst College, Clitheroe
Westholme School, Blackburn

LEICESTERSHIRE

The Dixie Grammar School, Market Bosworth
Fairfield Preparatory School, Loughborough
Grace Dieu Manor School, Leicester
Leicester Grammar School, Leicester
Leicester High School For Girls, Leicester
Loughborough Grammar School, Loughborough
Loughborough High School, Loughborough
Manor House School, Ashby-de-la-Zouch
Our Lady's Convent School, Loughborough
PNEU School, Loughborough
Ratcliffe College, Leicester
Stoneygate School, Great Glen

LINCOLNSHIRE

Copthill School, Stamford
Kirkstone House School, Bourne
Lincoln Minster School, Lincoln
St Hugh's School, Woodhall Spa
St Mary's Preparatory School, Lincoln
Stamford High School, Stamford
Stamford Junior School, Stamford
Stamford School, Stamford
Witham Hall, Bourne

NORTH EAST LINCOLNSHIRE

St James' School, Grimsby
St Martin's Preparatory School, Grimsby

NORTH LINCOLNSHIRE

Brigg Preparatory School, Brigg

LONDON

Abercorn School, NW8
Alleyn's School, SE22
Arnold House School, NW8
The Arts Educational School, W4
Avenue House School, London W13
Belmont (Mill Hill Preparatory School), NW7
Blackheath High School GDST, SE3
Broomwood Hall School, SW12
Bute House Preparatory School for Girls, W6
Cameron House School, SW3
The Cavendish School, NW1
Channing School, N6
City of London School, EC4V
City of London School for Girls, EC2Y
Colfe's School, SE12
Devonshire House Preparatory School, NW3
Dulwich College, SE21
Dulwich College Preparatory School, SE21
Durston House, W5

Ealing College Upper School, W13
Eltham College, SE9
Emanuel School, SW11
Falkner House, SW7
Finton House School, SW17
Forest School, E17
Francis Holland School, NW1
Francis Holland School, SW1W
Garden House School, SW3
Glendower Preparatory School, SW7
The Godolphin and Latymer School, W6
Grange Park Preparatory School, N21
Grangewood Independent School, E7
The Hall School, NW3
The Hampshire Schools (Kensington Gardens), W2
The Hampshire Schools (Knightsbridge Under School), SW7
The Hampshire Schools (Knightsbridge Upper School), SW7
Harvington School, W5
Hawkesdown House School, W8
Hellenic College of London, SW1X
Hendon Preparatory School, NW4
Hereward House School, NW3
Herne Hill School, SE24
Highfield School, SW18
Highgate School, N6
Hornsby House School, SW12
Ibstock Place School, SW15
The Italia Conti Academy of Theatre Arts, EC1M
James Allen's Girls' School, SE22
James Allen's Preparatory School, SE22
Keble Preparatory School, N21
Kensington Prep School, SW6
The King Alfred School, NW11
King's College Junior School, SW19
King's College School, SW19
Latymer Preparatory School, W6
Latymer Upper School, W6
Lyndhurst House Preparatory School, NW3
Mander Portman Woodward, SW7
Mill Hill School, NW7
More House, SW1X
The Mount School, NW7
Naima Jewish Preparatory School, NW6
Newton Prep, SW8
Norland Place School, W11
Normanhurst School, E4
Northcote Lodge School, SW11
Notting Hill and Ealing High School GDST, W13
Oakfield Preparatory School, SE21
Orchard House School, W4
Palmers Green High School, N21
Pembridge Hall, W2
Portland Place, W1B
Prospect House School, SW15
Putney High School GDST, SW15
Putney Park School, SW15
Queen's College, W1G
Queen's Gate School, SW7
Ravenscourt Park Preparatory School, W6
Redcliffe School, SW10
Riverston School, SE12

Rosemead Preparatory School, SE21
Royal Ballet School, WC2
The Royal School, Hampstead, NW3
St Anthony's Preparatory School, NW3
St Benedict's School, W5
St Christina's RC Preparatory School, NW8
St Christopher's School, NW3
St Dunstan's College, SE6
St James Independent School for Boys, W14
St James Independent School for Girls (Juniors), W14
St James Independent School for Senior Girls, W14
St Margaret's School, NW3
St Mary's School Hampstead, NW3
St Olave's Preparatory School, SE9
St Paul's Cathedral School, EC4M
St Paul's Girls' School, W6
St Paul's Preparatory School, SW13
St Paul's School, SW13
Salcombe Preparatory School, N14
Sarum Hall, NW3
Snaresbrook College Preparatory School, E18
South Hampstead High School, NW3
Southbank International School, Hampstead, NW3
Southbank International School, Kensington, W11
Streatham and Clapham High School, SW16
The Study Preparatory School, SW19
Sussex House School, SW1X
The Swaminarayan School, NW10
Sydenham High School GDST, SE26
Sylvia Young Theatre School, NW1
Tower House School, SW14
University College School, NW3
University College School, Junior Branch, NW3
Virgo Fidelis, SE19
Vita Et Pax School, N14
Westminster Abbey Choir School, SW1P
Westminster Cathedral Choir School, SW1P
Westminster School, SW1P
Westminster Under School, SW1P
Wimbledon High School GDST, SW19
Woodside Park International School, N11

GREATER MANCHESTER

Abbotsford Preparatory School, Manchester
Bridgewater School, Manchester
Chetham's School of Music, Manchester
The Manchester Grammar School, Manchester
Manchester High School for Girls, Manchester
Moor Allerton School, Manchester
St Bede's College, Manchester
William Hulme's Grammar School, Manchester
Withington Girls' School, Manchester

MERSEYSIDE

The Belvedere School GDST, Liverpool
Birkenhead High School GDST, Wirral
Birkenhead School, Wirral
Carleton House Preparatory School, Liverpool
Kingsmead School, Wirral
Liverpool College, Liverpool

Merchant Taylors' School, Liverpool
Merchant Taylors' School for Girls, Liverpool
Prenton Preparatory School, Wirral
Redcourt St Anselm's, Prenton
Runnymede St Edward's School, Liverpool
St Mary's College, Liverpool
Sunnymede School, Southport
Tower College, Prescot

MIDDLESEX

ACS Hillingdon International School, Hillingdon
Alpha Preparatory School, Harrow
Ashton House School, Isleworth
Buckingham College School, Harrow
Denmead School, Hampton
Halliford School, Shepperton
Hampton School, Hampton
Harrow School, Harrow on the Hill
Heathfield School, Pinner
Innellan House School, Pinner
The John Lyon School, Harrow
The Lady Eleanor Holles School, Hampton
The Mall School, Twickenham
Merchant Taylors' School, Northwood
Newland House School, Twickenham
North London Collegiate, Edgware
Northwood College, Northwood
Orley Farm School, Harrow
Peterborough & St Margaret's School, Stanmore
Quainton Hall School, Harrow
Reddiford, Pinner
St Catherine's School, Twickenham
St Christopher's School, Wembley
St David's School, Ashford
St Helen's College, Hillingdon
St Helen's School, Northwood
St James Independent School for Boys (Senior),
   Twickenham
St John's Northwood, Northwood
St Martin's School, Northwood
Staines Preparatory School, Staines
Twickenham Preparatory School, Hampton

NORFOLK

Beeston Hall School, Cromer
Glebe House School, Hunstanton
Gresham's Preparatory School, Holt
Gresham's School, Holt
Hethersett Old Hall School, Norwich
Langley Preparatory School & Nursery, Norwich
Langley School, Norwich
The New Eccles Hall School, Norwich
Norwich High School for Girls GDST, Norwich
Norwich School, Norwich
Notre Dame Preparatory School, Norwich
Riddlesworth Hall, Diss
Sacred Heart Convent School, Swaffham
St Christopher's School, Norwich
St Nicholas House Kindergarten and Prep School,
   North Walsham

Taverham Hall, Norwich
Thetford Grammar School, Thetford
Thorpe House School, Norwich
Town Close House Preparatory School, Norwich

NORTHAMPTONSHIRE

Beachborough School, Brackley
Great Houghton Preparatory School, Northampton
Laxton Junior School, Peterborough
Maidwell Hall, Northampton
Northampton High School, Northampton
Northamptonshire Grammar School, Pitsford
Oundle School, Peterborough
St Peter's School, Kettering
Spratton Hall, Northampton
Wellingborough School, Wellingborough
Winchester House School, Brackley

NORTHUMBERLAND

Longridge Towers School, Berwick-upon-Tweed
Mowden Hall School, Stocksfield

NOTTINGHAMSHIRE

Arley House PNEU School, East Leake
Bramcote Lorne School, Retford
Dagfa House School, Nottingham
Greenholme School, Nottingham
Grosvenor School, Nottingham
Highfields School, Newark
Hollygirt School, Nottingham
Mountford House School, Nottingham
Nottingham High Junior School, Nottingham
Nottingham High School, Nottingham
Nottingham High School for Girls GDST, Nottingham
Plumtree School, Nottingham
Ranby House, Retford
Rodney School, Newark
St Joseph's School, Nottingham
Salterford House School, Nottingham
Trent College, Nottingham
Waverley House PNEU School, Nottingham
Wellow House School, Newark
Worksop College, Worksop

OXFORDSHIRE

Abingdon School, Abingdon
Bloxham School, Banbury
The Carrdus School, Banbury
Chandlings Manor School, Oxford
Christ Church Cathedral School, Oxford
Cokethorpe, Witney
Cothill House Preparatory School, Abingdon
Cranford House School, Wallingford
d'Overbroeck's College, Oxford
Dragon School, Oxford
Ferndale Preparatory School, Faringdon
Headington School, Oxford
Kingham Hill School, Chipping Norton

Magdalen College School, Oxford
The Manor Preparatory School, Abingdon
Moulsford Preparatory School, Wallingford
New College School, Oxford
Our Lady's Convent Senior School, Abingdon
Oxford High School GDST, Oxford
Radley College, Abingdon
Rupert House, Henley-on-Thames
Rye St Antony School, Oxford
St Edward's School, Oxford
St Hugh's School, Faringdon
St John's Priory School, Banbury
St Mary's School, Henley-on-Thames
St Mary's School, Wantage
School of St Helen & St Katharine, Abingdon
Shiplake College, Henley-on-Thames
Sibford School, Banbury
Summer Fields, Oxford
Tudor Hall School, Banbury
Windrush Valley School, Chipping Norton
Wychwood School, Oxford

RUTLAND

Brooke Priory School, Oakham
Oakham School, Oakham
Uppingham School, Uppingham

SHROPSHIRE

Adcote School for Girls, Shrewsbury
Bedstone College, Bucknell
Castle House School, Newport
Concord College, Shrewsbury
Ellesmere College, Ellesmere
Kingsland Grange, Shrewsbury
Moor Park School, Ludlow
Moreton Hall, Oswestry
The Old Hall School, Telford
Oswestry School, Oswestry
Packwood Haugh School, Shrewsbury
Prestfelde Preparatory School, Shrewsbury
St Winefride's Convent School, Shrewsbury
Shrewsbury High School GDST, Shrewsbury
Shrewsbury School, Shrewsbury
Wrekin College, Telford

SOMERSET

All Hallows, Shepton Mallet
Bruton School for Girls, Bruton
Chilton Cantelo School, Yeovil
Downside School, Bath
Hazlegrove (King's Bruton Preparatory School), Yeovil
King's College, Taunton
King's Hall School, Taunton
King's School, Bruton
Millfield Preparatory School, Street
Millfield School, Street
The Park School, Yeovil
Perrott Hill School, Crewkerne
Queen's College, Taunton

Queen's College Junior and Pre-Preparatory Schools, Taunton
Taunton Preparatory School, Taunton
Taunton School, Taunton
Wellington School, Wellington
Wells Cathedral Junior School, Wells
Wells Cathedral School, Wells

BATH & NORTH EAST SOMERSET

King Edward's School, Bath
Kingswood Preparatory School, Bath
Kingswood School, Bath
Monkton Combe Junior School, Bath
Monkton Combe School, Bath
Paragon School, Bath
Prior Park College, Bath
The Royal High School, Bath

NORTH SOMERSET

Sidcot School, Winscombe

STAFFORDSHIRE

Abbots Bromley School for Girls, Abbots Bromley
Abbotsholme School, Uttoxeter
Brooklands School, Stafford
Chase Academy, Cannock
Denstone College, Uttoxeter
Edenhurst School, Newcastle-under-Lyme
Lichfield Cathedral School, Lichfield
Newcastle-under-Lyme School, Newcastle-under-Lyme
St Bede's School, Stafford
St Dominic's Priory School, Stone
St Dominic's School, Stafford
St Joseph's Preparatory School, Stoke-on-Trent
Smallwood Manor Preparatory School, Uttoxeter
Stafford Grammar School, Stafford
Vernon Lodge Preparatory School, Stafford
Yarlet School, Stafford

STOCKTON-ON-TEES

Red House School, Norton
Teesside Preparatory and High School, Eaglescliffe
Yarm School, Yarm

SUFFOLK

The Abbey, Woodbridge
Amberfield School, Ipswich
Barnardiston Hall Preparatory School, Haverhill
Cherry Trees School, Bury St Edmunds
Culford School, Bury St Edmunds
Fairstead House School, Newmarket
Finborough School, Stowmarket
Framlingham College, Woodbridge
Framlingham College Preparatory School, Brandeston
Hillcroft Preparatory School, Stowmarket
Ipswich High School GDST, Ipswich

Ipswich Preparatory School, Ipswich
Ipswich School, Ipswich
Moreton Hall Preparatory School, Bury St Edmunds
Old Buckenham Hall School, Ipswich
The Old School, Beccles
Orwell Park, Ipswich
Royal Hospital School, Ipswich
Saint Felix Schools, Southwold
St Joseph's College, Ipswich
South Lee Preparatory School, Bury St Edmunds
Stoke College, Sudbury
Woodbridge School, Woodbridge

SURREY

Aberdour School, Tadworth
ACS Cobham International School, Cobham
ACS Egham International School, Egham
Aldro School, Godalming
Amesbury, Hindhead
Barfield School, Farnham
Barrow Hills School, Godalming
Belmont School, Dorking
Bishopsgate School, Egham
Box Hill School, Dorking
Bramley School, Tadworth
Canbury School, Kingston-upon-Thames
Caterham Preparatory School, Caterham
Caterham School, Caterham
Charterhouse, Godalming
Chinthurst School, Tadworth
City of London Freemen's School, Ashtead
Claremont Fan Court School, Esher
Clewborough House School, Frimley
Collingwood School, Wallington
Coworth-Flexlands School, Woking
Cranleigh Preparatory School, Cranleigh
Cranleigh School, Cranleigh
Cranmore School, Leatherhead
Croham Hurst School, South Croydon
Croydon High School GDST, South Croydon
Cumnor House School, South Croydon
Danes Hill Preparatory School, Leatherhead
Downsend School, Leatherhead
Duke of Kent School, Ewhurst
Dunottar School, Reigate
Edgeborough, Farnham
Elmhurst School, South Croydon
Epsom College, Epsom
Ewell Castle School, Epsom
Feltonfleet School, Cobham
Frensham Heights School, Farnham
Glenesk School, Leatherhead
Greenacre School for Girls, Banstead
Greenfield School, Woking
Guildford High School, Guildford
Hall Grove School, Bagshot
Halstead Preparatory School, Woking
Haslemere Preparatory School, Haslemere
Hawley Place School, Camberley
The Hawthorns School, Redhill
Hazelwood School, Oxted
Hoe Bridge School, Woking

Holy Cross Preparatory School, Kingston-upon-Thames
Homefield School, Sutton
Hurtwood House, Dorking
King Edward's School Witley, Godalming
King's House School, Richmond
Kingston Grammar School, Kingston-upon-Thames
Kingswood House School, Epsom
Lanesborough, Guildford
Laverock School, Oxted
Lingfield Notre Dame School, Lingfield
Lodge School, Purley
Longacre School, Guildford
Lyndhurst School, Camberley
Manor House School, Leatherhead
Marymount International School, Kingston-upon-Thames
Micklefield School, Reigate
Milbourne Lodge School, Esher
Notre Dame Preparatory School, Cobham
Notre Dame Senior School, Cobham
Oakhyrst Grange School, Caterham
Old Palace School of John Whitgift, Croydon
Old Vicarage School, Richmond
Parkside School, Cobham
Parsons Mead, Ashtead
Prior's Field School, Godalming
Priory School, Banstead
Reed's School, Cobham
Reigate Grammar School, Reigate
Reigate St Mary's Preparatory and Choir School, Reigate
Ripley Court School, Woking
Rokeby School, Kingston-upon-Thames
Rowan Preparatory School, Esher
Royal Grammar School, Guildford
Royal Russell School, Croydon
The Royal School, Haslemere
Rydes Hill Preparatory School, Guildford
St Andrew's (Woking) School Trust, Woking
St Catherine's School, Guildford
St Christopher's School, Epsom
St David's School, Purley
St Edmund's School, Hindhead
St George's College, Weybridge
St George's College Junior School, Weybridge
St Hilary's School, Godalming
St Ives School, Haslemere
St John's School, Leatherhead
St Teresa's Preparatory School, Effingham
St Teresa's School, Dorking
Seaton House, Sutton
Shrewsbury House School, Surbiton
Sir William Perkins's School, Chertsey
Stowford College, Sutton
The Study School, New Malden
Surbiton High School, Kingston-upon-Thames
Surbiton Preparatory School, Surbiton
Sutton High School GDST, Sutton
Tormead School, Guildford
Trinity School, Croydon
Unicorn School, Richmond
West Dene School, Purley
Whitgift School, South Croydon
Wispers School for Girls, Haslemere
Woldingham School, Woldingham

Woodcote House School, Windlesham
Yehudi Menuhin School, Cobham

EAST SUSSEX

Ashdown House School, Forest Row
Battle Abbey School, Battle
Bodiam Manor School, Robertsbridge
Bricklehurst Manor Preparatory, Wadhurst
Brighton and Hove High School GDST, Brighton
Brighton College, Brighton
Brighton College Prep School, Brighton
Eastbourne College, Eastbourne
Greenfields School, Forest Row
Lancing College Preparatory School at Mowden, Hove
Lewes Old Grammar School, Lewes
Moira House Girls School, Eastbourne
Mowden School, Hove
Newlands Manor School, Seaford
Newlands Preparatory School, Seaford
Roedean School, Brighton
St Andrew's School, Eastbourne
St Aubyns School, Brighton
St Bede's Prep School, Eastbourne
St Bede's School, Hailsham
St Leonards-Mayfield School, Mayfield
St Mary's Hall, Brighton
Sacred Heart School, Wadhurst
Skippers Hill Manor Preparatory School, Mayfield
Vinehall School, Robertsbridge

WEST SUSSEX

Ardingly College, Haywards Heath
Ardingly College Junior School, Haywards Heath
Arundale Preparatory School, Pulborough
Brambletye School, East Grinstead
Broadwater Manor School, Worthing
Burgess Hill School for Girls, Burgess Hill
Christ's Hospital, Horsham
Copthorne Prep School, Copthorne
Cottesmore School, Pease Pottage
Cumnor House School, Haywards Heath
Dorset House School, Pulborough
Farlington School, Horsham
Fonthill Lodge, East Grinstead
Great Ballard School, Chichester
Great Walstead, Haywards Heath
Handcross Park School, Haywards Heath
Hurstpierpoint College, Hurstpierpoint
Lancing College, Lancing
Lavant House, Chichester
Oakwood School, Chichester
Our Lady of Sion School, Worthing
Pennthorpe School, Horsham
The Prebendal School, Chichester
St Margaret's School Convent of Mercy, Midhurst
Seaford College, Petworth
Shoreham College, Shoreham-by-Sea
Slindon College, Arundel
Sompting Abbotts School, Sompting
Stoke Brunswick, East Grinstead

The Towers Convent School, Steyning
Westbourne House School, Chichester
Windlesham House, Pulborough
Worth School, Turners Hill

TYNE AND WEAR

Argyle House School, Sunderland
Central Newcastle High School GDST,
    Newcastle upon Tyne
Dame Allan's Boys School, Newcastle upon Tyne
Dame Allan's Girls School, Newcastle upon Tyne
The King's School, Tynemouth
La Sagesse School, Newcastle upon Tyne
Newcastle Preparatory School, Newcastle upon Tyne
Newcastle Upon Tyne Church High School,
    Newcastle upon Tyne
Newlands School, Newcastle upon Tyne
Royal Grammar School, Newcastle upon Tyne
Sunderland High School, Sunderland
Westfield School, Newcastle upon Tyne

WARWICKSHIRE

Abbotsford School, Kenilworth
Arnold Lodge School, Leamington Spa
Bilton Grange, Rugby
The Crescent School, Rugby
The Croft Preparatory School, Stratford-upon-Avon
The King's High School for Girls, Warwick
The Kingsley School, Leamington Spa
Princethorpe College, Rugby
Rugby School, Rugby
Stratford Preparatory School, Stratford-upon-Avon
Twycross House School, Atherstone
Warwick Preparatory School, Warwick
Warwick School, Warwick

WEST MIDLANDS

Bablake School, Coventry
Birchfield School, Wolverhampton
The Blue Coat School, Birmingham
Coventry Prep School, Coventry
Crackley Hall School, Kenilworth
Davenport Lodge School, Coventry
Eastbourne House School, Birmingham
Edgbaston High School for Girls, Birmingham
Elmhurst School for Dance, Birmingham
Eversfield Preparatory School, Solihull
Hallfield School, Birmingham
Highclare School, Birmingham
Hydesville Tower School, Walsall
King Edward VI High School for Girls, Birmingham
King Edward's School, Birmingham
King Henry VIII School, Coventry
Mayfield Preparatory School, Walsall
Newbridge Preparatory School, Wolverhampton
Norfolk House School, Birmingham
Priory School, Birmingham
The Royal Wolverhampton Junior School,
    Wolverhampton

The Royal Wolverhampton School, Wolverhampton
Ruckleigh School, Solihull
St George's School, Edgbaston, Birmingham
St Martin's School, Solihull
Solihull School, Solihull
Tettenhall College, Wolverhampton
West House School, Birmingham
Wolverhampton Grammar School, Wolverhampton

WILTSHIRE

Chafyn Grove School, Salisbury
Dauntsey's School, Devizes
The Godolphin School, Salisbury
Heywood Preparatory School, Corsham
La Retraite Swan, Salisbury
Leaden Hall, Salisbury
Marlborough College, Marlborough
Norman Court Preparatory School, Salisbury
Pinewood School, Swindon
Prior Park Preparatory School, Cricklade
St Francis School, Pewsey
St Margaret's Preparatory School, Calne
St Mary's School, Calne
Salisbury Cathedral School, Salisbury
Sandroyd School, Salisbury
Stonar School, Melksham
Warminster School, Warminster

WORCESTERSHIRE

Abberley Hall, Worcester
The Alice Ottley School, Worcester
Bowbrook House School, Pershore
Bromsgrove Preparatory School, Bromsgrove
Bromsgrove School, Bromsgrove
Dodderhill School, Droitwich
The Downs School, Malvern
The Elms, Malvern
Green Hill School, Evesham
Hartlebury School, Kidderminster
Heathfield School, Kidderminster
Hillstone School (Malvern College), Malvern
Holy Trinity School, Kidderminster
King's Hawford, Worcester
The King's School, Worcester
The Knoll School, Kidderminster
Malvern College, Malvern
Malvern College Preparatory School, Malvern
Malvern Girls' College, Malvern
Moffats School, Bewdley
Royal Grammar School Worcester, Worcester
St James's School, Malvern
St Mary's Convent School, Worcester
Winterfold House, Kidderminster

EAST RIDING OF YORKSHIRE

Hull Collegiate School, Anlaby
Hymers College, Hull
Pocklington School, Pocklington

NORTH YORKSHIRE

Ampleforth College, York
Ashville College, Harrogate
Aysgarth Preparatory School, Bedale
Bootham School, York
Bramcote School, Scarborough
Catteral Hall School, Settle
Clifton Preparatory School, York
Fyling Hall School, Whitby
Giggleswick School, Settle
Harrogate Ladies' College, Harrogate
Howsham Hall, York
Lisvane, Scarborough College Junior School, Scarborough
Malsis School, Skipton
The Minster School, York
The Mount School, York
Queen Ethelburga's College, York
Queen Margaret's School, York
Queen Mary's School, Thirsk
Read School, Selby
Ripon Cathedral Choir School, Ripon
St Martin's Ampleforth, York
St Olave's School (Junior of St Peter's), York
St Peter's School, York
Scarborough College & Lisvane School, Scarborough
Terrington Hall, York
Woodleigh School, Malton

SOUTH YORKSHIRE

Ashdell Preparatory School, Sheffield
Birkdale School, Sheffield
Brantwood School for Girls, Sheffield

Hill House St Mary's School, Doncaster
Mylnhurst RC School & Nursery, Sheffield
Rudston Preparatory School, Rotherham
Sheffield High School GDST, Sheffield
Westbourne School, Sheffield

WEST YORKSHIRE

Ackworth School, Pontefract
Batley Grammar School, Batley
Bradford Girls' Grammar School, Bradford
Bradford Grammar School, Bradford
Bronte House School, Bradford
Cliff School, Wakefield
The Froebelian School, Leeds
Fulneck School, Pudsey
Gateways School, Leeds
The Gleddings School, Halifax
Hipperholme Grammar School, Halifax
Lady Lane Park School, Bingley
Leeds Girls' High School, Leeds
Leeds Grammar School, Leeds
Moorfield School, Ilkley
Moorlands School, Leeds
Queen Elizabeth Grammar School, Wakefield
The Rastrick Independent School, Brighouse
Richmond House School, Leeds
Rishworth School, Rishworth
Silcoates School, Wakefield
Sunny Hill House School, Wakefield
Wakefield Girls' High School, Wakefield
Westville House Preparatory School, Ilkley
Woodhouse Grove School, Apperley Bridge

NORTHERN IRELAND

COUNTY ANTRIM

Belfast Royal Academy, Belfast
Campbell College, Belfast
Methodist College, Belfast
Royal Belfast Academical Institution, Belfast

COUNTY DOWN

Bangor Grammar School, Bangor
Rockport School, Holywood

COUNTY FERMANAGH

Portora Royal School, Enniskillen

COUNTY LONDONDERRY

Coleraine Academical Institution, Coleraine

COUNTY TYRONE

The Royal School Dungannon, Dungannon

SCOTLAND

ABERDEENSHIRE

Robert Gordons College, Aberdeen
St Margaret's School for Girls, Aberdeen

ANGUS

The High School of Dundee, Dundee
Lathallan School, Montrose

ARGYLL AND BUTE

Lomond School, Helensburgh

CLACKMANNANSHIRE

Dollar Academy, Dollar

FIFE

St Leonard's School & VIth Form College, St Andrews

GLASGOW

Craigholme School, Glasgow
The Glasgow Academy, Glasgow
The High School of Glasgow, Glasgow
Hutchesons' Grammar School, Glasgow
Kelvinside Academy, Glasgow
St Aloysius Junior School, Glasgow

LOTHIAN

Belhaven Hill, Dunbar
Cargilfield, Edinburgh
Clifton Hall School, Edinburgh
The Edinburgh Academy, Edinburgh
Fettes College, Edinburgh
George Heriot's School, Edinburgh
George Watson's College, Edinburgh

Loretto School, Musselburgh
The Mary Erskine School, Edinburgh
Merchiston Castle School, Edinburgh
St George's School for Girls, Edinburgh
St Margaret's School, Edinburgh
Stewart's Melville College, Edinburgh

MORAYSHIRE

Gordonstoun School, Elgin

PERTH AND KINROSS

Ardvreck School, Crieff
Craigclowan Preparatory School, Perth
Glenalmond College, Perth
Kilgraston (A Sacred Heart School), Perth
Morrison's Academy, Crieff
Strathallan School, Perth

RENFREWSHIRE

St Columba's School, Kilmacolm

ROXBURGHSHIRE

St Mary's Preparatory School, Melrose

WALES

CARDIFF

The Cathedral School, Cardiff
Howell's School, Llandaff GDST, Cardiff
Kings Monkton School, Cardiff
Westbourne School, Cardiff

CARMARTHENSHIRE

Llandovery College, Llandovery
St Michael's School, Llanelli

CONWY

Lyndon Preparatory School, Colwyn Bay
Rydal Penrhos Senior School, Colwyn Bay
St David's College, Llandudno

DENBIGHSHIRE

Howell's School, Denbigh
Ruthin School, Ruthin

GWYNEDD

St Gerard's School, Bangor

MONMOUTHSHIRE

Haberdashers' Monmouth School For Girls, Monmouth
Monmouth School, Monmouth
St John's-on-the-Hill, Chepstow

NEWPORT

Rougemont School, Newport

POWYS

Christ College, Brecon

4.10
Educational Associations and Useful Addresses

The Allied Schools
Cross House
38 High Street
Banbury
Oxon OX16 5ET
Tel: (01295) 256441
Fax: (01295) 275350
E-mail: n.coulson@alliedschools.org.uk
Website: www.alliedschools.org.uk
General Manager: Nevil Coulson MA, MBA

The organization provides management, financial, helpline and other support services to member schools, as well as operating a communications network between school governors, heads, bursars and other staff for the exchange of information and ideas. The Allied Schools include:

Canford School	Harrogate Ladies' College
Riddlesworth Hall Preparatory School (associate)	Stowe School
Westonbirt School	Wrekin College

The Association for the Education and Guardianship of International Students (AEGIS)
Tel/Fax: (01453) 755160
E-mail: secretary@aegisuk.net
Website: www.aegisuk.net
Secretary: Janet Bowman

The Association promotes best and legal practice in all areas of guardianship and the care of international students, under 18 years of age, at school or college in the United Kingdom. All members, including school members, are required to adhere to the AEGIS Code of Practice and undertake to follow guidelines on caring for international students. Guardianship organizations are admitted to membership after a successful accreditation inspection.

Association of Governing Bodies of Independent Schools (AGBIS)
Field House
Newton Tony
Salisbury
Wiltshire SP4 0HF
Tel: (01980) 629831
Fax: (01980) 629774
E-mail: sec@agbis.org.uk
Website: www.agbis.org.uk
Secretary: Brigadier S Rutter-Jerome

The aim of the association is to advance education in independent schools, to promote good governance and administration in independent schools and to encourage co-operation between their governing bodies. For details please contact the Secretary.

Association of Heads of Independent Schools
St Nicholas School
Redfields House, Redfields Lane
Church Crookham
Fleet
Hampshire GU52 0RF
Honorary Secretary: Mrs A V Whatmough

Membership of AHIS is open to the Heads of girls' independent secondary schools and girls' co-educational junior independent schools which are accredited by the Independent Schools Council (see below).

Association of Nursery Training Colleges
The Chiltern College
16 Peppard Road
Caversham
Reading RG4 8JZ
Tel: (0118) 9471847

Provides information and advice on careers in childcare, as nannies and nursery workers. Also gives information on Diplomas, National Vocational Qualifications (NVQs) and Montessori training in childcare and education offered at Chiltern College in Reading (www.chilterncollege.com), the Norland College in Bath (www.norland.co.uk) and the Montessori Centre International, whose headquarters are in London (www.montessori.ac.uk).

Association of School and College Leaders (ASCL)
130 regent Road
Leicester LE1 7PG
Tel: (0116) 299 1122
Fax: (0116) 299 1123

E-mail: info@ascl.org.uk
Website: www.ascl.org.uk
General Secretary: J E Dunford

ASCL (the new name for the Secondary Heads Association) is the only professional association and trade union in Britain to speak exclusively for secondary school and college leaders, in both the independent and mainstream sectors.

The association has nearly 13,000 members including heads, deputy heads, assistant heads, bursars and business managers and others with school/college responsibility.

ASCL has strong ties with the Headmasters' Conference and Girls' School Association and their members are automatically part of ASCL.

Benefits of ASCL membership include access to legal support and advice, a telephone hotline for guidance on urgent issues, persoanl support from regional field officers, regular publications and guidance on courses and conferences, and pension advice.

Association of Tutors

Sunnycroft
63 King Edward Road
Northampton NN1 5LY
Tel: (01604) 624171
Fax: (01604) 624718
Website: www.tutor.co.uk
Secretary: Dr D J Cornelius

The professional body for independent private tutors. Members provide advice and individual tuition to students at all levels of education. The tutoring may be supplementary to full course provision or may be on a full course basis.

Boarding Schools' Association (BSA)

Grosvenor Gardens House
35–37 Grosvenor Gardens
London SW1W 0BS
Tel: (020) 7798 1580
Fax: (020) 7798 1581
E-mail: bsa@boarding.org.uk
Website: www.boarding.org.uk
National Director: Hilary Moriarty

The BSA has the twin objectives of promoting boarding education and developing quality boarding through high standards of pastoral care and boarding facilities.

A school can join the BSA only if it is a member of one of the constituent associations of the Independent Schools Council or, for state-maintained boarding schools, a member of SBSA (the State Boarding Schools Association). These two bodies require member schools to be regularly inspected by the Independent Schools Inspectorate (ISA) or OFSTED. Parents and prospective pupils choosing a boarding school can therefore be assured that BSA member schools are committed to providing the best possible boarding environment for their pupils.

For further information about the BSA Professional Development Programme please contact:

Tim Holgate BSc (Hons), MSc
BSA Director of Training
4 Manor Farm Cottages
Etchilhampton
Devizes
Wilts SN10 3JR
Tel/Fax: (01380) 860953
E-mail: training@boarding.org.uk

British Accreditation Council

The Chief Executive
44 Bedford Row
London WC1R 4LL
Tel: 0207 447 2554
Fax: 0207 447 2555
E-mail: info@the-bac.org
Website: www.the-bac.org

BAC is a registered charity organization which was established in 1984 to act as the national accrediting body for independent further and higher education. A college accredited by BAC undergoes a thorough inspection every five years which is followed up with an interim visit after 2–3 years. Accreditation means that a BAC college has achieved a satisfactory standard in the areas of *health and safety provision, administration and staffing, the management of quality, student welfare* and *teaching and learning.* BAC also attempts to take action to intercede for students if a conflict arises between the student and the accredited college.

At present BAC accredits over 200 colleges in the UK and nearly 20 overseas in 10 different countries: the Czech Republic, France, Spain, Pakistan, United Arab Emirates, Bulgaria, Greece, India, Germany and Switzerland.

British Association for Early Childhood Education (Early Education)

111 City View House
463 Bethnal Green Road
London E2 9QY
Tel: (020) 7739 7594
Fax: (020) 7613 5330

A charitable association which advises on the care and education of young children from birth to eight years. The association also publishes booklets and organizes conferences for those interested in early childhood education.

British Dyslexia Association
98 London Road
Reading
Berkshire RG1 5AU
Tel: (0118) 966 2871
Fax: (0118) 935 1927
E-mail: helpline@bdadyslexia.org.uk
Website: www.bdadyslexia.org.uk
(Helpline/Information Service 10am–12.45pm and 2pm–4.45pm Mondays, Wednesdays
and Fridays).

Children's Education Advisory Service
Trenchard Lines
Upavon
Pewsey
Wilts SN9 6BE
Tel: (01980) 618244
E-mail: enquiries.ceas@gtnet.gov.uk

To support Service families and entitled civilians in obtaining appropriate educational
facilities for their children and to provide high quality, impartial advice on all aspects of
education worldwide.

Choir Schools Association
Wolvesey
College Street
Winchester SO23 9ND
Tel: 01962 090530
Fax: 01962 869978
E-mail: info@choirschools.org.uk
Administrator: Susan Rees

An association of schools educating cathedral and collegiate boy and girl choristers.
Membership comprises the following schools:

Bristol Cathedral School, Bristol
The Cathedral School, Llandaff
Chetham's School of Music,
    Manchester
The Chorister School, Durham
Christ Church Cathedral School,
    Oxford

Exeter Cathedral School, Exeter
Hereford Cathedral Junior School,
    Hereford
King's College School, Cambridge
King's Preparatory School, Rochester
The King's School, Ely
The King's School, Gloucester

The King's School, Worcester
Lanesborough, Guildford
Lichfield Cathedral School, Lichfield
Lincoln Minster School, Lincoln
Magdalen College School, Oxford
The Minster School, Southwell
The Minster School, York
New College School, Oxford
Norwich School, Norwich
The Pilgrim's School, Winchester
Polwhele House, Truro
The Prebendal School, Chichester
Ripon Cathedral Choir School, Ripon
St Edmunds Junior School, Canterbury

St George's School, Windsor
St James's School, Grimsby
St John's College, Cardiff
St John's College School, Cambridge
St Mary's Music School, Edinburgh
St Paul's Cathedral Choir School,
    London EC4
Salisbury Cathedral School, Salisbury
Wells Cathedral School, Wells
Westminster Abbey Choir School,
    London SW1
Westminster Cathedral Choir School,
    London SW1

Associate Members
Ampleforth College, Ampleforth, North Yorkshire
The Cathedral School, Chelmsford
The King's School, Peterborough
Portsmouth Grammar School, Portsmouth
Queen Elizabeth Grammar School, Wakefield
Reigate St Mary's Preparatory and Choir School, Reigate
St Edward's College, Liverpool
Warwick School, Warwick

Council for Independent Education (CIFE)
Dr Norma R Ball
Executive Secretary
75 Foxbourne Road
London SW17 8EN
Tel: (020) 8767 8666
Fax: (020) 8767 9444

CIFE, founded in 1973, is a professional association for independent colleges of further education which specialize in preparing students (mainly over statutory school leaving age) for GCSEs, A and AS levels and university entrance. In addition, some colleges offer English language tuition for students from abroad and degree-level tuition. The aim of the association is to promote good practice and safeguard adherence to strict standards of professional conduct and ethical propriety. Full membership is open to colleges which have been accredited either by the British Accreditation Council for Independent Further and Higher Education (BAC) or by the Independent Schools Council. Candidate membership is available to colleges seeking accreditation by either body within three years which otherwise satisfy CIFE's own stringent criteria for membership. All CIFE colleges, of which there are currently 24 spread throughout England, with concentrations in London, Oxford and Cambridge, have to abide by exacting codes of conduct and practice; and the character and presentation of their published exam results are subject to regulation, the accuracy of the information presented requiring in addition to be validated by BAC as academic auditor to CIFE. Colleges in full membership are subject to re-inspection from time to time by their accrediting bodies. Further information and a list of colleges are available from the Secretary.

CReSTeD (Council for the Registration of Schools Teaching Dyslexic Pupils)
Registered Charity No: 1052103
Greygarth, Littleworth
Winchcombe
Cheltenham GL54 5BT
Tel/Fax: (01242) 604 852
E-mail: admin@crested.org.uk
Website: www.crested.org.uk
Chairman: Brendan Wignall

The CReSTeD Register is to help parents and those who advise them to choose schools for dyslexic children. Its main supporters are the British Dyslexia Association and Dyslexia Action who, with others, established CReSTeD to produce an authoritative list of schools, both maintained and independent, which have been through an established registration procedure, including a visit by the CReSTeD selected consultant.

Department for Education and Skills
Sanctuary Buildings
Great Smith Street
London SW1P 3BT
Tel: (08700) 012345
Website: www.dfes.gov.uk

The Dyslexia Institute: National Training and Resources Centre
Park House, Wick Road
Egham
Surrey TW20 0HH
Tel: (01784) 222300
Fax: (01784) 222333
E-mail: info@dyslexiaaction.org.uk
Website: www.dyslexiaaction.org.uk
Registered Charity No. 268502

Dyslexia Action is a national charity and the UK's leading provider of services and support for people with dyslexia and literacy difficulties. We specialize in assessment, teaching and training. We also develop and distribute teaching materials and undertake research.

Dyslexia Action is the working name of the Dyslexia Institute, created on its merger with the Hornsby International Dyslexia Centre and forming the largest supplier of specialist training in this field. We are committed to improving public policy and practice. We partner with schools, LEAs, colleges, universities, employers, voluntary sector organizations and Government to improve the quality and quantity of help for people with dyslexia and specific learning difficulties.

Our services are available through our 26 centres and 160 teaching locations around the UK. Over half a million people benefit from our work each year.

Gabbitas Educational Consultants

Carrington House
126–130 Regent Street
London W1B 5EE
Tel: (020) 7734 0161
Fax: (020) 7437 1764
E-mail: market@gabbitas.co.uk
Website: www.gabbitas.co.uk

Gabbitas offers independent, expert advice on all stages of education and careers:

- choice of independent schools and colleges;
- educational assessment services for parents concerned about their child's progress at school;
- Sixth Form options – A and AS level, International Baccalaureate and vocational courses;
- university and degree choices and UCAS applications;
- alternatives to university;
- careers assessment and guidance;
- extensive guidance for overseas students transferring into the British system;
- specialist services, including guardianship, for overseas students attending UK boarding schools.

Gabbitas also provides a full range of services for schools, including the appointment of Heads and staff as well as consultancy on any aspect of school management and development.

The Girls' Day School Trust (GDST)

100 Rochester Row
London SW1P 1JP
Tel: 020 7393 6666
Fax: 020 7393 6789
E-mail: info@wes.gdst.net

Website: www.gdst.net
The GDST is a registered Charity (no 306983).

The GDST is the largest group of independent schools in the UK, with 3,500 staff and 19,500 students. As a charity that owns and runs a family of 27 schools in England and Wales, it reinvests all its income for the benefit of the pupils. With a long history of pioneering innovation in the education of girls, the GDST now also educates boys aged three to seven in some of its all-through schools; has one educational Sixth Form College; and is developing a selective group of prep schools, some of which are co-educational.

The wide-ranging curricular and extra-curricular opportunities available in GDST schools encourage creativity, articulate self-expression and enterprise in students who are prepared to participate fully in the challenges of 21st century life.

Schools

The Belvedere School, Liverpool
Birkenhead High School, Birkenhead
Blackheath High School, London SE3
Brighton and Hove High School, Sussex
Bromley High School, Kent
Central Newcastle High School,
   Newcastle-upon-Tyne
Croydon High School, Croydon
Great Houghton Prep School,
   Northampton
Heathfield School, Pinner
Hilden Grange School, Tonbridge, Kent
Howell's School, Llandaff, Cardiff
Ipswich High School, Suffolk
Kensington Preparatory School,
   London SW6
Norwich High School for Girls, Norfolk
Notting Hill & Ealing High School,
   London W13

Nottingham High School for Girls,
   Nottingham
Oxford High School, Oxford
Portsmouth High School, Hampshire
Putney High School, London SW15
Royal High School, Bath
Sheffield High School, Sheffield
Shrewsbury High School, Shropshire
South Hampstead High School,
   London NW3
Streatham & Clapham High School,
   London SW16
Sutton High School, Surrey
Sydenham High School, London
   SE26
Wimbledon High School, London
   SW19

All GDST schools are non-denominational day schools, but The Royal High School, Bath, also takes boarders. The GDST's small group of prep schools – Great Houghton, Hilden Grange and Kensington – prepare pupils for entry to other schools at 11 or 13. All other schools in the group offer an 'all-through' education, catering for pupils from ages three or four to 18, with thriving Sixth Forms and, in many cases, nursery classes too.

Howell's School in Cardiff has a co-educational Sixth Form College and, in a new initiative, The Belvedere School in Liverpool is due to transfer from the independent sector to Academy status and open as The Belvedere Academy in September 2007.

The Girls' Schools Association (GSA)
130 Regent Road
Leicester LE1 7PG
Tel: (0116) 254 1619
Fax: (0116) 255 3792
E-mail: office@gsa.uk.com
President: Dr Brenda Despontin
General Secretary: Ms Sheila Cooper

The GSA exists to represent the 208 schools whose Heads are in membership. Its direct aim is to promote excellence in the education of girls. This is achieved through a clear understanding of the individual potential of girls and young women. Over 110,000 pupils are educated in schools which cover day and boarding, large and small, city and country, academically elite and broad based education. Scholarships and bursaries are available in most schools.

The Headmasters' and Headmistresses' Conference (HMC)
12 The Point
Rockingham Road
Market Harborough
Leicestershire LE16 2GU
Tel: 01858 469 059
Fax: 01858 469 532
Membership Secretary: R V Peel
Secretary: G H Lucas

The Headmasters' and Headmistresses' Conference (HMC) represents the headteachers of some 250 leading independent schools in the United Kingdom and the Republic of Ireland.

The Incorporated Association of Preparatory Schools (IAPS)
11 Waterloo Place
Leamington Spa
Warwickshire CV32 5LA
Tel: (01926) 887833
Fax: (01926) 888014
E-mail: hq@iaps.org.uk
General Secretary: John Morris

IAPS is the main professional association for Heads of independent preparatory and junior schools in the UK and overseas. There are some 570 schools whose Heads are in membership, accommodating over 130,000 children.

The Independent Schools Association (ISA)

Boys' British School
East Street
Saffron Walden
Essex CB10 1LS
Tel: (01799) 523619
Secretary: Timothy Ham

There are approximately 300 schools in membership of ISA. These are all schools which have been accredited by the Independent Schools Council Inspection Service. This and the requirement that the school should be good of its kind are the criteria for membership. ISA represents schools with pupils throughout the age range. The majority of schools are day schools, but a significant number also have boarders. Membership of the Association enables Heads to receive support from the Association in a number of ways and enables pupils to take part in many events organized by ISA.

The Independent Schools' Bursars Association (ISBA)

Unit 11–12, Manor Farm
Cliddesden, Basingstoke
Hants RG25 2JB
Tel: (01256) 330369
Fax: (01256) 330376
E-mail: office@theisba.org.uk
Website: www.theisba.org.uk
General Secretary: Mr Jonathan Cook

Membership of ISBA includes over 850 independent schools. The object of the ISBA is the advancement of education by the promotion and effective administration and ancillary services in independedent schools.

The Independent Schools Careers Organisation (ISCO)

12A Princess Way
Camberley, Surrey GU15 3SP
Tel: (01276) 211888
Fax: (01276) 691833
E-mail: admin@isco.org.uk
Website: www.isco.org.uk

ISCO is a not-for-profit organization established to help young people make informed decisions about higher education and career choices. It provides support to schools through its ISCO Membership and Information Service schemes and direct support to young people and their parents through the Futurewise scheme. This provides a range of career and higher education services, online and face-to-face, from enrolment to age 23.

ISCO delivers these schemes across the UK and internationally through a network of professionally qualified Regional Directors and Regional Advisers. Operations are supported centrally by the Careerscope team which ensures that up-to-date information is provided to members of the schemes through a range of publications, online services and the termly Careerscope Magazine, and the Expanding Horizons team which organizes a range of unique development opportunities for Futurewise members.

Independent Schools Council (ISC)
St Vincent House
30 Orange Street
London WC2H 7HH
Tel: (020) 7766 7070
Fax: (020) 7766 7071
General Secretary: Jonathan Shephard
ISC is a federation of the following associations:

The Association of Governing Bodies of Independent Schools (AGBIS)
The Girls' Schools Association (GSA)
The Headmasters' and Headmistresses' Conference (HMC)
The Incorporated Association of Preparatory Schools (IAPS)
The Independent Schools' Association (ISA)
The Independent Schools' Bursars Association (ISBA)
The Society of Headmasters and Headmistresses of Independent Schools (SHMIS)

The total membership of ISC comprises about 1,300 schools which are accredited by ISC and inspected on a six-year cycle by the Independent Schools Inspectorate (ISI) under arrangements agreed by the DfES and OFSTED. ISC deals with matters of policy and other issues common to its members and when required speaks collectively on their behalf. It represents its members in discussions with the Department for Education and Skills and with other organizations and represents the collective view of members on independent education.

Independent Schools Examinations Board
Jordan House, Christchurch Road
New Milton
Hants BH25 6QJ
Tel: (01425) 621111
E-mail: ce@iseb.co.uk
Website: iseb.co.uk

Details of the Common Entrance examinations (see the section on Examinations and Qualifications) and copies of past papers are available from the General Secretary at the address above.

The Round Square Schools
Braemar Lodge
Castle Hill, Hartley, Dartford
Kent DA3 7BH
Tel: 0147 470 6927
E-mail: andhow@braemarlodge.fsnet.com
Secretary: Mrs J Howson

An international group of schools which follow the principles of Kurt Hahn, founder of the Salem School in Germany and Gordonstoun in Scotland. There are now over 50 member schools in more than 12 countries: Australia, Canada, England, France, Germany, India, Japan, Kenya, Oman, Scotland, South Africa, Switzerland, Thailand and the United States. Member schools arrange regular exchange visits for pupils and undertake aid projects in India, Kenya, Eastern Europe and Thailand. All member schools uphold the five principles of outdoor adventure, community service, education for democracy, international understanding and environmental conservation. UK member schools are as follows:

Abbotsholme, Uttoxeter (Co-ed)
Box Hill, Dorking (Co-ed)
Cobham Hall, Gravesend (Girls')
Gordonstoun, Elgin (Co-ed)

Wellington College, Crowthorne
    (Boys', Girls in Sixth Form)
Westfield, Newcastle upon Tyne (Girls')
Windermere St Anne's (Co-ed)

SATIPS
Professional Support for Staff in Independent Schools
Cherry Trees, Stebbing
Great Dunmow
Essex CM6 3ST
Tel/Fax: (01371) 856823
E-mail: admin@satips.com
Website: www.satips.com
General Secretary: Andrew Davis
Administrator: Mrs P M Harrison

SATIPS – founded in 1952 – is a source of professional support and encouragement for staff in preparatory, and other schools. We are now one of the foremost providers of subject-based and cross-curricular INSET courses for prep school and other staff. SATIPS is a registered charity. In 1993 the Society widened its appeal by changing its emphasis from purely preparatory school teachers to any school staff, especially those in independent schools. In particular, teachers who have pupils in Key Stages 1, 2 and 3 will find the membership of SATIPS useful: we are particularly interested in making contact with colleagues in the maintained sector. The Society publishes 19 Broadsheets each term in all subject areas and runs conferences (mostly one-day) at various venues during the year. We offer school and individual membership.

The Society of Headmasters and Headmistresses of Independent Schools (SHMIS)
5 Tolethorpe Road
Oakham
Rutland LE15 6GF
Tel: (01572) 755426
Fax: (01572) 756234
E-mail: gensec@shmis.org.uk
Website: www.shmis.org.uk
General Secretary: David Richardson

A society of some 95 schools, most of which are co-educational, day and boarding, and all of which educate children up to the age of 18.

Steiner Waldorf Schools Fellowship
Kidbrooke Park
Forest Row
East Sussex RH18 5JA
Tel: (01342) 822115
Fax: (01342) 826004
E-mail: info@swsf.org.uk
Website: www.steinerwaldorf.org.uk
Chairman: Christopher Clouder

The Steiner Waldorf Schools Fellowship represents the 32 autonomous Steiner Waldorf Schools and 45 Early Years Centres in the UK and Eire. There are now over 890 schools worldwide. Key characteristics of the education include: careful balance in the artistic, practical and intellectual content of the international Steiner Waldorf curriculum; co-educational from 3 to 19 years. Shared Steiner Waldorf curriculum for all pupils. GCSE and A Level examinations. A broad education based on Steiner's approach to the holistic nature of the human being. Co-operative school management – usually a variable parent payment scheme. Steiner Waldorf education is rapidly gaining in popularity all over the world.

Woodard Schools (The Woodard Corporation)
High Street
Abbots Bromley
Rugeley
Staffordshire WS15 3BW
Tel: (01283) 840893

The Woodard Corporation has 40 schools throughout the country, including 17 Affiliated schools. All have an Anglican foundation and together they form the largest independent group of Church Schools in England and Wales.

Member Schools

Southern Area

Ardingly College, Haywards Heath
Ardingly College Junior School,
    Haywards Heath
Bloxham School, Banbury
Hurstpierpoint College, Hassocks
Hurstpierpoint Junior School, Hassocks
Lancing College, Lancing
Mowden School, Hove

Midland Area

Abbots Bromley School for Girls,
    Rugeley
Denstone College, Uttoxeter
Ellesmere College, Ellesmere
Prestfelde, Shrewsbury
Ranby House, Retford

Smallwood Manor Preparatory,
    Uttoxeter
Worksop College, Worksop

Eastern Area

Peterborough High School, Peterborough
St James's School, Grimsby

Western Area

The Cathedral School, Llandaff
Grenville College, Bideford
King's College, Taunton
King's Hall School, Taunton
St Margaret's School, Exeter

Northern Area

The King's School, Tynemouth
Queen Mary's School, Thirsk

Affiliated Schools

Alderley Edge School for Girls, Alderley Edge
Archbishop Michael Ramsey Technology College, London (Voluntary Aided)
Bishop of Hereford's Bluecoat School, Tupsley (Voluntary Aided)
Bishop Stopford School, Kettering
Bishop's Blue Coat Church of England High School, Chester
Bolitho School, Penzance
Crompton House Church of England School
Derby High School, Derby
Grammar School for Boys, Derby
The King's School, Wolverhampton
St Aidan's Church of England Technology College, Poulton le Fylde
St George's Church of England School, Gravesend
St Olaves Grammar School, Orpington
St Peter's Church of England High School, Stoke on Trent
St Peter's Collegiate School, Wolverhampton (Voluntary Aided)
St Saviour's and St Olave's Church of England School, Southwark
St Wilfred's Church of England High School and Technology College, Blackburn

4.11
Glossary of Abbreviations

ABRSM	Associated Board of the Royal Schools of Music
ADD	Attention Deficit Disorder
ADISR	Association des Directeurs d'Instituts de la Suisse Romande
AEB	Associated Examining Board
AGBIS	Association of Governing Bodies of Independent Schools
AHIS	Association of Heads of Independent Schools
ASCL	Association of School and College Leaders
AICE	Advanced International Certificate of Education
ANTC	Association of Nursery Training Colleges
ARCS	Accreditation, Review and Consultancy Service
ARELS	Association of Recognised English Language Services
AVDEP	Association Vaudoise des Ecoles Privees
BACIFHE	British Accreditation Council for Independent Further and Higher Education
BAGA	British Amateur Gymnastics Association
BAYS	British Association for the Advancement of Science
BHS	British Horse Society
BSA	Boarding Schools Association
CAE	Cambridge Certificate in Advanced English
CASE	Council for Advancement and Support of Education
CEE	Common Entrance Examination
CIFE	Council for Independent Further Education
COBISEC	Council of British International Schools in the European Community
CReSTeD	Council for the Registration of Schools Teaching Dyslexic Pupils
CSA	Choir Schools Association
DfES	Department for Education and Skills
ECIS	European Council for International Schools
EFL	English as a Foreign Language
ESL	English as a Second Language
ESOL	English for Speakers of Other Languages
FCE	Cambridge First Certificate in English

FOBISSEA	Federation of British International Schools in South-East Asia
FSEP	Federation Suisse des Ecoles Privees
GBA	Governing Bodies Association
GBGSA	Governing Bodies of Girls' Schools Association
GDST	Girls' Day School Trust
GSA	Girls' Schools Association
HAS	Head Teachers' Association of Scotland
HMC	Headmasters' and Headmistresses' Conference
IAPS	Incorporated Association of Preparatory Schools
IB	International Baccalaureate
IBO	International Baccalaureate Organisation
IBSCA	International Baccalaureate Schools and Colleges Association
IBTA	Independent Business Training Organisation
ICG	Independent Colleges Group
IGCSE	International General Certificate of Secondary Education
ISA	Independent Schools Association
ISBA	Independent Schools Bursars' Association
ISC	Independent Schools Council (formerly Independent Schools Joint Council or ISJC)
ISCIS	Independent Schools Council Information Service (formerly ISIS)
ISCO	Independent Schools Careers Organisation
ISI	Independent Schools Inspectorate
ISIS	Independent Schools Information Service
LAMDA	London Academy of Music and Dramatic Art
LISA	London International Schools Association
MSA	Middle States Association of Colleges and Schools (USA)
NABSS	National Association of British Schools in Spain
NAHT	National Association of Head Teachers
NAIS	National Association of Independent Schools
NE/SA	Near East/South Asia
NEAB	Northern Examinations and Assessment Board
NEASC	New England Association of Schools and Colleges
OFSTED	Office for Standards in Education
OUDLE	University of Oxford Delegacy of Local Examinations
PET	Cambridge Preliminary English Test
PSE	Personal and Social Education
RSA CLAIT	Computer Literacy and Information Technology
SATIPS	Society of Assistants Teaching in Preparatory Schools
SCIS	Scottish Council of Independent Schools
SGS	Scottish Girls' Schools
SHMIS	Society of Headmasters and Headmistresses of Independent Schools
SpLD	Specific Learning Difficulties
STABIS	State Boarding Schools Information Service
WJEC	Welsh Joint Education Committee

Abbreviations used to denote Special Needs provision in the profiles section are as follows:

Special needs support provided (independent mainstream schools)

Learning difficulties

CA   Some children with special needs receive help from classroom assistants

RA   There are currently very limited facilities for pupils with learning difficulties but reasonable adjustments can be made if necessary

SC   Some children with special needs are taught in separate classes for specific subjects

SNU   School has a dedicated Special Needs Unit, which provides specialist tuition on a one-to-one or small group basis by appropriately qualified teachers

WI   There is no dedicated Special Needs Unit but some children with special needs are withdrawn individually from certain lessons for one-to-one tuition

Behavioural disorders/emotional and behavioural difficulties/challenging behaviour

CA   Some children with behavioural problems receive help from classroom assistants

CO   Trained counsellors available for pupils

RA   There are currently very limited facilities for pupils with behavioural disorders but

reasonable adjustments can be made if necessary

ST   Behaviour management strategies identified in school's behaviour management policy

TS   Staff trained in behaviour management available

Physical impairments/medical conditions

AT   Adapted timetable for children with health problems

BL   Materials can be provided in Braille

CA   Some children receive help from classroom assistants

DS   Signing by staff and pupils

HL   Hearing loops available

IT   Specialist IT provision available

RA   There are currently very limited

facilities for pupils with physical impairments or medical conditions but reasonable adjustments can be made if necessary

SL   Stairlifts

SM   Staff with medical training available

TW   Accessible toilet and washing facilities

W   School has wheelchair access (unspecified)

WA1   School is fully wheelchair accessible

WA2   Main teaching areas are wheelchair accessible

WA3   No permanent access for wheelchairs; temporary ramps available

Special needs

ADD	Attention Deficit Disorder
ADHD	Attention Deficit/Hyperactivity Disorder
ASD	Autistic Spectrum Disorder
ASP	Asperger's Syndrome
BESD	Behavioural, Emotional and Social Disorders
CB	Challenging Behaviour
CP	Cerebral Palsy
DOW	Down's Syndrome
DYC	Dyscalculia
DYP	Dyspraxia
DYS	Dyslexia
EPI	Epilepsy
HEA	Health Problems (eg heart defect, asthma)
HI	Hearing Impairment
IM	Impaired Mobility
MLD	Moderate Learning Difficulties
PMLD	Profound and Multiple Learning Difficulties
SLD	Severe Learning Difficulties
SP&LD	Speech and Language Difficulties
TOU	Tourette's Syndrome
VI	Visual Impairment
WU	Wheelchair User

4.12
Further Reading

Schools and Further Education

Schools for Special Needs: A complete guide
12th Edition: Gabbitas Educational Consultants
*The definitive guide to special needs education in the UK
£19.99   Paperback   ISBN 978 0 7494 4696 3   600 pages   2006

How to Pass Secondary School Selection Tests
Contains over 600 Practice Questions
Mike Bryon
*Ideal for 11+ common entrance & SATS
£8.99   Paperback   ISBN 978 0 7494 4217 0   224 pages   2004

Everything You Need to Know about Going to University
3rd Edition: Sally Longson
"comprehensive resource to help you make the right choices." —Mandy Telford, former National President, National Union of Students,
£9.99   Paperback   ISBN 978 0 7494 3985 9   192 pages   2003

Educational Reference

British Qualifications
A complete guide to professional, vocational & academic qualifications in the United Kingdom
37th Edition
"The single best one-volume reference on British educational awards in print." —*World Education News & Reviews*
£48.00   Paperback   ISBN 978 0 7494 4803 5   1040 pages   2007
£70.00   Hardback   ISBN 978 0 4794 4802 8   1040 pages   2007

British Vocational Qualifications
A directory of vocational qualifications available in the United Kingdom
9th Edition
"Splendid. . . Every imaginable accessible procedure is packed into its pages." —*New Statesman*
£40.00   Paperback   ISBN 978 0 7494 4812 7   544 pages   2007

Careers

The A–Z of Careers & Jobs
13th Edition: published in association with *The Times*
"The perfect starting point for students and school leavers" *—Education & Training*
£14.99   Paperback   ISBN 978 0 7494 4627 7   416 pages   2006

also available:

Careers & Jobs in Hospitality & Catering £7.99 Paperback ISBN 978 0 7494 42246 8
128 pages 2005
Careers & Jobs in IT £7.99   Paperback   ISBN 978 0 7494 4245 X   144 pages   2004
Careers & Jobs in the Police Service £7.99   Paperback   ISBN 978 0 7494 4204 2
112 pages 2004
Careers & Jobs in Travel & Tourism £7.99 Paperback ISBN 978 0 7494 4205 0 112
pages 2004

What Next after School?
All you need to know about work, travel & study
4th Edition: Elizabeth Holmes, published in association with *The Times*
"A wealth of practical information about the world of work, training and higher-
education" *—Evening Standard*
£7.99   Paperback   ISBN 978 0 7494 4504 1   224 pages   2006

What Next after University?
Work, travel, education & life with a degree
2nd Edition: Simon Kent, published in association with *The Times*
"Covers everything from basic work, travel and education options and graduate recruitment tests to finding a home and personal finance." *—Girl About Town*
£8.99   Paperback   ISBN 978 0 7494 4251 4   224 pages   2004

Job Applications

Great Answers to Tough Interview Questions
6th Edition: Martin Yate
"The best book on job-hunting." *—Financial Times*
£8.99   Paperback   ISBN 978 0 7494 4356 6   240 pages   2005

The Ultimate CV Book
Write the perfect CV and get that job
Martin Yate
*Over 100 samples of job-winning CVs
£9.99   Paperback   ISBN 0 978 0 7494 3875 3   pages   2002

The Ultimate Job Search Letters Book
Write the perfect letter and get that job
Martin Yate
£9.99   Paperback   ISBN 978 0 7494 4069 5   256 pages   2003

Readymade Job Search Letters
Every type of letter for getting the job you want
3rd Edition: Lynn Williams, published in association with *The Times*
"The first book I've seen which specifically deals with letters. . . . A really useful resource."—*Phoenix Journal*, Keele University
£8.99   Paperback   ISBN 978 0 7494 4277 4   208 pages   2004

Readymade CVs
Sample CVs for every type of job
3rd Edition: Lynn Williams, published in association with *The Times*
"A resource book offering several ways to design your CV for a multitude of needs." —*All About Money Making*
£8.99   Paperback   ISBN 978 0 7494 4274 3   176 pages   2004

Property

The Complete Guide to Buying & Selling Property
How to get the best deal on your home
2nd Edition: Sarah O'Grady
Published in association with the *Daily Express*
"Valuable, no-nonsense information." —*Ideal Home*
£8.99   Paperback   ISBN 978 0 7494 4194 4   256 pages   2004

The Complete Guide to Renovating & Improving Your Property
2nd Edition: Liz Hodgkinson
"Focuses on major renovation work, from obtaining planning permission to employing and managing contractors."
—*What Mortgage*
£10.99   Paperback   ISBN 978 0 7494 4870 7   224 pages   2006

Also available:

The Complete Guide to Letting Property
6th Edition: Liz Hodgkinson
£10.99   Paperback   ISBN 978 0 7494 4804 2   264 pages   2006

The Complete Guide to Buying Property Abroad
5th Edition: Liz Hodgkinson
£12.99 Paperback ISBN 978 0 7494 4742 7   304 pages 2006

The Complete Guide to Buying Property in France
4th Edition: Charles Davey
£10.99   Paperback   ISBN 978 0 7494 4646 8   304 pages   2006

The Complete Guide to Buying Property in Italy
Barbara McMahon
£9.99   Paperback   ISBN 978 0 4794 4151 7   224 pages   2004

The Complete Guide to Buying Property in Portugal
Colin Barrow
£9.99   Paperback   ISBN 978 0 7494 4303 0   240 pages   2005

The Complete Guide to Buying Property in Spain
Charles Davey
£9.99 Paperback   ISBN 978 0 7494 4056 5   208 pages   2004

Personal Finance

A Complete Guide to Family Finance
Essential advice on everything from student loans to inheritance tax
Roderick Millar: published in association with the *Daily Express*
*Comprehensive and practical advice on everything you need to know about saving,
investing and insuring for the future.
£12.99   Paperback   ISBN 978 0 7494 4203 3   368 pages   2004

How the Stock Market Works
A beginner's guide to investment
2nd Edition: Michael Beckett
"Not just for investors, but for anyone who wishes to understand our financial system."
—Neil Collins, City Editor, *Daily Telegraph*
£8.99   Paperback   ISBN 978 0 7494 4190 6   208 pages   2004

How to Write Your Will
16th Edition: Marlene Garsia
"A practical and easy-to-read guide." —*Pensions World*
£8.99   Paperback   ISBN 978 0 7494 4868 4   200 pages   2006

Relocation

Working Abroad
The complete guide to overseas employment
27th Edition: Jonathan Reuvid
"Anyone involved in working abroad will quickly come to look upon this as their bible."
—*Personnel Today*
£12.99   Paperback   ISBN 978 0 7494 4644 4   464 pages   2006

Kogan Page publishes books on Business, Management, Marketing, HR, Training, Careers and Testing, Personal Finance, Property and more.

Visit our website for our full online catalogue:
www.kogan-page.co.uk

4.13

Main Index

A

Abacus College, Oxford   177, 428, 460, 481

Abberley Hall, Worcester   223, 432, 444, 462, 483, 495

Abbey College, Birmingham   214, 431, 444

The Abbey College, Malvern Wells   222, 432, 444, 462

Abbey College, Manchester   162, 427, 440

Abbey Gate College, Chester   90, 422, 436, 467, 486

Abbey Gate School, Chester   90, 422, 467, 478, 486

The Abbey School, Reading   77, 421, 435, 451, 467, 485

The Abbey School, Tewkesbury   488

The Abbey School, Torquay   100, 423

The Abbey, Woodbridge   190, 467, 493

Abbot's Hill School, Hemel Hempstead   120, 309, 425, 438, 452, 467, 488

Abbots Bromley School for Girls, Abbots Bromley   186, 429, 442, 454, 461, 467, 481, 493

Abbotsbury School, Newton Abbot   98, 467

Abbotsford Preparatory School, Manchester   162, 491

Abbotsford School, Kenilworth   212, 431, 482, 495

Abbotsholme School, Uttoxeter   188, 429, 461, 493

Abercorn School, London NW8   147, 318, 426, 490

Aberdeen Waldorf School, Aberdeen   236, 445

Aberdour School, Tadworth   202, 429, 442, 482, 493

Abingdon House School, London W8   159

Abingdon School, Abingdon   176, 428, 441, 450, 460, 467, 481, 492

Abinger Hammer Village School, Dorking   193, 465

Abu Bakr Independent School, Walsall   217, 471

The Academy School, London NW3   144

Ackworth School – International Study Centre, Pontefract   232, 432, 463, 472, 483

Ackworth School, Pontefract   232, 269, 432, 445, 463, 472, 483, 496

Acorn Independent College, Southall   167

Acorn School, Bedford   73, 477

Acorn School, Nailsworth   110, 467

ACS Cobham International School, Cobham   192, 360, 442, 461, 482, 493

ACS Egham International School, Egham   194, 360, 442, 482, 493

ACS Hillingdon International School, Hillingdon   166, 314, 440, 480, 491

Adcote School for Girls, Shrewsbury   181, 428, 441, 454, 461, 467, 481, 492

Aiglon College, Switzerland   255, 418

Airthrie School, Cheltenham   109, 467

Akeley Wood Lower School, Buckingham   83

Akeley Wood School, Buckingham   83, 436, 478

Akhurst Preparatory School, Newcastle upon Tyne   211

Akiva School, London N3   142, 471

Al-Aqsa Primary School, Leicester   135

Al-Burhan Grammar School, Birmingham   214, 455, 471

Al Hijrah School, Birmingham   214, 431, 450, 455, 471

Al-Islah School, Blackburn   130

Al-Islamia Primary, Leicester   135, 471

Al Jamiah Al Islamiyyah, Bolton   161, 449

Al Karam Secondary School, Retford   175, 450, 460, 471

Al-Mizan School, London E1   140, 449, 471

Al-Muntada Islamic School, London SW6   151, 471

Al-Sadiq and Al-Zahra Schools, London NW6   146, 449, 453

Albemarle Independent College, London W1   156, 426, 439, 467, 480

Albyn School, Aberdeen   236, 408, 433

Alcuin School, Leeds   231, 445

Aldenham School, Elstree   119, 309, 425, 438, 459, 467, 479, 488

Alder Bridge School, Reading   77

Alderley Edge School for Girls, Alderley Edge   89, 422, 436, 452, 465, 486

Aldro School, Godalming   195, 442, 450, 461, 467, 482, 493

Aldwickbury School, Harpenden   119, 449, 459, 467, 488

The Alice Ottley School, Worcester   223, 432, 444, 455, 467, 495

All Hallows, Shepton Mallet   183, 429, 441, 461, 472, 481, 492

All Saints School, Norwich   169, 428, 465

Alleyn Court Preparatory School, Southend-on-Sea   487

Alleyn's School, London SE22   149, 318, 426, 439, 467, 490

The Allied Schools   498

Alpha Preparatory School, Harrow   166, 440, 491

Alton Convent School, Alton   112, 424, 452, 472, 488

Altrincham Preparatory School, Altrincham   89, 448, 486

Amberfield School, Ipswich   189, 429, 442, 454, 465, 493

The American School in London, London NW8   147, 319, 439, 480

Amesbury, Hindhead   197, 429, 442, 467, 482, 493

Ampleforth College, York   226, 432, 444, 462, 472, 496

Annemount School, London N2   142

Appleford School, Salisbury   219, 462

Ardingly College Junior School, Haywards Heath   208, 431, 443, 462, 467, 482, 494

Ardingly College, Haywards Heath   208, 431, 443, 462, 467, 482, 494

Ardmore Montessori School, Lancing   209

Ardvreck School, Crieff   244, 433, 446, 463, 465, 497

Argyle House School, Sunderland   212, 495

The Ark School, Reading   77, 421, 435, 465, 477

Arley House PNEU School, East Leake   173, 492

Arnold House School, London NW8   147, 439, 449, 467, 490

Arnold Lodge School, Leamington Spa   212, 290, 465, 482, 495

Arnold School, Blackpool   131, 426, 439, 489

The Arts Educational School, Hertfordshire   447

The Arts Educational School, London W4   157, 319, 439, 490

Arts Educational School, Tring Park, Tring   122, 310, 425, 459, 479, 488

The Arts Educational Schools, London W4   447

Arundale Preparatory School, Pulborough   210, 431, 443, 482, 494

Ash-Shifa School, Banbury   176, 454

Ashbourne Independent Sixth Form College, London W8   159, 320, 426, 439, 460, 480

Ashbourne Middle School, London W8   159, 320, 426, 439, 480

Ashbridge Independent School, Preston   134

Ashbrooke House, Weston-Super-Mare   186

Ashdell Preparatory School, Sheffield   228, 444, 455, 465, 483, 496

Ashdown House School, Forest Row   205, 443, 462, 467, 482, 494

Ashfold School, Aylesbury   83, 436, 457, 465, 486

Ashford School, Ashford   124, 350, 425, 438, 459, 479, 489

Ashgrove School, Bromley   124

Ashton House School, Isleworth   167, 491

Ashville College, Harrogate   224, 432, 444, 462, 471, 483, 496

The Association for the Education and Guardianship of International Students (AEGIS)   498

Association of Governing Bodies of Independent Schools (AGBIS)   485, 499

Association of Heads of Independent Schools   499

Association of Nursery Training Colleges   499

Association of School and College Leaders (ASCL)   499

Association of Tutors   500

Aston House School, London W5   158, 480

Athelstan House School, Hampton   165

Atherton House School, Liverpool   163

Attenborough Preparatory School, Nottingham   173

Auckland College, Liverpool   163

Austin Friars St Monica's School, Carlisle   94, 423, 436, 472, 487

Avalon Preparatory School, Wirral   164, 427, 440

Avenue House School, London W13   160, 321, 490

Avon House, Woodford Green   108, 465, 475

Avondale School, Salisbury   219, 465
Ayscoughfee Hall School, Spalding   138
Aysgarth Preparatory School, Bedale   224, 432, 444, 450, 462, 467, 496

B

Babington House School, Chislehurst   125, 425, 452, 489
Bablake School, Coventry   216, 431, 444, 495
Badminton School, Bristol   81, 388, 422, 436, 451, 457, 477, 486
Bales College, London W10   159, 439, 460, 480
Balham Preparatory School, London SW12   153, 471
Ballard School, New Milton   114, 424, 438, 467, 488
Bancroft's School, Woodford Green   108, 424, 437, 467, 487
Bangor Grammar School, Bangor   234, 451, 496
Bangor Independent Christian School, Bangor   234, 465
Barbara Speake Stage School, London W3   157, 447, 480
Barfield School, Farnham   195, 429, 467, 493
Barlborough Hall School, Chesterfield   95, 265, 437, 472
Barnard Castle School, Barnard Castle   103, 423, 437, 458, 487
Barnardiston Hall Preparatory School, Haverhill   189, 442, 461, 467, 493
Barnardiston Hall, Havershill   475
Barnsley Christian School, Barnsley   228, 465
Barrow Hills School, Godalming   195, 472, 493
Basil Paterson Tutorial College, Edinburgh   242, 463, 484
Bassett House School, London W10   159, 322
Baston School, Bromley   124, 425, 438, 452, 467, 489
Bath Academy, Bath   185, 461, 481
Batley Grammar School, Batley   229, 445, 483, 496
Battle Abbey School, Battle   204, 374, 430, 443, 462, 482, 494
Beachborough School, Brackley   171, 428, 441, 460, 467, 492
The Beacon School, Amersham   83, 436, 448, 467, 486
Beaconhurst School, Stirling   246, 433, 446
Bearwood College, Wokingham   80, 297, 421, 435, 457, 467, 477, 485

Beaudesert Park School, Stroud   111, 458, 467, 488
Beaulieu Convent School, Jersey   88, 452
Bedales School, Petersfield   114, 424, 438, 459, 479, 488
Bedford High School, Bedford   73, 421, 435, 451, 457, 485
Bedford Modern School, Bedford   73, 421, 435, 485
Bedford Preparatory School, Bedford   73, 421, 435, 448, 457, 467, 485
Bedford School Study Centre, Bedford   73, 457
Bedford School, Bedford   73, 296, 421, 435, 448, 457, 467, 477, 485
Bedgebury School, Cranbrook   125, 452, 459, 475, 479, 489
Bedstone College, Bucknell   180, 428, 441, 461, 467, 481, 492
Beech Hall School, Macclesfield   91, 436, 467, 486
Beech House School, Rochdale   134, 439
Beechenhurst Preparatory School, Liverpool   163, 467
Beechwood Park School, St Albans   121, 459, 467, 488
Beechwood Sacred Heart School, Tunbridge Wells   130, 350, 425, 438, 453, 459, 472, 479, 489
Beehive Preparatory School, Ilford   106
Beeston Hall School, Cromer   169, 440, 460, 467, 481, 491
Beis Chinuch Lebanos Girls School, London N4   142, 453
Beis Hamedrash Elyon, London NW11   148, 449, 471
Beis Rochel D'Satmar Girls School, London N16   143, 453, 471
Belfast Royal Academy, Belfast   233, 496
Belhaven Hill, Dunbar   242, 445, 463, 484, 497
Bellerbys College & Embassy CES Cambridge, Cambridge   86, 422, 436, 458, 478
Bellerbys College, Hove   205, 430, 462
Belmont Grosvenor School, Harrogate   224, 432, 444
Belmont House, Newton Mearns   245
Belmont (Mill Hill Preparatory School), London NW7   147, 426, 439, 490
Belmont School, Dorking   193, 429, 461, 467, 476, 493
The Belvedere School GDST, Liverpool   491
Bendarroch School, Exeter   97
Benedict House Preparatory School, Sidcup   129, 465

Benenden School, Cranbrook   126, 425, 438, 453, 459, 467, 479, 489

The Bennett House School, Chorley   132

Berkhampstead School, Cheltenham   109, 424, 437, 467, 488

Berkhamsted Collegiate Preparatory School, Berkhamsted   118, 425, 438, 465, 488

Berkhamsted Collegiate School, Berkhamsted   118, 425, 438, 449, 452, 459, 465, 488

Beth Jacob Grammar for Girls, London NW4   146, 453

Bethany School, Cranbrook   126, 425, 438, 459, 467, 475, 479, 489

Bicker Preparatory School, Boston   137

Bickley Park School, Bromley   124, 425, 438, 449, 489

Bilton Grange, Rugby   213, 431, 443, 462, 467, 482, 495

Birchfield Independent Girls School, Birmingham   214, 455, 471

Birchfield School, Wolverhampton   217, 431, 444, 462, 467, 483, 495

Birkdale School, Sheffield   228, 432, 444, 450, 496

Birkenhead High School GDST, Wirral   164, 427, 440, 453, 491

Birkenhead School, Wirral   164, 427, 440, 449, 491

Bishop Challoner RC School, Bromley   124, 425, 472, 489

Bishop's Stortford College, Bishop's Stortford   118, 425, 438, 459, 479, 488

Bishopsgate School, Egham   194, 461, 493

Blackheath High School GDST, London SE3   148, 426, 439, 453, 490

Blackheath Preparatory School, London SE3   148, 426

Bloxham School, Banbury   176, 428, 441, 460, 467, 475, 481, 492

The Blue Coat School, Birmingham   214, 431, 444, 467, 483, 495

Blundell's Preparatory School, Tiverton   100, 465, 487

Blundell's School, Tiverton   100, 389, 423, 437, 458, 467, 478, 487

Boarding Schools' Association (BSA)   500

Bodiam Manor School, Robertsbridge   206, 467, 494

The Bolitho School, Penzance   93, 423, 436, 458, 467, 478, 487

Bolton Muslim Girls School, Bolton   131, 453, 471

Bolton School (Boys' Division), Bolton   131, 439, 449, 489

Bolton School (Girls' Division), Bolton   131, 439, 453, 479, 489

Bootham School, York   226, 432, 444, 462, 472, 483, 496

Bosworth Independent College, Northampton   171, 428, 441, 460, 481

Botton Village School, Whitby   226

Boundary Oak School, Fareham   112, 424, 459, 488

Bow School, Durham   487

Bowbrook House School, Pershore   222, 465, 483, 495

Bowdon Preparatory School For Girls, Altrincham   89, 452

Box Hill School, Dorking   193, 361, 429, 442, 461, 482, 493

Brabyns School, Stockport   91, 422, 486

Brackenfield School, Harrogate   225, 483

Bradfield College, Reading   77, 297, 421, 457, 467, 477, 485

Bradford Christian School, Bradford   229, 465

Bradford Girls' Grammar School, Bradford   229, 432, 445, 455, 496

Bradford Grammar School, Bradford   229, 432, 445, 496

Braeside School for Girls, Buckhurst Hill   104, 452, 487

Brambletye School, East Grinstead   208, 380, 431, 462, 467, 482, 494

Bramcote Lorne School, Retford   175, 267, 428, 441, 460, 467, 492

Bramcote School, Scarborough   225, 432, 444, 462, 467, 483, 496

Bramdean School, Exeter   97, 389, 423, 437, 458, 478

Bramley School, Tadworth   202, 430, 442, 454, 493

Brampton College, London NW4   146, 426, 480

The Branch Christian School, Heckmondwike   230, 465

Brantwood School for Girls, Sheffield   496

Brantwood School, Sheffield   228, 444, 455, 483

Branwood Preparatory School, Eccles   161, 427

Breaside Preparatory School, Bromley   124, 351, 425

Bredon School, Tewkesbury   111, 424, 437, 458, 467, 475, 479, 488

Brentwood School, Brentwood   104, 424, 437, 448, 452, 458, 467, 479, 487

Bricklehurst Manor Preparatory, Wadhurst   207, 430, 443, 494

Bridgewater School, Manchester   162, 427, 440, 491

Brigg Preparatory School, Brigg   139, 439, 467, 490

Brighton and Hove High School GDST, Brighton   204, 430, 443, 454, 494

Brighton College Pre-preparatory School, Brighton   204, 467

Brighton College Prep School, Brighton   204, 430, 467, 482, 494

Brighton College, Brighton   204, 430, 443, 462, 467, 482, 494

Brighton Steiner School Limited, Brighton   204

Brigidine School Windsor, Windsor   79, 421, 435, 451, 472, 485

Bristol Cathedral School, Bristol   81, 422, 436, 467, 486

Bristol Grammar School, Bristol   81, 422, 436, 486

Bristol Steiner School, Bristol   81

British Accreditation Council   501

British Association for Early Childhood Education (Early Education)   501

British Dyslexia Association   502

Broadhurst School, London NW6   147

Broadmead School, Luton   74

Broadwater Manor School, Worthing   210, 467, 494

Brockhurst & Marlston House Pre-Preparatory School, Thatcham   79, 467, 477

Brockhurst and Marlston House Schools, Newbury   76, 421, 448, 451, 457, 467, 477, 485

Brockwood Park School, Bramdean   112, 424, 459, 479

Bromley High School GDST, Bromley   124, 425, 438, 453, 465, 479, 489

Bromsgrove Pre-preparatory and Nursery School, Bromsgrove   221, 467

Bromsgrove Preparatory School, Bromsgrove   221, 432, 444, 462, 467, 483, 495

Bromsgrove School, Bromsgrove   221, 290, 432, 444, 462, 467, 483, 495

Brondesbury College For Boys, London NW6   147, 449, 471

Bronte House School, Bradford   229, 432, 445, 463, 471, 496

Bronte School, Gravesend   126, 467, 489

Brooke House College, Market Harborough   136, 275, 426, 460, 480

Brooke Priory School, Oakham   180, 492

Brooklands School & Little Brooklands Nursery, Stafford   187, 442

Brooklands School, Stafford   493

Broomfield House School, Richmond   200, 467

Broomwood Hall School, London SW12   154, 426, 465, 490

Brownberrie School, Leeds   231, 465

Bruern Abbey, Chesterton   476

Bruton School for Girls, Bruton   182, 429, 441, 454, 461, 481, 492

Bryanston School, Blandford Forum   101, 423, 437, 458, 467, 478, 487

Bryony School, Gillingham   126

The Buchan School, Castletown   123, 489

Buckholme Towers, Poole   102

Buckingham College Preparatory School, Pinner   167, 427, 449, 467

Buckingham College School, Harrow   166, 427, 449, 491

Buckswood School, Hastings   205, 374, 430, 443, 462, 482

Burgess Hill School for Girls, Burgess Hill   207, 381, 431, 443, 454, 462, 482, 494

Bury Catholic Preparatory School, Bury   131, 472

Bury Grammar School Girls, Bury   132, 426, 439, 453, 489

Bury Grammar School, Bury   132, 426, 439, 449, 489

Bury Lawn School, Milton Keynes   85, 422, 436, 486

Burys Court School, Reigate   199, 467

Bute House Preparatory School for Girls, London W6   158, 453, 490

Buxlow Preparatory School, Wembley   168

C

Cabin Hill School, Belfast   233, 445, 451, 463

Cademuir International School, Thornhill   239, 463

Caldicott School, Farnham Royal   83, 436, 448, 457, 467, 478, 486

Cambridge Arts & Sciences (CATS), Cambridge   86, 272, 436, 458, 478, 486

Cambridge Centre for Sixth-Form Studies, Cambridge   86, 272, 422, 436, 458, 478, 486

Cambridge Tutors College, Croydon   193, 430, 442, 461, 482

Cameron House School, London SW3   151, 323, 467, 480, 490

Campbell College, Belfast   233, 433, 451, 463, 496

Canbury School, Kingston-upon-Thames   197, 430, 442, 482, 493

Canford School, Wimborne   103, 423, 458, 467, 487

Canterbury Steiner School, Canterbury   124

The Cardiff Academy, Cardiff   248, 434, 484

Cargilfield, Edinburgh   242, 433, 445, 463, 497

Carleton House Preparatory School,
    Liverpool   163, 472, 491

Carmel Christian School, Bristol   81, 465

The Carrdus School, Banbury   176, 441, 454, 492

Casterton School, Kirkby Lonsdale   94, 423, 436,
    452, 458, 467, 487

Castle Court Preparatory School, Wimborne   103,
    423, 437, 465, 487

Castle House School, Newport   181, 465, 492

Caterham Preparatory School, Caterham   192, 442,
    465, 493

Caterham School, Caterham   192, 361, 430, 442,
    461, 473, 482, 493

The Cathedral School, Cardiff   248, 434, 446, 467,
    497

Catteral Hall School, Settle   226, 432, 444, 462,
    483, 496

The Cavendish School, London NW1   144, 323,
    453, 465, 490

Cavendish School, London SE16   149

Cedars School of Excellence, Greenock   241

Cedars School, Aldermaston   75, 465, 477

Central Newcastle High School GDST, Newcastle
    upon Tyne   211, 431, 443, 454, 482, 495

Centre Academy, London SW11   476

Chafyn Grove School, Salisbury   219, 431, 444,
    462, 467, 483, 495

Chandlings Manor School, Oxford   177, 467, 492

Channing Junior School, London N6   142, 453

Channing School, London N6   142, 426, 439, 453,
    490

Chard School, Chard   182, 441, 465, 481

Charterhouse Square School, London EC1   141

Charterhouse, Godalming   196, 430, 442, 450,
    461, 467, 482, 493

Chartfield School, Westgate-on-Sea   130

Chase Academy, Cannock   186, 429, 442, 461,
    465, 493

Chase School, Whickham   212

Chavagnes International College, France   254, 416

Cheadle Hulme School, Cheadle   89, 436, 448,
    486

Cheam School, Newbury   76, 298, 421, 457, 467,
    477, 485

Cheltenham College Junior School,
    Cheltenham   109, 424, 437, 458, 467, 479, 488

Cheltenham College, Cheltenham   109, 424, 437,
    458, 467, 479, 488

The Cheltenham Ladies' College,
    Cheltenham   109, 424, 437, 452, 458, 479, 488

Cherry Trees School, Bury St Edmunds   189, 429,
    493

Cherwell College, Oxford   177, 441, 460, 481

Chesham Preparatory School, Chesham   83, 486

Cheshunt Pre-preparatory School, Coventry   216

Chetham's School of Music, Manchester   162, 427,
    447, 460, 491

Chetwynde School, Barrow-in-Furness   94, 262,
    423, 436, 487

Chigwell School, Chigwell   105, 308, 424, 437,
    458, 467, 479, 488

Children's Education Advisory Service   502

Children's Montessori School, Sandy   74

Chiltern College School, Reading   77

Chilton Cantelo School, Yeovil   184, 429, 461,
    467, 481, 492

Chinthurst School, Tadworth   202, 450, 482, 493

Chiswick and Bedford Park Preparatory School,
    London W4   157

Choir Schools Association   502

The Chorister School, Durham   104, 266, 423, 437,
    458, 467, 487

Christ Church Cathedral School, Oxford   177, 428,
    450, 467, 481, 492

Christ College, Brecon   252, 434, 446, 464, 467,
    484, 497

Christ's Hospital, Horsham   209, 443, 462, 467,
    494

Christ the King School, Sale   91, 465

Churchers College Junior School, Liphook   114

Churchers College, Petersfield   114, 424, 438, 488

Citischool, Milton Keynes   85

City of London Freemen's School, Ashtead   191,
    430, 461, 482, 493

City of London School for Girls, London EC2   141,
    426, 439, 453, 490

City of London School, London EC4   142, 426, 439,
    449, 490

CKHR Immanuel College, Bushey   488

Claires Court School, Maidenhead   76, 421, 448,
    477, 485

Claires Court Schools, Ridgeway, Maidenhead   76,
    421, 448, 477, 485

Claires Court Schools, The College,
    Maidenhead   76, 421, 451, 472

Claremont Fan Court School, Esher   195, 362, 430,
    467, 493

Claremont School, St Leonards-on-Sea   206, 430,
    467

Clarence High School, Formby   163, 460

Clarendon Cottage School, Eccles   161, 480

Clarks Preparatory School, Ilford   106

Clayesmore Preparatory School, Blandford
   Forum   101, 423, 437, 458, 467, 475, 478, 487
Clayesmore School, Blandford Forum   101, 390,
   423, 437, 458, 467, 475, 478, 487
Cleve House School, Bristol   81
Clevelands Preparatory School, Bolton   131, 426,
   479, 489
Clewborough House School, Frimley   493
Cliff School, Wakefield   232, 496
Clifton College Pre-Prep – Butcombe, Bristol   81,
   422
Clifton College Pre-Prep, Bristol   486
Clifton College Preparatory School, Bristol   81,
   422, 436, 457, 467, 475, 477, 486
Clifton College, Bristol   81, 388, 422, 436, 457,
   467, 477, 486
Clifton Hall School, Edinburgh   242, 445, 484, 497
Clifton High School, Bristol   81, 422, 436, 457, 486
Clifton Lodge Preparatory School, London
   W5   158, 324, 426, 449, 465
Clifton Preparatory School, York   496
Cobham Hall, Gravesend   126, 351, 425, 438, 453,
   459, 475, 479, 489
Cokethorpe School, Witney   179, 286, 428, 441,
   481, 492
Colchester High School, Colchester   105, 424, 488
Coleraine Academical Institution, Coleraine   235,
   445, 451, 496
Colfe's School, London SE12   149, 426, 439, 467,
   490
College Saint-Pierre, Leigh-on-Sea   107, 424, 479
Collingham Independent GCSE and Sixth Form
   College, London SW5   151, 324, 439, 480
Collingwood School, Wallington   202, 493
Colston's Collegiate School, Bristol   81, 422, 436,
   457, 467, 486
Colston's Girls' School, Bristol   82, 422, 436, 451,
   486
Colston's Lower School, Bristol   82, 486
Combe Bank School, Nr Sevenoaks   127, 352, 425,
   438, 453, 472
Combe Bank School, Sevenoaks   489
The Compass School, Haddington   243, 445
Concord College, Shrewsbury   181, 428, 461, 492
Conifers School, Midhurst   209, 431, 443, 467
Connaught House, London W2   156, 426, 480
Convent of Mercy, Guernsey   88, 472
Convent Preparatory School, Gravesend   127
Conway Preparatory School, Boston   137, 467
Cooley Primary School, Sixmilecross   235
Coopersale Hall School, Epping   106, 467, 488
Copthill School, Stamford   138, 426, 480, 490

Copthorne Prep School, Copthorne   208, 431, 443,
   462, 468, 494
Coteswood House School, Nottingham   174, 428
Cothill House Preparatory School, Abingdon   176,
   450, 460, 468, 481, 492
Cottesmore School, Pease Pottage   209, 382, 443,
   462, 468, 482, 494
Council for Independent Education (CIFE)   503
Coventry Muslim School, Coventry   216, 455, 471
Coventry Prep School, Coventry   216, 431, 468,
   483, 495
Coworth-Flexlands School, Woking   203, 442, 493
Crackley Hall School, Kenilworth   212, 495
Craig-y-Nos School, Swansea   253
Craigclowan Preparatory School, Perth   244, 446,
   484, 497
Craigholme School, Glasgow   240, 433, 445, 455,
   497
Cranbrook College, Ilford   107, 437, 448, 488
Cranbrook School, Cranbrook   126, 352, 425, 459
Cranford House School, Wallingford   179, 428,
   441, 454, 468, 492
Cranleigh Preparatory School, Cranleigh   193, 430,
   461, 468, 493
Cranleigh School, Cranleigh   193, 430, 442, 461,
   468, 493
Cranmore School, Leatherhead   198, 450, 472, 493
Cransley School, Northwich   91, 422, 478, 486
The Crescent School, Rugby   213, 465, 495
CReSTeD (Council for the Registration of Schools
   Teaching Dyslexic Pupils)   504
The Croft Preparatory School,
   Stratford-upon-Avon   213, 431, 468, 495
Croham Hurst School, South Croydon   201, 363,
   430, 442, 454, 465, 482, 493
Crosfields School, Reading   77, 448, 485
Crown House School, High Wycombe   84, 486
Crowstone Preparatory School (Sutton Annexe),
   Rochford   107
Crowstone Preparatory School,
   Westcliff-on-Sea   108, 424, 488
Croydon High School GDST, South Croydon   201,
   430, 442, 454, 482, 493
Culcheth Hall, Altrincham   89, 422, 436, 452, 478,
   486
Culford School, Bury St Edmunds   189, 429, 442,
   461, 471, 482, 493
Cumnor House School, Haywards Heath   208, 462,
   468, 494
Cumnor House School, South Croydon   201, 430,
   450, 468, 493

Cundall Manor School, York   226, 432, 444, 462, 468

D

d'Overbroeck's College, Oxford   178, 286, 428, 460, 481, 492
Dagfa House School, Nottingham   174, 481, 492
The Daiglen School, Buckhurst Hill   105, 424, 465, 488
Dair House School Trust Ltd, Farnham Royal   84, 468, 486
Dale House School, Batley   229, 465
Dallington School, London EC1   141, 439
Dame Alice Harpur School, Bedford   74, 435, 451, 465, 485
Dame Allan's Boys School, Newcastle upon Tyne   211, 431, 443, 450, 495
Dame Allan's Girls School, Newcastle upon Tyne   211, 431, 443, 454, 495
Dame Johane Bradbury's School, Saffron Walden   108, 437, 488
Danes Hill Preparatory School, Leatherhead   493
Danes Hill School, Leatherhead   198, 430, 465, 475
Danesfield Manor School, Walton-on-Thames   202
Daneshill School, Basingstoke   112, 438, 468, 488
Darul Hadis Latifiah, London E2   140, 449, 471
Darul Uloom Islamic High School & College, Birmingham   214, 450, 455, 462, 471
Darul Uloom London, Chislehurst   125, 425, 449, 459
Darvell School, Robertsbridge   206, 465
Date Valley School, Mitcham   198, 471
Dauntsey's School, Devizes   219, 401, 431, 462, 483, 495
Davenies School, Beaconsfield   83, 422, 436, 448, 486
Davenport Lodge School, Coventry   216, 495
David Game College, London W11   160, 460
Davies Laing and Dick, London W1   156, 325, 426, 439, 480
Dean Close Preparatory School, Cheltenham   109, 282, 424, 437, 458, 468, 479, 488
Dean Close School, Cheltenham   109, 282, 424, 437, 458, 465, 479, 488
Deepdene School, Hove   205, 468
Denmead School, Hampton   165, 449, 468, 480, 491
Denstone College, Uttoxeter   188, 429, 442, 461, 468, 481, 493

Department for Education and Skills   504
Derby Grammar School for Boys, Derby   95, 423, 437, 448, 465, 487
Derby High School, Derby   95, 423, 437, 468, 478, 487
Derwent Lodge School for Girls, Tonbridge   129, 425, 453, 465, 489
Devonshire House Preparatory School, London NW3   144, 326, 426, 490
Dharma School, Brighton   204, 465
Ditcham Park School, Petersfield   114, 424, 465, 488
The Dixie Grammar Junior School, Nuneaton   213
The Dixie Grammar School, Market Bosworth   136, 426, 490
Dodderhill School, Droitwich Spa   221, 432, 455, 495
Dollar Academy, Dollar   238, 433, 463, 497
Dolphin School (Including Noah's Ark Nursery Schools), London SW11   153, 439, 465
The Dolphin School, Exmouth   98, 465
Dolphin School, Reading   77, 421, 435, 477, 485
The Dominie, London SW11   153
Donhead Prep School, London SW19   155, 449, 472, 480
Dorchester Preparatory and Independent Schools, Dorchester   102, 423, 437, 478
Dorchester Preparatory School, Dorchester   487
The Dormer House PNEU School, Moreton-in-Marsh   110, 468
Dorset House School, Pulborough   210, 431, 443, 450, 462, 468, 482, 494
Dover College, Dover   126, 353, 425, 438, 459, 468, 476, 479, 489
Dower House School, Bridgnorth   180, 428, 441, 465, 481
Downe House, Thatcham   79, 298, 421, 451, 457, 468, 485
Downham Prep School and Montessori Nursery, Kings Lynn   169, 465
The Downs School, Bristol   486
The Downs School, Malvern   222, 432, 444, 462, 483, 495
The Downs School, Wraxall, Bristol   82, 422, 436, 457, 468, 477
Downsend School, Ashtead Lodge, Ashtead   191
Downsend School, Leatherhead   493
Downsend School, Leatherhead Lodge, Leatherhead   198, 493
Downside School, Bath   182, 429, 441, 461, 472, 481, 492

Dragon School, Oxford   178, 441, 460, 468, 481, 492

Drayton House School, Guildford   196, 442

The Drive Prep School, Hove   206

The Drive Preparatory School, Wolverhampton   217

Dudley House School, Grantham   137, 473

Duff Miller, London SW7   152

Duke of Kent School, Ewhurst   195, 363, 430, 442, 461, 493

Duke of York's Royal Military School, Dover   126, 425, 459, 468, 489

Dulwich College Preparatory School, London SE21   149, 439, 449, 460, 468, 490

Dulwich College, London SE21   149, 426, 439, 449, 460, 468, 490

Dulwich Preparatory School, Cranbrook, Cranbrook   126, 353, 459, 468, 479, 489

Dumpton School, Wimborne   103, 423, 437, 468, 487

Duncombe School, Hertford   120, 468, 489

Dunedin School, Edinburgh   242

Dunhurst (Bedales Junior School), Petersfield   114, 424, 438, 459, 488

Dunottar School, Reigate   199, 430, 442, 454, 493

Durham High School For Girls, Durham   104, 423, 437, 452, 468, 487

Durham School, Durham   104, 423, 437, 458, 468, 478, 487

Durlston Court, New Milton   114, 424, 438, 468, 488

Durston House, London W5   158, 426, 449, 490

The Dyslexia Institute: National Training and Resources Centre   504

Eagle House, Sandhurst   79, 299, 421, 457, 468, 477, 485

Ealing College Upper School, London W13   160, 426, 439, 490

Ealing Independent College, London W5   158, 327, 426, 480

East Lodge School, Shefford   74

East London Christian Choir School, London E8   141, 465

Eastbourne College, Eastbourne   205, 430, 443, 462, 468, 482, 494

Eastbourne House School, Birmingham   214, 495

Eastcourt Independent School, Ilford   107

Eaton House School Belgravia, London SW1   150, 449, 480

Eaton House The Manor, London SW4   151, 426, 449, 480

Eaton House The Vale School, London SW7   152, 480

Eaton Square School, London SW1   150, 426, 480

Ebor Preparatory School, York   226

Ecole Francaise Jacques Prevert, London W6   158

Edenhurst School, Newcastle-under-Lyme   187, 429, 442, 468, 493

Edgbaston High School for Girls, Birmingham   214, 431, 444, 455, 495

Edge Grove, Aldenham   117, 438, 459, 468, 489

Edgeborough, Farnham   195, 430, 442, 461, 468, 493

Edgehill College, Bideford   97, 423, 437, 458, 471, 478, 487

The Edinburgh Academy, Edinburgh   242, 433, 445, 451, 463, 497

The Edinburgh Rudolf Steiner School, Edinburgh   242, 484

Egerton-Rothesay School, Berkhamsted   118, 425, 438, 465, 489

Elfin Pre-Prep & Nursery School, Stratford-upon-Avon   213

Elizabeth College, Guernsey   88, 422, 448, 468, 486

Ellesmere College, Ellesmere   180, 428, 441, 461, 468, 475, 481, 492

Elliott Park School, Sheerness   128, 425, 438

Elm Green Preparatory School, Chelmsford   105, 479, 488

Elm Tree House, Cardiff   248, 446

Elmhurst School for Dance, Birmingham   215, 431, 444, 447, 462, 468, 495

Elmhurst School, South Croydon   201, 450, 493

The Elms, Malvern   222, 432, 444, 462, 468, 495

Elstree School, Reading   78, 421, 435, 448, 457, 468, 477, 485

Eltham College, London SE9   490

The Elvian School, Reading   78, 421, 468, 477, 485

Emanuel School, London SW11   153, 426, 439, 468, 490

Emberhurst, Esher   195

Emmanuel Christian School, Oxford   178, 441, 465

Emmanuel Christian School, Poulton-Le-Fylde   134

Emmanuel School, Derby   96, 465

Emmanuel School, Exeter   97, 437, 465

Emmanuel School, Walsall   217, 465

Emmaus School, Trowbridge   220, 465

E

Emscote House School and Nursery, Leamington
  Spa   212
Epsom College, Epsom   194, 430, 442, 461, 468,
  482, 493
Eridge House Preparatory, London SW6   151
Essendene Lodge School, Caterham   192, 430, 442
Eton College, Windsor   79, 421, 435, 448, 457,
  468, 485
Eton End PNEU, Slough   79, 468, 485
Eveline Day School, London SW17   155
Eversfield Preparatory School, Solihull   216, 431,
  444, 465, 495
Ewell Castle School, Epsom   194, 430, 442, 450,
  468, 482, 493
Excel Preparatory School, London N17   143
Excelsior College, London N17   143
Exeter Cathedral School, Exeter   98, 423, 437, 458,
  468, 478, 487
Exeter Junior School, Exeter   98, 423, 437, 465
Exeter School, Exeter   98, 423, 437, 465, 487

F

Fairfield Preparatory School, Loughborough   136,
  490
Fairfield School, Backwell, Bristol   81, 422, 436,
  468, 486
Fairholme Preparatory School, St Asaph   250, 468,
  484
Fairstead House School, Newmarket   190, 429,
  493
The Falcons School for Boys, London W4   157, 449
The Falcons School for Girls, London W5   158, 453
Falkner House, London SW7   152, 453, 490
Farleigh School, Andover   112, 424, 459, 472, 488
Farlington School, Horsham   209, 383, 431, 443,
  454, 462, 468, 494
Farnborough Hill, Farnborough   113, 393, 424,
  438, 452, 472, 488
Farringtons School, Chislehurst   125, 354, 425,
  438, 459, 471, 479, 489
Farrowdale House Preparatory School,
  Oldham   133
FCJ Primary School, Jersey   88, 472
Felixstowe International College, Felixstowe   189,
  429, 461, 468, 482
Felsted Preparatory School, Dunmow   488
Felsted Preparatory School, Felsted   106, 424, 437,
  458, 468, 479
Felsted School, Dunmow   106, 424, 437, 458, 468,
  479, 488

Feltonfleet School, Cobham   192, 430, 442, 461,
  468, 493
Fen School, Sleaford   138, 426, 439, 468
Ferndale Preparatory School, Faringdon   177, 428,
  492
Fernhill School, Rutherglen   241, 455, 472
Fettes College, Edinburgh   242, 409, 433, 445, 463,
  484, 497
Ffynone House School, Swansea   253, 434, 446,
  465, 467, 484
Filgrave School, Newport Pagnell   85, 465
Finborough School, Stowmarket   190, 429, 461,
  475, 493
Finton House School, London SW17   155, 480, 490
The Firs School, Chester   90, 473, 478, 486
Firwood Manor Prep School, Oldham   133, 426
Fletewood School, Plymouth   99, 473
The Fold School, Hove   206, 430, 443
Fonthill Lodge, East Grinstead   208, 443, 450, 454,
  468, 494
Foremarke Hall School, Derby   96, 423, 437, 458,
  468, 487
Forest Park School, Sale   91, 478, 486
Forest School, Altrincham   89, 487
Forest School, London E17   141, 426, 439, 449,
  453, 468, 490
Forres Sandle Manor, Fordingbridge   113, 438,
  459, 468, 488
Fosse Bank Mountains School, Tonbridge   129, 466
Framlingham College Preparatory School,
  Brandeston   189, 429, 442, 461, 468, 482, 493
Framlingham College, Woodbridge   190, 279, 429,
  442, 461, 468, 482, 493
Francis Holland School, London NW1   144, 327,
  426, 439, 453, 468, 490
Francis Holland School, London SW1   150, 426,
  439, 453, 468, 480, 490
Francis House, Tring   122, 466, 489
Frensham Heights School, Farnham   195, 364, 430,
  442, 461, 493
Friars School, Ashford   489
Friends' School, Saffron Walden   108, 424, 437,
  458, 472, 479, 488
Friskney Private School, Boston   137
Froebel House School, Hull   224
The Froebelian School, Leeds   231, 432, 445, 466,
  496
Fulham Prep School (Pre-Prep), London SW6   152
Fulham Prep School (Prep Dept), London
  W14   160, 328, 426

Fulneck School, Pudsey   232, 432, 445, 463, 471, 475, 483, 496

Fyling Hall School, Whitby   226, 432, 462, 483, 496

G

Gabbitas Educational Consultants   505

Gad's Hill School, Rochester   127, 354, 425, 438, 489

Garden House Boys' School, London SW3   490

Garden House School, London SW3   151, 426, 439

Gatehouse School, London E2   140, 328, 466, 480

Gateway Christian School, Ilkeston   96, 466

Gateway School, Great Missenden   84, 422, 486

Gateways School, Leeds   231, 432, 445, 455, 483, 496

Gayhurst School, Gerrards Cross   84, 436, 448, 468, 486

George Heriot's School, Edinburgh   242, 433, 445, 497

George Watson's College, Edinburgh   242, 433, 445, 484, 497

The German School, Richmond   200

Ghyll Royd School, Ilkley   230, 432, 450, 466

Gidea Park College, Romford   107

Giggleswick School, Settle   226, 432, 444, 462, 468, 483, 496

The Girls' Day School Trust (GDST)   505

The Girls' Schools Association (GSA)   485, 507

The Glasgow Academy Dairsie, Glasgow   240

The Glasgow Academy, Glasgow   240, 433, 445, 471, 497

Glasgow Steiner School, Glasgow   240

Glebe House School, Hunstanton   169, 428, 440, 460, 468, 491

The Gleddings School, Halifax   230, 496

Glen House Montessori School, Hebden Bridge   230

Glenalmond College, Perth   244, 412, 433, 446, 463, 471, 484, 497

Glenarm College, Ilford   107, 466, 488

Glendower Preparatory School, London SW7   152, 329, 453, 490

Glenesk School, Leatherhead   198, 442, 493

Glenhurst School, Havant   113, 479

Gloucestershire Islamic Secondary School For Girls, Gloucester   110, 452, 471

The Godolphin and Latymer School, London W6   159, 426, 439, 453, 490

Godolphin Preparatory School, Salisbury   219, 431, 455, 466

The Godolphin School, Salisbury   219, 432, 444, 455, 462, 468, 495

Godstowe Preparatory School, High Wycombe   84, 422, 436, 451, 457, 468, 478, 486

Golders Hill School, London NW11   148

Goodrington School, Hornchurch   106

Goodwyn School, London NW7   147

Gordonstoun School, Elgin   244, 411, 433, 446, 463, 484, 497

Gosfield School, Halstead   106, 424, 458, 488

Gower House School, London NW9   148

Grace Dieu Manor School, Leicester   135, 426, 472, 490

Gracefield Preparatory School, Bristol   82, 466, 477

Grange Park Preparatory School, London N21   144, 453, 490

The Grange School, Northwich   91, 422, 436, 487

Grangewood Independent School, London E7   140, 466, 490

Grantchester House, Esher   195, 482

The Grantham Preparatory School, Grantham   137

The Granville School, Sevenoaks   128, 438, 453, 489

Grasscroft Independent School, Oldham   133

Great Ballard School, Chichester   207, 431, 443, 462, 468, 482, 494

Great Beginnings Montessori School, London W1   156

Great Houghton Preparatory School, Northampton   171, 428, 441, 492

Great Walstead, Haywards Heath   208, 431, 443, 462, 466, 494

Green Gables Montessori Primary School, London E1   140

Green Hill School, Evesham   221, 495

Greenacre School for Girls, Banstead   191, 430, 442, 454, 482, 493

Greenbank, Cheadle   89, 487

Greene's Tutorial College, Oxford   178, 460, 481

Greenfield School, Woking   203, 493

Greenfields School, Forest Row   205, 462, 482, 494

Greenholme School, Nottingham   174, 481, 492

Greenwich House Independent School, Louth   138

The Gregg School, Southampton   115, 424, 438, 488

Grenville College, Bideford   97, 423, 437, 458, 468, 475, 478, 487

Gresham's Preparatory School, Holt   169, 428, 440, 460, 468, 481, 491

Gresham's School, Holt   169, 428, 440, 460, 468, 481, 491

Grey House Preparatory School, Hook   113, 466

Grindon Hall Christian School, Sunderland   212, 443, 482

Grittleton House School, Chippenham   218, 401, 432, 483

Grosvenor School, Nottingham   174, 441, 492

Grove Independent School, Milton Keynes   85, 478

Guildford High School, Guildford   196, 430, 442, 454, 466, 493

Gyosei International School UK, Milton Keynes   85, 457

H

Haberdashers' Aske's Boys' School, Elstree   119, 425, 438, 449, 468, 489

Haberdashers' Aske's School for Girls, Elstree   119, 425, 438, 452, 468, 489

Haberdashers' Monmouth School For Girls, Monmouth   251, 434, 446, 456, 464, 497

Haberdashers' Redcap School, Hereford   117, 452, 488

Haddon Dene School, Broadstairs   124, 425

Haileybury, Hertford   120, 311, 425, 438, 459, 468, 479, 489

Hale Preparatory School, Altrincham   89, 478, 487

Hall Grove School, Bagshot   191, 461, 493

Hall School Wimbledon, London SW20   156, 426, 480

The Hall School, London NW3   145, 449, 468, 490

Hallfield School, Birmingham   215, 468, 495

Halliford School, Shepperton   167, 427, 440, 449, 480, 491

Halstead Preparatory School, Woking   203, 442, 454, 468, 493

Hamilton College, Hamilton   241, 433, 466

The Hamilton School, Aberdeen   236

Hammond School, Chester   90, 422, 447, 458, 468, 487

Hampshire Collegiate School (Embley Park), Romsey   115, 393, 424, 438, 459, 468, 479

Hampshire Collegiate School, Embley Park, Romsey   488

The Hampshire Schools (Kensington Gardens), London W2   156, 426, 490

The Hampshire Schools (Knightsbridge Under School), London SW7   152, 426, 490

The Hampshire Schools (Knightsbridge Upper School), London SW7   152, 426, 490

Hampstead College of Fine Arts, Independent College, London NW3   145, 329, 426, 440

Hampstead Hill Pre-Preparatory & Nursery School, London NW3   145, 426, 440

Hampton Court House, East Molesey   194, 430, 461, 482

Hampton School, Hampton   165, 427, 440, 449, 491

Handcross Park School, Haywards Heath   208, 431, 443, 462, 468, 494

Handel House Preparatory School, Gainsborough   137

Handsworth Christian School, Sheffield   228, 444, 466

Hanford School, Blandford Forum   101, 423, 452, 458, 468, 487

Harecroft Hall School, Seascale   94, 423, 436, 458, 478, 487

Harenc School Trust, Sidcup   129, 449, 479, 489

Haresfoot Preparatory School, Berkhamsted   118, 425, 489

Harpenden Preparatory School, Harpenden   119, 438

Harper Bell School, Birmingham   215

The Harrodian, London SW13   154

Harrogate Ladies' College, Harrogate   225, 432, 444, 455, 462, 468, 483, 496

Harrogate Tutorial College, Harrogate   225, 432, 444, 462, 483

Harrow School, Harrow on the Hill   166, 427, 440, 449, 460, 468, 480, 491

Hartlebury School, Kidderminster   221, 432, 444, 495

Harvington School, London W5   158, 426, 453, 490

Haslemere Preparatory School, Haslemere   197, 430, 442, 450, 466, 493

Hatherop Castle School, Cirencester   110, 424, 437, 458, 468, 479, 488

Hawkesdown House School, London W8   159, 330, 449, 490

Hawley Place School, Camberley   191, 430, 442, 482, 493

The Hawthorns School, Redhill   199, 430, 442, 493

Hazel Hurst School, Nottingham   174

Hazelwood School, Oxted   199, 430, 442, 468, 493

Hazlegrove (King's Bruton Preparatory School), Yeovil   184, 429, 441, 461, 468, 475, 481, 492

Headington School, Oxford   178, 428, 441, 454, 460, 468, 481, 492

The Headmasters' and Headmistresses' Conference (HMC)   485, 507

Heath House Preparatory School, London SE3   148, 466, 468, 480

Heath Mount School, Hertford   120, 425, 459, 468, 489

Heathcote School, Chelmsford   105, 488

Heatherton House School, Amersham   83, 451, 486

Heathfield House School, London W4   157

Heathfield School, Kidderminster   222, 495

Heathfield School, Pinner   167, 427, 440, 453, 491

Heathfield St Mary's School, Ascot   75, 300, 421, 435, 451, 457, 466, 477, 485

Heathland College, Accrington   130, 426, 439, 468

Heathside Preparatory School, London NW3   145, 426, 480

Hellenic College of London, London SW1   490

Hemdean House School, Reading   78, 421, 435, 468, 485

Hendon Preparatory School, London NW4   146, 426, 480, 490

The Hereford Cathedral Junior School, Hereford   117, 468, 488

The Hereford Cathedral School, Hereford   117, 424, 438, 468, 488

Hereward House School, London NW3   145, 440, 449, 490

Herington House School, Brentwood   104, 424

Herne Hill School, London SE24   150, 466, 490

Herries School, Maidenhead   76, 485

Hessle Mount School, Hessle   224

Heswall Preparatory School, Wirral   165, 466, 480

Hethersett Old Hall School, Norwich   169, 428, 440, 454, 460, 468, 481, 491

Heywood Preparatory School, Corsham   218, 495

High March School, Beaconsfield   83, 422, 436, 451, 486

The High School of Dundee, Dundee   237, 445, 496

The High School of Glasgow, Glasgow   240, 433, 445, 497

Highclare School, Birmingham   215, 431, 444, 455, 483, 495

Highfield Preparatory School, Harrogate   225, 444, 463, 468

Highfield Priory School, Preston   134, 489

Highfield School, Birkenhead   163, 440

Highfield School, Liphook   114, 394, 424, 438, 459, 468, 479, 488

Highfield School, London SW18   490

Highfield School, Maidenhead   76, 421, 435, 451, 477, 485

Highfields Private School, Redruth   93

Highfields School, Newark   173, 492

Highgate School, London N6   142, 426, 440, 468, 490

The Highlands School, Reading   78, 485

Hilden Grange School, Tonbridge   129, 425, 438, 468, 489

Hilden Oaks School, Tonbridge   129, 468, 489

Hill House International Junior School, London SW1   150, 426, 440, 480

Hill House St Mary's School, Doncaster   228, 432, 496

Hillcrest Grammar School, Stockport   91, 436, 487

Hillcroft Preparatory School, Stowmarket   190, 429, 442, 468, 475, 493

Hillgrove School, Bangor   250, 446, 466

Hillstone School (Malvern College), Malvern   495

Hipperholme Grammar School, Halifax   230, 432, 445, 496

Hoe Bridge School, Woking   203, 364, 430, 482, 493

Holland House, Edgware   165

Holland Park Pre-Preparatory School, London W14   161

Holly Park Montessori, London N4   142

Hollygirt School, Nottingham   174, 428, 454, 492

Holme Grange School, Wokingham   80, 421, 468, 477, 485

Holme Park School, Kendal   94, 423, 458, 468, 478

Holmewood House, Tunbridge Wells   130, 355, 425, 459, 479, 489

Holmwood House, Colchester   105, 424, 437, 458, 475, 488

Holy Cross Convent, Gerrards Cross   84, 422, 436, 451, 472, 478

Holy Cross Preparatory School, Kingston-upon-Thames   197, 442, 454, 472, 494

Holy Trinity School, Kidderminster   222, 432, 466, 495

The Holywood Rudolf Steiner School, Holywood   234, 445

Homefield School, Sutton   201, 365, 430, 450, 494

Homewood Independent School, St Albans   489

Homewood Pre-Preparatory School, St Albans   121

Honeybourne School, Birmingham   215, 466

Hopelands School, Stonehouse   110

Hordle Walhampton School, Lymington   114, 424, 438, 459, 468, 475, 479, 488

Horlers Pre-Preparatory School, Cambridge   486

Hornsby House School, London SW12   154, 490

Horris Hill School, Newbury   76, 421, 435, 448, 457, 477, 486

Howe Green House School, Bishop's Stortford   118, 489

Howell's School, Denbigh   250, 434, 446, 456, 464, 466, 484, 497

Howell's School, Llandaff GDST, Cardiff   248, 434, 446, 497

Howsham Hall, York   226, 432, 444, 463, 483, 496

Hubert Jewish High School for Girls, Salford   163, 453, 471

Huddersfield Grammar School, Huddersfield   230, 432, 445

Hull Collegiate School, Anlaby   224, 432, 444, 468, 495

Hull High School, Anlaby   455

The Hulme Grammar School for Girls, Oldham   133, 426, 439, 453, 489

Hulme Hall Schools (Junior Division), Cheadle   90, 487

Hulme Hall Schools, Cheadle   90, 422, 436, 487

Hunter Hall School, Penrith   94, 436

Hurlingham Private School, London SW15   154, 427, 440, 468

Hurst Lodge School, Ascot   75, 421, 435, 451, 457, 477, 486

Hurstpierpoint College, Hurstpierpoint   209, 431, 462, 468, 482, 494

Hurtwood House, Dorking   193, 366, 430, 461, 482, 494

Hurworth House School, Darlington   103, 424, 437, 448

Hutchesons' Grammar School, Glasgow   240, 445, 483, 497

Hutchesons' Lilybank Junior School, Glasgow   240

Hydesville Tower School, Walsall   217, 431, 466, 495

Hyland House, London E17   141, 473

Hylton Kindergarten & Pre-preparatory School, Exeter   98

Hymers College, Hull   224, 444, 495

I

Ibstock Place School, London SW15   154, 427, 490

Ilford Preparatory School, Ilford   107

Ilford Ursuline Preparatory School, Ilford   107, 452, 472, 488

Immanuel College, Bushey   118, 425, 471, 489

Immanuel School, Romford   107

The Incorporated Association of Preparatory Schools (IAPS)   485, 507

The Independent Schools Association (ISA)   485, 508

The Independent Schools' Bursars Association (ISBA)   485, 508

The Independent Schools Careers Organisation (ISCO)   508

Independent Schools Council (ISC)   509

Independent Schools Examinations Board   509

Inglebrook School, Pontefract   232

Ingleside PNEU School, Cirencester   437

Ingleside School, Cirencester   110

Innellan House School, Pinner   167, 468, 491

Instituto Espanol Vicente Canada Blanch, London W10   160

International College, Sherborne School, Sherborne   102, 391, 458, 478, 487

International Community School, London NW1   144, 331, 480

International School of Aberdeen, Aberdeen   236, 445, 483

International School of London, London W3   157, 331, 440, 480

Ipswich High School GDST, Ipswich   189, 429, 442, 454, 493

Ipswich Preparatory School, Ipswich   189, 493

Ipswich School, Ipswich   189, 429, 442, 461, 468, 482, 493

IQRA School, Oxford   178, 454, 471, 481

Irwin College, Leicester   135, 426, 460, 480

Islamia Girls High School, Huddersfield   230, 455, 471

Islamia Girls' School, London NW6   147, 453, 471

Islamic Shakhsiyah Foundation, Walthamstow   472

Islamiyah School, Blackburn   130, 453, 472

The Italia Conti Academy of Theatre Arts, London EC1   141, 427, 447, 490

J

Jack and Jill School, Hampton   166, 453, 466

Jamahiriya School, London SW3   151, 472

Jamea Al Kauthar, Lancaster   132, 453, 459, 472

James Allen's Girls' School, London SE22   150, 427, 440, 453, 468, 490

James Allen's Preparatory School, London SE22   150, 468, 490

Jamiah Madaniyah Primary School, Forest Gate   472

The Japanese School, London W3   157

The John Lyon School, Harrow   166, 427, 440, 449, 491

Josca's Preparatory School, Abingdon   176, 428, 441, 450, 466, 481

Joseph Rayner Independent School, Audenshaw   161, 466

Junior King's School, Canterbury   125, 438, 459, 468, 479, 489

The Junior School, Bishop's Stortford College, Bishop's Stortford   118, 425, 438, 459

The Junior School, St Lawrence College, Ramsgate   489

K

Kassim Darwish Grammar School for Boys, Manchester   162, 449

Keble Preparatory School, London N21   144, 427, 449, 490

Kelly College Preparatory School, Tavistock   99, 437, 458, 468, 487

Kelly College, Tavistock   99, 423, 437, 458, 468, 478, 487

Kelvinside Academy, Glasgow   240, 433, 497

Kensington Prep School, London SW6   152, 453, 490

Kent College Infant & Junior School, Canterbury   125, 459, 471, 479, 489

Kent College Pembury, Tunbridge Wells   130, 425, 438, 453, 459, 471, 479, 489

Kent College, Canterbury   125, 355, 425, 438, 459, 471, 479, 489

Kerem School, London N2   142, 440, 471, 480

Kew College, Richmond   200

Kew Green Preparatory School, Richmond   200, 367, 482

Kilgraston, Perth   244, 433, 446, 455, 463, 472, 476, 484, 497

Kimbolton School, Huntingdon   87, 422, 436, 458, 478, 486

The King Alfred School, London NW11   148, 490

King Edward's Junior School, Bath   185

King Edward's Pre-Prep School, Bath   185

King Edward's School Witley, Godalming   196, 430, 442, 461, 482, 494

King Edward's School, Bath, Bath   185, 429, 442, 493

King Edward's School, Birmingham   215, 431, 444, 450, 468, 495

King Edward VI High School for Girls, Birmingham   215, 431, 444, 455, 495

King Edward VI School, Southampton   115, 424, 438, 488

King Edward VII and Queen Mary School, Lytham St Annes   133, 426, 489

King Fahad Academy, London W3   157, 440, 472

King Henry VIII School, Coventry   216, 431, 444, 495

King of Kings School, Manchester   162, 466

King's Bruton, Bruton   182, 397, 429, 441, 461, 468, 475, 481

King's College Junior School, London SW19   155, 427, 440, 449, 468, 490

King's College Madrid, Madrid, Spain   255, 417

King's College School, London SW19   155, 427, 440, 449, 468, 490

King's College, Taunton   183, 429, 441, 461, 468, 481, 492

King's Hall School, Taunton   183, 429, 441, 461, 468, 481, 492

King's Hawford, Worcester   223, 432, 444, 468, 495

The King's High School for Girls, Warwick   495

King's High School, Warwick, Warwick   213, 431, 443, 455

King's House School, Richmond   200, 442, 450, 482, 494

King's Preparatory School, Rochester   127, 425, 439, 459, 468, 489

The King's School Ely, Ely   87, 273, 422, 436, 458, 469, 478, 486

King's School Rochester, Rochester   128, 425, 439, 459, 469, 475, 489

The King's School Senior, Eastleigh   112, 466

The King's School, Basingstoke   112

King's School, Bruton   492

The King's School, Canterbury   125, 425, 459, 469, 489

The King's School, Chester   90, 436, 469, 487

The King's School, Gloucester   110, 424, 438, 458, 469, 488

The King's School, Macclesfield   91, 422, 436, 448, 452, 469, 487

The King's School, Nottingham   174, 441, 466

King's School, Plymouth   99, 466

The King's School, Primary, Witney   179, 466

The King's School, Tynemouth   212, 431, 443, 482, 495

The King's School, Witney   179, 466

The King's School, Worcester   223, 432, 444, 469, 495

King William's College, Castletown   123, 425, 438, 459, 468, 479, 489

Kingham Hill School, Chipping Norton   177, 287, 428, 441, 460, 466, 475, 481, 492
Kings Monkton School, Cardiff   248, 434, 484, 497
Kings Primary School, Southampton   115, 466
Kings School, Harpenden   119, 466
Kingscote Pre-Preparatory School, Gerrards Cross   84, 448, 469, 486
Kingscourt School, Catherington   488
Kingshott School, Hitchin   120, 469, 489
Kingsland Grange, Shrewsbury   181, 428, 441, 450, 469, 481, 492
The Kingsley School, Leamington Spa   212, 431, 443, 455, 469, 482, 495
Kingsmead School, Wirral   165, 427, 440, 460, 466, 480, 491
Kingston Grammar School, Kingston-upon-Thames   197, 430, 442, 466, 494
Kingsway School, Wigan   134, 466
Kingswood College at Scarisbrick Hall, Ormskirk   134, 426, 439, 475, 479, 489
Kingswood House School, Epsom   194, 430, 443, 450, 475, 494
Kingswood Preparatory School, Bath   185, 442, 461, 471, 481, 493
Kingswood School, Bath   185, 398, 429, 442, 461, 471, 481, 493
Kingswood School, Solihull   216
Kirkham Grammar School, Preston   134, 426, 439, 459, 479, 489
Kirkstone House School, Bourne   137, 426, 439, 480, 490
Knighton House, Blandford Forum   101, 423, 437, 452, 458, 487
Knightsbridge School, London SW1   150, 427, 440, 471, 480
The Knoll School, Kidderminster   222, 432, 469, 495

L

L'Ecole Des Petits, London SW6   152
L'Ile Aux Enfants, London NW5   146
La Retraite Swan, Salisbury   220, 432, 444, 466, 495
La Sagesse School, Newcastle upon Tyne   211, 431, 443, 454, 466, 495
The Ladies' College, Guernsey   88, 452, 486
Lady Barn House School, Cheadle   90, 466, 487
The Lady Eleanor Holles School, Hampton   166, 427, 440, 453, 469, 491
Lady Lane Park School, Bingley   229, 496

Ladymede, Aylesbury   83, 422, 436, 478, 486
Laleham Lea School, Purley   199, 472
Lambrook Haileybury, Bracknell   75, 435, 457, 469, 486
Lambs Christian School, Birmingham   215, 466
Lammas School, Sutton in Ashfield   175
Lancaster House School, Weston-Super-Mare   186
Lancaster Steiner School, Lancaster   133
Lancing College Preparatory School at Mowden, Hove   206, 430, 443, 469, 482, 494
Lancing College, Lancing   209, 431, 443, 462, 494
Lanesborough, Guildford   196, 430, 450, 469, 494
Langdale Preparatory School, Blackpool   131, 479
Langley Manor School, Slough   79, 421, 466
Langley Preparatory School & Nursery, Norwich   169, 428, 440, 491
Langley School, Norwich   170, 277, 428, 441, 460, 481, 491
Lansdowne College, London W2   157, 332, 427, 440, 480
Lathallan School, Montrose   237, 433, 445, 463, 496
Latymer Preparatory School, London W6   159, 333, 427, 490
Latymer Upper School, London W6   159, 333, 427, 440, 490
Lavant House, Chichester   207, 431, 443, 454, 462, 469, 482, 494
Laverock School, Oxted   199, 454, 466, 494
Laxton Junior School, Nr Peterborough   172, 278, 469, 492
Le Herisson, London W6   159, 480
Leaden Hall School, Salisbury   220, 432, 444, 455, 462, 495
Leckford Place School, Oxford   178, 428, 481
Leeds Girls' High School, Leeds   231, 432, 445, 455, 496
Leeds Grammar School, Leeds   231, 432, 445, 450, 496
Leicester Grammar Junior School, Leicester   135, 469
Leicester Grammar School, Leicester   135, 426, 439, 466, 469, 480, 490
Leicester High School For Girls, Leicester   135, 426, 439, 469, 490
Leicester Montessori Grammar School, Leicester   135
Leicester Montessori School, Leicester   135
Leighton Park School, Reading   78, 421, 435, 457, 472, 477, 486
Lewes Old Grammar School, Lewes   206, 430, 494

The Leys School, Cambridge   86, 273, 422, 436, 458, 471, 478, 486

Licensed Victuallers' School, Ascot   75, 421, 435, 457, 477, 486

Lichfield Cathedral School, Lichfield   187, 429, 442, 461, 469, 481, 493

Lightcliffe Preparatory, Halifax   230, 466

Lighthouse Christian School, Manchester   162, 466

Lime House School, Carlisle   94, 262, 423, 437, 458, 475, 487

Lincoln Minster School, Lincoln   137, 426, 460, 466, 490

Linden School, Newcastle upon Tyne   211

Lingfield Notre Dame School, Lingfield   198, 430, 443, 466, 494

Linley House, Surbiton   201

Lion House School, London SW15   154, 480

Lisvane, Scarborough College Junior School, Scarborough   225, 432, 463, 466, 496

Little Acorns Montessori School, Bushey   118

Little Eden SDA School & Eden High SDA School, Hanworth   166, 480

Littlegarth School, Colchester   105, 437, 488

The Littlemead School, Chichester   207, 469

Liverpool College, Liverpool   163, 427, 440, 469, 480, 491

Llandovery College, Llandovery   249, 434, 446, 464, 467, 484, 497

Llangattock School, Monmouth   251, 434, 446

The Lloyd Williamson School, London W10   160, 334, 427, 480

Lochinver House School, Potters Bar   121, 449, 489

Lockers Park, Hemel Hempstead   120, 425, 438, 449, 459, 469, 479, 489

Locksley Christian School, Manby   138, 466

Lodge School, Purley   199, 430, 454, 482, 494

Lomond School, Helensburgh   237, 433, 463, 497

London East Academy, London E1   140, 449, 472

London Islamic School, London E1   140, 449, 472

London Jewish Girls' High School, London NW4   146, 453, 471

Long Close School, Slough   79

Long Close School, Upton   486

Longacre School, Guildford   196, 482, 494

Longridge Towers School, Berwick-upon-Tweed   173, 428, 441, 460, 481, 492

Longwood School, Bushey   118

Lord's College, Bolton   131

Lord Wandsworth College, Hook   113, 394, 424, 438, 459, 479, 488

Lorenden Preparatory School, Faversham   126, 439, 466

Loreto Preparatory School, Altrincham   89, 452, 472, 478, 487

Loretto Junior School, Musselburgh   243, 433, 463, 484

Loretto School, Musselburgh   243, 409, 433, 445, 463, 484, 497

Loughborough Grammar School, Loughborough   136, 426, 439, 449, 460, 490

Loughborough High School, Loughborough   136, 426, 439, 453, 490

Loyola Preparatory School, Buckhurst Hill   105, 424, 448, 472, 488

Lubavitch House School (Junior Boys), London E5   140, 449, 471

Lubavitch House Senior School for Girls, London N16   143, 453, 471

Luckley-Oakfield School, Wokingham   80, 301, 421, 435, 451, 457, 469, 477, 486

Lucton School, Leominster   117, 424, 438, 459, 466, 479, 488

Ludgrove, Wokingham   80, 448, 457, 469, 486

Lycee Francais Charles de Gaulle, London SW7   152, 427

The Lyceum, London EC2   141, 427, 466

Lyndhurst House Preparatory School, London NW3   145, 334, 440, 449, 490

Lyndhurst School, Camberley   191, 430, 443, 494

Lyndon Preparatory School, Colwyn Bay   249, 434, 446, 464, 471, 484, 497

Lynton Preparatory School, Scunthorpe   139

Lyonsdown School Trust Ltd, Barnet   117

M

Madingley Pre-Preparatory School, Cambridge   86, 436, 478

Madni Girls School, London E1   140, 453, 472

Madresfield Early Years Centre, Malvern   222

Magdalen College School, Oxford   178, 428, 441, 450, 492

Magdalen Court School, Exeter   98

Maidwell Hall School, Northampton   172, 428, 441, 450, 460, 469, 481, 492

Maldon Court Preparatory School, Maldon   107, 488

The Mall School, Twickenham   168, 440, 449, 480, 491

Malsis School, Skipton   226, 432, 444, 463, 496

Maltman's Green School, Gerrards Cross   84, 436, 451, 478, 486

Malvern College Preparatory and Pre-Prep School, Malvern   222, 432, 444, 462, 469, 476, 483

Malvern College Preparatory School, Malvern   495

Malvern College, Malvern   222, 291, 432, 444, 462, 469, 483, 495

Malvern Girls' College, Malvern   495

Malvern St James, Great Malvern   221, 291, 432, 444, 455, 462, 469, 475, 483

The Manchester Grammar School, Manchester   162, 440, 449, 491

Manchester High School for Girls, Manchester   162, 427, 440, 453, 491

Manchester Islamic High School, Manchester   162, 453, 472

Manchester Muslim Preparatory School, Manchester   162

Mander Portman Woodward, Birmingham   215, 483

Mander Portman Woodward, London SW7   152, 427, 440, 480, 490

Mannafields Christian School, Edinburgh   242, 466

Manor House School, Ashby-de-la-Zouch   135, 439, 490

Manor House School, Honiton   98, 487

Manor House School, Leatherhead   198, 430, 454, 494

Manor Lodge School, Radlett   489

Manor Lodge School, Shenley   121

The Manor Preparatory School, Abingdon   176, 287, 441, 469, 492

Mansfield Preparatory School, Mansfield   173

Maranatha Christian School, Swindon   220, 466

Maria Montessori School Hampstead, London NW3   145

Maria Montessori School, Exeter   98

The Marist Preparatory School, Ascot   75, 451, 472, 486

The Marist Senior School, Ascot   75, 421, 451, 472, 486

Markazul Uloom, Blackburn   131, 453, 472

Marlborough College, Marlborough   219, 432, 444, 462, 469, 495

Marlborough House School, Hawkhurst   127, 439, 459, 469, 489

The Mary Erskine School, Edinburgh   243, 433, 445, 455, 463, 497

Marycourt School, Gosport   113, 424

Marymount International School, Kingston-upon-Thames   197, 367, 430, 443, 454, 461, 472, 482, 494

Mayfield Preparatory School, Walsall   217, 495

The Maynard School, Exeter   98, 423, 437, 452, 478, 487

Maypole House School, Alford   137, 426, 439, 466

Mayville High School, Southsea   115, 424, 438, 475, 479, 488

The Mead School, Tunbridge Wells   130, 466, 489

Meadowbrook Montessori School, Bracknell   75, 469

Meadowpark Nursery & Pre-Prep School, Cricklade   218, 466

Mechinah Liyeshivah Zichron Moshe, London N16   143, 449, 471

Meoncross School, Fareham   112, 424, 488

Merchant Taylors' School for Girls, Liverpool   164, 427, 440, 453, 480, 491

Merchant Taylors' School, Liverpool   163, 427, 440, 449, 491

Merchant Taylors' School, Northwood   167, 427, 440, 449, 469, 491

Merchiston Castle School, Edinburgh   243, 410, 433, 445, 451, 463, 484, 497

The Merlin School, London SW15   154

Merton Court Preparatory School, Sidcup   129, 425, 439, 469

Merton House, Chester   90, 422, 469

Methodist College, Belfast   233, 433, 445, 463, 496

Michael Hall (Steiner Waldorf School), Forest Row   205, 375, 462, 466

Michael House Steiner School, Heanor   96, 437

Micklefield School, Reigate   200, 469, 494

Milbourne Lodge School, Esher   195, 430, 469, 494

Mill Hill School, London NW7   147, 335, 460, 490

The Mill School, Devizes   219

Millfield Preparatory School, Glastonbury   183, 429, 441, 461, 481, 492

Millfield School, Street   183, 429, 441, 461, 481, 492

Milton Abbey School, Blandford Forum   101, 392, 423, 437, 458, 469, 476, 478, 487

Milton Keynes Preparatory School, Milton Keynes   85, 422, 436, 478, 486

Milverton House School, Nuneaton   213

The Minster School, York   227, 432, 469, 496

Miss Morley's Nursery School, Newbury   77

Moffats School, Bewdley   221, 292, 432, 444, 462, 469, 483, 495

Moira House Girls School, Eastbourne   205, 430, 443, 454, 462, 482, 494

Moira House School, Eastbourne   205, 430, 443, 454, 462, 482

Monkton Combe Junior School, Bath   185, 429, 442, 461, 469, 493

Monkton Combe School, Bath   185, 429, 442, 461,
    469, 475, 481, 493
Monmouth School, Monmouth   251, 434, 446,
    451, 464, 467, 484, 497
The Montessori House School, London N10   142
Monton Prep School with Montessori Nurseries,
    Eccles   161, 440, 466
Moor Allerton School, Manchester   162, 491
Moor Park School, Ludlow   181, 428, 441, 461,
    472, 481, 492
Moorfield School, Ilkley   231, 455, 496
Moorland School, Clitheroe   132, 439, 459, 469
Moorlands School, Leeds   231, 445, 496
Moorlands School, Luton   74, 421, 435, 485
More House School, Farnham   195, 450, 461, 472
More House, London SW1   150, 336, 427, 440,
    453, 472, 490
Moreton Hall Preparatory School, Bury St
    Edmunds   189, 429, 442, 461, 472, 482, 493
Moreton Hall School, Oswestry   181, 289, 428,
    441, 454, 461, 469, 481, 492
Morley Hall Preparatory School, Derby   96, 469
Morrison's Academy, Crieff   244, 433, 446, 463,
    484, 497
Mostyn House School, South Wirral   91, 422, 436,
    475, 478, 487
Mougins School, France   254, 416
Moulsford Preparatory School, Wallingford   179,
    450, 460, 469, 492
Mount House School, Tavistock   99, 423, 437, 458,
    469, 478, 487
Mount School, Huddersfield   230
The Mount School, London NW7   147, 427, 453,
    480, 490
The Mount School, York   227, 432, 444, 455, 463,
    472, 483, 496
Mount St Mary's College, Spinkhill   96, 265, 423,
    437, 458, 472, 478, 487
Mountford House School, Nottingham   174, 492
Mountjoy House School, Huddersfield   230, 466
Mowden Hall School, Stocksfield   173, 428, 441,
    460, 469, 492
Mowden School, Hove   494
Moyles Court School, Ringwood   115, 459, 475,
    488
MPW (Mander Portman Woodward),
    Cambridge   86, 422, 436, 458, 478
The Mulberry House School, London NW2   144
Mylnhurst RC School & Nursery, Sheffield   228,
    472, 496

N

Naima Jewish Preparatory School, London
    NW6   147, 440, 471, 490
Netherleigh and Rossefield School, Bradford   229
Netherwood School, Saundersfoot   252, 434, 446,
    464, 469, 484
The New Beacon, Sevenoaks   128, 449, 469, 489
New College School, Oxford   178, 428, 450, 469,
    481, 492
The New Eccles Hall School, Norwich   170, 428,
    441, 460, 481, 491
New Hall School, Chelmsford   105, 424, 437, 458,
    472, 479, 488
New Horizon Community School, Leeds   231, 455,
    472, 483
New Life Christian School, Croydon   193, 466
New Lodge School, Dorking   194, 430, 443, 469,
    482
New School, Exeter   98, 469
Newbold School, Bracknell   75, 473
Newbridge Preparatory School,
    Wolverhampton   217, 444, 455, 495
Newcastle Preparatory School, Newcastle upon
    Tyne   211, 443, 495
Newcastle School for Boys, Newcastle upon
    Tyne   211, 431, 450
Newcastle-under-Lyme School, Newcastle-under-
    Lyme   187, 429, 442, 493
Newcastle Upon Tyne Church High School,
    Newcastle upon Tyne   211, 431, 443, 455, 469,
    495
Newland House School, Twickenham   168, 440,
    491
Newlands Manor School, Seaford   494
Newlands Preparatory School, Seaford   494
Newlands School, Newcastle upon Tyne   495
Newlands School, Seaford   206, 376, 430, 443,
    462, 475, 482
Newton Bank School, Newton-Le-Willows   164
Newton Prep School, London SW8   153, 427, 490
Noor Ul Islam Primary School, London E10   141,
    472
Norfolk House Preparatory & Kids Corner Nursery,
    Sandbach   91, 466
Norfolk House School, Birmingham   215, 431,
    466, 495
Norfolk House School, London N10   143
Norfolk Lodge Nursery & Preparatory School,
    Barnet   117
Norland Place School, London W11   160, 490

Norman Court Preparatory School, Salisbury   220, 432, 444, 462, 469, 483, 495

Normanhurst School, London E4   140, 427, 490

North Bridge House Junior School, London NW3   145

North Bridge House Lower Prep School, London NW1   144, 427

North Bridge House Nursery School, London NW3   145

North Bridge House Senior School, London NW1   144, 427, 480

North Bridge House Upper Prep School, London NW1   144, 449, 480

North Cestrian Grammar School, Altrincham   89, 422, 436, 448, 487

North London Collegiate, Edgware   165, 427, 440, 453, 491

North London Rudolf Steiner School, London E5   140

Northampton High School, Northampton   172, 428, 441, 454, 469, 492

Northamptonshire Grammar School, Pitsford   172, 428, 441, 481, 492

Northbourne Park School, Deal   126, 425, 439, 459, 469, 479, 489

Northcote Lodge School, London SW11   153, 427, 449, 469, 490

Northgate Preparatory, Rhyl   250

Northwood College, Northwood   167, 314, 427, 453, 491

Northwood Preparatory School, Rickmansworth   121, 449, 469, 489

The Norwegian School, London SW20   156, 440

Norwich High School for Girls GDST, Norwich   170, 428, 441, 454, 481, 491

Norwich School, Norwich   170, 428, 441, 450, 466, 491

Notre Dame Preparatory School, Cobham   192, 430, 443, 454, 472, 482, 494

Notre Dame Preparatory School, Norwich   170, 472, 481, 491

Notre Dame Senior School, Cobham   192, 430, 454, 472, 494

Notting Hill and Ealing High School GDST, London W13   160, 427, 440, 453, 490

Notting Hill Preparatory School, London W11   160

Nottingham High Junior School, Nottingham   174, 441, 450, 492

Nottingham High School for Girls GDST, Nottingham   174, 428, 441, 454, 492

Nottingham High School, Nottingham   174, 428, 441, 450, 492

O

Oakfield Preparatory School, London SE21   149, 490

Oakfield School, Woking   203, 430, 443

Oakfields Montessori Schools Ltd, Upminster   108

Oakham School, Oakham   180, 276, 428, 441, 460, 469, 481, 492

Oakhill College, Clitheroe   132, 472

Oakhyrst Grange School, Caterham   192, 494

Oaklands School, Loughton   107, 479, 488

Oakwood School & Nursery, Purley   199, 443, 472

Oakwood School, Chichester   207, 431, 469, 494

Ockbrook School, Derby   96, 423, 452, 458, 487

Old Buckenham Hall School, Ipswich   189, 442, 461, 469, 493

The Old Hall School, Telford   182, 428, 469, 492

The Old Malthouse, Swanage   103, 423, 458, 469, 478, 487

Old Palace School of John Whitgift, Croydon   193, 430, 454, 469, 482, 494

The Old School, Beccles   188, 469, 493

The Old Vicarage School, Derby   96

Old Vicarage School, Richmond   200, 454, 469, 494

The Oldham Hulme Grammar School, Oldham   133, 439, 449, 489

Oldham Hulme Kindergarten, Oldham   133

Olive Secondary, Bradford   229, 450

The Oratory Preparatory School, Reading   78, 301, 421, 435, 457, 472, 477, 486

The Oratory School, Reading   78, 422, 435, 448, 457, 472, 477, 486

Orchard House School, London W4   158, 322, 427, 490

Oriel Bank, Stockport   91, 422, 436, 452, 469

Orley Farm School, Harrow   166, 469, 491

Ormer House Preparatory School, Alderney   88, 422, 436

Orwell Park, Ipswich   190, 429, 442, 461, 482, 493

Oswestry School Bellan House, Oswestry   181, 429, 441, 469

Oswestry School, Oswestry   181, 428, 441, 461, 481, 492

Oundle School, Nr Peterborough   172, 428, 441, 460, 469, 492

Our Lady of Sion School, Worthing   210, 431, 443, 494

Our Lady's Convent Junior School, Abingdon   176, 472

Our Lady's Convent School, Loughborough   136, 453, 472, 490

Our Lady's Convent Senior School, Abingdon   176, 428, 441, 454, 472, 481, 492
Our Lady's Preparatory School, Crowthorne   76, 472
Overndale School, Bristol   82, 436
Oxford High School GDST, Oxford   178, 428, 441, 454, 492
Oxford House School, Colchester   106, 488
Oxford Montessori Schools, Oxford   178
Oxford Tutorial College, Oxford   178, 428, 441, 460, 481
OYH Primary School, London NW4   146, 471

P

Packwood Haugh School, Shrewsbury   181, 429, 441, 461, 469, 481, 492
Padworth College, Reading   78, 302, 422, 435, 457, 477
Palmers Green High School, London N21   144, 427, 440, 453, 490
Pangbourne College, Pangbourne   77, 422, 435, 457, 469, 486
Papplewick School, Ascot   75, 302, 422, 448, 457, 469, 477, 486
Paragon Christian Academy, London E5   140, 466
Paragon School, Bath   493
Paragon School, Prior Park College Junior, Bath   185, 429, 442
Pardes Grammar Boys' School, London N3   142, 449, 471
Park Hill School, Kingston-upon-Thames   198, 469, 482
Park School for Girls, Ilford   107, 424, 452, 488
The Park School, Bournemouth   101, 423, 437, 487
Park School, Totnes   100, 437
The Park School, Yeovil   184, 429, 442, 461, 466, 481, 492
Parkgate House School, London SW4   151, 336, 427, 480
Parkside Preparatory School, London N17   143
Parkside School, Cobham   192, 450, 494
Parsons Mead, Ashtead   494
Pattison College, Coventry   216, 444, 447
Peaslake School, Guildford   196, 469
Pembridge Hall, London W2   157, 453, 490
Pennthorpe School, Horsham   209, 443, 469, 494
Perrott Hill School, Crewkerne   183, 429, 442, 461, 469, 481, 492
The Perse School for Girls, Cambridge   86, 422, 436, 452, 486

The Perse School, Cambridge   86, 422, 486
Peterborough & St Margaret's School, Stanmore   168, 453, 469, 491
Peterborough High School, Peterborough   87, 422, 436, 452, 458, 469, 478, 486
The Phoenix School, London NW3   145
Pilgrims Pre-Preparatory School, Bedford   74, 469, 485
The Pilgrims' School, Winchester   116, 424, 438, 448, 459, 469, 488
Pinewood School, Shrivenham   220, 402, 432, 444, 462, 469
Pinewood School, Swindon   495
Pipers Corner School, High Wycombe   84, 307, 422, 436, 451, 457, 469, 478, 486
Plumtree School, Nottingham   174, 469, 492
Plymouth College, Plymouth   99, 423, 437, 458, 466, 478, 487
PNEU School, Loughborough   136, 490
Pocklington Montessori School, Pocklington   224
Pocklington School, Pocklington   224, 432, 444, 462, 469, 483, 495
The Pointer School, London SE3   148, 427, 440, 466
Polam Hall, Darlington   103, 424, 437, 452, 458, 478, 487
Polam School, Bedford   74
Polwhele House School, Truro   93, 423, 436, 458, 487
Port Regis School, Shaftesbury   102, 423, 437, 458, 478, 487
Portland Place School, London W1   156, 427, 490
Portora Royal School, Enniskillen   496
The Portsmouth Grammar School, Portsmouth   114, 424, 438, 466, 488
Portsmouth High School GDST, Southsea   116, 424, 438, 452, 488
The Potters House School, Bury   132, 466
Pownall Hall School, Wilmslow   92, 436, 487
Prebendal School (Northgate House), Chichester   208, 469
The Prebendal School, Chichester   207, 431, 443, 462, 469, 494
Prenton Preparatory School, Wirral   165, 491
Prestfelde Preparatory School, Shrewsbury   181, 429, 441, 461, 469, 492
Prestwich Preparatory School, Prestwich   163
Primrose Independent School, London N5   142, 480
Prince's Mead School, Winchester   116, 424, 469, 488

The Princess Helena College, Hitchin   120, 425, 438, 452, 459, 469, 479, 489

Princethorpe College, Rugby   213, 431, 472, 482, 495

Prins Willem-Alexander School, Woking   203

Prior Park College, Bath   185, 399, 429, 442, 461, 472, 481, 493

Prior Park Preparatory School, Cricklade   218, 444, 462, 472, 476, 483, 495

Prior's Field School, Godalming   196, 368, 430, 443, 454, 461, 482, 494

Priory School, Banstead   191, 450, 494

Priory School, Birmingham   215, 431, 444, 455, 472, 483, 495

Priory School, Shanklin   123, 466

Promised Land Academy, London E13   141, 466

Prospect House School, London SW15   154, 322, 427, 490

Prospect School, Brislington   82, 466

The Purcell School, Bushey   119, 425, 438, 447, 459, 489

Putney High School GDST, London SW15   154, 427, 440, 453, 490

Putney Park School, London SW15   155, 337, 480, 490

Q

Quainton Hall School, Harrow   166, 440, 450, 469, 491

Queen Anne's School, Reading   78, 303, 422, 435, 451, 457, 469, 477, 486

Queen Elizabeth Grammar School, Wakefield   232, 432, 445, 450, 496

Queen Elizabeth's Grammar School, Blackburn   131, 426, 439, 489

Queen Elizabeth's Hospital, Bristol   82, 422, 436, 448, 477, 486

Queen Ethelburga's College, York   227, 268, 432, 444, 463, 469, 483, 496

Queen Margaret's School, York   227, 432, 444, 455, 463, 469, 483, 496

Queen Mary's School, Thirsk   226, 432, 444, 455, 463, 469, 496

Queen's College Junior and Pre-Preparatory Schools, Taunton   183, 429, 442, 461, 471, 493

Queen's College Prep School, London W1   156, 453, 469

Queen's College, London W1   156, 427, 440, 453, 469, 490

Queen's College, Taunton   183, 429, 442, 461, 471, 481, 492

Queen's Gate School, London SW7   152, 337, 427, 453, 490

The Queen's School, Chester   90, 436, 452, 478, 487

Queen Victoria School, Dunblane   244, 446, 463

Queenswood School, Hatfield   119, 425, 438, 452, 459, 479, 489

Querns Westonbirt School, Tetbury   111, 284, 469

Quinton House School, Northampton   172, 428, 441, 481

Quwwatt Ul Islam Girls School, London E7   141, 453, 472

R

Radlett Preparatory School, Radlett   121

Radley College, Abingdon   176, 428, 441, 450, 460, 469, 492

Rainbow Montessori Junior School, London NW6   147

Ramillies Hall School, Cheadle   90, 436, 475, 487

Ranby House School, Retford   175, 428, 441, 460, 469, 481

Ranby House, Retford   492

Raphael Independent School, Hornchurch   106

Raphael Independent School, Romford   488

The Rastrick Independent School, Brighouse   230, 466, 483, 496

Ratcliffe College, Leicester   135, 426, 439, 460, 472, 480, 490

Rathvilly School, Birmingham   215, 469

Ravenscourt Park Preparatory School, London W6   159, 480, 490

Ravenscourt Theatre School, London W6   159, 447, 469

Ravenstone House Pre-preparatory and Nursery, London W2   157

Raventhorpe Preparatory School, Darlington   104, 424

Rawdha Tul Uloom, Blackburn   131, 472

Read School, Selby   225, 432, 444, 463, 469, 483, 496

Reading Blue Coat School, Reading   78, 303, 422, 435, 448, 469, 486

Red House School, Norton   188, 466, 493

The Red Maids' School, Bristol   82, 422, 436, 451, 477, 486

Redcliffe School, London SW10   153, 338, 466, 490

Redcourt- St Anselms, Prenton   164, 472, 491

Reddiford, Pinner   167, 469, 491

Redehall Preparatory School, Horley   197

Redemption Academy, Stevenage   122

Redland High School, Bristol   82, 422, 436, 451, 486

Redroofs Theatre School, Maidenhead   76

Reed's School, Cobham   192, 369, 430, 443, 450, 461, 469, 494

Regius Christian School, Edinburgh   243, 466

Reigate Grammar School, Reigate   200, 430, 443, 494

Reigate St Mary's Preparatory and Choir School, Reigate   200, 430, 469, 494

Rendcomb College, Cirencester   110, 283, 424, 438, 458, 469, 479, 488

Repton School, Derby   96, 423, 437, 458, 469, 478, 487

RGS The Grange, Worcester   223, 432

The Richard Pate School, Cheltenham   109, 424, 488

Richmond House School, Leeds   231, 432, 445, 466, 483, 496

Rickmansworth PNEU School, Rickmansworth   121, 452, 466, 489

Riddlesworth Hall, Diss   169, 441, 460, 469, 475, 481, 491

Ringwood Waldorf School, Ringwood   115

Ripley Court School, Woking   203, 430, 443, 494

Ripon Cathedral Choir School, Ripon   225, 432, 444, 463, 469, 496

Rishworth School, Rishworth   232, 432, 445, 463, 469, 483, 496

River House Montessori School, London E2   140

River School, Worcester   223, 444, 466

Riverston School, London SE12   149, 427, 440, 480, 490

Rivington Park Independent School, Horwich   132

Robert Gordons College, Aberdeen   236, 433, 445, 496

Rochdale Girls School, Rochdale   134, 453, 472

The Roche School, London SW18   155, 338, 427, 440, 480

Rochester Independent College, Rochester   128, 356, 425, 439, 459, 479

Rock Hall School, Alnwick   173, 469

Rockport School, Holywood   234, 463, 496

Rodney School, Newark   428, 441, 460, 469, 492

Roedean School, Brighton   204, 431, 443, 454, 462, 469, 482, 494

Rokeby School, Kingston-upon-Thames   198, 430, 450, 494

Rookesbury Park School, Portsmouth   114, 424, 438, 459, 479, 488

Rookwood School, Andover   112, 395, 424, 459, 488

Rose Hill School, Tunbridge Wells   489

Rose Hill School, Wotton-under-Edge   111, 424, 438, 469, 479, 488

Rosebrae School, Elgin   244, 446

Roselyon, Par   93, 423, 436, 469, 487

Rosemead Preparatory School, London SE21   149, 339, 491

Rosemeade School, Huddersfield   230

Rossall Junior School, Fleetwood   132, 426, 439, 459, 469, 489

Rossall School International Study Centre, Fleetwood   132, 459, 480

Rossall School, Fleetwood   132, 426, 439, 459, 469, 479, 489

Rosslyn School, Birmingham   215, 469

Rougemont School, Newport   251, 434, 446, 497

The Round Square Schools   510

Roundstone Preparatory School, Trowbridge   220, 466

Rowan Preparatory School, Esher   195, 454, 494

The Rowans School, London SW20   156, 480

Roxeth Mead School, Harrow on the Hill   166, 470

Royal Alexandra and Albert School, Reigate   200, 370, 443, 461, 470

Royal Ballet School, London WC2   161, 440, 447, 460, 491

Royal Ballet School, Richmond   200, 461, 482

Royal Belfast Academical Institution, Belfast   233, 445, 451, 496

Royal Grammar School Worcester, Worcester   223, 432, 444, 495

Royal Grammar School, Guildford   196, 430, 443, 450, 494

Royal Grammar School, Newcastle upon Tyne   211, 450, 495

The Royal High School, Bath   186, 399, 429, 442, 454, 461, 481, 493

The Royal Hospital School, Ipswich   190, 279, 429, 442, 461, 466, 482, 493

The Royal Masonic School for Girls, Rickmansworth   121, 311, 425, 438, 452, 459, 479, 489

Royal Russell School, Croydon   193, 430, 443, 461, 470, 482, 494

The Royal School Dungannon, Dungannon   235, 433, 445, 463, 483, 496

The Royal School, Armagh   234, 445, 463, 483

The Royal School, Hampstead, London NW3   145,
   340, 427, 440, 453, 460, 480, 491
The Royal School, Haslemere   197, 430, 443, 454,
   461, 470, 482, 494
The Royal Wolverhampton Junior School,
   Wolverhampton   217, 444, 462, 470, 495
The Royal Wolverhampton School,
   Wolverhampton   217, 431, 444, 462, 470, 483,
   495
Ruckleigh School, Solihull   216, 495
Rudolf Steiner School, Dartington   97
Rudolf Steiner School, Kings Langley   120
Rudston Preparatory School, Rotherham   228, 444,
   496
Rugby School, Rugby   213, 431, 443, 462, 470,
   482, 495
Runnymede St Edward's School, Liverpool   164,
   427, 472, 491
Rupert House, Henley-on-Thames   177, 492
Rushmoor School, Bedford   74, 470, 485
Russell House School, Sevenoaks   128, 470, 489
Ruthin School, Ruthin   250, 434, 446, 464, 484,
   497
Rydal Penrhos Senior School, Colwyn Bay   249,
   434, 446, 451, 456, 464, 471, 484, 497
Ryde School, Ryde   123, 425, 438, 459, 470, 479,
   489
Rydes Hill Preparatory School, Guildford   196, 494
Rye St Antony School, Oxford   179, 428, 441, 454,
   460, 472, 481, 492
The Ryleys, Alderley Edge   89, 423, 436, 448, 478,
   487

S

Sackville School, Tonbridge   129, 425, 439, 470,
   489
Sacred Heart Convent School, Swaffham   170, 428,
   441, 460, 472, 491
Sacred Heart Preparatory School, Chew Magna   82,
   422, 466, 486
Sacred Heart R.C. Primary School, Wadhurst   207,
   443, 472
Sacred Heart School, Wadhurst   494
Saddleworth Preparatory School, Oldham   133,
   470
Saint Felix School, Southwold   190, 429, 442, 461,
   482, 493
Saint Martin's School, Solihull   216, 431, 455
Saint Michael's College, Tenbury Wells   223, 432,
   462, 483

Salcombe Preparatory School, London N14   143,
   491
Salesian College, Farnborough   113, 438, 449, 473,
   488
Salisbury Cathedral School, Salisbury   220, 432,
   462, 470, 495
Salterford House School, Nottingham   175, 492
Sancton Wood School, Cambridge   87, 422, 436,
   470, 478
Sanderstead Junior School, South Croydon   201,
   443, 470
Sandhurst School, Worthing   210
Sandroyd School, Salisbury   220, 432, 462, 470,
   483, 495
Sands School, Ashburton   97, 437
Sarum Hall, London NW3   146, 440, 453, 470, 491
SATIPS   510
Saville House School, Mansfield   173, 470
Scarborough College & Lisvane School,
   Scarborough   225, 432, 444, 463, 483, 496
Sceptre School, Dunstable   74, 466
School of St Helen & St Katharine, Abingdon   492
The School of St Helen & St Katharine,
   Abingdon   176, 428, 441, 454, 470, 481
School of the Lion, Gloucester   110, 438, 466
Sea View Private School, Kirkcaldy   239, 445
Seaford College, Petworth   209, 384, 431, 443,
   462, 470, 482, 494
Seaton House School, Sutton   201, 430, 454, 494
Second Chances at The Vine Trust Walsall,
   Walsall   217, 466
Sedbergh Junior School, Lancaster   133, 426, 439,
   459, 466
Sedbergh School, Sedbergh   94, 423, 437, 458,
   470, 478, 487
Sefton Park School, Stoke Poges   85, 466
Sevenoaks Preparatory School, Sevenoaks   128,
   439, 489
Sevenoaks School, Sevenoaks   128, 356, 425, 439,
   459, 479, 489
Shaw House School, Bradford   229, 433, 445, 470
Shebbear College, Beaworthy   97, 423, 437, 458,
   471, 478, 487
Sheffield High School GDST, Sheffield   228, 432,
   444, 455, 483, 496
Sherborne House School, Eastleigh   112, 424, 438,
   479, 488
Sherborne Preparatory School, Sherborne   102,
   423, 437, 458, 466, 470, 478, 487
Sherborne School for Girls, Sherborne   103, 423,
   437, 452, 458, 470, 478, 487

Sherborne School, Sherborne   102, 423, 437, 448, 458, 470, 478, 487

Sherfield School, Hook   113, 424, 438

Shernold School, Maidstone   127, 470

Sherrardswood School, Welwyn   122, 425, 470, 489

Shiplake College, Henley-on-Thames   177, 428, 460, 470, 481, 492

Shoreham College, Shoreham-by-Sea   210, 431, 443, 470, 494

Shrewsbury High School GDST, Shrewsbury   182, 429, 441, 454, 492

Shrewsbury House School, Surbiton   201, 443, 450, 470, 494

Shrewsbury School, Shrewsbury   182, 429, 441, 450, 461, 470, 481, 492

The Shrubbery School, Sutton Coldfield   217

Sibford School, Banbury   176, 428, 441, 460, 472, 475, 481, 492

Sidcot School, Winscombe   186, 400, 429, 442, 461, 472, 475, 481, 493

Silcoates School, Wakefield   232, 433, 445, 473, 496

Silverhill School, Winterbourne   111, 424

Sinclair House School, London SW6   152, 427, 440, 473

Sir William Perkins's School, Chertsey   192, 430, 443, 454, 494

Skippers Hill Manor Preparatory School, Mayfield   494

Slapton Pre-Preparatory School, Towcester   172, 470

Slindon College, Arundel   207, 431, 443, 450, 462, 476, 482, 494

Smallwood Manor Preparatory School, Uttoxeter   188, 470, 493

Snaresbrook College Preparatory School, London E18   141, 470, 491

The Society of Headmasters and Headmistresses of Independent Schools (SHMIS)   485, 511

Solefield School, Sevenoaks   128, 425, 439, 449, 470, 489

Solihull School, Solihull   216, 431, 444, 470, 495

Somerhill Pre-Preparatory School, Tonbridge   129

Sompting Abbotts School, Sompting   210, 443, 462, 470, 494

South Hampstead High School, London NW3   146, 427, 440, 453, 491

South Hills School, Salisbury   220, 444

South Lee Preparatory School, Bury St Edmunds   189, 429, 493

Southbank International School, Hampstead, London NW3   146, 343, 480, 491

Southbank International School, Kensington, London W11   160, 343, 480, 491

Southbank International School, Westminster, London W1   156, 344, 427, 480

Southleigh Kindergarten, Burnham-on-Sea   182

Spratton Hall, Northampton   172, 470, 492

Spring Grove School, Ashford   124, 425

Springfield Christian School, London SE6   149, 466

St Agnes PNEU School, Leeds   231, 470

St Albans High School for Girls, St Albans   121, 312, 425, 438, 452, 470, 489

St Albans School, St Albans   122, 312, 425, 438, 449, 489

St Aloysius' College, Glasgow   240, 433, 445, 472

St Aloysius Junior School, Glasgow   240, 497

St Ambrose Preparatory School, Altrincham   89, 448, 472

St Andrew's Montessori School, Watford   122, 425, 438, 479

St Andrew's School, Bedford   74, 451, 485

St Andrew's School, Eastbourne   205, 431, 443, 462, 470, 482, 494

St Andrew's School, Reading   78, 435, 457, 470, 486

St Andrew's School, Rochester   128

St Andrew's (Woking) School Trust, Woking   203, 370, 430, 443, 470, 494

St Andrew's, Cambridge   86, 458

St Andrew's, Wantage   179, 428, 441

St Andrew School, Marlborough   219

St Anne's College Grammar School, Lytham St Annes   133, 426, 439, 459, 480

St Anne's Pre-School, Lee-on-the-Solent   114

St Anne's Preparatory School, Chelmsford   105, 488

St Anselm's School, Bakewell   95, 437, 458, 470, 478, 487

St Anthony's Preparatory School, London NW3   145, 449, 472, 491

St Anthonys School, Cinderford   109, 472

St Antony's Leweston School, Sherborne   102, 423, 437, 452, 458, 472, 478

St Antony's Leweston Schools, Sherborne   487

St Aubyn's School, Woodford Green   108, 424, 466, 488

St Aubyns School, Brighton   204, 431, 443, 462, 470, 482, 494

St Augustine's Priory, London W5   158, 427, 453, 472, 480

St Bede's College, Manchester   162, 427, 440, 472, 480, 491

St Bede's Prep School, Eastbourne   205, 431, 462, 475, 494

St Bede's School, Hailsham   205, 377, 431, 462, 475, 494

St Bede's School, Stafford   187, 461, 472, 481, 493

St Bees School, St Bees   94, 263, 423, 437, 458, 470, 475, 478, 487

St Benedict's Junior School, London W5   158, 427, 472

St Benedict's School, London W5   158, 427, 440, 449, 472, 491

St Bernard's Preparatory School, Slough   79, 472, 486

St Catherine's Preparatory School, Stockport   92, 472, 487

St Catherine's School, Guildford   196, 430, 454, 461, 470, 482, 494

St Catherine's School, Twickenham   168, 427, 453, 472, 491

St Cedd's School, Chelmsford   105, 488

St Christina's RC Preparatory School, London NW8   147, 453, 472, 491

St Christopher's School, Beckenham   124

St Christopher's School, Canterbury   125, 425, 439, 479

St Christopher's School, Epsom   194, 470, 494

St Christopher's School, Hove   206, 443, 470

St Christopher's School, London NW3   145, 427, 453, 470, 491

St Christopher's School, Norwich   170, 491

St Christopher's School, Wembley   168, 480, 491

St Christopher School, Letchworth   120, 425, 438, 459, 479, 489

St Christophers School, Totnes   100, 423, 437, 466

St Clare's School, Porthcawl   247, 434, 484

St Clare's, Oxford, Oxford   179, 288, 428, 441, 460, 481

St Colette's School, Cambridge   86, 486

St Columba's College, St Albans   122, 425, 438, 449, 472, 489

St Columba's School, Kilmacolm   241, 497

St Crispin's School (Leicester) Ltd., Leicester   135, 426, 439, 471, 476, 480

St David's College, Llandudno   249, 434, 446, 464, 466, 475, 484, 497

St David's College, West Wickham   130, 489

St David's School, Ashford   165, 428, 440, 453, 460, 470, 491

St David's School, Purley   199, 443, 470, 482, 494

St Dominic's Independent Junior School, Stoke-on-Trent   187, 429

St Dominic's Priory School, Stone   187, 429, 442, 454, 472, 493

St Dominic's School, Stafford   187, 429, 442, 454, 466, 481, 493

St Dunstan's Abbey–The Plymouth College Junior School, Plymouth   99, 478, 487

St Dunstan's College, London SE6   148, 491

St Edmund's College, Ware   122, 425, 438, 459, 472, 479, 489

St Edmund's School, Canterbury   125, 425, 439, 459, 470, 479, 489

St Edmund's School, Hindhead   197, 430, 443, 450, 461, 470, 494

St Edmunds Junior School, Canterbury   125, 425, 439, 459, 470, 479, 489

St Edward's School Cheltenham, Cheltenham   109, 424, 438, 472

St Edward's School, Cheltenham   488

St Edward's School, Oxford   179, 428, 441, 460, 470, 492

St Edward's School, Reading   78, 422, 448, 486

St Faith's at Ash School, Canterbury   125

St Faith's, Cambridge   86, 422, 486

St Francis' College, Letchworth   120, 425, 438, 452, 459, 466, 479, 489

St Francis School, Pewsey   219, 432, 444, 470, 495

St Gabriel's School, Newbury   77, 422, 435, 451, 470, 477, 486

St George's College Junior School, Weybridge   202, 472, 494

St George's College, Weybridge   202, 430, 472, 494

St George's Preparatory School, Jersey   88, 422, 436, 478

St George's School for Girls, Edinburgh   243, 445, 455, 463, 484, 497

St George's School, Ascot   75, 304, 422, 435, 451, 457, 470, 477, 486

St George's School, Edgbaston, Birmingham   215, 431, 444, 466, 483, 495

St George's School, Windsor   79, 422, 457, 470, 486

St George's, Dunstable   74

St Gerard's School, Bangor   250, 472, 497

St Helen's College, Hillingdon   166, 491

St Helen's School, Northwood   167, 315, 428, 440, 453, 460, 466, 480, 491

St Hilary's School, Godalming   196, 371, 430, 443, 482, 494

St Hilda's School, Bushey   119, 452, 489

St Hilda's School, Harpenden   119, 452, 470, 489
St Hilda's School, Wakefield   232, 470
St Hilda's School, Westcliff-on-Sea   108, 424, 437, 452, 466, 488
St Hugh's School, Faringdon   177, 460, 470, 492
St Hugh's School, Woodhall Spa   138, 439, 460, 470, 490
St Ia School, St Ives   93, 466, 478
St Ives School, Haslemere   197, 430, 443, 454, 470, 494
St James Independent School for Boys (Senior), Twickenham   168, 440, 450, 460, 491
St James Independent School for Boys, London W14   161, 440, 449, 491
St James Independent School for Girls (Juniors), London W14   161, 440, 453, 491
St James Independent School for Senior Girls, London W14   161, 440, 453, 491
St James's School, Malvern   495
St James' School, Grimsby   139, 426, 439, 460, 470, 480, 490
St John's Beaumont, Windsor   80, 304, 448, 457, 472, 477, 486
St John's College School, Cambridge   87, 422, 436, 458, 470, 486
St John's College, Cardiff   248
St John's College, Southsea   116, 424, 459, 472, 479, 488
St John's Northwood, Northwood   167, 450, 470, 491
St John's-on-the-Hill, Chepstow   251, 434, 446, 464, 470, 484, 497
St John's Preparatory School, Lichfield   187
St John's Preparatory School, Potters Bar   121
St John's Priory School, Banbury   176, 492
St John's School, Billericay   104, 479, 488
St John's School, Leatherhead   198, 430, 443, 450, 461, 470, 482, 494
St John's School, Porthcawl   247, 434, 446
St John's School, Sidmouth   99, 437, 458, 475, 478, 487
St John's Senior School, Enfield   165, 466
St Johns Wood Pre-Preparatory School, London NW8   148, 440, 480
St Joseph's College, Ipswich   190, 429, 442, 461, 466, 493
St Joseph's Convent School, Burnley   131, 426, 472
St Joseph's Convent School, London E11   141, 453, 472
St Joseph's Convent School, Reading   79, 422, 435, 451, 472, 477, 486
St Joseph's Convent, Chesterfield   95, 472

St Joseph's in the Park, Hertford   120, 425
St Joseph's Preparatory School, Stoke-on-Trent   187, 472, 493
St Joseph's School, Launceston   92, 423, 436, 452, 487
St Joseph's School, Nottingham   174, 472, 492
St Lawrence College Junior School, Ramsgate   127, 358, 425, 439, 459, 470, 479
St Lawrence College, Ramsgate   127, 358, 425, 439, 459, 470, 479, 489
St Leonards-Mayfield School, Mayfield   206, 378, 431, 443, 454, 462, 472, 482, 494
St Leonards School & VIth Form College, St Andrews   239, 433, 445, 463, 497
St Margaret's Preparatory School, Calne   218, 483, 495
St Margaret's School Convent of Mercy, Midhurst   209, 472, 494
St Margaret's School for Girls, Aberdeen   236, 433, 445, 455, 483, 496
St Margaret's School, Bushey   119, 313, 425, 438, 452, 459, 470, 479, 489
St Margaret's School, Edinburgh   243, 433, 445, 455, 497
St Margaret's School, Exeter   98, 423, 437, 452, 470, 487
St Margaret's School, Halstead   106, 424, 470, 479, 488
St Margaret's School, London NW3   145, 341, 427, 440, 453, 470, 480, 491
St Martha's Senior School, Barnet   118, 452, 472
St Martin's Ampleforth, York   227, 432, 444, 463, 473, 483, 496
St Martin's Preparatory School, Grimsby   139, 490
St Martin's School, Bournemouth   101, 423, 437, 470
St Martin's School, Northwood   167, 450, 470, 491
St Martin's School, Solihull   495
St Martin's, London NW7   147, 480
St Mary's College, Liverpool   164, 427, 440, 473, 491
St Mary's College, Southampton   115, 424, 470, 479
St Mary's Convent School, Worcester   223, 432, 444, 455, 473, 495
St Mary's Hall, Brighton   204, 379, 431, 443, 454, 462, 470, 482, 494
St Mary's Hall, Stonyhurst   134, 426, 459, 473, 490
St Mary's Hare Park School, Romford   108, 473
St Mary's Junior School, Cambridge   87, 452, 473, 486

St Mary's Music School, Edinburgh   243, 433, 447, 463

St Mary's Preparatory School, Lincoln   137, 466, 490

St Mary's Preparatory School, Melrose   245, 433, 463, 497

St Mary's School Hampstead, London NW3   146, 427, 440, 473, 480, 491

St Mary's School, Ascot, Ascot   75, 305, 422, 451, 457, 473, 486

St Mary's School, Calne   218, 402, 432, 444, 455, 462, 470, 483, 495

St Mary's School, Cambridge   87, 274, 422, 436, 452, 458, 473, 478, 486

St Mary's School, Colchester   106, 424, 452, 479, 488

St Mary's School, Gerrards Cross   84, 422, 436, 451, 470, 486

St Mary's School, Henley-on-Thames   177, 492

St Mary's School, Shaftesbury   102, 423, 452, 458, 473, 478, 487

St Mary's School, Wantage   179, 428, 441, 454, 460, 470, 481, 492

St Mary's Westbrook, Folkestone   489

St Matthews School, Northampton   172, 466

St Michael's Preparatory School, Jersey   88, 422, 436, 486

St Michael's School, Leigh-on-Sea   107, 437, 466, 470, 488

St Michael's School, Llanelli   249, 434, 446, 497

St Michael's School, Sevenoaks   128, 425, 439, 470, 479, 489

St Michael's, Barnstaple   97, 423, 437, 470, 487

St Michaels School, Newbury   77, 435, 448, 451, 457, 473

St Neot's School, Hook   113, 424, 438, 459, 470, 488

St Nicholas House Kindergarten & Prep School, North Walsham   169, 481

St Nicholas House Kindergarten and Prep School, North Walsham   491

St Nicholas Preparatory School, London SW7   152, 342

St Nicholas' School, Fleet   113, 395, 424, 438, 452, 470, 479, 488

St Nicholas School, Harlow   106, 424, 437, 488

St Nicholas School, London NW9   148

St Olave's Preparatory School, London SE9   149, 480, 491

St Olave's School (Junior of St Peter's), York   496

St Paul's Cathedral School, London EC4   142, 342, 427, 440, 460, 470, 491

St Paul's Girls' School, London W6   159, 427, 440, 453, 491

St Paul's Preparatory School, London SW13   154, 427, 440, 449, 470, 491

St Paul's School, London SW13   154, 427, 440, 449, 460, 470, 491

St Peter & St Paul School, Chesterfield   95

St Peter's Independent School, Blackthorn   171

St Peter's School, Burgess Hill   207, 443

St Peter's School, Exmouth   98, 423, 458, 487

St Peter's School, Kettering   171, 441, 470, 492

St Peter's School, York   227, 432, 444, 463, 470, 496

St Petroc's School, Bude   92, 423, 436, 470

St Philip's School, London SW7   153, 449, 473

St Philomena's Preparatory School, Frinton-on-Sea   106, 473, 488

St Piran's Preparatory School, Hayle   92

St Piran's Preparatory School, Maidenhead   76, 305, 422, 436, 470, 486

St Pius X Preparatory School, Preston   134, 473, 490

St Richard's, Bromyard   117, 424, 438, 459, 473, 488

St Ronan's School, Hawkhurst   127, 425, 459, 470, 489

St Serf's School, Edinburgh   243, 484

St Swithun's School, Winchester   116, 424, 438, 452, 459, 470, 488

St Teresa's Catholic Independent & Nursery School, Princes Risborough   85, 473, 486

St Teresa's Preparatory School, Effingham   194, 454, 461, 473, 494

St Teresa's School, Dorking   194, 372, 430, 443, 454, 461, 473, 482, 494

St Thomas Garnet's School, Bournemouth   101, 473

St Ursula's High School, Bristol   82, 422, 473, 477, 486

St Ursulas Convent School, Wigton   95, 437

St Wilfrid's School, Exeter   98, 423, 437, 470

St Winefride's Convent School, Shrewsbury   181, 473, 481, 492

St Winifred's School, Southampton   115, 488

St Wystan's School, Repton   96, 423, 437, 470, 487

Stafford Grammar School, Stafford   187, 429, 442, 493

Staines Preparatory School, Staines   167, 440, 480, 491

Stamford High School, Stamford   138, 426, 439, 453, 460, 490

Stamford Junior School, Stamford   138, 460, 490

Stamford School, Stamford   138, 426, 439, 449, 460, 470, 480, 490

Stanborough School, Watford   122, 425, 459, 473, 479, 489

Stanbridge Earls School, Romsey   115, 438, 459, 476, 479, 488

Station Education Centre, March   87

Steephill Independent School, Longfield   127, 357, 470

Steephill School, Longfield   489

Steiner Waldorf Schools Fellowship   511

Stella Maris Junior School, Stockport   92, 473

Stepping Stones Nursery and Pre-Preparatory School, Marlborough   219, 470

Stewart's Melville College, Edinburgh   243, 433, 445, 451, 463, 497

Stockport Grammar School, Stockport   92, 423, 436, 487

Stockton House School, Fleet   113, 424, 438

Stoke Brunswick, East Grinstead   208, 431, 443, 462, 470, 494

Stoke College, Sudbury   190, 429, 442, 461, 493

Stonar School, Melksham   219, 403, 432, 444, 455, 462, 483, 495

Stonehouse School, Leyland   133, 466

Stonelands School of Ballet & Theatre Arts, East Sussex   447

Stonelands School of Ballet & Theatre Arts, Hove   206, 431, 462, 482

Stoneygate College, Leicester   136, 466

Stoneygate School, Great Glen   490

Stoneygate School, Leicester   136, 426, 439, 470

Stonyhurst College, Clitheroe   132, 426, 439, 459, 473, 480, 490

Stoodley Knowle School, Torquay   100, 423, 452

Stormont, Potters Bar   121, 438, 452, 489

Stourbridge House School, Warminster   220, 470

Stover School, Newton Abbot   99, 423, 437, 458, 470, 478, 487

Stowe School, Buckingham   83, 422, 436, 457, 470, 478, 486

Stowford College, Sutton   201, 430, 443, 466, 476, 482, 494

Stratford Preparatory School, Stratford-upon-Avon   213, 495

Strathallan School, Perth   245, 412, 433, 446, 463, 484, 497

Streatham and Clapham High School, London SW16   155, 427, 440, 453, 491

Streatham House School, Liverpool   164, 427, 440, 453

Stretton School, Norwich   170

The Stroud School, Romsey   115, 424, 470, 488

The Study Preparatory School, London SW19   155, 453, 480, 491

The Study School, New Malden   199, 470, 494

Summer Fields, Oxford   179, 450, 460, 481, 492

Summerhill School, Leiston   190, 461, 482

Sunderland High School, Sunderland   212, 431, 443, 470, 482, 495

Sunflower Montessori School, Twickenham   168, 428, 440, 466, 480

Sunningdale School, Sunningdale   79, 436, 448, 457, 470, 486

Sunninghill Preparatory School, Dorchester   102, 466, 487

Sunny Hill House School, Wakefield   232, 473, 496

Sunnymede School, Southport   164, 440, 491

Surbiton High School, Kingston-upon-Thames   198, 430, 443, 454, 470, 482, 494

Surbiton Preparatory School, Surbiton   201, 450, 470, 482, 494

Sussex House School, London SW1   150, 427, 449, 470, 491

Sutton High School GDST, Sutton   201, 430, 443, 454, 482, 494

Sutton Valence Preparatory School, Maidstone   127, 470, 489

Sutton Valence School, Maidstone   127, 425, 439, 459, 470, 479, 489

Suzi Earnshaw Theatre School, Barnet   118

The Swaminarayan School, London NW10   491

Swanbourne House School, Milton Keynes   85, 307, 422, 436, 457, 470, 478, 486

Sycamore Hall Preparatory School, Doncaster   228

Sydenham High School GDST, London SE26   150, 427, 440, 453, 491

Sylvia Young Theatre School, London NW1   144, 427, 440, 447, 460, 480, 491

T

Tabernacle School, London W11   160, 466

Talbot Heath, Bournemouth   101, 423, 437, 452, 458, 470, 478, 487

Talbot House Preparatory School, Bournemouth   101

Talmud Torah Bobov Primary School, London N16   143, 449, 471

Tashbar School, Salford   134, 449, 471

TASIS The American School in England, Thorpe   202, 373, 443, 461, 482

Tauheedul Islam Girls High School,
    Blackburn   131, 453
Taunton International Study Centre (TISC),
    Taunton   183, 461, 481
Taunton Preparatory School, Taunton   184, 429,
    442, 461, 481, 493
Taunton School, Taunton   184, 429, 442, 461, 481,
    493
Taverham Hall, Norwich   170, 428, 441, 460, 470,
    481, 492
Tavistock & Summerhill School, Haywards
    Heath   209, 431, 443
Tawhid Boys School, Tawhid Educational Trust,
    London N16   143, 449, 472
Tayyibah Girls School, London N16   143, 453, 472
Teesside Preparatory and High School,
    Eaglescliffe   188, 429, 442, 493
Terra Nova School, Holmes Chapel   90, 423, 436,
    458, 478, 487
The Terrace School, Leamington Spa   213, 466
Terrington Hall, York   227, 432, 444, 463, 483, 496
Tettenhall College, Wolverhampton   218, 431,
    444, 462, 476, 483, 495
Thames Christian College, London SW11   153,
    440, 480
Theodore Mcleary Primary School, London
    SE22   150
Thetford Grammar School, Thetford   171, 428,
    441, 492
Thomas' Preparatory School Clapham, London
    SW11   153, 470
Thomas's Fulham, London SW6   152, 480
Thomas's Kindergarten, Battersea, London
    SW11   153, 470
Thomas's Kindergarten, London SW1   150, 466
Thomas's Preparatory School, London SW11   153,
    427, 470
Thomas's Preparatory School, London W8   159,
    466, 480
Thorngrove School, Newbury   77, 422
Thornlow Preparatory School, Weymouth   103,
    423, 487
Thornton College Convent of Jesus and Mary,
    Milton Keynes   85, 422, 436, 452, 458, 473, 478,
    486
Thorpe Hall School, Southend-on-Sea   108, 424,
    437, 466, 479, 488
Thorpe House School, Gerrards Cross   84, 422,
    436, 448, 470, 478, 486
Thorpe House School, Norwich   170, 454, 492
Tockington Manor School, Bristol   82, 436, 457,
    470, 478, 486

Tonbridge School, Tonbridge   129, 359, 425, 439,
    449, 459, 471, 479, 489
Tormead School, Guildford   196, 430, 454, 494
Torwood House School, Bristol   82, 422, 478
Tower College, Prescot   164, 427, 491
Tower Dene Preparatory School, Southport   164,
    427, 440
Tower House School, London SW14   154, 449, 491
Tower House School, Paignton   99, 423, 437, 478
The Towers Convent School, Steyning   210, 431,
    443, 454, 462, 473, 482, 495
Town Close House Preparatory School,
    Norwich   170, 428, 471, 492
Treffos School, Menai Bridge   247
Tregelles, York   227, 472
Treliske, Truro   487
Trent College, Nottingham   175, 428, 441, 460,
    466, 492
Trentvale Preparatory School, Keadby   139
Trevor Roberts', London NW3   146, 471
Trinity School, Croydon   193, 430, 443, 450, 466,
    494
Trinity School, Stalybridge   91, 466
Trinity School, Teignmouth   100, 423, 437, 458,
    473, 478, 487
Truro High School, Truro   93, 423, 436, 452, 458,
    471, 487
Truro School Preparatory School, Truro   93, 436,
    471
Truro School, Truro   93, 458, 478, 487
Tudor Hall School, Banbury   177, 428, 454, 460,
    471, 492
Twickenham Preparatory School, Hampton   166,
    466, 491
Twycross House School, Atherstone   212, 495
Twyford School, Winchester   116, 459, 471, 479,
    488

U

Unicorn School, Richmond   200, 494
University College School Junior Branch, London
    NW3   146, 449, 491
University College School, London NW3   146,
    427, 440, 449, 491
Uplands School, Poole   102, 423, 437, 466, 487
Uppingham School, Uppingham   180, 428, 441,
    460, 471, 492
Upton House School, Windsor   80, 306, 422, 436,
    471, 477, 486

The Urdang Academy of Ballet, London WC2   161, 447

Ursuline Preparatory School, Brentwood   104, 473, 488

Ursuline Preparatory School, London SW20   156, 453, 473

V

Vernon Lodge Preparatory School, Brewood   186, 429

Vernon Lodge Preparatory School, Stafford   493

Victoria College Belfast, Belfast   233, 455, 463, 483

Victoria College Preparatory School, Jersey   88, 448, 486

Victoria College, Jersey   88, 422, 436, 448, 466, 486

Viking School, Skegness   138

The Villa Pre-Preparatory School, London SE15   149

The Village School, London NW3   146, 453

Vine School, Southampton   115, 466

Vinehall School, Robertsbridge   206, 431, 443, 462, 471, 482, 494

Virgo Fidelis, London SE19   149, 427, 473, 491

Vita Et Pax School, London N14   143, 473, 491

W

Wakefield Girls' High School, Wakefield   232, 433, 445, 455, 496

Wakefield Independent School, Wakefield   232, 433, 471

Wakefield Tutorial Preparatory School, Leeds   231, 433, 467

Waldorf School of South West London, London SW16   155

The Walmer Road School, London W11   160

Walthamstow Hall, Sevenoaks   128, 359, 425, 439, 453, 479, 489

Walthamstow Montessori School, London E17   141

Warlingham Park School, Croydon   193, 443, 467

Warminster School, Warminster   220, 432, 444, 462, 471, 476, 483, 495

Warwick Preparatory School, Warwick   213, 467, 495

Warwick School, Warwick   214, 431, 443, 450, 462, 471, 495

Waverley House PNEU School, Nottingham   175, 492

Waverley School, Wokingham   80, 477, 486

Wellesley House School, Broadstairs   124, 426, 439, 459, 471, 479, 489

Wellingborough School, Wellingborough   172, 492

Wellington College, Crowthorne   76, 306, 422, 436, 457, 471, 486

Wellington School, Ayr   238, 445

Wellington School, Wellington   184, 429, 442, 461, 471, 481, 493

Wellow House School, Newark   173, 428, 441, 460, 492

Wells Cathedral Junior School, Wells   184, 429, 442, 461, 471, 493

Wells Cathedral School, Wells   184, 429, 442, 461, 471, 481, 493

Wellspring Christian School, Carlisle   94, 437, 467

Welsh School of London, London NW10   427, 480

Wentworth College, Bournemouth   102, 392, 423, 437, 452, 458, 478, 487

West Buckland Preparatory School, Barnstaple   97, 423, 437, 458, 471

West Buckland School, Barnstaple   97, 423, 437, 458, 471, 478, 487

West Dene School, Purley   199, 430, 494

West House School, Birmingham   216, 444, 450, 495

West Lodge Preparatory School, Sidcup   129, 479, 489

Westbourne House School, Chichester   208, 431, 462, 471, 495

Westbourne School, Cardiff   248, 484, 497

Westbourne School, Sheffield   228, 432, 444, 496

Westbrook Hay Preparatory School, Hemel Hempstead   120, 425, 438, 459, 471, 489

Westbury House School, New Malden   199, 482

Westfield School, Newcastle upon Tyne   211, 431, 443, 455, 482, 495

Westholme School, Blackburn   131, 426, 453, 490

Westminster Abbey Choir School, London SW1   151, 344, 427, 449, 460, 471, 491

Westminster Cathedral Choir School, London SW1   151, 427, 440, 449, 460, 473, 491

Westminster School, London SW1   151, 427, 440, 460, 471, 491

Westminster Tutors, London SW7   153, 345, 427, 440, 480

Westminster Under School, London SW1   151, 427, 440, 449, 471, 491

Weston Green School, Thames Ditton   202, 467

Westonbirt School, Tetbury   111, 284, 424, 438, 452, 459, 471, 479, 488

Westville House Preparatory School, Ilkley   231, 496

Westward Preparatory School, Walton-on-Thames   202

Westwood, Bushey Heath   119

Wetherby Preparatory School, London W11   160, 346, 449, 467, 480

Wetherby School, London W2   157, 346, 449

The White House Prep & Woodentops Kindergarten, London SW12   154, 427, 440

White House Preparatory School, Wokingham   80, 436, 451, 477, 486

White House School, Whitchurch   182

Whitehall School, Huntingdon   87, 486

Whitgift School, South Croydon   201, 430, 443, 450, 494

Wickham Court School, West Wickham   130, 467

Widford Lodge, Chelmsford   105, 471, 488

William Hulme's Grammar School, Manchester   162, 427, 440, 491

Willington School, London SW19   155, 427, 440, 449, 480

Willow Tree Montessori School, Crawley   208

Wilmslow Preparatory School, Wilmslow   92, 436, 452, 478, 487

Wimbledon Common Preparatory School, London SW19   155, 449

Wimbledon High School GDST, London SW19   155, 427, 453, 491

Winbury School, Maidenhead   76, 477, 486

Winchester College, Winchester   116, 396, 424, 438, 449, 459, 471, 488

Winchester House School, Brackley   171, 428, 460, 471, 492

Windermere St Anne's, Windermere   95, 264, 423, 437, 458, 478, 487

Windlesham House, Pulborough   210, 385, 431, 443, 462, 471, 482, 495

Windmill House School, Uppingham   180

Windrush Valley School, Chipping Norton   177, 441, 492

Winterfold House, Kidderminster   222, 432, 444, 473, 495

Wisbech Grammar School, Wisbech   87, 422, 436, 471, 486

Wispers School for Girls, Haslemere   197, 430, 443, 454, 461, 494

Witham Hall, Bourne   137, 426, 439, 460, 471, 490

Withington Girls' School, Manchester   163, 440, 453, 480, 491

Woldingham School, Woldingham   203, 430, 454, 462, 473, 482, 494

Wolverhampton Grammar School, Wolverhampton   218, 431, 444, 495

Wood Dene School, Norwich   170, 428, 441, 471

Woodard Schools (The Woodard Corporation)   511

Woodbridge School, Woodbridge   191, 429, 442, 461, 471, 482, 493

Woodcote House School, Windlesham   202, 430, 443, 450, 462, 482, 494

Woodford Green Preparatory School, Woodford Green   108, 467, 488

Woodhill Preparatory School, Southampton   115

Woodhill School, Chandler's Ford   112, 479

Woodhouse Grove School, Apperley Bridge   229, 433, 445, 463, 471, 483, 496

Woodlands Schools, Brentwood   104, 488

Woodleigh School, Malton   225, 432, 444, 463, 471, 476, 496

Woodside Park International School, London N11   143, 347, 427, 440, 476, 480, 491

Woodstock Girls' School, Birmingham   216, 455

Worksop College, Worksop   175, 428, 441, 460, 467, 471, 492

Worth School, Turners Hill   210, 431, 450, 462, 473, 482, 495

Wrekin College, Telford   182, 429, 441, 461, 471, 481, 492

Wychwood School, Oxford   179, 428, 441, 454, 460, 492

Wyclif Independent Christian School, Machen   248

Wycliffe College & Preparatory School, Stonehouse   476

Wycliffe College, Stonehouse   110, 285, 424, 438, 459, 479, 488

Wycliffe Preparatory School, Stonehouse   110, 285, 424, 438, 459, 476, 479, 488

Wycombe Abbey School, High Wycombe   84, 422, 452, 458, 471, 486

Wykeham House School, Fareham   113, 424, 438, 452, 471, 479, 488

Wynstones School, Gloucester   110, 438, 459, 479

Y

Yardley Court, Tonbridge   129, 426, 439, 449, 467, 489

Yarlet School, Stafford   187, 429, 442, 461, 493

Yarm School, Yarm   188, 429, 442, 467, 493

Yarrells School, Poole   102, 423, 437, 478, 487

Yateley Manor Preparatory School, Yateley   116,
424, 471, 488

Yehudi Menuhin School, Cobham   192, 430, 443,
447, 462, 482, 494

Yesodey Hatorah Jewish School, London N16   143,
449, 453, 471

Yetev Lev Day School for Boys, London N16   143,
449, 471

York House School, Rickmansworth   121, 425,
438, 449, 471, 489

Yorston Lodge School, Knutsford   91, 436, 471

Ysgol Gymraeg Llundain, The Welsh School,
London, London NW10   148

Ysgol Rhydygors, Carmarthen   476

ALSO AVAILABLE FROM KOGAN PAGE

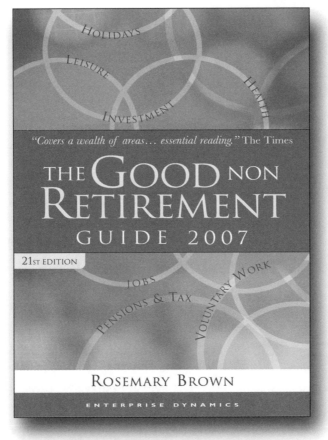

READER ENQUIRY CARD

If you would like further information about our Advisory, Guardianship or other services, please complete and return this card. No stamp necessary if posted within the United Kingdom.

Name: _____

Address: _____

_____ Tel: _____

Please indicate which area of our services might interest you:

_____

Please tell us where you obtained a copy of this Guide:

Bookshop/Library (name and town): _____

School/advisory service etc (please give details): _____

_____

Other (please give details): _____

READER ENQUIRY CARD

If you would like further information about our Advisory, Guardianship or other services, please complete and return this card. No stamp necessary if posted within the United Kingdom.

Name: _____

Address: _____

_____ Tel: _____

Please indicate which area of our services might interest you:

_____

Please tell us where you obtained a copy of this Guide:

Bookshop/Library (name and town): _____

School/advisory service etc (please give details): _____

_____

Other (please give details): _____

GGIS 13

GABBITAS EDUCATIONAL CONSULTANTS Ltd

CARRINGTON HOUSE

126–130 REGENT STREET

LONDON

W1B 5EE

BUSINESS REPLY SERVICE
Licence No WD 598

GGIS 13

GABBITAS EDUCATIONAL CONSULTANTS Ltd

CARRINGTON HOUSE

126–130 REGENT STREET

LONDON

W1B 5EE